DATE DUE

PRINTED IN U.S.A.

LAW ENFORCEMENT IN COLONIAL NEW YORK

PATTERSON SMITH REPRINT SERIES IN
CRIMINOLOGY, LAW ENFORCEMENT, AND SOCIAL PROBLEMS

A listing of publications in the SERIES *will be found at rear of volume*

PUBLICATION No. 122: PATTERSON SMITH REPRINT SERIES IN
CRIMINOLOGY, LAW ENFORCEMENT, AND SOCIAL PROBLEMS

LAW ENFORCEMENT IN COLONIAL NEW YORK

A STUDY IN CRIMINAL PROCEDURE
(1664–1776)

JULIUS GOEBEL JR.

George Welwood Murray Professor of Legal History
Columbia University School of Law

T. RAYMOND NAUGHTON

of the New York Bar

PATTERSON SMITH

MONTCLAIR, N. J.

1970

Copyright 1944 by The Commonwealth Fund
Reprinted 1970, with permission, by
Patterson Smith Publishing Corporation
Montclair, New Jersey 07042

SBN 87585–122–3

Library of Congress Catalog Card Number: 71–108239

This book is printed on three-hundred-year acid-free paper.

TABLE OF CONTENTS

FOREWORD

THE hand of time has not dealt gently with our colonial records. The decimation of war and fire has in many places been needlessly enhanced by indifferent custodianship. Nevertheless we have done what lay within our power to make our account complete, and since we have constantly had in mind the possible practical uses of materials bearing upon American conceptions of due process, we have included all details which seem to possess such significance. We know further that lawyers must be sure of what was normal practice and what was exceptional. Consequently we have sought to be scrupulous about established fact, inference and conjecture.

Many cases have been used in this volume, but no attempt has been made to cite every case we have found, for this would have involved a pedantic complication of an already unwieldy critical apparatus. Where a practice of long duration existed we have referred to representative cases scattered over the period in question. In certain instances prosecutions which we regard as contemporaneously important or about which an unusual amount of information is available have been repeatedly cited on various points of law. This has involved occasional repetition in text or notes but should ease the otherwise constant hue and cry after a *supra* or an *infra*. The Dutch law has been discussed only on points where it was possibly influential. Similarly we have noted any New England practices that may have affected the early law in New York.

We have done our best with proper names but it is often an indifferent best, for the variations in spelling in a polyglot eighteenth century community are staggering, and certain sources (as, for example, in Kings County) were available only in the form of modern office copies of the original manuscripts. There is consolation in the reflection that a work on criminal procedure is not likely to be a source book for family history.

When the research on this volume was initiated we were aware that our greatest problem was the dispersion of records. Mr. Naughton undertook to reduce to order the sources in New York and Kings counties, a task which included the difficult reconstruction of Supreme Court cases. I assumed responsibility for the sources in other provincial counties and in places outside the state of New York. We have each of us worked over certain collections in the Hall of Records and in the New-York Historical Society. We have both shared in the labor of writing this book. For the form in which it now stands and for the introduction I am alone responsible.

Our research could never have been done except for the help and cooperation of many people. We are especially indebted to Mr. Maxwell Volins, Chief Record Clerk, New York County Clerk's Office, who has done so much to restore and make usable the materials in the New York Hall of Records, and to Miss Edna Jacobsen, Chief of the Manuscripts Division, New York State Library, who has been doing a similar work at Albany. The New-York Historical Society has given us permission to use and quote from its manuscript collections and we have benefited by endless kindnesses at the hands of Director Alexander J. Wall and of the staff, Miss Dorothy Bark, Miss Susan Lyman and Mr. John T. Washbourn. Mr. Albert De Vito, Librarian of the Court of General Sessions, and Mr. Joseph M. O'Neill, in the office of the Clerk of that Court, have also done much to assist us. Our thanks are further due to Mr. Sidney B. Hill, Librarian of the Association of the Bar of the City of New York; to Mr. Fred Shipman, Director of the Franklin D. Roosevelt Library at Hyde Park; to Mrs. Amy Van Nooy of the Adriance Memorial Library, Poughkeepsie; to the staffs of the Manuscript Division of the New York Public Library and of the Museum of the City of New York; and to the officials at the Public Record Office, London. In all the various county and town offices we were received with great courtesy, and officials there have given freely of their time in ransacking attics, basements and vaults in the search for old files.

Mr. Morton Pennypacker, the late Mr. Augustus Van Cortlandt and the executor of the late Livingston Rutherfurd generously permitted examination of their private collections, and it is to the latter that we owe the privilege of publishing James Alexander's brief in *King* v. *Zenger*.

In the preparation of this manuscript our labors were greatly lightened by Mrs. Anne Naughton and by my assistants past and present—Dr. Donald Tilton, Lieutenant Joseph Henry Smith, U.S.N.R., and Miss Ruth McIntyre. The list of names and cases at the end of this volume was compiled by Miss McIntyre. Professors Elliott Cheatham, Dorothy Burne Goebel, Huger Jervey, Karl Llewellyn and Jerome Michael read and criticized the manuscript in whole or in part.

Finally, I desire to acknowledge my obligation to the Commonwealth Fund which has supported the work of the Foundation for Research in Legal History, to the Legal Research Committee of the Fund, and in particular to Mr. George Welwood Murray, Chairman of the Committee, who read our manuscript before his death. Mr. Murray's early experiences with title searching gave him a rueful understanding of research problems in local records; his command of the law's history and its administration, an acute awareness of the problems of colonial law. It was his custom to follow closely the progress of a research project and by his counsel and encouragement to take an active share in its unfolding. This is companionship hard to forfeit—*iucunda est praeteritorum laborum memoria.*

J. G. Jr.

July, 1943

GOVERNORS OF NEW YORK PROVINCE, 1664–1776

(*Calendar of Council Minutes* 6)

The dating in this list is on the basis of the first official act of a new Governor. Temporary administrations are dated from the departure of the Governor.

Richard Nicolls	August 29, 1664
Francis Lovelace	May 23, 1668
Cornelis Evertse Jr. and a council of war	July 30, 1673
Anthony Colve	September 9, 1673
Edmund Andros	October 31, 1674
Anthony Brockholls, Commander-in-Chief	November 16, 1677
Sir Edmund Andros	August 8, 1678
Anthony Brockholls, Commander-in-Chief	January 7, 1680/81
Thomas Dongan	August 27, 1683
Sir Edmund Andros	August 11, 1688
Francis Nicholson, Lieutenant-Governor	October 9, 1688
Jacob Leisler	June 3, 1689
Henry Sloughter	March 19, 1690/91
Richard Ingoldesby, Commander-in-Chief	July 26, 1691
Benjamin Fletcher	August 30, 1692
Richard Coote, Earl of Bellomont	April 2, 1698
John Nanfan, Lieutenant-Governor	May 16, 1699
Richard Coote, Earl of Bellomont	July 24, 1700
Col. William Smith Col. Abraham De Peyster ⎬ Councillors Col. Peter Schuyler	March 5, 1700/01 to May 19, 1701
John Nanfan, Lieutenant-Governor	May 19, 1701
Edward Hyde, Viscount Cornbury	May 3, 1702
John Lord Lovelace	December 18, 1708
Peter Schuyler, President of Council	May 6, 1709
Richard Ingoldesby, Lieutenant-Governor	May 9, 1709
Gerardus Beekman, President of Council	April 10, 1710
Robert Hunter	June 14, 1710
Peter Schuyler, President of Council	July 21, 1719
William Burnet	September 17, 1720
John Montgomerie	April 15, 1728
Rip Van Dam, President of Council	July 1, 1731
William Cosby	August 1, 1732
George Clarke, President of Council	March 10, 1735/36
George Clarke, Lieutenant-Governor	October 30, 1736
George Clinton	September 22, 1743

Sir Danvers Osborne . . . . October 10, 1753
James De Lancey, Lieutenant-Governor . . . October 12, 1753
Sir Charles Hardy . . . . September 3, 1755
James De Lancey, Lieutenant-Governor . . . June 3, 1757
Cadwallader Colden, President of Council . . August 4, 1760
Cadwallader Colden, Lieutenant-Governor . . August 8, 1761
Robert Monckton . . . . October 26, 1761
Cadwallader Colden, Lieutenant-Governor . . November 18, 1761
Robert Monckton . . . . June 14, 1762
Cadwallader Colden, Lieutenant-Governor . . June 28, 1763
Sir Henry Moore . . . . November 13, 1765
Cadwallader Colden, Lieutenant-Governor . . September 12, 1769
John Murray, Earl of Dunmore . . . . . . October 19, 1770
William Tryon . . . . July 9, 1771
Cadwallader Colden, Lieutenant-Governor . . April 7, 1774
William Tryon . . . . June 28, 1775

INTRODUCTION

THE prospects of independence so lately declared were dark, indeed, when in 1777 the embattled New Yorkers resolved as a part of their constitution that the acts of the provincial legislature, and such parts of the common law and the statutes of England and Great Britain as "together did form the law of the ·. . . colony" on the day of the battle of Lexington, were to be the law of the new state.[1] It is impossible not to believe that this was done for pressing immediate need, when one sees how the records of the country Sessions courts break off at various dates, with the "style" of the ensuing term written out ready for the next court, but never again to be held in the name of the King; when one reads how clerks of the peace inquire of the distracted Provincial Congress whether precepts should be sent out for grand juries; and when one reflects that while a Tory might demand justice no better and no worse than that which a county committee might accord him, those who were steadfast in rebellion must have a forum with a due process of law not different from that to which they were accustomed. The colonists were in no doubt as to their desires. They had declared in 1774 that they were entitled to the common law, and there had been a persistent sense of grievance that they were being ousted of their right by Crown and Parliament. Inevitably the new constitution of New York had to take care that there would be no tampering with something that seemed a part of the freedom for which men had shown themselves ready to die.

The article by which the constitution of 1777 declared the law of the new state was at the moment itself a terse bill of rights in its implicit assertion of what had hitherto been withheld—the declarations and statutes which protected the subject in England (yet which in spite of colonial claims did not extend overseas) and so much of constitutional right as was imbedded in the common law. Equally significant is the manner of expression—"as together did form the law of the said colony." This is not the triumphant cry of sudden victory after long denial. It is the sober recognition of achievement, an affirmation that New York would use in the future what it had wrought for itself in the past.

The People of the State, then, were compacting for nothing new. The judges of the Supreme Court of Judicature had long read in their commissions that

---

[1] Art. 35, 1 *Laws NY* (1813 rev.) 41.

they were to judge by the law of the Province as well as by the law of England. The rules of practice of the Circuit had stated explicitly the primacy of the former:

> That in all Such Cases that shall Come before this Court wherein there may arise any difficulty, whether the Same are to be Proceeded in according to ye Laws of This Province or according to ye Laws of England, itt is always to be understood, & itt is hereby declared, that this Court will Proceed in all Such Cases in manner following, that is to say: where ye Laws of this Province have made any Provision therein, that then in Such Cases ye Court will Proceed according and not otherwise and that wherein ye Laws of this Province are Silent ye Court will be regulated by ye Laws of England.[2]

No one who has troubled to look at the judicial records for the weeks when the up-river farmers were hurrying to humble Burgoyne,[3] and later when their Orange County brethren were weighing the misdeeds of Claudius Smith and his savage Cowboys,[4] can doubt that proceedings were conducted in a manner no different from that of a few years earlier. It could not be otherwise, for the judges who held court for the People and the lawyers who attended had been blooded in courts of the same name and the same jurisdiction when process still ran in the name of King George.

The reception article of 1777 was written at a time when the common law was still the stone from which the edifice of our law was built, and had not yet become the dab of mortar to mortise the strawless brick of unremitting statutory production. The provincials having labored for better than a century in the construction of this edifice were intent upon its preservation. For them there were no dreams of a formative era to come—a brave new world into which Americans were to march from out the thickets of a frontier jurisprudence. Their formative era was behind them, the years when the law of England had been molded to their needs, if not utterly to their desires. This they were committing to posterity, by good fortune unaware that scholars were to make of them and their knowledge figures as clownish as a Dogberry or a Justice Shallow.

With the passing of the years, the reception article, which has weathered successive constitutional revisions, has come to be regarded in the courts as a

[2] *Ms. Rules for the Court of Oyer and Terminer* (Redmond-Livingston Mss.).
[3] *Ms. Mins. SCJ 1775–81* (Engr.) 107, Sept. 9, 1777.
[4] *H.R. Pleadings* (unnumbered) "At a Court of Oyer and Terminer and General Gaol Delivery . . . in and for the County of Orange . . ." (Jan. 13, 1779). On the Cowboys, Ruttenber, *History of the County of Orange* (1875) 91.

sort of let-pass for judicial excursions into the realm of English law books instead of into the less easily penetrable reaches of our colonial legal practice. The explicit reference to the provincial status quo of 1775 has usually been conveniently overlooked. When it has been necessary to a decision that a common law rule be settled, it has been siphoned out of English books without reference to possible colonial aberrance, or has been sublimated out of that mythical general common law so beloved of legal sentimentalists. This is an affront to American tradition, no less than an evasion of what the New York constitution in no uncertain language has directed.

The judicial approach to legal-historical problems just described is quite general and is one of some antiquity, for it runs back to the time of unhappy succession when the dynasty of Blackstone lawyers finally took command of our courts. It has been subjected to virtually no criticism; indeed it has of late been connived at by scholars who have carelessly assumed that the cold facts of history are matters susceptible to the brilliant artifices of jurisprudence. One cannot otherwise charitably explain the striking and uttering of that false coinage, the "frontier theory" of American law, and that equally spurious piece, the "formative era," *post* 1783.

The conversion of Turner's frontier theory to the use and behoof of the law has been chiefly the doing of a distinguished jurist whose words, often and attentively listened to, merit examination.[5] He has averred that the history of the common law in America "begins for practical purposes after the Revolution" for he denies that the colonists brought with them and cultivated the common law in the New World, insisting that this doctrine has been overthrown by a study of colonial records and legislation. Beguiled by certain reflections of the sociologist Sumner, this jurist has asserted further that "many crudities in judicial organization and procedure are demonstrably legacies of the frontier."[6] Administration of justice in colonial America is described as "initially executive and legislative" and "these types of non-judicial justice persisted well into the last century." Indeed, the law of New York is alleged

[5] Professor Roscoe Pound first stated his views in *The Spirit of the Common Law* (1912) 112 *et seq.* This was followed by the article, Judge Story in the Making of the Law, 48 *American Law Rev.* 676, 680 (1914). Reiteration in *An Introduction to American Law* (1924) 20–21; Comparative Law in the Formation of American Common Law, 1 *Actorum Academiae Universalis Jurisprudentiae* 183 (1928); *History and System of the Common Law* (National Law Library, 1939) 98; What of Stare Decisis? 10 *Fordham Law Rev.* 1, 4 (1940). Professor Pound's views are canonized by Aumann, *The Changing American Legal System* (1940) c. IV. Pound has added further glosses in his *Contemporary Juristic Theory* (1940) 25 and in *Law and Federal Government, Federalism as a Democratic Process* (1942) 25. The most extraordinary of these recent additions is that the Privy Council deprived Pennsylvania of courts for twenty years!

[6] Pound, *The Spirit of the Common Law* 113 *et seq.*

by him to have been "so completely at large," as late as 1791, that "the genius of a Kent was needed to make the common law the law of the State."[7]

Having thus dismissed to outer darkness the century and more of colonial legal development, this same writer in a recent expansion of his thesis that the formative era of American law occurs after the Revolution has offered some further explanation of the ban. The colonists, he says, claimed in the year 1774 to be entitled to the common law, but "it was not easy in the colonies to find out what that law was."[8] This difficulty he ascribes to the fact that even by the year 1775 Americans themselves had published a mere handful of law books and there were available no printed reports of provincial decisions. The implications of this statement both as to what went before and as to what happened later are obvious.

The "frontier" and the "formative era" theories in combination result in this —that the law of the colonial period is relegated to the antiquarian, and the law of post-Revolutionary time is enthroned as the true American law. The emphasis laid upon the practicality of this severance has its attractions for lawyers, and so far as the profession is concerned this ruthless dichotomy will probably be assured a longer life than it deserves. Its acceptance by scholars is a question of a different order. For them no considerations of plausibility, of convenience or of practicality can validate an historical hypothesis or interpretation which is based upon inconclusive, or unexamined, data. There can be no dalliance with probability when proof positive may be lying grimly in wait. It is with facts, therefore, and their probative effect that we must concern ourselves. The details of these as they relate to the applicability of a frontier theory to New York are presented in the body of this volume. Here we shall merely enter a general denial, and outline our objections. But before we proceed to this, it is necessary that two fundamental questions of terminology be determined.

In the first place, it must be settled how the word "American" is properly used in connection with the development of our law. Since considerations of time and place, of motion and repose are involved, conventional juristic concepts are of little avail. If one nourishes a mystical belief in the essential unity

---

[7] *Ibid.* 11. Other adherents of the frontier theory: Radin, *History of Anglo-American Law* (1936) 22; Morris, *Studies in the History of American Law* (1930) 17; Paxson, Influence of Frontier Life on the Development of American Law, 13 *Reports State Bar Assn. of Wisconsin* 474 (1919–21). In Beutel, Colonial Sources of Negotiable Instruments Law, 34 *Illinois Law Rev.* 134 (1939), the variant "pioneer" society is used. Paxson has been widely cited. He is the leading lay preacher of "frontierism" but his paper shows no signs that professional data were examined.

[8] Pound, *The Formative Era of American Law* (1938) 8.

of the common law wherever carried,[9] this has implications of immutability or universality which obscure the effects of migration and stamp the law with an indelible Anglicism. If, less imaginatively, one regards the law as what the sovereign wills, this requires that the law of the colonies and English law be taken as identical, and the Revolution thus becomes the instant of transubstantiation. The problem, however, is one of accounting for historical reality and it is more profitably approached as one in the mutations of a transplanted culture. Like every bit of Old World civilization brought overseas, the law underwent a process of indenization, of acquiring a New World identity. This process was profoundly affected by the accidents of settlement, the separateness of the provinces and the intense particularism which prevailed, so that nowhere did it proceed at the same pace or run the same course. In some places the intellectual pull of the motherland was stronger; in others the effects of the sea change were more immediate. English officials did not delude themselves with a belief that the law which was being administered in the several plantations was identical with English law, and they were well aware of the differences between the various provincial systems. This sense of difference was no less acute in the colonies. Neither the continental label on the map nor the fact that the inhabitants were all subjects of the Crown supplied a *principium unitatis*. The culture of the settlers, and so their law, polarized in the jurisdictions where they lived. It is "American" because the history of these lusty polities is severally the history of America. Their several achievements even when they seem most English in substance and flavor are the blood and bone of American civilization and are not to be interred as a defunct bit of Empire history.

We must next inquire, what of the expression "common law"? No excursion into our colonial legal past can be undertaken unless the implications of the term are settled. It is a fact worth noticing that in the royal charters which from time to time passed the seals, the clauses dealing with the law invariably employ the expression "laws of England." The intendment of this, as we shall see, was not to effect an introduction of that law but to set a standard for colonial action. The phrase, owing to the extraordinary diversity of jurisdiction in England, actually implied an infinite variety of choice wider than if the expression "common law" had been used, and failure to take notice of this has been the undoing of many an unwary prowler into the past. A man presented

---

[9] For example, Pound, *The Spirit of the Common Law* 1 *et seq.*; Pound, What is the Common Law? in *The Future of the Common Law* (1937) 10 *et seq.*

at an English leet had rights different from a man presented at Sessions. A fellow tried at a Gaol Delivery must be alert that the powers of Oyer and Terminer were not used. The litigant in Common Bench faced a different *cursus curiae* from the one in King's Bench or Exchequer. No doubt a Yorkshireman who never attended a court more august than a Quarter Sessions or a County Court conceived that what he there learned was "common law," and so the Londoner who ventured into Old Bailey. The realm was a honeycomb of jurisdictions and the course of proceeding in inferior courts had not been reduced to uniformity any more than had the procedure of the central courts. It is true the law practiced in these latter courts is generally spoken of as the common law, a manner of thought which makes plausible the ever-ready "test" for anything colonial—is it to be found in Coke or Blackstone? For the provincials, however, the easy way of modern scholarship was not yet open. To the making of their law they could bring only the viewpoints of their generation and their immediate experience with some part of the "law of England." This last, we think, is a consideration of decisive importance as we come now to assess the validity of the frontier theory in relation to the law. Inevitably one asks, was that which an emigrant brought with him of his mind's goods so ephemeral, his hold upon it so tenuous, that it was promptly overwhelmed by the rigors of his place of settlement?

Both the first and second stages of the reception of English law in New York Province (the first, 1664–1683; the second, 1684–1776) that we are about to consider establish how tough-minded the settlers were, and how few concessions were made to the circumstances of place. Things were done during the first stage that to the uninitiated may seem to prove the disintegrating effects of the frontier, but the "true inwardness" of affairs (as the Puritans would put it) is not discovered by merely taking a view of the terrain and what was there built. This problem of approach was considered by us over a decade ago when we undertook in relation to a New England colony to examine the thesis that because of the grim dangers lurking in the American forests when the first settlements were made, a special frontier jurisprudence developed.[10] It was indicated that various dispositions at Plymouth resembled in remarkable degree the practices in English local courts—the manorial, the borough, the county and Sessions courts—the type of law-enforcing

---

[10] Goebel, King's Law and Local Custom in Seventeenth Century New England, 31 *Col. Law Rev.* 416 (1931). Our theory was first advanced in *Some Legal and Political Aspects of the Manors in New York* (1928) but without the full critical apparatus.

institution with which these humble people were familiar. In short, the characteristics of their law were mainly determined not by what was here but by what they had already experienced.

But the New England soil, despite its name, has too long been venerated as the seed-bed of American culture for our suggestion that there was less originality and spontaneity than is commonly supposed to be welcomed.[11] The offense of our suggestion may, therefore, be moderated by what is offered in this volume respecting the enforcement of the criminal law in New York during the first epoch following its conquest. Using, as a base, matter from New England codes that had its origin in English usages, the Duke of York's lieutenants with great skill promoted as the provincial law the little they knew of English local administration. One will find few reminiscences of Coke in what was done, but much of it will responsively footnote *The Countrey Justice*. The system of law thus introduced endured for two decades, and since in many details it revived, as was designed, "memories of old England," the new order of the conqueror operated acceptably.

This artless adaptation of the practices of English inferior courts by lay persons whose resources were mainly their recollections was without doubt intended to be an accommodation with the laws of England. New York's first book of laws directed that its provisions were to be supplemented by reference to the "lawes of England,"[12] and the provincial records are replete with particular proofs. In this process of unguided assimilation there inhered potentialities for a highly original development of provincial law. But the course of history was to be otherwise. Upon the arrival of Governor Thomas Dongan in 1683 an elected assembly enacted a new judicature law and during the following spring a change of profound importance occurred. Within a few short months the whole procedural apparatus is renovated, the practices and forms of the English central courts come into use—the second stage of reception which will endure until the Revolution is under way.

Although the growth of procedure after 1684 is of infinitely greater professional significance than the initial experiments with the law, we have dwelt upon the stage of first reception in New York because writers have failed to recognize that there was a reception of English law at so early a date. Hence

---

[11] Cf. 1 Chafee and Morison, *Records of the Suffolk County Court 1671–80* (1933) xxxii. But no effort was made to test our theory against the materials there edited. Aumann, in *The Changing American Legal System* 58, views our findings with great reserve. His verdict is a "not proven" so far as abandonment of the "accepted view" is concerned.

[12] 1 *Col. Laws NY* 45 (1665).

they have found in crudities imported from the County of Kent, or Bedford-shire or elsewhere, inspiration for the fantasm of the frontier. To the accomplished student of Coke, these crudities (which have their parallel in other provinces) have been so striking that they have even been made to speak for the remainder of the colonial period.[13] Since there exists no reliable record study of eighteenth century colonial law for any American jurisdiction, this assumption has gone unchallenged. Thus the developments after 1783 can be made to take on a quite overpowering, but none the less distorted, significance.

It is tempting if one lives in an oasis to imagine the surrounding desert green; yet we will not speak for other American plantations, we can speak only for New York. Illusions created and fostered respecting the state of colonial law that make the period following the Revolution the "formative era" of our law have no substance so far as this Province is concerned. To find the Exchequer process of "extent" employed in 1691 abandoned, resumed and again abandoned is warning of native experiment with ancient molds. To discover the medieval *distringas nuper vicecomitem* pounced on to force an errant ex-sheriff to account is no less enlightening. To observe the institution of nisi prius jurisdiction with the complicated panoply of issue rolls, fictive jury process and *posteas* let loose in the early 1700's against the yeomen of sparsely settled counties suggests that law enforcement even in the early eighteenth century is not in the hands of ignoramuses but of people who are using English law for the good government of the Province. If one must speak solemnly of a formative era, it begins in New York on that remote day in 1684 when English indictment, English process and English forms of recordation moved in to stay. There were few who at that moment knew the import of these devices or how they were to be used, but on all sides the magistrates and attorneys set about to cut a substantive law to fit what they had to use as due process.

No branch of the law has more to tell us in its working than the criminal law of how the business of adaptation and adjustment proceeded. This is especially true of the initial stages, for its matter was too urgent to await the immigration of skill and learning. Indeed, the criminal law remains something

---

[13] A striking example of this is the use by Thurman Arnold and Fleming James, Jr. (*Cases and Materials on Trials, Judgments and Appeals* [1936] 243–246) of excerpts and summary from an unpublished modern study on colonial procedure. From the matter printed and the author's conclusions it appears that only early seventeenth century materials were used, for it is averred that anything resembling English forms did not come into use until 1760! Arnold and James accept this without any qualification. Tricked by this bit of "history," Walton Hamilton, in The Law and Mr. Blackstone, 39 *Col. Law Rev.* 736 (1939) could say: "America was ready and waiting; the *Commentaries* appeared with no rival to dispute its claims; Blackstone mounted a waiting and empty throne."

to which learning comes slowly and sporadically, the provincial bar having but a casual connection with its growth, since it is only the Crown that is entitled to be invariably represented. The felonies were still a preserve as restricted to defense counsel as were the hunting grounds of the Indian to the colonists, and in the misdemeanor field the lawyers' pickings for a long time were as lean as the quitrents paid to the King. For all that, the procedural apparatus was set up with rapidity and nearly in its entirety, as if, wanting the protection of skilled judges, there was safeguard in the forms themselves. During the brief regime of Jacob Leisler (1689–1691) the common law forms which had been in use for five years were displaced by the earlier primitive types. The experience of those tragic months made the inhabitants glad enough to revert to the "known forms of English law." This welcome was no mere superstitious totemism. The freeman was perforce a courtgoer and was aware that justice not dispatched by tested instruments was vulnerable. It is impossible to read the case of *King v. Bayard* (1702)[14] and not be struck with this awareness that proper forms were the sinews of the individual's protection. And when one compares the account of this New York trial with the English cases in the same volume of the *State Trials* the conclusion is inescapable that the colonials were by this time almost as knowledgeable as the men at home. This report was not just a carefully prepared affair for the purpose of influencing opinion. Minutes of proceedings held a year or so later at the General Sessions for Ulster County with motions to postpone trial, presentments put into indictment form and a motion in arrest based upon nice technical reasons, testify to the extent of common law procedural reception.

Once common law forms become seated, the second stage of reception passes into a phase that may be described as one of selective reproduction of English legal institutions at large. This is essentially a process of imitation, quickened from time to time by the arrival of able craftsmen—the judge Mompesson, the lawyers Alexander, Murray and Smith, and the two Attorneys General, William and John Tabor Kempe. It is a process that can be measured and understood only by examination of the records, the minutes, *posteas,* judgment rolls, pleadings and briefs. And it can be assessed only by a painstaking scrutiny of everything available on contemporary English practice which, as to their Sessions and Assizes, is, alas, only too meager.

The records of the Supreme Court and the General Quarter Sessions of the Peace for the City and County of New York are the sources for appraising the

---

14 Cf. 14 Howell, *State Trials* 486.

best of professional development of provincial law. In the capital were congregated the most skillful lawyers, and from the beginning of the eighteenth century onward, these courts were peopled by men who had legal training. These urban sources standing alone are traverse enough of the stuff propagated as American legal history. They reveal that in one outpost of Europe litigation was conducted as skillfully as at York or Bristol, and that the picture of an oafish frontier jurisprudence is a mirage of writers who have never blown the dust from indictment, pleading or judgment roll.

The penetration of the countryside proceeds at greater leisure, but eventually with considerable completeness. From the records, the story there is obviously different and involves factors that have commonly been overlooked. The business of a General Sessions in the country was mainly the charge of the justices of the peace, and of those unsung heroes—the clerks of the peace. In the early eighteenth century, professional contacts were casual—a lawyer deputized by the Attorney General will now and again appear for the Crown, and occasionally a city barrister will make the arduous journey to Southold or to Kingston. After 1750 there is a Deputy Attorney General in most counties, and there are local lawyers like Moss Kent in Dutchess or Peter Yates in Albany who occasionally appear at Sessions although their chief business is in the local Common Pleas. By this time, however, the patterns are set and it has been largely the work of laymen, the squires on the bench, the clerks and the freeholders from whom the juries are picked.

In some few instances nearly all the documents relating to a prosecution in these inferior courts have been preserved—from the first complaint, through the meeting of the justices who examine witnesses, the warrant to take the offender, the indictment, subsequent process and the minutes of the General Sessions where trial is finally had. There is nothing very complex about the procedure. What is noteworthy is the businesslike way in which everything is done—the meeting minuted, the examinations carefully taken, the precepts in the correct form—no different from what it would have been in English Yorkshire or Sussex, and all without benefit of schools of law administration or watchful bar associations.

There is some inkling of how the *ordo judiciorum* spread. In 1738 James Livingston sent to "Cozen Henry" in Dutchess County a bill for Jacob's *Law Dictionary,* Bohun's *Declarations* and *The Clerk's Instructor.*[15] Henry Livingston had become clerk of the peace in 1737, and he was still in the office when

---

[15] In a letter of April 24, 1738, *Livingston Mss.* 1.

Howe's men came staggering into White Plains.[16] Henry's monument is unique—a formidable array of papers filed in the Dutchess County Court House and divers nicely written volumes of minutes. They bear witness as few muniments now can of the part that the ordinary man of substance had in the spread of English law and the English way of doing things. In this process, as we have suggested, the freeholders all shared. They were a minority in every county, but because they were propertied they had to bear responsibility. They were enormously litigious as the civil records show. That they had a canny flair for finding their way in procedure is indicated in the spread of the plea *nolo contendere,* and the development of appeals from justices' orders.

Sessions business on the judicial side, as already remarked, was not intricate in New York, but neither was it in the English shires. There was not an enormous amount to master, and the technicalities were not beyond the grasp of a persistent courtgoer. Furthermore, as we shall describe, a Supreme Court judge came down annually on circuit, with the hardier members of the bar at his heels, and at a Court of Oyer and Terminer and General Gaol Delivery and a Court of Causes brought to Issue in the Supreme Court gave demonstration of the metropolitan way. For things not rightly done at Sessions or beyond its jurisdiction, or likely to be muddled, there was the writ of certiorari, and by a diligently fostered system of removals the finger of the central authorities was kept upon local courts. For the foolish, incompetent or knavish official there was the information, the attachment for contempt or the Governor's power of removal. But all of this was monitory or corrective. The task of building a provincial law into the lives of the farmers and villagers was done chiefly by themselves. The motto which the Richmond clerk inscribed in his record book is testimony of their intentions:[17]

> *Quid faciunt Leges ubi sola pecunia regnat*
> *Aut ubi paupertas vincere nulla potest.*

The fact that attendance upon the courts and participation in the administration of the law, especially in the country, was an incident of the freeman's duty as much as the paying of rates, does not wholly account for the spread and assimilation of English practices. On both levels—the usage in inferior courts and the infinitely more intricate practice of superior courts—the reception of English law was furthered, as already noticed in the case of Henry Living-

---

[16] He was made clerk of the peace by the State May 8, 1777 (1 *Journal of the Provincial Congress* [1842] 917).

[17] *Ms. Mins. Richmond Co. Sess. 1710/11–1744* 45.

ston, by the use of English law books. Provincial patriotism in New York never went the length of exacting that only products from the presses of William Bradford or James Parker were to be studied and used in the courts. And since the intellectual home of colonial lawyers was still centered in the dingy streets about the Inns of Court, they read and cited what lawyers did at home. That is why James Alexander, William Smith, Joseph Murray, Richard Nicholls and other New York attorneys collected every book they could lay their hands on; why James De Lancey, Chief Justice of New York, was among the original subscribers to Viner's *Abridgment;* why nearly every early treatise used in the preparation of this volume bears the name of an eighteenth century New York practitioner. And lest this state of civilization here be thought exceptional, the library of Thomas Bordley of Maryland,[18] of William Samuel Johnson of Connecticut,[19] and the commonplace book of young Thomas Jefferson are thought-provoking exhibits to the contrary.

English law books were prized in New York because it was from English precedent that provincial law was built. To the extent, as in the case of General Sessions, that a virtual counterpart existed in England, the authority and jurisdiction of the colonial court could be developed into close resemblance with the aid of a Lambard, a Dalton, a Nelson or a Shaw. But in the case of the Supreme Court, endowed with the powers of King's Bench, Common Bench and Exchequer, the question of source was complicated. If a second process was needed to summon jurors, should it be the *distringas* of King's Bench or the *habeas corpus* of Common Bench? Should an Exchequer information be brought on a forfeited bond, or a *scire facias,* and if the latter what leeway should defendant have—that given by the Barons or that given by the Lords Justices? Such were the types of problem with which both lawyers and judges had to grapple, and inevitably they saw the springs from which they must draw as the sum of available learning on English law and practice.

The lawyers' solution of their immediate problem of accommodating the usage of English courts to a different jurisdictional scheme and altered circumstances posits for the legal historian the basic question of the second stage of reception in New York—how much was copied and what was innovation? To questions of this sort the answer is often difficult to give, but so far as our proof permits we have sought to show what the New Yorkers created and what was docilely accepted. The record in this relation is not a matter of

---

[18] To Mrs. J. Montgomery Gambrill who is preparing a biography of Bordley we are indebted for a view of this inventory.

[19] Now reposing in the Law Library, Columbia University.

boasting for those who honor the American genius for originality. The criminal law and procedure more than any other part of English law needed purging, but beyond abandoning some of the more barbarous incidents and making numerous small procedural changes the judiciary was acquiescent.

This matter of innovation during the eighteenth century is affected somewhat by acts of assembly. Some of these provincial statutes merely parroted Acts of Parliament which did not extend to the plantations, and some were novel. But it was unusual for anything markedly original to become law, for throughout the colonial period the spirit of adventure languished under the cloud of the royal power of disallowance. Notable, of course, in the criminal field are the provincial acts setting up special machinery for the trial of slaves, and those for the summary trial of offenses below the degree of grand larceny where the accused could not give bail (1732). These latter statutes are the most striking in a steady stream of legislation extending summary jurisdiction, a trend characteristic also of contemporary English penal enactment, which certainly affected thinking in New York. As matter of sheer bulk the multiplication of penal acts was perhaps the most important contribution of the provincial legislature to the criminal procedure, and it is this bulk which has led to misunderstanding and misinterpretation—indeed, has colored the whole approach of lawyers to the problem of colonial criminal law.

The valiant service which a massing of colonial statutes can perform is illustrated by the effects produced in an academic sortie made some years ago against a privilege of jury trial in misdemeanors.[20] A seemingly impressive record of colonial indifference was achieved by the mere volume of the matter cited on the extension of summary jurisdiction, but no effort at a serious investigation of the circumstances relating to these enactments was undertaken. Instead, certain conjectures were made, such as the explanation that the statutory development in New York was due to the efforts of the royal administrators to cope with a heterogeneous population. Considering the continuous state of tension in the relations between the governors of New York and the assemblies, this seems an unsupportable hypothesis and would hardly have been proffered if the authors had done more than shepherd their statutes. The legislation of another age has meaning only if examined in connection with the social, economic and political factors which conditioned the enactment. The material which we have examined indicates that the problem of

[20] Frankfurter and Corcoran, Petty Federal Offences and the Constitutional Guaranty of Trial by Jury, 39 *Harvard Law Rev.* 917, 945 (1926).

vagabondage and the desire to relieve legislators' local budgets of the costs of detention and relief led the New York legislators to favor summary trial.[21] Unquestionably, too, the limited franchise and the composition of the provincial legislature were factors of importance. The common man, who had no vote, had nothing to say about the making of these laws. It was he who felt the flick of summary justice, and his opinion about it is apparent in the mock trials of Justice Peters and Justice Hough conducted by the rioters in Dutchess and in Cumberland counties. Although when the war came he shouldered a musket to fight for his beliefs, he had nothing to say about the cautious "jury trial as heretofore used," the form in which the Constitution of 1777 guaranteed his right. And fifty years were to pass before his voice was entitled to be heard. Against this background one cannot help feeling uneasiness when historical research is confined to the text of enactments alone, particularly if the levy of defunct statutes is made for the defeasance of a living constitution.

This specimen of legal historiography with its one-sided emphasis upon statutes, its bland disregard of circumstance, is typical of a prevailing mode of history writing by lawyers. We are in such fundamental disagreement with this manner of approach that we must consider at some length the postulates of method. The historical writing to which we take exception (and other examples will shortly be given) is flawed by two assumptions, both tacit, both indefensible. In the first place, it is assumed that command of contemporary law qualifies for expert opinion on the law of Coke's day or of Holt's. This fallacy seems to stem from a confusion of the role of the scholar with that of the judge. In the case of the judge who is presumed to know the law and who, to determine what has been settled as law, must fix the genealogy of a rule, the fiction is tolerated that the law is ageless. So, if he has something to say about old law, not merely *obiter,* even if he is wrong as a matter of fact, his statement stands as valid until overruled, for the judge is making a pronouncement of law. On the other hand, no presumptions protect the historian of the law, and by no fiction can his mastery of Abbot's *Forms* validate what he may say about Coke's *Book of Entries.* The end of his inquiry is not to formulate a rule of law by reference to the past—it is to uncover the state of the law at a given time. He should know that this is but an inquiry into facts even although these facts are rules of law, incidents of practice and the circumstances relating to them. The legal historian is exactly in the position of a

---

[21] *Infra* 117, 382, 606 *et seq.*

witness on foreign law at trial—he must qualify for the time of which he speaks, as the foreign expert qualifies for the law of the place.

The second and no less unwarrantable assumption relates to the matter of proof. In the teeth of everything a lawyer knows about the nature and quantum of proof these writers, when they deal with historical matter, cleave to a scintilla of evidence theory. They take a proposition as proven with the minimum of citation. A rule of law will be bottomed on a single case or statute; judicial practices will be settled by reference to statutes alone. This is the way of advocacy, not of scholarship. It is the method of forensic combat, not the method of investigation. The ends of legal history are not served by the mere establishment of a *prima facie* case. There is no adversary to whom the burden of proof or the duty of going forward with the evidence can be shifted. A legal historical investigation is not to be conceived as the hasty assembling of matter for a trial memorandum, but as being in the nature of an inquest of office at which the available and relevant data will be collected and made of record.

Unhappily, relevance has been predetermined by availability and availability has come to mean what stands in cold print on library shelves. So it has happened that, because the acts of colonial legislatures are ordinarily accessible, lawyers who write about early American law are prone to regard a mere polling of colonial acts as an adequate method of composing legal history. No one writing today of the Volstead Act and its satellites would risk the criticism that would be properly his by failing to consider the actualities of enforcement, and the pathological aspects of the national thirst. That the judicial records of the colonial period should be overlooked by a brief writer is forgivable: that they should be ignored by lawyers who purport to write history is not.

The work of the provincial legislatures, considerable though it seems, was but a single factor in the complicated pattern of lawmaking, law transfer and law administration. If the New York Acts of 1732 are to be used as proof of a prevailing indifference to jury trial, surely the records of their enforcement are relevant, and equally the opinion of John Tabor Kempe. If one undertakes to give an account of the office of provincial Attorney General, clearly some reason must be offered for a failure to have fingered the papers of Alexander, Bradley and the two Kempes.[22] If an author devotes a long chapter to colonial appellate procedure, since matters of practice are involved, he does not discharge his burden by marshalling the statutes and leaving untouched the teeming records of what the courts were doing.[23] In the chancery of Clio there are no letters patent to pardon such misprisions.

That compositions which so depart from standards maintained in the discussions of contemporary legal problems should be tolerated by the bar is a strange circumstance which can only be attributed to the training which produces a peculiar confinement of lawyers' critical faculties. From incessant harping upon the distinction, the "common law rule" versus the present state of the law in a particular jurisdiction, lawyers have come to view the common law as a vast immobile corpus in which neither the pulse of time stirs, nor the nerves of circumstance. For anything so old, so ossified, awareness that the law in action and the law in the books are not always identical is of no moment. If Coke or Hale or Blackstone will yield a premise, a bit of dialectical skill can lend it momentary dynamic strength. To a profession which asks so little, a string of ancient statutes with a case or two thrown in is respectable historical achievement.

The lawyers having shown themselves indifferent to proving title to the rich and often exciting land of the law's past, it has become a sort of *res nullius* awaiting an occupant. Although these vacant acres can be properly husbanded only by those who are technically equipped for the task, lay historians, led on by the classification of the law as a social science, have attempted to take seisin.

We have in another place expressed our doubts on the competence of laymen to manage a task for which the lawyer alone is trained.[24] It is difficult enough for one who can step blithely through the mazes of the New York Civil Practice Act to overcome the ambuscades of William Tidd or John Impey. The layman who starts his march into seventeenth or eighteenth century procedure with a staff no stouter than Blackstone's *Commentaries* will soon discover himself in the thorns. To be sure there is no virtue in knowing that *po. se cul.* indorsed on the back of an indictment signifies that a defendant has pleaded the general issue and that a jury has convicted him, but one can make misleading generalizations if one is unaware.[25] There is no great harm in be-

---

[23] Pound, *Appellate Procedure in Civil Cases* (1941) c. III. The short page on the bill of exceptions (p. 94) is a particularly glaring example of how little the solution of hard problems is furthered by the employment of a bad method.

[24] In 43 *Amer. Hist. Rev.* 403 (1938), a review of *Records of the Vice-Admiralty Court of Rhode Island* (edited by D. S. Towle, with an introduction by C. M. Andrews, 1936).

[25] *Infra* 585 n. 147.

lieving that a cause initiated by presentment may be a civil action, but it is a belief an editor of legal records should not entertain.[26]

Our animadversions on the writing of legal history by laymen have earned us reprimand.[27] It is, of course, an American assumption of long standing that given a book or two a man of parts can qualify, if not as a lawyer, at least as a jurist. Lieutenant Governor Cadwallader Colden, in 1764, succumbed to this delusion,[28] but others have learned no lessons from his discomfiture.[29] The bracketing of the law with economics, politics, sociology and whatever other "social sciences" there be, has not *eo ipso* supplied a visa for that terrible and wonderful land charted by Williams in his notes to Saunders. Nevertheless, there have been passages undertaken within its borders and things have been told by these intrepid travellers that make strange listening to one accustomed to the tongue that lawyers speak.[30] Indeed, it is evident that having failed to master the language of the law these historians have failed to penetrate into the realm of its concepts and usages.

The misuse of legal terms is no small distemper which the physic of the dictionary will soon make right, for it casts an informed and critical reader into a mood of doubting the validity of any conclusions that may be offered on any points of law and practice. If one is bred in the law, this is disturbing, because inevitably one's judgment is affected by functional considerations. Our law is one of the few occupations of man where history is of direct and specific utility. Traditionally it is by an inquiry into what the law was or has been that the solution of present perplexities is sought. The further back in time this quest is pressed, the more difficult is the finding, and it is then that the aid of the legal historian is sought. Where such an historian, therefore, undertakes to speak of

---

[26] Morris, *Select Cases of the Mayor's Court of New York City 1674–1784* (1935) 742n.

[27] C. M. Andrews in 4 *Colonial Period of American History* (1938) 222 n. 1. Particulars of this replication to our criticisms in the *Amer. Hist. Rev.* (*supra* n. 16) are dealt with *infra* 44 n. 216; 307 n. 96. Mr. Andrews failed to grasp, and hence to answer, our objection to generalizations about colonial law at large on the basis of matter plucked here and there from various jurisdictions. His charge that we have not seen as many documents relating to the vice-admiralty jurisdiction as he has we admit. But we do not accept the inference he seems to draw that the mere viewing of a mass of material entitles one to speak with not-to-be-disputed authority on a technical subject. Mr. Fredrick Wiener, in a review of the same book (*supra* n. 16), expresses opin-

ions similar to ours (50 *Harvard Law Rev.* 1213 [1937]).

[28] In the case of Forsey v. Cunningham, *infra* 235 n. 37.

[29] Historians should find food for reflection in the comments of John Watts written to Governor Monckton January 10, 1765 (*Letter Book of John Watts* [61 *NYHS Colls.*] 321).

[30] A common law judged "estopped" a vice-admiralty court (*Records of the Vice-Admiralty Court of Rhode Island* 45). In English law before a man need answer a presentment a court officer "had to" frame an indictment (Scott, *Criminal Procedure in Colonial Virginia* [1930] 72). A sworn information in a rape case is referred to as a *qui tam!* (Farrell, *The Superior Court Diary of William Samuel Johnson* [4 American Legal Records, 1942] xxxix).

the past, since it is something a future court may need and use, he assumes a responsibility not lightly to be dismissed. This is a moral obligation the implications of which are far-reaching, for not only must the judge put trust in his word, but the parties litigant whose rights and whose fortunes will be affected by it. Once it is accepted and woven into the fabric of a precedent, it becomes something upon which still others will place reliance. This obligation is of a different order than any imposed by the self-discipline of scholars in the fields of political or economic history. Their code is their own to make and enforce. No man's rights are affected by their mistakes of facts or their misinterpretations of data. The social effects of their work lie beyond the horizon of the moment. A generation can be led by scholarly skepticism to an attitude of cynical irreverence for the achievements of its forefathers and no one can be made chargeable, for when conversion is complete, no one will by that time care. But the historian of the law must be mindful of the especial fealty which he owes. The penalties *pro stultiloquio* have long since vanished, but with digest and citator, those pitiless Mendelian registers of the law, the strain conceived by an historian's sin can be uncovered and his credit forever impaired.

Whether or not lay historians are sensible of the privity which exists between the work of legal scholars and the work of the courts, they have indicated unwillingness that the standards of the profession be applied to them. Apparently the immunity which they have properly enjoyed in their incidental use of legal materials for the writing of political history is supposed to extend to their ventures into the body of the law itself.[31] Indeed, it has been suggested that they are privileged because it is not legal, but institutional, history which they are writing. Such evasive pleading meets none of the issues we have raised respecting competence and responsibility. In the end they must be judged by what they do and not by what they may pretend to have been about.

American legal history is in its infancy, and if it is to be reared in accord with the high standards which have prevailed in the writing of English legal history, the matter of tutelage is crucial. We cannot aspire to Maitland's insight, his felicity of expression, but we can at least emulate his patience, his candor and his industry. These are the virtues essential to the study of our own law, for the first duty of those into whose cure it is committed must be the

---

[31] The distinction was clearly recognized by Herbert Osgood who used legal sources with the greatest discretion in the preparation of his incomparable institutional histories. His sober note on legal history (1 *The American Colonies in the Seventeenth Century* [1930 ed.] 182, n. 2) should be compared with C. M. Andrews' protestations of competence to write on "historical law" (4 *Colonial Period of American History* 222, n. 1).

reconstruction of the practice in each colony. All question of technical competence aside, the writings of institutional historians do not inspire confidence that such preliminary labor will be done. In their haste to exploit quickly the new and fascinating addition to the social science family, they have failed to hold discrete the legal developments in each colony, and seduced by their belief in a general colonial history they have indulged in dangerous generalization. We think this no less a demonstration of unfitness than the light-hearted misuse of legal terms. With their first footsteps in Contracts I, lawyers have been schooled to hold singular the several American jurisdictions, and the evidence is overwhelming that the same attitude prevailed in the plantations. Because the colonies each tapped in the same cellar is no reason to assume that each drew in the same amount and of the same vintage, or that the wine bottled in New York was identical with that in South Carolina. Process of New Jersey courts did not run in New York. Jefferson of Virginia, in his catalogue of 1783, classifies the statutes of Massachusetts, Connecticut and other states together with those of Barbados and Bermuda, and calls them "Foreign Law," because that is what they in fact were to him.[32]

Nevertheless, despite what is a basic postulate of our system of public and private law, the records of various colonies have been culled here and there to produce a never existent common American rule.[33] If something is practiced in Massachusetts, it is regarded as valid for any other jurisdiction.[34] The sour complaints of royal officials are whipped together to produce a composite and unflattering picture of the colonial bench and bar at large.[35] Even the barriers of time are lightly leapt, and the legal institutions of the seventeenth century settlers are spoken of as if they remained impervious to the changes which the next century brought.[36]

Synthesis of the sort described may be proper fare for the alimentation of the social historians who function in a pleasant anarchic world of their own.[37] What sustenance such confections can furnish to a lawyer who, for his bread, must settle whether the Statute of Frauds was observed in New York Province,

[32] I am indebted to Marie Kimball for the list. She informs me that the list is not later than 1783 and probably was compiled between that date and 1770 when Jefferson's first collection of books was destroyed by fire. On Jefferson's legal training cf. her excellent book, *Jefferson: The Road to Glory 1743–1776* (1943) c. V.

[33] Morris, *Studies in American Law* (1927) c. I.

[34] Hockett, *Constitutional History of the United States* (1939) 39 *et seq.*

[35] Labaree, *Royal Government in America* (1932) 382 *et seq.*

[36] Reinsch, The Common Law in the Early American Colonies in *Select Essays in Anglo-American Law* (1908) 367, 371, 410 *et seq.*

[37] Compare the matter set forth about the law in Adams, *Provincial Society 1690–1703* (1927) 14, 278; Wertenbaker, *The First Americans 1607–1690* (1929) 209 *et seq.*

or whether under the constitution there is historical warrant for a blue ribbon jury is open to doubt. Where the common law reception statute or constitutional article makes specific reference to the state of the law in the colony,
this calls for an inquiry into facts, which, once established, can be argued as a
once applicable rule of law. Such inquiry is not concluded by forays into the
pantries of other provinces. The judge who would accept in lieu of a documented statement of colonial practice in his own jurisdiction the mince of the
institutional historians or the fragile meringues of social historians does the
law no service.[38]

If we have seemed to speak sharply regarding the well-intentioned efforts of
amateurs in the law to re-create a part of culture that only the technician is
equipped to handle, this should be attributed to a certain pedantic attachment
to truth, and a fear that the already deplorable historiography of lawyers will
be worsened by acquaintance with the fantastic Pandects of colonial law fabricated in the studies of laymen. The practitioner has been criticized for the nar-
rowness of his approach to legal-historical problems, and rightly so. The ambit
of his researches has been fixed by the digests and so far as these will carry him,
he can produce something workmanlike for judicial advisement. In the limbo
of colonial practice on which digests are silent, the lawyer is nearly helpless.
He has consequently proceeded as if he were charged with the abatement of
a nuisance, rather than with the delicate task of reconstructing ideas and procedures at least as complicated as the present system of law. The pressure of
practice is such, however, that unless scholars trained in the law will undertake the burden of making available to the profession the record of colonial
achievement, the choice of American lawyers will remain between the chance
and unreliable gleanings of laymen, and the scarcely more reliable assumption
that the *Commentaries* of Blackstone are a summation of provincial American usage.

It is in discharge of what we conceive to be the duty of the lawyer-historian
that this book has been undertaken. Only one sector in the vast battlegrounds
of seventeenth and eighteenth century law—the enforcement of the criminal

---

[38] In National Labor Relations Board v. Air Associates Inc., 121 *Federal 2nd* 586 (1941) respondent claimed that the trial examiner had been
biassed and it had thus been deprived of a fair trial.
On the point of procedural due process the brief
of respondent referred to cases running back to the
sixteenth century, and cited considerable material
on colonial practice. The court brushed aside this
matter, and under a misapprehension that one case
(2 Rolle, *Abridgment* 668 H 1, *Dyer* 367, pl. 40)
involved the Statute of Liveries delivered a discourse on that statute buttressed by citation of a
galaxy of college textbooks. The method of this
opinion should be contrasted with the masterly historical exposition of Chief Justice Stone in C. J.
Hendry Co. v. Moore, 318 *U.S.* 133 (1943).

law—has been chosen for reduction. But it is one of perennial interest, for the basic problem of civilized people, the security of man's person and property against his predacious fellows, and the no less important corollary, the protections of the individual against whom the weapons of society may be directed, are still matters of lively concern. Two considerations determined the selection of this problem: in the first place the desirability of filling in what has hitherto been a blank; in the second place the fact that in this relation the provincial records are fecund sources of information. During the late seventeenth and the eighteenth centuries, the English Crown law, except as occasionally modified by statute, was nearly static. Its introduction and development in New York were consequently chiefly matters of practice and administrative detail. And since throughout the period the criminal law was still a first instance jurisprudence, that is to say, a part of the law rarely subjected to the corrective effects of the appellate process, the absence of those precious gems, the reasoned opinions of the judges hearing a cause by way of error, is of small consequence. Indeed, we believe that what has here been threshed out of the apparent chaff of minute books, pleadings, briefs and judgment rolls, should once and for all dispose of the fatuous preconception that colonial legal history cannot be written because there are not sufficient provincial decisions.

The manner in which the widely scattered sources upon which our conclusions are based has been reduced to order could no doubt have been improved upon. Indeed, we suspect that our regard for Serjeant Hawkins' *Pleas of the Crown* has predisposed us to his ideas of systematizing a subject not without its confusions even in England. The clarity of that eighteenth century practitioner's approach, as yet unhampered by the coils of juristic fashion—whether natural law, realism or sociological jurisprudence—inevitably possesses attractions to those who must establish a method for an historical enterprise of some complexity. Our problem was from the first complicated by the fact that since the death of Herbert Osgood, our greatest colonial historian, the study of political institutions on the basis of native materials has sadly languished. It therefore became necessary to settle numberless details, particularly of local administration, without which one cannot understand the actual functioning of royal government in America. What was begun as a study in procedure has thus overflowed into peripheral and incidental matter which a lawyer may think dispensable. He may find his solace, however, in the minutiae of process and similar matter which have been set forth in all their arid detail. Of such dull stuff as the use of *alias* and *pluries,* of bench warrants and estreats, the reception of English law consisted. It is futile to speak in generalities of reception, unless such prosy particulars of practice are first determined.

So far as the sources and the limitations of a procedural study have permitted, it has been sought in this work to take account of the various factors in the life of the colonists that helped to mold the criminal law, and which gradually gave a peculiar provincial cast to what was received. At this late date, however, too much has perished for us to answer with precision the exiguous command of the commission of oyer and terminer—*per quam vel per quem cui vel quibus quando qualiter et quomodo*—a formula for historical inquiry hard to excel, and hard to discharge.

Finally, it is proper we speak of our illusions regarding the utility of a study of this sort. The citizen must seek the most immediate protections of his right not in the federal constitution but in the fundamental law of his state. Whatever may be the case in other jurisdictions, the constitution of the state of New York in the article on jury trial, the article on the jurisdiction of the Supreme Court and others have raised a beckoning finger to the past and thus will not suffer the deeds of colonial lawyers and judges to sleep in death. The days of judgment when happenings in the reigns of our one-time Kings must be accounted for have become rarer than they were in the youth of the Republic, but they may still be days of moment. At no time, perhaps, since Sir Guy Carleton sailed out of New York Bay, is the substance of what was then joyfully celebrated more close to becoming shadow. Whatever of freedom we have sought to protect by law has been something wrested by the individual with or without benefit of judges, and it behooves us not to forget. Restless lie the bones of Martin Marprelate who printed his tracts under English hedges, of Francis Makemie whom Lord Cornbury had prosecuted for unlicensed preaching on Long Island, since Rosco Jones' conviction for peddling religious tracts without a license was sustained by the highest court in our land.[39]

It is the tradition of our law that examples may prevail, if reason does not suffice.[40] This we think is peculiarly apposite in respect of the citizen's right

[39] Jones v. City of Opelika, 316 *U.S.* 584 (1942). Since this volume went to press the Supreme Court on rehearing reversed the judgment in this case (63 *Sup. Ct. Rep.* 890 [1943]). We have not changed our text as we are not persuaded the disturbance precipitated in 1940 by the decision in Minersville School District v. Gobitis, 310 *U.S.* 586, has subsided. In the Gobitis case Mr. Justice Stone was the solitary dissenter. The court divided 5–4 in the first Jones case. Shortly thereafter Mr. Justice Byrnes, who had concurred with the majority, resigned. This judgment was reversed (5–4) when his successor, Mr. Justice Rutledge, sided with the previous dissenters. Under the circumstances one cannot yet be easy that the issue of religious liberty is safely placed beyond future unsettlement.

[40] *Dialogus de Scaccario* (Hughes, Crump and Johnson. eds., 1902) I, xii.

where the dry phrases in which his protections are cast will succumb to the compulsion of logic unless their meaning as the distillation of past happening is kept clear. Only thus can there be intelligent choice when the moment comes to decide whether there is more virtue in losing touch with the past than in harkening to its lessons. The alien corn which seems so ravishing to many of our generation may be more green than the fields so long and so toilfully ploughed, but there have been good harvests here and the tale of the reapings may move men to cherish the old seed.

CHAPTER I

THE BASIS OF JURISDICTION

THROUGHOUT the ages the history of the common law has been enlivened by disputes and struggles over jurisdiction. Some of the most spectacular battles were waged in the seventeenth century, and as this was the period when American law first comes into being, it was inevitable that echoes of jurisdictional strife should here be heard from the very beginning. In provincial New York the struggle revolved about the warring theories of Crown and colonists —on the one hand a policy of close control and centralized administration, on the other a strong predilection for local autonomy and decentralization. It was in disputes over the law and legal institutions that resentment was nurtured against what were conceived to be the oppressions and injustices of royal officials. It was in the courts that the colonists were indoctrinated to revolution.[1]

According to theories prevalent in 1664, the English Crown was the ultimate source of law and authority in the plantations of the New World. This legislative authority derived from the peculiar constitutional status of these lands which at common law were conceived to be dominions of the King in the right of his Crown, because they were deemed by a legal fiction to have been acquired by conquest, and the King, as conqueror, "seeing that he hath the power of life and death he may at his pleasure alter and change the laws."[2]

The Royal Charters

It is important to notice that the earliest and most important instrument dealing with the governance of New York, the charter to James, Duke of York,[3] issued before the reduction of the Dutch colony and was esteemed a valid conveyance of the territory involved because the English Crown regarded the lands as usurped by the Dutch. Charles II and his ministers were, of course, quite aware that a conquest in fact would have to be made, and that whatever might be pretended or advanced as a matter of English law respecting Crown's rights, Dutch claims could be extinguished only by force. And

---

[1] On the role of the common law in early Revolutionary doctrine cf. Goebel, Constitutional Hist. and Constitutional Law (38 *Col. Law Rev.* 555).

[2] Calvin's Case, 7 *Coke Rep.* 1, 17b. The King could obtain a kingdom only by descent or conquest. Conquest might be from a Christian king or from infidels, and with the latter, as they were

perpetui inimici, there was perpetual hostility. Cf. on the King's prerogative, the Case of the Earl of Derby, 2 *And.* 115. The notion of Englishmen taking their law with them is first announced in Blankard v. Galdy, *Holt, K.B.* 341; cf. also 2 *Peere Williams* 75.

[3] 1 *Col. Laws NY* 1, Mar. 12, 1663/64.

this was what was done. An expedition was dispatched, and New Netherland after brief resistance surrendered on August 29, 1664.

Until the year 1673 when the Dutch retook the province, English rights as to
the rest of the world were the result of a conquest by force of arms, ratified by
the Treaty of Breda[4] through the circumstance that the rule of *uti possidetis*
as to all territory was incorporated in the treaty. As a matter of English constitutional law the title rested, in respect to all the land claimed in North
America,[5] upon the fictitious conquest from the infidels by whom it was
peopled, for not otherwise could the letters patent to James be deemed valid.

By the Treaty of Westminster of 1674 the United Provinces restored New
York to the King of England[6] and the Treaty of Breda was explicitly confirmed and renewed. A second charter was issued to the Duke of York in
substantially the same form as the first, probably to cure any possible defects
in his title arising out of the mutations of seisin through conquest and formal
restoration to the Crown. Since the Treaty of Breda was confirmed and since
English law based nothing on any international doctrines of cession (if, indeed, these can be said to have existed at this time) the province was regarded
as conquered from the Dutch, and as late as 1774 Lord Mansfield in *Campbell*
v. *Hall* referred to New York as an example of the Crown's right in case of a
conquest.[7]

The charter of 1664 upon which the Duke of York's rights as proprietor
were grounded was granted by Charles II by virtue of his uncontested prerogative. This document being the vehicle whereby the nearly unlimited governmental powers of the Crown were delegated was of sovereign importance for
it was in a very literal sense the "fundamental law" of the colony.[8] It conveyed

> . . . full and absolute power and authority to Correct punish Pardon Governe
> and Rule all such the Subjects of us our heires and Successors as shall from
> tyme to tyme Adventure themselves into any the parts or Places aforesaid or that
> shall or doe att any tyme thereafter Inhabite within the same according to such
> Lawes Orders Ordinances direccons and Instruments as by our said dearest
> Brother or his Assignes shall bee established And in defect thereof in Cases of

[4] 2 Davenport, *Treaties Bearing on the Hist. of
the United States* (1929) 123.
[5] "For the Laws of England do not extend to
Virginia, being a conquered Country," per Holt,
C.J., in Smith v. Brown, 2 *Salkeld* 666. Cf. also the
argument of counsel in East India Co. v. Sandys,
1683 (10 Howell, *State Trials* 374, 391, 440).
[6] Davenport, *op. cit.* 229.
[7] 1 *Cowper* 204.

[8] This expression is used advisedly. Although
the colonists in New York during the proprietorship did not speak of the charter as a "fundamental
law" but based their claims to certain privileges
upon the common law, any legal analysis of jurisdiction perforce must treat the charter as the fundament. Cf. *infra* 325. For later references to a
"fundamental law," see *Ms. Mins. of the Debating
Club 1768–74.*

necessitie according to the good discreccons of his Deputyes Commissioners Officers or Assignes respectively as well in all Causes and matters Capitall and Criminall as Civill both Marine and others SOE ALLWAYES as the said Statutes Ordinances and Proceedings bee not contrary to but as neare as conveniently may bee agreeable to the Lawes Statutes and Governement of this our Realme of England AND SAVEING and reserveing to us our heirs and Successors the receiveing heareing and determineing of the Appeale and Appeales of all or any Person or Persons of in or belonging to the Territories or Islands aforesaid in or touching any Judgment or Sentence to bee there made or given AND FURTHER that it shall and may bee lawfull to and for our said dearest Brother his heires and Assignes by these presents from tyme to tyme to Nominate make Constitute Ordeyne and Confirme by such Name or Names Stile or Stiles as to him or them shall seeme good and likewise to revoke discharge Change and alter as well all and singuler Governors Officers and Ministers which hereafter shall bee by him or them thought fitt and needfull to bee made or used within the aforesaid Parts and Islands and alsoe to make Ordayne and Establish all manner of Orders Lawes direccons Instruccons formes and Ceremonies of Government and Magistracy fitt and necessary for and concerneing the Government of the Territories and Islands aforesaid soe allwayes as the same bee not contrary to the Lawes and Statutes of this our Realme of England butt as neare as may bee agreeable thereunto. . . .[9]

By its terms the charter granted absolute and supreme legislative, executive and judicial control to one authority, centering all power in the hands of the proprietor. But there were limits to the grant: the Duke was subject to the Crown's appellate supervision and to the necessity of conforming as nearly as possible to English law.

The exact significance of this last restriction is difficult to assess. Since the time of Henry VII, it had been usual to insert this or an equivalent clause in grants and charters to individuals or companies engaged in overseas enterprise,[10] partly because the exercise of by-law power was traditionally supposed

---

[9] 1 *Col. Laws NY* 2.

[10] The early charters to merchant groups trading abroad had contained no such limitation. Thus, the charters of Henry IV to the merchants in Prussia gave power to make reasonable ordinances with no further restrictions (8 Rymer, *Foedera* 360 [1404]). So too the charter to the Holland merchants (*ibid.* 464 [1406]) and those trading in Norway and Sweden—the later Eastland Co. (*ibid.* 511 [1408]). However, there are actually too few early charters of this type to have resulted in any policy formulation. The question of control over ordinance power comes into sharp focus as a domestic matter during the reign of Henry VI, when a statute was enacted forbidding the enactment by gilds, fraternities or companies of ordinances which diminished royal prerogative and were against the common weal, and charging the justices of the peace with supervisory powers (15 Hy. VI c.6). This statute was substantially reenacted during Henry VII's reign (19 Hy. VII c.7), but provided for assent to by-laws by the chancellor, treasurer, the chief justices or any three of them, or by the judges of assize for the county where the ordinance

to conform to common law standards, and partly because the government was already committed by statute to a policy of supervising the rules of domestic bodies. Consequently some warning of surveillance of activities conducted by Englishmen in regions beyond the reach of the statutory machinery was desirable. There is no evidence that the employment of the conformity formula was at all connected with the safeguarding of the royal prerogative over legislation, but the opinion in *Calvin's Case* (1608)[11] undoubtedly lent the charter clauses a new and important significance. This case, sometimes called the Case of the *Postnati,* was one of extraordinary constitutional importance for it determined the status of the Scots born after the accession of James I, and all the

had been made. It will be observed that this form of control was far from practical in dealing with any company operating outside of England, even if the traditions had been less liberal than they were in favoring such enterprises. It is not surprising therefore that none of the earliest English enterprises connected with the discovery and settlement of America were subjected to any restriction. The patents for Cabot being in the nature of licenses have nothing to say about ordinance powers (12 Rymer, *Foedera* 595; 2 Harrisse, *John and Sebastian Cabot* [1882] 393). However, the two patents to the Bristol syndicate (1501, 1502) were more grandly conceived and granted the fullest legislative powers with no restriction whatever (Biddle, *A Memoir of Sebastian Cabot* [1831] 306; 13 Rymer, *Foedera* 37).

The statute relating to by-laws was enacted in 1504, and the following year was granted the first charter we have seen to restrict the ordinance power of companies operating abroad—the charter to the powerful Merchant Adventurers (2 Schanz, *Englische Handelspolitik gegen Ende des Mittelalters* [1881] 549, 552; Cawston and Keane, *Early Chartered Companies* [1896] 249). It is significant that a policy which had developed in respect to a purely domestic problem should have thus been carried over to the regulation of companies operating overseas, and via the instrumentality of the charter. Twenty-five years later restriction in the form that ordinances against the "publique welthe" of the subjects were to be of no effect, is contained in the charter of Henry VIII to the Merchants trading to Andalusia (1531): Carr, *Select Charters of Trading Companies* (Selden Soc. 1913) 3. The charter to the Russia Company of 1555, possibly because of the success and importance of the enterprise, is the first to employ the phraseology which was to be used in the American charters (2 Hakluyt, *Principal Navigations, Voyages, etc.* [1903 ed.] 304) for the ordinance power was limited: "And so alwayes, that such their acts, statutes and ordinances bee not against our prerogative, lawes, statutes, and customes of our realm and Dominion . . ." (*ibid.* at 311).

Whether by accident or design, the limitation on the legislative authority of companies which were to conduct either trading or colonizing activities overseas thus came into being. In Elizabeth's reign the charters to important trading enterprises all have the formula of restriction; cf. the charter to the Merchant Adventurers of 1564 (Cawston and Keane, *op. cit.* 254), the charter to the Eastland Company (Sellers, *Acts and Ordinances of the Eastland Co.* [1906] 142, 145), the charter to the Levant Company of 1581 (5 Hakluyt, *op. cit.* 192, 194), the charter to the Barbary Merchants of 1585 (6 *ibid.* 419–421). Moreover, the purpose of exacting conformity to common law ceases to be associated primarily with groups of entrepreneurs or bodies corporate and is deemed an essential restriction upon plantations, for it is carried over to charters granted to individuals as, for example, that to Sir Humphrey Gilbert of 1578 (Shafter, *Sir Humfrey Gylberte* [Prince Soc. 1903] 95, 100), and that to Raleigh of 1584 (8 Hakluyt, *op. cit.* 289, 294).

The first important exception to what (in default of a complete diplomatic study of the Tudor charters) we may regard by 1600 as settled Chancery policy is the charter to the Virginia promoters, 1606 (1 Brown, *Genesis of the United States* [1897] 52 *et seq.*). This instrument did not convey legislative powers, but the instructions subsequently issued specifically permitted a limited authority to be exercised consonant with the laws of England "or the equity thereof," subject to royal review, and to the further reservation of royal ordinance power (*ibid.* 73, 74). When the London Company was incorporated in 1609, however, full ordinance power was granted "as near as conveniently may be agreeable to the laws, statutes, government and policy of our realm of England." Thereafter this formula or its equivalent is the rule for the American charters. The early history of this matter deserves a closer examination than it is here practical to make.

[11] 7 *Coke Rep.* 1a.

judges, the Lord Chancellor, the law officers of the Crown and certain leading barristers participated in the argument. Here in addition to the points immediately in issue were settled for generations to come the basic rules respecting the King's prerogative to make at his pleasure laws for conquered countries, and here was laid down the fateful proviso that once the law of England was introduced into a conquered Christian country it could not be altered except by Parliament. Since the words of the charter just quoted could hardly be taken as an explicit direction to introduce English law, and thereby to divest the Crown of its prerogative, this formula operated during the seventeenth century as a safeguard against Parliamentary interference and at the same time, since it was itself a declaration of royal policy, enabled the Crown to control unpalatable innovation. Not until just before the American Revolution was it even suggested by the courts that the royal prerogative in conquered countries was subordinate to the King in Parliament.[12]

The effect of the charter provision as respects the Crown was thus to reserve implicitly a control over legislation enacted by the proprietor. At the same time it set up a standard which was subsequently to be a chief canon in the policy of the Crown agencies for the administration of colonial affairs.[13] As far as the colonists were concerned, the charter provision was of no avail to them as a ground for demands regarding the laws of the province.[14] But subsequently, when James became king and the control over legislation depended simply upon royal policy, the requirement of conformity with the law of England was regarded by the provincials as much more than the imposition of a standard. With the progressive assimilation of common law doctrine and practice, the notion that the common law was a fundamental law, to the benefits of which the colonists were entitled, gained sway. The position of the extremists was essentially as illogical as that of the Crown. They desired everything in the way of benefit, and at the same time wished to be free to make innovation or change as might seem expedient. The Crown, on the other hand, was anxious to preserve its as yet unshorn prerogative abroad, and so, while it promoted the adoption of English law on all points which did not trench upon the prerogative, it resisted all efforts of the colonists to exploit the political implications of certain common law rules, and denied them the advantages of the legislative changes wrought by successive revolutions in England.[15]

---

12 Campbell v. Hall (1774), 1 *Cowp.* 204.
13 This matter will be considered exhaustively in J. H. Smith, *Appeals to the Privy Council from the American Plantations* shortly to be published for the Foundation for Research in Legal History.

14 Thus the petition of the Court of Assizes to the Duke of York (1681) makes no reference whatever to the charter provision (45 *NYHS Colls.* [1912] 15–17).
15 An example is the attitude of Andros toward

We have dwelt upon this matter because the whole question of jurisdiction and the scope of judicial power in New York Province was greatly affected by the various theories respecting the exact status of the common law. The old issue—was the prerogative under the law?—could only be drawn if it could be established that the common law was in fact the fundamental law of the Province. On this point even the colonists were not wholly in agreement, and the home authorities steadfastly clung to the view that as far as the colonies were concerned this law was not "fundamental" but merely embodied a policy over which the Crown possessed an administrative discretion.

The Proprietary and the Royal Commission and Instructions

At the time the Duke of York's charter passed the seals these controversies still lay in the future. The Crown made its reservations, but as yet no instrumentality had been developed to make these really effective. As a practical matter the Duke possessed and exercised a vast governmental authority and this he in large measure delegated by commission to his governors.[16] The Duke, however, did not wholly relinquish all his authority for his commissions obliged his deputies to follow such directions as he should issue from time to time.[17] The instructions to the Duke's first governor cannot be found,[18] but they undoubtedly gave Colonel Nicolls the power to set up courts and establish a system of justice.[19] The instructions to Nicolls' immediate successors, how-

the extension of the Habeas Corpus Act (31 Car. II c.2) to the colonies (1 *Andros Tracts* [Prince Soc. 1868] 15, 46).

[16] See Nicolls' commission of 1664, 2 Brodhead, *Hist. of NY* (1871) 653; Leaming and Spicer, *Grants, Concessions, etc. of New Jersey* 665. On Lovelace's commission, see 1 *Col. Laws NY* xiii; Fowler, *Bradford's Laws* (Grolier Club ed.) lviii. For Andros' commission of 1674 see 3 *Doc. Rel. Col. Hist. NY* 215, and for Dongan's commission of 1682, *ibid.* 328. There was no substantial variance in these commissions but, on the other hand, we shall see that the Governor's instructions undergo some changes.

[17] The commission to the Duke's first governor, Richard Nicolls, after reciting the Duke's charter provided that Nicolls as "deputy" governor was "to perform and execute all and every the powers which are by the said Letters Patents granted unto me, to be execute [*sic*] by my deputy, agent or assign. To have and to hold the said place . . . during my will and pleasure only . . . the inhabitants . . . to give obedience to him the said Richard Nicolls, in all things according to the tenor of his Majesty's said Letters Patents, and the said Richard Nicolls Esq. to observe follow and execute such

orders and instructions as he shall from time to time receive from myself" (Leaming and Spicer, *Grants, etc. New Jersey* 666).

[18] Cf. 2 Brodhead, *Hist. of NY* (1871) 18 n.

[19] The articles of capitulation (2 *Doc. Rel. Col. Hist. NY* 250) have nothing to say regarding the future system of law and the courts. They confirmed Dutch customs of inheritance and contained an agreement to leave previous judgments of Dutch courts undisturbed with a right of appeal to the States General. The articles have a stipulation that a copy of the grant to James and the latter's commission to Nicolls be delivered to the Dutch governor. On June 12, 1665, Nicolls issued a proclamation revoking the Dutch and establishing the English form of government in New York City. 1 *Doc. Hist. NY* 389, and 1 *Col. Laws NY* 100. In this proclamation Nicolls recited that "for the more Orderly establishment of his Majesties Royal authority as near as may be Agreeable to the Lawes and Customes of his Majesties Realme of England; upon Mature deliberacon. . . . I have thought it necessary to Revoke & discharge . . . fforme and Ceremony of Government of this his Majesties Towne of New Yorke." Also cf.

ever, carefully restricted the law-making power accorded by the commissions and expressly commanded the Governor to put into execution the same laws and to continue the same courts already established.[20]

In 1682/83 a change in the Duke's policies[21] resulted in the grant of additional powers to the new Governor, Dongan. The commission, like those issued earlier, conferred on the Governor the same powers granted to the Duke, subject to the Duke's further orders.[22] But the instructions[23] gave the Governor and Council, assisted by the newly created popular assembly,[24] the power to make all laws necessary for the "good weale and government" of the colony, subject, however, to veto by the Governor and the Duke, and subject also to the proviso that "noe man's life, member, freehold, or goods, be taken away or harmed . . . but by established and knowne laws not repugnant to but as nigh as may be agreeable to the lawes of the kingdome of England." This provision is a forerunner of our modern constitutional right to due process and is to be found in subsequent instructions to colonial governors of New York.[25]

Proclamation of 1664, Leaming and Spicer, *Grants, etc. New Jersey* 667.

In connection with the promulgation of the Duke's Laws it is to be noted that the "Lawes" were "Establisht by Authority of his Majesties Letters patents granted to . . . [the] Duke of York" and were "Published . . . by virtue of a Commission from . . . [the] Duke of Yorke . . . to Colonell . . . Nicolls Deputy Governeur" (1 *Col. Laws NY* 6, 7). Cf. also, "Whereas ye Laws Established in this Government & confirmed by his R. Highnesse though long since publist' yett have not beene put in practisse throughout his R. Highn[ss] his Territoryes, It is ordered that from & aft[er] ye Session of this Court of Assizes, ye body of Laws comprised in one Volume, allowed and confirmed as aforesaid, Togeth[er] wth ye Additions & Amendments be in force in all parts of this Government, & none others Contrary or Repugnant to y[e] Laws of England" (*Ms. Duke's Laws*, Van Cortlandt copy).

[20] The commission to Governor Lovelace in 1667 commanded him to continue the same courts and laws established under Nicolls (1 *Col. Laws NY* xiii; Fowler, *Bradford's Laws* lviii).

The second royal grant to the Duke of York effected no change in his powers (1 *Col. Laws NY* 104) and the latter's commission to Major Andros (1 *Col. Laws NY* 106) gave that Governor the full powers granted to the Duke himself, subject, however, to the instructions which expressly provided (3 *Doc. Rel. Col. Hist. NY* 216 at 218) that he was to continue such laws as were established by Nicolls and Lovelace. Andros could not vary those laws except "upon emergent necessity" with the advice of his council, and such emergency legislation was only to be of one year's duration unless con-

firmed by the Duke. The Governor was to continue the system of courts already established.

[21] In a communication to Lieutenant Governor Brockholls in 1681/82, the Duke announced his intention of establishing "such a form of Government at New York as shall have all ye advantages and privileges . . . wch his Majesties other plantations in America . . . enjoy, particularly in ye chooseing of an Assembly, and in all other things as nere as may be agreable to ye laws of England" (3 *Doc. Rel. Col. Hist. NY* 317).

[22] *Ibid.* 328.

[23] Instructions to Dongan of 1682/83; *ibid.* 331.

[24] Agitation had long been under way for a popular assembly (1 *Col. Laws NY* xiii, xiv) but the Duke writing to Andros in 1675 said that he was to discourage a general assembly since it was not provided for in the instructions or consistent with the government of the colony, and was unnecessary because the colonists had a general assize where the same persons, as justices, were present who would have been their representatives if they had had an assembly (3 *Doc. Rel. Col. Hist. NY* 230). As a further indication of the Duke's policy, a communication to Andros in 1676 (*ibid.* 235) stated that assemblies disturbed the peace of the government, that the Governor and Council alone were to govern according to the laws, and that redress from grievances could be had by appeal.

[25] Cf. 1 Labaree, *Royal Instructions to British Col. Governors* (1935) no. 414. In 1697, the "not repugnant" clause was dropped. It was restored in 1701. The last instruction with this provision was in 1761.

For reasons unknown but quite in harmony with James' sour opinion of legislative assemblies, the new assembly was to have no hand in making a judicial establishment, for the instructions of 1682/83 explicitly directed Dongan, with his Council's advice, to "elect and settle"[26] any courts deemed necessary, provided that the Duke confirmed such establishment and provided also that such courts should be "as nere answerable to ye laws and Courts of Justice in England as may be." This direction and the implicit exclusion of the assembly from a share in erecting the general system of courts remain cardinal rules of policy from this time forward.

It is beyond our purpose to consider all the clauses of these instructions to Dongan; we need notice only certain of the important functions connected with law enforcement that were expressly delegated. Thus, the Governor was given power to pardon before or after conviction all crimes save treason and wilful murder, and in the latter cases he could, in his discretion, submit recommendations for mercy to the Duke, granting a reprieve to the offender in the meantime. Orders were also given to Dongan to take care that drunkenness, debauchery, swearing and blasphemy be punished,[27] and he was advised to have an act passed by the assembly to set the qualifications of jurors.[28]

When the Duke of York became King in 1685 his rights as proprietor devolved upon the Crown and New York thus became a royal province and, being "annexed to our other dominions,"[29] supervision was committed to the agencies then handling the affairs of royal plantations. The charter, of course, was determined, and in its place the commission to the Governor becomes the fundamental source of authority in the Province.[30] The former short and broadly worded warrant under the hand and seal of the proprietor is succeeded by the long and explicit letters patent under the Great Seal that was at this time employed to commission royal governors.

English administrators,[31] and eventually even the judges, speak of the royal commission as the constitution[32] of a royal province, but at the start this expression is used only in the sense that a governmental establishment was thereby

---

[26] *Supra* n. 23.
[27] These and similar provisions appear in all subsequent instructions (2 Labaree, *Instructions* nos. 728, 729).
[28] In Dongan's instructions of 1686 and in all subsequent instructions until 1753 a direction of this sort is made (*ibid.* nos. 417–419).
[29] 3 *Doc. Rel. Hist. NY* 360.
[30] No adequate study of the instrument exists.

There is a brief statement in 1 Osgood, *Amer. Col. in the Eighteenth Century* (1924) 34, to which Labaree, *Royal Government in Amer.* (1930) 30, adds nothing material.
[31] For example, the opinion of the law officers (1747) in 1 Chalmers, *Opinions of Eminent Lawyers* 272; Pownall, *The Administration of the Colonies* (1765) 54.
[32] Campbell v. Hall, 20 Howell, *State Trials* 326.

instituted,[33] and not in the sense that it was a source of right in the colonists.[34] Nevertheless, it should be observed that the commission was in the form of letters patent and was published. Since in certain particulars it conveyed privileges to the inhabitants and contained clauses of limitation in the nature of privileges, it was subject to the rules governing grants of royal right.[35] The most important of these rules, so far as its constitutional implications were concerned, was that when privileges or jurisdictions were created by the King, they did not become extinct by accession of them to the Crown, but time and usage made them appendant.[36] In other words, even although the commission was at pleasure and expired six months after the demise of the Crown,[37] jurisdictional rights once created did not thereby again merge in the Crown. This rule of indefeasible delegation was not laid down with express reference to the colonies until 1774,[38] but it was a very ancient rule of law and was certainly known to colonial lawyers.

A further rule of considerable significance, since it tended to stabilize the form of delegation, was that which restrained commissions to known and stated forms,[39] a rule which was sometimes expressed in terms of the right of the subject.[40] This was initially no limitation upon the prerogative outside the realm, although it was later thought to be,[41] and it is doubtful how a colonial could have availed himself of it except in an action against a governor. Nevertheless, since the royal administration was conducted with some regard to common law rules,[42] and since the critical clauses of the commissions suffered negligible change or addition in point of form, it appears this rule was in fact observed.

The instructions, which issued under the sign manual, were on a different footing. They are sometimes mentioned with the commission as setting a provincial constitution,[43] but they were private directions to the Governor, and

[33] Cf. Report of the Board of Trade (1721), 5 Doc. Rel. Col. Hist. NY 595, 606.

[34] It should be noticed that in Process into Wales (Vaughan 400, 401) it is remarked regarding the plantations "most of them, at present [bound] by laws appointed and made by the King's letters patents." This report was first published in 1677. The dictum does not seem to have been noticed until much later.

[35] Compare the report on Jamaica (1679) in 1 Acts of the Privy Council, Colonial 832: ". . . they cannot pretend to farther Priviledges than have been granted to them either by Charter or some solemn Act under your Great Seal." It was claimed here only a temporary privilege was granted.

[36] Case of the Abbot of Strata Mercella, 9 Co. Rep. 24, 25 b.

[37] After 7 & 8 Wm. III c.27 §21; 1 Anne St. 1 c.8.

[38] Campbell v. Hall, supra n. 7.

[39] Coke, Fourth Institute 164.

[40] 2 Hawkins, Pleas of the Crown c. 1 §§3–8.

[41] Pownall, op. cit. 54.

[42] Compare here 1 Acts of the Privy Council, Colonial 638 (1675); and Bellomont's dispatch as reflecting common understanding (4 Doc. Rel. Col. Hist. NY 515).

[43] Thus Mansfield in Stamp Act Debate (16 Hansard, Parliamentary Hist. 175; 4 Acts of the Privy Council, Colonial 449 [1760]).

although they were on a few occasions read in court and some clauses were entered in the judicial minutes, it was not intended that they should be published at large. Obedience was expected, but obviously the instructions, being the peculiar vehicle of the prerogative, were scarcely an instrument on which the subject could base a claim of right.

The most material immediate changes in the basis of jurisdiction effected by the transformation of New York to a royal province were the shifting of matter from instructions to the commission and the abolition of a colonial assembly. In the matter of the judiciary, Dongan's commission of 1686[44] and that issued to Andros[45] when New York was incorporated into the Dominion of New England (1688) specifically limited the power to establish courts to the Governor and Council.[46] Furthermore, the instructions to Dongan ordered him not to erect courts not already established,[47] and although this admonition was wanting in the Dominion instructions, Andros was ordered to deliver an account of all courts to England for further instructions.[48] It is important to notice that after the Revolution of 1688 this curious combination—an authority in the commission to erect courts but a limitation in the instructions to courts already existing—was resumed and never abandoned.

The royal commission[49] was the vehicle for conveying the most basic legislative, executive and even judicial power. Here is to be found, from 1691 onward, the mandate to convene the assembly and to make laws "as near as conveniently may be agreeable to the laws and statutes of this our Kingdom of England," subject to royal approval and the Governor's veto. The commissions up to 1703 included, further, the clause allowing hearing of appeals by the Governor and Council and allowing appeal to the Privy Council if a cause involved £300 or more. The commission invested the Governor with the power of appointment and commission of judicial officers and the filling of vacancies in the

[44] 3 Doc. Rel. Col. Hist. NY 377.
[45] Ibid. 537.
[46] The style of enacting laws was to be by the Governor and Council "and noe other."
[47] 3 Doc. Rel. Col. Hist. NY 369.
[48] Ibid. 543.
[49] The royal commissions examined include, in addition to those of Dongan and Andros: Sloughter (3 Doc. Rel. Col. Hist. NY 623), Fletcher (ibid. 827), Bellomont (4 ibid. 266), Cornbury (Misc. Ms. Cornbury), Hunter (5 Doc. Rel. Col. Hist. NY 92, 391), Burnet (Ms. Jay Papers Box 3), Montgomerie (5 Doc. Rel. Col. Hist. NY 834), Clinton (6 ibid. 189), Osborne (Smith, History of NY [1814 ed.] 356). The Governors' commissions provided that the Lieutenant Governor was to exer-

cise the powers granted to the Governors: cf. instructions regarding Lt. Gov. Brockholls in 1674 and 1680 (3 Doc. Rel. Col. Hist. NY 219, 283). Cf. the commission to Geo. Clarke in 1736 (6 ibid. 71). The Duke sent special instructions to Lt. Gov. Brockholls in 1681/82 (3 ibid. 317) and the commission to Lt. Gov. Nicholson in 1689 (3 ibid. 606) gave him power to govern the province with the aid of the principal inhabitants. Lt. Gov. Nanfan was commissioned to follow the commission and instructions of Ld. Bellomont (4 ibid. 277) and received special instructions from Bellomont (ibid. 557) to cause impartial justice to be done, to preserve the King's peace and not to pardon without the Governor's consent.

Council. It also gave the powers of remitting fines and forfeitures and of re-prieve and pardon—wilful murder and treason only excepted, matters which the Crown reserved to itself. The seal of the province was committed to the Governor, and finally, in connection with the authority to erect courts, he was invested with a prerogative to make ordinances (with the advice of the Coun-cil) relating to the administration of justice.

There is no doubt that the commission delegated to the Governor the most substantial incidents of the royal prerogative, but the Crown did not intend the delegation to be absolute for the instrument contained the caveat respecting limitation by instruction and by orders which might occasionally issue under the privy seal. General instructions were issued when a governor was commis-sioned, a complex series of directions which were constructed upon a set pat-tern, altered only when for some reason a revision was essential. Supplemen-tary instructions on particular points would occasionally issue.

In relation to the problems with which we are concerned, it should be no-ticed that royal instructions from the year 1686 onward remain with certain few exceptions nearly static; in other words, royal policy respecting law en-forcement is consistent and subject to little change. We have noticed already the limitation upon the erection of any new courts by which the authority of the commission was confined, expressive of an obvious intention to assure the permanence of the judiciary. This was modified only by the addition in 1708[50] of a direction that the assembly take steps to provide a court for determining small causes. This was a move of especial political interest for it was the one concession made by the Crown to the provincial demand to have a voice in the creation of courts, and it was by virtue of this that the civil jurisdiction of the justices of the peace was progressively enlarged.

A second important particular in which royal instructions underwent change was in relation to appeals. In 1703 the mandate respecting appeals, re-ferred to above, was shifted from the commission to the instructions.[51] The article directed allowance of appeals to the Governor and Council in case of error in civil causes involving more than £100. A right of further appeal to the Privy Council of cases involving over £300 under certain conditions of security was also provided.[52] The Governor was also to permit appeals directly to the Privy Council in cases of misdemeanor if the fine exceeded £200.[53] In 1753 this instruction was rewritten, the jurisdictional limit for appeals to the

---

[50] Labaree, *Instructions* no. 435 where there is noted a circular to this effect sent out in 1703.
[51] *Ibid*. no. 448.

[52] *Ibid*. no. 449 and cf. the circular no. 450.
[53] *Ibid*. no. 458 from 1690 to the Revolution, ex-cept in Bellomont's instructions.

New York Council was set at £300 and for appeals to the Privy Council at £500. The words "in case of error" were dropped out, and as we shall see a violent controversy developed over the change.[54]

The instructions further limited the appointive power by requiring local, commissions to be issued without time limit, and later explicitly commanded that these were to issue only at pleasure.[55] The power to remit fines was held down to the sum of £10.[56]

The general instructions contained, further, a variety of miscellaneous and hortatory matter. Thus from 1686 until 1753 the Governor was in one formula or another adjured to get a law for the qualification of jurors;[57] there was a standing order that writs were to run in the King's name;[58] accounts of the courts were to be sent in;[59] with the advice of the Council, fees were to be settled.[60] Until 1761, the due process clause already spoken of was embraced in the instructions[61] and, after 1727, a sharp order respecting speedy and impartial administration of justice was added.[62]

The major points of Crown policy in the administration of New York were couched in the commissions and general instructions, but there was in addition a perennial bombardment of circular letters, special instructions, royal letters and proclamations, Orders in Council and special warrants or mandamuses, and lastly the more dilute forms of royal will expressed in letters from agencies like the Treasury or Admiralty and the Board of Trade. Considering the difficulties of distance and the perils of the sea, a close watch was kept on both the representatives of the Crown and the colonists through the powers of appointment and removal of officers, through the disallowance of provincial acts and through the appeals to the Privy Council.

Common Law and Acts of Parliament

As a matter of law the mandates and directions embodied in the several instruments noticed were the expression of the prerogative, that is to say, they were the articulation, as Holt, C.J., once put it, "of what the King pleases."[63] It is true that, by reiteration, publication and a nearly meticulous observation of certain common law rules by the English officials, an expectation of stability

---

[54] *Ibid.* no. 453 and cf. *infra* 235. The whole matter of appeals instructions is discussed in Smith, *Appeals to the Privy Council.*

[55] Labaree, *Instructions* nos. 512–514 where the variations and changes are noted.

[56] *Ibid.* no. 459.

[57] *Ibid.* nos. 417–419.

[58] *Ibid.* no. 420.

[59] *Ibid.* no. 423.

[60] *Ibid.* no. 521.

[61] *Ibid.* no. 414.

[62] *Ibid.* no. 411.

[63] Smith v. Brown, 2 *Salkeld* 666.

was created that the colonials often urged in terms of right. But it cannot be conceded that the prerogative overseas was under the law as the prerogative within the realm most certainly was in the eighteenth century, a circumstance which enkindled great warmth for the "liberties of Englishmen" and eventually for the rights of man. The assertion by King's Bench in 1693 that Englishmen carried their law with them,[64] built up, at least in New York, a firm belief that even a provincial Englishman possessed certain rights as a subject. The New Yorkers' monotonous harping upon the claim that the colonial was entitled to the common law was the inevitable response to a scheme of government that, in certain particulars, could not concede such a claim without imperilling the prerogative as exercised. By no trick of exegetic dexterity is it possible to twist the provisions of commissions or instructions into a grant of English law to the conquered province in the sense that any important incident of prerogative over law making was divested. The intendment of these instruments was to exact conformity with English law, but only to the extent the Crown saw fit. In other words, so far as the prerogative found it comfortable, the law of England was to be a standard, but it was not to be the possession of the provincials.

The posture which the Crown took with respect to the introduction of the law of England into New York has a most important bearing upon the role of Parliament in making law for the colony. It will be recalled that in *Calvin's Case* it was said that once the law of England was introduced into a conquered country it could only be changed by Act of Parliament. But it was also conceded that even as to dominions (where the law was what the King willed) an Act of Parliament[65] would apply if the dominions were expressly included. Two things about this doctrine are to be noticed. The first is the fact that in theory the English statute is the act of the King in Parliament, and the second is that a considerable body of medieval precedent supported the conception that Parliamentary legislation for dominions of the Crown was exceptional, and to be binding on the dominions an act had to name them specifically.[66] *Calvin's Case* left open the question whether statutes passed before conquest could apply.

When New York was conquered there had yet been no further judicial ruling respecting the vigor outside the realm of general acts of Parliament, al-

---

[64] Blankard v. Galdy, *Holt, K.B.* 341.
[65] And further emphasized by the opinion of the two chief justices and chief baron in "Parliament in Ireland," 12 *Co. Rep.* 109.

[66] The early statutes are discussed in Schuyler, *Parliament and the British Empire* c. 1; cf. also 30 *Col. Law Rev.* 273.

though soon after, in 1669, the Common Bench reiterated the rule regarding Parliament's capacity to legislate for conquered territory.[67] The admonition of the Duke's charter respecting the making of laws not repugnant to the laws of England implies inclusion of basic statutes in this standard, and there can be no doubt from the way the colonists proceeded to develop their law, that no distinctions were drawn between common law and general statutes. The English authorities on their part appear to have regarded the non-mention of plantations in statutes (and the consequent inapplicability) as a conclusive reason why the New Yorker could not claim to be governed by the laws of England,[68] a piece of reasoning which is unique.

The basis for further development of discussion respecting pre-conquest statutes was supplied by the remarks of Holt, in *Blankard* v. *Galdy* (1693).[69] It was said that in newly settled countries all the laws in force in England were in force, but in case of conquest, only when declared by the conqueror, thus indicating a widened base for statutory reception. Subsequently the law officers of the Crown expanded this opinion by the assertion that acts passed before settlement would apply, but not future acts unless the dominions were named.[70] This was in general the posture taken by the Privy Council in appeals cases although there are instances where the Lords Committee refused to treat as applicable laws enacted long before settlement.[71]

From the beginning, the New York lawyers and judges viewed the body of English statutes as a part of the law which they were putting into effect. Some of these statutes, such as those relating to the office of the peace, the riot and forcible entry statutes,[72] were extremely important in the founding and expansion of jurisdiction, and on the whole there seems to have been little attempt by the Crown to interfere with this mode of tacit adoption where the act was old enough and no political issues were involved. The attitude is well summarized in Governor Tryon's report of 1774.[73]

The New Yorkers were perfectly aware of the rule respecting the naming

---

[67] Craw v. Ramsey, *Vaughan* 274.

[68] 3 *Doc. Rel. Col. Hist. NY* 357. In the "Observations" on the so-called Charter of Liberties. "This privelege is not granted to any of his Matᵉ Plantations where the act of Habeas Corpus and all other such bills do not take place."

[69] *Supra* n. 2. Reported also 4 *Modern* 215; 2 *Salkeld* 411.

[70] The opinion of West in 1720, 1 Chalmers, *Opinions* 194; and of Yorke in 1724, *ibid.* 220 who regards reception as dependent on legislation or long usage.

[71] Discussed in Smith, *Appeals to the Privy Council* c. IX.

[72] *Infra* 121 *et seq.*

[73] "The Common Law of England is considered as the Fundamental law of the Province and . . . all the Statutes (not local in their Nature and which can be fitly applied to the circumstances of the Colony) enacted before the Province had a Legislature are binding upon the Colony; but that Statutes passed since do not affect the Colony, unless by being specially named" (8 *Doc. Rel. Col. Hist. NY* 434, 444).

of dominions; the difficulty was that they were named in the sort of statutes they did not like—the Navigation Act, the Act for Preventing Frauds, the acts directed against domestic manufacture. Nevertheless, some of these statutes made significant jurisdictional dispositions, such as the thrusting of excise cases into any court of record, inducing the founding of vice-admiralty courts (7 & 8 Wm. III c.22), and earmarking the trial of pirates for special authorization (11 & 12 Wm. III c.7). Parliamentary plantation legislation is consequently a factor of first importance in the complex pattern of "conusance." Many of the English statutes which were regarded as beneficial and which were not extended to the colonies for the obvious reason that it was not in the interest of the prerogative to have wholesale statutory interference, the colonists themselves attempted to put in effect. This was sometimes done by simply putting the innovation in practice.[74] More usually a badly disguised version of an English statute[75] was passed by the provincial legislature. And on one brave occasion an omnibus bill was attempted that was promptly disallowed.[76] Unquestionably, the body of post-conquest English statutes, for all it was *terra prohibita,* was influential both on colonial practice and on the statutory trends in the province.

The Provincial Judicial System; Acts of Assembly

We have next to inquire how, within the bounds set by the Crown, by the acts of Parliament and by the accepted judicial expositions respecting law transfer, the colonial law-enforcing agencies were set up and the process of

[74] *Infra* 540, 550.

[75] *Infra* 372 *et seq.*

[76] On this Act of Dec. 24, 1767 (4 *Col. Laws NY* 953) cf. the report by Richard Jackson, counsel to the Commissioners of Trade and Plantations, in P.R.O., C.O. 5/1075, 461: "It is with a good deal of Concern that I find myself obliged to represent to your Lordships that though the first of these acts introduces no Law or part of any law of this kingdom the substance of which upon a careful perusal does not appear of public utility to that province yet it does not seem fitting they should be thus adopted in Cumulo and that without stating more of the several Acts than the Title and the number Sections adopted That nothing can be more obvious than that such a Cumulative Act deprives both the Crown and the Governor of that distinct approbation or dis-approbation that is essential to the Constitution of the Province, and to all similar constitutions and that the perusal of the Acts of Parliament themselves, make it palpable that such an introduction by way of reference will frequently occasion great difficulties in the Construction, and those sometimes such as ought not to be left to a Court of Justice to decide.

"It is however with the less reluctance that I make these Objections to this Act because it seems to be in a great measure calculated for the guidance of those inferior Courts whose jurisdiction is so far extended by the Acts 3 and 4 [No. 3, May 20, 1769, Empowering J.P.s Mayors Alderman to try causes to the value of £10, 4 *Col. Laws NY* 1079] [No. 4, May 20, 1769, Prevent Suits at Supreme Court of sums not exceeding £50, *ibid.* 1088]. Although 2 acts did not actually pass till more than 2 years afterwards no great want of Uniformity being to be apprehended in the Devisions [*sic*] of the Supreme Court which two Acts I conceive to be no means proper in point of law in as much as they run directly counter to the Juridical Policy of this Country, and cannot but occasion Mischievous effects under the specious appearance of facilitating justice."

adapting English law was engineered, and we shall commence by considering the courts and the partition of jurisdiction.

Colonel Richard Nicolls,[77] upon whom lay the onus of reducing New Netherlands and planting his master's government, was an old soldier. The son of a barrister of good family, he had left his studies when nineteen to join the royal forces and, until the Restoration, had served with various commanders on the Continent. His experience with the working of English institutions was, under the circumstances, of the slightest, and one would not expect that a person of his background would be able to undertake a slavish application of common law rules and a general introduction of English governmental agencies. On the other hand, the Roundhead odor of what Nicolls and his fellow commissioners must have observed in New England before the expedition sailed on to New Amsterdam could hardly have predisposed him in favor of American notions about what was suitable in a colony. The consequence was that what was erected in New York was nostalgic of memories of old England, for it was indeed a creation of memory and not of exact knowledge.

The initial dispositions with respect to the provincial courts are contained in the code known as the Duke's Laws prepared in advance and submitted to an assembly of settlers at Hempstead, Long Island, March 1, 1664/65.[78] The Duke's new subjects appear to have had ambitions to make their own laws. Nicolls accepted some proposed amendments, but with great finesse suc-

---

[77] On Nicolls, 2 Brodhead, *Hist. of the State of NY* 17–18.

[78] On this assembly cf. 2 Brodhead, *Hist of NY* 67 *et seq.* The proceedings are in 2 *Ms. Deeds* (NY Sec. of State). There can be no question that the Duke's Laws were designed as a code for the province at large. This may be inferred from the presence of delegates for the Dutch towns of Long Island, and there is proof positive in *Ms. Bushwick Town Recs. 1660–1825*. In March 1665, Van Ruyven ordered the town to elect constables and overseers (*ibid.* 131–133). On April 19, 1665 he transmitted to the town so-called instructions which were in fact selections from the Duke's Laws (*Constables, Impressment, Publick Charges*, etc.) translated into Dutch (*ibid.* 135 *et seq.*). The amendments of 1666 were also sent to this town (*ibid.* 215 *et seq.*). This evidence should dispose once and for all of the contention that the Duke's Laws applied only to the English settlements (Fowler, *Bradford's Laws* lv). Andrews, in 3 *Col. Period of Amer. Hist.* (1937) 106, states that these laws "were designed especially for the population of Long Island—overwhelmingly English by race," etc. We have seen no evidence to support any part of this statement. Nicolls himself says that the laws had been collected out of the laws of other colonies "onely with such Alterations as may revive the Memory of old England amongst us," and that the Duke had "intended . . . the settlement of his Maties Authority in true English words and formes" (2 *NYHS Colls.* [1869] 119). No implications regarding the restriction to Long Island can be drawn from these remarks. Moreover, the laws were put in force in Staten Island, Westchester, and in June, 1665, in New York City (*supra* n. 19). The difficulties at Esopus caused a delay, but in 1669 the Esopus commissioners directed the place be governed by English laws (1 *Exec. Council Mins.* 281). Orders issued in 1671 indicate a partial introduction (2 *ibid.* 529), which in 1673 was made complete (1 *ibid.* 183). Albany alone does not appear to have been immediately ordered to put the laws in force. However, the proclamation of Andros of Nov. 9, 1674, declares the Duke's Laws to be generally in force (1 *Col. Laws NY* 107). Subsequently Andros, in reference to Schenectady and later to Albany, authorized continuation of former practice not repugnant to the laws of the province (2 *Ct. Mins. of Albany* 23 [1675], 130 [1676]). As to the Delaware lands cf. *infra* n. 88.

ceeded in quashing the proposals of the delegates that looked to a New England way of government, and the code as a whole was voted by the assembly. The tact and sagacity of this man are well brought out by the manner in which the delicate political problem of the moment was handled. It was not only essential to keep the Dutch inhabitants contented but to attach the English settlers to the new government. As a conquered people the Dutch were entitled to no further consideration than was laid down in the articles of capitulation,[79] but they considerably outnumbered the English population. The English plantations, which had enjoyed a considerable autonomy whether they were under Dutch rule[80] or under the loose arrangements with Connecticut and New Haven,[81] were a problem unto themselves. The new code, as a form of *douceur,* was professedly compiled out of existing colonial law and it made generous acknowledgment of the local predilection for self-government by conceding to the towns a court to be held by constable and overseers, where civil causes up to £5 and petty criminal offenses were to be cognizable.[82] In addition, the towns were conceded an ordinance power subject to supervision.[83] The laws, however, provided for a judicious yet hardly concealed control by means of the justices of the peace who were authorized to sit in town courts,[84] but who were appointed by the Governor, for Colonel Nicolls had refused to permit these magistrates to be elected.[85] The justices were granted certain summary powers,[86] but on the whole no attempt was made to make of this office the cornerstone of general administration which it was in England, and which it subsequently became in New York.

[79] There was no provision in the articles of capitulation for the continuation of the Dutch courts but inferior civil officers were to remain in office until the next election time. Actually there was an interim functioning of Dutch local courts. Cf. for New York City 5 *Recs. of New Amsterdam* 108 *et seq.;* for Flatbush, *Ms. Flatbush Town Recs.* Liber D. I. 1664–70. When the Delaware settlements surrendered the courts were permitted a six-month period to function (3 *Doc. Rel. Col. Hist. NY* 71). It seems likely that some general assurance had been given to all the Dutch in the province, for Cartwright writes to Nicolls from Boston on Feb. 4, 1664/65: "The Dutch expect the English lawes at their six months end, and it is probable they wil rather take that for oppression w[ch] shal be imposed on them afterwards, then, for the present acknowledge your indulgence in letting them for a while longer use their own lawes." In Leaming and Spicer, *Grants, etc. of New Jersey* 667, is printed the purport of a proclamation of Nicolls where among other things is recited a promise that the towns would have liberty of making "particular laws" and deciding small causes. The only proclamation now extant was made before conquest and was not so specific; cf. *Gen. Entries 1664–65 (NYSL Hist. Bull. no. 2)* 81. A letter of Nicolls Dec. 1, 1664, to Young and Howell simply directs that magistrates in office continue to function (*ibid.* 132; 1 *Southold Town Recs.* 357).

[80] *Laws and Ordinances of New Netherland 1638–74* 27, 43, 53, 97.

[81] On the relations of the Long Island towns with Connecticut and New Haven, cf. 1 Brodhead, *op. cit.* 670.

[82] 1 *Col. Laws NY* 7 (Actions), 63 (Townships), cf. the later amendments, *ibid.* 71, 74, 91.

[83] *Ibid.* 63.

[84] *Ibid.* 44 (Justice of Peace).

[85] 2 Brodhead, *op. cit.* 69.

[86] Chiefly in relation to commitment 1 *Col. Laws NY* 17 (Bayle), 28 (Constables), and to fugitives, *ibid.* 47 (Masters and Servants) and to correction of children and servants, *ibid.* 26 (Children and Servants).

For the general run of litigation the Duke's Laws set up what were described as Courts of Sessions.[87] Initially these courts were designated to be held only in the three main divisions of the province, the so-called ridings which embraced the towns of Long Island, Westchester and Staten Island. New York City, the Esopus, Albany and the Delaware plantations were not included in this arrangement, but in gradual succession all of these localities with the exception of Albany were given a Sessions jurisdiction.[88]

The Sessions were conceived of as intermediate tribunals. The scope of their jurisdiction was ill defined in the Duke's Laws, but by subsequent amendment and in practice their authority was limited in civil matters to cases involving over £5 and under £20, and to criminal causes not capital.[89] The courts were held by the justices of the peace, and the Duke's Laws contemplated that the Governor or a councillor was to be present.[90]

It should be observed that although the Duke's Laws provided for appeals, reviews and transfers of causes from one level of courts to another, the really effective linking of these institutions was not left to chance but was accomplished through the presence of officers who were agents of the central government. In practice this scheme of control was made to function because the Governor possessed a wide discretion in issuing warrants,[91] a discretion explicitly recognized in the Duke's Laws. It was still further fortified by the man-

---

[87] *Ibid.* 27.

[88] As to New York, *supra* n. 19; as to Esopus, *supra* n. 78. In the Delaware region the first directions are in the instructions to Carr in 12 *Doc. Rel. Col. Hist. NY* 457, and the "Resolutions and Directions" of 1668, *ibid.* 461. In the latter it was provided that the "Lawes of the Government Establisht by his Royall Highnes be shewed and frequently Communicated" to the local councillors so that through acquaintance with them these laws could be established. Certain changes were instituted in 1671, such as the appointment of constables, *ibid.* 481, and in 1672 "English Lawes" and a town court were ordered established, *ibid.* 496–497. Shortly after his arrival Andros recommissioned the former magistrates or commissaries, *ibid.* 513, 514, and authorized them to proceed as under Nicolls and Lovelace. In the spring of 1675 Andros visited Delaware and held court there, *ibid.* 524 *et seq.* It subsequently became necessary to make new arrangements. The Duke's Laws were introduced, "Except the Constables Courts, Country Rates, and some other things peculiar to Long Island." Then courts were instituted at Newcastle, Uplands (Chester) and at the Whorekill (Lewes Creek). These courts were to "have the Power of a Court of Sessions" with a civil jurisdiction and "for crime extending to life, limb or banishment to admit appeals to the Court of Assizes." Proceedings were to be entered in English and all "writts, Warrants & Proceedings at Law shall bee in his Maties Name." (Cf. the ordinance, *ibid.* 561–563.) The magistrates were commissioned as justices of the peace, three or more to "bee a Court of Judicature" (*ibid.* 557, 558). The court exercised the functions elsewhere left to town courts. Matters under £5 would be tried without a jury unless requested by parties, and it was recommended they be handled by arbitration. The jurisdiction over crimes involving death penalty was a considerable enlargement of normal Sessions jurisdiction. The minutes of this court at Newcastle are printed in *Recs. of the Ct. of New Castle on Delaware* (Col. Soc. of Pa. 1904). The Uplands records are in 7 *Memoirs of Pa. Hist. Soc.* (1860) 35. The Whorekill records from 1681 onward are in *Ms. Anc. Rec. Sussex Co.* (Pa. Hist. Soc.).

[89] The limitations in civil cases are set forth in the Duke's Laws, 1 *Col. Laws NY* 7 (Actions). There seems to have been doubt about this for Nicolls, in Feb. 1665/66, repeated the direction respecting jurisdiction, *ibid.* 88.

[90] 1 *Col. Laws NY* 28, 31 (Councell).

[91] *Infra* 389–390.

ner in which the supreme court of the province—the Court of Assizes—was organized.

The Court of Assizes was composed of the Governor, his Council and the several justices of the peace in the province.[92] The Duke's Laws have nothing to say about how the bench was constituted but the court records are clear on the point. The law provided for an annual meeting[93]—although it was subsequently enacted that the Assizes could be summoned for special sessions at any time.[94] The court exercised executive, legislative and judicial powers, some of which are particularly specified in the Duke's Laws. In its judicial capacity the Court of Assizes was apparently to have original jurisdiction over capital causes and appellate jurisdiction over Sessions cases.[95] It was further vested with power to deal with cases for which no special rule existed in the laws.[96]

To supplement the Court of Assizes, provision was made in the laws for the issuance of commissions of oyer and terminer in criminal cases,[97] but nothing was said respecting the functions of the Governor and Council in dealing with the business that could not await dispatch until the Assizes met. In practice this was of utmost importance, and the surviving collections of orders, warrants and minutes disclose that a mass of affairs which in England would have been dealt with judicially was actually disposed of by the Council acting in a quasi-judicial capacity.

The institutional structure introduced in 1665 and extended under Lovelace and again put in force under Andros (1674) remained in vigor until 1683, after the Duke had altered his instructions to allow the Governor and Council to erect a new system of courts.[98] Governor Dongan permitted the elected assembly to aid in framing an act for courts, despite the fact that nothing in his commission or instructions warranted such a gesture. To this act, James, having meantime ascended the throne, gave his royal assent.[99]

The Judicature Act of 1683[100] strengthened central authority by the creation of a Court of Oyer and Terminer and General Gaol Delivery which took the place of the Court of Assizes formally abolished in the following year. This

---

[92] 2 Brodhead, op. cit. 63 n., 70, "does not doubt" that the Court of Assizes was already an existing institution when the Duke's Laws were enacted. It is tempting to infer this from the offhand manner in which the court is mentioned in the code. The evidence Brodhead cites is not conclusive. We have seen nothing that can be regarded as proof on the point.

[93] 1 Col. Laws NY 16 (Assizes).

[94] Ibid. 77, amendment of 1665.

[95] Infra 61; 1 Col. Laws NY 12 (Appeal), 20 (Capitall Lawes), 36 (Fire or Burning), 65 (Witnesses).

[96] Ibid. 44 (Lawes).

[97] Ibid. 17 (Assizes).

[98] "I doe also hereby authorize you wth advice of my s^d Councill to elect and settle such and soe many Courts of Justice & in such places as you shall wth advice of my said Councill judge to be necessary . . ." (3 Doc. Rel. Col. Hist. NY 333).

[99] Ibid. 370.

[100] 1 Col. Laws NY 125.

new court was, however, a judicial body only, to be held by a judge and four justices of the peace especially commissioned and empowered to hear and determine "all matters Causes and Cases Capitall Criminall or civil and Causes tryable at Common Law." It was to sit twice a year at New York City and once a year in each of the counties into which the Province had newly been divided. Ostensibly the object of the circuit feature was to avoid "the inconvenience of bringing ye peace, Sheriffs, Constables & other p'sons concerned from the remote parts of this Government to New York."[101] But in view of the obvious ineffectiveness of the Assizes as an instrumentality for maintaining a close correspondence between local and central government it seems probable that the new court, like the eyres of medieval England, was designed as a mechanism for the close supervision of local affairs by the judges of a central court. As the Governor and Council were constituted a court of final resort in the province,[102] the notion of an executive or at least quasi-judicial supervision over proceedings that Colonel Nicolls had introduced into New York was kept alive.

The Act of 1683 provided further for the continuation of the Courts of Sessions thereafter to be held for each of the new counties at specified times. These courts were empowered to hear, try and determine all cases, civil as well as criminal, "there brought and Comenced." Since there is no further specification of the jurisdiction, it is to be inferred that it was to be without limit. This inference is strengthened by the further provision that causes involving more than £5 could be removed to Oyer and Terminer and that by warrant, writ of error or certiorari, any judgment, information or indictment could likewise be transferred. Quarterly Sessions were provided for New York City.

The most radical disturbance of the earlier institutional arrangements was in relation to the town courts. Here the civil jurisdiction was fixed at 40s., although in 1685 the £5 limit was restored and the superior courts were expressly excluded from taking cognizance of cases below this sum.[103] Nothing is said respecting criminal jurisdiction and it must be assumed that this was abolished. Furthermore, a first step was taken in withdrawing from the town government participation in the provincial law enforcement by the provision that the monthly town courts were to be held by three persons commissioned for this particular purpose. In the following year the Judicature Act was

101 3 Doc. Rel. Col. Hist. NY 389.
102 By the odd provision that there should be a Court of Chancery to be "Esteemed and accounted the Supreme Court of this province." The Gover-

nor and Council were to be the Court of Chancery. Appeals were to lie to the King from the Courts of Chancery or Oyer and Terminer.
103 1 Col. Laws NY 175.

amended to permit the election of these commissioners,[104] but even with this concession the effect of the change was to facilitate the eventual shift to an administration of petty local judicial matters by justices of the peace.

The state of the judiciary during the period 1688 to 1691 is obscure. By his commission and instructions of April, 1688, James II had ordered the inclusion of New York into the Dominion of New England.[105] Andros arrived in New York in August and proclaimed that existing officials, civil and military, remain in service,[106] but there is no record of any ordinance or decree with respect to the courts. In New England the judiciary had been reconstituted by Andros in March, 1686/87,[107] and the system had been extended to all the colonies there. The act had instituted quarterly Sessions Courts for every county charged with "conservation of the peace and the punishment of offenders" and "Inferiour Courts of Common Pleas" with jurisdiction over all cases not concerning freeholds where more than 40s. and not over £10 were involved.[108] Over these tribunals was the Superior Court of Judicature which had cognizance of all civil pleas and pleas of the Crown and was endowed with the powers of King's Bench, Common Pleas and Exchequer. This court was to sit at stated times in various parts of the Dominion. It had an error jurisdiction over cases appealed from Common Pleas, but in turn its judgments were subject to review by the Governor and Council if the amount in controversy exceeded the sum of £100. A Court of Chancery was likewise established, and then in a blanket provision all the judges of the several courts were empowered to make orders and establish rules of proceeding as fully and as amply as the judges of the three great courts at Westminster. Subsequently, by special enactment, justices of the peace were given jurisdiction over cases involving less than 40s.[109]

Despite the absence of any order putting this scheme into effect in New York, there is collateral proof that Andros in fact discarded the system erected by Dongan and instituted the Dominion Judicature Act. Andros stated this rather generally in his report,[110] and there has long been in print the evidence

---

[104] Ibid. 144.

[105] 3 Doc. Rel. Col. Hist. NY 537, 543.

[106] Ibid. 554; 1 Min. Com. Council NYC 198.

[107] 3 Pub. Recs. Conn. 411 et seq., 1 Laws of New Hampshire (Batchellor ed. 1904) 190. Some modifications were made in an act of Dec. 29, 1687, 3 Pub. Recs. Conn. 402.

[108] The Act of 1687 removed the £10 limit and gave unlimited jurisdiction to the Common Pleas courts except where title to land was involved, saving the right of removal by habeas corpus or

certiorari. Barnes (Dominion of New England [1923] 106–107) avers that the Common Pleas courts had a criminal jurisdiction. The statute does not provide this, and it would have left the Sessions with nothing to do.

[109] 3 Pub. Recs. Conn. 414.

[110] 3 Doc. Rel. Col. Hist. NY 722 et seq. "Courts of Judicature were setled in the severall parts, soe as might be most convenient for the ease and benefitt of the subject, and Judges appoynted to hold

for specific inference,[111] although the historians seem to have ignored it.[112] There is, moreover, direct evidence in the judicial records to show that the Dominion Act was actually put into operation in the form of commissions issued for the counties of Westchester, Kings and Queens on August 25, 1685, for both Courts of Sessions and Common Pleas.[113] Although there are extant no minutes of the courts for Westchester and Queens, in the records of both Kings and Richmond counties is proof that the Dominion Act was in fact put into operation. On October 27, 1688, Stephen Van Cortlandt, under a *dedimus potestatem,* opened the Sessions in Kings County, and on this occasion the commissions of the justices of the peace, the clerk and the judges of the Inferior Court of Common Pleas were read.[114] The court sat again on January 1, 1688/89, at which time three Dominion acts were proclaimed.[115] There were two further sessions in April and October at both of which the clerk carefully opened his record with the correct "style."[116]

The Richmond records are even stronger proof. There is a memorandum entry of "Pleas at Court before Thomas Lovelace Judge of the Inferior Court of Pleas, Richard Stillwell and Jacob Garrettson Justices of the Peace." There is a further formal record of a Court of Sessions held the same day where

the Terms and goe the Circuite throughout the Dominion . . ." (27 May 1690).

[111] Nicolson to the Lords of Trade (*ibid.* 576): "This part of the Governm^t is by occasion of said revolutions deprived from its free course of Justice since the Judges appointed for this circuit are also in custody at Boston, . . ." (15 May 1689). Robert Livingston, writing in Mar. 1688/89, to Edward Randolph regarding debts owed by Colonel Dongan, states that he had written his friends Graham and West [both in Boston] "for a writt from ye Superior Court & doe intend to goe to N: Yorke speedily & if he will not by faire means comply & give me security then I must arrest him or attach his estate as my friends best can advise me." (4 Toppan, *Edward Randolph* [Prince Soc. 1899] 261, 262.) Unless the Superior Court had jurisdiction in New York, the business of getting a writ out of the clerk's office in Boston to prosecute a claim against a New York resident would have been senseless.

It should be added that Mr. Edsall has found proof that the Dominion Judicature Act was put into effect in East Jersey (Edsall, *Jour. of the Cts. of Com. Right and Chancery* 25 n. 54).

[112] Neither of the two monographs that deal with this period in detail mentions the extension of the Judicature Act to New York (Barnes, *op. cit. supra* n. 108; Kimball, *Public Life of Joseph Dudley* [1911]). The fact is not reported by Brodhead on whom nearly all writers lean and is not

noted in the chronology in Stokes, *Iconography of New York*. Van Rensselaer, in 2 *Hist. of the City of NY* (1909) 248, states that the Dongan system was left intact. The latest book covering the period, 3 Andrews, *Col. Period of Amer. Hist.* (1937), has nothing on the matter.

[113] *Ms. Deeds Westch. Co.* Liber B, fols. 7 (Peace), 11 (Common Pleas); *Ms. Conveyances Kings Co.* Liber I, 129; *Ms. Deeds Queens Co.* Liber A, 736. Cf. also the entry of a probate by a *Court of Pleas* (Jan. 16, 1688/89) in *Ms. Deeds Suffolk Co.* Liber A, fol. 40 and the certificate of Arnold on the taking of oaths there by the justices: 129 *Mass. Archives* 322.

[114] *Ms. Kings Co. Ct. & Rd. Recs. 1668–1766* 379. The act respecting the raising of £2555 was read. This act had been passed by Dongan and his council and then suspended. It was revived at a council meeting at New York, Aug. 29, 1688. Cf. *Andros Rec.,* 13 *Proc. Am. Antiq. Soc.* (n.s.) 498. The *dedimus* is in *Ms. Conveyances Kings Co.* Liber I, 127.

[115] *Ms. Kings Co. Ct. & Rd. Recs. 1668–1766* 384. The acts read were the act empowering justices of the peace to try cases under 40s. (3 *Pub. Recs. Conn.* 414); the act regulating weights and measures (*ibid.* 420) and the act on militia (*ibid.* 429).

[116] "Att The Court off Common Pleas" etc. The October Session, 1689, reflects the difficulties of the moment "The actions off Sessions being concidred

"The Commission of the Peace under the Great Seale of Dominion of New England being read and silence commanded," the grand jury was called. At this court a recognizance for good behavior of Bethewell Langstaff was delivered, but Bethewell defaulted. It was ordered the default be recorded and "the Recognizance Kept safe in the hands of the Clerk of ye Peace and order the same Recognizance to be certifyed to the Superiour Courte when the judges comes the circuit."[117]

Sometime in the fall of 1689, after political power had passed to Leisler and his adherents, the Dominion Act was avoided and the judicial arrangements established by the Act of 1683 were at least partially restored.[118] The order making the change does not seem to have been preserved, but the revival of the Dongan act is clear from a commission of December 19, 1689.[119] There seems to have been some doubt as to the validity of this measure,[120] but in Kings County, at least, a Sessions Court was held under this new dispensation.[121] A number of oyer and terminer commissions were also issued but

and the Court nott ffounden according as hee must bee and the Grand Jurey nott compleath"—the cases depending referred to the next court. The same action taken respecting Common Pleas (*Ms. Kings Co. Ct. & Rd. Recs. 1668–1766* 393).

[117] *Ms. Deeds Richmond Co.* Liber A, fols. 639, 643.

[118] This conclusion rests upon inference and is based on the fact that the Andros commissions were vacated (2 *Doc. Hist. NY* 32) and new commissions issued, some with particular reference to the provincial act of 1683 (*infra* n. 119 and cf. Leisler's letters of Dec. 28, 1689, in 2 *Doc. Hist. NY* 30–31). The statute as a whole was regarded as being still in force not only because Leisler established an exchequer court but because he also issued commissions of oyer and terminer (*ibid.* 36), a court not provided for in the Dominion Act. The report of Leisler and his council of Jan. 7, 1688/89, states merely "the next step was to settle the Magistracy and appoint Com' of Judicature in the respective counties according to our Laws." Leisler's council revived the Revenue Act of 1683, and, from the terms of a proclamation of Dec. 20, 1689, apparently regarded the permanent act of the 1683 assembly to be in full vigor. Much of the confusion regarding the measures of the revolutionary government respecting the courts arises from the fact that Leisler, in his letter of Mar. 31, 1690, to the Bishop of Salisbury (3 *Doc. Rel. Col. Hist. NY* 700, 701), stated that "the courts of judicature" are suspended. As we have records of courts held in Albany, New York, Kings and Queens, and as Leisler would certainly have made no damaging admissions, this statement can have reference only to a suspension of the New York Mayor's Court. The Kings Sessions met only a few days later.

[119] 36 *NY Col. Mss.* 142, no. 65.

"By the Lieu.t Governo.r and Commander in Chief &c.a—

By Virtue of the Authority unto mee derived I doe hereby Constitute Authorize and appoint you his ma.ties Justices of the Peace for y.e County of Suffolk or the major part of you to Elect and appoint Three proper & fit persons to hold a Monethly Court within y.e Said County for determining Matters of Controversie of Small Causes & Cases of Debt & Trespasses to the Value of fforty Shillings or under according to An Act of Assembly (made 1683) Entitled An Act to Settle Courts of Justice And this Commission to Continue until I receive further orders from his Ma.ties King William. Given under my hand & Seale at Fort William In New York December the 19th, 1689. Jacob Leisler."

Cf. also *Ms. Deeds Westch. Co.* Liber B, fol. 70, Commission to John Pell, Oct. 30, 1690.

[120] At the Kings Sessions Jan. 28, 1689/90 "Questioned by Roeloff Schenck [a Justice of the Peace] iff this court did sitt by a Legall Power to the Judge and Sherriffe where upon Judge Beakman and Sherriff Meynd. Courten did answer that they satt by a Legall Power . . ." (*Ms. Kings Co. Ct. & Rd. Recs. 1668–1766* 394). Again in Apr. 1690, the court opened with a declaration that the court sat by "Legall Power" (*ibid.* 399). In the *Ms. Flatbush Town Recs. Misc.* 161 *et seq.* is a letter to Domine Varick accompanied by extracts from English statutes to support an attack on the proceedings of Leisler, specifically his commissioning of judges and the arbitrary arrests.

[121] *Ms. Kings Co. Ct. & Rd. Recs. 1668–1766* 396–403.

these from their terms must be deemed to have been special.[122] The administrative measures regarding the courts were ratified by the assembly in September, 1690, in an act which among other things provided that "all Courts of Judicature be duely Keept & observed according to the lawes of this province (not repugnant to the lawes of their Mat[ies] Realme of England)."[123] For what this enactment was worth it may be regarded as the accepted basis of jurisdiction for the few remaining months of Leisler's regime, which came to an end in March 1690/91.

The dispositions of Andros as Dominion governor and Leisler as rebel leader were transitory episodes in the judicial history of New York. Yet the Dominion Act by virtue of which the courts were briefly held was to leave its impress upon the structure of New York judiciary for generations to come.

The instructions to Governor Sloughter had specifically enjoined him not to erect any courts of judicature not theretofore established.[124] It is not clear whether or not the Crown projected any legislation, but it may be inferred from the fact that commissions of the peace were issued by the new governor on April 4, 1691[125] (in other words before the assembly had had an opportunity to act) that no radical change in local arrangements was contemplated. Furthermore Sloughter commissioned Henry Filkin of Kings "To be Clarke of the peace, generall Quarter sessions and court of Pleas within Kings County," indicating either that he regarded the Dominion Act to be in force or that it was to be confirmed.[126]

Shortly after the assembly had convened in this same month, Sloughter, in spite of his commission which left the creation of courts to the Governor and Council, recommended that a bill be expedited establishing courts of judica-

---

[122] 2 *Doc. Hist. NY* 36; *Cal. Eng. Mss.* 198, 199. Although in form special, it is possible the Oyer and Terminer Courts held a number of sessions under these commissions. An entry in 2 *Hempstead Town Recs.* 67 (Dec. 4, 1690) suggests this.

[123] The text of a bill is in 2 *Doc. Hist. NY* 200. What is apparently the official text with the endorsement of Leisler and certification by Gouverneur is in P.R.O., C.O. 5/170 II, 496. As this text differs from the bill it is worth quoting:

"A bill for administering & executing the lawes unto all persones within this province whereby no Just complainte may arise for want thereof.

Bee it Enacted & it is hereby enacted by the Geñall assembly & by the authority of the same that all & every the Inhabitants of this province may enjoy & receive the full privilege & benefit of the lawes of this province & that no freemen be taken or imprisoned but by warrant lawfully issued out & that

all Courts of Judicature be duly kept & observed according to the lawes of this province (not repugnant to the lawes of their Maties province of England) & for any such persones who are fled out of this province are hereby requyred to returne to their respective habitations without trouble or molestation whatsoever in three weeks after publication hereof, but if any crimes are by them committed that they be legally sued befor any Court of Judicature within this province as the lawes doe requyre & all persones so fleeing as aforesd & shall not returne in the tyme limited as aforesd shall be proceeded agt as the law in such cases directs."

[124] 3 *Doc. Rel. Col. Hist. NY* 687.

[125] *Ms. Deeds Westch. Co.* Liber B, fol. 77; *Ms. Conveyances Kings Co.* Liber I, 269.

[126] *Ms. Conveyances Kings Co.* Liber I, 264, Mar. 26, 1691.

ture and that the earlier act of assembly setting up courts of justice be taken into consideration.[127] The assembly appointed a committee to prepare a bill and revise former laws on the matter, but except for the few members who had served as justices of the peace, no one appears to have had the least qualification for the task. A report was made within twenty-four hours and it was ordered that the Attorney General draw up a bill. This order was presumably based on the committee report and laid down explicitly certain directions which followed in the main the Dominion Judicature Acts of Andros except that the circuit feature was eliminated.[128] George Farewell, acting for the absent Attorney General Newton, failed to produce a draft, and the assembly then directed its speaker, James Graham, who had been Attorney General under both Dongan and Andros, to prepare the bill. This was submitted the following day and was promptly passed. The Governor and Council made a few amendments, the most important of which was to fix the appellate jurisdiction of the Governor and Council. The statute was finally enacted May 6, 1691.

While the assembly was considering the judiciary, Sloughter made an attempt to assure the financial support of the superior court judges, and probably some other directions were included in the message to the assembly. This is indicated by the answer which stated that "this house had already on ye 15th Instant agreed to a method for settling of Courts of Judicature throughout this Province wherein they had Paid that Duty to there Majts. & to his Excelln as to leave ye Commissionating & appointing of ye Justices and Judges of these Courts unto his Excelln."[129]

In view of the prevailing hysteria concerning anything that had to do with the Stuart regime, it is somewhat remarkable that the assembly should have fastened upon Andros' Dominion scheme as a model for the newly liberated province. Indeed, a few days after the directions for the Judicature Act had been approved, the assembly by resolution (not concurred in by the Governor and Council) repudiated all antecedent Stuart legislation whether by assembly or Governor and Council.[130] Since this inconsistency transcends even what is normally to be expected of legislative bodies, an explanation of the provisions of the Judicature Act can only be found in the surmise that some direction was exercised by those leaders in the New York government who had been important figures in the Dominion government—Speaker Graham, Acting Attor-

[127] 1 *Jour. Gen. Assembly NY* (1764) 4b.
[128] *Ibid.* 5b, 8b.
[129] *Ibid.* 8b; 37 *NY Col. Mss.* 107b; 1 *Jour. Legis. Council* 3, 4, 6.
[130] *Ibid.* 8b.

ney General Farewell, the councillors Bayard, Dudley, Phillipse and Van Cortlandt.

It should be noted that the Judicature Act of 1691,[131] while not passed in accordance with the Governor's commission, may be viewed as a reasonably obedient execution of the instruction not to erect any courts "not before erected or established," because many chief features of the Dominion Act were enacted. Clearly the failure of the Governor and Council to concur in the assembly's resolution abrogating all antecedent Stuart legislation[132] indicates a disposition to maintain what was conceived to be the *status quo ante* Leisler. Most significant is the perpetuation of Andros' scheme of central control.

On the foundation of the local jurisdiction of justices of the peace, sitting singly or by two's and three's or in Courts of Common Pleas and Courts of Sessions, was erected a superstructure of central control which by means of the system of appellate and transfer jurisdiction and by means of the wide original jurisdiction of the Supreme Court of the Province was to be a watchtower over local affairs. Quasi-administrative supervision of judicial decision was provided for in this Act, in accordance with the Governor's instructions, by the appellate jurisdiction of the Governor and Council in cases over £100. There was a further appeal to the King in Council where the amount involved was over £300.[133] Nothing is said in this act about appeals in criminal cases.

All vestiges of the town courts were expunged by the new Judicature Act,[134] and instead the inferior jurisdiction was committed to single justices of the peace who were given the right to determine summarily cases of debt and trespass to the value of 40s.; and of course by the very recognition of the office of the peace, the petty criminal jurisdiction of the justice was implicitly confirmed. For "the Increase of Virtue and the Discouraging of Evil-doers" in every county, Sessions of the Peace were to be held four times a year in New York City, three times in Albany and semi-annually in the other counties. After 1692 the country courts were known as "General Sessions of the Peace," but the New York City court, since it had four annual terms, was known as the "General Quarter Sessions of the Peace." No differences in jurisdiction were

---

[131] 1 *Col. Laws NY* 226.

[132] 1 *Jour. Gen. Assembly NY* 8b. This resolution was not acted upon by the Council and consequently never became law. The question of the effect of this resolution is discussed by Fowler in his introduction to the Grolier Club edition of Bradford's *Laws* lxxviii. There are several proceedings in the records which indicate that the earlier laws were regarded as being in effect in the early eighteenth century. Cf. *Mins. SCJ 1693–1701* (45 *NYHS Colls.*) 43, 173; *Ms. Mins. NYCQS 1694–1731/32* fol. 193, Feb. 8, 1710/11.

[133] It should be observed, however, that the instructions from the Crown contained this limitation (1 Labaree, *op. cit.* nos. 446, 448, 453).

[134] Except as established by charter, e.g., in Kingston.

intended by the Act of 1691, the purpose obviously being to erect the Sessions courts substantially like the Quarter Sessions in England. For reasons of convenience we shall refer to the New York City court as Quarter Sessions, to the country courts as General Sessions. The local civil jurisdiction as in Andros' Dominion Act was to be heard in county Courts of Common Pleas and the Mayor's Courts of Albany and New York City. This jurisdiction was final in actions involving £20 or less, but the customary jurisdiction of the New York and Albany Mayor's Courts was confirmed.

A Supreme Court of Judicature was placed by this statute as the keystone of the judicial system in the province. This court, to be "constantly kept" at New York City and not elsewhere, was to be held by five justices commissioned for the purpose. It was "fully Impowered and Authorized to have cognizance of all pleas, Civill Criminall, and Mixt, as fully & amply to all Intents & purposes whatsoever, as the Courts of Kings Bench, Common Pleas, & Exchequer within their Majestyes Kingdome of England, have or ought to have."[135] The original jurisdiction of this tribunal was limited to cases involving more than £20, but the authority over criminal cases was complete. Furthermore, it was endowed with appellate and transfer jurisdiction over judgments (in civil

---

[135] The inclusion of Exchequer powers was apparently in conformance with royal instructions. A Court of Exchequer, called also the Court of Judicature, was first set up by an order of the Governor and Council, 14 Dec. 1685 (*Cal. Council Mins.* 47) which court heard cases involving lands, rents, rights and revenues (3 *Doc. Rel. Col. Hist. NY* 390). Andros' Judicature Act, however, had amalgamated this jurisdiction with that of the other central courts (*supra* 21), but there is no evidence of the exercise of these powers while New York was part of the Dominion. Presumably Leisler had set up a Court of Exchequer—he was charged with doing this without any commission from King William (3 *Doc. Rel. Col. Hist. NY* 683). Sloughter's instructions (*ibid.* 688) provide for the establishment of a Court of Exchequer for the determination of revenue cases (an instruction continued in all subsequent ones, Labaree, *Instructions* no. 436). In 1691 the Supreme Court sat as Exchequer (*infra* 530). Gov. Cosby in 1734 (6 *Doc. Rel. Col. Hist. NY* 6) refers to minutes of a Court of Exchequer held thirty years previously, but in 1698 Gov. Bellomont had complained that a Court of Exchequer could not be held because there was no one able to hold such a court (4 *ibid.* 442). The exchequer powers of the Supreme Court were brought sharply in issue in the Van Dam case (1733). There is a discussion of this episode in Daly, *Hist. of the Ct. of Com. Pleas,* 1 E. D. Smith, *Rep.,* introd. lvi.

Although we are not concerned with the equity jurisdiction, for the sake of completeness a word should be added respecting chancery. The act of assembly of 1683 (1 *Col. Laws NY* 125 at 128) had given chancery jurisdiction to the Governor and Council. (Cf. also Dongan's report of the "State of the Province," 3 *Doc. Rel. Col. Hist. NY* 389). The Act of 1691 (1 *Col. Laws NY* 226, 230) provides for a High Court of Chancery composed of the Governor and Council. This was not continued in Bellomont's Ordinance of 1699 (2 *NY Laws* [1813 rev.] App.) and in 1700 both Governor Bellomont (4 *Doc. Rel. Col. Hist. NY* 721) and Chief Justice Smith (*ibid.* 829) refer to the want of a Court of Chancery because no one rightly understood how to hold such a court. In 1702, Lt. Gov. Nanfan in a letter to the Lords of Trade encloses another ordinance specifically providing for a Court of Chancery. A further ordinance was made by Cornbury Nov. 7, 1704 (2 *NY Laws* [1813 rev.] App.). In 1711, Gov. Hunter stated that he was "pelted with petitions for a Court of Chancery" (5 *Doc. Rel. Col. Hist. NY* 208). The matter had been submitted to a committee of the Council (10 *Ms. Mins. Council* 574) and on Sept. 29, 1711, Hunter ordered the erection of a Chancery Court (11 *ibid.* 9). The extant *Ms. Order Books* show the court sitting Sept. 1701–May 1702; May 1705–Sept. 1708. The *Ms. Min. Books* run Jan. 1711/12–July 1719; Dec. 1720–Aug. 1748; May 1740–Mar. 1770; 1770–76.

cases over £20), indictments or informations removed from the inferior courts by warrant, certiorari or writ of error.

One of the most significant provisions of the 1691 Act was the broad grant to all the judges and justices of the several courts to make, order and establish all such rules and orders for the "more orderly practizeing & proceeding" in the courts as fully and amply as the judges of King's Bench, Common Pleas and Exchequer could "legally doe." The effect of this was to commit a wide discretion over the rules of procedure and assure an almost unbounded judicial control over the conduct of litigation, especially apparent when one considers the broad words by which both Sessions and the Supreme Court were instituted. The purport of these words "Courts of Sessions" as directed to the former, and "Kings Bench, Common Pleas and Exchequer" as directed to the latter, was a grant by reference to anything that had been embraced in the dominion of the several English prototypes.

Pursuant to this grant of power the Supreme Court formulated an order of business "At the Supream Court at ye first Sitting," a page of which is preserved and which from the minutes seems to have been thereafter followed. From time to time, particular rules of practice were promulgated which will be noticed at appropriate places in our discussion. An elaborate set of rules was made for the later Circuit, and the Mayor's Court in New York similarly formulated its own rules.[136] No trace of any corpus of Sessions rules has been found, although occasionally some special order would be made. In these courts it is probable that practice was guided by the justices' manuals when these became available.

The Act of 1691 by its terms was to endure two years, but instead of an automatic extension, the provincial assembly in 1692 proceeded to tinker with the machine it had helped to construct.[137] The chief change was made in respect of the Supreme Court. Its powers remained the same but terms were appointed—twice annually for New York and Orange counties together, and annually for all the other counties, with a joint term for Dutchess and Ulster. As stipulated in the previous act, five justices were to be commissioned, but the new statute expressly directed that a single justice should "goe the circuit" and

---

[136] The "first Sitting" rules are in 38 NY Col. Mss. 16. It begins with the formula for the Cryer, the demand for return of inquisitions, etc. and the call for the grand jury, and ends with oath for the inquest. The Rules for the Court of Oyer and Terminer are in the Redmond-Livingston Mss. The

Mayor's Court rules are in Ms. Mins. Mayor's Ct. NYC 1695–1705 (Apr. 8, 1701) fol. 199 et seq. There is a copy of the Mayor's Court rules in Ms. Deeds Westch. Co. Liber D, fols. 1–4.

[137] 1 Col. Laws NY 303.

at the places and times provided hold the Supreme Court assisted by two or more justices of the peace of the county where held.

The resemblance of this renovated Supreme Court to the Oyer and Terminer of Dongan's time is apparent. What is not clear is whether or not the colonists were attempting to erect a Supreme Court and give it circuit terms, or whether they were remaking the court into a Supreme Court for each county.[138] In any event this Act marks the commencement of the Circuit in the province. The legislative intention was not clarified when the Act was renewed in 1695,[139] but the design of the assemblymen to promote decentralization is apparent in the further innovation that the local justices in Common Pleas should have the power to try land titles, a move which the Council supported but which Governor Fletcher resented.[140] In 1697 the Judicature Act as amended was continued for another year[141] but upon the expiration of this act a political controversy of major importance developed. The courts were continued by proclamation[142] while the assembly struggled to agree on an acceptable statute. The bill which passed the assembly on April 11, 1699, was reported by Chief Justice Smith to be an attempt to make the Supreme Court a mere county court.[143] Governor Bellomont, upon a report that the act was contrary to English law, finally took matters in his own hands.[144] Taking advantage of his commission which empowered him with the advice of the Council to erect courts, Bellomont on May 15, 1699, issued an ordinance[145] establishing the judiciary along the lines of the earlier act of 1692. Henceforward it was upon executive fiat that the court establishment of New York Province rested.

Bellomont's ordinance had the virtue of making clear that the Supreme Court was to be "held and kept" at New York City twice a year, and that when a single justice went out to hold court in the country he was going the circuit. The rest of the judicial scheme remained unchanged except that the Common Pleas were shorn of their power to try titles.

Two further important changes were made by ordinance in the early eighteenth century. In 1704 Lord Cornbury increased the terms of the court to four

---

[138] The act says "there Shall be at New York, a Supreame Court of Judicature," but the words "and not elsewhere" of the previous statute are eliminated. The provision that two justices with the Chief Justice should be quorum, taken in connection with the circuit clause, indicates that the act intended only the addition of a circuit term for the counties.

[139] 1 *Col. Laws NY* 359.

[140] 1 *Jour. Legis. Council* 86, Oct. 24, 1695.

[141] 1 *Col. Laws NY* 380.

[142] 8 *Ms. Mins. Council* 83, Jan. 19, 1698/99.

[143] 1 *Jour. Legis. Council* 140, May 12, 1699.

[144] 4 *Doc. Rel. Col. Hist. NY* 515.

[145] 8 *Ms. Mins. Council* 127, text in 2 *NY Laws* (1813 rev.) App. A facsimile of the broadside issued by the Statute Law Book Co. 1932.

annually,[146] and in 1715 Governor Hunter put the nisi prius jurisdiction upon a firm and sensible footing.[147]

The colonists did not ungrudgingly accept the new dispensation. Again and again during the decades following the promulgation of Bellomont's ordinance, bills to establish courts were offered and even passed by the assembly.[148] The sense of grievance, moreover, was kept alive by the strong and continuous opposition to the exercise of the office of chancellor by the Governor. Opposition reached a peak during the governorship of Cosby, stirred partly by the wrangle over the exchequer powers of the Supreme Court, and partly over the unsuccessful challenge of the judges' commissions in *King* v. *Zenger*.[149] In 1734 the inhabitants of New York, Westchester and Queens counties drew up petitions praying the establishment of courts by act of assembly.[150] The assembly resolved to hear the opinions of William Smith and Joseph Murray, two of the leading provincial lawyers. The issue was discussed by these men with considerable learning but nothing came of the matter.[151] For years thereafter rumblings continued in the legislative halls.

Although the assembly after 1692 was never again successful in engineering past Governor and Council a comprehensive act on the judicial establishment, it was not without voice in matters relating to the legal institutions in the province. During the course of the eighteenth century a mass of legislation was enacted by which in one way or another the jurisdiction of the courts was altered in specific details. The net effect of these statutes in forming a characteristic provincial law was considerable, but they did not in any perceptible degree disturb the fundamentals of the existing judicial structure. It was chiefly in the lower brackets of civil and criminal litigation that the acts of assembly were important. Thus in particular were the powers of the justices of the peace enhanced by statute; the jurisdiction over civil actions was increased to £5;[152] by statute the justices were given jurisdiction over the ever growing class of *qui tam* actions;[153] by statute the power was extended to try summarily all

---

[146] 2 *NY Laws* (1813 rev.) App.

[147] *An Ordinance for Altering the Times of sitting of the Supream Court of Judicature in the City of New York and for Trying of Causes in the Respective Counties of the said Province*, brought to issue in the *Said Supream Court* (Broadside NYHS), and cf. *infra* 79.

[148] 1 *Jour. Legis. Council* 197 (1703); 1 *Jour. Gen. Assembly NY* 247 (1709), 334, 336, 338

(1713), 571 (1727), 703 (1737), 783 (1740), 815 (1741).

[149] *Infra* 49.

[150] 1 *Jour. Gen. Assembly NY* 662.

[151] *Mr. Smith's Opinion Humbly Offered to the General Assembly of the Colony of New York—Mr. Murray's Opinion Relating to Courts of Justice* (Bradford 1734).

[152] 3 *Col. Laws NY* 1011 (1754).

[153] Cf. *infra* 127 *et seq.*

criminal offenses under the degree of grand larceny where offenders could not within forty-eight hours furnish bail.[154]

The number and variety of the acts of the type just mentioned are to be explained as a permissive extension of the privilege conceded by the Crown to the assembly in respect of courts for small causes. So definitely was the scope of legislative activity controlled (at least in theory) by royal instructions and the eventual veto power, that not much enactment affecting the superior courts succeeded in clearing the double barrier of Governor and Council and King in Council where the final approval or rejection of all provincial legislation was had. The exact lines, however, within which an assembly was to be confined were never clearly marked. Thus, the attempts of the assembly to curb the use of informations were consistently opposed by governors over a long period of years,[155] yet it was permitted to enact statutes which, in the guise of shortening lawsuits, effected changes in rules of process and pleading and put limitations on transfer procedure.[156] It was not allowed to relieve defendants acquitted of crimes from paying costs,[157] but the Crown approved legislation prescribing how courts for the trial of negro slaves were to be constituted.[158] An act altering old common law practice with respect to the commissions of judges on circuit[159] was allowed, yet the Crown refused to permit alterations in the ancient process of outlawry[160] and promptly disallowed an act establishing fees.[161]

It is beyond our purpose to attempt here a catalogue of statutes which, in one way or another, affected the jurisdiction of the courts, but we shall from time to time in the succeeding chapters have occasion to refer to the more important legislative acts. With but few exceptions, no drastic changes in the jurisdictional ideas both explicit and implicit in Bellomont's ordinance of 1699, or even in the common law rules of criminal procedure, were accomplished by means of colonial statute. The record of frustrated legislative thrusts by the assembly is an impressive monument to unending accumulation of fugitive but successive dissatisfactions,[162] yet, surprisingly enough, the final epitaph

---

[154] 2 *Col. Laws NY* 745 (1732).

[155] *Infra* 372 *et seq.*

[156] 1 *Col. Laws NY* 841 (1714). This was repealed by the Crown in 1721. In 1728 another act was passed "to amend the practice of the law" covering some of the same points and making changes in rules respecting bail (2 *Col. Laws NY* 462). Compare also 4 *ibid.* 494 (1760), "Act for making process in courts of Equity Effectual. . . ."

[157] 1 *Col. Laws NY* 623 (1708).

[158] *Ibid.* 761 (1712).

[159] 3 *ibid.* 185, 191 (1741).

[160] 1 *ibid.* 476 (1702) and cf. 4 *Doc. Rel. Col. Hist. NY* 999.

[161] 1 *Col. Laws NY* 638 (1709). It was disallowed in the same year, cf. 5 *Doc. Rel. Col. Hist. NY* 157.

[162] *Bills Which Failed to Become Laws 1685–1776* (3 vols.).

written by the Constitution makers of 1777 was only a canonization of the status quo.[163]

The Ordinance and the Proclamation

As it had been made manifest both by the Crown and by its governors that matters relating to the judicial structure as a whole were not properly subject to popular will, the business of necessary enactment was, under the commissions and instructions, committed to the Governor and Council. This authority was exercised by ordinance. Most of these ordinances were essentially of an administrative nature, such as instituting courts in counties where none had before been held, fixing the time of circuits and, after the assembly had been denied the power to fix fees, setting these tariffs.[164] The ordinance power was actually greater in scope than historians have been willing to concede.[165] The Governor and Council were viewed as a microcosmic copy of the King and the Privy Council and, in relation to any matter reserved to it, necessarily had to be conceded power to make ordinances. This is explicitly recognized in the commission of the Governor in respect of the judiciary, the defense of the Province and the granting of lands.[166] Whatever may have been the situation in other provinces, there can be no question that in New York the ordinance was a legislative device of prime importance. For seventy-seven years the courts sat by virtue of an ordinance, the lawyers earned their bread by the schedules in another and the titles to the very land itself were recorded in obedience to still another.[167]

The ordinance power was exercised by the Governor in conjunction with the Council, but he possessed in addition his own proper prerogatives in relation to enactment. These powers were derived from the fact that he was the instrumentality for the exercise of the King's prerogative abroad, an authority implemented by committing to the Governor the custody of the great seal of the Province. This delegation, although delimited by commission and instructions, necessarily implied a considerable discretion and this the Crown officers

---

[163] *Constitution of 1777* Art. 35.

[164] Cf., for example, the ordinance establishing fees, *Acts of Assembly 1691–1725* (C.U.) App. For a court for Palatines (1710), 10 *Ms. Mins. Council* 522; the ordinance re courts for Dutchess County (1722), 13 *ibid.* 110; a further ordinance on the same matter (1727), 15 *ibid.* 133; an ordinance on "county" courts (1729), *ibid.* 317; an ordinance on courts for Orange County (1733) 16 *ibid.* 258; an ordinance re circuit courts (1738) 17 *ibid.* 232; an

ordinance re circuit courts in Dutchess County (1753) 23 *ibid.* 67; an ordinance for Tryon County courts, *Ms. Book of Commissions 1770–89* 42; an ordinance for Charlotte County courts, *ibid.* 87. We shall have occasion to refer to other ordinances.

[165] Labaree, *Royal Government* 175.

[166] Cf. here the Council's safeguarding of its prerogatives, 5 *Doc. Rel. Col. Hist. NY* 184, 292.

[167] *Acts of Assembly 1691–1725* App.

at home recognized. An example of how this discretion operated exists in relation to the manor grants of Nicolls and his successors.[168] There was nothing in any mandates from the Crown specifically authorizing the conveyance of judicial rights, yet under the explicit power to make grants of land a whole succession of governors assumed and exercised the prerogative of conveying the franchise of a court leet. An exercise of prerogative of far greater practical consequence was the issuance of charters of incorporation. Of these the charters of the two municipalities of New York and Albany are the most important for they contain a variety of provisions regulating the judiciary and the public officers.[169] These two cities were two of the most important jurisdictions in the province, and since all subsequent acts of assembly had to take account of the charter rights, the two Dongan charters (and of course the Montgomerie charter) are to be regarded as hardly less significant manifestations of prerogative in founding jurisdiction than the judiciary ordinance of 1699.

In addition to the ordinance power which was exercised with the advice and consent of the Council, the Governor possessed also the prerogative of proclamation.[170] The lines which separate these two law-making functions are by no means sharply defined, but it is reasonably clear that the Governor on his mere motion could issue proclamations.[171] In some instances these documents

[168] The matter is discussed in Goebel, *Some Legal and Political Aspects of the Manors in New York* (1928). There is no evidence that the grant of leet jurisdiction was more than a formality.

[169] 1 *Col. Laws NY* 181 (New York), 195 (Albany). Compare with these the much more limited charter granted by Dongan for the incorporation of Kingston, in Schoonmaker, *Hist. of Kingston* (1888) 510 *et seq.* The New York and Albany charters both set forth specifically the officers of the municipality: mayor, recorder, aldermen, assistants, sheriff, coroner, high and petty constables, marshal, chamberlain, clerks, etc. Both in Albany and in New York City, the mayor, recorder and aldermen were to sit in Courts of Sessions to hear, try and determine petit larceny, riot, rout, oppressions and extortion, and to punish such offenses as justices of the peace according to the laws of England and the province. Out of Sessions, the city justices had the power to apprehend by warrant those accused of high and petit treason, felony and misdemeanor, and to send them to prison until lawfully delivered. The Mayor's Courts were to act as courts of common pleas to hear and determine cases of debt, trespass, case, detinue and ejectment according to the rules of common law. In 1730/31 a new charter was granted to New York City by Gov. Montgomerie (Kent, *The Charters of the City of NY* [1836] 25) and was con-

firmed by act of assembly in 1732 (2 *Col. Laws NY* 752). This charter gave the mayor and aldermen additional powers (*infra* n. 241). Note also the power to try 40 shilling cases, to arrest vagabonds, send them to the workhouse for 40 days and thence to the bridewell for punishment, and in all other ways to act as justices in England could. Other charters to towns now part of Greater New York are collected in Seymann, *Colonial Charters, Patents and Grants to the Communities Comprising the City of New York* (1939).

[170] There is no complete list of these proclamations. The most extensive available bibliography is Hasse, *Some Materials for a Bibliography of the General Assembly 1669–1775*, 7 *Bulletin of NY Pub. Lib.* (1903) 51, 129, but the subject matter of the proclamation is not always stated.

[171] While there is no doubt from the terms of the governors' commissions that the Crown intended to give necessary executive discretion, it is doubtful whether it was proposed to convey a sole legislative power. So far as we are aware, however, the Board of Trade never questioned the propriety of issuing proclamations in New York, and it was fully cognizant of the extent to which this was being done. For a remarkable admission by a colonial lawyer of the Governor's prerogatives cf. the opinion of Lewis Morris in 14 *Ms. Mins. Council* 98 *et seq.*

are so phrased that they appear to be ordinances made with the advice and consent of the Council.[172] In most cases, however, it is stated only that the advice of the Council has been taken,[173] and there are many proclamations where the Council is not mentioned at all.[174] A great variety of subject matter is covered by these proclamations, and they appear in sufficient number to warrant regarding them with greater respect as an important source of law than historians have paid them in the past.[175] In view of the strong bonds which in England were put upon the royal power of proclamation during the seventeenth century,[176] it comes as a shock to discover that in New York prosecutions are initiated in the early eighteenth century for violations of the Governor's proclamation against immorality,[177] and that a mere decade before the Revolution a proceeding for contempt of a proclamation is undertaken where it seemed impossible to compel a defendant to answer an information.[178]

---

[172] Dongan's proclamation on coin (Feb. 23, 1683/84) is by the Governor and Council as is the one on taking affidavits (Aug. 6, 1685). Cf. 1 *Min. Com. Council NYC* 126, 166. The proclamation re deserters (Nov. 4, 1697) is with the advice and consent of Council (NYHS Broadsides). So, too, Clinton's proclamation of July 28, 1753, on N.H. and Mass. depredations is with advice and consent (NYHS Broadsides).

[173] E.g., the proclamation of May 31, 1697, re exportation of grain (NYHS Broadsides); Bellomont's proclamation re immorality in 4 Stokes, *Iconography of Manhattan Island* Plate 25b; De Lancey's proclamation for settlement of lands (4 *Doc. Hist. NY* 345); Colden's on the boundary (*ibid.* 346), against the rioters (*ibid.* 379); Tryon's against Ethan Allen (*ibid.* 526).

[174] The proclamations proroguing or dissolving the assembly are the most numerous. These are scattered through the *Jour. Legis. Council.* The proclamation by the Governor alone was a method first used by Nicolls (*Gen. Entries 1664–65* 157, 163, 171, 174). The confirmation of rights and the restoration of the Duke's Laws in 1674 were effected by proclamation (1 *Col. Laws NY* 107). Even Dongan, whose proclamations usually mention the Council, issued the important prohibition on carrying concealed weapons (Mar. 1684/85) as his own act (1 *Min. Com. Council NYC* 160). Cf. also the proclamation (Mar. 3, 1691/92) regarding seditious pamphlets (37 *NY Col. Mss.* 75); Nanfan's proclamation (Jan. 24, 1701/02) on the Bayard prosecution (NYHS Broadsides); Hunter's good morals proclamation of Jan. 12, 1711/12 (NYHS Broadsides).
A noteworthy example of the proclamation as from the Crown under *teste* of the Governor is Colden's proclamation against exorbitant fees (1 *Colden Letter Books* 343 [9 *NYHS Colls.* 1876]). Compare the proclamations of 1762 for the mili-

tary to protect an execution (*ibid.* 165, 166) and Moore's proclamation of 1762 re the Chancery (Bradford, *Acts of Assembly 1762* App. [Bar Ass'n]).

[175] This may be due to the fact that colonial history has been written as if only what happened in New England and particularly Massachusetts was significant, and the ululation of the Massachusetts proclamations in the seventeenth century suggests the camp meeting and not the law book. The more recent mode of writing colonial history from the materials in the Public Record Office has also tended to obscure what was of local significance (e.g. Labaree, *Royal Government in the Colonies,* a book which barely mentions the justice of the peace and has little to say about subsidiary legislative processes). The only attempt to describe the proclamation power we have seen is the slight discussion in Greene, *Provincial Governor* (1898) 159. Greene is apparently unaware of the fact that in English law the proclamation was a vehicle for enactment with a peculiar history that quite distinguishes it from the Order in Council. In New York at least, there is enough evidence to support the distinction. It is clear that Attorney General Kempe understood the proclamation to be a thing *sui generis,* cf. *infra* n. 178.

[176] 1 Steele, *Bibliography of Royal Proclamations of the Tudor and Stuart Sovereigns* (1910) cxiii.

[177] *Infra* 98 n. 175.

[178] Cf. *J. T. Kempe Lawsuits* L–O *sub nom.* John Henry Lydius, dated Jan. 18, 1762, endorsed "copy of proceedings of the Council with respect to John Henry Lydius received 18 January, 1762, in the afternoon, Fo. 38, at 72 words": "At a Council Held at Fort George on the third day of December 1760. . . . Whereas it is Represented to this Board by Affidavit that John Henry Lydius . . . pretends some right to a tract of land . . . on Hudson's River . . . Ordered by this

Regarded solely in terms of powers respecting enactment and leaving aside even the important judicial functions exercised in council, it is obvious that the office of Governor in New York was cut from Tudor or early Stuart patterns. No aspect of the political set-up illustrates more strikingly the contrast be-

Board, that the Sherif . . . of Albany do Notify to the said John Henry Lydius that he appear before this Board." The sheriff was also ordered to investigate surveying of the lands in dispute by John Henry Lydius or others and to warn all in his Majesty's name not to proceed further. At a Council held on February 18, 1761, it was ordered that a proclamation be issued by Lieutenant Governor Colden: "Whereas it appears that John Henry Lydius . . . claimeth Property . . . That the Said John Henry Lydius hath so far presumed upon his Right . . . as to assert that he hath collected 800 families and upwards to settle twelve towns . . . that the said John Henry Lydius . . . was notified to appear . . . in Council . . . to shew by what right he claims Lands in that part . . . and why a suit . . . for intruding . . . ought not to be prosecuted against him. That the said John Henry Lydius . . . hath not complied therewith by a personal attendance . . . I have therefore thought fit, with the advice of his Majesty's Council, to Issue this Proclamation, Hereby . . . prohibiting all Persons . . . to enter . . . On pain of being prosecuted as intruders on the Crown Lands . . . and . . . commanding all his Majesty's subjects . . . to be aiding and assisting . . . in the execution of all process in law and every legal measure. . . ." At a Council held on November 18, 1761, the high sheriff of Albany was ordered to take John Henry Lydius into custody and bring him to answer for his contempt in not appearing and this order "shall be to the said Sherif a sufficient warrant." Lydius appeared before the Council on December 15, 1761, in the custody of the sheriff and being asked why he did not appear "answered that he was indisposed . . . and the season of the year so very severe, . . . and being then asked why he did not appear as soon as these objections were removed, replyed that he thought the Board would not expect his attendance after the issuing of the Proclamation . . . And being then asked why he had presumed to survey . . . contrary to . . . the said Proclamation, he acknowledged that he had surveyed . . . not looking on the Premises as Lying within the Province of New York . . . John Henry Lydius . . . was informed that the Board would not suffer the Point of Jurisdiction or limits of the province . . . to be argued in this case . . . Mr. Hicks . . . for Mr. Lydius . . . Informed the Board that Mr. Lydius claimed no Title to the Premises under this Government. The said John Henry Lydius . . . produced . . . an Indian deed . . . dated 1732 and an Instrument in writing granted in the year 1744 by . . . the Governor of . . . Massachusetts Bay. The Board being of opinion that the said Indian Deed and Instrument,

vested no Title . . . ordered . . . that the High Sherif . . . of Albany . . . do keep the said John Henry Lydius in custody. . . ." On December 16, 1761, the Council ordered that John Henry Lydius be discharged from his contempt in not appearing and also be discharged out of the sheriff's custody on entering into a recognizance before Justice Horsmanden in the amount of £5000 for his appearance at the next Supreme Court to answer to an information "for his contempt in Surveying . . . contrary to the Proclamation of 18 February 1761 . . . and to an Information for Intruding on Crown Lands. . . ." The Lieutenant Governor and Council ordered that copies of the proceedings in Council be laid before the Attorney General to file informations against Lydius for his contempt and for the intrusion. Cf. also 1 *Colden Letter Books* 64–67.

Attorney General John Tabor Kempe on Mar. 8, 1762, having received the above order in Council, wrote a letter to Lieutenant Governor Colden, a rough draft of which is contained in the *J. T. Kempe Lawsuits* L–O and excerpts from which are as follows:

"In the last Term I filed an Information against him for the Intrusions and he . . . was compelled to plead instanter so that that suit is at Issue—But being in doubt whether an Information would lie merely for the contempt of this proclamation . . . [Kempe felt it his] duty to defer filing such Information

"I . . . beg leave to made some observations . . .

"A Proclamation creating a New Law or making an act punishable . . . not punishable before, is void because it would alter the Law which cannot be done but in Parliament.

"Where a proclamation forbids that . . . which before was unlawful, it changes not the Law but is a gracious Admonition . . . it makes not . . . a new Crime but makes the perpetration . . . more aggravated . . . The Contempt . . . shall not be punished as a new offence. . . .

"It is to be considered also that no person shall twice be punished for the same Crime Mr. Lydius is already charged with the Intrusion should he be again charged for his Contempt . . . and punished for both I conceive he would be twice punished for the same offence, For should it be objected that the Intrusion is one offence and the Contempt . . . another . . . I answer that . . . a general charge of Mr. Lydius for Contempt of this Proclamation would be faulty The particular act . . . must be set forth and in this case it must be his intruding on the King's Lands, For this Intrusion he is charged already . . . for as is common in these cases, he is charged with a continuation of his

tween the lush and unpruned "garland of prerogatives" which the King possessed overseas and the withered wreath which two revolutions had left him at home. Neither the existence of a continuously turbulent assembly nor the rapid and general reception of common law doctrine was an effective check upon prerogative, because the last word was always spoken at Whitehall. This is why, of course, it was usually futile to challenge executive acts by process of law, and why it was possible to introduce so many English administrative practices which, like the estreating of fines and amercements,[179] seem a little baroque for an infant community. This phase of institutional reproduction and the extent of the Governor's participation are unknown territory. Since it touches only the periphery of our own problems we can concern ourselves with it no further than to suggest that as a practical matter the mandate powers exercised by writ may be involved. During the proprietary period, precepts of an extraordinary nature—the so-called special warrant—were freely used for all manner of judicial and administrative business.[180] There is some evidence that the practice thus begun continued in the eighteenth century, and that the writ as a means of making prerogative effective was a weapon not to be despised.[181]

Local Ordinance

A source of jurisdiction that in the everyday life of the inhabitants was of as immediate importance as the acts of assembly or the ordinances of the Governor and Council was the local enactment. In the chartered cities, the mayor and aldermen sitting as a common council were empowered to pass ordinances, which were to be in force as law for a certain number of months or made perpetual on confirmation by the Governor. These ordinances were not

---

Trespass, to the day of the filing the Information agt. him. . . ."

In the *J. T. Kempe Lawsuits* L–O, a document of June 1762, containing a copy of the costs for putting off the trial has at the foot of the same the following notation in Mr. Kempe's handwriting: "3 inst. 163. Proclamations are of great force grounded on the laws of the Realm."

[179] Cf. *infra* 519 *et seq.*
[180] Cf. *infra* 389.
[181] For example, the issuance of writs of adjournment. The earliest entry is that in *Ms. Mins. SCJ 1710–14* 335, "The Queens writ for adjournment of this Term was read and allowed" on account of the Canadian expedition. In *Ms. Jay Papers* Box 3, 16a is a copy of the writ of adjournment Feb. 13, 1720/21, another version is in *H.R. Parch.* 209D2. There are notes for an argument in

the *Jay Mss.* where the writ is spoken of as a "new devised writ" and that there are no precedents for the adjournment of a whole term. The English proceeding of Elizabeth's time is described in 1 *Anderson* 278–279, where it is stated the Queen proclaims the adjournment which proclamation is a warrant for the keeper of the Great Seal to issue the writs. Cf. also *Cro. Car.* 11. 13, 27; 1 *Levinz* 176, 178. The 1721 writ above is described in the parchment as "his Majesty's closed writt."

Compare also the action staying a justice's precept upon prayer for a protection (19 *Ms. Mins. Council* 25 [1739]) and the attack on the Governor's warrants (14 *ibid.* 337). The most celebrated episode in the eighteenth century is Colden's writ for an appeal in Forsey v. Cunningham. The documents are in 29 *ibid.* 101, and cf. 1 *Colden Letter Books* 433; 2 *ibid.* 41 *et seq.*

to be derogative of the King's prerogative or repugnant to the laws of England or New York.[182] Under them jurisdiction was given to justices of the peace to enforce liquor laws, weights and measures and minor police regulations by means of fines and amercements leviable by warrants of distress.

Of the same general character as the city ordinances were the local town laws passed in town meetings.[183] These regulations covered such matters as fences, pounds, road building, health, and even traffic, and fines leviable by justices of the peace were imposed as sanctions. The town laws had to be confirmed in the Courts of Sessions[184] in order to be enforced, a rule of considerable importance for the purposes of central control.[185] It was, moreover, a

[182] In the Montgomerie Charter the royal prerogative is not expressed as a limitation on the liberties and powers granted to New York City and the only requirement is that they should not contradict the laws of England or of the province (Kent, *op. cit.* 55). The confirmation of the Montgomerie Charter by the assembly expressly states that this charter is to be good and effectual in law against the King.

It should further be noted that in 1694 a statute against unlawful by-laws was enacted (1 *Col. Laws NY* 326). This was directed against certain ordinances of New York City made "under colour and pretext of their Charter or Custom. . . ." This is the first attempt to control the by-law power by provincial statute. In 1735 an information was filed against the city of New York for a by-law which was alleged to be unreasonable and against law (*Ms. Mins. SCJ 1732–39* 186). The by-law was repealed.

[183] The town regulations are to be found in the various printed town records. Cf. the examples *infra* n. 185.

[184] The ordinance power of towns was recognized in the Duke's Laws and the requirement of confirmation by Sessions was there first laid down; cf. 1 *Col. Laws NY* 63 (Townships). In 1691 a statute (*ibid.* 225) was enacted requiring confirmation apparently only of ordinances for the "improvement" of lands but the requirement seems to have been regarded as covering any ordinance; see, for example, the swine ordinance in 2 *Huntington Town Recs.* 167; in 1723 the Queens justices refused to confirm a Flushing "town act" re straying horses, *Ms. Mins. Queens Co. Sess. 1722–87* May 21, 1723; in 1770 the Ulster justices confirmed an order of New Paltz re sheep, *Ms. Files Ulster Co.* Bundle E. In *Ms. Mins. Albany Co. Sess. 1717–23* are entries Oct. 2, 1717, June 8, 1720, confirming Schenectady ordinances.

[185] For examples of confirmation under the Duke's Laws cf. 1 *Southold Town Recs.* 384, 385 (1681/82); 1 *Huntington Town Recs.* 285 *et seq.* (1681/82).

The Kings County records afford a clear picture of the confirming process under the Act of 1691 and indicate the nature of town regulation. Thus a town law providing for the erection and repair of fences and gates was "confirmed and granted by the court of Sessions and [was ordered] to be recorded in the Register of Kings County. Per curia. Entered in Register for Kings County Liber A Folio 238/9 November 24, 1693 . . . Register" (*Ms. Kings Co. Ct. & Rd. Recs. 1692–1825* 75, Nov. 14, 1693). Cf. also the confirmation of town laws of Flatbush and Gravesend regarding fences (*ibid.* 15, Nov. 8, 1692), of Flatbush protecting young trees and regulating the ditching of meadows (*ibid.* 31, May 13, 1696), of Brooklyn for proportioning the commons (*ibid.* 37, May 11, 1697) and of Boswyck and Brooklyn providing for trustees to raise taxes and defend the town patents (*ibid.* May 11, 1703).

In a Gravesend rule about fences, it is entered that the town "agreement should be in Court Confirmeth and made as a Statute Law ffor ffuture time . . ." indicating a lofty opinion of local ordinance (*ibid.* 65, Nov. 12, 1700). A town law of Boswyck providing for a 3s. penalty for failure of its inhabitants to do their share of the work in repairing a highway was approved in Sessions on November 12, 1706 (*ibid.* 150). Another town law, that of Flatlands, made very elaborate provisions stating that its inhabitants could not sell any part of the common woods to outsiders, nor set up fences on these woods nor sell firewood from the commons to any outsider, nor cut green firewood, and was approved (*ibid.* 97, May 11, 1703).

On May 9, 1704 the town of Flatbush was ordered to have another meeting to make rules for fences and three or any two justices of the peace were "ordered to grant the warrant ffor the said towne Meeting and to take the votes . . . and to be Judges of the qualifications of the Inhabitants . . . and to bring said towne law . . . to the next Court of Sessions ffor a Conffirmation according to law" (*ibid.* 143).

The Courts of Sessions by no means confirmed every town law submitted, and oftentimes made regulations governing the manner and form which

tighter form of control than existed in England where the early statutes which had attempted the same policy of administrative supervision[186] were either never enforced or had fallen into desuetude so that only a judicial proceeding against unpalatable ordinances was practically available. The provincial rule, which depended on statute, made no exception of incorporated towns which had the ordinance power by charter, subject to conformity with English and New York law.[187] The confirmation at Sessions may have been only *pro forma* but it at least tended to avoid the dangers and nuisance of proceedings by information against illegal by-laws.

On a very different footing stood the regulations for the counties, the so-called orders made by the Courts of General Sessions. As in England, the legislative activity of the justices of the peace in Sessions was subject to no administrative control from above.[188] This ordinance power, moreover, was not expressly provided for in any of the judicature acts, and must, therefore, be regarded as one of the functions which through some mysterious osmotic process flows overseas from the homeland by virtue of the phrase "Sessions of the Peace," which the statutes employ. It is one of the most striking examples of unconscious institutional reception that we have. Colonel Nicolls' scheme of local government had been built about the town as the unit, and consequently matters best dealt with locally had been committed to the constable and overseers for regulation. The "ridings" were obviously not compact enough for the

---

such laws should take before being submitted to the court. So the Kings County Sessions, on May 9, 1704: "Ordered that noe towne lawes or orders be brought into this Court in dutch or any other language but English" (*ibid*. 144). Many town laws were rejected in Sessions and so, on May 11, 1703, in the Kings Sessions "ffor severall reasons offered . . . by some of the ffreeholders of said towne . . . [a fencing law of Flatbush was] rejected, and ordered . . . towne meeting . . . where the . . . ffarmers only shall have a free vote" (*ibid*. 96). Flatbush must have had some difficulty getting its various laws approved by the Court of Sessions, for on November 12, 1701, another regulation of fences made by that town was "Rejected by Reason that the Court do Nott ffind itt Conveniend that the old Law Should be Voyd" (*ibid*. 84). Because several freeholders were denied votes, the town laws of Boswyck and Flatbush were rejected by Kings Sessions on November 10, 1703 (*ibid*. 192).

Evidently unauthorized groups of town freeholders had been bringing town laws into Kings Sessions for confirmation, because on November 10,

1703, the court found it necessary to order "that hencefforward noe person . . . shall . . . bring in any towne law to this Court of Sessions ffor confirmation . . . or pleade ffor . . . any of the said townes without ffirst having Authority and power ffrom said town" (*ibid*. 193).

[186] The statute 15 Hy. VI c.6 contemplated supervision of guild and company statutes but it does not appear to have been enforced (cf. Putnam, *Proc. before Justices of the Peace* [1938] cx). The renewing act, 19 Hy. VII c.7, included cities, towns and boroughs (cf. *supra* n. 10). So far as we can discover this statute seems to have been ignored in the course of the seventeenth century. The judgment in the case of the Tailors of Ipswich (11 *Co. Rep.* 53) denied that compliance with the statute had corroborative effect on by-laws but left them to be "affirmed as good or disaffirmed as unlawful by the law." Compliance simply relieved the corporations of the penalty mentioned in the act.

[187] E.g., Fletcher's charter to Huntington Oct. 5, 1694, in 2 *Huntington Town Recs.* 140.

[188] Webb, *Eng. Local Government; Parish and County* (1906) 535.

institution of county legislation, and hence the Sessions' function was supervisory. But when, in 1683, the province was divided into counties, the Sessions became a county court and the stage was set for the development of county government on the English pattern. This process was furthered by the elimination of the old town courts and the enhancement of the functions of the justices of the peace. The use of the grand jury after 1683 was also an important factor in bringing about the change.[189] The meetings of General Sessions came to be regarded as meetings of the whole county, especially as provincial acts directed the dispatch of certain county business at such Sessions,[190] although for some matters special meetings of county freeholders were authorized.[191] These freeholder meetings were exceptional, however, for most county orders were made by the justices. The matters regulated in Sessions and sometimes at "meetings" of the justices embraced such perennial problems as fencing[192] and impounding of cattle[193] and in these particulars were to some extent preventive in intent, for there were constant disputes arising over boundaries and loose animals. We have found also ordinances regarding common woods,[194] against the racing of horses in the streets,[195] the convivial assembly of negroes,[196] and even one requiring the repair of houses.[197] The collection of taxes

---

[189] This is shown clearly in the *Ms. Mins. Albany Co. Sess. 1685–89* 49 where the grand jury presents "that ye Bakers may be ordered to make there bread of a Due Assise and that ye price may be diminished since wheat is so cheap." The suggestion can come from other officers as in *ibid.* 57 (Jan. 1688/89) where the sheriff requests the price of wheat be fixed for the purpose of rate paying.

[190] E.g., 1 *Col. Laws NY* 456 (1701).

[191] Thus the act for the Dutchess courthouse, *ibid.* 868; the warrant for the auction, *Book of Supervisors Dutchess Co. 1718–22* 6; the act re fences, 2 *Col. Laws NY* 64 (1721), 481 (1728) and cf. the regulation made in *Ms. Deeds Richmond Co.* Liber C, 446, 447 (1733).

[192] *Ms. Mins. Ulster Co. Sess. 1693–98* Sept. 4, 1694. In Kings an order was made by the court on November 15, 1704, fixing the height of fences at four feet, three inches (*Ms. Kings Co. Ct. & Rd. Recs. 1692–1825* 145) while some years earlier, on May 19, 1691, the same court had set six shillings as the penalty for failure to keep fences in repair (*Ms. Kings Co. Ct. & Rd. Recs. 1668–1766* 66). Christopher Rousby was indicted in New York City Quarter Sessions on Nov. 7, 1705, for "not keeping his fences in repair next the Commons" and a *venire facias* was issued against him returnable next Sessions (*Ms. Mins. NYCQS 1694–1731/32* 106). Compare the Albany order regarding roads in *Ms.*

Mins. Albany Co. Sess. 1717–23 Feb. 4, 1718/19.

[193] The Kings County rules for impounding of stray cattle obliged owners to pay fines and poundage fees: *Ms. Kings Co. Ct. & Rd. Recs. 1692–1825* 146, Nov. 15, 1704 (stray horses); *ibid.* 71, July 14, 1692 (swine running at large). John Griggs was presented on May 9, 1693, "for breaking open the pound and fencing the King's Highway at Gravesend," and for this offense he was fined 10s. "to the use of their Majestys" (*ibid.* 15). The poundmaster complained to Kings County Sessions on Nov. 10, 1696 that he had stray horses in the pound for several weeks and no owner claimed them. He also stated that the horses had done great damage on a neighbor's corn, and the court therefore ordered that the poundmaster make sale of the horses to satisfy costs and damages, the overplus to be returned to the owner if he showed up within a year and a day (*ibid.* 34).

[194] In orders made defining the extent of common woods and forbidding encroachment, fines were set and damages exacted for failure to observe the regulations made in Sessions (*ibid.* 146, Nov. 15, 1704).

[195] *Ms. Mins. Ulster Co. Sess. 1711/12–1720* Mar. 27, 1719.

[196] *Ms. Mins. Ulster Co. Sess. 1693–98* Sept. 4, 1694.

[197] *Ms. Mins. Ulster Co. Sess. 1737–50* Nov. 4, 1744.

and rates[198] and the retailing of liquor were also the constant concern of general county orders.[199]

A great deal of the enactment by Sessions was of a supplementary type, that is to say it was issued to reinforce locally an existing statute, and some of it was transitory. The decrees issued for the general preservation of the peace[200] and for the observance of the Sabbath are among the most interesting examples of the efforts to safeguard the manners and morals of the counties.

For obvious reasons the regulation of trade constituted a most important

[198] On Dec. 14, 1693, the Kings County Sessions made an order setting the county rates (*Ms. Kings Co. Ct. & Rd. Recs. 1692–1825* 23) and on Nov. 10, 1703, the same court set taxes and apportioned the share payable by each town (*ibid.* 193). The grand jurors of New York County on Nov. 4, 1696, presented Tymon Van Borson and Andries Marschalk, assessors of the North Ward, for "not duly assessing the inhabitants of the Ward," on house, ground and estate. A capias was ordered against these defendants but when they appeared on Feb. 2, 1696/97, they prayed their discharge, claiming that "the not assessing of Cornelius Plevier was wholly through Ignorance Omitted and not willfully." The court, however, wished to advise on the case and we have not learned what subsequently happened to the delinquent assessors (*Ms. Mins. NYCQS 1694–1731/32* 17–19). *Ms. Mins. Westch. Co. Sess. 1710–23* contains a great number of these. Cf. also *Ms. Mins. Ulster Co. Sess. 1737–50* Sept. 1747.

[199] *Ms. Mins. Richmond Co. Sess. 1710/11–1744/45* Sept. 13, 1717; *Ms. Mins. Westch. Co. Sess. 1710–23* June 7, 1715. For text of such an order of Kings County cf. Nov. 8, 1692: "The Court doe order that noe Retaylers of liquors . . . doe presume to retayle . . . or kepp any publique house . . . without having a license under the hands and seales of two Justices of peace . . . and be bound by recognizances . . . with two sufficient suretys on the penalty of ten pounds each for their good order and rule in their house as the law directs in such Cases, ordered likewise that all Retaylers as aforesd. shall Come to the Clerck of the peace of the County . . . to take out their licenses according to law" (*Ms. Kings Co. Ct. & Rd. Recs. 1692–1825* 14; see also *ibid.* 88, May 13, 1702).

Sessions also exercised a summary power to suppress disorderly ale houses and to revoke retail liquor licenses. Thus John Gardner was, on Aug. 6, 1706, "suppressed" from retailing liquors because he had "entertained" slaves in his ale house (Queen v. John Gardner, *Ms. Mins. NYCQS 1694–1731/32* 110). Likewise John Webb, having been indicted for keeping a disorderly "tipling" house, was found guilty by the jury and fined 3s. 4d., and while his case was pending, he was ordered to close his establishment (Queen v. John Webb, *Ms.*

Mins. NYCQS 1694–1731/32 170, 248–250, 252, 254–256, Aug. 6, 1712, Nov. 4, 1712, Feb. 3, 1712/13). After Webb had paid a fine for keeping the disorderly house, he apparently pulled some wires to have his license reinstated, because on May 6, 1713, the justices in Quarter Sessions recommended that "the Mayor . . . Grant A Lycence to John Webb for Retailing of Strong Liquors," he giving sureties and certificates from his neighbors and stating that he would keep an orderly "tipling" house (*ibid.* 260).

[200] *Ms. Mins. Albany Co. Sess. 1685–89* 28, order increasing the number of constables. Note the recital in a regulation made in New York City Quarter Sessions on Feb. 4, 1718/19: "For the better Preservation of the Peace and Preventing Tumults Disorders and Other Mischiefs that Commonly happen . . . on Shrove Tuesday by Great Numbers of Youth Apprentices and Slaves that Assemble together in throwing at Cocks and for Suppressing that Cruel Usage and Custom . . . Ordered . . . that there be no throwing at Cocks . . . on that day" (*Ms. Mins. NYCQS 1694–1731/32* 359).

Frequently in New York City Quarter Sessions, the following entry appears: "Proclamation made and his Excellency's Proclamation Dated the Third of May last against Immorality and Prophaneness was published in open court" (*ibid.* 70, Nov. 3, 1702; see also *ibid.* 258, May 5, 1713).

The justices also enforced rigid observance of feasts and holidays, and William Bickley and Daniel Latham were "presented for keeping open shop and working on the thirtieth day of January. . . ." Capias was issued against these two, and finally William Bickley pleaded guilty, but said that he "did not know it was an offense against the law." Bickley was released on the payment of a 6s. fine, but Latham, a more hardened offender, "appeared in his proper person and the indictment being read, he refused to plead." Cf. *infra* 595 n. 189.

In Ulster County the Sessions had apparently made an order against Sabbath breach. In Queen v. Livingston (*Ms. Mins. Ulster Co. Sess. 1711/12–1720* Sept. 2, 1712) the defendant indicted for Sunday riding claimed first that he had had fever and ague and had gone out for air. Subsequently, on motion of the attorney for the defendant averring that an act of assembly regulated the matter (indi-

part of Sessions ordinance power, especially in New York and Kings counties. Nothing illustrates more decisively how rulemaking was regarded as a Sessions function than the orders of the New York Quarter Sessions respecting the assize of bread[201]—even although the city was chartered and the ordinance power was normally exercised by the common council. The regulatory power of Sessions extended also to matters of health[202] and it likewise comprehended the important business of maintaining proper weights and measures.[203] The

cating thus the procedure was based on an ordinance, and that the indictment did not name the arresting officer), the indictment was quashed. Cf. also the list of fines (March 26, 1718) for Sabbath breach.

[201] On February 1, 1697/98 the Court of Quarter Sessions for New York City made a general order setting the assize of bread as follows: "Order'd the Assize of Bread be till further Order as followeth (Vizt) A White loaf of the finest flower to weigh ten ounces for three half pence. A Wheaten loaf the Coarsest bran only taken out and Not Otherwise to weigh three pound and a Quarter for four pence halfe peny and that no other bread be made for sale than what above specifyed Ordered that all Bakers within this City doe keep bread in their shops that the Inhabitants be supplyed accordingly" (Ms. Mins. NYCQS 1694–1731/32 34, Feb. 1, 1697/98).

Despite this order Jacob Bratt and other bakers were presented on Feb. 8, 1699/1700, for "vending bread of unlawful assize," but when they appeared on May 1, 1700, they were discharged, having been fined before for the same fact (Ms. Mins. NYCQS 1694–1731/32 51, 53). In 1715, Garret Van Laer and Ralph Thurman were fined 22s. each; Peter Fosborgh, James Bergeron and Magdalen Salnave were fined 3s. each, while Joost Lynsen was fined 20s. and John Harris 15s. when these defendants pleaded guilty to indictments for breaking the assize of bread (ibid. 285–311, May 3, Aug. 2, 1715). Coenraet and Jacob Ten Eyck were also indicted for breaking the assize of bread on May 3, 1715 (ibid. 287, 288, 295, 312, 313) and cf. also King v. Walling (ibid. 443, 444, Aug. 5, 1724); and King v. John Bogert, Jr., and George Remsen (Ms. Mins. NYCQS 1732–62 163, 164, May 3, 4, 1744).

We have also noted indictments for unmerchantable flour, and in one, that against Cornelius Sebring, viewers were appointed to determine the condition of the flour. When it was found not merchantable, the defendant, pleading not guilty, was tried, found guilty "of the fraud and nuisance" and fined £8 (Ms. Mins. NYCQS 1694–1731/32 37–39, May 3, 4, 1698). Likewise Elias Nean and Ezekiel Grazeillier, on recognizance to answer for nuisance in packing unmerchantable flour, appeared in court and "declared they intended no fraud . . . believed it was good and pray the

court to remitt any prosecution." They were apparently discharged without paying any fine (ibid. 56, Nov. 5, 1700; NY Misc. Mss. Box 3, no. 19, Aug. 30, 1700). In the New York City Quarter Sessions minutes for 1751, the names, addresses and brands of bakers were entered in accordance with an act of assembly to prevent the exportation of unmerchantable flour and false taring of bread and flour casks (Ms. Mins. NYCQS 1732–62 291, 292, Mar. 21, June 4, 1751; 3 Col. Laws NY 788, 883). In one case a person was indicted for a cheat in selling as good flour certain unmerchantable flour (Ms. Mins. NYCQS 1732–62 282, 283).

The regulation of bread and flour was of great interest to the New York merchants. In the New York Common Council Minutes are petitions to the King and the Governor requesting that the City of New York have the sole right of "bolting flower" (e.g., 1 Min. Com. Council NYC 142; 2 ibid. 6–8, 25–54).

[202] Thus Benjamin Disbrow was indicted in Westchester County Sessions on Dec. 5, 1693, for "offring Carrion beefe to saile," and on May 14, 1696, for "Stincking Beefe" (Mins. Westch. Ct. Sess. 1657–96 85, 86, 128). There being no provincial statute this probably was for violating a county ordinance. On May 7, 1701, Peter Marks was indicted in New York for selling "putrid and unwholesome flesh" and being found guilty was fined £3 and sentenced to three months' imprisonment "without bail or mainprize" (Ms. Mins. NYCQS 1694–1731/32 63, 64). George Norton, butcher, on indictment for "selling corrupt flesh," was somewhat more fortunate in that he was found not guilty (ibid. 90–92, Aug. 1, Nov. 8, 1704). James Rusthead, indicted for "exposing to sale unwholesome and corrupt flesh," pleaded guilty and was apparently discharged simply on the payment of fees (Ms. Mins. NYCQS 1732–62 101–103, May 3, Aug. 7–9, 1739; see also King v. John Poor, ibid. 163, 165, 170, May 2, 3, Aug. 8, 1744).

[203] Cf. a Kings County order, establishing weights and measures according to English laws, by which the constable and freeholder of each town were to seize unlawful weights (Ms. Kings Co. Ct. & Rd. Recs. 1692–1825 98, May 11, 1703). A provincial statute was passed a month later (1 Col. Laws NY 554). Prior to this the situation in New York City, where one would expect regulation, is obscure. Thus on Feb. 5, 1700/01, Jellis Provoost

extraordinary amount and variety of these subordinate legislative acts can be compared only with the modern mizzle of administrative rescripts. The matter has been quite overlooked by historians, but there was no one in eighteenth century New York who did not have to tread carefully because of these orders.

The Judicial Commissions

We have thus far considered the basis of jurisdiction in New York Province chiefly in terms of the location of enacting power and its various manifestations, for we are dealing with a system of law which in its inception depended directly upon fiat. So far as there were any elements of prescription in the early provincial law these were borrowed, and it was long before the colonists were mindful of the fact. The ordinance power of Sessions just considered is one of these borrowings, and we have now to consider the most significant of them all as respects jurisdiction—the commission.

In those remote years when the King's justice had yet to establish its utter preeminence in England, and when the struggle over jurisdiction was widely and bitterly waged, the commission was focal because it was invariably the first point of attack. Much of the learning on jurisdiction had grown up about these instruments and it was used with telling effect in the early seventeenth century when the common law courts were seeking to establish their superiority over the tribunals created by the Tudors.

The judicial commission was originally conceived as the medium whereby the Crown had delegated its prerogative in matters judicial.[204] Although Sir

---

and seven other defendants were presented by the grand jury for using false weights, and capias issued against them. Cornelius Lodge, one of the defendants, offered a rather naive excuse in that he "informed the court that his wife used a Yard not his," and praying the court's mercy he was released on the payment of a 6s. fine. Richard Potter, another of these defendants, also confessed the indictment offering an excuse similar to that given by Lodge. Potter explained that "the weight was borrowed from one of his neighbors," but he was also fined 6s. as were two other defendants who simply pleaded guilty without bothering to offer defense (King v. Jellis Provoost et al., Ms. Mins. NYCQS 1694–1731/32, 60, 61). On Nov. 4, 1702, the grand jury presented sixteen for using false weights. Capias was issued against the defendants, and on Feb. 2, 1702/03, they pleaded not guilty but submitted to a fine and were released on the payment of 6s. (Queen v. Joseph Isaacs et al., ibid. 73–75). However, one of these defendants pleaded guilty on Nov. 4, 1702 (Queen v. Caleb Cooper,

ibid. 73). It is difficult to determine whether in this case violation of a city ordinance or Sessions order is involved. Thus the indictments in the cases above recited that each of the defendants "not minding or Regarding an honest upright & Conscientious dealing & behavior towards . . . his Neighbors . . . but wholly contriving . . . for his own private and unlawful gains to foster advance and . . . did keep false and deceitful weights . . . to the great loss & damage & in deceit of the Leige subjects of . . . the Queen and others having occasion to buy the same contrary to the forme of several statutes in such case made and provided and ags'. the peace of . . . the Queen that now is" (H.R. Pleadings Pl. Q. 40, Pl. Q. 41). We have found no provincial acts earlier than 1703. See also Queen v. John Basford (Ms. Mins. NYCQS 1694–1731/32 190, 191, 199–201, Feb. 6, 7, 1710/11, May 1, 1711) and King v. David Lyell (ibid. 288, May 3, 1715).

[204] Bracton, De Legibus fols. 107b–108.

Edward Coke had minimized this aspect by defining the commission as a delegation by warrant of an Act of Parliament or of the common law where jurisdiction or authority was conferred,[205] the older view was a closer description of theory respecting commissions in a royal province where the prerogative was nearly paramount.[206] Traditionally, the powers of English judges were sought in their commissions, so that it was impossible to use in America instruments of the same or similar type without reference to the law and practice that had grown up with respect to them. It is obvious, therefore, that no discussion of the basis of jurisdiction can dispense with a consideration of these forms.

The most remarkable fact in connection with the earliest judicial commissions in New York is their failure to conform to English models. During the first twenty years of English rule in the province, even an approximation of such a usual document as a commission of the peace was not thought necessary, and as a result the persons commissioned were either cast upon their own discretion or were obliged to turn to the Governor for help.[207] A striking example of this is the Nicolls commission to the mayor and aldermen of New York,[208] whose functions among other things included the exercise of Sessions jurisdiction for the city. In respect of their status as provincial officers, it is clear that they ranked as justices of the peace, for in this capacity they sat in the Court of Assizes, yet they are directed by the commission merely that they are to "rule and governe" according to the law of "this government" and that the commission shall be a sufficient warrant for the "due administration of Justice."[209] The first commissions to the justices of the peace in the country have fortunately been preserved.[210] They, like those issued subsequently by

---

[205] Coke, *Fourth Institute* 163.

[206] The justice of the peace handbooks are partial to the time-honored theory; cf. Lambard, *Eirenarcha* Bk i. c.5; Dalton, *Countrey Justice* (1677) c.1 §1; c.3 §4. It is interesting to note that the doctrine of the handbooks is much affected by the statute 27 Hy. VIII c.24 which was enacted for the recontinuation of liberties in the Crown. Even in the eighteenth century, Hawkins in 2 *Pleas of the Crown* c.5 takes this statute as his point of departure in the discussion of commissions. The importance of this view of the commission as deriving directly from the Crown is illustrated in 1 Chalmers, *Opinions of Eminent Lawyers* (1814) 240, 244 *et seq.*

[207] The wide authority left to the Governor by the Duke's Laws in the matter of the special warrant (1 *Col. Laws NY* 66) and the constant intervention of the early governors in the smallest details of law enforcement lead one to infer that the vagueness of the commissions was intentional. An

English form of peace commission is in Dalton, *op. cit.* 16.

[208] *Gen. Entries 1664–65* 172.

[209] The revocation of the Dutch form of government (*ibid.* 171) indicates Nicolls intended the change to conform with English borough practice.

[210] The form:

"A Commission for a Justice of the Peace.

Whereas I have conceived a good opinion of the Ability prudence and integrity of You Daniel Denton of Jamaica in the North Riding of Yorkshire upon Long Island, for the carrying on of Publique affaires, I have therefore thought fitt to Constitute and appoint, And by these presents do Constitute and appoint you Daniel Denton, to bee a Justice of the Peace within the said Riding, with full Power and Authority to Execute all such Lawes as are made, or shall hereafter bee made for the good Government of those parts of his Royal Highenesse, the Duke of York his Territoryes, hereby

Governor Lovelace,[211] were couched in words so general as to bewilder the patentee. For although the justice is given full power and authority to execute the provincial laws, he is required to discharge his duty as a "Justice of ye peace ought to do." The Lovelace commission added a command that such rules as the Governor might from time to time send be observed.[212]

The early years of proprietary government saw a considerable use of the *ad hoc* commission[213] for the settlement of particular controversies—a device that is reminiscent of the commissions of inquiry in England. There is great variation in the terms of these commissions, for which no particular authority except the Governor's general prerogatives appears to have existed.[214] These commissions are a passing phase, for as the judiciary becomes better organized they disappear. The only exception to this is the oyer and terminer commission, the use of which was authorized by the Duke's Laws. This commission, however, is not in the English form;[215] indeed, were it not for the clerk's label and the use of the operative words "hear and determine" it would hardly be recognized for what it purported to be.

The provincial variants, which Andros took no pains to alter,[216] were sup-

---

willing and requiring you, Strictly to discharge yo'
Duty as a Justice of the Peace ought to do. And all
other Persons within this Government, are hereby
Strictly Charged and required to take notice hereof,
and to beare respect and give obedience according
to Law unto You Daniel Denton in the performance
of your Office as a Justice of the Peace appointed by
the Authority of his Royall Highnesse the Duke of
York, Given under my hand at ffort James in New
York this 16th day of March 1664.
                                    Rich Nicolls."
2 *Ms. Book of Deeds* 17 (Sec. of State's Office,
Albany).
   [211] 2 *Exec. Council Mins.* 526, Justice of Peace
Commission to Chambers, 1671.
   [212] *Ibid.* On Chambers' difficulties cf. *infra* 65.
   [213] E.g., 14 *Doc. Rel. Col. Hist. NY* 617; *Exec.
Council Mins.* 262 (1669), 313 (1669), 333
(1670).
   [214] The curious commissions to Coffin and to
Mayhew as chief magistrates respectively of Nantucket and Martha's Vineyard rest upon the same
ground (*Exec. Council Mins.* 363, 368).
   [215] Cf. the oyer and terminer commission for the
murderer of Jn° Steward, *Exec. Council Mins.* 758,
and the similar commission for trial of Johnson
et al. (*ibid.* 761). A form of the English oyer and
terminer commission is in *Office of Clerk of Assize*
(1682) 8, and cf. Coke, *Fourth Institute* 162.
   [216] Cf. the justice of the peace commission in 12
Doc. Rel. Col. Hist. NY 604; the Nantucket commission in *Ms. Warrants Orders and Passes 1674–79*
137; the admiralty commission (*ibid.* 160); the spe-

cial commission for the Newcastle court (*ibid.* 180);
the commissary commission for Schenectady (*ibid.*
205); for Albany (2 *Mins. of the Ct. of Albany,*
etc. 143). The New York City mayor and aldermen
commission is in 1 *Mins. Com. Council NYC* 1.
   The admiralty commissions deserve particular attention because they throw considerable light on
the question of the limits of the Governor's authority in this field of jurisdiction. The commissions
together with the records of the courts held by virtue of them indicate clearly enough that the jurisdiction was regarded to be as full and as ample
as that exercised by the High Court of Admiralty
at home. Indeed, the recital in an information
(1684) goes as far as to describe the New York
court as "the High Court of Admiralty for his
Royal Highness James Duke of York and Albany
for his Territoryes in America" (34 *NY Col. Mss.*
pt. I, 21. Cf. also *H.R. Ms. Wills* Liber I, 282, 295;
34 *NY Col. Mss.* pt. II *passim*). Between 1664 and
1673 the sessions of the admiralty court were apparently all held by special commission. Andros attempted to put the court on a more permanent
basis. He was instructed by the Duke in 1678 to appoint a judge, register and marshal (3 *Doc. Rel.
Col. Hist. NY* 268). All of these documents are
relevant exhibits for the purpose of correcting
C. M. Andrews, who in 4 *Col. Period of Am. Hist.*
222 n. 1, states *inter alia*, "probably no colonial
governor, proprietary or royal ever exercised plenary jurisdiction in vice-admiralty matters certainly
not before 1692, *up to which time no governor was
legally authorized to appoint a single judge, regis-*

planted during the governorship of Dongan by forms which obviously were drawn to conform with common law practice. There were difficulties, however, implicit in the idiosyncrasies of the judicial structure in New York. A peace commission could parrot an English prototype in respect of criminal jurisdiction, but then, because of the civil jurisdiction under the Judicature Act of 1683, it was necessary to improvise.[217] As far as the commission for the New York Oyer and Terminer and General Gaol Delivery Courts was concerned, since the judges were endowed with a greater power than a judge with English commissions of those names, the New York commission consequently had to be drawn specially,[218] but for each session in a particular county a commission after the English model was supplied.[219]

ter or marshal . . ." (italics ours). This is part of a statement written to traverse certain animadversions in 43 Amer. Hist. Rev. 403 regarding the accuracy of Mr. Andrews' legal history; the remarks quoted above now raise the issue of the reliability of his facts.

[217] 34 NY Col. Mss. pt. I, 74, 75. It is drawn for the city and county of New York but the record indicates the same form was used for Kings County.

[218] 34 NY Col. Mss. pt. I, 14:
"Thomas Dongan Lieu[t] Governor and Vic. Admirall—&c.
Whereas by an act of the Generale Assembly Entituled an act to Settle Courts of Justice bearing date the first day of November 1683 it is Enacted that Annually and Every yeare there shall be within the Province of New Yorke and in Each Respective County Within the same a Court of oyer and Terminer and Generale Gaole delivery the members of which Court shall be a Judge with four of the Justices of the Peace of the County. I do therefore hereby by virtue of the authority derived unto me Constitute authorise and appoint you Cap[t] Matthias Nicholls together with Cap[t] John Palmer Judge of the said Court Giveing you and Either of you Joyntly and severally full Power to keep the Said Court at the time and Place appointed in the said act then and there to try and and [sic] determine all matters Causes and Cases Capitall Criminall or Civill Tryable at Comon Law and to act and do all those things Appertaining to the office and Place of a Judge according to the Lawes Established by his Royal High[sse] and the General Assembly and where the said Lawes are defective according to the best of your Knowledge and conscience not repugnant to the Lawes of England and this Commission to be of force during my will and Pleasure only Given under my hand and seal and sealed with the Seale of the Province att Fortt James the 2nd december in the 35th year of the Reigne of our Soveraigne Lord Charles the Second . . . 1683."

[219] Ibid. 43 tres.
"James Duke of York and Albany & Lord Proprietor of this Province to John Palmer Esq[e] one of the Judges of our Court of Oyer and Terminer and Generall Gaole Delivery, John Pell and Lieut. John Palmer Justices of the Peace for the County of Westchester Greeting Know YEE that wee have assigned you and any two of you whereofe the said John Palmer Judge of our said Court of Oyer and Terminer to be one our Justices to Enquire by the Oath of good and Lawfull men of our County of Westchester and by other ways, manners and methods by which the truth may be the better known as well within Liberties as without of all manner of Treasons misprisons of Treasons, murthers, Homicides fellonyes burglarys and all other Crimes offences, and Injuryes Whatsoever, and of theire accessoryes within the County aforesaid by whomsoever, or in what manner soever had done Perpetrated or Comitted and by whom to whom: or with whom when in what manner and of how and other articles and Circumstances aforesaid and anything: Concerning the same and the Said Treasons fellonyes and all other the Premissesse for this time to hear Try and Determine according to the Lawes of this our Province and the Lawes and Customes of his Majesties Kingdome of England, and therefore we Comãnd you that you or any two of you whereof the Said John Palmer Judge of our Court of Oyer and Terminer and Generall Gaole Delivery to be one on Wednesday Thursday and Fryday the 18, 19, and 20 Dayes of this Instant ffebb[ry] at the Publique Court House of the Said County of Westchester make dilligent Enquiry into the Premisses and all and Singular the Said Premisses to here try and determine in manner and forme aforesaid soe farr as it oppertaineth [sic] to Justice according to the said Lawes of this our Province and the Lawes and Customes of his Majestyes Kingdome of England wee have therefore Comanded the Sheriffe of the Said County on the said 18th day of Febb[ry] to cause to come before you such and soe many good and Lawfull men of his Bailiwyke as well without

The adoption in New York of commissions closely approximating English forms was an event of considerable significance in the growth of the law. On the one hand, although the New York peace commission sedulously avoided reference to English law, the acceptance of the ancient English form portended the eventual reception of the body of law which had grown up about this commission. This lay in the cards, for the country justice who sought guidance would soon learn to turn to those common textbooks which existed in such profusion and which, because they conveniently trussed up the black letter learning on the justices and their commissions, enjoyed even in England an authority beyond their juristic merit.[220] On the other hand, the Dongan oyer and terminer commission, by its mandate that it be exercised according to the "laws of this our Province and the laws and customs of . . . England," specifically makes of English law the residual authority to which immediate reference was unavoidable in view of the slender and confused body of endemic law.[221]

Curiously enough, Dongan and his advisers elected to do some rewriting even of the clauses relating to the conservation of the peace and the scope of criminal jurisdiction. The English form then in use gave the justice authority to inquire into "Felonies, Witchcraft, Enchantments, Sorceries, Magick Arts, Trespasses, Forestalling Regratings Engrossing and Extortions" and all other offenses into which a justice might lawfully inquire, and to hear and determine the same list, with unlawful assemblies added. In New York the reference to the dark arts was sensibly omitted, and the justices were empowered to inquire into "petty larcenies, trespasses, extortions and other misdeeds" and offenses subject to inquest by the justices, and to hear and determine the named offenses. This was a significant change because only the least of the felonies was left to the Sessions to try. The English commission was an assignment to keep and cause to be kept all "ordinances and statutes." The New York com-

---

Liberties as within by whom the truth of things may be the better known and Enquired in Testimony whereof we have caused the Seale of our Said Province to be Affixed   New York Febb^ry 13th 1684/85

              Test: Tho: Dongan."

The form follows closely the English oyer and terminer commission, although specification of office is different.

[220] These books were designed as aids to the local justices, but it is clear from works of such scientific pretensions as 2 Hawkins, *Pleas of the Crown* c.8, which is peppered with citations to Lambard, *Eirenarcha*, Crompton, *L'Office et Auctoryte des Justyces de Pees*, and Dalton, *Countrey Justice*, that the leading justices' handbooks were treated as possessing a juristic value equivalent to Coke's *Institutes*. Compare here also Bacon, *Abridgment*.

We have not been able to establish the presence in New York of a copy of Dalton before 1689. Cf. the inventory of Alderman William Coxe in *H.R. Ms. Wills* Liber 14A, 405.

[221] On the importance of the simultaneous introduction of English process cf. *infra* 406 *et seq.*

mission reads "all lawes and ordinances." The latter omitted the inspection of indictments, the continuation of process and the final charge to the justices. The New York justices were not told to reserve cases of difficulty, but were given an entirely novel paragraph respecting civil jurisdiction. In other respects the language follows the form in Dalton's *Countrey Justice*.

The mode being thus set under Dongan eventually became fixed despite the political vicissitudes of the years 1687 to 1691. The peace commission[222] used by Andros when New York was annexed to the Dominion of New England resembles that of Dongan, but the inquiry clause reads "petty larcenies, thefts, trespasses, forestallings regratings engrossings and extortions," and the "hear and determine" clause adds, as in England's, "unlawful assemblies." The inspection of indictments and continuation of process is added, as well as the general charge. There is no chastisement clause or caution to reserve difficult cases and of course the paragraph on civil jurisdiction is omitted. This form was abandoned by Leisler, who had his own ideas on the matter. A large number of his commissions survive. His oyer and terminer commissions are in the same form as those used under Dongan,[223] but the peace commissions,[224] perhaps because Leisler wished the justices to function only in the monthly courts, are of the crude variety used after the conquest.

A precise history of the commission after the Revolution of 1688 can no longer be written since the volumes where these were enrolled before 1770 were destroyed by fire. It is obvious, however, from the few examples which in one way or another have survived, that some effort was made to cleave to common law forms. To be sure, in the case of the Supreme Court this was an unattainable objective since this tribunal was endowed with the powers of King's Bench, Common Bench and Exchequer. The letters patent by which, for example, in England a judge of the Common Bench was appointed,[225]

---

[222] *Ms. Conveyances Kings Co.* Liber I, 129, Aug. 25, 1688; *Ms. Deeds Queens Co.* Liber A, 36, Aug. 25, 1688; *Ms. Deeds Westch. Co.* Liber B, 7, Aug. 25, 1688.

[223] *2 Doc. Hist. NY* 36.

[224] 36 *NY Col. Mss.* 142 no. 65, no. 62. A commission in somewhat different form was issued to Andrew Cannon of Staten Island (Oct. 14, 1690): "By virtue of the authority derived from his most sacred Maj^{tie} King William I do hereby Constitute authorize and apoint you Andrè Canon to be a Justice of ye peace for ye County of Richmond on Staten Island Giving you full power and authority to act therein as a Justice of Peace may or ought to do for the good and welfare of ye Government and

the due administration of Justice according to Law and this Commission to continue until I receive futher orders from his said majtie Given under my hand and seald at Fort William" (*Misc. Mss. Andrew Canon, Staten Island*). Cf. also *Ms. Conveyances Kings Co.* Liber I, 199, where Beekman was commissioned to preside at all courts of judicature held by justices of the peace.

[225] Clarke reported in 1738 that the chief justice was usually appointed at home and by the King's warrant to the Governor and was commissioned under the seal of the province. The puisne justices were appointed without warrant (4 *Doc. Hist. NY* 116). We have not attempted to check this procedure. Mompesson was first appointed without war-

were exceedingly terse and uninformative respecting powers. The colonial Supreme Court commission was, on the other hand, considerably fuller. The commission was granted by the Crown, tested by the Governor.[226] In all the eighteenth century forms examined, power was conferred to hear, try and determine all pleas civil, criminal and mixed, according to the laws, statutes and customs of England and the laws and usages of New York, not being repugnant thereto, a curious inversion which, by its order of words, placed English law in the position of primacy.[227] A rulemaking power as "neare as may be agreable" to the rules of the three central courts was included, and tenure was, as a rule, at pleasure. The later commissions[228] make an important addition: "to

rant. The Solicitor General reported on July 6, 1718, that no warrant for the place of chief justice had been brought to the Office of Trade and Plantations since Atwood's appointment. But Cornbury, on Nov. 6, 1704, writes that upon the death of Dr. Bridges "whom her majesty has been pleased to appoint Chief Justice," by virtue of his commission he had designated Mompesson. Cf. *Misc. Mss. Atwood* and 9 *Ms. Mins. Council* 456.

[226] The form of the commission in the name of the Crown tested merely by the Governor appears to have been followed to avoid the vacating of commissions by the death or removal of the Governor. Cf. the opinion of Morris, C.J., in 1 Chalmers, *Opinions* 250.

[227] The earliest of these documents issued after 1692 which we have seen is the badly injured fragment of a draft commission to William Smith, C.J., William Pinhorne, etc. (39 *NY Col. Mss.* 23). This apparently followed Dongan's form for the oyer and terminer justices. The first complete commission discovered is the following:

"GEORGE by the grace of God of Great Britain France & Ireland King defender of the faith &c. To our trusty and Welbeloved LEWIS MORRIS Esqr. GREETING. We reposing Special trust and Confidence in your Integrity and ability have Assigned Constituted and appointed and we do by these presents Assigne constitute and appoint you the Said LEWIS MORRIS to be CHIEF JUSTICE in and over our Province of NEW YORKE in America in the room of ROGER MOMPESSON Esqr. deceased our late chief Justice of our Said Province GIVING and by these presents granting unto you full power And Lawfull Authority to heare try and determine all Pleas whatsoever Civill criminall and mixt According to the Laws, Statutes and customes of England and the Laws and usages of our said Province of New Yorke not being repugnant thereto And Execution of all Judgments of the said court to Award and make such rules and orders in the said court as may be found convenient and useful and as neare as may be Agreeable to the Rules and orders of our Courts of Kings bench comon Pleas and Exchequer in England To HAVE HOLD AND ENJOY

the Said office or Place of Chief Justice in and over our Said Province with all and Singular the Rights privileges, proffits, advantages Sallaries fees & perquisites unto the Said place belonging or any waies Appertaining in as full and ample manner as any person heretofore Chief Justice of our Said province hath held and Enjoyed or of right ought to have held and Enjoyed the Same. To you the said LEWIS MORRIS during Our will and pleasure In Testimony whereof we have caused these our letters to be made patent and the Seale of our Said Province of New Yorke to these our letters patent to be affixed WITNESSE (by our Especiall direction) our trusty and wellbeloved ROBERT HUNTER Esqr. our captain Generall and Governour in chief of the Province of New York New Jersey and Territories depending thereon in America & Vice Admirall of the Same &c. this ffirst day of July in the ffourth Yeare of our reigne Annoq.Dni. 1718. By Vertue of his Majesties Special Warrant bearing date . . . September, 1715" (*Misc. Mss. Morris*).

The De Lancey commission of August 21, 1733, is in the *Trial of John Peter Zenger* (London, 1765) 6, 7; Phillipse's commission is in 2 *Ms. Rutherfurd Coll.* 197.

[228] "GEORGE THE THIRD by the Grace of God of Great Britain France and Ireland King Defender of the Faith and so forth To our trusty and welbeloved THOMAS JONES Esquire GREETING We reposing especial Trust and Confidence in your Loyalty Learning and Integrity HAVE assigned constituted and appointed And We Do by these Presents assign constitute and appoint you the said THOMAS JONES to be one of our Justices of our Supreme Court of Judicature of and in our Province of New York in America giving and by these Presents granting unto you the said Thomas Jones full Power and Authority in our Said Supreme Court to hear try and determine all Pleas whatsoever Civil Criminal and mixed according to the Laws Statutes and Customes of that Part of our Kingdom of Great Britain called England and the Laws of our said Province of New York not being repugnant thereto And Executions of all Judgments of our said Court to award and to act and do all

act and do all things which any of our Justices of either Bench or Barons of the Exchequer in that part of our Kingdom of Great Britain called England may or ought to do." When this was added we do not know but we surmise it followed upon the acrid controversy over the exchequer powers and the well-known case of *King* v. *Zenger* (1735).

It will be desirable to consider this controversy at this point not only because, as we have conjectured, it may have led to a change in the form of the commission, but also because the episode illustrates the great importance which was attached to these instruments in founding jurisdiction. The attack on the commissions had been preceded by a wrangle over the exchequer powers of the Supreme Court that had resulted in the resignation of Chief Justice Morris. Not long after this proceedings were instituted against John Peter Zenger for printing allegedly seditious matter. As a preliminary move to forestall a trial, James Alexander and William Smith, counsel for the defendant, excepted to the commission of Chief Justice De Lancey on the ground that it was granted during pleasure and not during good behavior as was the commission of a judge of King's Bench (by virtue of which cognizance in the cause was claimed). Secondly, that the jurisdiction and authority of a judge of Common Bench were granted De Lancey, a power which would not be granted to or exercised by any justice of King's Bench. Thirdly, that the form of the New York commission was not warranted by common law or any English or provincial statute. Lastly, that it did not appear that the commission was granted by and with the advice of the Council without which the Governor could not grant the same. The same exceptions were offered to Justice Phillipse's commissions. The Chief Justice said after argument that the court

Things which any of our Justices of either Bench or Barons of the Exchequer in that part of our Kingdom of Great Britain called England may or ought to do And to make such Rules and Orders in our said Court as shall be judged convenient and useful and as near as may be agreeable to the Rules and Orders of our Courts of Kings Bench Common Pleas and Exchequer in that Part of our Kingdom of Great Britain called England To Have And To Hold the said Office and Place of one of our Justices of our said Supreme Court of Judicature of and in our said Province of New York in America with all and singular the Rights Privileges Advantages Salaries Profits Fees and Perquisites unto the said Office belonging or in any wise appertaining or which of right ought to belong or appertain to the said Office in as full and ample Manner as any of our said Justices of our said Supreme Court heretofore hath or of right ought to have enjoyed the same To you the said THOMAS JONES for and during our Pleasure IN TESTIMONY whereof We have caused these our Letters to be made Patent and the Great Seal of our Province of New York to be hereunto affixed Witness our trusty and welbeloved WILLIAM TRYON Esquire our Captain General and Governor in Chief in and over our Province of New York and the Territories depending thereon in America Chancellor and Vice Admiral of the same by and with the Advice of our Council of our said Province At our Fort in our City of New York the twenty ninth day of September in the Year of our Lord one thousand seven hundred and seventy three and of our Reign the Thirteenth" (6 *Ms. Book of Commissions 1770–89* 91). Cf. the commission, in identical form, of Whitehead Hicks, Feb. 14, 1776 (*NY Misc. Mss.* Box 12 no. 12).

would neither hear nor allow the exceptions; "for (said he) you thought to have gained a great deal of applause and popularity by opposing this court as you did the court of Exchequer; but you have brought it to that point that either we must go from the bench or you from the bar and therefore we exclude you and Mr. Alexander from the bar."[229]

For the holding of circuits the Supreme Court commission alone was not adequate warrant of authority. In England,[230] the practice was to arm the judges going on circuit with an assize commission, commissions of oyer and terminer, of general gaol delivery, of the peace and of association, and a writ of admittance, a writ *si non omnes* and a writ of nisi prius. With this battery of authority the business of the King's courts in the country could be attacked. We are concerned here only with the criminal commissions, and we have already noted that Dongan had introduced the oyer and terminer commission for the particular sessions of the Court of Oyer and Terminer and General Gaol Delivery in the several counties. When the circuit feature was again added to the judicial scheme in 1692, it apparently was deemed necessary to issue commissions for the exercise of this function. The solitary examples we have found are drafts of an oyer and terminer and a gaol delivery commission of April 10, 1705, for the county of Queens.[231] The body of these commissions, except for one or two minor changes, are almost exact copies of the English forms. In the test clause, however, they are explicitly stated to be in force for the period of one year, a provision which does not appear to have been common law usage.[232] No other examples of commissions for the circuit have been available, but it is beyond doubt that they were issued for they are frequently mentioned in the Council minutes and there are references to them in O'Callaghan's *Calendar of Commissions*.[233] After 1741 the justices did not need an assize commission but by provincial act sat ex officio at nisi prius.[234] Judging from the recitals in other records[235] there is some reason to believe that eventu-

[229] On the Exchequer row cf. Daly, "Hist. of the Court of Common Pleas," in 1 E. D. Smith, *Rep.*, Introd. lvi *et seq.* A summary of Chief Justice Morris' dissenting views regarding the commission is in 2 Smith, *Hist. of NY* 11. The Zenger case is in *Trial of John Peter Zenger* (London, 1765) 7 *et seq.*, Rutherfurd, *John Peter Zenger, his Press, his Trial and a Bibliography of Zenger Imprints* (1904). Proceedings on the exceptions in 2 *Ms. Rutherfurd Coll.* 25. Cf. also Rutherfurd, *Family Letters and Events* (1894) c. I.

[230] The text of these several commissions (except peace) and writs (except nisi prius) is in *Office of the Clerk of Assize* (1682) 4–11.

[231] 50 NY *Col. Mss.* 61, 68. For the text cf. Appendix *infra* 771 *et seq.*

[232] Cf. the forms in *Office of the Clerk of Assize*, and the statement, *ibid.* 1. For the learning on determination, 2 Hawkins, *Pleas of the Crown* c.5 §§7, 8.

[233] *Cal. of NY Col. Comm.* (NYHS 1929) 16, 67, 76.

[234] 3 *Col. Laws NY* 191. The assize commission supplied the authority for nisi prius, *infra* 81.

[235] Thus in the pardon granted to Isaac Jacobs in 1722 this recital appears: "At a Court of Oyer and Terminer and General Gaol Delivery holden for the County of Westchester the Eleventh day of

ally a composite form was used joining in one instrument power to hear, try and determine felonies, trespasses and misdemeanors and also to deliver gaols. There is some further collateral basis for inference in the executive minutes of

August in the Eighth Year of our Reign Before Lewis Morris Esqr. Chief Justice of the Province of New York in America, William Willet, Josiah Hunt, Oliver Besley, Joseph Hunt and Joseph Budd Esqrs Justices of our Peace of the County of Westchester our Justices and Commissioners Assigned and Lawfully authorized by Virtue of our Commission under our Great Seal of our Province of New York to them Directed bearing date at our Fort in New York the Twenty ninth day of July in the Seventh Year of our Reign to Enquire by the Oaths of honest and Lawfull men of our County of Westchester of all treasons, Misprisions of Treasons, Insurrections, Rebellions, murthers felonies homicides killings, Assaults batteries, woundings Congregations and unlawfull meetings, words Spoken Trespasses Riots Routs, oppressions Confederacies false Allegiance and other misdoings offences and Injuries and also all Accessories thereunto within the County aforesaid by whomsoever had done perpetrated or Committed to hear and Determine according to the Laws and Custom of the Kingdom of Great Britain and the Province of New York and our goal [sic] at Westchester in the County aforesaid of the Prisoners therein being for that time to Deliver as by the Said Commission may more fully appear" (H.R. Parch. 223 A 4). Compare also another recital of the same commission in the indictment against William Moras, Westchester, 1721: "Province of New York, Inquisition taken at Westchester in the County of Westchester the ninth day of August in the Eight year of the Reign of George over Great Brittain France and Ireland King Defender of the faith &c. before Lewis Morris Esqr. Chief Justice of the province of New York in America William Willet Josiah Hunt [sic] Oliver Beasly Joseph Budd & Joseph Hunt Esqrs Justices of ye peace for the County of Westchester Justices & Commissioners of our Said Lord the King assigned and Lawfully authorized by vertue of a Commission of the Same our Lord the King under his great Seal of the province of Newyork to them directed bearing date at Fort George in Newyork the 29th day of July in the Seventh year of the Reign of our Said Lord the King to Inquire by the oaths of honest and Lawful men of the County of Westchester of all Treasons misprisions of Treasons Insurrections rebellions murthers fellonies—homicides Killings assaults batteries woundings Congregations and unlawfull meetings words spoken Trespasses Riots Routs oppressions Confederacies false allegiance and other misdoings offences &. Injuries and also of all accessories thereunto within the county aforesaid by whomsoever and howsoever had done perpetrated or Committed to hear & determine according to the Law and Custom of the Kingdom of Great Britain and the province of Newyork and his

Majesty's Goal at Westchester in the County of Westchester aforesaid of the prisoners therein being for this time to Deliver as by the said Commission more fully appears." (Ms. James Alexander Papers Box 60 no. 3.) It will be observed that the minute entries of this court have also been preserved and the heading reads as follows: "At a Court of Oyer and Terminer and General Gaol Delivery held for the County of Westchester at the House of Mr. Daniell Clark in Westchester on the Second Tuesday in August being the 8th day. . . . Present Lewis Morris Esqr. Chief Justice of the Province of New York . . . [four named justices of peace] Esqrs. Justices The Commission of Oyer and Terminer Proclaim'd" (Ms. Mins. Cir. 1721–49 1, Aug. 8, 1721).

Another recital of a regular oyer and terminer and general gaol delivery commission is to be found in a presentment in 1756 at Albany against Edmond Mathews for altering the muster rolls: "Att a Court of Oyer & Terminer and General Gaol Delivery held for the County of Albany at the Hall of the said County By Virtue of his Majestys Commission under the Great seal of the province of New York Before James DeLancey Esqr. Chief Justice of the Supreme Court of Judicature for the province of New York John Chambers Esqr. second Justice of the said Court Sybrant G. Van Schaick & others Justices of our said Lord the King his Gaol in the County afd & the prisoners in the same being to Deliver and also Divers felonies Murders falsities, deceits & the [obliterated line] . . . County perpetrated to hear & Determine assigned on Tuesday the 27th Day of July in the Thirtyeth Year of the Reign of . . . King George the Second &c. of Great Britain &c. Anno Dom. 1756" (H.R. Parch. 200 G 10).

We have also seen a rough draft of an indictment of George Borne at a Court of Oyer and Terminer and General Gaol Delivery in New York City in 1722/23 but the recital therein contained indicates that this was possibly a special commission especially since such courts did not ordinarily sit in New York City: "At a Court of our Lord the King of Oyer and Terminer and General Gaol Delivery holden for the City and County of New York at the City Hall of the same City and County the — day of January in the Ninth year of . . . George . . . before Lewis Morris Esqr. Chief Justice of the Province of New York—Justices of his Majestys peace of the said City and County [sic] by Virtue of his Majestys Commission of Oyer and Terminer and General Gaol Delivery under the Great Seal of the Province of New York to them directed bearing date the — day of —— and to remain and be in force for one month after the Date thereof as by the same Commission more fully appears" (James Alexander Papers Box 44).

the Council which during the last decades of the colonial period, when mention is made of oyer and terminer and gaol delivery, use the singular form "commission." This taken in connection with the record recitals and with the fact that after the Revolution a single composite commission was used seems to us fairly conclusive on the point.[236]

Throughout the eighteenth century special commissions of oyer and terminer issued. For these special occasions, a gaol delivery commission as well did not necessarily issue. So for the Leisler trial (1691) and for that of Nicholas Bayard and John Hutchins the oyer and terminer alone was thought sufficient. In certain other instances the record will read as if both commissions were used. Where the defendants were already in custody and had been indicted, the normal expectancy would be for a gaol delivery commission to be used. But on the special commission it is impossible to speak with certainty.

The pride which led the descendants of ensigns, lieutenants or captains in the provincial militia to preserve their ancestors' commissions did not apparently animate the clerks of the peace or the offspring of the justices of the peace. Considering the number of these officers, accessible commissions of the peace are relatively few, and in county offices the clerks ceased to enroll these instruments after the reign of Anne.

The Dominion form of peace commission was determinative after the Leisler Rebellion, possibly because Governor Sloughter used this form to commission justices of the peace before even the Judicature Act of 1691 was enacted.[237] In any event, the peace commissions issued by him, by Fletcher, by Bellomont and by Cornbury for the several outlying counties are in substantially the same form as those which Andros sealed in the name of the execrated James II. The Provincial Secretary reports in 1693 that in "Quarter Sessions" the justices have "all such powers and authorities as are granted in a commission of ye peace in England,"[238] but the commissions certainly did not give them the exact equivalent for the only felonies included were petit larcenies and thefts.

---

[236] For example, 26 *Ms. Mins. Council* 116, 122. In a letter from Justices Robert Livingston and George Ludlow to Gov. Tryon Sept. 9, 1773, it is stated that the Oyer and Terminer had opened but owing to the departure of the other judges no adjournment could be made and the commission was determined without finishing the King's business. A new commission is requested so that "we might still go through what is necessary to be done here and discharge the gaol." (*Ms. Penn. Hist. Soc. Gratz*

Coll.) For the post-Revolutionary practice cf. the printed commission to Richard Morris *et al.* (1786) for the Suffolk Circuit, *Misc. Mss. Suffolk.*

[237] *Ms. Conveyances Kings Co.* Liber I, 264, Apr. 7, 1691; 301, Feb. 6, 1692/93; Liber II, 187, Oct. 11, 1698; 245, Oct. 14, 1702; *Ms. Deeds Orange Co.* Liber A, 4, Mar. 8, 1702/03; 44, Oct. 6, 1707; *Ms. Deeds Westch. Co.* Liber B, 77, Apr. 4, 1691; 137, Jan. 27, 1692/93; Liber C, 1, Oct. 11, 1698.

[238] 1 *Doc. Hist. NY* 202.

Unfortunately, the evidence as to the exact form of later peace commissions in the early eighteenth century is most incomplete. There are extant commissions for the city and county of New York but owing to the limitations of the Dongan Charter the peace commissions initially gave no power beyond petit larceny.[239] They follow otherwise the form of contemporary English peace commissions except they do not include the chastisement provision or the proviso for adjournment of difficult cases.[240] After the Montgomerie Charter (1731) the justices of the peace in New York City possessed jurisdiction over felonies at large. The charter itself provided that the mayor, deputy mayor, recorder and aldermen were assigned to be ex officio justices of the peace with all the powers of any justice of the peace in the province including the power to inquire of, hear and determine felonies, riots, trespasses and the like, and were to be "justices assigned" of oyer and terminer and gaol delivery to be named in such commissions issued for the city and county.[241] The charter it-

[239] The 1702 commission from Queen Anne to the mayor, recorder and aldermen of New York is in *NY Misc. Mss.* Box 3 no. 26. The 1711 commission is in the same language; *NY Misc. Mss.* Box 4 no. 2. The 1715 commission is in *ibid.* no. 28.

[240] According to Dongan's Charter to New York City, 1686, the mayor, recorder and aldermen were to be justices of the peace "to hear and Determine all . . . manner of Petty Larcenyes Riots Routs Oppressions Extorcons and other trespasses and Offences" (1 *Col. Laws NY* 190), and until the Montgomerie Charter of 1730, the powers of New York City justices of peace were always expressed in this language. Thus in the 1702, 1711 and 1715 commissions referred to above (n. 239), the justices of peace were to hear and determine "petty larcenies, thefts, trespasses, forstallings, regratings, Extorcons . . . and . . . other misdeeds and offences" (*NY Misc. Mss.* Box 3 no. 26, Box 4 nos. 2 and 28). See also the precept for Quarter Sessions, dated Oct. 25, 1712, which recites: "Her majestys Justices for the conservation of the peace in the City and County of New York and of divers thefts trespasses and other offences . . . perpetrated to hear and determine assigned" (*NY Misc. Mss.* Box 4 no. 8).

[241] In the Montgomerie Charter the mayor, deputy mayor, recorder and aldermen were assigned to be justices of the peace and were to hold Courts of General Quarter Sessions in which they were authorized to "Enquire of and hear and determine . . . all manner of ffelonies Imprisonments Riots Routs Oppressions Extortions fforestallings Regratings trespasses Offences and all and singular other Evil Deeds and Offences . . ." (2 *Col. Laws NY* 621).

Subsequent to 1731 we note that in the recitals contained in precepts, indictments and memorandum entries, the following language is used to de-scribe the powers of New York City justices of peace: "Divers Felonys, Imprisonments, Riots, Routs, Oppressions, Extortions, Forestallings, Regratings, Trespasses and other offences . . . to hear and Determine Assigned" (King v. Hugh and Jane Munro and John Welch, *Memorandum Entry, Ms. Mins.* NYCQS 1732–62 6–8, May 1732; precept for Feb. Sessions, N.Y. City, Jan. 14, 1745, *NY Legal Mss.* Box 43; indictment of George Beatty, Aug. 7, 1745, *NY Misc. Mss.* Box 35, also recorded in *Ms. Mins.* NYCQS 1732–62 188; precept for Nov. Sessions 1762, N.Y. City, *H.R. Pleadings* Pl. P. 2769; precept for May Sessions 1765, N.Y.C. *H.R. Pleadings* Pl. P. 2768).

The headings on the Quarter Sessions Minutes for New York City accord with the powers expressed in the Montgomerie Charter. Thus, the heading for Nov. 7, 1769, contains this language: "Att a Court of General Quarter Sessions of the peace . . . Before . . . Justices . . . assigned to keep the peace . . . and also to hear and determine divers felonies, Trespasses, and other Misdemeanors" (*Ms. Mins.* NYCQS 1760–72 293; see also the headings for Feb. 2 and Feb. 4, 1773, *Ms. Mins.* NYCQS 1772–91 33, 40).

The heading sometimes refers explicitly to the charter. Thus, in the heading for May 1, 1733, this appears: "Att a Court of General Quarter Sessions of the Peace for the City and County of New York . . . before the Mayor, Deputy Mayor, Recorder and Aldermen of New York City Justices of the Peace assigned by his Majestys royal Charter granted to the Mayor and Commonalty of New York" (*Ms. Mins.* NYCQS 1732–62 72; see also the same heading for May 1, 1770, *Ms. Mins.* NYCQS 1760–72 309, and for May 5, 1772, *Ms. Mins.* NYCQS 1772–91 1).

We have, however, noted one New York City indictment of 1771 which uses the old form em-

self was the equivalent of the commission for the peace.[242] The effect of this, except as to the appointive officers like the mayor and recorder, was that in New York City the magistrates were elected and were justices of the peace ex officio. How jealously this privilege was regarded may be deduced from the protest of the corporation in 1764 after it had been ordered in Council that, owing to the increase of business and for the ease of the magistrates, seven persons, one for each ward, be commissioned as justices of the peace. The letter of objection was ordered to be filed but it must have been effective, for we do not find that the additional justices were in fact commissioned.[243]

Whether or not the change in the jurisdiction of the New York City Quarter Sessions incident upon the new charter led also to a change in the form of the country commissions we do not know. There are early recitals in a riot record and indictments to the effect that the justices are assigned to hear and determine felonies but such recitals are obviously not a reproduction of the terms of the commission.[243a] But the late commissions of 1772 do give the general felony jurisdiction, and we must assume that at some time between 1707 and 1772 this was added. These peace commissions of the year 1772[244] conformed substantially to the English form in the 1742 edition of Dalton's *Countrey Justice,* except for the following: 1) the excision of witchcraft, sorcery, enchantments and magic arts as a head of jurisdiction; 2) the assignment of a minimum of three instead of two justices to inquire or hear and determine; 3) the excision of the clause "as in like case been used or ought to be done" in the hear and determine clause; 4) the excision of the chastisement clause and

ployed before 1730: "At a Court of General Quarter Sessions of the Peace . . . before . . . Justices . . . for the Conservation of the peace . . . and of all manner of petty Larcenies, Thefts, Trespasses, Riots, Routs, Assaults, Batteries, and divers other offences . . . to hear and Determine, assigned" (King v. Henry Brasher, Feb. Sessions, 1771, New York City, *H.R. Pleadings* Pl. K. 905).

[242] For a late opinion on this cf. Kent, *The Charter of the City of New York* n. xl. The only officers appointed by the Governor were the mayor, recorder, sheriff and coroner (Charter, §§2, 10). It is clear from the recorder's commission (4 *Min. Common Council NYC* 255) that the charter itself was the commission for the justice of the peace. That the words of assignment in the charter operated as a commission is to be deduced from the difference in the post-election proceedings before and after the Montgomerie Charter. Compare the proceedings in 1730, where the mayor and several aldermen were handed commissions (*ibid.* 29), with those after the charter took effect where no

commissions are mentioned (*ibid.* 73, 158, 198). On the English practice here, cf. Webb, *Manor and Borough* 349.

[243] 25 *Ms. Mins. Council* 534, 537, Dec. 5, 20, 1764.

[243a] Cf. the recital in Kings County riot record "for the keeping of the peace . . . as alsoe to inquire of heare and determine ffellonyes trespasses Riotts and other misdemeanours" (*Ms. Kings Co. Ct. & Rd. Recs. 1692–1825* 38, Sept. 18, 1696). Cf. the form of a return on a certiorari "Suffolk Cty. SS. I . . . one of the Justices of the peace of our Lord the King in the County of Suffolk to keep and also diverse felonies Trespasses and other misdeeds in the said County of Suffolk to hear and determine . . ." (*Ms. Precedent Book Joseph Murray* 11). The earliest country indictment we have found with this phrase is one of 1725 (*Ms. Files Ulster Co.* Bundle F, King v. Bruyn).

[244] 6 *Ms. Book of Com. 1770–89* 66. For the text cf. Appendix *infra* 772 *et seq.*

proviso for difficult cases clause; 5) the addition in the clause relating to Sessions of the words, "or by law shall be appointed." These commissions like the earlier ones were drawn for the county,[245] and other names were added as new justices were appointed,[246] or by a patent of association proper authority was conveyed.[247] Initially the first person named in the commission presided at Common Pleas[248] but later special commissions for this court were issued.[249]

Although both in England and in New York legislative enactment heaped upon the justices of the peace an overwhelming mass of administrative and judicial duties, yet there was virtually no change in the form that had been used generations earlier. Apparently when powers such as sureties for the peace, committal and riots were not specified in the commissions the statutory additions were all to be referred to the "general charge" section of the commission.

It is beyond our purpose to inquire into the various types of commissions issued to sheriffs,[250] clerks of the Supreme Court, circuit and peace, the Attor-

---

[245] *Ibid.*

[246] Cf. Beekman to Henry Livingston (Nov. 12, 1744): "it is requested by som of frinds to writ to you to send me the Dutches county comission of the peace in order to have Joseph Cranie made a Justice and his name aded wch they say can be done by haveing fur that purpos it here to have it a new toutch given with the Seale" (*Misc. Mss. Beekman*).

[247] "George the Third by the Grace of God of Great Britain France and Ireland King Defender of the Faith and so forth To our beloved and faithful John Van Alen of Claverack, John Watson, Robert Lewis, and Benjamin Spencer, Esquires Greeting Whereas on the Eighteenth Day of April in the Tenth year of our Reign Letters patent and Commission of the Peace did Issue for our County of Albany in our Province of New York under the Great Seal of our Province of New York bearing date the same Day and year, thereby appointing the Members of our Council for our Province of New York, our Attorney General of our said Province, and the Seventy nine persons therein after named Justices to keep our Peace in our County of Albany in our said Province of New York and thereby also appointing the said Members of our said Council, our said Attorney General and the thirty one Justices therein after named of the Quorum, as by the said Letters Patent or Commission or the Record thereof in our Secretary's Office for our said Province may more fully and at large appear Now Know Ye that We have authorized and Assigned you the said John Van Alen, John Watson, Robert Lewis and Benjamin Spencer, and every or you Jointly and severally also our Justices to keep our Peace in our said County of Albany hereby associating you for that purpose with our said Justices appointed in and by our said in part recited Letters Patent and Commission, And hereby fully and Effectually giv-

ing and Granting to you and each of you all and every the like Powers and Authorities Granted in and by our said in part recited Letters Patent and Commission to our Justices therein named as fully and amply to all Intents and purposes as if the same were herein and hereby particularly expressed, hereby Commanding all our Justices in our said Recited Commission Named to admit and receive you the said John Van Alen, John Watson, Robert Lewis, and Benjamin Spencer, our said Justices Assigned by these Presents as their Associates, and further Commanding our sherif of our said County and all Constables and other our Peace Officers in our said County and all others to pay due Obedience to you our said Justices by these Presents Assigned. In Testimony whereof We have caused these our Letters to be made Patent and the Great Seal of our said Province of New York to be hereunto affixed. Witness our Right Trusty and Right Well beloved Cousin John Earl of Dunmore our Captain General and Governor in Chief in and over our Province of New York and the Territories depending thereon in America Chancellor and Vice-Admiral of the same. At our Fort in our City of New York the Twelfth Day of December in Year of our Lord one thousand seven hundred and Seventy and in the Eleventh year of our Reign. Clarke."

6 *Ms. Book of Com. 1770–89* 5.

[248] 1 *Doc. Hist. NY* 200, although Andros issued special commissions (*Ms. Deeds Queens Co. Liber A*).

[249] *Cal. Col. Com.* 7 (1702). For text, cf. 6 *Ms. Book of Com. 1770–89* 87.

[250] See, for example, *H.R. Parch.* 194 K 1, commission of 1753 to B. Hinchman, high sheriff of Queens County.

neys and Advocates General[251] and to coroners.[252] In all of these the hand of royal authority was to be seen and the necessity for conformity to English law was provided for either directly or by inference. Just as the judicial commissions were subjected to scrutiny, so too were the commissions of other officers examined to determine just what degree of power was conferred by these instruments,[253] and everywhere English practice was called in to aid in determining conflicts.[254] So, for example, when a justice of the peace was elected coroner and attempted to exercise his powers in both offices he was reminded that one occupying the ministerial office of coroner could not act in a judicial capacity according to English law. This case is doubly interesting because in the Albany Charter of 1686 the mayor, who was ex officio a justice of the peace, was also named as coroner.[255]

In the uprooting and transplanting to New York of common law forms, it was inevitable that the soil of common law substance should cling to the matter thus removed. It was not even necessary, as we have seen in case of the justices of the peace, to await the arrival of those who had read in the Inns of Court for the absorption of English legal doctrine to begin. It was only necessary for books to arrive and men shrewd enough to use them, however ineptly. The castigation of Leisler's proceedings compiled by an unknown hand in 1690 on the basis of English statutes is an example of the process in its early stages. The learning displayed in the Bayard trial a decade later is evidence how far familiarity with the sources of common law had progressed. No one who has examined the memoranda and citations of any first-rate New York lawyer of the 1730's can doubt the general availability or spread of these sources or the competency to use them.

We shall have occasion in the succeeding sections to examine in detail how common law doctrine became seated in New York Province. In advance of this specification of particulars, however, it is desirable to emphasize how directly familiarity with common law doctrine affected the matter of jurisdiction. During the first two decades of English rule, there are only a few in-

[251] A draft of James Alexander's commission as Attorney General is in *James Alexander Papers* Box 10 no. 172.

[252] Commission to Teunis Roelossen to be coroner (Oct. 8, 1698), *Misc. Ms. Orange Co.*

[253] The critical examination of commissions was not limited to those of inferior officers. Cf. here the animadversions of Dr. Daniel Coxe against the renewal of Hunter's commission because, contrary to the laws of Great Britain and without regard to his instructions and his commission, he had among

other things dispensed with acts of assembly, appointed justices of the peace, and turned out sheriffs before the end of their term (*Ms. Jay Papers* Box 3 no. 16D).

[254] For example, the discussion over the question whether the Albany city charter empowered the magistrates to sit as justices of oyer and terminer, in 26 *Ms. Mins. Council* 293.

[255] "Alderman Blagge's Case," Nov. 19, 1772 (*J. T. Kempe Lawsuits* B).

stances of reference to ideas such as reasonable notice, which we generally consider as basic to the common law system, and there was no effort to solve jurisdictional questions by resort to English analogy. But as the judicial structure came more closely to approximate the English, and as the forms in use at home were adopted in the colony, the oracles of Westminster became the law and the prophets in the provincial courts. The broad outlines of jurisdiction set forth in royal orders and colonial legislation were inadequate to care for the manifold minutiae of judicial action not articulated in any official pronouncements. Courts and judges in New York exercised most of their powers as functions presumed to be inherent in their offices. Thus, the Supreme Court was endowed with all the powers of King's Bench, Common Pleas and Exchequer and under this broad jurisdictional grant heard cases from treason to nuisance; and since it employed virtually all the procedures used in English central courts, it could hardly avoid the injunction laid down by Crown orders and colonial legislation alike—that the law practiced and procedure followed were to conform as closely as possible to English law. Thus English law was not merely, in Coke's phrase, a "golden metewand" by which to measure the validity of colonial action but was also a source for the exercise of many judicial powers which were otherwise unspecified in any official document.

It is a fact of considerable significance for the development of the law in New York that, although nearly every royal act and every instrument upon which jurisdiction in the colony was founded at one time or another were subjected to attack by the colonists, the common law itself as a source of authority was never challenged but, on the contrary, was regarded as the shield and buckler of constitutional right. At the same time, the adherents of the Crown while not under the same necessities of justification found convenient support for prerogative action in the same inexhaustible well. It thus came about that despite the intense political fervor of the contest between the two groups, the discussions were conducted in the legalistic idiom of an argument on a plea to the jurisdiction. The blow which was never forgiven was the Governor's ordinance on the courts. This was tilted at, as we have seen, in the recurrent attempt of the assembly to recapture the right to set up courts. It was brought to issue in an attack on the legality of an exchequer court and in the periodic assaults upon the Chancery. This dissatisfaction with the whole basis of jurisdiction was manifested further in such episodes as the challenge of the judges' commissions in *King* v. *Zenger,* the right of the Governor and Council to hear appeals from jury verdicts and the appointment of judges to serve at pleasure instead of good behavior. So strongly are these contests colored by underlying political differences arising from two theories of government, a notion of representative government versus government by prerogative, that their effect upon the law itself is easily overlooked. In this respect the recurrent forensic alarums and excursions which enliven the history of provincial law from the indictment of Captain Dyer in 1681 to the day of independence recall the judicial battles in England of the early seventeenth century. However fugitive their political effect may have been, what was accomplished in defining jurisdiction, in settling the forms by which it was exercised and, above all, in the establishment of the common law was enduring.

CHAPTER II

ORIGINAL AND CONCURRENT JURISDICTION

IT is a characteristic of legal systems that no matter how neatly the plans for their operation may be drawn, no matter how clearly the framework can be pictured from statutes, charters, commissions and the like, the actual functioning is something unto itself. Since this depends upon three intensely volatile elements—human judges dealing with relations of human litigants in terms of ideas—the stabilizing tendencies of the written word, whether this be in statute, writ or judicial decision, are often enough set at naught. The vagaries of the law in action increase as professional competency diminishes or as expert control lessens, so that in any given civilization there may be the widest variations in the actualities of law enforcement. This was, of course, the situation in England during the seventeenth and eighteenth centuries where, despite a high degree of professional skill, things were done even at Westminster for which there was no warrant in the books. And in the country, the justice of the peace was equally swayed by the winds of circumstance for he appears as one creature in the Acts of Parliament and as quite another in Sessions and without, as the records themselves show.

It is necessary to bear in mind these considerations as we move to examine the working of the judicial machinery as it existed in New York Province between the years 1664 and 1776. In the early decades of English rule, the divergencies between the statutory outline of jurisdiction and what, in fact, went on in the several tribunals are very striking and run far beyond the sort of divagation from common usage that was tolerated in the English country courts. The Province being conquered, the magistracy was at first commissioned not for competency so much as for loyalty. It was handed the book and left to compose its own sermons, with occasional admonition or helpful hint from the Governor and his councillors. But as familiarity with forms of common law procedure spread, and as a gradual mastery of common law doctrine was acquired by practitioners, law administration in New York rapidly comes to resemble that in England. The standard of practice in the highest court becomes really comparable with that in King's Bench, and the inferior criminal jurisdiction is administered in much the same way as it is in English Quarter Sessions. In other words, for nearly everything done in the New York Supreme Court precedent can be found in Sergeant Hawkins' *Pleas of the Crown;* and the New York City Sessions Court, since it is not scorned by either the Attorney General or the metropolitan bar, treads as closely as it may the path of the superior court. In the rural counties, some justice's manual like Dalton, Nelson or Shaw is the magistrate's *vade mecum,* but there is no slavish obedience to the word, for there is variation enough to be found on the themes set in manual, statute and commission. And what is more, each county developed some peculiarities of its own. The differences between the Sessions records of Ulster and Suffolk, or Dutchess and Richmond are as noticeable as those exemplified in the contrast between the records of English Middlesex and York. It is only as the colonial period drew to a close that the practice in the several counties began to assume some uniformity, a result due chiefly to closer supervision by the Attorney General; but to the very end certain established local characteristics remain.

We shall be concerned in this and succeeding chapters with the basic problem of how the law in fact functioned in the demesnes marked out by statute, charter, ordinance, commissions and the like, a marking as we have seen not always precise, that often leaves us halting like bewildered surveyors questing for the blasted oak tree or the big stone of an ancient conveyance. The metes and bounds of these jurisdiction-founding instruments with all their defects must nevertheless remain our constants, for the variables of practice are otherwise unmanageable. From decade to decade, and from court to court the judges and lawyers will sometimes do things differently; the tempo of common law infiltration will vary; a new English statute not extended to the colony will produce a shift in judicial attitude. Out of such uneasy ingredients we must reduce the normal *cursus curiae* for city and country, for superior and inferior courts.

The Courts under the Duke's Laws

The initial dispositions with respect to criminal jurisdiction in New York were evidently not made with an intention of creating a simulacrum of the English system; or if any such intention was nursed it was based upon defective recollections of how authority was partitioned at home. Neither in the Duke's Laws nor the subsequent amendments thereto, nor in the commissions issued to justices of the peace during the first two decades after the conquest were any clear lines laid down as to the competence of the courts. And the reorganization of the judiciary under Dongan advanced the clarification of authority but little. The process of definition was consequently one entirely of practice, and for this reason had an influence upon subsequent developments that outlived the early founding statutes. This influence was one of principle rather than of particulars, and consisted chiefly in the firm seating of the notion that major offenses were properly cognizable only by the highest tribunal of the Province, and that, excepting petit larceny, the competence of inferior courts did not extend beyond the trial of misdemeanors. This division was not clearly formulated in any of the enactments before 1691, but it was a principle well rooted in practice.

To one familiar with the fortuitous manner in which the jurisdiction of English courts had come to be marked out, and with the number of problems of this variety still unsettled in Charles II's reign, it comes as no surprise that colonial legislation should be unprecise in defining the authority of any court. At the same time, it is difficult to account for the vague and casual manner in which the Duke's Laws allude to the powers of the several tribunals which they were instituting in a conquered country. At no point is there an explicit enumeration of the powers either of Assizes or the Sessions courts.

Many of the vagaries of the original code were due to the fact that it was patched together from New England codes which themselves were peppered with inconsistencies or obscurities. Furthermore, in respect of causes criminal, the New England codes were heavily weighted with policy provisions that grew out of the intense biblicism of those settlements. The inclusion of this matter in the Duke's Laws,[1] while such homely crimes as manslaughter, theft, burglary[2] and rape (all of which were to confront the courts) were unmentioned, made it difficult for the newly appointed magistrates to act without special advice from the Governor. It seems probable, however, that only the highest provincial tribunal or one of equivalent stature specially constituted was conceived to be the proper forum for the trial of capital offenses. The laws provide that upon notification from Sessions to the Governor and Council of any capital offender the cause would be tried at Assizes if it should sit within two months, otherwise an oyer and terminer commission was to issue.[3] The seemingly equivocal passage in the *Appeals* section of the Duke's Laws which provides that "if the case be capital and the person condemned shall appeal; he shall be kept in Gaole till the Next Assizes and then prosecuted and tried accordingly,"[4] must be taken to have reference not to appeals from Sessions,

---

[1] 1 *Col. Laws NY* 20.
[2] Laws regarding burglary, robbery and larceny were added by Nicolls to the code in an undated amendment (*ibid.* 73).

[3] *Ibid.* 16.
[4] *Ibid.* 12.

which are not there mentioned, but to appeals from convictions at the special Oyer and Terminer Courts.

There are other provisions of the Duke's Laws which point to the Assizes as the forum for serious crimes. Thus the court was particularly authorized to stipulate the punishment in certain cases of sodomy and where single persons were convicted of copulating with a married man or woman.[5] It was vested with the power in cases of arson to pronounce judgment even although trial might occur in Sessions.[6] Finally and most important of all it was to determine "matters of Equity" or award punishment agreeable to English law in criminal cases for which no provision in the law was made.[7] The Assize Court was given concurrent jurisdiction with Sessions over cases of injuries to and by Indians.[8]

An examination of the extant Assizes records[9] discloses actually a small amount of criminal business. Since the Assizes met but once a year a great deal of matter that might have come before the court was disposed of by the Governor and Council, and where a cause was serious it was handled by an Oyer and Terminer Court commissioned *ad hoc*.[10] At the first session of the Assizes in 1665 a homicide and a witchcraft case were tried.[11] In the succeeding year there were no felonies tried, but three misdemeanor cases and three cases of political character.[12] The score varied year to year, but the policy was followed of remanding misdemeanors to Sessions and trying only the serious crimes and political offenders.[13] Toward the end, the civil appeal jurisdiction over-

---

[5] *Ibid.* 20, 21.
[6] *Ibid.* 36.
[7] *Ibid.* 44.
[8] The injuries to Indians were made cognizable in any court, and Indian injuries to cattle were cognizable in Assizes or Sessions.
[9] *Ms. Cal. of Proc. Ct. Assizes 1665–72; Ms. Mins. Ct. Assizes 1665–72;* 2 *Rep. NY State Historian* 381 *et seq.* (1675); 25 *NY Col. Mss.* 181, 192, 196, 205 (1676); *Proc. Gen. Ct. Assizes 1680–82* (45 *NYHS Colls.* [1912]).
[10] No such commissions appear to have been issued by Nicolls although a special commission of inquiry was sent to Esopus (1 *Rep. NY State Historian* 204). Extraordinary cases were apparently handled by Nicolls and his Council, cf. *H.R. Ms. Wills* Liber I, 285, 287–291. For the Oyer and Terminer Courts under Lovelace, cf. 1 *Rep. NY State Historian,* for a burglary, *ibid.* 237 (Apr. 1669), for a murder, 243 (July 1669), for a burglary, 319 (Jan. 1672/73). A special commission was issued in 1670 for an alleged homicide (*Ms. Gen. Entries 1665–72* 543). Under Andros a few such commissions were issued, cf. *Ms. Warrants Orders Passes 1674–79* 180, a commission to Newcastle justices to

try a rape case (1675) and *ibid.* 242, an oyer and terminer for the East Riding (1677); 28 *NY Col. Mss.* 79, a commission to try a murder (1679); *Ms. Mins. Mayor's Ct. NYC 1677–82* fol. 154, a commission to try a larceny (1679). Andros also used a special Court of Assizes to try Fenwick (1676) and Carteret (1680), 1 *New Jersey Archives* 230–239, 303. This was again used in proceedings against Dyer (1681), *Proc. Gen. Ct. Assizes 1680–82* (45 *NYHS Colls.*) 8.
[11] *Ms. Cal. Proc. Ct. Assizes 1665–72* Oct. 2, the trial of Cornelienson for homicide, and of Hall and wife for witchcraft. The witchcraft proceedings are in 4 *Doc. Hist. NY* 84 *et seq.*
[12] *Ms. Mins. Ct. Assizes 1665–72* misdemeanor, 54, 81; threats to kill, 86; liquor violation, 87; denying King's authority, 82; resisting constable, 83; seditious words, 84.
[13] In 1667 an assault and battery (*ibid.* 106) was referred back. Two fines were remitted, one for certain "miscarriages" (*ibid.* 142) and one for abuse of a justice (*ibid.* 143), apparently on petition and not by way of new trial or appeal. A presentment against Oyster Bay for not taking out a patent was suspended (*ibid.* 156). Only one case (seditious

shadowed all else, for in the last years of the Assizes' existence criminal business was negligible.[14]

The definition of jurisdiction as a practical matter was effected in two ways. A Sessions Court would bind over a defendant for Assizes whenever the case seemed to be beyond the competence of the immediate tribunal.[15] The question of jurisdiction could be settled when the Assize court met or it could be disposed of beforehand by the Governor.[16] The other method consisted in obtaining an opinion in advance from the central authorities and proceeding in accordance therewith.[17] This was a most unsatisfactory mode of dealing with a basic problem of law administration because issues were not necessarily settled judicially but could be determined by the executive. It would have been simpler to have resorted to a statutory definition, but this would have limited

words) came to trial (*ibid.* 141). In 1668 a homicide (*ibid.* 179), a case of breaking and entering (*ibid.* 184), a theft (*ibid.* 187), and an unlawful cohabitation case (*ibid.* 189) were tried. An order was made for a contempt of Sessions (*ibid.* 192). The calendar for 1669 shows a burglary and a rape case withdrawn. In 1670 apparently only a larceny and a breach of the peace were held over for trial (1 *Rep. NY State Historian* 359), but the *Ms. Cal.* in the New York Public Library shows two adultery cases. In 1671 apparently only a case of "suspicion of felony" came to trial. In 1672, two "suspicion of felony," an unlawful marriage and two cases of seditious words appear on the calendar (*ibid.* 362). The *Ms. Cal.* shows further a case of divorce on the ground of bigamy where the defendant was sentenced to be burned through the tongue, fined and imprisoned.

The available records for the years 1674 to 1679 inclusive are scarcely sufficient for any conclusions. The rough minutes of the session for 1675 (2 *Rep. NY State Historian* 381 *et seq.*) show a homicide, an incest and a larceny were tried (*ibid.* 393, 399, 406). Of less serious offenses are the two proceedings against Quakers (*ibid.* 411, 428), and a case of blasphemy (*ibid.* 421, 422). One Quaker case was not tried and a case of holiday breach and "reproachful" words was remanded (*ibid.* 429). The big trial of this session was that of Steenwyck for sedition, viz., refusing to take the oath and hence tending to rebellion (*ibid.* 422, 431). The fragments of the 1676 minutes show the trial of two homicide cases (25 *NY Col. Mss.* 181a), one Quaker (*ibid.* 196[2]), one seditious words (*ibid.* 191), one false news (*ibid.*), one maladministration of a court (*ibid.* 205[6]).

[14] The minutes for 1680 have no criminal cases entered although an information was brought by one of the justices (*Proc. Gen. Ct. Assizes* 8). The court was specially called in July 1681 to sit in the Dyer and Rumbouts treason cases. At the regular

fall term Rumbouts was discharged. A case of maladministration of justice was tried and the defendant acquitted. In 1682 five negroes were tried for prison breach and stealing a boat.

[15] Cf. *infra* 391 n. 34. The Calendar (1665–72) in 1 *Rep. NY State Historian* 351 *et seq.* shows conveniently the cases where defendants were bound over by Sessions and were held for trial at Assizes. Occasionally, as in the 1676 Assizes, petitions from persons injured came before the court and the matters were referred to the proper court. Cf. 25 *NY Col. Mss.* 197[1]. Where persons were bound over and no prosecuting witnesses appeared the court would usually discharge (*ibid.* 196) and cf. the 1682 Assizes (*Proc. Gen. Ct. Assizes* 35).

[16] The extent of the Governor's powers in Council are best illustrated by the civil cases and the constant occupation of Council with such matters is shown by the minutes. A great deal of this jurisdiction arose by petition which among other things was necessary to secure an appeal (e.g., 1 *Exec. Council Mins.* 42). Sometimes, where no settlement could be reached a cause would be referred to Assizes (*ibid.* 31). The special commission mentioned *supra* n. 10 was another method of determining jurisdiction as, for example, in the case of the Delaware insurrection (*ibid.* 38, 309 *et seq.*). Note in this connection the instructions to a commission for investigating a petition for divorce; the power to bind over to Sessions to answer for contempt (*ibid.* 335). The Harrison witchcraft case was referred to Assizes (*ibid.* 55), but a special commission was issued to deal with the "high misdemeanour" of boarding the ship *Expectation* (*ibid.* 103); and in the case of Groenendijke, the Council sat with the mayor and aldermen (*ibid.* 169). There is some material on this phase of "settling" jurisdiction in 3 *Ms. Mins. Council* pt. ii, 13 (1674/75) 17, 21, 25, 105. Cf. also *Ms. Warrants Orders Passes 1674–79* 111.

[17] Cf. *infra* nn. 52, 71; 396 n. 60.

the Governor's discretion, and evidently no Governor was ready to tolerate such a notion.

Particulars respecting the original jurisdiction of Sessions are scattered through the Duke's Laws, and on the criminal side the picture that emerges is one not dissimilar from the Quarter Sessions of England. The jurisdiction over assaults, batteries and breaches of the peace initiated by private complaint is placed here,[18] a provision which fostered a borderline quasi-criminal authority since a general civil jurisdiction in causes involving between £5 and £20 was conferred on the courts. In Sessions, however, the churchwardens, and later, in their place, the constables are to present cases of swearing, drunkenness, Sabbath breach, profaneness, fornication and adultery.[19] The men who fire woods,[20] and those who spread false news[21] and those who maltreat their servants[22] are all to be tried here. It is a strange medley of matter that the compiler of the Duke's Laws sees fit to mention, but there is enough basis for inference that a sort of combined English County Court and Sessions jurisdiction was to be created.

The code provisions have to be treated as a mere outline of a pattern of Sessions jurisdiction. Not only because they are sketchy but because of the character of the population, it was not possible to introduce into each settled region intermediate tribunals with substantially uniform jurisdiction. Probably the Sessions held in the three ridings came closest to official preconceptions of a proper tribunal of this type, for these courts were frequently attended by either the Governor or a member of the Council,[23] and petty matters, both civil and criminal, were handled in town courts. In New York City, however, the Mayor's Court combined both the inferior and intermediate jurisdiction,[24] and

[18] On the penal aspects of actions begun by private suit, cf. *infra* 331 n. 20; 560.

[19] 1 *Col. Laws NY* 26, 78.

[20] *Ibid.* 36.

[21] *Ibid.* 45. The Governor is given concurrent jurisdiction.

[22] *Ibid.* 48.

[23] This appears in the North and West Ridings from the presence on the bench of Van Ruyven (1668/69), collector of customs, of Secretary Matthias Nicolls (1669 and 1670), of the Governor (1672), of M. Nicolls (1675). The West Riding Sessions were held at Gravesend and the North Riding at Jamaica. The former included the East River towns and Staten Island. The latter included Westchester (as is clear from certain orders regarding this region) and the northwestern towns of Long Island. The following records of these ridings have been consulted: 1) *Ms. Kings Co. Ct. & Rd. Recs. 1668–1766*, where the first Sessions recorded

is that for March 1668/69. Between Dec. 1671 and June 1675 no Sessions minutes are entered; 2) 2 *Rep. NY State Historian* 244–260, 317–345, where are minutes for the years 1674 and 1675—apparently the clerk's rough notes; 3) the minutes in 25 *NY Col. Mss.* 55 (1675), 129 (1676), 130–133 (1675), 252 (1676); 26 *ibid.* 159, 160 (1678); 27 *ibid.* 127–129 (1678); 28 *ibid.* 23 (1678), 110 (1679), 164 (1679); 29 *ibid.* 88 (1680); 4) *Ms. Conveyances Kings Co.* Liber I (at the end), Sessions from Dec. 1676–Dec. 1679. All that remains of the East Riding Sessions records is in *Ms. Suffolk Co. Sess. 1668–87*.

[24] Nicolls' commission to the mayor and aldermen, of June 12, 1665, declares the city to be a body corporate and authorizes the mayor and aldermen or any four of them to rule and govern according to the laws of the province (5 *Recs. of New Amsterdam* 249). In Lovelace's report to the Duke the court is referred to as a "City Court" (3 *Doc.*

the same combination was made in the case of the Delaware courts.[25] A theoretical division of authority along the lines of the ridings was instituted in the Esopus, but the records show that the local officers were apparently unable to maintain this division.[26] Down to the Judicature Act of 1683 Albany remained a jurisdiction in all respects *sui generis*.[27]

Although the early laws and communications emanating from the Governor's office both indicate that the mere maintenance and functioning of a court rather than the drawing of fine jurisdictional distinctions were the prime considerations of policy, the practice of the courts themselves discloses a sense of caution regarding the observance of proper limits of authority. It was due chiefly to this that lines of separation developed. Of the offenses mentioned in the Duke's Laws the West Riding records show cases of assault and battery,[28] drunkenness,[29] fornication[30] and Sabbath breach.[31] There are a number of cases of "abuse,"[32] and "misdemeanor"[33] the nature of which is undisclosed. Bastardy cases could be handled as a logical extension of the fornication jurisdiction,[34] but theft, pound breach, highway violations[35] and the considerable number of cases relating to the proper enforcement of justice such as interferences with constables are all instances of jurisdiction for which no explicit statutory authority existed.[36] In one case this Sessions dealt with an infraction of liquor regulations,[37] a matter the Duke's Laws had reserved for the town courts. In some instances (adultery[38] and Quakers[39]), Sessions made preliminary investigation before binding over to the Assizes.

Rel. Col. Hist. NY 188). Andros' first commission of Oct. 17, 1675, conveys authority to "Administer Justice as a Court of Sessions" (1 *Mins. Com. Council NYC* 1). The commission of 1677 uses the phrase "as a Cort of Mayor and Aldermen or Sessions" (*ibid.* 63). This expression is used in the succeeding commissions of 1678 and 1679 (*ibid.* 69, 74).

25 Cf. *supra* 18 n. 88.

26 The commission to Captain Chambers as justice of the peace (2 *Exec. Council Mins.* 526) provided that it was not to diminish the "usual Authority & course of Judicature now in being administreed in ye Towne of Kingston by ye Schout and Commissaryes there." As town courts were authorized at the same time, and it was not made clear whether the Commissary Court had the status of a town court or something more, the local officers were naturally confused; cf. Chambers' letter to Lovelace explaining that he had not sat in the Commissary Court because he was to sit twice a year at Sessions (*Ms. Deeds Ulster Co.* Liber I, 621). In February 1672/73, however, the justice of the peace is sitting in the Commissary Court insisting

on Sessions jurisdiction over a case and being overruled (*ibid.* Liber II, 3).

27 Cf. *infra* 395 n. 55.

28 *Ms. Kings Co. Ct. & Rd. Recs. 1668–1766* 201, 355.

29 *Ibid.* 209, 214; 26 *NY Col. Mss.* 160.

30 *Ms. Kings Co. Ct. & Rd. Recs. 1668–1766* 24, 179.

31 *Ibid.* 217.

32 E.g., *ibid.* 56, 63.

33 *Ibid.* 18.

34 *Ibid.* 302; 25 *NY Col. Mss.* 57.

35 Theft: 27 *NY Col. Mss.* 129; 29 *ibid.* 88. Pound breach: *Ms. Kings Co. Ct. & Rd. Recs. 1668–1766* 281, 328. Blocking highways: 25 *NY Col. Mss.* 133. Fences: 2 *Rep. NY State Historian* 341, 342.

36 These are of all varieties, such as abuses of constables, refusing to aid an officer, and other petty contempts (*Ms. Kings Co. Ct. & Rd. Recs. 1668–1766* 18, 50, 111, 130, 198, 248, 299, 301, 324; 27 *NY Col. Mss.* 129a).

37 *Ms. Kings Co. Ct. & Rd. Recs. 1668–1766* 6.

38 *Ibid.* 6, 35.

39 *Ibid.* 73; 2 *Rep. NY State Historian* 341.

The picture is much the same in the North Riding although the records are not very informing.[40] There are certain variations such as prosecutions for violation of marriage laws,[41] unlawful cohabitation,[42] breach of the peace,[43] selling rum to Indians,[44] killing hogs[45] and illegal marking of livestock.[46] The scanty records of the East Riding are to the same effect[47] but with one striking departure from the accepted pattern of jurisdiction—a prosecution for forging a warrant.[48]

As one might expect, a great deal more criminal business passed through the Mayor's Court of New York City than through any of the country courts, for not only was this the most populous jurisdiction but it was the most heterogeneous. Yet even allowing for the lacunae in surviving records[49] the number of prosecutions compared with a Massachusetts jurisdiction like Essex County are surprisingly few. Whether this was due to a lack of popular vigilance and of effort on the part of officials, or whether the inhabitants being less vociferously godly were less susceptible of temptation, it is impossible to say, but it is clear that in the seventeenth century the devil had not yet come to roost in Manhattan.

During the first period of English occupation (1664–1673) most of the prosecutions in the Mayor's Court relate to offenses against property—the many variations of theft, receiving stolen goods, breaking and entering and arson.[50] No attempt appears to have been made to distinguish between grand and petit larceny.[51] In general there is no indication that any distinction was made between felonies and lesser crimes. Occasionally, where there was doubt, the Governor would order the court to proceed,[52] but apparently the only test seems to have been the elusive one of capital or not capital.[53] Next in order of

---

[40] Abuses: 25 NY Col. Mss. 130. Bastardy: ibid. 252; 26 ibid. 159. Cursing: 27 ibid. 127. Fences: 3 Rep. NY State Historian 326. Misdemeanor: 25 NY Col. Mss. 55, 157. Theft: 25 NY Col. Mss. 55, 133, 252. Offenses against public officers: ibid. 252; 2 Rep. NY State Historian 318.
[41] 28 NY Col. Mss. 110.
[42] Ibid. 23.
[43] Ibid.
[44] Ibid. 110.
[45] 25 NY Col. Mss. 55, 150.
[46] 28 ibid. 110. There is one complaint by an Indian (2 Rep. NY State Historian 257) for theft of hogs.
[47] Breach of attachment: Ms. Suffolk Co. Sess. 1668–87 31. Fornication: ibid. 2, 30. Abuse of a Justice: ibid. 32. Misdemeanor: ibid. 6.
[48] Ibid. 7.
[49] The proceedings of the Mayor's Court, 1665–74, are published in Recs. of New Amsterdam

(Fernow ed.) vols. 5, 6, and 7. There are many gaps in the minutes. Some entries refer to previous judicial action which is not entered in the extant minutes and may have been of record elsewhere. The proceedings after the reoccupation in 1674 are in manuscript. Here, too, there is considerable matter missing.
[50] Theft: 5 Recs. of New Amsterdam 314, 317, 335, 340; 6 ibid. 49, 226, 279. Receiving: ibid. 31, 32, 64, 113. Breaking and entering: ibid. 99. Arson: ibid. 94.
[51] We have not attempted to classify these cases but have bulked them under the rubric "theft."
[52] As in the case of Engle Hendricks (6 Recs. of New Amsterdam 34) who had attempted to kill her child, and in the case of Pieter Wolfertsen who had spoken in contempt of the Assize Court (ibid. 56).
[53] On punishments, cf. infra 686, 688 et seq.

frequency were the assaults, riots and breaches of the peace, and the violations of the liquor regulations.[54] Presentments for offenses against morals such as fornication, drunkenness and Sabbath breach were rare,[55] but there are a number of cases involving Indians—entertaining them or selling them rum.[56] The Mayor's Court enforced the Assize of Bread, the maintenance of proper weights, and the rules about carmen. It suppressed disorderly houses and occasionally had to do with damage by cattle and failure to fence.[57] Curiously enough there are only a few cases of resisting or refusing to aid peace officers, and only two cases of seditious words.[58] By special warrant this court took an inquest of death and dealt with a case of attempted homicide.[59]

During the brief period of Dutch reoccupation the records show an increased number of prosecutions for petty matters, but when the English again resumed control there appears to have been a falling off of criminal cases. The calendar has much the same complexion as it had earlier. The prosecutions for thefts, burglaries and receiving preponderate.[60] Assaults and infractions of the licensing laws fall off[61] but there are more cases of contempt of court and seditious words.[62] Between 1674 and 1683 there is only a trickle of complaints for bastardy, drunkenness and Sabbath breach.[63] But again we find an attempted homicide presented[64] and the first proceedings to enforce the English Navigation Acts appear.[65] In contrast with the considerable bulk of civil liti-

---

[54] Assaults: 5 *Recs. of New Amsterdam* 328, 332; 6 *ibid.* 11, 54, 62, 87. Wounds: *ibid.* 25, 34. Breach of peace: *ibid.* 102. Liquor violations: 5 *ibid.* 311, 341; 6 *ibid.* 37, 87, 176, 220, 344.

[55] Fornication: *ibid.* 93; and note in this connection the control over disorderly women, *ibid.* 10, 101. Sabbath breach: 5 *ibid.* 290; 6 *ibid.* 43, 139.

[56] 5 *ibid.* 346, 354; 6 *ibid.* 32, 65, 72, 100, 142, 143.

[57] Assize of Bread: 6 *ibid.* 30, 95, 111, 266. Weights: *ibid.* 374. Carmen: 5 *ibid.* 316; 6 *ibid.* 123. Disorderly houses: 5 *ibid.* 338. Cattle damage: 5 *ibid.* 295. Fences: 6 *ibid.* 71. Apparently the overseers of the highways dealt with all matters related to roads and imposed fines directly, *ibid.* 146.

[58] Offenses relating to officers: 5 *ibid.* 331; 6 *ibid.* 233. Seditious words: *ibid.* 56, 371.

[59] Inquest: *ibid.* 228. Attempted homicide: *ibid.* 35.

[60] Theft: *Ms. Mins. Mayor's Ct. NYC 1674-75* fols. 51, 63; *Ms. Mins. Mayor's Ct. NYC 1677-82* fols. 49b, 131, 226b, 227, 228, 230, 244b, 270b, 302, 331b. Receiving: *Ms. Mins. Mayor's Ct. NYC 1674-75* fol. 26; *Ms. Mins. Mayor's Ct. NYC 1677-82* fols. 183, 227. Burglary: *ibid.* fol. 125. Cheats: *ibid.* fols. 173b, 391b.

[61] Assaults and brawling: *Ms. Mins. Mayor's Ct. NYC 1674-75* fol. 10; *Ms. Mins. Mayor's Ct. NYC*

1677-82 60, 192; *H.R. Ms. Wills* Liber 19b, fol. 295, and the presentment for immoderate correction, *ibid.* fol. 306; *Ms. Decl. Book 1675-77* fol. 6. Liquor violations: *Ms. Mins. Mayor's Ct. NYC 1674-75* fol. 25; *Ms. Mins. Mayor's Ct. NYC 1677-82* fol. 44; *H.R. Ms. Wills* Liber 19b, fol. 207.

[62] Contempt: *Ms. Mins. Mayor's Ct. NYC 1677-82* fols. 178, 188b, 278; *Ms. Decl. Book 1675-77* fols. 123, 335. Seditious words: *Ms. Mins. Mayor's Ct. NYC 1674-75* 29; *Ms. Decl. Book 1675-77* 104, 334. Connected with this are the prosecutions for abusive words, e.g., *Ms. Mins. Mayor's Ct. NYC 1677-82* fols. 205, 227.

[63] Bastardy: *Ms. Mins. Mayor's Ct. NYC 1677-82* 197, 260b. Drunkenness: *ibid.* 201. Sabbath breach: *Ms. Mins. Mayor's Ct. NYC 1674-75* 25. Fornication: *Ms. Mins. Mayor's Ct. NYC 1677-82* 188, Oct. 16, 1678; *H.R. Ms. Wills* Liber 19b, 205. It should be noted that the deacons prosecuted fornication cases. Compare here the order of April 26, 1681, that the deacons were to make visitations to find out and return persons fit to be or continue inhabitants, who are idle and vagrant (*Ms. Mins. Mayor's Ct. NYC 1677-82* 268b).

[64] *Ibid.* 246.

[65] *Ms. Mins. Mayor's Ct. NYC 1674-75* 61; *Ms. Decl. Book 1675-77* 98, 214, 279; and cf. the pro-

gation, criminal justice is small beer, indeed, and one is led to wonder whether it was not overreadiness of the settlers to go to law with a thrifty eye to damages that brought many a quarrel before the court in its incipient stages before it had festered into deeds of violence. There is evidence to indicate that by 1683 the Mayor's Court was conscious of the felony concept, but not as a limitation upon its powers for it exercised a jurisdiction over grand larceny.[66] Since the court did not, however, attempt to inflict capital punishments, no great jurisdictional significance is to be attached to the use in the records of the word felony.

In general the type of jurisdiction exercised in the Delaware courts[67] and at Kingston[68] conforms to that in other Sessions Courts. At Newcastle, it is true, a rape case was tried in 1676,[69] but subsequently for another such case an oyer and terminer commission was obtained[70] and the officers did not hesitate to ask advice when jurisdictional issues arose.[71] For the most part the crime in these outlying regions was petty and there was little occasion for seeking enlightenment on the obscurities of the Duke's Laws as to the proper office of Sessions.

Along what lines the powers of justices of the peace out of Sessions, acting singly or doubly, developed during this early period it is difficult to make an accurate judgment, for there is little of record except a few orders and warrants.[72] As a matter of fact the town court, where authorized, was calculated to absorb a great deal of business which in England, and later in New York, was handled by the justices out of Sessions. So, for example, the business of

ceedings in *Ms. Mins. Mayor's Ct. NYC 1677–82* Jan. 25, 1680/81 and again August 23, 1682.

[66] Cf. *Ms. Mins. Mayor's Ct. NYC 1680–83* 200, Apr. 3, 1683. The defendant was indicted for stealing goods. He was "acquitted of the fellony." But as he had confessed he had found some goods and concealed them without public outcry, he was sentenced to pay thirty shillings or receive five stripes. It is difficult to understand exactly what lines the court drew, for in September 1683 (*ibid.* 158) appears the entry that the matter with which a defendant was charged (viz., breaking into a house) "being above the cognizance of this court" defendant bound for Assizes. Yet the Mayor's Court had previously tried such cases.

[67] *Recs. Ct. of New Castle*: attempted arson, 19; assault, 32, 287; bastardy, 289, 320, 440; breach of peace, 60; cheats, 302; challenge to duel, 91; fornication, 263; receiving, 203; theft, 104, 492; offenses to officers, 128, 226, 469. *Upland Ct. Rec.*: assault, 54, 59; sale of liquor to Indians, 194.

[68] The following examples from the Kingston records will indicate the type of cases. *Ms. Deeds Ulster Co.* Liber II: assault and battery, 48, 49, 329, 457; fence violations, 59, 549; obstructing high-

ways, 52; receiving, 456; Sabbath breach, 49, 544, 594; seditious words, 547; smuggling, 475; wife beating, 464.

[69] *Recs. Ct. of New Castle* 16. The victim was the sheriff's maid, a fact which may explain why jurisdiction was taken.

[70] *Ibid.* 85, and cf. *Ms. Warrants Orders Passes 1674–79* 180.

[71] *Recs. Ct. of New Castle* 330, 421; 12 *Doc. Rel. Col. Hist. NY* 621; *Ms. Deeds Ulster Co.* Liber II, 4, 312, 461.

[72] For example, *Ms. Gravesend Town Rec.* Liber IV: 25 (1669), a justice of the peace order putting an idler at service; 28 (1670), an order re fines for military training; 32 (1671), a warrant reciting the examination of a *mittimus* by justices and binding Thos. Applegate for the Assizes. Compare also *Ms. Kings Co. Ct. & Rd. Recs. 1668–1766* 355 where on a complaint of threats, one justice is authorized by Sessions to examine and bind over. In *Ms. Misc. Recs. Richmond Co.* 68 is a warrant re rates (1681), and in *Stillwell Mss.* an order of the constables and overseers of Feb. 5, 1682/83, is signed by Stillwell (J.P.) on Oct. 21, 1683.

making preliminary examinations was committed to constable and overseers,[73] and likewise the enforcement of liquor regulations.[74] Town court business on the criminal side was of the same character as the pettiest Sessions business, but there are not many criminal cases entered in the town books. Since there is no ground to suppose that the Long Island Puritans were more angelic than their brethren across the Sound, one suspects that the independency of these settlers, who abominated the very name of a justice of the peace,[75] led them to prefer an off-the-record justice. Sabbath breach, incontinence, setting woods on fire, assaults, abusive words, failure to fence and the like is the routine of what is entered.[76] There was no reason why most of this could not equally well have been handled at Sessions except for the expedience of quick dispatch, and this qualification was to apply equally to the eventual substitute—the justice of the peace.

The Judiciary under Dongan

The extent to which the pattern of jurisdiction established by the practice of nearly two decades was disturbed by the Judicature Act of 1683 cannot be exactly determined because the records for the years immediately following the statutory change are very incomplete.[77] The Act itself was so poorly drafted that it was inevitably necessary to have some further definition of the jurisdictional boundaries of the several courts, and in this process practice was bound to be of importance. Furthermore, as we shall presently discover,[78] the introduction at this time of common law procedural forms and removal devices such as the habeas corpus made decision upon jurisdictional issues a much

---

[73] Compare here *Ms. Mins. Mayor's Ct. NYC 1677–82* 184 where the constable and overseers submit testimony taken from a New York lawsuit (Jan. 21, 1679/80); *Ms. Flatbush Town Recs.* Liber AA, 71, evidence taken on the order of justices of the peace (1678); *ibid.* 131, evidence in a fornication case (1679); arbitration by a warrant, *Ms. Flatbush Town Recs.* Liber C, 3; examination on order of Van Ruyven, J., *ibid.* Liber D, 107.

[74] 1 *Col. Laws NY* 40. The licensing was done by justices in Sessions but offenses were tried by constables with two or more overseers. On the later practice, cf. *infra* 129 *et seq.*

[75] Nicolls to the Earl of Clarendon (1666) in 2 *NYHS Coll.* (1869) 119.

[76] Abusive words: *Ms. Flatbush Town Recs.* Liber D, 231, 375; Liber D II, 317, 363; 1 *Hempstead Town Recs.* 285; 1 *Huntington Town Recs.* 119. (These cases include those where a fine was imposed although the action was at the suit of the party.) Abuse of authority: 1 *Hempstead Town Recs.* 293. Breach of peace: 1 *Easthampton Town*

Recs. 423. Contempt: *Ms. Flatbush Town Recs.* Liber D, 377; *Ms. Gravesend Town Recs.* Liber IV, 16; 1 *Easthampton Town Recs.* 326. Fences: *Ms. Flatbush Town Recs.* Liber D, 175, 303, 305. Incontinence: *Ms. Flatbush Town Recs.* Liber D, 147; 1 *Easthampton Town Recs.* 369. Speeding: *Ms. Flatbush Town Recs.* Liber D, 339, 365. Sabbath breach: *ibid.* 153, 175; *Ms. Gravesend Town Recs.* Liber IV, 14; 1 *Huntington Town Recs.* 333.

[77] The minutes of the Council are only partially preserved. Volumes 31, 32, 33 and part of volume 34 of the *Col. Mss.* are totally destroyed. No trace of Oyer and Terminer minutes for any counties except New York, Ulster and Albany have been found. The minutes for some counties were contained in the destroyed volumes of *Col. Mss.* No Sessions minutes for Queens, Richmond or Dutchess counties during Dongan's regime have been found. The Suffolk Sessions records contain only wills. Only one page of Ulster Sessions minutes appears to have been preserved.

[78] *Infra* 406 *et seq.*

more immediate and lively matter. Previously these issues appear in the records to have been raised not at the instance of the parties but by the judges, and were usually resolved by letting the superior court settle the problem. With the advent of devices whereby a defendant could force a preliminary judicial settlement of the question where he was to be tried,[79] one looks for a much greater clarification of the limits of authority than had theretofore existed.

The first step in the more accurate definition of the courts' authority was effected by the commissions to the judges. In the case of the Oyer and Terminer Court, authority was thereby extended over treasons, felonies and misdemeanors, but the peace commission, since it did not follow the terms of its English prototype, did not go beyond a jurisdiction over petit larceny which, while still technically a felony, was usually punished as a misdemeanor.[80] Measured by these instruments, therefore, the Sessions Courts would be excluded from trying serious crimes.

The Oyer and Terminer records disclose that jurisdiction was taken over cases from homicide to nuisance.[81] The statutory authority of the court was sufficient for the exercise of concurrent jurisdiction in any matter. Why, in a session for the county of New York, where Quarter Sessions was competent to try such matters as false weights and nuisance, the Oyer and Terminer should have troubled itself with such causes but remitted a case of bastardy is not to be explained.

It is fortunate that for the two localities where a real change was made respecting intermediate jurisdiction we still have records—the Quarter Sessions for New York County and the Sessions for Albany where the old Commissary Court was done away with.

The New York Quarter Sessions was destined to take over the criminal business theretofore exercised by the Mayor's Court,[82] but for a time consider-

[79] For example, King v. Dean, in *Ms. Mins. NYCQS 1683/84–1694* 3, May 6, 1684. The writ of habeas corpus to remove cases is first used in civil cases; cf. *Ms. Mins. Mayor's Ct. NYC 1680–83* (no foliation) under dates of Nov. 20, 1683, and Feb. 26, 1683/84.

[80] *Infra* 691 n. 91.

[81] At the Oyer and Terminer session for New York County, April 1684, a homicide and three grand larcenies were tried. There was one case of enticement of servants, five cases of false weights and three indictments for nuisance. Apparently no criminal cases were on the calendar for the October term, 1684 (7 *Ms. Mins. Council* [Reverse]). At the Albany Oyer and Terminer, May term, 1687, no criminal cases were tried (35 *NY Col. Mss.* 86). A parchment (*H.R. Parch.* 221 B 2) has the record of

a burglary tried Sept. 10, 1686, in New York by a special Oyer and Terminer. At the Oyer and Terminer for Ulster County, June 4–7, 1684, were tried four indictments for seditious attempts to subvert the laws. The offense was recited to be a trespass and misdemeanor (*Ms. Mins. Oyer and Terminer Ulster Co.* fols. 1–8).

[82] The Judicature Act of 1683 had provided for town courts and Sessions Courts, stipulating for New York City quarterly sessions of the latter. From a petition of November 9, 1683, it appears that the city authorities wished to continue the old scheme of a single court (1 *Mins. Com. Council* 102–105). The answer of the Governor (*ibid.* 105) was ambiguous, indicating, however, that two courts should be held. On November 24, 1683, a commission was issued authorizing the holding of

able civil litigation came before it, and the Mayor's Court occasionally handled police matters.[83] A similar confusion respecting jurisdiction prevailed in respect of the criminal cases brought to trial, for an indictment for burglary was tried at a Special Sessions,[84] and the indictments are not free from technical words of felony.[85] In several instances prisoners were held for Oyer and Terminer,[86] but there is nothing to show what this court supposed the boundaries of its authority to be. The bulk of the business related to misdemeanors: assaults, bastardy and nuisance.[87] The most important head of jurisdiction in point of frequency was the trial of informations for violation of the Navigation Acts.[88] Inquests upon deaths were also held here.[89]

The Albany Sessions business is of a similar type. The assault cases predominated. Cases of maltreating servants, trading with Indians or selling them rum, enforcement of licensing regulations, the assize of bread and highway obstruction all appear on the records.[90] New county ordinances are made upon presentment by the grand jury,[91] but on the whole the proceedings in this court are already assuming the aspect they were to have in the eighteenth century. The surviving records of the Sessions Court for Westchester County have virtually no criminal cases brought to trial,[92] and the entries in the Kings County records show almost no criminal business.[93]

a "Court of Mayor and aldermen and sessions" (*ibid.* 107). In December, Dongan commissioned James Graham as recorder (*ibid.* 117) and on February 1, 1683/84, the common council voted to hold a Court of Sessions. The Governor disputed this action but ordered court be held until the Duke's pleasure be known (*ibid.* 119). It may be inferred from the fact that the city authorities resolved that a grand jury be impanelled for Sessions that they intended this court for criminal business. This inference is strengthened by the direction of the Governor and Council that the recorder give a charge (5 *Ms. Mins. Council* 45): "Ordered by the Governo͏ʳ & Council that Mr. Recorder be spoken to so he give the Charge to the grand jury, & that if any of the Council go thither they are to take places before the Mayor & Aldermen, the Mayor representing no more than a Justice of the Peace at the Quarter Sessions of the City & County Ordered that Mͬ West at present serve as Clarke of the Sessions

"The Recorder is in his Charge to presse for the Clearing of the lands in this County & to give notice that no one shall plead in any Court that hath not been an Inhabitant here five years; & paid scot and lot in this province" (Jan. 31, 1683/84).

[83] E.g., *Ms. Mins. Mayor's Ct. NYC 1682–95*, under date of May 12, 1687, a complaint against butchers, and Nov. 6, 1687, a proceeding against a keeper of a disorderly house.

[84] *Ms. Mins. NYCQS 1683/84–1694* 69, King v. Thomassen, Nov. 13, 1685.

[85] E.g., *Ms. Mins. NYCQS 1683/84–1694*, King v. Edmonds, 71, Nov. 13, 1685; King v. Hubbart, 31, Feb. 3, 1684/85; King v. Thomassen, 69, Nov. 13, 1685.

[86] *Ibid.* 32, 141.

[87] Assault: *ibid.* 82, Feb. 2, 1685/86. Bastardy: *ibid.* 141, 142, 147, Nov. 1, 1688. Breaking: *ibid.* 89, May 4, 1686. Larceny: *ibid.* 71, 73, Nov. 13, 1685. Misdemeanor: *ibid.* 148, Aug. 1, 1689. Nuisance: *ibid.* 112, May 3, 1686.

[88] *Ibid.* 33, 40, 48, 50 *et seq.*, 93, 95, May 5, Aug. 4, 1685, Aug. 3, 1686. Cf. also the minutes of Aug. 4, 1685, *H.R. Papers* (no number).

[89] *Ms. Mins. NYCQS 1683/84–1694* 142, 148, Nov. 1, 1688, Aug. 1, 1689.

[90] *Ms. Mins. Albany Co. Sess. 1685–89*. Assault: 14, 16, 18, 20. Maltreatment of servant: 28. Indians: 18, 38. License violation: 36. Assize of bread: 49. Highways: 57.

[91] For example, on Dec. 4, 1688, the grand jury presents that all persons who sell strong drink by retail must keep lodging for horse and man.

[92] *Mins. Westch. Ct. of Sess.* 58, an unspecified charge and a complaint for violating liquor regulations (1688). These records have some data on the supervisory control of Oyer and Terminer.

[93] The meager entries in *Ms. Kings Co. Ct. & Rd. Recs. 1668–1766* are clearly not a full record

The manner in which the practical definition of jurisdiction was effected over the long stretch of years during which the judicial machinery set up by the Judicature Act of 1691 and its successors was in operation was one of selective reproduction. The foundation for this was laid when in Dongan's time common law enrollment, forms of process, indictments, informations and the like displaced the earlier homemade forms. The use of these instruments in the proper way (and by proper is meant accepted common law usage) was necessarily a slow business, involving the education not only of country justices but of the judges of the superior courts, the clerks and old-resident attorneys. What takes place cannot be described as a development in the sense of an evolution where the ideas are native born and are molded by the courts into rules which in turn become the substance for further procreation. Rather is the process one of becoming familiar with and adopting a gradually increasing number of details from the existing body of common law dogma, the practice of English courts and the professional traditions. In specific instances, as we shall see, the course of the courts is not hard to trace. Thus the English form of indictment falls suddenly into the stream of provincial administration, and bit by bit as learning from English books is washed about it —the motion to quash, the limitations on quashing, the removal by certiorari, the *procedendo,* the record function and a myriad other details—a firm corpus of common law is built up. From the standpoint of English lawyers or officials this must have seemed simply a process of imitation, but the colonists, who were under some limitation and control in their law-building, would have been justified in regarding what their courts were about in the light of our own figure, as a process of accretion, for as Englishmen they regarded themselves as entitled to the common law, and the courts were simply making it their own as need arose. Indeed, the eighteenth century is well along before there are signs that provincial law is conceived as something discrete.

Although the sources run thin for the years after Leisler's Rebellion, there can be no question that appropriation of common law devices and traditions proceeded apace and with increasing completeness. This is demonstrated not only by the appearance of artful pleading in the Supreme Court, and by the employment of learned citation,[94] but also by the changing character of proceed-

---

of proceedings as witness the indictments for the county of Kings (1687) in 35 *NY Col. Mss.* 1. In *Ms. Gravesend Town Recs.* Liber IV, 38–45, are some civil proceedings before justices between 1687–92. These are important in showing the tran-

sition from town court to justice of the peace jurisdiction.

[94] Cf. the authorities cited in King v. Bayard (1702), 14 Howell, *State Trials* 47.

ings in the country courts. The evidence of the records of criminal proceedings is strongly corroborated by the fuller record of civil litigation. This general and wholehearted reception of an old and, as respects criminal procedure, nearly static jurisprudence was itself enough to eliminate the hazards of native experiment. And when, by reference, the chief court of the province was made coordinate in power with the three great courts at Westminster the destiny of provincial law as a science of imitation was fixed. Aside from the improvement of expert knowledge, this process was encouraged by the stability of the institutional structure over three quarters of a century. There was no need of those recurrent basic adjustments in respect to jurisdiction that had previously been unavoidable, and with this problem of general demarcation settled, the courts were faced with issues no more difficult than those of determining within the framework of statutes, ordinances and commissions some particular conflict of authority by the application of common law rules. On the procedural side this results in a body of colonial precedent in the sense that forms and practices once employed become indenizened, but substantive precedent remains to the end English precedent. Thus the whole process of defining jurisdiction in the eighteenth century, indeed the settlement of practice generally, assumes the aspect of a sporadic but unceasing addition of colonial marginal glosses to the second book of Hawkins' *Pleas of the Crown*.

We have dwelt upon these characteristics of the provincial courts and criminal procedure in the eighteenth century because we propose to discuss the matter of jurisdiction in terms of the sum of powers exercised in particular tribunals over this period, indicating so far as possible the sequence of particular accretions and of the regional variations. The objections to this method for the purposes of an historical account are obvious, but as we have remarked it is with accretion by imitation and not with evolution that we have to do, and we shall therefore pursue a method whereby the process of imitation is best depicted.

The Supreme Court

The partition of original jurisdiction in the system inaugurated by the Judicature Act of 1691 must properly commence with a consideration of the Supreme Court, not only because it was, except for a few appeals by writ of error, the court of final instance in criminal cases, but because there was consolidated in it the sum of the powers exercised by the three great English courts,

the King's Bench, Common Pleas and Exchequer.[95] It was thus the highest
court of original jurisdiction in New York Colony and enjoyed almost unlimited power to hear,[96] try and determine Crown pleas no matter how serious
or how trivial.[97]

In practice, however, the Supreme Court *en banc* did not handle the bulk of
routine criminal business but left such matters to be heard at Circuit or in
Quarter and General Sessions or by the justices of the peace. It is true that
Governor Hunter's Ordinance of 1715 stipulated with respect to nisi prius
trials that all persons "having any issues depending" in the Supreme Court
might try them at bar,[98] but this does not seem to have affected criminal jurisdiction, so that, as we shall see, the Court alone settled the question whether
such causes were to be tried at bar.

In relation to the city and county of New York certain exceptions must be
noticed to this rule that criminal causes would normally not be tried at bar
because, as a matter of practice, offenses committed in that county, both capital and sometimes very minor ones, were tried in the Supreme Court. This
came about as a result of the provincial Act of 1692 by which the circuit system was instituted.[99] The theory of this statute was that a Supreme Court was
to be held in and for each county, so that every sitting of the Supreme Court
was in effect an Oyer and Terminer for the county where it convened. Two
sessions a year were to be held for New York and Orange counties jointly. By
Bellomont's ordinance, however, the Supreme Court was settled in New York
City, and the outlying counties were put on a circuit like the English Assizes.
No stipulation was made respecting a circuit term for New York and Orange
counties, so that, as to these two localities the Supreme Court remained the
competent Court of Oyer and Terminer and General Gaol Delivery. In consequence, the New York City and County cases continued to be tried at bar, and
in 1704 the circuit was extended to Orange.[100]

We do not know whether or not the arrangements thus made were influenced by the old practice which had prevailed in England respecting cases
arising in Middlesex County where the King's Bench sat. Anciently these cases
had always been tried in King's Bench at bar. But in 1576, since the business

[95] 1 *Col. Laws NY* 226, 229.
[96] Cf. *infra* 299 *et seq.*
[97] Original and transfer jurisdiction in civil matters was limited to cases where the amount involved was more than £20, cf. 1 *Col. Laws NY*
226, 229, 303, 306, 359, 380; 2 *Rev. Statutes NY*
(1813) App. no. v.

[98] *An Ordinance for Altering the Time of Sitting
in the Supreme Court* (Broadside, NYHS).
[99] 1 *Col. Laws NY* 306.
[100] 49 *NY Col. Mss.* 87–89; 9 *Ms. Mins. Council*
394.

of the court had thereby become obstructed, it was provided by statute that the chief justice or two puisne judges were authorized to try issues in Middlesex as a nisi prius court.[101] The New York judges could hardly have been unaware of the parallel between Middlesex and New York County; indeed, there is some late evidence to show acceptance of the rule of *Lord Sanchar's Case*[102] which held that when King's Bench was sitting the powers of other courts in the county were suspended.[103]

There was no reason to carry out in New York the English nisi prius statute of 1576. If it were necessary to dispose of cases out of term, special commissions of oyer and terminer and general gaol delivery would be issued.[104] We believe that prior to 1768 all commissions for New York City of which there is a record were special although the destruction of the books of enrolled commissions makes a certain answer impossible. Certainly, if the court in addition to its eventual four regular terms had had regular circuit session in that county, this would have appeared in the several ordinances relating to the times of sitting. In other words, these were emergency occasions, for what may be called the normal circuit business of New York County was dispatched at the regular terms.

Early in the year 1768, however, there was an abrupt change in the situation. At a meeting of the Council on February 10 it was considered that the time allowed for the continuance of the several Supreme Court terms was often found insufficient for the trial of causes. Since the business of the Crown had a pref-

---

[101] 18 Eliz. c.12.

[102] 9 *Co. Rep.* 117, and cf. 2 Hawkins, *Pleas of the Crown* c. III §11: ". . . As to the third Point, viz. How far the Presence of this Court suspends the Power of all other Courts, it is certain, That this being the supreme court of Oyer and Terminer, Gaol Delivery and Eyre, doth so far suspend the Power of all other Justices of this Kind . . . that all Proceedings commenced before any such Justices during such Time are void . . ."

[103] In the *Ms. Mins. NYCQS 1760–72* 264, Nov. 1, 1768, this statement is made: "It appearing to this Court, that the Supreme Court of Oyer and Terminer and General Gaol Delivery for this province, is now sitting, which Suspends the power of all proceedings of this Court in Criminal matters, It is therefore ordered that the Grand Jurors . . . be discharged." Cf. also *Ms. Mins. Queens Co. Sess. 1722–87*: at the session of May 21, 1760, no grand jury was sworn because an Oyer and Terminer was sitting at Jamaica.

[104] See, for example, the cases of Milward Thorpe, George Borne, Ann Sawyer and Domingus Crea, all of whom were indicted and tried for felony before Lewis Morris and Robert Walter, justices of the Supreme Court of Judicature, sitting at New York City under a commission of oyer and terminer and general gaol delivery on January 15, 16, 17, 18, 19, 23, 25, 1722/23 (*Ms. Mins. Cir. 1721–49* 26–31). Cf. also *Ms. James Alexander Papers* Box 44, *Mayor's Ct. Papers*, for an indictment against George Borne and Millward Thorpe at Oyer and Terminer and General Gaol Delivery, 1722, New York City. The examination of George Borne is in *Ms. James Alexander Papers* Box 45, *Quarter Sessions Papers*. The minutes do not state that this was a special commission but this fact is established from 3 *Mins. Com. Council* 308. See also a presentment for burglary at Oyer and Terminer in New York City, Jan. 26, 1768, King v. John Dupe (*J. T. Kempe Lawsuits* C–F). On Jan. 20, 1764, Horsmanden and Smith requested that the term of the Supreme Court be enlarged as the time was not sufficient to deliver the gaol and dispatch pending business. An ordinance was therefore issued (25 *Ms. Mins. Council* 505). Nevertheless, at the February 2 meeting a special commission was ordered because the Mayor of New York and the magistrates represented that various felons had been caught since the Supreme Court had sat.

erence by law, civil causes frequently went off for want of time. Consequently it was ordered by the Governor with the unanimous advice of the Council that in the future "a Commission of Oyer and Terminer and General Gaol Delivery for the City and County of New York do issue thirty Days before the Commencement of the respective Terms of the Said Supreme Court and that such Commission be directed to the Justices of the Supreme Court and the Mayor Recorder and Aldermen of the City of New York for the time being and the Powers thereof vested in them or any three of them whereof either of the said Justices of the Supreme Court to be one." No commissions for these regular sessions have been found but in the margin is set forth some collateral evidence. It should be noticed that the order of 1768 did not subtract any criminal jurisdiction from the Supreme Court which continued to try crimes at its regular terms, and further that special commissions were sometimes issued when necessary.[105]

The jurisdiction exercised prior to 1768 because of the important exception *ratione loci* was the ground of proceeding in nearly all of the capital cases which came before the Supreme Court, and most of the minor offenses there dealt with, such as breaches of the peace, assaults, disorderly houses, nuisances, receiving and petit larceny, were likewise New York City cases. As to the rest of provincial crime the Supreme Court ordinarily took cognizance only of cases involving Crown rights, offenses committed by public officers, matters of general welfare, unusual or difficult cases and serious riots and disturbances.[105a]

It may be inferred from the early records of the Supreme Court, and it is increasingly clear as the sources become fuller, that in relation to criminal jurisdiction this tribunal was patterning itself upon King's Bench. The percentage

---

[105] The order is in 26 *Ms. Mins. Council* 116. The first commission is probably that of Mar. 14, 1768 (*Cal. NY Col. Com. 1680–1770* 70). The parchment estreat (*H.R. Parch.* 179 A 9) mentions fines against Cornelius Edison and others for a disorderly house paid at a Court of Oyer and Terminer and General Gaol Delivery held in New York City, Mar. 25, 1768. We are not at all sure that thereafter an Oyer and Terminer was held prior to each term. The roll of estreats (*H.R. Parch.* 211 C 2) lists such a court, Dec. 15, 1775 (viz. a month before January term, 1776) but we have seen no other estreats. These have not, of course, all been preserved.

The court mentioned *supra* n. 103, as held Nov. 1, 1768, must have been special as it was held after the October term of the Supreme Court. Again in Nov. 1769 another special commission for New York City issued (26 *Ms. Mins. Council* 166). At the request of Mayor Hicks a special commission issued Nov. 30, 1774 (*ibid.* 414).

[105a] Excluding from consideration 933 miscellaneous cases (appearances, jurors' and constables' contempts, debt on bonds, and unidentified offenses), material exists on 1280 Supreme Court criminal cases handled *en banc* from 1691 to 1776. Of these 281 were matters of Crown interest; 52 involved matters of general public welfare or unusual or difficult cases or cases which, like perjury and forgery, were presumably not triable at Sessions (". . . justices of peace have no jurisdiction over forgery and perjury at the common law." 2 Hawkins, *Pleas of the Crown* c.8 §38); 271 cases concerned riot or resistance to authority; 28 were moral offenses such as rape; 25 were *qui tams* in excise cases or under statutes regulating trade, mar-

of cases tried at bar was in all probability higher[106] than in England, and the supervision over country crime was more concentrated since the total number of judges available for circuit was fewer than in England,[107] and since it was continually necessary, for political reasons, to take cognizance of matters which in England would never have been taken to Westminster. In general, these cases fall into two classes: those where local grand juries could not or would not present, or the complaints on which it was felt that true bills would not be found; and those where immediate central court supervision was deemed desirable. In both situations these matters were brought up from the counties for the Supreme Court's attention by Crown informations framed by the Attorney General.[108] Certiorari was employed to bring up indictments already found in cases in which superintendence by the central authorities was believed to be necessary.[109] Great care was taken that all such cases be tried by jury, and by a jury of the vicinage at that,[110] and therefore, cases transferred from the counties by certiorari[111] or by Crown information[112] were tried by juries of the vicinage[113] either at bar or at nisi prius.

kets and commodities. There were 303 minor offenses. It is difficult to determine the exact number of capital cases but there appear to have been roughly 348 cases.

The cases of Crown interest included: treason, sedition, maladministration by public officials, high misdemeanors, extortion, false imprisonment, intrusion on Crown lands, counterfeiting, champerty, maintenance, embracery, contempt, usurping the office of Mayor of Westchester, and interfering with the Indians.

The unusual crimes or those not triable in Sessions or concerning public welfare included bigamy, blasphemy, sacrilege, usury, maintaining unlawful lotteries, dissenters preaching without a license, forgery, perjury, embezzlement, libel, and giving a challenge.

Riot cases comprised riot, rescue, gaol break, forcible entry, assaulting officers, obstructing officers in the performance of their duties, interfering with land surveyors, preventing partition of lands, refusing to aid officers in apprehending criminals, harboring felons, burning fences, breaking lamps and windows in New York City contrary to act of assembly, obstructing roads and the King's highways and slandering jurors.

The capital cases included murder, grand larceny and the 1741 slave conspiracy.

The minor offenses were breaches of the peace, assault and battery, trespass, disorderly houses, nuisances, receiving stolen goods and petit larceny.

106 1 Stephen, *Hist. Criminal Law* 93, 95, regarding the practical exercise of the King's Bench criminal jurisdiction.

107 Where the judges of all the central courts were subject to circuit duty, 1 Holdsworth, *Hist. of Eng. Law* (1927) 279.

108 *Infra* 163.

109 *Infra* 154.

110 The New York "Charter of Liberties" of Oct. 30, 1683 (1 *Col. Laws NY* 113) demanded that all trials be by verdict of twelve men "of the neighborhood and in the County Shire or Division where the fact Shall arise or grow Whether the Same be by Indictment Infermacon Declaracon or otherwise. . . ." The provincial statute of May 13, 1691 (1 *Col. Laws NY* 244 at 247) enacted this demand in similar language. The Judicature Acts of 1691 and 1692 provided for trial by jury of the vicinage (*ibid.* 230, 307) and a similar provision was contained in Bellomont's ordinance. Cf. also 2 Hawkins, *Pleas of the Crown* c.40 §1; Coke, *Third Institute* (1809 ed.) 34.

111 Certiorari, employed also as a method of appellate review (*infra* 261), was frequently used to transfer indictments from New York City Quarter Sessions and the country Sessions to the Supreme Court (*infra* 154). In some cases of perjury and capital offenses, the indictments were transferred *a propria manu* without writ from Quarter Sessions to the Supreme Court (*infra* 147).

112 Crown informations were framed on private complaints, on informal grand jury presentments, on the Attorney General's own knowledge, on order of the court, and on order of the Governor and Council. This was the commonest method of removal and we shall see (*infra* 172 *et seq.*) that this device afforded an excellent method for central supervision of the local administration of justice. (See also *infra* 372 *et seq.*)

113 Commonly, trials at bar or at nisi prius were

The whole matter of transfers will be discussed in the next chapter, but it is desirable at this point to consider the workings of the nisi prius machinery not only because the King's Bench character of the Supreme Court's jurisdiction will be clarified thereby, but also because the authority exercised in respect of the nisi prius cause is in certain particulars part of original jurisdiction.

The nisi prius causes were initiated either by information filed in the Supreme Court itself or by indictment found in an inferior court and removed to the Supreme Court. The cause would remain in the Supreme Court until pleading to issue at which point the case would be sent down for actual trial in the county where the offense had been perpetrated. Trial would be held at Circuit, the judges of which initially derived their authority from imitation of the English rule that the Assize commission, although civil in nature, through the operation of statute conveyed the necessary criminal jurisdiction.[114] In 1741, by provincial act, the judges of the Supreme Court were given nisi prius jurisdiction ex officio.[115] The distinctive character of the jurisdiction is indicated by the fact that the plea roll, viz., minute entries of nisi prius causes, is kept under a special style: "A Court for the Trial of Causes brought to Issue in the Supreme Court." After verdict a formal account of the proceedings at trial, the *postea,* would be returned to the Supreme Court where judgment on the verdict would be rendered at bar. Since the pleading and the final proceedings took place in the Supreme Court, the cases handled in this way have to be regarded as *pro tanto* a part of the Supreme Court's original jurisdiction.

The imitation of this particular English procedural *tour de force* may seem a somewhat pedantic gesture, since the Supreme Court judges themselves rode the circuit and were thus able to control what went on at an Oyer and Terminer session. The chief advantage lay in the fact that the technically most complicated aspects of a prosecution—the initial and final proceedings—took place before the full bench of the court and that the trouble and expense of bringing witnesses and jury to town were avoided. Furthermore, the lay justices of the peace who were included in the circuit commissions were not present at junctures where their local interests might enable them effectively to block the central authorities. This last consideration is suggested by the type of cases handled in this way. They embrace matters of Crown interest and offenses constituting interference with Crown officials or with the due admin-

---

by jury of the vicinage unless it was alleged that an impartial jury could not be drawn from the county. In such cases a change of venue was authorized. Cf. *infra* 144 n. 33; 170.

[114] 1 Chitty, *Criminal Law* 142; Bullock v. Parsons, 1 *Salkeld* 454.
[115] 3 *Col. Laws NY* 191.

istration of justice, such as intrusion on Crown lands, making false deeds, interfering with Indians, sedition, champerty, maintenance, embracery, obstructing or assaulting officers in the execution of their offices and maladministration on the part of public officials.[116]

The nisi prius system was put into operation in the last years of the seventeenth century. This appears from the case of *King* v. *Schermerhorn* (1696) where upon information read in the Supreme Court the defendant pleaded not guilty and it was ordered "that the deft. be bound for his appearance to abide the determinacon of this Court upon tryall in the circuite of Albany."[117] Whether or not the machinery just described was then operating in all its details is, however, open to doubt, for the Supreme Court ordinance of Governor Hunter (1715)[118] recites the grievance that the inhabitants of the province had been put to excessive charges at trials in the Supreme Court "for want of a Regular Establishment for the Tryal of Causes in the respective Counties brought to issue in the said Supream Court." Consequently it was ordained that at certain times there be held "a court for the Tryal of Causes brought to Issue in the Supream Court," at the circuit terms "as near to the Methods and Proceedings in England as the circumstances of the Province will admit." Judgment on any verdict was not to be given in the country but was reserved to the Supreme Court.[119]

---

[116] Out of 86 nisi prius cases which have been examined, there were nisi prius trials on 21 informations for riot, 3 informations and 1 commitment for assaulting officers, 1 information for intrusion on Crown lands, 1 information for making false deeds against the Indians, 2 informations for preventing partition of lands under an assembly act of 1762 (4 *Col. Laws NY* 584, 612, 1036), 2 informations for seditious words, 2 informations for "obstructing the King's Highway," and a single information each for perjury, for attempted poisoning, for maintenance, for bribery of a jury, for harboring a felon, for false weights, for taking a steer from a town common, for making a fraudulent deed, and for champerty. There were 8 informations for assault and battery, 6 informations for unidentified offenses, 3 informations for forcible entry, 1 inquisition for forcible entry taken before two justices of the peace (removed to the Supreme Court by certiorari and thence sent down for trial at nisi prius), and one Sessions indictment for setting fire to a jail (removed to the Supreme Court by certiorari and thence sent down for trial at nisi prius). Ten of the cases at nisi prius involved offenses of jurors and constables, and these were punished summarily by fines. There are serious gaps in the nisi prius records.

[117] *Mins. SCJ 1693–1701* (45 *NYHS Colls.*

[1912]) 105. Nisi prius did not occur in this early period as a matter of course. Cf. the petition (50 *NY Col. Mss.* 66) and the Council action (9 *Ms. Mins. Council* 516 [1705]).

[118] *An Ordinance for Altering the Time*, etc.

[119] Although the statute 14 Henry VI c.1 gave power to justices of nisi prius to give judgment on the verdict (see 2 Hale, *Pleas of the Crown* 403, 404) the New York practice after 1715 was for judgment to be given *en banc* on the *postea* returned from nisi prius. We have seen but two very doubtful exceptions to this rule, Samuel Moffett v. Cleare Everett, and E. Underdonck v. Abraham Herring. Regarding Moffett v. Everett, the following entry appears in the *en banc* minute entries of the Supreme Court: "Whereas at the Circuit Court held in June . . . for the County of Dutchess It was by Rule of the said Court Ordered . . . that this cause be referred to [three named referees] . . . the Defendant . . . Confess Judgment for the damages" [according to the referees' report]. "Ordered that the said Rule entered . . . at the Circuit be made a Rule of this Court accordingly" (*Ms. Mins. SCJ 1764–66* [Engr.] 264, July 1765). A similar *en banc* rule adopting an order of the Circuit Court was made in Underdonck v. Herring: "Whereas at the last Court of Nisiprius in Orange County . . . by consent of both Parties

The potentialities of nisi prius developed only as the various counties became more populous and as the information procedure came into use as a means of administrative policing. Richard Bradley, who was Attorney General from 1723 to 1751, seems to have been largely responsible for this last development,[120] and during his incumbency the combination of information, removal proceedings and nisi prius reached a high degree of technical perfection. It should be added that much of the success of the nisi prius jurisdiction was due to the benefit which the country litigant derived from the trial of civil pleas in his own district. This matter lies without the scope of our study but it deserves to be thoroughly explored.

The Circuit and Special Commissions

The powers of superintendence vested in the judges of the Supreme Court extended beyond the jurisdiction exercised at bar and through nisi prius, since one or more of these judges were required to "go the circuit and hold and keep the Supreme Court for the several counties." The matter of nomenclature will be examined in the next chapter, but it should be stated at once that the court held pursuant to this mandate was not identical with the Supreme Court. In the first place its several functions were exercised pursuant to particular commissions; and secondly the attendance of at least two justices of the peace included in the commissions was a dilution of the judicial personnel that quite destroyed the identity of the tribunal with the Supreme Court. What the provincial authorities had in mind, of course, was a reproduction of the English Assizes, a creation which, like the mythological beasts of the Greeks, combined the best parts of so many animals that even in 1861 the Common Bench could do no better than describe it as a "superior court."[121] The criminal jurisdiction of the Circuit[122] was exercised pursuant to commissions of the peace,

. . . it was ordered that this Cause should be left to the final determination of . . . [three named justices as referees] and it was thereby agreed that the said rule be . . . made a Rule of the next Court . . . Ordered . . . that said Rule . . . be made a Rule of this Court" (*ibid*. 298, July 1765). It will be noted, however, that it was considered necessary even in these two civil cases to have the rule of the Circuit adopted and ratified by being made a rule of the Supreme Court *en banc*.

[120] Cf. *infra* 372 *et seq*.

[121] *Ex parte Fernandez*, 10 *C.B.* (n.s.) 3.

[122] No special peace commission issued in New York Province for the Circuit judges, the county commission apparently being deemed sufficient. We have found no assize commission, but from a

Council minute it appears such were issued (9 *Ms. Mins. Council* 516).

The chief extant Circuit records comprise the following:

(i) 1716–1717—Two bound manuscript volumes "Courts of Oyer and Terminer and Supreme, August 7, 1716, to September 5, 1717," containing 52 pages; "Courts of Oyer and Terminer and Supreme, September 6, 1716, to September 11, 1717," containing 21 pages. These two volumes are on file on the seventh floor of the Hall of Records, New York City.

(ii) 1721–1749—Two bound manuscript copies made in 1911 of original Circuit minutes in private hands from August 8, 1721, to September 26, 1749. These two volumes are continuously numbered and

of oyer and terminer, of gaol delivery, and of assize (upon which the nisi prius depended). Each of these instruments conveyed distinct powers, because, having in the past not invariably been issued in combination, discrete rules had been developed as to each. The assize commission by force of various statutes conveyed the authority merely to conduct the actual trial of causes previously brought to issue. The gaol delivery empowered the judge to deliver the jail in a particular place or county on the basis of indictments already found, usually by inferior courts whose powers of trial did not extend to the grade of offenses presented. By virtue of an oyer and terminer commission, however, the grand jury had to be impanelled, which could present, or return indictments that could then be tried. The effect of these several instruments in combination was to convey a general criminal jurisdiction in respect to offenses occurring in the designated county, and consequently in New York Province, where the judge rode armed with all the necessary jurisdiction-giving instruments, the original jurisdiction over both felonies and misdemeanors was plenary.

What part of the Circuit Courts' functions in fact were exercised originally is a very technical question the answer to which depends partly on the traditional rules about the commissions themselves, and partly upon the implications of the word "original" in relation to the juncture at which the Circuit took cognizance of a case. As we have seen, the nisi prius cause belongs to the original jurisdiction of the Supreme Court since the Circuit's function in rela-

total 357 pages. The copies are on file in the Library of the Bar Association of the City of New York, 42 W. 44th St. It will be noted that the Oyer and Terminer and General Gaol Delivery minutes are entered under the heading "Minutes of the Circuit" and cover pp. 1–128, while pp. 231–357 contain "Minutes of the Court for the Trial of Causes," i.e., the nisi prius entries. Pages 128–230 are blank.

(iii) 1765–1767—H.R. Parch. 218 D 1 contains "Estreats of Issues" at Oyer and Terminer and General Gaol Delivery for various counties.

(iv) 1767—A parchment "Estreat of Issues," etc. from Sessions and Oyer and Terminer and General Gaol Delivery for Suffolk. This is on file in the Hall of Records and once bore the number 175 H 1, but at present it has no number.

(v) 1766–1771—H.R. Parch. 179 A 9 contains some "Estreats of Issues," etc. at Oyer and Terminer and General Gaol Delivery for the Counties of Albany, Queens, Westchester, Dutchess and New York.

(vi) 1769–1775—H.R. Parch. 211 C 2, estreat of issues, etc. at Oyer and Terminer and General

Gaol Delivery for various counties during these years.

(vii) Miscellaneous references to Oyer and Terminer and General Gaol Delivery cases—H.R. Parch. 169 K 5; 156 L 10; H.R. Pleadings K 367, 368, 423, 683, 685, 704, 716, 71°· J. T. Kempe Lawsuits C–F, King v. Hugh Cairns, King v. Mary Cavenaugh, King v. Abraham De Witt; ibid. G–J, King v. John Hunt; Misc. Mss. Albany 1691–1799 Folder 1750–69, King v. Four Negroes, Folder 1770–79, King v. Peet, a slave, and King v. John Snyder; Misc. Mss. Ulster, a form of capias issued out of Ulster Oyer and Terminer and General Gaol Delivery, ca. 1723; Horsmanden Papers 1714–47 NYHS, September Circuit at Jamaica; James Alexander Papers Box 59, "Callendar of Persons in Custody," and several attached papers relating to Suffolk Oyer and Terminer and General Gaol Delivery, 1722; ibid. Box 44, King v. Borne, King v. Thorpe, NYC Oyer and Terminer and General Gaol Delivery, 1722; ibid. Box 46, King v. Isaac Jacobs; ibid. Box 60, King v. the Hunts and Baxter, King v. Slaughter, King v. Moras.

tion thereto was circumscribed. On the other hand, the proceedings upon indictments found by grand juries impanelled pursuant to the oyer and terminer commission were clearly original. As to indictments transmitted by the General Sessions Courts, proceedings may be viewed as a part of the transfer jurisdiction of the Circuit Court or as a part of the original jurisdiction of a Gaol Delivery. For reasons of convenience, and because a removal was involved, we shall consider the latter in relation to transfer jurisdiction (to be discussed in the next chapter), although the proceedings can with propriety be treated as an exercise of original jurisdiction.

The criminal business of the Circuit in the county was ordinarily the desultory occasional crime of regions where the population increased but slowly. The minutes for the earlier years of its existence show a small amount of business but the score mounts in step with colonization, and as the homogeneous character of early backwoods settlement is succeeded by the heterogeneity of eighteenth century immigration. The crimes tried ranged from murder and grand larceny down to mere petty nuisance, although the Circuit frequently did not proceed in minor cases, preferring to remand such causes to the Sessions Courts.[123] This was in accord with the practice that prevailed in the Supreme Court with respect to misdemeanors and was even more of a necessity in the case of the Circuit since the latter sat but briefly once a year in each county.

The significance of the Circuit, both political and as an agency of law enforcement, cannot be accurately assessed until its functions in respect of transfer jurisdiction have been considered. We shall see in the next chapter how it served as a bridge between the Supreme Court *en banc* and the General Sessions Courts, but it should be noticed here that the Circuit was designed as the forum for major crimes in the country and its original jurisdiction as to this was equivalent to that of the Supreme Court. The accumulation of this business, however, was not considerable, not only because there was less serious crime in the country than in the city, but because it frequently was found necessary and expedient to issue special commissions of oyer and terminer where it was dangerous or undesirable to delay trial until the Circuit was due on its annual visit.

The employment of such special commissions has been remarked upon in

---

[123] Some 689 cases heard, tried and determined at Oyer and Terminer and General Gaol Delivery have been examined. Murder, grand larceny, riot and assault and battery cases were the most numerous.

connection with the original jurisdiction of the Supreme Court in New York City. They were an extremely important supplement of ordinary jurisdiction, and the occasions upon which they were used may be roughly divided into political causes and those where, for the relief of the prisoner on the court calendar or for public security, speedy trial was desirable.

The special oyer and terminer commission has a history in New York running back to the Duke's Laws, and the motives for its issue were consistently identical during the whole of the colonial period. We shall consider first the instances where this commission was used for political reasons.

The tradition had been established in the early years of the colony that cases of political importance were handled by special commissions of oyer and terminer or by special meetings of the Court of Assizes.[124] So the insurrection of the Delaware plantations was dealt with, the proceedings against Fenwick and the trial of Captain Dyer for treason. This practice of special commission was adhered to in the two early *causes célèbres* of Leisler and of Bayard. In the case of Leisler and his associates there was justification other than political for the use of a special commission since the judicial system was in a state of suspension owing to the collapse of the Dominion of New England and the impossibility of accepting the dispositions made under Leisler. The advantage of a special commission may be deduced from the way that the trial in these two cases was conducted, and the disadvantages were soon perceptible from the acute political results of these proceedings. The record of the Leisler case,[125] to which we shall again advert, is disconcerting. The prisoners had pleaded to the jurisdiction and the court instead of itself ruling on this had submitted the matter to the Governor for decision.[126] Upon the subsequent refusal of the court to entertain the plea and Leisler's refusing to plead further, he was eventually sentenced[127] and executed under circumstances which no amount of explanation has justified.

The Bayard trial for treason in 1702 was a more or less inevitable result of the Leisler affair, as the province had been rent for ten years by quarrels between two political groups, the Leislerians and the anti-Leislerians. In January 1701/02, the provincial council, then controlled by the Leislerians, was apprised that certain addresses derogatory to the government were being circulated by the opposing party and that Colonel Nicholas Bayard and his son

<hr />

124 *Supra* n. 10.
125 P.R.O., C.O. 5/1082; 5/1037, King v. Leisler. Milborne, Delanoy, Gouverneur, Beekman.

126 2 *Doc. Hist. NY* 207.
127 P.R.O., C.O. 5/1082, fol. 6. Cf. further *infra* 582, 692.

Samuel were the chief movers in the affair. It was reported that at the tavern of Alderman John Hutchins signatures had been obtained by misrepresentation and by the even then traditional free drinks.[128] The Bayards refused to produce the addresses and were ordered to furnish security to appear in the Supreme Court to answer.[129] Hutchins, who likewise claimed to be unable to produce the addresses, was arrested after the Council resolved he was in contempt and had violated the Act of 1691 for quieting recent disorders.[130]

The Attorney General, Sampson Shelton Broughton, was of the opinion that no criminal acts were involved, but the Council, which initially seems to have contemplated only a prosecution for misdemeanor, took the bit in its teeth and, conceiving that a case for treason could be sustained, on February 4 ordered a special commission of oyer and terminer to be prepared.[131] There was a certain irony in the Council's decision, for the alleged treason was not the violation of the ancient statute 25 Edward III c.2 but of the provincial statute which the anti-Leislerians had themselves enacted and which provided that "whatsoever person or persons shall by any manner of way or upon any pretence whatsoever Endeavor by force of arms or otherwise to disturbe the peace good and quiet of this their Majestyes Government as it is now Established shall be Deemed and Isteemed as Rebells and Traitors unto their Majestyes and incur the penalities and forfeitures provided by the law of England for such offences."[132]

Since the addresses in question had been circulated upon news of the imminent arrival of the new governor, Lord Cornbury, and were allegedly petitions directed to him, Bayard, fighting for time, petitioned to have his trial respited until the usual term of the Supreme Court. This was refused, and the local law officers of the Crown were ordered to prosecute for high treason.[133] On February 12 the commission of oyer and terminer issued[134] and three weeks later the trial began. Both Bayard and Hutchins were convicted and their cases were appealed to the Privy Council. The details of the proceedings will be considered later in connection with the various aspects of colonial procedure. The trial created a tremendous stir and although it was not accurately reported, at least two separate accounts were printed and in this way came to

[128] Cal. S.P., Colonial 1702 nos. 35, 41, 343. Case of William Atwood, 13 NYHS Colls. (1880) 264, 265.
[129] Cal. S.P., Colonial 1702 no. 373; 8 Ms. Mins. Council I, 297; 4 Doc. Rel. Col. Hist. NY 947.
[130] Cal. S.P., Colonial 1702 no. 41; 8 Ms. Mins. Council I, 299, 300.
[131] Cal. S.P., Colonial 1702 no. 91; 8 Ms. Mins.

Council I, 308; Case of William Atwood (13 NYHS Colls.) 275–276.
[132] 1 Col. Laws NY 223, 224. And see Atwood's jeering comment, Case of William Atwood 244, 245.
[133] Cal. S.P., Colonial 1702 no. 104.
[134] Ibid. no. 112; 8 Ms. Mins. Council I, 310. The commission is in 14 Howell, State Trials 476.

be embalmed in the *State Trials*.[135] The judicial conduct of the case was prejudiced and unfair, even although Chief Justice Atwood who presided was a well-trained lawyer who should have better known how to demean himself. *King* v. *Bayard* is, nonetheless, a landmark in New York law not merely because the reports demonstrate a familiarity with a rather remarkable range of English precedents, but because despite the unfairness of the bench, the trial discloses a much closer adherence to common law usage than had been the case a decade earlier.

In the years immediately following this episode which convulsed the colony at the time and left its marks upon provincial politics for decades to come, the special commission of oyer and terminer was not often used.[136] It is possible

---

[135] The narrative by Bayard and Jamison was printed in 1702 in New York (*British Museum* C. 71 g. 3). In the Library of the NYHS there is a copy of the second edition (London, 1703) printed by the Bayard sympathizers. The report in 14 Howell, *State Trials* 471, follows the 1703 London edition. In answer to the Bayard version, Atwood anonymously printed, in 1703, his side of the trial (viz., *The Case of William Atwood, supra* n. 131), a garbled document which does not give a running account. The rough manuscript minutes of the Supreme Court of Judicature from 1701–1704 coincide in almost every detail with Bayard's report. Cornbury, however, in a letter to the Lords of Trade, in 4 *Doc. Rel. Col. Hist. NY* 972, says: "Mr. Atwood would not permit any minutes to be taken in court. Not even court practitioners could take notes." On the title page of Bayard's account is the recital that this report was based on "several memorials taken by divers persons privately the commissioners having strictly prohibited the taking of trial in open court." In the Bayard report (14 Howell, *State Trials* 484) we find that Jamison was ordered not to take notes because until he was purged of signing the treasonable addresses he was not considered an attorney of the court. Atwood refused to allow two clerks to take notes for the prisoner. However, Atwood did permit prisoner's solicitor assigned to take notes (*ibid.* 483); Atwood in his own defense (*Case of William Atwood* 299) asserts: "The Title Page says, the taking the Tryal was strictly prohibited; the Preface will have it that that were no Notes but what were taken privately unknown to the Court . . . yet according to their own account of the Tryal, the Chief Justice upon denying to admit a Stranger . . . [to take notes] said, You have a Sollicitor allowed, he may take notes . . ."; and finally we have the order by Atwood (given in Bayard's report, 14 Howell, *State Trials* at 484) that "a minute be made that it appears to the court that the attorney general hath neglected his Majesty's service." (This minute is actually entered in *Ms. Mins. SCJ 1701–04* 43, Mar. 7, 1701/02.) Also in Bayard's report (14

Howell, *State Trials* 485) a minute of the reading of Bayard's petition was ordered to be entered and in the minutes the petition is read "but it does appear to this court that the Grand Jury did find the Bill by above the number of twelve" (*Ms. Mins. SCJ 1701–04* 43, Mar. 7, 1701/02).

Atwood (*Case of William Atwood* 279) calls attention to the fact that "It appeared in Court, that private Applications by warm Men of the Party, had been made to several in the Pannel of the Petty Jury. . . ." In a marginal note, Atwood says, "No notice of this is in their print." This remark is true and we find in the *Ms. Mins. SCJ 1701–04* 45, Mar. 9, 1701/02, this entry: "Thomas E . . . and William P . . . entered and sworn. . . . It does appear in this Court that a paper was some way given to one of the Jury by Johannes Cortlandt and that a paper was found with ye Jury which paper was against finding the bill and that J . . . C . . . was one of them that was dismissed from the Grand Jury." In other respects the manuscript minutes and the Bayard account tally in their description of the procedure observed at the trial. Atwood's charges are more against omission than error in the Bayard report. On Atwood cf. Charles Daly's account, 7 *Green Bag* (1895) 121.

[136] It has not been possible to compile a complete and satisfactory list of the several special commissions of oyer and terminer and gaol delivery. They appear to have been more frequent in the fifteen years following the Leisler Rebellion than later. The following cases relate to those years. *Treason:* King v. Cornelius Jacobs, NYC, indictment *ignoramus* (*Mins. SCJ 1693–1700* 56, July 20, 1694). *Murder:* Queen v. Richard Davis, John Bell, Wm. Smith and Wm. Douler, NYC, acquitted (*Ms. Mins. SCJ 1701–04* 100, May 22, 1703); King v. William Simpson, Albany, sentenced to death but Governor requested pardon, 1698 (4 *Doc. Rel. Col. Hist. NY* 428); King v. Martinus Lambris, NYC, acquitted (*Mins. SCJ 1693–1700* 193, May 16, 1700); King v. Fred Platt, Westchester, acquitted (*Mins. SCJ 1693–1700* 195, June 5, 1700). *Burglary:* King v.

that the Bayard case had given rise to prejudice respecting the creation of special commissions for the trial of cases about which there was public excitement. In the emergency of the Negro Conspiracy of 1741 the problem of the proper court was debated by the judges and lawyers and it was determined the matter should be handled in the Supreme Court. A special ordinance was therefore issued enlarging the term.[137] The few occasions where special commissions were issued after 1702 were only for the expedition of ordinary criminal cases that were not allowed to await term time. But in the troubles which arose after 1763 the advantages of special commission were presently rediscovered. The impression one gains from the records of criminal courts for the period after the French and Indian War is one of a general and nearly continuous state of riot throughout the province. The tumults which arose in connection with the Stamp Act are familiar history. But provincial discontent was more deeply founded, as the land riots in Dutchess County and the proceedings along what became the Vermont border demonstrate. The Crown officers had long been in the habit of referring to the "levelling spirit" and to the Levellers[138] of the colony, by which phrases they characterized all aspects of dis-

---

John Wood, NYC, acquitted (*Ms. Mins. SC] 1701–04* I, Aug. 11, 1701). *Grand larceny:* King v. Geo. Jefferson and Richard Clifford, NYC, found guilty, granted clergy (*Mins. SC] 1693–1701* 51, 52, Dec. 15, 1693); King v. Geo. Jefferson, NYC, indictment *ignoramus* (*ibid.* 77, July 19, 1695). *Miscellaneous:* King v. John Johnson, NYC, discharged by proclamation (*Ms. Mins. SC] 1701–04* I, Aug. 11, 1701); King v. Le Reaux, NYC, acquitted (*Mins. SC] 1693–1701* 76, 77, July 19, 1695).
    Instances for the years immediately following the Bayard case are: Albany (1706), Queen v. Woodcock (murder), Queen v. Roach (manslaughter), 51 *NY Col. Mss.* 184; Albany (1710), Queen v. Yanke (burglary), 54 *ibid.* 11. Cf. also 11 *Ms. Mins. Council* 19 (1711), a gaol delivery for Westchester ordered.
    There are references to commissions of oyer and terminer, most of them certainly special, in the *Cal. Col. Com. 1680–1770.* This calendar may have been a complete inventory of the commission books, but if so there was no rule about filing special commissions. For example, the calendar does not list a special commission for Ulster County November, 1714, yet the minutes of the County Sessions show a special Oyer and Terminer was then held (*Ms. Mins. Ulster Co. Sess. 1711/12–1720,* King v. Bart Noxon, Nov. 24, 1714).
    [137] Horsmanden, *The NY Conspiracy* (1810) 40, 41; 19 *Ms. Mins. Council* I, 107; *infra* 120.
    [138] The term "Levellers" was used in England during the Civil War and apparently first appears

in a letter of November 1, 1647 (3 Gardiner, *Hist. of the Great Civil War* [1891] 216 n. 1. See also Pease, *The Leveller Movement* [1916]). It was a party nickname describing a group with radical proclivities. From that time on, the term "Levellers" was used to describe radical and revolutionary elements in the population. So Richard Bradley, Attorney General of New York, writing to the Duke of Newcastle on Jan. 4, 1727/28, in opposition to the act of assembly of Nov. 25, 1727, for preventing informations, remarked that Crown informations "seem to be almost the only means His Majesty has to check that levelling spirit that too plainly appears among the genallity [*sic*] of the people of these countrys . . ." (P.R.O., C.O. 5/1092/64).
    John Tomkins was informed against by the Attorney General in 1735 for beating the high sheriff of Westchester, and in the course of the information it was recited that the defendant was "of an arrogant, audacious, and levelling Spirit; and a Contemner of Majestracy, and of all Persons in power and Authority under . . . the King" (*H.R. Parch.* 116 L 10).
    Governor Clinton, in his letter of Nov. 30, 1745, complained to the Board of Trade because the assembly had not attended to the building of forts on the frontier, and the Governor explained further "That as they are jealous of the power of the Crown, and are Levellers by principle, nothing but an Independent Govr could bring them to a just sence of their duty" (6 *Doc. Rel. Col. Hist. NY* 647).

content and failed in consequence to realize that there were important differences between the political radicalism of the merchants and the social radicalism of the upstate farmers.

The Dutchess County land riots furnished the occasions for the first important quasi-political use of a special commission of oyer and terminer since the Bayard trial. From 1751 onward there had been trouble simmering among the tenants of the great land barons flaring up in sporadic breaches of the peace. The story of what occurred in 1766 is tersely told by James Duane in a letter to his brother, Captain Abraham Duane:[139]

> Inhabitants of the manor of Livingston and other tracts in Albany and Dutchess Counties holding by lease have lately given great disturbance by writing [rioting], to oppose their Landlords and defend themselves against a course of Justice. Their object was to intimidate the Proprietors to give them the fee of their farms—But in executing it they acted with so much violence that they threw themselves very soon into the crimes of Treason and Murder—Vigorous measures have been pursued against them particularly two chiefs are apprehended and a grand court appointed for their trial. The Governor has done me the honor of Counsel for the King on this Occasion which, . . . but a feather, may be of future use.

Duane goes on to relate that he had recently bought 30,000 acres of land.

> A valuable tract I hold . . . is in possession of some of this riotous crew so that a settler . . . was whipped and sent back—I hope soon to have it in my power to abate this insolence.

The Dutchess crisis was handled with great severity. The Governor, by proclamation, declared the participants had committed high treason and sent out a regiment to suppress them.[140] Several skirmishes occurred which resulted in some soldiers being wounded, but the rioters were dispersed and many of them taken.[141] Fresh outbreaks ensued both in Albany and Dutchess counties and more troops were poured into the disturbed districts.[142]

The trial of the captured ringleaders was obviously not to be held at the bar

---

[139] *James Duane Mss.* Box 10, I, 57. On the Dutchess riots, see further 7 *Doc. Rel. Col. Hist. NY* 825, 833, 845, 846, 849, 867, 879. There were also riots in Westchester (7 *Doc. Rel. Col. Hist. NY* 825), and in Orange (*J. T. Kempe Lawsuits* G–J, "List from Judge Harrington of the Rioters at Orange Town, Mar. 21, 1769"). There is a detailed account of the movement in Mark, *Agrarian Conflicts in Col. NY 1711–75* (1940) 131 *et seq.*

[140] 2 *Colden Letter Books* (10 *NYHS Colls.* [1877]) 115; 1 Carter, *Correspondence of Thomas Gage* (1931–33) 95. See also the Council proceedings (26 *Ms. Mins. Council* 51, 53).

[141] *The Montresor Jours.* (14 *NYHS Colls.* [1881]) 376; 2 Carter, *Correspondence of Thomas Gage* 312.

[142] *The Montresor Jours.* 378.

of the Supreme Court if the salutary medicine of public prosecution was to have the desired deterrent effect upon the local rebels. And it was equally un-desirable to hold the prisoners for the Circuit where the court would be com-posed of one or two Supreme Court judges sitting with justices of the peace of the county. Consequently the oyer and terminer commission was decided upon since this enabled the government to make up a hand-picked bench.[143] The picking was done with great care, for the commission included the Chief Justice, Daniel Horsmanden, and the puisne justice, William Smith, three members of the provincial council, and two prominent lawyers, Whitehead Hicks and John Morin Scott.[144] A number of the leading lawyers assisted the Attorney General at the trials as there was a staggering array of indictments outstanding. In a few of the cases notes are preserved of the trials—notably the trials of William Prendergast, the mob leader, for treason and of Edmond Green, Alexander McArthur, Daniel McArthur and others for murder. These notes show the trials to have been fair, and although a city newspaper con-tained some intimations of prejudice, we have a signed statement of Thomas Jones, of counsel for the Crown, that the newspaper account was untrue. Many of the defendants confessed the indictments and were sentenced to imprison-ment, whipping or pillory. A total of ninety-four fines were inflicted ranging from £200 to 6d. for assaults, riots, rescue, forcible entry and harboring.[145] Prendergast, the leader, was convicted of high treason and was sentenced to be hanged, drawn and quartered. The judges on the commission unanimously joined in soliciting pardon for him. In forwarding this petition to the Crown, Governor Moore explained that Prendergast and his associates, in order to in-timidate some persons who refused to join with them, had made some regula-tions and laws of their own by which they threatened to try all persons who

[143] Commissions of oyer and terminer and gen-eral gaol delivery were issued for Dutchess on July 8 and for Albany on July 11, 1766 (*Cal. Col. Com. 1680–1770* 67; 26 *Ms. Mins. Council* 58).

[144] It is incorrectly stated by Mark (*op. cit.* 145) that this was a session of the Supreme Court. He also remarks of the bench, "All these were amongst the greatest landlords and land speculators of the Colony at least two of the judges, if we include Justice Robert R. Livingston who was present though not sitting, were related to the landlords against whom the prisoners had rebelled." Liv-ingston was not on the commission and hence was not one of the judges. Mr. Mark's comments be-long to the school of historiography which tends to make much of our past seem disgraceful. He ob-viously does not comprehend that firing on sol-diers, breaking open jails and violent assaults on

citizens, however such acts may be viewed by lay-men interested in social problems, were then, as they still are, crimes.

[145] *Notes on July Assizes 1766* (36 ms. pages), *Misc. Mss. Dutchess Co. 1752–1870*. The estreats of fines are in *H.R. Parch.* 218 D 1. Cf. also *J. T. Kempe Lawsuits* C–F, "Complaint against Wil-liam Pindergass [*sic*], Samuel Monroe Jr. *et al.*"; *ibid.* P–R *sub nom.* William Prendergast, a draft in-formation for rioting in Westchester.

The NY Gazette or Weekly Postboy, Sept. 4, 1766, has a brief account of the trial. Jones's note is written in the margin. An example of a lay his-torian's weighing of evidence is the acceptance of the newspaper account in the text of Mark, *op. cit.* 147, and Jones's comment is relegated to footnotes. Cf. *infra* 626, 643.

disagreed. "This being adjudged treason he was try'd and convicted upon it." As a result of this favorable presentation of the case Prendergast was presently pardoned.[146] The estreats of fines imposed by the Dutchess Assizes show that only a small percentage of the persons involved in the riots were rounded up, and there were probably a great many offenders still at large when the court adjourned. Some of these men were later caught and were tried at the next Circuit in June, 1767. The minutes for this session are missing, but there are still preserved the minutes of the trial of Elisha Cole for high treason and the estreat of fines. Cole was apparently acquitted. His name appears in the list of persons fined for riot, and it is unlikely that he would have been arraigned on this charge if he had been convicted of the treason.[147]

The situation in Albany County was hardly less parlous than in Dutchess, for in addition to the tenant rioting there were the constant outbreaks on the New Hampshire border. A special commission was therefore issued for Albany in 1766.[148] The authorities apparently regarded the special oyer and terminer as the best means of speedily bringing a condign punishment to the restless farmers for another commission issued for that county in 1768 and again four years later.[149] In 1774 special commissions issued for Dutchess where riots had again become serious[150] and for New York County.[151] The rioters in Cumberland County[152] compelled the courts there to suspend and

[146] Moore to Shelburne, Oct. 11, 1766 (P.R.O., C.O. 5/1098 fol. 257). Shelburne to Moore, Dec. 11, 1766 (7 Doc. Rel. Col. Hist. NY 879). It is worth noting that in Ms. Deeds Dutchess Co. Liber G is entered a conveyance of 1774 by Morris, Robinson and Phillipse to William Prendergast. The McArthurs seem to have been acquitted. The estreat for the Albany Oyer and Terminer Aug. 1766 (H.R. Parch. 179 A 9) shows that they were there fined for riot and forcible entry. It is unlikely they would have been arraigned on these indictments if they had been convicted of murder. A descendant, Dr. Selim McArthur of Chicago, tells us these men had been brought over from Scotland by Livingston to work in his iron foundry.
[147] Cf. the estreats 218 D 1. In J. T. Kempe Lawsuits C–F are Notes on the Trial of Elisha Cole and a subpoena for appearance of witnesses. The mob of 1766 is supposed to have been 500 strong.
[148] The commission issued July 11, 1766 (Cal. NY Col. Coms. 67). The estreat (H.R. Parch. 179 A 9) shows a total of 54 fines for riot, rescue, assault etc. Cf. also J. T. Kempe Lawsuits V, sub nom. "Van Schooack's case respecting the abuse he met with from the Roiters at Albany" (attempted to collect stamp tax; J. T. Kempe Lawsuits G–J

sub nom. "Rex v. Rioters at Albany"). On the earlier riots of 1755, cf. 3 Doc. Hist. NY 463–473. For the rioting in New York City, see the description in "Mr. Colden's account of the State of the Province of New York" (7 Doc. Rel. Col. Hist. NY 795–800).
[149] 26 Ms. Mins. Council 138, 293, 326.
[150] Ibid. 412, and cf. Ms. Mins. Dutchess Co. Sess. Liber E, May 17, 1774, Oct. 14, 1774.
[151] 26 Ms. Mins. Council 414.
[152] These riots arose out of boundary disputes between New York, New Hampshire and Massachusetts and began at an early date; cf. the references to the Massachusetts and New Hampshire rioters of 1753 (NY Misc. Mss. 1741–59 Box 7 no. 38). There is a large collection of material in 4 Doc. Hist. of NY 331 et seq.
The Duane papers are replete with materials on the rioters in the districts which later became part of Vermont. John Munroe, writing to James Duane in April 1772, said of them that they denied God and would not even allow a Bible (James Duane Mss. Box 2, 1767–72, II, 154, ms. 472). Rewards had been offered for apprehending the ringleaders of the Bennington rioters (cf. "Act for preventing . . . riotous assemblies . . .," 5 Col. Laws NY 651) and yet Ethan Allen, one of the ringleaders

even took prisoner a sheriff and a judge. Colden reported cheerfully that he would presently have an Oyer and Terminer there, little realizing that events had moved too far by 1775 for this device to stem the tide of disaffection.

There is a certain flamboyance about the occasions, here discussed, when the special Court of Oyer and Terminer was employed that may deceive us into a misleading view of the institution. In spite of the sometimes extraordinary role that it was made to play for political reasons or for remarkable occasions, such as the trial of offenses committed on the high seas,[153] the special commission was normally a mere adjunct to the regular Circuit. As we have already remarked, the fact that the Circuit Court made only an annual visit might be a matter of considerable hardship, especially if there was pending a charge for a non-bailable offense, or if a defendant in custody was not able to put up bail. Furthermore the local jails were not places greatly to be relied upon. Every Sessions minute book is studded with complaints by the sheriff on the insufficiency of the jail, and sometimes also grand juries found it necessary to make presentments on the subject. For example, in Ulster County on September 3, 1752, a presentment was made alleging that the doors of the courthouse were left open so that prisoners could be furnished by "relatives friends and negros with Iron Crows and chisels" to break out, that no guard was kept and that when a felon had recently been brought for detention, the key to the prison itself could not be found.[154] All the jails may not have been as bad as this one, but we have found a Dutchess petition for a gaol delivery of some counterfeiters because the jail was insecure and it was too expensive to maintain the suspects, and even for New York City a special commission issued because the sheriff thought the prisoner might decamp.[155] We have seen an in-

of the "Green Mountain Boys" had the "insolence" to post the following reward notice: "Advertisement. £25 Reward. Whereas James Duane & John Kemp, [Attorney General John Tabor Kempe] . . . have, by their Menaces and Threats, greatly disturbed the public Peace and repose of the honest Peasants of Bennington, . . . which Peasants now, and ever have been, in the Peace of God & the King, and are patriotic and leige Subjects of George the third—Any Person that will apprehend those common disturbers . . . and bring them to Landlord Fay's . . . shall have £15 Reward for James Duane and £10 for John Kemp paid by, Ethan Allen . . . ." (*James Duane Mss.* Box 2, 1767–72, II, 149 *et seq.*, ms. 454 *et seq.*). The act of assembly of 1774 for putting down the rioters (5 *Col. Laws NY* 647) was probably the result of a complaint by Benjamin Hough and many inhabitants of Charlotte and North East Albany to

the general assembly, in February, 1774, of many acts of cruelty and oppression by the "Bennington Mob" (*James Duane Undated Mss.* Box 10, IV, 44, ms. 123, *Draft of Resolution of Committee of the Gen. Assembly of NY;* also see on the Bennington rioters: *James Duane Undated Mss.,* now marked *Social, Boro and Vermont* IV, 44, 50, 61, 62, 63, mss. 123–126, 145–148, 173–176, 177–180, 181, 182, and add, *ibid.* mss. 157–160 [no modern numbering]; *J. T. Kempe Lawsuits* A–B *sub nom.* "Albany Riot, Information of Benjamin Garner on Oath").

[153] *Infra* 306 *et seq.*

[154] *Ms. Files Ulster Co.* Bundle N. Cf. also the Meeting of the Justices, Aug. 1–5, 1729, re repairs (*ibid.* Bundle G); the Meeting, Sept. 19, 1743, re iron work on the prison (*ibid.*).

[155] 85 *NY Col. Mss.* 38 (1757). The supervisor's accounts of Dutchess County have numerous en-

stance where a child had committed homicide by misadventure when the commission issued obviously for humanitarian reasons;[156] and another occasion where trouble with the Indians was feared.[157] All of this may account for the fact that although the issuance of these commissions was one of the important prerogatives of the Governor, there was virtually no grumbling about his exercise of this power. As a rule advice of the Council was taken[158] and thus a check upon an arbitrary action was present.

General Sessions

The practical importance of the Circuit and of the occasional commission in respect of the trial of serious crime becomes apparent as we move down the scale of jurisdiction to consider the courts of General Sessions of the Peace (in New York City, Quarter Sessions) kept by the small army of justices of the peace.[159] Although the peace commissions were in terms most comprehensive, at first empowering the justices to inquire into and to hear and determine petit larceny, trespasses and other misdemeanors, and later extending to felonies generally, the records indicate that after 1691 the justices did not try any felonies of a degree greater than petit larceny. The only exceptions to this that we have found are the special courts for the trial of negro slaves like the extraordinary special court of 1712 held under a colonial statute for the trial of slave conspirators.[160]

The fact that Sessions jurisdiction was thus restricted in spite of the broad

tries for the repair of the jail locks. In 1730 the sheriff was paid 8s. "for a Lock and menden the Wall of the Prison" after an escape (*Old Misc. Recs. Dutchess Co.* [1911] 24). The New York City commission ordered in 1719 (12 *Ms. Mins. Council* 7).

[156] So the special Oyer and Terminer in Ulster County to try a child for homicide by misadventure: King v. Noxon, Nov. 24, 1714 (*Ms. Mins. Ulster Co. Sess. 1711/12–1720*).

[157] 4 *Doc. Rel. Col. Hist. NY* 428, 454.

[158] Which the commission to the Governor required. Cf. the commission to Bellomont (*ibid.* 268).

[159] A list of justices of the peace in 1763 (*NY Misc. Mss.* Box 8, no. 32) shows a total of 134 *quorum* justices and 194 other justices for all counties except New York. The distribution was as follows: Albany, 15 *quorum*, 41 others; Ulster, 14 *quorum*, 20 others; Orange, 13 *quorum*, 10 others; Dutchess, 18 *quorum*, 32 others; Westchester, 23 *quorum*, 27 others; Suffolk, 17 *quorum*, 26 others; Queens, 13 *quorum*, 22 others; Kings, 11 *quorum*, 10 others; Richmond, 10 *quorum*, 6 others. Jus-

tices named of the *quorum* were assumed to have legal knowledge.

The above figures represent a total of 328 justices of the peace for all counties exclusive of New York, and, estimating the population of the counties concerned as being about 114,500 in 1763, it will be seen that there was an approximate ratio of one justice of the peace to 350 people, one-seventh of whom were negro slaves. The figures on which the above estimate of population is based may be found in the 1749 New York census (6 *Doc. Rel. Col. Hist. NY* 550) and in the 1771 census and estimate of population increase contained in Governor Tryon's report on the state of the Province of New York (8 *Doc. Rel. Col. Hist. NY* 457).

The report of Clarkson in 1693 lists a total of 49 justices of the peace exclusive of New York City and the city officers of Albany (1 *Doc. Hist. NY* 200). According to Bellomont's census figures of 1698, viz., 13,130 inhabitants exclusive of New York City, the relative number of justices was much higher than in 1763 (*ibid.* 465).

[160] *Infra* 118.

language of the later peace commissions requires some explanation. We have already adverted to the fact that before 1691 the then Sessions Courts had dealt only with non-capital cases, and although this was not the equivalent of a less-than-felony jurisdiction, the notion had become seated that serious crime was the business of the highest provincial tribunal. The Judicature Act of 1691 and its successors had stipulated nothing respecting the limits of Sessions jurisdiction, for these acts and ordinances spoke only of "Sessions of the Peace," or "General Sessions of the Peace." The inference to be drawn from this language is that there was designed a Sessions in accordance with English usage[161] and this was how in practice the jurisdiction of Sessions became defined. The chief guides here, as we have suggested, were the contemporary textbooks, but it seems beyond doubt that some firsthand knowledge of English Quarter Sessions practice prevailed in New York at an early date, for the records disclose a clearer understanding of the nature and scope of Sessions business than any mere study of manuals would yield. This is most persuasively demonstrated by the imitation of the English practice in respect of felonies.

In the textbooks where the powers of the justices of the peace are discussed there is considerable confusion respecting jurisdiction over felonies.[162] On their face the English commissions appeared to be reasonably explicit, and there can

161 Clarkson's report in 1693 indicates this was how the powers of Sessions were interpreted (1 Doc. Hist. NY 202).

162 The discussions related either to the power of inquiry or of hearing and determining. So Fitzherbert (L'office . . . des Justyces de peas), fol. 22 (1538): "Le Commission de peas done auctorite as Justices de peas de enquerer de toutes maners de felonies . . . par le come ley et . . . par divers statutes," but (fol. 16) ". . . ils nount power denquerer de murdour, pour ceo que il nest en lour commission par cest terme (Murdre) mes ils poient enquerer de ceo come felonie, et manslaughter. . . ." But see Fitzherbert, Abridgement, Corone, no. 457, justices of the peace have no power to inquire of the death of a man. Apparently Coke was of the same view; cf. Second Institute 316, where it is stated that justices of the peace could not take an indictment of killing a man se defendendo because it was not taken to be within their commission. Lambard (op. cit. Bk. 4, c.7) says: "In the rest (so farre as I have found) their power of Enquirie is accompanied with the authoritie to heare and determine also. For this want of Jurisdiction is not found in the Commission of the Peace itselfe, but only in certain statutes, that (for waighty causes) doe restraine this further proceeding." But in Bk. 4, c.14, he remarks: ". . . it seemeth by Marr. [Marowe] and M. Fitzherbert fol. 16 that albeit two Justices of the Peace (the one of them being of the Quorum) may

heare and trie felonies: yet no Justices of the Peace have aucthoritie to deliver Felons by proclamation." Lambard also states (loc. cit.) that although in his day justices of the peace were not "much occupied [in the trial of felonies] the rather because they commonly defer it till the comming of the Justices of the Assise . . . Nevertheless their power is no whit restrained, to proceede before the coming of those Justices."

Hale, 2 Pleas of the Crown (1778 ed.) 45, states "although the commission of the peace mentions not murders by express name but only felonies generally, yet by these general words in these statutes . . . they have power to hear and determine murders or manslaughter . . . [p. 46] but though the justices have this power, yet they do not ordinarily proceed to the hearing and determining of murder or manslaughter and rarely of other offences without clergy. . . ."

Hawkins, 2 Pleas of the Crown (1787 ed.) c.8 §33, avers that the commission expressly gives the justices of peace (one to be of the quorum) power to inquire of, hear and determine felonies and trespasses, but he further comments: "It hath been generally thought advisable for Justices of Peace to proceed no farther in Relation to any Felonies [than to take examination of offenders and information of others and certify the same to gaol delivery] though within their commissions, except only Petit Larcenies."

be no doubt that in the fourteenth and fifteenth centuries all types of felonies were tried at Sessions.[163] But in the late sixteenth and seventeenth centuries the records now in print show that it was unusual for capital cases to be there tried; indeed, in some English counties there is no evidence that any such cases were handled in Sessions.[164] As to the probative value of these records, however, it must be observed that many of them are calendared to the point of virtual uselessness, and in some of them the lay compilers have quite ignored the difference between Gaol Delivery and Sessions rolls. Allowing even for these defects, however, it is apparent that "grand felony" had ceased to be a head of jurisdiction in the English Sessions Courts. On the other hand, the textbooks, compiled as aids for the squires who were to administer justice in the King's name, present a quite different picture, for a reader, unaware of how in fact the Quarter Sessions were conducted, is led to assume that almost any felony could be tried in those courts. But if one comes to examine the manner in which these manuals are constructed, it is quite evident that except

---

[163] Putnam, *Proc. before Justices of the Peace* (1938) cxii *et seq.*
[164] Cf. *Middlesex Co. Recs.* (1886) xxii, xxv, comment by editor Jeaffreson.
The Middlesex Sessions records for 1612–15 and for 1689–1709 also indicate that Quarter Sessions was concerned with the trial and punishment of minor offenses. In examining the printed Middlesex Sessions records it must be borne in mind that the editors of the later volumes have indiscriminately grouped Sessions and Gaol Delivery minutes together without indicating which part of the action took place in which court. In *Sess. Rolls for Hertford 1581–1689* (1 *Hertford Co. Recs.* [1905]) the editor (xxvii) refers to prisoners pleading benefit of clergy at Sessions but an examination of his references to cases on pages 2 and 17 indicates that these pleadings appear on Gaol Delivery and not Sessions Rolls. An examination of the volume cited above and of *Cal. Sess. Books, Sess. Min. Books, etc. 1619–57* (5 *Hertford Co. Recs.* [1928]) indicates no capital cases tried and determined in Sessions. The reader will observe by references to pages xxx–xxxii of *Cal., etc. 1658–1700* (6 *Hertford Co. Recs.* [1930]) that the calendar therein contained shows no punishment more severe than whipping in Quarter Sessions. Likewise the schedule of offenses and punishments on pages xxxiv–xxxvi of *Cal., etc. 1700–52* (7 *Hertford Co. Recs.* [1931]) discloses no capital cases tried in Sessions.
The first volume of *Surrey Quarter Sessions Recs.* (32 *Surrey Rec. Soc. Pubs.* [1931]) contains merely extracts of the records and is therefore not useful for making any generalizations as to the kind of cases tried. In 35 *Surrey Rec. Soc. Pubs.* (1934) the editor, on p. xvii, n. 6, states: "No ex-

ample of Grand Felony has appeared in these early Surrey [Quarter Sessions] rolls." The period covered is 1659–61.
In 1 *Worcestershire Recs.* (1900) xcv, the editor draws certain conclusions for endorsements on indictments, but this evidence is not to be relied on. Thus in the colonial material it is not unusual to find a Sessions indictment endorsed by a Supreme Court or Circuit clerk when the trial took place in the Supreme Court or at Circuit. See, for example, The King v. John King alias Edward King (*Ms. Mins. NYCQS 1760–72* 303, Feb. 9, 1770) where indictments for grand larceny and burglary were handed in by the grand jury at Quarter Sessions. The case was tried in the Supreme Court of Judicature where prisoner was found guilty (*Ms. Mins. SCJ 1769–72* [Engr.] 170, 174, 182, 198, Apr. 17, 18, 23, 28, 1770). In the pleadings in the Hall of Records are two indictments in Quarter Sessions for the above offense (Pl. K. 475, 484) and these two indictments were endorsed as true bills with the following additional notations: "Po. se" (on K. 475) and "Po. se cul" (on K. 484). To the uninitiated or to one who had not seen the Supreme Court Minute Book, these would appear to have been two indictments heard, tried and determined in Quarter Sessions. Cf., to the same effect, King v. John Quain *et al.* for grand larceny (*Ms. Mins. NYCQS 1772–91* 175, Feb. 8, 1776; *Ms. Mins. SCJ 1775–81* [Engr.] 85–87, Apr. 24, 26, 27, 1776; H.R. *Pleadings* Pl. K. 338); King v. Susanne Mitchell for grand larceny (*Ms. Mins. NYCQS 1760–72* 313, May 4, 1770; *Ms. Mins. SCJ 1769–72* [Engr.] 233, 240, 241, Aug. 1, 3, 1770; H.R. *Pleadings* Pl. K. 465).

for an occasional reference to actual practice, the compiler has built his book chiefly from details culled from the long array of statutes reaching back to the time of Edward III; and since these acts were in many particulars inconsistent and irreconcilable, the textbooks necessarily reflect the disorders of the statutory structure. It should further be noticed that the bulk of such books as Lambard's *Eirenarcha* and Dalton's *Countrey Justice* is devoted to the powers of the justice of the peace out of Sessions. Indeed, it was not until Dalton's work had been through several editions that a special section was devoted to the Quarter Sessions.

The evolution of Sessions practice under the Tudors is still *terra incognita.* We are disposed to believe, however, that the change in practice respecting "grand felonies" came about as a result of statutes enacted during the reign of Mary which had the indirect effect of ousting justices of the peace from this jurisdiction.[165] The commission of the peace as revised in 1590 does not take account of this change.[166] Nevertheless, the country courts as a matter of practical expedience continued to abstain from meddling with grand felonies; indeed, from certain remarks of Williams, J., at the Cambridge Assizes regarding the propriety of trying petty felonies at Sessions, a hard and fast rule seems to have been maintained in despite of the language of statutes or commissions.[167] A realization of this limitation upon Sessions could hardly have been acquired from the ambiguities of the textbooks. It could have become settled in New York Province only as a result of familiarity with the actual functioning of Quarter Sessions in England.

We do not know whether or not in New York the initial exclusion of the word "felony" from the commissions of the peace was a deliberate recognition of what in fact was the course of practice in England. It is, in any event, curious that at a time when English forms were carefully copied, so important an omission should have been made. What is more significant, however, is

---

[165] 1 & 2 Ph. & Mary c.13 provided that persons arrested for manslaughter or felony or suspicion thereof could only be let to bail by two justices in open session. The justices were to take the examination of the prisoner and "the information of them that bring him," put into writing the material evidence against the prisoner, all of which should be certified by the justices at the next Gaol Delivery. In the following year a statute required examination of prisoners not let to bail and the certification thereof to Gaol Delivery where the trial was to be. A failure to comply entailed a fine: cf. also 2 & 3 Ph. and Mary c.10, and the earlier statute 3 Hy. VII c.3.

Dalton (*Countrey Justice* [1619] c.40 §3) treats the statute as if limited to cases initiated by information, for he asserts (with later particular exceptions) the "authority" of the justice to hear and determine felonies where the person was indicted before the justices. The records indicate the statute of Philip and Mary in fact had a broader effect.

[166] Lambard, *Eirenarcha* (1614) Bk. 1, c.9; Coke, *Fourth Institute* 171. On the earlier commissions cf. Putnam, *op. cit.* xx. It is possible that the proviso clause, which directed the reservation of difficult cases for justice of the bench at the Assizes, was effective in steering "grand felonies" to the Assizes. This clause was not contained in the New York commissions.

[167] Dalton, *op. cit.* (1619) 48.

that even after the word "felony" was inserted, there was no attempt on the part of the General Sessions courts to move beyond the boundaries of jurisdiction previously set.

In the face of the bewildering vagaries of the English courts and text writers on the subject of the classification of crime—the unspecified difference between grand and small felony, the occasional escape of homicide from the felony category, the division of clergiable and non-clergiable felonies, the permutations of misdemeanors—the New York colonists took the short road and drew their lines as they had from the first, in terms of capital and non-capital crime, and the Sessions trial jurisdiction in practice was over non-capital cases.

In the main, the common law rules regarding what were capital offenses were observed, but there were some occasional deviations which threw into Sessions the trial of causes that in England would have been handled at Assizes. The most important of these colonial aberrations was the offense of counterfeiting coin. The English law was complex. Counterfeiting the King's coin or foreign coin if made current in the realm by royal consent was high treason. But counterfeiting foreign coin not made current by proclamation was only punishable as a cheat. Innocently passing counterfeit was also only punishable as a cheat. It was misprision of treason if the person uttering knew who the counterfeiter was. The colonists apparently elected to treat coinage counterfeiters as cheats for they prosecuted persons so charged for misdemeanors.[168] The cases all stem from the turn of the century and in all but two of them it is clear that foreign coin was involved.

The cases could be explained on the basis of the distinctions just mentioned

[168] For the English law 1 Hale, *Pleas of the Crown* 210 *et seq.*, 225. In the case of King v. William Fowler, bound to answer for uttering "clipt" coins, the defendant "Offered to make Oath that the Ryalls which were Clipt were intermixt with a large sum of Money . . . and does believe he Received the said Money from Rhode Island Whereupon several persons of Note Vouching for the honesty of the said William Fowler and . . . he be discharged" (*Ms. Mins. NYCQS 1694–1731/32* 68, Feb. 4, 1701/02). In this case apparently no formal indictment was had and evidently this proceeding was a preliminary examination before the justices. On the other hand, Garrett Onclebagg, on indictment for coining and uttering false money, "Protest he is not Guilty of the fraud of Coyning and uttering false Money of base & mixt metalls . . . yett . . . submitts himselfe to a fine." The defendant was fined £20 and ordered to give surety for good behavior in £100 for one year (*ibid.* 70, 71, 74, 77, Feb. 2, 3, 1702/03).

In two other cases from New York Quarter Sessions, one for "uttering of Clipt and Fyled Spanish Money" and the other for "having clipt money in her possession," each of the defendants "demurs to the insufficiency [*sic*] of the indictment." The Attorney General joined in the demurrers and upon hearing the argument "itt is considered by the court" that the said indictments were "insufficient and ordered the same be quashed," Queen v. Sophia Thomas (*ibid.* 71, 72, 78, Nov. 4, 1702, Feb. 3, 1702/03) and Queen v. Anna Vanderspigel (*ibid.* 78, 79, Feb. 3, 1702/03). On the other hand, we have seen one indictment for "uttering and putting away Clipt and hammer[ed] Money,"

except for the fact that a report made some years later by Cadwallader Colden, Master in Chancery, discloses that a persistent debasement of the coinage had been practiced in the colony and that by proclamation the Governor and Council in 1692 and 1693 had fixed the current value of some of these foreign coins. The Master's report did not touch on the question whether or not these proclamations were to be treated as the equivalent of a royal proclamation so that clipping or hammering would be treason.[169] In 1704 Queen Anne issued a proclamation establishing the value of foreign coins, an event which precipitated a long-drawn-out struggle in New York, as the shilling values were less than those theretofore established. But even this proclamation did not effect a change in the New Yorker's attitude about the nature of the offense of clip-

and in this case the defendant brought a writ of certiorari for removing the indictment and record to the Supreme Court. The Supreme Court minutes indicate an order in the case that the "record be brought up from Quarter Sessions," King v. Susannah Elliott (*Ms. Mins. NYCQS 1694–1731/32* 60, 61, Feb. 5, 1700/01; *Ms. Mins. SCJ 1701–04* 7, Oct. 1701). From the latter case it would appear that the indictment for "clipt" money was cognizable in Sessions since, in order to effect transfer to the Supreme Court, it was necessary to obtain a writ of certiorari. Had the case not been cognizable in Quarter Sessions, the indictment would have been automatically removed *a propria manu* without writ (*infra* 147). Cf. also the case of Richard Thomas, indicted for uttering counterfeit dollars and tried in Quarter Sessions where he was found not guilty (*Ms. Mins. NYCQS 1694–1731/32* 63, May 6, 7, 1701).

[169] *H.R. Chancery*, BM 7 K, King v. Peter Fauconier, "Master's Report Setling the Currency before ye Year 1704 Fyled Dec. ye 11, 1724." ". . . Do find that Sr Edmund Andros the first time he was Governor of the Province of New York Encouraged Severall persons Residing within the Said Province to Trade to fforeign parts, By Means of which Trade Gold and Silver Moneys were first Imported into the Said Province, And from that time Spanish Gold and Silver Coins became Current within the Same Province (Vizt.) Peeces of Eight at Six Shillings, halfe Pieces at three Shillings, Double Reals or Double Bitts at Eighteen pence, Single Reals at Nine pence & Pistoles at twenty four Shillings. And that Some time before the Year Sixteen hundred Ninety three the Current Money of the Said Province began to be very much diminished in its Intrinsick Value by Clipping, The light and heavy Money then passing Indifferently & in Common Payments The Merchants then Residing within the Said Province began to give an Advanced price for heavy pieces of Eight in Order to export them to Other parts where they Disposed of them at a higher rate according to their weight; And that the Said Merchants likewise made an Advantage in Exporting—those that were very light to Other parts where they passed by tale, which Practices Occasioned the lessening as well as Debasing of the then Current Coin within the said Province and Several Other Other [*sic*] Inconveniencys To Remedy which I find [one or two words illegible] Minute of the then Council for the Said Province, Dated the Twenty third of March in the Year of our Lord Sixteen hundred Ninety two, That & a Proclamation was Order'd by the then Governour and Council to Issue for fixing the Currency of pieces of Eight, to a Certain Standard of Weight And do find that a Proclamation dated the Twenty fifth day of March Sixteen hundred Ninety three Issued Accordingly— Whereby the Said Governour Did Direct Order and Declare in the following word, That Whereas whole pieces of Eight of the Coins of Sevill, Mexico, and Pillar, pieces of the Weight of fifteen Weight not plugg'd, are Current and Pass in all payments of Money at the Rate of Six Shillings per piece.—All pieces of Eight of the Coins above Exprest of Greater Weight than fifteen penny weight not pluggd Shall be Current and pass at the Rate of four pence halfe penny for Each penny weight more than fifteen penny weight not plugg'd over and above Six Shillings as aforesaid, And also That all pieces of Eight of the Coins above Named of lesser weight than fifteen penny weight not plugg'd Shall be Current and pass as aforesaid at the rate of Six Shillings abating only four pence halfe penny for Each penny weight they Shall be under and wanting of fifteen penny weight as aforesaid And further that all whole pieces of Eight of the Coin of Peru not plugged Shall be Current and pass at the rate of four pence for Each penny weight Such pieces of Eight of Peru Shall Weigh and I find by the Same Proclamation That Dollars Called Dog Dollars were made Current at five Shillings & Six pence Each, At which rates pieces of Eight Continued Current till after the Year Seventeen hundred and four.—But that Reals and Double Reals or Quarterpieces Continued (as then formerly) to pass at the rate of Six Shillings ₱ piece

ping or counterfeiting foreign coin, for we find that in 1705 Mary Barnes and John Kingston were prosecuted in the New York Quarter Sessions for clipping Spanish "ryalls," and the gist of the charge was the allegation of fraud. Probably the colonial authorities regarded as determinative their own act of 1702 which punished this crime by imprisonment for a year and a day and forfeiture of chattels. This act had not been repealed by the Crown and it remained in effect until partially repealed in 1710.[170]

An extremely interesting insight into the workings of the provincial psyche is afforded by the legislation on bills of credit which were destined to become the current legal tender. In the very first of these acts the counterfeiting of bills of credit was made a felony without benefit of clergy and this penalty was repeated in succeeding acts until 1756 when a special act regarding the counterfeiting of bills of credit was passed. Ten years later the counterfeiting of the bills of credit of any colony current in New York was likewise made a felony without benefit of clergy. Under the influence possibly of the changed attitude respecting counterfeiting (and as we shall have occasion to see there were many settlers with an illicit talent for engraving) the legislature in 1745 made the counterfeiting of certain foreign gold and silver coins a felony without benefit of clergy. It need hardly be added that any counterfeiting thus explicitly made a capital felony was not within the jurisdiction of the Sessions Courts.[171]

The early coinage cases in New York City are the most striking deviation from English practice to be found, for although we sometimes discover a

of Eight without weighing And that Pistoles did likewise pass at Twenty four Shillings Each till after the Year Seventeen hundred and four." [170] In Queen v. Mary Barnes and John Kingston: "Memorandum that . . . itt stands presented that Mary Barnes . . . no ways regarding an upright & Conscientious dealing and behaviour . . . but Contriving . . . to abuse and deceive . . . did fraudulently . . . Clip . . . pieces of Spanish Moneys Called Ryalls [etc.] and the Clippings . . . did . . . utter and make payment of in the Room and stead of lawful Money. . . ." The jury ". . . Say upon their Oath that the said Mary Barnes is not Guilty of the Misdemeanors Contempt and Offenses Whereof She Stands indicted . . . Therefore . . . discharged . . . paying fees" (*Ms. Mins. NYCQS 1694–1731/32* 96–99, 102–104, May 1, 2, Aug. 7, 8, 1705). The Act of 1702 is in 1 *Col. Laws NY* 521; revived (1708) *ibid.* 621; partly repealed (1710) *ibid.* 714. On the coinage situation in New York cf. Nettels, *The Money Supply of the Amer. Col. before 1720* (1934) 240 *et seq.* [171] The first bill of credit act (1709), 1 *Col.*

Laws NY 666. See also *ibid.* 689, 695, 737, 938; 2 *ibid.* 25, 205. We are not listing the many re-enactments. The Act of 1756 (4 *ibid.* 92) was induced by the case of Owen Sullivan and a Dutchess counterfeiting ring (*infra* 296). The Act of 1745 is in 3 *ibid.* 511. Note also the Act of 1753 re the importing and passing of counterfeit British halfpence and farthings (*ibid.* 948).

After the statute respecting counterfeiting of bills of other colonies (4 *ibid.* 907) the offense of "altering a bill of credit of the colony of New Jersey from 3*s.* to £3 and passing same" was considered not cognizable in Sessions. When an indictment was brought against Peter Lynch for that offense, it was "Ordered that the clerk deliver the same into the next Supreme Court." The case was accordingly transferred without writ (indicating therefore that it was not considered cognizable in Sessions). The defendant was tried in the Supreme Court where he was acquitted (*Ms. Mins. NYCQS 1760–72* 289, Aug. 4, 1769; *Ms. Mins. SCJ 1769–72* [Engr.] 104, 120, 143, Oct. 18, 28, 1769, Jan. 17, 1770).

country clerk entering a felonious taking of an object obviously worth more than 12*d.*, the Sessions Courts seem to have stepped beyond traditional boundaries only in these larceny cases, but all such thefts were treated as petit larcenies.[172] And once the transfer system was in gear the supervision from above made for a careful observance of jurisdictional proprieties as to all questions of trial. On the other hand, no limitation was put upon the power to indict. In the early provincial commissions the inquiry clause and the hear and determine clause of the commissions were not quite identical, for although both clauses convey power to inquire or to hear and determine petit larcenies, thefts, trespasses etc., the inquiry clause adds "and all and singular the misdeeds and offences of which Justice of the peace may or ought lawfully to enquire." And from the first (viz., during Dongan's governorship) indictments were taken for major offenses and as we shall later see were sent to the superior courts for trial.

The number of offenses for which indictments were found or presentments were made in these inferior courts over a period of eighty-five years runs into thousands and includes nearly all those fruits of man's iniquity as the common law conceived them. From this harvest what was grist for trial at Sessions was chiefly the crimes of petit larceny, receiving stolen goods, assault and battery, riots, nuisances,[173] disorderly houses, market offenses, bastardy and fraud.[174] There crop up in the records occasional exceptional cases such as the early indictments for adultery, for gaming and lotteries,[175] for barratry,[176]

---

[172] E.g., King v. John Horton, "feloniously marking a lamb," *Ms. Mins. Westch. Co. Sess. 1710–23* June 7, 1714 (discharged by proc.); King v. Sam Horton, "feloniously taking a ewe," *ibid.* Dec. 7, 1714 (discharged by proc.); Tim Knapp indicted for carrying away a dead cow was acquitted, *ibid.* June 2, 1713. In this last case no words of felony, but obviously even a dead cow was worth more than 12*d.* Cf. also Queen v. U. Springsteen, "feloniously taking a mare worth 30*s.*," *Ms. Mins. Orange Co. Sess. 1703–08* Apr. 27, 1703.

[173] Under "nuisance" were classed the most diverse offenses: stopping roads, unmerchantable flour, a mill obstructing navigation, failure to put up gates, horses running at large, keeping a hog sty, operating tan pits, tanning, fire hazards such as having a fire in a tar cellar, a vessel aground in the Hudson River, having a liquor still, flax dressing, fences and streets in disrepair, digging holes in the public street, and ruinous houses and chimneys in danger of falling down. Objection was made not only to fire dangers, but also to "noysome" smells.

[174] Under fraud, cheats and deceit, we have included such offenses as altering the tax rolls (King

v. Stephen Buckenhoven, *Ms. Mins. NYCQS 1694–1731/32* 64–66, May 7, Aug. 5, 1701), improperly gauging casks, selling unmerchantable flour (sometimes referred to as "nuisance"), altering the weighmaster's books, pledging a brass ring as gold, tearing and defacing or cancelling bonds and notes, and falsely returning votes for an alderman.

[175] Cf. the three indictments for lotteries held in contempt of "his Excellency's proclamation": King v. Abraham Hart (*Ms. Mins. NYCQS 1694–1731/32* 61, Feb. 5, 1700/01) pleaded guilty, fined £2 6*s.*; King v. Janneke Van Duerson, and King v. Daniel Jonett (*ibid.* Feb. 5, 1700/01); also one indictment in New York City Quarter Sessions for "unlawful games," Queen v. William Barclay (*ibid.* 118, 122, 135, 136, Nov. 6, 1706, Feb. 4, 1706/07, Feb. 4, 1707/08); and one indictment in Queens Sessions for keeping a gaming house (*H.R. Pleadings* Pl. K. 449, Sept. 1760). See also King v. Homan—gaming (*Ms. Mins. Queens Co. Sess. 1722–87* Sept. 15, 1761); King v. Brown, King v. Tallowball, King v. Owen—lotteries (*Ms. Mins. Suffolk Co. Sess. 1760–75* Mar. 28, 1775).

[176] E.g., an indictment for "barretry" was handed up in Richmond General Sessions and the

maladministration of justice,[177] seditious words,[178] and toward the end of the colonial period for criminal attempts. A sprinkling of indictments for violations of certain peculiar colonial statutes are also to be found.[179] The distribution of the offenses which constituted the chief business of Sessions varies from period to period, and there are likewise certain noticeable differences between city and country. Throughout the eighteenth century petit larceny appears as the bugbear of the law enforcement agencies, but it is most prevalent in New York City. Even after provision was made for summary trial at special Sessions or meetings, the General Sessions Courts continued to handle the cases of persons able to furnish bail. Riot, which in the early 1700's is relatively occasional, after 1763 became a major head of jurisdiction especially in Albany, Dutchess and New York counties. Assault, on the other hand, is constantly and in every county the most frequent offense. The highest incidence seems to be in Richmond where roughly one-half the prosecutions were assaults or batteries. The percentage also is high in New York City and

defendant pleaded guilty, paying a 40s. fine (King v. John Le Conte, Sept. 1756, *James Duane Ms. Register 1755–69* 15). Hawkins (2 *Pleas of the Crown* [1787 ed.] c.8 §39) states that justices of the peace have jurisdiction over barrators.

[177] Under maladministration we have included: offenses by justices of the peace (not tried in Sessions), cases of neglect of duty or refusal to serve in office by constables, tax collectors, assessors, deputy sheriffs and surveyors, and presentments of constables and other officers for allowing prisoners to escape. We have seen one case of extortion by a jailer: King v. James Mills (*Ms. Mins. NYCQS 1760–72* 52–57, 65, May 4, Nov. 4, 1762). Hawkins (2 *Pleas of the Crown* c.8 §39) states that justices of the peace may take indictments of extortion.

[178] Under the heading "seditious words" and "contempt of authority" we have grouped offenses denominated under one or the other of these headings as well as contempt of court, scandal to the court, abuse of justices of the peace, resisting officers, slandering a grand jury (the latter indictment in Ulster, 1766, *H.R. Pleadings* Pl. K. 918), and "singing in praise of the Pretender" (*Ms. Mins. NYCQS 1732–62* 181, May 8, 1745). The following is a typical entry: "Johannes Tiebout . . . Turner being bound to his good behaviour and for his personall appearance . . . for Contempt of Authority and Speaking seditious Words . . . appeared in his proper person and says he did not think ill in speaking of the said Words and prays the Mercy of the Court. Whereupon the Court . . . doe fine the said Johannes Tiebout fifteen Shillings for the said Misdemeanor with fees of Court & Ordered . . . Committed till he pay the same" (*Ms. Mins. NYCQS 1694–1731/32* 10, Feb. 4, 1694/95).

[179] For example, King v. John Ten Eyck (*Ms. Mins. NYCQS 1732–62* 104, 114–117, Aug. 9, 10, 1739, May 6, 7, 1740), the defendant, having been indicted for "pulling down and impairing of the fortifications called the Battery," pleaded guilty and was fined 10s. In 1711, an act of assembly had been passed "to prevent the Impairing of Fortifications" (1 *Col. Laws NY* 745), but the statute gave any one justice of the peace power summarily to convict on the oath of one witness and to impose fine or imprisonment in his discretion. Yet here we find an indictment in Quarter Sessions, and no mention is made of the statute but the offense is declared to be against the peace.

Philip Riche was indicted for breaking glass windows, pleaded guilty and was fined 5s. (*Ms. Mins. NYCQS 1732–62* 164, 170, 171, May 4, Aug. 8, 1744). Apparently this offense was a crying abuse of the times for in 1771 the assembly was finally obliged to pass an act for the punishment of persons guilty of trespasses (5 *Col. Laws NY* 237) under which act any person who should break glass windows, porches, knockers, signs, etc. was to be summarily convicted on the oath of one witness and fined £10.

John Ryne was indicted for a "misdemeanor" in throwing squibs and attempting to set fire to a stable; he pleaded guilty and was fined 6s. 8d. (*Ms. Mins. NYCQS 1732–62* 192, 193, Nov. 6, 7, 1745). In 1771, this offense was taken care of by an act against squibs and fireworks which provided for summary conviction on the oath of one witness before a justice of the peace and a 20s. fine (5 *Col. Laws NY* 244).

about one-fifth of the assault indictments there are for attacks on public officers.

The disorderly house is a persistent metropolitan crime; it is now and then that country courts have to deal with a "wide house." The term "disorderly" is an elastic one comprehending not merely houses where fights and brawls took place, but brothels, places where inordinate drinking was done and at unseasonable hours, unlicensed alehouses, "tippling" houses and dives where slaves, negroes, servants, apprentices and sailors were entertained and often given credit when they could not pay cash.[180] There is some reason to suspect that the city authorities used the disorderly house charge as a catch-all to deal with disorderly conduct generally, the expression serving the same end for which in early times the vague and loose expression "misdemeanor" had been used. Possibly, too, since the disorderly house was the club room of un-

---

[180] In New York City Quarter Sessions over 128 defendants were presented for these offenses between 1691 and 1776. Ordinarily fines were meted out for the offense of keeping disorderly houses. So William Barclay on Nov. 6, 1706, was indicted for "suffering tipling" and, on Feb. 4, 1707/08, found guilty and fined £5 (Ms. Mins. NYCQS 1694–1731/32 118, 122, 124, 135–139); also see King v. Mary Brown, indicted for entertaining negroes and keeping a disorderly house, pleaded guilty and fined £5 (ibid. 497–498, 501–503, Aug. 7, Nov. 5, 6, 1728). Joan Griffiths on indictment for the same offense was fined only 40s. on a judgment by default (Ms. Mins. NYCQS 1760–72 360, Nov. 7, 1771) while Thomas Noble, on indictment for selling strong liquors to slaves and trading with them was fined only 1s. when he pleaded guilty (Ms. Mins. NYCQS 1694–1731/32 288, 296, 297, 305–307, May 3, Aug. 2, 1715).

We have seen, however, an indictment against Hannah Bond for disorderly house and entertaining vagabonds and when the jurors found her "guilty of the misdemeanors of which she stands charged in the indictment," it was ordered by the court that she "be stripped from the waste up and receive 31 lashes" for her offense (Ms. Mins. NYCQS 1732–62 94, 98, 104, 107–109, Nov. 10, 1738, Feb. 6, 1738/39, Aug. 9, Nov. 7, 1739). Catherine O'Niel was for the same offense sentenced to one hour in the stocks and to give surety for good behavior for one year or spend that year in jail (Ms. Mins. NYCQS 1760–72 226, 230, 233, Nov. 3, 4, 1767).

The offenses of entertaining negro slaves, of entertaining apprentices and servants, and of entertaining sailors were based upon acts of assembly. Thus, an indictment against Judith Peters, who was on Nov. 6, 1723, presented for "selling strong liquors to negroes contrary to the Act of Assembly"

(King v. Judith Peters, Ms. Mins. NYCQS 1694–1731/32 428); the act is in 1 Col. Laws NY 519, 588, 1023, Acts of 1702 and 1705 continued to 1726.

On the other hand, indictments simply for disorderly houses did not recite that they were kept in violation of any statute. The following indictment against one William Powers for keeping a disorderly house is typical: "The Jurors for our said Lord the King, for the Body of the City & County of New York upon their Oath do present William Powers late of the said City Labourer on the ninth day of february in the ninth year of the reign of our Sovereign Lord George the Third, now King of Great Britain etc. & divers other days and times between that day: and the day of the taking this Inquisition with force and Arms . . . at Montgomery ward of the Same City & County did keep & maintain and yet doth keep and maintain a certain common ill governed, and disorderly house, and then and the said other days and times there for his own Lucre and gain unlawfully and willfully did cause and procure certain evil and ill disposed persons of evil name and fame, and of dishonest Conversation to frequent & Come together in the said House of him the said William Powers and then and the said other days and Times there unlawfully and willfully did permit and yet doth permit the said persons of evil name and fame and dishonest Conversation at unlawful times as well in the night as in the day to be and remain in the house of the said William Powers drinking, Tipling, Quarrelling, fighting, gaming and misbehaving themselves to the great Damage and Common Nuisance of all the liege Subjects of our said Lord the King, and against the peace of our said Lord the King his Crown & Dignity" (H.R. Pleadings Pl. K. 460).

desirables the prosecutions were undertaken as a crude medium of crime prevention.[181]

The jurisdiction of the Sessions Courts over bastardy is complicated in the sense that this court exercised an original and concurrent as well as an appellate authority. The matter was viewed as an aspect of the control over vagrancy and poor relief and was closely related to the criminal law because it was linked with the difficult task of suppressing and punishing immorality. This is clearly indicated in the first of the Elizabethan statutes[182] to commit the jurisdiction to secular hands, and it may here be noticed that the colonists regarded their own jurisdiction as resting directly upon the English legislation.[183] Originally, the statutes provided that two justices of the peace should make orders upon examination for the support of the bastard child and for the punishment of the mother and reputed father, and take security for the performance of the order or appearance at Quarter Sessions.[184] This court itself was first given authority to make orders in Sessions by statute 3 Car. I c.4 §15.

Bastardy was dealt with in New York exactly as it was in England. The bulk of the orders were made by two justices out of Sessions, a circumstance which makes difficult any attempt to estimate the scope of this problem for such orders unless contested would not ordinarily be entered in the minutes, but merely filed with the clerk. Only in Dutchess County did the clerks usually enter the orders—as if the bastard being *terrae filius* must perforce be duly enrolled in their libers.

Bastardy proceedings might be originated in General Sessions in a variety of ways. The grand jury might present a suspected party or parties for having a

---

[181] For the occasional disorderly house indictments in the county, cf. Philip Travis indicted for keeping a "wide house" (*Ms. Mins. Westch. Co. Sess. 1710–23* Dec. 7, 1714); King v. Slecht (*Ms. Mins. Ulster Co. Sess. 1711/12–1720* Sept. 4, 1716); King v. Mary Tiler (*Ms. Mins. Suffolk Co. Sess. 1760–75* Mar. 28, 1775). Cf. also the general summons to retailers of liquor (*Ms. Mins. Richmond Co. Sess. 1710/11–1744/45* Sept. 3, 1717).

[182] 18 Eliz. c.3.

[183] Cf. *Ms. Deeds Richmond Co.* Liber B, fol. 189, an indenture of apprenticeship of a bastard child (1692) citing 43 Eliz. c.2, and compare the late statute (5 *Col. Laws NY* 689) which refers to 18 Eliz. c.3. The Kings County minutes of May 8, 1694, set forth the substance of 18 Eliz. c.3: "It is ordained and enacted—that two Justices of the

peace one to be of the Quorum may by their discreçon take ordr. for the punishment of the reputed father and mother of a bastard child and saving the parish harmles and alsoe may by their discreçon charge . . . soe much mony weekly for the sustenance of said child, and for non preformance of the sd Justices ordr. . . . the father and mother making default shall be sent to the Common gaole without bayll or mainprize, till they give security to performe said Justices Ordr. or else to appear at the next sessions, and then and there to stand and abide the ordr. of the sd. Court or the ordr. before made by the Justices, if the Court of Sessions thinks ffitt" (*Ms. Kings Co. Ct. & Rd. Recs. 1692–1825* 26).

[184] *Supra* n. 182 and 7 Jac. I c.4.

bastard,[185] or even present the mother for refusing "to father" a bastard.[186] Sometimes the cause would be initiated by the mother of the bastard or some other person appearing in court and making complaint[187] and sometimes the overseers of the poor whose concern it was to see that the unwanted child did not become a public charge would initiate proceedings.[188]

Presentments of bastardy become very rare after the middle of the eighteenth century, and the making of orders is regularly performed by the justices out of Sessions. At the same time, however, the records show a sharp increase in the numbers of appeals taken to General Sessions, a matter which

[185] Thus, Queen v. Catherine Springsteen (*Ms. Mins. Orange Co. Sess. 1703–08* Apr. 27, 1703, and again Oct. 26, 1703); Queen v. Ab. Johnson's daughter (*Ms. Mins. Richmond Co. Sess. 1710/11– 1744/45* Mar. 2, 1713/14); King v. Sarah Jamison (*ibid.* Sept. 5, 1721); King v. Van Pelt (*ibid.* Sept. 15, 1742); King v. Wm. Morril (*ibid.* Mar. 15, 1742/43); King v. Rachel van Aken (*Ms. Mins. Ulster Co. Sess. 1711/12–1720* Mar. 6, 1715/16); King v. Rosekrans (*Ms. Mins. Ulster Co. Sess. 1737–50* Nov. 1, 1737). In Westchester "The jurors present Philip Travers for cohabiting with Darcas Travers his brother's wife . . . for having carnal copulation with Darcas by having gotten a bastard on her." This presentment was returned "billa vera" and "put in execution for further process" (King v. Philip Travers, *Mins. Westch. Ct. of Sess. 1657–96* 66, 126, June 8, 1692, May 12, 1694). Also see King v. Eliz. Lounsbury (*ibid.* 85, 126, Dec. 6, 1693, May 12, 1694); King v. Susannah Galpin (*ibid.* 65, 68, 126, June 8, 1692, May 12, 1694); Queen v. Jonathan Horton (*Ms. Mins. Westch. Co. Sess. 1710–23* June 5, 1711); King v. Holmes (*ibid.* June 7, 1715); Queen v. Sarah Brewer (*Ms. Kings Co. Ct. & Rd. Recs. 1692–1825* 161, May 9, 10, 1710); Queen v. Ben Aske, Queen v. Isaac Gabay, Queen v. Eliz. Piles, Queen v. John Chollwell (*Ms. Mins. NYCQS 1694–1731/32* 101, Aug. 8, 1705). Anna Maria Cockin was presented at Albany Sessions for having two black bastards. She claimed that she was led to fornication through poverty. Thirty-one lashes and banished (*Ms. Mins. Albany Co. Sess. 1717–23* Feb. 4, 1718/19, June 3, 1719).
[186] Queen v. Elizabeth Springsteen (*Ms. Mins. Orange Co. Sess. 1703–08* Oct. 29, 1706); Queen v. Emilie Hays (*ibid.* Apr. 29, 1707). Later, reluctant women might be handled roughly as in New York: "Defendant been brought to Court by the Constable and it appearing to the Court by Divers Examinations that Mary Lawrence . . . is a Common Prostitute of Notorious and Lewd behavior and of evil Name and fame and was lately Delivered of . . . a bastard . . . she not discovering . . . the Reputed father . . . Ordered . . . one and thirty Lashes . . . and then . . . Committed to the House of Correction for a Year and kept to hard Labor unless she give Security to keep the parish Harmless from the maintenance of the said Bas-

tard," King v. Mary Lawrence (*Ms. Mins. NYCQS 1732–62* 87, May 4, 1738).
[187] For example, *Ms. Mins. Ulster Co. Sess. 1693–98:* Geertruy Hendrix against Barent Cool, Mar. 3, 1694/95 (*Ms. Mins. NYCQS 1694–1731/32* 101, Aug. 8, 1705). "Elizabeth Chick single woman Maketh Oath that Peter Morin, . . . later her master is the father of the Child of which she now goes with. Ordered a Warrant issued agt. . . . Peter Morin to Oblige him to give Bond to save the parish harmless" (King v. Peter Morin, *ibid.* 270, Aug. 3, 1714). Most pathetic is the graphic language of one Abigail Lancaster's petition "which was read and contened these . . . words, That whereas She having beene beguiled through the Protestations and Oath of one Joseph Budd . . . who did promise yt ye whole world should not part us, And that the Solemnity of marriage should forthwith be done between Us but after he had satisfied his Lust with me: Left me in a poore Miserable and Disstressed Condition: and my poore Child which came out of his Loynes must be cald a Bastard. . . . Relying upon Yer Worships compassion . . . Humbly prayes your Worships will . . . order that the said Joseph Budd may be healpful in the bringeing upp said Child. . . . Whereupon the Court order that two or three Justices of Peace . . . doe Examen in said Petiton and Give Reliefe as the Law directs" (King v. Joseph Budd, *Mins. Westch. Ct. of Sess. 1657–96* 107, Dec. 3, 1695).
[188] "Whereas it appears upon complaint by . . . one of the overseers of the poor . . . that Elizabeth Burns . . . single woman, hath lately been delivered of a female bastard . . . likely to become chargeable to the parish . . . and whereas upon the Examination of the said Elizabeth Burns on oath, it appeared . . . that Caleb Ogden, an apprentice . . . was the father . . . Ordered . . . according to the statute that . . . Caleb Ogden . . . pay weekly . . . unto the Churchwardens . . . two shillings towards the maintenance of the said bastard . . . and Elizabeth Burns shall pay weekly . . . three shillings . . . Caleb Ogden to give Recognizance to perform this order" (King v. Caleb Ogden, *Ms. Mins. NYCQS 1732–62* 427, Feb. 8, 1758).

will be discussed in connection with appellate jurisdiction.[189] The disappearance of presentments is due largely, we think, to the increasingly effective employment of the recognizance device which was another means of putting a bastardy case before the Sessions Court. A single justice had the power to bind over a man suspected of fathering a bastard to answer at Sessions,[190] and this would be done when the mother had not yet been delivered, when there was some question of pregnancy, or where the person accused resisted the charge or refused to give the necessary bond to save the parish harmless. If the defendant appeared at Sessions he might be ordered to post a bond to indemnify the parish, and if he complied would be discharged.[191] If there were any reason why he should not be held responsible the court would examine into the matter.[192] Failure to appear would entail forfeiture of the recognizance.[193] Implicit in the recognizance to answer at Sessions was not merely the matter of being ordered to support but likewise the latent danger of being prosecuted for fornication.[194] The use of capias and imprisonment as mesne process indicated clearly the criminal cast of this jurisdiction.[195]

[189] *Infra* 269 *et seq.*
[190] This practice is in effect at an early date. So John Sharpe was "bound to answer for begetting a bastard on Mehetabell Mahany" (*infra* 487 n. 9). See also *Ms. Mins. Ulster Co. Sess. 1693–98* Sept. 27, 1693.
[191] Examples of discharge from recognizance for appearance on producing the bond: King v. Thomas Carmer (*Ms. Mins. NYCQS 1732–62* 365, 369, 375, 381, May 6, Aug. 5, Nov. 4, 1755, Feb. 3, 4, 1756); King v. Isaac De Costa (*ibid.* 289, 290, 294, 299, 300, 301, 305, Feb. 6, 7, 1750/51, May 7, Aug. 6–8, Nov. 6, 1751); King v. James Sackett (*ibid.* 381, Feb. 3, 1756); King v. Edward Menzie (*ibid.* 264, Nov. 10, 1749); King v. Thomas Quill (*ibid.* 449, Feb. 6, 1759); King v. Jacobus Davis (*Ms. Mins. NYCQS 1694–1731/32* 48, Aug. 1, 1699); King v. John Norwood (*Ms. Mins. NYCQS 1760–72* 147, Nov. 7, 1765). The accused might be discharged when the churchwardens sent in a certificate that he had posted bond to indemnify the parish: King v. Jas. Ketcham (*ibid.* 359, Nov. 7, 1771); King v. Neal Shaw (*Ms. Mins. NYCQS 1732–62* 442, Nov. 7, 1758); King v. Jos. Bary (*Ms. Mins. NYCQS 1772–91* 16, Aug. 6, 1772).
One defendant, either already on recognizance to indemnify the parish for a bastard or on recognizance to answer for a bastard and having not yet posted a bond of indemnity, was continued on recognizance through every sitting of the Court of General Sessions from May 1768 to Nov. 1772, being finally discharged in the latter month: King v. Isaac Winn (*Ms. Mins. NYCQS 1760–72* 280, 282, 302, 308, 314, 323, 331, 338, 345; *Ms. Mins. NYCQS 1772–91* 2, 16, 23); see also King v. William Latham (*Ms. Mins. NYCQS 1760–72* 106,

111, 113, 118, May, Aug., Nov. 1764).
[192] In one instance we have seen the father discharged because he had since married the mother (King v. Edward Thorne, *Ms. Mins. NYCQS 1732–62* 331, 334, May 1, 1753). Another putative father was released when it was shown that the mother was a non-resident (case of Jeofry Yellerton, *Ms. Mins. NYCQS 1694–1731/32* 53, May 2, 1700), and still another was discharged when it was found that the child was dead (King v. Garret Onclebagg, *ibid.* 192, Feb. 7, 1710/11).
[193] In the early minute books the orders to forfeit are blanket and single cases cannot be identified. When regular estreats are the rule (after 1763) the orders are easily identifiable. Thus the estreats of the Dutchess General Sessions, Jan. 1775, indicate that one Willcocks and his surety each forfeited £ 20, "the principal because he did not appear and the surety because he had him not here to answer" (*H.R. Pleadings* Pl. K. 364, Pl. M. 876).
[194] Daniel Willcocks and his surety, Joseph Sheldon, were bound in £ 20 each before one justice of peace of Dutchess County on Mar. 12, 1774, "Conditioned that if the said Daniel Willcocks Shall Appear at the Next Court of General Sessions of the peace . . . at Poughkeepsie . . . To Answer what Shall be Objected against him Touching his being Charged with fornication in begetting a Child On the body of Mary Burch Singlewoman and shall not depart from the said Court without leave then this Recognizance to be Void otherwise to remain in full force . . ." (*H.R. Pleadings* Pl. K. 503); see also recognizance of William Latham in £ 100 before an alderman of New York City (*H.R. Pleadings* Pl. K. 1000).
[195] King v. John Sharpe (*Ms. Mins. NYCQS*

The proceedings in Sessions bore most heavily upon the putative fathers because of the prevailing anxiety that the burden of public relief should not be increased by these unexpected and illegitimate additions to the population. But there were no tears shed for the unmarried mother. If she did not reside in a particular county she was liable to immediate deportation to her place of domicile.[196] If she had not already given birth to the child, she might suffer the indignity of examination by a jury of women[197] and depending upon circumstances might be ordered into custody.

We have discussed the bastardy jurisdiction at such length because of the procedural ramifications and because it has a direct relation to the problem of where in the New World the control of morals (exercised in England by the ecclesiastical courts) was to be placed. The English bastardy legislation was one of the first breaches struck in the monopoly of the church, the disintegration of which was furthered by Puritan attacks. In the opening years of the eighteenth century, due chiefly to royal pressure, civil magistrates in England were active in suppressing various forms of vice,[198] and it is possible the proclamations of Bellomont, Cornbury and Hunter are related to this English movement.[199] In any event, it is worth noticing that most of the prose-

---

1694–1731/32 21, Feb. 3, *1696/97*); King v. Teneick (*Ms. Mins. Orange Co. Sess. 1703–08* Oct. 22, 1703); King v. Van Aken (*Ms. Mins. Ulster Co. Sess. 1711/12–1720* Mar. 6, 1715/16).

One recalcitrant, having been ordered to enter £100 bond to pay 4*s.* a week for the child for three years and £3 for the woman's confinement, failed to enter a recognizance and was committed into the constable's hands "by a mittimus." But he ran away from the constable and an order was made in General Sessions that "if he can be found within this County" he be committed to the common gaol "by a mittimus from any of the justices of the quorum" (King v. Johannes Laquire, Jr., *Ms. Kings Co. Ct. & Rd. Recs. 1692–1825* 29, Nov. 12, 1695).

In one instance where a father appeared on recognizance to answer for a bastard the court used this unusual language in ordering him to provide maintenance for his child: "Ordered that John Finey shall pay as A Fine towards the maintenance of A Bastard Child by him begott six pounds . . . and that he pay itt into the Treasurers hands; in the space of fourteen days" (King v. John Finey, *Ms. Mins. NYCQS 1683/84–1694* 158, Nov. 1, 1692). When bastardy is regularly handled out of Sessions the process entries in the minute books disappear.

[196] E.g., *Ms. Mins. Mayor's Ct. NYC 1724/25–1729.* On April 5, 1726, Charity Yeomans of Orange Co., who comes in with a bastard child, ordered deported to Orange Co.

[197] *Ms. Mins. Ulster Co. Sess. 1711/12–1720* Dec. 8, 1715. In a Dutchess case a woman was suspect of a bastard by a negro, and a jury of women was summoned to examine the child (*Ms. Mins. Dutchess Co. Sess. Liber B,* May 18, 1756). The bastardy act of 1774 apparently attempted to limit the justices' power to compel examination before delivery (5 *Col. Laws* NY 691).

[198] It is stated in 1 Webb, *English Local Government; The Parish and the County* (1906) 335: "It was in vain that the pious Queen Mary and the decorous Queen Anne successively gave their patronage to Societies for the Reformation of Manners and allowed proclamations to be made . . . enjoining the magistrates to put in operation the laws against swearing, profanation of the Lord's day, drunkenness, vice and immorality . . . the popular prejudice against a compulsory reformation of manners . . . was throughout the first half of the 18th century too strong to be overcome by such means. . . ." Yet on page 391 speaking of the justices' work it is stated "Between 1689 and 1714 . . . we find them 'goaded on by the Societies for the Reformation of Manners,' . . . very active in putting down Sunday desecration, gaming-houses, profane swearing and 'vice and immorality.' . . ."

[199] Bellomont's proclamation in the NYHS collection of broadsides. On Nov. 3, 1702, Cornbury's proclamation of May 3, 1702, against immorality and profaneness had been published in court (*Ms. Mins. NYCQS 1694–1731/32* 70; *Ms. Kings Co. Ct. & Rd. Recs. 1692–1825* 88, May 13, 1702).

cutions for adulterous activity occur in the reign of virtuous Anne. The minutes of the country Sessions at this time, however, do not show any remarkable enterprise respecting this type of law enforcement. In February, 1705/06, the Albany grand jury sought to secure county regulation when it presented Sabbath breach, meetings of negroes and other such derelictions, but the Court said that there were acts of assembly on these matters and ordered the sheriff to enforce the laws.[199a]

It may be supposed that most of what was undertaken was done out of Sessions, since a provincial act of 1708[200] specifically conferred upon single justices the power to deal with immorality. In this connection the dilemma of the justices of Suffolk, a godly Puritan county, is illuminating. Petitioning Governor Hunter the bench complains:

> Humbly Sheweth: That whereas there are severall Instances of persons Cohabiting together as man and wife (being not Legally Marryed) and frequent Instances of fornication Committed and other Crimes of Like Nature done in ye County and that upon useing our Endeavours to Suppress these views we have been in a great measure obstructed by means of an opinion spread amongst ye people that we have no power to Inflict any punishment upon Such persons as are Guilty of the Crimes above Named for that they are only Cognizable in a Spirituall Court Therefore your petitioners Humbly Crave your assistance herein and that you will be pleased to give us Such Directions as to your Excy shall Seem meet for us to Govern ourselves by for ye suppression Hereof and as in Dutie Bound Shall ever Pray.[201]

This effusion was laid before the Council which advised that a letter be written telling the justices that "these vices are punishable by law," presentable by the grand jury and within the powers of the justices.

With the accession of the Hanoverians the war on vice, except for the dis-

Hunter's proclamation of Jan. 11, 1711/12, is in the NYHS Coll. This prolation was to be read before the charge to the grand jury who were to be encouraged to present breaches of the laws against immorality.

[199a] In 51 NY Col. Mss. 77.

[200] 1 Col. Laws NY 617. Cf. the prosecution for adultery, Queen v. Henry Cordus (Ms. Mins. NYCQS 1694–1731/32 157, 159, 163, 167, 169, 170, 173, 176, 185, 191, 193–196, Feb. 2, 1708/09, May 3, Aug. 2, Nov. 1, 1709, Feb. 7, 8, 1709/10, May 2, Aug. 2, Nov. 8, 1710, Feb. 6, 7, 1710/11, May 1, 1711); we shall discuss this case infra 445. Four other cases were all brought into Quarter Sessions on Aug. 8, 1705, when Paroculus Parmyter

was presented for buying and entertaining Richard Hunter's wife; Gyles Shelley for keeping Charles Peters' wife; Jacob Deporto for "entertaining publickly a woman att his house at the Bowry," and Richard Rowe for entertaining Rebeckah Haines, "a Marryed woman." "Due process" was issued against these defendants but no further proceedings are found on any of the cases except that of Richard Rowe, who appeared in Quarter Sessions on Nov. 6, 1706, and was discharged because "Rebeckah Haines who swore the peace against him," had not appeared (ibid. 100, 101, 117).

[201] The petition is in 60 NY Col. Mss. 136, Nov. 1, 1716. The answer is in 11 Ms. Mins. Council 386.

orderly house cases in the city and an occasional country prosecution for immoderate drinking, gambling or the like,[202] is confined chiefly to the bastardy cases. There is a brief renascence of Puritan fervor in Dutchess during the French and Indian War. In 1756 Thomas Young was indicted for blasphemy[203] and in 1759 Samuel Shaw is indicted "as a person of ill fame, a whoremonger and adulterer."[204] Then at the May Session, 1762, John Pierce is indicted for adultery and the grand jury likewise presents that Hezekiah Willcocks had left his wife and children and was living with Abigail Scribner and the court is asked to take measures.[205] The Court, "having taken so hainous an offence into consideration and in order to suppress such wicked and abominable crimes against the law of God and in open violation of the Law of the Kingdom of Great Brittain and this province to prevent licentiousness Adultery fornication and other crying sins," ordered the couple apprehended, heard, punished and bound to good behavior.

One other phase of original jurisdiction of the General Sessions deserves particular mention—the appearance toward the end of the colonial period of indictments for attempts. This is a reflection of the practice in the Supreme Court rather than a deliberate effort to broaden the base of Sessions jurisdiction. There are not many of these cases,[206] but the fact that jurisdiction is assumed by inferior courts indicates that in the colony the attempt was recognized as a special category of misdemeanor.[207]

In addition to what may be described as the common law criminal business of General Sessions, a considerable bulk of cases came before these courts in connection with violations of orders made by the justices of the peace for their respective counties.[208] Related to this jurisdiction was the authority exercised

[202] King v. Thos. Pitts—Sabbath breach (Ms. Mins. Dutchess Co. Sess. Liber A, Oct. 21, 1729); King v. Cole—Sabbath breach (Ms. Mins. Orange Co. Sess. 1727–79 Oct. 25, 1737); King v. Gale —Sabbath breach (ibid. Oct. 1756); Queen v. Marshill—drunkenness (Ms. Mins. Richmond Co. Sess. 1710/11–1744/45 Sept. 1713); King v. Sarah Hillyard—adultery (ibid. Mar. 1719/20); King v. Heath—fornication (ibid.); King v. Sunderland —Sabbath breach (ibid. Sept. 1742); Queen v. Livingston—Sabbath breach (Ms. Mins. Ulster Co. Sess. 1711/12–1720 Sept. 2, 1712), and cf. the grievance against a Sunday barber (ibid. Sept. 4, 1716).
[203] Ms. Mins. Dutchess Co. Sess. Liber B, Oct. 19, 1756.
[204] Ms. Mins. Dutchess Co. Sess. Liber C, Oct. 16, 1759.
[205] Ibid. May 18, 1762.

[206] For example, King v. Bastarr—attempted buggery (Ms. Mins. NYCQS 1760–72 290, 295, 297, Aug. 4, Nov. 8, 9, 1769); King v. Nath. Cooley —attempted murder (Ms. Mins. NYCQS 1772–91 80, 91, 95, Feb. 5, May 4, 6, 1774); King v. Berwick—attempted rape (ibid. 183, May 10, 1776); King v. Joseph Lace—attempted rape (Ms. Mins. Albany Co. Sess. 1763–82 Oct. 2–5, 1764); King v. Archibald McNeal—attempted rape (Ms. Mins. Dutchess Co. Sess. Liber E, Oct. 14, 1774).
[207] Apparently more sharply defined than in England, cf. Sayre, Criminal Attempts, 41 Harvard Law Rev. 821, 834; Hall, Criminal Attempt, 49 Yale Law Jour. 789. But note that neither of these writers has examined Assize or Quarter Sessions records, the only material properly comparable with the New York records.
[208] Supra 39.

as a part of what may be described as public works. Already under Dongan the Sessions had assumed jurisdiction over the maintenance of highways,[209] and, although by statute in 1691[210] local surveyors were authorized to supervise highways, they were subjected to control of the Sessions of the Peace. In 1703 a statute was enacted dealing in considerable detail with highway problems and appointing commissioners.[211] The enforcement was centered in the Sessions Courts, and consisted either in presentments of highways by grand juries or in prosecutions for encroachments.[212] Similarly, the maintenance of jails, stocks and whipping posts was Sessions business.[213]

The picture of General Sessions in action is not complete without some reference to the duties it performed in the matter of poor relief.[214] This jurisdic-

---

[209] E.g., *Ms. Mins. Albany Co. Sess. 1685–89* 57.

[210] 1 *Col. Laws NY* 225.

[211] *Ibid.* 532, and cf. the return, dated June 21, 1707, of the "commissions for laying on highways in New York City remaining on record in the office of the clerk of the peace of the City and County of New York in the Book of Minutes of General Quarter Sessions of the Peace begun August 7, 1694" (*James Alexander Papers* Box 46 A).

[212] In New York City Quarter Sessions surveyors were ordered to view and repair roads and bridges (*Ms. Mins. NYCQS 1694–1731/32* 124, 132, May 7, Nov. 4, 1707), and overseers of the highways were also appointed who were to lay out or repair roads and prevent encroachments (*ibid.* 433, Feb. 5, 1723/24; *ibid.* 127, 128, Aug. 1707; *Ms. Mins. NYCQS 1722–42/43* [Rough] 16, Feb. 6, 1722/23; *ibid.* 33, Feb. 5, 1723/24; *ibid.* 51, Feb. 3, 1724/25; *ibid.* 65, Feb. 2, 1725/26).

In Kings County Sessions, also, surveyors of the highways were appointed and it was provided that those who should encroach upon the highway would not only pay court costs and civil damages but would also be "amersed to the King" (*Ms. Kings Co. Ct. & Rd. Recs. 1692–1825* 23, Dec. 14, 1693). On Nov. 12, 1695, this same court made two road orders, violations of which were punishable by a £5 fine which was to be paid to the poor (*ibid.* 28).

Delinquent surveyors were the subject of Sessions regulations. So, on Nov. 12, 1695, the Brooklyn town surveyors were fined 12s. each for not making a return of a warrant for laying out the King's Highway, and it was ordered that if the surveyors refused to pay the fines, there should be levies by "duress and sale of the offendrs goods and chatteles . . . by a warrant from this Court" (*ibid.* 28).

"Carmen" or "carters" were ordered to keep in repair roads and streets over which their wagons passed, and penalties were provided in the event of their failure to do so, and in some instances their licenses were revoked (*Ms. Mins. NYCQS 1683/84–1694* 158, Nov. 1, 1692; *Ms. Mins. NYCQS 1694–*

1731/32 168, May 1, 1695; *ibid.* 395–396, Feb. 7, 1721/22; *ibid.* 265, 267, 433, 434, 472).

In some instances whole towns were ordered to repair and keep up roads, and in Kings County Sessions for Nov. 10, 1696, the towns of Broockland and Buswyck were ordered to repair the roads within their jurisdiction or be subject to fines for their failure to do so (*Ms. Kings Co. Ct. & Rd. Recs. 1692–1825* 32). The grand jury often presented defective roads and bridges; cf. *Ms. Mins. NYCQS 1694–1731/32* 124, May 7, 1707.

Examples of presentments of encroachments, *Ms. Mins. Suffolk Co. Sess. 1723–51* Oct. 5, 1736; *Ms. Mins. NYCQS 1732–62* Aug. 7, 1746; *Ms. Mins. Ulster Co. Sess. 1737–50* Nov. 1, 1743.

References to other road orders are the following: *Ms. Kings Co. Ct. & Rd. Recs. 1692–1825* 28, 31, 33, 37, 40, 64, Nov. 12, 1695, May 13, Nov. 10, 1696, May 11, Nov. 9, 1697, Nov. 12, 1700; *Ms. Mins. NYCQS 1694–1731/32* 208, Feb. 5, 1711/12.

[213] Thus in Kings County Sessions for Nov. 8, 1692, is the entry: "The Court doe order That there be a good pr of stocks and a good pound . . . in every town within Kings County and to be always kept in sufficient repaire and that there be warrants issued out by the Cleark of the Court to the Constables of every towne to see the order of Court performed as they will answer to the Contrary at their perill" (*Ms. Kings Co. Ct. & Rd. Recs. 1692–1825* 14); see also *ibid.* 151, 154, May 13, Nov. 12, 1707.

On Nov. 12, 1707, an order was made in Kings County Sessions for the repair of the local jail (*ibid.* 154), and in New York City Quarter Sessions on May 7, 1707, an order was made to erect a "Bridewell" for the suppression of vice and the maintenance of the poor (*Ms. Mins. NYCQS 1694–1731/32* 124). Cf. also the order re jails (*Ms. Mins. Westch. Co. Sess. 1710–23* June 7, 1720), and see *supra* n. 154. The prosecution of the Albany justices for neglect of the jail is discussed *infra* 173.

[214] This is not explored in the latest work, Schneider, *Hist. of Public Welfare in New York*

tion was not strictly criminal but, as it was connected with the general and perplexing problem of vagrancy as well as with the matter of bastardy, it is related to the criminal law both in its remedial and preventive aspects. There is not much evidence of any warm eleemosynary spirit, for the records indicate that terror of having some wretch as a charge upon the local budget was the compelling motive for many of the orders.[215] Of a similar character was the control over the indentured servants and slaves.[216] Even in the early days of English rule in New York the many hue and cry warrants for servants suggests the quasi-criminal character of this jurisdiction. And the necessity of

State (1938). Schneider has examined few records and has no inkling of the common functions exercised by the justices of the peace.

[215] On the English practice, cf. Webb, 1 *English Local Government; The Parish and the County* 420 n. 1, 477. For examples in New York, cf. the order made obliging a husband to permit his wife and children to live in his house in order to prevent their becoming a charge on the parish, and ordering him to be put on surety for good behavior for his contempt if he refused to do so (Queen v. Vincent Delamontagne, *Ms. Mins. NYCQS 1731/32* 160, 199, 202, May 4, 1709, May 1, Aug. 7, 1711). Another defendant was obliged to enter a bond with two sureties in £100 each to "save the city harmless against his wife becoming a charge to the city" (King v. Thomas Willson, *Ms. Mins. NYCQS 1732–62* 218, May 6, 1747). On complaint of the churchwardens a mother was ordered to support her child and pay 6s. a week for its maintenance on penalty of 20s. for every month she neglected to do so (King v. Olive Burgess, *Ms. Mins. NYCQS 1772–91* 29, Nov. 6, 1772). On complaint of the churchwardens a son-in-law was ordered to support Abraham Ackerman and his wife with 20s. a month until further notice (*ibid.* 29, 30, Nov. 6, 1772).

Sessions did not confine itself to ordering relatives to provide support for the indigent but might make orders as to the disposition of children and household goods by the churchwardens when these children were deserted by their fathers (*Ms. Mins. NYCQS 1694–1731/32* 498, 499, Aug. 7, 1728). In another case it ordered the churchwardens to pay for the maintenance of Ann Sawyer, a poor prisoner (*ibid.* 425, Aug. 7, 1723), and in still another the court ordered that four and one half ounces of plate, unclaimed and supposedly feloniously stolen by one Thomas Codman, should be "delivered to Hannah Anderson [who] is very sick and weak in a Dour condition and a great object of charity" (*ibid.* 384, Nov. 2, 1720).

A footnote on colonial educators is afforded by the following poor relief entry: "Whereas Mitchell Sommersett, schoolmaster is lately Absconded & hath left upon the Parish two Small female Children . . . Ordered by the Court that the Church

Wardens do Receive the said Children & Household goods from . . . Mary Kelly, and . . . put them to Nurse to Antie Cross or . . . Other Orderly family . . . on the most Easy Terms they can agree for" (*Ms. Mins. NYCQS 1722–1742/43* [Rough] 102, 103, Aug. 7, 1728).

In Kings County Sessions an order was made providing that the estate of an orphan's father be kept by the "chest keepers" of Boswyck until the orphan come of age or be married (Petition of Peter Witt v. Phillip Volkertse, *Kings Co. Ct. & Rd. Recs. 1692–1825* 147, 148, May 8, 9, 1705). In a New York City case, Joseph Johnson, the six-year-old child of a felon "fled from Justice," was by order of Quarter Sessions apprenticed by the churchwardens to William Bradford, printer (*Ms. Mins. NYCQS 1732–62* 51, May 6, 1735). Cf. also the presentment of the Grand Jury regarding the maintenance of Peter Pieter by "the town he belongs to" (*Ms. Mins. Ulster Co. Sess. 1693–98* Sept. 1, 1696).

[216] References to indentured servants in New York colonial court records are not abundant, but cf. the complaint by Robert Ellis through his attorneys concerning "divers indented servands" who had deserted his service. The Court of Quarter Sessions found by the confession and oath of the suspected servants that they were paid for by Robert Ellis and put on a sloop for Philadelphia, but that the ship having been captured by pirates and the indenture papers destroyed, the alleged servants had refused to serve. The Court ordered that the servants be "Committed to . . . Gaol . . . untill they Shall Respectively be bound . . . to Serve . . . for the Term mentioned . . . in their . . . indentures" (*Ms. Mins. NYCQS 1694–1731/32* 338, Nov. 6, 1717). Another "covenant servant" refusing to serve out his remaining three years in Pennsylvania was ordered committed to jail for three months unless his alleged master convey him to Pennsylvania or discharge his imprisonment (King v. John Welsh, *ibid.* 541, 542, Nov. 2, 1731). Alice Kerney confessed an indictment of perjury, was released by her master and ordered out of the county (*Ms. Mins. Dutchess Co. Sess.* Liber A, May 19, 1741).

affording the servant some measure of protection against immoderate correction by the master made the Sessions a forum for domestic discipline.[217] The vagabond, on the other hand, did not ordinarily achieve the distinction of appearance at Sessions for his case was customarily dealt with summarily by a single justice or at the so-called "meetings" of justices.[218]

The miscellaneous county business which was crammed into General Sessions grew constantly in bulk during the eighteenth century. Such matters as reports by road supervisors, tax assessors and collectors, overseers of the poor, pound masters, fence viewers and road commissioners,[219] had little or nothing

[217] These cases were often handled summarily. Thus Patrick Smith, "an unruly servant," was without formal trial sent to the House of Correction "to receive thirty one lashes" for having abused the watch (*Ms. Mins. NYCQS 1732–62* 155, Aug. 4, 1743; see also King v. Margaret Robinson, *Ms. Mins. NYCQS 1694–1731/32* 517, Nov. 5, 1729). On the other hand, the master and mistress of a maid servant were indicted for "beating and bruising" her "in a cruel and barbarous manner" and on their plea of guilty fined five shillings (King v. Rice and Dorothy Williams, *Ms. Mins. NYCQS 1732–62* 391, 395, 396, Aug. 4, 1756). However, Anne Sewell, a "Widdow," who pleaded guilty when charged with "keeping in Chains and Irons for several Weeks upon bread and water . . . and . . . Cruelly beating A Certain servant Maid," was released simply on the payment of fees when she "Confessed the matter of fact & says she did not know itt was the breach of any Law her . . . servant having highly Offended her" (*Ms. Mins. NYCQS 1694–1731/32* 9, Nov. 6, 1695). When apprentices were dissatisfied with conditions, they made complaint to Sessions, and the master was ordered to show "his apprentice cause why he should not be discharged from his apprenticeship" (King v. John Marshall, *Ms. Mins. NYCQS 1732–62* 300, Aug. 7, 1751). When Anthony Smith and John Job, apprentices, made complaint against their masters they were not so fortunate since it was ordered that they each "returne to his master The charge . . . not being fully proved to the Court" (King v. John Gilliland, King v. Alexander Lessly, *Ms. Mins. NYCQS 1772–91* 78, 79, Feb. 2, 3, 1773). On the other hand, Samuel Magee was discharged from apprenticeship upon the court's "hearing the parties and seeing the marks upon the head, arms and body" (King v. Thomas Hall, *Ms. Mins. NYCQS 1694–1731/32* 535, May 5, 1731) and James Jamison won his release on the court's discovery that he was "grievously disfigured in his face and . . . in danger of loosing his eyes thereby" (King v. Henry Brughman, *ibid.* 333, 336, 342, 343, Aug. 6, Nov. 6, 1717, Feb. 4, 1717/18). See also King v. Benjamin Peck (*ibid.* 374, 376, Aug. 2, 1720) and King v. Benjamin Bate (*Ms. Mins. NYCQS 1722–1742/43* [Rough] 109, Feb. 5, 1728/29). We have seen another apprentice dis-

charged for "misdemeanors against his master" (*Ms. Mins. NYCQS 1772–91* 11, May 8, 1772), while several were discharged when their masters abandoned them (*Ms. Mins. NYCQS 1732–62* 77, Aug. 3, 1737; *ibid.* 181, 182, May 8, 1745. Cf. also, 1764; *Ms. Mins. NYCQS 1732–62* 316, May 6, 1752; *Ms. Mins. NYCQS 1694–1731/32* 374, 376, 478, 484, 485, 502, 503).

We have seen a few orders respecting lunatics in Sessions. In Kings County Sessions an order was made for keeping "mad James" by the whole county, the Deacons to consider the proportions each parish was to pay for his maintenance (*Ms. Kings Co. Ct. & Rd. Recs. 1692–1825* 28), while in New York City Quarter Sessions, "Robert Bullman . . . committed to the Common gaol . . . as A Lunatick and Dangerous Madman the High Sheriff having Represented . . . that [he is] recovered . . . Ordered . . . Discharged from . . . Imprisonment" (*Ms. Mins. NYCQS 1722–1742/43* [Rough] 71, May 4, 1726). In Westchester, Dinah Kirkpatrick was complained of as a common disturber. As she was supposed to be a lunatic her husband was ordered to keep her home (*Ms. Mins. Westch. Co. Sess. 1710–23* 63, 64).

[218] Susanna Norton was, by Quarter Sessions Court, summarily "Sent to the House of Correction and be there confined . . . till further order She being an Idle Wandring Vagabond" (*Ms. Mins. NYCQS 1732–62* 169, Aug. 7, 1744); see also King v. Ann Butler (*Ms. Mins. NYCQS 1694–1731/32* 524, May 6, 1730).

[219] The entries in judicial minutes gradually become infrequent as this business comes to be handled out of Sessions. However, when Tryon County was carved out of Albany, for some reason this administrative business was handled in General Sessions. The records for the years 1772 to 1776 show returns were made by districts to the court once every year by road supervisors, tax assessors and collectors, pound masters, fence viewers and road commissioners, a truly formidable array of assistants in the local administrative machinery (*Ms. Mins. Tryon Co. Sess. 1772–76* Quarto I, 1772, Sept. 8, 1772 [*Misc. Mss. Tryon County*]).

to do with matters criminal, but some of the miscellaneous orders with which the records are peppered had a relation to the duties of law enforcement and crime prevention.[220] It is quite outside the scope of this study, however, to enter upon the details of county government not related to the administration of criminal law. We must content ourselves with the observation that in New York as in England the justices of the peace were in Maitland's phrase the "rulers of the county." By provincial statute, by usage and by imitation of English practice, a staggering complex of duties was gradually loaded upon or assumed by the officials. They supervised churchwardens, constables, coroners, tax collectors and assessors, road commissioners and overseers of the poor. They had some part in the enforcement of laws relating to ferriage, militia, fortifications, poor relief, fencing, roads, traffic, peddling, revenue, maritime matters, Indians, slaves, hunting and game, nuisances, fire, health and medicine. No matter was too small for them, none was so important that they did not have some part in its enforcement.

Special Sessions and Justices' Meetings

The performance of this bewildering array of tasks was by no means all of it a matter for General Sessions. This was not because the colonists any more than their brethren at home had convictions about the separation of powers (and on this the Sessions minutes are clear enough) but because the system of local law administration was largely a projection of the English. This had

---

[220] We cannot go further into detail regarding the miscellaneous county business handled in General Sessions, but we have seen the court appoint a board of arbitration in a civil dispute (*Ms. Mins. NYCQS 1683/84–1694* 161, 162, May 2, 1693), make an order to sell at "publick outcry" the estate of a man found dead by a jury of inquest (*Mins. Westch. Ct. of Sess. 1657–96* 86, 88, 91, Dec. 5, 1693); and make orders for the burning or destruction of counterfeit coin (*Ms. Mins. NYCQS 1694–1731/32* 385, 422, 423, 437, Nov. 2, 1720, May 8, 1723, May 5, 1724; *Ms. Mins. NYCQS 1732–62* 127, Feb. 4, 1740/41).
Under the Act of Parliament, 1 William and Mary c.18 §2, non-conformists were obliged to certify their places of worship, and so on February 7, 1704/05, certain Quakers certified their meeting house to be recorded by the Court of Quarter Sessions and their request was granted (*Ms. Mins. NYCQS 1694–1731/32* 93). Likewise the English Presbyterian church was allowed to be registered and recorded at Fort George in 1720 (*ibid.* 390, 391).

Orders of naturalization of foreigners were made. Typical is an order of November 4, 1766, in New York City Quarter Sessions (*Ms. Mins. NYCQS 1760–72* 188).
On November 3, 1714, James Du Pré, one of the clerks of the Court of Chancery, appeared in Quarter Sessions to take the oath to His Majesty King George and the test oath (*Ms. Mins. NYCQS 1694–1731/32* 276).
We have seen that the sheriff's accounts for hangings, repairing jails and emptying prison tubs were reported to, and allowed by, the Court of Quarter Sessions (*ibid.* 22, 36, 117). One interesting account rendered was that by the Attorney General who asked allowance for services in prosecuting felonies on indictments found by grand juries in the Supreme Court, and the Court of Quarter Sessions was "of opinion that the said Attorney General . . . having no sallary, the Court humbly recommend his case to the General Assembly . . . for his relief therein" (*ibid.* 527, Aug. 5, 1730). Cf. *infra* 721, 735 *et seq.*

been built up by using the individual justice of the peace as the integer for the delegation of authority and, depending upon usage or statute, this authority was exercised jointly, severally or collectively. In other words, a major portion of the magistrate's function was in terms of his commission to be done in fulfilment of the clauses relating to the conservation of the peace, rather than in execution of the court-keeping clauses, viz., those relating to the hearing and determining of offenses. It was no part of the general design that the quarterly Sessions of the Peace were to be the chief instrumentalities of law administration,[221] and the early manuals certainly do not so regard them. The English Quarter Sessions are not even specifically mentioned in the commission of the peace, and they gradually acquire status as the most important locus for the discharge of business because they are a general sitting for the whole county, that is to say, all the justices were summoned to form a court and the whole county was supposed to appear.

Although the English statutes by which the duties of the justices of the peace were persistently enlarged sometimes specifically designate the Quarter Sessions as the forum, for the most part they confer jurisdiction upon one, two, three or four justices. The basis upon which the Acts of Parliament distinguished between matters cognizable by a single justice and those to be handled by two or more defies analysis. Lambard's famous manual is drawn in terms of the combinations and permutations[222]—a bold departure from the prudential English philosophy of an alphabetical catalogue—but no principle of legislative wisdom can be extracted. These statutory designations, however, were only minimum requirements and were not intended to exclude a larger number from attendance.[223] Furthermore, by the terms of the commission, the justices or any two of them had the power to appoint a session, and matters that might by statute be committed to two or three justices and even Quarter Sessions business could be disposed of there. These sessions held out of term came to be known as "Special Sessions" and we shall have to inquire somewhat into their status.

As with everything else related to the office of justice of the peace there is a gap between the textbook descriptions of Special Sessions and what in fact was

---

[221] Quarterly Sessions were instituted by statute (36 Edw. III St. 1 c.12; 12 R. II c.10; 2 Hy. V St. 1 c.4).

[222] The second book of the *Eirenarcha* (in the 1614 edition, pp. 72–304) deals with the authority

of the single justice out of Sessions. On p. 305 *et seq.* is a table of functions. The third book (pp. 309–375) deals with what two or more justices may do.

[223] Lambard, *op. cit.* Bk. 3 c.1.

practiced. Lambard thought the chief difference between the Quarter and Special Sessions was the circumstance that the latter were held at pleasure and usually summoned for special business although he admitted that all the articles within the commission were inquirable and determinable at Special Sessions.[224] Hawkins, however, distinguished between the general Quarter Sessions appointed by statute, the General Sessions held at any other time for the general execution of the authority of justice of the peace and the Sessions held on a special occasion for the execution of some particular branch of their authority.[225] It has been shown, however, by the Webbs, on the basis of their study of the records, that this textbook classification is much too sharp.[226] In certain places regional sessions were held for special purposes such as licensing alehouses or for highway regulation, and the term "Special Sessions" was only gradually adopted. Furthermore, no sharp lines were drawn between "meetings" of the justices and the more or less regular divisional Sessions.[227]

While there can be no doubt that English usage, and even its confusion, greatly influenced the dispositions of the New Yorkers with respect to the settlement of inferior criminal jurisdiction, the colonists did not exactly imitate it. Here the office of justice of the peace was a matter that did not rest upon local statute but upon the exercise of the Governor's appointive power. This is apparent as well from the fact that Sloughter commissioned justices at a time when no judicature act was in effect,[228] some weeks before the statute of 1691 was passed, as from the assumptions of that act itself. This statute intended no diminution of the traditional judicial authority of the single justice but actually increased it by the addition of civil jurisdiction. The provisions as to regular Courts of Sessions have an important bearing on the special courts, for quarterly Sessions were instituted only for New York City, and semi-annual Sessions for all the other counties except Albany where three Sessions a year were to be held. In the Act of 1692 and in Bellomont's Ordinance the Sessions are described as General Sessions, and although the point does not ever seem to have been raised, the statutory description (since the precise time and place of holding are stated) would seem to have excluded any other General Session. In other words a session convened by the justices or any three of them by virtue of the commission would necessarily be a Special Session.

224 *Ibid*. Bk. 4 cc.19, 20.
225 2 Hawkins, *Pleas of the Crown* c.8 §47.
226 Webb, *English Local Government; The Parish and the County* 396 *et seq*.
227 *Ibid*. 406.

228 *Ms. Deeds Westch. Co*. Liber B, 77, commission of the peace dated Apr. 4, 1691; *Ms. Conveyances Kings Co*. Liber I, 269, commission of the peace dated April 7, 1691.

For some reason, and probably because English nomenclature was not set-tled, "Special Session" did not become the *terminus technicus* for any and all sessions of justices held out of term even if judicial business was dispatched. Extant records of these meetings are most numerous for the last years of the seventeenth and the early eighteenth centuries. The greatest variety of designations is used in the County of Kings. In 1692 a local tempest over the detention of the schoolhouse key was examined into by four justices at what was called "This Special Sessions Court."[229] In the following year a contempt case is disposed of "At a Meeting" of the justices.[230] This expression is used for various sessions held in 1698 and 1699 to deal with administrative matters,[231] but in September, 1700, Jurian Bries is heard "Att a Quorum,"[232] and the next month a petition is disposed of "Att a Session."[233] A number of miscellaneous complaints were heard at "a Special Court of Sessions,"[234] June 30, 1701, and the court which tried nine slaves accused by the sheriff was also held by this style.[235]

In New York City one "Speciall Court of Sessions" was held in 1685 to try a burglary case[236] and then not again until 1693 at a "Special Session" when certain administrative orders were issued.[237] However, in 1696, the new commission of the peace was proclaimed at a "Meeting of the Justices,"[238] and the following year, also at a "meeting" a negro was sentenced to be whipped on complaint of a magistrate,[239] while a forcible entry case was settled at a "Special Sessions."[240] On October 12, 1698, another "Special Sessions" was called to deal with Gabriel Ludlow, charged with counterfeiting. The Supreme Court had adjourned and the grand jury of its own volition recommended the case to the justices of the peace. Ludlow was examined by the justices and, admitting receipt and payment of counterfeit, was ordered to make restitution to

229 *Ms. Kings Co. Ct. & Rd. Recs. 1692–1825* 6–9.
230 *Ibid.* 19.
231 *Ibid.* 46–48.
232 *Ibid.* 62.
233 *Ibid.* 63.
234 *Ibid.* 79.
235 The complaint was for beating and wounding another slave and for "Swearing Drinking ffighting Realing and hollowing all The said night to the Disturbance off his Maijtis. Subjects and against the Peace." The court examined the "actions and ffacts" and finding that Jack (the victim) "was beated" gave judgment that Jack and two of the other slaves be whipped "with thirten Laces uppon thire Nakett back" and their masters

pay fines of 20s. each for them. The master of another slave paid 6s. as his fine and the masters of the rest of the culprits, "being bounden to the sherriff by Verbaell Promising to bring thire Slaves" and failing to appear, were fined 8s. each. At this same Special Sessions an "ordinary keepster" was fined 20s. for selling liquor to slaves (*ibid.* 81, 82).
236 *Ms. Mins. NYCQS 1683/84–1694*, King v. Thomassen.
237 *Ibid.* Oct. 28, Nov. 2, 1693.
238 *Ms. Mins. NYCQS 1694–1731/32* 13, May 14, 1696. Curiously enough, this was regarded as a meeting of the whole county: "The Inhabitants of the county being present according to summons."
239 *Ibid.* 28, June 10, 1697.
240 *Ibid.* 26, Aug. 11, 1697.

the payees.[241] Two months later, proceedings to revoke a license because of disorderly conduct were had at a "Meeting of the Justices."[242]

Two Special Sessions were held in December, 1700. At one an order was made regarding an indentured servant;[243] the other was held to deal with the complaint of a lieutenant of the garrison who was having trouble getting his men to bed.[244] This Special Session after examining into the matter proceeded to deal very severely with the ladies of the town who had led the soldiers astray.

The records of the Westchester justices for the years 1710–1723 do not indicate that any style for the casual meetings was settled, for these are sometimes called a Special Sessions, a Special Court and sometimes a Meeting.[245] In Ulster County and in Dutchess the scattered records of the justices sitting together are almost invariably called "meetings" and this as late as 1755.[246] The business done is various, and we have seen no indication that the purpose for which the meeting is held had anything to do with the style. Furthermore, after 1725,

241 Ludlow prayed the court's "favorable construction" in the premises and alleged his hitherto "unstained reputation." The court appointed a goldsmith to assay the metal who reported it to be "Aspers melted down which is very little worse than the current dollars." On this finding the defendant was ordered to pay good money for the debt in lieu of the counterfeit, to give security in £50 for his good behavior for three months, to pay a £3 fine for the use of Trinity Church and to defray the costs of the Special Sessions (King v. Gabriel Ludlow, Ms. Mins. NYCQS 1694–1731/32 42 [Spec. Sess.] Oct. 12, 1698).

242 Ibid. 44, Dec. 8, 1698.

243 Ibid. 64.

244 The minute reads: "Whereas Information hath been given to this Court by Charles Oliver . . . one of the Lieuts. of his Majesty's Forces . . . that last Night several soldiers being missed out of the said Garrison he the Depon.ᵗ tooke some soldiers . . . and went in search of those missing . . . and there found two . . . soldiers in bed in . . . [Jannica Inmin's] house . . . found Elizabeth Stoaks and Isabell Aggott who . . . had been in bed also but had gott from thence into the Cellar without Shoes or Stockings and also in another bed found A man with the children of the said Jannica Inmin And in a backhouse found one of the soldiers and Katherine Didlow together the soldier being in bed and she just gott out from thence . . . and . . . the Depon't . . . went into the house of —— in Beaver Street and their [sic] found in bed to-gether one of the said soldiers and one Jane Connell in a very beastly unseemly posture . . . and Whereupon . . . [the accused women] being all Examined made frivolous Excuses to the said Information . . . Ordered . . .

that . . . [the women] being persons of Evil Name and fame and wicked lifes & Conversations be . . . tyed upon a Cart or Carts and publickly Carted throughout all the Streets of the City and that they be afterwards discharged paying fees" (ibid. 56, 57, Dec. 13, 1700).

245 Ms. Mins. Westch. Co. Sess. 1710–23 Jan. 25, 1711/12, May 5, 1712, "at a Special Court held by ye Justices"; Jan. 7, 1713/14, "Special Court of Sessions"; Apr. 13, 1714, "At a Special Court"; Aug. 22, 1714, "At a Special Sessions"; Apr. 7, 1718, "At a Justices Meeting"; Apr. 5, 1720, "At a Special Court."

246 For Ulster, cf. the Ms. Mins. Ulster Co. Sess. 1711/12–1720, where even an inquiry into a homicide is a "Meeting." Some later "Meetings" are in the collection NYSL Misc. Ms. 7460, but in one instance (1738) a "Special Session" is held on the matter of elections at Hurley. See also Ms. Files Ulster Co. Bundle C, Meeting Apr. 10, 1730; Bundle D, Meeting Jan. 3, 1738/39, June 19, 1741; Bundle F, Meeting June 22, 1728; Bundle G, Meeting Aug. 1729; Bundle H, Sept. 19, 1743; Bundle J, Oct. 9, 1744; Bundle O, Meeting Dec. 28, 1727. Cf. in Dutchess the Book of Supervisors 1718–22, which shows (p. 8) a "meeting" Jan. 15, 1717/18 but a "Special Sesions" Feb. 19, 1717/18 (p. 7). On Nov. 29, 1721, a meeting is had "Att a Sessions" (p. 47). Some later minutes of meetings are in Ms. Files Dutchess Co. 1755 Apr. 24, 1749, and Sept. 7, 1755. In Ms. Mins. Albany Co. Sess. 1717–23, "Meetings" are entered for June 20, 1719 (bastardy) June 8, 1722 (complaint of arson). In the Ms. Mins. Albany Co. Sess. 1763–82, "Special Sessions" held Oct. 22, Nov. 2, Nov. 21, 1766 on a nuisance. Another held Jan. 3, 1767 to consider an assault on an alderman.

it is unusual to find the designation "Special Session" in the country records (although the term is used in the Excise Act of 1741) and the clerk of the peace ceases to enter in his regular minutes the sittings of justices out of term time, a fact which leads us to infer that the notion of a Special Sessions as it was crystallizing in England did not gain footing in New York. On the other hand, it is obvious that barring the style of a sitting, the provincial justices were exercising most of the powers of the present-day Special Sessions and along the same procedural lines.

To understand the relation of the colonial jurisdiction to today's Special Sessions now regulated by the Code of Criminal Procedure and the Inferior Criminal Courts Act, it is necessary to point out that as a matter of state institutional development Special Sessions rests upon a statute of 1801[247] which was a substantial reenactment of certain colonial acts. To the powers granted in this act eventually there was laminated the jurisdiction once exercised by the justices of the peace, singly, by twos or by threes. We shall speak first of the basic colonial acts, since these provided the spool on which the loose and tangled threads of earlier authority were wound.

In 1732 the provincial legislature passed two statutes, one for New York City, the other for the rest of the province,[248] providing that in cases where persons were accused of misdemeanors, breaches of the peace and other criminal offenses under the degree of grand larceny, if the accused could not furnish bail within forty-eight hours, they could be tried summarily without a jury and could be sentenced to corporal punishment. In the country the justice committing the offender was authorized to certify the cause of commitment to two other justices and require them to associate themselves with him to hear and determine the case. In New York City, the mayor, deputy mayor, recorder and alderman or any three of them (the mayor, deputy or recorder to be one) were authorized to try these cases. The acts were "revived" in 1736[249] and again in 1744.[250] In 1762 the procedure was extended to persons obtaining goods under false pretences in New York City,[251] and in 1768 an additional jurisdiction over larcenies up to £5 was confirmed.[252]

---

247 1 *Revised Laws NY* (1807) c.70 §9 (NYC); §11 (rest of state). C.110 §4, however, gave the New York City Special Sessions powers of General Sessions. It is that court alone which by this statute can be regarded as a Special Sessions in the English usage.

248 2 *Col. Laws NY* 766, 745. For some reason Suffolk and Albany counties were not included. This oversight was corrected in 1736 (*ibid.* 933).

249 *Ibid.* 920, 933. This latter act gave discretion to impose a fine not exceeding forty shillings.

250 *Ibid.* 379, 377. A fine not exceeding £3 could be imposed in lieu of corporal punishment outside of New York. The acts provided for the banishment of non-residents from the county or colony.

251 4 *ibid.* 669; continued to 1780 5 *ibid.* 10.

252 4 *ibid.* 969. The act recited that whereas the Supreme Court had but four terms a year and the

The chief muniment of the jurisdiction thus created is the record of the proceedings had in New York County between the years 1733 and 1743, where there were heard, tried and summarily determined on the oaths of accusing witnesses some seventy-five cases.[253] The offenses included petit larceny, for-

"Assizes for the Delivery of Jails" were only held once a year, and whereas the act for speedy releasing of those guilty of offenses less than grand larceny was not sufficient for the purpose, it was enacted that those guilty of felonious and fraudulent taking and carrying away of personal goods or money to the value of £5 might (except where benefit of clergy was taken away) be proceeded against as offenders in petit larceny.

[253] These cases are entered in the *Mins. of the Meeting of the Mayor, Deputy Mayor and Aldermen of NYC 1733–43*, which are bound with a volume of *Ms. Mins. NYCQS 1722–42/43* (Rough) and comprise pages 328–377 of the latter. We shall refer to a few cases. James Brown, a wandering vagabond, was accused by Elizabeth Schuyler of feloniously stealing goods to the amount of 10*d*. He was "heard in his defense and having made only trifling Excuses and Evasive pretensions . . . [by sufficient witnesses] being convicted" and ordered to receive twenty-one lashes (*ibid*. 336, July 15, 1735). Philip Anderson and Elizabeth Allen were accused of stealing to the amount of 9*d*. and H. and Elizabeth Bell of receiving stolen goods. Elizabeth Allen confessed and was sentenced to twenty-one lashes but "in Regard . . . [to her] Voluntary Confession and no Other Evidence appearing against her Ordered the Punishmt be Remitted." Philip Anderson and H. Bell were found not guilty on the court's examination and although the court was of the opinion that Elizabeth Bell was guilty of receiving stolen goods knowingly, yet they "Considering all the Circumstances do remit all punishments for the Same" (*ibid*. 375, May 19, 1742). Patrick Butler, a "wandering tincker" of Westchester, was accused of uttering false counterfeit dollars and being seen with counterfeiting materials "whereby to deceive and defraud his Majesty's Liege People which might prove of dangerous Consequence to all." It was also found that Patrick Butler was a wandering vagabond of evil fame and reputation and a dangerous person who traveled under fictitious names. Although he pleaded not guilty, he was convicted by the evidence of credible witnesses, and the court "upon full proof declare him . . . to be Guilty of the accusations against him and of divers Other crimes and Misdemeanors agt. his Majesties peace & thereof to be Convict." Butler was sentenced to ¼ hour in the pillory, to carting and to 39 lashes. It was further ordered that he be conveyed from constable to constable until he be delivered to the Westchester constable, and if he were to return to the city in six months he was to be forthwith apprehended and further corporal punishment given to him in accordance with provisions of the act of as-

sembly (*ibid*. 343, 344, Mar. 3, 1736/37). Elizabeth Carlow, accused of petit larceny, was convicted by "sufficient evidence" and was ordered to be fastened to the whipping post for ¼ hour and then to depart from the city within five days on pain of suffering corporal punishment (*ibid*. 335, Apr. 29, 1735). Jane Clark, alias Robinson, was accused by John Vanderspiegel of stealing linen, and she confessed "that she was prompted by liquor and the Old Boy and prays mercy." Unfortunately, Jane Clark's excuse did not succeed in alleviating the harshness of her punishment since she was sentenced to 15 lashes on the naked back and ordered to depart the town in 48 hours with her child. Apparently this defendant was not sufficiently chastened by her punishment, since three years later she was again convicted of petit larceny, sentenced to lashing and ordered to depart the city with her child on pain of further punishment. Less than a month later Jane was in again, charged with being a "notorious wandering vagabond and notorious thief," having stolen linen to the amount of 10*d*. She was again convicted by "sufficient proof and evidences" and ordered to be fastened to the tail of a cart, stripped to the waist, and drawn through public places. She was to receive lashes at each public place but the lashes were not to exceed 31. She was then to be imprisoned for a week at the end of which time she was to receive the same punishment again, and then imprisoned for another week when she was again to receive a like punishment. Twenty-four hours after her last punishment she was ordered to depart the colony. A memorandum entry appears in the minutes stating that "there was also found of Jane one dozen knives and forks and linen, etc. supposed to be stolen." The exemplary punishments meted out to Jane did not, however, discourage her for, two years later, she was again brought in for petit larceny and sentenced to 31 lashes and, a week later, 31 more (*ibid*. 338, 359, 360, 368, Aug. 14, 1735, Aug. 24, Sept. 13, 1738, Aug. 28, 1740).

William Dickson, accused of petit larceny, was convicted "by sufficient Proof, as by his own tacit confession." He was sentenced to 35 lashes (*ibid*. 339, Oct. 21, 1735). Samuel Flood of Massachusetts was "accused for . . . attempt to . . . seduce Mr John Hastier . . . to make and counterfeit . . . Bills [of] Massachusetts Bay all which . . . Hastier Informed a Magistrate of & caused the said Samuel Flood to be apprehended, to Which accusation the said Samuel Flood pleaded Guilty and said he was now sensible of his Error and hoped God would give him more Grace for the future." Flood was convicted of the crime and misdemeanor

gery, assault and battery, passing counterfeit and receiving stolen goods. The court was held under the style "Meeting of the Mayor, Deputy Mayor and Aldermen of New York City." No later minutes for the city have been found and we do not know, therefore, whether or not there was any subsequent change in name.

With one exception, which will be considered in a moment, no records of the exercise of this jurisdiction in the country have been found. The considerable files still preserved in Dutchess and Ulster counties have yielded no minutes and we must suppose that for record purposes the jurisdiction was on the same footing as the summary proceedings before a single justice. This supposition finds some support in the exception just spoken of, which is also a piece of evidence bearing on the post-Revolutionary designation of the jurisdiction —the book kept for the years 1774–1779 by Daniel Howel, justice of the peace in Suffolk County. This volume contains the cases, both civil and criminal, in which Howel held court, and it is, we think, significant that the cases where he was competent to sit alone are entered "At a courte held before me . . ." or "At a courte before Daniel Howel," but the cases heard pursuant to the less-than-grand larceny statute are entered "At a Court of Special Sessions."[254] Possibly this had become by the time of the Revolution the technical style for such courts elsewhere in the province, and the statute of 1801 merely recognized the general state of affairs when it baptized the court for the trial of cases less than grand larceny.

The colonial acts of 1732 were motivated by the necessity of dealing sternly with the serious problem of vagrancy, and of sparing the local rate payers the cost of supporting a vagrant in custody while he awaited General Sessions, or the family of the petty offender without means. The transplanted Englishmen entertained no sentimental feelings with regard to persons without substance who were of no potential value to the community and elected to treat those who transgressed on a sort of nuisance theory. Trial by jury was eliminated partly because it was traditional for petty crime to be handled summarily and partly because the right to jury trial was still viewed as a privilege of free men of reputation and property, at least to the amount of a recognizance to answer

by his own confession and full proof, was sentenced to 39 lashes, and ordered to depart the province in 48 hours on pain of like punishment (*ibid.* 362, May 3, 1739). Catherine Morely was accused of assaulting and beating Mary Rabbit and stealing her child, and carrying it away with her to go begging. For this offense Catherine received 31 lashes (*ibid.*

357, Apr. 11, 1738). William Young, accused of petit larceny, pleaded guilty and was sentenced to receive 39 lashes once a week for three weeks (*ibid.* 361, Nov. 21, 1738).

[254] *Daniel Howels Book of Recs.* (Pennypacker Coll., Easthampton Library).

—usually in £20, with two sureties good for the same amount. We shall have more to say about this jurisdiction in Chapter X.

The dispositions with regard to the trial of slaves, that somewhat resemble the jurisdiction created in 1732, rest on a different footing. Here we find, at first, trial in the regular courts or summarily at "Special Courts."[255] But in 1708, by act of assembly, trials of slaves accused of murder, homicide or of conspiring to kill were ordered to be held by three or more justices of peace (one of whom was to be of the quorum) who could hear and determine such cases and give judgment of death.[256] As the slaves were mere chattels there was no question of any right to indictment or jury trial. Furthermore, the New Yorkers were patently nervous about their negro and Indian chattels, as witness the very considerable bulk of local ordinances regarding their entertainment or the mere meeting together of these unfortunates. From every point of view it was deemed desirable that proceedings on crimes committed by them be dispatched immediately and summarily.

The first meeting under this statute was held in New York City under the style of "Att a Court for the Tryal of Slaves."[257] Four years later, when the city was trembling at the news of a great conspiracy, a protracted session was had in April and May, 1712, when over forty slaves were tried for murder and conspiring against their masters. Allen Jarrat's slave, Claus, being found guilty, was ordered "to be broke upon a wheel and so to continue languishing until he is dead and his head and quarters to be at the Queen's disposal,"[258] while Adrian Hoghlandt's slave, Robin, more fortunate, was mercifully sentenced "to be hung in chains alive and so continue from lack of any sustainance until he be dead."[259] Abraham Provoost's slave, Quaco, was sentenced "to be burnt with fire until he be dead and consumed,"[260] while Nicholas Roosevelt's slave, Tom, and Sheppard's slave, Furnis, were sentenced "to be burned with fire (Tom gradually to continue in torment for eight or ten hours) and to continue in fire until they be consumed to ashes."[261] Fifteen other slaves were sentenced to be hanged for murder[262] while two or more were hanged as "ac-

---

[255] For example in Ulster, cf. Jan. 7, 8, 1695/96. Tham, a negro, was tried at a special court held by seven justices (*Ms. Mins. Ulster Co. Sess. 1693–98*); in New York City Prince, a negro, was tried and ordered whipped at a meeting Aug. 20, 1696 (*Ms. Mins. NYCQS 1694–1731/32* 15; *Mins. SCJ 1693–1701* 42, 43).

[256] Or before any court of Oyer and Terminer or General Gaol Delivery and should be put to death by judgment of the justices (1 *Col. Laws NY* 631).

[257] *Ms. Mins. NYCQS 1694–1731/32* 153, Dec. 8, 1708.

[258] *Ms. Mins. NYCQS 1705/06–1714/15* 76, 78, Apr. 11, 1712.

[259] *Ibid.* 77, Apr. 11, 1712.

[260] *Ibid.*

[261] *Ibid.* 78, 82, 83, Apr. 12, 14, 15, 1712.

[262] The slaves were Peter Fauconnier's slave, Sam; Isaac Gouverneur's Kitto, Mrs. Norwood's Caesar, John Barberie's Mingo, Rip Van Dam's

cessarys before the fact for murder"[263] and the rest were discharged being found not guilty.[264]

The act of assembly of 1708 was silent on a trial by a jury in slave cases; nevertheless we note in the slave trials of 1712 that all of the conspirators were tried by such a jury. Probably as a result of this scare just related, another act of assembly was passed on December 10, 1712,[265] which provided that certain offenses by slaves including murder, homicide (except by misadventure), arson, rape, mayhem, attempts or conspiracy to commit these crimes upon free persons, as well as murder of slaves should be tried before three or more justices of the peace (one of whom was of the quorum) in conjunction with five of the principal freeholders and without a grand jury or before any Court of Oyer and Terminer or General Gaol Delivery. The act is badly drawn but it did not intend a trial by jury as a rule since it was especially stipulated that jury trial could be had at the request of a master of a slave if he would pay the costs.

Although courts held pursuant to this act and its successors, at which were heard, tried and determined murders, rapes, larcenies and minor offenses committed by slaves,[266] resemble Special Sessions, under the less-than-grand-lar-

---

Quais and Quaco, John Dehoneur's Tom, Andrew Huckey's Hannibal, John Cure's Toby, Peter Morin's Caesar, Richard Ray's Titus, David Lyell's Tom, Will Walton's Coffee, Walter Thong's Quaco, Stephen Pell's Sarah (*ibid.* 76–79, 81–89, 95–98, Apr. 11, 12, 14–19, May 6, 27, 1712).
[263] Queen v. Abigail and Tom (*ibid.* 97), May 27, 1712.
[264] *Ibid.* 76–89, 95–99, Apr. 11–19, May 6, 27, 30. See also *Ms. Mins. NYCQS 1694–1731/32* 212–231. In the latter is a long memorandum entry (pp. 229–231, June 10, 1712) which recites that "at a Court held for the tryal of Negro and Indian slaves . . . by vertue of . . . An Act for preventing the Conspiracy of Slaves by the Oath of twelve Jurors it is presented that [Claus, Robin, Quaco and Sam] . . . did make an assault . . . and that . . . Robin with . . . a Dagger . . . in the back Voluntarily Trayterously and feloniously and of his Malice aforethought . . . did give . . . to Adrian Hoghlandt a certain Mortal wound."
[265] 1 *Col. Laws NY* 761. For a proceeding under this act cf. the prosecution of Abraham Kip's negress at a Meeting June 8, 1722 (*Ms. Mins. Albany Co. Sess. 1717–23*). The summons to the freeholders is there set forth. The Act of 1712 was repealed by the Act of Oct. 29, 1730 (2 *ibid.* 679–687) to which new matter was added. The provision for the special court was retained. An interesting sidelight on the enforcement of the Act of 1730 against negro slaves is furnished in an act for building the

Ulster County courthouse and jail, and defraying the expense of executing a negro, Oct. 14, 1732 (*ibid.* 763): "And Whereas . . . a negroe man Called Jack being convicted of burning a barne and a Barrack with wheat . . . was Condemned to be burnt . . . but the Justices not being able to procure an Executioner to performe the sentence at the rate limited in an Act . . . for Preventing . . . the Conspiracy . . . of Negroes . . . were obliged . . . to hire one at a much great price . . . Be it Enacted . . . that the Supervizors shall . . . Levy . . . such . . . mony as has been Actually payd by the said Justices. . . ."
Other acts regulating slaves were an Act for Regulating of Slaves, Nov. 27, 1702 (1 *ibid.* 519); an Act to Continue the Regulation of slaves and to Subject such Persons as Trade with them to a Presentment and Prosecution, June 17, 1726 (2 *ibid.* 310); two acts of Aug. 4, 1705 and May 14, 1745, to prevent slaves from running away to Canada (1 *ibid.* 582, 3 *ibid.* 448); and an act of Mar. 8, 1773, which provided that if any owner of a slave was convicted before "two Magistrates" on the oath of an informer of allowing his slave to go begging, such master should forfeit £10, half to be paid to the informer and half to the poor (5 *ibid.* 533).
[266] For example, under the Act of 1730 a meeting of the chief justice, justices of the peace and five freeholders was held on July 20, 1738, for the trial of Jannean, a negro slave accused of rape. The following oath was administered to the freeholders:

ceny acts of 1732, the association of five freeholders makes them a court *sui generis*. The sittings pursuant to the slave conspiracy legislation are held under different styles. In New York City at the trial of *King* v. *Cato*[267] accused of attempted rape in January, 1733/34, the court which was convened was called a "Meeting of the Justices for the Conservation of the Peace—pursuant to . . . an Act of General Assembly." In Dutchess a few years before it was styled "At a Court of three Justices of the Peace aided with five freeholders . . ."[268] but later in that county and in Ulster the designation "Meeting" is used.[269]

The most terrible of all the witchhunts of criminous slaves, the so-called plot of 1741, was not held under the provision of the Conspiracy Act, but, as indicated, the prosecutions were conducted in the Supreme Court. The reason

"You Shall well and truly try and Judge According to evidence if . . . Jannean . . . be Guilty of the Crimes whereof he is accused or Not Guilty So help You God." William Sharpas, the town clerk, was appointed prosecutor and he exhibited an accusation in writing giving the justices and freeholders "here to understand and be Informed that . . . [the defendant] being Moved and seduced by the Instigation of the Devil . . . in and upon Ann Carr . . . with force and Arms Violently did attempt to Commit A Rape . . . against the form of an Act of General Assembly . . . and against the Peace of . . . the King his Crown and dignity." Jannean pleaded not guilty, and several witnesses having been examined and the defendant having nothing more to say than absolutely denying all the facts and offering nothing in his defense, the justices "do declare and Pronounce, that . . . Jannean is not Guilty . . . of attempting . . . Rape . . . [but] guilty of Assaulting [and battery]." The slave was fastened to a cart's tail and given 39 lashes with a cowskin whip at three different times (*Ms. Mins. NYCQS 1722–1742/43* [Rough] 348–350).
   [267] On Jan. 21, 1733/34, a warrant was issued to apprehend him (text *infra* 418 n. 192). Cato was arrested by virtue of this warrant and on Jan. 22, 1733/34, a *mittimus* was issued in the following words: "City of New York, ss: Robert Lurting Esq. Mayor . . . To the Keeper of . . . Gaol . . . Greeting. By Vertue of An Act [1730] . . . I send you herewithal the body of Cato . . . brought before me this present day and Charged with attempting to Committ a Rape upon . . . Susannah Sylvester . . . (which crime upon conviction is capital) hereby Straightly charging & Commanding you in his Majesties Name to Receive the said Cato into your Custody, and him Safely to keep in . . . Gaol until he Shall thence be delivered by due Course of Law and hereof fail not at Your Perill." Having safely committed Cato to jail, the Mayor issued his "Certificate" to three other justices, and

this certificate was evidently a writ of association since it was couched in the following words: "City of New York ss: Robert Lurting Esq. Mayor . . . To [3 named justices of peace of New York City] . . . By Vertue of an Act of General Assembly . . . I do hereby Certifie unto you that . . . Cato . . . was brought before me and Charged . . . [with attempted rape] which Cato I have Committed to the Common Gaol, and therefore hereby Require you to Associate yourselves with me . . . [on Jan. 23, 1733/34] in Order to proceed on the Tryal of the said . . . Slave for the Offence aforesaid, Dated in New York the 22d. January. . . ."
   On January 23, at a "Meeting of the Justices for the conservation of the Peace . . . Pursuant to the Directions of an Act of General Assembly," Chief Justice De Lancey and Frederick Phillipse, second judge of the Supreme Court, met with the Mayor and Deputy Mayor as justices of the quorum, to whom were associated two other justices of the peace and "the Justices aforesaid Issued their summons to . . . five of the Principal Freeholders . . . to meet them . . . to hear and determine if . . . Cato be Guilty of the Offense Aforesaid. . . ." The justices then issued summons to five freeholders (cf. *infra* 473 n. 390). The culprit was set at the bar by the jailer, and the justices and freeholders appointed an attorney to prosecute Cato, and he presented an "Accusation in writing." Unfortunately a page of the Minute Book is missing, but we assume from a fragment of an order for payment to the officers of the court by the justices of May 10, 1734, that Cato was convicted and sentenced (*Ms. Mins. NYCQS 1722–1742/43* [Rough] 329–334).
   [268] *Ms. Mins. Dutchess Co. Sess.* Liber A, June 10, 1735.
   [269] *Ms. Files Dutchess Co. 1755* Meeting Apr. 24, 1749; Meeting Sept. 17, 1755. *Ms. Files Ulster Co.* Bundle O, Meeting June 19–30, 1741; Bundle F, Meeting June 22, 1728.

for this was partly the peculiar way in which the "plot" unfolded and a panic of fear gripped the city and even the whole province.[270]

The episode began as a routine prosecution in New York City of a burglary in which a negro was implicated. About this time some fires occurred, and upon investigation testimony was given that seemed to indicate a widespread plot to murder the white population and destroy the city. A condition of such hysteria was presently aroused that large numbers of people deserted the town. There were wholesale arrests including a number of white persons with the inevitable papist villain of the period. As we have seen, the Supreme Court judges took the advice of leading counsel in the city and determined, despite the provincial act for the trial of negroes, since white persons were confederated with the blacks and since the affair seemed a conspiracy of deeper design than negroes were capable of contriving, that it was advisable for jurisdiction to be assumed by the Supreme Court.[271] A lengthy account of the trials was written by the gullible puisne judge of the Supreme Court, Daniel Horsmanden, the chief virtue of which is that it furnishes us with considerable data regarding the procedure at the time.

Double and Single Justice

We come at length to consider the incidents of jurisdiction exercised by the justices of peace out of Sessions in pursuance of their authority as conservators of the peace, where they proceeded not as a Sessions but by virtue of the powers delegated to them individually and where, depending upon the terms of statute, they performed alone or jointly. For the most part these duties, where judicial, were discharged in a summary way; that is to say, upon complaint or information, process issued, and the cause was tried before one or more justices without a jury, the testimony of two or even one witness being sufficient to sustain a conviction. The two most important exceptions to the usual *modus judicandi* were the cases of riot and forcible entry, a jurisdiction sufficiently complicated to need some explanation.

The powers of the justices of the peace in riots have a hoary statutory lineage running back to the reign of Edward III[272] and are closely related to those respecting forcible entry.[273] Both are of a piece with the legislation respecting

[270] Horsmanden, *The NY Conspiracy* (1810 ed.) *passim*.
[271] *Ibid.* 41.
[272] 34 Edw. III c.1.

[273] The distinctions lie chiefly in the fact that a forcible entry could be effected by one man, and only one justice need make the record on which the offender was convicted and held for fine. Cf. Lam-

livery, maintenance and unlawful assembly designed to aid in the conservation of the peace.[274] The authority exercised in New York was assumed on the basis of the ancient Acts of Parliament, for in the provincial records the most basic of all the acts, the statute of 13 Henry IV c.7, is in fact recited. The colonial officials treated the English statutory precedents as if they were the equivalent of the common law precedent which they were free to imitate.[275]

It is unnecessary to enter into the ramifications of the learning on riot and the intricacies of the various statutory provisions, since the New York justices saw fit to accept only some of the main features of English practice. Most important was the so-called record upon view and the inquest of riot. As to the former the statutes empowered two justices with the sheriff to proceed to the fracas and make a record of the riot upon view, to convict summarily on the basis thereof and to incarcerate the offenders until they made fine and ransom. If the rioters had dispersed, the record was sent to King's Bench for process to issue. In the event that the sheriff was not present, and but a single justice appeared, this summary proceeding could not be had. The single justice could only attempt to disperse the rioters, cause fresh suit to be made and an inquest to be had by a jury. This inquest was in the nature of an inquest of office, a mere determination of the circumstances. Upon the basis of this the justices in Sessions could then issue process and proceed to fine the offenders.

The earliest evidence of the use of riot powers in New York dates from the year 1696 and it is apparent that the justices did not comprehend the distinction between the record made upon view and the inquest proceedings. The provincial record opens in accordance with forms of a record upon view in Lambard and Dalton,[276] but as it proceeds the relation indicates an inquiry by the justices upon which the defendants were fined.[277]

---

bard, *Eirenarcha* (1614) 136 *et seq.;* 5 Rich. II St. 1 c.7; 15 Rich. II c.2; 8 Hy. VI c.9; 1 Hawkins, *Pleas of the Crown* c.64, for the later statutes. The relation is clearly indicated in the statute 13 Hy. IV c.7 which prescribes the conviction on the record as in the statute of forcible entries.

[274] 2 Holdsworth, *Hist. Eng. Law* 452, 453.

[275] Cf. the report of Attorney General Smith on the Livingston Manor riots (1752): ". . . the Statutes of England being duly put in Execution will sufficiently punish the offenders, and afford a speedy Relief to the Petitioner and give him an adequate Remedy in a way strictly conformable to Law" (3 *Doc. Hist. NY* 438).

[276] Lambard, *Eirenarcha* (1614) 320; Dalton, *Countrey Justice* (1677) 525.

[277] "Kings County ss: Memorandum that . . . we Joseph Hegeman and Henry ffilkin two of the Jus-

tices of the peace . . . and Quorum for Kings . . . for the keeping of the peace . . . assigned as alsoe to inquire of heare and determin ffellonyes trepases Riotts and other misdemeanours And Jeremiah Stillwell Esqr. high sherriff . . . (upon the heavy Complaint and humble petition & request of Barne ffullman of fflatbush . . . keeper of the King's gaole and Court house . . . that on . . . [Sept. 14 at 8 P.M.] John Rapalje I. Remsen J. Vannesten J. Danielse . . . [and 9 others named] with force and armes, viz. with swords guns and pistolls Came into the Kings Courthouse . . . and then and there riotously routously and unlawfully being gathered . . . the Kings Armes . . . hanging up in said Courthouse did shoott burne disfigure and deface Contrary to their loyalty . . . and to the great dishonour and affront to his . . . Majesty his Crown and dignity etc. and severall . . . harmes to

Considering the frequency and persistence of the riots and unlawful assemblages during the eighteenth century, the instances of summary conviction on a riot record are surprisingly few. For the most part the cases were tried on inquisitions delivered into the Supreme Court[278] or were handled by transfer at Circuit.[279] It seems to us that this was the counsel of caution in dealing with a robust and turbulent population, or, as the justices of Queens County wrote to Governor Hunter in 1719 justifying their action in imposing fines after the church riots: "The petitioners might have been ffined on the View of the Justices, But in favor to them, and that they might have no manner of reason to Complain of any hasty, or otherwise severe way of proceeding; This of doing it by a Jury was made use of."[280]

There was so obvious a savagery about many of the riots of which accounts are preserved that attempts to proceed summarily would only have invited more trouble. The English legislation dated from a time when the justices were feudal lords who could ride to an outbreak with their men-at-arms and have some hope of quelling the disturbance. It was quite a different thing to expect some country squire or storekeeper to brave a brawling mob. Curiously

the people . . . there did to the great breach of . . . peace, the terror of his people, and against the form of the statute of Henry the fourth . . . in the 13th yeare of his Reigne and other statutes in such case made and provided) Came thereupon in our owne proper persons to the said Courthouse, and then and there made enquiry of the truth of the said Riott and high misdemeanoer by the oaths of three evidences, & found by the oaths of said evidences . . . [the 13 defendants] guilty of the said riott breach of the peace & high misdemeanor as aforesd. and therefore we . . . [2 justices of the peace and sheriff] . . . the . . . [said defendants] have caused to be arrested and Committed to the Common gaole of the County . . . being Convicted by our Record by their owne Confession and the testimony . . . aforesaid . . . there to remaine till they . . . each . . . have paid a fine to . . . the King, but the said . . . [13] by their humble petition . . . and begging pardon . . . we the said Justices have caused them to be dismissed . . . each for a fine to his Majesty with all Costs and charges expended about the enquiry and suppressing said riott according to their demerritts and greatness of their Crimes as ffolloweth, viz. . . . [2 to pay 20s. each fine and 40s. each costs and damages; 2 fined each 10s. and 30s. costs; 9 fined each 6s. and 12s. costs] In Witness Whereof to this our present Record we have put to our hands and seales the day and yeare first above written" (*Ms. Kings Co. Ct. & Rd. Recs. 1692–1825* Riot Record, 38, 39, Sept. 18, 1696).

In the New York City Quarter Sessions minutes for August 20, 1696, is what appears to be a Spe-

cial Sessions or riot justice's entry in the case of King ex rel. William Morrett, Mayor, v. Prince and other negroes. This record was in the following form: "William Morrett Esq. Mayor . . . of his own knowledge Informed this Board that last Night . . . severall Negro slaves were making a great Noise and disturbance in the street near his dwelling house and were Uttering several Oaths and Execrations whereupon the said Mayor went out and Ordered them to disperse and goe home . . . which they Refused . . . and thereupon he Offered to strike some of them and tooke them into Custody upon which a Negro man slave Named Prince assaulted the . . . Mayor upon the face but some Persons . . . seized the said Negro . . . and he was Committed to Gaol and Upon our Examination of the fact and the pernicious and Evil Example thereof. Wee doe Order that the said Negro man slave . . . Prince be by the publick Whipper forthwith Carryed to the publick whipping post . . . and there to be stripped . . . from the middle upwards and then there be tyed to the tale of A Carte and being soe stripped and tyed shall be drawn round this City . . . and at the Corner of Every street shall Receive Eleven lashes upon his body for the said Misdemeanor" (*Ms. Mins. NYCQS 1694–1731/32* 15).

[278] Apparently, where objection was had to the inquisition of riot found by the justices of the peace, the inquisitions were delivered into the Supreme Court and judgment was pronounced or the inquisition was quashed.

[279] *Infra* 190 *et seq.*

[280] 3 *Doc. Hist. NY* 174.

enough there are occasional references in New York to what in the vernacular is described as "reading the riot act."[281] But this seems to have been merely a precaution and not what it was in England—a necessary condition to a prosecution of the rioters as felons.[282]

The related forcible entry legislation was directed chiefly at violent disseisins and was bifurcate, that is to say, it set up a machinery for punishing riot and a procedure for restoration of the disseisee. A single justice upon notice of a violent entry, holding or detainer was empowered to proceed to the premises, arrest the offenders if the force continued and make a record of the force upon view. This record would be a sufficient conviction on the basis of which the offenders could be imprisoned and make fine. The justice was also supposed to make inquiry by a sufficient jury of the forcible entry, for it was only upon such inquest that restitution could be made.

The earliest record of forcible entry proceedings in New York appears to be an inquiry made in Westchester County on July 31, 1688, before two justices of the peace and the high sheriff.[283] The record consists of the inquiry, the precept and the testimony. The judgment does not indicate what was done to the defendants or that an order of restitution was made.

Some years later (1697) in New York County, on the sworn complaint of

[281] 4 Doc. Hist. NY 548 (1775).

[282] By 1 Geo. I c.5, if proclamation to disperse was made and the rioters to the number of twelve or more did not do so, they could be tried as felons. We have seen no evidence of any attempt to treat the statute 1 Geo. I c.5 as in force. It did not extend to the plantations. The proceedings occasioned by the riots in the Livingston Manor indicate that the colonial authorities resorted to the device of a governor's proclamation as a means of intimidation and conservation of the peace (3 Doc. Hist. NY 449, 462, 472, 490, 493, 494).

It should be noted that the procedure of "reading the riot act" is much older than 1 Geo. I c.5. This procedure had been authorized by a statute 3 and 4 Edw. VI c.5 which had made it high treason for twelve or more persons assembled to attempt to kill or imprison the King's council or to alter any laws and to continue together after command by a justice to return, and made it felony when the design was for destruction of property or the reduction of rent, etc. The Act of 1 Mary c.12 had repealed this statute and had uniformly made the failure to disperse a felony. This act was continued by 1 Eliz. c.16 for the life of the Queen and until the end of the succeeding session of Parliament. Lambard, Eirenarcha (1614) 183, gives the form of the proclamation which is substantially identical with the form in 1 Geo. I c.5.

[283] Ms. Deeds Westch. Co. Liber C, 265:
"WESTCHESTER COUNTY, July 31th 1688 and in the fourth year of the reigne of James the Second of England Kinge &c. Present then upon enquirey of a ryott and force entry &c., lately made in said County; James Palmer, Esqre. Wm. Richardson, Esqre. both Justices of the Peace in Comm. & Benjamin Collier Esqe. High Sherrife of said County with his Under Sherrife &c. There being returned 24 good & lawfull men of the Baylywick by said Sherrife these wher emparnelled & sworne by ye names of which Jurors being sworn by the said Justices to inquire for our Souerigne Lord the King according to Evedences of R. Ryott & force entry & lately made in said County which evidences being duly examined & sworne to gaither with the Complaint warrants & all other papers relateing thereunto wite ye laws & statutes in that case made. The charge was given ye jury the Justices adjurned for two houres being returned in the afternoone the Jury come in and being all called over answering to their names being all agreed of their verdict gave it thuss in by their foreman redd. The Jury being 24 men finds the cause yt was brought before them to be a ryott & force entry made in said County the 16th Instant by Ryor Michaile, Henrick Heirses and other &c. upon and at the houses of Elijah Barton, Robert Barton and Edward Hubbard, within said County &c."

Penelope Attkins against one Fransa and others for forcible entry and detainer, the justices and jurymen went to the scene and, on Fransa's second refusal to relinquish possession, order was made for the sheriff and constable to break down the door. When this was done in the presence of the justices the complainant was restored to possession and the defendant fined forty shillings.[284]

Neither the Westchester record nor that in the Attkins case conforms to the precedents of the English form books, and it appears that although the provincial justices were familiar with the rules of the riot and forcible entry proceedings (as later inquests indicate)[285] they felt free to make their own variations in despite of the explicit distinctions and rules of the textbooks. The manner in which the jury was associated in Mrs. Attkins' case appears to have been one persistent variant. As late as 1754, in Albany County, the inquest jury was thus used as moral backing in a summary proceeding. The matter is related in the complaint of one Sybilla Berckenmyer:

> The complaint of Mrs. . . . Sybilla Berckenmyer . . . that she has lived in the Church House . . . Lutheran . . . at Loonenburgh and held the peacable possession . . . 26 years and that in December . . . some . . . did with force and violence Break Open the said House carried out her goods Laid them on the Street . . . and put another person in the said house which force was removed by two Justices with a Jury of Enquiry. The Rioters were indicted by the Grand Jury and afterwards cleared by the court after that Jacob Frees and Johannis

[284] "Penelope Attkins Widdow . . . hath Complained to the King's Justices that Hendrick Fransa with several Other Evil Doers . . . did with force and Arms break Open and forcibly Enter into a Certain dwelling house of . . . the Complainant . . . and doth with Armed force detain the same against the peace . . . Whereupon . . . Penelope Attkins humbly prayeth the assistance of the King's Justices . . . and that she be restored to the Possession of the said Tenement. Whereupon the Justices directed a Writt to the Sheriff . . . to return twenty four Freeholders who have Each fourty shillings p. Annum, etc. . . . And the said Penelope Attkins being sworn did declare . . . [that the defendants] did break open the door . . . and with force and Arms did Enter therein and with armed force did turn her out . . . and did strike and beat [her] . . . and Hendrick Fransa did . . . say he would kill any person that Came to the door. Whereupon the . . . Justices and Jury went to the place . . . and did finde the said Hendrick . . . with force and Arms in the said house, and the said Hendrick . . . was Ordered by the said Justices to Open the Doors . . . and lett them in which he Refused upon which the Inquest did Re-

turn . . . that the said Hendrick . . . did . . . Enter . . . and with power and Armed force did hold out the said Penelope . . . until the taking the inquisition. . . . [Defendant was again ordered to come out and again he refused]. . . . Whereupon the Justices gave Order to the Sheriff and Constable to break Open the Door and Restitution be made in their presence . . . [so done] and the said Justices made Restitution and put her into quiet possession . . . and doe fine the said Hendrick Fransa fourty shillings . . . and . . . a Mittmus to be directed to the Sheriff to keep him in . . . Gaol till he shall pay the said fine or give sufficient surety for itt and . . . pay the Costs Expended by . . . Penelope . . . in the Recovery of her possession" ("Att a Special Sessions of the Peace," May 11, 1697, *Ms. Mins. NYCQS 1694–1731/32* 26, 27). In *Ms. Deeds Queens Co.* Liber A, 83 is a hearing at Special Sessions on a forcible entry where the record was produced, Nov. 4, 1695. Cf. also 40 *NY Col. Mss.* 86–89.

[285] Cf., for example, King v. Tackert, 1763 (*Ms. Files Ulster Co.* Bundle K); Hunt v. Jonathan Hoegg (*Ms. Files Dutchess Co.* 1740–50 IV, Inquest July 25, 1748).

Provoost Esqr. who had been by the first riotous Entry had caused a Jury to be summoned and had a Trial among them without giving me any timely notice Tried an action of Title Put me and my goods out of the house and another person in possession thereof Witness my hand January 29, 1754.[286]

The forcible entry statutes seem a strange importation into a new country with enormous reaches of unsettled territory. But cleared land was prized, and even the grantees of whole sections of virgin forest were unsympathetic to squatters. When the agrarian and border troubles broke out in the 'fifties with riotous incursions upon farms, the forcible entry procedure came into its own and there was a sharp increase in its use, especially in Dutchess County. There were also numerous indictments preferred and tried in General Sessions.[287]

In none of the other proceedings out of Sessions where one, two or three justices were competent, was there any use of a jury. The colonists, in spite of their vociferous advocacy of jury trial, seem to have accepted without noticeable resistance the English way of doing things. When the justices of the peace were first commissioned the town courts absorbed most of the petty criminal business. There is little early evidence of independent meetings of justices,[288] but the Sessions records show that the Court referred matters to one or two justices.[289] Thus the inhabitants gradually were conditioned to the government by magistrates, so that when the town courts were abolished there does not appear to have been much objection to the loss of judicial authority by the locally elected officers.

The business of statutory assignment of functions to two justices of the peace had begun under Dongan,[290] and it was resumed after the Revolution of 1688.[291] As far as the justices themselves were concerned, the stipulations of the statutes appear to have been simply the fixing of a minimum number of

---

[286] J. T. Kempe Lawsuits A–B. The entry made by the justices of the peace after Mrs. Berckenmyer's complaint against the previous riot justices' finding was as follows: "Whereupon Wee went to the said House [Feb. 11] wherein we found Anna . . . Knoll and . . . family, Wee required her (her husband . . . not at home) to remove out of the house by the next day . . . and restore possession to . . . Sybilla Berckenmyer . . . which she refused, upon that we went from thence and sent for Jacob Freese Esqr. who . . . refused to [be our assistant] . . . then we commanded him in the King's name to be there next day. [Went with assistance and two constables but not Freese. Then broke in] and restored the possession thereof to . . . Sybilla Berckenmyer on the 12th February 1754 Henry Van Rensselaer, Jur. Abraham Fonda, Jur." (ibid.).

[287] Thus at the October 1751 Sessions seven indictments were preferred. Cf. the rough minutes in Ms. Files Dutchess Co. 1741–50.
[288] Cf. the warrant in Ms. Gravesend Town Recs. Liber IV, 32 (1671) which issued in the name of three justices and recites a meeting where a prisoner was examined.
[289] Ms. Kings Co. Ct. & Rd. Recs. 1668–1766 56 (1670) "abuses" to be settled by one J.P.; 75 (1675) a fine to be mitigated before 2 J.P.'s; 255 (1683) threats to be examined by one J.P. Of course the reference of matters to constables and overseers was the equivalent of considerable "out of sessions" jurisdiction.
[290] 1 Col. Laws NY 147, 152.
[291] The earliest statute is in 1691, 1 ibid. 261.

justices for purposes of acting. There are not a great number of records of these meetings, but it is clear from an exceptionally detailed minute book of Ulster County[292] that as many as ten or twelve justices would assemble and deal with matter for which two or three acting together were competent.[293] The lack of any settled rule is illustrated by a pair of early cases in Kings County. In one case (1693) four justices committed a defendant "for diverse scandalous and abusive words" against the justices of the peace. The defendant submitted and was discharged upon payment of fees and on giving surety for his good behavior until the next Court of Sessions.[294] In the other case, only a few weeks later, an accused was examined by three justices for raising "dissention, strife and a mutiny," and committed until he should post bond for his good behavior and appearance at Sessions.[295]

It would be tedious to enumerate the long array of provincial statutes which empowered the justices to perform various duties out of Sessions by threes or twos, but it may be remarked that in general the provincial statutes seem to have preferred the duo over the trio.[296] And so to two justices (one being of the quorum) wide authority was conveyed to proceed, often summarily, on the sworn informations of accusing witnesses or on the knowledge of the justices themselves. A sampling of the accretions by statute will indicate the diversity of matter dealt with.[297] Thus two justices of the peace were authorized to examine cases of vagrants and vagabonds; if they found that such persons would become a charge on the parish, they were authorized to order that the vagrants be conveyed from constable to constable to their original place of settlement; if the vagabond returned, the constable was to see to it that the vagrant was lashed.[298] Any householder harboring a suspected vagrant for more than three days was to post bond to save the parish harmless or to go to jail until he did.[299] Those who should stop roads in Dutchess County would forfeit £40 before two justices of peace on the oath of two witnesses.[300] Suspected gamblers were to be summoned before two justices of the peace and if they could not clear

---

[292] *Ms. Mins. Ulster Co. Sess. 1711/12–1720.*

[293] The following matters were dealt with at Ulster meetings: inquiry into a death by misadventure; bastardy; theft by negroes, larceny, common disturbance, harboring negroes, burglary by negroes, quarrelling, shooting hogs, cutting fences, racing horses, rescue.

[294] King v. John Bibou (*Ms. Kings Co. Ct. & Rd. Recs. 1692–1825* 19, Oct. 11, 1693).

[295] King v. Hendrick Cloysse Yechte (*ibid.* 20, Oct. 28, 1693).

[296] For a three justice jurisdiction, cf. the act (1701) re condemnation for roads (1 *Col. Laws*

NY 471) and the Private Lotteries Act (5 *ibid.* 351).

[297] Since the statutes are readily available we have not attempted to give an exhaustive chronological account of additions. No principle of growth is involved.

[298] 2 *Col. Laws NY* 56, 210, and 5 *ibid.* 513, which latter act also provides for an appeal from the order of the two justices of the peace to General or Quarter Sessions.

[299] 2 *ibid.* 57.

[300] 2 *ibid.* 967, 969.

themselves they were obliged to post bond for twelve months or go to jail. If the gamblers violated the surety for good behavior by gambling involving over 20*s.*, the surety was forfeited.[301] Failure of the inhabitants of Albany to repair their fences involved a forfeiture leviable by the constable and if this were not paid in fourteen days, or if the fences were not mended, then on complaint to two justices of the peace the offenders were to go to jail until the forfeiture was paid.[302] Alehouse keepers in New York City who should give seamen credit beyond 6*s.* were to lose the amount in excess, and if a clerk issued a writ against seamen so credited he would forfeit £5 before two justices of the peace, half of which penalty was to go to the poor and half to the informer.[303] Those who should furnish rum to Indians in Albany and be convicted on the oath of one Christian or the affirmation of one Indian would forfeit £3 before two justices of the peace and half the penalty should go to the informer and half to the County of Albany.[304] Constables of New York City who failed to collect or to account for poor relief money should forfeit such money before the mayor or recorder and one alderman proceeding in a summary way, and if the constable had no goods which could be levied on, then he was to go to jail until he repaid the money.[305] Unlicensed liquor retailers would forfeit £10 before two justices of the peace proceeding in a summary way and half this penalty was to go to the informer and half to the poor. If the liquor retailer was unable to pay the penalty, he was to spend three months in jail.[306]

Of course the mere enactment of these colonial acts signifies nothing respecting their enforcement, and the paucity of material on the functioning of the "double justices"[307] renders it difficult to formulate conclusions. There are occasional records which throw some light on enforcement like the Ulster proceedings of the year 1766 regarding the difficulties of enforcing the statute respecting vagrancy.[308] One Nancy Smith was examined by two justices at

---

[301] 5 *ibid.* 621, 624.

[302] 1 *ibid.* 605, 606.

[303] 1 *ibid.* 345, 346. The reenactment of 1700 expressly provided that there should be no further appeal from the judgment of the mayor, recorder or two justices of the peace (*ibid.* 438). Note also that in some other statutes dealing with New York City the mayor or recorder was treated as the equivalent of two ordinary justices.

[304] *Ibid.* 657.

[305] 4 *ibid.* 37.

[306] 3 *ibid.* 750.

[307] The Webbs (*op. cit.* 392) state that the expression is "contemporary lawyers' slang."

[308] The proceedings in this case are in a deposition of Jacobus Bruyn, an overseer of the poor of Ulster County. Nancy Smith was taken upon the road on the complaint of an inhabitant of Shawangunk that she was likely to become a charge on the parish, and on Aug. 17 the justices resolved to transport her out of Shawangunk. The warrant to convey Nancy Smith (or Smit) to Kingston was as follows: "To the Constable of . . . Shawangonck . . . And Also to all constables whom it may Concern To Receive and Convey and to Obey Whereas we [two justices of the peace] Being informed of Nancy Smith A Stranger . . . Not being an inhabitant . . . of Shawangunk And

Shawangunk and found not to be an inhabitant. She was ordered to be passed along from constable to constable until she reached Kingston. This was done. But the justices at Kingston decided that Shawangunk was Nancy's domicile and had her reconveyed for delivery to the overseers of the poor at Shawangunk.[309] The evidence respecting the "common law" jurisdiction of the justices out, of Sessions, that is to say, the jurisdiction exercised because it was regarded by the colonists as inherent in the office, is somewhat more satisfactory. Thus the jurisdiction over bastardy was in this wise assumed and, as we have seen, it was usual for two justices to convict and make a summary order for support on the oath of one accusing witness.[310] Since these orders involved the fiscal interests of the community, a considerable number of examinations, recognizances and orders to support have survived.[311] Similarly the licensing of the retailing of liquor may be regarded as based on English precedent. The Duke's Laws[312] copied the English rule of license by double justices, and when this code was in

suspect . . . Nancy Smit, Not to be of Sufficient Abilities and Likely to Become A Charge . . . These are therefore in [the King's] Name to Command you forthwith to bring . . . Nancy Smit (sic) to the Constable of the New paltz, and . . . warrant . . . and so to be Carried to some place in which she Has Remained Forty Days, which She Said upon Examination to be in . . . Kingston Hereof Neither of you Are to fail . . . 20th day of August 1766." In the indictment against Jacobus Bruyn it is recited that when Nancy Smith was brought to Kingston two justices of the peace there (both of the quorum) received a complaint from the overseers that Nancy Smith had not gained a legal settlement in Kingston nor produced a certificate showing that she was settled elsewhere. On due examination of Nancy Smith on oath and finding that her last place of legal settlement was in Shawangunk, the justices of the peace of Kingston ordered the constable to convey her from Kingston to the next constable of Hurley, and thence from constable to constable until she be delivered to the overseers of the poor of Shawangunk, who were to provide for her as one that had gained legal settlement in that precinct. Apparently, on the basis of the Kingston justices' order, Nancy Smith was delivered from Hurley to New Paltz and thence to Jacobus Bruyn, an overseer of the poor of Shawangunk. Jacobus Bruyn "unlawfully wilfully, Obstinately & Contemptuously did refuse to receive the said Order and the said Nancy Smith . . . or to provide for the said Nancy Smith" although she was delivered to him on two separate occasions. The proceedings in the above case are contained in the H.R. Pleadings Pl. K. 929, and see also Ms. Mins. SCJ 1766–69 (Engr.) 339, Oct. 31,

1767. The order to convey of Aug. 22, 1766, is in Ms. Files Ulster Co. Bundle B.

[309] Compare further the New York City ordinance (1731) requiring masters of vessels to give the names of strangers to the Mayor within twenty-four hours after arrival (4 Mins. Com. Council NYC 80) later changed to a period of two hours (5 ibid. 476), and the ordinance for searching out strangers (4 ibid. 80).

[310] The jurisdiction was related to the functions respecting poor relief as the statutory history in England shows. The matter is not discussed in Schneider, Hist. of Public Welfare in NYS. From the earliest days the support of bastards was a constant problem as the Sessions minute books show. An adequate study of the welfare problem is at present possible only by a thorough search of local records.

[311] There are dozens of these in the files of Ulster and Dutchess counties. The following is a specimen examination of Jan. 9, 1739/40, before two Albany justices of the peace: "The Examination of Clara Marinus . . . who upon oath sayeth that she liveth with her Grant father . . . about middle of June . . . one Jermie Swart living next door as its where [sic] one family (no person being present and promiseing . . . he would marry her . . .) prevailed with her and then had the Carnall knowledge of her body and has had tree [sic] Several times since and at one of the times . . . begot her with the bastard child with which she is now pregnant . . . and . . . is the only true father . . . Sworn before us the day and year aforesaid" (Misc. Mss. Albany 1691–1799).

[312] 1 Col. Laws NY 39.

popular opinion no longer operative, in one county (1692) an order was made requiring licenses signed by two justices.[313] The matter stood on this footing of local regulation until 1741 when the assembly, in an act dealing with the farming of excise, put the existing practice in statutory form and authorized the granting of licenses by two justices and the power of suppressing the licenses of offenders in General or Special Sessions of the peace.[314] But even before this measure the violators of the liquor licensing rules were dealt with at special courts or meetings of justices.[315]

When we turn to the powers exercised by justices of the peace singly out of Sessions, we are presented with a bewildering array of statutory and ex-officio jurisdiction over civil, criminal and quasi-criminal cases as well as administrative powers the most various. To the powers granted by Acts of Parliament before the occupation of New York (which were treated as if they were powers at common law) must be added the manifold business committed to the care of one justice of the peace by the colonial assembly. The enforcement of game regulations, such as those dealing with the killing of deer, gathering of oysters out of season, the killing of English pheasants, and fishing for salmon in the Hudson, was one of his duties.[316] Not only the wild but also the do-

---

[313] "The Court doe order that noe Retaylers of liquors within . . . Kings . . . doe presum to retayll . . . or kepp any publique house . . . without having a license under the hands and seales of two Justices of the peace . . . and be bound by Recognizances to their Majties with two sufficient suretys on the penalty of ten pounds each for their good order and rule in their house as the law directs in such Cases, ordered likewise that all Retaylers as afores⁴., shall Come to the Clerck of the peace of the County . . . to take out their licenses according to law . . ." (Ms. Kings Co. Ct. & Rd. Recs. 1692–1825 14).

[314] 3 Col. Laws NY 152. The provision is in the renewal acts and was continued after farming the excise was abandoned (3 ibid. 951). In New York City the mayor granted the licenses. In 1736 a dispute arose over the destination of the fees (4 Mins. Com. Council NYC 317) that continued for over twenty years (5 ibid. 116, 323; 6 ibid. 190). A fine of £5 was exacted for failure to secure a license (4 ibid. 81). There were relatively more grog shops per capita than justices of the peace, for in 1772 a total of 396 liquor licenses were issued in New York City (7 ibid. 420). In 1776, 268 licensed and unlicensed vendors of liquor were reported (1 Cal. Historical Mss. Relating to the Revolution [1868] 287).

[315] Book of Supervisors, Dutchess Co. 1718–22 (Platt ed.) 7, 8, 22, 47. The taverns in Dutchess

reached the stage of a major nuisance in 1763 when the assembly enacted that every justice, supervisor, assessor and overseer of the poor was to be a commissioner for licensing inns and taverns. The penalty of £20 was recoverable in any court of record, half to the informer and half to the use of the poor. The act expired in 1766 (4 Col. Laws NY 729).

[316] The penalty for killing a deer out of season was 20s. or twenty days in jail and later, 30s. or thirty days, enforceable summarily by a single justice of the peace on the oath of an informant; half the penalty if collectible went to the prosecutor and half to the poor (1 Col. Laws NY 585, 618). Digging pits to catch deer was punishable by a £5 fine (half to the prosecutor, half to the poor) or one month in jail and a six man jury was optional on costs (4 ibid. 688). Gathering oysters out of season was punishable by a 20s. fine and a single justice of the peace could finally determine the case without right of further appeal (1 ibid. 845; but see infra 267, where the right of the justice of the peace finally to determine such cases was called into question). The sum of £10 was payable to the informer when an offender should fish for salmon in the Hudson (5 ibid. 211). Killing English pheasants was punishable by a 10s. fine (half to the prosecutor, half to the poor) or five days in jail (2 ibid. 825).

mestic animals of the province were committed to the care of one justice of the peace who was vested with both administrative and judicial functions.[317] Since the responsibility for the government of the county devolved upon the justices, the regulation of lesser public officers, constables, supervisors, overseers of the poor, road surveyors and overseers, was of course included among their manifold duties.[318] Tradesmen and professional men, ferrymen, pilots, peddlers, liquor retailers and physicians were some of the classes concerning whose offenses the acts of assembly required the justice of the peace to inquire and punish.[319] Market regulations were enforceable in General Sessions, but single justices of the peace were charged with the enforcement of statutes regulating the sale of bricks, bar iron, leather, rawhides, flax and bread.[320]

[317] Where dogs destroyed sheep, damages were payable on the oath of one witness and if the dog owner failed to pay damages he was to spend ten days in jail. The owner was also to kill the dog making such depredations or else pay 6s. to an informer. Later the penalty was raised to 20s. and a six man jury optional on costs (2 Col. Laws NY 667, 735; 3 ibid. 402). Gelding horses without the approval of a justice of the peace was punishable by one month in jail and treble damages to the owner (2 ibid. 832; cf. 1 ibid. 996). The failure to return cattle to owners was punishable by 20s. for cattle and 3s. for sheep, which was to be paid to the owner on his oath (ibid. 1003). Later it was provided that for this offense the offender should lose his right to poundage and pay 20s. to the owner of the cattle (3 ibid. 202). Penning sheep in Hempstead was punishable on the oath of one witness in the amount of 40s., half to the prosecutor, half to the poor (2 ibid. 822).

[318] Poor overseers of New York City failing in their duty forfeited £5 on warrant of the mayor, recorder or two aldermen (1 Col. Laws NY 351). Later, by statute, if they failed to register vagrants, then on the oath of two witnesses they forfeited 40s. or spent twenty days in jail (5 ibid. 513). Road surveyors and overseers forfeited 40s., on the oath of one witness or on the view of the justice of the peace for their delinquencies (2 ibid. 68 at p. 78, 972; 3 ibid. 482, 487). Constables refusing to serve in office forfeited £5 by warrant of the justice of the peace (4 ibid. 977; 5 ibid. 389). Constables failing to deliver recognizances and examinations to the clerk of the peace forfeited £10 on being informed against before one justice of the peace (5 ibid. 209). For failure to collect the dog tax in New York, Albany, Queens or Suffolk, constables forfeited £5 in an action of debt before one justice of the peace (5 ibid. 659).

[319] Those who should ferry without authority forfeited 20s. to the nearest ferryman, and ferrymen who themselves broke the ferriage regulations forfeited £5, half of these penalties to go to the informer and half for the county tax (5 Col. Laws NY 592). Unlicensed pilots forfeited £3, half to the informer and half to the King, on the oath of the informer (1 ibid. 1001). Those practicing medicine without a license in New York City forfeited £5 and one justice of the peace (viz., mayor, recorder or any alderman) was expressly ordered to hear, try and determine such cases summarily (4 ibid. 455). Those who should inoculate against smallpox would, on the oath of two witnesses before a single justice of the peace, forfeit £20 (one third to the "prosecutor," two thirds to the poor) or spend six months in jail (4 ibid. 707). Unlicensed liquor retailers forfeited £5 on the oath of one witness, one third to the informer, one third to the governor, one third to the King (1 ibid. 424). This penalty was later raised to £6 and distributed one third each to the informer, the poor and the commissioners of excise (3 ibid. 951). Sheriffs or constables who neglected to detect unlicensed peddlers forfeited 40s. (half to the informer, half to the poor) and could be convicted on the oath of one witness. Unlicensed peddlers forfeited £30 before a single justice of the peace on the confession or oath of one witness (1 ibid. 807). Later, refusal by peddler to produce his license to a justice of the peace or to the sheriff on demand involved a £5 forfeiture to the poor or a month in jail on the oath of one witness before a single justice of the peace (2 ibid. 571). There were a series of later acts increasing the penalties and risks of unlicensed hawking; cf. 3 ibid. 61; 4 ibid. 388; 5 ibid. 68, 788. Selling to a slave involved a forfeiture of £5 (5 ibid. 643).

[320] Unmerchantable bricks were forfeitable by order of the mayor, recorder or aldermen (J.P.'s) of New York City to the hospital which, at the time of the act (1773), was under construction (5 ibid. 546). For frauds in bar iron, 3s. a bar was forfeitable before one justice of the peace, half the penalty to the informer and half to the poor (5 ibid. 65). A forfeiture of 40s. was levied for selling uninspected leather and was collectible by action

Fraudulently repacking meat, selling unmerchantable flour and violating the act setting the assize of casks and weights and measures for wine, flour and bread were also made punishable before one justice of the peace.[321] Similarly, conducting vendues, outcries and auctions at night, or selling liquor at such sales, or sales by transients of property not their own, were within the scope of the single justice's authority,[322] and likewise good moral legislation such as that dealing with profaning the Sabbath, drinking and swearing, maintaining gaming houses, dealing in lottery tickets and furnishing liquor to apprentices.[323]

Road and fence orders as well as traffic regulations were enforceable by the justices of the peace.[324] Such trespasses as cutting timber, breaking glass lamps

of debt in a summary way before a single justice of the peace, half to the informer and half to the poor (5 *ibid.* 71, 267). Exporting rawhides was punishable on the oath of an informer by a fine of 20*s.* a hide, half to the informer, and half to the King (1 *ibid.* 991). Selling uninspected flax rated a forfeiture of 3*d.* a pound and was collectible in an action of debt before one justice of the peace, while counterfeiting labels on flax was punishable by a £5 fine collectible in debt before one justice of the peace (5 *ibid.* 361). Frauds in the sale of bread were by an Act of 1773 punishable by a 40*s.* fine before one justice of the peace proceeding in a summary way (5 *ibid.* 545).

[321] An Act of 1740 for fraudulently repacking meat provided that violators should forfeit £5 on the oath of one witness, half the penalty to be paid to the informer and half to the poor. The act also provided, as to unmerchantable or misbranded meat, for forfeiture of the meat and fine before a single justice of the peace. In addition, the offender should be prosecuted in the usual way for a cheat—presumably in Sessions (3 *ibid.* 79); see also 5 *ibid.* 201 with respect to beef and pork inspection. An Act of 1750 provided that those who should violate the statute against unmerchantable flour should forfeit 40*s.* before a single justice of the peace, by virtue of the Act of 1737 (2 *ibid.* 964); but if the penalty was over that amount, the forfeiture would be collectible in a court of record by the officials (3 *ibid.* 788). The act setting the assize of casks, weights and measures for wine, flour and bread provided that the penalty was enforceable by an information in any court of record (half the penalty to the poor and half to the informer) or on conviction by oath of one witness before a single justice of the peace (1 *ibid.* 554). Selling rum and liquor without gauging entailed a 40*s.* fine collected as debts under £5, before a justice of the peace (4 *ibid.* 739; 5 *ibid.* 523).

[322] Vendues at night in New York City were punishable in debt to the amount of £5 before a justice of the peace proceeding in a summary way, half to the informer, half to the poor (5 *ibid.* 547).

The same penalty was entailed for selling liquor at auctions in Orange and Ulster counties (4 *ibid.* 1068, 1113; 5 *ibid.* 300). Transients selling the goods of another in Albany, Westchester, Richmond and Dutchess forfeited £10 to the poor and could be convicted on the oath of an informer or on the view of the justice of the peace himself (4 *ibid.* 674; see also *ibid.* 579).

[323] Profaning the Lord's Day: 6*s.* to the poor on the view of a justice of the peace or on confession or on the oath of one witness. On failure to pay fine, three hours in stocks; thirteen lashes if the offender was a slave (1 *Col. Laws NY* 356). Drinking and swearing: conviction on confession, the oath of one witness or the constable's information. Fined 3*s.* or four hours in the stocks for drinking or two hours for swearing. Not over forty lashes for slaves (1 *ibid.* 617). Gaming houses: youths, servants or sailors who should frequent the same forfeited 6*s.* (half to informer, half to the poor) or six days in jail (3 *ibid.* 194). Dealing in lottery tickets: £10 fine. Summarily tried before one justice of the peace (5 *ibid.* 351). Furnishing liquor to apprentices: 40*s.* fine (3 *ibid.* 756).

[324] Acts setting the width of wagon tracks provided for the forfeiture of fines from 10*s.* to 20*s.* to the informer, before one justice of the peace, whenever the wagons made wider tracks than four feet ten inches (2 *Col. Laws NY* 75, 515, 834). Obstructing highways in Albany was punishable by a 40*s.* fine on the oath of one witness (2 *ibid.* 519). A previous act had provided for a £5 forfeiture in all counties on the oath of one witness (2 *ibid.* 70, 661). Cf. 40*s.* fine for obstructing roads in the counties of Kings, Queens, Richmond and Orange (2 *ibid.* 661). In New York City, a 40*s.* fine was recoverable in debt before a single justice of the peace for this offense. For letting a dead horse lie on the streets or having a scarecrow on the roadside, a 40*s.* fine was leviable, while 10*s.* was allotted if a dead dog was allowed to lie on the street (4 *ibid.* 840; 5 *ibid.* 655). In 1713, failure to help mend roads cost the offender 6*s.* per diem on the warrant of a justice of the peace to a constable (1 *ibid.*

in New York City, breaking glass windows and milestones, impairing the city fortifications and riding over another's lands, as well as fire regulations prohibiting the burning of brush, the firing of guns and fireworks or hunting with firearms in New York City, were also punishable or to be given effect by single justices of the peace.[325] Those who failed to pay tonnage duties and the liquor excise, those who passed counterfeit British halfpence or farthings, those who refused to billet soldiers and those who took out writs of certiorari or of error more than one month after judgment or without affidavits were punishable before a single justice.[326] In certain cases such jurisdiction was given by statutes regarding vagabonds and runaway servants.[327]

794), while after 1721, a 3s. fine per diem was collectible on the warrant of commissioners or surveyors of highways (2 ibid. 71; 3 ibid. 485). Failure to mend fences entailed enforced contribution (1 ibid. 832). Failure to help clear the snow off Albany roads involved a forfeiture of 9s. for each day of neglect, leviable by warrant of one justice of the peace, and the penalty was used to keep up roads (2 ibid. 518). An Act of 1774 provided that where two wagons met on any of the roads leading into New York City, those going out of the city were obliged to give way before those coming into the city, and failure to do so merited a 40s. fine before one justice of the peace (5 ibid. 657).

[325] Cutting timber on another's lands was punishable in an action that may be denominated as a quasi-criminal proceeding. On information to one justice of the peace the offender was ordered to pay damages of between 6s. and 20s. a tree to the owner, and for the second offense was to pay 40s. or spend a month in jail. If the offense involved a penalty of over £5, the case was to be sued in Common Pleas (Act of 1699, 1 ibid. 402). In the case of cutting timber on public roads, 10s. a tree was leviable before one justice of the peace, half to the poor, half to the complainant (1 ibid. 533). For breaking glass lamps in New York City conviction was had by confession or the oath of one witness and a £20 fine leviable, part of which was to be used to recompense the owner of the lamp, and the remainder was to be paid half to the poor and half to the informer. On failure to pay the fine, three months in jail was the alternative (3 ibid. 855). In later acts two justices were empowered (4 ibid. 575, 672, 824; 5 ibid. 55). For breaking glass windows and porches in New York City, Albany and Schenectady, a £10 fine, half to the poor and half to the informer, was leviable on confession or oath of one witness before a justice of the peace, and on failure to pay the fine one month in jail was the alternative. Slaves who should offend against this act were to receive thirty-nine lashes (5 ibid. 237). The "misdemeanor" of breaking milestones cost the offender £3 or two months in jail (5 ibid. 647). Riding over another's lands in Albany was punishable by a 6s. fine and damages,

and the judgment of a single justice of the peace was final (2 ibid. 229). On conviction by the oath of one witness of the offense of impairing fortifications a single justice of the peace might levy a fine in his discretion (1 ibid. 745). But we have seen that the case of King v. John Ten Eyck (supra n. 179) was handled by indictment.

We have seen some fire regulations; so, in an Act of 1710, it was provided that those who should burn brush in certain counties would forfeit 40s. on the oath of one witness or go to jail (1 Col. Laws NY 716). Hunting with firearms in New York City was punishable by a 20s. fine or three months in jail (4 ibid. 748), while firing guns, throwing squibs or using fireworks was punishable by 20s. or one month in jail (5 ibid. 244). In Albany and Ulster, the failure of the inhabitants to aid in extinguishing fires in woods entailed a 3s. fine leviable on the oath of a fireman before one justice of the peace (4 ibid. 508).

[326] Passing counterfeit British halfpence or farthings: forfeit ten times the value on the oath of an informer, the justice of the peace having full power if the amount involved no more than £6 current money. In disputes over such counterfeit, if the sum was under 40s., the goodness could be determined by the justice. If it exceeded this sum the justice on request must take two freeholders to assist him in hearing and determining (3 ibid. 948). Failure to pay liquor excise: forfeit of liquor three times its value and liberty to appeal to the next Sessions (1 ibid. 664). Failure to pay tonnage duties: forfeit £20, conviction before the mayor on the oath of one witness (1 ibid. 675). Refusal to billet soldiers: penalty of £5 a soldier (4 ibid. 638). Taking out certiorari or writ of error more than a month after judgment or without affidavit: £5 to the adverse party leviable on the order of one justice of the peace (ibid. 861).

[327] In Ulster and Orange counties a justice of the peace was authorized on examination to bind vagabonds to their good behavior for a year or send them to jail for lack of bond (2 Col. Laws NY 210). Runaway servants were punishable by being obliged to serve double time until the expiration of their contract (4 ibid. 924).

In the records themselves, which are by no means abundant on the activities of the single justices, there have been preserved some orders regarding vagrants and apprentices, as well as numerous examinations of suspected persons and depositions of witnesses.[328] We shall later consider the warrants issued by single justices and the infinite variety of recognizances for appearance, peace, good behavior and the performance of public duties.[329] Justices of the peace presided at town meetings,[330] supervised church affairs

[328] An order regarding a vagrant was that of November 4, 1774: "City of New York ss: William Waddell Alderman of . . . City . . . and Justice of the Peace. . . . To the Constables or Marshals of . . . city Whereas Complaint hath been made before me upon oath of Solomon Townsend . . . That John Willson, Wetheston and Joseph Young . . . [refused to work &c.] These are therefore in his Majesty's name to command you . . . to apprehend . . . and convey them to the House of Correction and deliver them to the Keeper thereof commanding You also the said Keeper to Receive into your said House of Correction the Bodys of the said [&c] . . . and them safely keep to hard Labour not exceeding 30 days nor less than 14 hereof Fail not Given under my hand and seal this &c." (*J. T. Kempe Lawsuits* W–Y).

We have also seen a *mittimus* made up by one justice of the peace committing one Mary Atkins to jail: "To the Keeper of the House of Correction You are hereby Required and Commanded to take into the Bridewell the Body of Mary Atkins and her [to] keep to Hard Labor During . . . 40 days given under my hand and seal this 19th Day of December . . . 1772 . . . John Dykeman." Mary Atkins' mother's letter asking Attorney General J. T. Kempe for relief against this order is of interest: "Worthy Sir.—My daughter . . . of 16 . . . although poor yet I do my best to bring her up, was sent to the Bridewell by Mr. Dickman without any crime The good Alderman Brewerton hearing of it released her. Mr. Dickman hearing sent since that sent [*sic*] a warrant for her and sent her there again . . . hindered from her service besides hurting her Carecter which is tender to those that live by their Labour Beg your known goodness to relieve the distress . . ." (*J. T. Kempe Lawsuits* A–B).

With regard to examinations of suspected persons, see King v. Pat Moore (*H.R. Pleadings* Pl. K. 725). With respect to examinations of witnesses on oath against accused persons, we quote the examination of Mrs. Swift against Captain Davies: "Jur Septimo die feb. A.D. 1714 Coram me John Johnston City of New York ss: Elizabeth Swift . . . being duly sworn and examined saith . . . (Captain Daniell &. Mr. Henderson began) to quarrel with the Defendt and called her abundance of scandalous names as Bitch Whore Newgate Bridewell & several other . . . threw some parings of Po-

tatoes in her face which stood in a Chafing dish and that Dr. Henderson said he would lye her behind the fire and thereupon . . . he and the Lieut. took hold of her one by one arm and the other by tother upon which the Depont. and the Children Cried out . . . that Mr. Dahariette & some Frenchmen were in another Room in the house who hearing the noise came out, that Captain Davies had then his sword drawn and was striking and thrusting with itt . . . that she heard Mr. [John] Cruger Call out I Command the peace . . . [broke her windows that night &c.] and further this Depont. saith not" (*NY Misc. Mss.* Box 4, no. 19).

Such examinations might be made by two justices; cf. King v. John Wright (*J. T. Kempe Lawsuits* W–Y, Aug. 25, 1767). John Wright was indicted and pleaded not guilty on Oct. 23, 1767, in the Supreme Court and on Oct. 24, the jury found him not guilty (*Ms. Mins. SCJ 1764–67* [Rough] 273, 274).

From Queens in August, 1769, comes a report by a justice of the peace to the Attorney General regarding the treatment and character of an apprentice: "Upon the whole I have heard the boy's general carrecter from Deponents above and the neighbors in general say he was a very good boy and deserved better treatment from his Master Yr Humble Servant Samuel Smith Justice" (*Misc. Mss. Queens Co.*).

[329] On warrants, *infra* c. VII. A specimen is that issued on Jan. 10, 1767, by a Dutchess justice of the peace, to one of the constables to apprehend a suspected robber: "Whereas Bazaliet Tyler . . . hath this present day complained unto me John Rider justice of the peace . . . and upon oath Chargeth Thomes Minzey with Robbing him of Divers Cattel and Sheep . . . these are therefore to Command you to apprehend the Said Thomes Minzey and him bring forthwith before me or some other of his majestyes [*sic*] of the peace to be Examined Concerning the pramises with which he is Charged and further to be Dealt with according to Law Given under my hand and Seal . . ." (*J. T. Kempe Lawsuits* L–O sub nom. Minzey). Compare the hue and cry warrants for the same county, *Book of Supervisors Dutchess Co. 1718–22* 21, 46; *Old Miscellaneous Recs. of Dutchess* (1722–42) 147, 148, 195. On recognizances, *infra* c. VIII.

[330] See, for example, the minutes of town meetings 1701–62 in Libers A, B, C, D, *Ms. Flatbush Town Recs.* where are recorded town elections by

(the latter at meetings with churchwardens and vestrymen)[331] and sat with the Supreme Court judges at Circuit. We cannot here enter into the civil authority exercised by the justices of the peace, but suffice it to say that the justices' courts, from the time of the Duke's Laws onward, were popular tribunals, and the colonists themselves by the Forty Shillings, Five Pound and Ten Pound Acts committed a large jurisdiction in minor civil cases to them.[332] Colonial predilection for local tribunals is illustrated by the wide jurisdiction conferred by the Court Act of 1691 which gave to the Courts of Common Pleas, to which justices of the peace were specially commissioned, power "to hear, try and determine All actions . . . Tryable att the Common Law of what nature or kind soever."[333] In the short-lived Court Act of 1695 the Court of Common Pleas was given the power to try title to land[334] although the royal governor, no doubt well aware of colonial aspirations to local home rule, stated that it was altogether indefensible to have local justices, untrained in the law, trying such matters.[335]

If one weighs with the ponderous catalogue of matter listed (all of which was the contrivance of the colonists themselves) the scarcely less considerable impedimenta from English statutes that were regarded as inherent in the office of the peace, one can only wonder at the extraordinary credulity of lawgivers who believed that so much could be effectively executed by mortal man. The justices were beyond shadow of a doubt the foundation stones of the whole scheme of law enforcement, and although this role was certainly not distasteful to the squirearchy of the colony, there were sober critics who viewed such

the People of Midwout, 1703–62. The people were called by warrant of a justice of the peace of the town to choose such men as the act of assembly prescribed. At these elections were chosen assessors, collectors, supervisors, constables, town trustees, road overseers, poundmasters, meadow inspectors, fence and ditch supervisors, poor overseers and arbitrators. In 1711, churchwardens were elected to take care of church and school affairs and town lands. At the election in 1755, two townspeople were elected to engage a schoolmaster "in accordance with the old custom of the town of Flatbush." In Liber C, in 1773, Justice of the Peace Nagel and two townspeople who had been appointed to call a schoolmaster announced that they had agreed upon one and that he was to hold school in a prescribed manner opening with prayers. He was to receive 5s. for each Dutch pupil and 6s. for each English one. Also see *Gravesend Town Meeting Mins. 1699–1872, Ms. Gravesend Town Recs.* Liber VII.
[331] See above, and see also *First Book of Mins. of the Parish of Rye, Book of Vestrymen and*

Churchwardens, 1710–95. Here at parish meetings were administered matters involving parish rates and poor relief (*ibid.* 19, 24).
[332] By the Act of May 6, 1691 (1 *Col. Laws NY* 226) every justice of the peace had cognizance of all causes, cases of debt or trespass 40s. or under, and such cases were triable without jury with the assistance of one freeholder. On Dec. 16, 1737, an act was passed providing that a justice of peace (with a jury of six if requested) might try debt, detinue, trespass and replevin where the matter in controversy amounted to less than 40s. (2 *ibid.* 964). In 1754 the jurisdiction was enlarged to include causes up to £5 (3 *ibid.* 1011; see also 4 *ibid.* 296, 372) and, in 1769, was extended to causes up to £10, but this was repealed by the King in 1770 (4 *ibid.* 1079).
[333] 1 *Col. Laws NY* 230.
[334] 1 *Col. Laws NY* 360.
[335] 1 *Legis. Council Mins. 1691–1743* 86, Oct. 24, 1695.

overgenerous delegation of power with jaundiced eyes. Thus William Smith, Jr., in his *History of New York*, remarked:

> Justices of the Peace are appointed by commission from the governours who . . . sometimes grant . . . the administration to particular favourites in each county . . . There are instances of some who can neither write nor read. These genii, besides their ordinary powers, are by acts of assembly enabled to hold courts for the determination of small causes of £5 and under; but the parties are privileged, if they choose it, with a jury of six men. The proceedings are in a summary way, and the conduct of the justices has given just cause to innumerable complaints. . . .[336]

We shall later have occasion to speak of particular derelictions and malfeasances of the justices, but it is right that some tribute of respect should precede the bill of complaint. No one who has examined the now fragmentary records of how the body of justices applied themselves to their duties can fail to marvel at the pains taken by so many of them to discharge their office. Indeed, these papers disclose a devotion to public service for little recompense that no longer exists. To view the warrants or examinations, laboriously penned by some Dutchess Dutchman fumbling with his English, or to read how a dozen Ulstermen would assemble from the ends of a huge county in the dead of winter to inquire into some petty crime inevitably stirs some feeling of admiration. The city lawyers who inveighed against the country magistrates and the proclivity for holding of court in taverns[337] rarely frequented country Sessions, although they did not themselves hesitate to confer on their cases over the comfort of a bowl.[338] It was not the barristers who had to deal with niggling poor officers, patiently to extract the story of some overtrusting wench, boldly to face a mob of outraged rent payers or to cope with the indignation of neighboring Indians.[339] Better means of local law enforcement

---

[336] Smith, *Hist. of NY* (1814) pt. VI c.6, "On Our Laws and Courts," 373, 374.

[337] In 1758, fifteen prominent New York attorneys (of whom William Smith was one) offered objections against a proposed extension of the power of single justices to try causes to the amount of £5 (2 *Jour. Legis. Council* 1323). The justices of the peace in New York were stated to be men neither of rank nor of education. The bill would confine the distribution of justice to private house and dram shops "And how often these petty Courts have ended in Drunkenness, Revels, Games and Horse races, Tumults, Quarrels and Breaches of the Peace, we must submit to the Knowledge even of several members of this Honourable House." On

the latter point made by the attorneys, it is interesting to note an act of assembly, passed on April 1, 1775, to prevent causes being tried in taverns by justices of peace in Cumberland County (5 *Col. Laws NY* 780).

[338] *Wm. Smith Jr. Supream Ct. Register A.*

[339] E.g., *Ms. Mins. Ulster Co. Sess. 1737-50* May 7, 1745. The Esopus Indians complained there were too many taverns and their produce too cheap and commodities they wanted too dear. The justices told them they could lessen the number of taverns by being sober and that prices depended on agreement of the parties. They then proceeded to order rum, beer, bread and bacon to be given the Indians.

might possibly have been devised, but in a land "newly found out," a government of laws is perforce a government of men, and if the justices brought modest learning to their office, their virtues of industry and zeal lie fast on the record.

CHAPTER III

TRANSFER JURISDICTION

IN England judicial supervision over the administration of criminal justice at large was effected chiefly by means of a highly elaborate system of transfer jurisdiction rather than by means of error proceedings, and before the seventeenth century was out, this conception of control and a part of the machinery became operative in New York. From the viewpoint of the English rulers of New York there were many advantages in the transfer scheme, for the practice of inferior tribunals could thereby be kept in order and the procedure of the Province made uniform. It also was an aid in superintending the conduct of Crown officials, the local justices, sheriffs, coroners and constables, as well as in overseeing the verdicts of juries and the general administration of Crown pleas and law enforcement in the counties. To comprehend the exact scope of this jurisdiction, as well as the devices whereby it was exercised, it is desirable to take a brief view of how the system in England, upon which that in New York was modeled, had developed.

The English system was based upon the device of judicial circuits which had been instituted in response to problems not entirely unlike those in provincial New York, and these institutions had persisted into the seventeenth and eighteenth centuries long after the circumstances which had originally called them into being had disappeared. The circuits were made a regular part of the administration of justice in the twelfth century at a time when the dispersal of jurisdiction through infeudation and franchise and the decentralization even of royal authority had stalemated the effectual functioning of the central government. The scheme was founded upon the ingenious notion of sending into the country the officers of the Crown to administer the King's law and to adjudicate in accordance therewith, relying upon local agencies to supply the factual data necessary for intelligent law enforcement. As the system developed into the so-called General Eyre, the whole range of public business in particular counties came before the eyes of the visiting justices, and since their functions included as well the hearing of civil pleas, the visitations worked out into a measure of control which had political implications far beyond the mere adjudication of disputes, the hanging of felons and the increase of revenue.[1]

---

[1] When a General Eyre sat in any English county to handle criminal, civil and administrative business, "no court, no judge might do aught that should detract from the solitary supremacy of the

The circuit idea had from the first been forwarded also by means of occasional commissions of gaol delivery, oyer and terminer, and assize.[2] Since the General Eyres were, in theory at least, held but once every seven years for each county, the employment of casual commissions was important both for the dispatch of business and to maintain an even tempo of royal law enforcement. During the reign of Edward I, by ordinance and statute, regular circuits were established for the realm and the beginnings of the nisi prius system instituted.[3] Judges from the central courts who rode the circuit were armed with commissions which enabled them to deal with criminal cases,[4] and consequently when the General Eyres fell into desuetude toward the middle of the fourteenth century their functions on the plea side were carried on at these regular circuits which came to be called "the Assizes." It is also clear from statutes and from Privy Council records that certain duties of a general administrative and supervisory sort were also performed at Assizes.[5]

Apart from the fact that the English circuit system tended to bring about uniformity in the law and to establish the superiority of King's law over local custom, it proved an effective means of superintending local government. These advantages were clearly perceived in the seventeenth century although few would have put their thoughts in the candied phrases of Sir Francis Bacon: "This manner of justices itinerant carrieth with it the majesty of the king to the people and the love of people to the king; for the judges in their circuits are sent *a latere regis* to feel the pulse of the subject and to cure his disease."[6]

It is hardly to be doubted that the Duke of York and his representatives were unaware of the utility of employing a similar system in New York where the problem of governing through a lay officialdom and of combatting tendencies toward particularism were considerable. The solution found by Colonel Nicolls after the conquest suggests a lively appreciation of the importance of propagating the law as the proprietor's agents viewed it, for, as we have seen,

---

Eyre over all persons and all causes within and touching the county" (1 *Eyre of Kent 1313–14* [24 *Selden Soc. Pub.*] xviii).

[2] Cf. 1 Stephen, *History of the Criminal Law of England* (1883) 99, 102.

[3] St. Westminster II, 13 Edw. I c.10, 30; 27 Edw. I, st. 1, *de finibus*, c.3; 1 Pollock and Maitland, *History of English Law* (2 ed.) 200 *et seq.*; 2 Hale, *Pleas of the Crown* (1778 ed.) 39–41; 2 Hawkins, *Pleas of the Crown* c.7.

[4] On the criminal side, commissions of oyer and terminer and general gaol delivery had been occasionally issued at the King's will. 27 Edw. I, st. 1, c.3; 2 Edw. III c.2 and 4 Edw. III c.2 provided

that Assize or central judges should be on the commissions. "Thus, although the king did not abandon his right to issue these commissions on special occasions, they were generally issued on the occasions upon which the justices of assize travelled around the country, and these justices were always among the commissioners" (1 Holdsworth, *Hist. Eng. Law* 277, 278).

[5] Cf. 18 *Acts of the Privy Council* 242; Hawarde, *Les Reportes del Cases in Camera Stellata* (1894) 187; James I, *Works* (1616 ed.) 562, 563.

[6] 6 Spedding, *Life and Letters of Sir Francis Bacon* 303.

the Courts of Sessions were to be held with the Governor or a councillor present, and the Court of Assizes was to be an annual meeting of all the justices of the peace with the Governor and Council. This scheme of having members of the Council at Sessions approximated the English Assizes, although the jurisdiction was more limited. The notion of the annual round-up of justices of the peace, at a meeting where both legislative and the most important judicial business was transacted, reminds one vaguely of the old King's Council although it was but a crude replica thereof. During the period 1664–1684, however, there was no development of any system of transfer jurisdiction. Colonial procedure did not move beyond the device of binding over by recognizance offenders (who, for one reason or another, an inferior court thought should be tried by a higher tribunal),[7] or the issuance of a special warrant by the Governor. If the superior tribunal did not wish to take cognizance of a cause it was simply remanded.

Curiously enough, it was not at the instance of the royal proprietor but of the colonists that a step which brought colonial arrangements closer to the English system was taken. As we have already noted, "Because of the inconvenience of bringing ye peace sheriffs constables and other persons from the remote parts of this government to New York"[8] the assembly in 1683 provided for the Court of Oyer and Terminer and General Gaol Delivery which was to sit twice a year at New York City, and once a year in each of the counties. The statute is strangely worded and the ambiguous phrasing can be taken as manifesting an intention to give the new court only a transfer and error jurisdiction, although, as we have seen, this court in fact exercised a broad original criminal jurisdiction. The whole purport of the act, however, was to decentralize the judicial administration. This tribunal cannot, in view of the Act, be regarded as a central supreme court, for another section of the same statute providing for the Chancery Court adds that this "shall bee Esteemed and accounted the Supreme Court of this province." Since there is nothing to indicate the nature of the Chancery Court's jurisdiction, and since it was provided that appeals were to go directly from Oyer and Terminer to the Crown, the colonists apparently intended to have no closer supervision than it was possible to exert by a circuit at which the local justices were to be a majority. Governor Dongan regarded the Chancery Court as one to which appeals were to be taken, but there is nothing in the statute to justify this view.

The surviving records of the Oyer and Terminer are too few to furnish an adequate picture of transfer jurisdiction. In civil cases habeas corpus was used to remove causes, and in one criminal case the same device was resorted to for the purpose of transferring a case from Quarter Sessions to Oyer and Terminer.[9] The recognizance for appearance at that court is also employed,[10] but we have seen nothing which resembles a certiorari. Oyer and Terminer ordered cases to be sent down to Sessions but there is no indication of the process.[11]

The Circuit

After 1691 the whole picture changes, for the new Judicature Act makes no mention whatever of a circuit.[12] On the contrary there is a swing back to the single central court idea. Between 1691 and 1692 there may have been discussion of a circuit court in the house, but some of the assembly minutes for that period are unfortunately missing.[13] In any case, as we have seen, it was expressly enacted in 1692 that there should be a Supreme Court in New York and that the Supreme Court should "be holden" at the various counties at certain times.[14] The difficulty of ascertaining whether or not it was intended to have a court sitting *en banc* and holding mere circuit terms has been commented upon. The minute book for these early years shows that the country sittings were held under a variety of styles: "At A Court of Nisi Prius," "The Circuite of King's County," "at a Supreme Court of Judicature in nisi prius," and "att a Supream Court of Judicture for the Province of New Yorke held at Jamaica."[15] Unfortunately, we have not found any commissions for this period,

[9] *Supra* 70 n. 79. There are a number of entries of habeas corpus in the burned volume 32 of the *NY Col. Mss.;* cf. the *Cal. Eng. Mss.* 112 *et seq.*

[10] *Ms. Mins. Albany Co. Sess. 1685–89* 22; *Ms. Mins. NYCQS 1683/84–1694* 32.

[11] 7 *Ms. Mins. Council* (Reverse) 32.

[12] 1 *Col. Laws NY* 226; see also 1 *Jour. Gen. Assembly* 5, Apr. 17, 1691. Apparently a circuit had been held under the Dominion Judicature Act, for Joseph Dudley was captured on his return from Southold where he is said to have held court.

[13] "The minutes of the Sessions beginning April 20th and ending 29 April, 1692, are, with others of a later period, missing" (Fowler, *Bradford's Laws* lxxix).
Note that later in the year 1692 an assembly committee, which met to confer on the Governor's amendments to the proposed bill for courts, was of the opinion that these were not amendments but articles defeating the whole design of the bill (1 *Jour. Gen. Assembly* 26, Nov. 10, 11, 1692). In the legislative council minutes it is indicated that the Governor's proposed amendments were as follows:

"That for the ease benefite and releife of any poor man injured or oppressed by an erroneous or false judgment in the County Courts or Courts of Comon pleas & Mayor and Aldermen, Appeales be permitted for the smallest sume. The bill to be amended throughout accordingly.

"That the Courts of Mayor & Aldermen in the Citty of Newyorke & Albany, shall have noe jurisdiccōn over the Countyes of Newyorke & Albany by virtue of such Office; that Clause therefore to be omitted.

"That instead of these words, vizt: for the hearing & determining all Accōns and Cause of accōns arising within the libertyes of the town of Kingstown to the value of five pounds and under (be inserted) granted them in their Charter.

"And that the Act for Courts of Judicature shall continue in force for five years or soe long as the Revenue shall be granted" (1 *Jour. Legis. Council* 30, Nov. 9, 1692).

[14] 1 *Col. Laws NY* 303.

[15] *Mins. SCJ 1693–1701* (45 *NYHS Colls.*) 56 (1694), 77 (1695), 97 (1696), 139 (1698).

and it is not even certain that special commissions were issued for holding court in the country, although some instrument must have been necessary to qualify the local justices who were associated with the Supreme Court judge. The matter of commissions was discussed in the Council in 1695 but the report on the matter is not enlightening.[16]

The status of the country visitation was somewhat clarified by Bellomont's Ordinance of 1699, for as already noticed, the Supreme Court was to be held and kept at New York, and the judges were to "go the circuit" when necessary, and hold and keep the Supreme Court for the several counties.[17] It is true that Cornbury's ordinance for Orange ordains "That a Supreme Court of Judicature is and shall from henceforth be established in the said county . . ." yet the style of the Ulster County sitting of 1700—"At a Supream Court held in ye Circuit at Kingstown"[18]—seems to us to make fairly explicit that the court so held was a circuit term of the Supreme Court. Bellomont was very probably attempting to set up a replica of the English scheme of a central judiciary and Assizes in the country, but the final ordering and execution of the intention were not effected until Hunter, in 1715, regulated the nisi prius jurisdiction.[19] It was this final step which made possible the successful exploitation of the ramified system of removal we are about to examine. If the natives' notion of a separate Supreme Court for each county had been carried out, the transfer system would never have come into being.

Whatever the citizenry may have thought about the eyres thus promulgated—and the references to Supreme Courts of Judicature are frequent—the fact that the country sittings depended upon a battery of special commissions tended to establish for them a particular identity. The commission of oyer and

---

[16] The executive minutes of the Council for June and August, 1695, indicate that there had been discussion as to the form of a commission for holding courts of judicature and the Council finally advised the Governor that he should draw up the commissions in the manner appointed by the assembly in 1692: "At a Council held at ffort William Henry the 27th of June, 1695. Present, His Excellency Benjamin Fletcher . . . His Excellency did appoint Col. William Smith Chief Justice William Pinhorne Esqr Justice Chidley Brooke Esqr and Coll. Caleb Heathcote a Committee to consider of the form of a Commission for holding of Courts of Judicature throughout the Province who are to report their opinion to his Excellency in Council in writing. The Attorney Genll is to joyn to assist this Committee. . . . At a Council the 29th of August 1695 . . . His Excellency did appoint . . . Cortlandt to joyne the Committee to consider of the form of a Commission for Establishing Courts of Judicature . . . Pursuant to yr Excellency's Order in Council of the 25th of June 1695, we whose names are subscribed, having considered of the form of a commission for holding Courts of judicature throughout the Province, Humbly offer it as our opinion, That yr Excellency would please to grant Commissions for the Holding Courts of Kings Bench Comon pleas and Excheqr at such Times and Places as were appointed pr a late Act of Assembly Held in the City of New York In the fourth year of Oʳ Sovoreign Lord—and Lady King William and Queen Mary. Which is humbly submitted pr Yr Excellency's Most Obidient Svts. William Pinhorne, Caleb Heathcote, W. Nicolls, Chid. Brooke, V. Cortlandt" (7 Ms. Mins. Council [1693–97] 141, 155).

[17] Supra 29.

[18] Mins. SCJ 1693–1701 194. On the Orange Ordinance, 49 NY Col. Mss. 27.

[19] Supra 79.

terminer was proclaimed at the opening of court, and the nisi prius part was begun by publication of the ordinance,[20] a formality no longer necessary after the Act of 1741 which dispensed with a special commission for the "Court for the trial of Causes Brought to Issue in the Supreme Court."[21] The acts of assembly themselves use the greatest variety of names. In the statute just referred to, the expression "Circuit Courts" is used; in other acts reference is made to Courts of Oyer and Terminer and Gaol Delivery,[22] or to Assizes for the Delivery of Jails.[23] The same confusion obtains in the Sessions records.[24] Judging, however, from the elaborate schedule of rules which the judges drew up for Circuit headed "Rules and orders for ye court of Oyer and Terminer throughout this Province,"[25] the official name was Court of Oyer and Terminer. Nevertheless, in the Council records, in Colden's Ordinance of 1761[26] where the terms of Circuit Courts are fixed, and again in Moore's ordinance prolonging the Albany Circuit Court, the expression "Annual Circuit Court" is used.[27] The usage is not settled even at the end of the colonial period.[28]

It is not, of course, the name so much as the acquisition of a distinct identity, which is significant, for with an identity of its own, the Circuit achieves a special place in the hierarchy of provincial courts. As a "Court for the Trial of Causes brought to Issue in the Supreme Court," it functions as the representative of the Supreme Court; but under its criminal commissions it is *sui juris*.[29] In both its roles the Circuit performs the important and valuable task of intermediary between the inferior courts and the Supreme Court sitting *en banc*

---

20 "The Commission of Oyer and Terminer Proclaim'd" at the opening of Westchester Circuit (*Ms. Mins. Cir. 1721-49* I, Aug. 8, 1721). In the minutes for the trial of causes brought to issue: "His Majesties Ordinance published" at the sitting for September 12, 1721 (*ibid.*).

21 3 *Col. Laws NY* 185 at 191.

22 1 *Col. Laws NY* 765 (1712); 2 *ibid.* 684 (1730); 4 *ibid.* 1001 (1768).

23 4 *ibid.* 969 (1768).

24 E.g., *Ms. Mins. Queens Co. Sess. 1722-87* May 17, 1726 (Oyer and Terminer); *ibid.* May 21, 1760; *Ms. Mins. Ulster Co. Sess. 1737-50* May 7, 1745 (General Gaol Delivery); *Ms. Mins. Dutchess Co. Sess.* Liber A, Oct. 17, 1727 (Gaol Delivery), Liber E, May 17, 1774 (Oyer and Terminer).

25 *Livingston-Redmond Mss.*

26 Cf. 17 *Ms. Mins. Council* 226 (1737/38); 23 *ibid.* 67 (fixing a six day limit on sessions); *An Ordinance Declaring the Commencement and Duration of the Several Terms,* etc. (Broadside, Bar Assn.).

27 *An Ordinance for Prolonging the Annual*

Circuit Court for the County of Albany (Broadside, Bar Assn.).

28 "The Judges of the Supreme Court . . . are Judges of *Nisi prius* of Course by Act of Assembly, & annually perform a Circuit thro' the Counties. . . . The Judges when they go the Circuit have A Commission of Oyer and Terminer and General Gaol Delivery." (Report of Governor Tryon on the State of the Province of New York, June 11, 1774, 8 *Doc. Rel. Col. Hist. NY* 444, 445.) "The judges of this court according to an act of assembly are judges of *Nisi Prius* of course; and agreeably to an ordinance of the governour and council, perform a circuit through the counties once every year. They carry with them, at the same time, a commission of oyer and terminer and general gaol delivery, in which some of the county justices are joined" (1 Smith, *Hist. of NY* [1814 ed.] 380-382). The newspaper announcements of the terms of the court consistently use the expression "Circuit Courts."

29 *Supra* 82.

at New York City. The notion of associating the local justices and the use of local juries was, as had been the original purpose in England, to make available local advice and local knowledge on both sides of the bench, and doubtless it was also conceived as some concession to the prevailing passion for local self-government. But for all that, the annual perambulation of the shires inspired the unease of a domiciliary visit among a yeomanry which did not take in good part extensions of the Crown's authority.[30]

However objectionable the colonists may have deemed the circuits to be because of the opportunity offered the central authorities to mix into matters of local concern,[31] the periodic visitations were at least preferable to the nuisance of trials at bar in a period when a trip to New York City had not yet the fascination for the rustics that it was to acquire.[32] On the other hand, it is beyond doubt that the judges themselves viewed with acute distaste the prospect of arduous journeys through the wilds. That they were not above resorting to subterfuge to avoid a sojourn in some dull provincial village is sometimes apparent even in the records. Thus the entry in an Ulster ejectment action:[33]

[30] Cf. *infra* 363, the presentment of the Attorney General for Sabbath breach; 735 on the question of costs.

[31] And there are occasional flagrant examples such as a case in 1748. Certain soldiers had sued their captain for their pay but the Governor had ordered the Dutchess County judge handling the case to put a stop to the case, and the clerk was ordered not to issue the writs. The assembly claimed this act by the Governor was a violation of law and a grievance, but the Governor asserted that he had only made a recommendation to the judges and had not given any orders (1 *Jour. Gen. Assembly* 240). In 1749 the assembly renewed its complaints in this case, but the Governor stated he had already acknowledged his error and had offered redress. The Governor quaintly remarked that it was not "becoming" for the assembly "to renew this Complaint" (*ibid.* 272, Aug. 4, 1749).

[32] Cf. the assembly's objections (June 11, 1713) to trials at bar in small causes: "The House . . . resolved itself into a Committee of the whole House for the Redress of Grievances. . . . Resolved, that the bringing of Actions of small Value into the Supreme Court at New-York against the Inhabitants of the remote Counties is a great Burthen . . . and a Grievance to the People of this Colony. Resolved, that Tryals at Bar by Juries brought out of remote counties to New-York is a vast Charge . . . and a Grievance" (1 *Jour. Gen. Assembly* 336).

[33] James Jackson ex dem. Daniel Terboss v. Peter DuBois (*Ms. Mins. SCJ 1764–66* [Engr.] 240, July 1765).

The motion on which the order in the above cases

was granted was grounded on an affidavit made by T. McCullum, Daniel Terboss and Nathaniel Sackett, who deposed that Thomas Beaty's and Benjamin Hayne's farms lay within the lands claimed by the plaintiffs under Saunder's patents; that these two farms were mortgaged to the loan office of Ulster; that Abraham Hasbrouck's brother held some of the lands claimed by the plaintiffs; that Abraham Hasbrouck and Jacobus Bruyn (a relative of the Hasbroucks) were representatives in the assembly and persons of influence in Ulster County, and that therefore the trial should be had by a jury outside of the county of Ulster. To these arguments, opposing counsel claimed that the ejectments were "local" actions "such as the policy of our laws made triable by a Jury of the County only." It was argued further by the defendant's counsel that the form of the venire supported a trial by a jury of the locality; that the "neighborhood" should be the "judges" because the people of the locality were supposed to be best acquainted with the facts, and that the subject had a right to be tried by a jury of the vicinage. To have the injury tried by persons not supposed to be so well acquainted with the merits of the controversy and the character of the witnesses would be "full of danger," would aggravate "the Expence to Excess," and would be an "Intolerable Burthen." Defendant's counsel went on to point out that the two farms mortgaged to the loan office of Ulster were not in suit and were not held under the same titles as the farms which were in suit, nor was the county as a whole interested in the outcome of the suit, for the county was not answerable for anything taken up on the defendant's farms. It was hence

It appearing to the court that an impartial Jury cannot be had in Ulster . . . and that the cause will require great Examination both on account of the value of the lands in controversy and the length and difficulty of the tryal, and because from the peculiar State of this Country to which the Practice of this court has been adopted, for the advancement of Justice Tryalls at Barr have been frequently allowed on reasons not so urgent as those now offered,

and because it was supposedly easier for the old and infirm to come to New York City by boat than to the Ulster county seat by land, the court ordered, "a tryal at Barr . . . that jurors be summoned from the County of Orange to have a view previous to tryal."

No more poignant picture of how the miseries of a circuit affected the judges can be found than in the malicious tale, which Governor Cosby reported to the Lords of Trade, of the Chief Justice who, compelled to lodge apart from the lawyers, his natural companions, sought solace in the bowl. Oversleeping "till near sunsett," his very bedchamber beset with impatient townspeople, "his friends or his servants awaked him, he got up and Company being admitted unto his Chamber, he asked what hour it was, they answered almost night; how can that be, said the Chief Justice, the sun is but just risen, and saying so, he took up his Fiddle and played the Company a tune."[34]

"unreasonable we should be deprived of our natural and legal Trials because my neighbor chooses to mortgage his farms even if held under the same title I hold." If lands could be mortgaged in order to obtain a change of venue or other legal advantages a door for frauds would be opened. With regard to the interest which the county had in the outcome of the suit "it does not appear what this mighty interest is." The sums involved were not great, and the securities held in the loan office would certainly protect the county in any event. Referring to the argument that Hasbrouck and Bruyn were persons of influence, it was not to be presumed that these people would interfere "to byass the jury," and it was a reflection on the characters of men of worth to make any such supposition. Defendant's counsel asked: "Will the court suppose all this and without the most urgent necessity drive us to submit our property to triers out of the Common and known Rules and the policy of the Law framed with so much wisdom by our ancestors? What is this pretended Influence? . . . Would this be allowed as a Reason to change the Venue in England? . . . It would not. It should at least be shown there [sic] influence was so great as to render a fair Tryal almost impossible. . . . If allowed for such reasons as these the Natural Venue is at an End in this Country." In opposition to the part of the plaintiff's motion requesting a trial at bar, it was argued that there was no sufficient rea-son to induce such a trial, since the rule in England was that the premises should be worth at least £100 annual income (citing 1 Barnad. 141) and here the lands in controversy were not worth £100 a year. The plaintiff's arguments, grounded on the interest of the judges, the complicated nature of the question, the great examination necessary, &c. &c. were circumstances common to all such cases, and "if this is sufficient the Circuits may be soon useless [sic] Tryals at Bar may be had in all cases." Citing "Andrews 273," defendant's counsel stated that the motion for the trial at bar was "contrary to Law and Reason . . . [and] against the Practise in England." To the request for a view, defendant's counsel intended to make no opposition. (For a recital of the affidavit by McCullum, Terboss and Sackett, and for the argument of defendant's counsel in opposition to the motion, see "Notes on Motion for foreign Jury, Tryal at Bar and for a view" in Peter DuBois ads. James Jackson ex dem. Daniel Terboss et al., J. T. Kempe Lawsuits S–U sub nom. Daniel Terboss.)

[34] 6 Doc. Rel. Col. Hist. NY 8 et seq. Governor Cosby complained bitterly against Lewis Morris who another time delayed so long in getting to Albany "that he had much ado to reach the nearest part of the County on the day which by ordinance it [the court] was to be opened, but getting just within the borders, he opened the court and adjourned it to the City of Albany the next day, . . .

It is to the credit of the New York judiciary that prejudice against an unpleasant duty did not lead to an inefficient performance thereof. So completely
did the judges take over the whole English mechanism of transfer whereby
detailed supervision of minor jurisdiction and the handling of important cases
was assured, that one is led to suspect a constant and exacting study of the
Crown Circuit Companion and of the *Office of the Clerk of Assize*.[35] Exercising the ancient role of the King's Bench of general superintendence over
the administration of justice, the New York Supreme Court sitting *en banc*
stood at the head of the hierarchy of tribunals between which transfer of
cases was effected. Since the judges who rode the circuit were chosen from this
court alone, and not as in England from the three common law courts, it was
possible to preserve a tighter control over county business than in England.
The presence of justices of the peace on the commissions at circuit was no
effective counterbalance against this tight centralization since these justices, although nominally of the quorum, possessed ordinarily little or no legal training. Practically, therefore, the personnel of the Supreme Court wielded an
authority that was nearly unlimited. The opportunity for the assembly to interfere was slight, both because of the Governors' instructions and because of
the Crown's ultimate authority to disallow legislation. Moreover, as far as the
administration of the criminal law was concerned, the common law restrictions upon review were such that there was little chance of upsetting what the
judges did. For the inhabitants at large the only corrective against abuse was
the jury, and it is possible that American confidence in this institution stems
in some degree from this fact.[36] The records actually show little or nothing to

and there again . . . adjourned [it] to the . . .
third [day]; on that day likewise he opened it
but doubting whether the first opening . . . was
regular . . ., he left the Bench without doing any
business" (*ibid*. 9). Some excuse may be made for
the Chief Justice's dereliction of his duty in the instance mentioned by Cosby, for we note in the
minutes that Morris gave the following excuse for
this delay: "The Chief Justice by Reason of Contrary Winds was Disappointed in Getting up to
Albany to hold ye Court on the first Day appointed
for that purpose Did therefore think fit, as Soon as
he got within ye County of Albany to open the
Court for the Tryal of Causes and adjourn it to ye
City of Albany" (*Ms. Mins. Cir. 1716–17* 47, Sept.
3, 1717, at the "Manor of Livingston").

Other examples of Morris's "maladministration"
are mentioned by Cosby. In an ejectment action, the
Chief Justice was partial to a church in which he
preached. He delayed justice, oppressed the people,
and adjourned court after keeping everyone waiting
all day. "In the Circuits it is still more intolerable,

for there, these hours of adjournment and sitting
are not only like those, but the people . . . go 40
or 50 miles from their habitations, . . . and sometimes after Jurys . . . summoned, witnesses subpened, partys attended and all the Justices of Peace
. . . and other Officers have gone to the place
appointed . . . as by ordinance of Morris's own
procuring, they are . . . waited [*sic*] their several
days in expectation of the Chief Justice who . . .
has not come to hold the Court" (5 *Doc. Rel. Col.
Hist. NY* 942, May 3, 1733).

[35] Those interested in the survival of now meaningless tradition will discover in MacKinnon, *On
Circuit 1924–1937* (1941) how much of the ritual
current in eighteenth century New York lingers on
in England, and how MacKinnon must constantly
advert to the *Office of the Clerk of Assize* to give
point to this ritual. His querulous comments about
lodgings and waste of time recall the grumblings
of the New York provincial judges.

[36] On the jury cf. also *infra* 603 *et seq*.

suggest that the judges of the Supreme Court acted arbitrarily. It was clearly understood that one purpose of the system of removals was to maintain established jurisdictional divisions, and this was carefully executed in New York. The advantage to the subject of a trial in his own county was in general respected. As we shall see, the inferior courts frequently on their own motion diverted prosecutions begun there into the Supreme Court, and in view of the pronounced sentiment for local autonomy this fact indicates a spirit of cooperation which existed only because the superintending tribunal was respected as a fair court.

Perhaps the most important aspect of the transfer jurisdiction relates to the capital cases. The English practice, as we have seen, had come to the point that Quarter Sessions were not to hear and determine "grand" felonies, an expression that embraced capital common law and certain statutory crimes.[37] This practice had become so well settled that the trial of capital offenders was regarded as properly held only when a trained judge was present. It is possible that a desire to afford a defendant, whose life was in jeopardy and whose right to counsel was restricted, some measure of legal security may have been involved. But whatever the reasons for the rule, it had resulted in certain practices respecting transfers, well summarized by Hale,[38] that were accepted in New York, where all capital cases were brought before Supreme Court justices sitting *en banc* at New York City or on circuit under commissions of oyer and terminer and gaol delivery in the counties.

Transfers by Hand

The New York provincial transfer procedure was grounded upon the fact that General Sessions took indictments and presentments of capital cases, although it did not try them. Moreover, although the New York peace commission did not have the proviso for reserving difficult cases for the Assizes, the justices of the peace in practice would refer such cases to the Supreme Court or to the Circuit. The transfer was made in a variety of ways, by handing over the indictment *a propria manu,* that is to say by delivery at the hands of a justice or clerk of the peace, by writ of certiorari, by taking a recognizance to answer at the superior court, or by framing a Crown information upon a county presentment.

It is a curious circumstance that although Hale, writing toward the end of

---

[37] *Supra* 94 n. 165.

[38] 2 Hale, *Pleas of the Crown* (1778 ed.) 210 *et seq.*

the seventeenth century, states the usual manner of transfer to be by certiorari and implies delivery of indictments *a propria manu* to be exceptional,[39] yet in New York the practice of manual transfer was frequent whenever the justices of the peace decided on their own initiative that a case was beyond their competence. Indictments in capital cases that were found in Sessions were brought into the Supreme Court by a justice or the clerk of the peace, and in many instances indictments for perjury and forgery were so transferred. In the opinion of eighteenth century text writers, General Sessions courts were not competent in either of these last two crimes,[40] and except for one indictment, the Sessions in New York City appears to have followed this rule.[41] In the country, however, there is some confusion, for there are cases both of perjury and forgery where the court took jurisdiction,[42] and at the spring, 1775, Sessions in Suffolk one defendant was bound to Oyer and Terminer, while a plea of *nolo contendere* was accepted from another and he was fined.[43]

The range, then, of crimes for which indictments were found in General Sessions and subsequently delivered into the Supreme Court by hand includes murder, rape, perjury, forgery, grand larceny and counterfeiting bills of credit.[44] The removal of these indictments was supposed to take place as of course and without writ. The justices' manuals, which were reluctant to admit

[39] Hale states that "tho this be usual to remove records of indictments by *certiorari*, yet . . . the justices of peace or other commissioners of *oyer* and *terminer* or gaol-delivery may deliver indictments taken before them *manibus propriis* without writ, and such a record so removed, and a record made of it removes the record" (*ibid.* 210, 213, 214; cf. also Lambard, *Eirenarcha* Bk. 4 c.7, 18).

[40] The statute 5 Elizabeth c.14, on forgery, limited the punishment of this offense to special judges or the justices of oyer and terminer, and hence the justices of the peace had no jurisdiction to determine the offense (2 Hale, *Pleas of the Crown* [1778 ed.] 44; 2 Hawkins, *Pleas of the Crown* c.8 §33). Hawkins also states "Yet it hath been of late settled, that Justices of Peace have no Jurisdiction over Forgery or Perjury at the Common Law, the principal Reason of which Resolution, as I apprehended, was, that inasmuch as the chief End of the Institution of the Office of these Justices, was for the Preservation of the Peace against personal wrongs and open Violence" (*ibid.* c.8 §38).

[41] In this case, the jurors in Quarter Sessions found the defendant not guilty. This defendant at a trial in the Mayor's Court "did falsely and maliciously swear upon oath" regarding the disposition of ten barrels of "strong beer" (*Ms. Mins. NYCQS 1694–1731/32* 370, 374, 376, 378, Feb. 3, 1719/20, Aug. 2, 3, 1720).

[42] King v. Alice Kerney, convicted of perjury

(*Ms. Mins. Dutchess Co. Sess.* Liber A, May 19, 1741); King v. Mace, forgery—security for appearance (*ibid.* Liber C, Oct. 17, 1758). But when Sheriff Louis Dubois was indicted of false swearing, the indictment was sent to the Attorney General (*ibid.* Liber E, Oct. 1, 1771). Cf. also King v. Mersereau, perjury—process issued (*Ms. Mins. Richmond Co. Sess. 1745–75* May 7, 1765).

[43] King v. Oakes, bound over, and King v. Penny, convicted (*Ms. Mins. Suffolk Co. Sess. 1760–75* Mar. 28, 1775).

[44] See, for example, the following cases: MURDER: John Moore and John Riggs were indicted for murder in Quarter Sessions, August 8, 1711, and capias was issued. On October 11, 1711, Moore was arraigned in the Supreme Court and pleaded not guilty, and on March 12, 1711, he was found not guilty of murder but of "killing . . . by misadventure." On the same day John Riggs was acquitted in the Supreme Court (*Ms. Mins. NYCQS 1694–1731/32* 203; *Ms. Mins. SCJ 1710–14* 343, 346, 356, 358, 359, Oct. 11, 12, 1711, Mar. 11, 12, 1711/12; *NY Misc. Mss.* Box 4, no. 3). Godfrey Swan was indicted on May 9, 1765, at Quarter Sessions for murdering his child and it was "Ordered that this Court deliver this indictment into the next Sessions of the Supreme Court" (*Ms. Mins. NYCQS 1760–72* 134). On July 31, 1765, the defendant appeared in the Supreme Court on "Indictment for the murder of Jacob Swan found by the

that the jurisdiction of Sessions as a practical matter was less than the words of the peace commission supposedly imparted, nevertheless, contain cautions that the justices should not proceed where they do not possess authority. These

Grand Jury of the Quarter Sessions . . . and Delivered by the Mayor of the said City with his own Hands into this Court and filed" (*Ms. Mins. SCJ 1764–67* [Rough] 82).

RAPE: In King v. Wm. Craighan, the defendant being indicted in Quarter Sessions, the clerk of the peace was ordered to deliver the indictments into the Supreme Court, but we have found no subsequent Supreme Court proceedings (*Ms. Mins. NYCQS 1760–72* 350, Aug. 8, 1771).

BURGLARY: Richard Healey, alias Heiley, indicted for burglary, Feb. 9, 1770, in Quarter Sessions (*Ms. Mins. NYCQS 1760–72* 303), appeared in the Supreme Court on October 20, 1770, was tried and found not guilty (*Ms. Mins. SCJ 1769–72* [Engr.] 276). In *H.R. Pleadings* Pl. K. 471, is the Sessions indictment against Healey which is endorsed on the back "Po. se non cul.," i.e., the subsequent verdict found in the Supreme Court was endorsed on the original record made up in Sessions.

Two indictments at Sessions were found against John King, alias Edward King, one for grand larceny and one for burglary, on Feb. 9, 1770 (*Ms. Mins. NYCQS 1760–72* 303). Cf. *supra* 93 n. 164.

GRAND LARCENY: Susanne Mitchell was indicted for grand larceny at Quarter Sessions and the clerk of the peace was ordered to deliver the indictment into the next Supreme Court (*supra* 93 n. 164).

John Dailey (Daley) was indicted at Quarter Sessions for grand larceny and the clerk of the peace was ordered to deliver the indictment into the next Supreme Court to be proceeded upon. In the Supreme Court the defendant pleaded not guilty, was convicted, prayed his clergy which was granted, and being burned in the left thumb he was discharged (*Ms. Mins. NYCQS 1760–72* 372, Feb. 6, 1772; *Ms. Mins. SCJ 1769–72* [Engr.] 516, 520, Apr. 28, May 1, 1772; *H.R. Pleadings* Pl. K. 468; *J. T. Kempe Lawsuits* P–R).

John Bentley, indicted for grand larceny at Quarter Sessions, was arraigned in the Supreme Court on the indictment "returned from Quarter Sessions," and on pleading not guilty he was tried and acquitted (*Ms. Mins. NYCQS 1760–72* 303, 304, Feb. 9, 1770; *Ms. Mins. SCJ 1769–72* [Engr.] 170, 174, Apr. 17, 18, 1770). See also indictment for grand larceny at February Sessions, 1770, endorsed "Po: so non cul." (*H.R. Pleadings* Pl. K. 477).

Patrick Smith, alias Pat Pollen, alias Pat Collen, was indicted at Quarter Sessions on November 4, 1774, for grand larceny and arraigned in the Supreme Court, pleaded not guilty, and was acquitted (*Ms. Mins. NYCQS 1772–91* 117; *Ms. Mins. SCJ 1772–76* [Rough] 221, 243, [Leaf 192b] Jan. 21, Apr. 1775; *H.R. Pleadings* Pl. K. 39).

John Quain, Robert Fall and John Harriot were indicted at Quarter Sessions for grand larceny on Feb. 8, 1776 (*supra* 93 n. 164).

William Seville, Edward Warren and Nicholas Doran were indicted at Quarter Sessions for grand larceny and the clerk of the peace was ordered to deliver the indictments into the next Supreme Court to be proceeded upon. When Seville and Doran appeared in the Supreme Court and pleaded not guilty, they were found guilty, prayed their clergy which was granted. Warren was discharged for lack of prosecution (King v. Seville, Warren and Doran, *Ms. Mins. NYCQS 1760–72* 372, Feb. 6, 1772; *Ms. Mins. SCJ 1769–72* [Engr.] 516, 520, 523, Apr. 28, May 1, 2, 1772; *Ms. Mins. SCJ 1772–76* [Rough] 60, Oct. 31, 1772; *H.R. Pleadings* Pl. K. 530, K. 506, 526).

For slave cases transferred, King v. Fortune, 1724 (*Ms. Mins. NYCQS 1694–1731/32* 438; *Ms. Mins. SCJ 1723–27* 87, 93). Cf. also the case of Juba (*Ms. Mins. NYCQS 1772–91* 7, May 8, 1772; *Ms. Mins. SCJ 1772–76* [Rough] 29, 37, July 30, Aug. 1, 1772; *H.R. Pleadings* Pl. K. 470).

PERJURY: Catherine Garret was indicted for perjury in Sessions and pleaded not guilty in the Supreme Court. However, her "cause went off for want of jurors" and it was "Ordered that the venire in this cause be quashed and that a venire de novo issue." No further proceedings can be found in the case (*Ms. Mins. NYCQS 1772–91* 95, May 6, 1774; *Ms. Mins. SCJ 1772–76* [Rough] 184, 185, 201, 207, July 30, Oct. 26, 1774; *H.R. Pleadings* Pl. K. 309).

Sarah Kennedy was indicted at Sessions on May 6, 1774, for "wilfull and corrupt Perjury" and this indictment was ordered to be delivered to the Supreme Court for further proceedings (*Ms. Mins. NYCQS 1772–91* 95). On July 30, 1774, the indictment for perjury against Sarah Kennedy was entered on the Supreme Court records (*Ms. Mins. SCJ 1772–76* [Rough] 184), but a venire facias, issued on July 30, 1774, to answer the indictment in the October Supreme Court, was endorsed "not found" (*H.R. Parch.* 185 D 2). On April 18, 1775, however, the defendant appeared by her attorney, James Duane, and pleaded not guilty. No further proceedings on this case can be found (*Ms. Mins. SCJ 1772–76* [Rough] 222). Other papers in this case: *H.R. Pleadings* Pl. K. 324 (Sessions indictment written on paper and dated May Sessions, 1774); K. 326 (£100 recognizance for appearance in Supreme Court); K. 870 (another indictment for the same offense written on parchment and marked July Term, 1774); *James Alexander Papers* Box 45 (certified copy of indictment of Sarah Kennedy which was dated Mar. 10, 1784, and was apparently used in a post-Revolution lawsuit).

COUNTERFEITING: Peter Lynch (*supra* 97 n. 171).

caveats were particularly apposite in New York where the peace commission did not at first extend beyond petit larceny, and judging from the records the practice of removal as settled in the early eighteenth century was not altered even after the word "felonies" was added to the commissions.

The order for transfer is sometimes to be found in the minutes of General Sessions, and sometimes the Supreme Court minutes will note that the case was "brought up" from Sessions. But frequently it is only from the absence of a certiorari and the change in the locus of the pleading that the procedure can be traced. The loss and dispersal of records has been so great that it is often difficult to track the peregrinations of an indictment and its ultimate fate.[45] Furthermore, mere presentments made at Sessions or at Circuit, that is to say, accusations not put in the form of an indictment, when delivered into the Supreme Court would often be handed over to the Attorney General with orders to proceed. Usually informations were framed upon such presentments, and these country presentments were transferred without writ no matter what the type of offense. Apparently this was due to the fact that not being "in form" as indictments the presentments were not a "record" of the lower court.[46]

Most of the cases of transfers *a propria manu* are removals from the New York City Sessions to the Supreme Court. Indictments for capital offenses found at country Sessions were delivered *a propria manu* to the county Circuits. The earliest example we have seen is at the Ulster County Oyer and Terminer of September, 1722.[47] Delivery was effected either by the clerk of the

---

[45] In the following cases indictments for capital offenses or perjury were handed up in Sessions, but while there is no indication that they were transferred to the Supreme Court there is, on the other hand, no indication that they were tried in Sessions either: Mathew Lake for grand larceny (*Ms. Mins. NYCQS 1760–72* 245, Feb. 5, 1768); William Dupe and Alexander Coumneron for burglary and grand larceny (*ibid.* 245, Feb. 5, 1767/68); Adam Burget for being an accessory before the fact to the burglary committed by Dupe and Coumneron (*ibid.* 245); Ed Walsh for "wilfull and corrupt perjury" (*Ms. Mins. NYCQS 1772–91* 157, Aug. 4, 1775); Isaac Bratt, for perjury (*ibid.* 117, Nov. 4, 1774). In King v. Robert Pealing alias Rice indicted for grand larceny (*ibid.* 304, Feb. 9, 1770) the explanation for the failure further to prosecute is contained in *H.R. Pleadings* Pl. K. 476, which is the Sessions indictment against the defendant and is endorsed "died in gaol a few days ago."

In one instance a defendant on indictment in Quarter Sessions for perjury pleaded guilty but nevertheless "the indictment in this cause appearing insufficient, the Clerk of the Peace enters a nolo prosequi." Apparently since the indictment was found irregular, defendant's plea of guilty was ignored and there was no necessity for transferring the case to the Supreme Court (King v. Abraham Van der Voort, *Ms. Mins. NYCQS 1760–72* 73, 82, Feb. 2, Aug. 3, 1763; *H.R. Pleadings* Pl. K. 476).

[46] *Infra* 167.

[47] Gilbert Livingston, "Clerk of the county," delivered into court five indictments, evidently found at Ulster Sessions, against Maria Boss (Brass) for murder, negro Jack and Hartman Hine for stealing, Gritie Boss (Brass) and Augentie Brass (Boss) for carnal copulation with negroes by which they had bastards, and Huybert Lambertson for jail break. The ultimate disposition of the Maria Boss, Gritie Boss and Huybert Lambertson cases does not appear but negro Jack was found guilty and sentenced to thirty lashes "at the Court house door forthwith"; Hartman Hine, though acquitted, was ordered to find recognizance in £30 with two sureties of £15 each for his good behavior for a year; Augentie Brass pleaded guilty and the court, finding "that she was seduced under promise of marriage and something out of her sences," discharged her (*Ms. Mins. Cir. 1721–49* 18–22).

peace, a justice[48] or as in the case of Manas Carlan (indicted at Albany Sessions for murder) by the three justices who were sitting at Circuit.[49] In only one case have we seen a transfer by hand from Oyer and Terminer to the Supreme Court.[50] The country minute books do not often contain entries respecting disposition of indictments for offenses beyond the competence of the General Sessions. Orders have been found that an indictment should be certified to the next Oyer and Terminer, or to the Attorney General[51] (a direction in accord with advice in the handbooks) but no indication of the form of certification has been found. It may have been no more than an endorsement on the indictment[52] or the direction may have signified only that the clerk of the peace turn the bill over to the clerk of the Circuit when the court came down.

The Case of Difficulty or Doubt

In cases less than capital and other than perjury and forgery, the normal method of transferring indictments from General Sessions to the Supreme Court was by writ of certiorari. This rule was consistently observed for it was exceptional that a minor case was ever brought up without writ.[53] But it was a rule which occasioned some perplexity when a case arose which was considered one of difficulty or doubt, and which, therefore, the ancient text writers

---

[48] On June 29, 1733, John de Peyster, the mayor of Albany and a justice of the peace, delivered at Albany Oyer and Terminer and General Gaol Delivery a bill of indictment against William Hogan Jr. and Bernardus and Johannes Bratt for feloniously killing John Griffes of Oswego which indictment had been found at the Albany Sessions of the Peace on October 6, 1732 (Ms. Mins. Cir. 1721-49 60-62).

[49] The reference to this case can be found in the certiorari bringing up the judgment from Gaol Delivery to the Supreme Court (H.R. Parch. 169 K. 5). At the Court of Oyer and Terminer and General Gaol Delivery for Albany June 9, 10, 1747, Manas Carlan pleaded not guilty. The jury convicted him; the court ordered him "to be hanged by the neck until he be dead and the Lord have mercy on his soul" (Ms. Mins. Cir. 1721-49 120, 121).

[50] "On indictment at the last court of Oyer and Terminer in the City and County of Albany Mr. Justice Chambers delivered the Indictment into Court with his own hand . . . Process ordered" (King v. James McMasters, Ms. Mins. SCJ 1750-54 [Engr.] 164, Aug. 1, 1752).

[51] E.g., King v. William Moyles (Ms. Mins. Queens Co. Sess. 1727-87 May 17, 1726); Queen v. Nodine (Ms. Mins. Westch. Co. Sess. 1710-23 Dec. 5, 1710).

[52] In King v. Oakes, indicted for perjury, the minutes order him bound to Oyer and Terminer (Ms. Mins. Suffolk Co. Sess. 1760-75 Mar. 28, 1775). The indictment is endorsed "Bound to the Supreme Court" (Ms. Files Suffolk Co. Indictments 1773-1839).

[53] The cases of Jacob Moses, James Brown and Elizabeth Robins (alias Philipse) may be instances of misdemeanor indictments moved up without certiorari. The indictment was for knowingly receiving stolen goods, and the Court of Quarter Sessions "Ordered that the clerke deliver the above several indictments in at the next Supreme Court." Defendant Brown appeared in the Supreme Court on "indictment for misdemeanor" in receiving stolen goods and was bound in recognizance with two sureties of £15 each for his appearance at the next Supreme Court. He subsequently turned King's evidence. Moses was convicted (Ms. Mins. NYCQS 1772-91 7, May 8, 1772; Ms. Mins. SCJ 1769-72 [Engr.] 441, 448, Oct. 23, 25, 1771; Ms. Mins. SCJ 1772-76 [Rough] 28, July 30, 1772; H.R. Pleadings Pl. K. 345, K. 510 [infra 586 n. 149, 759 n. 479]. Also note H.R. Pleadings Pl. K. 528 for Sessions indictment against Jacob Moses "filed May 8, 1772." H.R. Pleadings Pl. K. 505 is endorsed "Filed in Supreme Court July 30, 1772— Po. Se: Cul").

had advised should be referred to a higher court.[54] In England the peace commission explicitly directed such a reference, but in New York the transfer of difficult cases was entirely voluntary since, as already stated, the New York peace commissions did not contain the proviso of the English commission respecting the *casus difficultatis*. Possibly the General Sessions Courts in New York were moved to caution by the admonitions of the text writers, but more probably it was the presence of a King's attorney that was responsible. In any event, on numerous occasions from 1695 onwards, hard cases were removed out of Sessions.

The selection of a means to transfer misdemeanors out of Sessions on the motion of the justices themselves appears to have been determined by the practice settled during the proprietary period, viz., the taking of bail to appear at the superior tribunal. A pair of early cases are illustrative.

In 1695 Attorney General Graham informed the Westchester Sessions that Peter Chocke had spoken seditious words. A witness was sworn who declared that he had heard Chocke say

> that Ye Governor's comition is out and he was no more Governor than Peter Chocke is, Now the Queen is Dead . . . I wonder the Assembly doe not Send home with his Accusations with him And the said Peter did also say if the Kinge of England had don as Ill a thinge as our Governor had done—They would have shortened him by the head, And further he said that this Governor is the worst Governor that Ever was in New Yorke.

There is no doubt that at this time seditious words were punishable at common law[55] but it is not clear whether in England the Sessions were competent.[56] Traditionally, in New York Province, cases of this sort had been taken to the highest tribunal.[57] In consequence Sessions refused to hear the case because it found "the words Vented by the said Chocke to be highly Criminall And not within their Cognizance." The court, therefore, ordered the defendant committed to jail until delivered by due course of law, but on the defendant's request bail was taken for his appearance at the next Supreme Court where he was discharged for want of prosecution.[58]

---

[54] See, for example, Lambard's statement quoted *supra* 92 n. 162.

[55] 1 Hawkins, *Pleas of the Crown* c.23.

[56] Under the doctrine of de Libellis Famosis (5 *Co. Rep.* 125), spoken seditious words came under the heading of libel. These matters had been handled by Star Chamber (Hudson, *Treatise on the Star Chamber* 101). The common law courts took over this jurisdiction and even at the opening of

the eighteenth century were hardly less strict than the Star Chamber; cf. Reg. v. Tutchin (14 Howell, *State Trials* [1704] 1095, 1128) and cf. also the cases in *Carthew* 6, 14. The justices of the peace had jurisdiction over written libels (2 Hawkins, *op. cit.* c.8) but not necessarily over spoken words of sedition.

[57] *Supra* 62 nn. 12, 13.

[58] King v. Chocke [Clocke] (*Mins. Westch. Ct.*

At an Ulster County Sessions in this same year one Richard Wilson was also bound over to the Supreme Court because he had said, in the presence of a grand juryman, that the Dutch could get justice but the English could not.[59] It may be remarked here that only reflections on the magistracy were viewed as seditious, for a few years later an outraged grand jury informed the Ulster court that Hellegonda Van Slechtenhorst had said they were "damned doggs and a cursed jury." Plaintively the foreman queried, "Is this a grievance or nott?" But the court did nothing.[60]

Throughout the eighteenth century the recognizance to answer in the Supreme Court or Oyer and Terminer was the usual method by which the country *casus difficultatis* was handled, although in one exceptional instance—an indictment against some soldiers for an affray—the clerk was ordered to send copies of the indictment and examination to the Lieutenant Governor advising him that the justices wished to be free of keeping the prisoners and that the commanding general should arrange for punishment.[61]

The first departure from the established practice of binding over in a difficult minor case appears to have been the prosecution of the printer, James Parker, for blasphemous libel. Parker and another were indicted at New York Quarter Sessions on May 8, 1752. Despite authorities which averred that libel was cognizable by the justices of the peace, the Sessions ordered that the mayor deliver the indictment into the Supreme Court. The entry apparently indicates a transfer *a propria manu*,[62] although the cause was one where jurisdiction would be ousted only by a certiorari from the Supreme Court. Apparently the city fathers were in a panic to be rid of the case and were unwilling to await the issuance of the writ. The Supreme Court's rough minute book recounts the delivery of the indictment by the recorder, but this matter is crossed out and the engrossed version is to the effect that a certiorari was issued.[63]

Parker, who had been apprenticed to Bradford and was a partner of Frank-

Sess. 102, 103). It should be noted that three months before the Attorney General had appeared in the Supreme Court and had moved the court that the defendant had spoken seditious words. Chocke had been bound to good behavior until the next term (*Mins. SCJ 1693–1701* 68, 72). Apparently the Supreme Court prosecution was dropped, and the proceedings begun anew at General Sessions.

[59] *Ms. Mins. Ulster Co. Sess. 1693–98* Sept. 4, 1695.

[60] *Ms. Mins. Ulster Co. Sess. 1703–05* Sept. 5, 1705.

[61] *Ms. Mins. Dutchess Co. Sess.* Liber C, Oct. 20, 1761.

[62] "Ordered . . . that . . . the mayor . . . Do Deliver the said Indictments in the Supream Court . . . Agreed that . . . the Mayor Do Issue his Warrant to apprehend the said James Parker [to give recognizance in £500 with two sureties in £250 each for his appearance at the next Supreme Court]" (*Ms. Mins. NYCQS 1732–62* 318, May 8, 1752).

[63] *Ms. Mins. SCJ 1750–56* (Rough) 96, July 28, 1752; *Ms. Mins. SCJ 1750–54* (Engr.) 155, 158, 159, July 28, 31, 1752.

lin,[64] was never brought to trial. In addition to publishing the *New York Ga-zette* and the *Independent Reflector,* Parker was the public printer of the Province and the librarian of the corporation. He had powerful friends, and in due course the Attorney General appeared with a warrant for a nolle prosequi from the Governor who "in compassion to the frailty of the petitioners extended his Majesties Grace and Mercy."[65] Only two other instances of transfer *a propria manu* of a minor offense have been found.

Certiorari

In England certiorari was used in cases less than capital and other than forgery and perjury and not of difficulty, doubt or ambiguity, for the purpose, as Hale explains, of determining the validity of indictments or of having the defendant tried at bar or at nisi prius instead of at Sessions.[66] Since certiorari was grantable as of right at the instance of the King,[67] this device was of great utility in promoting surveillance of the business in local courts. In New York the cases which were moved up on motion of the Attorney General usually involved Crown interest or were cases where there was some doubt as to whether a fair trial could be had in the country. The Attorney General did not always move on his own initiative but might act at the request of the Governor or interested parties. The evidence on this matter of initiative is unsatisfactory and rests on inferences drawn from a letter of Attorney General John Tabor Kempe relative to a case where the defendant had been presented at Albany General Sessions for detaining a sloop unlawfully. Kempe states that he had entered a certiorari to remove the presentment against the defendant

[64] Van Doren, *Benjamin Franklin* (1938) 120.
[65] "The several Indictments of the Defendants being returned on severall Writts of Certiorari from the Court of Sessions . . . [the] Attorney General . . . pursuant to a Warrant from . . . the Governor . . . Reciting That Whereas James Parker . . . printer at the last general Sessions of the Peace . . . had been indicted for printing and publishing in his weekly newspaper [the *NY Gazette*] . . . a Writing containing scandalous Reflections against the Christian Religion And the said James Parker . . . had set forth That at the Solicitation of a Certain Gentleman he had been induced inadvertently to insert the same in his paper which . . . had affected some tender minds and the said petitioner was heartily sorry . . . and promised to be more upon his Guard for the future And humbly prayed that he would be favorably pleased to grant him a Noli prosequi on that Indictment. And

Whereas Patrick Carryl . . . Apothecary, having been the person who induced the said James Parker to insert . . . [the blasphemy and who said he was sorry] That his Excellency therefore in compassion to the frailty of the said Petitioners and being willing to believe that they are heartily sorry . . . and depending on their promise . . . for the future had thought fit . . . to extend his Majesty's Grace and Mercy . . . [on payment of all] fees that then were and should be due on the said prosecution and until such Noli prosequi in each Suit should be entered . . . I therefore . . . in obedience to his Excellency's said Order and Warrant do hereby declare that I for . . . the King . . . will not any further prosecute" (*Ms. Mins. SCJ 1750–54* [Engr.] 158, 159, July 31, 1752).
[66] 2 Hale, *Pleas of the Crown* (1778 ed.) 210.
[67] 2 Hawkins, *Pleas of the Crown* c.27 §§27–39.

but he could not recall that the Governor had desired him to do so. Kempe went on to say:

I cannot see the end that is to be answered by the removal of these proceedings but that of mere expence to the persons accused, because I am as much bound to prosecute here as the magistrates are at Albany. However, if it will be any satisfaction to them to be tried at the Supreme Court I have no objection.[68]

It is perhaps because of the fact that the Attorney General did not always solicit certiorari on his own initiative that we have noted cases where the defendant was discharged because of the Attorney General's failure to bring on his case after an indictment had been removed by certiorari.[69] It lay within the discretion of the court whether or not certiorari would be granted on motion by the defendant. This rule obtained in England[70] and the provincial judiciary adopted the strict attitude of the English courts. This may possibly have been due to the fact that habeas corpus as a means of removal was available to defendants, but actually cases of record in New York where habeas corpus was so used in criminal cases are rare,[71] and it therefore appears

---

[68] *J. T. Kempe Lawsuits* C. The Supreme Court minutes in this case (King v. Cairns) indicate that the Attorney General did have a certiorari issued, for we note that the Supreme Court "Ordered the justices of Albany return the certiorari" (*Ms. Mins. SCJ 1762–64* [Engr.] 91, Jan. 22, 1763).

In the case of King v. Johannis Luyk, "Ed Collins memorandum for Richard Morris Clerk of the Circuits" states that he (Collins) was sending down with Morris a copy of the indictment in King v. Peter and Johannis Luyk. Collins further stated that Peter, having been taken, laid himself on the mercy of the court and was discharged, while Johannis was not taken and Collins had been ordered to send down to the Attorney General a copy of the indictment "in order, I suppose, that a certiorari do issue" (*H.R. Pleadings* Pl. K. 687). Note also in *H.R. Pleadings* Pl. K. 504, that Peter and Johannis Luyk had been indicted for assault and battery and the endorsement on the indictment indicates that "Peter Luyk is discharged from the within indictment by the court."

[69] Thus, in King v. Remsen & Thomas, the case was brought to the Supreme Court on November 30, 1730, on a certiorari and process was ordered to issue. On March 16, 1730/31, the sheriff of Kings returned *cepi corpus* and was ordered to bring in the defendant's body or forfeit 40s. However, the defendant's attorney, Smith, entered his appearance for the defendant, and the defendant was ordered to plead in twenty days or suffer judgment. On June 13, 1732, the Remsen case was ordered to

be tried the following term or the defendant was to be discharged, and on October 11, 1732, after the lapse of nearly two years since the case had been transferred, the defendant was discharged "because the Attorney General has not brought up his case" (*Ms. Mins. SCJ 1727–32* 245, 261, 351, 354).

[70] Hawkins states "That it is left to the Discretion of the Court either to grant or deny it [certiorari] at the prayer of the defendant" and he goes on to enumerate certain instances in which the court was not wont to grant it: "The Court will never grant it for the Removal of an Indictment before Justices of Gaol Delivery" unless the court is unreasonably prejudiced against the defendant or where the case is a very critical one or where the prosecution is for a "Matter not properly criminal"; nor is certiorari ordinarily grantable at the prayer of defendant for removal of perjury, forgery or heinous misdemeanor nor for removal of a conviction of recusancy on a default at Sessions nor when issue joined in the court below and a venire issued for trial. Hawkins adds references to many other restrictions on the issuance of certiorari at the prayer of defendant (2 *Pleas of the Crown* [1787 ed.] c.27 §§27–39).

[71] Cf. the early case where Thomas Spurr "being summoned from the hands of the Sheriffe by a habeas corpus from the judge of the Supreame Court and being cleared at the Supreame court by proclamation," the Court of Quarter Sessions in New York City was obliged also to discharge the recognizance of Rip Van Dam who had been

we have to do simply with a matter of mere imitation. In any event, only a sprinkling of cases have been found where certiorari to remove indictments were granted on motion of the defendant.[72] When this was allowed a recognizance was always required, apparently by virtue of the statute 21 James I c.8. This act provided that writs of certiorari should be delivered at Quarter Sessions in open court and that before the allowance there, the persons indicted be bound to the prosecutor in £10, on the condition that the person removing the indictment pay the prosecutors, within a month after conviction, such costs and damages as the justices of the peace should allow. When no recognizance was posted it was lawful for justices of the peace to proceed to trial of the indictment despite any writ of certiorari.

It is difficult to escape the conclusion that the writ of certiorari was not invariably used to promote justice.[73] The extraordinary delays that sometimes ensued after a case had been removed to the Supreme Court, and the occasional

bound to prosecute the offender (*Ms. Mins. NYCQS 1683/84–1694* 153, Nov. 3, 1691). In Queen v. John La Rou, Bickley, for the defendant, prayed a "habeas corpus to the Sheriff to bring ye defendant immediate" and the court granted his prayer (*Ms. Mins. SCJ 1701–04* 149, Sept. 5, 1704). In King v. John Johnson, a special Court of Oyer and Terminer and General Gaol Delivery "Ordered that the Sheriff bring John Johnson, the prisoner in his custody immediately to the Barr" and the prisoner was thereupon discharged by proclamation (*ibid.* 1, Aug. 11, 1701).

On January 18, 1754, Benjamin Ferguson was brought before the Supreme Court on habeas corpus and "on Motion of Mr. Nicoll Ordered that the Habeas Corpus be returned at the opening of the Court To morrow and that a copy of the return be delivered to defendant's Council [*sic*] . . . this evening." On the following day the habeas corpus to the gaoler of Orange County was returned and filed by Nicoll, and thereupon the defendant gave a bond of £40, with two sureties in £20 each, for his appearance at the next Court of Oyer and Terminer and General Gaol Delivery for Orange County and for his good behavior in the meantime (*Ms. Mins. SCJ 1750–54* [Engr.] 346, 349, Jan. 18, 19, 1754). See also King v. Sackett, *infra* 317 n. 135, where a habeas corpus was used to remove a case from a justice of the peace to the Supreme Court of Judicature.

For a form of habeas corpus from the Supreme Court to the Common Pleas Court of Suffolk, in a civil case in August 1765, see *H.R. Parch.* 194 C 3.

[72] Cf. the following example: Thomas Clarke, indicted for a misdemeanor at NY Quarter Sessions, pleaded not guilty and then appeared "in his proper person and produced his Majesties Writt of Certiorari for Removing the Indictment to the next Supream Court." The certiorari was read and al-

lowed and the defendant put in recognizance of £20 with one surety in £10 to "procure the issue to be tryed the next Supreme Court after the return of the said Writt" (*Ms. Mins. NYCQS 1694–1731/32* 317, 318, 323, 326, 329, Feb. 8, 1715/16, Nov. 6, 1716, Feb. 5, 1716/17).

An indictment of "Rescous" was found by the grand jury at an Orange County Sessions on Oct. 25, 1727, and the defendant appeared in the Supreme Court on a certiorari removing the indictment (King v. John Little, *Ms. Mins. SCJ 1727–32* 18, 19, 34, Nov. 29, Dec. 1, 1727, Mar. 15, 1727/28 [*infra* 600 n. 211]).

Four defendants were indicted at Quarter Sessions on Aug. 5, 1773, for a trespass, but on Nov. 4, 1773, "Kissam pro defendant produced His Majesty's writ of certiorari" which was read and return ordered to be made (King v. Stephen Tippet, Vanderclyff Norwood, Marmaduke Forster and James Hill, *Ms. Mins. NYCQS 1772–91* 58, 73). On January 18, 1774, the defendants appeared in the Supreme Court and they were tried, April 29, 1774, on "the indictment for burning the Fence . . . of Cornelius Bogardus to the danger of firing the house of Bogardus Removed by Writ from the court of Common Pleas [*sic* for Quarter Sessions?]." The jury found them guilty of pulling down and burning the fence "but that they are not guilty of the charge of endangering the buildings in the neighbourhood by the Said Fire." The defendants were discharged without any punishment, the court being of the opinion that "the offense is not fineable" (*Ms. Mins. SCJ 1772–76* [Rough] 139, 167 [fol. 155a], 170 [fol. 156b]; *J. T. Kempe Lawsuits* S–U; *H.R. Pleadings* Pl. K. 435 [notes on trial]).

[73] Cf. here the proceedings against Allison, *infra* 183 *et seq.*

mysterious disappearance of a cause from the records, like those rivers which vanish into desert sands, lead one to suspect that the process of removal was sometimes a convenient device for the arrangement of a deal between defendant and prosecuting authority.[74] In at least one instance a defendant had resort to certiorari as a procedural trick to avoid punishment. One Ewing, indicted for "beating and abusing a poor woman . . . [and] knowing that the

[74] Thomas Carrol was indicted at Quarter Sessions for assault and battery and pleaded not guilty, but the Attorney General brought certiorari removing the indictment into the Supreme Court. We cannot find the Supreme Court of Judicature minutes on this case, but it is curious that the defendant appeared at the next Quarter Sessions and no prosecutor appearing against him he was discharged (*Ms. Mins. NYCQS 1694–1731/32* 101, 106, Aug. 8, Nov. 6, 1705; *Ms. Mins. NYCQS 1705/06–1714/15* [Rough] 2, Feb. 7, 1705/06). If the defendant in this case appeared in Quarter Sessions on the indictment already transferred to the Supreme Court by certiorari, it would appear that the indictment was remanded in violation of the rule expressed by the English law text writers. See, for example, 2 Hale, *Pleas of the Crown* (1778 ed.) 3, where he says that "if a record of an indictment . . . come into the court before the filing thereof, the court may remand it . . . but if it be once filed, it is not to be remanded." It is possible, however, that in the Carrol case the indictment had not actually been filed in the Supreme Court and hence there are no minute entries. On the same day that Thomas Carrol was indicted at Quarter Sessions one Evert Byvanke appeared in Quarter Sessions, pleaded not guilty to an indictment for assault, and gave recognizance in £20 and one surety in £10 to appear at the next Sessions to prosecute his traverse. At the next Sessions, that is, on November 6, 1705, the same day that the certiorari was allowed in the Carrol case, the Attorney General brought a writ of certiorari for removing the indictment and record in the Byvanke case into the Supreme Court. The certiorari returnable the second Tuesday in March was read and allowed. In the Supreme Court minutes for March 15, 1705/06, the entry *cessat processus* appears in connection with the Byvanke case. It is possible that the process or proceedings of the Carrol case in the Supreme Court were terminated in the same manner as in the Byvanke case. On the Byvanke case see *Ms. Mins. NYCQS 1694–1731/32* 101, 105, Aug. 8, Nov. 6, 1705; *Ms. Mins. SCJ 1704/05–1709* 58, Mar. 15, 1705/06.

On August 4, 1751, David Provoost was indicted for nuisance at Quarter Sessions and the clerk of the peace on behalf of the Attorney General produced his Majesty's writ of certiorari which was read, and on the clerk's motion, it was ordered that return be made. The certiorari was returned and filed in the Supreme Court on January 21, 1758, and process was ordered to issue. It is curious that

in this case a lapse of some seven years occurred between the issuance and return of the certiorari. In April, 1758, the sheriff of New York made his return on a venire facias that he had caused the defendant to come as commanded, and the defendant endorsed his appearance on the writ. The court ordered that the defendant plead within twenty days or suffer judgment, and this is the last entry that can be found regarding this case (*Ms. Mins. NYCQS 1732–62* 414, 421, Aug. 4, Nov. 2, 1751; *Ms. Mins. SCJ 1756–61* [Rough] 90, Jan. 21, 1758; *Ms. Mins. SCJ 1757–60* [Engr.] 114, Apr. 1758).

John Provoost was presented for assault at Quarter Sessions, and the presentment being put in form as an indictment, process was ordered to issue. The sheriff returned the defendant taken and he was ordered to plead within twenty days or suffer judgment for want of a plea. The deputy clerk of the peace on behalf of the Attorney General produced a writ of certiorari which was read and return ordered to be made. Thereafter, upon motion of the Attorney General it was ordered that the mayor and aldermen of New York City return the certiorari. The defendant later appearing in the Supreme Court, he was ordered to plead within twenty days or suffer judgment. At the next term of the Supreme Court Nicoll appeared for the defendant—the last entry we have on this case (*Ms. Mins. NYCQS 1732–62* 339, 340, 342, Nov. 7, 1753, Feb. 5, 1754; *Ms. Mins. SCJ 1754–57* [Engr.] 42, 53, 122, Apr. 25, Aug. 3, 1754, Jan. 25, 1755).

John Keating was indicted for assault and battery in Quarter Sessions on Aug. 8, 1765, and the Attorney General produced his Majesty's writ of certiorari which was read and filed and return ordered to be made (*Ms. Mins. NYCQS 1760–72* 141–146; *H.R. Pleadings* Pl. K. 305 [Sessions indictment for assault Aug. 1765]; *NY Misc. Mss. 1758–66* no. 62 [sworn deposition against the defendant by Dr. Magra before Justice of the Peace Whitehead Hicks, July 29, 1765]; *H.R. Pleadings* Pl. K. 325 [certiorari]). Nearly a year and a half later, the defendant appeared "in proper person" in the Supreme Court (Jan. 23, 1767) saying he would "not contend with the King. . . . Whereupon the court set a fine upon the defendant of 6s. 8d. which he paid to the prothonotary in court" (*Ms. Mins. SCJ 1764–67* [Rough] 207; *Misc. Mss. Supreme Ct.* 4th folder [parchment copy of indictment in Supreme Court, Jan. 23, 1767]). The delay and the small fine here indicate composition.

woman is not able to defend herself, removes it to the Supreme Court en banc in order to escape Justice." Two of the Albany justices of the peace wrote to Attorney General Kempe on March 14, 1763, asking him to prevent such a miscarriage of justice "which we cannot help saying is acting that ought not to escape in that manner. . . . We beg your interposition in behalf of the poor woman who has no other remedy." Ewing, having tried his trick, was undone by the Attorney General's superior strategy. Kempe proceeded to move for a *procedendo* since no recognizance as prescribed in the statute had been entered into, and the case remained at General Sessions.[75]

Having considered the policy aspects of certiorari and what may be described as the pathological aspects of the proceeding, we shall next review the administrative details. The writ of certiorari transferring proceedings before trial was, of course, issued out of the higher court directing the judges or justices of the lower court to send the indictment or presentment along with the writ itself into the higher court for further proceedings. In the margin are set forth two examples of the form commonly used in the province.[76] When a

[75] King v. William Ewing (*Ms. Mins. SC] 1762–64* [Engr.] 106, 176, Jan. 22, Apr. 30, 1763; *J. T. Kempe Lawsuits* C *sub nom.* Campbell and Duncan, Albany justices of the peace, letters of Mar. 14, 1763, Feb. 24, 1764). In *Ms. Files Indictments Suffolk Co. 1773–1839* is a draft of an indictment against Mathew Welles for swearing falsely to secure a certiorari.

[76] "George the Third by the Grace of God . . . to John Cruger Mayor and to all other Justices assigned to keep the peace and also to hear and determine divers felonies, Trespasses and other misdeeds . . . and to everyone of them Greeting We being willing for certain causes to be certified of an Indictment or Presentment before you . . . made concerning certain trespasses and misdemeanors whereof John Keating . . . is indicted or presented Therefore We command you . . . that the said indictment or presentment with all things touching or concerning the same to us under your seals . . . You distinctly and openly send together with this writ so that we may have the same before us in our Supreme Court of Judicature . . . in January next that upon view of the said Indictment or presentment We may further cause to be done therein that which of Right and according to Law ought to be done Witness Daniel Horsmanden . . . 26 October 6 George III. . . .
"John Tabor Kempe, Attorney General   Clarke
"Allowed 5 November, 1765, Daniel Horsmanden." This writ was endorsed "The execution of the within writ appears by the return hereunto annexed," but unfortunately the annexed return is missing (King v. John Keating, *H.R. Pleadings* Pl. K. 325). Compare the recital of a writ of cer-

tiorari in King v. George Harrison in the following "Roll, ex^d":
"City and County of New York ss: George Harrison puts in his place James Duane his attorney . . . in a plea of trespass and Contempt whereof he stands Indicted . . . Be it remembered that . . . a Writ of . . . the King under the Seal of the Supreme Court of Judicature . . . issued in these words: . . . King to . . . Mayor of our City of New York and to all other our Justices [of the Peace] of New York . . . Greeting We being willing for certain Causes to be certified of all and Singular Indictments and Presentments . . . before you or some of you taken . . . concerning certain Trespasses and Misdemeanors whereof George Harrison . . . Merchant Indicted or Presented Therefore . . . command you . . . that the said Indictments . . . with all things touching . . . the same to us under your hands and seals . . . you distinctly and openly send together with this Writ, so that We may have them before us . . . [at the April term of the Supreme Court] that upon view of the said Indictments or Presentments we may further cause to be done therein that which of Right and according to Law ought to be done, Witness . . . [our hands and seals etc. Jan. 19, 1760].
"At which day . . . [the] Mayor . . . [and one justice of the peace] returned the Writ thus indorsed The Execution of this Writ appears in a Certain schedule to this Writ annexed . . .: City and County of New York ss.: By Virtue of his Majesty's Writ of Certiorari hereunto annexed and delivered unto me John Cruger Mayor . . . . a Certain Indictment whereof mention is made in the

certiorari was received in the lower court, it was usually read and allowed by the judges of the lower court and a return ordered to be made.[77] In some instances, however, the lower court justices failed to make a return to the certiorari, and repeated orders would then be made by the higher court.[78] Toward the end of the colonial period there are instances where an order would issue for the delinquent justices to show cause why attachment should not be brought against them for their failure to make a return. Thus, in the case of *King* v. *Hendrick Groatfelt,* the following entry appears in the minutes of the Supreme Court for April 23, 1770: "On motion of William Smith [presumably the defendant's attorney] Ordered peremptorily that David Pye Esq. make return to the *certiorari* in this cause by the first day of next term or show cause why an attachment should not issue against him."[79] Apparently in this case, difficulty was experienced even in serving the justice of peace with the order to show cause, for, in the October Term of the Supreme Court for 1770, the above-recited order was again repeated and in the January Term for 1772 an

affidavit of service of the former rule of October Term 1770 being read and filed Ordered that Justice David Pye do lodge the certiorari delivered to him in

said writ . . . I . . . John Cruger distinctly and openly send under my seal as by the said Writ is commanded . . . the Tenor of which Indictment follows . . . [then is stated the purport of the indictment against John Lawrence, George Harrison and others]" (*H.R. Parch.* 136 E 7). This appears to be one of the rare cases where a tenor of a record was sent up from the court below. On the case *King* v. *Lawrence, Harrison et al.,* cf. *infra* 280 *et seq.*

[77] So in Queen v. David Provoost, Jr.: "Emott pro Defend'. produced her Majesty's writt of Certiorari Returnable the Next Supream Court which was read and Allowed & Ordered Return be made thereof Accordingly" (*Ms. Mins. NYCQS 1694–1731/32* 77, Feb. 2, 1702/03). Cf. King v. John Little—"Shasherara read and allowed" (*Ms. Mins. Orange Co. Sess. 1727–79* Oct. 1722); King v. Thomas Pepper (*Ms. Mins. Dutchess Co. Sess.* Liber A, Oct. 18, 1737); King v. Hendrick Therman (*Ms. Mins. Dutchess Co. Sess.* Liber C, Oct. 20, 1760); King v. Barnes (*Ms. Mins. Richmond Co. Sess. 1745–1812* Sept. 28, 1762); King v. Griffiths (*Ms. Mins. Albany Co. Sess. 1763–82* Oct. 14, 1766).

[78] In King v. Johannes Isaacse Lansing, the Supreme Court on April 26, 1737, ordered that the justices return the certiorari by next term, but on August 2, 1737, the justices had apparently not returned the certiorari because the Supreme Court again ordered "on motion of Murray the justices of Albany to return the certiorari by next term" (*Ms.*

Mins. SCJ 1732–39 261, 272). In King v. Susannah Bond, "Ordered judges and justices of Ulster return the certiorari by the first day of next term on motion of Alsop" (*Ms. Mins. SCJ 1750–54* [Engr.] 289, Aug. 4, 1753). In King v. Thomas Forsey, "Ordered the justices of . . . Albany return the certiorari . . . next term" (*Ms. Mins. SCJ 1757–60* [Engr.] 284, Jan. 1760). In King v. Thomas Walton, "Justices of Queens Ordered to return the certiorari by next term" (*Ms. Mins. SCJ 1754–57* [Engr.] 284, July 30, 1756). In King v. William Parks, "Ordered that the Judges and Justices of Dutchess County return the certiorari by the first day of April term" (*ibid.* 124, Jan. 25, 1755). In King v. Jacob Vrooman, an order for the return of a certiorari by the justices of Albany was made on the Attorney General's motion (*ibid.* 53, Aug. 3, 1754).

Compare the early case of Queen v. Hugh Crow where the Attorney General, though anxious to remove the case, was unable to do so because the lower court refused him permission, "Defendant's prayer for discharge from recognizance on bill found *ignoramus* granted," despite the Attorney General's prayer that the recognizance be continued to Supreme Court (*Ms. Mins. NYCQS 1694–1731/32* 108, Feb. 8, 1705/06).

[79] *Ms. Mins. SCJ 1769–72* (Engr.) 203, 294, 479, Apr. 28, Oct. 26, 1770, Jan. 25, 1772. Unfortunately we have been unable to learn the subsequent proceedings in this case.

this cause with his return in the clerk's office in twenty days after service of a copy of this rule on him or that an attachment issue against him.[80]

Sometimes the judges of the lower court, having been ordered to return a certiorari, would offer excuses explaining their failure to do so. Thus Justice Richard Esselstyne "having appeared in court offered reasons for his not returning the certiorari agreable to the rules of this court" and the court "Ordered that he be discharged upon the payment of the reasonable costs."[81] In another case where the certiorari had been returned and filed by Mr. Murray (evidently the attorney for the defendant), "the judge being indisposed and not able to attend the argument in this cause, Ordered the same to be put off until next term."[82]

In the practice just before the Revolution, attachment apparently issued not only when the justices failed to make any return of a certiorari, but also when they made an imperfect return. Thus, in the case of *King* v. *Andrew Lyon:* "Justice Abraham Hetfield having made a return to the Certiorari in this Cause; On Motion of Mr. Witmar Ordered that the Return being imperfet is set aside and that the said Justice do make a proper return to the said Certiorari by . . . next term or shew Cause why an Attachment should not issue against him."[83]

When the certiorari had been read and allowed by the lower court, and the judges of the lower court had ordered a return to be made to it, the writ was then returned or delivered into the higher court. Apparently the original record was attached thereto.[84] The colonial judiciary does not seem to have paid

---

[80] Cf. John Heughan and others adv. the King: "On reading the affidavit of Joseph Moore Ordered attachment issue against John Duncan for returning the certiorari in this cause" (*Ms. Mins. SCJ* 1775–81 [Engr.] 45, Oct. 28, 1775).

[81] *Ms. Mins. SCJ* 1772–76 (Rough) 220, Jan. 21, 1775.

[82] It is to be noted that in this case an order was made eight months later that the justices of Queens return the certiorari by the next succeeding term. However, we have failed to discover any subsequent proceedings in the case: King v. John Batty (*Ms. Mins. SCJ* 1754–57 [Engr.] 196, 197, 284, Oct. 21, 22, 1755, July 30, 1756).

[83] *Ms. Mins. SCJ* 1772–76 (Rough) 221 (fol. 182a), Jan. 21, 1775.

[84] Thus in King v. John Willet Jr.: "Certiorari and return in this cause is this day lodged in court by Mr. Whitehead Hicks" (*Ms. Mins. SCJ* 1764–67 [Rough] 107, Oct. 16, 1765). In King v. Abraham De Peyster: "The certiorari returned and filed with the clerk in the court by Jones" (*Ms. Mins. SCJ* 1756–61 [Rough] 107, July 29, 1758). It is

to be observed that in the latter case, Justice Jones, who returned the certiorari, was one of the judges of the Supreme Court and it is entirely possible that the certiorari in this case had been issued to the Court of Oyer and Terminer and General Gaol Delivery in which Justice Jones had probably been sitting on his yearly circuit. In King v. Wate Hopkins, the following entry appears: "Certiorari delivered into court" (*Ms. Mins. SCJ* 1762–64 [Engr.] 300, Oct. 29, 1763; see also King v. Manuel Myers, King v. William Van Neuys, *Ms. Mins. SCJ* 1756–61 [Rough] 106, July 28, 1758). Indicative of the fact that the record was removed with the certiorari is Queen v. Jacobus Van Cortlandt *et al.* where the record and certiorari were entered, and during the course of the argument in the higher court "a word of the record [was] read" (*Ms. Mins. SCJ* 1710–14 509, 512, 521, 526, 531, Mar. 10, 11, 13, 1713/14, June 2, 5, 1714; Bickley's Supreme Court docket, March, June, September, October Terms, 1714, March, June, September Terms, 1715; F. A. DePeyster Mss. no. 3B).

any attention to the precious distinctions respecting the propriety of transferring a record or a tenor of a record or a tenor of a tenor of a record that fascinated the English text writers.[85] The New York judicial records have suffered great destruction, but even so the remnants would offer some evidence if transcripts had usually been sent in removals by certiorari. There are only one or two cases where it is possible that a tenor of a record was sent up, and we must therefore assume that as a rule the record itself was removed and so, when certiorari was used, the transfer was complete.

Recognizance and Information as Removal Devices

Before proceeding to discuss the disposition of causes transferred by hand or by certiorari,[86] it is desirable, for the sake of completeness, to consider briefly the function of the recognizance and the information procedure as means of removal. These devices will later be considered more fully in connections where they were of greater importance—the recognizance in relation to its general law enforcing function; the information as a type of initiatory mechanism.

We have already pointed out that subsequent to the conquest, and for some years thereafter, transfers from a lower to a higher court were effected chiefly by means of the inferior court binding over an offender for appearance at a superior tribunal.[87] This practice continued during the eighteenth century, and was the simplest and least technical method of removal. Of course, if a defendant was not bailable or could not furnish security he was simply held in custody for the next delivery of the jail.[88] Occasionally a defendant would be

[85] While Dalton states that "the *Certiorari* may be sometimes to remove and send up the Record it self, and sometimes but onely the Tenor of the Record" (*The Countrey Justice* [1677 ed.] 553), Hale takes a different position. "And *note* the difference between a *certiorari* in the king's bench and chancery: In the king's bench the very record itself is removed, and that which remains in the court below is but a scroll. But usually in chancery . . . they remove but the tenor of the record and therefore if the tenor of a record of an indictment . . . be removed by *certiorari* into the chancery, and thence sent by *mittimus* into the king's bench, they cannot thereupon proceed either to judgment or execution, because they have only the tenor of the record before them . . ." (2 *Pleas of the Crown* [1778 ed.] 215).

[86] The following cases were also removed by certiorari in addition to cases cited in other parts of this work: King v. John Van Zandt, removed to

the Supreme Court from New York City Quarter Sessions, Nov. 3, 1748 (*Ms. Mins. NYCQS 1732–62* 240; cf. other references *ibid.* 239, 245, 248, Nov. 2, 1748, Feb. 7, 9, 1748/49); King v. Roger Barnes, removed to the Supreme Court from Richmond Sessions (*Ms. Mins. SCJ 1762–64* [Engr.] 65, 91, Oct. 30, 1762, Jan. 22, 1763); King v. Floyd, removed into the Supreme Court, Apr. 5, 1699 (*Mins. SCJ 1693–1701* 157).

[87] *Supra* 140–141.

[88] In King v. Ker (treasonable words) and King v. Turner (grand larceny) both defendants ordered in custody until next gaol delivery (*Ms. Mins. Ulster Co. Sess. 1737–50* May 7, 1745). Cf. also King v. Noxon (homicide) (*Ms. Mins. Ulster Co. Sess. 1711/12–1720* Aug. 19, 1714), where the defendant, an infant, was kept in jail, and compare King v. Aerie Roosa (homicide) where the child was bailed (*Ms. Mins. Dutchess Co. Sess. Liber A,* Oct. 7, 1727).

bound by recognizance to appear both at Sessions and at the Supreme Court. The latter, by discharging the recognizance for appearance there, could thus in effect remand to Sessions without the necessity even of an order or minute entry.[89] Furthermore in some cases, recognizances were taken in the Supreme Court for the appearance of the defendants to answer "at the next court of Oyer and Terminer and General Gaol Delivery,"[90] and in one early instance the defendant, having already appeared on recognizance in the Supreme Court to answer for the death of an Indian boy, was bound over to appear at a special Court of Oyer and Terminer and Gaol Delivery.[91]

The importance of this device and its manipulation as a means of shuttling cases from one jurisdiction to another can hardly be overemphasized. The eventual control over recognizances was vested in the Supreme Court, for when an offender had been bound in any court for appearance, peace or good behavior, and failed to abide by the conditions of his bond, this was forfeited and the forfeiture was estreated into the Supreme Court. Here would be brought the actions of debt on the bond, and at this juncture the circumstances of binding the offender would often come before the Supreme Court which would thus be enabled to scrutinize the original proceedings. Moreover, the recognizances were occasionally delivered into the Supreme Court *a propria manu*[92] or by certiorari,[93] and by this means, too, a transfer could be ef-

---

[89] E.g., King v. Thomas Lawrence and Ellinor Blackington (*Ms. Mins. SCJ 1723–27* 188, Mar. 15, 1725/26).

[90] Queen v. Zachariah Roberts (*Ms. Mins. SCJ 1704/05–1709* 20, June 2, 1705); Queen v. John Jones (*ibid.* 20, June 2, 4, 1705); King v. Mark Christie (*Ms. Mins. SCJ 1756–61* [Rough] 137, Apr. 20, 1759).

[91] King v. Fred Platt (*Mins. SCJ 1693–1701* 175, 191, 195, 196, Oct. 17, 1699, Apr. 6, 1700, special Court of Oyer and Terminer and General Gaol Delivery in Westchester for June 5, 1700). Cf. also King v. Martinus Lambris, where the prisoner, having pleaded not guilty to the murder of a white woman and a negress and having asked the court to "recommend his Pettition to his Excellency for a special commission that he may come to a speedy tryall," the court ordered that the "Chief Justice do recommend it to my lord." In this case a special Court of Oyer and Terminer was held for the defendant's trial and he was acquitted (*Mins. SCJ 1693–1701* 188, 189, 192, 193, Apr. 6, May 16, 1700).

[92] E.g. in King v. Joseph Taylor, Mr. Justice Chambers "with his own hand delivers into Court the Recognizance taken for the Appearance of the defendant at the Court of Oyer and Terminer &

General Gaol Delivery held in and for the County of Westchester in the month of September last." Process was ordered against this defendant, and later the sheriff of Dutchess returned the first *scire facias* "Nichil." Taylor subsequently filed an affidavit showing that he had been disabled by sickness and hence was unable to attend the Westchester Oyer and Terminer and General Gaol Delivery pursuant to the recognizance. It was therefore ordered that the recognizance be discharged on the defendant's promising to pay the costs occasioned "by his delay in not giving satisfaction to this court sooner" (*Ms. Mins. SCJ 1750–54* [Engr.] 106, 148, 164, Jan. 25, 1751/52, Apr. 30, Aug. 1, 1752). "A Justice of the Peace may deliver or send into the Kings Bench . . . a Recognizance of the Peace taken by him . . . without any *Certiorari*" (Dalton, *The Countrey Justice* [1677 ed.] 553).

[93] King v. Nath. Osborn (*Ms. Mins. SCJ 1727–32* 158, Oct. 21, 1729). ". . . by the statute III H. 7 c. I. It is now enacted, That every Recognizance taken for the Peace, by the Justice of Peace, and Ex Officio, shall be certified (sc. Sent or brought in) at the next Sessions of the Peace" (Dalton, *The Countrey Justice* [1677 ed.] 277). ". . . he that demanded this Surety, 'or he that is bound to

fected and a decision reached by the highest provincial court as to further proceedings.[94]

The manner in which the information was used as a medium of removal may have been a peculiarity of New York procedure, for too little is known about how the information was employed and manipulated in contemporary England for us to relate colonial usage with that in England. Briefly, the system in New York was for the Attorney General to frame an information upon informal presentment made by a local grand jury in lieu of having the presentment drawn up in form as an indictment. County presentments returned into the Circuits or the Supreme Court *en banc* were frequently delivered to the Attorney General with orders to proceed on them. This ordinarily meant that an information would be filed. The types of cases where this occurred were similar to those where Crown informations would have been used in the first instance. Such were matters relating to the administration of justice, Crown revenues, intrusions on Crown lands, interference with Indians and the like. The advantages of the system lay primarily in the greater flexibility of the information and its freedom from the technicalities with which the indictment was loaded, and secondarily, in the circumstance that causes thus informally transferred were committed to the guidance of the chief law officers of the Crown and to the chief court of the province. Even if the case were sent down for trial at nisi prius—a second transfer—the superintendence of the central authority was preserved.

---

the peace,' may by a *Certiorari*, remove such Recognizance into the *Chancery* or *Kings Bench*, before the Justice hath certified the same to the Sessions" (*ibid.* 278).

[94] The following instances indicate how the Crown authorities kept their fingers on the recognizance.

On August 16, 1760, John Surnan was bound over to the peace by Alderman Mesier and thereafter, on August 25, he assaulted John Hunter, allegedly breaking the conditions of his bond, but on Oct. 14, 1760, Attorney General Kempe wrote to Alderman Mesier stating: "I received the enclosed . . . [affidavits regarding the breach of the bond] but I want to know whether they were bound to keep the peace or to their good behavior. . . . If the recognizances are drawn up in form, be pleased to let me see them or a copy . . . if . . . not yet drawn up in form, be pleased to certify whether the conditions of the recognizances are to keep the peace or be of good behavior." (*J. T. Kempe Lawsuits* S–V.) On September 20, 1760, Kempe wrote to Alderman Mesier stating

that he understood that Thomas Yates (Yeats) had been bound over to the good behavior by the alderman and had several times since broken the King's peace, and Kempe asked what amount of security Yates had to post so that he, the Attorney General, might proceed against him according to law. On August 18, 1760, Mesier told Kempe that Yates had been bound to the King in £20. On October 15, 1760, Elizabeth Yates wrote to Kempe stating that Elizabeth Lugg (Sugg) had maliciously sworn the peace against her husband Thomas Yates, and she asked Kempe's protection. On October 18, 1760, Kempe wrote to Mesier asking who swore the peace against Thomas Yates and Mesier told him that Elizabeth Lugg had done so. Evidently as a result of the doubt regarding the affidavits and recognizances in the Surnan and Yates cases, certiorari issued to transfer both cases to the Supreme Court: King v. Surnan, King v. Thomas Yates (*Ms. Mins. NYCQS 1732–62* 488, Nov. 4, 1760). See also the cases of King v. Cornelius and Lawrence Kortright, and King v. Joseph Rodman, cited *infra* 548 *et seq.*; 439 n. 271; 510 n. 100.

The Disposition of Cases Transferred

The transfer jurisdiction of the Supreme Court embraced not merely its authority to act upon causes removed to it by the various methods we have described; it possessed also the inherent power to order the removal of cases where prosecution had been initiated at bar. The implications of this latter power will become obvious when we come to consider the actual functioning of the transfer system in terms of particular types of prosecution. For the moment it will suffice to point out that by moving out cases as well as by drawing them in, the Supreme Court maintained a jurisdictional balance and did not use the transfer system to overextend its own jurisdiction.

The dominance of this notion of balance is apparent from the way in which cases were disposed of. In general, regardless of the method by which the case was brought before the Supreme Court, the various courses open to the court were as follows: 1) if the case had not been properly removed, a writ of *procedendo* would issue whereby the lower court would be ordered to proceed; 2) cases would be remanded or referred if the Supreme Court did not wish to handle them; 3) the case removed could be tried at bar; 4) the case could be sent down for trial at nisi prius.

The New York Supreme Court appears to have followed its own ideas both in regard to *procedendo* and remandings, for here again, the technical rules as set forth by Hale[95] were disregarded. The practice respecting *procedendo* was settled at an early date in a case which caused considerable commotion because it was connected with the episode that gave rise to the Bayard treason trial.[96]

The remote cause of the proceedings was a heated dispute between the Leislerians and their opponents over an election in New York City. On October 10, 1701, the grand jury offered a presentment in the Supreme Court against Johann De Peyster, David Provoost Jr. and Nicholas Roosevelt for "corruptly, maliciously, falsely, fraudulently and deceitfully" returning aldermen, assistant tax collectors and constables "when the majority of the . . . several wards were for other persons." Such was the influence of the defendants that when their attorney, Bickley, moved on October 11, 1701, that the grand jury presentment be quashed, the motion was granted and the defendants discharged.[97] The locus of attack was then shifted, for in the following year, on November 4, 1702, the grand jury presented David Provoost Jr. in Quarter

---

95 2 Hale, *Pleas of the Crown* 213.
96 *Supra* 83 *et seq.*

97 *Ms. Mins. SCJ 1701–04* 20, 21, Oct. 10, 11, 1701.

Sessions "for falsely and Malitiously returning himselfe Alderman . . . contrary to the plurality of voices to the utter overthrow of the liberties and privileges of this city." The defendant's attorney on February 2, 1702/03 produced her Majesty's writ of certiorari returnable in the next Supreme Court. The writ was read and allowed in Quarter Sessions and a return was ordered to be made accordingly. The defendant failed to appear in the Supreme Court in the following term, and the Attorney General on April 6, 1703, prayed that "if defendant doe not appear during the sitting of the court tomorrow . . . *procedendo* to be ordered." Evidently the writ issued, for on May 4, 1703 we find the defendant's attorney, Emott, appearing in the Court of Quarter Sessions and asking time to plead until the next court. The defendant appeared in Quarter Sessions in June 1703 and being tried on his plea of not guilty was acquitted.[98]

There is not much material on the use of *procedendo,* but an entry of 1768[99] shows the early rule applied to a defendant who did not appear to argue in support of a certiorari, and in the case of *King* v. *Ewing,*[100] referred to above, the writ was used where the defendant had failed to post a recognizance.[101]

It will be noticed that in both the Provoost and Salisbury cases just cited although a *procedendo* was used, what in effect took place was a remand, since in both instances the record appears to have been removed. In so acting the Supreme Court seems to have departed from the traditions of King's Bench of which Coke had remarked: "so Supream is the jurisdiction of this court, that if any record be removed into this court, it cannot (being as it were in his centre) be remaunded back unlesse it be by act of parliament.[102] . . . The justices of the King's Bench . . . may grant a nisi prius because only a transcript of the record goes down and they may refuse to receive indictments re-

---

[98] *Ms. Mins. NYCQS 1694–1731/32* 72, 77, Nov. 4, 1702, Feb. 2, 1702/03; *Ms. Mins. SCJ 1701–04* 68, Apr. 6, 1703; *Ms. Mins. NYCQS 1694–1731/32* 79, 81, May 4, 1703, June 1703. The case was apparently not closed at this point for, on October 12, 1703, an indictment was found against David Provoost by the grand jury in the Supreme Court for a false return of an alderman for the West Ward of New York City. The defendant pleaded not guilty, and on April 4, 1704, the Attorney General prayed that a trial take place. Although his motion was granted, nevertheless on October 12, 1704, the Attorney General entered a *nolle prosequi (Ms. Mins. SCJ 1701–04* 120, 130, 168).
[99] King v. Salisbury (*Ms. Mins. SCJ 1766–69* [Engr.] 511, July 30, 1768).
[100] *Supra* 157.

[101] We have also noted cases where indictments were removed at the instance of the defendant and judgment against the defendant was threatened because of his failure to plead. So, in the case of Nicholas Brittain, an indictment found in Richmond (*Ms. Mins. Richmond Co. Sess. 1710/11–1744/45* Mar. 25, 1738) was, on Jan. 23, 1738/39, removed into the Supreme Court by certiorari and, Smith as defendant's attorney appearing on his behalf, the court ordered that the defendant plead within twenty days or suffer judgment. For further proceedings, *infra* 579 n. 122.
[102] *Fourth Institute* (1809 ed.) 73. Hawkins adds the further limitation "It is certain that they [the justices of the peace] cannot proceed on an indictment taken before a coroner or justices of oyer and terminer or gaol delivery . . ." (2 *Pleas of the Crown* [1787 ed.] 56).

moved by practise or delay."[103] Both Coke and Hale, however, regarded the statute 6 Henry VIII c.6 as authorizing remand[104] in cases of "felons and murders," but the Provoost and Salisbury cases indicate that if this statute was known it was not regarded. We have no other clear cases of remand. What the records do show, however, are cases of remitting to Sessions for prosecution presentments found in the Supreme Court. Since this also involves the supposedly sacrosanct quality of King's Bench records and since this must be distinguished from remand, it will be convenient to consider it here. The New York practice for which some justification can be found in Hale,[105] appears to have developed as a result of a pedantic insistence on indictments as a foundation for a record, since the cases of remitting to Sessions which we have noticed were informal grand jury presentments which had not yet been drawn up "in form" and on which true bills had evidently not been found.

The practice of reference in cases of petty crime where the magistrates were clothed with statutory or common law powers to hear and determine, grew up in New York at a time when the professional knowledge of the bench was inconsiderable. The proprietary Court of Assizes and the later Court of Oyer and Terminer had established this usage,[106] and it was followed by the Supreme Court after the Judicature Act of 1691. Thus in 1693, a presentment of three persons for entertaining negroes was referred by the Supreme Court to the mayor and aldermen of New York City at the next Quarter Sessions.[107] Two defendants subsequently pleaded guilty and were fined at Sessions but the third defendant, who had been bound over, was ordered to be tried in the Mayor's Court.[108] In the succeeding years presentments for the same offense[109] and for profaning the Sabbath[110] were likewise remitted to the mayor of New York City for further action.

[103] Coke, *Fourth Institute* 74.

[104] 2 Hale, *Pleas of the Crown* 41.

[105] "At common law, if a record of an indictment, or other thing, come into the court [King's Bench] before the filing thereof, the court may remand it; for 'till it be filed it is no record of the court; but if it be once filed; it is not to be remanded" (2 Hale, *Pleas of the Crown* 3).

[106] *Supra* 140, 141.

[107] King v. Hutchins, Marchand and Roos (*Mins. SCJ 1693–1701* 43, Apr. 6, 1693).

[108] *Ms. Mins. NYCQS 1683/84–1694* 160, 161, 163.

[109] King v. Rachel Hunt (*Mins. SCJ 1693–1701* 192, Apr. 6, 1700).

[110] "The Bench having sent for the Mayr and Aldermen did cause to be read . . . an Addresse from the Grand Jury setting forth a Genll Breach of the Lords day and urged their diligence in causing the constables to go about during divine service" (*Mins. SCJ 1693–1701* 128, 129, Oct. 9, 1697). "King v. New York City. The Grand Jury present the Citty of New York for suffering and conniving at the Generall breach and profanation of the Sabbath by the frequent meeting of negroes in tumultuous crowds the common playing of children upon the street, the frequenting of publick taverns and ale houses. Ordered this Presentment be recommended to the Mayor of the Citty of New York" (*ibid.* 192, Apr. 6, 1700). "King v. Magistrates of New York City. Ordered that the presentment of the Grand Jury be sent to ye Magistrates of this City and that they be directed to take care that the laws be put in due execution for the future, relating to the prophaneing of the sabath and regulating the streets of the City" (*Ms. Mins. SCJ 1701–04* 60, Apr. 10, 1702).

At Circuit the presentments of trivial offenses were remitted during the eighteenth century,[111] and it is from an entry respecting a presentment of a negro for attempted rape at an Ulster Oyer and Terminer for July 9, 1748, that we discover how a technical justification of the New York practice was eventually found: "The court being informed the fellow had left the county and that the crime was tryable by the justices of the peace pursuant to the act of the Assembly, they did not order the presentment to be put in form."[112] In other words the Court of Oyer and Terminer in this instance, by not permitting a record to be made up, in effect remitted the case.

In the causes where the Supreme Court did not relinquish jurisdiction after the removal, the initial problem was that of the locus of trial, viz., at bar or at Circuit. Since in either case control was maintained, although it was more immediate where the trial was at bar, reasons of convenience and of expense were the chief considerations involved. Convenience here was the complicated balancing of the state of the calendar, the desirability of speedy trial and the judges' dislike of extended circuits. The matter of expense was perhaps a more weighty factor and needs some explanation.

The chief expense in connection with trials at bar was that of transporting the witnesses to New York City as well as a jury of the vicinage which the common law, as accepted in the Province, made mandatory. In England, the nisi prius system owed much of its success to the fact that it saved the subject the expense of a trial at bar, but in New York, geography, the wilderness and the conditions of colonial travel combined to make the expense of a circuit trial sometimes greater than a trial before the court *en banc*. This was re-

---

[111] Cf. the minutes of the Suffolk County Oyer and Terminer for August 21, 1717, when the grand jury "made the following presentments, viz.: Wee the Grand Jurors for our Sovereign Lord the King do present . . . John Goodwin . . . for profane Swearing yesterday by saying By God . . . [here are named two witnesses] Benjamin Nicoll for Vain swearing and Cursing four or five times at least the last night . . . [here are named two witnesses] Joseph Hawkins . . . and Benjamin Ketcham . . . for profane Swearing this day . . . [here are named three witnesses] Nathaniel Woodol . . . for Breach of the peace for Striking of Aaron Owen and other abuses on the Road Between Obadiah Smith's & Brookhaven about a fortnight or three weeks ago . . . [one witness named] Daniel Turner for profane swearing yesterday . . . [one witness named] . . . [these presentments were signed by the foreman of the grand jury]." The court then made the following order remitting these cases to Sessions: "All Wh^ch presentm^ts are Recommended to ye Justices of the peace of ye Gen-

eral Quarter Sessions in order to have ye offenders prosecuted" (1 *Ms. Mins. Cir. 1716–17* 46).

Thomas Hunt, Mansfield Hunt and Thomas Baxter were each arraigned on three indictments at Westchester Oyer and Terminer on August 12, 1721, for riotously taking geese, for a "trespass" in taking a pig and for entering J.W.'s close and taking his leather. The defendants, Thomas Hunt and Thomas Baxter, pleaded guilty and were fined 5*s.* each on each indictment. These two defendants were also ordered to post recognizances in £10, with one surety each in £10, for their good behavior until the next General Sessions of the peace where they were ordered to appear again—a partial remit.

[112] King v. Robin (*Ms. Mins. Cir. 1721–49* 123). The offense for which Robin was presented was that of "attempting to commit rape on the body of Elizabeth Davenport, wife of Gerrit Davenport." The act of assembly referred to by the court is probably that passed by the assembly on October 29, 1730 (2 *Col. Laws NY* 679).

marked upon, as we have seen, by the court in the case of *DuBois* v. *Terboss*. In certain instances the difficulties of transporting a large panel of jurymen seem to have been met by the device of using a struck jury. The earliest evidence we have seen on this is an order in a case of 1728[113] where the sheriff of Queens was ordered to return a list of freeholders and a special jury to be chosen from the list.[114]

Of course even the economies effected by using a special jury did not eliminate expenses and necessities of finding money to conduct a trial at bar. When George Klock was informed against as a disturber of the peace and of Indian relations, Attorney General John Tabor Kempe, writing to Sir William Johnson on January 3, 1763, stated that Klock "has not got over the prosecution ordered against him by the Governor and Council, . . . I would wish to try it next April in New York could I fall on a means of defraying expenses of a Jury from the county of Albany here, but as there is no fund in the Provinces for these contingent expenses I believe it must be putt off till the next Circuit at Albany."[115]

Not the least of the expenses at Circuit was the problem of examining witnesses remote from the county seat. Attorney General Kempe, writing to the Lieutenant Governor on March 8, 1762, regarding the prosecution of John Henry Lydius for intrusion on Crown lands, stated:

113 King v. Adam & Thos. Smith *et al.*, debt for breach of recognizance (*Ms. Mins. SCJ 1723–27* 279; *Ms. Mins. SCJ 1727–32* 22, 27, 37, 45, 68, Dec. 5, 1727, Mar. 15, 19, 1727/28, June 11, 1728). It will be noted that on October 8, 1728, upon the sheriff's failure to return the *scire facias, scire feci*, judgment was ordered. However, on Oct. 12 and 15, 1728, on the *sci. fa.*, the rule was enlarged in favor of the defendant and he was ordered to plead in twenty days or judgment to be rendered against him (*ibid.* 72, 83, 88).

114 The procedure is discussed *infra* c. X 619. For the moment compare the account in the case of King v. Vanderveer, an information for perjury (*H.R. Parch.* 141 E 6). On July 30, 1752, on the motion of the defendant's attorney in the Supreme Court *en banc*, the court "Ordered that unless the Attorney General bring this cause to tryal the next circuit Coᵗ at Kings County that the defendant be discharged." The court also ordered that the former rule for a struck jury in this cause be revived, "that the sheriff of Kings return a Book of the Freeholders of the said county into the clerk's office on or before Tuesday August 24 and that on Friday August 28, the Clerk in the presence of one of the judges shall, strike 48 names out of the said Book of Freeholders that each party strike out 12 of the said 48 names and the remaining 24 to try the cause, and if either [party] neglect giv-

ing their attendance the Clerk strike [out the names] for the absent party" (*Ms. Mins. SCJ 1750–54* [Engr.] 157, July 30, 1752). The writ for the struck jury is to be found in *H.R. Parch.* 160 G 5, and was an order from the King to the Sheriff of Westchester: "Greeting We Command you that You Cause to Come before Us . . . [at the Supreme Court *en banc* or at Kings County *nisi prius*] . . . the bodies of the several persons named in the pannel . . . annexed . . . [with property worth] Sixty pounds . . . being a struck Jury . . . specially appointed . . . by the Information of . . . Attorney General . . . Witness . . . James De Lancey Chief Justice . . ." Endorsed on the back of the writ is the following entry: "The execution of this writ appears in the pannel." The annexed panel was endorsed: "Our sovereign Lord the King v. Dominicus Vanderveer Esqr the jury called appear and say . . . [that they find the defendant] not guilty—a list of the struck jury." The panel itself contained a list of the jury in the above cause struck before the chief and second justices of the Supreme Court on August 29, 1752 (*Ms. Mins. SCJ 1750–54* [Engr.] 188, Oct. 24, 1752; *Ms. Mins. SCJ 1750–56* [Rough] 114, Oct. 25, 1752). The defendant was acquitted, cf. the *postea, H.R. Parch.* 141 E 6.

115 *J. T. Kempe Lawsuits* J–L.

The prosecution . . . for the Intrusion being now at Issue may be brought to tryal next Circuit in Albany but I am yet uninformed of the Proofs . . . I would beg leave to propose . . . that the Mayor of Albany or some person of Integrity . . . be directed to enquire out the witnesses and take their Examinations . . . and as the Witnesses . . . live . . . at a great Distance from the City of New York, that the Sheriff of the County . . . may be directed to serve them with Subpoenas, for . . . your honor will not think it incumbent on me at my own expense to hire Persons to do this Service for the Crown.[116]

This, to be sure, was a case of considerable difficulty and importance, and ordinarily trials at Circuit would not involve great outlays. It is significant, however, in illustrating budgetary difficulties in handling prosecutions for violation of Crown rights.

When cases removed were actually put on the calendar for trial at bar, they suffered any variety of fate. Thus the indictment might be quashed,[117] or a rule entered that the defendant plead within a certain period or suffer judgment for want of a plea,[118] or if the Attorney General failed to move, the defendant could be discharged.[119] Sometimes the defendant would plead guilty[120] or *nolo contendere*[121] and judgment would then be entered. In many instances, of course, the case would actually come to trial by jury. This happened most frequently in the causes where informations were brought although, as we shall presently see, these would also be sent down for trial at nisi prius.

[116] *J. T. Kempe Lawsuits* L–O *sub nom*. John Henry Lydius, letter of Mar. 8, 1762.

[117] King v. John Little (*Ms. Mins. SCJ 1727–32* 18, 34, Mar. 15, 1727/28).

[118] Thus in King v. Moses Owen, *infra* 179.

[119] King v. Remsen and Thomas (*Ms. Mins. SCJ 1727–32* 245, 261, 321, 354).

[120] King v. Terboss, Sackett *et al.*, "The following presentment &. Indictments were delivered into court and the court delivered it to the Atty. General with orders to proceed thereupon vizt. presentment of the grand jury of Ulster for forcible entry" (*Ms. Mins. SCJ 1764–67* [Rough] 85, Aug. 1, 1765). "Information read and filed for a Riot, by Order of the Court on a Presentment in Ulster County at the Circuit Court in June last . . . Ordered Process to issue" (*Ms. Mins. SCJ 1764–66* [Engr.] 368, Oct. 1765). ". . . it appearing to the Court, that Nathaniel Sackett the other defendant was attending as a Grand Juror in Dutches, Ordered that his appearance be dispensed with for this Term and the Defendants to have time until . . . next Term to produce Depositions in Mitigation of Fine" (*ibid.* 404, Aug. 1766). "Daniel Terboss and Nathaniel Sackett fined 20 shillings

each paid into prothonotary . . . and discharged" (*Ms. Mins. SCJ 1764–67* [Rough] 171, Oct. 24, 1766). See also King v. Ambrose Jones, George Elms, William Henderson, Michael Brenner, and David Day. Judgment for want of a plea was found against Elms, while Ambrose Jones was fined 6s. 8d. on a plea of guilty. Michael Brenner died and William Henderson ran away (*Ms. Mins. SCJ 1766–69* [Engr.] 78, 94, 304, Oct.–Nov. 1, 1766, Jan. 24, 1767, Oct. 21, 1767; *H.R. Parch.* 184 E 4, 185 G 2, 194 H 5, 221 B 4; *J. T. Kempe Lawsuits* C–F).

[121] King v. Van Schaick and Ten Eyck, an information for preventing a partition under the Act of 1762 for collecting the quitrents. The information is in *H.R. Parch.* 165 H 8, and this document also contains the defendant's plea and the writ to summon the jury to bar. The nisi prius roll in King v. Anthony Van Schaick is to be found in *J. T. Kempe Lawsuits* V. The Supreme Court minute entries are as follows: *Ms. Mins. SCJ 1762–64* (Engr.) 361, Jan. 28, 1764; *Ms. Mins. SCJ 1764–67* (Rough) 11, 46, Aug. 4, 1764, Apr. 1765. Also see Kempe's Rules, Apr. 16, 1765, *H.R. Pleadings* Pl. K. 733.

Some of the information cases tried at bar are interesting for the light they throw upon the way in which prosecutions that presented difficulties in securing convictions were managed. Thus, when the justices of Queens County were informed against by Attorney General Bradley in 1723 for failing to keep the county jail in repair, the Attorney General moved that the venue be changed from Queens to Westchester County and that the case be tried at bar. Obviously, here considerations more important than geography and expense dictated the advisability of trying the case at bar rather than at nisi prius.[122]

The same tactics were employed against the justices of Albany who were also informed against in 1723 for the non-repair of the Albany jail, and again it was ordered that the information be tried at bar the following term.[123] The case dragged on without coming to trial, and Bradley appears to have exacted some money from the defendants. The matter was aired in the assembly in 1727, and Bradley made a formal defense to the charges against him.[124] Probably as a result of this pressure the case was finally sent down for trial at nisi prius in 1729.[125]

Of a somewhat different type was the information against John Shakemaple of Suffolk County who was charged with trespass in taking away fourteen tierces of rum and ten casks of brandy belonging to the King. It was ordered that the cause be tried at bar and a petit jury in the Supreme Court found for the plaintiff, that is, the King, 5s. damages and costs and also found that the defendant had taken away two "cagges of brandy, part of the goods in the Declaration mentioned."[126]

---

[122] *Ms. Mins. SCJ 1723–27* 72, Mar. 17, 1723/24. Attorney General Bradley's information charged that under an act of assembly of June 24, 1719 (1 *Col. Laws NY* 1025), authorizing and empowering the justices of the peace on the presentment of the grand jury or on their own view to issue warrants to collect moneys for the building and repair of jails, the grand juries at the Queens Sessions and Court of General Gaol Delivery presented the Queens jail as being ruinous and in disrepair. But the justices, "the said act of assembly not minding or their duty regarding but the same wholly dispising, &. contending the common gaol for the county aforesd. by the manifest neglect &. default of them the s^{d.} Justices is . . . very ruinous . . . to the great impoverishment of many his Maties liege subjects &. more especially such as reside in the county . . . &. also in breach of the publick Credit of the province" (*H.R. Parch.* 102 G 8). On June 5, 1724, the jury was sworn for the trial of the Queens County justices, and on motion of the Attorney General the act for repair of jails, the information

of the Attorney General, a rule of the court, the minutes of the justices and the "representation of the grand jury" were read. However, the defendants were found not guilty by the jury at bar (*Ms. Mins. SCJ 1723–27* 83, 84; also see *ibid.* 23, Oct. 9, 1723).

[123] *Ms. Mins. SCJ 1723–27* 72, Mar. 17, 1723/24.

[124] 1 *Jour. Gen. Assembly* 569, 599.

[125] *Infra* 173.

[126] On October 9, 1723, it was ordered on the Attorney General's motion that the sheriff of New York bring in the body of the defendant Shakemaple or be amerced 40s., and on March 17, 1723/24, the defendant was ordered to plead in five weeks' time or suffer judgment. On October 15, 1724, on the motion of the Attorney General, it was ordered "that this cause be tryed at Barr the next Terme," and on November 27, 1724, the jury made the finding quoted in the text *supra* (*Ms. Mins. SCJ 1723–27* 23, 71, 103, 116). For the information against this defendant, see *H.R. Parch.*

It is virtually impossible to formulate any conclusions respecting the policy of sending down cases removed for trial at nisi prius. Most of the transfers by certiorari to the Supreme Court were from New York City, and it is only occasionally that cases were removed to the Supreme Court from the country. This explains, perhaps, why we have found no clear case of a double removal of an indictment, viz., from Sessions to the Supreme Court and thence remitted for trial at Circuit. All the examples we have of such double removal relate to inquests on forcible entries, which are not in any strict sense indictments. There is, however, no evidence that the Supreme Court felt hampered by the text writers' admonitions respecting the remitting of a record once transferred. On the contrary, some correspondence of John Tabor Kempe indicates that such objections were not even thought of.[127]

For the most part the nisi prius system on the criminal side was used in connection with the information procedure, that is to say, where the Attorney General exhibited an information originally in the Supreme Court, or where he had drawn it upon an informal presentment, and the causes were sent down for trial in the country. We have already outlined[128] how nisi prius operated, with the Supreme Court controlling the pleading to issue,[129] the remission for

120 G 5. It is also interesting to note that in James Alexander's papers he has the following note for November Term, 1724: "Drew the writ and declaration [sic] for . . . Bradley . . . and assisted him in making up the issue tried this term. The jury fined 5/ damages 6d. costs and they find he carried away two Kegs of brandy part of the goods . . . and being asked if they gave damages for the value of the brandy they answered No but only for the trespass done. Mr. Bradley owes me for the services done by me in this action for the King" (James Alexander, *Supreme Ct. Reg. 1721–42* no. 10). It is interesting that the Supreme Court minutes do not contain any reference to the jury's statement that they had not given damages for the value of the brandy but simply "damages" for the trespass done.

127 In King v. William Chase, one Lake complained to the Attorney General on Oct. 30, 1761, requesting that Chase be prosecuted for assaulting Lake's mulatto cook, and in order to support his complaint, Lake submitted John Farrel's affidavit that Chase had broken the cook's leg and said, "Dam the black bitch I will kill her." Chase was thereafter indicted for assault and battery in Albany Sessions, 1762, but on Jan. 30, 1762, Peter Sylvester of Albany wrote to Attorney General Kempe as follows: "As the assault and battery was a very severe one, and . . . attended with many acts of cruelty, I thought best to acquaint you of it that

the indictment may be removed by certiorari and be proceeded against in the Supreme Court. If you think fit otherwise process shall be issued out of our court here." Apparently Kempe felt that if the indictment were to be transferred to the Supreme Court by certiorari, it would have to be tried at nisi prius, for on March 19, 1763, he wrote to Sylvester saying: "I received your letter of 30 January . . . relating to the Indictment found against William Chase, and the suits intended to be brought for the damages sustained by the assault and battery. . . . As to the removal of the indictment, it cannot possibly be returned into the Supreme Court time enough to be tried next Circuit, as your next Quarter Sessions is not till after the next Supreme Court, so that I must wait till after next court before I can issue the certiorari" (*J. T. Kempe Lawsuits* C–F sub nom. King v. William Chase).

128 Supra 78.

129 Upon joinder, a venire would go out for trial at the Supreme Court, but by the usual fiction the jurors would not appear; another day would be given, and finally a *distringas* or *habeas corpus juratorum* would issue for trial at bar unless before that date the Supreme Court justices should come to the county for the "trial of causes brought to issue in the Supreme Court." Cf. here the recital in the judgment roll, King v. John Henry Lydius (*H.R. Parch.* 219 D 4).

trial at the Circuit,[130] the return of the proceedings in the form of a *postea*[131] to the Supreme Court and the rendering of judgment at bar,[132] when the judgment roll was finally made up. Obviously the Crown derived certain advantages from the fact that actual prosecution of misdemeanors committed in any part of the province could be initiated at bar even if locally presented, and from the fact that those phases of a prosecution where technical skill was needed were conducted at the provincial capital. The out-of-town defendant was in this relation at a disadvantage unless he could afford to retain counsel; but, as the outcome of many cases shows, he might derive benefit from the fact that the actual trial was held locally.

The Transfer System at Work

The information and the nisi prius system in combination had implications, however, that ran far beyond the immediate balance of advantage in individual cases, for as administered they possessed a political importance which cannot be deduced from an account of the mechanics alone. It is only from a scrutiny of the cases that it becomes apparent how the transfer system in this and its other phases functioned as a main gear in the machinery of law enforcement operated by the royal officials. For this reason, therefore, we shall consider a number of prosecutions which should bring into focus the manifold utility of this jurisdiction and at the same time illustrate the procedure at

[130] The jury's verdict was entered both on the minutes of the Circuit as well as endorsed in transcript of the record sent down; cf. for example, King v. Albertson (*Ms. Mins. Cir. 1721–49* 322; *Ms. Mins. SCJ 1732–39* 351, Aug. 6, 1739).

[131] The usual entry appeared in the Supreme Court minutes thus: "Postea returned read and filed," and on motion either of the Attorney General or of the defendant, depending in whose favor the verdict was found, judgment was ordered unless cause were shown to the contrary. See, for example, King v. Isaac Lent *et al.* (*Ms. Mins. SCJ 1764–67* [Rough] 81, July 31, 1765).

In the Lydius case the *postea* was returned and filed in the Supreme Court on the Attorney General's motion on Oct. 20, 1763, and on Jan. 17, 1764, the record was read and filed and a *concilium* made (*Ms. Mins. SCJ 1762–64* [Engr.] 277, 342). On Jan. 28, 1764, the defendant was ordered to reply to the Attorney General on the first Thursday of the following term, and on April 18, 1764, the defendant made his argument (*ibid.* 361, 411). Cf. *infra* 215.

[132] It would appear that the original record was not sent down to the court at nisi prius but merely

a transcript, and the *postea* endorsed thereon. Thus in the judgment roll in King v. John Henry Lydius, after the trial at nisi prius on June 23, 1763, "it is told to the said John Henry Lydius that he Expect his day before the above said Judges or Justices or some or one of them at the said day and place [i.e., June 23, 1763] and that he be here [that is, in the Supreme Court *en banc*] on the said last Tuesday in July to hear his Judgement if &c.

"AT which said last Tuesday in July before our said Lord the King at the City of New York comes as well the aforesaid John Tabor Kempe Attorney General for our said Lord the King &c. who prosecutes &c. as the Said John Henry Lidius in his own proper Person and David Jones Esqr our Said Lord the Kings Second Justice of the said Supreme Court . . . and Robert R. Livingston Esqr. our Said Lord the Kings fourth Justice of the said Supreme Court before whom &c. Sent hither the Tenor of the Record aforesaid thus Indorsed to wit AFTERWARDS . . ." (*H.R. Parch.* 219 D 4).

It will be noted in this judgment roll (which is the formal record in the case) that it is clearly stated that the tenor of the record was returned with the *postea* endorsed thereon.

work. The details of practice will not make enlivening reading; but they are indispensable to an understanding of the mechanics. Attention to the chronology of particular cases may seem overmeticulous; but not otherwise can one sense the sluggish pulse beat of superior court procedure in the eighteenth century.

The cases selected are many of them interesting for the glimpses they give into the seamy sides of colonial life. They fall into four main categories: 1) those relating to public officers in the administration of justice; 2) a miscellaneous group; 3) those dealing with assaults, forcible entries and riots; 4) those involving Crown lands.

Cases Relating to Public Officers

The cases in the first group are of course of particular importance since they concerned matters that touched the very heart of effective law enforcement. Here, one would suppose, both subject and royal officer would see eye to eye, and yet the record of the several Attorneys General, measured in terms of convictions, was one of frustration at the hands of the freeholders in the jury box. It is possible that this was due to the unfortunate circumstance that the first important prosecutions of magistrates by Attorney General Richard Bradley were regarded as persecutory. We have already referred to the proceedings against the justices of Queens (where the trial was at bar) and against the Albany magistrates where the information was sent down for trial at Circuit.[133] In this last case, after all the delays in coming to trial, Bradley dropped proceedings against two justices and he suffered the discomfiture of an acquittal as to the others. The political repercussions of the Albany case were considerable and, as we shall later see, led to an attempt to restrict the use of informations. The colonists patently resented employment of the criminal machinery against local magistrates for what amounted to mere negligence in the execution of certain statutory duties.[134] Indeed, the pressure of opinion was such that prosecution for this type of misfeasance thereafter languished[135] and

---

[133] The information is in *Misc. Mss. Albany 1691–1792.* Cf. also *Ms. Mins. SCJ 1727–32* 23, 29, 32, 36, 72, 132, 133, 253, 265, 279; *Ms. Mins. Cir. 1721–49* 252, 253; *H.R. Parch.* 67 B 2, 123 L 1, 1 G 1.

[134] There are various entries in *Ms. Mins. Albany Co. Sess. 1717–23* on the jail, and although orders had been made, there was a lack of vigor on the part of the magistrates.

[135] After the Albany justices had been acquitted, it was ordered on Dec. 2, 1729, that the Attorney General have leave to file informations anew (*Ms. Mins. SCJ 1727–32* 141, 177). This was done and a capias ordered to issue (*ibid.* 188, 191). Another order of process was made in August, 1734 (*Ms. Mins. SCJ 1732–39* 116). There is no further entry. We are disposed to believe the matter was abandoned for reasons of political expediency.

for a space the complaints against justices of the peace were mainly handled in the Council.[136]

The outcry against informations did not affect the prosecutions for malfeasance. Bradley, who appears throughout his career as a nemesis of the justice of the peace, in July, 1735, filed an information against one Moses Fowler, a Westchester justice, as a "person of unpeaceable Turbulent and domineering spirit, a stirrer up of strife and arrogantly assuming to himself a power above the rest of the justices of the peace." Fowler's brother had brought an action of debt for a penalty for cutting one of his geldings and although the witnesses swore that the defendant was not guilty, yet Fowler, "craftily and wickedly devising to perswade" one of the witnesses to give "corrupt evidence" against the defendant, adjourned the action and stated that he would try to get what evidence he could against the defendant. Later Fowler gave judgment against the defendant contrary to the opinion of the other justices.[137] On August 4, 1735, process was ordered to issue out against Justice Fowler from the Supreme Court *en banc*.[138] On January 24, 1735/36, the sheriff of Westchester returned *venire feci,* and on motion of the Attorney General the defendant, Fowler, was ordered to plead in twenty days or suffer judgment against him for want of a plea.[139] On January 27, 1735/36, a venire issued to the sheriff of Westchester to summon a jury for the trial of the defendant.[140] The Circuit minutes for Westchester for March 23 and March 24, 1735/36, contain the trial of Moses Fowler at nisi prius. There it was ordered that two witnesses have the court's protection to give evidence, an indication that local feeling was inflamed. The witnesses for the King (including several justices of the peace) and for the defendant were sworn. The jury at Circuit found Moses Fowler not guilty.[141] The Circuit jury's verdict was endorsed as a *postea* on the transcript of the record sent down to nisi prius,[142] and on April 20, 1736, Chambers moved that the clerk of the Circuit return the *postea* by the following Saturday. On Saturday, April 22, 1736, the *postea* was returned and filed in the Supreme Court *en banc* and the court ordered "judgment thereupon unless cause shewn."[143]

<hr/>

[136] See, for example, 16 *Ms. Mins. Council* 189 (1732); 17 *ibid.* 87 (1736); 19 *ibid.* 25 (1739), 137, 141 (1741).

[137] *H.R. Parch.* 75 F 5. This document also contains the defendant's plea of not guilty to the information.

[138] *Ms. Mins. SCJ 1732–39* 178.

[139] *Ibid.* 200.

[140] The venire, containing the usual fictional

command for the jurors to be summoned to the Supreme Court *en banc* in April, 1736, unless before that time the justices should come to the court for the trial of causes in Westchester in March, 1735/36, is to be found in a parchment strip attached to *H.R. Parch.* 113 F 2.

[141] *Ms. Mins. Cir. 1721–49* 299.

[142] For the *postea,* see *H.R. Parch.* 113 F 2.

[143] *Ms. Mins. SCJ 1732–39* 208, 210. On August

In the proceedings against Fowler, the interest of the Crown was merely that justice should be fairly administered. But in certain prosecutions initiated years later by John Tabor Kempe against various Dutchess officials for malfeasance, the issues involved affected the Crown much more painfully, since then it was a matter of revenue. The case involved the collection of recognizances which were in default, a matter that will be further discussed in Chapter VIII. Suffice it here to remark that Kempe was at this time attempting to put the collection of these revenues on a sound footing and consequently the Dutchess cases were of trenchant importance. In the first prosecution, as the information relates, Jacobus Terboss and eighteen other justices of the peace on May 15, 1764, at the Court of General Sessions of the Peace of Dutchess County "craftily and illegally intending under color of their offices to usurp the powers of the Supreme Court of Judicature as a court of Exchequer" caused recognizances on which there had been defaults to be put in suit in the General Sessions of the Peace. They had then issued process against the defaulters causing them to appear in the General Sessions of the Peace to answer the King in a plea to render several sums of money. Under the law, these recognizances should have been estreated into the Supreme Court of Judicature as a court of Exchequer. But these justices of the peace, yielding to the prevailing dislike for collecting the direct revenues of the Crown, had permitted the money due to be collected locally, and possibly had also benefited financially.[144] A total of four informations were filed against these nineteen delin-

7, 1733, another information had been filed in the Supreme Court *en banc* against Moses Fowler and process issued against him, but we have been unable to find the subsequent disposition of that case (*ibid.* 44, 46). Fowler was again in the toils of the law on Aug. 3, 1736, when process was ordered to issue against him out of the Supreme Court *en banc* "for divers misdemeanors," and on October 20, 1736, the defendant entered his appearance in the Supreme Court *en banc* and was ordered to plead in twenty days or suffer judgment against him for want of a plea (*ibid.* 228, 232). On March 22, 1736/37, the Circuit minutes for Westchester contain the trial of Moses Fowler for divers misdemeanors, and Clowes and Chambers appeared for the King while Joseph Murray appeared for the defendant. In this case "the court ruled yt ye person was one William —— Justice Fowler had given judgment against which judgment was charged as a crime in said justice by ye information. He might be an evidence." It would appear from this statement in the course of the Circuit trial that Moses Fowler had again been guilty of maladministration as a justice of the peace. However, the jury at the Westchester Circuit again found this justice of the peace of the county not guilty (*Ms. Mins. Cir. 1721–49* 304, 305). On April 20, 1737, a *postea* embodying the Circuit verdict was read and filed in the Supreme Court *en banc* (*Ms. Mins. SCJ 1732–39* 253).

144 For a very detailed description of the offenses of these remiss justices of the peace, see *H.R. Pleadings* Pl. K. 795, containing the Attorney General's information against them. Cf. also *infra* c. VIII 526, for the Supreme Court rule respecting estreats. For some sample estreats returned from the various courts, see the following: *H.R. Parch.* 192 A 2 (a return from Suffolk Sessions of the Peace for Mar. and Oct., 1764); 218 D 1 (an estreat of issues forfeited at Ulster and Dutchess Oyer and Terminer and General Gaol Delivery, 1765, 1766, 1767). *H.R. Pleadings* Pl. K. 449 contains an account of estreats of issues from Queens Sessions of the Peace from 1757 to 1763, and this was filed on Oct. 18, 1763, probably as a result of the order of July, 1763. The offenses mentioned in this estreat were: an insult and assault and battery on justices of the peace, £6 and £10 fines; assaults, 5s., £1, £5 fines; disorderly gaming houses, 2s. and £4 fines; and delinquent grand jurors, 16s. fines. At-

quent justices of the peace for maladministration in office, and in August, 1765, the defendants were ordered to plead in twenty days or suffer judgment. In October, 1765, the sheriff of Dutchess returned the defendants taken and on May 2, 1767, judgment for want of a plea was ordered against Anthony Yelverton and John Bogardus. The other defendants were tried at the Dutchess Circuit Court for June, 1767, and were found not guilty. The verdict was undoubtedly against the weight of the evidence, for against Justice James Smith it was shown that he failed to record the default of a defendant who did not appear at the Court of Oyer and Terminer for Dutchess. Against Justice Mathew DuBois it was shown that he had taken a £200 recognizance for the appearance of a witness against one James Cook, held for passing a counterfeit, and that DuBois had failed to return the recognizance, thus causing a bill against Cook to be quashed because the court did not know that the material witness had been summoned (even though he was present).[145]

The opportunity for misfeasance was not confined to magistrates, for Kempe's second prosecution was directed against Henry Livingston, clerk of the peace of Dutchess County. An information was filed against Livingston for his failure to return recognizances into the Supreme Court of Judicature as a court of Exchequer and

> the Duty of his said office . . . little regarding and the Trust and Confidence in him reposed entirely perverting and devising and intending craftilly and unlawfully the King to defraud . . . for his own private Lucre and Gain unlawfully to oppress . . . the persons bound in the said Recognizances . . . with force and arms . . . did make frame seal and issue writs and cause to be Served and Executed . . . in Manifest Contempt of . . . the King and his Laws to the great hindrance and delay of Common Justice to the grievous Damages . . . [of those bound] to the Evil Example of all others in like Case offending and against the Peace of . . . the King his Crown and Dignity.[146]

tached to this estreat is the following certificate: "City of New York ss.: Whitehead Hicks Clerk of the Court of General Quarter Sessions of the Peace and . . . Commonpleas . . . of Queens . . . Duly Sworn Deposeth . . . That the Aforegoing Contains an Account or Estreat of all the fines and Amerciaments . . . Set by the . . . Sessions of the Peace as appears by the Minutes of the said Sessions during the time . . . he . . . hath been Clerke . . . and that he knows of no fines or amerciaments . . . in the Court of Common Pleas. . . ." This deposition was taken before R. R. Livingston, justice of the Supreme Court, on Oct. 18, 1763. For other estreats from Quarter Sessions and Oyer and Terminer Courts, see the fol-

lowing: *H.R. Pleadings* Pl. K. 47, 361, 368, 369, 447, 448, M. 874, M. 877, F. 335, L. 1533, L. 1429; *H.R. Parch.* 19 D 2, 156 L 10, 179 A 9. For returns of estreats from the clerk of the Supreme Court of Judicature returning issues, &c. forfeited in the Supreme Court *en banc* between the years 1765 and 1775, see *H.R. Parch.* 193 H 2, 192 G 10, 209 G 6, 221 B 4.

[145] For an information against the defendants, see *H.R. Parch.* 222 C 3, and for the *postea* stating that the defendants had been found not guilty, see *H.R. Parch.* 77 D 9. For the details regarding the offenses of Smith and DuBois, see *H.R. Pleadings* Pl. K. 734.

[146] For the information, see *H.R. Pleadings* Pl.

On January 24, 1767, a copy of the notice of trial at the Poughkeepsie court was served on William Smith, Jr., the defendant's attorney, but at the June Circuit Court for Dutchess before Justice David Jones, it appears from "minuets [*sic*] taken from Mr. Morris the 11th of June, 1767" that when the Attorney General moved to bring on the action, "William Smith Jr . . . for the defendant withdraws his plea and prays an entry that the defendant will not contend with . . . the King but submits to such fine as the court above shall impose."

It will be observed in this case that the plea of *nolo contendere* was made at Circuit although the usual procedure, we have noted, is that the plea as a rule was made at bar before the case had been sent down for trial at nisi prius. In this instance, despite the fact that the plea was made at Circuit, judgment was not rendered there but in accordance with the usual practice was to be given *en banc*.[147] The defendant's plea at Circuit was entered upon the *postea* in the same manner as the jury's verdict would have been had there been a trial of the issue. On July 28, 1767, the clerk of the Circuit was ordered on the Attorney General's motion to return the *postea* by the following Thursday, and on July 31, the *postea* having been read and filed on the Attorney General's motion, judgment was ordered unless cause was shown to the contrary by the defendant. The defendant, on the same day

appeared at Bar and agreeable to the *Postea* Submitted to a Fine, and it appearing to the Court that the Proceedings which gave Rise to the Prosecution were all owing merely to Error and mistake, and not to any Corrupt designs and all the Recognizances mentioned in the information being by him now delivered to the Clerk of this Court, it is Ordered that the Fine . . . be but 50s. . . .

The defendant paid the fine and fees and was discharged.[148]

K. 784 and *H.R. Parch.* 91 A 4. See further on this case *infra* 529.

[147] For the copy of the notice of trial and for the minutes referred to in the text, see *J. T. Kempe Lawsuits* L–O *sub nom.* Henry Livingston. For copies of the *postea*, see *H.R. Parch.* 91 A 4, 217 B 5, and *J. T. Kempe Lawsuits* L–O *sub nom.* Henry Livingston. Note also that in the citations last given, the *postea* entry reads as follows: "Afterwards at the day and place . . . before David Jones . . . according to the form of the ordinance and the act of the Lieutenant Governor . . . came as well . . . John Tabor Kempe . . . who for . . . the King . . . prosecutes as . . . Henry Livingston Esq. in his own proper person whereupon the said Kempe . . . prayed leave to proceed to the tryal

of the issue . . . and thereupon the said Henry Livingston withdrew his plea of not guilty . . . and prayed an entry might be then there made of Record that he . . . would not further contend . . . but that he submitted himself to the Payment of such fine as should be imposed on him by the said Supreme Court of Judicature for the matter within upon him charged as aforesaid."

[148] *Ms. Mins. SCJ 1766–69* (Engr.) 246, 256, 259, July 28, 31, 1767. Indicative of the fact that the judgment on the *postea* was always rendered *en banc*, even in civil cases, see John Doe ex demise Samuel Honeywell v. Jonathan Tyler where "the clerk of the Assize returns the postea which is filed . . . Ordered that no judgment be entered against the plaintiff till the first Thursday in

In addition to prosecutions for defrauding the Crown of revenue we have found a proceeding for "misdemeanor" against certain justices of Kings which throws some interesting light on the conduct of public business. Samuel Gerritson, Stephen Williams, Abraham Schenck and seven others were informed against "for misdemeanor" on January 19, 1754, and process was ordered to issue against the defendants. On April 25, 1754, the sheriff of Kings County returned *cepi corpora* and the defendants' appearance was ordered to be entered, and a rule made to plead in twenty days or suffer judgment for want of a plea.[149]

There is no record that any plea was filed, but there is some evidence that the defendants were overanxious to avoid trial. The sheriff of Kings County, Jacobus Rider, executed an affidavit on October 4, 1754, to the effect that when he had served process on Stephen Williams, this worthy had asked Rider "to accommodate the matter for him with the Attorney General" offering the not persuasive sum of twenty shillings. Sheriff Rider approached the Attorney General and endeavored to put a stop to the prosecution. He denied, however, accepting a bribe, claiming that his fees had amounted to no more than 24s. including his journey, that he had charged for only ten miles' travel and had taken a mere 15s. from Williams for an extra copy of process.[150]

The Attorney General appears to have credited the sheriff's protestations for no proceedings were initiated against Rider. Nearly a year later, on August 2, 1755, judgment for want of a plea was rendered against all the defendants in this action, and *capias pro redemptione* was ordered to issue. The sheriff of Kings, on October 27, 1755, was ordered to return the writs *pro redemptione* by the following term, but on January 22, 1756, the court, on reading two affidavits, ordered that judgments in the causes against the defendants be set aside on the payment by them of costs. A new rule to plead in twenty days was given, but nothing further happened until July 27, 1756, when on the motion of Murray, the defendants' attorney, certain affidavits were read. For some reason Attorney General Kempe was not prepared to proceed because at the next term of the Supreme Court it was ordered that unless the Attorney General try the case "before or at the next Circuit of Kings County the defendants be discharged." The Circuit minutes for these years are missing, but as this rule was not vacated it seems probable that trial was had at nisi prius. In any event

---

next term he having till that time to show cause" (*Ms. Mins. SCJ 1756–61* [Rough] 205, Oct. 25, 1760).

[149] *Ms. Mins. SCJ 1750–54* (Engr.) 348; *Ms. Mins. SCJ 1754–57* (Engr.) 40, 41.

[150] *J. T. Kempe Lawsuits* S–U *sub nom.* King v. Abraham Schenck, Kings County.

in the October Term, 1759, the defendants appeared in the Supreme Court *en banc* and were discharged.[151]

The Crown was more successful in the sole case we have found of a prosecution for perjury and maladministration against a justice of the peace. On October 29, 1763, J. T. Kempe filed two informations against Moses Owen, a justice of the peace of Westchester. Owen's offense consisted in the following breach of his duty. Two litigants in a lawsuit before Benjamin Fowler, a justice of the peace, having disputed the value of some grain, Fowler had appointed arbitrators to value the grain. The arbitrators found that the grain belonged to one of the litigants; Justice Owen, in order to prevent that litigant from recovering, falsely swore that only two arbitrators had been appointed instead of the three who should have been appointed.[152]

On January 18 and August 1, 1764, Justice Owen having appeared on recognizance was each time respited to the next term; but on October 23, 1764, judgment for want of a plea was ordered against him. However, later on in the same day, the defendant, having appeared on his recognizance, pleaded guilty to the information for maladministration in the execution of his office and was fined £10. The perjury charge had been sent down for trial at nisi prius in Westchester. There Owen had been found not guilty; consequently, on October 24, 1764, the Supreme Court on this charge ordered judgment for the defendant unless cause shown to the contrary. The remarkable result was thus reached that an official acquitted of perjury, the gravamen of the concomitant prosecution for maladministration, nevertheless pleaded guilty to the second charge. Possibly Kempe had other evidence on maladministration. In any event, Owen was already out of office when the trial took place, for from the Executive Council minutes we learn that before trial, on September 19, 1764, Mr. Chief Justice Horsmanden represented to the Lieutenant Governor that Owen was under prosecution for perjury and maladministration in office for which he was to be tried at the next Circuit Court. The Lieutenant Governor with the advice of the Council ordered that "a supersedeas do issue to amove and discharge the said Moses Owen from his said office of one of his Majesty's justices of the peace of the county of Westchester."[153]

The action of the Council in Owen's case needs some comment, for while it

[151] *Ms. Mins. SCJ 1754–57* (Engr.) 177, 200, 220, 283, 320; *Ms. Mins. SCJ 1757–60* (Engr.) 263.

[152] For the *en banc* minutes on this case see *Ms. Mins. SCJ 1762–64* (Engr.) 298, 348; *Ms. Mins. SCJ 1764–67* (Rough) 5, 15, 24, 27, 30. For the

information and *postea* in this case see *H.R. Parch.* 153 H 1. For a copy of the notice of trial see *J. T. Kempe Lawsuits* L–O, King v. Moses Owen, Sept. 10, 1764.

[153] *25 Ms. Mins. Council* 525.

is not immediately related to the transfer jurisdiction, Council proceedings might affect the initiation or cessation of prosecutions. It has been noticed how in Bradley's day, complaints were directed to the Council and this practice continued down to the Revolution. Indeed the cases became so frequent and the Council was bothered with so many trivial grievances that on December 5, 1764, it was ordered a complainant against a justice of the peace or other officer must post a bond of £100 for costs and charges in case of no prosecution or dismissal. The proceedings before the Council do not appear to have been contingent upon the outcome of a pending prosecution as the Owen case shows. Sometimes it had the effect that a prosecution would be dropped, as we shall later observe in the case of Nicholas DeLavergne. Possibly also the hearings had the effect of a preliminary examination. When Justice John Sleght was accused of maladministration, the Attorney General made elaborate notes of the testimony, obviously to be used in the event of an order to prosecute.[154]

The proceedings against justices of the peace were not the only cases involving officers where transfers took place. There were also cases of assaults on officers, three of which will be considered here.

In 1735 an information was filed in the Supreme Court *en banc* against John Tompkins for assaulting and beating the high sheriff of Westchester.[155] On August 4, 1735, process was ordered to issue out of the Supreme Court *en banc* against the defendant. Subsequently, on January 24, 1735/36, Chambers having appeared for Tompkins, the latter was ordered to plead in twenty days or suffer judgment for want of a plea. Since the sheriff was the complainant, a venire was ordered to issue to the coroner of Westchester to summon a jury for the defendant's trial,[156] and on March 25, 1736, Tompkins was tried at the Westchester Circuit and found not guilty.[157] The following month the Supreme Court *en banc* ordered that judgment be given for the defendant unless cause shown "this sitting."[158]

A second case of this sort was brought in 1763 when Peter DeWitt was in-

[154] For the 1764 order, 25 *Ms. Mins. Council* 534. For further cases of malfeasance and other complaints against justices cf. Justice Honeywell informed against for perjury, removed (1753), 23 *ibid.* 129; Justice Sherwood charged with malfeasance, removed (1760), 25 *ibid.* 307; Justice DeLavergne accused of selling Massachusetts titles, case dismissed (1761), *ibid.* 366; Justice Sands removed (1765), 26 *ibid.* 20; Justices Pawling and Hardenbergh, maladministration, case dismissed (1767), *ibid.* 103, 107; Justices Elsworth, Dumont and John Sleght, maladministration, case dismissed (1770), *ibid.* 216; the second DeLavergne case discussed

infra 530. The Kempe notes on the Sleght case are in *J. T. Kempe Lawsuits* C–F.

The preliminary examination character of the Council hearings is further brought out in the case of Sheriff Rosekrans (1771) where the Attorney General after hearing was ordered to prosecute (26 *Ms. Mins. Council* 251).

[155] For the information cf. *H.R. Parch.* 116 L 10.

[156] *Ms. Mins. SCJ 1732–39* 177, 200.

[157] *Ms. Mins. Cir. 1721–49* 300. For the *postea*, see *H.R. Parch.* 116 L 10.

[158] *Ms. Mins. SCJ 1732–39* 211.

formed against for attacking and beating a constable and process was ordered to issue. On October 29, 1763, the sheriff of Dutchess returned the precept, and the defendant, having endorsed his appearance on the writ, was ordered to plead in twenty days or suffer judgment. We do not know whether this case was finally tried or not as the Circuit minutes are lost, but we note that on March 7, 1764, the aggrieved constable wrote to Attorney General John Tabor Kempe stating that the defendant did not "make up with him" and the constable also stated, "But if you intend to bring on my suite this next Supreme Court at Pughkeepsie . . . give me time to get there with my witnesses."[159]

A case involving both harboring and assault arose in Orange County where the royal officials were constantly having difficulties over the enforcement of the law. The grand jury at an Oyer and Terminer on July 22, 1763, presented John Peterse Smith for harboring James Campbell, a "felon" charged with counterfeiting, and also presented Robert Campbell and Archibald Livingston for refusing to assist the constable in taking the "felon" and for the offenses of assaulting the undersheriff and attempting a rescue.[160]

Smith, Campbell and Livingston were apparently bound over by recognizance to appear at the Supreme Court for on July 26, 1763, they appeared at bar and their recognizances were respited to the next term. Four days later, the clerk of the Circuit returned "the presentment offered by the grand jury of Orange County to the Court of Oyer and Terminer there" and this was filed in the Supreme Court en banc. Evidently the Attorney General framed informations on the presentment, because on October 29, 1763, an information was filed against Smith for a misdemeanor in harboring a felon, while Campbell and Livingston were informed against for assaulting an undersheriff in office. The defendants were ordered to plead in twenty days or suffer judgment for want of a plea, and process was ordered out against Livingston who had not made an appearance. The right hand of the law does not always know what the left hand has been doing, for it appears from an affidavit filed on behalf of Livingston that he had been confined in the Orange County jail on a civil process for debt. The court, therefore, ordered that the recognizances be continued until the next Sessions.[161] Kissam pleaded not guilty for Campbell and Livingston and a plea of not guilty was also filed for John Peterse Smith.

[159] For the information see H.R. Pleadings Pl. K. 780. For the minute entry see Ms. Mins. SCJ 1762–64 (Engr.) 177, 298. The Attorney General's brief in this case is to be found in J. T. Kempe Lawsuits C–F sub nom. King v. Peter DeWitt, and in this same set of papers is also to be found the constable's letter of Mar. 7, 1764, to Kempe.

[160] H.R. Pleadings Pl. K. 789.

[161] H.R. Pleadings Pl. K. 789; Ms. Mins. SCJ 1762–64 (Engr.) 213, 224, 298, 344. For John

On May 14, 1764, J. T. Kempe sent a notice of trial to Kissam,[162] the sub-poena for the Crown witnesses having been issued a month earlier.[163] The defendants were placed on trial June 6, 1764, at Orangetown. As the evidence developed in the two prosecutions, it was apparent that the Crown had a bad case. James Campbell, the *casus belli*, was merely under indictment, and was living at the house of John Peterse Smith. The latter had been a justice of the peace but he had recently been removed on charges for embezzlement of army blankets which he had brought back from the wars. This fact was not mentioned at the trial but it was probably what had emboldened the undersheriff to show a certain truculence. Livingston was out of jail "on the word" of Robert Campbell who alone seems to have been a solid citizen.

The undersheriff, one Martling, had come to Smith's house looking for James Campbell who, on the alert, evaporated into the woods. Subsequently Martling came upon James riding a horse and as the latter put his hand in his pocket, Martling suspected a pistol. A scuffle ensued and Martling called for straps to secure the prisoners. Robert Campbell who was present was unwilling to see his brother manacled and pitched in to help. Apparently no actual rescue was effected.

Attorney Kissam handled the two cases adroitly. In Smith's case he emphasized the fact that the defendant's house was the home of the wanted James Campbell and that Smith's duty was no more than that of any citizen. He also brought out the bad feeling of the undersheriff against the defendant. Said Kissam, the law never meant that an officer should treat a prisoner ill. James Campbell had put away his pistol and "the weight of the evidence" should be given to defendant's witnesses. Kissam pointed out a "high crime" was charged here and he cleverly emphasized the serious consequences to the defendants as they would be fined "at the discretion of the Crown."[164] This

Peterse Smith's affidavit that Livingston was confined in jail, see *H.R. Pleadings* Pl. K. 1003.

[162] For Kissam's plea on behalf of Campbell and Livingston, see *H.R. Pleadings* Pl. K. 1062. For Smith's plea, see *ibid.* Pl. K. 615. The notice of trial from J. T. Kempe to Kissam read as follows: "Sr. be pleased to take notice that I intend to bring this cause to tryal at the court for the Tryal of Causes in Orange" (*ibid.* Pl. K. 1063). For the notice of trial sent to Smith, see *ibid.* Pl. K. 777.

[163] *H.R. Parch.* 186 D 3. *H.R. Pleadings* Pl. K. 1061 contains the Attorney General's "brief" which states that the information had been filed on Oct. 29, 1763, and that the defendants Campbell and Livingston had pleaded not guilty. The brief also states "the case" that the defendant's brother, James

Campbell, had been indicted at the Orange Sessions of the Peace for counterfeiting "which is felony" citing "Vol. 1st Laws N.Y. Pa: 370 Cha: 815" (cf. 3 *Col. Laws NY.* 511). This statute made it felony without benefit of clergy to counterfeit French, Spanish or Portuguese gold and silver coin. For the brief in the John Peterse Smith case, see *H.R. Pleadings* Pl. K. 774.

[164] *H.R. Pleadings* Pl. K. 1064 contains the notes on the evidence and arguments of counsel. They are unfortunately fragmentary. Also see *H.R. Pleadings* Pl. K. 1002 for the notes on the trial of John Peterse Smith. The documents relating to Smith's removal from office are in 90 *NY Col. Mss.* 33, the order in *Cal. Council Mins.* 456.

was the right sort of talk for a jury in turbulent Orange. Campbell and Livingston were acquitted and the erstwhile justice, Smith, was equally fortunate in being found not guilty of harboring. On July 31, 1764, the defendants, Smith, Livingston and Campbell, all appeared at bar for judgment and, on motion of Kissam, judgment was ordered *nisi causa*.[165]

In a later chapter we shall consider the attachment for contempt, and the rule to show cause, as these devices were employed against local officials charged with delinquencies. We do not know whether or not the difficulties in getting juries to convict magistrates on information proceedings stimulated the use of this more summary method of handling complaints, but it is apparent from the cases just related that there may be a causal relation. As to the assaults on officers it may be remarked that although the sheriffs were picked from the same lot of squires as the justices, their duties were such that no class feeling was strong enough to overcome the quite human prejudice against police officers.

Miscellaneous Prosecutions

In the category of miscellaneous cases[166] handled by removal we have elected to consider two series of prosecutions: a long-drawn-out duel between Attorney General Bradley and John Allison, a tavern keeper of Orange County, and a series of cases relating to a certain Ferris family.

The *affaire* Allison is an altogether remarkable example of official persistence in trying to net a very small fish in a very complicated procedural seine. It runs along for some fifteen years, so long, indeed, that it ceases to be episodic and like the legal adventures of the Abbot of Croyland[167] attains almost saga-like dimensions.

On the last Tuesday in October, 1729, Allison was indicted for false weights and measures by the grand jury of Orange County at the General Sessions of the Peace, but "by his craft and contrivance the said Indictment being afterwards mislaid and not as yet found," he evidently eluded trial and continued his misdeeds.[168] Two years later he appears, among others, in what seems to

[165] For the information and *postea* on the Campbell and Livingston case, see *H.R. Parch.* 160 G 10. For the *postea* on the Smith case, see *ibid.* 130 K 8. For the court's judgment *en banc*, see *Ms. Mins. SCJ 1764–67* (Rough) 4.

[166] Two other miscellaneous cases are worth noticing: King v. Tillet, highway obstruction (*Ms. Mins. SCJ 1732–39* 65, 80, 125, 126; *Ms. Mins. Cir. 1721–49* 281 *et seq.*; the *postea* is in *H.R. Parch.*

[171] C 6, the issue roll in *H.R. Parch.* 136 C 3); King v. Caleb Pell, fraud (*Ms. Mins. SCJ 1754–57* [Engr.] 42, 45, 72, 74, 87, 118, Apr. 25, 1754— Jan. 25, 1755; the information is in *H.R. Parch.* 210 F 8, the brief in *H.R. Pleadings* Pl. K. 441).

[167] *Historiae Croylandensis Continuatio* (1 Fulman, *Rerum Anglicarum Scriptorum Veterum* [1684] 453 *et seq.*).

[168] *Ms. Mins. Orange Co. Sess. 1727–79* Oct.

be a conspiracy to oust Lancaster Symes, Jr., a justice of the peace.[169] Whether for this reason, or because the Attorney General apparently decided to take no more chances with the public-spiritedness of the local enforcement agencies, an information for false weights and measures was filed by the Attorney General against Allison and eight other defendants in the Supreme Court *en banc* on December 6, 1731. On March 21, 1731/32, the Orange County coroner returned *cepi* on the capias issued against the defendants and William Smith entered an appearance as their attorney. They were ordered to plead in a month's time or suffer judgment for want of a plea, and on June 13, 1732 and again on March 20, 1732/33, Smith appeared for the defendants on the information for false weights.[170]

In the meantime, on April 27, 1732, at a Court of Oyer and Terminer and General Gaol Delivery held at Haverstraw in Orange County before Chief Justice James De Lancey and the Orange County justices of the peace, Allison was indicted for maintenance, and process ordered to issue against him. But when he appeared on May 27 before the same court, sitting by adjournment at Tappan in Orange County, "The Court was served with a certificate to move up the indictment against John Allison for maintenance to the Supreme Court."[171] On June 6, 1732, "A certiorari being returned and filed for the Attorney General," the Supreme Court *en banc* ordered process to issue against the defendant, but Smith's appearance was "entered for the defendant Gratis" and, on June 9, the defendant was ordered to plead in twenty days or suffer judgment for want of a plea. On December 5, 1732, Allison and ten others appeared "on the indictment moved from the court of Oyer and Terminer in Orange County" and it was ordered that the Attorney General file issue or the defendants be discharged. This the Attorney General apparently failed to do and the defendants were discharged at the succeeding March term "pursuant to a rule of this court made last term."[172] The Attorney General was probably not satisfied with the manner in which the indictment had been drawn and therefore failed to file issue, for a month later he filed an information against Allison for maintenance, and on Jan. 22, 1733/34, a venire issued to the coroner on the Attorney General's motion. On Smith's motion for the defendant, a

Term, 1729, Apr. 1730. The details are in an information, King v. Allison (1735–36), in *Misc. Mss. Orange Co.*

169 *Cal. of Eng. Mss.* 516.

170 *Ms. Mins. SCJ 1727–32* 303, 320, 344; *Ms. Mins. SCJ 1732–39* 17.

171 *Ms. Mins. Cir. 1721–49* 55–57.

172 *Ms. Mins. SCJ 1727–32* 326, 337, 343, 396; *Ms. Mins. SCJ 1732–39* 18.

view was ordered of the premises—apparently in connection with the false weights and information of 1731 which had still been pending.[173]

Finally, on June 5, 1735, the defendant was brought to trial at a "Court for the Trial of Causes brought to issue in the Supreme Court" (the technical expression for nisi prius) held at Haverstraw in Orange County and he was tried on the information for maintenance and for false weights and measures.[174]

When Allison appeared at nisi prius, a witness was sworn to prove that "Thomas Smith, Jr., ought not to be a juror having differed with the defendant" and "three of the first jurors sworn to try whether Thomas Smith ought to be an indifferent man," but it was "allowed by the defendant that he should be sworn." So strong was the grip of this early racketeer on the county of Orange that it was necessary in the course of the trial for the court to order "that Samuel Concklin and Thomas Miller have the protection of the Court to give the evidence." The final upshot of the whole trial was that Allison was found "not guilty of maintenance nor of a cheat," the latter offense referring to the information for false weights and measures.[175] On July 29, 1735, the nisi prius verdict was returned as a *postea*[176] into the Supreme Court *en banc* where it was "read and filed and judgment *nisi causa ad contrarium in quattuor diebus.*"[177]

Attorney General Bradley was not abashed by his previous failures to bring to book for his misdeeds this threat to the Province because, on July 20, 1735, the very day the nisi prius verdict of acquittal was returned, Bradley brought a fresh information against Allison for forgery, averring that the culprit had "knowingly, fraudulently and deceitfully" forged the word "denes" on an "acquittance" before an alderman in New York City.[178] This information for

---

[173] This view was ordered to be at the cost of the defendant (*Ms. Mins. SCJ 1732–39* 26, 28, 49, 81).

[174] The first information recited that the defendant "being a contentious vexatious & avaritious, malitious and disorderly person and intending to create differences between his Neighbours . . . did unlawfully and vexatiously excite persuade and encourage one John Yeomans to Sue Thomas Cullen . . . Sheriff . . . in the Supream Court . . . in an action of trespass upon the case . . . to the great loss and damage of . . . [the sheriff] in manifest contempt of . . . the King and his Laws and against the peace of . . . the King his Crown and dignity . . ." (*H.R. Parch.* 165 B 5). The information for false weights and measures accused Allison of "falsly . . . Intending the Subjects of

. . . the King by false weights and measures and by other Unlawful Ways and means to Deceive and Defraud, and himself to Enrich by Dishonest and Unjust Gain . . . In Great Deciet and to the Great Damage of Divers of the Subjects of . . . the King In Manifest Contempt of . . . the King and his Laws In Evil and pernicious Example of all others In the Like case offending And against the peace of . . . the King his Crown and Dignity . . ." (King v. Allison, 1735–36, *Misc. Mss. Orange Co.*).

[175] *Ms. Mins. Cir. 1721–49* 294–297; *H.R. Parch.* 165 B 5 and 183 E 6.

[176] *H.R. Parch.* 165 B 5.

[177] *Ms. Mins. SCJ 1732–39* 167.

[178] *Ibid.* 168; *Misc. Mss. Supreme Ct.* folder 4.

forgery was followed up on August 4, 1735, by another one for false weights and measures,[179] and these were still pending when the Attorney General brought two further informations, on August 3, 1736, for stopping up three highways "with force and arms . . . voluntarily, audaciously, arrogantly [and] unlawfully"[180] and for an assault and battery.[181] Even with these the roster of Allison's evil doings was not yet told, for in October, 1736, the Attorney General brought an information for slandering a jury, alleging that Allison was "a most audacious, Impudent, Deceitful and abusive person, a contemner of Magistracy and authority and a daily stirrer up of strife and discord among his neighbors" and that he had "Published and with a loud voice that the Jury that Tryed that Cause were all forsworn in bringing in their verdict as they did . . . and that John Allison . . . declared that there was not above two or three honest men in the County."[182] Having delivered this blast, the Attorney General, like the King of France in the nursery rhyme, effected a strategic retreat. On January 10, 1736/37, Bradley sent John Chambers (who had meanwhile become defendant's attorney) notice of a motion to alter all the informations outstanding:

> Sir I hereby give you notice that I intend to move . . . for leave to alter and amend three informations . . . against John Allison . . . One . . . for false weights . . . another for forgery and the other for slandering . . . a jury. And that I hereby (on your recommendation) promise to Drop and proceed no further upon . . . the rest of the Informations . . . except that for his stopping up . . . the Highways and that . . . for a Riot . . . which . . . [information] for the Riot . . . if John Allison do . . . pay . . . what I am out of pocket therein . . . I will likewise Drop that.[183]

It is not clear whether Bradley made a deal with Chambers or whether he felt he could not hope to maintain the actions and simply wanted to get his fees out of them. But on April 26, 1737, the *en banc* Supreme Court minutes contain this entry: "On five several informations by consent of Mr. Attorney General Ordered . . . defendant . . . discharged from . . . same."[184]

On January 20, 1737/38, Allison was in trouble again, for "an indictment in Orange" was removed into the Supreme Court *en banc*. What this indictment was we do not know, but it may have been identical with one noticed in the

---

[179] *Ms. Mins. SCJ 1732–39* 178.
[180] King v. Allison, Oct. Term, 1736 (*Misc. Mss. Orange Co.*).
[181] *Ms. Mins. SCJ 1732–39* 228, 243.

[182] King v. Allison, Oct. Term, 1736 (*Misc. Mss. Orange Co.*).
[183] *Ibid.*
[184] *Ms. Mins. SCJ 1732–39* 260.

April minutes for the Orange General Sessions for scandalizing the jury in a civil case by saying they were perjured.[185] For reasons not apparent on the record, the Attorney General, on August 1, 1738, moved that the indictment in Orange which had come up by certiorari into the Supreme Court be quashed for want of sufficiency. This motion was granted as was his request "that he might be admitted to file an information upon the merits of the case." However, on April 20, 1739, the Attorney General was again defeated in his attempt to snare Allison, for "on motion of Chambers for the defendant ordered defendant discharged being for the fact that he was formerly informed against and discharged with the consent of Mr. Attorney General."[186]

In the meantime, Allison had also escaped the toils of the law at Circuit when, on June 8, 1738, a jury at nisi prius in Orange found him not guilty of an offense the nature of which is undisclosed.[187]

Unfortunately, we have been unable to locate any further Supreme Court proceedings against this redoubtable antagonist of Attorney General Bradley, for the minutes of that court from 1739 to 1750 are missing. There is, however, a grand jury presentment of June 2, 1740, made at a Court of Oyer and Terminer and General Gaol Delivery for Orange County against John and four other Allisons for a "violent and dangerous assault and battery." Ten witnesses were bound in £30 each, while John Allison himself was bound in £60 to answer and meantime to be of good behavior, especially to William James on whom he had made the assault. At last, on April 24, 1744, Allison was presented at Orange Sessions for a cheat in that he had forged the handwriting of one Conkling to a note. This indictment was quashed at the next term of the court.[188]

Aside from their value as an illustration of the nisi prius jurisdiction in action, the proceedings against Allison afford a vivid glimpse of the obstacles which beset the central authorities in enforcing the law. The elaborate machinery imported from England functioned perfectly in all its parts but in these prosecutions arrived exactly nowhere, either because Allison's political power was too great or because the succession of informations smacked of persecution.

The Ferris cases are of quite a different *genre,* being a most curious example

[185] The Supreme Court entry (*ibid.* 290; cf. *Ms. Mins. Orange Co. Sess. 1727–79* Apr. 15, 1738).
[186] *Ms. Mins. SC] 1732–39* 317, 336, 339.
[187] *Ms. Mins. Cir. 1721–49* 307.
[188] *Ms. Mins. Orange Co. Sess. 1727–79* Apr. 24,

1744, Oct. 30, 1749. There are entries for April, 1752 and Oct., 1752 of appearance on an indictment by a John Allison and discharge. The offense is not stated.

of domestic pathology. In the year 1750, an interesting advertisement appeared in the *New York Gazette,* inserted by Hannah Ferris. She stated that whereas Gilbert Ferris had lately ·notified the public that she, Hannah Ferris, had eloped from him, she thought it "proper to make known in what manner he forced me to leave him." Hannah Ferris went on to say that Gilbert's father, Peter, was the first cause and instigator of the family rift. Gilbert, a black-smith, had married Hannah on February 27, 1748, and about a month after-wards Gilbert's father, Peter, "noted for mischief and wicked devices," came to Hannah's father and said that he would part Hannah and Gilbert. Peter also ordered his son not to see Hannah any more or he would "use him in the worst manner he could and would disown him." Peter was later alleged to have promoted intimacy between Gilbert and a young woman, "an orphan" named Sarah Fowler. Sarah "proved pregnant by my husband" and Gilbert then left Hannah. In the advertisement Hannah expressed her fear that Gil-bert Ferris or Sarah Fowler would murder her and she also stated that Gilbert and Sarah lived in open adultery and had several children. As a result of the advertisement in the *New York Gazette* an information for libel was filed against Hannah Ferris and her father Hugh Rider on October 25, 1753, and on January 18, 1754, she pleaded guilty in the Supreme Court *en banc* and was fined 13s. 4d.[189]

Apparently the Ferris matter was not closed there, for in January Term, 1754, Hugh Rider, co-defendant with Hannah Ferris in the previous libel action, had the Attorney General file an information against Peter Ferris for libel, and this information was read and filed in the Supreme Court *en banc* on January 15, 1754.[190] This case was evidently tried at Circuit for on October 21, 1755, the Supreme Court *en banc* ordered the clerk of the circuits to return the *postea* in this action by the following Thursday, but we have found neither the *postea* nor any further Supreme Court minute entries, and we therefore do not know whether or not Peter Ferris was convicted.[191]

A more serious aspect of the Ferris family troubles had come to light shortly before this when Hannah Ferris, on October 30, 1753, informed the Attorney

[189] For the information against Hannah and the recital of the advertisement appearing in the *New York Gazette,* see *H.R. Pleadings* Pl. K. 1103. For the *en banc* minute entries, see *Ms. Mins. SCJ 1750–54* (Engr.) 315, 346. For Peter Ferris' complaint in order to have the Attorney General file an informa-tion against Hannah Ferris, see *H.R. Pleadings* Pl. K. 605.

[190] *H.R. Pleadings* Pl. K. 871; *Ms. Mins. SCJ*

1750–54 (Engr.) 341. Also see *Ms. Mins. SCJ 1754–57* (Engr.) 84, 147, Oct. 22, 1754, Apr. 19, 1755, where *venire feci* was returned and the defendant ordered to plead in twenty days or suffer judgment and where, in April, trial was postponed until the next term.

[191] *Ms. Mins. SCJ 1754–57* (Engr.) 197, Oct. 21, 1755.

General on examination that Gilbert Ferris had attempted to poison her. She stated that

> ye 31st June 1749 She saw Gilbert Ferris . . . hiding in the woods . . . for fear of being arrested in a criminal prosecution, she this Informant carryed . . . to him a pot of tea . . . there being some Tea left . . . Gilbert Ferris told this Informant he had left enough tea in the pot for her breakfast . . . says she . . . drank it, not suspecting . . . neither did she find any ill effects but . . . says . . . Gilbert Ferris . . . acquainted several there had been a design to poison this Informant and . . . Sarah Fowler had given him Ratsbane . . . and . . . he told . . . [one woman] he put a lump of Ratsbane as he apprehended into the Teapot, in order to poison his wife, but it had not the intended effect and therefore he supposed that what he put into the teapot was Borax . . . and . . . [Hannah Ferris] prays an Information, 30th October, 1753.[192]

On the basis of this complaint, the Attorney General filed an information against Gilbert Ferris for attempting to poison his wife, "not having the fear of God before his eyes, but being moved and seduced by the instigation of the devil . . . unlawfully & wickedly and designing contriving and intending the death . . . of Hannah his wife."[193] On January 15, 1754, the Attorney General's information was read and filed in the Supreme Court *en banc* and process was ordered to issue out against the defendant. The defendant was ordered on April 25, 1754, to plead in twenty days or judgment would be taken against him by default. However, on that date the sheriff of Westchester returned the defendant taken and William Smith appeared for the amorous blacksmith.

On October 22, 1754, the Attorney General moved to have leave to amend the information and his motion was granted.[194] On this information of the Attorney General, William Smith, the defendant's attorney, filed the following paper in the Supreme Court: "I plead for the defendant not guilty modo et Forma &c. William Smith attorney for defendant. City of New York ss.: Gilbert Ferris puts in his place William Smith his attorney at the suit of our Lord the King in the plea aforesaid."[195] Trial was had at the Westchester Cir-

---

192 *J. T. Kempe Lawsuits* C–F *sub nom.* Gilbert Ferris.

193 *H.R. Parch.* 52 E 4; *H.R. Pleadings* Pl. K. 537. Also note *ibid.* Pl. K. 605, which is an entry in the Attorney General's handwriting stating that an information was to be drawn up on the presentment by the jurors of Westchester against the defendant. In the *J. T. Kempe Lawsuits* C–F *sub nom.* Gilbert Ferris, the following presentment by the grand jury of Westchester appears: "Westches-

ter County ss.: The Grand Jury of Westchester Doe Present Gilbert Ferris of Eastchester for attempting to poison his wife Hannah Ferris . . . on ye 25th day of June or thereabouts in ye year 1749 And pray ye court to put it in form."

194 *Ms. Mins. SCJ 1750–54* (Engr.) 341; *Ms. Mins. SCJ 1754–57* (Engr.) 41, 83; cf. also *infra* 116.

195 *J. T. Kempe Lawsuits* C–F *sub nom.* Gilbert Ferris. Also see Attorney General William Kempe's

cuit Court and at this "proclamation is made whether any would inform the King of the within contents and Benjamin Nicoll offered himself for the King," apparently as the deputy for the Attorney General. There are no minutes of the trial but the defendant was found guilty[196] as appears from the *postea* returned, read and filed in the Supreme Court *en banc* on October 28, 1755. Benjamin Nicoll, on behalf of the Attorney General, moved and it was ordered that judgment be given for the King unless cause shown to the contrary, but "Mr. Smith having fyled Reasons in arrest of judgment Ordered on the same motion that he argue the same the second day of next term." On January 23, 1756, "the court having heard the arguments on both sides upon a motion in arrest of judgment, the court is of the opinion that Judgment be entered according to the Verdict." The following day the Attorney General moved for judgment on the verdict, and the court set a fine of £80 on the defendant and ordered him discharged on the payment of his fine and fees. Apparently Ferris did not pay the fine in court for we note that it was "ordered a *capias pro fine* issue."[197]

The evidence in this last case would scarcely have led to a conviction on an indictment for conspiracy or for attempted homicide. But since the penalties for conviction on an information ordinarily ran only to a fine, the Ferris poisoning case may be viewed as an exemplification of the utility of this device for purposes of law enforcement in a system of law still suffering from the intractability of the felony concept. The usefulness of the information procedure is even more clearly apparent in the way it came to be employed in assault and riot cases.

Assaults and Riots

We have already described how the riot problem became focal in New York during the last decades of the colonial period, and we have seen how special oyer and terminer commissions were employed to cope with it, and how, at an

brief summarizing the information, stating that the defendant had pleaded not guilty, giving "the case," and summarizing the evidence of the witnesses (*ibid.*).

[196] *H.R. Parch.* 52 E 4, for record and *postea*. Also note William Kempe's notes on the trial where it is stated that in July, 1748, Gilbert Ferris had assaulted Hannah by presenting a pistol and threatening to shoot her as well as attempting to poison her. It was stated that Ferris had confessed to Mrs. Hunt that he had thought he had put a lump of ratsbane in his wife's tea to poison her, but when

it did not have the desired effect he supposed it was not ratsbane but "Borax which is like Ratsbane" (*J. T. Kempe Lawsuits* C–F *sub nom.* Gilbert Ferris).

[197] *Ms. Mins. SCJ 1754–57* (Engr.) 203, 223, 240. See also the information against Solomon Fowler for assaulting Peter Ferris in the execution of his office. Nicoll pleaded not guilty for this defendant but we cannot learn the subsequent disposition of this case (*Ms. Mins. SCJ 1750–54* [Engr.] 68, 102, 148, 167, Aug. 3, 1751, Jan. 21, 1751/52, Aug. 1, 1752).

early date, the riot powers of single justices were used.[198] To understand how the information and nisi prius system fitted into the whole policy of law enforcement regarding this troublesome matter it is necessary to consider again the dimensions and persistence of the problem. The normal course of dealing with assaults and riots was to prosecute by indictment in General Sessions[199] or in the Supreme Court.[200] There was also available, as we have seen in the previous chapter, the peculiar proceedings under the old English statutes respecting forcible entries and riots. Unless an offense could be treated as having achieved the status of a "high misdemeanor"

[198] *Supra* 86.

[199] *Supra* 98, 99. Cf. e.g. King v. Benson *et al.*, 1721 (*James Alexander Papers* Box 45 Q.S. Papers); King v. Haskell *et al.* (*Ms. Mins. NYCQS 1694–1731/32* 409, 412, 422, 423, Aug. 7, 8, 1722, May 7, 8, 1723; *James Alexander Papers* Box 45 Q.S. Papers); King v. De Hart (*Ms. Mins. NYCQS 1694–1731/32* 409, 412, Aug. 7, 8, 1722; *James Alexander Papers* Box 45 Q.S. Papers); King v. Nathan and Isaac Levy *et al.*, 1729 (*Ms. Mins. NYCQS 1694–1731/32* 515–518, Aug. 6, Nov. 4, 1729); King v. Doakes *et al.*, 1760 (*Ms. Mins. NYCQS 1732–62* 447, May 7, 1760); King v. Lieutenant William Jones (*Ms. Mins. NYCQS 1760–72* 268, 271, 273, 277, Feb. 8–10, 1769; *H.R. Pleadings* Pl. K. 515). John and Elizabeth Dowers, indicted for riot on Aug. 4, 1763, pleaded guilty and were fined £5, which they paid in court (*Ms. Mins. NYCQS 1760–72* 79, 81, 83, 84, Aug. 2–4, 1763).

[200] The indictments and trials were so frequent here, it is impossible to go into the cases *in extenso.* A great deal of this business was city rioting as, for example, King v. Wendall Ham *et al.* (1754), indicted for riot when the merchants refused to take copper money at standard rates. The defendants pleaded *nolo* and were fined 13s. 4d. each (*Ms. Mins. SCJ 1750–54* [Engr.] 340, 344, 346, 349, Jan. 15, 17–19, 1754; *Ms. Mins. SCJ 1754–57* [Engr.] 1, 9, Apr. 16, 18, 1754; *H.R. Pleadings* Pl. K. 535, 644, 727; *NY Misc. Mss.* Box 7; also see 23 *Ms. Mins. Council* 133). Another, and unusual, case was King v. McMon, Larkin *et al.* where the defendants were convicted and sentenced to be whipped (*Ms. Mins. SCJ 1769–72* [Engr.] 315, 317, 318, Jan. 17, 18, 1771; *H.R. Pleadings* Pl. K. 346; *J. T. Kempe Lawsuits* L–O *sub nom.* Patrick Larkin).

References to other indictments for riot handed into the Supreme Court *en banc* are as follows:

King v. Nicholas Augur, Lucas Stevenson, Stephen Buckenhoven, Jacob Cornellisen, Jacob Frederycksen, James Simms and Thomas Cooper; Cooper pleaded guilty; the others pleading not guilty were tried and found not guilty (*Mins. SCJ 1693–1701* 92, 93, 95, 103, 107, 112, Apr. 9, 11, 1696, Oct. 8, 1696, Apr. 10, 1697). King v. Ma-

thias Knight, Johannes Andries, Conrad Noble and Abraham Huyswalt; pleaded guilty; Knight fined 40s.; the rest fined 20s. (*Ms. Mins. SCJ 1754–57* [Engr.] 47, 49, 84, 154, July 31, Aug. 1, Oct. 22, 1754, Apr. 24, 1755; *H.R. Pleadings* Pl. K. 648, 662, 706, Pl. H. 816 no. 9). King v. Walter Lukridge, found not guilty (*Ms. Mins. SCJ 1756–61* [Rough] 80, 84, 88, 134, 138, Oct. 21, 25, 1757, Jan. 19, Apr. 17, 20, 1759). King v. James Hawkins, Barney McClosky and John Boswick, process to issue (*ibid.* 80, 84, Oct. 21, 25, 1757). King v. Thomas Martin and Ed. Groomes, "not found" (*Ms. Mins. SCJ 1764–67* [Rough] 59, Apr. 22, 1765; *Ms. Mins. SCJ 1764–66* [Engr.] 179, Apr. 27, 1765; *Ms. Mins. SCJ 1766–69* [Engr.] 186, 187, May 2, 1767; *H.R. Pleadings* Pl. K. 788, 792). King v. John Coats *et al.*; pleaded *ore tenus* not guilty to riot (*Ms. Mins. SCJ 1764–67* [Rough] 134–136, 139, 140, Jan. 24, 25, Apr. 17, 1766; *J. T. Kempe Lawsuits* C–F *sub nom.* Campbell and Coats). King v. Andrew Hamilton and Charles Smith; pleaded guilty to riot but not to breaking lamps (*Ms. Mins. SCJ 1764–67* [Rough] 155, 157, Aug. 1, 2, 1766). King v. George Clark and James McKinney; Clark pleaded guilty, fined 6s. 8d. (*Ms. Mins. SCJ 1766–69* [Engr.] 317, 318, 329, 374, Oct. 29, 31, 1767, Jan. 19, 1768; *H.R. Parch.* 221 B 4; *H.R. Pleadings* Pl. K. 472, 502; *J. T. Kempe Lawsuits* C–F *sub nom.* George Clark). King v. Major Henry Pullen; pleaded not guilty, found guilty, fined £10 (*Ms. Mins. SCJ 1769–72* [Engr.] 11, 114, 119, Apr. 21, Oct. 24, 28, 1769; *H.R. Pleadings* Pl. K. 1034; *J. T. Kempe Lawsuits* P–R; *H.R. Parch.* 209 G 6). King v. James and Peter Van Kleeck and John Russell, process to issue (*Ms. Mins. SCJ 1772–76* [Rough] 67, Jan. 22, 1773; *H.R. Parch.* 184 D 2; *H.R. Pleadings* Pl. K. 394; *J. T. Kempe Lawsuits* V *sub nom.* Van Kleeck). King v. Edward Webb and James Baker; pleaded *nolo*, fined £10 (*Ms. Mins. SCJ 1772–76* [Rough] 132, 137, Oct. 28, 30, 1773; *J. T. Kempe Lawsuits* W–Y *sub nom.* Edward Webb). King v. Sam and John Dobbins, James and Thomas McLaughlin; the sheriff ordered to apprehend the defendants (*Ms. Mins. SCJ 1772–76* [Rough] 199, Oct. 24, 1774; *H.R. Parch.* 185 H 7; *H.R. Pleadings* Pl. K. 316).

it would not be the subject of an information. For this reason, the complicated machinery of informing and then sending a case down for trial at nisi prius was not often used in cases of simple assault.[201] During the first half of the eighteenth century, the same reasoning applied to the occasional riots. But thereafter, as the outbreaks grew more frequent and were increasingly difficult to handle, it became more common to use the information than to resort to indictment. As we shall presently see, the information was a decidedly more flexible means of initiating a procedure than indictment, and in the turbulent years before the Revolution it had the additional advantage of avoiding the obstacle of a grand jury agreement to a bill of indictment.

It was not necessary, of course, for the information to be tried at nisi prius, and in the case of riots in the provincial capital, it was usual for the case when so initiated to be tried at bar.[202] During the period when Bradley was Attorney

[201] But see King v. Jacob Lewis, 1735 (*Ms. Mins. SCJ* 1732–39 79, 120, 122, 141, 185, 201; *Ms. Mins. Cir.* 1721–49 297; *H.R. Parch.* 12 H 7). Lewis was convicted by a jury of inquest upon default and fined £20. King v. Barnes and McHugh, 1754 (*Ms. Mins. SCJ* 1750–56 [Rough] 218; *H.R. Pleadings* Pl. K. 214, Pl. K. 642). The precept for summoning the jurors at nisi prius is in *J. T. Kempe Lawsuits* B. The final disposition does not appear in the records. King v. De Bevois, 1760 (*Ms. Mins. SCJ* 1756–61 [Rough] 180, 197; *Ms. Mins. SCJ* 1764–67 [Rough] 140). For the *postea,* see *H.R. Parch.* 170 C 1. Convicted and fined 20s., six years after the *postea* was returned. King v. Solomon Seaman, 1765 (*H.R. Pleadings* Pl. K. 735; *H.R. Parch.* 185 H 2, 193 K 3; *Ms. Mins. SCJ* 1764–67 [Rough] 177; *Ms. Mins. SCJ* 1764–66 [Engr.] 177). This case was compromised; cf. *J. T. Kempe Lawsuits* S–U.
   It should be noted that in this last case the complaining witness entered a recognizance to pay to the Attorney General such fees as were usually paid in the province by clients for appearance at Queens Co. nisi prius. This may explain why the proceedings were begun by information in assault cases.
[202] Compare the following cases: King v. William Dykos, John Ellit, Thomas Bowells, David Burgher and Nicholas de Moyan, discharged, no prosecution (*Ms. Mins. SCJ* 1723–27 185, 196, 197, 199, 200, 211, 220, 234, Mar. 15, 1725/26, June 10, 13, Oct. 14, 18, Dec. 6, 1726). King v. Nathan Potter, Joseph Deane *et al.,* riot in taking the King's goods, process to issue (*Ms. Mins. SCJ* 1723–27 235, 276, Dec. 6, 1726, June 13, 1727). King v. Henry Willse, process ordered to issue (*Ms. Mins. SCJ* 1732–39 270, 297, Aug. 1, 1737, Jan. 24, 1737/38). King v. Jacob Halinbeck *et al.,* ordered to plead in twenty days or suffer judgment (*Ms. Mins. SCJ* 1750–54 [Engr.] 28, 53, Jan. 19, 1750/51, Apr. 25, 1751). King v. Thomas and

John Armstrong, Wessell Wessells, and others, the defendants returned on *pluries venire facias* (*ibid.* 348, Jan. 19, 1754; *Ms. Mins. SCJ* 1754–57 [Engr.] 41, 42, 53, 84, 155, 177, Apr. 25, Aug. 3, Oct. 22, 1754, Apr. 24, Aug. 2, 1755). King v. James Wilks, James Smith, Joseph Higginbotham, Moses Lord, Mary Allison, Ephraim Lockwood, Hendrick Suydam, David and Jane Robinson, Mary Mucklewain, John Christie, Mathew Woolsey, Printz Van Tollinsel *et al.;* two of these defendants pleaded not guilty; six of them being tried were found guilty and *capias pro redemptione* issued against them; three of the defendants pleaded guilty; judgment being entered against three others, *capias pro fine* was entered against the latter three (*Ms. Mins. SCJ* 1750–54 [Engr.] 348, Jan. 19, 1754; *Ms. Mins. SCJ* 1754–57 [Engr.] 41, 42, 52, 53, 84, 94, 118, 119, 128, 148, 156, Apr. 25, July 30, Aug. 3, Oct. 24, 1754, Jan. 25, Apr. 21, 24, 1755; *J. T. Kempe Lawsuits* L–O *sub nom.* Ephraim Lockwood; *ibid.* A *sub nom.* Mary Allison; *H.R. Pleadings* Pl. K. 639, 659, Pl. H. 816). King v. Hannah Caldwell, Peter Hart and seven others, process ordered to issue (*Ms. Mins. SCJ* 1750–54 [Engr.] 274, 315, 316, July 31, Oct. 24, 1753; *H.R. Pleadings* Pl. K. 585, 629, 928, 948, 949, 953, 956, 971; *H.R. Parch.* 121 E 6). King v. James Daniel Denton, Joseph Bloomer, Jr., John Mornell and Stephen Albertson, ordered to plead in twenty days or suffer judgment (*Ms. Mins. SCJ* 1750–54 [Engr.] 274, 315, July 31, Oct. 25, 1753; *Ms. Mins. SCJ* 1754–57 [Engr.] Apr. 25, Oct. 22, 1754; *H.R. Pleadings* Pl. K. 951). King v. Edward Savage, Francis Welsh and Alexander Brown, ordered to plead in twenty days or suffer judgment (*Ms. Mins. SCJ* 1750–54 [Engr.] 348, Jan. 19, 1754; *Ms. Mins. SCJ* 1754–57 [Engr.] 41, 53, Apr. 25, Aug. 3, 1754; *H.R. Pleadings* Pl. K. 548, 634, 705, Pl. H. 816). King v. Cornelius Symason *et al.,* process ordered to issue (*Ms. Mins. SCJ* 1750–54

General, there were not many occasions where the information procedure was used to prosecute riots, and as this officer seems to have had a penchant for compounding cases where he could, it was rarely that these informations were brought to trial. Bradley, moreover, appears to have preferred to keep proceedings before the court *en banc,* tactics which were not calculated either to expedite matters or to bring them to a successful conclusion. His correspondence with Evert Wendell, his deputy in Albany, over a riot case in that county[203] is an amusing illustration of the disadvantages of trying to enforce the King's law by remote control. Wendell, who was engaged in preparing for a civil suit which had arisen out of the riot, was apparently too preoccupied with his clients' affairs to attend properly to his official duties, particularly as he was suing the defendants to the Crown's prosecution and was no doubt reluctant to have the King's suit determined in advance of the civil action.[204] But despite the bitter and censorious admonitions of the Attorney General[205]

[Engr.] 341, Jan. 15, 1754; H.R. Pleadings Pl. K. 543). King v. John Merrick and seven others for riot and driving cattle, process ordered to issue (Ms. Mins. SCJ 1750–54 [Engr.] 275, July 31, 1753; H.R. Pleadings Pl. K. 681, 952, 955; H.R. Parch. 192 L 9). King v. Lewis Morris, Richard Ayscough and John Knox, process ordered to issue (Ms. Mins. SCJ 1754–57 [Engr.] 40, Apr. 24, 1754). King v. Green et al., fined (Ms. Mins. SCJ 1762–64 [Engr.] 91, Jan. 22, 1763; Ms. Mins. SCJ 1764–67 [Rough] 40, 68, Jan. 16, Apr. 27, 1765; Ms. Mins. SCJ 1764–66 [Engr.] 88, Oct. 27, 1764). King v. McCarty et al., judgment for want of a plea (Ms. Mins. SCJ 1762–64 [Engr.] 223, 299, July 30, Oct. 29, 1763; Ms. Mins. SCJ 1764–67 [Rough] 15, Oct. 16, 1764; H.R. Pleadings Pl. K. 754). King v. Petrus and John J. Haring, John Peterse Smith, Neal MacDaniel and seven others; MacDaniel pleaded guilty, fined 6s. 8d. (Ms. Mins. SCJ 1762–64 [Engr.] 362 et seq., Jan. 28, Apr. 28, 1764; Ms. Mins. SCJ 1764–67 [Rough] 3, 5, 35, 71, July 31, Aug. 1, Oct. 27, 1764, Jan. 19, July 30, 1765; H.R. Pleadings Pl. K. 245, 757). King v. Regnier Quackenbush, pleaded nolo (Ms. Mins. SCJ 1764–67 [Rough] 40, Jan. 16, 1765). King v. George Elms, judgment for want of a plea, fined 20s. on subsequent appearance (Ms. Mins. SCJ 1769–72 [Engr.] 275, Oct. 18, 1770). King v. Robinson (1771), fined (H.R. Pleadings Pl. K. 386; J. T. Kempe Lawsuits P–R sub nom. Silas Robinson).

203 King v. Jan Bronck et al. (Ms. Mins. SCJ 1723–27 219, Oct. 18, 1726).

204 Cf. Evert Wendell's Account Book fols. 29, 34 and 40. Wendell was attorney for J. C. Halenbeck, who was suing the Broncks for trespass, for forcible entry and riotously taking away his wheat and corn. Evidently Wendell was so interested in

the civil lawsuit that his notes on this case between July 14, 1726, and Oct. 6, 1727, fail to reveal one word regarding the Crown's case against these defendants for the same offense for which he was suing them on the civil side. Yet on the civil side he expended much learning, quoting 1 Lilly's Abridgement 143, Wood's Institutes 423–429, Stiles' Practical Register 189, 190, Dalton's Countrey Justice 311 and many other authorities. In Wendell's notes in his Account Book folio 40, for October 6, 1727, is a reference to a provincial precedent, a rare occurrence: "See in the Bundell of the Mayor and Aldermen a precedent to challenge the array."

205 On November 19, 1726, Richard Bradley was constrained to write to Wendell in the following language: "I have yᵉ letter of the 10th instant and think it very strange you shd trifle with me thus; do you think I don't see through all this? I am not to be deceived, Sʳ with words; I regard nothing but deeds. Did not the Chief Justice Order you and Casperse in my hearing, to attend me; in order to my prosecuteing the Rioters; and did not you give me the necessary Instructions in order thereto; and have not I told you already, more than once, that I have fyled an Information here agt. the Rioters; and sent up process to the Sherriffe of Albany agt. them; and did I not order you . . . that all proceedings in your Court be Stop'd. That Defᵗˢ may not Complaine of their being prosecuted in two several Courts at the same time for the same offense; and that I may have no further cause of Complaint?

"As to Mr. Smith, he is retained some time ago for the Defts. and no device shall hinder my proceedings in the Supream Court agt. them. Is this enough?

"I desire once more you'll send me the names of the Justices who d/d' [delivered?] up Arenout Valck's recogn* and when they did so, and to

the criminal proceedings dragged on for years and eventually disappear from the records without having come to trial.[206]

There can be no doubt that about the time when William Kempe took over the duties of Attorney General, the judicial machinery was operating more effectively than earlier, and it is not to be denied that Kempe, and later his son, brought a greater degree of skill to the office than had their predecessors. Such skill was then needed, for on the political side the task of law enforcement became increasingly difficult. Even before the outbreak of the French and Indian War, when the presence of large bodies of troops led to constant violence, disorders in various parts of the province were not infrequent. It was at this time that information began to supplant indictment in the riot cases, and trial at nisi prius became more usual.

The rioting in New York Province was not all due to economic or political causes. Many of the outbreaks were small affairs and were riots only in the technical sense of the word. These cases were due to a prevailing attitude of lawlessness which subsequently underwent transfiguration into the spirit of liberty. Three cases which arose after 1750 are illustrative.

In the environs of Southold, Timothy Hudson was living at daggers' ends

whome; as to the ffees w^h are justly due they ought to be pd."

On January 21, 1726, Bradley wrote again to his deputy in Albany, putting a little stricter tone in his letter: "Pray trifle no more with me with such odd kind of letters; sure you must believe I have not comon sense to credit y^r pretence of not knowing the Justices Names; when they are y^r Neighbours . . . and when you not only saw and heard w^t they did and ordered; were of Council for the King in that very case? I know yr. meaning very well; you don't care to name them to me lest they should blame you for their prosecution; If you only want my promise never to disclose it, that you gave me their names; I hereby promise you I never will; but if this wont do, pray give Mr. Hopkins 6s. for their Names and sirnames (as they write them themselves) of those who ordered the Recognizance to be delivered up; (if less than 6s. etc.).

"Surely you must believe me to be void of [?] when you so often tell me you do the business more for my sake etc. than for y^r own; will any man in his witts believe it? Ther's no such thing in the world.

"You hint as if you repented doing the Business; Pray whenever you are weary of it tell me so; and I'll soon provide another; and then you are allways vindicateing y^r honesty; which looks very odd to any man of but comon understanding w^n you are not accused in that pticular. . . .

". . . pray send me no more such Queer letters, I can't abide 'em. . . .

"And I desire you to get Jan Casperse Halenbeck &. his wife bound by recog^e before two Justices of y^r County (and 2 or 3 more if so many to be found) to give evidence for the King, agt. the Broncks &, on the Informat fyled agt., them here in the Supream Court; (If you Can find 2 or 3 more as aforesd. who saw the riot &. assault on Halenbeck & his wife). They must pay you for such trouble; & if I recover I'll repay them . . . or the Defts. shall; and pray send me such recognizances as soon as you can; (to witt) by the first Vessel. If you take more than Ordinary pains herein, I'll see you handsomely gratifyd; If we recover and there Can be no doubt we shall if the riot shall be proved and you know who can do that besides Halenbeck and his wife; . . ." (Misc. Mss. Richard Bradley).

[206] On Mar. 21, 1726/27, the sheriff of Albany was peremptorily ordered to return the writ by the following term, and when on June 13, 1727, he failed to return the writ, attachment was ordered to issue against him. On June 10, 1729, this case was still before the Supreme Court, and on Oct. 21, 1729, the sheriff of Albany returned cepi corpus as to Casperus Bronck and Jacob Collier. On June 9, 1730, cepi corpus was returned as to Peter Winn. We note from the minutes that the case was still before the court on Oct. 17, 1732, when Smith entered his appearance for Jan Bronck. Cf. Ms. Mins. SCJ 1723–27 226, 252, 280, Dec. 1, 1726, Mar. 21, 1726/27, June 13, 1727; Ms. Mins. SCJ 1727–32 130, 160, 210, 229, 372, June 10, Oct. 21, 1729, June 9, Oct. 20, 1730, Oct. 17, 1732.

with some of his neighbors. According to a draft of an information, in March, 1751, Josiah Rayner and others proceeded to eliminate some of Hudson's sheep by mixing and boiling ratsbane with water and Indian corn and strewing it on the grass. Some months later, for reasons unknown, Rayner, William Reeves Senior, William Reeves Junior, James Lupton and about twenty others blacked their faces and with "drums beating and colors flying" beset the house of Hudson making divers indecent and obscene speeches.[207] This assemblage has the earmarks of a charivari or shivaree, unless in view of the earlier sheep incident a more malicious purpose must be supposed.

Owing to personnel shifts in the office of the Attorney General, prosecution was not gotten under way until the spring term, 1753, when two informations were filed, one for poisoning the sheep and the other for riot.[208] Process was at once ordered to issue out of the Supreme Court *en banc.*[209] On August 25, 1753, a notice of trial at the Suffolk County Circuit Court in September was served and an affidavit of service was filed. There was some doubt whether the cause would be heard, for on September 8, 1753, Sheriff George Muirson wrote to Attorney General William Kempe saying: "I received your venires at the suit of the King v. Rayner, Lupton and Reeves, the younger. I will do my endeavor to return an . . . impartial Jury wch will be difficult as the Country is very Sikly."[210] However, the sheriff was apparently able to find enough able-bodied freeholders because on return of the writ ordering him to obtain a jury he annexed a panel.[211] On September 11, the Circuit jury at nisi prius found William Reeves Jr. guilty and Josiah Rayner not guilty of the sheep poisoning.[212] The papers on the riot case are missing but it appears from the Supreme Court minutes that the defendants were convicted. On October 17, 1753 the Attorney General moved the clerk of circuits return the *postea,* and it later ordered that judgment be given unless cause shown to the contrary. William Smith then appeared for the defendants and on October 20, 1753

[207] Cf. H.R. *Pleadings* Pl. K. 1099, in which is contained the Attorney General's brief, "the case" and the proofs. Also see *ibid.* K. 984 and 578.
[208] For copies of the information, see H.R. *Pleadings* Pl. K. 588, 934, 944.
[209] *Ms. Mins. SCJ 1750-56* (Rough) 137, Apr. 27, 1753. On Apr. 29, 1753, a return to a certiorari in this case was filed in the Supreme Court *en banc* by the justices of the peace of Suffolk County (*ibid.* 140). On August 4, 1753, Smith appeared on behalf of the defendants, who were then ordered to plead within twenty days or suffer judgment against them for want of a plea (*Ms. Mins. SCJ 1750-54* [Engr.] 286).

[210] For the notice of trial and the affidavit of service of notice of trial, see H.R. *Pleadings* Pl. K. 422, 1008. Cf. also *J. T. Kempe Lawsuits* V.
[211] H.E. *Parch.* 210 E 6. This document also contained the Attorney General's information against the defendant, the defendant's plea of not guilty, the Attorney General's joinder therein, the writ of nisi prius, and endorsed on the back of the parchment containing the information, joinder etc. is a *postea* stating that William Reeves Jr. had been found guilty by the jury while Josiah Rayner had been found not guilty. The *postea* was signed by the clerk of Assizes per his deputy.
[212] H.R. *Parch.* 210 E 6.

moved in arrest, filing reasons in support. The court, however, decided Smith's reasons in arrest of judgment were insufficient and ordered that the judgment stand confirmed. Josiah Rayner was fined £20, William Reeves Jr. was fined £5, and James Lupton fined 10s. William Reeves, the elder, was fined £40 and obliged to find security for his good behavior for twelve months.[213]

A riot with a certain quality of modern gangsterism occurred some years later in Westchester. It appears from an affidavit signed by one of the defendants, Augustine Reynolds, a New York tailor, that he had been approached by Esther Hadden (wife of Joseph Hadden) who told him that she was offering £30 to anyone who would recoup certain mulatto children whom "Thomas Hadden had by his wench Rose." After Thomas Hadden's death the wench Rose had been purchased by Judge Thomas who apparently took the progeny as a part of the bargain. Mrs. Hadden claimed "the rest of the judges" had said the children belonged to the Haddens and she would "vindicate" anyone who would take the children. It was to capture the Haddens' colored kinfolk that the riot was fomented. Reynolds, together with four others, broke into the house of Daniel Ferris to whom one of the negroes had been bound and carried off Ferris and the boy. They next broke into Caleb Hyat's house and captured Caleb and two other children. They also broke into the house of Benjamin Lyon and committed an assault there. According to the information all three of the mulatto children had been manumitted by the will of Thomas Hadden. The defendants pleaded not guilty but at the Westchester Circuit, September 13, 1763, they were duly convicted. On October 18, 1763, on motion of the Attorney General, it was ordered that the clerk of the Circuit return the *postea* by the following day. Nothing further came of the case until January 19, 1764, when the Attorney General moved for judgment and also informed the court that the defendants had "repurchased" the negroes whom they had riotously taken away, brought them back and set them at liberty. Since the defendants "had also satisfied the charges of the prosecution and made the fullest discovery in respect to the instigation of the riot, the court . . . in consideration of the poverty of the defendants" set a fine of 20s. upon them. This was paid and they were discharged.[214]

A riot of quite different character took place a year later in Dutchess County,

[213] *Ms. Mins. SCJ 1750–56* (Rough) 151, 152, 165; *Ms. Mins. SCJ 1750–54* (Engr.) 306, 308, 317.
[214] For the information and *postea*, see *H.R. Parch.* 178 H 4. For the minute entries, see *Ms.*

Mins. SCJ 1762–64 (Engr.) 4, 266, 349. Also see *H.R. Parch.* 189 G 2 and *J. T. Kempe Lawsuits* P–R *sub nom.* King v. Augustine Reynolds *et al.* for the affidavit.

in connection with a "ride skimmington," an ancient and bawdy English custom[215] which was transplanted to New York and appears to have thrived among the yokelry of Dutchess and Westchester Counties.[216] On November 30, 1764, a Mrs. Clarke of Dutchess who made her living baking gingerbread executed an affidavit to the effect that she and her son William had been beaten by some young people of Dutchess County who had attempted at a local wedding a ride skimmington.[217] It appears that one of the participants had come to Mrs. Clarke's asking for gingerbread. The wedding guests including the groom were in pursuit, for a number of them, minus their coats and carrying clubs, arrived at the Clarke house and forced their way in. The rioters took prisoner one Vandervoort, who was in the house, stating that they had a commission which empowered them to do so. They also beat Vandervoort and stripped and beat Mrs. Clarke and disposed of a lot of gingerbread. A few days later another fracas ensued at which William Clarke was attacked and a dog set on him. Mrs. Clarke and her son "being in fear of their lives" went before Justice William Humphrey and swore the peace against the rioters. Humphrey granted a "warrant of the peace" and thereupon, one of the rioters being taken by the constable, the others went before Justice Humphrey who took them as sureties for each other, and the offenders demanded that Mrs. Clarke give se-

215 Thomas Hardy, in *The Mayor of Casterbridge* (Modern Library) 247, 254, 263, gives a graphic account of this custom and its meaning: " 'Tis an old foolish thing they do in these parts when a man's wife is—well, not too particularly his own. . . ." "two images on a donkey back to back their elbows tied to one another! She's facing the head and he's facing the tail. . . ." The skimmingtoners accompanied the effigies on the donkey in a great and riotous assembly, beating on drums, dishpans and the like. Hogarth's illustration of Hudibras suffering the ride skimmington depicts the ritual. Cf. also Murray, *New English Dictionary*, *s.v.* skimmington, and for the law, Rex v. Roberts, where the defendant was fined £40 for riding skimmington (3 *Keble* 578); also see *H.R. Pleadings* Pl. K. 962 where the case of Rex v. Roberts was cited by Attorney General Kempe in the case of King v. Lynch, Branson and Wade, as precedent for the fine set in notorious riots.

216 Thus Ebenezer Kniffin wrote to the Attorney General from Rye, N.Y., on Mar. 2, 1758, on behalf of Hezekiah Holdridge, stating that John Slater and others of Rye had "carried him [Holdridge] on a rail which they call riding Scimiton." Holdridge himself in his complaint stated that Slater and others of Rye had formed a riotous assembly, had assaulted, beaten and abused him, burned his hair, "rode him on a rail," and walked him two miles, "and this . . . done on pretence of punishing complainant for his keeping with and having criminal conversation with one Rachel Jameson as they pretend." References to this case are to be found in the *J. T. Kempe Lawsuits* G–J *sub nom.* Hezekiah Holdridge.

On April 24, 1751, an information for a riot was filed against Jeremiah Hunt, his wife, and 11 others, for riot in Dutchess, for throwing down fences and for "riding skimmington" (*H.R. Pleadings* Pl. K. 813; *Ms. Mins. SCJ 1750–54* [Engr.] 45, 68, 93, Apr. 24, Aug. 3, Oct. 24, 1751).

It will be noted that the riding on the rail accorded to Hezekiah Holdridge was referred to as "riding skimmington," although later in America riding on a rail usually was combined with a tarring and feathering. Tarring and feathering was also employed in colonial New York but was not part of the skimmington ritual. Cf. a draft of an information drawn up by J. T. Kempe in Jan. 1763, against John Franklin for carting, wounding, tarring and feathering one John Jones, although no prosecution was finally made against this defendant (King v. John Franklin, *J. T. Kempe Lawsuits* C–F; *Ms. Mins. SCJ 1769–72* [Engr.] 99, 110, 113, 142, 148, Oct. 17, 23, 24, 1769, Jan. 16, 20, 1770).

217 *J. T. Kempe Lawsuits* C–F *sub nom.* Elizabeth Clarke.

curity to continue the prosecution. Justice Humphrey refused to accept any surety from Mrs. Clarke unless such surety were a freeholder. Chief Justice Horsmanden of the Supreme Court wrote to Humphrey about the riot in Dutchess County stating that he had

> received Complaint on the oath of Elizabeth Clarke sent to me by the Attorney General . . . that severall persons of your place were guilty of Enormious Riots to the great injury of the said Elizabeth Clarke and her Son . . . that you have taken the Offenders Securities the one for the other for their Appearance at your next Court of Quarter Sessions . . . the Circumstances attending this Riot appear to be very bad and . . . you ought not to have taken the Offenders themselves as Securities . . . nor demanded any other than the Woman's personal Security.
>
> The Attorney General intends to prosecute the offenders in the Supreme Court according to their deserts . . . [you are therefore to] cause the offenders to be bound with good Security . . . in such sums as shall be adequate to the enormity of the offense. . . .[218]

In January, 1765 Mrs. Clarke wrote to Attorney General Kempe stating that the rioters had had her indicted for an unknown charge

> and as I am a poor widow and the snow so exceeding deep That I cannot come to New York this court, but hope nevertheless to be ready . . . and also I offered to bring my evidence . . . to prove myself innocent of doing anything to the Skimmiltoners—the Judges . . . (being against me and sideing the rioters being their relations) would not take any notice of me So I with the Lord assisting, The Honble imperjial Court at New York will hear and do me justice.[219]

As a result of Mrs. Clarke's complaint, the Attorney General drew two informations, one against James Higby, Abraham Lent, Peter Johnson, Andrew Mick, John Van Vleck Junior, Jonas Schoonover, Lewis Vandewater, Korah Myers and Daniel Hausbrook for the skimmington riot; another against Isaac Lent, Peter Johnson, James Higby, Andrew Mick, Abraham Lent, John Van Vleck Jr. and Peter Vanderwater for the second outbreak. These were read and filed in the Supreme Court on January 19, 1765, and process was ordered to issue out against the defendants. Ludlow, on behalf of the defendants, moved that their appearance be dispensed with and their recognizances respited because

---

[218] *Misc. Mss. Dutchess Co. 1752–1870.* This letter from Horsmanden to Humphrey is undated but was probably written in the early part of December 1764.

[219] *J. T. Kempe Lawsuits* C–F, Elizabeth Clarke to Kempe, Jan. 1765.

"the defendants have not had small pox" (an epidemic was apparently raging in New York City) and they might contract that disease.[220] *Venire feci* was returned in this case on April 27, 1765, and the defendants' appearance having been entered, they were ordered to plead in twenty days or suffer judgment. At the same time, subpoenas were issued summoning witnesses.[221] A copy of the notice of trial to be held at Poughkeepsie was served on May 17, 1765, on the defendants, Isaac Lent, James Higby *et al.*, by Jarvis on behalf of Attorney General John Tabor Kempe. The two informations were tried at the June Circuit, 1765. In the skimmington case the jury found the defendants guilty "except John Van Vleck the Younger and Daniel Hausbrook who they find not Guilty." On the second information Peter Johnson and Abraham Lent were found guilty only of assault and the other defendants were acquitted.[222] On July 31, 1765, the *postea* was returned, read and filed in the Supreme Court *en banc,* and on motion of the Attorney General, judgment *nisi* was ordered as to those defendants found not guilty. With a fine sense of anticlimax the court "sets a fine of 6*s.* each on James Higby, Abraham Lent, Peter Johnson, Andrew Mick and Korah Myers. The court sets a fine of 6/8 on Peter Johnson and Abraham Lent."[223]

In addition to the prosecutions initiated by information, riot cases were also handled by a different mode of transfer, viz., when the inquisitions taken before justices out of Sessions were delivered to the Supreme Court either for defendants to be fined or where they had traversed the inquest. Under the English statutes the justices had the power to fine and to hear and determine the traverse, but as Dalton remarks, "they shall do well to send such indictment . . . into Kings Bench."[224] During the early eighteenth century in New York it was usual for inquisitions to be delivered *a propria manu* on the initiative of the justices of the peace themselves. Thus, in *Queen* v. *William, Samuel, Jonathan and John Lawrence, John Whitehead et al.,* "Ryoters," on March 12,

220 For the information, see *H.R. Pleadings* Pl. K. 341. For the minute entries, see *Ms. Mins. SCJ 1764–67* (Rough) 37, Jan. 15, 1765; *Ms. Mins. SCJ 1764–66* (Engr.) 117, Jan. 19, 1765.

221 *Ms. Mins. SCJ 1764–66* (Engr.) 177, 210. On the same day, subpoenas were issued commanding the appearance of four witnesses, Zachariah Bush, Powel Vanderwoort, William and Frederick Scuff (*J. T. Kempe Lawsuits* C–F *sub nom.* Elizabeth Clarke).

222 For copies of the notice of trial in King v. James Higby *et al.*, and King v. Isaac Lent *et al.*, see *J. T. Kempe Lawsuits sub nom.* James Higby, and *ibid.* L–O *sub nom.* Isaac Lent. Note that the

latter citation also contains the names of the persons Mr. Ludlow was concerned with as attorney in the riot case, as well as the defendants' plea of not guilty, the names of the witnesses subpoenaed, and the witnesses' testimony. For the copies of the minutes of the verdict quoted in the text, see *H.R. Pleadings* Pl. K. 806, June Circuit, 1765. For "the nisi prius record" with the *postea* in the second assault endorsed on the back of the issue roll see *H.R. Parch.* 140 B 4. Notes on trials in *J. T. Kempe Lawsuits* L–O.

223 *Ms. Mins. SCJ 1764–67* (Rough) 81, July 31, 1765.

224 Dalton, *Countrey Justice* (1677) c. 82 §24.

1705/06, "Inquisicon of a Riott taken in Queens County before Salin Mars and others was delivered into this court by . . . a justice of the peace of the said county and ordered to be filed." On March 15, 1705/06, process was ordered to issue against the defendants, and on June 5 the sheriff of Queens County was ordered to bring their bodies into court the following Saturday or be amerced. The court admitted the defendants "to a traverse" and they were bound each with two sureties in £40 to prosecute their traverse with effect. On October 9, 1706, the jury, being sworn, found all the defendants not guilty and they were discharged.[225]

On June 5, 1706, Jonathan Whitehead, justice of the peace in Queens County, in *Queen v. Peter Pra, Garrett Sprung et al.,* "in his proper person delivered . . . to the court [that is, the Supreme Court *en banc*] an inquisition of a riott against the defendants . . . which was ordered to be filed." The Attorney General prayed process against the several defendants in the inquisition named, but on September 7, 1706, all seven of the defendants having been called, they failed to appear. On September 10, 1708, the following entry appears in the Supreme Court minutes: "Mr. Attorney General enters by orders from his Excellency Lord Cornbury a nol. pr͞os," and the defendants were thereupon discharged from their recognizances.[226]

We have seen only one case of the later eighteenth century where an inquisition was delivered by hand,[227] and possibly one removal was had by certiorari.[228] But by this time it had become more usual to handle riots by information. As has been pointed out, the later riots were ferocious affairs conducted in a manner which would have made it impossible to make a record on view and even by inquisition. The adventures of Justice Henry Van Rensselaer

---

[225] It is amusing to note that on Oct. 11, 1706, the high sheriff of Queens made an affidavit that one John Hunt "who was summoned to serve as a Juryman in this cause" tried to avoid serving in the cause "by declaring he would give his inquest beforehand in the cause and by that means should find a way to get off." An attachment was ordered to issue against Hunt, "returnable immediate," but on Oct. 12, 1706, Hunt was discharged from the attachment (*Ms. Mins. SCJ 1704/05–1709* 49, 57, 66, 71, 76, 86, 91, 92, 100, 103, 105, 108).

[226] *Ms. Mins. SCJ 1704/05–1709* 66, 70, 95, 96, 191. Cf. also Queen v. Cornelia Burroughs *et al.,* 1706 (*Ms. Mins. SCJ 1704/05–1709* 86, 95), where one defendant was fined and put on bond; Queen v. Erasmus Wilkins *et al.,* 1705 (*ibid.* 37, 46). The court ordered the defendants imprisoned for six months without bail, apparently because an indictment for murder was pending.

[227] In King v. Flemming Colgan, Thomas Payer and Francis Smith, an inquisition of riot by the defendants was returned on Jan. 20, 1759, into the Supreme Court by a justice of the peace of Queens County and process was ordered to issue against the defendants (*Ms. Mins. SCJ 1756–61* [Rough] 131, Jan. 20, 1759).

[228] This we infer from the certiorari entry in King v. Rayner *et al.* after the information had been filed (*Ms. Mins. SCJ 1750–54* [Engr.] 249, 253, Apr. 27, 29, 1753). Cf. further James Straten's complaint against rioters, Dec. 27, 1762 (*J. T. Kempe Lawsuits* S–U *sub nom.* Straten); Judge Harrington's list of rioters at Orange Town, Mar. 21, 1769 (*ibid.* G–J *sub nom.* Harrington); Van Schaack's case respecting the abuse he met with from Albany rioters when the Sons of Liberty accused him of seeking the office of stamp distributor, January 1766 (*ibid.* V *sub nom.* Van Schaack).

in 1765 are instructive on this point. Van Rensselaer had attempted to suppress an alleged riot and the persons charged with riot complained to the Attorney General in the following language: "The several violent and arbitrary steps so manifestly tending to the Subversion of the inviolable privileges of English Subjects they Conceive ought not to pass unnoticed; and as the Law undoubtedly wisely guarded against the enormous abuse thereof by its Ministers—they Submit the above state of their Case to those whose province it is, to take Cognizance thereof."[229] On April 10, 1765, Van Rensselaer wrote to the Attorney General stating that the complaint was false and groundless, that he had attempted with the aid of the local overseers to get some stones to build a church, but when he and the overseers reached the place where the stones were, several riotous persons attempted to prevent his getting the stones. Van Rensselaer went on to explain: "When I came to the place where the stone was, I found seven or eight persons where I maid my proclamation to depart and not to make a riot and then there came five men more to joyn the rest and . . . affronted me and I dasen't not Speach. At last I ordered Samuel Ten Broeck to load stone to try their motion. . . ." It appears, however, from Kempe's draft of an information against Van Rensselaer that the stones were on land that did not belong to him, and that he had come up with some negroes, a fact which he carefully suppressed. Van Rensselaer loaded his stone but he claimed the "rioters" attacked him and compelled him to withdraw. The worthy justice then proceeded to have his witnesses bound over to give evidence, and with two other justices issued a warrant. At a sort of Star Chamber session, witnesses and defendants were browbeaten into making statements regarding the affair which Van Rensselaer seems to have held over them as a club.[230]

As a result of the complaint against the proceedings of the Albany justices of the peace in this case, informations for riot were filed on April 27, 1765, by the Attorney General against Henry Van Rensselaer, John and Samuel Ten Broeck, Gabriel Eyselstyne and Hendrick Rowe; and for maladministration in office against Henry Van Rensselaer, Jacob Freeze and Stephen Van Dyke. In August term, 1765, the sheriff of Albany returned *venire feci* as to all the defendants except Rowe who was "not found." The defendants were ordered to plead in twenty days or suffer judgment for want of a plea, and in October

---

[229] *Ibid. sub nom.* Henry Van Rensselaer. There is one early case (1721) of attempted interference; cf. *James Alexander Papers* Box 45, Q.S. Papers; Box 44, Supreme Court Papers.

[230] Letter of Apr. 10, 1765, from Henry Van Rensselaer to John Tabor Kempe (*J. T. Kempe Lawsuits V sub nom.* Henry Van Rensselaer).

term, 1765, default judgment was rendered against all except Rowe and Van Rensselaer who later pleaded *nolo*. On April 19 and August 2, 1766, on the riot information, William Smith, Jr., the defendants' attorney, moved to have affidavits read in mitigation of fine and these being read, the court fined each defendant 6s. 8d., which was paid. On the maladministration charge the fine was 20s.[231]

This case occurred at a time when the up-river revolt against the great landlords was seething, and from Van Rensselaer's account, it is apparent a record upon view would have been a greater act of daring than even so overbearing a person as he would have undertaken. It is not clear why a charge of riot was laid against the various justices, for the gravamen of the information was the maladministration and the evidence on this was damaging. In spite of the small fine, the tenants of the worthy justice must have found some grim satisfaction in seeing him hoist with his own petard.[232]

Under the forcible entry statutes which were designed to deal with a particular type of riotous behavior, a practice of transfer similar to the riot cases developed. In the late seventeenth century, as we have seen, the English summary procedure was being used in New York, for the problem was regarded as a type of inferior jurisdiction, and the magistrates also proceeded by indictment in Sessions.[233] It is only later that forcible entries become Supreme Court business and are prosecuted there by indictment,[234] although there was at least

[231] *Ms. Mins. SCJ 1764–66* (Engr.) 177, 282, 283, 367; *Ms. Mins. SCJ 1764–67* (Rough) 141, 157; *H.R. Pleadings* Pl. K. 804, Pl. K. 781. The *J. T. Kempe Lawsuits* (V *sub nom.* Henry Van Rensselaer) contain an amusing letter dated May 13, 1766, from Stephen Van Dyke, one of the defendants, to J. T. Kempe, in which Van Dyke stated that he had "acted in the affair according to the absolute demand of Henry Van Renselaer . . . and not knowing but that I was obliged to do as he demanded (he being one of the quorum) . . . think . . . it should be but just that Van Renselaer should pay the whole [fine] as he was the only instigator of the matter."

[232] On abuse of riot charges, compare also Stephen Case's letter to John Tabor Kempe dated at Newburgh, N.Y., June 14, 1769, in which Case stated that Jacob Teachout wanted to make a complaint against him. Case explained to Kempe that everyone was lawless in his section of the country and that Teachout "would swear a riot against me" for serving a precept on him (*J. T. Kempe Lawsuits* C–F *sub nom.* Stephen Case).

[233] Thus Elizabeth Sydenham *et al.* were indicted for forcible entry in New York City Quarter Sessions, and Elizabeth, having been found guilty, was committed to the city jail for three months,

fined £5, and ordered to pay costs (*Ms. Mins. NYCQS 1694–1731/32* 135, 146–148, Feb. 4, 1707/08, May 5, 1708). The case of Abraham Rideout to be discussed *infra* c. VII 444, was another case of forcible entry on which an indictment was returned in New York City Quarter Sessions on Feb. 4, 1707/08, but as we shall have occasion to notice, defendant was outlawed since he could not be apprehended (*ibid.* 135, 146, 150, 152, 160, 163, 170, 174).

[234] Thus Thomas Flood, Patrick Mulvanie, William Wilson, Tim Hurst, Tom Mulliner, John Grime and Sylvester Cavendish were indicted in the Supreme Court *en banc* for forcibly entering a house with drawn swords, threats and other abuses against the peace. Wilson and Grime were found guilty, the former paying a fine of £100 and the latter a fine of 10s. Judgment for want of a plea was rendered against Mulvanie, Tim Hurst was found not guilty, and *non est* was returned on the process against Mulvanie and Cavendish. We have been unable to learn anything regarding the further proceedings in the cases of Flood and Mulliner (*Ms. Mins. SCJ 1762–64* [Engr.] 177, 227, 284, 285, 296, 297, Apr. 30, July 30, Oct. 18, 25, 29, 1763; *Ms. Mins. SCJ 1766–69* [Engr.] 94, 187, Jan. 24, May 2, 1767; *H.R. Pleadings* Pl. K. 752; *J. T.*

one occasion (1735) when Bradley brought an information in such a case.[235] Inevitably, however, the information was employed in the period when rioting became acute and on those occasions when the objective of the outbreaks was the dispossession of some individual. Thus it was used in connection with the Terboss litigation already spoken of[236] and in the agrarian uprisings of 1766. On April 19, 1766, Joshua Bishop, Isaac Wright, R. Satterly, Daniel and Richard Cornell, Solomon and Joseph Tidd, Jr., Samuel Rutt, Daniel Chapman, Daniel and Nathaniel Brundage, Ed Gonen and nine other rioters of Westchester were brought into the Supreme Court *en banc* by the sheriff of Westchester "in virtue of Mr. Chief Justice's warrant." The affidavit of one Joseph Golding being read and filed, the court ordered that each defendant post a recognizance of £200 with two sureties in £100 each for their appearance to answer at the Court of Oyer and Terminer and General Gaol Delivery at Westchester and meantime to be of their good behavior. On April 25, 1766, the defendants posted the required bonds for their appearance at Circuit, but in the meantime the Attorney General had filed four informations against them in the Supreme Court *en banc* for riotously assembling and turning Joseph Golding out of his farm at Cortlandt Manor.[237] In August, 1766, and on January 24, May 2 and August 1, 1767, judgments for want of a plea were filed against Bishop, Wright, Daniel Brundage, the Tidds and Richard Cornell, and process was returned against the others, not found.[238] On May 2, 1767, *capias pro fine* was ordered against Wright, Bishop and Daniel Brundage, and the sheriff of Westchester was ordered to return the process by the next term or suffer attachment. In the following term (August, 1767), the sheriff returned Wright not found, and Bishop "taken but rescued." The sheriff was accordingly ordered to show cause why attachment should not issue against him for his suffering the rescue.[239] On October 26, 1767, Rutt and the Tidds were each fined 20s., and on July 26, 1768, James Duane on behalf of Attorney General Kempe moved for judgment against Bishop, but "the court waived judgment" and the defendant was committed. However, on the following day

Kempe Lawsuits C–F *sub nom.* Thomas Flood; *ibid.* L–O *sub nom.* Mulvanie).

[235] The information was brought against Evert Wendell, Bradley's deputy. The case was eventually settled; cf. *Ms. Mins. SCJ 1732–39* 162, 190, 204, 211, 226, 270, 343, 350, Apr. 21, Oct. 27, 1735, Jan. 27, 1735/36, Apr. 23, Aug. 2, 1736, Aug. 1, 1737, Apr. 24, Aug. 4, 1739.

[236] *Supra* 144. The citations in this case are *Ms. Mins. SCJ 1764–66* (Engr.) 368, 404; *Ms. Mins. SCJ 1764–67* (Rough) 85, 171, 268; *Ms. Mins.*

SCJ 1766–69 (Engr.) 78, 94; *H.R. Parch.* 221 B 4, 184 E 4, 185 G 2, 194 H 5; *J. T. Kempe Lawsuits* C–F *sub nom.* Terboss.

[237] *Ms. Mins. SCJ 1764–67* (Rough) 141, 144, 145; *J. T. Kempe Lawsuits* C–F *sub nom.* Joshua Bishop *et al.; ibid.* W–Y *sub nom.* Isaac Wright *et al.*, violent entry and riotous dispossession.

[238] *Ms. Mins. SCJ 1764–66* (Engr.) 44; *Ms. Mins. SCJ 1766–69* (Engr.) 94, 95, 186–188, 253.

[239] *Ms. Mins. SCJ 1766–69* (Engr.) 187, 188, 253.

Bishop was fined £3 6s. 8d. on each information and was ordered to post a bond in the amount of £100 New York money to keep the peace for five years.[240]

The trifling penalties exacted in the Bishop case, as in other instances where convictions were obtained for riot, are somewhat ludicrous in contrast with the staggering recognizances exacted for appearance and the terrific effort expended in getting the case to trial. The result of these cases conveys the impression that the authorities were using a battery of artillery to slay a mouse, yet they had no choice because the simple and summary machinery of dealing with riots and forcible entries was no longer effective. This seems to have been particularly true of the summary proceedings on forcible entry, judging from the disposition of inquisitions removed to the Supreme Court. In English law, as we have seen, a justice of the peace could upon an inquest fine and award restitution of the premises entered or detained.[241] Where a traverse of the record was made the case could be removed to King's Bench or the justice could by certification shift the duty of determining fine and restitution to that court. Such a transfer occurred in New York as early as 1703,[242] but it was only after 1750 that it was much used. These late cases illustrate the various situations where transfer of the record of forcible entry was effected.

In *King ex rel. Jonathan Hoegg v. Nathaniel Burdsall Jr.*,[243] a certiorari for the removal of the proceedings of William Doughty and Nicholas De-Lavergne, two justices of the peace of Dutchess, was, in August, 1760, issued out of the Supreme Court *en banc* ordering these justices to make return of the record of forcible entry and detainer found before them. On October 22, 1761, the court being of the opinion that the proceedings in this cause before the justices should be set aside, it was ordered that the inquisition be quashed and a writ of "rerestitution" awarded.[244]

Likewise in the case of Archibald Campbell, the record of a conviction of forcible entry and detainer was found against the defendant and brought up to the Supreme Court by certiorari. There, on hearing counsel on both sides

240 *Ibid.* 253, 312, 501, 503; for the estreat by the clerk of the Supreme Court on the fine of Rutt and the Tidds, see *H.R. Parch.* 221 B 4.

241 But not upon the proceeding where a justice merely viewed the forcible entry and removed the force (Dalton, *Countrey Justice* [1677] c.44 §3).

242 Queen v. Onclebagg, 1703 (*Ms. Mins. SCJ 1701–04* 111, 116, 122, 129. The inquisition was filed in the Supreme Court on motion of defendant's attorney, and was quashed.

243 *Ms. Mins. SCJ 1757–60* (Engr.) 346; *Ms. Mins. SCJ 1756–61* (Rough) 254.

244 The Court of King's Bench might restore the premises to the defendant in the original forcible entry action if the indictment or inquisition were quashed there. If restitution had been awarded on insufficient indictment and removed to the King's Bench, "the court there will cause the Party to be restored, that before was put out by the justices of the peace . . ." (Dalton, *op. cit.* c.133).

and on motion of Duane for the defendant, the record of the conviction was ordered to be quashed and a writ of restitution awarded to Campbell.[245]

A forcible entry case interesting for procedural detail is that of *King* v. *George Janeway and John Waters* for it is one of the rare examples where the certiorari has been preserved as well as the record of the inquest of forcible entry taken before two New York City justices of the peace.[246] On January 19, 1773, the certiorari and justices' return were filed in the Supreme Court *en banc* and on motion of the defendant's attorney, Ludlow, the court ordered that the inquisition for forcible detainer be quashed for defective jurors, two of the jurors not being freeholders. This order must have been set aside for on October 22, 1773, Attorney General Kempe secured a rule that this case be tried in the Supreme Court *en banc,* and on October 26 the defendant being tried was found not guilty.[247]

In *King* v. *Benjamin Ferris* we have an example of a forcible entry and detainer removed from the hands of two justices of the peace of Westchester to the Supreme Court *en banc* by certiorari and thence sent down for trial at Circuit. In 1771 an inquisition was taken at the scene of a forcible entry in Westchester County on the oath of twenty-one jurors before two justices of the peace of that county. The jurors said on their oath that the defendant and other malefactors with force and arms and with strong and armed power did enter into certain tenements and "expelled and disseized and do yet keep out" the lawful owners "to the great disturbance of the peace of our Lord the King and against the form of the statutes in such case made and provided."[248] On October 26, 1771, a certiorari and return on the same were filed in the Supreme

<hr/>

[245] *Ms. Mins. SCJ 1764–67* (Rough) 244, 245, May 2, 1767. Also see King v. Gilliad Hunt, where, on Jan. 22, 1763, a certiorari and a copy of the record being returned, the court on motion of Mr. Morris ordered a writ of "rerestitution" (*Ms. Mins. SCJ 1762–64* [Engr.] 109).

[246] *H.R. Parch.* 111 K 7, which is the judgment roll in this case. The judgment roll begins: "Pleas . . . April . . . one thousand seven hundred seventy three . . . [issued upon an inquisition] City and County of New York ss: Be It Remembered that a writ of . . . the King under the Seal of this Court [issued] . . ." At this point in the judgment roll the certiorari is recited and then the return of the justices of the peace to the certiorari. The judgment roll then recites the schedule annexed by the justices of the peace to the return on the certiorari, and this schedule contains the inquisition. The roll then continues: "And the Tenor of the said plea of him the said George Janeway . . .

defends the said force and Injury and . . . he says that he is nowise Guilty . . . puts himself on the country and . . . [the] Attorney General . . . in like manner and now . . . [all the parties] comes here . . . [that is, into the Supreme Court *en banc*] George Janeway by Samuel Jones his attorney and the . . . Attorney General . . . [and] prays a writ of . . . the King to cause to come here . . . [12 jurors] to try whether the said George Janeway is guilty." The judgment roll recites that the jury found George Janeway not guilty and therefore he was discharged *sine die* and judgment was signed on Mar. 19, 1774. The judgment roll was filed on Mar. 21, 1774 (*H.R. Parch.* 111 K 7).

[247] *Ms. Mins. SCJ 1772–76* (Rough) 63, 123, 129. Also see *H.R. Parch.* 111 K 7 and see also *J. T. Kempe Lawsuits sub nom.* George Janeway, where is to be found a notice of trial sent from Kempe to Samuel Jones, attorney for the defendants.

[248] *H.R. Pleadings* Pl. K. 1076.

Court *en banc*.[249] Subsequent to the return of the certiorari, it appears that a trial was had at Circuit in Westchester, for we have found John Tabor Kempe's notes on the trial held at White Plains on September 9, 1773. The Kempe papers indicate that Benjamin Ferris had able defenders, Richard Morris, Benjamin Kissam and Gouverneur Morris, who had been admitted to the bar two years earlier.[250] The defense took the line that no evidence had been produced proving an actual possession in the landlord, and it was argued that only the tenant had been dispossessed and actual disseisin had not been shown.[251] The defendant's attorneys evidently succeeded at the Circuit trial since on October 25, 1773, we find that the *postea* was read and filed in the Supreme Court and "on motion of Mr. Morris, ordered judgment for the defendant *nisi*."[252]

It should be observed that where the inquest was traversed, it served as an indictment or information in the court to which it was transferred. This is apparent from the record in *King* v. *Janeway* discussed above and from the proceedings in *King* v. *Nobles and Bogardus,* a case involving a forcible entry upon property of Trinity Church.[253] The tender of a traverse did not necessarily mean the cause would be transferred. If the justice of the peace wished he could impanel a jury and proceed to trial. But where it led to removal, the opportunity for preliminary motions was presented; in other words, by transfer the defendant was given more latitude in managing his defense than if the cause was settled by a magistrate and jury.

We have treated forcible entry as a phase of the riot problem for this is how the jurisdiction was originally conceived, and there is no doubt that in the words of the inquest the "strong hand and armed force" were frequently real enough. At the same time, this jurisdiction should be viewed also in connection with the general legal administrative problem which arose out of controversies over the land and its issues, the fourth category of cases where transfer procedure was vital.

The Land Cases

Bitter and continual were the disputes over land in New York Province. From the moment Colonel Nicolls in the capitulation of New Netherland

---

[249] *Ms. Mins. SCJ 1769–72* (Engr.) 458.
[250] *Ibid.* 484.
[251] The attorneys' arguments and the testimony of the witnesses at the Circuit trial are to be found in *J. T. Kempe Lawsuits* C–F *sub nom.* Benjamin Ferris. The attorneys cited the following authorities:

"Hawk. 141; Bacon 548; Hawk. 151, Section 46; Hawk. 145 Section 25; Bacon 558."
[252] *Ms. Mins. SCJ 1772–76* (Rough) 127.
[253] *J. T. Kempe Lawsuits* L–O *sub nom.* John Nobles; *Ms. Mins. SCJ 1772–76* (Rough) 231, Apr. 19, 1775.

confirmed the ancient Dutch grants and recognized the Dutch system of in-heritance to the final suspension of the colonial judiciary in 1776, battles, skir-mishes, alarums and excursions raged over grants, leases, mortgages and the like. The lack of any carefully considered policy in respect of Crown lands, the failure to pursue with consistency an equitable course in respect both to large scale promotion and individual farm settlement, led not only to incessant litigation but to acrid political controversy. The basic difficulty lay in the cir-cumstance that the Crown never abandoned a feudal attitude, and the mass of inhabitants clung to the ideal of the unincumbered freehold. The establish-ment of manors by the Duke of York's lieutenants and by some of the later royal governors facilitated the growth of the huge semi-baronial estates like those of the Phillipses, the Livingstons and others where the tenants could never acquire title and in due course rose in rebellion.[254] Governors, like the complaisant Fletcher, for trifling consideration made extravagant grants which were sometimes vacated, leaving the grantees of the original patentee with defective titles.[255] In some cases, promoters[256] or land-greedy magnates like John Van Rensselaer,[257] made intrusions upon Crown lands with little or no color of right, and in others, enterprising individuals fostered questionable title by securing fraudulent deeds or by deluding Indians into making con-veyances.[258] Toward the end of the colonial period boundary quarrels with Massachusetts and New Hampshire led to the impugning of individual titles in the disputed areas and, as we have seen, to the use of armed force to effect evictions.

[254] There is a superficial discussion of the land problem in 3 *Hist. State NY* (Flick ed.) 147 *et seq.*

[255] See an Act of May 16, 1699, "Vacateing Breaking & Annulling Several Extravagant Grants of Land made by Coll Fletcher, the late Govr." (1 *Col. Laws NY* 412). This law was repealed by the assembly on Nov. 27, 1702 (*ibid.* 523), but the repealing act was repealed by the Queen and the original vacating act confirmed by the Crown on June 26, 1708 (*ibid.* 412, editor's head note to the Act of 1699). In April, 1714, Queen Anne or-dered that the Governor of New York discontinue the prosecution in Chancery against the corporation of Trinity Church, whose land grant was one of those vacated by the Act of 1699 (*John Jay Papers* Box 3 no. 16 B).

[256] King v. Lydius, *infra* 209.

[257] King v. Van Rensselaer, *infra* 249.

[258] King v. Klock, *infra* 218. There is consider-able matter in the records relating to the swindling of Indians. For example, in October Term, 1722, the Attorney General filed a Crown information against John Baptist Van Eps for spreading false reports among the Indians that Margaret Vedder had included three lots instead of one in a deed which the Indians had signed giving her certain land (*H.R. Parch.* 153 G 10). In 1765 an informa-tion was filed against Samuel Monroe for a "great" misdemeanor in exciting the Indians to claim cer-tain Dutchess lands (*H.R. Pleadings* Pl. K. 796). In January Term, 1765, Richard Nicholls brought a *qui tam* action against James Pine, Jonathan Valentine and Daniel Terboss for buying and sell-ing pretended land titles (*ibid.* Pl. N. 106) while Beverly Robinson, on April 27, 1765, brought a *qui tam* against James Crane, Jr., Daniel Monroe and Stephen Willcocks for the same offense (*Ms. Mins. SCJ 1764–66* [Engr.] 180; *H.R. Parch.* 193 L 10). Beverly Robinson in Aug. 1765 also brought a *qui tam* against Joseph Fowler, Jr., Ben Palmer and Ed. Gray for buying and selling pretended land titles (*Ms. Mins. SCJ 1764–66* [Engr.] 285; *J. T. Kempe Lawsuits* P–R *sub nom.* Beverly Robinson). In the latter case, tampering with the Indians was considered as the crime of maintenance.

The law enforcing officers of the Crown were faced with a variety of perplexing problems in connection with the struggle over lands. First among these was the harassing task of securing payment of quitrents, one which does not here concern us.[259] In the second place, there was the control of litigations over title, which sometimes involved criminal procedure. And finally there was the question of intrusions. Transfer jurisdiction was involved in the handling of both the latter problems because of the practical necessity of trying land cases locally, but even more so because of the pressure of colonial opinion that such matters should be handled where they arose.

The question of control over title litigation in possessory actions can be briefly disposed of. Except where the forcible entry procedure was used it was only occasionally that resort was had to criminal sanctions. The favorite action for trying title was ejectment, and more than sixty per cent of the civil cases tried at nisi prius were of this form.[260] Litigants were not invariably happy at the outcome of a case and so it was sometimes necessary to resort to attach-

[259] For some cases with regard to the difficulty of collecting quitrents, see David Jameson Qui pro Domina Regina &c. v. Engelbert Lott and Daniel Polhemus, in Chancery, 1713. Here Jameson in his information set forth the great omissions and neglect of the freeholders and inhabitants of New York in paying their quitrents "to the great disappointment and prejudice of her Majesty's Service and that for want of a quit-rent roll Her Majesty's Receiver General is not enabled to make a full and true discovery of the soil already patent in the province and of the arrearages of quit-rent." Jameson pointed out that the defendants had not given an account of how many lots there were, nor did they set forth their receipts for the quitrent, etc. We note that the defendants paid the money into court in the amount of £44 11s. on June 25, 1713 (James Alexander Papers Box 44 Supreme and Mayor's Court Papers; Flatbush Town Recs. Misc. Liber B, 194, 195 et seq.).
Cf. also King in Exchequer on the equity side, bill against Scott and York for his Majesty's quitrents, in which case on Mar. 21, 1731/32, a bill was read and filed against the defendants and process was ordered to issue, returnable the first day of the following term (Ms. Mins. SCJ 1727–32 322).
Attorney General Richard Bradley complained to Evert Wendell on Aug. 5, 1725: "If you ever see one George Syden[ham . . .] you would oblige me if you would tell [him] unless he speedily sends his qu[it-rent and] charges he will be fetched down [to New York by the] Seargeant at Arms several writts [. . .] having been sent against him . . . without effect and he not [answering . . .] to the bill fyled against him in Canc. though served with a spa [subpoena] a writt of Rebellion will go out agt. him If he does not prevent it by

speedy payment of quit-rent and charges" (King v. George Sydenham, Misc. Mss. Richard Bradley).
Also see the James Alexander Papers Box 45 Chancery Papers, for several quitrent cases between 1718 and 1732.
On Nov. 2, 1721, Byerly wrote to James Alexander as follows: "I hereby require you as Attorney General to prosecute according to law the persons hereunder written who are considerably indebted to His Majesty for Quitt Rent . . . I do not think fit to wait any longer, nor . . . incur the displeasure of the Lords of the treasury which would be the consequence of my not discharging my office of Receiver General. . . . These that follow are by his Excellency's order so I would have Mr Elliston search the Rent Rolls for what they are indebted for whaleing without licence" (James Alexander Papers Box 2, B, no. 92). Also see Byerly's letter to Alexander on Nov. 27, 1726 (ibid. no. 91).
[260] The following are among the interesting cases tried at nisi prius: Hendrickson v. Hallet, Kings court for the trial of causes brought to issue at the Supreme Court, Aug. 8, 1716 (1 Ms. Mins. Cir. 1716–17 6, 7) (a civil action for forcible entry); Barnes ex dem. Plainson v. Hallet, Queens Court for the trial of causes brought to issue &c. Aug. 15, 1716 (ibid. 15, 16) (ejectment action); "En. on ye demise of Coeman v. Schuyler," Albany court for the trial of causes &c. Sept. 4, 1717 (ibid. 47–50) (ejectment); Hanson v. Van Isaack and Smith ex dem. Chambers v. Nottingham, Albany court for the trial of causes &c., Sept. 6, 1716 (ibid. 1, 2) (both ejectment actions); John Smith ex dem. Casper Van Heusen v. Hendrick Van Rensalaer, Albany court for the trial of causes &c., Sept. 15, 16, 18, 1721 (Ms. Mins. Cir. 1721–49 232, 233) (ejectment).

ment against persons who forcibly resisted execution.[261] More difficult was the task of assuring that cases would be properly tried. Changes of venue were frequently had for this reason, and on one occasion an information was filed for embracery against one Swart who had endeavored to influence a jury.[262]

A problem of much greater dimensions and of real political import was the intrusion on Crown lands. We cannot enter into an extensive examination of the cases[263] but we shall deal with two, *King* v. *Lydius,* and *King* v. *Klock,* which in their time were regarded as causes of the first magnitude, not only because Crown interests were at stake but because the much contested validity of Indian deeds was in issue.

John Henry Lydius was brought before the Council in December, 1760, for intrusion on Crown lands and pretending a right to such lands in violation not only of the common law but also of a Governor's proclamation.[264] The Attorney General was ordered to frame informations against Lydius for intrusion and for contempt of the Governor's proclamation, but as Kempe doubted whether a new law could be made by a proclamation he decided to

261 For example, King v. Edward McNeal (*Ms. Mins. SCJ 1762–64* [Engr.] 357, Jan. 26, 1764).
262 King v. Dirck Swart (*Ms. Mins. SCJ 1766–69* [Engr.] 326, 388, Oct. 31, 1767, Jan. 23, 1768). For the information see *J. T. Kempe Lawsuits* S–U *sub nom.* Dirck Swart. This copy of the information was to be sent to James Duane, who was evidently the attorney for the defendant, and the copy of the information bears the following expense account: "folio 41 at 9*d.*—£ 1, 10*s.*"
263 Compare the following informations for intrusion on Crown lands filed at various times during the colonial period: Queen v. Jacob Carsen *et al.,* "Information of intrusion" (*Ms. Mins. SCJ 1701–04* 130, Apr. 4, 1704); Queen v. John Kirchison *et al.* (*ibid.* 132, Apr. 5, 1704); King v. Bedford and Shaw, information for intrusion on Crown lands in Ulster (*Ms. Mins. SCJ 1723–27* 252, Mar. 21, 1726/27; *Ms. Mins. SCJ 1727–32* 6, 43, 158, 377, Oct. 11, 1727, Mar. 19, 1727/28, Oct. 21, 1729, Oct. 17, 1732); King v. John Henry Lydius, Jan. 1763, discussed in the text; King v. David Moore, Samuel Wickham and William Cox (*Ms. Mins. SCJ 1764–67* [Rough] 141, Apr. 19, 1766; *Ms. Mins. SCJ 1764–66* [Engr.] 178, 284, Apr. 27, Aug. 1765; *H.R. Parch.* 193 B 9; *J. T. Kempe Lawsuits* L–O *sub nom.* Moore); King v. Joshua Smith, Nathan Owen and George McNeish, Ulster, Aug. 1765 (*Ms. Mins. SCJ 1764–67* [Engr.] 178, 284, Apr. 27, Aug. 1765; *J. T. Kempe Lawsuits* S–U *sub nom.* Smith; *H.R. Pleadings* Pl. K. 803, 1088); King v. Robert Ferguson and Jabes Cooley, Aug. 1766 (*H.R. Parch.* 193 L 9); King v. John Van Rensselaer, discussed *infra* 249.

In the *James Alexander Papers* Box 48 is an interesting note, apparently made by James Alexander, regarding English authorities on intrusion to be used in the case of King v. the Intruders into Evans Patent:

"Fitzherbert N.B. 200. For trespass done on the King's soil The use is to have an information of intrusion in the Exchequer and when he appeareth the course is to bind him in recognizance at his peril to leave the possession to the King. Plowden 547 There is a good form of an information of intrusion with the pleadings and arguments at large upon it and in the same case fol. 561b there is the judgment against the intruders and the form of a writ to oust them

"Hardress 460 concerning form of the judgment and Execution in Intrusion and there adjudged not bind a stranger to the Suit

"Dyer 238b pl 37 Deft. in an intrusion ought to set forth a title in This plea otherwise by the course of the Exchequer he will be dispossessed Theres many cases cited in the margin whose effect I have not lookt for

"Savill 48 how the Deft. in intrusion ought to plead and there a general Information in urbis [?] ter [?] and tenement is held good and for it the case of mines in Plowden is cited

"Savill 64 if deft. pleads a grant a lease etc. the King need only deny title of deft. without maintaining his right for he acknowledges title in the King if what he pleads gives him not the title

"Deft. ought to plead his letters patents Savil 48."
264 *Supra* 34 n. 178.

file an information against Lydius merely for intrusion and to bring the case to trial at the next Albany Circuit.[265] Owing to various delays and postponements, it was not until January term, 1763, that the Supreme Court made a peremptory rule that Lydius plead to the information which charged that defendant,

> the Laws of . . . the King now little fearing but unlawfully and wickedly devising and intending the Exheridation and Disherison . . . of the said Tract or Parcel of Land with force and Arms did Enter and Intrude . . . and let to farm and Issue and the profits thereof . . . to his own proper use . . . by cutting and taking Twenty Thousand car Loads of wood . . . and also in pasturing . . . cattle . . . in contempt of . . . the now King and his Laws and Dignity.[266]

On April 30, 1763, a subpoena was issued for witnesses and an order made for trial at the Albany Circuit on June 23.[267] On May 23, 1763, the Attorney General wrote to the sheriff of Albany saying:

[265] *J. T. Kempe Lawsuits* L–O *sub nom.* King v. John Henry Lydius, letter of Mar. 8, 1762. Cf. *supra* 34 n. 178.

[266] For copies of the information, see *H.R. Parch.* 219 D 4, 226 C 4. Filed in the *J. T. Kempe Lawsuits* (L–O *sub nom.* John Henry Lydius) is a notice of trial of Lydius dated May, 1762, indicating that a trial was to be held in Albany in June, 1762. It is also to be noted that on May 16, 1762, the sheriff of Albany wrote to Kempe stating: "I can't return the book of freeholders of the county as there are only two days left . . . there is no book . . . and it would take a week to prepare one" (*ibid.*). On May 24, 1762, Kempe replied to Harmanus Schuyler, the sheriff of Albany, stating: "You receive herewith a *venire* and *distringas* . . . which you will be pleased to execute and return to court at the Supreme Court which will sit at Albany on 24 June next. I have annexed to each writ a parchment for the Jurors names to be wrote on—I have received your letter informing me that you could not return a book of freeholders. It seems very extraordinary you should have no such book . . . next post you will receive from me some subpoenas to be served on the witnesses . . ." (*ibid.*).

The trial was not held at Albany Circuit for June, 1762, for on June 24, 1762, the defendant, Lydius, made an affidavit before David Jones, Justice of the Supreme Court, to put off the trial: "John Henry Lydius . . . being duly sworn maketh oath that . . . he received a copy of a notice of trial . . . and that he . . . sent . . . a messenger to go to . . . New Hampshire . . . for one Benjamin Sumner a meterial witness . . . this deponent haes not heard from said messenger . . . and has great reason to believe that he shall be able at the next court for Tryale of causes . . . in . . . Albany . . . to procure the said Benjn Sumner as a witness . . . and verily believes that he cannot proceed to Tryale with safety without the Benefit of said witness's testimony" (*ibid.*). See also a copy of J. T. Kempe's "Costs for putting off trial," *infra* Appendix 775.

On July 7, 1762, J. T. Kempe reported to Governor Monckton relating to the putting off of Lydius' trial: "By order of the Lieutenant Governor in Council . . . I was directed to prosecute John Henry Lydius . . . I immediately commenced the prosecution and attended at Albany at the Circuit Court. . . . On my moving there to bring on the Tryal the Council for Mr. Lydius offered to the court an affidavit . . . and . . . grounded a motion for putting it off which the court thought proper to grant overuling the objections made to the insufficiency of the affidavit. . . . As the consequences . . . may extremely affect the good of this Province and His Majesty's interest and as the proceedings originated at the Council board I thought it my Duty to acquaint your Excellency with the steps" (*ibid.*). It will be noted that the minute entries of the Supreme Court indicate that on October 19, 29 and 30, 1762, the defendant's recognizance was respited and continued, the final continuance being until the next term (*Ms. Mins. SCJ 1762–64* [Engr.] 4, 20, 23). The judgment roll in the Lydius case (*H.R. Parch.* 219 D 4) reflects the postponements of the trial in a series of continuances.

Apparently impatient at the postponements and delays in this case, the Attorney General on Jan. 22, 1763, moved that the defendant plead by next term and the court "Ordered peremptorily that the defendant plead by next term" (*Ms. Mins. SCJ 1762–64* [Engr.] 90).

[267] For a parchment form of the subpoena, see *J. T. Kempe Lawsuits* L–O *sub nom.* John Henry

You receive herewith a venire and distringas in . . . King v. John Henry Lydius which you will be pleased to execute and return to the court at the Assizes at Albany 23 June next . . . I also enclose four subpoenas and 20 tickets to be served on the witnesses. . . . The method of serving the subpoenas is by showing the witness the subpoena in which his name is wrote so that he may see the seal and deliver him the ticket directed to him. . . . Pray subpoena Baltus Lydius . . . [and two others named] before you summon the others and before it is known the venire is come as they are material witnesses and may get out of the way.[268]

Apparently the Attorney General was still having considerable difficulty bringing Lydius to trial because not only did the defendant make all kinds of excuses, but Goldsbrow Banyar, one of the witnesses, wrote to the Attorney General on June 10, 1763, stating that the Governor did not want him to go to Albany for the trial, and on June 13, Banyar asked to be excused of the subpoena served on him because he was on the Governor's business, saying "Mr. Brash can prove everything you wanted my testimony for."[269] The trial of John Henry Lydius was finally had at the Albany Circuit for June 23, 1763. The minutes are missing but we have seen copies of the *postea* which was returned as well as of notices of trial.[270]

The Attorney General's notes for his brief are most interesting. He indicates that by order of the Governor in Council he had filed an information charging the defendant with intrusion into two tracts of land vested in the King, one near Fort Edward and the other near Otter Creek, that the defendant had pleaded not guilty, and that the facts to be proven were: (1) that the lands were the King's; (2) that they lay in Albany County; and (3) that the facts of the intrusion were as charged in the information. Addressing himself to the first point, Kempe proposed to prove "the general principle of law" that all lands are held from the Crown and that the original proprietorship by the Crown of all lands is, "according to the policy of the Constitution," sufficient proof of "right" unless the King granted them away. Kempe indicated

Lydius, dated Apr. 30, 1763, and for the order for the trial at Albany Circuit, see *H.R. Parch.* 219 D 4.
268 *J. T. Kempe Lawsuits* L–O *sub nom.* J. H. Lydius, May 23, 1763.
269 *Ibid.*
270 For copies of the *postea*, see *H.R. Parch.* 219 D 4, 158 E 6, 226 C 4. For the notice of trial at Albany Circuit, June 23, 1763, see *J. T. Kempe Lawsuits* L–O *sub nom.* J. H. Lydius. A note attached to one of the copies of the notice of trial at Albany Circuit is as follows: "N.B. The cause above

mentioned intended to be brought to tryal is for intrusion into the Crown lands . . . that was noticed for tryal last year and put off . . . on your [i.e. Lydius'] affidavit the prosecution of which . . . in the Supreme Court commenced in Jan. Term, 1762," the information being then filed. Endorsed on the notice of trial is the statement of Jarvis Daft dated May 30, 1763: "Served a notice of trial of which the within is a true copy on the within named John Henry Lydius" (*ibid.*).

that the proof of title in such case would rest upon the defendant. He considered a possible objection which the defense might make, namely, that while this principle held good as to lands within the realm of England, nevertheless the King had no right to lands "belonging to native Indians who . . . shall be presumed to have a right to and . . . cant be divested but by Conquest, Surrender or Sale. . . . It lies on the King to prove a conveyance from the Indians. . . ." Kempe's proposed answer to this objection on the part of the defendants was that the discovery of land by a subject of the King in parts of the world inhabited only by savages gave the kingdom a right to the lands. The King's subjects were estopped from saying that the lands belonged to the Indians, warning that "if this Doctrine that Indian Titles are good against the Crown shall be of any force the Inconveniency will be almost incredible." Addressing himself further to the first point, the matter of the King's title, Kempe pointed out that the defendant's plea of not guilty admitted the jurisdiction of the court and went on to say that "in admitting the Jurisdiction he has admitted it to be within this province."

The Attorney General also considered the defendant's supposed defenses based on an Indian deed, on a grant from the Governor of Massachusetts Bay, and on the argument that the lands lay out of the Province of New York. With reference to the argument based on the Indian deed, Kempe pointed out that such matter "shall not be given in evidence it being contrary to the Constitution for a subject to derive any title . . . but through the Crown." Considering the defendant's possible argument based on the grant from Governor Shirley of Massachusetts, Kempe argued:

> This can with no propriety be given in evidence on his plea of not guilty as it tends to prove that the lands lie out of this province . . . [this matter] should have been pleaded to the Jurisdiction in abatement for it is a rule in law that whatever can be pleaded in abatement shall not be given in evidence on the general Issue and this . . . [rule exists] to prevent a surprise on the plaintiff for which End Special pleading was first introduced to drive the controversy to a single point.

To the objection the defendant might make that he only offered the Shirley grant in evidence in order to prove a grant from the King and not to show that the lands lay out of the province, Kempe proposed to make answer that the Massachusetts Bay title denied the jurisdiction of the Supreme Court of New York. To another possible objection by the defendant that the King by special commission could empower any grants, Kempe intended to argue that it would be necessary to show such special commission, and that the Governor of Massachusetts Bay, merely as governor, had no power to grant lands not lying within his jurisdiction. Furthermore that the defendant by a plea of not guilty and a submission to the jurisdiction could not falsify his plea and that a plea of any grant not under the Great Seal of this Province or the Seal of Great Britain would tend to falsify his plea.[271]

Kempe's argument continued that the defendant could not give special matter in evidence in bar "for it is the prerogative of the Crown that in informations for intrusion on Crown Lands, Deft shall plea title specially (17 Vin. Tit. Prerog. p. 218; 4 Inst. 116)." Against the argument that the prerogative was taken away by 21 James I c.14, Kempe countered that this statute did not extend to affect the wastes in America belonging to the Crown

of which no one takes the profits. . . . The drift of that act was to ease the subject in suits brought by the Crown on Titles long dormant and where possession had been against the Crown for a number of years. . . . It lies on the defendant to prove the King [was] out of possession 20 years before the Intrusion brought and that he hath not taken the profits of the lands during all that time, or he cannot (supposing the Stat. extends to the present case) give any special matter in evidence it being expressly limited to where the King has been out of possession 20 years.

Anticipating the possibility that the verdict might not show that Lydius personally made the intrusions, Kempe added to his brief the following:

If it appears on the evidence that Mr. Lydius has been in any wise concerned in any intrusion made on these lands it will be sufficient to convict him, for in treasons and trespass there are no accessories and it is a rule that whatever will make a man an accessory before the fact in felony makes him a principal in trespass. After a crime hath been proved in the Count in which . . . laid, evidence may be given of other instances of the same crime in another count in order to satisfy the jury. 2 Hawk. Pl. Cr. 436; Keiling 33.15 N L Ev.[272]

Undoubtedly the extreme technicality of the law and the facts involved in this prosecution for intrusion bewildered the simple farmers sitting on the jury at Albany Circuit, and in consequence they found a special verdict of more

271 Kempe stated that the King cannot grant lands but under his Great Seal, quoting "Viner's Abridgement 17, p. 70. title Prerogative, Section 1, 2, County Lanes case 16.6; 2 Coke's Institutes 552."

272 The drafts of the brief of the Attorney General are to be found in J. T. Kempe Lawsuits L-O sub nom. J. H. Lydius.

than four thousand words. The jury recited that in 1732 Lydius built a house south of Fort Edward and built on and cleared land, residing there until 1745, during which time he received the profits. The jury found that this was part of the land described in the information and they also found that in 1745 the French and Indian savages, making a "hostile eruption" into the northern part of the province, burned the house and drove Lydius to Albany where he stayed until 1749, during which time the ground remained unpossessed by anyone. In 1749 Lydius built a new house on the said ground and resided there with his family receiving the profits of the surrounding land until the outbreak of the French and Indian War in 1754, when Lydius returned to the city of Albany where he had resided ever since. In addition, the jurors found that, in 1760, Lydius published in the city of Albany an instrument inviting British subjects to the number of one hundred to settle a township in the land on which he had formerly resided, and did also make a lease of the profits in pitch to Nicholas DeLavergne, Samuel Doty, Platt & Co. of Dutchess, of certain lands six miles square alleged in the lease to be in Massachusetts Bay. This land was also mentioned in the Attorney General's information. Other leases and assertions of ownership were also stated by the jury to have been made by Lydius:

> But whether upon the whole matter aforesaid by . . . the said Jurors in form aforesaid found the said Entries into possession receiving the profits Leasing and granting of the Premises . . . [&c] and other the actings and doings of him the said John Henry Lydius . . . [are found to be so by the jurors it] will make the said John Henry Lydius guilty of the Intrusion as charged in the said Information . . . the Jurors aforesaid are Entirely Ignorant and pray the advisement of the said Justices in the premises. And if upon the whole matter aforesaid . . . it shall seem to the court here that the said Entries . . . [&c] makes the said John Henry Lydius guilty of the Intrusion as charged in the Information . . . then the same Jurors upon their oath do say that the said John Henry Lydius in and upon the possession of our said Lord the King . . . did Enter, Intrude and make Entry in manner and form as by the said Information is within alledged. And if upon the whole matter . . . it shall seem to the Court here that the aforesaid Entries . . . do not make the said John Henry Lydius guilty of an Intrusion . . . then the same jurors say upon their oath that the aforesaid John Henry Lydius in and upon the possession of our said Lord the King . . . did not Enter, Intrude nor make Entry. . . .[273]

[273] For the special verdict, see the *postea* entered on the judgment roll in *H.R. Parch.* 219 D 4.   Also see *J. T. Kempe Lawsuits* L–O *sub nom.* J. H. Lydius, for another copy of the *postea*.

On July 25, 1763, the Attorney General moved for judgment against the defendant for want of a plea. Although the court ordered that the clerk of the Assizes return the *postea* by the following Thursday, on July 28 the rule for the *postea* was enlarged to the following term. On October 20, 1763, the *postea* was returned and read and filed on the Attorney General's motion. On January 17, 1764, the judgment roll had evidently been made up, for the "record" was read and filed in the Supreme Court *en banc* and on the Attorney General's motion it was ordered that it be made a *concilium*. The Attorney General having argued on behalf of the Crown, the defendant was ordered to reply to the Attorney General on the first Thursday in the following term. On April 18, 1764, Ogden for the defendant filed his argument.[274]

The arguments are extremely interesting exhibits on the state of legal learning, and it is therefore desirable to consider them at some length. Defendant's first argument was made by Whitehead Hicks who stated that counsel, conceiving the evidence of the Crown to be insufficient in law, had requested the court to recommend to the jury to find the matter specially that "the law upon the point might be more deliberately and solemnly concidered by the court above than it could be by a Hasty Tryal at a circuit." Hicks recited the information and the allegations contained therein and next said "then comes the Doubt of the Jury." Hicks pointed out that only such facts as showed the defendant guilty of an intrusion since October 20, 1760 deserved notice. He also claimed that the defendant had not received any of the profits of the lands mentioned in the information and no title had been found in the King, and then pointed out that no judgment for the King could be rendered unless "office found."[275] Citing Gilbert's *Exchequer* (pp. 109, 110), Hicks pointed out that the King could not take except by matter of record and that it was a part of the liberty of England "that the King's officers might not enter . . . until the jury form the King's title." Hicks admitted that where lands belonged to no one the King's officers might enter, because by the law the possession of such lands was in the Crown; nevertheless, the King's title to land ought to appear of record,[276] and the King could not seize the land of an offender until it appeared, by the return of an inquisition, of precisely which lands the King was seised. Therefore, since the defendant was in possession at the time of the pretended

[274] *Ms. Mins. SCJ 1762–64* (Engr.) 215, 219, 227, 277, 342, 361, 411.
[275] Citing "2 Lilly's *Abridgement* 75, Title Intrusion; Moor's case 440, folio 295, Viner's *Abridgement* title Prerogative 218 N 1: 'An infor-

mation of intrusion lies for the King in Exchequer upon office found though the Record be not there.' "
[276] Citing 1 Hawkins, *Pleas of the Crown* 20 §45.

intrusion, he was not liable to an information "before an office first found." Admitting the Attorney General's argument that all title to lands must be derived from the Crown, Hicks argued that nevertheless an information for intrusion could not lie until office found.[277]

Arguing next for the defendant, Ogden asserted that the facts found by the jury's special verdict were insufficient since there was no finding that the late George II had title at the time of the alleged entry, nor that the defendant had cut wood or taken the profits as alleged in the information. Ogden claimed further that surveying the lands was not an intrusion for which an information would lie. Neither had there been any mention made of the fact that the King was in actual possession of the lands. Ogden admitted the court's jurisdiction to try the cause because of the defendant's plea of not guilty. He insisted, however, that the verdict did not show that the Crown had received the profits of the land for twenty years prior to the bringing of the information, and therefore the defendant had the right to plead the general issue, it being the duty of the Crown to prove a clear title to support the information. It was also stated by Ogden that "My lord Coke in his First Institute, 277, says he that entereth upon any of the King's demesne and taketh the profits is said to intrude." Ogden admitted that Wood, in his *Institutes* abridging Coke's *Institutes,* omitted the expression "and taketh the profits," but he argued:

> the authority of my Lord Coke cannot be lessened by Wood's wrong abridgement, and it is conceived there is no room for the Attorney General to suppose two authorities from Coke and Wood's Institutes, and that the sense of both . . . together is that entering . . . animo Possidendi is an Intrusion but . . . Lord Coke remains unshaken.

The "Historical view of the court of Exchequer p. 132, 133" was also cited to the effect that it was part of the liberty of England that the King's officers could not enter upon any other man's possession until the jury had found the King's title unless the King's title appeared of record, and quotations from Jacob's *Law Dictionary,* Tit. *Intrusion,* citing Moor's *Reports,* 295 ("which

---

[277] Hicks argued that Viner's *Abridgement,* title Prerogative, 70, and Coke, *Second Institute* 166, 552, showing that the King's rights could not be disposed of except by patent under the Great Seal, were not applicable, nor the authorities in *Hobart* 322. Hicks claimed that these authorities merely stated that the King could not be disseised in the same manner as a common subject because the King was not in actual possession. But, Hicks argued, it by no means followed that where a subject was in possession and the King claimed a right, the King was not put to a regular proceeding in law to prove his title. Hicks therefore prayed judgment for the defendant.

book I have not"), were offered to support the thesis that the person who occupied land before office found was not an intruder.[278]

Reciting that "it is now my duty to complete the debate by answering their
argument" the Attorney General filed his second argument on the part of the
Crown in answer to the defendant's argument. In reply to the point advanced
by the defendant, namely, that the verdict was insufficient, Kempe conceded
that "as to the principle itself, it is certainly law in general that the judges shall
not presume a fact not found in a special verdict . . . but this holds as to mere
facts only of which the jurors are only to answer and does not extend to such
things as arise by operation of law . . ." and he insisted the question of the
Crown's proprietorship resting upon diverse public instruments was a matter
of which the court should take judicial notice. Kempe also pointed out that
mere entry *animo possidendi* was sufficient "notwithstanding what is inferred
from my Lord Coke . . . who is certainly misunderstood." Kempe continued
that

> an information for intrusion . . . is in the nature of an action of trespass and is
> principally intended to try the title of any person entring . . . lands in the pos-
> session of the Crown and is used in the case of the Crown in the Room of an
> ejectment in the case of a common person for the King being considered in law
> as always in possession and not liable to be disseised cannot bring an action of
> ejectment . . . the same effect is produced by an information of intrusion for
> the Crown as by ejectment for a common person. In the case of the Crown, the
> intruder is fined and removed. In the case of the subject there is also a fine and
> the possession is recovered.[279]

Addressing himself to Ogden's argument regarding the interpretation of
Coke and the paraphrase of the same in Wood's *Institute,* Kempe went on:

> I take the plain meaning of my Lord Coke to be that though a person does not
> actually set himself on the Crown lands as would drive a common person to
> ejectment but only enters . . . and takes . . . the profits and goes off again he is
> liable to be punished for intrusion, the taking of the profits in such case being
> only evidence of the intent . . . to possess [the lands].

Arguing to the defendant's point that the King could only take by matter
of record, it was urged that this rule only related to such lands as had left the

[278] For the arguments of Hicks and Ogden on behalf of the defendant, see *J. T. Kempe Lawsuits* L–O *sub nom.* J. H. Lydius.

[279] Citing 1 Coke, *Reports* 40, where there is a judgment in intrusion.

possession of the Crown and related only to causes where an office had to be found entitling the King to enter. Citing Gilbert's *Exchequer,* 109, 110, and 9 Coke, *Reports,* 95b, 96, Kempe insisted that in many cases the King might enter without office found. Such doctrine of office found would not apply to cases like that of Lydius where the lands had never left the possession of the Crown. As to the defendant's assertion that where the lands belonged to no one, then title could only be divested from the person entering the land by matter of record, Kempe stated that land was always conceived as being possessed by someone and therefore, in this case, the one who had been holding the land prior to the defendant's intrusion was the Crown.[280]

On August 4, 1764, "On a Special Verdict found on an Information for Intrusion" the Supreme Court gave "Judgment for . . . the King. Mr. Attorney General moved that the Defendant [be] solemnly called three times by proclamation and not appearing . . . his sureties were in like manner called to bring him . . . also made default."[281] In another place, we shall go into the further details and subsequent outcome of the Lydius case after suit was brought on the forfeited recognizance for £5000 due to the failure of the defendant to appear.[282]

Concomitant with the offense of intrusion on Crown lands and frequently one of the bases on which intruders attempted to support claims to unoccupied lands, was the device of procuring Indian deeds. This was a persistently troublesome problem, but although it was pregnant with such grave dangers the matter was not dealt with vigorously or consistently. During the French and Indian Wars George Klock, an enterprising settler in the Mohawk Valley, engineered a *coup de main* which brought down on him the wrath of Sir William Johnson. The Indians who complained staged for the authorities a graphic representation of the swindle that is irresistibly comic because, as the conference was acted out, it was punctuated by frequent "token" potations to show how Klock had overcome the aboriginal sales resistance. The information against Klock, filed on May 1, 1762, tells the story more soberly. It charged that Klock,

> wickedly and illegally by wicked and undue means and practices devising and intending to cheat defraud and disposses the . . . Indians of the Mohawk Tribe or people, Inhabitants of Conajoharie, of their lands and lawful possession . . . [and] little considering the Treaties . . . between the . . . King . . . and the

---

[280] For the Crown's argument, see *J. T. Kempe Lawsuits* L–O *sub nom.* John Henry Lydius.

[281] *Ms. Mins. SC] 1764–67* (Rough) 11.

[282] *Infra* 729.

said Indian Tribe . . . and utterly regardless of . . . the King and his laws, and of the fatal consequences . . . [of] destroying the peace friendship and good harmony [with] the Indians . . . did cause . . . a writing . . . [granting land from George Klock and Jellis Fonda as native owners to Van Horne, Livingston and others] . . . and [afterwards] George Klock . . . with Force and Arms did intoxicate . . . the named Indians . . . and persuaded . . . them to seal and deliver the deed . . . To the Grievous Damage Deception and Impoverishment of the same Indians And manifestly tending to Create war and hostilitys between the said Indians and . . . the King and grievously endangering the Lives of the liege subjects of . . . the King . . .[283]

John Tabor Kempe, on September 13, 1762, writing to Sir William Johnson, commented on the Klock prosecution as follows:

I do not wonder the Indians are so very uneasy when their very Habitations are taking [sic] from them . . . and I am afraid no legal Process (situated as We are at present,) will be sufficient.

The Interests of the Original Patentees, is now subdivided among Many, several of whom reside out of this province. . . .

Mr. Smith as well as myself is of opinion that in these Ejectments . . . the Plaintiffs will produce a Title by the Kings Patent, against which no Indian Right can by the Policy of the Constitution be heard of in the Kings Court, The King being Lord Paramount. . . .

I could wish for the sake of doing the Indians that Justice they seem really entitled to that we were in this case less tied down to the observance of these rules which though in general are just and equitable seem here something contrary to natural Justice and I fear the Indians not seeing it in its proper light will . . . have reason to think little of our Honesty and the Publick Faith.

Again on November 15, 1762, Kempe, writing to Sir William Johnson, stated:

I cannot think any steps can be taken in the court of Chancery for the relief of the Indians for the same reasons as take place in the courts of common pleas— nor can I think of anything that will be of service except an Act of Assembly.

On May 9, 1763, Kempe, advising Johnson how to serve the subpoenas in the Klock case, also took the opportunity to point out that it would be difficult to prove that the Indians were drunk and he stated that "we have a hard case."[284]

---

[283] For the information, see H.R. Parch. 228 B 2; also see Misc. Mss. Canajoharie. There are details in 4 Papers of Sir William Johnson (1925) 50, 78, 108, 112, 114.

[284] For the above quotations see J. T. Kempe Lawsuits J–L sub nom. George Klock. These papers also contain affidavits of witnesses, pleadings, notices of trial, etc.

Klock was tried at the Albany Circuit on June 23, 1763, and found not guilty, and on July 29, 1763, a *postea* having been read and filed in the Supreme Court, it was ordered on motion of Livingston for the defendant that the said defendant have judgment *nisi causa*.

Official interest did not, however, cease with this trial, for George Klock, relying upon his acquittal, continued in the ways of iniquity. On July 29, 1767, at an Executive Council before Governor Moore and his Council, a letter from Sir William Johnson was read regarding the trouble caused by Klock among the Canajoharie Indians. Johnson demanded that Klock execute a deed of release to the Indians according to the agreement he had made. The Governor and Council thereupon ordered that Johnson's letter be delivered to the Attorney General in order that he might file an information against Klock as a common disturber of the peace, and also a bill in Chancery to force the defendant to execute a release. Attorney General Kempe then drafted an information alleging Klock

being a person of evil name and fame and of dishonest conversation and devising and intending unlawfully and wickedly and contrary to the duty of a good subject of our Lord the King to disturb the Peace . . . and that Harmony and Friendship which . . . has continued between the King and his liege subjects and confederated Indians . . . and to alienate the affections of the said Indians did publish false rumors among . . . the Indians.

Appended to this draft is the following comment by the Attorney General:

The charges against him are the best I could frame upon the general order given me by the Governor in Council which was to prosecute him as a common disturber of the peace—I have added . . . general charges respecting his malpractise with the Indians I have added . . . a note of what is barretry by our law imagining it might serve as a clue . . . in collecting the necessary proofs.

On February 28, 1768, Klock, by his attorney, William Smith Jr., pleaded not guilty, and on April 29, 1769, a notice of trial at the Albany Circuit Court for June 27, 1769, was served on the defendant's attorney by J. T. Kempe. We have not, however, found any other papers on this case, nor have we been able to learn the outcome of this second prosecution.[285]

285 For the *postea*, see *H.R. Parch.* 228 B 2. For the minute entries, see *Ms. Mins. SCJ 1762–64* (Engr.) 4, 69, 221, Oct. 19, 1762, Jan. 18, July 29, 1763. For J. T. Kempe's brief for the Circuit trial, see *Misc. Mss. Canajoharie,* where Kempe recites the information, the testimony of the witnesses, the fact that the information had been filed by order of the Council, etc. Also see the same citation for a parchment subpoena to Casper Keller and three others to appear as witnesses at the Albany Circuit,

It is not easy to assess the exact value of the transfer system as it was used in New York Province. For the purposes of political supervision it was undoubtedly an indispensable device, and as there was no developed system of criminal appeals in the eighteenth century, the scheme of permitting motions in arrest of judgment in the Supreme Court *en banc,* after the removal of the *postea* and before final judgment was there pronounced, served to promote justice. But whether or not its achievements in the actual enforcement of the law were better than mediocre can scarcely be determined. The chief obstacle here was the necessity of using (even for trials at bar) juries of the vicinage who did not always convict when they should have. In many of the cases where Crown rights were involved, the defendant was a person of power and standing in the community. The juries were picked from the freeholders, as we have intimated the very class most likely to entertain the reasonable doubt when a squire-in-chief was in the dock. If one contrasts the verdicts in the prosecutions against justices of the peace with those in riot cases where usually the defendants were of a lower social stratum, the inference of partiality is hard to escape. There is no doubt that persons of property regarded the circuit system as a pillar of security. Robert Livingston Jr., writing from Livingston Manor to his son-in-law, James Duane, on May 26, 1768, was moved to complain:

> I am so uneasy at the disappointment of the Judges not comeing up to hold the Circuit Court that I can hardly Express it, as its not only a loss and damage to me but to numbers of people in the country, though as I possess a large estate into which a Rascall has presumed to Enter and now he finds I cannot bring him to trial he will encourage other Villins to do the same by which I may be ruined . . . I can but lament my hard faith [*sic*] that we have no prospect of Tryal this year and God knows if next, or ever and all the while must lay at the mercy of any dareing interloper. Pray why cant I go and pull down this fence of Houser and every fellow who presumes to fix any [fence] within my lines without any leave?[286]

June 23, 1763. The subpoena was dated April 30, 1763. On the later prosecution, cf. also Kempe to Johnson, May 5, 1769 (6 *Johnson Papers* 743). The costs in the George Klock case certified by Livingston to the defendant from January Vacation, 1762 to October 4, 1763, found in the *James Alexander Papers* Box 19A, printed *infra* Appendix 775 *et seq.*

[286] *James Duane Papers* Box 2, 1767–72, III, 27, 28, under date May 26, 1768.

Cf. King v. Abraham DeWitt, a petition to Attorney General John Tabor Kempe, dated at Go-

shen, April 7, 1762, by "Sundry persons" in behalf of Abraham DeWitt who was charged with counterfeiting, his first offense, and lay in Goshen gaol a year "and we fear there will be no circuit court this year which in case it should not would be the means of his confinement another year . . . we therefore pray he may be admitted to Bail if any ways consistant with justice" (*J. T. Kempe Lawsuits* C–F *sub nom.* Abraham DeWitt). Cf. also King v. Theodorus Snedeker, John and William Coe, Paulus Vandervoort, Francis Garnier, G. and

Whether or not the small men in the province were equally attached to the Circuit and all its works is nearly impossible to determine. As we have seen, they were initially anxious to have a Supreme Court in every county, yet they probably never envisaged the juggernaut that was set upon them. But it is evidence of general opinion, not without some retrospective significance, that when the new state was founded the Circuit was preserved.

John Cuyper, Jonas Halstead, Ben Allison and nine others: "March 6, 1765 At a Council held at Fort George . . . On Reading the Affidavit of Shadrack Chatterdon . . . that . . . John Coe . . . [and two other justices of the peace of Orange] . . . came to the Deponents house with John De Noyeles and pretending a Right to Deponents possession under the Kakiate Patent. . . ." The justices of peace said "it would not do to let such Fellows come to live upon their Lands: . . . That then the said John Parsells with the Consent of the Other two Justices as Deponent understood made a Mittimus to send the Deponent to Goal and Commanded Assistance to turn out Deponents Family and Household Goods out of the House," and afterwards deponent agreed with Noyelles and Parsells to deliver the same possessions as they had had when he came upon the land. Ordered by the "Lieutenant Governor with the Advice of the Council that they the said John Coe John Parsells and John Vander Voort, do on the service on them respectively of a Copy hereof, on or before the 18th Instant shew Cause . . . why they should not be removed from their Office of Justice of the Peace for having thus Exercised Jurisdiction in a Cause wherein they themselves were Interested" (*NY Misc. Mss.* Box 8 no. 60).

On April 26, 1759, these defendants had appeared in the Supreme Court and "it appearing to the court by affidavits that . . . two several assembly has been had at Haverstraw in Orange County by about twenty men who came to a lot of . . . Smith and entered and with force and arms carried off posts and rails. Ordered that the Attorney General do forthwith proceed by information against the parties that assembled for said unlawful purposes." On October 25, 1759, an information for riot was filed against the defendants, and in April, 1760 a struck jury was ordered and the sheriff of Orange County commanded to return a list of the freeholders of the County into the office of the clerk of the court. Alsop, by virtue of a warrant of attorney, appeared for Theodorus Snedeker and pleaded not guilty. On August 4, 1764, an information having been filed against these defendants "five years past" and not brought on to trial, on motion of Duane, the defendants were ordered to be discharged (*Ms. Mins. SCJ 1756–61* [Rough] 145, 165; *Ms. Mins. SCJ 1757–60* [Engr.] 311, 319; *Ms. Mins. SCJ 1764–67* [Rough] 12); subpoena for trial at Orange Circuit, June 3, 1762 (*H.R. Pleadings* Pl. K. 378, and *J. T. Kempe Lawsuits* C–F sub nom. John Coe; *H.R. Pleadings* Pl. K. 1082, Pl. K. 1050).

CHAPTER IV

APPEALS, ERROR, REVIEW

THE constitutional importance of political control through the agency of the judicial establishment was a matter of which the English officials were well aware. This notion was implicit in the early proposals that English judges should ride the circuit in the colonies.[1] It lay at the basis of the later attempts to have colonial judges directly dependent on the will of the Crown.[2] It was involved in the final desperate effort to suppress the rising tide of revolt by the transfer of trial of officials and soldiers out of Massachusetts Bay to England or to some other colony.[3] As the scheme of imperial control was first developed, however, and as it was executed during the eighteenth century, it was by supervision rather than by the direct exercise of authority that the Crown kept its finger on legislation and litigation.

Curiously enough the exercise of supervisory authority by means of appellate review was never adequately exploited. The legislative process was kept under strict superintendence, but owing to the limitations of common law rules respecting judicial review and the imperial policy of admitting to appeal only cases involving large sums of money, the number of cases per colony that came before the King in Council in relation to the prodigious amount of litigation and prosecution was few.[4]

---

[1] Sir William Keith wrote to the Board of Trade in 1728 as follows: "It is generally acknowledged in the Plantations that the subject is entitled by birthright unto the benefit of the Common Law of England; But, as the Common Law has been altered from time to time and restricted by statute it is still a question in many of the American Courts of Judicature whether any of the English statutes, which do not particularly mention the Plantations, can be of force there until they be brought over by some act of Assembly in the Colony where they are pleaded—and this creates confusion—so that according to the art and influence of the lawyers, the judges who by their election are indifferently qualified—sometimes allow the force of particular statutes and of others reject the whole—The People here are not so well qualified even to serve upon juries, and much less to act upon a Bench of Judicature—it seems impractible to provide a remedy until a sufficient revenue be found out amongst them to support the charge of sending judges from England to take the Circuits—by turn in the several Colonies on the main" (P.R.O., C.O. 5/4 no. 37).

Also compare the Andros report of 1690 on the administration of New England in which he re-

fers to the early attempt to centralize the administration of justice for the Dominion: "Courts of Judicature were setled in the severall parts . . . for the . . . benefitt of the subject, and Judges appoynted to hold the Terms and goe the Circuite throughout the Dominion, to administer justice in the best manner and forme, and according to the lawes, Customes and statutes of the realme of England, and some peculiar locall prudentiall laws of the Country, not repugnant therto" (3 Doc. Rel. Col. Hist. NY 723).

[2] On the efforts to have colonial judges appointed during pleasure instead of during good behavior and the colonists' protests against this, see 7 Doc. Rel. Col. Hist. NY 466, 471, 479, 483, 489, 503, 705; 6 ibid. 792, 951.

[3] 14 Geo. III c.39.

[4] The only presently available monograph is Washburn, Imperial Control of Judicial Administration (1923). This is a most unsatisfactory study and is unreliable on the legal and procedural aspects. These matters are fully dealt with in Joseph Henry Smith, Appeals to the Privy Council from the American Plantations, shortly to be published.

Appeals to the King in Council

Prior to the year 1696 the control of the Crown over political activities in the colonies was limited. Under Charles II, machinery for the review of colonial legislation had been brought into existence and, in the case of the royal plantations, had gradually acquired some administrative effectiveness. As far as the continental colonies were concerned, however, the review of judicial proceedings by the Crown was inconsequential.[5] The New York charter was the first to incorporate a provision for appeals to the Crown, but the Duke of York does not appear to have taken steps to implement the privilege. Nevertheless, it was presumably in reliance upon the charter that the first criminal case to be taken to the Privy Council from a New York court was transmitted in 1681. In that year at the instance of Samuel Winder, an attorney, an indictment of treason was procured against Captain William Dyer, the Duke's Collector, on the ground he was collecting without authority of an Act of Parliament. At a special Court of Assizes Dyer objected to the jurisdiction of the court, and after some debate it was decided to send the defendant to England, take security of Winder to prosecute and refer the matter to the Privy Council. Dyer petitioned the Council and the matter was referred to the Lords Committee. In due course the case was dismissed as Winder did not appear to prosecute.[6]

Since there was no final judgment in the Court of Assizes, this case can hardly be considered an appeal in any technical sense, and the manner in which it was finally liquidated was not calculated to give the cause value as precedent.

It is beyond our purpose to inquire into the general development of the appeals jurisdiction in the years that followed. But it should be noticed that with the initiation of quo warranto proceedings against Massachusetts Bay, the way began to be cleared for a broader exercise of power and on a larger scale than had previously been possible. Yet it was not until the establishment of the Board of Trade and Plantations in May, 1696, that the system of control to which law administration in the American colonies was subject until the Revolution was brought into being.[7] In December of the same year a further Order in Council directed that all appeals from the plantations be heard "as

---

[5] The records in the Public Record Office show a total of some eighty-seven appeals from all the American colonies before 1696. Most of these were from the West India plantations, and many cases never were in fact heard as, e.g., the cases appealed from Massachusetts by Randolph.

[6] Cf. *infra* 334. *Proc. Gen. Ct. of Assizes 1680–82* (45 *NYHS Colls.*) 10; 3 *Doc. Rel. Col. Hist. NY* 318–321; 2 *Acts of the Privy Council, Colonial* 24. Winder was later excluded from practice (*Ms. Entries Letters Warrants 1680–83* 65).

[7] 4 *Doc. Rel. Col. Hist. NY* 145.

formerly" by a committee on which all the Lords of the Council or any three or more of them were appointed.[8] The committee was thereafter the agency which handled appeals and reported to the Privy Council for the rendering of a final decision.

By virtue of these dispositions the King in Council exercised a power of judicial review and although the notion still obtained in the early eighteenth century that appeal to the Crown was an inherent right of the subject,[9] this "right" was of infinitely greater significance to the Crown than to the subject. In conjunction with the review of colonial legislation the appellate judicial power aided the home authorities in keeping colonial experiments within bounds already defined by the common law. To be sure the Crown was moved by considerations of policy which, particularly in regard to the prerogative, were not in harmony with the law of England as it had been adjusted to internal constitutional changes in England.[10] Yet, at least in respect of judicial review, it cannot be doubted that the common law was regarded as a basic standard. Herein lies, of course, the similarity between the judicial functions of the King in Council and the United States Supreme Court.

It should be observed that both the jurisdiction of the Council and the manner of its exercise were matters peculiar to the dominions of the Crown. The exercise by the Council of any judicial functions within the realm itself had been effectively expunged by the statute of 1641,[11] so that during the period with which we are here concerned, appellate powers were lodged in the courts at Westminster with an eventual resort to the House of Lords. The scope of these powers was limited. During the early seventeenth century the English courts had sought to make of the common law a fundamental law to which even Acts of Parliament would be subordinate, but by the end of that century the supremacy of Parliament was settled. As far as legislation was concerned it was only to local customs and to by-laws enacted by bodies corporate that his Majesty's courts could apply the tests of conformity with the common law. On the other hand, the whole theory of error jurisdiction, exercised by writs of error or certiorari, rested upon the necessity of courts below acting in agreement with the common law, and hence, in so far as no Act of Parliament had effected changes, the common law remained the standard of judicial performance. To this extent, then, appellate jurisdiction as it was exercised within

[8] 2 *Acts of the Privy Council, Colonial* no. 657.
[9] Williams' arguments in Christian v. Corren, 1716 (1 *P. Wms.* 329).
[10] Russell, *Review of American Colonial Legislation* 176 *et seq.*
[11] 16 Charles I c.10.

the kingdom approximated that which was wielded by the King in Council with the further important exception that the functions of the Council, since it was primarily an administrative body, could be performed by persons with no qualification for the judicial office.

Although the King in Council stood at the apex of the colonial hierarchy of courts, exercising a power of appellate supervision over colonial judgments, this jurisdiction was narrowly conceived. The opportunity had existed for creating an effective weapon of control, but by the Crown's own orders the limitations on the civil side were such as to bring cases of monetary rather than legal importance to the attention of home authorities. We have already spoken of the directions respecting appeals[12] but it is desirable at this point to recapitulate. When New York first became a royal province, it was provided in Dongan's commission that appeals be permitted "in cases of error from our courts of New York unto the Governor and Council in civil causes, provided the value appealed for" exceed £100. Appeals to the King in Council were allowed from the Governor and Council where the amount in controversy exceeded £300.[13] These provisions were repeated in subsequent commissions[14] until 1703. In that year the article respecting the matter was shifted to the instructions.[15] The language here was more general until the revision of 1753, but it is clear from the text of the early commissions that civil cases alone were involved.[16] As we have seen, criminal cases were on a very different footing.

---

[12] Supra 11.

[13] Dongan's commission of 1686, Andros' commission of 1688 and Sloughter's commission of 1689 provided that civil cases in error over the amount of £300 might be appealed to the King in Council on security for costs being posted by appellant (3 Doc. Rel. Col. Hist. NY 377, 537, 623).

[14] Fletcher's commission of 1691/92 contained a provision similar to that in Dongan's (3 ibid. 827), and cf. also Bellomont's commission of 1697 (4 ibid. 266).

[15] In 1702/03, when the instructions became the vehicle for authorization respecting appeals, the section was removed from the commission as it stood in 1697. Cf. Labaree, Royal Instructions to British Colonial Governors 322 et seq. (over £100 to Governor and Council; over £300 to the Privy Council). The appeal limit to Governor and Council is incorrect in Labaree, op. cit., as our next following reference indicates. In 1727 a further change was made for while all the previous practice had been that only the appellant need give security for costs on an appeal, the instructions to Burnet in 1726/27 provided that the appellee must also give security for costs (5 Doc. Rel. Col. Hist. NY 816). Although Burnet's instructions provided as before,

that appeal should be to the King in Council only in cases over £300, nevertheless Thomas Byerly, writing to James Alexander on November 27, 1720, referring to a prosecution for the quitrents, seems to have been under the impression that no appeal could be allowed to England unless the amount involved was at least £400 (James Alexander Papers Box 2, B, no. 91).

With reference to appeals to England in civil cases, Montgomerie's, Cosby's and Clinton's instructions were in the same form as the earlier ones, that is, they expressed a limit of £300 as the amount which should determine whether the case could be appealed; cf. 1 Labaree, op. cit. no. 449.

[16] Cf. the instructions to Sir Danvers Osborne in 1753, no. 26 mentioned in 6 Doc. Rel. Col. Hist. NY 788; Labaree, op. cit. no. 453. On April 18, 1754, the following entry appears in the Supreme Court minutes concerning this instruction: "Mr. Banyar Deputy Clerk of the Council of this Province delivered to the Court a copy of the 26th and 27th Articles of His Majesty's Instructions to Sir Danvers Osborn, relating to appeals, which he acquainted the court he was directed to lay before them by . . . the Lieutenant Governor in Council in order that the same might be entered in the

In convictions for treason and wilful murder the Governor might, in his discretion on extraordinary occasions, grant reprieve until the King's pleasure should be known.[17] The Governor was also instructed to permit appeals to the King in Council in all cases of fines over £200 imposed for misdemeanors.[18]

Minutes of this Court . . . .: Instruction 26. Our Will and pleasure is that you [i.e. the Governor] . . . do in all civil causes . . . permit and allow appeals from any of the courts of Common Law in our said Province . . . and you are for that purpose to issue a writt . . . returnable before yourself and the Council . . . who are to proceed to hear and determine such appeal . . ." (*Ms. Mins. SCJ 1754-57* [Engr.] 6, 7).

[17] Dongan's commission of 1686 and Andros' commission of 1688 gave the Governor power to pardon capital and criminal offenders and remit fines and forfeitures except in cases of treason and wilful murder. On extraordinary occasions the Governors were permitted to grant reprieves until the King's pleasure might be known (3 *Doc. Rel. Col. Hist. NY* 377, 537). It should be noted that Dongan's instructions of 1682/83 had given him power to pardon and remit fines imposed by the courts of the province and pardon and remit all crimes before or after conviction except treason and wilful murder. In the latter cases the Governor was given the power to reprieve execution and transmit to the Duke of York "the true state of the matter and the grounds and reasons which incline you to judge the persons objects of mercy" (3 *ibid.* 331). However, Dongan's instructions of 1686 and Andros' instructions of 1689 specifically provided that the Governor was not to remit fines and forfeitures over the amount of £10 nor escheats until notice had been given in Dongan's case to the Treasurer or Commissioners of the Treasury and in Andros' case to these officers and the Committee on Trade and on Plantations of the nature of the offense and the sums involved. These Governors were to wait until they received the King's instructions (3 *ibid.* 369, 543). Sloughter's commission of 1689 gave him power to pardon capital and criminal offenders and to remit fines and forfeitures except in cases of treason and murder, and in these cases he was permitted to grant reprieves until the King's pleasure might be known (*ibid.* 623). Sloughter's instructions (1689/90) provided, however, that he was not to remit fines or forfeitures over the amount of £10 until he received instructions from England, although the Governor could in the meantime suspend the fines (*ibid.* 685). The commissions and/or instructions to Fletcher, Bellomont, Cornbury, Hunter and Burnet were the same as Sloughter's respecting the pardoning of offenders, the remitting of fines, etc. (except in treason and murder) and granting reprieves, but the clause forbidding the remission of fines and forfeitures over £10 until the receipt of instructions from England was omitted (3 *ibid.* 827; 4 *ibid.* 266; *Misc. Mss. Corn-*

bury; 5 *Doc. Rel. Col. Hist. NY* 92, 124, 391; *John Jay Papers* Box 3 no. 16K).

It is interesting to note that Governor Bellomont's instructions to Lieutenant Governor Nanfan contained a provision that the latter should not pardon any offenders without the Governor's consent (4 *Doc. Rel. Col. Hist. NY* 557). It may be that Governor Bellomont had gotten into difficulties regarding the pardoning of offenders, for in a letter to the Lords of Trade on November 12, 1698, he says: "I formerly acquainted your Lordships in my letter of the 14th September, that William Simpson a soldier had killed an Indian Sachem and wounded one or two more at Albany and was tried and lay under sentence of death, and then I was of opinion he ought to suffer accordingly notwithstanding the intercession of the Indians for his pardon when I mett them at Albany, and I desired your Lordships would direct me what course to take with him; but now I must make an humble request that the man may be pardoned, least I should be brought into a praemunire myself—The matter is this. The King's commission restrains me from erecting Courts of Judicature in criminal cases without consent of his Majesty's Councill; now I can be deposed that to the best of my knowledge and remembrance I did acquaint the Councell with the notice sent me of the murder of that Indian, and Colonel Cortlandt and the Attorney Generall both say they are confident I did so, and a commission of Oyer and Terminer was sent up to Albany to try that soldier that murdered the Indian: but it seems M' Jamison the late Clerke of the Councill, who lay upon the watch to betray me has omitted to minute my taking the concurrence of the Council in the said Commission, and I am told 'tis intended to be made the ground of a hainous complaint against me. But however false the thing be in itself Jamison is capable of swearing any thing" (*ibid.* 428–429).

[18] The appeals to the King in Council in cases of fines over £200 imposed for misdemeanors are first provided for in Sloughter's instructions of 1689 (3 *ibid.* 685). The same provision does not appear in Fletcher's instructions of 1691/92 (*ibid.* 818) or in Bellomont's of 1697 (4 *ibid.* 284). On the other hand, Cornbury's instructions of 1702/03 restored the provision relating to appeals to the King in Council of misdemeanor cases involving over £200, and that provision is continued in all subsequent instructions. The appellant was required to give good security that he would effectually prosecute the appeal and answer the condemnation, if the sentence by which such fines were imposed should be confirmed.

No mention was made regarding the method of bringing such cases before the Crown.

The scope of the power to review, as it appears in the eighteenth century commissions and instructions, can only be understood in the light of the phrase "as formerly" in the Order in Council of December, 1696. This undoubtedly referred to the practice respecting the American plantations as it existed immediately before the Order. But this in turn was patterned to a considerable degree upon the practices which had been used for the review of causes appealed from the ancient medieval dominions of the Crown. Since the fifteenth century, if not before, the Council had been hearing appeals from the Channel Islands. The procedure in these cases was not in any technical sense the equivalent of English error procedure at law but approximated more nearly the Chancery appeal. This was inevitable since the Channel Islands courts administered a customary law by methods peculiar to the Islands. The problem of reviewing these was thus not parallel to that where the cause came up from a jurisdiction in which the common law forms and rules were used. It is possible the officials at Whitehall were aware of this, but the use of the word "appeals" in the Order of 1696 does not indicate it. Conceivably a general right of petition may have been contemplated, but it is fair to infer from the early commissions to the governors that a strict common law procedure up to the last hearing in the colony was essential.[19] The expression "cases of error"

[19] We have seen no early discussion of this but a report of the Solicitor and Attorney General on the New York instructions of 1753 supports our view: "But we presume to say further to your lordships that we are of opinion that the alteration made in the instruction to the Governor of New York in 1753 did not vary the sense of them as they stood before that time. The words *in cases of error only* appear to us to have been struck from these instructions as superfluous and improper. For how or in what case can an appeal lie *but in cases of error only?* That is error in law upon the record of a judgment given in a Court of common law . . ." (P.R.O., P.C. 1/51).

For a colonial discussion compare the following: ". . . As to the Instructions for permitting appeals to the King and Council, we take it that there is nothing of the like nature either from the courts of Law or Equity in England, for the method to the dernier Resort in Law affairs is by Writt of error retournable in Parliament and there its the writ of *error* that is the Stay of proceedings but writt of error will never discharge one out of Execution or undo any one step done on the execution of the Judgment but stays doing further.

"As to the method to the Dernier Resort from the Chancery it is not by writt of error but by peti-

tion of appeal to the Lords in Parliament which petition, being granted by the Lords and served, will prove a stay of further proceeding to execution on a decree in chancery but that petition granted will not undoe any one step before taken towards the execution nor deliver the person in custody upon execution out of custody.

"It is to be observed that there is no such thing in England as a petition directed to the chancellor himself for appealing from his decree to the Lords in Parliament or to stay the execution of his decree untill the Parliament sits and if we remember right it is one of the Grievances Complained of in the Latter end of King Charles the Second's time that by the infrequent meeting of Parliaments the Subject was debarred of all relief by appeal against decrees in Chancery—petitions of appeal to Chancellor against the Decrees of the master of the Rolls are frequent but against the chancellor's own decrees nothing can be done before him but by way of rehearing before the decree is sealed and by bill of Review after the Decree is Sealed.

"Now as theres no practice of the Courts of Law or Equity in England upon which this Instruction is founded, we conceive the reason of the instruction is, that the parties might be much injured by the execution of judgments and decrees before it

can, in the case of New York, only refer to causes brought up by writ of error to the Governor and Council. On the other hand, neither the commissions nor the instructions use any words in the clauses that deal with appeal to the Crown to indicate that this final stage was to be by writ of error. The reason for this silence was possibly the old rule that this writ did not run from the King's courts to the dominions of the Crown,[20] but it is also possible that the Privy Council merely wished to maintain a flexible procedure not restricted by rules regulating ancient forms. We are disposed to believe, however, that the traditions regarding error jurisdiction were determinative, particularly because of the limitations set upon criminal appeals.

In England review of causes criminal by writ of error was rarely had. This was due to the common law rule that where judgment was for the King a writ of error could not be granted except as an act of grace by the Crown.[21] A relaxation of this stringent practice had been effected in the case of outlawries where the court determined if the writ was to be granted.[22] A bill of exceptions was under no circumstances allowable[23] and hence, even where the Crown consented that a writ of error be brought, only the record (indictment, plea, verdict, etc.) came up for review and not that part of the proceedings which were likely to have been most prejudicial to the defendant. An effort to remedy this defect was made in 1690 but the proposed legislative action came to naught.[24]

Throughout the seventeenth century the medieval rule respecting the Crown's discretion over the grant of writs of error was rigidly observed. But early in the reign of Anne (1704) the question of error in a misdemeanor case was referred to the judges and it was held by ten out of twelve of them that in

was possible (by reason of the great distance of place) to obtain and bring a writt of error or to petition the Lords in parliament and to obtain and bring their order thereon for stay of Execution—wherefore we conceive this Instruction to be a new remedy in its nature founded on that reason and which does no way deprive the subject of any remedy that he had before neither doth or can this instruction leave the subject to apply to the dernier resort for Relief in the usual way in England or from Ireland or any other way that he thinks proper —But if the Subject will claim the benefit of this instruction he must comply with the terms and conditions therof both in point of time and security and if he neglects either he is not entitled by it but is still left to his course as if no such instruction were, we mean by petition to Lords in Parliament or King and Council as he shall be best advised . . ." (Drafts of a letter from James Alexander to Mr.

Cox, dated July 12 and 15, 1742, in answer to Mr. Alexander's letter of July 4, in re: Courtlandt and Stoutenbergh v. Thoumes, *James Alexander Papers* Box 2 Letters A–D no. 33).

[20] There is a discussion of this problem in 30 *Col. Law Rev.* 273.

[21] *Yearbook* 23 Edward III, 22 pl. 14. The rule was reiterated (*Rolle* 175) and in The Rioters Case, 1683 (1 *Vern.* 175). If the Crown was willing to grant the writ, the Attorney General would be ordered to grant his fiat, but without this fiat the writ would not issue, Crawle v. Crawle, 1683 (1 *Vern.* 170). The learning is summarized by Mansfield in Rex v. Wilkes (4 *Burr.* 2527, 2550).

[22] Cf. 2 Hawkins, *Pleas of the Crown* c.50.

[23] Sir Henry Vane's Case (1 *State Trials* [1719] 938).

[24] *Hist. Mss. Commission, Thirteenth Rep.* App. Pt. V, no. 244 (House of Lords Mss.).

such cases the writ should issue as of right.[25] The practice then changed, although the textbooks are so reticent on this point that it cannot have been resorted to very frequently. In any event, the discretion was shifted to the courts to determine as to misdemeanors whether there was probable cause for the writ of error to issue. In felony cases no changes in the old procedure were made.

In respect of criminal causes the instructions to governors may be regarded as reflecting the state of the law at the outset of the eighteenth century. No review by the King in felony cases generally was contemplated, but an opportunity was left open in treasons and murder for the Crown to exercise its prerogative of pardon. In these instructions the relaxation of the earlier harsh rule respecting misdemeanors did not go as far as the change in English practice, since only cases where heavy money penalties were inflicted were to be reviewed, and no discretion whatever was intended in misdemeanors for which imprisonment or infamous punishment was adjudged. What is even more striking is the failure of the English officials to instruct as to the class of those Crown pleas which were not conventionally regarded as either felonies or misdemeanors, that is to say, the quasi-criminal proceedings like intrusions, for these proceedings one would expect to have been covered by something more explicit than the omnibus civil appeal or misdemeanor instructions. Finally, it should be noticed that the Crown did not delegate to the Governor its own discretion respecting the allowance of writs of error in criminal cases, although it did convey a power to pardon. The implied limitation upon the Governor's authority to interfere in the course of a criminal prosecution by allowing writs of error was to have its effect upon the development of appellate jurisdiction in the colonies by keeping matters strictly within traditional common law boundaries.

As a result of these various restrictions the records show a minimum of Crown interference in the judicial administration of the criminal law. After Leisler and Milborne were found guilty of high treason and were executed, Parliament reversed the attainders[26] and restored the heirs to the forfeited property. This was more in the nature of a pardon than a rehearing of the case

---

[25] Paty's Case (2 *Salkeld* 503, 504). The procedure on writ of error as used in the late eighteenth century is best set forth in Hands, *The Solicitors Practice on the Crown Side of the Court of Kings Bench* (1803) 47 *et seq.*, Mansfield apparently regarded the discretion over probable cause in misdemeanor cases to lie with the court: Rex v. Wilkes (4 *Burr.* 2527, 2551).

[26] For the Act of Parliament reversing Leisler's attainder, see 1 *Jour. Gen. Assembly* App.

on the law or the facts, although it may be that a reconsideration of the facts formed a basis for granting the reversal.

On the conviction and sentence of Bayard and Hutchins (1702) for high treason and on the denial of their motion in arrest of judgment, the Lieutenant Governor, conceiving certain aspects of the trial to warrant action, granted a reprieve to the defendants in accordance with his instructions, until the Queen's pleasure might be known.[27] Meantime Bayard's friends had been active in England and at their instance, the Board of Trade had obtained an opinion of the Attorney General, Northey, that the New York Council's warrant of commitment against Bayard was sufficient but that Hutchins could only have been charged with misdemeanor.[28] On April 28, 1702, the Board recommended that the Crown order respite of the sentences,[29] and a letter to that effect under the sign manual was dispatched to Cornbury.[30] Some days later the Board further decided the case was one for conciliar[31] action and in consequence Bayard's friends, Adderley and Lodwick, petitioned the King in Council for a writ of error.[32] The law officers of the Crown reported favorably as they found the proceedings very extraordinary. They recommended leave be given Bayard to appeal and that minutes of the evidence, if available, be sent with the record. An Order in Council embodying these recommendations issued and it was directed that Bayard be let to bail.[33] Hutchins was likewise admitted to appeal.[34]

[27] Reprieve to Col. Bayard from Lieut. Gov. John Nanfan, April 2, 1702: "Whereas Colonell Nicholas Bayard . . . now lyes under sentence of condemnation for high treason and by his humble petition p'ferred to me hath submitted himself acknowledging his offence and . . . imploring his Majesty's mercy I do hereby in pursuance of the power and authority given . . . me by his . . . Majesty under the Great Seale of England Require and Command the said com. [commissioners] to desist from granting or signing any warrant for the Execution of . . . the said Bayard But in case the same be already issued I do hereby require and command the high sheriff . . . of New York and all other . . . persons . . . impowered to execute . . . the sentence . . . to desist from making . . . any progresse in the p'misses hereby repriveing . . . the said Nicholas Bayard for the offense he hath been guilty of as aforesaid untill his Majesty's pleasure shall be further known . . . and hereof all persons concerned are to take notice at their perill Given under my hand and seal" (Bayard Papers 1698–1710).

[28] Cal. S.P. Colonial 1702 no. 379; 4 Doc. Rel. Col. Hist. NY 954.

[29] Cal. S.P. Colonial 1702 no. 392.

[30] Reprieve from Queen Anne, May 3, 1702: "To . . . Viscount Cornbury . . . and in his absence to the Commander in Chief or President and Council . . . We greete you well Whereas . . . Nicholas Bayard . . . has been committed within our Colony . . . for high treason and Captain Hutchins . . . for high Crimes and misdemeanors upon a Prosecution w^ch . . . appears to our Commissioners . . . not sufficiently Grounded . . . We do hereby Command that upon sight hereof the Execution of any . . . sentences . . . past . . . be respited and surceased untill our further Pleasure . . . for which this shall be to you . . . a sufficient warrant and direction Given att our Court att St. James. . . . By Her Majesty's Command Nottingham" (Bayard Papers 1698–1710).

[31] Cal. S.P. Colonial 1702 nos. 397, 399–401, 423.

[32] P.R.O., P.C. 2/79/156.

[33] P.R.O., P.C. 2/79/169; Cal. S.P. Colonial 1702 no. 755.

[34] P.R.O., P.C. 2/79/170.

The request for the minutes of evidence is significant, because such matter was not embraced in the record and it may therefore be conjectured that the law officers either envisaged a new and unusual form of review or were desirous of having some basis for a royal act of grace.

Upon receipt of the Order in Council in New York a recognizance in £1500 was taken from Bayard,[35] and Governor Cornbury commissioned his new Chief Justice, Bridges, and Attorney General Broughton to receive all records, notes and minutes of evidence, and to take testimony of all persons able to give evidence of the trial.[36] Some weeks later a similar writ issued as to the Hutchins trial, to which on December 1, 1702, a return was made to the Governor and Council.[37] The Bayard evidence alone seems to have reached England in time for the hearing.

In the interim Bayard had petitioned the Queen in Council, and this document was referred to the Lords Committee on December 17, 1702.[38] The usual

[35] 9 *Ms. Mins. Council* 97, 102, 106.

[36] "Anne by the Grace of God of England, Scotland, France and Ireland Queen defender of the Faith &c. To Dr. John Bridges . . . and Samson Shelton Broughton Members of the Council . . . Greeting We being Willing to be informed of all proceedings in the courts of New York against Co. Nicholas Bayard and relating to any criminal offences for which he stands accused or condemned Have unto that end given him leave to appeal unto us in our Privy Council and have admitted him to bail giving sufficient security to answer before us in our said Court to what shall be objected against him and to abide to our dterm. therein. We therefore reposing especial trust and confidence in y^r ability Fidelity Prudence and integrity Have thought fit to constitute and appoynt and do hereby constitute and appoint you to receive all such records and notes of the tryall of the said Col. Bayard and of such examinations or minutes of the evidence taken therein together with all such other evidence and Informations by which ye truth in y^t matter may best appear as also to examine on oath all such . . . persons who are able to give any evidence in relation to the said prosecution and to put the same into method and order and lay them before our Captain General and Governor in . . . New York in Council That the same may be transmitted to us in our Privy Council under our seal of . . . New York to the end that we may thereby be fully informed of the said Col. Bayard's case Witness . . . Cornbury . . . 28 October 1702 . . ." (*Misc. Mss. Bayard*).

[37] 9 *Ms. Mins. Council* 97, 98, 102, 106; *Bayard Papers 1698–1710*.

[38] The petition and appeal of Bayard were in the following language:
"To the Queen's most Excellent Majesty   The Humble Peticōn and Appeal of Nicholas Bayard

. . . Sheweth   That upon 21 January last . . . yor Petitioner was committed by . . . the Governor and Council . . . for High Treason under pretence that your Pet^r had signed . . . scandalous libells . . . subverting the government ther and on 19 February . . . brought to tryall before the Special Commissioners appointed for that purpose and though the Indictment against the petitioner was not found by twelve Ju^r but only eleven (several of whom were aliens) and though . . . the pretended libells . . . were only addresses to William 3^d, to the Comōns . . . and to Lord Cornbury and were not produced at the tryall for the judgment of the court and though no full proof that the petitioner signed or caused any others to sign 'em [*sic*] and if he had done so he . . . was not . . . guilty of High Treason . . . (. . . only . . . just complaints Lawful for English Subjects to make . . . and congratulations . . . on his Excellency's safe arrival) yet y^r pet^r by the direction of the court and the particular artifice of Atwood then Chief Judge of New York and in that comission, was convicted by an illegal petty jury of Aliens and Dutch unduly returned and very ignorant of the English Laws and Language after which verdict yor pet^r offered by his Council severall material reasons in arrest of judgment which were not answered but overruled by the Judges and y^r petitioner on the 16th March . . . received the sentence of death as in cases of High Treason
"Which proceedings and sentence being . . . erroneous, unjust and contrary to law y^r petitioner and pursuant to y^r Majesty's gracious permission by an order in council made on the 2^d July last hath appealed from said Judgment to yor sacred Majesty the Fountain of Justice and mercy for relief and gives security to abide by yor Majesty's determ. therein.
"That the Judges before whom yor petitioner was

course of a committee report did not ensue, for instead the appeals of both Bayard and Hutchins were heard *coram concilio* on January 21, 1702/03, the appellants being represented by counsel. The New York Solicitor General Weaver and former Chief Justice Atwood appeared in person and with counsel, for various irregularities had been charged to them.[39] The Privy Council decided that the prosecution had been illegal, and Cornbury was ordered to direct the Attorney General to consent to a reversal of the sentence and to do all acts necessary to restore appellants.[40]

When the Order in Council reached New York the Supreme Court was not sitting and Bayard was in a heat to get back his property. After some discussion a bill was enacted by the provincial legislature declaring the proceedings against Bayard and Hutchins null and void,[41] and at the ensuing October term of the Supreme Court, upon motion of Jamison for the defendants, the judgments were ordered reversed and the defendants restored.[42]

---

tryd having strictly prohibited all persons from taking the tryall in writing, some very short minutes and only such as the Judges thought fitt to allow were taken by the Clerk who dyed before yo[r] Majesty's order in council arrived at New York and . . . Cornbury being then gone up to Albany . . . the said minutes with the Records of your Commission, Indictment and sentence were sent up to Albany for the Governor's Examination who perused and signed a copy thereof, but the publick seal being at New York could not be affixed to it, by reason of the speedy departure of the ships before his Excellency's return from Albany.

"Wherefore yo[r] pet[r] most humbly prays that yo[r] Majesty will be graciously pleased to receive his said appeal and to appoint a day for the hearing thereof and that said Copys of Records and minutes of said tryall soe attested by his Excellency Lord Cornbury (though not under public Seal) together with such Witnesses viva voce and copys of Depositions relating to tryal and proceedings may be received as Evidence upon said Hearing and that yo[r] Majesty's Attorney General may be ordered to attend such hearing under such directions as yo[r] Majesty shall think fit and also that William Atwood Chief Judge and Thomas Weaver Esq. Chief prosecutor who are both fled to London may be ordered to attend the same

And yo[r] Pet[r] as in Duty Bound shall ever pray &c."

(*Bayard Papers 1698–1710*.) The order of reference is in P.R.O., P.C. 2/79/268.

In *Bayard Papers 1698–1710* July 2, 1702, is a report from the Attorney General and Solicitor General to the Queen in Council on the petition of Bayard and the Queen's order of reference: "May it please yo[r] Majesty In obedience to y[or] . . . order of reference: We have considered . . . the annexed Petition . . . and have heard the petitions

on behalf of Colonel Nicholas Bayard and perused severall letters . . . from New York by which it appears that the proceedings are very extraordinary and may be proper for yo[r] Majesty's Consideration and are therefore humbly of the opinion that it is reasonable . . . to give leave to Colonel Bayard to be heard before yo[r] Majesty in Council touching the treason . . . and to give leave for him to appeal from the proceedings in New York and that the minutes of the Evidences taken by the Officer of the court there (if any such bee) may be transmitted with the record . . . 20 June 1702 Submitted to Yo[r] Royall Wisdom. . . ."

"Her Majesty with the advice of the Privy Council approves the said report . . . and it is ordered that the said Nicholas Bayard be admitted to Appeal to her Majesty at this Board from all proceedings against him in courts of New York relating to the criminal offences for which he stands accused or condemned and that he be admitted to baile giving sufficient security to answer . . . at this Board to what shall be objected against him and to abide by her Majesty's Determinations therein and . . . order that authentic copies under the publick seal of all proceedings against him in New York and of such Examinations or minutes of evidences . . . be transmitted to this Board . . . Whereof the Governor and Council and all others whom it may concern are to take notice and govern themselves accordingly."

[39] P.R.O., P.C. 2/79/295; 4 *Doc. Rel. Col. Hist. NY* 1023.

[40] *Ibid.*

[41] 1 *Col. Laws NY* 531.

[42] The Supreme Court minutes for October 16, 1703, contain the following entry: "Jamison pro defendant moves to have judgment reversed that past against the defendant for high treason severall errors brought by direction of ye Queen in Council

Judged by the strict standards of English error proceedings the course followed in these two cases is utterly aberrant, and it is clear there was no intention to cleave to old rules, for the order to assemble minutes of the evidence indicates that the Crown did not propose to be limited by the narrow record available in review by writ of error. Some precedent for the Crown's action existed in the case of certain earlier misdemeanor appeals to the King in Council from other plantations,[43] but unless the manner in which these appeals were conducted can be viewed as an instance of what Sergeant Hawkins calls an avoidance of judgment "without writ of error for matters *dehors* the record" there is no English precedent for what was done. Hawkins refers to the falsifying of judgment without writ because the commission was void.[44] In the Bayard case the commission was not defective, yet the proceedings ran over the time to which it was limited. This objection was urged at the trial,[45] but there is no evidence that the English authorities considered it or that their course was influenced by any technical considerations of this sort.

were read and allowed by the court and consented to by the Attorney General Ordered judgment be reversed accordingly y^t the defendant Bayard be restored &c." (*Ms. Mins. SCJ 1701–04* 128). The entry as to Hutchins then follows.

[43] Compare the following cases:

One Samuel Hanson appealed to the King in Council from a fine of £150 imposed at a Barbados Court of General Sessions of August 16, 1681 (*Cal. S.P. Colonial 1681–85* no. 469). Upon hearing the appeal (*ibid.* nos. 1290, 1301, 1341, 1352) the Lords Committee of Trade and Plantations reported to the King in Council that the fine was irregularly inflicted by Sir Richard Dutton, Governor, but that the charge against Hanson was so serious that it should be again examined and heard by the said Lords Committee and that five months be allowed to collect the necessary evidence in the island (*ibid.* no. 1368). But this rehearing never took place. In March, 1685, Sir John Witham appealed to the King in Council from the imposition of three fines totalling £11,000 in the Barbados Court of General Sessions (*Cal. S.P. Colonial 1685–88* no. 94). For the nature of the high crimes and misdemeanors and bribery involved see *Cal. S.P. Colonial 1681–85* no. 2023. The prosecution arose from the personal animosity of Sir Richard Dutton, the Governor. Upon admission of the appeal it was ordered that liberty be given without discouragement to taking the necessary evidence in Barbados (*Cal. S.P. Colonial 1685–88* no. 97). For appointment of commissioners to take evidence by the Council of Barbados, see *ibid.* nos. 247, 248. For the execution of the commission and interference therewith, see nos. 254, 256, 265, 270, 300, 308, 336, 358. Upon the hearing of the appeal by the Lords Committee (*ibid.* nos. 400, 430, 440) it was

represented to the King in Council that the proceedings against Witham were malicious, that Witham be restored to all his dignities, that the fines imposed be remitted (*ibid.* no. 439) and ordered in Council accordingly (P.R.O., P.C. 2/71/151 [Nov. 13, 1685]).

See also the case of George Lillington who in October, 1705, petitioned the Privy Council complaining of the proceedings of a Court of Oyer and Terminer held June 4–15, 1705, at Barbados at which petitioner was fined £2000 for scandalous and seditious words against the Governor (P.R.O., P.C. 2/81/5. For accounts of the trial, compare *Cal. S.P. Colonial 1704–05* no. 1251, with *ibid.* no. 1368). Upon advice of the Board of Trade (*ibid.* no. 1387) it was ordered in Council that Governor Granville transmit under seal an exemplification of the commission under which the said court sat, the summons and return of jurors, and that four justices of the peace nominated by the parties be authorized to take depositions and examine upon the particular wrongs complained of; each party interchangeably giving notice of the taking of such depositions, so that the other parties could be present to cross-examine if desired, such depositions and examinations to be transmitted to the Council Board (P.R.O., P.C. 2/81/9). Upon objections of the parties (P.R.O., P.C. 2/81/17; *Cal. S.P. Colonial 1704–05* nos. 1427, 1483) this Order in Council was vacated and petitioner Lillington left at liberty to appeal from the said sentence, but the provision for taking evidence was not repeated (P.R.O., P.C. 2/81/33). When finally heard, the sentence was reversed and all issues declared null and void (*ibid.* 283).

[44] 2 Hawkins, *Pleas of the Crown* c.50.
[45] *Infra* 274, 312.

It is interesting to speculate what would have been the repercussion if the appeals of Bayard and Hutchins had been followed by others like it, for the Privy Council was holding what was substantially an inquest into matter traditionally the province of the jury. And although it was agreeable that in the exercise of the pardoning power, investigations of facts be made,[46] the colonists were extremely jealous of the jury's prerogatives. Years later, in 1764, when an attempt was made to bring the civil trespass action of *Forsey* v. *Cunningham* before the Governor and Council by a so-called writ of appeal after a motion for a new trial was denied, the most violent controversy developed. The use of an "appeal" was proclaimed to be an infringement of constitutional right since it was a civil law procedure which would bring up the facts, and by putting a jury verdict to the test would deprive the subject of his right to trial by jury.[47] No such protest was made in the case of Bayard and Hutchins, chiefly because the episode was generally regarded as a miscarriage of justice, and fortunately for the peaceful development of the criminal law, issue over the matter was never drawn.

There was only one further occasion in New York when a Crown case was appealed and heard by the King in Council, the case of *Kennedy q.t.* v. *Fowles*. This case can be described as criminal only in the sense that there was involved a prosecution for penalties and forfeitures under the acts of trade, but a most important question of jurisdiction was involved since the locus for

---

[46] *Infra* 757.

[47] There is a voluminous mass of material on this case. The chief matter in print is in 7 *Doc. Rel. Col. Hist. NY* 676, 696, 797; *The Report of an Action . . . between Forsey Plaintiff and Cunningham Defendant* (NY 1764); 1 *Colden Letter Books* (9 *NYHS Colls.* 1876) 425, 427, 446–469. Cf. also 29 *Ms. Mins. Council* 7–17, 33–57, 101 *et seq.*; 93 *NY Col. Mss.* 103, 139.

The Supreme Court minute entries on the Forsey v. Cunningham case indicate that on October 25, 1764, a trial for assault and battery was had before a struck jury, and the court, having instructed the jury to seal up the verdict, adjourned. On October 26, 1764, the jury found for the plaintiff £1500 damages, 6d. costs. On October 27, Duane made a motion that the court set aside the verdict and grant a new trial, but the court was of the opinion that it could not mitigate the damages nor order a new trial. Therefore judgment was awarded to the plaintiff (*Ms. Mins. SCJ* 1764–67 [Rough] 32, 35). A writ was sent on November 2, 1764, from the Governor to the Chief Justice of the Supreme Court and was in the following language: "George the Third to the Chief Justice . . . of the Supreme Court—Greeting Whereas by our writ to you—We lately commanded—that all further pro-

ceedings be stay'd on the Verdict against Waddel Cunningham in Trespass and assault tried at the last Supreme Court—until the merits be heard before the Governor and Council on the appeal of the said Waddel Cunningham . . . Further command you cause all proceedings whereon the said Verdict was obtained to be brought before the Governor and Council . . . Answer at your Perill Witness Governor" (*J. T. Kempe Lawsuits* C–F *sub nom.* Forsey v. Cunningham).

On October 22, 1765, R. R. Waddel, on behalf of Waddel Cunningham, presented a petition but the court called upon him to show his authority for presenting the petition, and Waddel produced a power of attorney. However, the court "unanimously declare their opinion to be First that the said Letter of attorney here produced does not give sufficient authority to . . . Waddel . . . Secondly . . . this Court cannot comply with the prayer of the petition because no proper Writ to Authorize their sending up the Record has been brought, nor do they know of any Power they have to Assign Counsel to Transact business in a Court where they have no Jurisdiction" (*Ms. Mins. SCJ* 1764–67 [Rough] 125). This case is discussed at length in Smith, *Appeals to the Privy Council* c. VII.

proceeding in such cases was the subject of dispute. There was in New York a stout tradition of common law cognizance. Our old friend Captain Dyer and others had brought various informations in the Mayor's Court of New York City for it was not usual before 1684 to convene an admiralty court. After the arrival of Dongan and the reconstitution of the judiciary the bulk of the cases were tried in the New York Quarter Sessions Court although the Admiralty Court set up by Dongan met frequently and some cases were tried there.[48] This division of authority between common law and admiralty courts continued even after the changes induced by the English "Act to Prevent Frauds" and the establishment of a Vice-Admiralty Court in New York.[49] As the statute 15 Car. II c.7 provided for *qui tam* procedure the jurisdiction was essentially quasi-criminal, but as far back as the reign of Edward III, the Crown had assented to the employment of the writ of error in such cases.[50]

In 1739, Archibald Kennedy, Collector of Customs, seized the sloop *Mary and Margaret* on information for importing goods not of English origin and not laden in England. To the subsequent libel in the Vice-Admiralty Court, Thomas Fowles, who was represented by William Smith and Joseph Murray, pleaded to the jurisdiction that the offense was not committed on the high seas and was therefore not within the court's jurisdiction. The plea was overruled and Fowles then moved the Supreme Court in October term for a writ of prohibition, which issued in November. At the January term of the Supreme Court, James Alexander moved and had a rule for Fowles to declare in a month or a consultation to issue. In his declaration Fowles averred that the seizure was made within the body of the city and county of New York and therefore, under the statutes 13 R. II c.5, 15 R. II c.3 and 2 Hy. IV c.11, an admiralty court had no jurisdiction. Archibald Kennedy, the libellant, demurred, but the com-

---

48 For early cases Rodney and Lee v. Gerritz (*Ms. Mins. Mayor's Ct. NYC 1674–75* 61, July 27, 1675); Dyer v. Pattishall, 1677 (*Ms. Decl. Book Mayor's Ct. NYC 1675–77* fol. 214); Dyer v. Barnes, 1677 (*ibid.* fol. 279); Mann v. Sloop *Newport*, 1680–81 (*Ms. Mins. Mayor's Ct. NYC 1677–82* fol. 251); Mann v. Van Horne (*ibid.*); Antill q.t. v. the Pink *New York* (*ibid.* fol. 351). For Admiralty proceedings at this time cf. *H.R. Ms. Wills* Libers 1 and 2, 282 (Sloop *Hope*, 1666), 285 (Ship *Cedar*, 1668).

For Quarter Sessions cases cf. Larkin q.t. v. Sloop *Lewis* (*H.R. Pleadings* Pl. K. 456, 452); Ludgar q.t. v. Sloop *Fortune* (*Ms. Mins. NYCQS 1683/84–1694* fol. 40, May 5, 1685); Meine q.t. v. Sloop *Unity* (*ibid.* fol. 93, Aug. 3, 1683); Santen q.t. v. *The Two Sisters* (*ibid.* Aug. 2, 1686); Lud-

gar q.t. v. the Pink *Charles* (*ibid.* fols. 48–50, Aug. 4, 1685). For Admiralty proceedings, *H.R. Ms. Wills* Libers 1 and 2, fol. 316, Oct. 11, 1683; 34 NY Col. Mss. 22 (1684), 34 (1684), 40 (1686), 64 (1687).

49 For the common law cases cf.: Van Cortlandt q.t. v. Ship *Fortune*, 1698 (*H.R. Parch.* 210 G 1); Hungerford q.t. v. Swift, 1699 (*Mins. SCJ 1693–1701* 154); Hungerford q.t. v. East Indian Goods, 1699 (*ibid.* 166); Lott q.t. v. Sundry Goods, 1700 (*ibid.* 168, 173, 183, 184); Weaver q.t. v. Wake, 1701 (*Ms. Mins. SCJ 1701–04* 3, 4); Hammond q.t. v. Sloop *Carolina*, 1735 (*Ms. Mins. SCJ 1732–39* 172–175, *H.R. Parch.* 159 D 2). There are numerous cases also in the Mayor's Court minutes.

50 2 *Rot. Parl.* (1347) 168.

plainant's declaration was found good and sufficient, and a writ of consultation was denied.[51] The Supreme Court took the position that by 15 Car. II c.7 forfeitures were to be sued for "in any of his Majesty's Courts" in the colony, and that this meant courts of record, which the admiralty courts were not, and that 7 and 8 Wm. III c.22 indicated that prosecutions were to be brought in courts of record. The effect of this view, as Kennedy had foreseen (writing to Acting Governor Clarke while the cause was pending), would mean trial of navigation cases at common law by juries "who perhaps are equally concerned in illicit trade and it is hardly to be expected they will find each other guilty."[52]

On writ of error to the Governor and Council the judgment of the Supreme Court was affirmed[53] April 18, 1741. Alexander then moved for an appeal to the King in Council, and the motion was granted upon £100 security. The petition and appeal was referred to the Committee of the Council in March, 1741/42. Ryder and Forrester argued the cause for the appellant and took the position that the various Acts of Parliament had altered the general jurisdiction of the admiralty courts in the colonies in order to supply the lack of courts of exchequer, and further that to abridge the powers of the admiralty courts would be fatal to enforcement. A clever interpretation to get around the Supreme Court's view of 15 Car. II c.7 was proffered, but the Committee advised affirmance of the judgment, and it was so ordered on March 23, 1742/43, the effect of the confirming order being, of course, to uphold the Supreme Court's ruling as to 15 Car. II c.7.[54]

The decision was of great importance for purposes of imperial policy as there had earlier been a doubt whether an appeal lay in such cases.[55] It adds

[51] Archibald Kennedy q.t. v. Thos. Fowles, 1739–44 (H.R. Parch. 225 D 1, 230 A 2; James Alexander, Ms. Letters Earl to Lynne, Box 4; James Alexander, Supreme Ct. Register 1721–42 no. 42; James Alexander, Admiralty Papers Box 45 nos. 4, 5). Cf. also Hough, Cases in Vice Admiralty (1925) 16; Mins. Vice-Admiralty Court NY Province 1715–46 104–109 (L. C. transcript).

[52] P.R.O., C.O. 5/1059/45.

[53] The proceedings are in 19 Ms. Mins. Council (Reverse) 81, 96, 98, 102.

[54] P.R.O., P.C. 2/97/107, 314, 345; 3 Acts of Privy Council, Colonial no. 528. Draft of appellant's case is in NYSL Misc. Mss. no. A2705. A similar jurisdictional issue was raised in the case of Vincent Pearse q.t. v. George Cummings (under an order regarding reprisals against Spain). On this case cf. Hough, op. cit. 17; H.R. Parch. 42 G 6 (prayer for writ of prohibition to the Supreme Court); James Alexander, Admiralty Papers Box

45 (recognizance by Vincent Pearse to pay costs and damages if awarded against him on his appeal to the King in Privy Council); H.R. Parch. 217 B 3 and 227 C 3 (which two parchments contain a full description of the case, including the writ of error). In this case the Privy Council reversed the Governor and Council's affirmance of the Supreme Court's allowance of a prohibition (P.R.O., P.C. 2/97/305–310, 344–345) probably because a matter of prize was involved.

[55] Wm. Popple, writing to the Attorney General (1700) sending an extract from proceedings of the admiralty court of Carolina relating to an appeal from the condemnation of Cole and Bean, galley, states:

"Mr. Henry Wiggington, in behalf of Mr. Butler made a motion for an appeal, but being able to produce to the Court neither law nor precedent for an appeal, where a ship and goods were condemned and disposed of by a penal statute, the

nothing to the meager learning respecting criminal appeals, for the jurisdictional point was obviously settled along lines of strict statutory construction. But, as the growing number of *qui tams* in the common law courts indicates,[56] the decision had the effect of increasing the bulk of their business. The conciliar appeal cannot be said to have determined the broad point that appeals involving a penal statute were necessarily admissible nor was this issue, so far as we know, ever directly settled in any case arising in New York Province. It was unusual for an issue regarding jurisdiction to be raised in criminal cases, and with the well-organized battery of transfer devices it would have been virtually impossible to have drawn such an issue in a way to have led to an appeal. Moreover, as it was exceptional for large fines to be imposed even in cases where circumstances would seem to have justified them, there was little occasion for the use of the appeal in misdemeanor cases. One is inevitably moved to conjecture whether the lightness of fines may not have been due to design—a desire to have criminal cases settled in the Province and not to open the avenue of appeal to the Crown.

Appeals to the Governor and Council

If policy and circumstances combined to preserve the administration of criminal law in New York from the direct ministrations of the Crown officers in England, the same considerations prevented the exercise of review powers by the Governor and Council. Prior to 1683, there was no question of the Governor and Council acting as an appellate tribunal for these powers were vested in the Court of Assizes. But in the Judicature Act of 1683 which constituted the Governor and Council a Court of Chancery to be "esteemed and accounted the Supreme Court" of the Province, a general right of "appeal" was granted from "any judgment or decree" in the Court of Chancery or the Court of Oyer and Terminer,[57] but the language of the act shows that only civil cases could have been embraced in this provision. If the assembly was bent upon continuing the loose appeal procedure of the Assizes, the contem-

---

Judge was of opinion that there lay no appeal in this case, where a vessel and goods were condemned and distributed by a law where no essoin, protection or wager of law was to be allowed."

Asked about appeals to either King in Council or High Court of Admiralty at appellant's volition, Trevor wrote, "I am of opinion that an appeal in this case doth properly lie before the King in Council" (*Cal. S.P. Colonial 1700* no. 574).

[56] Thus Harison q.t. v. Two Bundles of Tobacco, 1752 (*Ms. Mins. SCJ 1750–54* [Engr.] 124, 127,

130); Kennedy q.t. v. Seventy-Seven Cases of Bottles etc., 1756 (*ibid.* 254, 260); Allen q.t. v. Two Tons of Sugar, 1769 (*Ms. Mins. SCJ 1766–69* [Engr.] 607); Elliot & Moore q.t. v. Six Hogsheads, 1768 (*Ms. Mins. SCJ 1766–69* [Engr.] 505–507); Elliot & Moore q.t. v. Seven Casks Tea, 1772 (*H.R. Pleadings* Pl. K. 474, *H.R. Parch.* 120 G 1); Elliot & Moore q.t. v. Twenty Pipes of Wine, 1772 (*H.R. Parch.* 93 H 2). There are also cases in the Mayor's Court.

[57] 1 *Col. Laws NY* 128.

porary introduction of the writ of error[58] must certainly have put a sharp limitation upon earlier procedure. Unfortunately the almost complete destruction of the Council records for Dongan's administration makes it impossible to speak with certainty about the practice.[59]

With the change in New York's status to a royal colony the restrictions in the commissions and instructions respecting appeals already discussed came into effect. The essence of the Governor's power in criminal cases was executive. Since recourse in treason, murder and large fines was directly from the trial court to the Crown, the Governor was authorized only to grant the necessary reprieve, or in the case of fines over £200 to "permit appeals." The Judicature Act of 1691 added nothing to this power, for the statute merely enacted what was contained in Sloughter's commission, that is to say, it conveyed an error jurisdiction only in cases where the judgment exceeded the sum of £100.[59a] This provision was repeated in the Act of 1692 and in Bellomont's Ordinance.

There is no evidence that the legislature intended the word "judgments" to comprehend fines for misdemeanors; indeed, in contemporary statutory usage these are always referred to explicitly as fines and forfeitures. Furthermore, at the time the judicature was settled in New York all reviews of criminal cases were still a matter of royal grace, and the limits of this grace were stated in the instruction respecting fines in excess of £200. What was not determined, either in these instructions or by statute or ordinance, was the status of the causes which lay in the twilight zone of quasi-criminal prosecutions like the informations for intrusion or the suits on penal bonds. Probably because these matters were Exchequer business in England they came to be regarded in the colony as properly the subject of review in spite of the fact that proceedings were pursued for penal purposes. Otherwise, however, there is very little evidence of a desire to break through the limitations upon the use of error in criminal cases, and this complaisance may be attributed to the rapid and complete acceptance of common law procedure and ideas respecting criminal practice.

In 1714, in the case of *Queen* v. *Howard,* an attempt was made to "appeal" a criminal case where there had been a demurrer and judgment for the defendant. The Attorney General moved the Supreme Court "for an appeal to

---

[58] Cf. the writ of error, assignments of error and proceedings in *Ms. Mins. O. & T. Ulster Co.* fols. 8, 10–12.

[59] There are some proceedings in error before the Council. Cf. 35 *NY Col. Mss.* 39; 5 *Ms. Mins. Council* 171, 179, 225.

[59a] 1 *Col. Laws NY* 230, 231.

the Governor and Council" but although the Supreme Court granted the motion there is no record of any further proceedings.[60] With the exception of this one case, where the records are so meager that we do not even know the nature of the offense charged, there seem to have been no further attempts to secure review by the Governor and Council of causes criminal until the French and Indian War when the Attorney General, faced with the most blatant violations of the laws against trading with the enemy, sought to bring the New York merchants to book.

The law in the background of these cases is complicated. In the first place there was the general common law rule against trading with the enemy which at this period was regarded as a misdemeanor.[61] Shortly after the war broke out in the colonies the New York assembly passed a statute against trade with the French[62] and required that vessels exporting provisions post a bond as security. In 1756 the Board of Trade ordered an embargo upon all trade to any except British colonies,[63] and in December of that year Governor Hardy by proclamation declared this embargo and required a bond of all vessels clearing New York.[64] Early in the following year the English Parliament enacted an elaborate embargo law with the same provisions respecting bonds and imposed heavy penalties for violation, running up even to imprisonment.[65] The choice of weapons against violators was consequently wide indeed.

In spite of this fearsome barrier, the colonial merchants, who were hardened in the business of misprision, carried on a lively and lucrative trade under the rose.[66] It was in the words of a contemporary "an odd kind of mungrell commerce"[67] which the lawyers declared to have been legal, but which flourished only because of evasions, irregularities and illegal practices.[68] To a considerable extent the enforcement problem was a matter for the Court of Vice-Admiralty, but as proceedings there affected only single vessels and cargoes the prosecution of the fomenters of illegal trade could only be conducted in the common law courts.

---

[60] *Ms. Mins. SCJ 1710–14* 433, 447, 479, 491, 513, 531. Also see an entry in Bickley's Supreme Court Docket for March Term, 1713/14, which is as follows: "Rule for time for bayle 1/6" (F. A. De Peyster Mss. Box 2 no. 3 A).

[61] Cf. the opinion of Ryder and Murray quoted in Pares, *War and Trade in the West Indies* (1936) 421.

[62] 3 *Col. Laws NY* 1050, 1077 (continuation), 1121 (revision). All three acts were passed in 1755.

[63] 7 *Doc. Rel. Col. Hist. NY* 162; and cf. Beer, *British Colonial Policy 1754–65* (1922) 81 *et seq.*

[64] *H.R. Pleadings* Pl. K. 440.

[65] 30 Geo. II c.9. On the background cf. Beer, *op. cit.*; Pares, *op. cit.* 437 *et seq.*

[66] On this cf. Harrington, *The New York Merchant on the Eve of the Revolution* (1935) 254 *et seq.* The judicial records, however, are quite overlooked.

[67] *Letter Book of John Watts* (61 NYHS Colls.) 27.

[68] Kempe to Monckton (1762) in *The Aspinwall Papers* (Mass. Hist. Soc. Colls.) 469.

The problem of prosecution was complicated by various factors. In the first place the merchants were some of them the ornaments of provincial society. Many of them were outfitting and operating privateers which were preying on enemy commerce, and consequently, as in the case of the modern munitions maker who reaps large profits but buys great blocks of government securities, the balance of convenience was difficult for the eighteenth century conscience to weigh. Finally it should be noticed that so many persons were involved that the production of convicting evidence was extremely difficult.

The first important prosecution was begun in 1756 against Samuel Stillwell who was informed against for illegally exporting provisions on a vessel that had not posted bond under a provincial act prohibiting trade with the French.[69] The defendant was convicted and fined £500 and committed until he satisfied the penalty. On the same day the Attorney General filed another information charging generally that Stillwell had furnished the enemy with provisions. As this second information was not grounded on the New York statute, Stillwell could not plead *autrefoits convict*. He accordingly memorialized the Governor for a nolle prosequi on the ground, among others, that he had already "been fined on this offense." Governor Hardy seems to have ignored the petition and Stillwell accordingly appeared, pleaded guilty and paid a second fine.[70] The use of the memorial as an appeal device will be considered presently.

The Attorney General's success in the Stillwell case was no deterrent upon the traders, but it is certain from the elaborate measures taken to cover evasions that there was increasing difficulty in securing proof sufficient to convict.[71] In the year 1759 there emerged upon the legal stage a character as strange as any yet encountered. This was George Spencer. He seems to have been some sort of unprosperous man of business and was insolvent at the time

[69] 3 *Col. Laws NY* 1121. The order to prosecute Stillwell is in 25 *Ms. Mins. Council* 122.

[70] For the Supreme Court minutes on this case, see *Ms. Mins. SCJ* 1754–57 (Engr.) 282, 286, 305, 307, 314, 317, 336, 348, July 27, 31, Oct. 19, 20, 25–28, 1756, Jan. 18, 21, 1757. For the information, the framing of the issue and the summoning of the jury, see the issue roll in *H.R. Pleadings* Pl. K. 321, and *H.R. Parch.* 31 A 2. For the venire for the jury see *H.R. Pleadings* Pl. K. 904. In *ibid.* K. 443, is to be found a draft of the information of Oct. 28, 1756, the defendant's plea of not guilty, the examinations and informations of several witnesses, the Attorney General's brief, the "case," the proofs and the order of the Council to prosecute Stillwell for exporting provisions contrary to the

act of assembly. This document also contains the defendant's reasons in arrest of judgment in which the defendant pointed out that the act was only "barely prohibitory" for which reason no information would lie, and that the defendant was not guilty of the crime because it had not been averred that the defendant had had an intent to violate the provisions of the act. This document also contains Stillwell's memorial to Governor Hardy of Jan. 10, 1757, referred to in the text, *supra*.

[71] Kempe to Monckton, *supra* n. 68 and his letter in 6 *Letters and Papers of Cadwallader Colden* 171. Cf. Pares, *op. cit.* 439 *et seq.* There are some data in Harrington, *op. cit.* 254, but that writer does not mention the embargo legislation.

of which we are speaking, but from his letters it is obvious that he was a person of more than usual education. It was undoubtedly to remedy his fortunes that Spencer turned informer and set in train the most important prosecutions of the war. The New York merchants undertook very promptly to deal with this menace to the more abundant life. We shall consider the ensuing riot later in this chapter. The indignities which Spencer suffered only hardened his resolution, and succeeded in getting the ear of the Council. A long report on the illegal trade was presented by William Smith on December 4, 1760. Kempe was ordered to prosecute Spencer's attackers, and the informer under these auspices was able to get on with his *qui tams*. In May, 1762, condemnations of several vessels and cargoes for trading were decreed in the Vice-Admiralty Court.[72] The testimony disclosed the implication of many leading citizens. Kempe thereupon proceeded to inform against sixteen of these men: Waddel Cunningham, Thomas White, Godardus Van Solingen, Thomas Livingston, Thomas Smith, Philip Smith, Theunis Thew, William Williams, William Dobbs, Jacob Van Zandt, George Moore, John Keating, Abraham Lott, James Bell and John Fox.[73] They were severally charged by the Crown with

> devising and intending unlawfully and corruptly to have keep and maintain an illegal communication and correspondence with the enemies of . . . the King [when they illegally shipped food and provisions to the French] in manifest contempt of . . . the King and his laws to the great assistance of the enemy To the great damage and injury of . . . [the King's] subjects To the most pernicious example of all others in like case offending . . . and against the peace of the King his crown and his dignity.[74]

On April 21, 1763, the jury found Waddel Cunningham and Thomas White guilty, and on April 23, Duane for the defendants moved in arrest of judgment; but on January 28, 1764,

> on motion of Mr. Attorney General for judgment the court gives judgment for the King and an attested copy of the decree of the court of Vice-Admiralty be-

---

[72] The papers on these admiralty cases are in J. T. *Kempe Lawsuits* S–U. There are also a number of letters from Spencer to Kempe. See also Hough, *Reps. of Cases in the Vice Admiralty of the Province of NY* (1925) 196–199.

[73] *Ms. Mins. SCJ* 1762–64 (Engr.) 2, 23–25, 42, 43, 64, 65, 73, 82, 83, 91, 129, 136–138, 151, 224, Oct. 19, 30, 1762, Jan. 18, 20, 22, Apr. 19–21, 26, July 30, 1763; *H.R. Parch.* 165 A 1 (information),

196 K 3 (subpoena *duces tecum*); *H.R. Pleadings* Pl. K. 308, 313, 767, 1032, 1040; *J. T. Kempe Lawsuits* J–L *sub nom.* William Kennedy.

[74] The Attorney General's brief in these cases (*H.R. Pleadings* Pl. K. 1023) is interesting. He sets forth the information for trading with the enemy, the case and the proofs, and then deals with the qualifications of the witness; cf. *infra* 646.

ing produced by the defendants' counsel whereby it appears that the vessell and cargo for which the defendants are prosecuted were adjudged as prize and the court being informed that the defendants had paid the charges of prosecution and had been at great expence for council the court set a fine of £100 on each defendant.[75]

Jacob Van Zandt and Abraham Lott were tried on October 26, 1763 in the Supreme Court and Theunis Thew, one of the original offenders, was sworn as a witness in the cause after his pardon was "first read and tendered to him." However, Thew refused to answer several questions put to him "which the Court were of opinion were pertinent to the said issue," and it was therefore "ordered that the said Theunis Thew stand committed." Evidently it was impossible to get a conviction against Van Zandt and Lott due to Thew's refusal to answer, and the defendants were acquitted, but Thew, not so fortunate, was on October 29, 1763, fined £200 for contempt in refusing to answer the questions put to him.[76]

John Keating and William Kennedy were tried on October 28, 1763 and found not guilty. The same difficulty was experienced in getting evidence against Keating and Kennedy as in the case of Van Zandt and Lott for

William Dobbs who was sworn as a witness . . . for the King in an issue of traverse . . . refusing to answer several questions put to him . . . pertinent to the said issue . . . Ordered . . . committed. William Paulding . . . called as a witness . . . for the King in said Issue and on the Book being offered and the oath repeated by the clerk he said he understood he was not to declare anything that might affect himself—he was then told he had the King's pardon whereupon he declared he would not accept the pardon.

Dobbs and Paulding were fined £200 for refusing to answer the court's questions in the case.[77]

The Crown officials evidently decided to make an example of Cunningham

[75] Ms. Mins. SCJ 1762–64 (Engr.) 138–141, 149, 150, 157, 222, 223, 276, 360, Apr. 23, 25, 28, July 29, 30, Oct. 20, 1763, Jan. 28, 1764.
[76] Ms. Mins. SCJ 1762–64 (Engr.) 289–291, 297.
[77] Ibid. 273, 274, 297. Dobbs, Thew and Paulding were on January 28, 1764, each fined £5 for trading with the enemy, on their pleas of guilty and the court's taking into consideration their poverty. Evidently all three defendants refused to accept the pardons granted to them in order to have them act as witnesses.
Godardus Van Solingen does not appear in the minutes subsequent to the original information

filed against him until May 2, 1767, when an order was made that John Roberts, the high sheriff of the city of New York, return the capias against the defendant or suffer attachment. A similar order was made on July 28, 1767. On the 29th of July, the sheriff returned the defendant taken and was ordered to bring in the body or be amerced 40s. On July 31 the sheriff was ordered to bring in the body or be amerced £4. On May 2 and Oct. 31, 1767, the sheriff was ordered to bring in the body or show cause why attachment should not issue against him. These are the only minute entries on this case and we do not know what the subsequent disposi-

for the Governor directed the Attorney General to prosecute a bill for debt on the bond required by statute. Cunningham promptly addressed a memorial to the Governor for relief against a double prosecution for trading with the enemy. Unfortunately this document has been destroyed[78] but its purport can be deduced from the report of the Attorney General in answer.[79] Cunningham averred that the action on the bond was a fresh prosecution for the same offense and had been set on foot to punish him twice for the same transgression "an instance of rigor altogether unexampled" and that it was "oppressive, contrary to the spirit of government and the dictates of law and reason." He claimed further that this was a second information, that the prosecutor (as in *qui tam* cases) was claiming one half the forfeiture, and he prayed a nolle prosequi.

In his report the Attorney General denied that this was a double prosecution. The information on which Cunningham had been convicted charged an offense at common law, for illegal communication and correspondence with the enemy. The proceeding of which Cunningham was complaining was for a violation of the provision act which consisted in lading or exporting provisions before security given pursuant to the statute, an offense entirely distinct from trading with the enemy. Moreover, replied Kempe, this was not an information but an action of debt for the penalty incurred on the statute. It was brought for the King alone, and the Attorney General received no benefit in the prosecution. Kempe admitted that the "facts as far as relate to the commodities shipped charged in both suits were the same" but he insisted that a person was punishable not for one fact but, "if in perpetrating that fact he commits several offences," for every offense committed.

Unfortunately we have not succeeded in discovering the final disposition of this case. But this and the Stillwell memorials are interesting exhibits on the confusion respecting the nature of the various forms of proceeding which the Crown could bring. The action on the bond, while in form civil, was actually

tion of the case was (*Ms. Mins. SCJ 1764–67* [Rough] 247, 250, 329; *Ms. Mins. SCJ 1766–69* [Engr.] 186, 255; *J. T. Kempe Lawsuits* V *sub nom.* Godardus Van Solingen).

On June 25, 1762, John Fox, a "mariner," informed the Governor of some of the facts in connection with the shipping of provisions to the enemy by the defendants in the action discussed in the text. There is also a memorandum by Governor Moore indicating that Broockman, Fox, Crew and Lane were interested in the *Charming Polly*, Keating and Kennedy in the *Susannah and Anne*, Van Zandt in the *Iron Hester*, and Van Solingen and

Livingston in the *York Castle*, all boats which shipped provisions to the enemy (*J. T. Kempe Lawsuits* C–F *sub nom.* Fox *sub nom.* Cunningham). Among these papers are several drafts of information, notices of trial and notes on English authorities to be cited.

[78] Cf. *Cal. Eng. Mss.* 745. The manuscript volume was destroyed by fire.

[79] *H.R. Pleadings* Pl. K. 451. Also see *ibid.* Pl. K. 1051, in which an analysis is made by the Attorney General of Cunningham's memorial and Kempe's proposed answers.

grounded upon the violation of a penal statute. It is to be classed with those devices which were an important means of enforcement collateral to the criminal law, since a sanction was exacted by a civil proceeding in lieu of an information.[80]

The proceedings against Stillwell and Cunningham did nothing to settle the somewhat indeterminate line between a Crown action on a penal bond and a Crown plea begun by information, and the twilight was deepened in a series of actions brought against another set of merchants for violations of the proclamation of 1756. Theophilact Bache, Ennis Graham, George Folliott, Joseph Forman, Charles Tillinghast and James De Peyster were New York City merchants engaged in an import and export business in liquors and between 1760 and 1762 these merchants posted bonds as required by the proclamation. According to a report of Governor Colden[81] all the wines consumed in New York came from Spanish colonies and were paid for by an exchange of provisions. Apparently Bache and the other merchants violated the embargo and the Attorney General brought an action of debt on the bonds.[82] April 1, 1760, narrations in debt on a bond were filed severally against George Folliott and Charles Tillinghast by the Attorney General claiming that a £1,000 customs bond was forfeited.[83] The defendants demurred and the Attorney General joined in the demurrer. Subsequently a declaration was filed against Forman, Graham and Bache[84] who also demurred to the declarations.[85] In their argument on the demurrer, counsel for Bache admitted the bond and the condition, but the exaction of the bond was attacked on the general ground that the Crown had no prerogative to restrain trade and that at common law trade was free and restrictions on it were void.[86] It was further claimed only Parliament could place restrictions upon trade and, in support, counsel for the defendant relied upon a supposed statute (10 Henry VIII c.6) which gave the King power to restrict trade to particular places, thus implying

[80] Traditionally the procedure for debts to the Crown was by information (Robertson, *Civil Proceedings by and against the Crown* [1908] 142). Where the debt was of record it was also possible to proceed in Exchequer where *scire facias* was the first process (Gilbert, *Treatise on the Court of Exchequer* [1758] 125). Cf. further *infra* 530 *et seq.*

[81] 1 *Colden Letter Books* 50.

[82] *H.R. Pleadings* Pl. K. 709.

[83] *J. T. Kempe Lawsuits* C–F *sub nom.* George Folliott, and cf. *H.R. Pleadings* Pl. K. 599.

[84] *H.R. Pleadings* Pl. K. 599.

[85] *H.R. Pleadings* Pl. K. 1047. Cf. *infra* n. 92.

[86] A declaration was also filed against Bache be-

cause he had failed to pay £142 customs duty on distilled spirits. The defendant pleaded *nil debet*. It seems that in this case the treasurer took a promissory note from Bache on January 20, 1762, to pay the customs duty within three months, but Bache later refused to pay the note, claiming that the act of assembly laying a duty on British goods was repugnant to an Act of Parliament which gave a bounty on English goods imported from Great Britain. The defendant relied on 7 and 8 William III c.22 §9, because the Act of Parliament overrode a repugnant act of assembly (*H.R. Pleadings* Pl. K. 603).

that without such an Act of Parliament he would have had no power to restrict trade. The defendant pointed out that no act of assembly or Act of Parliament had restricted trade, and yet a customs bond had been exacted.[87] On October 30, 1762, the Attorney General argued against Bache's demurrer, and on April 30, 1763, defendant's counsel was ordered to reply to the argument of the Crown by the following term or be precluded.[88] On April 18, 1765, Bache moved for judgment,[89] and on October 22, judgment was given in his favor.[90] The Attorney General thereupon obtained a writ of error directed to the justices of the Supreme Court returnable before the Governor and Council on January 8, 1765.[91]

The arguments of the Crown in the Bache case are not available but in the similar action against Graham,[92] whose contentions appear to have paralleled those of Bache, a rough draft of Kempe's argument has been preserved. With a great show of learning and considerable skill the Attorney General first traversed the defendant's claims that no power lay in the Crown in default of legislation to control trade, and then proceeded to set forth the wide powers which inured to the King in war times. Starting with the proposition that the Crown possessed a prerogative to restrain trade without the consent of the legislature, and referring to the comforting maxim *salus populi est suprema lex,* Kempe averred that the King might restrain trade for the public good, and while "it cannot be denied but that the King is restrained from granting monopolies," nevertheless the regulation of trade was not a monopoly according to 3 Coke's *Institutes* 181. Kempe further argued that ordinarily the

[87] Citing 1 Rolle's *Reports* 4. The defendant also quoted the various statutes of merchants, citing Magna Carta c.30, 2 Edw. III c.9; 9 Edw. III c.1; 11 Richard II c.17; 14 Edw. III c.2 St. 9 [*sic*]; 27 Edw. III c.2 St. 2; 28 Edw. III c.13 §3; 38 Edw. III c.2 (*H.R. Pleadings* Pl. K. 610).

[88] *Ms. Mins. SCJ* 1762–64 (Engr.) 65, 90, 176, Oct. 30, 1762, Jan. 22, Apr. 30, 1763.

[89] *H.R. Pleadings* Pl. K. 787.

[90] *Ms. Mins. SCJ* 1764–67 (Rough) 124, Oct. 22, 1765.

[91] The writ of error read as follows: "George the Third . . . to our trusty and well beloved Daniel Horsmanden . . . David Jones . . . William Smith . . . and Robert R. Livingston . . . of our Supreme Court . . . Greeting Because in the Record and process and also in the rendering of judgment of a Plaint which was in our said court before you brought by John Tabor Kempe . . . who for us in that behalf prosecuted against Theophilact Bache for that the said Theophilact Bache should render to us £ 2,000 of good and lawful money of Great Britain / as is said / manifest Error hath intervened to the grievous damage of us, as of the complaint of the said John Tabor Kempe . . . we have received We willing the Error (if any has been) should in due manner be corrected and that to us and the same Theophilact Bache full and speedy justice be done . . . do command you that if Judgment be rendered then the Record and Process aforesaid with all and singular those things thereunto relating . . . under your hands and seals . . . you send and this writ so that we may have the same before our Governor and Council . . . that the record and process aforesaid being inspected we may further do thereupon for correcting that Error what of right and according to the Laws and customs of . . . England and our Province of New York ought to be done Witness ourself [at Fort George, Oct. 31, 6 George III]."

This document was found in a bin in the Hall of Records, New York City. It had no parchment number assigned to it when our research was done.

[92] Cf. *J. T. Kempe Lawsuits* G–J *sub nom.* Ennis Graham; *Ms. Mins. SCJ* 1762–64 (Engr.) 65, Oct. 30, 1762; *H.R. Pleadings* Pl. K. 1047. For Kempe's argument cf. *ibid.* K. 440.

Crown should not grant monopolies without the consent of the legislature because it would be injurious to the individual, preventing his earning his bread, and would be injurious to the commonwealth "by promoting idleness." However, the restraint of trade in particular instances was "for the good of the state." Referring to the defendant's second argument, in which the defendant asserted that trade was free under laws passed from Magna Carta to Richard II, Kempe said that he admitted that trade in England was free, but "that it is in some measure restrained cannot admit of a doubt." As for the defendant's argument that the passage of a statute (10 Henry VIII c.6) giving the King power to restrain trade indicated that without such a statute the King would not have had such power, Kempe replied that a statute of this type was not an enabling statute, but was merely a statute in "affirmance of the common law." He continued: "That many statutes have been made in affirmance of the common law is too notorious to be disputed," but he insisted that no such statute as 10 Henry VIII c.6 had ever been made. The Attorney General pointed out that there was a statute 26 Henry VIII c.10, giving the King power to permit the importation of wines from Gascony and repealing the statute of 23 Henry VIII c.7, which had forbidden the importation of these wines. The Attorney General said that the act to which the defendant was referring was in fact the act of 26 Henry VIII c.10, but that the defendant had misquoted the statute, that in any event this statue was obsolete, and had not been set forth at length in the statutes at large. It is amusing to note that Kempe adds the following professorial comment: "I presume the gentlemen had not read it but trusted to some books where it is misquoted."

Kempe's arguments respecting the war powers of the Crown are reminiscent of those advanced in the famous *Ship Money Case* (1637). The Crown, he said, can lay embargoes for public good in war time for in "our constitution" the defense and safety of the realm are in the King. The embargo proclamation of 1756 was levied pursuant to this power and no legislative authorization was necessary. The Crown could lay an absolute embargo, and therefore could lay a conditional embargo, viz., through the medium of a bond.

On April 18, 1765, the defendant, Graham, moved for judgment which was given for him on October 22 of that year.[93] However, on June 21, 1766, John Tabor Kempe sent a notice to William Smith Jr., who was Graham's attorney, stating that a writ of error had been issued in the case.[94]

---

[93] H.R. *Pleadings* Pl. K. 787; *Ms. Mins. SCJ* 1764–67 (Rough) 124, Oct. 22, 1765.

[94] H.R. *Pleadings* Pl. K. 1047. For this writ of error see H.R. *Parch.* 156 B 7. The record in error

The proceedings in error before the Council were long drawn out and the record as it stands is not very informative. On January 8, 1766[95] the Chief Justice informed "his Excellency and the Court" that writs of error had been received in the cases of *King* v. *Bache, King* v. *Graham* and *King* v. *Forman*,[96] but he had been unable to make the returns. It was accordingly ordered that these be made on May 7 following. The returns were not made until July 9, 1766 when Kempe delivered an assignment of errors and upon his motion a *scire facias ad audiendum errores* was ordered returnable October 8.[97] A number of postponements ensued and finally on January 7, 1767,[98] the *scire facias* was returned in the Graham case and the defendant ordered to plead in fourteen days. The record was returned, read and filed in Council on January 21, and it was ordered that it be made a *consilium*.[99] In the meantime the Bache case disappears from the records. Colden had ordered a *nolle prosequi* in 1764[100] but this does not appear to have been served on the Attorney General. It is possible that Governor Moore had finally made the order effective, for Bache was a rich and influential man.

On May 7, 1767 the Council on motion of Kempe made a show cause order in the Graham and Forman cases,[101] and a week later it nolle prossed the Forman case,[102] but ordered that Graham be given six weeks to produce proofs of landing at Jamaica provisions mentioned in the bond on which the case was grounded. In this Graham was successful and it was accordingly ordered on February 10, 1768, that a *nolle prosequi* issue upon the defendant's paying the Attorney General a reasonable allowance for his trouble.[103]

It should be observed that the procedure in error before the Council conformed generally with that in the English courts,[104] although the form of

in this case was filed on Jan. 21, 1767, and is contained in *ibid.* 233 D 1. This document recites the writ of error, the return and record annexed and also contains the Attorney General's statement before the Governor and Council that manifest error in the record and process and judgment had appeared.

In the case of Joseph Forman, this defendant was also sued on a £1,000 bond and judgment given for him on the demurrer (*Ms. Mins. SCJ 1762–64* [Engr.] 90, 239, Jan. 22, July 30, 1763; *Ms. Mins. SCJ 1764–67* [Rough] 12, Aug. 4, 1764; *Ms. Mins. SCJ 1764–66* [Engr.] 117, Jan. 19, 1765; *Ms. Mins. SCJ 1764–67* [Rough] 124, Oct. 22, 1765; *H.R. Pleadings* Pl. K. 609, 787; *H.R. Parch.* 160 D 9). On Jan. 21, 1765, the Attorney General notified Forman that the writ of error was issued (*H.R. Pleadings* Pl. K. 166). For the writ of error see *H.R. Parch.* 237 A 3.

For the citations on the Tillinghast case, on which

evidently no writ of error had been issued, see the minute entries above cited and also *H.R. Pleadings* Pl. K. 541, 906, 908. Also see the "roll" filed in January term, 1767, which is to be found in *H.R. Parch.* 90 K 3.

95 *29 Ms. Mins. Council* 103.
96 There had been actions on two bonds against Forman.
97 *29 Ms. Mins. Council* 143.
98 *Ibid.* 201.
99 *Ibid.* 204.
100 *6 Letters and Papers of Cadwallader Colden* (55 *NYHS Colls.*) 300, 301. The sealing of the writ of error Oct. 31, 1765, is endorsed on it.
101 *29 Ms. Mins. Council* 241.
102 *Ibid.*
103 *Ibid.* 254.
104 Compare Hands, *Solicitors Practice on the Crown Side* 47 *et seq.*

judgment was peculiar. The assignments of error have not been preserved, but the scanty minutes indicate that in the Graham case at least, the issue raised by demurrer was not dealt with, for the defendant was allowed to produce matter in bar that had presumably been admitted by the demurrer. No question as to the propriety of the error proceedings was raised, and we may therefore take as accepted the contention of Kempe that an action on a bond was not in the nature of an information.

The handling of the provision bond cases by the Governor and Council must have been a grievous disappointment to the Attorney General, and in particular the unpleasant surprise of having a court of errors transform itself into an administrative body. This had implications which directly affected other phases of Kempe's activities in law enforcement. We shall later see how the Attorney General was at this time endeavoring to assure the collection of all forfeited recognizances and was constantly being frustrated by demurrers which the Supreme Court sustained. If Kempe entertained any notions that his position would be improved by error proceedings to the Council the Graham and Forman cases must have disabused him.

Shortly after this episode the Crown sustained a further defeat, and this time at the hands of the Supreme Court. The case in question, *King* v. *Van Rensselaer*, did not go to the Governor and Council, but it is so instructive on the difficulties inherent in common law error proceedings that it will be considered at this point. The cause arose as a result of complaints by one Campbell who discovered that lands allotted to him for his military services were claimed by one of the land-greedy Hudson River patroons. As a result of representations to the Crown a special instruction was issued to the Governor of New York directing that a suit for intrusion be brought, and ordering further that if the case went against the Crown an appeal should be taken to the Privy Council.

Pursuant to this mandate, on October 31, 1767, an information was filed against John Van Rensselaer for intruding on Crown lands, and on January 23, 1768, the sheriff returned the defendant taken, and the latter was ordered to plead in twenty days or suffer judgment for want of a plea. On April 30, 1768, Kissam on behalf of the Attorney General moved that there be a view of the premises

by six or a greater number of jurors who are to try the same and that Lucas Van Veghte and Thomas Yates . . . [of Albany and Schenectady] be elisores to summon the jury to try the said cause. And that they return a pannel of 48 jurors into the clerk's office on or before the 21st day of May next and that the Jurors for the view be balloted before one of the judges of this court on the usual notice of time and place and that Alexander Colden . . . Surveyor General . . . shew the premises on the part of the Crown and that . . . [two named persons] survey and shew the premises on the part of the defendant and that on both sides leave be given to name other shewers and surveyors at the time of the balloting.[105]

On July 30, 1768

on the motion of Mr. Duane in behalf of Mr. Attorney General it is ordered that there be a tryal at Bar . . . & that Dirck Swart . . . of Albany be appointed one of the Elizors to summon the Jury who shall try the same instead of Lucas Van Vaghte heretofore appointed . . . Ordered . . . that said cause be tryed by a Struck Jury That the Elizors return a book of the persons qualified to serve as jurors within . . . the county of Albany into the office of the clerk of this court . . . That the Jury . . . be struck before one of the judges of this court . . . That the Clerk of the court . . . make a Pannel of 48 jurors out of the book so to be returned by the Elizors That each Party shall strike 12 names out of said Pannel and that the remaining 24 shall be the Jurors who are to try the said cause and that if the Attorney General or Defendant's attorney shall neglect to attend the striking the Clerk shall strike 12 names for the absentee. Ordered that the jurors who are to have a view of the premises . . . previous to the tryall . . . be balloted before one of the judges of this court immediately after the striking the said jury. [On October 25, 1768 it appeared to the court] that the Jury would not be able to go through the trial of this cause without rest and refreshment and the parties on both sides agreeing to an adjournment of the Jury and that they should be committed to the care of the Elizors the court ordered adjournement to tomorrow.[106]

On October 26, 1768, the trial of this cause was had. It lasted over several days and there were many pages of evidence, including even such ancient records as those of the County of Albany of 1672 and 1678. On November 5, 1768 the jury found the defendant not guilty.[107]

[105] Ms. Mins. SCJ 1766–69 (Engr.) 329, 388, 481, 482. In H.R. Pleadings Pl. K. 608, is a letter from James Duane to the elisors enclosing a venire, returnable October 24, to have a jury for a view.

[106] Ms. Mins. SCJ 1766–69 (Engr.) 519, 520, 557. For an interesting account of the expenses of the "rest and refreshment" of the jurors including an expensive wine bill, see J. T. Kempe Lawsuits V

sub nom. John Van Rensselaer. The total bill from October 21 to November 5, 1768, came to £58 7s. 3d. and the liquor bill alone amounted to £28.

[107] Ms. Mins. SCJ 1766–69 (Engr.) 558, 574. Also see H.R. Pleadings Pl. K. 281, quoted infra 650 n. 159.

In J. T. Kempe Lawsuits V sub nom. John Van Rensselaer, is to be found the Attorney General's

It is to be noted that in the course of the trial the Attorney General excepted to a ruling excluding certain Crown witnesses and later excepted to the admission of certain evidence for the defendant. Finally, on October 25, 1768 he made certain exceptions to the judge's charges to the jury, and John Tabor Kempe's papers contain a recital of what took place:

> Memorandum that on October 25 . . . before David Jones, Second Justice of the Supreme Court . . . in a plea of intrusion, trespass and contempt . . . John Tabor Kempe . . . did give in evidence to the jurors aforesaid as follows (prout all the evidence of the Crown) and the said William Smith Junior . . . for the defendant did further give in evidence . . . whereupon . . . the said Attorney General did request the said Justice to give in charge to the Jurors . . . that the law is that where a grant of the Crown for lands is doubtful and will admit of two constructions such construction . . . [shall be adopted] as will pass the least land . . . and said grants . . . to Killian Van Rensalaer . . . given in evidence on the part of the defendant . . . are void in law for uncertainty . . . and . . . [the Attorney General] requested the said Justice [so] to charge . . . and the Attorney General did further request the said Justice to direct the Jurors to find their verdict specially . . . [but Justice Jones did not so charge] wherefore the said Attorney General prayed his bill of exceptions to the opinions and charge of the said justice.[108]

On January 21, 1769, Justice David Jones wrote to Attorney General Kempe in connection with his request to have the bills of exceptions sealed, stating as follows:

> I have been long in Suspence about sealing the exceptions . . . It was made a question before the trial was concluded whether the King was entitled to have his exceptions or not. Since I came home I have examined into the matter from the 13th Edward I, by which the bill of exceptions is given and find by all the authorities I have which treat on the subject that they are to be allowed only in civil but not in criminal causes and I take an information for an intrusion into crown lands to be as much a criminal cause as an information for assault and battery . . . But however as the case does not appear to be quite clear I have sealed two of the bills of exceptions but the third on my charge to the jury I cannot seal without allowing that I said what I am confident I did not say viz. . . .

---

information against the defendant for intrusion and in the margin of the information are the following entries: "Coke's Entries Title Information 376, 372, 385, another precedent when intrusion made in the reign of two kings and the trespass particularized, 378–9, 383–5." *J. T. Kempe Lawsuits* V also con-

tain an abstract of evidence on the part of the defendant, a draft of additional instructions for the view (the latter document dated Sept. 17, 1768), a notice of trial dated Oct. 24, 1768, and the defendant's plea of not guilty.

[108] On this exception, *infra* 665.

[Jones here discusses the various boundary lines] . . . and that another line should be supplied by the jury . . . This I am very confident I did not say and therefore do not think myselfe obliged to seal the exceptions especially as I find some other matters therein not rightly represented.[109]

On January 27, 1769, John Tabor Kempe replied to Judge Jones and stated that he was sorry that the latter "should imagine that anything is inserted in the bill which you did not give in charge to the jury . . . which I was afraid might be the case and therefore the more strenuously requested your signing the bills before you left the bench."[110]

On April 29, 1769, the Attorney General moved in the Supreme Court that the defendant within six weeks deliver to the clerk of the court all the written evidence of the defendant given in the trial in October "which were withdrawn out of the court after the Bill of Exceptions tendered to the judge's charge by the council on the part of the Crown."[111]

The Attorney General never brought the writ of error. On February 10, 1773, he reported to Governor Tryon and the Council giving his reasons why no writ of error in prosecution for intrusion on the Claverack lands had been prosecuted. In his explanation Kempe recited that prior to the suit for intrusion, John Van Rensselaer had prayed a grant in confirmation of the lands in his Claverack tract, but no grant could be given to him "until further Directions from Home," and the King suspended the grant until it was determined by due course of law whether the lands were vacant or not. Meantime under the instructions to Sir Henry Moore ordering that intrusions on Crown lands be restrained, the Attorney General brought his information of intrusion against John Van Rensselaer: "And a very solemn trial afterwards was had thereon at the bar of the Supreme Court . . . for ten days and at last . . . a verdict for the defendant agreeable to the charge of the Court" in October term, 1768. Since in 1773 the Council was preparing to confirm Van Rensselaer's tract of land, the Attorney General desired to make certain observations to the Governor and Council explaining why he did not prosecute the writ of error in the previous prosecution for intrusion:

As the not prosecuting a Writ of error on the part of the Crown in that suit is urged by the Council as a Reason for their conclusion above stated . . . and as

---

[109] J. T. Kempe Lawsuits V.
[110] Ibid. Note infra 253, the variation in Kempe's report to the Governor.

[111] Ms. Mins. SCJ 1769–72 (Engr.) 22, Apr. 29, 1769. Same rule on July 29, 1769, ibid. 70.

the . . . want of such proceeding may expose me to blame . . . I . . . conceive it . . . incumbent on me . . . to state my conduct herein.

During the trial of this cause, the Council concerned for the crown with me thought it proper to take several exceptions to the opinion of Mr. Justice Jones who alone sat on the trial—the first exception was for his refusing to admit evidence on the part of the Crown which we conceived ought by law to have been admitted, the 2nd was for his admitting evidence on the part of the defendant which we conceived ought not to have been given to the jury and the last was to the Judge's charge which we thought erroneous . . . [on] which we principally depended for setting aside the judgment.

. . . Evidence consisting of numerous deeds and writings, besides the testimony of . . . 60 witnesses the delivery of which to the Jury took . . . 10 days, could not be inserted at length in the Bills of Exceptions taken during the Trial even had we on the part of the Crown been possessed of the Deeds and Writings . . . in Evidence . . . We therefore contented ourselves as is usual here with drawing up the Exceptions complete except the stating the Evidence given which was nevertheless referred to in the Drafts with a Prout &c.

As soon as the charge was given by the Judge and we had begged leave to except to it, the court having set up all night adjourned for a short space I think only for one hour, during which we were to draw up the exceptions to the charge. Before the rough draft was completed . . . we received a message from Justice Jones that the court was sitting and that he was in haste to leave town and thereupon we finished the rough draft in the utmost haste . . . I tendered these Bills of Exceptions observing that there had been no time to insert the Evidence and praying him to stay till that could be done . . . but the Judge declared he would not stay longer in time. I prayed . . . he would . . . put his seal to the Bills as they then stood which has been the usual practice here, intending without loss of time to have redrawn them at large and to have applied to him to put his Seal to the Engrossed Bills, but his Honor hesitated . . . when William Smith . . . for the defendant intimated to the court that he doubted whether a Bill of Exceptions would lie in this case it being a Crown cause on which Jones desired he would speak to that point and . . . Smith entered into the argument, which we . . . replied to and . . . the Judge . . . refused . . . to seal and sign any of the Bills of Exceptions, left the court and went home, having first been desired by me to endeavor to settle his opinion as soon as possible because a delay might occasion his forgetting the facts and if Council on both sides should disagree it might defeat the exceptions which was drawn up in the words following. . . .

Kempe stated that he did not press Jones to sign the bills of exceptions but waited until January term for his opinion, but when Jones failed to attend court on January 17, 1769, Kempe sent to him for the bills of exceptions and on January 21, 1769, Jones sent two bills of exceptions sealed with the letter which was quoted above.

In his explanation to the Governor and Council Kempe went on to say that on January 27, 1769, he replied to Judge Jones as follows: "I am very sorry you should imagine that anything is inserted in the Bill of Exceptions which you did not give in the charge to the jury . . . and can only account for it by supposing . . . your memory failed in this instance which I was afraid might be the case." Kempe furthermore asked Jones to point out what misrepresentations had been made and to send him a copy of the third and unsealed bill of exceptions as he had no copy, but Jones failed to reply until March 13, 1769, when he sent Kempe the third bill of exceptions unsealed. Kempe then went on to explain to the Governor and Council as follows: "Upon the whole not being able to obtain this most material Exception against the charge we thought it improper without further Directions to risque the Cause on the other 2 exceptions which would have incurred a very great expense." Kempe also pointed out that since a year had passed before he got back the written evidence from the defendant (so that he might go on with the writ of error), it would have been impracticable to get the judge to supply from his memory and to get the parties to supply from their memories the testimony of the witnesses. Soon after the trial Kempe transmitted to his Majesty's ministers a full account of all the proceedings and evidence on the trial and he also explained the case to Governor Moore. Concluding his explanation, Kempe stated: "These Sir are the reasons why I have not prosecuted a writ of error . . . and I humbly beg leave to request your Excellency favorably to direct this my representation to be entered at large upon the minutes of the court."[112]

It should be observed that despite the common law rule that a bill of exceptions did not lie in a criminal case Justice Jones, nevertheless, signed and sealed two such bills. It is true that a meager trickle of authority supported bills of exception in quo warranto and Exchequer cases,[113] but Jones had not treated this as such a proceeding. Neither, for that matter, had Attorney General Kempe, who took the line that the King could take the benefit of any act

[112] Kempe's report to the Governor and Council is contained in *Misc. Mss. Claverack* and 31 *Ms. Mins. Council* 60 *et seq.* Kempe signed this report on Jan. 10, 1773, and on Feb. 6, 1773, James Duane entered the following certification on the report: "This I think is a just representation." Benjamin Kissam on Feb. 8, 1773, signed his name to the following certification: "To the best of my remembrance I think the above representation of facts to be just."

[113] Rex v. Higgins (1 *Ventris* 366); Rex v. Preston (*Cases temp. Hardwicke* 249).

where he was not especially named.[114] The point, whether in any event the Crown would be entitled to a writ of error, was seemingly not raised.

The abandonment of the error proceedings in *King* v. *Van Rensselaer* is interesting for the light it throws upon the deficiencies of review jurisdiction in New York Province. At home, intrusions were primarily justiciable in Exchequer and the Crown's suit was at best only quasi-criminal in character. The colonial lawyers, however, were prone to regard any proceeding by the Crown as virtually synonymous with a criminal proceeding, and hence the limitations which restrained the review of a prosecution, whether by indictment or information, were deemed to apply equally to any suit which the Crown might bring.[115]

It should be noticed that to some extent, and very occasionally, the deficiencies of the Governor and Council as a court of errors were supplied by the use of petition as a substitute. The Stillwell and Cunningham cases discussed above are examples of this petition practice which we think were induced by the limitations upon error proceedings in criminal cases. Others of these petitions were for an order that a nolle prosequi issue before trial as the defendants could not otherwise bring their cases before the highest authority in the province,[116] and in a few instances the order was made after trial.[117] In still other cases the petitions took the form of complaints against a judge or other officer.[118] The action here was essentially in the nature of an administrative re-

114 *J. T. Kempe Lawsuits* V *sub nom.* John Van Rensselaer contain "some notes on . . . bills of exceptions in Crown Causes" where the Attorney General has written the following comments: "It is said that bills of exceptions will not lie for the King in this case 1 Because the statute of Westminster giving bills of exceptions does not mention the King. Answer. The King may take the benefit of any particular act though he be not especially named 4 Bac. 198, 1 Blackstone 262, 1 Leonard 150, 7 Coke Rep: 32, 11 Coke Rep: 68b."
115 The basis of these ideas may have been the fact that proceedings on penal bonds often involved the trial of facts which had caused the recognizance to be exacted. Furthermore, as in King v. Forman, the bill of the Attorney General was patterned closely on the criminal information, viz.: "John Tabor Kempe Esq. Attorney General for the Province of New York, who for the same Lord the King prosecutes, complains, etc." (*H.R. Parch.* 160 D 9).
116 These will be considered later in c. VI. For the moment compare the nolle prosequi granted to certain Albany justices against whom Bradley was proceeding, Nov. 7, 1728 (14 *Ms. Mins. Council*

308); and the nolle prosequi granted in 1732 to Justice Wickham who was informed against for not attending court but who was ill (16 *ibid.* 189).
117 Cf. Queen v. Oncklebagg and Bogardus indicted for champerty (1712–13). The defendants were found guilty and continued on recognizances. Meantime Oncklebagg had secured a nolle pros order from the Governor and Council and on June 5, 1713, Jamison entered a *non vult ulterius pros* (*Ms. Mins. SCJ 1710–14* 409, 426, 430, 444, 460; 11 *Ms. Mins. Council* 165). Cf. also *H.R. Pleadings* Pl. C. 844 where the fees for getting the nolle prosequi are stated to be £1/14/0. In Queen v. Makemie and Hampton indicted for preaching without a license in March, 1706/07, the defendant Makemie was acquitted on June 6, 1707. On Sept. 4, 1710, the Attorney General entered a nolle prosequi (cf. *Ms. Mins. SCJ 1704/05–1709* 111, 115, 121–123, 130, 132; *Ms. Mins. SCJ 1710–14* 280). The record here is very puzzling as it does not appear why a nolle pros was entered. On the licensing row, cf. 3 *Papers of the Amer. Soc. of Church Hist.* (2d ser.) 102 *et seq.*
118 For example, the schoolmaster's complaint against Justice Codwise who was charged with pro-

view, but the circumstances of some of the cases indicate that the petitioners were seeking equitable redress for a proceeding not otherwise to be attacked.

Error and Appeal in the Supreme Court

While the appellate powers of the Governor and Council over criminal cases were limited both by royal instructions and common law rules, it was only the latter that controlled the judicature of the Supreme Court of the Province, vested as it was with the powers of the English King's Bench. Prior to 1691 the colonial legislators appear to have contemplated lodging review powers in the highest provincial tribunal. Under the judicial arrangements of the Duke's Laws the possibility of "appeal" in criminal cases was provided for,[119] but the records afford no examples of the exercise of this jurisdiction, for, as we have seen, difficult cases were invariably transferred by recognizance or prosecuted originally before the Assizes.[120] It should be noted that the Duke's Laws used the word "appeal" in a very loose sense and if the practice is any index of interpretation seem merely to have intended a claim to be tried at Assizes in the first instance. Under Dongan the English form of writ of error and the error proceeding at common law are introduced. The only cases we have seen are civil[121] although the Judicature Act of 1683 is explicit on the removal of indictments and informations to the Oyer and Terminer Court by writ of error or certiorari.[122]

It is possible that these early ideas respecting the function of the chief court may have influenced the later legislation, for the Judicature Act of 1691 provided that all persons might by "Warrant Writt of Error or certiorari, Remove" out of the inferior courts any "Judgment Information or Indictment" and that the Supreme Court might "Correct Errors in Judgment or Reverse the same." Since a succeeding section on appeals in case of error speaks of judgments above the value of £20,[123] it would appear that only removal proceedings before trial were intended in criminal cases. This confusion was clarified somewhat by the Act of 1692 where the words "by warrant or certiorari"[124] alone were used, and nothing was said about error. Nevertheless, the

---

curing a complaint and then issuing a warrant (19 Ms. Mins. Council 25, 28 [1739]). In 1765 a complaint was made against a justice for being interested in a case. It was dismissed (26 ibid. 13). Again in 1767 a clergyman arrested for disturbing the peace complained against the justices and the latter were admonished (ibid. 106–108).

[119] 1 Col. Laws NY 12.

[120] Supra 62, 63.

[121] Ms. Mins. O. & T. Ulster Co. fols. 8–15, where the writ of error, assignments of error and record are set forth.

[122] 1 Col. Laws NY 127.

[123] The appellant was obliged to pay the costs in the lower court and enter a bond, with two sureties in double the amount, to prosecute his appeal with effect within twelve months (1 Col. Laws NY 226).

[124] Ibid. 306; 359, 380 (continuations). The Or-

Supreme Court, in despite of statute and common law restrictions, proceeded to hear a number of cases brought up from Sessions by way of error. The earliest of the cases where error was brought in a Crown prosecution occurs in the year 1693. Unfortunately only the bare minute entry is available. In *King* v. *Brett* [*Burt*] on "Ltre de Error," Emott on October 3, 1693, in the Supreme Court, prayed that a day might be assigned to bring in the record, and on October 5 the record was filed. On October 6, 1693, the court took the case under advisement and on the following day decided that it had no cognizance of the case, "the debt and damages being under £20."[125]

A second case, *King* v. *Leggett*,[126] came up from Sessions by way of error,

dinance of 1699 continued the provisions of the previous acts respecting appeal (2 *NY Laws* [Rev. 1813] App. V).

On December 23, 1765, an act of assembly was made to restrain the bringing of writs of certiorari and writs of error for the removal of judgments given before justices of the peace within the colony. The act recited that it had been found by experience that many people on the most frivolous pretenses had procured writs of certiorari removing judgments of justices of the peace into the Supreme Court "which tends to the great Delay of Justice and to the Damage and oppression of many of the People in this Colony; there being no Costs given by Law in such Cases against the Party unjustly bringing such Certiorari." The act therefore provided that no case might be removed unless the appellant first made an affidavit before one of the judges of the Supreme Court complaining of the judgment of the justice of the peace. The judge of the Supreme Court was then to determine whether the certiorari or writ of error should be allowed. The affidavit should show reasonable cause for granting removal either for error or for some unfair practice by the justice. If the person making this affidavit swore falsely, he should pay all costs and damages and be punished for perjury. If anyone obtained a removal of a case without making the required affidavit, the person so procuring the writ of certiorari or writ of error should forfeit £5, recoverable with costs of suit before any one justice of the peace by the adverse party (4 *Col. Laws NY* 861).

On May 20, 1769, an act of assembly empowering justices of peace to determine cases to the amount of £10 also provided that no writ of error or of certiorari should issue out of the Supreme Court in any civil matter unless an affidavit were made showing reasonable cause for granting the writ (*ibid*. 1086). This act was subsequently disallowed by the Crown.

On the same day an act of assembly was passed providing that no suits should be brought in the Supreme Court either originally or in error, if the sums involved did not exceed £50, but this act

was repealed by the King in 1770. It should be noted that this act did, however, provide that it was not to extend to suits where the party sued on behalf of the Crown as well as on his own behalf, nor did it apply to suits brought in the King's name, nor to suits where the title to land was in question. The act further allowed the bringing of writs of error or attaint to remove causes into the Supreme Court where the amount involved was less than £50 (*ibid*. 1088, 1089).

For other acts providing that removal to the Supreme Court should only be made on affidavits of reasonable cause, see 5 *ibid*. 304, 313. An Act of March 8, 1773, provided that "for the preventing great Vexation from suing out defective Writs of Error BE IT ENACTED . . . That upon the quashing any Writ of Error . . . for Variance from the Original Record or other Defect, the Defendant in such Writ of Error shall recover against the Plaintiff . . . his Costs as he should have had if the Judgment has been affirmed . . ." (*ibid*. 537, 542).

[125] *Mins. SCJ 1693–1701* 46, 48, 49, 51.

[126] *Mins. Westch. Ct. of Sess.* 1657–96 86 *et seq.*; *Mins. SCJ 1693–1701* 73, 81, 95, 106. The entire record on this case has fortunately been preserved in H.R. *Parch.* 209 C 8 and is as follows:

"PROVINCE OF NEW YORK ss.: MEMORANDUM that on the Sixth day of Aprill in the seaventh year of the Reigne of our Soveraigne Lord William the third by the Grace of God King of England Scotland ffrance and Ireland Defender of the Faith &c. Before William Smith Esqr. Cheife Justice William Pinhorne Esqr. Second Justice Coll Stephen Cortlandt and John Lawrence Esqr. Justices of his Matyes Supreme Court of Judicature for his Majesties Province of New York in America the Justices of the Sessions of the Peace in the County of Westchester in the said Province did returne his Majtyes writt of Errour to them directed together with the record and processe upon a certaine Indictment had moved and presented Before the said Justices of the Sessions att Westchester on the fifth and Sixth dayes of December in the fifth year of the reigne of Our Said Soveraigne Lord the King

two years later. Leggett had been presented on December 5, 1693 in Westchester County for feloniously stealing a hog and the defendant appearing "pleads in abatement of indictment for yt there wanted a sufficient addition in the indictment according to the statute, and the court advise about the same." Leggett finally "owns ye matter of fact but pleads ye act of general pardon for his relief," but the court was of the opinion that the act of general pardon had no relation to anything that happened prior to the time of the Jacob Leisler disorders. Leggett next claimed that the indictment was insufficient in law, that the prosecutor, Thomas Williams, who was sworn as a witness against Leggett in the hearing before the grand jury, had been convicted and attainted of high treason and was incapable of owning chattels. The Sessions Court sustained the indictment, and Leggett then sued out a writ of error. On April 6, and in October, 1695, we note from the Supreme Court records that the writ of error was continued and Nicoll on behalf of Leggett having filed "Errours in a judgment against him . . . prays a time of hearing." On October

against Gabriell Leggitt of the County and Town of Westchester Yeoman for felonously Stealing a certaine Barrow hogg belonging to Thomas Williams of the same place Yoeman of the Value of twelve pence which said writt of Errour and process and record aforesaid are in these words following (to witt) WILLIAM the third by the Grace of God King of England Scotland France and Ireland Defender of the Faith &c. to Our Justices of Our Court of Sessions of our County of Westchester Greeting Because in the Record and processe and alsoe in giving judgment of a Suite which was lately Before you at the Town of Westchester in the said County between us and Gabriel Leggitt of the County Town of Westchester Yeoman upon an indictment for his felonously Stealing a barrow hogg of the proper goods and chattells of Thomas Williams of the Value of one Shilling Errour manifest Doth appear to have intervened to the grievous damage of the said Gabriell Leggitt as of his Complaint we have received WEE, being willing that Errour if any there bee, beg in this Behalfe in due manner be corrected and speedy justice to the said Gabriell therein done as it becometh us Command you that if Judgement be thereupon Given the Record and processe of the Suite aforesaid and all things touching the same in any manner you have before Our Justices of Our Supreme Court of Judicature at New York The first Tuesday in Aprill next ensueing under your Seale So that our Justices of Our Said Supreme Court of Judicature may then there have the processe and Record aforesaid and all things touching the Same and being inspected may further doe therein what of right ought to be done WITNESSE our trusty and Wel beloved Coll. Benjamin Fletcher Our Captaine Generall and

Governour in Cheife of Our province of New York in America &c.—the Sixth day of December in the Sixth Year of Our Reigne—Jamison Westchester County ss: At a Court of Sessions held at Westchester for the County of Westchester by there Majesties authority December the fifth and Sixth 1695 present the Honorable Coll. Caleb Heathcote One of their Majesties Councill for the Province of New York Judge of the Court of Common Pleas and president of this Court of Sessions for the County aforesaid William Barnes Esqr. Justice of the peace and quorum Daniel Streinge John Hunt William Chadderton and Thomas Putney Esqr. Justice of the Peace &c. the jurors for Our Soveriagne Lord and Lady the King and Queen upon their Oaths doe present Gabriell Leggitt of the County Town of Westchester Yeoman haveing not the fear of God before his eyes and by the instigation of the Devill at or about the first day of November in the third year of the reigne of Our Soveriagne Lord and Lady the King and Queen that now is feloniously did Steale a certaine Barrow hogge of a white Spoted colour of the proper Goods and Chattels of Thomas Williams of the Towne aforesaid of the value of twelve pence and at Westchester aforesaid in the day and date aforesaid the said hogg did take and carry away which is contrary to the peace of Soveriagne Lord and Lady the King and Queen their Crown and dignity and the publique peace &c. and the Law in that case made and provided the above said Gabriell Leggitt being called to the barr and the above said indictment being publicly read the said Gabriell being required to plead to the Same Sayd that he owned the matter of fact contained therein and pleaded in barr to the Said Indictment the late act of Generall Assembly Entituled An Act for the

10, 1696, the following entry appears in the Supreme Court minutes: "In errour the Justices having considered the whole matter see cause to reverse the judgment and it is reversed accordingly."

On March 15, 1711/12, in the case of *Queen* v. *Soaper et al.*, a writ of error having been brought to the Supreme Court an order was made by that court that "the judgment in ye inferior court to be reversed." On October 16, 1713, however, the Supreme Court ordered that "unless ye defendants appear this term and enter into such recognizances as the court shall direct, a procedendo to be awarded to ye justices of ye peace for Suffolk County."[127]

In *Queen* v. *Polhemus*, brought into the Supreme Court on writ of error, an order was made on June 6, 1713, that the plaintiff bring up the transcript of the record and on October 16, 1713, the Supreme Court gave judgment that "the judgment in ye county court of Queens County . . . be reversed unless cause be shown to the contrary ye first day of next term upon notice of this

pardoning of Such as have been active in the late disorders whereupon the Court haveing fully weighed and perused the said act and it being Owned by the said Gabriell Leggitt that the fact in the indictment committed was done and acted in the time of Sir Edmund Androsse was Governour . . . THEREFORE To the Judgment of the Court that the matter of fact in the indictment committed doth not come within the benefite of the abovesaid act nor was thereby ever intended by the said act to be pardoned as the said Gabriell hath above pleaded Therefore it is considered by the Said Court that the said Gabriell Leggitt for the abovesaid Offence Shall pay the charges of the Court . . . and alsoe before two of their Sd Majestyes Justices of the Peace of the County give in sufficient Security for his *Good Behaviour* for one whole year and untill the abovesaid costs be paid and Security given as above the said Gabriell Leggitt to remaine a prisoner in the Sherriffes custody who is hereby ordered him safely to keep untill he have performed the same March the 28th 1695 A true copy taken out of the Court Rolls and truely Examined by one Joseph Lee And the said Gabriell Leggitt came in his propper person and saith that in the Record and processe aforesaid and alsoe in rendering of Judgment as aforesaid there is manifest Errour in this that is to Say that by the Record aforesaid it appears that the indictment aforesaid is viccous [*sic*] wants forme and is not sufficient in the Law to cause the Said Gabriel thereunto to answer therefore in this it is manifest Errour Also it is manifest Errour in that one Thomas Williams a person convicted and attainted of high Treason was admitted and sworne as a Wittnesse for the finding of the Bill against the said Gabriell therefore in that it is manifest Errour alsoe in this it is manifest Errour that in the said

indictment is sett forth that the said Gabriell at or about the first day of November in the third year of the reign of our Lord and Lady the King and Queen that now are did Steal a barrow hogg of the Goods and chattells of the said Thomas Williams Where the said Tho: Williams at that time Stood convicted and attainted of high Treason by the due course to the Law and thereby was incapacitated to be owner of any Goods and Chattells whatsoever and in this it is manifest Errour also it is manifest Errour in this that judgement thereupon was given and Entered against the said Gabriell Leggitt whereby the Law of the Land judgement ought to have been that the said Gabriell should goe quitt there without day and in this it is manifest Errour and thereupon the said Gabriell prayed that the judgement aforesaid for the Errours aforesaid and others in the Same Record contained may be Reversed annulled and utterly made void and that he to all that by reason of the Said Judgement he hath lost may be restored &c. [The record then recites adjournments. Then, on October 10, 1696] . . . before William Smith Esqr. Chief Justice and William Pinhorne Esqur. Second Justice &c. Justices of the Supreme Court of Judicature . . . [came] the said Gabriel Leggit in his own proper person and hereupon as well the Record and Process and Judgement of the Court of Sessions aforesaid as all and singular the Errours aforesaid by the said Gabriell Leggitt Alleaged and brought into Court being seen and heard also by the sd Court here fully understood upon mature consideration it appeareth to the said Justices that in the record & process aforesd . . . the Judgement . . . against sd Gabriel Leggit is manifest Errour therefore . . . the Judgement aforesaid for the Errour . . . is hereby reversed &c. . . . . sine die."

127 *Ms. Mins. SCJ 1710–14* 368, 493.

rule." On March 13, 1713/14, the Attorney General was ordered to join in error by the following term,[128] but there is no further record.

It is notable that this is the last instance where a Crown plea was brought by writ of error from an inferior court to the Supreme Court. So far as we are aware there was no adjudication on the propriety of error and it is probable that as transfer jurisdiction was well developed by 1715 it operated to make error proceedings unnecessary. It is also possible that the desire to conform with common law precedent was effective here, for although Salkeld's *Reports* in which *Paty's Case* (1704) was reported were widely used we have never seen this case cited by colonial lawyers in New York.[129]

In view of the general unavailability of a writ of error in criminal cases it is quite remarkable that practically no use was made of habeas corpus. In the eighteenth century English writers referred to this writ as in the nature of a writ of error,[130] but as the so-called Habeas Corpus Act was not deemed to apply to the colonies, the possibility of a free and generous employment of this remedy for purposes of testing the legality of a commitment after conviction was foreclosed. We have found only one early case approaching an error use of habeas corpus—that of Hendrick Fransa—but this was an attack on the form of a mittimus and cannot, therefore, be regarded as in the nature of a proceeding in error.[131] The other occasions where the writ was used appear by the records to have been for the purpose of transfer before trial or to compel bail.[132]

The very conservative policy of the New York judiciary both in respect of writ of error practice and the habeas corpus is still further exemplified by its initial attitude toward the use of certiorari for review, particularly of summary proceedings. It had been held by Holt, C.J., that when Parliament created a new jurisdiction and the court acted as a court of record, a writ of error would lie, but where the court proceeded summarily or in a manner different from the common law, a certiorari was proper.[133] This broad proposition, was, however, modified by the rule in other cases that certiorari would not be awarded after conviction in a criminal case except for some very special reason.[134]

---

[128] *Ms. Mins. SCJ 1710–14* 459, 495, 517; "Bickley's Dogget," *F. A. De Peyster Mss.* Box 2 no. 3B.

[129] There is, moreover, no evidence before the case of Forsey v. Cunningham of any attempt to develop an "appeal." But see the curious entry in *Ms. Mins. NYCQS 1694–1731/32* 84, Nov. 2, 1703, where one Thurman "appealed" to the Supreme Court from a commitment by the Chief Justice.

It should be noted further that error was often used in civil cases. Cf., for example, the references in *Evert Wendell's Account Book* fols. 45–191. For a sample of the writ of error in a civil case, cf. *H.R. Parch.* 102 D 9.

[130] 1 Hale, *Pleas of the Crown* 584; Bacon, *Abridgment s.v. Habeas Corpus* A.

[131] *Infra* 504 n. 76.

[132] *Supra* 155 n. 71.

[133] Groenvelt v. Burwell (1 *Salk.* 263).

[134] Reg. v. Porter (*ibid.* 149); Reg. v. Bothell (6 *Mod.* 17). Cf. King v. Baker (*Carthew* 6).

The New York courts appear to have been guided chiefly by this last rule in their employment of certiorari after conviction, but our evidence is not very conclusive for the record entries in many certiorari cases are not sufficiently full for any conclusions whether the writ was used for a transfer or review of a cause.[135] Only one felony case has been found where the Supreme Court used a certiorari after conviction.

Manas Carlan had on June 9, 1747, been sentenced to be hanged for murder at the Albany Court of Oyer and Terminer and General Gaol Delivery,[136] but a certiorari was issued out of the Supreme Court ordering that the justices of gaol delivery send up the record and judgment to the Supreme Court *en banc*. The certiorari was directed to Daniel Horsmanden and the other justices of gaol delivery and was in the form given below.[137] Horsmanden made his return to the certiorari, sending the record of the conviction and attainder. The record annexed indicated that an inquisition had been taken at Albany General Sessions on January 20, 1747, at which Carlan was accused of murder, and that afterwards at a Court of Gaol Delivery the justices of the peace delivered

---

135 Cf. the following: King v. Roger Barnes (*Ms. Mins. SCJ 1762–64* [Engr.] 65, 91, Oct. 30, 1762, Jan. 22, 1763 [from Richmond County]); King v. Hendrick Groatfelt (*Ms. Mins. SCJ 1769–72* [Engr.] 203, 294, 479, Apr. 28, Oct. 26, 1770, Jan. 25, 1772); King v. Michael Brannin (*Ms. Mins. SCJ 1764–66* [Engr.] 215, Aug. 1765); Queen v. Jacobus Van Cortlandt, Joseph Drake and Henry Fowler (*Ms. Mins. SCJ 1710–14* 509, 512, 521, 526, 531, Mar. 10, 11, 13, 1713/14, June 2, 5, 1714) and Bickley's docket (*F. A. De Peyster Mss.* no. 3B); King v. Andrew Lyon (*Ms. Mins. SCJ 1772–76* [Rough] 221, Jan. 21, 1775); King v. John Heugan *et al.* (*Ms. Mins. SCJ 1775–81* [Engr.] 45, Oct. 28, 1775); King v. T. Way (*Ms. Mins. SCJ 1754–57* [Engr.] 208, Jan. 1756); King v. Thomas Walton (*ibid.* 284, July 30, 1756); King v. Jacob Vrooman (*ibid.* 53, Aug. 3, 1754 [from Albany]); King v. William Parks (*ibid.* 124, Jan. 25, 1755); King v. William Van Neuys (*Ms. Mins. SCJ 1756–61* [Rough] 106, July 28, 1758); King v. County of Richmond (*ibid.* 56, Apr. 19, 1757); King v. Manuel Myers (*ibid.* 106, July 28, 1758); King v. Johannis Lansing (*Ms. Mins. SCJ 1732–39* 261, 272, Apr. 26, Aug. 2, 1737 [from Albany]); King v. Wate Hopkins (*Ms. Mins. SCJ 1762–64* [Engr.] 300, Oct. 29, 1763); King v. Thomas Forsey (*Ms. Mins. SCJ 1757–60* [Engr.] 284, Jan. 1760); King v. Richard Floyd and Richard Woodhul (*Ms. Mins. SCJ 1754–57* [Engr.] 324, Oct. 28, 1756); King v. Abraham De Peyster (*Ms. Mins. SCJ 1756–61* [Rough] 107, July 29, 1758). It will be noticed that some of the above cases were cited *supra* 159 n. 79 on the mechanics of certiorari practice which was in certain points

the same whether the writ was used for transfer or review.

In Queen v. Jacobus Stricker, a certiorari was returned and filed with the proceedings below in the Supreme Court on September 2, 1712, and on Sept. 6, 1712, the following Supreme Court minute entry appears: "The order of Sessions qualified" (*Ms. Mins. SCJ 1710–14* 401, 408, 416, Sept. 2, 4, 6, 1712).

Certiorari was of course also used to bring up the judgments in civil cases. For the form, cf. Haviland v. Elwell, Jan. 20, 1753 (*J. T. Kempe Lawsuits* G–J). Cf. also the certiorari in Sleght v. Ten Broeck (*H.R. Pleadings* Pl. S. 1411). Also see Supreme Court minutes for Jan. 18, 1775, where the return on a certiorari in the case of Griffiths v. Thorne was quashed (*Ms. Mins. SCJ 1772–76* [Rough] 216).

136 *Ms. Mins. Cir. 1721–49* 120, 121. Carlan was indicted at the Albany Quarter Sessions but since the crime was murder he was tried at Albany Oyer and Terminer and General Gaol Delivery. See *H.R. Parch.* 169 K 5.

137 "Wee willir ᵣor certain Causes to be certified of the record and judgment in your custody remaining by which Manas Carlan . . . is attainted of felony and murder Command you . . . that the record and judgment . . . before us . . . under your hands and Seals . . . you send together with this writ that further thereupon we may cause to be done what of Right and according to the Laws and Customs of . . . England and this our province of New York Witness James DeLancey Chief Justice" (*H.R. Parch.* 169 K 5).

the indictment by their own hands into the latter court as a court of record to be determined. Carlan, pleading not guilty, was tried and convicted. Unfortunately the Supreme Court minutes are missing for this year and the ultimate disposition of the case is not known.[138]

In the case of misdemeanors, the employment of certiorari seems to have depended chiefly upon the extent to which a specific English practice was well settled and thus well known. Thus we find the writ used for review of bastardy proceedings, which were summary, but unavailable in other summary proceedings for which there was no precedent at home. The most interesting situation of the latter category was the conviction under the famous colonial statutes of 1732 enacted to deal with vagrants and petty thieves. There are no examples of certiorari to review these proceedings, for the reason that the Special Sessions or meetings in such cases were not regarded as courts of record. We have found no direct adjudication on this point but the official view was set forth collaterally in a brief of the Attorney General in an assault case. The exclusion from review of cases under the 1732 statutes is so important that we must consider the circumstances in some detail, even though no question of review was directly involved.

John Lawrence Jr., Charles Arding, Cornelius Livingston and Henry Oudenarde had been informed against for assault and battery.[139] The facts as related by the prosecution were not nice. The Attorney General charged

> that John Lawrence . . . [and others] with force and Arms . . . upon One Mary Anderson . . . did make an Assault . . . To this the Defendts have pleaded Not Guilty and thereupon Issue is joined. Although this prosecution is no more than for an Assault, yet . . . it will appear to be . . . A Crime that deserves the severest Reprehension . . . Now to come the matter immediately relating to the Cause of this prosecution.

The Attorney General then proceeded to describe how these young men about town had attacked Mary Anderson.[140] "Upon the Discovery to her Mother of what had happened to her, her Mother brought her the same day to the Attorney General and . . . made a Complaint against the Defendts . . . and

---

[138] The certiorari, Horsmanden's return and the record annexed are to be found in *H.R. Parch.* 169 K 5.

[139] The Attorney General's brief is printed in the Appendix *infra* 786. The proceedings are in *Ms. Mins. SCJ 1754–57* (Engr.) 49, 53, 118, 125, 145, 146, Aug. 1, 3, 1754, Jan. 25, Apr. 18, 1755; *H.R. Pleadings* Pl. K. 650.

[140] The facts as set forth in *H.R. Pleadings* Pl. K. 501 give a remarkable picture of the brutal and abandoned behavior of the young bloods of the town. A similar complaint in another case (1753) involving Robert Livingston, Philip Phillip, Captain Thomas French and Captain Johnson is in *H.R. Parch.* 48 K 5.

prayed a prosecution against them." In the interim the defendants proceeded to arrange a "frame up."

> The Defendts said they would have them [i.e. Mary and her mother] whipped, and accused the Mother of buying stoln Goods, . . . And in order to draw her in to be guilty of these offences, that they might have a handle agt. her [defendants, with the aid of one Sullivan, succeeded in "planting" a petticoat on Mrs. Anderson] . . . And thereupon Sulivan . . . was encouraged by the Defendts. to prosecute Mrs. Anderson for stealing ye pettycoat upon the presumption of Theft, . . . But to take away this presumption Mary Anderson related and offered to prove how her Mother came by the pettycoat. . . . But the Recorder gave no Attention to it, told Mary Anderson of her prosecuting the Defendts and threatened her and ordered Mrs. Anderson to be whipt; And Arding and Lawrence gave the Executioner Money to whip her severely and she was whipped inhumanly till she fell several times into Convulsions. . . .

The Crown needed to meet the anticipated objection that Mrs. Anderson had become disqualified by reason of having suffered an infamous punishment. The Attorney General admitted that Hawkins in his *Pleas of the Crown* had stated a witness could be excepted to where a court with jurisdiction had adjudged such punishment but he insisted that no such conviction could be used to this purpose unless the record be actually produced in court.[141] He went on to say:

> But the Maior Recorder and Aldermen proceeding in a Summary way by Witnesses without a Jury, upon the Act of Assembly intitled an Act for the speedy punishing and releasing such persons from Imprisonmt as shall commit any criminal offence in the City and County of New York under the Degree of Grand Larceny, are *no Court of Record* [italics ours] and in the 2nd place had no power by Vertue of that Act of Assembly to order Mrs. Anderson to be whipt. For that Act gives them power only where a person shall commit an Offence under the Degree of Grand Larceny and being taken and committed to Gaol shall not within 48 hours give Bail to answer at ye Sessions then they may hear and determine the Offence, and the Offender being convicted by Confession or on the Oath of one or more credible Witnesses they may in their Discretion order such corporal punishment not extending to life or Limb as they shall think proper and discharge the offender. . . .

Despite the damaging character of the evidence, and unfortunately for the future security of virtue, the defendants were eventually acquitted.

141 2 Hawkins, *Pleas of the Crown* c.46 §§19, 20.

The employment of certiorari to review bastardy orders came about because the statute, 18 Elizabeth c.3, which had committed bastardy to secular authority was regarded as being in force in New York.[142] The statute provided for the support of the child and also for the punishment of the mother and father. If the parties failed to perform they were to be committed unless they put in security to perform or personally appeared at the next General Sessions. This latter procedure came to be known as an "appeal" although the statute did not use the expression. Since the practice of reviewing Sessions orders by certiorari was already in existence in Elizabeth's time this device was also applied to bastardy cases, the King's Bench being the proper forum. During the seventeenth century a considerable body of authority had developed on bastardy so that it was more or less inevitable the New York Supreme Court would follow English practice.

We do not know at what date certiorari first came to be used to review bastardy orders of the provincial Sessions Court. We may suppose the writ was here more frequently used than the records show, since we have so many unspecified certiorari entries in the court minutes.[143] The presence of particular forms in lawyers' precedent books is suggestive also of common use.[144] The first case found on the matter is *King* v. *Broadhurst* (1725) where the Sessions minute entry shows the succession of appeal and certiorari:

> The Defendant upon his appeal being bound to appear here to answer Relating to an Order made by Francis Harison and John Cruger Esqs for the Maintenance of a Bastard Child by him begot on Mekiora Norwood . . . Personally appears and by Council moves to quash the Order. Cur advisare . . . Ordered by the Court that an Order made by Francis Harison and John Cruger . . . whereof one is of the Quorum . . . be confirmed from the performance of which order the Defendant appealed to this Court . . . Murray pro Defendant produced his Majestys Writt of Certiorari for removing an order of this court . . . which was read and allowed and ordered Return be made thereof.

We note that the Supreme Court minutes contain the following entry on this case: "On motion of Murray for the defendant ordered that a certiorari issue to the justices of the peace of New York County to certify to this court an order made by them relating to bastardy."[145]

---

142 *Supra* 101.
143 *Supra* n. 135.
144 *Ms. Precedent Book Joseph Murray* 12; *Brevia Selecta (Van Cortlandt Mss.)* 34.

145 *Ms. Mins. NYCQS 1694–1731/32* 450, 452, 464, May 4, 5, Aug. 3, 1725, May 3, 1726; *Ms. Mins. SCJ 1723–27* 184, Mar. 14, 1725/26.

In view of modern agitation over judicial review of administrative acts it is interesting to observe how certiorari to review the bastardy orders was handled. The certiorari would be returned by the justices of the particular county[146] and a show cause order would issue to the defendant.[147] If the latter appeared the matter would then be argued[148] and the Supreme Court would either confirm or quash the order. In one late case, a *procedendo* was directed to issue.[149] Sometimes the order to show cause would be directed to town officers or overseers of the poor. So in *King v. Thomas Hemsted,* the town of Hempstead was ordered to show that the defendant had been duly summoned,[150] and in *King v. Martin Van Buren,*[151] the overseers of the manor of Rensselaer were ordered to show cause why the bastardy order should not be quashed.[152]

The certiorari was used also to review other types of Sessions orders, and notably in the matter of settlement. A few examples will suffice. On October 28, 1756, two justices of the peace were ordered to return a certiorari and on July 29, 1756, the "court having considered the two warrants or orders for transporting . . . [a pauper] from Brookhaven out of this province and the

146 E.g., King v. Brewerton (*Ms. Mins. SCJ 1754–57* [Engr.] 276, 284, 298, 319, 328, 354, Apr. 29, July 30, 31, Oct. 28, 1756, Jan. 21, 1757; *Ms. Mins. SCJ 1757–60* [Engr.] 24, Apr. 1757; *Ms. Mins. SCJ 1756–61* [Rough] 59, 63, 74, Apr. 20, 23, July 29, 1757); cf. also the Orange County case (*Ms. Mins. SCJ 1769–72* [Engr.] 491, 513, 534; *Ms. Mins. SCJ 1772–76* [Rough] 27); King v. Van Buren (*H.R. Parch.* 25 D 5, *Ms. Mins. SCJ 1775–81* [Engr.] 95, Apr. 27, 1776).
On October 18, 1757, Zachariah Snyder appeared in the Supreme Court and on Jan. 20, 1758, two justices of the peace of Ulster certified that they could not return the order of bastardy mentioned in the certiorari because the clerk refused to deliver it to them. The court therefore ordered the clerk to deliver the bastardy order to the justices or show cause. On April 24, the order, evidently being returned, was confirmed by the Supreme Court (*Ms. Mins. SCJ 1757–60* [Engr.] 77, 87, 92, 93, 95, 97, 102, 112, 128, Oct. 18, 1757, Jan. 17, 20, Apr. 18–20, 22, 24, Oct. 17, 1758).
147 King v. Brewerton (*supra* n. 146); King v. James Thorn (*Ms. Mins. SCJ 1756–61* [Rough] 74, 82, July 29, Aug. 24, 1757; *Ms. Mins. SCJ 1757–60* [Engr.] 46, 89, 119, July 1757, Jan. 1758, Apr. 1758).
148 King v. Brewerton (*supra* n. 146); and the Orange County case there cited (*Ms. Mins. SCJ 1769–72* [Engr.] 534). King v. Cornelius Van Ransen in bastardy where it was ordered that the defendant plead by the next term (*Ms. Mins. SCJ 1757–60* [Engr.] 357, Aug. 1760). Also see King v. Cornelius Van Hoesen where on July 31, 1756, a certiorari was returned and filed and on Jan. 21,

1761, the defendant was ordered to argue on the order in bastardy (*ibid.* 295; *Ms. Mins. SCJ 1756–61* [Rough] 218). But in King v. Henry Heermans, on Oct. 30, 1762, the Supreme Court ordered that this defendant be precluded from arguing against the order in bastardy and that the said order stand confirmed (*Ms. Mins. SCJ 1762–64* [Engr.] 28).
149 King v. Robert Boys (*Ms. Mins. SCJ 1772–76* [Rough] 27).
150 *Ms. Mins. SCJ 1754–57* (Engr.) 284, 285, July 29, 30, 1756; *Ms. Mins. SCJ 1757–60* (Engr.) 78, Oct. 1757.
151 *Supra* n. 146.
152 On the practice see also the following cases: King v. Gilbert Williams where an order of bastardy was on April 19, 1770, confirmed in the Supreme Court, but at the same time, on reading the affidavits of the defendants, the court ordered that the justices who made the return to the certiorari show cause by the first day of the following term why an information should not be filed against them (*Ms. Mins. SCJ 1769–72* [Engr.] 159, 175, 176, Jan. 20, Apr. 19, 1770).
In King v. James Leggett a certiorari was returned and filed in Oct. 1754 on a bastardy order, and on Jan. 24, 1756 it was ordered that the order of bastardy against the defendant be quashed for the exceptions made against it in the Supreme Court (*Ms. Mins. SCJ 1754–57* [Engr.] 91, 230). In King v. Joseph Hunt, return of orders in bastardy were filed in the Supreme Court on Oct. 17, 1739 (*Ms. Mins. SCJ 1732–39* 360). King v. Dance (*Ms. Mins. SCJ 1732–39* 338, 341, Apr. 20, 23, 1739).

other made by the defendants for bringing him back Ordered the last warrant be quashed."[153] And again in the case of the unhappy Nancy Smith who had been shuttled about the county of Ulster as a vagrant the record was brought up by certiorari for review.[154] In 1758 three justices of the peace of Richmond County returned a certiorari and were ordered to show cause why their return for stopping up a road in Richmond County should not be quashed. In April, 1759, the order to show cause was set aside and the defendants discharged.[155]

One gains the impression from the records that in the years immediately prior to the Revolution the certiorari was coming to be employed with greater frequency. A case arising under one of the curious quasi-penal statutes of the province illustrates how lawyers were attempting to loosen old restrictions.

An assembly act of 1744[156] had provided that if any dogs killed sheep, the owners of such dogs were liable to the sheep owners for the full value of the sheep, recoverable before any one justice of the peace fully empowered to hear and finally determine the case, and on non-payment within three days after judgment, a warrant would issue to the constable to distrain the offender's goods, and on *nihil habet* to commit the dog owner to jail for ten days unless paid. Right was given to plaintiff or defendant to have a six-man jury, and the dog owner was to kill the dog in forty-eight hours or be liable to the further penalty of 20s. recoverable before one justice of the peace empowered to finally determine the same, and the penalty payable to the person who would sue for the same.

Joseph Green came before Jacobus Terboss, a justice of the peace of Dutchess County, complaining against John Cooper in a plea of trespass claiming damages of £10, and prayed process. The justice of the peace, in pursuance of the above recited act, issued a summons ordering the constable to command John Cooper to appear and answer Joseph Green in a plea of trespass on the case.

<hr />

[153] *Ms. Mins. SCJ 1754–57* (Engr.) 324, 352, Oct. 28, 1756, Jan. 21, 1757; *Ms. Mins. SCJ 1756–61* (Rough) 74, July 29, 1757.

[154] *Supra* 128.

[155] *Ms. Mins. SCJ 1756–61* (Rough) 81, Oct. 24, 1757; *Ms. Mins. SCJ 1757–60* (Engr.) 120, 190, 213, Apr. 1758, Jan. 1759, Apr. 1759. Also see King v. Michael Jackson, Dan Cooley Jr. and Peter Kykendal, commissioners of the highways of Minisink, where the defendants were ordered to show cause why attachments should not issue against them, evidently for failure to return a certiorari on a road order (*ibid.* 171, Apr. 24, 1755); King v. John Willet Jr., where a certiorari and return on a road order were filed in the Supreme Court by Whitehead Hicks on Oct. 16, 1765 (*Ms.*

Mins. SCJ 1764–66 [Engr.] 107; *J. T. Kempe Lawsuits* L–O *sub nom.* Nordstrandt).

In King v. Roger Barnes and Richard Conner, on July 28, 1773, the Supreme Court, on reading the affidavit of Samuel Ward, ordered that the defendants show cause by next term why an information should not be filed against them for convicting Samuel Ward for stopping up the road mentioned in the said affidavit without summoning him to make his defense (*Ms. Mins. SCJ 1772–76* [Rough] 95). The latter case would seem to have been one where instead of bringing up the case on certiorari, a complaint for an information was made against the justices of the peace.

[156] 3 *Col. Laws NY* 402.

The constable returned the summons and the defendant appeared. The plaintiff complained that Cooper's dog had killed two sheep and two lambs and the defendant by way of plea alleged that he was not chargeable because the sheep were not killed by his dog. Issue was joined and, no jury being demanded, the justice of the peace heard the case and adjudged that the plaintiff should recover 12*s.* damages. Then the justice of the peace issued his warrant of execution to the constable.

The defendant obtained a certiorari from the Supreme Court and swore that he had served the writ on the justice of the peace. The justice of the peace returned the certiorari and the record, and recited the case. John Tabor Kempe, acting as attorney for the appellant, argued to quash the proceedings, claiming that this was a certiorari for a wrong judgment, and therefore the Supreme Court should have the grounds of judgment delivered up: "This being a special power to commit in a summary way, contrary to the common law, nothing shall be presumed in favor of the proceedings, but the intendment will be against it. 1 Burns Justice, 330, 31." Kempe argued that this was a penal law contrary to the common law, since dogs were not accustomed to bite sheep. He further argued that even though it were not penal law, the same reasons which compel a return of the evidence on convictions on penal laws apply here, namely, that the Court of King's Bench may judge of its sufficiency. Finally he claimed the execution was bad since it was for debt, although the declaration and summons were for trespass on the case.[157] The case was presumably compromised, for the Supreme Court minutes do not show any final ruling.

Another unusual use of certiorari was in the case of *Deree v. the Trustees of Brookhaven,* where a motion was made to quash the proceedings before a justice of the peace. On December 27, 1686, Dongan's charter constituted the trustees of Brookhaven as a body politic; on November 27, 1768, a local by-law provided that oysters might not be caught in certain seasons or places. Deree caught oysters contrary to the by-law and having made no defense was found guilty by a single justice of the peace who fined the defendant 20*s.* On April 29, 1769, the justice of the peace was ordered to return the certiorari in this

[157] J. T. *Kempe Lawsuits* C–F *sub nom.* Green v. Cooper. The certiorari in this case was in the following form: "Greeting We being willing for certain causes to be certified of a certain Plaint or Action before you made [in Cooper v. Green] . . . Therefore we command you the said Plaint . . . and Judgment . . . with all . . . proceedings . . . in as full and ample Manner as possible as the same remain before you to us under your Seal you distinctly and openly send together with this Writ So that we may have the same before us in our Supreme Court for . . . New York [in October] . . . that upon View thereof we may further cause to be done therein that which of right and according to Law ought to be done Witness Daniel Horsmanden Esquire Our Chief Justice August 4, 1770 Clarke" Kempe Attorney

(*H.R. Parch.* 23 H 5; see also *ibid.* 24 G 1, 80 K 10, 80 E 10; cf. also the following acts of assembly: 2 *Col. Laws NY* 735, 667; 3 *ibid.* 402).

cause. Judging from a paper in the Kempe manuscripts a motion was made to quash the proceedings on the ground that there was no showing that the trustees had been elected by proper authority and that the by-law was bad since it gave costs. It was also alleged that the justice was a party interested. We do not know the subsequent disposition of the case.[158] It is possible that settlement was made out of term in chambers. To all appearances the habeas corpus cases[159] were thus dealt with and we have one exhibit on the quashing of a justices' order, by Lewis Morris, C.J., and Robert Walter, J., issued in chambers in 1722. Nicholas Schoonover had been fined £8 and costs for obstructing the sheriff of Ulster. "This was ordered on bare complaint without tryall." On certiorari, counsel was heard for both Schoonover and the justices and the order to quash was then made.[160]

If the cases just cited illustrate a tendency on the part of the lawyers to experiment with certiorari, the acts of assembly in 1765 and after[161] indicate a desire to restrict review and to make final the proceedings of inferior courts. It may be inferred from the language of these acts that the American passion for appealing cases was already inflamed but, from what we know of the capacities of certain justices of the peace, not unjustifiably so. Since more and more of the detail of law enforcement was committed to Sessions and to justices, it was inevitable that a means of checking stupidity or arbitrary action should be sought, and the certiorari was the device best adapted to this end.

Review Jurisdiction of Sessions

The appellate powers committed to Sessions were attenuated, and for the most part were concerned with the review of orders made by single or double justices. The origin of these powers has never been explored, but they were in existence in the sixteenth century. During the eighteenth century in England they formed a most important part of the Sessions jurisdiction,[162] and the manner of their exercise gave rise to much criticism. Indeed, even in the reign of Charles II the editor of Dalton (1677) was moved to speak a word of warning regarding the reversal of orders respecting bastardy and settlement.[163] The jurisdiction was *sui generis* in that it embraced not only administrative orders, as in the case of settling paupers, but quasi-penal orders as in bastardy and

[158] J. T. Kempe Lawsuits C–F sub nom. Deree; Ms. Mins. SCJ 1769–72 (Engr.) 55. See also various acts of the colonial assembly regulating the digging of oysters (1 Col. Laws NY 845; 2 ibid. 655, 1068).
[159] Infra 506. Costs were taxed in chambers.
[160] Ms. Files Ulster Co. Bundle L. This is a parchment and is badly faded.
[161] Supra 257 n. 124.
[162] 1 Webb, English Local Government; The Parish and the County 420, 437, 438.
[163] Dalton, Countrey Justice (1677) 538.

commitments under the summary powers of single justices. The common law judges seem to have been puzzled by the procedure, for in *Pridgeon's Case*[164] a Sessions order was referred to as being as final as an order by the Lord Keeper, an analogy which suggests they had difficulty in describing the jurisdiction in common law terms.

The English practice was imitated in New York probably from the beginning. We have seen how the Duke's Laws required confirmation at Sessions of town orders,[165] and there is at least one early case where a judicial order of these bodies is of record.[166] There have remained too few early justices' orders for us to form any further conclusions.

During the eighteenth century the appeal practice in bastardy cases becomes a usual part of Sessions jurisdiction, as the certiorari cases already cited indicate. This supervisory jurisdiction is not always clearly an appeal, especially in the early eighteenth century, for it appears from the minute books that the defendant would make an appearance at the Sessions when the order and recognizance were delivered and the court would then either confirm or quash. In two cases the woman appeared as a complainant[167] and the order was then examined; and on Long Island toward the end of the colonial period the overseers of the poor sometimes appeared as complainants to secure confirmation.[168] In one unusual case in Orange County, counsel for the defendant appeared with a certiorari,[169] and the justices decided to set aside the previous confirmation and ordered a new hearing.[170]

---

164 *Croke Car.* 341, 350.

165 *Supra* 37 n. 184.

166 1 *Huntington Town Recs.* 185. It will be recalled that in the period after the conquest the town officials handled part of the work done by single and double justices in England. There are, of course, numerous minutes of such orders.

167 Sarah Golding v. Nathl. Lewis (*Ms. Mins. Queens Co. Sess. 1722–87* May 19, 1724); Hannah Read v. Isaac Reads (*ibid.* May 18, 1725).

168 Hempstead v. Rayner, Hempstead v. Mitchell (*ibid.* May 21, 1766); Hempstead v. Hopkins (*ibid.* Sept. 17, 1771); Jamaica v. Lane (*ibid.* May 19, 1772); Southold Overseers v. Wells (*Ms. Mins. Suffolk Co. Sess. 1766–75* Oct. 1767).

169 King v. John Wood (*Ms. Mins. Orange Co. Sess. 1727–79* Apr. 1754).

170 For other examples which are typical of Sessions proceedings, cf. King v. Barhuyt (*Ms. Mins. Albany Co. Sess. 1763–82* Oct. 4, 1765); King v. Gunsale (*ibid.* Jan. 22, 1772, June 4, 1772); King v. Peter P. Bogert and King v. Peter Swart (*ibid.* Oct. 6, 1773); King v. Malhorn (*ibid.* Oct. 7, 1774); King v. Doolittle (*ibid.* Jan. 18, 1774); King v. Wolfram (*ibid.* Jan. 18, 1776); King v.

Hoff (*Ms. Mins. Dutchess Co. Sess.* Liber A, May 15, 1739); King v. Martin Eberle (*ibid.* May 17, 1743); King v. Joseph Muncey (*ibid.* May 21, 1745); King v. William Parks (*ibid.* Liber B, May 21, 1754); King v. James Thoner (*ibid.* Oct. 19, 1756); King v. Ed. Terry (*ibid.* Liber F, Oct. 8, 1773); King v. James Little (*Ms. Mins. Orange Co. Sess. 1727–79* Oct. 25, 1737); King v. De Kay (*ibid.* Oct. 1747); King v. Brooks (*Ms. Mins. Queens Co. Sess. 1722–87* Sept. 21, 1742); King v. Guildersleeve (*ibid.* May 21, 1751); King v. Batty (*ibid.* May 25, 1755); King v. Thomas May (*ibid.* Sept. 16, 1755); King v. Gilbert Lawrence (*ibid.* May 19, 1767); King v. Daniel Tremaine (*Ms. Mins. Richmond Co. Sess. 1710/11–1744/45* Mar. 17, 1729/30); King v. Merril (*ibid.* Sept. 24, 1743); King v. Obadiah Smith (*Ms. Mins. Suffolk Co. Sess. 1723–51* May 29, 1743); King v. Negric (*ibid.* Mar. 25, 1751); King v. Leak (*Ms. Mins. Suffolk Co. Sess. 1760–75* Oct. 4, 1763); King v. John Miller (*ibid.* Oct. 1, 1765); King v. Brewster (*ibid.* Oct. 6, 1772, Oct. 5, 1775); King v. Rosekrans (*Ms. Mins. Ulster Co. Sess. 1737–50* Nov. 1, 1737, May 2, 1738).

The country minute books which bulge with bastardy cases are not lucid on the procedure which was followed in the so-called appeals. It appears, however, from a late case that license to appeal had to be obtained. Thus on January 21, 1773, an order in bastardy was made against Martin Van Buren by Rensselaer Nicoll and Killian Van Rensselaer, one of whom was of the quorum, on the complaint of Cornelius Schuyler and Andrus Houck and on the oath of Tishe Schermerhorn, the mother. The justices of peace found that the woman was delivered of a male bastard, that the said child was chargeable to the district and that Martin Van Buren "did beget the said bastard . . . on the body of . . . Tishe Schermerhorn." The justices of peace furthermore found that Van Buren was not able to show that he was not the father, and therefore ordered him "as well for the better relief of the said district as for the sustentation and relief of the said bastard child" to pay to the overseers of the poor £5 toward the lying-in of the said Tishe Schermerhorn and the maintenance of the said child, and as well he was to pay 3s. a week toward keeping the child until it should be no longer chargeable to the district.[171] On January 19, 1773, Van Buren prayed license of the General Sessions of the Peace of Albany to appeal to that court from an order of bastardy made against him by the two justices of peace. The appeal was allowed

and the same with the said order filed and entered in the clerk's office of the said court of record . . . and the said Martin Van Buren on such his appeal prayed of the said court that the same order by reason of being defective bothe in form and substance might be quashed but because the said court now here to give their judgment . . . are not yet advised, day therefore is given . . . [at which day came the said Van Buren] whereupon on all . . . the premises being seen and . . . understood and considered . . . the said court ordered the following amendments to be made in the said order . . . [several words were changed] which said amendments were accordingly made Whereupon it seems to the said court that the Order aforesaid and the matter therein contained are good and sufficient in law Wherefore it is considered by the said court now here that the same order be confirmed and it is thereupon ordered . . . that the said defendant . . . stand committed until he obey the said order of bastardy so confirmed.[172]

It was also possible on occasion to obtain a rehearing of appeal as another late case shows. On May 28, 1773, two justices of the peace of Albany made a bastardy order against Peter P. Bogert causing him to pay 3s. a week for the

[171] H.R. Parch. 25 D 5. Cf. Ms. Mins. Albany Co. Sess. 1763–82 Jan. 22, 1773, June, 1773.

[172] H.R. Parch. 25 D 5. See supra 265 for the certiorari on this order to the Supreme Court.

maintenance of his bastard. This order was at first quashed in General Sessions, but afterward the Court of General Sessions "proceeded to reconsider the judgment so given . . . and . . . ordered the following amendment in the said order . . . that the words 'relief of the said district of Albany as for the sustentation and' be added . . . whereupon it was considered by the said court that the said order be confirmed." A certiorari was on April 30, 1774, directed to the Court of General Sessions of Albany ordering that court to certify the order against Bogert and to return the orders "with all things . . . concerning the same as fully . . . as the same before you remain" together with the writ.[173] On April 27, 1776, on motion of Yates for the defendant, the overseers of the poor of the district of Albany were to show cause by the following term why the order of bastardy brought up by certiorari should not be quashed.[174]

The appeals in bastardy cases, which come to be very numerous, are curious affairs because they are essentially an equitable proceeding in a common law court. Defendants, especially when they were prominent persons who had had mistaken ideas about the *droit de seigneur,* were often represented by counsel, for although no grievous social stigma attached to the production of what was delicately called a "by blow" the matter of financial support was more uncomfortable. It was when counsel appeared that battles over form or amount would ensue. But the court would also take evidence—a procedure which indicates the equitable character of the review—and would permit matter to be offered for scaling down the allowance. This, as a rule, was a miserable and nearly standard pittance—a sort of minimum wages of sin. Nevertheless, exertion to shift the onus on the rate payers was constant and sometimes even successful.

It does not appear that the New York Sessions Courts interfered with justices' orders to the extent that prevailed in England. Various statutes specifi-

---

[173] *H.R. Parch.* 146 K 3 contains the original bastardy order, the Quarter Sessions decision and the certiorari. Cf. also *Ms. Mins. Albany Co. Sess. 1763–82* Oct. 6, 1773.

[174] *Ms. Mins. SCJ 1775–81* (Engr.) 95. In Queen v. Garret Onclebagg, the defendant appeared in New York City Quarter Sessions on Feb. 7, 1710/11, and prayed discharge from his recognizance for the care of his bastard and it appearing to the court that the said bastard was dead, he was ordered to be discharged from his recognizance on paying to the churchwardens £3 for the maintenance and burying of the said child (*Ms. Mins. NYCQS 1694–1731/32* 65).
We have also seen in the *Ms. Mins. NYCQS*

1721/22–1743 (Rough) 327, authorization "to set aside an order for the maintenance of a Bastard Child Crook Carolus 436 Salter ver Brown—Stat 18 Eliz.—7th James Chap. 4—Nelson's Justice 79 —Styles Reports 14.386—2d Keeble's Report 349—Cumberback's Report 103, the King agt. Colbert—Blackerbies Justice 39—Nelson's Justice 82."
An act of assembly of 1774 providing for the relief of parishes from bastards provided that any one or more justices of peace might commit a putative father to appear at Quarter Sessions to confirm such orders as were there made in pursuance to the Act of Parliament passed in the 18th year of Queen Elizabeth. The act prescribed very minutely the procedure which should be followed.

cally denied the right of appeal;[175] in other instances, such as the 1709 act to enforce the payment of liquor excise,[176] the 1772 act against private lotteries[177] and the poor relief statute of 1773, appeals were permitted.[178] The jurisdiction was, in any event, exercised with sufficient frequency to call forth an act in 1772[179] requiring justices to determine appeals according to the merits of the case, notwithstanding defects in form in the original proceedings.

Any discussion of appellate procedure at common law is incomplete without some consideration of the several devices which had grown up to remedy the hardships which the restricted employment of writ of error made inevitable. The most important of these palliatives were the motion in arrest of judgment and the motion for a new trial. Only the first of these was freely used in the colonies, but there are not adequate data for comparison with English practice since, as Lord Mansfield pointed out, the old reports "do not give accounts of determinations made by the courts upon motions."[180]

Motion in Arrest of Judgment

The motion in arrest was made possible by the rule in King's Bench that four days were to elapse between the verdict and the sentence,[181] and by the circumstance that the formula for judgment required asking the defendant whether he had anything to say why judgment should not be pronounced.[182] In trial at Assizes the motion could be made there immediately upon conviction, and it could also be made at bar in the proceedings before judgment after the *postea* had been delivered. In New York colony, where the bench at a particular Circuit was preponderantly lay, it was of considerable benefit to defendants that the opportunity existed for making motions before the court *en banc* if the trial was at nisi prius.

The motion in arrest appears for the first time in a Crown case involving an information for breach of the navigation laws, *Brooke qui tam* v. *Barquenteen Orange*. On October 2, 1694, Graham, on behalf of the King, moved for judgment in the Supreme Court of Judicature against the barquentine *Orange* "if noe person appear to Defend her." The court ordered that if no one appeared

---

[175] 1 *Col. Laws NY* 346 (1695); 2 *ibid.* 229 (1724); 5 *ibid.* 378 (1772) succeeded by *ibid.* 471 (1773).
[176] 1 *ibid.* 664, 665.
[177] 5 *ibid.* 352.
[178] *Ibid.* 514.

[179] *Ibid.* 357, 785.
[180] Bright v. Eynon, 1757 (1 *Burr.* 390 at 394).
[181] 2 Hawkins, *Pleas of the Crown* c.48 §1.
[182] Rex v. Speke (*Comberbach* 144); Batsomb's Case [Anonymous] (3 *Mod.* 265).

on the following day to defend, judgment should pass. On October 3, 1694, Cornelius Jacobs (the owner) evidently appeared, for we note his name in the title of the case and we also note that the Attorney General on his motion was granted a *tales*. Emott, on behalf of Jacobs, moved that Mr. John Morris should not be on the jury "& offers to prove prejudice." Morris was set aside, another *tales* was granted on the Attorney General's motion, and the jury was sworn, as well as the defendant's and informant's witnesses. On October 5, 1694, the jury gave in a written and sealed verdict finding for the informant, and "Nicoll pr Defte moves in arrest of Judgment." On October 6, "Emott pr Defte moves the causes of arrest be heard," and "Graham, Attorney Genll demurrs to the reasons of arrest of Judgement. Arguments heard. Curia avisare vult in postmeridiem." The court later that day put the case over for the following term. On April 2, 1695, Graham prayed that judgment might be given but Emott, on behalf of the defendant, "prays a rule for refreshing the argumt." On the following day the arguments on both sides were heard in the Chief Justice's chambers, and on April 6, 1695, the court gave judgment for the informant according to the verdict.[183]

The next Crown case where the motion was used concerned a suit on a bond, if we may judge from the very meager information we have on the case. On April 7, 1699, the sheriff of Ulster County was ordered to bring the body of one DeMeyer into court the last day of the term. On October 2, 1700, the defendant DeMeyer was ordered to plead, Cosens having appeared for the Crown and Tuder appearing for the defendant. On October 4, 1700, Tuder, on behalf of the defendant, pleaded *nihil debet*.[184] On October 7, 1701, the defendant was ordered to be prepared for trial at the next adjournment of the court, which was to be about six weeks hence, but on November 27, 1701, the defendant having made an affidavit that "material evidences are wanting," the case was put over for trial the following term. On April 10, 1702, Cosens, on behalf of the King, moved for a *tales* which was granted. The jurors, witnesses and constables having been sworn, "the Jury find for the King £217, 10s. 10d. and costs." At this point Tuder, on behalf of the defendant, "moves in arrest of Judgmt," and was ordered to file his reasons the following day, but the next day the court entered its judgment in accordance with the jury's verdict.[185]

[183] *Mins. SCJ 1693–1701* 59, 62, 63, 65, 68, 73.   [185] *Ms. Mins. SCJ 1701–04* 11, 27, 54, 58, 61.
[184] *Ibid.* 157, 160, 204, 210.

In neither of these two cases is there any indication of the reasons offered in arrest. Such are available for the first time in the great treason case, *King* v. *Bayard*.

After the jury had retired and it was found they could not agree they were sent for. The foreman requested some direction respecting notes he had taken on the evidence. The Chief Justice declined to do this but said if the jury were under any doubt whether the matters alleged in the indictment and which were proved were treason, they could find the prisoner guilty, because he had his advantage in moving in arrest. This remark drew forth the liveliest protest from counsel, and after a bitter exchange with the bench the jury again were sent out and later brought in the verdict of guilty.

Counsel for the defendant at once asked time to offer reasons in arrest of judgment and were directed to do so the next day.[186] According to the report in Howell's *State Trials* two reasons were urged: 1) that no overt act was proved as required by 7 Wm. III c.3; 2) if the overt act as alleged were admitted to be proved, neither by the act of assembly nor the law of England could any of the overt acts amount to treason. Atwood remarked that he could answer these offhand but would permit argument. This took place on March 11. As to the first reason, the Chief Justice decided this had been settled by the verdict. Emott for the prisoner proceeded to argue the second point and then offered the further reasons: 1) that two of the jury were aliens; 2) that the venire in the precept was wrongly awarded, or "rather not awarded at all"; 3) that the precept was not returned by the sheriff and not endorsed and signed contra to the laws of England and the Statute of York 12 Ed. II c.5. The Chief Justice then stated that what the Solicitor General had offered was sufficient to overrule the reasons exhibited, but before formally making a decision allowed a motion to offer other reasons *ore tenus*. On March 16 the argument was resumed, but it consisted only in a further pressing of the three last reasons offered which Emott elaborated with great show of learning.

In the 1702 New York edition of the printed account of the Bayard trial,[187] a third reason in arrest of judgment is presented which does not appear in the 1703 London or any subsequent editions. This was as follows:

That the Special Commission of Oyer and Terminer (to which he humbly refers) whereupon this Court had proceeded is expressly limited. On the 19th

---

[186] 14 Howell, *State Trials* 506 *et seq.*

[187] This is in the British Museum C.71 g.4 (old number $\frac{515 \text{ K } 17}{4}$) p. 33. Cf. also *infra* 312.

of February to enquire of whatsoever Treasons &c. committed by the Prisoner and John Hutchins and on the said day to make Enquiry upon the Premises and all and singular the Premises to hear and determine Which hath not been performed accordingly: so that both the enquiry and the hearing and determining, has and of necessity must be after the expiration of the said Commission.

It was insisted that since the commission was limited to February 19, whatever had since been done was *coram non judice*. Two cases from Plowden's reports were cited in support, but the Solicitor General replied that a day in law was not construed according to the "vulgar acceptation or literal sense," but according to legal understanding. The motion in arrest was overruled and the prisoner sentenced.

The manuscript minute entries on the Bayard case are interesting in connection with the reasons offered in arrest of judgment and support the contentions of the defendant, despite Atwood's statement in his account of the trial.[188] On February 19, 1701/02, the special commission of oyer and terminer was read, the court was opened by proclamation and the grand jury was called, two being absent. The grand jury was sworn and the charge was given to them. On February 20, 1701/02, the grand jurors were listed and a note was placed opposite the names of eight of the grand jurors as follows: "The 8 above marked said they did not find the bill for Treason." At 4 P.M. that day four of the grand jurors were ordered to be "discharged . . . for refusing to observe the Charge given them by the Bench," and at 7 P.M. the grand jury presented Bayard and Hutchins for high treason. On March 2, 1701/02, Nicoll on behalf of the prisoners moved that the presentment be quashed, but his motion was overruled, and the defendants pleaded not guilty, putting themselves on God and the country. On March 7 the Attorney General was called and when he failed to appear, the court found "that the Attorney General does neglect his duty." Col. Bayard's petition was read (evidently the petition mentioned in the printed account of the trial but not quoted in the minutes of the court). However, the court found that the grand jury "did find the Bill by above the number of 12." On March 9, 1701/02, the jury was asked whether they had agreed upon a verdict, but they replied in the negative, asking for some directions from the court, which were given. The jury then found the prisoner Bayard guilty and "the prisoner moves in arrest of Judgment. Ordered that the reasons be offered tomorrow morning." Two witnesses were then sworn and evidently on their testimony the court made the following

[188] For the Atwood account of the trial, see 13 *NYHS Colls.* 243 *et seq.*

finding: "It does appear to this court that a paper was some way given to the Jury by Johannes Cortlandt and that a paper was found with ye jury which paper was against finding the bill and that Johannes Cortlandt was one of them that was dismissed from the grand jury." On the following day, that is, on March 10, reasons were offered in arrest of judgment, but on March 11, the reasons in arrest of judgment were argued and overruled. On March 16, the "second reasons in arrest . . . argued and over-ruled." The Solicitor General thereupon moved for judgment against the prisoner, and judgment of death was pronounced against him. On March 27 and 28, Hutchins was tried and found guilty of treason, and "Atwood [probably the Chief Justice's son] p. prisoner moves for arrest of judgment." The Hutchins case was adjourned from March 30 to April 6 because Hutchins was ill, but on the latter date sentence of death was passed upon the prisoner.[189]

We have discussed at length the proceedings in the Bayard case for they afford the most complete available data on the procedure where a motion in arrest was made. For the most part the minute entries of the Supreme Court record only that a motion was made. The practice came to be settled that the reasons be filed and the court would then give a day for the argument.[190] In some instances when judgment had been stayed the argument on arrest was put over until the following term.[191] It is interesting to note that in one of these cases[192] the prisoner personally offered his reasons in arrest and the court assigned counsel to argue for the prisoner.

The motion in arrest was used also to enable the defendants to plead a pardon. Thus Samuel and Ephraim Rose appeared on recognizance at Suffolk Oyer and Terminer and General Gaol Delivery on June 27, 1728, and were on June 28 presented for petit larceny. Ephraim was found not guilty and discharged, while the "jury find Samuel Rose guilty of the petty larceny." How-

[189] Ms. Mins. SCJ 1701–04 40–50.
[190] Cf. King v. Rayner et al., 1753 (Ms. Mins. SCJ 1750–56 [Rough] 137, 151, 306, 317; Ms. Mins. SCJ 1750–54 [Engr.] 286); King v. Ferris, 1755 (Ms. Mins. SCJ 1750–56 [Rough] 169, 258, 267, 273); King v. Peter Clewes et al., 1765–67 (Ms. Mins. SCJ 1764–67 [Rough] 47, 62, 110, Apr. 16, 23, Oct. 17, 1765; Ms. Mins. SCJ 1764–66 [Engr.] 107, Jan. 1767; Ms. Mins. SCJ 1764–67 [Rough] 245, May 2, 1767). Cf. H.R. Parch. 58 D 1. For the demurrers by the defendant, see H.R. Pleadings Pl. K. 833, 850. H.R. Pleadings Pl. K. 733 contains "Kempe's rules, April 16, 1765. Peter Clewes and Christopher Snedeker. Roll filed. Ordered to be made a concilium and defendant argue his demurrer next term. Paper books to Judge."

Later (April 23) Scott for defendant filed reasons in arrest. King v. Keyser, 1767–68, where the defendant had pleaded guilty to false swearing (Ms. Mins. SCJ 1764–67 [Rough] 273, Oct. 24, 1767; Ms. Mins. SCJ 1766–69 [Engr.] 443, 444, 449, 529, 554, Apr. 22, 26, July 30, Oct. 22, 1768; Ms. Mins. SCJ 1769–72 [Engr.] 22, 24, 313, Apr. 28, 29, 1769, Jan. 16, 1771).
[191] Queen v. Sinclair (Ms. Mins. SCJ 1701–04 69, 84, 104, 126, 130, 147, 154, Apr. 6, 8, Oct. 7, 13, 1703, Apr. 4, Sept. 5, 7, 1704); King v. Byng (Ms. Mins. SCJ 1723–27 159, 160, 164, 166, 169, Oct. 16, 18, 19, Dec. 2, 4, 1725).
[192] King v. Byng—Murder (ut supra n. 191, at 164).

ever, "on motion of the prisoner that Judgment be arrested, because he is informed there is an act of grace passed by his Majesty to which act he takes himself to be intitled," the court finding "by the presentment that the fact was committed 13 years since and that he was but a youth at the time of the fact committed . . . respite judgment by Consent of Blagge pro Rege." The court ordered that the prisoner enter a £50 recognizance with two sureties in £25 each for his good behavior for a year.[193]

In two cases the pardon was produced without motion: once, when the court saw fit to repeat the traditional formula whether the defendant had anything to say why judgment should not be pronounced,[194] and again, when it elaborated by asking whether there was any reason why the defendant should not be executed according to sentence.[195]

Only two certain instances where the motion in arrest was employed in the Sessions Courts have been found. Thurman, Gurney and Kingston were indicted on February 2, 1703/04 for breaking the assize of bread, and capias was ordered to issue against them. However, Ralph Thurman appeared and entered a £20 recognizance with one surety in £10 for his appearance at the next Sessions to answer indictment. On May 2, 1704, Thurman and Gurney pleaded not guilty, and on May 3, Thurman was found not guilty, while Gurney was found guilty of making bread of undue assize. But the court "considered that . . . his bread was very good and his offense not grevious" and he was therefore only obliged to pay a fine of 1s. and costs. On the other hand, John Kingston was also found guilty of selling bread of "undue assize," and "Bickley p. defendant moves in arrest of Judgment and prays time until the next court to file his reasons." The court ordered that he file his reasons fourteen days before the following court, and on August 1, 1704, "the reasons in arrest of judgment were argued and the court are of opinion they were not sufficient to stay judgment." The defendant was therefore fined 1s. and costs.[196]

The second Sessions case occurred in Ulster County in 1705.[197] Alexander Rosekrans was tried and convicted of an unnamed offense and moved in arrest. Barne Cosens appeared to argue for him and offered:

1. For yt noe venire facies issued for summoning of a jury for ye tryall of ye Issue Joyned in ye cause. 2. For yt noe venire facies was Returned or pannel of

193 Ms. Mins. Cir. 1721–49 50, 51.
194 Queen v. Berry & Mark, counterfeiting (Ms. Mins. SCJ 1710–14 475, 476, 500).
195 King v. Brown (Ms. Mins. Cir. 1721–49 95).
196 Ms. Mins. NYCQS 1694–1731/32 86–89.
197 Ms. Mins. Ulster Co. Sess. 1703–05 Sept 1705.

the Jury annexed thereto as by law the same ought to have been done with the officers name sett to the Returne. 3. For yt one of ye Jurors to witt Gerrit Van Whit after hee had taken his oath to try the Issue joined and the same was on tryall seperated from the Rest of ye Jurors with ye leave of ye court. 4. For yt most of ye Jurors did not understand ye English tongue.

This argument is interesting for the three technical reasons offered and comes as something of a surprise in a backwoods jurisdiction. The court "approved" the reasons but there is no minute of the defendant's discharge. The sheriff, however, quick to see the advantage of having a foxy city lawyer on the Queen's side, moved that Cosens be admitted "to plead in this court on Behalf of the Queen." The motion was granted.

It is puzzling that no further use was made of the motion in arrest in the inferior courts. We do not think the silence of the minutes is due to a failure to make note of motions, for motions to quash and others are usually entered. And even in the Supreme Court it was only occasionally that an effort was made to arrest judgment. One is not justified in inferring that proceedings were invariably so correct that there was ordinarily no ground for making such motions. On the contrary, there is considerable evidence of flaws such as mistakes in return of process, but there is at the same time indication that the provincial courts were not bound down by the utter deference for form that prevailed in England. The strongest proof of this is the fact that we have seen no instances of the writ of error *coram nobis* which would unquestionably have been employed if the Supreme Court had been tolerant of objections to formal error which was not substantial. In any event it must be remembered that even although on a motion sustained the proceedings would be set aside, this was no bar to a subsequent indictment and the prosecutor might immediately prefer a new indictment; consequently the device may have been deemed of not sufficient use.[198]

Motion for a New Trial

The motion for a new trial was *avis rara* in New York criminal procedure. One reason for this was the fact that it was a novel thing and the English practice was not clearly settled, even in Hawkins' time.[199] It was, however, agreed

[198] Rex v. Burridge (3 P. Wms. 439, 500).
[199] The most complete account of the history of the motion for a new trial is in Thayer, *Preliminary Treatise on Evidence* (1898) 170 *et seq.*, although Thayer fails to take account of criminal practice in respect of *venire facias de novo*. In the early 18th century all that seems to have been settled was that a verdict of acquittal would not be set aside for being contrary to the evidence (2 Hawkins, *Pleas of the Crown* c.47 §11).

that this motion did not lie after acquittal. In certain particular types of prosecution such as perjury, a new trial was allowed after conviction.[200] The rule that no new trial would in any event be granted in case of felony or treason was not fixed until the end of the eighteenth century.[201] The slowness with which this practice developed was due partly to the fact that a very ancient remedy, the *venire facias de novo,* existed. This not exact equivalent was available only when a mistake appeared on the record, whereas the motion for the new trial could be granted for improper direction, misconduct of jurors or other causes which did not appear on the face of the proceedings.[202] The *venire facias de novo* was also used when a juror was withdrawn with consent either to let the defendant into a ground of defense not otherwise open before evidence was given, or where the indictment was defective, or a material witness was ill.[203]

During the eighteenth century most of this information was still imbedded in the reports and was not conveniently collected in treatises. Only direct contact with English Crown practice would have led to imitation in New York, and this probably explains why the motion for new trial and *venire facias de novo* were so esoteric.

We have seen only one clear case of a motion for a new trial, and this was allowed contrary to what even then was probably English practice in capital cases. In *King v. Mulatto Will, alias Will Archer,* the defendant was on October 19, 1730, tried in the Supreme Court for the murder of Thomas Cox and was found guilty as charged in the indictment. On October 20, 1730, judgment was respited to the following term, and on November 30, 1730, "on the defendant's motion for a new trial, Ordered Murray to be his counsel and judgment to be respited until the first Wednesday of next term." On March 12, 1730/31, "verdict against the defendant set aside. New trial granted." On June 7, 1731, the defendant was tried again and this time was found guilty of manslaughter. The defendant prayed the benefit of his clergy, and on the Attorney General's motion judgment was respited until the following morning.[204]

There are a few instances of a *venire facias de novo* in New York where a cause "remained" for want of jurors or where witnesses were absent, but there is only one example where this device was used for the purpose of effecting a new trial after verdict.

[200] King v. Smith (*T. Jones* 163) and cf. King v. Bear (2 *Salkeld* 646).
[201] Cf. the remarks of Lord Kenyon in King v. Mawbey, 1796 (6 *Term Rep.* 619 at 638).
[202] Witham v. Lewis (1 *Wils. K.B.* 48 at 55, 56).
[203] Foster, *Crown Law* (1762) 31.
[204] *Ms. Mins. SCJ* 1727-32 220, 223, 227, 232, 245, 257, 279, 282.

On November 2, 1759, a "notorious" riot occurred in New York City precipitated by the impending suppression of the illicit trading which had been carried on with the French by New York City merchants during the French and Indian War.[205] George Spencer, whose activities as an informer[206] had struck terror in the hearts of the merchants, was settled upon by his victims who determined they would intimidate him and "render him infamous" in order to invalidate any testimony he might offer against them. They therefore approached one Alderman Bogert with a view to carrying out their plan by "framing" Spencer. Attorney General Kempe in relating this story indicates that Bogert was a particularly susceptible subject for the machinations of the merchants. He was always in financial straits for, as Kempe put it, Alderman Bogert's wife spent his money as fast as he earned it. The merchants obtained from Alderman Bogert a bond which George Spencer had posted to secure a debt owed Bogert. It was the latter's understanding that the merchants would go to the Supreme Court in order to prosecute the bond, but instead they went to August Van Cortlandt, the clerk of the Mayor's Court, and got process against Spencer. Bogert had given no warrant of attorney permitting them to put his bond in suit, and it would have taken too long for the merchants to go back to him for the warrant and then go to the Supreme Court to have the writ made out, to send it to the office to be sealed and next to deliver it to the sheriff to be served on Spencer. Van Cortlandt signed the writ with Bogert's name without his consent and delivered the writ to Philip Branson, a deputy sheriff, to serve on Spencer.

The deputy was unable to break into Spencer's house to serve the writ and therefore on a subterfuge brought Spencer to the door and he was taken in custody, was made a prisoner and marched to jail. One George Harrison came up, and with the deputy brought Spencer into Adam Van den Berg's house where they forced Spencer to drink wine "against his will." The plotters next got some sailors together to start a riot and hired a cart from Michael Wade. The sailors then attempted to capture Spencer from Van den Berg's house in order to take him to a neighboring pump, where they intended to "pump George Spencer." A mob of over a hundred people surrounded Van den Berg's house, and Philip Branson, instead of preventing the mob from rescuing the prisoner, as a good officer should have done, let the mob in. The mob captured Spencer

[205] For an account of this riot cf. *H.R. Pleadings* Pl. K. 930, 976.
[206] Spencer was at large when the riot occurred but spent the next two years in jail for debt; cf.

1 *Colden Letter Books* 49; 6 *Letters and Papers of Colden* 89 *et seq.* In the latter is the story of Spencer's financial troubles.

and put him in the cart. He was dragged through the streets "showered with filth and offal, much to the disgrace and annoyance of the said George Spencer and the peace and quiet of the inhabitants of the said city."[207]

There appears to have been some question as to the locus of prosecution. The Quarter Sessions Court took jurisdiction on November 6, 1759, but on the same day, the riot being reported to the Council by affidavit, the Lieutenant Governor inquired whether or not the Supreme Court could properly order recognizances and the Attorney General to prosecute. The Council made an order to that effect on November 6, 1759. Three days later Spencer complained to two aldermen accusing George Harrison, John Lawrence, Peter Lynch, Mr. and Mrs. Philip Branson, Michael Wade, William Kelly and Waddell Cunningham of riot.[208] The defendants, Harrison, Lawrence, Lynch, the Bransons and Wade were indicted in New York City Quarter Sessions on November 9, 1759, for a "notorious riott" and for an assault and battery on Spencer. They were ordered to plead in twenty days or suffer judgment.[209] On January 15, 1760, an entry appears in the Supreme Court minutes indicating that Wade was continued on recognizance to the next term of the Supreme Court.[210] On February 6, 1760, the clerk of the peace produced in New York City Quarter Sessions a certiorari from the Supreme Court which was read and filed in Sessions and a return thereto ordered to be made.[211] On April 22, 1760, the certiorari was returned and filed in the Supreme Court, and process was ordered to issue out against all the above named defendants.[212] Shortly thereafter all the defendants except Wade were discharged from their recognizances in the Quarter Sessions.[213]

In August, 1760, Duane appeared for all the defendants except Lawrence "on process of indictment" and the sheriff of New York endorsed on a venire facias against Lawrence the return that the defendant's body had been "taken." Lawrence's appearance was endorsed on the return and he was ordered to plead in twenty days or suffer judgment.[214] On October 21, 1760, Harrison, Branson, Wade and Lynch appeared in the Supreme Court and an affidavit was read in court that Harrison was related to the high sheriff. The court therefore ordered that the venire for the trial jury should issue to the coroner instead

[207] In addition to the accounts in *H.R. Pleadings* Pl. K. 930 and 976, cf. the information of November 2, 1760, against Kelly, Lynch, Branson, Wade, Harrison, Lawrence and five others (*Misc. Mss. Supreme Ct.*).

[208] The Council proceedings are in 25 *Ms. Mins. Council* fol. 300; the affidavit, in *H.R. Pleadings* Pl. K. 980.

[209] *Ms. Mins. NYCQS 1732–62* 461–465, Nov. 6–9, 1759.

[210] *Ms. Mins. SCJ 1756–61* (Rough) 166.

[211] *Ms. Mins. NYCQS 1732–62* 468, 470.

[212] *Ms. Mins. SCJ 1756–61* (Rough) 180.

[213] *Ms. Mins. NYCQS 1732–62* 477, May 6, 1760.

[214] *Ms. Mins. SCJ 1757–60* (Engr.) 357, 361.

of to the sheriff.[215] The Attorney General on the same day made a motion that a *habeas corpus ad testificandum* issue to bring in George Spencer, the victim of the riot, to be examined as a witness.[216] When on this same day, October 21, one of the defendants, Lynch, failed to appear, "judgment for want of a plea" was "confirmed" and a *capias pro redemptione* was ordered to issue against Lynch.[217] On October 22, 1760, the jury in the Supreme Court found Branson and Wade guilty.[218]

At the same time that a verdict had been found against Branson and Wade and a default judgment rendered against Lynch on the riot indictment returned by certiorari from Quarter Sessions into the Supreme Court, William Kelly and Waddell Cunningham were arraigned on informations for riot and misdemeanor. These informations had been filed against Kelly and Cunningham in the January term of the Supreme Court, 1760, and Kelly's offense was that of effrontery to the riot justices when he said before them that he would reward the carter who had carted George Spencer.[219] On October 22, 1760, Kelly was placed on trial in the Supreme Court, but a juror was withdrawn on the Attorney General's motion and the rest of the jurors discharged.[220]

On November 2, 1760, a new information for riot was drawn up by the Attorney General against all the unconvicted defendants except Cunningham, and Kempe prayed leave to withdraw the earlier information so that he might file a new information and include Cunningham.[221] Apparently he changed his mind, for a grand jury indictment was found against all the defendants for riot.[222] On April 22, 1761, John Lawrence, having been indicted for riot, was brought to trial. The jurors were sworn, but having returned to the court without finding a verdict, two constables were sworn to keep the jury in this cause "without meat, drink, fire or light." On the next day, April 23, when the court sent for the jury, they said they were not agreed on a verdict, and "were inclined to find a special verdict Whereupon the court ordered pen, ink and paper to be delivered to the jury." The jury then being returned found a special verdict in which they stated that Lawrence had been present at the riot and had said that the rioters ought to cart George Spencer around the town, but the jury left it to the court to say whether these acts on the part of the de-

[215] *Ms. Mins. SCJ 1756–61* (Rough) 198; H.R. *Pleadings* Pl. K. 979.

[216] *Ms. Mins. SCJ 1756–61* (Rough) 198.

[217] *Ibid.*

[218] *Ibid.* 198, 199; notes on trial, H.R. *Pleadings* Pl. K. 425; witnesses and their evidence, Pl. K. 978; notes of fines set in notorious riots, Pl. K. 962.

[219] *Ms. Mins. SCJ 1756–61* (Rough) 170, 180; *Ms. Mins. SCJ 1757–60* (Engr.) 276, 277, 361; H.R. *Parch.* 170 B 2, 139 C 3.

[220] *Ms. Mins. SCJ 1756–61* (Rough) 199.

[221] *Misc. Mss. Supreme Ct.*

[222] *Ms. Mins. SCJ 1756–61* (Rough) 228, Apr. 24, 1761.

fendant constituted riot.[223] On April 24, 1761 the Attorney General, evidently feeling that the jury's special verdict in the Lawrence case was irregular and would perhaps damage the prosecution of the other defendants, moved to have a juror withdrawn on the indictments of all the other defendants for riot, and this motion was granted.[224] On April 30, 1761, the Attorney General having filed a motion that a *venire facias de novo* issue, the court gave defendant Lawrence time until next term to answer.[225]

The greatest confusion must have existed regarding the status of the prosecutions against the defendants in this riot, because we note on August 4 and 5, 1761, Michael Wade was continued on recognizance in New York City Quarter Sessions,[226] but in April, 1762, subpoenas and subpoena tickets were issued for witnesses in trials proposed to be had of all the defendants in the Supreme Court, and we note also that the defendants' attorney made a motion to put off the trial in 1762.[227] On the ruling respecting the motion for a *venire facias de novo*, the minutes for the succeeding terms of 1761 are silent, and the minutes for the first three terms of 1762 are missing. The issue of subpoenas in April, 1762, indicates, however, that the Attorney General's motion was granted.

We have devoted more attention to the problem of the correction of errors in pleas of the Crown than it in fact received in colonial New York. The situation is a striking example of the degree to which provincial practice lagged behind the advances which were being made in England, timid though these were. This is notably exemplified in the failure to use error in misdemeanor

---

[223] *Ibid*. 224–226; H.R. *Pleadings* Pl. K. 976.
[224] *Ibid*. 228. The entry is ambiguous, seeming to apply only to the trial of Cunningham and Kelly. However, the entry, *ibid*. 239, indicates that all defendants were involved.
[225] *Ibid*.
The notes of Kempe for the motion are an interesting example of his technique in argument. The indictment and plea were to be read; then the point in issue stated—whether Lawrence was not guilty of riot as in the indictment. The special verdict was to be attacked as insufficient and ambiguous, because 1) it did not show the riot to be the same as that in the indictment; 2) that the George Spencer of the indictment was not shown to be identical with the Spencer of the verdict; 3) there might have been other riots on the day and at the place; 4) there may have been more George Spencers; 5) the riot found in the verdict was different from that charged in the indictment, for the indictment charged a "riotous carting" and the verdict found "a riot occasioned by the carting," a distinct offense not charged in the indictment. The court in judging on a special verdict is bound to facts found

and cannot supply anything. Verdicts must answer points in issue or are not good and must be positively, not ambiguously, found. Arrest of judgment would lie if the verdict is uncertain, but if a verdict was so imperfectly found that a court cannot give judgment on it a *venire facias de novo* shall issue (H.R. *Pleadings* Pl. K. 926).
[226] *Ms. Mins. NYCQS 1732–62* 505, 507, 509.
[227] H.R. *Pleadings* Pl. K. 960; J. T. Kempe *Lawsuits* G–J *sub nom*. George Harrison. In April, 1760, George Spencer had made a petition to the Supreme Court asking that that court assign him counsel and an attorney to assist him in carrying on the several prosecutions he had commenced against Harrison, Wade and others. Spencer alleged "that most of the attorneys and council here are retained against him by several defendants in those causes so that he is destitute of help unless the court shall interpose. Ordered that Attorney General Kempe be . . . appointed as of council for the said George Spencer and John Alsop attorney for the said George Spencer to assist him in carrying on the several prosecutions and suits" (*Ms. Mins. SCJ 1757–60* [Engr.] 308).

cases and the rarity of the motion for new trial. True, the exploitation of transfer devices eliminated in considerable degree the opportunity for appellate review, especially since royal instructions restricted recourse to the Governor and
Council. Yet there was still a margin where some means of correction would
have been desirable. The neglecting of this opportunity may be attributed in
part to the circumstance that counsel played a restricted role in criminal cases,
particularly as the bulk of those who were tried for serious crimes were persons to whose fate most persons were indifferent. In part, also, the lag behind
English practice may be laid to the fact that there existed no adequate and
comprehensive textbook discussion of procedures to correct errors in criminal
cases. The scattered cases in the reports gave a most inadequate picture of
practice in England, that is to say, they offered occasional precedents but they
gave no clue as to how generally such precedents were representative of ordinary usage at Assizes.[228] Since in New York, on the whole the exceptional was
discreetly avoided, and the patterns of practice were cut after the designs of
Hawkins, Hale and the *Crown Circuit Companion,* it was only the bold lawyer who would attempt now and then a *tour de force* in defiance of these
tutelary geniuses. Only in respect of certiorari did the provincial bar eventually exhibit a disposition to indulge in experiment and amplify somewhat the
exiguous error jurisdiction. In this, as we have indicated, New York was a half
century or more behind the motherland, but it was a first breach in a rigid
standard which was soon to crumble when the mastery of Blackstone in lieu
of Coke became the measure of professional accomplishment.

[228] Cf. here the details of practice at Newgate set forth in Foster, *Crown Law* 31 *et seq.*

CHAPTER V

CONFLICTS AND OTHER JURISDICTIONAL PROBLEMS

THE conflicts of jurisdiction which concern American courts today are largely the result of our political system with its multiple sovereignty, although occasionally they occur within a state because of imperfectly drawn statutes. In English law, however, these conflicts arose originally because judicial power was dispersed through enfeoffment and franchise, while coexistent and in competition with these jurisdictions were the public tribunals. Since the agencies of public authority came into existence at different times and in a variety of ways, by statute, ordinance or through immemorial usage, a further order of problems was presented by the lack of any clear definition of competence as between these tribunals. During the thirteenth and fourteenth centuries the subjection of private jurisdiction to the King's courts was settled, although the pressure of claims to prescriptive right and the efforts to evade restrictive rules were still evident in the seventeenth century. As to the public courts, however, the process of definition was far from complete even at the time of the Restoration. To be sure, through the distinctions constantly pressed between the inferior and superior courts, between the courts of record and those not of record, the primacy of the central courts at Westminster had long been fixed. But since the sphere within which these courts might act was so largely a question of usage and tradition, their respective preserves were separated not by hedgerows but by occasional landmarks, so that there were large areas of overlapping competence and many a corner where tenancy was in dispute.[1]

It cannot be denied that one of the factors which contributed largely to the recurrence of conflicts of jurisdiction was the untidy English habit of creating new agencies to deal with matter incompetently handled by older agencies without bothering particularly to liquidate the latter. Thus at certain points justices of the peace and the Assizes had an overlapping judicial authority which might only be determined at the expense of some unhappy defendant, but over which no reformer appears to have bestirred himself. Situations of this sort were manifold. Indeed, a most cursory perusal of Crompton's *L'Authoritie et Jurisdiction des Courts* or of Coke's *Fourth Institute* will disclose

---

[1] As, for example, the right of Common Pleas to issue the writ of habeas corpus or to review causes on writ of error, and of the King's Bench to take assizes where the case was begun by *latitat*.

a degree of disorder that only an intense veneration for established things could have made tolerable.

Since it was not until the early nineteenth century that a systematic effort at reform was undertaken by Parliament,[2] the business of defining jurisdiction was chiefly the task of the central courts. This task was assumed and pursued less from motives of reform or classification than for reasons of profit and prestige, two characteristics of jurisdiction which were a heritage of the Middle Ages and which tended to foment discord. The process of definition in the courts was based upon two major principles: what was settled must be kept, and what could be filched must be made colorable. In the execution of these precepts, rules and procedures were fabricated to safeguard the matter of which a court had become seised and equally to facilitate encroachments upon rival jurisdictions.[3] The learning which grew up about these rules and procedures, being promptly collected and abridged under the rubrics *Conusans, Jurisdiction,* etc. became the general postulates of jurisdictional discussion.

The administration of the criminal law was little affected by the rivalries of the central courts, for once the Star Chamber was abolished, the Court of King's Bench was left in undisputed possession of its ancient bailiwick, except for certain Crown cases, such as intrusion (over which the Exchequer had cognizance) and the quasi-criminal *qui tam* actions. In the field of criminal procedure the jurisdictional problems were chiefly those of maintaining a supervision over inferior courts and defining the boundaries of their competence. Here such general rules were applied, as that nothing would be intended to be out of the jurisdiction of a superior court except what expressly appears to be so, nor within the jurisdiction of an inferior court except what is expressly alleged to be so,[4] and more frequently the doctrine of *coram non judice.*[5] This last was perhaps the most important of the safeguarding rules. Specifically it meant that where a judge had no jurisdiction the proceeding was void, and actions would lie against the officers of the court who had executed process. This was based on the notion that there was no necessity of obeying one not a judge in the cause, any more than a stranger. A long line of precedent supported this, although the Latin tag was not used until the latter part of the fifteenth century.[6] With the characteristic predilection of the English bench for a com-

---

[2] There is a brief discussion in 1 Holdsworth, *Hist. Eng. Law* 634 *et seq*.

[3] Cf. the curiously frank discussion by Hale in *A Discourse Concerning the Courts of Kings Bench and Common Pleas* in 1 Hargrave, *Collection of Tracts* (1787) 367, 368.

[4] Peacock v. Bell (1 *Wms. Saund.* 74); Winford v. Powell (2 *Ld. Raymond* 1310); cf. Bacon, *Abridgment,* Courts D.

[5] The Case of the Marshalsea (10 *Co. Rep.* 76a).

[6] *Yearbook* 22 Edw. IV 33b. It is quickly popular, cf. *Yearbook* 1 Ric. III 1; *Yearbook* 2 Ric. III 2.

pact cliché, the phrase *coram non judice* came to enjoy a lengthy vogue in discussions over jurisdiction.

It has been necessary to sketch the contours of the problems of jurisdiction in England because the situation in New York Province was affected by the doctrines as well as the general confusion which prevailed at home. From the beginning, in New York, the judicial establishment rested upon enactment, but it was always enactment loosely drawn, and with only the vaguest specifications respecting jurisdiction. From 1691 onwards, the generous but unhelpful references to the courts of King's Bench, Common Pleas and Exchequer, in the case of the Supreme Court, and the equally broad and unspecific mention of Sessions of the Peace in the case of the provincial Sessions Courts, invited, indeed made essential, the spelling out of provincial jurisdiction in terms of English practice. The greatest source of schism, to be sure, was avoided by endowing a single court with the powers of the three rivals at Westminster. But, as we have seen, other jealousies were transplanted, as in the case of the Admiralty jurisdiction,[7] and similarly the contested sphere of equity jurisdiction between Exchequer and Chancery.[8] Due to the relative simplicity of the judicial structure in New York, and due also to the restricted use of writ of error to the Governor and Council even in civil cases, the Supreme Court of New York Province enjoyed a primacy which rendered the settlement of disputes over jurisdiction a fairly simple matter of applying the rules which had been evolved in England for the governance of inferior tribunals. In only one particular were the colonial authorities faced with problems that were without exact parallel in England—the matter of extraterritorial crime committed in other common law jurisdictions. We shall consider this matter before proceeding to examine the jurisdictional problems which arose within the Province.

Extraterritorial Crime and Extradition

Until the seventeenth century in England there had been no recognition that extradition might be a problem. It had been asserted flatly by Coke that there was no duty to surrender fugitives to friendly powers.[9] Within the

That the absence of jurisdiction is premised upon the fact the judge is not competent, seems to us to have been derived from the canon law where the doctrines of judicial competency were a large part of the learning on jurisdiction; cf. 1 München, *Das Kanonische Gerichtsverfahren* (1874) *passim*.

[7] *Supra* 235 *et seq.*

[8] *Infra* 310 n. 117.

[9] Coke, *Third Institute* 180. In the case of treason done out of the realm the English law permitted trial in the Court of the Constable and Marshal (Coke, *Fourth Institute* 124). On appeals for things done out of the realm generally, 1 Hy. IV c.14 gave this court jurisdiction.

realm the courts had settled that the once highly immune palatine jurisdictions were not insulated against royal process.[10] In the case of Wales a statute of Henry VIII had given concurrent jurisdiction over felons to contiguous English shires.[11] After the accession of James I, it had been enacted that where Englishmen committed felonies in Scotland, the judges of Assize, Gaol Delivery or justices of the peace in Sessions were empowered to examine evidence and surrender the persons charged.[12] No further changes were made in the law until the Habeas Corpus Act, 31 Charles II.[13] It was there provided that if any person resident in the realm should have committed any capital offense in Scotland, Ireland or any island or foreign plantations of the King where the offense was triable, such person might be sent to that place for trial. A few cases arose under this act where English courts had supported the power of the government to send malefactors abroad for trial or at least to give opportunity for them to be taken.[14]

The Habeas Corpus Act did not extend to the colonies, but the policy of the Crown was clearly indicated by both the statutes and judicial decisions. As to the situation of the colonies *inter se,* however, it did not exactly correspond with the situations dealt with by statute. In all the colonies jurisdiction depended from the Crown, but each was supplied with a "government" quite distinct.[15] Unlike the liberties and privileged localities in England there was no process, unless it was a prerogative writ, which would run from Westminster, and certainly no process of any provincial court would have vigor without the boundaries of a colony, as might capias and exigent issuing for a particular English county. Therefore extraterritorial crime and the fugitive offender presented in America peculiar problems of jurisdiction.

To understand how the law enforcing agencies in New York dealt with the rendition of offenders it is necessary to consider how they regarded the au-

---

[10] *Yearbook* 19 Hy. VI 1b, 2.

[11] 26 Hy. VIII c.6. For earlier legislation, cf. 2 Hy. IV c.17; 9 Hy. IV cc.3, 4. As to Chester, cf. 1 Hy. IV c.18.

[12] In 4 Jac. I c.1, the surrender of Englishmen was forbidden but by 7 Jac. I c.1 the procedure set forth in the text was instituted.

[13] 31 Car. II c.2 §16.

[14] Rex v. Lundy, 1690 (2 *Vent.* 314) held a fugitive from Ireland could be sent there for trial under the Habeas Corpus Act. It was noted in the case that before the Act an offender was sent over to Barbados. Cf. Rex v. Kimberley, 1731 (2 *Strange* 848); East India Co. v. Campbell, 1749 (1 *Ves. sen.* 246).

[15] In 1693 Solicitor General Trevor reported on the Connecticut and New Jersey charters "there Majesties by virtue of their Prerogative and Soverainty over those Colonies which is not granted from the Crown to the Governor and Company nor to the proprietors by any of the charters may appoint Governors for those places," etc. (4 *Doc. Rel. Col. Hist. NY* 1). The surrender in 1701 by certain proprietors of East Jersey refers to the grant by the Duke of York of "Powers Jurisdictions and Governments" and the surrendering clause is of "jurisdictions and powers of government" (2 *NJ Archives* 387). Cf. also Lewis Morris's letter of 1701 (*ibid.* 412), the letter of the Lords of Trade (*ibid.* 448) and the final surrender (*ibid.* 452).

thority of their own and other provinces. Political authority is spoken of in terms of jurisdiction and never in terms of sovereignty or quasi-sovereignty. Throughout the eighteenth century the expression "Government" of New York or New Jersey or Massachusetts is used in official correspondence,[16] and there is no doubt that by this was meant the sum of political powers delegated by charter, governors' commissions and the like, which were in a sense the constitution of a particular province.[17] The ultimate jurisdiction was conceived to lie in the Crown, so there was no question that claims to sovereignty would be advanced.[18] This is clearly shown by the discussions in boundary disputes[19] where on one occasion Lieutenant Governor De Lancey speaks of the desirability of avoiding civil war, an expression that excludes any conception of provincial sovereignty;[20] and on another, the New York Commissioners refer to the service of process by Hampshire County (Mass.) officers in Livingston Manor as "criminal acts,"[21] viz., as an intrusion upon a jurisdiction. The status of the several provinces resembled that of bodies corporate at common law, a view advanced by Thomas Pownall[22] and concurred in by William Smith Jr., a leading New York lawyer.[23]

Within its territorial limits the jurisdiction of a particular province as prescribed by its frame of government was exclusive. Since there was no immediate political connection between the several provinces each one made its own decisions on the trial or rendition of fugitive criminals with reference to its own interests. If it were important to conserve jurisdictional rights there would be no surrender; if nothing were at stake, a spirit of comity would prevail. At the end of the seventeenth century, the spirit of independence, so far as New York and its neighbors were concerned, was pronounced. Governor Bellomont, for example, had difficulties in securing from New Jersey[24] the

---

[16] There is a curious intimation of status, however, in Chambers' and Richard's report (1753) on the Massachusetts boundary where New York is described as "his Majesty's Immediate Government which theirs is not" and where the suggestion is made that initiative more properly lay with New York (3 *Doc. Hist. NY* 457).

[17] *Supra* 8 *et seq.*

[18] 1 *Colden Letter Books* 241 (1763). The Council of New York to Monckton: "The Jurisdiction as well as the property of the soil yet unappropriated in both governments appertain to his Majesty," etc. Compare the recital in the New York act on the New Jersey boundary, 1754 (3 *Col. Laws NY* 1036).

[19] Compare the report of Attorney General Bradley on the New Hampshire grants where the

"Government" of a province is treated as a jurisdiction grantable by the Crown (4 *Doc. Hist. NY* 334).

[20] 3 *Doc. Hist. NY* 465 (1755).

[21] *Ibid.* 457. And compare also the language in the report of William Smith Jr. regarding the colonies "tho independent of each other are nevertheless connected by the indissoluble ties of Interest and subject to the same sovereign," 1773 (26 *Ms. Mins. Council* 344). Smith's draft of the report is in *NYSL Mss.* no. 9704.

[22] Pownall, *op. cit.* 31, 33.

[23] 1 Smith, *Hist. NY* 369 n.

[24] 2 *NJ Archives* (1 ser.) 229; 4 *Doc. Rel. Col. Hist. NY* 359. Basse requested the recording of the admiralty commission in New Jersey.

surrender of certain pirates for trial by the Vice-Admiralty Court (which at that time had authority over New Jersey), and experienced reluctance on the part of Connecticut in the extradition of one of Captain Kidd's noxious associates.[25] That these episodes were not exceptional, and that the difficulty of securing extradition was a matter of real and general concern may be inferred from the fact that William Penn's Plan of Union contained a provision for the surrender of fugitive malefactors.[26]

As the eighteenth century wore on, evidence of an occasional disposition toward comity between the provinces is here and there perceptible. The Governor of New York urges the government of Pennsylvania to proceed against John Henry Lydius, because the case against Lydius is not sufficient in New York to secure a conviction.[27] The New York Assembly enacts a statute making punishable the counterfeiting of bills of credit emitted by other provinces,[28] and a statute to cooperate with New Jersey in the prosecution of trespassers on the premises of the Sandy Hook Lighthouse.[29] But despite the growth of inter-colonial cooperation the business of extradition remains a matter of policy where immediate jurisdictional interests are paramount.

The vagaries of extradition policy were due largely to the fact that from the first it was handled by the executive.[30] This came about because of the insulation of provincial jurisdictions and because there was no judicial process that would have vigor outside of a particular colony. Inevitably, if the law enforcing authorities wanted a man they could hope to secure him lawfully only through the intermediacy of the Governor.

[25] 4 Doc. Rel. Col. Hist. NY 595.

[26] Ibid. 296. In Pennsylvania arrangements were made as early as 1684 with West Jersey for the extradition of offenders through the device of validating the hue and cry warrants of the prosecuting province. Cf. 1 Mins. Provincial Council of Pennsylvania 101; Charter and Laws of Pennsylvania (1879) 168; Leaming and Spicer, Grants and Concessions 488. The validation was effected by affixing the seal of the province where the fugitive was supposed to lurk (1 Mins. Prov. Council Pa. 147 [1685]).

In connection with Penn's scheme should be noted also the provision made by the New England Confederation in 1643 (Brigham, Compact Charters and Laws of New Plymouth [1836] 312) and the later confederation of 1672 (ibid. 317).

[27] De Lancey to Morris, 1755 (2 Pa. Archives 273).

[28] 4 Col. Laws NY 906 (1766). For cases under the act, cf. King v. Zachariah Smith Allen, indicted for passing a counterfeit bill of credit of Pennsylvania, knowing it to be counterfeit (Ms. Mins. SCJ

1775–81 [Engr.] 62, 63, Jan. 19, 1776; H.R. Pleadings Pl. K. 240, 241); King v. Samuel Mount, indicted for attempting to pass a Jersey bill of credit which was altered, and also indicted for altering two Jersey bills of credit and passing one of them, found not guilty on both indictments (Ms. Mins. SCJ 1769–72 [Engr.] 444–447, Oct. 25, 1771; H.R. Pleadings Pl. K. 237, 350; J. T. Kempe Lawsuits L–O sub nom. Samuel Mount); King v. Peter Lynch, indicted for altering a bill of credit of the colony of New Jersey from 3s. to £3 and passing the same (Ms. Mins. NYCQS 1760–72 289, Aug. 4, 1769).

[29] 4 Col. Laws NY 624 (1762).

[30] The standard book on the colonial governor, Greene, Provincial Governor, mentions the matter in a note (p. 101) citing two instances—in one of which the facts are misrepresented. Greene states that extradition was very rare, but his conclusion is obviously not grounded upon a thorough examination of the evidence.

It should be noticed that in Rhode Island, that

The records are scattered and unsatisfactory on the development of extradition procedure in New York. As early as 1691 we find the Council of New York passing on to the Governor of Pennsylvania a counterfeiter, taken in Jamaica and shipped to New York for trial at the place where the offense was committed,[31] but except for the pirates mentioned above, there is nothing to indicate how the extradition process was initiated. The New Jersey pirate case shows the requisition made by the Governor writing to the Governor of the province where the wanted men were in custody, and the executive of that jurisdiction deciding what course it would pursue. And a few years later we come upon a request sent by Secretary Stanley of Connecticut to the Lieutenant Governor of New York for the rendition of Hannah Taylor whose husband had petitioned for a divorce on account of adultery. The executive request was accompanied by an order of the Superior Court at Hartford that application be made for the arrest and rendition of Hannah and by an affidavit to the effect that this woman was living in New York with a negro servant of one Sacket. The request was laid before the Council but we do not find that anything was done.[32] Usually, however, where the malefactor was at large the procedure was followed of issuing a proclamation for his apprehension. The Governor would then write to adjoining provinces requesting that proclamation be made for the offender. So far as we know this procedure was first used in the case of Thomas Weaver, the Receiver General of Customs in New York who took to his heels in 1702.[33] There are various examples of this procedure during the eighteenth century. Thus in 1720, when one Robert Moore escaped from New York to Pennsylvania, the Governor of New York having requested a proclamation, hue and cry warrants and then a proclamation were issued.[34] Again in 1760 when some of the crew of the *Winchester* were killed by men of the ship *Sampson,* Colden made proclamation and sent it about to his brother governors.[35] Similarly Governor Moore of New York, at the request of the Governor of New Jersey, issued a proclamation in 1768 for the apprehension of the persons who had robbed the treasurer of New Jersey.[36]

Where a fugitive was actually laid by the heels in a neighboring province, the matter of physical transfer presented a problem of its own. In the 1691 counterfeiting case mentioned above, the Council's warrant for deportation as

seat of aberration, the legislature exercised some authority in extradition.

[31] 37 *NY Col. Mss.* 173.
[32] 53 *NY Col. Mss.* 110; 10 *Ms. Mins. Council* 702, Sept. 8, 1710.
[33] 4 *Doc. Rel. Col. Hist. NY* 960.

[34] 3 *Pennsylvania Colonial Records* 108.
[35] 1 *Colden Letter Books* 11, 16. The proclamation of August 20, 1760 is in NY Hist. Soc. *Collection of Broadsides.*
[36] 9 *NJ Archives* (1 ser.) 564.

far as Elizabethtown has been preserved.[37] Apparently not enough cases arose to establish a practice, for we find Governor Clinton instructing President Palmer of Pennsylvania on the proper procedure according to the opinion of a New York judge:[38]

> . . . I waited for the opinion of the Judge, who try'd the Criminal, said to be in your Jaol, he being out of Town, and he tells me the only way of conveying him hither, is to send him properly guarded from Philadelphia to Trentown by water, to be delivered up to the care of the Sheriff of that County, and so on to Brunswick by Land, & from thence to New York by water. If you approve of this method, I will send the Deputy Sheriff of this City to Philadelphia, to assist in escorting him, and shall write to Gov[r] Belcher, to give directions to receive him at Trentown, & to pass him thro' his Government. . . .

In a later case where an Indian accused of murder was caught by Massachusetts authorities, Justice Horsmanden of the Supreme Court, apparently at the instance of the Council, sent his precept to the sheriff of Albany to go to the frontier to receive the offender from the officers of Massachusetts.[39]

The fact that a requisition was made did not necessarily mean that an offender, if captured, would be surrendered. In the troubles which arose over boundaries the provinces, in order to preserve their claims, were very stiff-necked. Lieutenant Governor De Lancey flatly refused to surrender persons demanded by Phipps of Massachusetts,[40] and similarly Colden denied a request from Wentworth of New Hampshire.[41] On other occasions, too, the New York executive was not inclined to comity. Thus, in 1745, Governor Shirley of Massachusetts sent out a round robin regarding a gang of counterfeiters.[42] The Connecticut authorities found evidence of their activities and sent on the captives, but a person apprehended in New York was not arrested because the

---

[37] "Whereas John Rush hath been taken up and Imprisoned in Jamaica being suspected of Coyning Counterfeit money found with him to the sume of nine pounds fifteen shillings Pennsilvania And Whereas the said John Rush is sent from Jamaica hither [illegible] to be conveyed to the place where the fact is (as is said) Committed. These are therefore in the name of our Soveraign to Command you to Deliver the said prisoner John Rush unto the next Constable with the said bagg of Counterfeit money to be Conveyed from Constable to Constable unto Elizabethtowne in East Jersey And to Desire that the Justices of the peace or some of them in Elizabethtowne to cause the said prisoner to be conveyed by those Constables to West Jersey to some Justices of peace those of whom Wee Desire the like service untill he be Delivered unto the Governor or Cheife Magistrate in Philadelphia with the said bagg of money to be proceeded against according to Law and for soe Doing this shall be your sufficient Warrant Given under our hands and seales at Newyorke this 24 day of June 1691 . . ." (37 NY Col. Mss. 173 b).

[38] 2 Pa. Archives 16 (1748).

[39] 6 Letters and Papers of Cadwallader Colden 152; 1 Colden Letter Books 207 (1762).

[40] 3 Doc. Hist. NY 471, 474 (1755).

[41] 6 Letters and Papers of Cadwallader Colden 342; 1 Colden Letter Books 358 (1764).

[42] 1 Law Papers (Conn. Hist. Soc. Colls.) 284. The same document, badly scorched, is in 74 NY Col. Mss. 196. The New York authorities collected a large number of affidavits for a list; cf. Cal. Eng. Mss. 572.

Council thought the evidence, being merely hearsay, did not justify a war-rant.[43] Again, in 1773 the Massachusetts government requested of Governor Tryon that sentence upon certain convicted counterfeiters in New York be not executed unless it was established that the offense was committed in New York.[44] The criminal acts had been committed in the disputed border regions and a confederacy of some magnitude had been uncovered, for thirty-five indictments were found. One Sheriff Williams and Justice Ashley of Massachusetts Bay, who had been instrumental in apprehending the offenders, were summoned to attend both branches of the Massachusetts legislature to answer for their conduct, and Governor Hutchinson's demand was made pursuant to a vote of that body. Apart from the issue as to territorial jurisdiction over the locus of the offense, the case was complicated by the fact that in New York counterfeiting foreign bills was a felony without benefit of clergy, whereas in Massachusetts it was a mere trespass for which the party injured had his damages.

The matter was submitted by the New York Council to a committee of which William Smith Jr. was chairman. In its report the committee asserted in strong terms the right of a colony to protect its currency, claiming jurisdiction over the act of counterfeiting wherever it might be committed. Said the report:

> That the Committee conceive this Practice (which has prevailed here for many Years past) is founded upon the aggravated Nature of the Offence, and the great and invincible Law of Necessity for if the mere Circumstance of Counterfeiting the Coin of any Country, beyond the precise Line of its Territory, will render the Agent dispunishable, the Power of providing for the publick safety, a Power essential to every Legislative Body, cannot be enjoyed in its proper Extent, and this pernicious Practice will receive such Countenance and Encouragement, as must be subversive of Commerce and Confidence, and all the Security of Civil Society.
>
> Of several Acts passed here for this purpose, not one of them was ever disallowed by the Crown, nor until now do we learn that they have given the least Umbrage to any of the Neighbouring Colonies, some of which have on the contrary assisted in the Surrender of the Offenders to our Justice. . . .
>
> Had the Jurisdiction and Title of that Province to a Line of twenty Miles East from Hudson's River been uncontrovertable, it might have been expected that an Excess of Eagerness on the Part of the Officers of this Government in the

---

[43] 1 *Law Papers* 302, 312, 345.   [44] 26 *Ms. Mins. Council* 339.

Caption of the Criminals, would scarce have exposed them to censure, since the Guilt of such Offenders ought to render them obnoxious as Pirates are by the Law of Nations to be proceeded against in the Courts of all States to what Prince soever they may be Subject—And tho' the Committee do not mean to assert that a Counterfeiter of public Coin of any Country is Subject to the same universal Law, yet from the peculiar Malignity of the Crime and its extensive and pestilent Effects the Obligation upon Colonies (which tho' independent of each other are nevertheless connected by the indissoluble Ties of Interest and Subject to the same Sovereign) to Act upon a Principle of mutual Sympathy, seems to stand upon so solid and immovable a Foundation, as that which justifies independent Nations in proceeding against the Subjects of any other State for such Crimes as are incompatible with human Safety—Instead therefore of complaining of the Execution of our Laws against such enormous Offenders, we might rather have expected the Aid of the Massachusetts Bay for their punishment, and that by Laws of their own they would have conspired to prevent the Infraction of ours.

It reinforced this claim by reiterating the rights of New York to the regions where the offense had been done, and in a succession of strong policy arguments rejected the demands of the neighboring province. The Council having already decided not to interfere, on the ground that the offense was a bad one and the law should take its course, ordered the report to be entered in the minutes.

From the evidence we have examined, it cannot be said a consistent policy was evolved in extradition; rather, as requisitions were sporadic, cases were settled as they came up. The absence of any strong and steadily increasing feeling of cooperation among the colonies in matters of law enforcement affected the whole question. Twice in Connecticut, excuses were found (probably because of the expense) for not sending necessary witnesses to Massachusetts where men were being tried for forging Connecticut bills,[45] and the Rhode Island Assembly indignantly repudiated any financial responsibility for the prosecution out of their province of persons counterfeiting Rhode Island bills.[46] Clinton of New York notifies Law of Connecticut that a suspect is about to "stroll" to New London, but when he indignantly demands

[45] 1 *Talcott Papers* (*Conn. Hist. Soc. Colls.*) 322, 325, 330; 3 *Law Papers* 381, 384, 385. Connecticut passed a statute in 1720 providing for expulsion of foreign offenders (*Acts and Laws of Conn.* 258). The request for evidence and witnesses was not covered by the act. The question of expense is mere inference, but there is some evidence in other connections on the point; cf. 2 *Pa. Archives* 272 (rendition of deserters), 1 *Talcott Papers* 322 n. (expense of messenger service).

[46] 2 *Law Papers* 64 (1745).

that the clergyman who married his eloping daughter be prosecuted Governor Law replies blandly that it does not "fall in my province to intermeddle in it."[47]

Undoubtedly a decision to extradite or not depended partly upon the personal relations of the governors involved and partly upon the state of local pride. Clinton had not endeared himself to the Connecticut government, so that when he was succeeded by the politic De Lancey who was at pains to show his good will, Governor Wolcott expressed his gratification over the change. Consequently when it came to the ears of the Council that one Key had been caught with counterfeit New York bills and Connecticut had requested a genuine £20 bill for the prosecution, the Council advised a request for extradition on the ground that Key would only be corporally punished in Connecticut and further that once in New York he could identify his accomplices. The Council suggested assurances "that any request of the like nature will be readily complied with on the part of this Government." De Lancey made the requisition, to which Wolcott answered that he would have been glad to comply but Key had escaped from New London jail.[47a] We shall see in a moment how fragile the New York assurances of cooperation turned out to be.

The most difficult point to determine in colonial extradition proceedings is the role of the courts. We have seen that judicial warrants were obtained when offenders were to be received, but there is little information as to what the courts did if an application came to them or if an offender was requisitioned who was already in their jurisdiction.

About the middle of the eighteenth century we pick up evidence tending to show that the courts were attempting to evolve some simplification of the business of rendition. The first exhibit is a so-called "escape warrant" entered in the precedent book of John Van Cortlandt.[48] This warrant, dated August 15, 1746, was issued by Robert H. Morris, Chief Justice of New Jersey, requesting the assistance of all officers in New York in apprehending John Hopkins "as they would expect the like assistance from us." This is followed by a form of bench warrant issued by De Lancey, Chief Justice of New York, which recites that "it being reasonable for the officers of his Majesties provinces to assist each other in bringing offendors to justice, I do therefore in his Majesties name

[47] 3 ibid. 298, 320; 2 ibid. 28.
[47a] 23 Ms. Mins. Council 166, Mar. 8, 1754; Wolcott Papers (Conn. Hist. Soc. Colls.) 437, 438.
[48] Brevia Selecta 34 (Van Cortlandt Mss.). We have seen one evidence of local cooperation. At a meeting of the Ulster justices Aug. 20–21, 1728,

Justice Mackintosh reported he had a hue and cry from Orange for fellows who had committed a robbery in Bergen County, New Jersey. Apparently the Orange warrant issued upon the receipt of a Jersey hue and cry (Ms. Files Ulster Co. Bundle E).

hereby require all sheriffs constables and other officers to be aiding and assisting" the New Jersey sheriff in apprehending the offender.

Forms were not casually put into manuscript precedent books, and we think,
therefore, the above entry, which recalls the backed warrants of England,[49]
implies a usage better established than the records show. An episode which occurred some ten years after the above warrant issued appears to be an example
of its continued employment.

In 1756, a ring of counterfeiters was operating in Dutchess County and one
Eliphalet Beecher, a Connecticut catchpoll, was promised a reward by the
assembly of his province if he apprehended persons alleged to be counterfeiting Connecticut, New York, Rhode Island and New Hampshire bills at Dover
in Dutchess County.[50] Beecher repaired to New York and secured from De
Lancey and two puisne justices of the Supreme Court what we believe must
have been a warrant like the one just described. On February 9, 1756, he apprehended in Dutchess County two persons suspected of counterfeiting, viz.,
Samuel Griswold and Jacob Mace. He brought these men before Justices Haviland and Humphrey who proceeded to take their examinations. Beecher,
however, was required to give security to prosecute. After much delay the
justices refused to grant a warrant to send either of the suspects out of the colony without sufficient proof that these men had committed the offense. This
Beecher was unable to do and consequently Griswold and Mace were required
to give bail to appear at the next Circuit in Poughkeepsie, while Beecher was
saddled with all the costs.[51]

The Connecticut Assembly, feeling that there had been "want of encouragement" on the part of the civil authorities in Dutchess, desired the Governor to
write Governor Hardy acquainting him with Beecher's troubles and requesting that further authority be given Beecher or that the suspects be sent to Connecticut for trial or be tried in New York if the case were cognizable there.[52]
In spite of the New York Council's assurances made two years before, it does
not appear that anything was done, for Mace who had been under indictment
in Dutchess for forgery since 1751 appears in the records of that county to have
been kept on recognizance until October, 1761, when his case disappears from
the records.[53] However, Owen Sullivan who was supposed to have been the

---

[49] A warrant issued by a justice of the peace was
good only in the county where issued, but by "backing," viz., endorsement by a justice in a neighboring county, it had vigor in the latter.
[50] 10 *Pub. Recs. Conn.* 455; *Conn. Archives,* 4
Crimes and Misdemeanors 264.

[51] *Conn. Archives,* 4 *Crimes and Misdemeanors*
265, a deposition of Beecher.
[52] *Ibid.* 266; 10 *Pub. Recs. Conn.* 462.
[53] *Ms. Mins. Dutchess Co. Sess.* Liber B, Oct. 15,
1751. The case was ordered for trial at the next
court on Oct. 17, 1758 (*Ms. Mins. Dutchess Co.*

leader of the gang was convicted in New York in May, 1756.[54] Beecher who claimed to be out £134 3s. ¼d. petitioned for his reward alleging that Sullivan was "as much out of mischief in the New York Gaol as in Connecticut."[55]

This case illustrates the weakness of the mere "backed warrant" as against an order from the Governor. The local justices were in duty bound to examine suspects and determine questions of probable cause to protect their own citizenry when the mandate of their own court merely ordered assistance in apprehending. But a writ or warrant from the Governor, being a prerogative precept, was not to be parleyed with by inferior magistrates. Where, however, a suspect was actually in the jurisdiction of the Supreme Court the direct action of that court without intervention of the executive could be effective, since the court having once taken jurisdiction, the disposition of his person (except for pardon or reprieve) was a matter entirely within the court's cognizance. Two cases bearing on the matter of extradition are illustrative.

Abraham Arie Ackerman was indicted by the grand jury of Orange County for knowingly passing a piece of base metal as a true Spanish milled dollar and was then bound on recognizance to appear at the New York Supreme Court. When Ackerman appeared in the New York Supreme Court, that tribunal "ordered that the same be Notified to the Judges of the Supreme Court in the province of New Jersey where the offense was Committed and it is requested that . . . the Chief Justice of this Court do signify the same accordingly and transmit a Copy of the Indictment."[56] Apparently the communication was made directly by the court to the New Jersey government without executive intervention. Possibly the same course was followed in a case that arose a few years later—the court again acting upon its own motion. On April 27, 1767, one David Smith was indicted for burglary in the Supreme Court, but on April 29 he was found not guilty. The Supreme Court then made the following order: "The Court orders that the Prisoner David Smith stand Committed until he can be delivered to the sheriff of Philadelphia. He stands Charged with divers Felonies Committed by him in that City."[57]

Sess. Liber C) but no further steps appear to have been taken. Mace had been informed against for forgery of bills of Rhode Island on the basis of a Dutchess presentment (*H.R. Parch.* 189 A 4; *H.R. Pleadings* Pl. K. 957). A plea was filed Oct. 24, 1754 but no further action was taken (*Ms. Mins. SCJ 1750–54* [Engr.] 274, 349).

[54] *Ms. Mins. SCJ 1754–56* (Engr.) 255, 261. *Conn. Archives,* 5 *Crimes and Misdemeanors* 16, 17. The Rhode Island authorities had warned New

York about Sullivan in 1754 and stated a reward of £400 was out for him (*Cal. Eng. Mss.* 614).

[55] *Conn. Archives,* 5 *Crimes and Misdemeanors* 18. Cf. also the references (297, 298) to a later gang of counterfeiters (1769). Beecher was first voted £10 (10 *Pub. Recs. Conn.* 515) and later £58 7s. 6d. (*ibid.* 539).

[56] *Ms. Mins. SCJ 1762–64* (Engr.) 224, July 30, 1763.

[57] *Ms. Mins. SCJ 1764–67* (Rough) 228, 234, 235.

The practice of initiating correspondence with judicial officers of other provinces was not confined to New York. In 1772, Chief Justice Horsmanden appeared in Council with a letter from a Rhode Island Assize judge notifying him of the capture of two men who had counterfeited New York bills. The Council ordered the Chief Justice to take steps to have the offenders brought to New York, a most exceptional waiver of executive prerogative.[58] This episode is otherwise interesting in that it tends to show that where the Supreme Court acted on its own motion actually to render offenders, this was based entirely upon its immediate and actual jurisdiction over the person, for otherwise no reference would have been made in this case to the Council. Its powers of direct rendition are accordingly to be viewed as an aspect of the wide control it had in the matter of banishment, rather than as an attempt to trench upon executive authority.

The practice of expelling undesirables goes back to the early days of English occupation and was regarded as inhering in the power to inflict final sanctions.[59] Not until the seventeen-twenties was much use made of this device, but from then on a steady stream of orders for deportation is to be found.[60] The

---

[58] 26 Ms. Mins. Council 302.

[59] Infra 686, 688, 690.

[60] Frances Sutton was brought into Quarter Sessions on May 8, 1723, by the jailer into whose custody she had been committed for want of surety for her good behavior, and the court ordered that she be sent back to the government of New Jersey from which she had lately come. Evidently the lure of the metropolis was too strong for Frances because she was indicted there on Feb. 5, 1723/24 for assault and breach of the peace (Ms. Mins. NYCQS 1694–1731/32 423, 431, 438–440).

Cf. the order re Ann Butler (infra c. VIII 495): "Whereas it appeareth to this court that one Ann Butler . . . a Wandering Idle Vagrant . . . privately Conveyed herself into this City . . . and was of lewd life and Behavior for which Reason the Justices Ordered her to be Transported out of this Province as a Vagrant from Constable to Constable but upon her application (she being weakly in body & constitution) Indulged her so far as to lett her Transport herself out . . . to the Colony of Connecticut where she pretended she had friends & Moneys . . . [but she] is since Returned privately into this City where she follows a lewd Course of life as this Court is Credibly Informed and the said Ann Butler . . . humbly prays the Court not to inflict any Corporal punishment on her and she will again Transport herself out." Evidently the court "indulged" Ann again, for her humble prayer was granted, but she was warned that if she was again found in the colony of New York she would be whipped under the act of assembly of 7 George I (ibid. 517, 524).

When Rose, a mulatto slave, was committed to the common jail for divers misdemeanors and for "damning the white people's throats," the N.Y.C. Court of Quarter Sessions on Feb. 1, 1736/37, ordered that Rose be given thirty-nine lashes and transported out of the colony, and immediately before being transported she was to be carted and receive thirty-nine more lashes (Ms. Mins. NYCQS 1732–62 74).

See also the N.Y.C. Quarter Sessions minutes for May 8, 1745, where a culprit was given 11 lashes for singing in praise of the Pretender and acknowledging himself to be a Roman Catholic. This culprit was then sent to Elizabethtown, New Jersey, from whence he came, and it was ordered that as often as he came back to New York he should be punished in the discretion of the justices of peace (ibid. 181). Compare a later case where an order was made transporting a pauper from Brookhaven out of the province, and another order made by the justices of peace of Richmond bringing the pauper back. The Supreme Court in this instance ordered that the last warrant be quashed (King v. Joseph Ralph and Aaron Van Name, justices of peace, Ms. Mins. SCJ 1757–60 [Engr.] 74, July 29, 1757).

Bridget Clarke, on Feb. 9, 1748/49, pleaded guilty in New York City Quarter Sessions to an indictment for petit larceny and was sentenced to twenty-nine lashes and to depart town, and if found in the town thereafter to be sent to the house of correction for further punishment (Ms. Mins. NYCQS 1732–62 248).

David Hannion on November 9, 1769, pleaded guilty in New York City Quarter Sessions to an in-

inherent power of the courts was further fortified by the acts for the summary trial of vagrants which were specifically grounded on the circumstance that "many vagrant persons passing through" the counties of New York "from neighboring colonies have often committed diverse misdemeanors breaches of the peace and other criminal offenses."[61] Provision was made not only for summary punishment but also for transportation out of the colonies. The practice was in no sense an extradition, for deportation ensued after trial. It was motivated in part, like poor laws, by the desire to prevent settlement of persons likely to be public charges, and in part to keep the colony free of undesirables.

Since so broad a control over the bodies of persons in custody resided in the courts, it is remarkable that instances of direct extraditions by the courts are rare. Executive prerogative in this matter had, however, been established long before the courts first saw fit to act, and the Governor and Council esteemed themselves fully competent to deal with the problem without necessarily consulting with the judiciary.[62] On several occasions governors expressed their uneasiness that there was nothing to prevent encroachments of jurisdiction by the Supreme Court,[63] but there never seems to have been a collision over extradition in New York and hence no necessity to obtain a final ruling from the Crown on the matter of competence.

Conflicts within the Province

In the first decades of English rule in New York when a clear separation of governmental functions had not yet come into existence, contests over jurisdiction were resolved by the simple expedient of reference to the Governor and his Council which exercised a large discretion in all matters of law enforcement. Under Dongan, when the process of separation began, it is possible that issues respecting cognizance may have arisen, but if so, the fragmentary records tell us nothing. It is only after 1691 when the frame of provincial gov-

dictment for petit larceny and was sentenced to thirty-nine lashes and ordered to leave the city on pain of like punishment, but it is not clear whether he simply had to leave the city of New York or whether he was also obliged to leave the colony (*Ms. Mins. NYCQS 1760–72 296*).

[61] Acts were passed in 1732 for the rural counties (*2 Col. Laws NY 745*) and for New York City (*2 ibid. 766*) and in both language such as quoted above is used. The assembly first enacted a vagrancy act in 1683 (*1 ibid. 131*) requiring security for persons without visible estate or a craft if they were to be admitted as inhabitants. This was substantially reenacted in 1691 (*ibid. 238*). An

elaborate vagrancy act was passed in 1721 (*2 ibid. 56*) which gave to the justices of the peace the power to examine and transport. It is probable that the increase in deportations noted above was due to this statute.

[62] Compare for example the Council's order that the sheriff of Orange proceed to Sussex County, New Jersey, and arrest certain persons who had intruded on Swartout's lands. The return was apparently to the Council (*9 NJ Archives [1 ser.] 178*).

[63] Cf. Clinton's remarks in *6 Doc. Rel. Col. Hist. NY 576*, and Colden in *2 Colden Letter Books 89, 141, 449, 450; 9 Letters and Papers of Cadwallader Colden 295, 296*.

ernment which was to last until 1776 came into being, that the business of fixing the sometimes indeterminate boundaries of authority led to collision.

We have already adverted to the fact that in respect of criminal jurisdiction the Supreme Court of New York enjoyed a position of supremacy in the judicial system that was greater in fact than even the King's Bench possessed in England, since the possibility of a review of its judgments was very restricted. There were, however, two spheres of authority where its powers could be challenged—the admiralty where the court depended upon Act of Parliament and special commission, and the jurisdiction over the naval establishment which had been specifically reserved by the Crown's commission to the Governor.[64] Inevitably, common law traditions respecting jurisdiction being what they were, the Supreme Court ventured into these forbidden waters.

The settlement of the Vice-Admiralty jurisdiction in New York after the English statute of 1696[65] and the adjustment of jurisdiction in relation to pre-existing tribunals were handled with great care, for the opinion of the Council was sought on several occasions.[66] The prosecutions for violation of the Navigation Acts, however, was by statute an area of concurrent jurisdiction[67] so that there was both opportunity for cooperation as well as for conflict. The first occasion when the Supreme Court interfered in admiralty jurisdiction was an example of attempted cooperation. The vessel of one John Wake was libelled by Paroculus Parmyter, the local naval officer, in July, 1699 under the "Act for Preventing Frauds" (7 & 8 Wm. III c.22) for failure to possess a register.[68] Wake executed a bond conditioned to produce the register and the ship was released. Two years later Collector Weaver seized the ship and proceeded by information in the Vice-Admiralty Court for the infraction of the act. The sentence of the court being in favor of Wake and the ship discharged, a special session of the Supreme Court was obtained[69] and Weaver procured one Collins to bring an information in the Supreme Court against Wake and at the same time the Collector applied to the Supreme Court for a prohibition against the Admiralty sentence.[70] This was granted. In other words, Chief Justice Atwood directed a prohibition to himself as Vice-Admiralty judge, the purport

---

[64] Cf. the commission to Dongan in 3 *Doc. Rel. Col. Hist. NY* 380.

[65] 7 & 8 Wm. III c.22.

[66] See, for example, in cases in 1697 and 1698, 8 *Ms. Mins. Council* 15 (appeals), 51 (jurisdiction), 75 (jurisdiction), 119 (jurisdiction).

[67] 7 & 8 Wm. III c.22 §§2, 7.

[68] The facts and a transcript of the Vice-Admiralty proceedings are in P.R.O., C.O. 5/1047.

[69] 8 *Ms. Mins. Council* I, 264.

[70] These proceedings are in *Ms. Mins. SCJ 1701-04* Aug. 23, 27, 1701. After the second Admiralty case was begun Collins' information was withdrawn.

of which was to annul and void the previous sentence discharging Wake's ship. This device was resorted to because the previous discharge in Admiralty was a bar to a fresh information there. The case was taken by error to the Governor and Council which sustained the prohibition.[71] An appeal is said to have been taken to the King in Council, but no trace of such has been found in the Privy Council records.[72] Meanwhile Atwood, sitting in the Vice-Admiralty in a fresh prosecution which the prohibition made possible, condemned Wake's ship to be forfeit. This case was in fact appealed to England but the appeal was not further prosecuted.[73] The whole affair has an air of collusion and was so highly irregular that it contributed to the charges made against Atwood.[74] It was not motivated by any desire to trench upon the Admiralty jurisdiction but rather to victimize Wake.[75] The case seems not to have been a precedent for we have seen no other like it.

Not until 1740 in the case of *Kennedy* v. *Fowles,* discussed in the previous chapter,[76] did the relations of the Supreme Court and the Vice-Admiralty reach a stage of conflict. The Supreme Court became involved here because the Admiralty Court refused to entertain a plea to the jurisdiction. As we have seen, the offense consisted in importing non-English goods not laden in England, but the seizure was made when the vessel was docked within the high water mark—as Fowles claimed, within the County of New York.[77] The libellant denied that the place of seizure was material to jurisdiction any more than in any other criminal case.[78] The decision of the Supreme Court by inference rejected this contention, although it was put on the ground that the provincial Vice-Admiralty Courts were not included in the words, "any of his Majesty's courts," used in the act (15 Car. II c.7). The affirmance by the Privy Council did not remove the possibility of friction, but in 1754 the Vice-Admiralty in New York itself decided that the statute 7 & 8 William III c.22 did not give it

---

[71] 8 *Ms. Mins. Council* 282; P.R.O., C.O. 5/1047/596.
[72] *Case of William Atwood* (13 *NYHS Colls.* 253); 4 *Doc. Rel. Col. Hist. NY* 924.
[73] C. M. Andrews, in his introduction to *Recs. of the Vice Admiralty Ct. of Rhode Island* (Towle ed. 1936) 46, with characteristic sportive misuse of legal terminology, states that the New York "verdict" was reversed by the Privy Council. We have examined the *Privy Council Register* in the Public Record Office and all the available papers in this case and have found nothing to substantiate Mr. Andrews' assertion. The petition to the Council was referred (P.R.O., P.C. 2/79/148). In 1703 Wake's

widow petitioned for admission to appeal (*ibid.* 2/79/352).
[74] Cf. the report in 4 *Doc. Rel. Col. Hist. NY* 1010, and the charges against Weaver, *ibid.* 1013; *Cal. S.P. Colonial 1702* 1206 xi. There is further material on this case in 4 *Doc. Rel. Col. Hist. NY* 886, 923, 930, 944. Atwood's defense is in the *Case of William Atwood* (13 *NYHS Colls.* 252).
[75] 4 *Doc. Rel. Col. Hist. NY* 817.
[76] *Supra* 235 *et seq.*
[77] *James Alexander, Admiralty Papers* Box 45; H.R. *Parch.* 230 A 2.
[78] *James Alexander, Admiralty Papers* Box 45 no. 5.

jurisdiction over seizures within the body of the county,[79] and there were no further direct collisions with the common law courts.

Where members of the naval establishment (exempt from local jurisdiction by the Governor's commission) were charged with crimes, the Supreme Court on two widely separate occasions undertook to demonstrate its independence. On October 6, 1697, Lieutenant John Lawrence and John Le Reaux were indicted for fraudulently and feloniously stealing goods to the amount of £15, and having pleaded not guilty were placed on trial. However, Captain John Evans "appearing did declare that his lieutenant [that is, Lawrence] was under confinement aboard His Majesty's ship . . . for the crime and did say he would give him to the court of Admiralty in England." The court resolved that his Excellency be made acquainted with this plea and the court decided to await his Excellency's direction thereon. Meantime, however, the jury on October 7, 1697, found Le Reaux guilty, and on October 8, Tuder on behalf of Le Reaux

> offers for the quashing of the Indictment and verdict that the prisoner is belonging to the ship Richmond under the King's pay and there is a provision in his Majesty's Letters Patent that such shall not be tryed but by comicion under the broad seal of England . . . and prays the Court will crave oyer of his Excellency's letters patents for the government under the Great seal.

The court thereupon had the letters patent obtained and read and took the case under advisement. On October 9, 1697, Le Reaux being asked what he had to offer why judgment should not pass according to the verdict, requested counsel who gave in writing the reasons for quashing the verdict and among other things said that Captain Evans of the *Richmond* required the prisoner "as being one of his Ship's Crew to be put on board his Majesty's ship. The Court do consider that the proceedings of this court in this matter indictment and said verdict be . . . quashed." However, the court ordered "that his Excellency the Captain Generall and vice admirall be acquainted from this Court with the crime for which those proceedings have been had against Le Reaux as all the grand jury's presentment of Lieutenant John Lawrence for the same fact and that the prisoner be not discharged until his Excellency's purpose be herein knowne."[80] The proceedings here were remarkable in that the court

---

[79] Kennedy q.t. v. Thirty-Two Barrells of Gunpowder (Hough, *Cases in Vice Admiralty* 82). Note also the case, Spencer q.t. v. Richardson *et al.* (*ibid.* 181), where the Vice-Admiralty denied this court possessed jurisdiction under 30 George II c.9.

[80] *Mins. SCJ 1693–1701* 120, 121, 124–128; *H.R. Parch.* 209 G 9. Le Reaux had prayed that, not understanding English himself, he might be heard

permitted the case to go to a verdict before the Governor had a chance to act, although what there was to gain by an assertion of jurisdiction is not obvious. The final disposition is curiously phrased, for although a verdict of conviction could be set aside,[81] it was unusual to speak of quashing it. Still, the case occurred when the common law learning was not yet a completely open book and fine distinctions of language were yet to be appreciated.

Many years elapsed before there was again occasion for a conflict of jurisdiction of the sort just described. The Supreme Court appears to have acquired after 1697 a new standard of *noblesse oblige* in respect of the King's own establishments, for in 1699 when Simon Smith, chaplain of the fort, was presented by the grand jury in the Supreme Court for marrying Elizabeth Buckmaster, married woman, to Adam Baldridge, without a license for so doing, the court ordered that the presentment be recommended to the Lieutenant Governor. And

> upon reading the said presentment the said Smith did contemptuously utter several scurrilous expressions to the scandal of his function the abuse of ye grand jurors and diminution to the dignity of the court. But in regard he executing the office of Priest in the church of England and chaplain to the Earl of Bellomont, the court would not put any censure on him for this contempt but recommend the same to the Lieutenant Governor to do therein what in his prudence and discretion he shall think convenient.[82]

There was no legal reason why jurisdiction should have been waived here, unless the court was moved by considerations of courtesy. No such feelings prevailed, however, when the second engagement of the provincial Supreme

by his counsel, who set forth "that the prisoner has no knowledge of the law nor Jurisdiccon of this court that the fact . . . on which the said verdict was grounded was alleged to be done upon the water out of a prize ship and the goods taken never brought to shoare That the governor's letters patent restrained all such offenses to the High Court of Admiralty That said LeReaux was born in his Majesty's pay and service on board his Majesty's ships . . . for which reasons his Council did alleage the verdict and prosecution of LeReaux ought to be allowed as coram non judice . . . the court having duly considered that part [of the Governor's letters patent] which restrains all offenses . . . done on the seas . . . creeks, havens, coves, rivers or harbours within the Province by any person . . . in his Majesty's service . . . are of opinion that the said Indictment and the prosesse and verdict . . . be quashed" (*Mins. SCJ 1693–1701* 127, 128).

[81] 2 Hawkins, *Pleas of the Crown* c.47 §11. The "quashing of convictions" was an expression limited usually to convictions on summary trial.

[82] *Mins. SCJ 1693–1701* 173, 174. Chaplain Smith was suspended in August, 1700 for "living a scandalous life, in neglecting his cure," parting with his wife and cohabiting with another woman (4 *Doc. Rel. Col. Hist. NY* 719). The trick whereby Smith secured the license to marry Elizabeth Buckmaster and Baldridge (a pirate) is related by Bellomont in *ibid.* 766. Compare also the case of John Winn, a soldier indicted for felony in stealing a parcel of linen and lace reserved for the Governor, as the defendant was a soldier in the garrison, 1694 (*Mins. Westch. Ct. of Sess. 1657–96* 92). Cf. also King v. James (*infra* 355) where indictment was quashed. In a Dutchess case (King v. Cassady *et al.*) the indictment of soldiers for an affray was sent down to the Lieutenant Governor (*Ms. Mins. Dutchess Co. Sess.* Liber C, Oct. 20, 1761).

Court with his Majesty's naval forces occurred in 1750.[83] Major William Ricketts was sailing with his wife and family in New York ·Bay. The sailboat was flying a pennon and Ricketts, who was evidently not up on naval etiquette, neglected to dip his flag as his boat passed H.M.S. *Greyhound*. This audacity was observed by a young officer and the gunner's mate, who apparently conceived a lesson in manners was indicated. A shot was fired from a swivel gun that unfortunately struck and killed Abigail Stibbins, the Ricketts' maid servant. James Parks, the gunner's mate, in an examination before the coroner,[84] confessed to having fired the gun and Chief Justice De Lancey then issued a warrant to arrest the offender. Captain Roddam of the *Greyhound* made two requests for the surrender of his man, but De Lancey refused. Roddam again demanded Parks stating he was sending home for trial Lieutenant How who had given the order to fire. He likewise addressed the Attorney General requesting an explanation of his conduct. When Bradley denied he had any power in the matter, Roddam turned to Governor Clinton who sought manfully to assist. He proceeded to publish in the *New York Gazette* that part of his commission relating to the trial of naval officers,[85] no doubt expecting thereby to influence opinion. He attempted further to bring pressure to bear

[83] The Supreme Court minutes for this term are missing. Our account is based upon the documents in 6 *Doc. Rel. Col. Hist.* NY 572 *et seq.*; 4 *Letters and Papers of Cadwallader Colden* 210 *et seq.*; *NY Jour.* June 11, 1750; P.R.O., Admiralty 1/3676/ 236 *et seq.*

[84] *Ms. Mins. Coroner NYC 1747–58* fols. 26–28, June 8, 1750: "The Jurors upon their Oaths Do say that John How Lieutenant of his Majesties Ship Greyhound and James Parks Gunners Mate of the Said Ship on Thursday the Seventh day of this present Month of June In the year aforesaid being then On Board his Majesties Said Ship Greyhound (the Said Ship then and there being and Lying in the North River otherwise called Hudsons's River in the City and County of New York and the Said John How being then and there Commanding officer on Board the Said Ship) between two and three O'Clock in the afternoon of the Same day Not having the fear of God before their Eyes but being Moved and Seduced by the Instigation of the Devill and as felons of Our Said Lord the King in and upon her the Said Abigail Stibbins in the peace of God and of Our Said Lord the King then and there being An Assault did make and he the Said John How did feloniously Voluntarily and of his Malice forethought point and the Said James Parks Did also feloniously Voluntarily and of his Malice forethought put the Match too and fire a Swivell Gun from On Board his Majesties Said Ship Greyhound which Said Swivell Gun was Loaded with Gunpowder and one Iron Bullet of about half a pound

Weight being of the Value of One Penny Current Money of New York which Said Swivell Gun the Said John How did then and there feloniously Order to be fired at a Small Boat belonging to William Ricketts of Elizabeth Town aforesaid Gent which Gun the Said James Parks did feloniously fire at the Said Boat (the Said Abigail Stibbins being then and there on Board the Said Boat So that the Iron Bullet So as aforesaid Loaden And Discharged from the Swivell Gun aforesaid feloniously Voluntarily and of their Malice aforethought did strike and Wound the Said Abigail Stibbins Above the Orbit of her Right Eye which Penetrated into her Scull Giving her a Mortal Wound of the Breadth of One Inch and an half and of the Depth of three Inches of which Said Mortal Wound the Said Abigail Stibbins Lived and Languished for about two hours— And then And there Died and So the Jurors aforesaid Upon their Oath aforesaid Say that the aforesaid John How and James Parks and Each of them feloniously and of their Malice forethought within the City and County of New York the Said Abigail Stebbins did then and there Kill and Murder Against the peace of Our Said Lord the King his Crown and Dignity and the Jurors aforesaid upon their Oath aforesaid Do further Say that the aforesaid John How and James Parks or Either of them had no Goods or Chattells Lands and Tenements within the City and County of New York to their knowledge."

[85] *New York Gazette* June 11, 1750.

upon De Lancey, C.J., with whom his political relations were not good, and failing, conceived that De Lancey's action was part of a plot to discredit him, because Roddam was his son-in-law.[86] He reported the matter to the Admiralty, but De Lancey remained adamant.

Parks was brought to trial and found guilty of manslaughter.[87] When called to judgment he produced the Governor's pardon which was allowed and he was discharged. Apparently the question of jurisdiction was raised, but De Lancey would have none of it "saying he was fully persuaded that it was cognizable in Banco Regis and he proceeded to trial."[88]

There can be no doubt that the Supreme Court's insistence on proceeding in the face of the explicit letter of the Governor's commission was improper, and, in view of the Chief Justice's political relations with Clinton,[89] it is possible that the latter's suspicions were a correct assessment of De Lancey's motives. In the competition for popular support then going on, one must take account also of the state of feeling respecting the naval establishment (which was not in good odor because of impressments and interferences with commerce) and the effects of a decision to make a salutary example. But whatever his motives, one cannot but commend De Lancey's determination to proceed when one considers what later took place in England.

After Clinton's report to the Admiralty arrived, opinions were sought on the question of jurisdiction. Despite the fact that in relation to a closely similar

[86] 4 *Letters and Papers of Cadwallader Colden* 213.

[87] *Ibid.* 222. *New York Gazette* Aug. 13, 1750.

[88] 4 *Letters and Papers of Cadwallader Colden* 223.

[89] 2 Smith, *Hist. NY* (*NYHS Colls.* 1826) 143. That Clinton took his revenge of the coroner, cf. the following entry:
"Memorandum that on the 29th day of September 1750 His Excellency Governor Clinton appointed Anthony Rutgers Esq. Coroner of the City and County of New York, in my Room—I having displeased his Excellency the Governor in not following and pursuing his Directions Concerning an Inquest Taken upon View of the Body of Abigaile Stibbins on the Eighth day of June Last past who was Killed by a Swivell Gun Shot from his Majesties Ship Greyhound under the Command of Robert Roddam Son in Law to the aforesaid Governor Clinton the said Ship being then Lying in the North river. 1st. his Directions to me were to keep the Jury till they were Cool 2ndly that I should follow the advice of a particular Man in the City of New York. Neither of which According to my Oath Could I Comply with, it being out of my power to keep the Jury after the Inquest found and as they are Sworn it is Certain if they be Honest Men they will find the Inquest on Evidence & the Dictates of their own Conscience without being Influenced by any Governour" (*Ms. Mins. Coroner NYC 1747-58* fol. 32).

The political turmoil in August, 1750 is the subject of a pasquinade by William Livingston:
"Political Bill of Mortality for the month of August, in the year 1750, in a certain quarter of the town near the Bowling-Green.

Burst with malice,	4
Over-fatigued with writing dialogues,	2
Grumbling,	3
Of vain expectations,	10
For want of pay,	5
Of roaring against the four members,	7
Of Madeira,	4
Nocturnal consultations,	3
Of the Cacoethes,	12
Running about for votes,	14
Of Probity,	1
Impolitic blunders,	6
Of a letter to the freeholders,	39

In all 110"
(Sedgwick, *Memoir of the Life of William Livingston* [1833] 65).

case in Portsmouth harbor in 1747 the holding of a county inquest had been treated as founding common law jurisdiction,[90] the pundits of Doctors Commons regarded the New York case as within the Admiralty jurisdiction. All were agreed it was not murder as the guns had been fired to make Ricketts strike his pennon.[91] Samuel Seddon went so far as to remark that "Captain Roddam has acted very prudently in recommending it to the Attorney General to prosecute Mr. Ricketts" for his insolence in having hoisted the flag.[92]

Lieutenant John How who had put the match to the gun was tried at an Oyer and Terminer for Admiralty causes at the Old Bailey in February, 1752. Seddon, who prosecuted for the Crown, reported that all the witnesses—three midshipmen, a gunner and the second quartermaster of the *Greyhound*— testified that they had never seen the corpse, that they had heard a woman had been killed but did not know of their own knowledge that she had been. The convenient absence of the *corpus delicti,* and the failure to establish that there was one (for the New York coroner's inquest although sent over was apparently not available) moved an indulgent judge to assert that no murder had been proved and that the jury must acquit.[93] Accordingly Lieutenant How was acquitted. If the Supreme Court judges entertained any lingering doubts about their action in *King* v. *Parks,* the news of this English trial must have quieted them. And we may add a final gloss, for the benefit of the economic interpreters of colonial disaffection, that one episode of this character did more damage than a baker's dozen of excise *qui tams.*

Ten years after the excitement caused by the shooting of Abigail Stibbins, the provincial authorities were faced by a new problem relating to maritime jurisdiction. Four sailors of H.M.S. *Winchester* were killed outside New York Harbor by members of the crew of the Bristol privateer, *Sampson.* The shooting took place because the *Winchester* sailors were mistaken for a press gang. Captain Hale of the *Winchester* made his complaint and warrants were issued, but the crew of the *Sampson,* which had come into port, armed themselves and defied capture. When Captain Hale brought up his ship to assist in the arrest the *Sampson* men took to their boats and escaped. The Lieutenant Governor then issued a proclamation for their arrest. Osborn Greatrakes, the master, and his mate were taken into custody and some of the crew were later captured.[94]

[90] P.R.O., Adm. 7/298/394. Conceded because the Admiralty coroner did nothing.
[91] P.R.O., Adm. 1/3676/236, 241, 242.
[92] *Ibid.* 248.

[93] Report of Seddon, Feb. 24, 1752 (*ibid.* 248).
[94] 7 *Doc. Rel. Col. Hist.* NY 446, 454. The proclamation of August 20, 1760 is in the NYHS collection of broadsides. On this episode cf. also 1

When these events took place the war with France was raging and the feeling about the impressment of seamen by the Navy was intense. At the October term of the Supreme Court indictments against the master and mate were submitted to the grand jury but this body refused to vote a true bill on the ground the offense was without the body of the county. Greatrakes then petitioned to be discharged or tried by special commission.[95]

At this moment the question of jurisdiction was a matter of considerable complexity. In England the trial of offenses on the high seas had been regulated by 28 Henry VIII c.15 which provided for the issuance of commissions of oyer and terminer under the Great Seal and trial according to the course of the common law.[96] The troubles with piracy at the end of the seventeenth century had led to the enactment of 11 and 12 William III c.7, designed to remove "Piracies, Felonies and Robberies upon the Sea" from the sphere of common law procedure. This act provided for the issue of commissions under the Great Seal or the seal of the Admiralty, and a method of proceeding without inquest or trial juries was stipulated. As the statute was made with reference to the colonial problem and expressly extended to the plantations, commissions were from time to time sent to New York for the trial of pirates.[97]

Colden, *Letter Books* 16, 62; *Ms. Mins. SCJ 1756–61* (Rough) 200, Oct. 24, 1760, 209, Oct. 28, 1760, 215, Oct. 30, 1760; *H.R. Pleadings* Pl. K. 375, Pl. K. 334.

[95] 25 *Ms. Mins. Council* 331.

[96] C. M. Andrews, in *Recs. of the Vice Admiralty Ct. of Rhode Island* (Towle ed. 1936) 3, states that jurisdiction over felonies on the high seas was exercised in "the criminal division of the High Court [of Admiralty] sitting as a common law court." In 43 *Amer. Hist. Rev.* 405, we explained that by virtue of 28 Henry VIII c.15 a commission of oyer and terminer under the Great Seal *ex necessitate* made the jurisdiction one at common law. Although Mr. Andrews subsequently admitted (4 *Col. Period Amer. Hist.* 223 n.) that "from a strictly legal point of view" he might have been more "technically precise," nevertheless, he there avers that the High Court of Admiralty "appointed special commissioners to sit as a court of oyer and terminer for the High Court of Admiralty in Justice Hall, Old Bailey, there to try with a jury all criminal cases arising on the high seas involving life and death." Mr. Andrews further avers that his statements were based upon oyer and terminer records that he has seen. There are no references given to these records or to any commissions. Such references would have been desirable since every reputable writer from Browne (2 *Civil and Admiralty Law* [1802] 55) down to Holdsworth (1 *Hist. Eng. Law* [1922] 551) has asserted that criminal jurisdiction over felonies on the high seas was exercised as set forth

above in the text. In 1720 the law officers of the Crown stated that 28 Henry VIII c.15 had taken away the admiralty jurisdiction even over piracy (2 Marsden, *Law and Custom of the Sea* 252, 253), and in 1833 Dr. Lushington, the eminent civilian, told a Parliamentary committee that jurisdiction over offenses at sea was "administered in effect by the courts of common law" (*Report from the Select Committee on Admiralty Courts* [1833] 58). The basic jurisdiction established by 28 Henry VIII c.15 remained unaltered until the nineteenth century, except for the procedure established by 11 & 12 Wm. III c.7 and later amending acts.

[97] For specimen commissions cf. that issued to Bellomont in Benedict, *American Admiralty* (5 ed.) 802; cf. also the list in 5 *NJ Archives* (1 ser.) 196. We do not know whether or not Mr. Andrews has seen any of these commissions. He states (4 *Col. Period Amer. Hist.* 229): "Piracies and other felonies committed on the high seas lay outside the categories [*sic*] of the civil law as they involved life and limb and required a jury. This need was met in the colonies by the Governors' appointments of special commissions sometimes construed as special courts of oyer and terminer, in both cases with a jury authorized under an Act of 11–12 William III." If Mr. Andrews refers to 11 & 12 Wm. III c.7, he has either not read the statute or he has not understood it. The Act gave no powers to the governors to issue commissions. As to accessories it provided trial according to 28 Henry VIII c.15, and until 1727 when by statute all persons were made

The latest of the commissions had been received in 1758, but owing to the demise of George II this instrument had determined, and there was consequently no warrant for trying the *Sampson* men by commission for the trial of pirates.[98] Authority to issue a special commission had to be found either in the general prerogatives of the Governor or justified out of the statutes which through constant amendment had reached a state of inconsistency typical of eighteenth century legislative patching.[99] Since the statute 28 Henry VIII c.15 was law long before colonization it presumably extended to the plantations. The Piracy Act of William III has language which seems to affirm such extension, and this was certainly the effect of 4 Geo. I c.11 §7. Nevertheless, in 1720 Counsel Richard West expressed the opinion that the Tudor statute did not extend to the West Indies.[100] The reasons are not given, but it should be noticed that since commissions of oyer and terminer for offenses on the high seas had to issue under the Great Seal there was no means of effective execution of the statute except in the form provided—without a royal commission, no trial possible.

There were some provincial precedents but they were of doubtful effect. Dongan had issued a commission of oyer and terminer in 1683 for the trial of offenses on the ship *Camellion*.[101] Less than ten years later (1692) the New Yorkers had enacted a statute patterned on 28 Henry VIII c.15 and making

principals, the royal instructions required that such defendants be sent to England' (Labaree, *Royal Instructions* no. 647). As to principals the statute eliminated jury trial by making the commissioners appointed under the Great Seal or the Admiralty seal the sole judges of both facts and law. The New York trials of Joseph Andrews (1769) and Wood (1774), reported by William Smith Jr. in 4 *Ms. Jour. Wm. Smith Jr.*, prove that the statutory mandate was exactly executed (cf. *infra* 609). Note also Stokes, *View of the Constitution of the British Colonies* (1783) 233, commenting that at one trial in the West Indies under 11 & 12 Wm. III c.7 prisoners "escaped because they were tried according to the course of the Civil Law."

R. B. Morris (The Ghost of Captain Kidd, 19 *NY History* 294 n. 26) referring to certain trials for piracy states: "Goebel (*Amer. Hist. Rev.* XLIII, 406) gives the impression these trials were common law trials, but it is quite clear that Admiralty judges generally took a leading rôle in such proceedings in the colonies." Our remarks were addressed to trials under commissions of oyer and terminer, and at no point did we refer to trials for piracy under 11 & 12 Wm. III c.7. As we had read that Act we were aware that in trials conducted pursuant to its provision no juries were used.

[98] The reception of the commission is noted in 25 *Ms. Mins. Council* 259, Oct. 4, 1758.

[99] As the Act 11 & 12 Wm. III c.7 was a temporary statute it was continued by 5 Anne c.34 §3, and 1 Geo. I st. 2 c.25 §17. Then intervened 4 Geo. I c.11 §7. William's Act was made perpetual by 6 Geo. I c.19. Nevertheless the subject was overhauled in 8 Geo. II c.24, the most important effect of which was to lay down that accessories were to be deemed principals. This act also appears to restrict the words "piracy felony and robbery" to acts related or connected with piracy (viz., the taking of ships or goods *animo furandi*). The instructions to the Governor certainly imply this (Labaree, *Royal Instructions* no. 647). Cf. also the later acts 2 Geo. II c.28 §7; 18 Geo. II c.30; 32 Geo. II c.25.

That the colonists were bewildered by the statutory kaleidoscope is shown by the dilemma caused by the arrest in 1717 of William Dobs, sexton of Trinity Church, accused of aiding pirates. The Council thought the outstanding commission had expired with the Act (11 *Ms. Mins. Council* 420 *et seq.* July 4, 11, 1717; *ibid.* 448, Nov. 14, 1717) and decided to await orders.

[100] 2 Chalmers, *Opinions of Eminent Lawyers* 204.

[101] H.R. *Ms. Wills* Libers 1 and 2, 306.

express reference thereto.[102] This act empowered the Governor to issue special commissions, and we think the Oyer and Terminer held for the trial of Cornelius Jacobs in 1694 was issued pursuant to this law.[103] Jacobs was accused of comforting and abetting the French in Hispaniola, a form of treason covered by 28 Henry VIII c.15.[104] The grand jury, of which ironically enough William Kidd was foreman, found the indictment *ignoramus* and Jacobs was discharged.[105] Subsequently in March, 1697/98 the Board of Trade attempted to get a model piracy law passed,[106] but the next provincial statute of 1699 was substantially identical with the 1692 act.[107] This new statute was disallowed in 1700, and the 1692 act was repealed by the Crown eight years later. It is important to notice that the Act of 1699 was printed by Smith and Livingston in their revision of the laws with no indications of disallowance.

Faced with this bewildering network of statutes the New York Council submitted the *Sampson* case to the Attorney General, who advised that a commission could be issued under the provincial Act of 1699.[108] The colonial authorities were under the impression that this act had never been disallowed; indeed, we have the testimony of the commissioners that no record of disallowance was available.[109] The special commission of oyer and terminer was accordingly issued on November 5, 1760.[110] The court convened on November 11, 1760 but the grand jury, no less intractable than their predecessors in the Supreme Court, returned the bill *non sumus informati*.[111] With a fine but deplorable sense of irony the Council then advised Lieutenant Governor Colden to order that William Mackey, John Callahan and John Phillipse of the *Sampson* and then in custody be delivered to H.M.S. *Dover* for service.[112]

102 1 *Col. Laws NY* 279.
103 *Mins. SCJ 1693–1701* 56.
104 7 *Ms. Mins. Council* 72. Chidley Brooke, writing to Blathwayt, states that Jacobs had been carrying on an illicit trade at Hispaniola and that provisions carried thence on the ship *Orange* had enabled Ducasse, the Governor of Hispaniola, to invade Jamaica (*Cal. S.P. Colonial 1693–96* no. 1546).
105 *Mins. SCJ 1693–1701* 56.
106 4 *Doc. Rel. Col. Hist. NY* 299.
107 1 *Col. Laws NY* 389.
108 25 *Ms. Mins. Council* 331; 7 *Doc. Rel. Col. Hist. NY* 455.
109 Wm. Smith, Jr., who had edited the 1750 revision of the New York laws, laid before the commissioners a 1718 London edition by Basket according to which the Act of April 19, 1699 upon which the commission was grounded had been repealed Sept. 5, 1700. The commissioners wrote to the Board of Trade Nov. 25, 1761: "No such dis-

allowance is to be found as we are informed, in our offices, not any copy of it, or note concerning it, upon the minutes of council, nor in the journals of the General Assembly; by which minutes & journals alone the editors of the edition made here, were to be directed in distinguishing what laws have had the Royal assent, & which of them are repealed. Nevertheless, upon this discovery, & the great probability that the London ed. was compiled from the exemplified copies of our laws, in the Board of Trade Office; and that Basket the compiler and King's printer, had access to the minutes of council in England, and of the Lords of Trade for his information, the Commissioners thought not safe to meet upon their last adjournment, and therefore the other seamen of the ship Sampson still remain in custody of the sheriff of N.Y." (P.R.O., C.O. 5/1070/O034).
110 *Cal. NY Col. Commissions* 55.
111 *Ms. Mins. SCJ 1756–61* [at the end] 1–6.
112 25 *Ms. Mins. Council* 335.

The aftermath of this case is interesting. It was reported to Whitehall, where the Order in Council repealing the Act of 1699 was known. The Board of Trade having doubts whether or not murder committed on the high seas could be tried in the colonies,[113] the Crown law officers advised that 28 Henry VIII c.15 extended to the colonies, but that the trial would have to be before commissioners in England. They were further of the opinion that the provisions of 11 and 12 Wm. III c.7 did not extend to murder. "They relate merely to such felonies as are equal or inferior to the species particularly mentioned."[114]

The English authorities promised a new statute (which was not forthcoming) and sent over a new commission for the trial of pirates.[115] It is significant that the effect of the opinion of the Crown law officers was to lead in New York to a restrictive interpretation of the statute of 11 and 12 Wm. III c.7, for in 1774 a defendant was acquitted by a "Commission for the Trial of Pirates" because in the robbery with which he was charged the evidence did not present the elements of piracy.[116]

It is unfortunate that we do not know more about the initial gambits in the *Sampson* case. Recourse to the Act of 1699 was obviously an afterthought once the effort had failed to found jurisdiction in the Supreme Court by procuring the indictment there of Greatrakes and his men. That this tribunal was chosen in the first instance as the proper forum for the trial of an offense outside New York Harbor indicates that the Supreme Court's pretensions to a sort of *summa potestas* in the Province were no longer to be questioned unless by the Crown itself. The English King's Bench was the court's exemplar, and it is not mere accident that it is sometimes so referred to in official correspondence. After the successful vindication of its powers as a Court of Exchequer during Cosby's regime the prestige of the Supreme Court was greatly enhanced[117] and it was certainly not lessened by the affirmance of its judg-

---

[113] 7 *Doc. Rel. Col. Hist. NY* 504.

[114] 2 Chalmers, *Opinions of Eminent Lawyers* 219–221.

[115] 4 *Acts of the Privy Council, Colonial* 485–487.

[116] 4 *Ms. Jour. Wm. Smith Jr.* Oct. 15, 1774.

[117] As early as 1702 Thomas Wright and Philip French, presented for high misdemeanors, were ordered to plead "at a court of Exchequer held for the province of New York" (*Ms. Mins. SCJ 1701–04* 56, 63, 64). Again in 1722 an English Exchequer decree was sued on in the New York Supreme Court as a Court of Exchequer (*H.R. Parch.* 235 D 2), and seven years later Samuel Heath, deputy weighmaster, was proceeded against there as in Exchequer (*Ms. Mins. SCJ 1722–32* 176; *James*

Alexander Papers Box 2 nos. 60, 118, 121, 124, 131, Box 4 no. 26). The exercise of these powers became an acute issue in the salary controversy between Van Dam and Governor Cosby.

~~Letters patent~~
On Dec. 5, 1732, "~~An Ordinance~~ [*sic*] for Es-
~~being produced~~
tablishing the Court of Exchequer in this province
~~& It is~~
read ordered that unless there be printed copys of
~~Letters patent~~
Said ~~Ordinances~~ [*sic*] delivered to Each of the Judges of this Court ~~the said Judges be Each of~~ ~~them served with a written one by the Clerk of~~ ~~this Court~~ [*sic*] that y⁰ Clerk of the Court deliver

ment by the Privy Council in *Kennedy* v. *Fowles*. In every successive *cause célèbre* down to the outbreak of the Revolution it proceeded with an Olympian certainty of the prerogative implicit in its very name. The defeat sustained in 1761–62 on commissions during good behavior was a matter of the judges, as individuals, succumbing to pressure. The independence and courage of the court were soon enough demonstrated in the issue over appeals from jury verdicts in the *Forsey* v. *Cunningham* controversy (1764).

The Supreme Court Supreme

While the various episodes related exemplify more or less dramatically the primacy of the Supreme Court its standing in the province was achieved no less by the constancy with which it superintended the inferior common law courts and by the diligent husbanding of the generous endowment of jurisdiction conveyed to it by ordinance and statute. As we have already had occasion to observe, provincial enactment was not specific in relation to the administration of the criminal law, so it was a matter of great moment for the enforcement of the law that the King's Bench powers of supervision be exploited to their fullest extent. In the years immediately following the introduction of common law forms (1684) the definition of the respective spheres of judicial authority in Crown cases was effected by reference to the prevailing pattern of practice in England so far as this was known to the judges. This process of applying concrete examples continued well into the eighteenth

to each of them a written one." [Interlineations and last clause beginning "that y⁰ Clerk . . ." are written in a different hand and darker ink.] (*Ms. Mins. SCJ 1727–32* 396.) This entry appears as a result of the bill filed by the Attorney General against Rip Van Dam, and on Mar. 20, 1732/33, the following Supreme Court entry appears in the Van Dam case: "Ordered that if Mr. Justice Phillips be of Opinion that this Court can hear & determine Matters on the Equity Side of the Exchequer that the plea and Demurrer in this Cause be Argued on Thursday in next Terme." On April 19, 1733, the court decided that it could hear and determine matters on the equity side of Exchequer and it was therefore ordered that Van Dam's plea be set aside without further arguing. But before the plea was set aside a parchment writing was filed which was "a further exception offered by the defendant to the power of judging of this court." However, the court was of the opinion that that exception ought not to be received. On Oct. 16, 1733, attachment was returned into the Court of Exchequer by the high sheriff of New York and in his return the sheriff said that the defendant was in his bailiwick.

On Oct. 23, 1733, the second attachment was returned not found, and on Jan. 19, 1733/34, "The Comⁿ of Rebellion returnable this day, was returned by the persons in the Said Commission Named & Appointed that the Said Rip Van Dam is Not found," and on Jan. 22, 1733/34, a warrant was ordered to issue to the sergeant-at-arms (*Ms. Mins. SCJ 1727–32* 396; *Ms. Mins. SCJ 1732–39* 18, 23, 26, 50, 51, 65, 76, 82, 88, 93). In the *James Alexander Papers* Box 44, Apr. 1733, we note that Alexander had asked that Judge Phillipse make a finding whether the Supreme Court had the power "to cognize in a course of equity." Phillipse had said that the Supreme Court had this power, and Alexander had offered to argue the plea but was opposed by the other side, and the court had said that it would be at his peril if he did. The court had further said that it could not but overrule the plea with resentment if Alexander argued the motion. The Chief Justice resigned as a result of this case and De Lancey was appointed in his place. For further details on the Rip Van Dam case, see *Horsmanden Papers 1714–47* nos. 5–7, 10.

century but it does not seem at first to have been subject to much centralized control. Thus, as we have seen, the justices of the peace adopted and exercised the powers and functions of the office as exemplified in the textbooks without guidance from the superior courts. It is only when common law theories respecting jurisdiction become current in the province that a basis for rationalized control is available. Here again, the case of *King* v. *Bayard* is our starting point, for it is in the arguments of counsel that the first evidence of a grasp of theory is perceptible.

It will be recalled that in the argument on the motion on arrest of judgment, counsel for Bayard had raised the point regarding the commission of oyer and terminer being limited to one day. Said Emott for the defendant: "I pass now to the words of the Commission which are strictly limited to the 19th of February so that whatever has been done since I humbly conceive has been *Coram non Iudice* and therefore void."[118] He then went on to say in reply to the Solicitor General:

> As to the special commission of oyer and terminer, that it is long since expired by its own limitation is very plain and self-evident, for it empowers your Honours to meet and make inquiry at the City Hall on the 19th of February, and upon the said Day, all and singular the premises to hear and determine. This indeed may be called a special commission for it is not in the Common Form of Commissions of Oyer and Terminer, as ye Books direct, for if we look at the form of this Commission in the Register, in Fitzherbert's Natura Brevium and in the Fourth Part of Sir Edward Coke in his Institutes they all agree in one form and are very different from this Commission for by those Commissions the Times and Places of their Meeting are left to the discretion of the Commissioners. . . . Yet in this special Commission both the time and place of your Meeting, Enquiring, hearing and determining are specially limited to the 19th of February so that I am of opinion that your Honors are strictly tyed up to by the words of your Commission and all your proceedings since the 19th of February are unwarrantable as being *coram non judice.*

Citing a case in Plowden, Emott proceeded to distinguish between persons acting by special commission and *virtute officii:*

> Persons appointed to act by special commission only . . . have no authority but what is specially given them by the very words of their Commission . . . but if persons do act anything by virtue of their office, as the Chief Justice of

[118] See page 33 of the 1702 New York edition of the Bayard trial, British Museum C.71 g.4.

the Kings Bench or Common Pleas, the Common Law in a great measure explains their authority and Power.[119]

It is evident from the tenor of this argument that the common law approach to questions of jurisdiction was well understood in New York at the turn of the century. Thereafter, certainly, issues of this sort were discussed in this idiom, but, we may say, uniformly without success when the powers of the Supreme Court were challenged. Some years after the Bayard case, in another prosecution of a political character, the Supreme Court itself had occasion to turn a deaf ear to an attempt to impugn its jurisdiction.

Samuel Mulford, a member of the assembly for Suffolk County, was informed against by the Attorney General for printing and publishing a malicious libel entitled "Samuel Mulford's speech to the Assembly at New York." Mulford's second plea to the information was "that whatever offenses (if any there be) are contained in the said speech, the same were done and committed in the general assembly where it ought to be examined and punished and not elsewhere, and that the courts of law have no jurisdiction thereof." The Attorney General demurred to the plea, alleging that the information was not for anything done or spoken by Mulford in the General Assembly as a member for the County of Suffolk, but for drawing up, compiling, framing, printing and publishing and promulgating a libel.[120] The demurrer also stated that

[119] Cf. also *supra* 274.

[120] For Mulford's speech see *NY Misc. Mss.* Box 4, 1711–16, no. 23. Also see Mulford's memorial of grievances contained in 3 *Doc. Hist. NY* 363. In *Horsmanden Papers* nos. 2 and 3 are the information, plea, demurrer and joinder, which are as follows:

"Of the Terme at June In the first year of . . . King George Witness Lewis Morris Esqr Chief Justice

Samuel Mulford putteth in his place May Bickley his Attorney at the Suit of . . . the King On an Information exhibited agt him for his Misdemeanor:

Be it Remembered That David Jamison Esqr Comissr for Executing the Office of Attorney Genl . . . who for . . . the King presents . . . Gives the Court to understand & be Informed That Samuel Mulford . . . well knowing his Excell^{en} Robert Hunter . . . to be . . . Governor [and to have] . . . used . . . much frugallity and Good Husbandry in the creating . . . and publick Debts . . . But maliciously & wickedly Contriving the s^d Robt Hunter Esq. of all tht his aforesaid Good & Deserved fame name and esteem to Deprive . . . & to bring . . . the same Robt Hunter into great Disesteem & Comtempt & the Displeasure of his sd

Majty . . . and the Disregard of the Subjects . . . intending to move & Stir up Sedition & Rebellion . . . Did then & there draw up [etc.] . . . a certain false Scandalous & malicious Scurrilous Libell . . . Some of wch Relations are wholly false & untrue & others of the same so artfully Deceitfully & maliciously disguised wth falsehood & misrepresentation to render, them effectual towards his own s^d Evil purposes . . . & Giving Colour & umbrage to the Inhitants . . . to Dread & expect the like Malladmcons . . . to what are in the af^d Libell Setforth . . . contrary to his Duty of Allegiance in manifest Contempt of his Majty & the Govr . . . To the Obstruction & hindrance of the future support of the Governt. . . . To the evil Example of others & agt the peace of Our sd Ld the King his Crown & Dignity and agt ye form of the Statutes made & provided Whereupon the sd David Jamison . . . prays Advice of this Court in the premes And that the sd Samuell Mulford be attached by his Body Wheresoever &c. to answer . . . the King . . . Therefore Comand is to the Sheriff That he attach &c So that he have the Body of the sd Samuel Mulford before his Majtys Justices of the Supreme Court of Judicature at the Citty of N. York on the first Tuesday of Sepb^r in [1716] . . . At wch day . . . before the same Justices . . . came ye sd

314 LAW ENFORCEMENT IN COLONIAL NEW YORK

Mulford's plea was evasive and sophistical. The Supreme Court minutes are not available for the date when the demurrer was ruled upon, but Mulford in a printed account states that the demurrer was overruled.[121] Before the case was settled he removed to England and was able to secure an order for cessation of further proceedings against him.[122]

The policy of refusing to give ear to challenge of its jurisdiction once settled, the Supreme Court steadfastly and with remarkable consistency adhered thereto. This tended eventually to obliterate any questions of conflicts where the powers of the Supreme Court might be in issue, for these were foredoomed to be determined in just one way.[123] Indeed, so assertive did this court become of its prerogative that upon one occasion it went so far as to deny that it possessed certain powers simply for the purpose of maintaining the finality of

David Jamison who &c And the Sheriff did bring into Court the Body of the sd Saml Mulford And the afd Samuel Mulford Cravd Oyer of the Information & it is read unto him wch being read & he heard The sd Saml Mulford in his own proper pson came and did Defend the Contempt Trespasses & Misdemeanors & whatsoever &c.

"And saith . . . he . . . was one of the members of the Genl Assembly . . . by virtue of his [?] patt[n] of . . . [Queen] Ann . . . And because the Supposed Libell in the sd Information mentioned is entitled in the sd Information his . . . Speech to the Assembly . . . he saith that whatsoever offences . . . contained in the sd Speech, the same were done & comitted in Genl Assembly afd And that the Court here ought not to have Conazance thereof because all such offences . . . in Genl Assembly . . . Ought in ye same Genl Assembly to be examined & punished and not elsewhere By wch he doth not intend That . . . the King will in Court hereof such Trespasses Contempts & misdemeanor & offences Done in the Genl Assembly be answered &c.

"And the sd David Jamison . . . Saith That . . . the King by anything by the afd Saml Mulford above in pleading alledgd for his Action afd thereof agt the sd Saml Mulford have ought not to be precluded Because . . . the plea afd by the sd Saml in manner &c. form afd above pleaded & the m̅re [matters?] therein contained are not sufft in the Law . . . the King from his Action afd agt the sd Samuel to have to preclude . . . Wherefore for want of a sufft answer . . . [the Attorney General for] the King asketh Judgmt And tht he . . . Samuel Mulford . . . be convicted And for Causes of Demur[r] in Law upon that plea the sd David Jamison who &c. for . . . the King according to the forms of Statute in tht Case made & provided Sheweth . . . ye following Clauses [causes?] . . . First . . . the afd Information . . . is not for anything done . . . in the Genl Assembly. . . .

But for drawing up Compileing framing printing publishing & promulgatg . . . a . . . libell . . . Intitled Samuel Mulfords Speech to Assembly . . . April the 2[d], 1714 and Secondly For that the same plea is altogether Evasive & Sophistical &c.

"And the sd Saml Mulford by May Bickley his Attrny Saith That forasmuch as the sd David Jamison who &c ffor Our sd Ld the King To that plea hath not answered Nor the same in any manner of way Gainsaid But altogether hath refused to admit that verification Which certain plea the m̅re contained the same Samuel Mulford is ready to Verify He prayeth Judgmt & that he of the prem̅es of the Court be dismissed &c."

For further material on this case, see *John Jay Papers* Box 3 nos. 16, A, G, J; *Horsmanden Papers 1714–47* nos. 1–3, etc.; *Ms. Mins. SCJ 1710–14* 367, 395, 412, 424, 427, 439, 445, 478, 531, Mar. 14, 1711/12, June 7, Sept. 6, Oct. 17, 18, 1712, Mar. 14, 1712/13, June 2, Sept. 5, 1713, June 5, 1714 (on the latter date the court took the case into advisement); *F. A. DePeyster Mss.* Box 2 no. 3B, Bickley's Docket for Mar. 1711/12, Sept. 1715.

[121] In 3 *Doc. Hist. NY* 330.

[122] 5 *Doc. Rel. Col. Hist. NY* 505.

[123] We have seen only one case of major importance where no ruling appears to have been made. This was a proceeding against Richard Gardener, a New Jersey justice, and others in the course of the boundary troubles. The defendants were indicted in Orange County and the case was removed by certiorari. They pleaded to the jurisdiction and claimed the locus of the alleged offense was in New Jersey (*Ms. Mins. SCJ 1754–57* [Engr.] 44, 49, 97, July 30, Aug. 1, Oct. 24, 1754; *J. T. Kempe Lawsuits* G–J, Aug. 3, 1754, *sub nom.* Richard Gardener; *ibid.* W–Y *sub nom.* Westbrook; *Wm. Smith Jr. Ms. Supream Court Register A* 101; *Ms. Mins. Orange Co. Sess. 1727–79* Apr. 1754). The minutes show nothing as to the final disposition of this case.

proceedings before itself. This occurred when the defendant in *Forsey* v. *Cunningham* sought to have the record sent up to the Governor and Council under the disputed "appeal" provision in the Governor's instructions. The court declared it would not comply with the prayer in the petition because no proper writ authorized it to send up the record nor did it know of any power it had to assign counsel to transact business in a court where it had no jurisdiction.[124]

The effect of these periodic assertions of sovereignty upon the relations with the inferior tribunals was not inconsiderable. The design of the Judicature Act of 1691 and its successors had been a hierarchy in which the Supreme Court (except for the limited right of appeal) was to be the final arbiter, but the practical working of the scheme depended actually upon how vigorously the supervisory authority was wielded. Since agitation for decentralization was never entirely dormant, a Supreme Court jealous of its predominance was consequently a decisive factor in the reception of those common law rules and theories which would make for a hierarchy and not for a congeries of jurisdictions with competitive ambitions. We have already examined in detail how greatly the transfer system as it was administered in New York contributed to a tightly held control. Similarly, the execution of other common law rules regarding jurisdictions of limited authority, such as the suspension of inferior courts in the county where the Supreme Court was sitting[125] and the application of the court of record theory to limit Special Sessions,[126] tended to fix the status of the various judicial agencies.[127]

There was surprisingly little friction in the settlement of these matters. This is best shown by the absence of conflict in the cases where defendants were bound by recognizances to appear both in Sessions or the Supreme Court for the same offense. The practice in these cases was invariably for the inferior court to surrender the case by discharging the recognizance.[128] If the offense

---

[124] *Ms. Mins. SCJ 1764–67* (Rough) 125, Oct. 22, 1765.
[125] E.g., the entry in *Ms. Mins. NYCQS 1766–72* 264, Nov. 1, 1768.
[126] *Supra* 263.
[127] An interesting sidelight on the currency of English doctrine is contained in a memorandum of authorities to be used in arguing a plea to the jurisdiction in the case of Murphy v. Sandrys, apparently in the Mayor's Court of New York City. Some of the authorities given were as follows: 2 Lilly's *Abridgement* 384, as authority for the statement that prohibition lies to an inferior court to prohibit them from meddling in what they have not cognizance of; 2 Lilly's *Abridgement* 385, 2nd paragraph, "for this court is to regulate all other

courts in their jurisdiction and not to suffer them to usurp authority where they have none"; 1 *Keble* 336; *Raymond* 189; 8 & 9 Wm. III c.10; Register 33, 34; *Natura Brevium* 102; "Register 90 [98?] is the form of the prohibition suited to the suggestion in Lutwych 1023, Turner v. Weston. There's a president for a prohibition in point with this case C.N:B. 89 bottom is form to partys who sue Second Inst. 220" (*James Alexander Papers* Box 44 no. 19).
[128] For example, see the following cases:
Henry Slyck was on Feb. 6, 1735/36, presented in N.Y.C. Quarter Sessions for entertaining and crediting apprentices and encouraging them to defraud their masters in order to pay him. He was bound in £20 with one surety in £10 to appear

was of a minor nature, however, the Supreme Court might relinquish juris-diction in favor of the inferior jurisdiction.[129] The authorities were careful not to give cause of complaint of simultaneous prosecutions in several courts for the same offense.[130] If a defendant under double recognizance was convicted in one court he would be discharged in the other.[131] In one curious case where the defendant was taken on process in a lower court, he prayed the protection of the higher court. This occurred on September 3, 1723, at the Court of Oyer and Terminer and General Gaol Delivery for Ulster County. The entry is as follows: "On Mr. Vernon's motion on reading the affidavit of Arien Vander-merken touching Nicholas Schoonhaven who being ordered to attend this court was taken into custody by the sheriff on execution from ye inferiour court prays the protection of this court . . . discharged."[132]

It is not necessary to recapitulate the various steps and the several devices employed in the eventual definition of the jurisdictional boundaries of the New York courts. Before the middle of the eighteenth century these were well settled. The inferior courts discovered that encroachments were perilous, as in the efforts to avoid estreating fines into the Supreme Court;[133] and at the

---

at the next Sessions and meantime be on his good behavior (*Ms. Mins. NYCQS 1732–62* 60). In the meantime, however, on April 23, 1736, process was ordered to issue against him out of the Supreme Court of Judicature (*Ms. Mins. SCJ 1732–39* 213), and therefore when the defendant appeared in Quarter Sessions on May 6, 1736, he was discharged from that court "forasmuch as he is indicted in the Supreme Court for the same offenses" (*Ms. Mins. NYCQS 1732–62* 62). Slyck appeared in the Supreme Court on July 30 and 31, 1736, and on April 25, 1737, and was found guilty as to the general charge of entertaining servants and apprentices, but not guilty as to crediting them. He was therefore fined £20 on April 26, 1737 (*Ms. Mins. SCJ 1732–39* 222, 224, 257, 258, 261).

In the case of George Clark, on Oct. 19, 1767, John Lyons made an affidavit before a single justice of the peace regarding a riot and assault and battery in which Clark was involved (*H.R. Pleadings* Pl. K. 472, 502). On Oct. 29, 1767, Clark was indicted in the Supreme Court for misdemeanor and for riot, and pleaded not guilty (*Ms. Mins. SCJ 1766–69* [Engr.] 317, 318; for the presentment see *J. T. Kempe Lawsuits* C–F *sub nom.* George Clark). Meantime, however, on November 3, 1767, the defendant having been called, appeared in New York City Quarter Sessions and alleged he was bound over to the Supreme Court for the same cause for which he was bound over to Quarter Sessions, and "it appearing to this court to be true it is therefore ordered he be discharged from his Recognizance" (*Ms. Mins. NYCQS 1760–*

72 225). On January 19, 1768, Clark pleaded guilty in the Supreme Court, was fined 6s. 8d. and discharged (*Ms. Mins. SCJ 1766–69* [Engr.] 374). For the return of the estreats of the Supreme Court on this case indicating that the 6s. 8d. fine was paid, see *H.R. Parch.* 221 B 4.

The spirit of comity was carried to considerable lengths, for when Cornelius Bogart was indicted in New York City Quarter Sessions for assault and battery and pleaded guilty, "The Court having Considered of the offense, and being Informed that the said Patrick Wood hath brought a private Suit agt. the Defendt in the Supreme Court do assess his fine at 2/6 . . ." (*Ms. Mins. NYCQS 1772–91* 16, 24, Aug. 6, Nov. 5, 1772). Cf. also King v. Griffith (*Ms. Mins. Dutchess Co. Sess.* Liber E, May 17, 1774).

[129] King v. Thomas Lawrence and Ellinor Blackington, alias Irish Nell. They appeared in the Supreme Court on Mar. 15, 1725/26, and were ordered to be discharged from their recognizances because they had been bound by recognizance to appear also in the Court of Quarter Sessions for New York City (*Ms. Mins. SCJ 1723–27* 188; also see *Ms. Mins. NYCQS 1694–1731/32* 458–466, 478–482, Feb. 2, May 3, 4, 1726, where it appears that the defendants were tried for petit larceny).

[130] E.g., *supra* 193 n. 205.

[131] E.g., King v. Klock (*Ms. Mins. SCJ 1766–69* [Engr.] 504, 505).

[132] *Ms. Mins. Cir. 1721–49* 35, 36.

[133] *Supra* 175 *et seq.*; *infra* 528 *et seq.*

same time that tribunal found it convenient to remit cases if it conceived a lower court should have cognizance.[134] The occasions when it became necessary to rule on jurisdictional questions were chiefly when these were presented by some act of assembly conveying powers to a court or justice. An example of this type of case is *King* v. *Sackett*.[135] The complaint here was before a single justice for cutting trees contrary to an act of assembly. The defendants pleading title had a record made up and returned to the "Orange County Court." They then removed the case to the Supreme Court, but the plaintiff moved for a *procedendo,* arguing that the act of assembly only gave authority to the justices of peace in the county courts to try such cases, but gave no authority to the Supreme Court. The defendant's counsel, on the other hand, argued that the King's Bench and Common Pleas, being courts of general jurisdiction, had cognizance of all causes "by their institution," and that such cognizance could not be taken away, even by act of Parliament, without plain, express, and clear negativing words. According to Smith, nothing in the act of assembly negatived the jurisdiction of the Supreme Court, and evidently the Chief Justice agreed with Smith in this case for he refused the *procedendo.*

In addition to the supervision exercised over the inferior courts that there be no transgression of the limits of their authority, the Supreme Court assumed a sort of watch and ward over administrative officers. The first instance of this sort of control occurred in 1702 in connection with the Bayard case. Sampson Shelton Broughton, the Attorney General, had refused to go on with the prosecution and he was accordingly presented for high misdemeanor in neglecting his duty as Attorney General. The grand jury prayed the court to put the presentment in form, "but the Attorney Generall says the court here has no authority over him unless he affronts ye court he is answerable to none but the King and Governor for any neglect of his office." The court ordered the Solicitor General to put the presentment in form, but two days later on April 11, 1702, ordered that the grand jury's presentment of the Attorney General "with the minuits of this court be laid before the Governor and Council."[136] Broughton was able to avoid suspension but was not suffered to handle any business.[137] After Cornbury's arrival the Board of Trade, believing Broughton had been suspended, ordered he be restored to his office.[138] The affair was obviously contrived by Chief Justice Atwood who had an inflated view of his authority. At

[134] *Supra* 166.
[135] *James Alexander Papers* Box 2 Letters A–D no. 57, Jan. 22, 1749/50. Cf. also 4 *Letters and Papers of Cadwallader Colden* 132, 139, 192.
[136] *Ms. Mins. SCJ 1701–04* 56, 62.
[137] 4 *Doc. Rel. Col. Hist. NY* 1018.
[138] *Ibid.* 963.

the time it was debatable whether an officer appointed immediately by the Crown could be held accountable in a provincial court. An Act of Parliament had provided that governors, lieutenant governors, deputy governors or commanders in chief when charged with oppressive acts or crimes were triable before the King's Bench in England, but no provision was made respecting other officers commissioned under the Great Seal.[139] In 1702/03, Attorney General Northey reported his opinion in connection with a complaint against Nanfan, that a governor "when discontinued" could be proceeded against in the plantations for illegal acts.[140]

The question of jurisdiction over officers commissioned by the Crown came up again in 1754 when Attorney General William Kempe was indicted for maladministration. It is interesting to note that although Kempe was an experienced lawyer he did not raise the issue of the manner of his appointment, although he remarked in his brief that it "is a high presumption for any One to accuse him criminally, for what he legally does by Virtue of his Office . . . 'tis falling upon the king's prerogative."[141] The Supreme Court quashed the indictment, but for "incertainty and insufficiency."[142] The failure to raise the issue of privilege because of the form of appointment indicates that, by the middle of the eighteenth century, officials beneath the rank of lieutenant governor were not regarded as exempt from prosecution in the province.

Control by the courts over officers commissioned by the Governor and particularly over the justices of the peace was, as we have already had reason to notice, extensive. It was exercised as well by the medium of certiorari, whereby proceedings were reviewed or taken out of the hands of justices of the peace, as by criminal proceedings through indictment or information and by attachment for contempt. For obvious reasons the activity of General Sessions was confined to supervision of the work of single or double justices, for although there was no legal impediment to criminal proceedings against a justice the very practical one of personal relations existed. This difficulty is illustrated by a case in the County of Kings. Hendrick Claaese Van Vegte, a justice of the peace of Kings County, was on November 15, 1710, presented in Kings Quarter Sessions for a breach of the peace "ffor Coming into Broockland Church . . . with his pen & Ink . . . taking up of peoples names and taking up one particular man's hatt . . . in disturbance of the minister and people in the service of God." The justice of peace

---

[139] 11 & 12 Wm. III c.12.
[140] 4 Doc. Rel. Col. Hist. NY 1032, 1033.
[141] H.R. Pleadings Pl. K. 421.

[142] Ms. Mins. SCJ 1754–57 (Engr.) 82, 87, 118, 155; cf. infra 377.

ffor plea to the presentmt saith that in obedience to . . . the Governor's order and a duty Incumbent . . . in his office ffor the preservation of the peace he did goe into the Church . . . to take notice of the persons that were guilty of the forcible Entry made into said Church that day . . . and that he is in noe manner of way guilty of the breach of the peace, y^t it was done in pursuance of his Excellency's order and his duty as a Justice of the peace.

The court was, of course, disinclined to proceed against a colleague, however ill advised his conduct, for it found that he was "noe manner of way guilty . . . by doeing of his duty."[143]

This case occurred in the period when jurisdictional lines were not completely settled, and when the grand jury's proceedings were not yet adequately managed. The supervision of what a grand jury could with propriety present was really the business of the Attorney General, and although we have seen an early deputization by him for Orange County,[144] a contemporary *ad hoc* appointment by the Sessions court itself in Ulster[145] indicates the matter was not on any regular footing. Bradley commissioned deputies,[146] but even during his regime the justices of the peace would have to name someone, usually the clerk of the peace, to act for the Crown.[147] It is not until the office of Attorney General was held in succession by William and John Tabor Kempe that the supervision of Crown business was kept in hand by deputies regularly appointed by the Attorney General.[148] Whenever an appointee was responsible

[143] Ms. Kings Co. Ct. & Rd. Recs. 1692–1825 163. Compare the case of Van Ditmars, Lott and Johnson, who were informed against by the Attorney General for taking away the school-house key in Flatbush. Johnson and Lott on examination defended themselves by saying "they are appointed by the people and towne of flatbush to looke to their priviledges . . . and that it was their priviledge to choose a schoolmaster, and the minister and Justice did wt. they pleased against the priviledge of the towne and there was another schoolm^r put upon them by the Commandr. in Chief & Councell. . . ." However, the plea offered by Lott and Johnson did not avail them because the justices, having considered "ye premises and alsoe the rude & Contemptuous behavior of the said persons . . . at this Special sessions doe order . . . that they be Committed . . . until they find sufficient surety . . . for their good behaviour until the next sessions of the peace . . ." (ibid. 5). Cf. further on this case infra 371 n. 180.

[144] Ms. Deeds Orange Co. Liber A, 27, deputization by S. S. Broughton of his son Sampson Broughton, Oct. 23, 1703.

[145] Ms. Mins. Ulster Co. Sess. 1703–05, designation of Barne Cosens, Sept. 4, 1705. Cf. also Ms. Mins. Richmond Co. Sess. 1710/11–1744/45 Mar.

1, 1714/15, Sept. 2, 1718, designation of Henry Vernon.

[146] NY State Lib. Misc. Mss. 8074, deputization of Evert Wendell, May 28, 1725. Cf. also Ms. Mins. Orange Co. Sess. 1727–29 Apr. 25, 1727, Wickham produced his deputization; Ms. Mins. Dutchess Co. Sess. Liber A, Oct. 18, 1737, Livingston mentioned as deputy; Ms. Mins. Richmond Co. Sess. 1710/11–1744/45 Sept. 5, 1727, Walter Dongan mentioned as deputy; Ms. Mins. Suffolk Co. Sess. 1723–51 Oct. 5, 1736, Clowes (a J.P. in Queens and attorney) appears for the King.

[147] Ms. Mins. Richmond Co. Sess. 1710/11–1744/45, Clerk of the Peace Adam Mott designated Mar. 4, 1728/29, Mar. 18, 1734/35; Ms. Mins. Ulster Co. Sess. 1737–50 Sept. 16, 1746, Clerk of the Peace John Crooke designated. Note also in Dutchess when Deputy Livingston refused to put an indictment in form the court ordered the clerk of the peace to do so (Ms. Mins. Dutchess Co. Sess. Liber A, May 16, 1738). Compare the ad hoc appointment of the clerk to prosecute a negro at a special court (ibid. June 10, 1735).

[148] Infra 366 n. 154 on fee arrangements. Cf. also Peter Sylvester in Albany to Kempe July 14, 1773 (Kempe Letters A–Z).

to the latter officer it was possible to exercise some control over prosecutions with the inevitable result that proceedings to make accountable the justices of the peace centered in the Supreme Court. As we have seen, the information came to be the favored method of proceeding, although on rare occasions a grand jury in Sessions would break bounds by bringing in a presentment, as it did in 1734 against Francis Harison, the recorder of New York. Harison had arrested one Truesdale "Imprisoning and Detaining him in Gaol during the Space of Nine weaks at the Sute of Joseph Weldon of Boston without the Consent Assent Agreement of the said Joseph Weldon."[149] In this instance Harison, as a councillor, was virtually immune to information proceedings. He had made himself obnoxious to many persons, and in consequence found it prudent to disappear. The case, therefore, never came to trial.[150]

The political agitation caused by Attorney General Bradley's proceedings against justices of the peace[151] and the consequent abatement of the use of informations against justices did not result in any increase in indictments but actually had the effect of throwing many complaints against law enforcement officials into the Council. After the arrival of William Kempe in 1753 the courts again became the scene of action and the records show a greater variety of procedures than earlier.[152]

It is obvious from some of the cases in and after 1753 that a criminal sanction might be thought proper where a justice had exceeded his jurisdiction, by treating this as maladministration. Thus, in the case of *King* v. *Doughty,* one

---

[149] *Ms. Mins. NYCQS 1732–62* 43, 49, 52, May 9, 1734, Feb. 6, 1734/35, May 7, 1735.

[150] *2 Letters and Papers of Cadwallader Colden* 142, and cf. 8 *ibid.* 232.

[151] *Supra* 173; *infra* 372.

[152] The method of relief was sometimes difficult to settle upon. Cf. Emanuel Smelliger's complaint against Charles Clinton, James McClaghry and Samuel Sands, justices of the peace. Smelliger had hired a mill from one Steward for £40 a year and had also agreed to keep the neighbors' hogs out of Steward's land. Smelliger was unable to keep one Davis' hogs out of Steward's land, and finally set a dog on one of Davis' hogs. Subsequently some of Davis' relatives brought wheat to be ground at Smelliger's mill, and although the latter charged no more than the usual rate, nevertheless a warrant was brought for Smelliger's arrest on Davis' complaint that Smelliger had stolen some of the wheat. Smelliger was jailed in a tavern and the three justices of peace "without examining witnesses . . . sentenced him to be publickly whipped." Kempe, writing on the matter to Justice of the Peace Charles Clinton, said he hoped that Clinton had not done this because Clinton had no legal authority so to proceed against Smelliger "and at no rate was it justifiable to sentence him [Smelliger] without examining witnesses in his presents that he might cross examine them." Kempe considered several remedies which Smelliger might have against the justices of peace, and debated either bringing trespass against the justices and constable or an information against the justices for maladministration. Kempe considered an action on the case or an action for forcible entry against Davis' relatives for holding Smelliger's mill and an action of trover against them for holding his goods (*J. T. Kempe Lawsuits* S–U *sub nom.* Smelliger).

For another case in which justices of peace proceeded illegally, see proceedings against John Dumont and William Elsworth, Dec. 22, 1770 (*J. T. Kempe Lawsuits* C–F *sub nom.* Dumont). Also see Mr. Hatton's Case, Aug. 10, 1771 (*ibid.* G–J) and King v. Joseph (John) Forman, informed against for assault, false imprisonment and pretending to serve a writ without any warrant (*ibid.* C–F *sub nom.* J. Forman; *Ms. Mins. SCJ 1754–57* [Engr.] 54, 84, Aug. 3, Oct. 22, 1754; *H.R. Pleadings* Pl. K. 593, 636, 637, 697).

Halleck had been complained of for cutting timber on land alleged to be the complainant's. Halleck had set up title and desired adjournment to the Common Pleas, offering security with a bond. Justice Doughty had refused unless the bond contained a condition that no more timber be cut until the title was settled. This demand was beyond what the statute authorized, so on the complaint of Halleck an information was filed in the Supreme Court. Doughty was ordered on October 25, 1753, to plead in twenty days or suffer judgment. The case then disappears from the records.[153]

Again in 1763, one Strickland proffered an affidavit in the Supreme Court alleging he had been robbed by divers persons in the house of John Edwards. He had informed before Justice Van Kleeck of Dutchess who had refused to do anything and later applied to Justice Vanderbergh who issued a precept only for Edwards and then released the man after allowing him to take an oath he was innocent. This was clearly beyond the power of a single justice, so the Supreme Court ordered the two justices to show cause why an information should not be filed. This case too was later dropped.[154]

The procedure employed in *King* v. *Van Kleeck and Vanderbergh* should be noted, for it illustrates the accretion of power to the Supreme Court over the administration of the law effected by the colonial Act of 1754.[155] This act, the background of which will be discussed in the next chapter,[156] provided that no information could be filed without a recognizance to prosecute except by express order of the Supreme Court. So far as the supervision of inferior judges and officers was concerned, this meant in effect that an important share in the directing control passed from the Attorney General to the Supreme Court. The complaining witness applied directly to the court which then by a show cause order could have a preliminary hearing. On the rule to show cause the usual procedure was to produce affidavits in defense. Thus the charge of the two Brush sisters against Justice Jervis for holding court in his tavern and letting the jurors be "treated with strong liquors" by one of the parties to an action was so dealt with. Thus the prosecution of Justice Carpenter for "malpractice" in 1771.[157]

It was of course possible for the defendant official to appear in proper person. In an amusing case involving an affront to the dignity of Mr. Justice Jones of

[153] King v. Doughty (*Ms. Mins. SC*] *1750–54* [Engr.] 274, July 31, 1753, 315, Oct. 25, 1753; H.R. Parch. 16 K 4; H.R. Pleadings Pl. K. 963).
[154] King v. Laurence Van Kleeck and Henry Vanderbergh (*Ms. Mins. SC] 1762–64* [Engr.] 175, 176, 225).

[155] 3 *Col. Laws NY* 1007.
[156] *Infra* 372 et seq.
[157] King v. Jervis (*Ms. Mins. SC*] *1764–67* [Rough] 227, 247, Apr.–July 1767). Compare also King v. Carpenter (*Ms. Mins. SC] 1769–72* [Engr.] 313, 342, 349).

the Supreme Court, the offending officer personally made his *amende hono-rable*. Justice Jones, while on the "river circuit," had been ordered by one of the overseers of highways for the Southern District of Oyster Bay where he owned property to help repair the public highways of the district. When Jones refused and neglected to do so, the overseer ordered that he be fined and issued a war-rant for levying the said fine on Jones' goods and chattels. Jones complained to the Supreme Court *en banc* on July 28, 1767, and the court ordered that Ben Birdsall, the overseer, appear in the Supreme Court to show cause why an in-formation should not be filed against him (Birdsall) for this offense. A copy of this order was sent by the clerk of the Supreme Court to the sheriff of Queens County to serve the same Birdsall, and on July 31, 1767, Birdsall ap-peared in the Supreme Court and said that he was "sorry for his offense and asking pardon of the court particularly of Justice Jones" prayed that he might be discharged. The court granted his request on the payment of fees.[158]

It is not necessary to elaborate with further examples upon the efforts of the Supreme Court to maintain jurisdictional discipline in the province, beyond noticing the fact that it also used the attachment for contempt, of which more hereafter. The burden of inherited and of novel statutory duties hoisted upon the inferior judicial officers was onerous, and by the end of the colonial era had become difficult certainly to ascertain, what with inadequate publication, ex-pired statutes and acts disallowed by the Crown. Inevitably an authority was needed to reduce this chaos to occasional order, and above all to prevent un-warranted actions by local officials endowed with such broad and unmixed powers that individual extensions of authority might easily pass unnoticed. To a large degree the justice of the peace functioned administratively, as it would today be called. In the eighteenth century, belief in the expediency of a judi-cial vigil over administrative acts was as yet unshaken. On the contrary, any discretionary act of an official that departed from accepted patterns was open to question, and it can hardly be doubted that the latent threat of an informa-tion proceeding in the Supreme Court must have led many a country justice to tread with care when he acted administratively. This policy did not make for efficiency, a virtue not known to colonial governments, as the conduct of their wars discloses, but it had the effect of at least minimizing in the pro-vincial local government the sort of abuses which flourished in England.

Beyond what was achieved in respect of control over local officials, the man-ner in which jurisdictional problems were solved, and especially the concen-

---

[158] *Ms. Mins. SCJ 1766–69* (Engr.) 247, 255.

tration of authority in these matters, had a profound influence upon the direction of institutional development and generally upon the law. Operating with the same body of precedent used in England that had come into existence in response to conditions different from those which obtained in America, a judicial system was evolved infinitely better articulated than that in England. The chief reason for this was the fact that, in New York, the common law courts were founded upon enactment, and with the possible exception of Sessions, no single tribunal was an exact copy of any single English court. The supreme judicial authority was not partitioned, the ecclesiastical jurisdiction was non-existent and, despite the warrant of charters, independent franchise jurisdictions did not develop in the manors, cities or incorporated towns. In these circumstances, common law rules about jurisdiction were simply rules of law, like the rules respecting malice prepense in murder, or asportation in robbery, and were no longer associated with the institutions for which they had been fashioned. No more cogent proof could be desired than the action of the Supreme Court in *King* v. *Zenger* when the objections to the judges' commissions were brushed aside. The New York courts could pick what they wished from the books and within the gaunt framework of the founding statute make of the judicial system what seemed most suitable.

In this process of selection and adaptation a factor of paramount significance was the recurrent involvement of the judiciary in constitutional struggles, and the fact that in its work it was frequently embroiled in political controversy. Matters which in England had so long been settled as to be beyond challenge, had a way in New York of becoming issues which excited public debate and which in consequence kept public attention focussed upon the functioning of the courts and the reasons why these functioned as they did. From the time of Fletcher's quarrels with the assembly over the Judicature Act down to the "Intolerable Acts" of 1774, there was a disposition to read into questions of jurisdiction implications of common law or constitutional right, and to this the judges, who in many cases were credited by contemporaries with a lively appreciation of popular opinion, could not have been wholly indifferent. Otherwise it would be hard to explain how the Supreme Court became the political power it did under the long chief justiceship of De Lancey.

Once the assembly had been excluded from any real voice in shaping the judicial system, the judges were left the arbiters of its destiny. The only pressure which the colonists could exert was through the medium of public discussion, or via the bar. This last was a means more effective than one might today suppose, for the lawyers dominated provincial politics, and wherever a case assumed the color of a "state trial," which often happened, the briefs, where they survive, are loaded with matter that can be recognized as the stuff of current debate. Thus the defendant's attack on the King's right to regulate trade in *King* v. *Graham*[159] when stripped of its garnishing of citation, and thus Smith's argument in *King* v. *Sackett* noted above.[160] When the constitutional history of the colonies comes to be written, the plea to the jurisdiction will have its chapter.

[159] *Supra* 246.
[160] The argument is in essence that of Joseph Murray before the assembly in 1734 on the question of the basis of the judicial establishment.

CHAPTER VI

PROSECUTION

THE colonial passion for the political chase and for flushing constitutional questions out of the most unlikely coverts was by no means confined to the general fields of the establishment of courts and the definition of jurisdiction. Since the common law was the forest where all manner of constitutional rights had first grown and were duly sheltered, the American, tender of his liberties, was forever coursing in its precincts.[1] The various problems of jurisdiction which we considered in the preceding chapters were deemed to involve the general political rights of the inhabitants, issues of how far the Crown's plans

[1] In view of the overemphasis which has been placed upon the natural law as the source of libertarian thought in the colonies it is desirable to reiterate what was pointed out in Goebel, Constitutional History and Constitutional Law, 38 *Col. Law Rev.* 558 *et seq.*, viz., that prior to 1776 the common law basis of constitutional rights was in the forefront of discussion. The Declaration of Rights (1774) was the culmination of this intellectual trend. There is interesting material on this in the shape of a rough draft of proposals to be offered at the Congress in *James Duane Papers, Undated Mss.* Box 10, IV, 65, no. 201 *et seq.* In these notes it is indicated that the committee referred to in the document was to state the rights of the colonies, their grievances and the means of redress. In the first place it was proposed to establish the colonists' rights "on solid principle." Already the detested Stamp Act and other statutes had been repealed "excepting the article of Tax which has been the fatal cause of our present misfortunes." However, it was considered "essential to place our Rights on a broader & firmer Basis to advance and adhere to some solid and constitutional[?] Principle which will preserve us from future Violation" and it was suggested that "it be founded upon Reason and Justice, and satisfy the Consciences of our Countrymen." More, the committee insisted that "England is governed by a limited Monarchy and a free Constitution But if the Subject is bound by a Law to which he does not assent either personally or by his Representatives, he is no longer free but under an arbitrary power. . . . It is admitted by the English Judicatories and has been solemnly [rendered?] by the King in privy Council: that the Common Law of England and such statutes as existed prior to our Emigration are fundamentals in our Colony Constitution. Upon this Grand Basis prerogatives of the Crown & the Rights of the Subject . . . are as fully ascertained in the Plantations as in the parent State.
"By the same Constitution the King has the Execu-

tive power and is the Fountain of Title offices[?] prerogative and Honours. Hence arises his royal *authority* [*sic*] in the formation[?] of Colonies to establish a System of Government legislative juridical and executive suitable to the Circumstances of a People who are blessed with the Privileges which they never meant nor were supposed nor could forfeit, by removing to a more remote part of the English Empire by altering their local situation within the same Empire. The privileges of Englishmen were inherent They were their Birthright and of which they coud only be deprived by their free consent. . . ."

In the *Duane Undated Mss.* Box 10, IV, 70, 227 *et seq.*, Mr. Kittredge's resolution carries the argument further: "The Colonists in the several Colonies are bound by and entitled to the Benefit of those parts of the Common Law of England, of the Civil & maritime Law used there; and of the statutes of that Kingdom of Force there at the Settlement of the Colonies which are applicable to them and from their local Circumstances are not impracticable there. And the like parts of the statutes of Great Britain made from that time for securing the Rights & Liberties of the Subject.

"We do not however admit into this Collection but absolutely reject the statutes of Henry the 8 and Edward 6 respecting Treasons and Misprisions of Treasons.

"They are also entitled to the [rights?] and priviledges which have been from ti[me] to time granted to them respectively by royal Charters; and to a free and exclusive power of Legislation *in all cases of Taxation and internal policy* Such parts of the Common Civil & maritime Law and the Statutes of Great Brittain, the Acts of our several assemblies & the Charters granted to the Colonies & these[?] only constitute the Laws of the Land and the Rights and priviledges of the peoples in the Colonies. These cannot be altered or abridged by any authority but our respective Legislatures."

of government collided with provincial ideas, and whether the law could be bent to suit the political desires of the colonists. The development in New York of procedures for the prosecution of offenders raised a different order of question—that which related to the civil rights of the individual.

In English law the lines beyond which constituted authority might not penetrate in its efforts to root out the wrongdoer were traditionally believed to be laid in Magna Carta. The struggles in England during the seventeenth century had had the effect of revivifying this document, of apotheosizing it as the palladium of constitutional privilege, and the extraordinary amount of pamphleteering in this period had given a popular vogue to the great charter that in America, at least, was profound and lasting. We are not concerned here with the historical correctness of these notions, but solely with the nature of vulgar belief and its activity, the eagerness with which the glosses, the pious opinions of publicists, and even the newer revelations like the Petition of Right and the Bill of Rights were related to the basic document. The time was to come when a sort of *Harmony of the Pentateuch* would be achieved in the constitution of the state, but this was made possible only because, from the day of New Amsterdam's surrender onward, the provincial inhabitants sustained a steadfast if not always united front in their battle for proper forms of accusation, trial by jury, fair notice and the procedural safeguards implicit in the expression, "due process of law."

We speak of the undercurrent of anxiety respecting the maintenance of the individual's constitutional protections at the outset of our discussion of criminal practice, for the matter is one that is easily lost to view when the prosy details of procedure come to be considered. The adoption and application of common law rules by the New York courts began early and was very complete. These rules had come into existence in England when the problem of crime was approached as a nuisance to the state, and the stern ethics of the medieval church had leavened this attitude with little mercy. Wanting a pressure of opinion from without, it was possible for the machinery of criminal procedure to move with unbearable relentlessness. In the colonies this was a danger of particular moment, for as the tide of emigration brought increasing numbers of adventurous and sometimes lawless persons, too often with little or no substance, the temptation of the propertied and established classes to deal harshly was great. The popular concern with the liberties of Englishmen supplied, in New York, a correcting influence. It was not utterly effective, nor was it all-embracing, as the vagrants, bawds and slaves could testify, but it kept green a part of common law tradition that could easily have been allowed to wither.

The earliest comprehensive expression of constitutional principles in New York is to be found in the so-called "Charter of Liberties" enacted by Dongan's first assembly in 1683. This enactment was approved by the Duke of York but upon his accession to the throne was forthwith disallowed.[2] After the Leisler troubles, in 1691, another "Charter" in almost the same form was enacted, but this too was repealed by the Crown after the lapse of six years.[3] These two provincial acts embodied various provisions which were regarded as fundamental to the liberty of the subject, and which in some instances can be traced to chapters in Magna Carta. They indicate a certain grasp of the notion of due process in the procedural sense and a definite desire for specific safeguards in criminal proceedings—grand jury presentment for capital and "criminal" causes, petit jury for the trial of indictments, informations "or otherwise," bail, and the right to challenge. Many of the items in the two "Charters" derive from the common law itself, and such the royal disallowance of necessity left with vigor unimpaired. We have already seen how the lawyers had recourse to some of these particulars, traditional in the law, and in the present chapter we shall have occasion to observe the persistence of colonial claims in the matter of prosecution.

Prosecution under the Duke's Laws

The "Charter" of 1683, for all its appearance of a conventional seventeenth century libertarian manifesto, owed something to the politics of the colony itself. The desire that the "Liberties of Englishmen" should in some way be assured may be referred to the first political disappointment of the colonists—the refusal of Colonel Nicolls in 1665 to permit the assembly at Hempstead any legislative initiative.[4] During the intervening period before 1683 the disgruntled Englishmen of the province took occasion periodically, as some crisis arose, to invoke these "liberties,"[5] but most of their claims were either vague

---

[2] 1 Col. Laws NY 111; 3 Doc. Rel. Col. Hist NY 357.

[3] 1 Col. Laws NY 244. Cf. the Order in Council, Cal. S.P. Colonial 1696–97 no. 1012.

[4] Supra c. I 16. Greene, Prov. Governor (1898) 78, remarks that "complete political authority" was vested in Nicolls. The instructions to Nicolls have never been found. From collateral evidence, however, we know that they provided that laws not confirmed by the Duke within a year were to be void (cf. Nicolls to Clarendon, 2 NYHS Colls.

[1869] 119). This indicates an authority somewhat less than complete.

[5] The earliest statement of what the eastern Long Islanders regarded as liberties under the Duke is in 1 Southold Town Recs. (1882) 358. These include right to lands in "free sockedge"; choice of civil officers; right of soldiers to choose their own officers; three courts per year; consent to taxation. In 1667, the inhabitants of Oyster Bay protest they should have free choice of magistrates and invoke English laws (1 Oyster Bay Town Records [1916]

or for greater political freedom. There is nothing to show that there was ever involved any issue respecting the enforcement of the criminal law. The Duke's Laws had made adequate provision for jury trial;[6] they had dealt reservedly with bail[7] and had indicated in somewhat obscure language that the law of England was a general guide where the laws were not specific.[8] Nothing was said respecting the manner of accusation beyond the curious adoption of the English practice of having churchwardens present in writing at Sessions all misdemeanors, "namely Swearing, prophaness, Sabbath breaking Drunkeness, fornication, Adultery, and all such abominable Sinnes."[9]

It seems not improbable that the failure to deal more adequately with the problem of accusation in the case of common law crimes was intentional. Certainly the situation immediately after the conquest was such as to induce a certain prudence with regard to the use of grand juries, for the device was not used by the Dutch, and Nicolls' own suspicion of the democratically minded but refractory and peevish English settlers[10] was sufficient to have made him hesitate to commit the enforcement of criminal law to mere groups of neighbors; nor would it have been politic to have forced the information upon them by express statute. The solution reached as shown by the records was typical of Nicolls' genius for shrewd compromise. He had apparently in-

33–35). In 1669, petitions from Westchester and various Long Island towns for privileges of His Majesty's subjects presented to the Court of Assizes (2 Brodhead, *Hist. State NY* [1 ed.] 160). In 1670 the inhabitants of Huntington, L.I., refuse to contribute to the repair of the New York fort because they are deprived of the liberties of Englishmen and have little or no benefit of the law (1 *Huntington Town Records* 163, 164; 2 Brodhead, *Hist. State NY* 172, and 1 *Mins. Exec. Council NY* 68; 2 *ibid.* no. xxx). In 1672 a similar refusal comes from Oyster Bay (1 *Oyster Bay Town Recs.* 680). The inhabitants of Easthampton agree to contribute if they might have the "priveledges . . . of his Majestie's subjects" (1 *Records Town of Easthampton* [1887] 346). Some notion of what the colonists on Long Island had in mind can be gained from the conditions upon which they were willing to accept Dutch sovereignty in 1673 (*Whitaker's Southold* [1931] 113; Howell, *History of Southampton* [1887] 60).

After the resumption of sovereignty by the Duke in 1674, there is less available evidence of disaffection although Andros seems to have reported on this; cf. the Duke of York to Andros, Apr. 6, 1675 (3 *Doc. Rel. Col. Hist. NY* 231). The "liberties" issue is again raised by Southampton in 1678 (2 *Records Town of Southampton* [1877] 357) and cf. the order of the Court of Assizes (*ibid.* 65–66).

Compare further the Oyster Bay protest of 1681 in 1 *Oyster Bay Town Recs.* 245, 246 and the amusing testimony of Antill regarding the juryman at Carteret's trial who hoped "that they had the same Privileges as the other Plantations, The Gover[r] answered that their Privileges hung on a slender thread . . ." (3 *Doc. Rel. Col. Hist. NY* 315).

[6] 1 *Col. Laws NY* 42. The mode of selection was as follows: the clerk of Sessions was to certify to the sheriff what and how many causes were entered. The sheriff was then to issue warrants to the constables of the towns for jurymen "proportionable to the Causes with regard to the equality of the number from each Town." The constable was to warn so many of the overseers (elected by the freeholders) to attend as jurymen, but if this were not sufficient the justices should require the sheriff to supply the lack with "able and discreet men" at court or from the town where court was held. In 1666 this provision was amended so that any two justices of the peace could summon a sufficient jury (*ibid.* 91).

[7] 1 *Col. Laws NY* 17. The provision does not exactly specify the crimes or circumstances under which bail would be granted.

[8] *Ibid.* 44.

[9] *Ibid.* 26.

[10] Nicolls to the Earl of Clarendon, Apr. 7, 1666, in 2 *NYHS Colls.* 113, 119.

tended to employ the churchwardens as they had been used in England for the civil business in the parishes.[11] This office, however, was one which was connected with the Anglican church. As there were no Anglican churches except in New York City, the provision was impractical. Accordingly in September, 1665, the Court of Assizes amended the Duke's Laws, to the effect that the "office" of churchwarden was to be performed by the constable and all the overseers.[12] This is the only enactment respecting accusation to be found. The practice in the Province grew up on this foundation, but it appears from the records that something may have been owed to the procedures prevailing before the conquest.

The effect of earlier practice is most obvious in New York City. Prosecution of crimes among the Dutch had been committed to the schout, an officer who combined the functions of sheriff and prosecutor.[13] In the English settlements on Long Island, proceedings appear to have been initiated by a complaint, although in Southampton a grand jury was contemplated, and in all of them the magistrates appear to have possessed a certain discretion to deal with wrong-doers without a complainant appearing.[14] The accusatory machinery which developed after 1665 retained certain features of the earlier system. Thus in

---

[11] By various Acts of Parliament, e.g., 27 Hy. VIII c.25; 5 and 6 Edw. VI. c.2; 2 and 3 Ph. & Mar. c.8; 14 Eliz. c.5; 18 Eliz. c.10; 4 Jac. I c.5; 3 Car. I c.3. The churchwarden provision in the Duke's Laws is strongly reminiscent of the *Constitutions and Canons of 1604* §CIX. Examples of churchwarden presentments in matters of morality may be found in Peyton, *Churchwardens Presentments in Oxfordshire Peculiars* (1928) *passim*.

[12] 1 *Col. Laws NY* 78.

[13] On this office in Holland, 1 Van Leeuwen, *Commentaries on Roman-Dutch Law* (Decker-Kotze eds. 1921) 15, 473; 2 *ibid*. 353. Cf. the instructions for the schout of New Amsterdam in 1 *Doc. Hist. NY* 388.

[14] For the grand jury provision in Southampton, cf. 1 *Recs. Town of Southampton* 24 (1641). It does not appear, however, from the records that such a jury was ever impanelled. The local records are generally written in such form as to make it difficult exactly to determine how proceedings against offenders were initiated. Compare for Southampton, 1 *ibid*. 39, 40, 123, 124; 2 *ibid*. 20, 30. Many misdemeanors were dealt with in the form of actions for assault or battery; and in defamation actions the court sometimes added a corporal penalty or fine, cf. 1 *ibid*. 80, 2 *ibid*. 29. A curious feature is the action, apparently civil, where felony is found by the jury (2 *ibid*. 29), or an "action of felony" was brought (2 *ibid*. 31), in which the defendant "convicted" is ordered to pay damages and suffer a corporal penalty. We have found a similar type of action in the *Ms. Town Recs. of Huntington—Court Records*, old page 17, Budde v. Skidmore, Mar. 28, 1661, an "action of ye case in suspition of felonious taking away hoggs and piggs. . . ." The court found the suspicion to be proved by evidence and thought the cause might have been tried at New Haven. Curiously enough there is an entry in *Recs. of New Haven 1653–65* 348, of an action "upon suspicion of felony" between the same parties on May 28, 1660, where the defendant was attached but did not appear. In Easthampton, no grand jury seems to have been used, although the inhabitants had taken the trouble in 1651 to obtain a copy of the laws of Connecticut where this institution was employed (1 *Recs. Town of Easthampton* 12, 30). Apparently offenses were prosecuted on complaint of the injured person or some informer (1 *ibid*. 47, 48, 83, 89). In the Garlick witchcraft case a number of depositions are entered. This case was sent to Connecticut for trial. At a special court of magistrates held on May 5, 1658, the defendant was acquitted. The record begins "Elizabeth Garlick thou art indited," etc. There is nothing to indicate that any grand jury anywhere found this indictment; cf. *Records Particular Court of Connecticut 1639–63*, 22 *Conn. Hist. Soc. Colls.* (1928) 188. In Huntington the early actions are all civil with the exception above noted and the proceeding against Mary Suten (1 *Huntington Town Recs.* 24)

New York City in the Mayor's Court, which exercised Sessions' criminal jurisdiction there, the sheriff ordinarily complained and prosecuted substantially as the schout had done before him.[15] In one case the court required the presence also of a complaining witness,[16] but the records do not show this to have been the rule. There is evidence during the Andros regime that the sheriff's complaints were put in form of a presentment. The documents, where made of record, are not artful and resemble the formless grand jury presentments of a later period. The sheriff's presentments are actually not very different from the "informations" which Andros' revenue officers submitted for violations of the navigation laws.[17] There seems to have been a vague notion that an accusation ought to have a certain form but there was no certainty as to what was substantial. One case has been found where the prisoner was discharged because the sheriff had not properly drawn the presentment. If the presentment still of record with phrases excised is the one objected to, it would appear that use of an early English statute was not regarded as proper.[18] In

on Apr. 13, 1660. This opens "Mary Suten indited to the corte. . . ." There is no evidence of an indictment by grand jury and the charge is so informally phrased as to suggest a mere complaint by the person injured.

There are no criminal cases recorded in the early Oyster Bay records, and there is also nothing in the early Southold records. The latter plantation was under the dominion of New Haven which did not use either grand or petit juries. In Liber B (1 *Southold Town Recs.* 466) are various depositions in civil cases, but no indications of criminal proceedings. In the cases sent over to New Haven for trial, the proceedings were taken on the basis of "writings" transmitted (*Recs. of New Haven 1653–65* 51, 97, 233, 291). In the English town of Gravesend the Dutch procedure of prosecution by the schout was followed (*Ms. Gravesend Town Recs. 1646–53* 107).

[15] The change to the English forms was made on June 12, 1665 (5 *Recs. of New Amsterdam* 248). The first prosecution by the sheriff is on June 27, 1665 (*ibid.* 268). This procedure continues, the prosecutions sometimes being made by a constable (6 *ibid.* 220, 233). In the period immediately following the conquest the records indicate considerable irregularity in procedure. Oral complaint by the prosecutor is apparently the rule but a written "declaration" is sometimes used (5 *ibid.* 354). After Manning becomes sheriff (July 1667) the word "presentment" appears (6 *ibid.* 93, 123, 129) and "represents" (*ibid.* 102, 176). It should be further noted that "presentments" by injured parties were also used (*ibid.* 194, 218). Apparently it is only after 1674 that the written presentment becomes usual but not invariable.

[16] 6 *Recs. of New Amsterdam* 20, 72, 130.

[17] When written the presentments were entered in the declaration or complaint books. Cf. the *Ms. Decl. Book Mayor's Ct. NYC 1675–77; H.R. Ms. Wills* Liber 19B where complaints and presentments 1677–81 are entered. For specimen "informations," Dyer v. Pattishall (*Ms. Decl. Book Mayor's Ct. NYC 1675–77* fol. 214); Dyer v. Barnes (*ibid.* fol. 279). The following are typical presentments:

"John Archer Sherrif of ye sd Citty p'sents to this worshipfull Court Peter Steephenson of ye Same City for y^t on ye 7th of this Instant ffeb^r 1679 he did assault & batter Hugh Sampson in ye open Streete contrary to ye Peace of our Sovereigne Lord ye King & a breach of ye Civill Lawes of this Governm^t wch I leave to ye Serious consideration of this worshipfull Court to Act in ye premises as they shall see most meete wth Costs &c."

"Citty of New Yorke

"Thomas Ashton Sherriffe of the said Citty Presenteth John Cooley of the said Citty Black-Smith ffor that hee the seaventeenth day of January 1677 here att New Yorke within ye Jurisdicōn of this Co^rt did violently and Immoderately correct chastise beate and Wound a Negroe man belonging unto him by which said Immoderate and unlawfull correction the said Negroe the Nyneteenth day of the same Instant departed this life. Therefore the said Sherriffe conceiving that the same being contrary to Law of this Goverment and against his May^tie^s peace &c Presents the same to the Co^rt and Leaves the same to their Judgemts therein &c

Tho. Ashton

Sherriffe"

(*H.R. Ms. Wills* Liber 19B, 222, 306).

[18] *Ms. Mins. Mayor's Ct. NYC 1677–82* fol. 186, Dec. 2, 1679.

"Citie of Newe York

"John Archer Sheriff of the City aforesd doth

the Sessions for the ridings the presentments were made by the constable.[19] These were also reduced to writing, but the brevity of the minutes makes it impossible to tell whether or not this rule was invariably followed.

Due perhaps to the fact that the more serious crimes were reserved for the Court of Assizes, the form of accusation there was ordinarily by presentment of the constable and town overseers together. But the constable alone might present and there are instances of complainants proffering a presentment.[20] The minutes of the Assizes have reference also to indictments,[21] but there is

present John Tuder for keeping unlaw[11] Gaming in his house or yard and in the Citie of New York aforesd from the first of Septbr 1679 untill the 18th day of November last as aforesd a common bowling and place for Reel-playing for his own proper gaine and then and ther to play with boules and Reels unlaw[11]y did keepe and maintaine contrary to law ~~the form of a statute in parliam^t in the 33 year of King Henry the 8th in that case made and provided~~ and that one Abrah. Smith upon Long Island within the territories of his Royall Highness James Duke of Yorke &c and other persons unknown about the 15th of November Last past in the year aforesd the sd Common Alley did frequent and then and there with boule and Reels unlawfully did play ~~at the sd unlaw[11] Game~~ and then and there the sd Tuder and Rich. Man did gett an Ox and some money of the sd Abr. Smith at the sd Un-lawfull Game which is contrary to Law ~~the form of the Statute aforesd~~ and agst the peace of our Soverayn Lord the King And a Statute reveived in the 16th year of our said Soveraigne Charles the 2nd pag 78 etc" (H.R. Ms. Wills Liber 19B, 205).

[19] There are examples in Ms. Kings Co. Ct. & Rd. Recs. 1668–1766 for the Sessions of Mar. 17, 1668/69 (ibid. 6), presentment by constable of Bushwick for retailing liquor without a license; (ibid. 7) constable of Newtown presents one for suspicion of adultery; (ibid. 11), constable of Gravesend presents one for suspicion of receiving stolen goods. At the Sessions Dec. 15, 1669 (ibid. 21) the constable of Flatbush presents one for fornication. Cf. also ibid. 25 (1669), ibid. 47 (1670), ibid. 60 (1671); ibid. 56 is a presentment by one of the justices for not repairing highways. In the West Riding, Dec. 15, 1675 "Mr. Sam. Leet Attorney etc. indicteth the Inhabitants of Flatbush etc." (ibid. 82). Cf. also for the Sessions of Dec. 1675, 25 NY Col. Mss. 55, 133; Sessions of 1676, ibid. 57, 129, 130; Sessions of 1677, 26 ibid. 160; Sessions of 1678, 27 ibid. 129a, 28 ibid. 23; Sessions of 1679, ibid. 110. In the Upland court in one case the sheriff "indicts" (1677), in one the constable "complains" (1680), and in one the same officer "informs" (Record of the Upland Court [7 Memoirs of Pa. Hist. Soc.] 51, 182, 194).

During the early period at Albany there appears to have been no change in the Dutch procedure (cf. 1 Ct. Mins. of Albany, Rensselaerswyck, and Schenectady [1926]). The prosecutions were made by

the schout exactly as under the Dutch. At the Court of Oyer and Terminer held in February, 1673 for the trial of an Indian an "indictment" was used (ibid. 328), but there is no evidence of a grand jury. During the Andros regime, the Governor ordered that the law and former practice of the place were to be followed in so far as not contrary to the laws of the Province (2 ibid. 23, 130). The Duke's Laws were in force (ibid. 89) but the practice remained unchanged except that written complaints or "declarations" were often used (e.g., 2 ibid. 181, 352, 367, etc.).

[20] The present remnant of the record (Ms. Mins. Ct. Assizes) begins with the session for September, 1666. Cf. on presentments by the constable and overseers of Brookhaven, etc., fol. 54; of Seatalcott, fols. 81–83; Flushing, fol. 84. At the 1668 session apparently no criminal cases were tried. At the 1668 session one Dufour "presents by way of indictment" John Cooperstaffe for the homicide of Dufour's son (fol. 160) and Bernard Smith is "accused and indicted" for breaking into a house (ibid.). The text of the Cooperstaffe "indictment" is at fol. 180: "David Dufour an Inhabitant upon this Island Manhatans doth present on ye behalf of our Soveraign Lord the King. . . ." The complaint in the Smith case is made by the householder (fol. 184). There were also two actions, civil in form, for theft at this sessions. The pages after 205 are burned. At present there is kept with this volume a fragment (fols. 520–739) which appears to be the remains of a General Entries Ms. At fol. 547 is a list of articles of business among which is the taking of presentments of misdemeanors from old constables. This list resembles the articles of a general charge to a grand jury.

The session for October, 1675 is published in 2 Rep. NY State Historian 381 et seq. On the presentments, loc. cit.; for a form of constable presentment, ibid. 406, 411. At this session Samuel Leet appears as prosecutor for the Crown (ibid. 431).

[21] Cf. supra n. 20. In the printed record of 1675, cited supra n. 20, there is mentioned an indictment brought by the constable of Newtown (p. 386), an indictment by one Samuel Barker, apparently a private person, for a homicide (p. 393); an indictment brought without naming the "indictor." The printed records of Assizes for 1680–82 (45 NYHS Colls.) mention four "indictments" of negroes (pp. 34, 35). At the session for October, 1681 the court

nothing to indicate that these indictments were found by a grand jury. Indeed, the distinction between a presentment and indictment in this court seems to lie only in a choice of words. At the special Courts of Oyer and Terminer in 1669 for the trial of one Frizzell and others, and of Engel Hendricks for murder,[22] and again in 1672 at that held for the trial of Johnson and Faulx,[23] so-called indictments were used. Crude in form, they have no caption or mention of jurors, and they are not endorsed as true bills. One is therefore led to conclude that they were actually informations or complaints cast in what was mistakenly thought to be the form of an indictment.

It must not be assumed that the practice of presentment by peace officers was an American innovation or that it was merely an adaptation of Dutch usage. In England, the constable had performed similar functions, at first solely with reference to the enforcement of the Assize of Arms and the Statute of Winchester[24] and then gradually with reference to other offenses. During the sixteenth century the presenting function of the constable had become increasingly important,[25] and an examination of the printed English Sessions records for the seventeenth century indicates a constant and general practice of constables' presentments.[26] It is possible that Nicolls was familiar with the Eng-

ordered that, whereas several persons had presumed, contrary to the known laws and practice of England, to exhibit and prefer causeless and vexatious accusations and indictments against magistrates and public officials, thereafter such accusations and indictments could not be brought in to any court unless the matter, cause and ground of such accusations were first heard before two justices of the peace who would be required to bind over the parties and make a record of their proceedings and examinations (*ibid.* 24).

[22] 1 *Rep. NY State Historian* (1897) 234 *et seq.* and 242. In the Hendricks case an inquest was held on the body of the child but the inquest jury did not attempt to frame an indictment.

[23] *Ibid.* 319. The "indictments" are also in 2 *Exec. Council Mins.* 767–769. Compare with these the presentment against Fenwick at the Special Court of Assizes, January 12, 1676/77 (1 *NJ Archives* 186, 236); and the presentment against Philip Carteret at a special Court of Assizes, May 27, 28, 1680 (*ibid.* 303).

[24] 13 Edw. I st. ii c.6.

[25] Lambard (*The Duties of Constables* [1614 ed.]) has little to say about the presenting function, but cf. pp. 40, 59. Already in the fourteenth century, the constables were presenting infractions of the Statute of Laborers (Putnam, *Enforcement of the Statute of Labourers* 67, 68), and various statutes increased the load of duties to which a presenting function attached. For a list of matter for which the constable must answer, cf. *Cal. S.P. Domestic 1598–1601* no. cclxxvi. As procedure by information grew, there is no doubt that this facilitated the displacement of communal presentment by presentment made by a representative—in effect, an information. On the expansion of the constable's function see the Webbs, *English Local Government; The Parish and the County* 463 *et seq.* It is not clear from their rambling account whether or not it was general practice for a grand jury to endorse the constable's presentment, although some evidence to this effect is published.

[26] There are a great many in 1 *Worcestershire County Recs., Cal. Quarter Sess. Papers* (Bund ed. 1900) and can be readily found by consulting Index *s.v.* presentment. There are many in *Quarter Sess. Recs. Co. of Northampton* (Wake ed. 1924) 60, 63, 124–126, 130, and cf. the presentments of constables and churchwardens at 161–164. Compare also 1 *North Riding Quarter Sess. Recs.* 14, 15, 18, 22, 24, 25, etc.; Gretton, *Oxfordshire Justices of the Peace in the 17th Century*. In some cases the manner in which the records are edited make it difficult to determine the source of a presentment. Thus in the many presentments listed in the *Hertfordshire Co. Recs.* we have found only one that can be identified (*Cal. to Sess. Book 1619–57* [Hardy ed. 1928] 3). The same comment applies to Tait, *Lancashire Quarter Sess. Recs.* (Chetham Soc. 1917). In the *Manchester Sessions* (Rec. Soc. 1901), 49 *et seq.* is a set of articles re recusants, alehouses, etc. (1618) and also (p. 54) articles whereof the high constable was to inquire. The

lish usage, a possibility which is fortified by the laws which sought to establish the parish system in New York and the temporal function of churchwardens.[27] The association of the overseers with the constable on presentments of serious offenses appears, however, to have been a new departure. It suggests a policy of rather tight official control over the accusatory process while seemingly conceding something to the more democratic notion of group presentment.[28] In view of the peculiar circumstances of the Province it was, in theory at least, a sounder method of achieving law enforcement than the leet practice of Plymouth where the presentment by the grand jury was tantamount to a conviction, unless a traverse of the presentment was had and the cause then tried by petit jury.[29] In New York by the employment of offi-

form in which certain entries are made (pp. 120, 124) suggests presentment by constables, but these may have been informations (cf. the entries at pp. 182, 185).

Some of the difficulty in identifying constables' presentments is due to the practice of having the grand jury re-present or return a true bill (e.g., 1 *Worcestershire Co. Recs.* 31, 32). Mr. Bund (*ibid.* lii) indicates, however, that many of the constables' presentments are not included in the matter presented by the grand jury. Occasionally, as in 3 *Middlesex Co. Recs.* (Jeaffreson ed. 1888) 270, 336, the recognizance indicates the prisoner was to answer matter "objected against" him by the arresting officer. It seems to us possible that the constable's presentment was effective as a charge on which the defendant would "take a plea" before any grand jury action was taken. The entries "exon." in *Surrey Quarter Sess. Recs.* 1661–63 (Powell and Jenckinson eds. 1935) 108, 109 suggest this.

[27] In the Duke's Laws—*Church*, an approximation of the English parish system is attempted. The law contemplates a church in every parish and the election of eight overseers from which number the constable and the overseers were annually to elect two churchwardens (1 *Col. Laws NY* 24). It will be noted that the laws also provided for eight overseers in each town (*ibid.* 55). On their face, then, the laws had provided for two sets of overseers. Apparently Nicolls discovered that the parish system was not practicable and that the town organization was sufficient. Churchwardens were chosen by the court in New York City (6 *Recs. of New Amsterdam* 18, 103, etc.) but this office had already existed under the Dutch (7 *ibid.* 142, 175, 237). We have not found any such officers elsewhere. The amendment of September–October, 1665 (1 *Col. Laws NY* 78) indicates clearly enough that the town organization was to take over the civil functions originally intended to be performed by the parish. Further evidence of Nicolls' acceptance of existing town organizations is in his manor grants (Goebel, *Some Legal and Political Aspects of*

the Manors in NY [1928] 14, 20). It is interesting to note that although later in 1665 the presenting function of the churchwardens was transferred to constable and overseers, in 1678 Darrall and Lawrence, deacons, presented William Phillips for fornication (*Ms. Mins. Mayor's Ct. NYC 1677–82* Oct. 16, 1678).

[28] It resembles the procedure which existed in certain parts of England where the grand jury was composed entirely of constables. Already in Lambard's time, in Kent the grand jury for the shire was made up largely of constables (*Eirenarcha* [1614 ed.] 398). On the practice elsewhere, cf. the Webbs, *op. cit.* 464. It should also be noted that the same notion pervades the Duke's Laws' provision respecting petit juries discussed *supra* n. 6.

[29] Discussed in Goebel, King's Law and Local Custom 31 *Col. Law Rev.* 441, 442. In Massachusetts Bay the earliest juries are inquests on deaths (1 *Recs. of Massachusetts Bay* 77, 78). One of the inquests accused, but not in form. The early entries in criminal cases in these records do not indicate how accusations were made. In 1633 it was ordered that the secretary was to direct process to the beadle for warning of twenty-four jurors to be named by the court, but it is not stated whether these were to serve as petit or grand jurors (*ibid.* 110). In the following year the further order is made that process was to issue from the secretary to the constable who was to notify the freemen of his locality to send as many of their members as the process directed, to attend upon public service, and all trials for life or banishment were to be by a jury so summoned (*ibid.* 118). Nearly a year later it was ordered that two grand juries should be summoned annually to make presentments (*ibid.* 143) but nothing further is said as to how these should be chosen. Apparently some further legislation about grand juries was enacted for they are used both in the county courts set up in March, 1635/36 and at the great quarter courts (*ibid.* 193, 198, 202). The Body of Liberties, c.50 (Dec. 1641) provided that all jurors were to be elected by the freemen (*Colonial Laws of Massachusetts* [Whit-

cial persons as accusers the administration was reasonably certain to get an accusation, and the wrongdoer was promised a jury for trial. We shall later see that in minor cases defendants did not make demands for juries, preferring the less costly method of summary procedure. The important thing from the standpoint of the colonists, however, was the assurance in the laws.

So far as existing records show no grand jury ever functioned in New York before 1681. None of the so-called "indictments" which we have examined was found by a grand jury. This body was first employed in the extraordinary case of Captain Dyer against whom an indictment of treason was so found.[30] But it is obvious from the loose manner in which the document is drawn, the deviation even from the so-called "indictments" commonly used in provincial

more ed. 1889] 45). The code of 1660 is somewhat more explicit (*ibid*. 167). The Essex County court records first list the names of a grand jury which sat at the session for November 25, 1641, viz., before the Body of Liberties was formally enacted (1 *Recs. and Files of the Quarterly Courts of Essex County Mass.* [1911] 33). An entry (Oct. 25, 1638) mentions an indictment but there is nothing to show how it was found (*ibid*. 9). At the session for Nov. 1, 1639, one H. is "presented by the grand jury" (*ibid*. 15), and an order from the *Waste Book* indicates that a grand jury was already a functioning institution.

The form for the oath for constable, dated Jan. 1, 1637, includes the following: "You shall endeuor to find out and p'esent all disorders in common victualling howses and all offence of drunkeness . . ." (*ibid*. 1). This was apparently inserted pursuant to a law enacted in 1637 (1 *Recs. of Mass. Bay* 214) although the form of constables' oath in the *Records* does not include this phrase (*ibid*. 252).

The grand jury is introduced in Connecticut by an order of July 5, 1643 which provides for an annual summons or oftener if the Governor or court should see fit (1 *Pub. Recs. Conn.* 91). Compare the Code of 1650 (*ibid*. 536). Two entries of 1660 and 1662 (*ibid*. 349, 379) suggest that the grand jury was either elected or appointed at the Court of Elections. The earliest records are much too bare to enable us to determine how accusations were brought prior to 1643. Apparently the order of that year applied only to the general court, for ever after that date in the Particular Courts no grand juries are mentioned. An information is mentioned in 1645 (*Recs. of Particular Ct. 1639–63* 34), and in 1647 an indictment is mentioned but nothing to show whether it was voted by a grand jury (*ibid*. 49). After March, 1650, the grand jury is used in the Particular Courts (*ibid*. 77 *et seq*.). We have found no order respecting this. It should be added that there are many instances of prosecutions on the basis of individual complaint. In March, 1662/63, the general assembly approved the practice of summons by magistrates of persons

suspected upon "a fame or report of misdemeanour" and authorized sentence upon examination (1 *Pub. Recs. Conn.* 394). In the 1650 Code the constable was given broad powers to search and complain (*ibid*. 534) and in 1658/59 the constable was authorized to present "disordered meetings of persons in private houses to tiple together" (*ibid*. 333).

In New Haven, as we have noted, juries both grand and petit were dispensed with because of reasons urged by Gov. Eaton (6 *Mass. Hist. Soc. Colls.* [2 ser.] 320). Accusation appears to have been by individual complaint (cf. here 1 *Recs. of New Haven 1638–47*). In one case the complaint is described as a "note of information" (*ibid*. 46). There are numerous cases in the records which show the procedure to have been information, examination, confession and then a public proceeding culminating in sentence (e.g., *ibid*. 62–66, 233, 253; *Recs. of New Haven 1653–65* 139, 169, 384; *New Haven Town Recs. 1649–62* [1917] 178, 246, 528). This bears a close similarity to the summary practice of the justice of the peace in England in petit misdemeanor cases, although in New Haven it was used in capital cases.

[30] The indictment is printed in 3 *Doc. Rel. Col. Hist. NY* 289, and in 45 *NYHS Colls.* 11. The proceedings at the Special Court of Assizes were instituted after an unsuccessful attempt to bring the case before the Mayor's Court of New York City (cf. *Ms. Mins. Mayor's Ct. NYC 1677–82* fol. 272b): "Samuell Winder haueing Charged Capt Wm Dyre in Open Court with High Treason for Imposing & Demanding Customs without an act of Parliamt. The Court thereupon withdrew Ordering Winder to be secured to be forthcomeing when the Court shall require & after Some Shorte & Debate sent the Clerke to acquaint Capt Brookholls with the Said Charge & to know his Pleasure when they should waite on him & the Counsell to give him a perticuler account & information thereof It being a Matter of to high a nature for them to act in who Returned for Answer. That ye Counsell could not be called together to night but tomorrow

felony cases, that the employment of the grand jury was unprecedented. It is curious that once having been employed at Assizes, the grand jury was not used at the succeeding session, nor did this bold innovation affect the courts in the ridings. We have noticed, however, that in March, 1681/82 in far-off Deale, after Penn's charter had passed the seals, a grand jury was impanelled and made presentments.[31] This was probably not in imitation of what had been done in the previous summer at New York but in anticipation of expected change.

The Dyer case was, however, destined to produce change, for the smoldering issue of the "fundamental laws" was again fanned to flame and was soon after to blaze in the "Charter of Liberties" of 1683.[32] The causal connection is suggested by the fact that the grand jury in cooking up what it fondly conceived amounted to an accusation of treason charged the unhappy collector with acting in defiance of fundamental laws such as Magna Carta and the Petition of Right. Having thus disclosed its preoccupation with the basis of English liberty, this same jury next proceeded to present the manifold grievances under

morning would Advise thereupon But on a Second Message Cap[t] Brockholls Came to ye Court & Expressed the Matter to be of High Concerne & that tomorrow morning he would Call the Counsell when he Desired the Court to Attend & Ord[ered] should be taken therein.—
Ordered that the Court be Adjourned till tomorrow morning eight a clock." The matter was then taken up by the Council which rapidly remitted the case to the Mayor's Court. At a special meeting of the City Council held June 2, 1681, it was decided the Mayor's Court had no jurisdiction. On this compare H.R. Ms. Wills Liber 19b, 15:
"Att a meeting att the City Hall the 2nd Day of June, 1681.

Present {
William Beakman
Peter Jacobs
Sam[ll] Wilson
James Graham
} Aldermen

"The Impeachment of Capt W[m] Dyre being Remitted to the Mayo[rs] Court from the Councell for further Examinacon & Proceedings thereon taken into Consideracon Resolved that this Court never did nor have they any power to punish any Capitall Crime that the Charge Declared in this Court ag[t] Cap[t] W[m] is High treason in General which they find by an Express Law of this Government to be punishable with Death and he being of the Councell Mayo[r] of this City and Chiefe member of the Court they Cannot further Meddle therein or Examine the same and thinke themselves fully to have Discharged their Duty and tryst by Delivering the p'sons and Cause to the Councell who alone they conceive are authorized and have power to make further Examinacon or proceedings thereupon and

to call a Court of Assizes if they Judge Needfull. And this is O[r] unanimous Opinion.
Signed by the above."
We have no information regarding the steps taken to have the trial before the Assizes beyond the recital in a letter that it was by virtue of a special warrant from the acting Governor and Council (45 NYHS Colls. 11). Note also that at this court Francis Rumbouts was indicted for subverting English laws (infra 566), but this case was continued.
How the notion of using a grand jury originated and was carried through is hard to explain, although Brockholls intimates the merchants had intimidated the court (3 Doc. Rel. Col. Hist. NY 289 n.). Since in East Jersey the grand juries were already authorized by law (Leaming and Spicer, Grants, Concessions, etc., of NJ 101) it is possible the practice there suggested the measure.

[31] Ms. Ancient Records of Sussex Co. (Pa. Hist. Soc.) fol. 43.

[32] This is suggested by the role which the Dyer jury assumed in championing the "fundamental laws." The East Jersey Assembly had enacted in 1678 that no person was to be deprived of the benefits of the common law (Leaming and Spicer, Grants, Concessions, etc. 129) and had already enacted the grand jury provisions and various protective statutes such as limitations upon distraint (ibid. 100), arrests for debt (ibid. 117). When Andros met with the assembly in 1680 and attempted to talk that body into accepting the Duke's Laws they voted in favor of keeping the liberties of Englishmen and confirmed their old laws (1 NJ Archives 308, 311, 312).

which the province "still Doth Groan," praying that the colony might be made "Equall sharers of that Imparraled Governmt of England" as in other plantations and given an elected assembly, so that "wee may Enjoy the benefitt of the Good and wholsome Laws of the Realme of England." This "writing" was made the basis for a petition which the court directed be drawn and which was sent to the Duke of York.[33]

The specific benefits which the colonists had in mind were set forth at large in the Charter of Liberties, and the "Grand Inquest" for all cases capital or criminal was expressly mentioned. The Judicature Act which was passed by the same assembly two days later does not mention the grand jury, but where it refers to indictments we must take it that the legislators intended indictment as stipulated in the Charter of Liberties and not to the sort of complaints previously used. The disallowance of the Charter had no effect upon the institution of the grand jury, for having been put into operation when the new system of courts began to function the grand inquest remained a regular part of the accusatory machinery and no question of its abolition was ever bruited.

How novel a thing the grand jury seemed to the New Yorkers in 1684 is indicated by doubts as to how the body was to be impanelled. At the Suffolk Sessions in March 1683/84 the justices ordered that three substantial men be chosen in each town by the freeholders to serve as grand jurymen and to present misdemeanors committed in their respective towns.[34] This method was apparently patterned after the New Jersey or Massachusetts method of electing grand jurors. In Kings County, however, the justices ordered "that there being a new way of proceeding in this Court that the Justices Do Consider of against ye next court and that a venire Do Issue returnaable then for a Grand Jury and yt Ye Clerk do Draw up a Charge proper to be given them."[35] The English usage respecting the functioning of the grand jury soon became current practice in the Province, but for a time the old manner of presentment by officers did not utterly disappear. The New Yorkers over a period of twenty years (and, if they were Dutchmen, for much longer) had become used to accusations ex officio, and it took some time for old ways to subside. What is a particularly interesting effect of this early process of induration to official complaint is the apparent complaisance toward the information. As we have

---

[33] Printed in 45 NYHS Colls. 14–17.
[34] In 1 Huntington Town Recs. 387. Cf. 2 Recs. Town of Easthampton 147, where this order is referred to and the election of three men noted. Cf. also 2 Recs. Town of Southampton 99.
[35] Ms. Kings Co. Ct. & Rd. Recs. 1668–1766 fol. 360 Apr. 1684.

said, there had been no real difference between a presentment by a sheriff and an information by a revenue officer. In misdemeanors the peace officer demanded a fine, and in violations of the trade acts the collector demanded forfeiture. The revenue cases were unaffected by the introduction of the grand jury and, as before, were prosecuted by information, the form of the document alone undergoing change in 1684 to conform exactly with English forms. Although the acts of trade were resented, proceeding by information was initially not subjected to attack, a surprising oversight by a population perpetually in terror of having their "libertyes and freedomes entharled."

Once settled in New York, accusation by grand jury became the predominant method of initiating prosecution of persons suspected not only of felonies but of the more serious misdemeanors. It was not the sole means of beginning criminal proceedings for as we have had occasion to notice in the cases where the Crown had some particular stake, or where there was reason to suppose an indictment would not be returned, there was the alternative of an information brought by the Attorney General. About this there will presently be more to say. There was, too, the vast area of petty misdoing and non-doing where for reasons of convenience and quick dispatch, methods less deliberate than the periodic ponderings of the neighborhood were thought desirable. In certain types of cases complaints would be brought by sheriffs, coroners, road commissioners, overseers of the poor, constables and other minor officials.[36] These, except for the representations on the sufficiency of jails, are most numerous

---

[36] The sheriff seems to have been a regular complainant with respect to the "insufficiency of the gaol." Thus on Oct. 9, 1697 in the Supreme Court, "Emot moves in the name of the sheriff that the Judges do move to the city the insufficiency of the City Hall and prison . . ." (*Mins. SCJ 1693–1701* 127). Cf. the sheriff's complaint of March 16, 1723/24 regarding the New York City jail (*Ms. Mins. SCJ 1723–27* 69).

In Suffolk Oyer and Terminer and General Gaol Delivery of July 27, 1722, the sheriff of that county "protests the insufficiency of the gaol" (*Ms. Mins. Cir. 1721–49* 13). Complaints are also made in Sessions, as e.g., that of the sheriff of Kings in 1707 (*Ms. Kings. Co. Ct. & Rd. Recs. 1692–1825* 154). In the Ulster County Sessions between 1738 and 1750 the sheriff's complaint of the jail was regularly made (*Ms. Mins. Ulster Co. Sess. 1738–50 passim*).

In one Kings County case the sheriff complained to Sessions of what amounted to a contempt of authority: "Upon Informacoñ to this Court by the sheriff . . . & Isaak Haselbury as they were at the house of Myndert Courten . . . to serve order of this Court upon a negro . . . Corning for breach of

the sabbath that said Myndert Courten did speake . . . to them then the Courts officers these factious seditious mutinous & threatening words viz. that he did not value the Court's order a ffart . . . and they that sent for his negro . . . shall answer for it and yt he would not obey none of their orders . . . orderd . . . sent for before this Court to answer to his Contempt. Isaac Haselbury being sent for as the sheriff's deputy with an order . . . to bring sd Myndert . . . made this returne that the s^d Myndert Kept his doors lock^t . . . and told him that he would not Come to the Court . . . upon Consideratoñ of the premises the Court orders that the sheriff shall immediately take him into his Custody and him safely to keep till he give a bond & security for his good behaviour till the next Sessions . . . then & there to answer for his Contempt aforesaid" (*Ms. Kings Co. Ct. & Rd. Recs. 1692–1825* 33, Nov. 10, 1696). A constable's complaint of seditious words is in *Ms. Mins. Ulster Co. Sess. 1693–98* Sept. 30, 1693.

For a complaint by a coroner, see, for example, a minute entry in Westchester Oyer and Terminer and General Gaol Delivery for Dec. 17, 1726, "The Coroner prays his protest may be entered against

in the latter seventeenth and early eighteenth century. Since the subject matter of complaint usually required only administrative action or was dealt with summarily, we think the disappearance of such matter from the judicial minutes was due to the shifting of business from General Sessions to the meetings of justices. The complaints by inferior officers thus came to be absorbed into the welter of summary jurisdiction where proceedings for misdemeanor were most often initiated by private informers and where magistrates made orders, or a conviction was had without trial by jury. Included here are statutory *qui tams,* complaints in bastardy, matters involving apprentices, paupers, the poor law, highway orders and the like.[37] Riot and forcible entries, however, when handled summarily had, as we have already noted, an initiatory procedure of their own;[38] and by statute special provision was made for the accusation and trial of slaves.[39] Lastly we must include among the devices for initiating prosecution certain types of recognizance. Persons brought before magistrates charged with some offense were, if bailable, required to post security for appearance at Sessions, Circuit or the Supreme Court. Where the bond included provision for good behavior, proceedings upon breach were almost automatic. These cases, and those where the "peace was sworn"[40] will be considered in the chapter on recognizances.[41]

the gaol for insufficiency" (*Ms. Mins. Cir. 1721–49* 48, 49).

For complaints by poor officers compare the case of Caleb Ogden, *supra* 102 n. 188.

Also compare the complaint by the overseers of the poor against Nancy Smith, a vagrant, referred to *supra* 128–129.

For complaints by town officers compare the town of Brooklyn's complaint to Sessions (1706) that Jacob Fardon, a constable, contrary to his oath and in disobedience to a warrant from Justice of the Peace Aerson, failed to summon all the inhabitants of Brooklyn to a town meeting. Two freeholders of Brooklyn having sworn that they were not summoned to the meeting, the court ordered that Fardon "ffor his neglect and Contempt . . . be ffined ffive pounds ffor the use of her Majesty," and it was also ordered that another warrant issue for calling a town meeting and another constable be chosen (*Ms. Kings Co. Ct. & Rd. Recs. 1692–1825* 149). Cf. the complaint of Josiah Hunt, member of the Westchester Mayor's Court (*Ms. Mins. Westch. Co. Sess. 1710–23* June 4, 1723).

On Nov. 10, 1696, Urian Nageell, poundmaster, complained to Kings County Sessions "yt he has had a stray horse this severall weekes in the pound . . . & noe owner [claimed it] . . . and that they have done great damage in his neighbours Corne . . . yt. if there be noe Care taken . . . they will still trespass . . . The Court . . . order that . . .

Nageell . . . make sale of said horses & . . . satisfye all Costs & damages . . . and if any owner appeare within a yeare or a day the overplus . . . to be returned to him" (*ibid.* 34).

[37] *Infra* 382.

[38] *Supra* 121, 124 and see 199 *et seq.*

[39] *Infra* 382.

[40] See, for example, the deposition of Dr. Joseph Magra against John Keating, ". . . maketh oath that . . . John Keating . . . came into his house . . . and asked Deponent if he had any furs to sell . . . abused deponent . . . assaulted . . . beat . . . threatened . . . him . . . and this deponent further sayth that he is afraid the said John Keating will do him some bodily hurt and mischief and that he requires sureties of the peace against the said John Keating not through malice or ill will But for the cause aforesaid Sworn to the 29th day of July 1765 before me Whitehead Hicks" (*NY Misc. Mss. 1758–66* no. 62).

[41] *Infra* c. VIII 488, 544. For the moment compare the typical entry, King v. Richard Baglin, N.Y. Quarter Sessions, Aug. 7, 1740: "The Deft. being Accused of a Misdemeanor in keeping a Disorderly house and Selling Strong drink Without a Lycence Order'd . . . Committed till he find Security for his Appearance at the Next sessions in the Mean time to be of Good behavior" (*Ms. Mins. NYCQS 1732–62* 122).

Although the list of causes handled summarily is numerically more formidable than the roster of offenses which came before grand juries, the colonists attached such importance to the inquest and it came in fact to assume a role of such constitutional significance in the matter of law enforcement that we shall have to devote some attention to the details of how it operated. We shall be less concerned with questions of what went into indictments than with the mechanics of this accusatory process. So far as we can ascertain there was little that took place which can be described as a development, for throughout the period with which we are now concerned, these mechanics change very little. Constitutionally the most notable factor is the extent to which the New York grand juries followed the English medieval tradition rather than the less democratic procedures then prevailing in England. With great tenacity the freemen of the Province held fast to their prerogatives as the accusers for their respective counties. And if the reader gains the impression that grand jury procedure in New York consisted of a great deal of passing about of papers, it is well to remember that the passage of these documents was watched with jealous eyes and that but for this the ex-officio information would have crowded out popular participation.

Preliminary Proceedings

The engines of the law were usually set in motion against persons accused of minor and sometimes of serious offenses when the injured person would appear before a committing magistrate alleging the commission of a crime. The accusing witness would then enter his accusation in the form of an affidavit which was in the nature of an information on oath.[42] The accused very

[42] For example, Catherine Corgall's petition to the "Lord Mayor of Albany" on Aug. 29, 1768 in which she says that one Abraham Person "forsed your petitioner . . . against her will" and she was terribly distraught. The justices of the peace "didn't chose to midel with the afers." She asked for a letter from the Mayor to Justice Van Dyck to look into this matter (*J. T. Kempe Lawsuits* C–F *sub nom.* Corgall).

These depositions, affidavits and "informations on oath" are so numerous that we can offer only a few examples: "City of New York ss: Daniel Ebbetts . . . being sworn upon the Holy Evangelists . . . Deposeth and Saith That . . . he . . . was Standing at the Door of Wm Bradford . . . & Saw James Jenkins in a Cart & Arnout Hendricks in a Slay running as fast as they Could . . . Deponent . . . looked after them . . . and Saw One of the Staves of the Cart Strike a Woman [Mary Nicholls]

upon her hip & threw her Down, And run Over her legg & brake it . . . And further this Deponent Saith not Daniel Ebbetts Jure Vicesimo Octavo Die Novembris Anno Dom. 1721 Coram Nobis . . . Walter . . . Cruger . . . Coorlandt" (*James Alexander Papers* Box 46). These defendants appeared in Quarter Sessions on Feb. 7, 1721/22, and no prosecutor appearing against them they were discharged (*Ms. Mins. NYCQS 1694-1731/32* 398). See also H.R. *Pleadings* Pl. K. 594, 687, 714, 708, 595, and H.R. *Parch.* 183 A 90. If the magistrates first approached did not act, it was not unusual to turn to others. Cf. the cases of King v. Van Kleeck & Vanderbergh, *supra* 321 *et seq.* and Catherine Corgall, cited above.

See also the examination of John Daley Feb. 4, 1772: "Defendant's Examination City of New York ss: The Examination of John Daily . . . charged with having broken open the Store of Wil-

often was called into court by the constable or sheriff, perhaps at the behest of the accuser, and the committing magistrate would then take an "examination" of the accused. These examinations were evidently not on oath and might be taken by one or more justices of the peace. Sometimes the examinations contained the accused's admission of the facts alleged against him, and in these cases such "examinations" are often referred to as "confessions."

Apart from their function in getting a prosecution under way the examinations or confessions were important for the conduct of trials and they were sometimes even read in evidence against the accused. Where this happened in the course of a trial by jury, no inferior probative force seems to have been attached to the examinations than to other evidence against the accused. It should be noted here that in point of form the language of "informations" and "examinations" taken before committing magistrates was at times undistinguishable from the informations and examinations in *qui tam* cases and cases of summary trial under statutory provisions. In the first situation the accused was accorded an indictment and trial jury, and in the other he was very often convicted solely on the information of witnesses and his own examination.

Sometimes the complaints before committing magistrates and the like took the form of "petitions" requesting redress of grievances or praying for some action to be taken against an offender,[43] and sometimes complaints were made directly to the Attorney General asking his intervention in cases of wrongdoing.[44] Such complaints the Attorney General might use either to com-

---

liam Neilson . . . and stealing thereout, sundry pieces of Woolen Cloths, the Examinant upon his Examination saith, that he lived about four years . . . at Newburgh . . . that he came to this city two or three weeks before Christmas and . . . got acquainted with William Seville and Edward Warren: that . . . [they] . . . worked on board of vessells; that one night . . . [they] were drinking . . . on Captain Clarke's vessel; that, after leaving . . . as they were passing by the Store of the said William Neilson, [Nicholas] Foran [who was with them] informed the Examinant . . . that he had worked in that store and that there were a great many goods in it; whereupon the said Warren proposed breaking open the said store, which he . . . did." The examination goes on at great length to explain how Warren and Seville took the goods out of the store and gave them to Daley to carry. The examination concludes as follows: "John Daley Taken 4th Febry 1772 before Mr. Whitehead Hicks Mayor" (*H.R. Pleadings* Pl. K. 468. Cf. also Pl. K. 726). Archilaus Lewis was

"overpersuaded" by John Higgins knowingly to accept counterfeit money (*ibid.* Pl. K. 791). Examination of Eliz. Burns (*J. T. Kempe Lawsuits* L–O *sub nom.* William Morrell [window breaking]).

[43] See *supra* n. 42, and also see John Walker's complaint and petition to Chief Justice Horsmanden against Captain Lovett for assaulting and wounding Walker. "To the Honorable Daniel Horsmanden Esquire Chief Justice . . . The Petition of John Walker . . . Humbly Sheweth . . . [explains facts of case] Your petitioner therefore humbly prays that your Honor would be pleased to order the said William Love [*sic*] to be held to Bail in such Sum as may be adequate to the Damages your Petitioner has received . . . least by the said Love's & leaving the Province your Petitioner be deprived of securing that Recompense for his Injury the Laws of his Country affords him" (*J. T. Kempe Lawsuits* W–Y).

[44] See the "Information of Rymer Van Hoese the younger . . . made to William Kempe Esquire

mence proceedings before the grand jury to obtain an indictment or to furnish the basis for Crown informations.

Ordinarily, after the magistrate had taken the deposition of the accusing witness and the examination of the accused, he would, if he found sufficient cause commit or bind over the offender to the next Sessions of Peace, Oyer and Terminer, or the Supreme Court, where proceedings before the grand jury would take place. But in many instances persons who were bound over by recognizance to answer charges, or who were brought into court by other means, were discharged in court before any presentment or true bill of indictment had been found against them. What usually occurred was that no one would appear against the defendant and his discharge would then follow as a matter of course.[45] This frequently happened even when witnesses had been bound over by recognizances to give evidence.[46] On other occasions where the Attorney General had initiated proceedings a nolle prosequi would be entered for reasons unknown,[47] or it might happen that even after a true bill had been obtained, circumstances would make further prosecution inadvisable.

The judicial procedure employed where no accuser or prosecutor appeared against a defendant was the so-called discharge by proclamation. A typical record entry is that in *Queen* v. *Brooke:*

proclamation was three times made for ye Defend[t] to Appear according to his recognizance. The Defend[t] accordingly appeared and proclamation was three times made and no person appearing to alleadge anything against. Ordered the

. . . Attorney General . . . August 3, 1756" in which the informant states that he set out in his sloop the *Jolly* from Poughkeepsie to New York. Van Hoese owed Tim Northam £50 on a bond and the latter threatened to seize his sloop for the debt. Northam then fired a shot at Van Hoese's wife, seized the boat and sent the informant and his wife ashore (*H.R. Pleadings* Pl. K. 1052). We shall discuss the complaints for informations *infra*.

[45] E.g., King v. Bulkley (*Ms. Mins. NYCQS 1694–1731/32* 5, Feb. 5, 1694/95). See also King v. Farmer (*Ms. Mins. NYCQS 1683/84–1694* 167, May 1, 1694). Compare, on the other hand, the case of John Bradon who appeared in New York City Quarter Sessions on February 3, 1701/02, but "on motion of Jeofrey Yellerton who complained against him the defendant is discharged" (*Ms. Mins. NYCQS 1694–1731/32* 67). The cases of discharge where no complaining witnesses appeared are legion. Typical country entries are King v. Mary Norton (*Ms. Mins. Suffolk Co. Sess. 1723–51* Oct. 2, 1739); King v. Allison (*Ms. Mins. Orange Co. Sess. 1727–79* Oct. 1752); King v. Simson (*Ms. Mins. Dutchess Co. Sess.* Liber A, May 18, 1742).

[46] As in King v. Kennedy, 1753. *H.R. Pleadings* Pl. K. 1065 contains the witness's recognizances. The minute entry is in *Ms. Mins. SCJ 1750–54* (Engr.) 221, Jan. 20, 1753.

[47] E.g., Queen v. Peter King (*Ms. Mins. NYCQS 1694–1731/32* Aug. 6, 1706). Discharged by consent of Attorney General. There is a later entry in this case—"Bickley p' Dom' Reg' enters noli pros." (*ibid.* 115). In the case of Isaac Rodrico Marques, "the Attorney General enters a non pros." on Apr. 10, 1697 in the Supreme Court (*Mins. SCJ 1693–1701* 114). John Town appeared in the Supreme Court on Oct. 13, 1705, and "by consent of ye Att Gen[11] . . . it is ordered that the deft be discharged paying fees" (*Ms. Mins. SCJ 1704/05–1709* 46). Stephen Bayly's appearance was entered in the Supreme Court at his request on Mar. 10, 1707/08, but on Mar. 13, 1707/08, the court "ordered that the defendant be discharged, the Attorney Gen[11] having nothing to object agt. him" (*ibid.* 160, 168). Cf. also King v. Miller (*Ms. Mins. Orange Co. Sess. 1727–79* Apr. 25, 1727); King v. Glen (*Ms. Mins. Albany Co. Sess. 1763–82* Jan. 11, 1764, June 5, 1764).

said John Brooke & William Waldron & Henry Freeman his Securities be discharged.[48]

No provincial formula of proclamation has been found but it was probably patterned upon that used in the English Assizes:[49]

If any man can inform my lords the King's Justices, the King's Serjeant or the King's Attorney of any Treason Murder Felony or any other Misdemeanour committed or done by A B &c. or any of them now prisoners at the Bar, let him come forth and he shall be heard for the Prisoners stand upon their deliverance.

The currency of this ceremony is best attested in the Supreme Court records, for the entries are not always explicit in the Sessions minute books.[50] Nevertheless, it may have been more usual than the evidence shows, for in Dutchess the court made a rule on May 15, 1744, "That the court alows for fees to the

[48] *Ms. Mins. SCJ 1710–14* 501, Oct. 16, 1713. In the case of King v. Peter King, the defendant appeared in NYC Quarter Sessions on Feb. 8, 1699/1700, and "Tuder p' Defend'. prays he be discharged from his Recognizance there being no prosecution agt. him." This motion was granted and the defendant was discharged (*Ms. Mins. NYCQS 1694–1731/32* 52).

[49] *Office of the Clerk of Assizes* (1682) 52. The entry in King v. Mary Norton (*supra* n. 45) is a simplified version of this.

[50] In the following Supreme Court cases the triple proclamation was made and discharge ordered:

Queen v. Francis Cowenhoven, Sept. 9, 1704 (*Ms. Mins. SCJ 1701–04* 160); Queen v. Negro man Frank, Oct. 12, 1706 (*Ms. Mins. SCJ 1704/05–1709* 108); King v. Francis Carruthers and King v. James Davis, July 31, 1756 (*Ms. Mins. SCJ 1754–57* [Engr.] 286); King v. Tim Bryan, Oct. 26, 1758 (*Ms. Mins. SCJ 1756–61* [Rough] 125); King v. Elizabeth Young and Thomas Jones, Nov. 1, 1766 (*Ms. Mins. SCJ 1764–67* [Rough] 194); King v. Ben Eaton and James Askin, Jan. 19, 1765 (*ibid.* 45); King v. negro slave of John Thomas, Apr. 27, 1765 (*ibid.* 68); King v. Philip Abrahams *et al.*, Aug. 2, 1765 (*ibid.* 88); King v. Callam Smith, May 1, 1767 (*ibid.* 244); King v. Mary Calwell *et al.*, May 2, 1767 (*ibid.* 244); King v. Elias Carter *et al.*, Aug. 1, 1767 (*ibid.* 257); King v. John Marter, Oct. 31, 1767 (*Ms. Mins. SCJ 1766–69* [Engr.] 327); King v. John Young, Mary Dailey and Lydia a mulatto wench, July 30, 1768 (*ibid.* 508); King v. Dan Morey, Jan. 21, 1769 (*ibid.* 608); King v. Tobias Sims, July 29, 1769 (*Ms. Mins. SCJ 1769–72* [Engr.] 68); King v. Robert Buchanan *et al.*, Apr. 28, 1770 (*ibid.* 198); King v. Jacob Osborn, Jan. 18, 1771 (*ibid.* 319); King v. William Kell and Thomas

Gilmore, Oct. 25, 1771 (*ibid.* 448); King v. Patrick McDonald, John Sullivan and Nicholas Doran, Jan. 25, 1772 (*ibid.* 477); King v. Mary Doran *et al.*, May 2, 1772 (*ibid.* 523); King v. Ed Warren, Oct. 31, 1772 (*Ms. Mins. SCJ 1772–76* [Rough] 60); King v. Henry Remsen, July 31, 1773 (*ibid.* 112); King v. Dick a slave, Oct. 30, 1773 (*ibid.* 137); King v. Joseph Shepherd *et al.*, July 30, 1774 (*ibid.* 185).

For Sessions, cf. the following: King v. James Travers, King v. Hannah Travers, who were "Cleared by Proclamation" on the payment of costs at Westchester Court of Sessions on June 5, 1694 (*Mins. Westch. Ct. of Sess. 1657–96* 92); King v. Sam Horton (*Ms. Mins. Westch. Co. Sess. 1710–23* Dec. 1715). In Kings County Sessions John Griggs was discharged on May 10, 1698, "no prosecutor appearing against him" (*Ms. Kings Co. Ct. & Rd. Recs. 1692–1825* 42), and on November 12, 1701, Nicholas Brouwer, accused of breaking his Majesty's peace, was discharged after 3 proclamations because no accuser appeared against him (*ibid.* 84). John Johnson, who appeared in NYC Quarter Sessions on Feb. 2, 1691/92, was "cleared by proclamation . . . no one appearing against him" (*Ms. Mins. NYCQS 1683/84–1694* 154). John Colon was discharged by proclamation in New York City Quarter Sessions on May 7, 1695, when no one appeared to prosecute him (*Ms. Mins. NYCQS 1694–1731/32* 6), and Abigail Heath was discharged on the payment of fees on Feb. 7, 1704/05, when no prosecutor appeared (*ibid.* 93). Cf. also King v. Jeccard (*Ms. Mins. Richmond Co. Sess. 1710/11–1744/45* Mar. 4, 1717/18, and the entries Sept. 1, 1719, Sept. 1, 1724; *Ms. Mins. Ulster Co. Sess. 1737–50* May 6, 1740, May 3, 1743, May 1, 1744, Sept. 20, 1748; *Ms. Mins. Albany Co. Sess. 1763–82* Oct. 4, 1763, Jan. 17, 1764).

clerk and cryer seven shillings to be paid by every defendant who is or shall be discharged of a recognizance by proclamation or otherwise."[51]

It is not clear under what circumstances a discharge by proclamation was regarded as necessary or proper. There are many cases where discharge seems to have been effected without this formality, and there is that army of defendants who vanish from the records without a line to show that the finger of suspicion was no longer directed at them. There is, too, some evidence of a practice equivalent to proclamation procedure where the accused was represented by counsel and by motion would pray for discharge. The court could either grant the motion[52] or make a rule *nisi* and, if no prosecution were forthcoming, order the discharge of the defendant.[53] This procedure was not often used, for ordinarily offenders were not represented. Suspects, unless they possessed means, were more or less at the mercy of the law enforcing authorities. Thus Hester Crutch (Crudge) appeared in the Supreme Court on June 5, 1729, petitioning for her discharge, stating that she had been in jail in the custody of the sheriff of New York for the preceding two terms. The court thereupon ordered her discharged since the Attorney General had nothing to charge against her.[54] Sometimes, too, the grand jury, unable to find a bill, would nevertheless have the defendant kept in custody in the hope of developing at a later time sufficient evidence on which to charge the accused. Thus Robert Willson appeared in the Supreme Court on March 19, 1727/28, and "the Grand Jury not having sufficient witnesses brought before them to find a bill of Indictmt but in as much as they can see strong cause of suspicion of ffelony agt him, they pray that the Ct o'd him to be kept confined 'till the next Term."[55] In another case where the grand jury held a defendant in jail pending the finding of a bill against him, "the Defendt being Committed to the Gaol . . . and no prosecution agt him (two Grand Jurys having been Charged to Examine into his Offence . . . & finding no Bill or presentment agt him) It is Ordered . . . discharged from his Imprisonment by Proclamation paying his fees."[56]

---

[51] *Ms. Mins. Dutchess Co. Sess.* Liber A.

[52] Cf. Queen v. Elias D'Grange. The defendant appeared in the Supreme Court on Sept. 3, 1706 and again on Sept. 7, 1706, when he was continued on his recognizance. On Oct. 12, 1706, "the defts appearance recorded on Mr. Regniers moĉon. Mr. Regnier prays the deft be discharged there being no prosecution, & it being consented to by the Attorney Gen[11]." This motion was granted and the defendant was discharged (*Ms. Mins. SC] 1704/05–1709* 76, 96, 108). Cf. for country cases King v.

Jarman Pick (*Ms. Mins. Ulster Co. Sess. 1737–50* Nov. 6, 1739); King v. Maxfield (*Ms. Mins. Dutchess Co. Sess.* Liber A, 1739).

[53] As in King v. Filkin. The motion by Murray on Oct. 15, 1750 for discharge on the first day of the following term unless cause shown to the contrary. The discharge was ordered Apr. 25, 1751 (*Ms. Mins. SC] 1750–54* [Engr.] 17, 47).

[54] *Ms. Mins. SC] 1727–32* 122, June 5, 1729.

[55] *Ibid.* 44.

[56] *Ms. Mins. NYCQS 1694–1731/32* 459, Feb.

Procedure before the Grand Jury

Procedure before the grand jury was essentially the same in the Courts of General Sessions, Oyer and Terminer and General Gaol Delivery and the Supreme Court, and we shall therefore consider this matter with reference to cases in all these courts. At the opening of every court day, proclamation was made for the sheriff to return the writs and precepts of the court which had been directed to him,[57] and at this time the precept for the grand jury and the panel was returned.[58] As in England, the precept to summon a grand jury for an Oyer and Terminer was contained in the commission; for General Sessions, in the precept to convene the court. In the case of the Supreme Court the summons was in the form of a judicial writ.[59] When the grand jury had been summoned, it oftentimes happened that a number of the grand jurors would default. Indeed, despite the prevailing solicitude for the preservation of the liberties of Englishmen, the records disclose that there was seldom a sitting of any of the courts in which grand jurors did not exhibit that age-old reluctance to the performance of this public duty. The usual penalty for the contempt of grand jurors in defaulting on their appearance was 13s. 4d.[60]

Before calling the grand jury, it was customary to make the following proclamation identical in form with that used in England: "You good men who

2, 1725/26. Cf. also the note wrapped in an indictment for perjury, King v. Hagaman (12 Geo. II): "To the honorable Court we have nothing to present att present but that Mr. Francis Hagaman has made his complaint afore us that they have the last year found a bill against him and according to the evidence apeared before us we cant find anything against him. John Bayly foreman" (*Ms. Files Dutchess Co. 1726–41*).

[57] See, for example, *Ms. Mins. NYCQS 1694–1731/32* 121, Feb. 4, 1706/07: "Proclamation made and the sheriff ordered to return the precept and other process returnable today that the justices of peace may proceed thereon. Proclamation made for all coroners, constables, petty constables and Bayliffs to answer . . . at the first call and save their fines." In *Ms. Mins. SCJ 1704/05–1709* 7, Mar. 15, 1704/05, the following Supreme Court rules indicate that the grand jury came into that court on the first day of each term: "General Rules to be observed ffirst day of . . . Terme for the Grand Jury and the Doggett, Second day for Tryalls if, y^t be not sufficient for all ye tryalls those remaining to be tryed the last day but one by special order—Notice of tryall within 40 miles of this City to be 8 days exclusive—above 40 miles 14 days —notice to countermand tryalls four days exclusive —a salvo in EXtraordinary cases, Third day for argument—fourth day for judgem^t of the Court

All Declarations to be filed sitting the Court the Second Terme inclusive after ye return of ye writt."

[58] *Ms. Mins. NYCQS 1683/84–1694* 166, Nov. 7, 1693.

[59] For Oyer and Terminer, *infra* Appendix 771; King v. Bayard, 14 Howell, *State Trials* 476. For Sessions, cf. *infra* 465 n. 365.

The Supreme Court form reads: "George . . . To our sherriff . . . Greeting: We Command you that you Cause to come before our Justices of our Supreme Court of Judicature . . . twenty four principal Freeholders of your Bailiwick to serve us and our Said City and County as Grand Jurors during the said Term, and have you then and there the Names of those Jurors and this Writ: Witness Daniel Horsmanden Esqr Chief Justice. . . ." This instrument is endorsed: "the Execution of this Writ appears by the Pannel hereunto annexed, John Roberts Sheriff." Cf. *H.R. Parch.* 191 H 1, 194 B 1, and an unnumbered parchment of Oct. 27, 1764, bearing the names of Justice Horsmanden and Sheriff Roberts. For the fees for "taking a grand jury for the court of Oyer and Terminer and Gaol Delivery for Suffolk County," dated Sept. 16, 1766, see *H.R. Pleadings* Pl. K. 368, where it is to be noted that the charge was 13s.

[60] E.g., *Ms. Mins. NYCQS 1694–1731/32* 118, where on Nov. 6, 1706, two grand jurors were each "amerced 13s. 4d. for their contempt in not appear-

be returned to Inquire for . . . the King and the Body of the City and County of New York answer to your names every Man at the first Call and save your Fines."[61] When a sufficient number of grand jurors appeared, proclamation was made and the panel was called over and the jurors sworn.[62] The oath administered to the grand jurors was in the following form:

> You as foreman of the Grand Inquest for the body of the City and County of New York, Shall Well and truly Enquire, and true presentment make, of all such matters and things, as Shall be Given you in Charge, his Majesty's Counsel, your fellows, and your own, you Shall keep Secret, you Shall present no man for Envy, hatred, or malice, neither Shall you Leave anyone, unpresented, for Love, fear, favour Affection, or hope of Reward, but you Shall present things truly, as they Come to your knowledge, according to the best of your understanding, So Help You God . . . The Rest of the Jury by four . . . The Same Oath which A. B. your foreman hath taken on his behalf, you and every of you, shall well and truly observe and keep, on your parts, so help you God.[63]

When the jurors were sworn, the following court order was made: "Silence commanded while ye charge is given to the grand jury."[64]

The importance attached in England to the general charge is reflected by the inclusion of specimens in early practice manuals. For the most part these are rather dreary catalogues of offenses that the grand jury was to present, decorated now and again with some moral reflections. The earliest New York

ing on the grand jury." However, we have seen higher penalties meted out. Thus on July 28, 1772, the Supreme Court fined grand jurors £5 for their failure to appear (*Ms. Mins. SCJ 1772–76* [Rough] 25). On July 31, 1773, seven persons who were summoned as grand jurors failed to appear, and their defaults being entered, they were fined £10 each. Whereupon, the court ordered the sheriff of New York to "levy the Sum of Ten pounds on the Goods and Chattels of each of the persons and bring the Money into Court on the first Day of the next Term" (*ibid.* 112). Occasionally the lack of grand jurors was so great that a panel could not be made up and the following entry is typical: "The Grand Jury Called and a Sufficient Number not appearing, those that appeared are ordered to attend again to Morrow Morning" (*Ms. Mins. NYCQS 1772–91* 1, May 5, 1772).

[61] *Ms. Mins. SCJ 1756–61* (Rough) flyleaves. For the English form, *Office of the Clerk of Assize* 29.

[62] *Ms. Mins. NYCQS 1694–1731/32* 122, Feb. 4, 1706/07; *Ms. Mins. NYCQS 1705/06–1714/15* (Rough) 1, Feb. 7, 1705/06; Kings County Sessions, May 19, 1692, *Kings Co. Ct. & Rd. Recs. 1692–1825* 2.

[63] *Ms. Mins. NYCQS 1760–72* on back of cover. In the flyleaf of the rough minute book of the S.C.J. for 1756–61, the grand jurors' oath appears and a marginal notation indicates that this form was intended as part of the instructions for the proceedings of the Supreme Court *en banc* and at Circuit. The following counties were named: New York, Albany, Ulster, Dutchess, Orange, Westchester, Richmond, Kings, Queens, Suffolk. The oath is substantially identical with that quoted above. The form then proceeds: "N.B. if any Juror is not present when the Foreman is sworn say thus, you as one of the Grand Jurors shall diligently enquire &c. . . . all maner of persons . . . to keep silence while charge is giving to the grand jury." These forms correspond with that in *Office of the Clerk of Assize* 31.

[64] *Ms. Mins. NYCQS 1683/84–1694* 166, Nov. 7, 1693; Kings County Sessions, May 19, 1692, *Kings Co. Ct. & Rd. Recs. 1692–1825* 2. In the *Ms. Mins. NYCQS 1694–1731/32* 122, Feb. 4, 1706/07, the following entry appears: "Proclamation made and silence Commanded on pain of Imprisonment while the Charge is Giving to the Grand Jurors."

specimen we have seen is preserved in the late seventeenth century minutes of Westchester County and is little more than a recital of matter in the peace commission.[65] Occasionally some judge would utilize the charge as opportunity for literary composition or political harangue. Two specimens of Sessions charges delivered in New York that we have seen are not at all in the technical tradition of the handbooks. The one which appears to have been written sometime between 1730 and 1740 is a brief, sober admonition reinforced with some biblical citation.[66] The other, a more elaborate affair penned about the same time by Mr. Justice Honeywell of Westchester County, is an amusing confection of political sycophancy in its praise of the existing political order and of popular placation in its reference to Magna Carta and the subjects' liberties.[67]

[65] *Mins. Westch. Ct. of Sess. 1657–96* 121.

[66] It reads as follows: "Gentlemen the oath that hath been administered unto you itself, but that its so general, would else be instruction as well as Obligation Sufficient, but the better to Explain it to you 1st you are diligently to Enquire according to your notice or knowledge, or and concerning all offenses committed against the King's Majesty, Your Country, and your fellow Subjects, in the doing whereof you must take care to accuse noe person Innocent 2nd the Scripture teaches one his Duty upon oath, it says one must swear in Truth, in Judgment, and in Righteousness Jeremiah Chap. 4: Exodus C. 20, Zach. 5 Acts ch. 5 and in several places more 3dly as you are sworn to keep all things secret to your selves is meant and Intended not only while you are assembled together in a body of the grand Inquest but even after you are dismissed from that service, otherwise you . . . may . . . cause great disorder and confusion among your neighbors and his Majesty's Subjects and may be the means to give Light to the Guilty to escape and Evade . . . Justice hereafter; although better proof might be afterwards given to some other grand Inquest and . . . by your Discoursing of what appeared before you, you forgett your oath that you were not to discover any Secret that appeared to you. So hoping you will be mindful of those things Gentlemen I leave you to doe your duty—" (*NY Legal Mss.* Box 44).

[67] "Gentlemen / It is usual upon these occasions to Expect a Charge from yᵉ Bench—I could heartily wish an abler person had been appointed to ye place I am in to Give it; but to preserve at least the Formality; and to keep up a sence of the Important Trust Committed to you Gentlemen of ye Grand Jury I will offer a few words which I hope will be accepted with ye same Candour with which they are spoken—and as you here Represent your Countrey I cant forbear in the first place to Congratulate with you the present happy security of our affairs owing to the very seasonable Interposition of Divine providence upon a Crisis of Distraction when (you

are all sensible) the political Disputes of unquiet persons had brought on such a Ferment upon the State that not only threatned the suspension of all Law and Justice but a speedy inundation of Confusion and misery through the whole Countrey—as our Deliverance has been Remarkable So I know it to be Joyful both as to matter and manner to the main Body of this County which I hope will always Express a Dutifull Submission to our most Gracious Soveraign with a sense of the happiness we enjoy under his most wise and Just administration: and shew themselves forward to Esteem and Reverence the Representatives of his majesties person and authority; both from a sense of Duty to almighty God and our most Gracious Soveraign—and then Let me intimate to you how highly we ought to prize and Esteem the happy Constitution we are under that Distinguishes us from most other nations; by such Immunities and priviledges as make us in Reality a *free people;* The happiness of which freedom depends upon the uninterrupted Course of *Justice* according to the most Excellent Laws which we have the Happiness to be ourselves the *Devisors* of; to hedge in and secure our Liberties in whatsoever is most dear and valuable to us—and amongst all our valuable priviledges as *Englishmen;* it is Justly esteemed one of the Greatest and has all the securities of *Magna Charta* that the King who holds the sword of Justice (from whom all power is Derived to Execute Justice and Judgment for ye protection of Innocence and for the terrour of Evil doers) will yet Give sentence upon no mans Person or Property but by Tryal of his Equals: and the method prescribed of putting the Law in Execution by *presentment* of a *Grand Jury;* who Represent the Countrey as well as by Living in it; must be acquainted both with persons and actions and their true Chara*cters;* ought to be esteemed a Great priviledge to the Subject: and to Render it so indeed you must imploy the trust Reposed in you to Give Life and force to all our wholsome Laws intended to suppress all sorts of vice and disorders;

The Supreme Court charges to the grand jury are considerably more in the professional tradition, but even here there is a disposition to speak in a manner intended to elevate or sometimes even inflame the freemen about to frame their accusations.[68] Generations earlier William Lambard had expressed the pious wish that a sermon "uttered by some learned man" be preached as well at Sessions as at Assizes,[69] and a hortatory style may accordingly have become the mode. The matter is of no legal importance but it deserves further study by students of American rhetoric.

After the charge had been delivered the grand jury would consider pending business. If there was nothing to be undertaken, the body was to be discharged.[70] This was probably a more frequent occurrence than the records show, for often at a country Sessions no indictments or presentments would be made, yet there is no notation in the minutes of the grand jury's discharge.[71]

We are badly informed as to how the work of the grand jury was managed when there were cases pending. From correspondence of both Attorney General Bradley and John Tabor Kempe it is clear that when the chief Crown officer was not present at a court, he endeavored in cases of importance to instruct his deputy. For the most part, however, the administrative responsibility rested with the clerk of the Supreme Court, clerk of the Circuits or the clerks of the peace, particularly as the latter frequently acted in the country as King's attorneys. In England the task of getting matter before the grand jury was handled by the clerks, and it seems likely that some modification of the procedure there used and so meticulously described in the handbooks was followed in New York.[72]

The bulk of the cases which would come up for consideration by the grand jury were those where the magistrates had bound over to the court persons complained against or examined before them. Occasionally complaint would

which weaken and infeeble a Commonwealth— The Solemnity of your oath I hope will be a Spur to you, and you will take care not to involve your selves and Countrey in the Guilt of such misdemeanours as are suffered to go unpunished, by your neglect of an impartial Enquiery and, faithful presentment of, according to the Direction of your oath:—And this Bench according to their Duty and the Trust reposed in them by our soveraign Lord the King, will be most ready to perform their Proper parte" (*John Chambers Mss.* no. 46).

[68] Cf., for example, *The Charge Given by the Chief Justice . . . to the Grand Jury . . . In March Term 1726–27* (1727); *The Trial of John Peter Zenger* (1765) 1, 2; Horsmanden, *The New York Conspiracy* 35–37.

[69] Lambard, *Eirenarcha* (1614) 404.

[70] Thus in Kings County Sessions: "The Grand Jurry Retorned and ffinding No Misdemines or Complaints are dismist . . ." (*Ms. Kings Co. Ct. & Rd. Recs. 1692–1825* 66, Nov. 12, 1700). Cf. also similar entries at Dutchess Oyer and Terminer and General Gaol Delivery for Sept. 19, 1716 (*Ms. Mins. Cir. 1716–17* 32) and Richmond Oyer and Terminer and General Gaol Delivery for April 9, 1717 (*ibid.* 37; *Ms. Mins. NYCQS 1683/84–1694* 163).

[71] For example, *Ms. Mins. Ulster Co. Sess. 1737–50* the Sessions for Nov. 3, 1741, May 4, 1742, Sept. 18, 1746, May 1750.

[72] *Office of Clerk of Assize* 32 *et seq.* (for Assizes), 139 *et seq.* (for Sessions).

be made directly to the grand jury by individuals aggrieved. Thus in 1714 the suspected members of an alleged "Atheisticall Club" who had been subjected to examination by the grand jury petitioned that body for action against their traducers as disturbers of the peace.[73] Again in 1754 residents of New York City by affidavit sought and secured an indictment against Elizabeth Anderson for keeping a disorderly house.[74] And some years later, John Knapp, an attorney who was alleged by John Watts to have been a transported convict and who alone of the bar carried flamboyant advertisements of his business in the gazettes, complained directly to the grand jury of John Morin Scott, John McKesson and Gilbert Burger.[75]

To what extent New York grand juries in the deliberations had before them all the written evidence collected by the magistrates in their preliminary investigations we do not know. Under the English statutes the primary purpose in taking evidence in cases of felony was for transmittal to the Gaol Delivery

[73] Delivered by Riggs, Graham and others, on March 14, 1713/14: "To the Gentlemen of the Grand Inquest of New York City and County . . . The Humble Representation of the Subscribers Sheweth That the subscribers justly conceiving that their being cited this morning and Examined before this inquest under the suspition of their being parties . . . to an Atheisticall Club or meeting kept within this City beg leave to express their utter abhorrence of any such abominable offence and although their lives and conversations will undoubtedly vindicate them from such an aspersion to all those that know them yet notwithstanding their Innocency ye very imputation may be a stain upon them to strangers Therefore they humbly pray that this inquest will do them that Right as to present to take notice of such . . . Persons as Disturbers of the peace who have thus falsely malitiously and groundlessly been the Occasion of this Imputation upon them whereby their reputations may be vindicated and persons deter'd from such vile practices for the future 14 March 1713/4" (*John Jay Mss.* Box 3 no. 14a). Cf. also *supra* n. 56, King v. Hagaman.

[74] For the affidavit see *H.R. Pleadings* Pl. K. 1022. For the presentment see *ibid.* Pl. K. 664, and for the indictment Pl. K. 638. The minute entries are contained in *Ms. Mins. SCJ 1754–57* (Engr.) 47, 49, July 31, Aug. 1, 1754.

[75] "Mr. Knaps Complaint against Mr. Scott, McKesson and Burger (Clerks) City of New York ss: The King against John Morin Scott, John McKesson and Gilbert Burger To the Gentlemen of the Grand Inquest Sitting on the Body of the said City of New York John Coghill Knapp . . . Attorney at Law most humbly Presents, and on the Holy Evangelist of Almighty God Deposeth that . . . [describes dealings with Simeon and William Coley, Lawsuit, debt owed, John Morin Scott refused to accept it and beat and abused deponent] And Lastly This Deponent saith that neither out of Enmity or any other reason whatever (save to prevent ill-treatment for the future) doth he this Deponent Apply to this Inquest, to present his hard Case for such relief as in Justice he shall be Intituled unto" (*J. T. Kempe Lawsuits S–V sub nom.* Scott; *Letter Book of John Watts* [61 *NYHS Colls.*] 521).

Sent to the grand jury, care of Attorney General John Tabor Kempe, was the following petition: "To the Worshipful The Jurors of Our Sovereign Lord the King now Sitting

The Humble Petition of Ann Gordon Maiden Woman now Living at Kinderhook in the County of Albany

Humble Sheweth

"That your poor Pet[r] being upon the 19th Day of July Last without any manner of Provocation abused and beat by Cornelius Van Schaak Jun[r] in Said Township Batchellor She your Pet[r] applyed to Henry Van Rensselaer Esq. One of his Majesties Justices of the Peace (Quorum unus) and made her Complaint unto him Upon w[ch] The Said M[r] Rensselaer granted to your Pet: Such Warrant and proceedings as the Law requires in Such Cases but the Defend[t] applying to the next Justice Isaac Van Alstyn Esq[r] to Determine the Matter upon which Your Pet[r] rested Satisfied as being a Stranger and Alien in the afores[d] place hoping to have Justice Done to me by the Said Mr. Van Allstyn of which Your Pet[r] has not received any Satisfaction hitherto and Much Less and return upon the affair

Your poor Pet[r] therefore humbly Prays your Worsh: to grant and admit y[r] Pet[r] to a hearing upon her grievances and She Shall Ever Pray
                                        Ann Gordon"

for use at the trial. The best evidence rule demanded, of course, examination of the witnesses by the grand jury, but it was not until late in the eighteenth century that English courts made a positive assertion to this effect.[76] Immediately after the grand jury was instituted in New York an entry in the Quarter Sessions minutes of New York states explicitly that the examinations of witnesses were submitted to the grand jury,[77] but thereafter there is little to show what the practice in fact grew to be, although it may be inferred from the numerous instances of binding persons to appear before the grand jury that personal appearance was thought desirable. This coincides with the English reluctance to have written examinations of witnesses submitted to the grand jury; but both in England and New York a prisoner's confession was always available. We have seen one late case in New York where a presentment was explicitly based on the accused's own confession,[78] and there are many indictments endorsed "prisoners confession" as well as with the names of witnesses. Nevertheless, it cannot be stated categorically that depositions of witnesses were never used except at trial. One difficulty in determining this question of the use of written testimony is the ambiguity of the term "evidences" in the eighteenth century. This is clearly brought out in a memorandum found in the Kempe papers:[79]

> The grand jury being met at Brocke . . . proceeded to examine the several evidences against Edward Dillon of New York City now in custody committed by Alderman Van Horn for breaking open and entering . . . it appears to the jury there is sufficient cause to find a bill also for stealing a Firkin of butter . . . Therefore desire you . . . the King's Attorney General to draw up an indictment against the said Edward.

The function of the written deposition in other than summary proceedings was its use at the trial chiefly for the control of testimony. For the purpose of securing an indictment the witnesses who informed or were examined by a magistrate were ordinarily bound over to give evidence to the grand inquest, and this was the usual practice in New York throughout the eighteenth century.[80] The condition of the recognizance could be solely to give evidence at

[76] Denby's Case, 1789 (2 Leach, *Crown Cases* 580).

[77] King v. Thomassen (*Ms. Mins. NYCQS 1683/84–1694* 2, Feb. 5, 1683/84).

[78] King v. Bratt (*H.R. Pleadings* Pl. K. 692, July 3, 1766).

[79] *J. T. Kempe Lawsuit* C–F *sub nom.* Dillon.

[80] The records use the expression "sworn to give evidence" which we take to mean some form of binding device. Thus four witnesses were sworn to give evidence to the grand jury in King v. Henry Lewis at a Special Court of Oyer and Terminer and General Gaol Delivery on Aug. 11, 1701 (*Ms. Mins. SCJ 1701–04* 1).

In Queen v. Daniel De Hart, a witness was sworn to give evidence to the grand jury in the Supreme

the grand inquest or to prefer an indictment and it could require also attendance at the trial.[81] This matter is of great importance because of the necessity that there be a prosecuting witness.

The grand jury was of course not confined to any prepared menu of evidence and witnesses but was clothed with vast prerogatives in respect of summons and examination. This power extended so far that even persons in the custody of other courts would be ordered to attend an inquest.[82] If an individual did not dare venture abroad for fear of arrest, his protection from arrest by virtue of any writ would be formally commanded.[83] But, where a refusal to appear was merely wilful, representations would be made to the court and the offender would either be taken into custody[84] or would be brought into court to answer for contempt.[85]

As to the actual proceedings before the grand jury we know little more than that the witnesses were put under oath.[86] Judging from entries in some country

Court of Judicature on Sept. 4, 1705 (*Ms. Mins. SCJ 1704/05–1709* 26).

In Queen v. Peter Rose, Attorney General Bickley on March 14, 1710/11, prayed the Supreme Court that Thomas Latham "may be sworn to give evidence to the grand jury," and Bickley's prayer being granted, Latham was accordingly sworn as well as Joseph Lush and Charles Pinkerton (*Ms. Mins. SCJ 1710–14* 312). Five witnesses sworn to give evidence to the grand jury on behalf of the King at Westchester Oyer and Terminer and General Gaol Delivery, Aug. 8, 1721 (*Ms. Mins. Cir. 1721–49* 1). Cf. further the entry (*ibid.* 97) where Justice Seaman delivered into Westchester Oyer and Terminer several recognizances to give evidence (1739).

[81] Cf. the recognizance of Abraham de Lucena to prosecute Moses and Solomon Levy for an affray (*NY Misc. Mss.* Box 4 no. 15). "The condition of this recognizance is such that if . . . De Lucena do personally appear . . . before her Majesties Justices Assigned to keep the peace . . . and . . . do then & there prefer or Cause to be preferred a Bill of Indictment . . . against Moses Levy Moses Hart and Solomon Ehel[?] Levy . . . and do also then and there give such Evidence as he knoweth Concerning the affray assault and breach of the peace . . . as well to the Jurors that shall enquire thereof on the behalf of . . . the Queen as also to the Jurors that shall pass upon the trial of the said Moses Levy Moses Hart and Solomon Ehel[?] Levy. . . ." It should be noted that while De Lucena initiated a prosecution against Moses Levy, the latter also prosecuted De Lucena. On Feb. 5, 1711/12, Moses Levy confessed the indictment and was fined 6s., while De Lucena, having pleaded not guilty, was found guilty and fined £6 (*Ms. Mins. NYCQS 1694–1731/32* 208–211). For further discussion, *infra* 509.

[82] *Ms. Mins. SCJ 1772–74* (Rough) 179, Apr. 28, 1774. Cf. also the following entry: "The High Sheriff representing that Simon Stevens, a Prisoner in his Custody upon Execution is required to attend the Grand Jury as a Witness: The Court Orders that the Sheriff do bring Simon Stevens, and Frederick Groome, also in his Custody, to attend the Grand Jury accordingly and that they after such their Examination, be immediately remanded to Prison" (*Ms. Mins. SCJ 1769–72* [Engr.] 474, Jan. 24, 1772).

[83] *Ms. Mins. SCJ 1727–32* 197, June 24, 1730.

[84] *Mins. SCJ 1693–1701* 122.

[85] *Ms. Mins. SCJ 1766–69* (Engr.) 317, Oct. 29, 1767. The witnesses later appeared and entered recognizances in £50 each to give evidence to the grand jury (*ibid.* 319).

[86] For example, *Mins. SCJ 1693–1701* 87 (1695); an Oyer and Terminer, Albany, Nov. 1706 (*51 NY Col. Mss.* 184; *Ms. Mins. Suffolk Co. Sess. 1723–51* Mar. 26, 1723). There are innumerable such entries. In 1764 "the Grand Jury representing to the court that John Lasher, John Stout, Joseph Griggs, Abraham Anthony, John King, John Anthony and Mathias Vredenburgh, had appeared before them, and on the usual Oath to give Evidence in behalf of the . . . King . . . they . . . had refused to take such Oath, or give any Evidence in behalf of the King. Whereupon the Court doth order the Sheriff . . . to take the said several Persons into his Custody, and bring them into Court to be examined . . . and dealt with according to Law" (*Ms. Mins. SCJ 1764–67* [Rough] 23, Oct. 22, 1764). When these witnesses were finally brought in on Oct. 25, 1764, an indictment was found against them for obstructing the King's highway, and on Jan. 17, 1765, the defendants pleaded guilty and were fined £5 each (*ibid.* 31, 41). Also see *H.R. Pleadings* Pl. K. 739, for the indictment

minute books the grand jury would sometimes ask for witnesses while it was deliberating and the court would swear them to give evidence.[87] In the Ulster County files we have found two "Notes of Grand Jury," one for the May term, 1767,[88] the other for the May term, 1769.[89] The former notices: "Bill vs. John Dick breaking gaol and stealing, John Woolsey for assault and swearing by His Maker he would take Daniel Sherwoods life." The 1769 notes state:

> Thomas Wood complains of Petrus Van Leuwen on fryday 1769, 7 day of April at the House of Art Van Waggonnen did assault and beat said Wood. Bill / Witness Petrus de Witt / Cornelius Van Wagenen / John Person complaines of Petrus Van Leuwen at the house of Petrus DeWitt was Beaten and Ill treated this Happn on 27 Day of April 1769. Bill / Witness Petrus Dewitt / Cornelius Van Wagenen.

Some other notes are enclosed. This last memorandum indicates that, even if a bill were prepared in advance, there was consideration of the testimony. At Circuit and at Sessions the judges were apparently always in great haste to conclude pending business. It seems likely, therefore, that the deliberations of the inquest were ordinarily pushed through with great rapidity, and consequently no more was considered than was necessary to secure a true bill.

Presentment and Indictment

Since the prime function of the grand jury was to make an accusation upon which a suspected offender would have to stand his trial, the mode and form of the accusation were matters of importance. Where an indictment had not been prepared beforehand it was the invariable practice in New York for the grand jury to make an informal presentment. This was always drawn on paper and was often couched in untechnical language. An early example is the following: "We the grand jurors for . . . the Queen Doe present Mary Wickham for Keeping a disorderly house to the Disturbance . . . of the neighborhood and entertaining of negroes. . . ."[90] The informal presentment, as we shall shortly see, was sometimes used as the basis for further proceedings, but the

which recited that the defendants stopped up the King's highway with force and arms unlawfully and injuriously to the great damage and common nuisance of the King's subjects and against the peace.

[87] For example, *Ms. Mins. Orange Co. Sess. 1727–79* Apr. 1728; *Ms. Mins. Queens Co. Sess. 1722–87* May 18, 1739, where subpoenas were sent out; *Ms. Mins. Richmond Co. Sess. 1710/11–1744/*

45 Sept. 6, 1720, Mar. 6, 1721/22, Sept. 4, 1722; *Ms. Mins. Ulster Co. Sess. 1737–50* Sept. 1747.

[88] *Ms. Files Ulster Co.* Bundle B.

[89] *Ms. Files Ulster Co.* Bundle E.

[90] *NY Misc. Mss.* Box 4 no. 10. This defendant under the name of Mary Wakeman pleaded not guilty and was acquitted Feb. 2, 1714/15 (*Ms. Mins. NYCQS 1694–1731/32* 270, 278, 280–282). The indictment is set forth in the last entry.

usual next step was for the presentment to be "put in form." This practice had come into existence in England because of the requirement that the written accusation be in Latin, and it was further desirable that a skilled hand be set to the drafting because of the stringency with which the form of indictments was scrutinized.[91] In New York, the Latin indictment was never used, but the vast bulk of law respecting perfection of form was current. Since it was impossible to expect a body of men not always even lettered to frame an acceptable indictment, the English practice was used of having an officer undertake the task of drafting.[92] This was usual but it was not mandatory.

The directions in the English handbooks respecting presentments indicate that the procedure was for the clerk of the court to request the presentments to be delivered and then to inquire whether the grand jury was content to have the court amend the form, altering no matter of substance.[93] In New York the records show merely the formality of delivery and next a prayer by the grand jury that the presentments be put in form.[94] The court would then make an order to this effect. This practice was adhered to until the Revolution, although in some cases the clerk entered simply an order that an indictment be "prepared."[95]

In the Supreme Court the task of transmitting the informal compositions of the grand jurors into the stiff and resistant phrases of an indictment was allotted to the Attorney General. There are only occasional orders indicating

[91] Compare the learning on false Latin in 2 Hawkins, *Pleas of the Crown* c.25 §86. The change to English was effected by 4 Geo. II c.26; 6 Geo. II c.6.

[92] The prayer to put in form is found in presentments as early as 1693; cf. 39 *NY Col. Mss.* 100.

[93] *Office of the Clerk of Assize* 37; *Crown Circuit Companion* (4 ed.) 11.

[94] The minute books do not reflect the extent of the practice for in the Hall of Records and among the Kempe papers are numberless scraps of paper on which the grand jury has written its presentment and asked that the court put the same into form. We shall cite examples to show the prevalence of the practice. In the Supreme Court, cf. King v. Paulus Turk and Robert Blackwell, 1695 (*Mins. SCJ 1693–1701* 87, 88); King v. Wynkey Lawrence, 1699 (*ibid.* 161); King v. Finlinson (*ibid.* 161); King v. Barber, 1699 (*ibid.* 172); King v. Baker, 1702 (*Ms. Mins. SCJ 1701–04* 56); King v. Joseph Prosser, 1702 (*ibid.* 56, 59); Queen v. Leisler, 1706 (*Ms. Mins. SCJ 1704/05–1709* 52, 75, 76); Queen v. Marquese, 1706 (*ibid.* 102, 108); Queen v. Jonas Wood, 1707 (*ibid.* 126, 134, 145); Queen v. Riggs, 1711 (*Ms. Mins. SCJ 1710–14* 359); King v. Trump, Nicolls *et al.*, 1716 (*Ms. Mins. Cir. 1716–17* 17); King v. Adrianson, 1724

(*Ms. Mins. Cir. 1721–49* 40, 41); King v. Edward King, 1733 (*ibid.* 65); King v. Honey, 1734 (*ibid.* 69, 70); King v. James Whey, 1753 (*H.R. Parch.* 183 A 10); King v. Dan Sherwood, 1753 (*H.R. Pleadings* Pl. K. 626; *H.R. Parch.* 183 B 4); King v. Christie, 1755 (*H.R. Pleadings* Pl. K. 360); King v. Magra, 1755 (*H.R. Parch.* 197 E 10); King v. Mulvanie, 1763 (*J. T. Kempe Lawsuits* L–O; *H.R. Pleadings* Pl. K. 752); King v. Catus and Spike, 1765 (*H.R. Pleadings* Pl. K. 786); King v. Moses Sherwood *et al.*, 1769 (*J. T. Kempe Lawsuits* S–U; *Ms. Mins. SCJ 1766–69* [Engr.] 605); King v. Wm. Smith, 1773 (*J. T. Kempe Lawsuits* S–U; *H.R. Pleadings* Pl. K. 28; *Ms. Mins. SCJ 1772–76* [Rough] 135). For examples in Sessions, cf. *Ms. Mins. NYCQS 1694–1731/32* 110, May 8, 1706, 125, May 7, 1707; *Ms. Mins. NYCQS 1732–62* 104, Aug. 9, 1739, 164, May 3, 1744, 184, Aug. 7, 1745, 212, Nov. 6, 1746; *Ms. Kings Co. Ct. & Rd. Recs. 1692–1825* 157; *H.R. Pleadings* Pl. K. 918 (Ulster Co.); *Ms. Mins. Dutchess Co. Sess.* Liber A, Oct. 17, 1738, May 15, 1739, Oct. 18, 1742; *Ms. Mins. Suffolk Co. Sess. 1723–51* Mar. 1725; *Ms. Mins. Ulster Co. Sess. 1737–50* Sept. 1747. The entries are too numerous to set forth at large.

[95] E.g., *Ms. Mins. NYCQS 1732–62* 163, 164, May 3, 1744.

this in the minute books,[96] but the presence among Kempe's manuscripts of many chits containing the presentments is evidence that for the Supreme Court this responsibility was normally discharged by the chief law officer of the Province.[97] In the country the task came to be done either by a deputy attorney general or the clerk of the peace. The Courts of Sessions appear to have exercised considerable discretion over the presentment, for there are various cases where these are quashed before put in form.[98] If the Crown's representative refused to draw the indictment, the court would order someone else to do so.[99] In Suffolk County we have found a rule of 1744 to the effect that the justices in different towns were to see that various presentments were to be prosecuted "according to the crimes therein specified," indicating that minor cases within the cognizance of single or double justices were there assigned for further action.[100]

The framing of a charge that would survive attacks upon its form was no inconsiderable undertaking. It is true that the clerks' and justices' manuals were bulging with forms for nearly every conceivable type of human transgression, but the hazards of too literal a trust in these guides are obvious from the welter of tedious detail respecting certainty, repugnancy, surplusage and the like in the chapters on indictment in treatises and abridgments. James Alexander reveals in his *Register* the toil and troubles of the draftsman:

> For counterfeiting a York bill, for issuing and passing a counterfeit, for altering a York bill, for passing an altered bill—which 4 indictments cost me a great

[96] The earliest reference is in 1694 (*Mins. SCJ 1693–1701* 64). In this case the defendant was ordered in custody "forasmuch as the Attorney General is not provided to present him at present." Cf. King v. Hunt, 1735 (*Ms. Mins. SCJ 1732–39* 190, 205, Oct. 27, 1735, Jan. 27, 1735/36).

[97] On Aug. 1, 1765, the following entry appears in the Supreme Court minutes: "The following presentments & Indictments were delivered into Court and the Court delivered to the Atty General with orders to proceed thereupon viz[t]: The King @ [against] Gale Yelverton—presentment of Grand Jury of Dutchess for Forgery—The King @ Archotunken Havenburgh—Presentment of Grand Jury of Dutchess for an Assault—The King @ Gale Yelverton—Indictment by the Grand Jury of D[t]uchess for Perjury—The King @ Francis Bogardus—Indictment by the Grand Jury of Dutchess for Perjury" (*Ms. Mins. SCJ 1764–67* [Rough] 85). In January Term, 1771, the grand jury presented William McMon, Patrick Larkin and two others for a riot and "desired the Attorney General to put in form a bill" against these defendants for riot (*J. T. Kempe Lawsuits* L–O sub nom. Mc-

Mon). Thereupon a true bill of indictment engrossed on parchment was drawn up against these defendants for unlawfully, riotously and routously breaking windows, besetting and entering a house and assaulting its inhabitants to the great damage of such inhabitants and against the peace of the King, his Crown and dignity (*H.R. Pleadings* Pl. K. 346). This indictment was filed in the Supreme Court on Jan. 17, 1771 (*Ms. Mins. SCJ 1769–72* [Engr.] 315).

[98] For example, in Queen v. John Horton a justice objected because he had found nothing against the defendant at preliminary examination (*Ms. Mins. Westch. Co. Sess. 1710–23* June 1, 1714). Cf. *Ms. Mins. Dutchess Co. Sess.* Liber A, Oct. 20, 1725, where the court ordered no further action on eleven presentments; also King v. Van Kleeck (*ibid.* Oct. 19, 1742) where on prayer to put in form, after deliberation ordered quashed.

[99] *Ms. Mins. Richmond Co. Sess. 1710/11–1744/ 45* Mar. 1, 1714/15; King v. Maxfield (*Ms. Mins. Dutchess Co. Sess.* Liber A, Oct. 16, 1739).

[100] *Ms. Mins. Suffolk Co. Sess. 1723–51* Mar. 27, 1744.

deal of thought, pains and care to draw them, all returned billa vera whereon he was arraigned and pleaded not guilty and at the trial I assisted as council for the King.[101]

During the first half of the eighteenth century, when the presentment had been delivered to the Attorney General or assigned to the clerk of the court to be put in form, it seems to have been forthwith engrossed. Attorney General William Kempe, however, appears to have introduced a more painstaking procedure, for after 1753 a preliminary draft was made of the indictment,[102] and finally this instrument was engrossed—in the Supreme Court, on parchment, in Sessions, on paper.[103] As this document was the basis of the record it had to be filed, and this fact was then entered in the minutes.[104]

At what stage the formal accusation was transfigured from a mere bill into an indictment through the mystical process of the endorsement as *billa vera* it is impossible to say. From Dongan's time onward it was customary, where the indictment was set forth in minute books, to add the notation *billa vera,* and the extant indictments framed upon a presentment are always so endorsed. Little evidence is available on the question whether or not grand juries after presentment went through the process of voting either the draft or engrossed instrument a true bill. There is an equivocal Ulster record where one DeWitt was presented for assault and battery, and later the minutes state that an indictment in form was "brought in."[105] Some years later, at the September, 1720

---

[101] King v. Mene (*James Alexander Supreme Ct. Register 1721–42* March Term, 1724/25).

[102] For an example see the draft of an indictment against Michael Smith for passing counterfeit Jersey bills (*J. T. Kempe Lawsuits* S–U). In many cases the informal presentment is endorsed "Bill drawn and filed," or "done"; cf. *ibid.* C–F *sub nom.* Eliz Clarke and the *Ms. Mins. SCJ 1764–67* (Rough) 225; King v. Barnet (*H.R. Pleadings* Pl. K. 300; *Ms. Mins. SCJ 1764–67* [Rough] 276); King v. Smith a negress (*J. T. Kempe Lawsuits* S–U, for the presentment, *H.R. Pleadings* Pl. K. 179 for the indictment, *Ms. Mins. SCJ 1764–67* [Rough] 279 for the minute entry). The paper draft is frequently endorsed "Ingrossed"; cf. King v. Kreamer (*H.R. Pleadings* Pl. K. 596, *Ms. Mins. SCJ 1754–57* [Engr.] 49); King v. Adam King (*H.R. Pleadings* Pl. K. 572 for the presentment, *ibid.* K. 575 for the draft, *Ms. Mins. SCJ 1750–54* [Rough] 317, 342 for the minute entries).

[103] For example, King v. Thomas Clay, Jacobus Osborn and John Galloway (*H.R. Pleadings* Pl. K. 538), a true bill of indictment for burglary engrossed on parchment, the "record" indictment in this case, for endorsed on the back of this parchment is the expression "po. se cul." (cf. *infra* c. IX

585). For the informal grand jury presentment in this case, see *J. T. Kempe Lawsuits* C–F and for the filing of the indictment in Supreme Court, see *Ms. Mins. SCJ 1769–72* (Engr.) 182, Apr. 23, 1770.

In King v. John Carey (1774) two indictments were prepared and each was endorsed with defendant's plea and verdict (*H.R. Pleadings* Pl. K. 337, Pl. K. 357). The latitude of the Attorney General's discretion is indicated by the procedure followed when William Thompson and John Burn were presented jointly for robbery in a dwelling house (*H.R. Pleadings* Pl. K. 1001 [1772]). Indictments against these men severally were prepared (*ibid.* Pl. K. 512, Pl. K. 513).

[104] Compare the note from Van Cortlandt to Kempe reporting a search for an indictment: "I have this day examined the Record of Quarter Sessions and don't find any Entry of an indictment found against Joseph Mensell nor is there any in the files of court" (*J. T. Kempe Lawsuits* C–F *sub nom.* Fagan [1770]). In 1756 a prosecution for perjury was held up because an indictment had disappeared (*ibid.* L–O *sub nom.* Evan Meyers).

[105] *Ms. Mins. Ulster Co. Sess. 1703–05* Sept. 4, 1705.

Richmond Sessions, Roger James, a soldier, was presented for stealing. At the succeeding March Sessions the minutes state an indictment was found *billa vera* and, after the grand jury was discharged, it was discovered it had not been found to be the major part of the jury. Hence the indictment was quashed.[106] The most decisive proof of early country practice comes from Albany in the following year. There Captain John Warren was presented and the court ordered "that an Indictment be drawn up in form against Captain John Warren and sent to the grand jury who send the same back signed by their foreman Billa vera."[107] In New York Quarter Sessions a presentment against one Lanyon was brought in on May 3, 1727, but on August 2, 1727 the grand jurors returned the bill "ignoramus."[107a] An actual vote was evidently taken in this second case, but it should be noticed that it was at a later term, and ordinarily a session was too brief for second deliberations on the same case.

It had been laid down by Lord Chief Justice Holt at the trial of Ambrose Rookwood for treason that "if the Jury upon examining the Witnesses would only present a Matter of Fact with Time and Place, the Court might cause it to be drawn up into Form without carrying it to the jury."[108] We do not know whether this precedent was known in New York but we are disposed to believe that eventually once the presentment was agreed upon, the endorsement of the bill by the foreman was the only further step needed.[109] It would have been absurd to have insisted upon a formal vote on an instrument the substance of which had already been agreed upon. The fact that, in some instances, the presentment with the request that it be put in form is endorsed *billa vera* or a "true presentment" tends to show that signing the bill when drafted was a mere clerical act.[110]

When one compares the records of New York with the material available on English practice, it is obvious that in the Province, the grand jury had a much greater independence of action. In England, the initiative in making

[106] *Ms. Mins. Richmond Co. Sess. 1710/11–1744/45* Sept. 20, 1720, Mar. 7, 1720/21. And defacement of the foreman's signature was regarded as implying disagreement.

[107] *Ms. Mins. Albany Co. Sess. 1717–23* Feb. 7, 1721/22.

[107a] *Ms. Mins. NYCQS 1694–1731/32* 485, 487.

[108] King v. Rookwood, 1696 (4 *State Trials* 107).

[109] This supposition is based upon the curious instance of an information for making a challenge which is endorsed "A true bill. J. J. Maloney foreman Grand Jury," King v. Benjamin Payne (*H.R. Pleadings* Pl. K. 356). This endorsement could

have been made, we think, only because endorsement was automatically executed, for any examination or deliberation upon the document would have disclosed its true nature.

[110] For example, King v. Stephen Case, 1769 (*Ms. Files Ulster Co.* Bundle E); King v. Harvey (*NY Misc. Mss.* Box 6, 1731–39); King v. Sherwood, 1753 (*H.R. Parch.* 183 B 4, *H.R. Pleadings* Pl. K. 626); King v. Sands, 1765 (*H.R. Pleadings* Pl. K. 919, Pl. K. 917). In the case of Mother O'Neal, presented for keeping a disorderly house, the document states "agreed that a bill be found against her for keeping a disorderly house" (*J. T. Kempe Lawsuits* L–O [1765]).

accusations had passed largely to the chief and petty constables whose presentments were referred to the grand jury to be voted upon, or alternatively, bills of indictment already prepared were submitted.[111] In New York, constables' presentments in the manner and form current in the years after the conquest disappeared by the end of the seventeenth century[112] and the grand jury recaptured its ancient autonomy in the process of accusation, so that in the majority of cases presentment preceded the forming of a bill of indictment.

The peculiarities of grand jury procedure in New York were due, we believe, to the fact that the colonists were intent upon preserving the maximum of liberty for the inquest and the maximum control over accusations, neither of which objectives was achieved by merely voting on what authority had made ready in advance. It is true that the prepared bill was employed in the Province but it was apparently never favored. This is the more remarkable since in general English practices were unresistingly duplicated. When the grand jury was first instituted in New York the prepared bill was likewise introduced. This appears clearly from the minutes of the New York City Quarter Sessions of February, 1683/84.[113] But in some manner which defies detection this practice was replaced by the more popular presentment. After the reconstitution of the judiciary in 1691, there are only occasional references in the minute books of the Sessions courts to bills referred to the grand jury.[114]

As Sessions practice usually followed patterns set in superior courts, it is probable that prepared bills were at first used in the proprietary Oyer and Terminer Court and subsequently in the Supreme Court, although it is not until 1694 that the minutes have entries to this effect.[115] The earliest bill of in-

---

[111] This is obvious from the directions in manuals like the *Office of the Clerk of Assize* and the *Crown Circuit Companion*. Considerable information on this is in the Webbs' *English Local Government; The Parish and the County*.

[112] Last vestiges can be seen in *Ms. Mins. Ulster Co. Sess. 1693–98*, in entries under Sept. 30, 1693, a constable's complaint; Sept. 3, 1695, a sheriff's complaint; March 3, 1695/96, a justice's complaint. Of course the type of complaint mentioned *supra* n. 36 continued.

[113] Cf. King v. Thomassen: "The Bill Against him was Committed to the Grand Jury wth the Exam^{con} of the Wittnesses and the Court Adjourned . . . the Indictm^t agst Henry Thomassen was Returned by the Grand Jury Billa Vera" (*Ms. Mins. NYCQS 1683/84–1694* 2, Feb. 5, 1683/84). The earliest indictments proper are for the year 1687 from Kings Co. in 35 *NY Col. Mss.* 1. Cf. also *Ms. Deeds Suffolk Co.* Liber A, 39, King v. Jenner (1688).

[114] *Mins. Westch. Ct. of Sess. 1657–96* 69 (1692) "a bill inditend being presented against J.D. for taking and stealing a certaine horse Colt which the Grand Jury found . . . ignoramus." Compare the entry (*ibid.* 66) respecting a presentment for bastardy at the same session where "the court orders the business returned billa vera." See also King v. Urian Nagell, 1694 (*Ms. Kings Co. Ct. & Rd. Recs. 1692–1825* 25) where Nagell "being presented to the Grand Jury . . . the bill was brought in ignoramus." In Oct. 1748 (*Ms. Mins. Orange Co. Sess. 1727–79*) the grand jury "delivers bill of indictment" in several cases, a presentment in another. *Ms. Mins. Richmond Co. Sess. 1745–1812* May 5, 1761, King v. Jacob Johnson, "indictment presented and filed."

[115] On April 4, 1694, in the Supreme Court, "the Grand jury doe present a bill of indictment against Leonard Lewis, Walter Vanderse and David Provoost endorsed ignoramus," and on April 5, the defendants "being cleared by the grand jurors En-

dictment we have found that we believe to have been drafted in advance is dated January 14, 1699/1700 and is endorsed "ignoramus."[116]

The proof respecting the practice of submitting prepared bills to the grand jury consists largely of instances where this body refused to indict, for, in view of the usual practice of presentment and subsequent putting in form, it is impossible to identify any indictment endorsed "true bill" as one drawn in advance of grand jury deliberations. That the bills found *ignoramus* were not indictments drawn after presentment on which a vote was taken appears from certain minute entries, as in *King* v. *Owen*[117] where the record speaks of a bill "exhibited" to the grand jury and in *King* v. *Greatrakes* where at the special Oyer and Terminer for the Admiralty the grand jury returned "we are not informed of the facts in this bill."[118]

From the files of the country Sessions of the Peace comes certain additional information. This consists chiefly of indictments which are in two hands, that is to say, the chief part of the instrument is drawn by one person, and in the handwriting of another is inserted matter like the names of jurors or additional data that would scarcely have been done in this way if the bill had been one put in form after presentment.[119] These indictments are endorsed with the names of witnesses and marked *billa vera* with the foreman's signature. Some of them can only be described as of sloppy appearance, and it may be that the not infrequent quashing was due to objections arising from this fact.

Certain inferences can also be made from the presence in the county files of certain indictments for offenses beyond the jurisdiction of General Sessions.[120]

---

tered their appearance and were cleared by Proclamacon" (*Mins. SCJ 1693–1701* 54).

Again on July 20, 1694, "The Grand Jury return an Indictmt against Cornelius Jacobs sur proditiore ignoramus. Ordered the Sheriffe sett the prisoner to the barr. Ordered Proclamation be made for the discharge of the prisoner no person appearing against him to Give informacon the prisoner is discharged paying fees being called at the prisoners express instance" (*ibid.* 56).

In King v. George Jefferson, at a special Court of Oyer and Terminer held in New York City on July 19, 1695, "the Grand Jury bring in the indictment against George Jefferson endorsed ignoramus" (*ibid.* 77).

[116] *H.R. Pleadings* Pl. K. 554.
[117] *Ms. Mins. Cir. 1721–49* 54.
[118] *Ms. Mins. SCJ 1756–61* (Rough) at end. Compare also King v. Praal (1724) where a bill was returned *ignoramus* and again recommended by the court (*Ms. Mins. Cir. 1721–49* 39, 40); King v. Halstead, 1733: "Bill against James Halstead for burning a barn the grand jury return

they could not find it" (*ibid.* 65); King v. Charles Warner, Jr., 1736/37 (*ibid.* 87); King v. Alier, 1763 (*Ms. Mins. SCJ 1762–64* [Engr.] 73, 87); King v. Van Sice, 1768 (*Ms. Mins. SCJ 1766–69* [Engr.] 64, 69). An interesting indictment against one Leonard Coons for blasphemy and endorsed *ignoramus* is in *Misc. Mss. Supreme Ct.* no. 4.

[119] For example, King v. Abraham Springsteen —larceny, 1734; King v. Ostrander—aiding escape of felon, 1739; King v. Wm. Smith—assault and battery, 1741 (*Ms. Files Dutchess Co. 1726–40*); King v. Lester—entertaining negroes, 1748 (*Ms. Files Dutchess Co. 1741–50*); King v. Young— blasphemy (*Ms. Files Dutchess Co. 1756*); King v. De Lamatre—assault and battery, 1743 (*Ms. Files Ulster Co.* Bundle H); King v. Matt. Wells— sheep stealing, 1773 (*Ms. Files Suffolk Co., Indictments 1773–1839*).

[120] King v. Thomas Turner—burglary, 1745 (*Ms. Files Ulster Co.* Bundle C); King v. Moran— burglary, 1752 (*ibid.*); King v. Oakes—perjury, 1774 (*Ms. Files Suffolk Co., Indictments 1773–*

These indictments we think were prepared in advance, because the Sessions minutes say nothing of "presentment,"[121] and the instruments bear none of the usual Supreme Court endorsements when they were used for trial.[122] If these were indictments drawn after presentment it seems unlikely that they would not have been delivered to the clerk of the circuits.

An episode which occurred in Dutchess County at the May Sessions, 1739 throws interesting light on the feeling respecting prepared bills. On May 15 an indictment was proffered the grand jury that was certainly prepared beforehand as the jurors' names are written in a handwriting different from that which penned the body of the indictment. This instrument charged John Maxfield, a local bad hat, with assaulting his wife and tying her to a horse's tail.[123] The jury found this bill *ignoramus,* yet the next day made a presentment in nearly the same language. But Henry Livingston, clerk of the peace, obviously irritated at this procedure, moved the discharge of the defendant and the court so ordered.[124]

No open protest, such as was made in New Jersey about the bills prepared in advance,[125] has been found for New York, but the proceedings consequent upon a coroner's inquest furnish some insight into the matter. In the cases where it was deemed inexpedient to arraign a defendant solely upon the finding of the coroner's inquest (which was legally the equivalent of a grand jury's finding[126]) the normal expectancy would be for a bill to be exhibited to the grand jury, yet there is only one case which is clear on the point.[127] Moreover, there are instances where despite the existence of an inquest finding, the grand jury nevertheless proceeded to make a presentment and left it to the Attorney

1839). In King v. Dubois (*Ms. Mins. Dutchess Co. Sess.* Liber E), defendant was indicted Oct. 1, 1771 for false swearing and for corruptly summoning a jury. The court ordered the clerk to send copies of the indictments to the Attorney General. We infer from this that the indictment was laid before the grand jury and voted a true bill; otherwise there would have been a "put in form" order by the court.

121 E.g., King v. Turner (*Ms. Mins. Ulster Co. Sess. 1737–50* May 7, 1745); King v. Oakes (*Ms. Mins. Suffolk Co. Sess. 1760–75* Mar. 29, 1774).

122 Turner (*ut supra*) was tried at Circuit and acquitted (*Ms. Mins. Cir. 1721–49* 115).

123 *Ms. Files Dutchess Co. 1726–40.*

124 *Ms. Mins. Dutchess Co. Sess.* Liber A, May 15, 1739.

125 *James Alexander Papers* Letters E–L, Grandin to Alexander, Oct. 13, 1724.

126 Thus King v. Gale arraigned on a coroner's inquest for murder in September, 1722 (*Ms. Mins.*

Cir. 1721–49 25); King v. Hailey and Hamilton, 1767, the same (*Ms. Mins. SCJ 1764–67* [Rough] 279, 316); King v. Brazier, tried for manslaughter on a coroner's inquest for murder in 1769 (*Ms. Mins. SCJ 1769–72* [Engr.] 16, 20).

127 In King v. Hinton a bill for murder was brought in *ignoramus* (1734). Hinton was then arraigned on a coroner's inquest for shooting one Weeks (*Ms. Mins. Cir. 1721–49* 71). There are other minute entries of arraignment both on indictments and inquests where we are disposed to believe the indictments were prepared in advance; cf. King v. James Wilks—murder, 1755–56 (*Ms. Mins. SCJ 1754–57* [Engr.] 200, 218, 221, 222); King v. Daniel Stagnier, King v. Godfrey Batcar—murder, 1757 (*ibid.* 338–340); King v. Boyd et al.—indictment for manslaughter, inquest for murder, 1758 (*Ms. Mins. SCJ 1756–61* [Rough] 100, 103–105); King v. Locidon—indicted for homicide *se defendendo,* inquest for manslaughter, 1764 (*Ms. Mins. SCJ 1764–67* [Rough] 7, 8); King v.

General to draft an indictment.[128] Where a coroner's findings were inconclusive, of course, some further investigation was necessary, but in such an event there would have been no arraignment on the coroner's inquest.

The cases where the grand jury on its own account presented persons whom a coroner's inquest had already accused exemplify the vigorous independency of the grand jury as an agency of provincial law administration. They aid, too, in understanding why the English preference for the prepared bill did not gain currency in New York. It was not merely that the colonists for constitutional reasons believed in the free functioning of this body, but in the absence of an effective constabulary a resumption of the "neighbor-witness" character of the grand jury was inescapable. As long as the function of responsible investigation devolved upon it[129] the prepared bill was of no utility, for it implied an end of inquiry the probable correctness of which the grand jury need only affirm.

Whether or not the manner in which the indictment process was conducted in New York tended toward the avoidance of the sort of technical objection which seems to have flourished in England cannot be determined, for it is not until the eighteenth century is well advanced that provincial counsel were much employed in misdemeanors, and felons could rarely afford the luxury of legal advice. This is illustrated by the state of the record entries on the amendment of indictments for these show that it was the court or the Attorney General who was usually the agent for ferreting out error.

It was settled English law by the end of the seventeenth century that indictments were not within any statutes of amendment.[130] Since at both Assizes and Sessions in England consent was given by the grand jury to altera-

---

Murphy—indictment for manslaughter, inquest for murder, guilty of manslaughter, 1773 (*Ms. Mins. SCJ 1772–76* [Rough] 128, 132, 136; *H.R. Pleadings* Pl. K. 32; *J. T. Kempe Lawsuits* L–O *sub nom.* Murphy).

[128] On July 31, 1754, Patrick Kreamer was presented for manslaughter and on August 1 indicted for manslaughter. At the same time he was arraigned on the coroner's inquest for murder (*Ms. Mins. SCJ 1754–57* [Engr.] 47, 49, 50; cf. also *infra* 675).

In October Term, 1766, the grand jury presented Josiah Sheater and two others for the murder of George Henry, and the Attorney General's marginal notation was "The indictment to be drawn the same in substance as the coroner's inquest" (*J. T. Kempe Lawsuits* S–U). The indictment for murder in this case was filed in the Supreme Court on October 31, 1766 (*Ms. Mins. SCJ 1766–69* [Engr.] 192). Also see King v. Belinda, a slave

(*ibid.* 175, Oct. 28, 1766; *J. T. Kempe Lawsuits* A–B *sub nom.* Belinda).

[129] Compare here *Ms. Mins. SCJ 1764–67* (Rough) 7, Aug. 2, 1764: "The Court having laid before the Grand Jury an Inquisition . . . on Thomas Tyrrel Lieutenant . . . who it appears by the Inquest . . . was killed . . . by . . . a Stone thrown . . . being then in a certain Boat . . . in order to press Men for the said Vessel—The Grand Jury informed the Court that after the most diligent Enquiry into this matter they find the said Thomas Tyrrel was murdered, but have not been able to discover any one Person concerned therein. The Grand Jury further informed the Court that they had made the Strictest Enquiry as to the person or Persons who burned the King's Boat, but had not been able to discover the perpetrator."

[130] 2 Hawkins, *Pleas of the Crown* c.25 §§97, 98.

tions in form, errors of this type could be corrected by the clerk. But where the indictment was insufficient in any point of substance, it could not be amended without the concurrence of the body by which it had been presented.

Common law rules about amendment were apparently accepted in New York only some time after procedure by indictment was adopted. The early indictments, especially in Sessions, while satisfying in general the ancient prerequisites of *quis, quando, ubi, quid, cuius, quomodo et quare,* were not artful,[131] and it was only when provincial lawyers acquired the characteristic professional conviction that only the artful was right that conditions were ripe for the general employment of the verbose and utterly explicit English forms. This occurred around the beginning of the eighteenth century, and the first order of the Supreme Court that an indictment be amended was made in 1702, but unfortunately the record is silent upon the subsequent procedure.[132]

Although motions to quash became a normal incident in provincial criminal procedure,[133] the cases where the grand jury was ordered to amend were relatively few, chiefly we believe because the inquest had been discharged before the plea would be ruled on. Thus, in November, 1724, in *King* v. *Munro,* a counterfeiting case, the Attorney General moved that the indictment "be qualified for insufficiency," but not until March, 1725 did the grand jury bring in a new bill.[134]

By the middle of the eighteenth century the records show that the courts were familiar with English practice respecting amendment. There are a handful of cases which may be said to establish a rule that an indictment would be resubmitted to the grand jury whenever the court gave leave to amend.[135] On

---

[131] Cf., for example, the following indictment made against two defendants in Kings County Sessions on May 8, 1694: "The Jurors . . . present Rachell Laquiee . . . and Ionica Schamp . . . to the worshipfull Court for breach of their Majesty's peace and signd billa vera . . . for that . . . [they] with force & armes the body of peter praw . . . did assault beat, wound, and evill entreat, & other enormities to him did, soe that of his life he despaird; all which being ag.st the peace of our sovereigne lord & lady the King and Queen . . . & the publique peace etc. as alsoe the laws and statutes in that Case made and provided . . ." (*Ms. Kings Co. Ct. & Rd. Recs. 1692–1825* 25).

[132] King v. Baker (*Ms. Mins. SCJ 1701–04* 59).

[133] Cf. *infra* 600.

[134] *Ms. Mins. SCJ 1723–27* 118, 121, 131. It should be noted that on March 15, 1724/25, the jury found the prisoner not guilty on both indict-

ments, and on Mar. 16 the prisoner was discharged (*ibid.* 134, 136).

[135] On July 31, 1754, one Mary Anderson was presented for keeping a disorderly house and on Aug. 1, 1754, an indictment was filed. However, on Aug. 2, 1754, "the grand jury having found a Bill of Indictment against the Defendant by the name of Mary Anderson . . . and offered a New Indictment against the Defendant Elizabeth Anderson for keeping a common disordered house of Baudry and Tipling House." For the informal presentment, see *H.R. Pleadings* Pl. K. 664; for the engrossed indictment written on parchment, see *H.R. Pleadings* Pl. K. 638; *Ms. Mins. SCJ 1754–57* (Engr.) 47, 49, 50. The amended indictment was quashed (*ibid.* 155, Apr. 24, 1755).

In the case of Sam Beatty, indicted for burglary on Oct. 19, 1769, the defendant pleaded not guilty to this indictment but on Oct. 20, "a mistake ap-

one occasion when the fault was discovered after plea and in the course of trial, a juror was withdrawn, the remainder of the petit jury discharged and a new indictment asked.[136] It is possible that the employment of technical practice of this description may have been due to the influence of the two Kempes who brought to the office of attorney general a much higher degree of proficiency in the arts of procedure than any of their predecessors.

An account of the grand jury's work is not complete without some further reference to the presentments which were made on the jurors' own knowledge,[137] and those on which some action was taken without their being put in form.[138] From the time of institution in New York the inquests acted as the voice of the county and at first seem to have had a mistaken idea of their powers. Thus we have noted at Albany Sessions in 1688 a "presentment" that persons selling spirits must keep lodgings for horse and man,[139] and later, a general presentment against persons who "ride over corn fields,"[140] both of

pearing in the former Indictment in this Cause the Grand Jury amended the same and then presented it to the Court." The defendant thereupon pleaded not guilty but on trial was found guilty (*Ms. Mins. SCJ 1769–72* [Engr.] 106–108).

On April 19, 1771, Margaret Higgins was indicted "for stealing from the person privilly and an error appearing therein the same was returned to the Grand Jury to be amended." On April 22 the defendant pleaded not guilty to the amended indictment, and on April 24 she was found guilty by the petit jury. On April 27 she was sentenced to be hanged (*ibid.* 351, 352, 356, 362).

On Jan. 23, 1772, Catherine Longworth was indicted for housebreaking "and a Mistake appearing therein, the Court orders that the same be amended and represented by the Grand Jury" (*ibid.* 471).

[136] King v. McDaniel and Kilfoy (*Ms. Mins. SCJ 1754–57* [Engr.] 338, 339). Evidently the indictment was amended, for on the same day the prisoners pleaded not guilty, and on Jan. 21, "The Jury . . . find the Defendants severally Guilty and that they had no goods or Chattels, Lands or Tenements at the time of the Felony Committed or at any time since to their knowledge." The Attorney General thereupon moved for judgment and the prisoners were sentenced to be hanged (*ibid.* 339, 341, 342).

[137] The cases where the presentment was on the grand jury's own knowledge are most obviously the blanket presentments, viz., of the general breach of the Lord's Day in 1694 (*Mins. SCJ 1693–1701* 128, 129); and again in 1700 (*ibid.* 197), the presentment of New York City for not clearing the city dock and for the constables not preventing youths and negroes playing in the streets on Sunday (*ibid.* 159). In 1702 the Supreme Court on a presentment ordered the laws for Sab-

bath breach to be put into execution (*Ms. Mins. SCJ 1701–04* 60). Compare further the presentment May 4, 1698 in Quarter Sessions of a parcel of unmerchantable flour "exposed with heads open" (*Ms. Mins. NYCQS 1694–1731/32* 37–39); and the presentment of a breach of the assize of bread Aug. 5, 1724 where the grand jury brought the loaves into court (*ibid.* 45). In Westchester, after complaint about the jail, the grand jury took a view and made a return, 1726 (*Ms. Mins. Cir. 1721–49* 48, 49), and later (1733) made a presentment (*ibid.* 58). See also the presentment of the insufficiency of the jail (*Ms. Mins. Albany Co. Sess. 1717–23* Feb. 6, 1722/23).

[138] The minutes of Oyer and Terminer and General Gaol Delivery, 1716–17, show that only five presentments were not drawn up "in form" and these were delivered to the justice of the peace for further action. Five bills were found *ignoramus* and there were five indictments on which true bills were found. In Oyer and Terminer and General Gaol Delivery minutes for 1721–49, there appear to have been fifteen presentments which were not drawn up "in form," and of these, one for rape by a negro was delivered to the justices of the peace and was expressly not drawn up "in form" because, under the act of assembly, the justices of the peace had the power to hear such a case (King v. Robin, a slave, *Ms. Mins. Cir. 1721–49* 123, Ulster Oyer and Terminer and General Gaol Delivery, July 9, 1748). Six of the fifteen presentments which were not drawn up "in form" were delivered to the Attorney General in order that he might frame informations thereon. There were 136 true bills of indictment and thirteen bills endorsed *ignoramus*.

[139] *Ms. Mins. Albany Co. Sess. 1685–89* 49.
[140] *Ibid.* 57.

them in effect an arrogation of the ordinance powers of justices. In the records of Kings County there is evidence that the country inquests regarded themselves as true neighbor-witnesses and their findings as a verdict, for in 1699 the grand jury "bring in their verdict that the niger . . . did confess the theft which they will prove . . ."[141] and in the next year another "verdict" is brought in that no horse might run in the woods, negroes run or meet together, and that the King's Highway be repaired.[142] In Ulster County (1696), the grand jury, more cautious, "brings in" that Peter Pieter be maintained by his own town[143] as well as grievances against the dilapidation of highways and pounds.

As the justices became aware of their powers and took a firm hold on ordinance making in their counties, the function of the grand jury became clarified as one of mere presentment. By this means all manner of matter was brought to the justices' attention and orders made pursuant to the tenor of the presentments. Where the grievance was of a nature which called for general regulation, such as Sunday observance, highways and the like, the justices would either make some preliminary order[144] or would promulgate an ordinance forthwith.[145] Frequently, however, some specific nuisance would be

141 Ms. Kings Co. Ct. & Rd. Recs. 1692–1825 50.

142 Ibid. 60. Cf. the verdict against Hans Fryman (1702) at p. 87.

143 Ms. Mins. Ulster Co. Sess. 1693–98 session of Sept. 1, 1696.

144 Thus in 1693 the jurors of Kings Co. presented a highway. The court appointed three men to view who later reported (Ms. Kings Co. Ct. & Rd. Recs. 1692–1825 12). Cf. the similar order in 1697 (ibid. 40, 41). In 1707, the Freshwater-Kingsbridge highways were presented by New York jurors and the surveyors ordered to view. They apparently failed to act and on a new presentment were ordered to repair or process to issue (Ms. Mins. NYCQS 1694–1731/32 124, 132, May 7, Nov. 4, 1707). Also note that on Feb. 5, 1711/12, the grand jurors presented the insufficiency of the common jail and also "the want of the reparation of the highways through the island to Queensbridge" (ibid. 208). With reference to highway repair, it is interesting to note the following minute entry in the NYCQS minutes for Nov. 1, 1692: "Ordered that all the Carmen of this Citty shall forthwith Repair the Highways between the said Citty and the fresh water . . . [and] do diligently Attend, and see to the Performance of this Order; and upon refusal thereof by any of said carmen . . . [to perform the order] they shall be liable to such penalty and Fines as the Mayor shall Judge required for the said Contempt" (Ms. Mins. NYCQS 1683/84–1694 158); also see a similar order for carmen to repair the highways, May 1, 1694 (ibid. 168). On Feb. 5, 1723/24, under an act of general assembly of 12 Anne for the repair of the post road from New York to Kingsbridge and another act of 7 Geo. I, the Court of Quarter Sessions appointed three surveyors who were to cause the roads and bridges to be repaired and also to take care that there were no encroachments made on the King's roads or bridges. At least two of the surveyors were to make certificates evidencing the performance of these orders at the next Quarter Sessions of the Peace on pain of prosecution for their neglect (Ms. Mins. NYCQS 1722–1742/43 [Rough] 33; also see similar orders and appointments of Feb. 6, 1722/23, Feb. 3, 1724/25, Feb. 2, 1725/26, ibid. 16, 51, 65).

With reference to the preliminary orders, note also the unusual procedure in Ulster Co. where a jury of women was ordered to examine a girl charged with bastardy (Ms. Mins. Ulster Co. Sess. 1711/12–1720 Sept. 15, Nov. 12, Dec. 8, 1715).

145 For example, Ms. Mins. Ulster Co. Sess. 1693–98 Mar. 6, 1693/94, a regulation for the collection of taxes; session of Sept. 4, 1694, an order re fencing; Ms. Mins. Ulster Co. Sess. 1711/12–1720 Mar. 27, 1719, an order re horse racing; Ms. Mins. Ulster Co. Sess. 1737–50 Nov. 1743, order re blocking highways; Ms. Kings Co. Ct. & Rd. Recs. 1692–1825 46, 47, orders re negroes meeting, selling liquors and Sabbath breach; Ms. Mins. Albany Co. Sess. 1763–82 Oct. 22, 1766, presentment of

complained of which would require the presence of a defendant or some action taken respecting him. It was in these cases which, generally speaking, fell within the scope of the justices' summary jurisdiction, that the presentment was not put in form.

The presentment not reduced to form was disposed of in a variety of ways. It could in the first place be ignored, like the presentment for Sabbath breach of Attorney General Bradley and Henry Vernon, a leading city barrister, who had apparently tried to alleviate the miseries of going the circuit to the indignation of the righteous men of Suffolk at the July Oyer and Terminer of 1724.[146] If it was a matter on which some hearing was deemed desirable, process would be ordered to secure the attendance of the persons concerned, usually a summons but on occasion a capias.[147] In many of the cases, however, where nuisances were presented, the courts do not appear to have bothered

---

storehouses—ordered removed; presentment of Ulster Gaol (1752), *Ms. Files Ulster Co.* Bundle N. Cf. also *supra* 38, 106.

[146] *Ms. Mins. Cir. 1721–49* 43. There are many examples of these presentments which were never prosecuted. Thus Martha Brekon, alias Bryant, was presented by the grand jury on Oct. 7, 1701 (*Ms. Mins. SCJ 1701–04* 9). Geo. Sanders and Ed. Attkins presented June 4, 1725, for stealing a box of sundry goods from a canoe at the Dock Ward in New York City (*Ms. Mins. SCJ 1723–27* 142, 143, June 4, 1724). On Aug. 2, 1751, James Bill was presented by the grand jury for counterfeiting a bill of credit (*Ms. Mins. SCJ 1750–54* [Engr.] 66). In June Term, 1722, Resolvert Waldron was presented by the grand jurors for assaulting J. Delamontagne and driving on his hedge, damaging his trees and property (*James Alexander Papers* Box 44 no. 34). On Apr. 26, 1753, in the Supreme Court of Judicature, "the grand jury . . . offered a presentment against John Ayscough, Esq., sheriff of the city of New York, for illegally discharging one Barnabas Morgan who was ordered by the justices to be whipped" (*Ms. Mins. SCJ 1750–54* [Engr.] 253; *H.R. Pleadings* Pl. K. 598). Michael Nestel [Nestal?] was presented for perjury in joining in a petition to Daniel Horsmanden and William Smith, judges of the Supreme Court, requesting the discharge of Frederick Staple, an insolvent debtor (*J. T. Kempe Lawsuits* L–O; *Ms. Mins. SCJ 1769–72* [Engr.] 287, Oct. 25, 1770). In October Term, 1773, Peter Kenney was presented for petit larceny and for mixing base metal with gold and silver (*J. T. Kempe Lawsuits* J–L).

[147] Cf. King v. Griffit presented for a false beam in the weighhouse (*Mins. SCJ 1693–1701* 49, Oct. 6, 1693). On Apr. 9, 1696, Jacob Teller and Philip Schuyler were presented by the grand jury in the Supreme Court "for playing at deys on the Sabbath and Francis Hulin for entertaining of them at play in his house." On this presentment a "warrant"

was ordered to issue against the defendants (*ibid.* 93). Dr. Samuel Staats and John Windower were presented in the Supreme Court by the grand jury for an unnamed offense, and on the following day "Emmott pr Dne Rege moves that Capias issue against Dr. Staats and Mr. Windower being presented by the Grand Jury to be brought to answer next terme" (*ibid.* 125, 127, Oct. 7, 9, 1697). Johannes Tiebout, being presented in the Supreme Court by the grand jury on Apr. 9, 1703, "for a misdemeanor in refusing to assist the constable in the execution of his office . . . Mr. Attorney General prays the court to award process against him to oblige him to answer" (*Ms. Mins. SCJ 1701–04* 87). Sarah Brower was presented by the grand jury in Kings Co. Sessions on May 9, 1710, for having a bastard and "the court ordered that the constable of Brooklyn should bring her before this court." However, on May 10 the constable made a return on his warrant that Sarah Brower was not to be found (*Kings Co. Ct. & Rd. Recs. 1692–1825* 161). On a grand jury presentment against James Jones for assault and battery, the Attorney General moved in the Supreme Court that process be issued against Jones and this motion was granted (*Ms. Mins. SCJ 1732–39* 142, Oct. 22, 1734). Again, on the Attorney General's motion, the Supreme Court on Jan. 25, 1734/35, ordered process to issue against Joseph Stephenson who had been presented by the grand jury for assaulting Anne Williams (*ibid.* 147). John DeWitt Peterson was presented by the grand jury "for cursing the Governour" and on the Attorney General's motion, it was ordered that process issue against him. In this case Mr. Murray was assigned as the defendant's counsel, but no other information appears on the case (*ibid.* 147, 189, Jan. 25, 1734/35, Oct. 24, 1735). In all of the above cases, the only entries that have been found are those recited, and it is not known whether or in what manner these presentments were continued or ended.

with defendants, but proceeded summarily by issuing orders for abatement. These were rarely in the alternative, viz., giving a property owner the opportunity to act first, for usually the sheriff was ordered to remove the nuisance and compensate himself from the materials.[148] This method of dealing with nuisances was not confined to Sessions, but, as the cases already cited indicate, was also the rule in the Supreme Court and at Circuit.

Even prior to the enactment of the statutes which dispensed with jury trial in cases less than grand larceny, the New York courts were exercising a discretion in proceeding upon presentments without troubling to have them put into form. After the appearance of a defendant had been secured, he would be permitted to plead to the presentment. Most of the early cases are instances where the defendants would confess the fact and offer something in extenua-

---

[148] In 1723/24 the grand jury presented to the Supreme Court a dilapidated house and the court ordered the house repaired or pulled down by the sheriff (*Ms. Mins. SCJ 1723–27* 69, Mar. 16, 1723/24). Compare also a summary order by the Supreme Court that the owner remove two old houses presented by the grand jury on June 9, 1729, as a public nuisance (*Ms. Mins. SCJ 1727–32* 127). Again, on Mar. 17, 1729/30, the grand jury in the Supreme Court presented a house lately belonging to Jane Smith "as a publick nuisance being in danger of falling into the Streete to the hurt of his Maties Liege Subjects Ordered that the Sherriff do take care that the said house . . . be within the space of a month pulled down paying himself . . . out of the materials of ye house" (*ibid.* 193). See also orders of June 5, 1730, for removal of several dwellings and a warehouse (*ibid.* 202). On Apr. 29, 1752, the grand jury presented as a nuisance a house in danger of falling down and, there being no tenant in the house, the Supreme Court ordered the sheriff to remove it and pay himself out of the materials (*Ms. Mins. SCJ 1750–56* [Rough] 92). Charles Beekman's house was presented by the grand jury on Oct. 25, 1757, as being out of repair and "likely to fall down endangering the lives of his majestys subjects" and the Supreme Court ordered that it be removed (*Ms. Mins. SCJ 1756–61* [Rough] 84).

The Sessions practice was similar: cf. the order in N.Y. Quarter Sessions, Aug. 7, 1723 (*Ms. Mins. NYCQS 1694–1731/32* 426). On Aug. 6, 1729, the Quarter Sessions grand jury presented a house as ready to fall down and the court ordered that the nuisance be removed in 14 days or else that the sheriff remove it (*ibid.* 515). On Aug. 5, 1730, the grand jury presented a house as dangerous and the court ordered that it be repaired forthwith or the sheriff was to pull it down (*ibid.* 527). Abraham Bickley's house was presented as a dangerous public nuisance, likely to fall down, and on Aug. 4, 1731, the court ordered that the sheriff remove it as

a public nuisance within a month, paying himself out of the materials (*ibid.* 538, 539). On Aug. 3, 1732, the New York grand jury "recommended" to Quarter Sessions that certain places were nuisances "as they now lye," and it was thereupon ordered that the aldermen of each ward where the nuisances were located should inspect the same and take such proper methods for their removal as the laws directed (*Ms. Mins. NYCQS 1732–62* 15). On May 7, 1735, the grand jurors "represented" to the court that the digging of a hill near the windmill on the common and the digging of William Street were public nuisances. The grand jury therefore prayed that the court "take some effectual method to remove the same" (*ibid.* 52).

For other summary orders for the removal of nuisances, see the orders in Quarter Sessions on the following dates: Nov. 10, 1738, a ruinous house (*ibid.* 94); Feb. 4, 1740/41, a house and well as a common nuisance (*ibid.* 127); Feb. 9, 1743/44, the chimney of a small shed as a very dangerous nuisance (*ibid.* 161); Nov. 6, 1746, 2 individuals presented for maintaining a nuisance (*ibid.* 212); Feb. 9, 1748/49, a house (*ibid.* 249); Nov. 8, 1752, a chimney (*ibid.* 324); May 7, 1760, four ruinous houses (*ibid.* 478); May 7, 1760, Nathaniel Ogden for an old house in South Street (*ibid.* 478); May 4, 1763, a house (*Ms. Mins. NYCQS 1760–72* 76); Nov. 7, 1768, a house (*ibid.* 148), and May 6, 1774, another (*Ms. Mins. NYCQS 1772–91* 99). In practically all of the next above references the sheriff was summarily ordered to remove these nuisances and to pay himself out of the materials. Country practice was identical; cf., for example, *Ms. Mins. Ulster Co. Sess. 1737–50* May 2, 1738, Nov. 6, 1744; *Ms. Mins. Albany Co. Sess. 1763–82* Oct. 22, 1766. In Suffolk a person regarded as a nuisance allowed to be taken out of the county (*Ms. Mins. Suffolk Co. Sess. 1760–75* Oct. 7, 1760). Cf. the presentments at Circuit, Albany, 1742 (*Ms. Mins. Cir. 1721–49* 109, 111), and Dutchess, 1749 (*ibid.* 126).

tion or put themselves at the mercy of the court. The minute entries suggest that the proceedings in court were informal; indeed, they seem to have been conducted more or less upon the style of a "meeting" of the justices.[149] Possibly in certain instances, when the presentment was made upon the knowledge of the grand jurors, the bench, before venturing upon a trial of the charge, would deem it prudent to make some further examination. This is very clearly indicated in the case of Stephen Buckenhoven who was presented on May 7, 1701, in New York City Sessions for altering the tax rolls. Buckenhoven appeared on August 5, 1701, and the minutes state: "The Court having Considered the presentment agt. the Defendt. and since which upon further Examination itt appeareth unto them that the said Defendt. has not Committed the fraud whereof he is presented doe therefore Order the said Stephen Buckenhoven be not any further prosecuted."[150]

The limits of discretion are not apparent from the records.[151] The charge against Buckenhoven was serious enough to have been put in form and tried, since the action of the grand jury put the case on a much more substantial footing than an individual complaint. The truth of the matter seems to be

[149] So John Vincent presented in 1697 for keeping tan pits, confessed and discharged (*Ms. Mins. NYCQS 1694-1731/32* 25, 26, May 4, 5, 1697). Albertus Ringo presented for selling drink to negroes, confessed but claimed ignorance of the law, fined 50s. (*ibid.* 51, 52, Feb. 8, 1698/99). In Kings County (1696), Isaac Haselbury "being bound over to this Court for a Certaine misdeamean[r] for carrying away the minister's horse . . . upon the presentment of the grand Jury," made a "humble submission to this Court & Craving their mercy." Cleared by proclamation on paying the costs of the court (*Kings Co. Ct. & Rd. Recs. 1692-1825* 31, 33). When Gabriel Sprung was presented by the grand jury on May 10, 1704, for "Gaming & playing on the Sabbath day," he "craved ffavour of the Court it being done agt. his will & Consent; The Court upon his submission & promise of not being guilty of the like offense ordered him to be discharged" (*ibid.* 143). Likewise Teunis Janse, presented on May 10, 1704 by the Kings County grand jury for "unlawfully taking and carrying away a parcell of ffirewood," appeared in court on Nov. 14, 1704, "and Conffesses the ffact & submits himself to the mercy of the Court," ordered dismissed on paying the costs of the court (*ibid.* 144, 145). William Brower, on Nov. 10, 1708, pleaded not guilty to presentments brought in against him by the Kings County grand jury for harboring and selling drink to negro slaves, as well as for not obeying a warrant by a justice of the peace. On May 10, 1709, Brower withdrew his plea and "referred himself

to this court." On May 11, "The Court having Considered of the presentmt. of William Brower by the Grand Jury ffor Contempt of Authority in not obeying Justice Strycker's warrant, and he refferring himself to this Court, doe order that he pay a ffine of twenty shillings for the use of her Majesty," and the court "having Considered of the presentmt. . . . ffor harbouring & selling of drink to negro slaves, doe Order . . . [that Brower] pay . . . ten shillings as a ffine ffor the use of her Majestye" (*ibid.* 157, 160). Sarah Knight and Martha Brower were presented on May 12, 1708 in Kings County Sessions because they had "sworne ffalse in their oaths taken before a speciall Court held at Bedfford . . . ffor the Inquiry and tryall of a Certaine Riott said to be Committed at the house of Sarah Knights . . . by Hans Jorisse Bergen . . . [and others] as pr the Record of said Court . . . Ordered [the defendants] appeare before this Court next Nov[r] to answer to the premises. . . ." On November 9, 1708, the defendants appeared "upon a venire facias," but on Nov. 10 they were "discharged by proclamation noe body appearing to prosecute them" (*ibid.* 156, 157).

[150] *Ms. Mins. NYCQS 1694-1731/32* 64, 66; *NY Misc. Mss.* Box 3 no. 2.

[151] On Mar. 21, 1726/27, John Wood, presented in the Supreme Court for an assault and wounding, was fined £9 (*Ms. Mins. SCJ 1723-27* 256). This is the most remarkable case of extended discretion.

that the courts were disposed to treat the presentment not yet put in form as if it were no more than a sworn information of an individual, and, as we have noticed in Suffolk, presentments were referred to single justices. So far as we are aware, in only one of the early cases was there a jury trial upon a formless presentment.[152] Of course, after the courts were empowered to deal summarily with defendants charged with crimes less than grand larceny, presentments of such offenses could be lawfully treated as equivalent to mere complaints.[153]

The Management of Prosecutions

One of the most puzzling aspects of the accusatory process in New York is the question of the directing control, and more particularly, the division of authority between the Attorney General and the courts. In the country the administrative responsibility of the clerks of the peace in respect to the preparation of cases for the grand inquest was considerable, and we have seen no evidence to indicate that the Attorney General possessed any authority over these officials. He might appoint his own deputy in a county, but this was no exclusive prerogative, for, as we have seen, the courts frequently designated persons to act in his room. This trenched, of course, upon one of the chief sources of the Attorney General's income, which was largely derived from fees,[154] yet only once was any real controversy over the court's powers raised.

[152] It is possible there was an indictment here, for the minutes refer to a "bill of presentment" brought into the Kings County Sessions by the grand jury against Jacob Fardon. It was ordered that he "be legally ordered to appear at the next court of Sessions to answer to the said presentment." On Nov. 8, 1709, Fardon "being summoned by a venire to this court upon a presentment . . . found against him the last court appeared. . . . Upon motion to this court by the clerke of the peace that an attorney may be permitted to speak on the behalf of the Queen in the presentment . . . Ordered that Henry Filkin be an attorney on behalf of the Queen in this case. Referred to a jury who ffind Jacob Fardon not guilty" (*ibid.* 160, 161).

[153] Compare the cases cited *supra* n. 149 with the entry in King v. Cash after the Act of 1732. On May 2, 1733, Martha Cash was presented by the grand jury in New York City Quarter Sessions "for setting the Prison Doors on fire in the City Hall of this City . . . Whereupon the Defendant was Ordered to the Bar and Confessed her only Design was to Gett out of Goal and prays the Mercy . . . and that She may be delivered out of Goal and that She will then immediately depart this province and never Return again." In this case, the court acted "(by Virtue of an Act of General

Assembly . . . Entituled An Act for the Speedy punishing and Releasing such Persons from imprisonment as shall commit any Criminal Offense in the City of New York under the Degree of Grand Larceny)" and found that the defendant was guilty of the crime and "is convict thereof." Accordingly she was sentenced to eleven lashes and then ordered to be discharged from custody (*Ms. Mins. NYCQS 1732–62* 25).

[154] Cf. the letter of Bradley to Wendell, Sept. 6, 1725, regarding the latter's acting at Albany. Bradley promised to engage Wendell "if you'd be faithful to me and allow as is usual both in England and here the half of the fees to be had and received in prosecuting for the Crown or in Crown business" (*Misc. Mss. Richard Bradley*). Note also the correspondence of Kempe and Duane. On April 28, 1757, Duane wrote to Kempe as follows: "The hard terms on which I obtained your Warrant to act for you in Richmond County . . . have occasioned me more attentively to consider the Force and Efficacy of your Appoint[ment] and I am perfectly satisfied that it endues me with no greater Power than I already had in acting in the Crown Causes in your Absence by the Order and Direction of the Court; who have undoubtedly the sole Right by Law, to appoint any Council they think proper

This occurred in 1734 when a prosecution of Recorder Harison of New York City was instituted.[155] The magistrates of the city ordered that the three leaders of the bar, James Alexander, Joseph Murray and William Smith, be requested to attend the court and advise whether it had the power to appoint persons to prosecute presentments where the Attorney General neglected to proceed. The answer was presumably in the affirmative for the clerk of the peace was ordered to prosecute and the three lawyers appointed to assist.[156]

The Supreme Court never had any doubt of its powers and did not hesitate to name someone to act as counsel for the Crown.[157] The judges of this court do not seem to have recognized any discretion to have been vested in the Attorney General with regard to the question whether or not a case should be tried. Thus in March, 1735/36 at the Westchester Circuit the Attorney General refused to put a presentment in form, and the court promptly ordered the clerk to do so.[158] In respect to the discontinuance of proceedings, too, the Supreme Court appears to have exercised a broader authority than even the King's Bench, for in England the consent of the Attorney General was indispensable to a nolle prosequi[159] whereas in New York the court did not regard this as necessary.

The discontinuance of prosecutions is one of the more obscure chapters in provincial criminal procedure, for the discretion of the minute entries effectively shrouds what went on behind the scenes. Occasionally, as in the prosecution of David Provoost Jr., one may suspect influence was at work.[160] Sometimes, particularly where the order emanated from the Governor, the action was to mitigate hardship resulting from the impossibility of error proceedings.[161] But even in the highest quarters it was possible to induce a liberal view

to assist their Clerk of the Peace in the Business of the Sessions when the Attorney General is not himself present, I therefore beg leave to return you your warrant as cou'd I not prosecute for the Crown in your Absence without it, it wou'd not now be worth my while to continue in that Office on the unreasonable Condition of accounting to you for one half of the Profits, when the whole are [so inade]quate to the Trouble and Expence of Time . . . ." (*James Duane Papers* Box 1, 1680–1766, I, 50, Ms. 151). Peter Sylvester wrote to Kempe July 14, 1773 from Albany that the deputy must have the drawing of indictments, the managing and the perquisites "otherwise it is not worth the trouble" (*Kempe Letters* A–Z). See also *infra* 734.
[155] *Supra* 320.
[156] *James Alexander Papers* Box 45. Q.S. Papers; *Ms. Mins. NYCQS 1732–62* 43, 49, 52, May 9, 1734, Feb. 6, 1734/35, May 7, 1735.
[157] So in the prosecution of Attorney General

Broughton (*supra* 317) the court ordered the Solicitor General to proceed (*Ms. Mins. SCJ 1701–04* 56, Apr. 9, 1702).
[158] *Ms. Mins. Cir. 1721–49* 83, 84.
[159] *Rex v. Cranmer* (1 *Ld. Raymond* 721).
[160] Indicted for making a false return in an election. On April 4, 1704, the Attorney General prayed Provoost might be tried but on Oct. 12, 1704, he entered the nolle prosequi (*Ms. Mins. SCJ 1701–04* 120, 130, 168); cf. *supra* 164. Compare the later case, King v. Oliver De Lancey, where the greatest efforts were made by Clinton to have the prosecution forwarded. Here the court, presided over by the defendant's brother, ordered a discharge but on motion of the Attorney General, "*salvo jure regis*" (*Ms. Mins. SCJ 1750–54* [Engr.] 95; 6 *Doc. Rel. Col. Hist. NY* 693, 695, 697, 766).
[161] *Supra* 255.

of public interest and to stop proceedings before trial.[162] This amenability is amusingly illustrated by the case of Isaac Jacobs who had been indicted in 1721 at Westchester Oyer and Terminer for felony in taking violently from one Moras £25 which the latter had stolen from Jonathan Merritt.[163] Jacobs had escaped to Connecticut and his creditors, merchants of New York, petitioned Governor Burnet for a nolle prosequi in order that Jacobs could return and settle with them.[164] So far as a governor's order was concerned, the Attorney General's cooperation was necessary.[165] In this particular case, the latter presumably did not agree, and as a result a formal pardon was issued.[166] It is conceivable that palms were crossed in this case, for the evidence of Jacobs' guilt seems clear, but there is no proof of the fact.[167]

Apart from cases where there are signs of irregularities, or where the court itself intervened, the Attorny General would enter a nolle prosequi either because his evidence would not lead to a conviction,[168] or because a case had been compounded and the prosecuting witness desired a discontinuance.[169] The no-

[162] In cases before trial see, for example, King v. Marques indicted for altering the weighhouse books, 1701 (*Ms. Mins. SCJ 1701–04* 20, 33); King v. French indicted for "high misdemeanors," 1702 (*ibid.* 55, 56, 63, 64). Queen v. Peter Pra *et al.,* 1706 (*Ms. Mins. SCJ 1704/05–1709* 66, 191, June 5, 1706, Sept. 10, 1708).

[163] A true bill had been found against William Moras at Oyer and Terminer and General Gaol Delivery for Westchester on Aug. 9, 1721, and on Aug. 10, Moras was tried and convicted. On Aug. 19, 1721, he was sentenced to be hanged. In the meantime, on Aug. 12, 1721, J. Lion Jr. and Joseph Budd entered a recognizance in £20 at Westchester Oyer and Terminer and General Gaol Delivery for Lion's appearance "at this or any other Gaol Delivery held in this County where and when Isaac Jacobs, indicted for felony, shall be apprehended and brought to tryall Notice whereof being left at his house to give Evidence against him." Likewise Deliverance Brown and one surety were also bound in £20 each for Deliverance Brown's appearance to give evidence against Jacobs (*Ms. Mins. Cir. 1721–49* 1–9).

[164] *James Alexander Papers* Box 46.

[165] Cf. *supra* 248, re the case of Theophylact Bache. In the case of King v. Glen, J. T. Kempe on Feb. 6, 1764 notified Peter Silvester that the Lieut. Governor had directed a nolle pros. to be entered against Glen, indicted at Albany for a trespass connected with billeting troops, and enclosed a warrant for that purpose (*J. T. Kempe Lawsuits* C–F *sub nom.* Fonda; G–J *sub nom.* John Glenn). The necessity of a warrant where the Attorney General was not personally at the trial indicates that his consent was essential (*Ms. Mins. Albany Co. Sess. 1763–82* Jan. 4, June 4, 1764).

[166] *H.R. Parch.* 223 A 4.

[167] Cf. the deposition of Robert Harrison, taken before "James Alexander one of his Majestys Councill" on Aug. 26, 1721. Harrison stated that just before Moras was committed to prison for stealing from Jonathan Merritt as he was returning to York, "one Isaac Jacobs a Jew overtook him at Rye and Ride along with him . . . and . . . told the Deponent that he had met Morras . . . and told him that he had authority to take up Pyrates [such as Moras] and hang them . . . and so he would do by him if he did not deliver him his money" (*James Alexander Papers* Box 46).

[168] King v. William Richardson, 1729 (*Ms. Mins. SCJ 1727–32* 102, 105, 124); King v. Anne Hall, 1739, where the defendant was an accessory and the principal was at large (*Ms. Mins. SCJ 1732–39* 341, 365). Cf. King v. Humphrey, *infra* 527.

[169] King v. Nathan and Isaac Levy, Meers and Isaacs (*Ms. Mins. NYCQS 1694–1731/32* 515–517, Aug. 6, Nov. 4, 1729); King v. William Proctor, 1756 (*Ms. Mins. SCJ 1754–57* [Engr.] 284, 318). In *J. T. Kempe Lawsuits* P–R is a letter from Wells, the prosecuting witness. Some of the cases which stop abruptly in the records were undoubtedly discontinued by a nolle pros. after compounding. So in King v. Armstrong (*Ms. Mins. SCJ 1769–72* [Engr.] 242) the defendant was indicted for assault and battery. No further entries appear, but in a letter from one Pierson to Kempe it is stated the "difference" with Armstrong was settled. In one case, King v. John Thorn, there was a settlement but the court fined the defendant 1s. (*Ms. Mins. SCJ 1732–39* 122, 137).

Many of the entries are simply to the effect that a nolle prosequi was entered: cf. Queen v. Boudinot

tion that a composition could only be effected with leave of the court was not current in New York, for the cases indicate that the consent of the Attorney General was sufficient. On the other hand, as we shall later see, the courts eventually got to mitigating fines if defendants took care of the complainants' costs and they did not hesitate to order the discharge of prisoners without consulting the Attorney General when for one reason or another they thought it desirable.[170]

At common law neither a discharge by proclamation nor a nolle prosequi protected a defendant from being indicted afresh. The rules about these matters were, therefore, essentially designed for administrative convenience and to maintain a balance in the exercise of discretion. This does not seem to have been understood in New York. The nolle prosequi was presumably a privilege of the Crown to be exercised through its counsel. But the governors obviously regarded it as an aspect of the pardoning power and the courts seem to have confused the privilege with their own prerogative to discharge where prosecution failed.[171] It is no wonder that the clerks would sometimes make their own contribution to confusion by simply entering the word "ended."[172]

(*Ms. Mins. NYCQS 1694–1731/32* 109–111, May 8, Aug. 6, 1706); Queen v. Anthony Young (*ibid.* 167, 170, Nov. 2, 1709, Feb. 8, 1709/10); Queen v. Frourt (*ibid.* 164, 167, 170–172, Aug. 3, Nov. 1, 2, 1709, Feb. 8, 1709/10); Queen v. P. Ronsby, 1713–14 (*Ms. Mins. SCJ 1710–14* 516, 537); King v. Chapman and Morer (*Ms. Mins. NYCQS 1732–62* 83, 84); King v. Lefferts et al., 1736–37 (*Ms. Mins. SCJ 1732–39* 242, 249, 260); King v. Constable (*Ms. Mins. Albany Co. Sess. 1763–82* June, 1766); King v. Miller (*Ms. Mins. Orange Co. Sess. 1727–79* Apr. 25, 1727); King v. Lakeman (*Ms. Mins. Richmond Co. Sess. 1710/11–1744/45* Sept. 1, 1719 [*cessat processus*]).

[170] So in King v. Mary Ball (1734–36) there was a rule entered of judgment for the defendant unless the case was brought to trial next term. "Mr. Attorney General not having brought in this cause, ordered that she be discharged" (*Ms. Mins. SCJ 1732–39* 121, 142, 161, 169, 179, 230). See also King v. Pat. Sealy and John Smith, 1763 (*Ms. Mins. SCJ 1762–64* [Engr.] 151, 174). In King v. Van der Voort after a plea of guilty "nolo prosequi" entered by the clerk because the indictment was insufficient (*Ms. Mins. NYCQS 1760–72* 73, 82, Feb. 2, 1763, Aug. 3, 1763). But note King v. et al. where there is a notation of the Attorney General's consent to discharge (*Ms. Mins. SCJ 1732–39* 242, 249, 260).

[171] The courts usually discharged by proclamation. The practice of ordering a discontinuance of process did not gain a foothold. We have seen only a few cases, all early: Queen v. Ellison (*Ms. Mins. NYCQS 1694–1731/32* 106, 108, 112, Nov. 7,

1705, Feb. 8, 1705/06, Aug. 6, 1706); Queen v. Purser, 1707 (*Ms. Mins. SCJ 1704/05–1709* 139, 144, 152); King v. Dowa Johnson (*Ms. Mins. Richmond Co. Sess. 1745–1812* May 4, 1773). The fee ordinances of 1710 and 1768 both have an item for *cessat processus*.

[172] King v. Gordon (*Ms. Mins. NYCQS 1732–62* 258, 261, Aug. 3, Nov. 9, 1749); King v. Mary Gifford (1758). For the minute entry see *Ms. Mins. NYCQS 1732–62* 437, May 3, 1758, and for the indictment with the "ended" endorsement, see *H.R. Pleadings* Pl. K. 1041. In King v. Luke Ament, indicted on Nov. 9, 1759, for keeping a disorderly house (*Ms. Mins. NYCQS 1732–62* 465), the true bill of indictment (*H.R. Pleadings* Pl. K. 966) is endorsed "Ended." Also compare King v. Cornelius Campbell, assault and battery, "ended," Nov. 9, 1759 (*Ms. Mins. NYCQS 1732–62* 465; *H.R. Pleadings* Pl. K. 974); King v. Abraham and Rachel Elberson, receiving stolen goods, "ended," Nov. 9, 1759 (*Ms. Mins. NYCQS 1732–62* 465; *H.R. Pleadings* Pl. K. 954).

For a complaint for an information endorsed "ended," see Hannah George's complaint against Thomas McCarty for assault and battery and her prayer for an information against him dated May 2, 1753. This complaint endorsed "ended" appears in *H.R. Parch.* 25 D 3. It should be noted that on April 25, 1753, the grand jury had presented McCarty for assaulting Hannah George, and on April 26, an indictment was filed against him, while on Aug. 4, 1753, the defendant was ordered to plead in twenty days or suffer judgment (*Ms. Mins. SCJ 1750–54* [Engr.] 250, 253, 286; *H.R. Pleadings*

The Information

While the provincial judiciary in respect of the indictment process often did not hesitate to treat the Attorney General as a mere officer of the courts rather than the direct representative of the Crown entrusted with the management and prosecution of Crown pleas, it was not able to exert its authority to the same degree in the prosecutions by information. This continued to be so even after the provincial Act of 1754, although that statute gave the Supreme Court a share of the discretion hitherto almost the sole cure of the Attorney General.

The information was a procedure where traditionally the Attorney General had wielded large powers in the initiation of proceedings, and in control over them up to judgment. Informations were of two kinds, those in the name of the King and those at the suit of an informer. For an offense against the Crown the English Attorney General could exhibit an information ex officio without any leave of the court; in other words, he was the sole judge of what public misdemeanors he would prosecute, and in England it was held in the late seventeenth century that the courts would never quash but would compel a defendant to demur or plead.[173] The Attorney General might, moreover, at any time enter a nolle prosequi, and file a new charge, and judgment was not pronounced until moved for by him.[174] In general, the cases where this proceeding was used in England were the so-called high misdemeanors, libels, bribery, interference with the revenue and the like. In the misdemeanors less immediately concerning the Crown the practice was for the Master of the Crown Office[175] to file informations, and until 1692 proceedings initiated by this officer were on the same footing as those begun ex officio by the Attorney General. In that year, however, by Act of Parliament[176] the express leave of King's Bench was required for the exhibition of any information of this class, and as affidavits were required to secure this permission, the control over this type of prosecution passed to that court.

Pl. K. 690, 920), but no further proceedings appear in this case. Possibly the "ended" endorsement on Hannah George's complaint for an information was entered at a date later than May 2, 1753.

The ended endorsement did not always mean discharge. Thus in King v. Anderson the defendant pleaded guilty to an assault and was fined (*Ms. Mins. NYCQS 1732–62* 445, Nov. 9, 1758) but the indictment is endorsed "Ended and done with" (*H.R. Pleadings* Pl. K. 432). Note finally the indictment in King v. Wm. Smith (*Ms. Mins. NYCQS*

1732–62 465, Nov. 9, 1759) endorsed "gone off by order of the Justices" (*H.R. Pleadings* Pl. K. 975).

[173] 1 *Salkeld* 372.

[174] The learning on informations is collected in 2 Hawkins, *Pleas of the Crown* c.26; Bacon, *Abridgment s.v.* Information.

[175] On the Crown Office cf. Hands, *Solicitor's Practice on the Crown Side of Kings Bench* xxiii.

[176] 4 & 5 Wm. and Mary c.18. Security to prosecute was required. This was also security for costs.

It is obvious from this brief outline that before the accession of William and Mary a large authority over the prosecution of misdemeanors was vested in the Attorney General and Crown Office, and that the courts had little or no directive control. The statute of 1692 did not apply to the plantations, and no Crown Office was set up in New York. At the outset, therefore, the provincial Attorney General was endowed with the powers exercised by the Master of the Crown Office[177] so that in effect every information begun by him in New York was prosecuted ex officio.

We have seen that the information was introduced in New York under the proprietor, but so far as can be determined from existing records it was employed only in revenue cases, particularly the violations of acts of trade.[178] We have also noticed that this method of initiating a prosecution differed little from the system of presentment by officials that had flourished for two decades,[179] and that for this reason, and because there was no immediate or noteworthy encroachment upon the activities of grand juries,[180] no immediate public objection to the information was made. Indeed, the information was

[177] Cf. 2 Smith, *Hist. NY* 202.

[178] E.g., *supra* n. 17; Santen q.t. v. Pattishall (*Ms. Mins. NYCQS 1683/84–1694* 33, May 5, 1685); Ludgar q.t. v. Garrett (*ibid.* 40, May 5, 1685); Livingston v. Hoogeboom, 1687 (*Ms. Mins. Albany Co. Sess. 1685–89* 38).

[179] In 1699 it was held by the Supreme Court in an information for violation of acts of trade that the sheriff of Kings "hath the right of information" (Lott q.t. v. Sundry Goods, *Mins. SCJ 1693–1701* 173).

[180] See, however, two cases, one in Kings County Sessions and one in Westchester County Sessions. In Kings, J. J. Van Ditmars, Ouchey Johnson and Englebert Lott had been examined before four justices of the peace for keeping the schoolhouse key despite the warrant issued by Justice Hegeman for them to deliver it up. Behaving contemptuously before the examining justices, the defendants were bound over in £100 each for their good behavior and for their appearance at the next Sessions (*supra* 319 n. 143). On May 19, 1692 the defendants appeared in Sessions, and Van Ditmars was "Cleard by proclamacoñ" but "An Informatoñ" was "exhibited by James Graham Esqr. . . . attorny generall" against the other two defendants. "The Informacoñ being read in Court in behalf of our Sovereigne lord & lady the King & Queen . . . The Court askt . . . whether they would plead to the Informacoñ guilty or not guilty . . . [the defendants] answered that they were not provided and desired time . . . to put their plea. The Court Consents yt . . . [they] shall have time till to morrow . . . [On May 20, Court opened] . . . The Court demanded whether they were guilty or not guilty

of the Informacoñ put in agst them by the attorney generall Who [the defendants] answered not guilty . . . desird the favour of the Court that their tryall may defer'd till next Court." In the November Sessions, 1692, the Attorney General was speaker of the assembly and couldn't attend court and a delay was granted. But on May 9, 1693 the defendants again appeared and "Informacoñ being read & an indictmt. drawn up was referd to a petty jury upon their pleading not guilty to Informacoñ for breach of the peace & Contempt of their Majestys authority." The defendants having pleaded not guilty "to Informacoñ & indictmt. And put themselves upon their Country" were found guilty "according to Informacoñ & The Court agreed wth. the verdict of the jury." The defendants were fined 50 shillings each for their contempt and ordered to pay the costs of this and the former court totalling £10 14s. 6d. (*Kings Co. Ct. & Rd. Recs. 1692–1825* 1–12). The case may perhaps be explained as a throwback to the earlier official presentments since an indictment was evidently framed on the information.

The Westchester case was that of Peter Chocke to which we have referred in Chapter III. It will be remembered that in that case Attorney General Graham "informs this court that . . . Peter Chocke had lately spoken . . . seditious words to the disturbance of his majesties government and that he had now ready . . . [a witness] who upon oath will declare the perticulars." However, the Court of Sessions in this case found that the words spoken were highly criminal and without their cognizance (*Mins. Westch. Ct. of Sess. 1657–96* 102, 103, June 4, 5, 1695).

explicitly recognized to be a valid method of procedure in the section of the 1683 Charter of Liberties dealing with jury trial, and this was repeated in the statute of 1691.

Despite the temptation to assume responsibility for prosecution in the lush pastures of misdemeanor, the early Attorneys General in New York wielded their potential authority with circumspection. Possibly this was due to the fact that in 1699 the Council had ordered no informations were to be filed without informing the Governor, and he was likewise to be advised what was charged in informations pending in order to prevent "vexation."[180a] It is doubtful how long orders of this sort were remembered, but in any event it was not until after Richard Bradley was appointed Attorney General that real political opposition to the information procedure developed. The causes of this opposition are complicated. Governor Burnet ascribed it to a dislike of Bradley's methods,[181] and it is hardly to be doubted that the prosecutions of various justices of the peace were an inciting factor.

In November, 1727 a provincial act[182] was passed requiring that all pending informations be quashed and prohibiting the exhibition of any information in the future except by order of the Governor signed in Council. In such cases the cause was to be tried in the county where the offense was committed, and the defendant when acquitted was to be discharged without costs. As a *douceur* to the Crown, the English penal acts mentioning the plantations were excepted. A penalty of £100 for infractions was provided.

Although the language of the statute strongly suggests it to be "An Act against the Attorney General," it will be recalled that the same assembly had staged a vicious attack upon the Chancery,[183] and we are therefore disposed to view the matter as a phase of colonial dislike of prerogative. The Crown information was peculiarly the means of securing a criminal sanction for violations of the King's rights. Local grand juries would not present in many instances because they had local sympathies or because they were prejudiced against Crown objectives or Crown officials. The popular preference for inquest procedure because of constitutional reasons was thereby given strength. Of these considerations Attorney General Bradley was fully aware. In his protest against the act of assembly and in a later letter to the Lords of Trade he called attention to the "levelling" spirit of the colonists and their attempts to

180a 8 *Ms. Mins. Council* 137.

181 P.R.O., C.O. 5/1092/62: "This is levelled at the Attorney General who has indeed been very vexatious and industrious to make use of trifling pretenses to bring him business in a very mean and sordid manner." Compare the proceedings in the Assembly (1 *Jour. NY Assembly* 566, 568).

182 2 *Col. Laws NY* 406.

183 1 *Jour. NY Assembly* 571.

set up assemblies and a system of law and procedure independent of Crown control.[184]

The home authorities found the act as bad as Bradley had represented it to be. In his report to the Board of Trade, June 5, 1728, Francis Fane described it as a "violent and extraordinary attack on the king's prerogative" and recommended that it be repealed,[185] which was accordingly done on November 5, 1728.[186]

[184] P.R.O., C.O. 5/1092 no. 64. He states the act to be ". . . repugnant to, and a notorious infringement on his Majesty's undoubted prerogative of prosecuting by Informations, without the leave or Order of any of His Majesty's Subjects whatsoever and the Governor and Council having sent me a copy of the Bill for my opinion thereon soon after it had been brought to the Council for their concurrence, I presented a memorial to the Governor and Council dated the 14th day of November last (a copy whereof and other papers I now send to Mr. Popple, ye Lordships Secretary, for your Lordships) Representing the dangerous tendency of such law, and they seemed to approve of wt I offered against the Bill, and inclined to reject it, but the leading men in the Assembly understanding this determined that unless the bill passed they w'd not Pass the Money Bill then before them, relating to a place called Oswege, and the Governor and Council being unwilling to give up the money bill, the Council made such amendments to the bill against Informations as they thought would prevent the ill Tendency of it, and hoped the Assembly would consent to these Amendments, but they utterly refusing them, the Governor and Council then found they would lose the money bill, if they did not pass the other agt. informations, they passed it. And Whereas it may be pretended by some persons that His Majesty's Prerogative will not be affected by such a law in regard informations may be still brought with the Governor and Council's order, yet I humbly beg leave to observe that in many cases, prosecution may be necessary where they may be very inconvenient for the Governor and Council to order: As when they may affect leading men in the Assembly (or their friends) who seem to have formed a designe, not only to screen themselves by this law but their friends also (which includes almost everybody, when all that do but vote for them will no doubt be tho't of that number) from such prosecutions tho never so just or necessary, And also to weaken His Majesty's Government here, by attempting to take away the remedy the law gives His Majesty of prosecuting by Information, without any leave or restraint whatsoever (which seems to be almost the only means His Majesty has to Check the levelling spirit that too plainly appears among the Genallity of the people of these countrys) and likewise to make all the officers of the Crown entirely dependent on the Assembly, who by haveing the sole power of granting money are able thus to influence even the Governor and Council to Consent to such Bills which they would otherwise reject."

[185] P.R.O., C.O. 5/1054/279. Opinion of F. Fane to the Board of Trade, June 5, 1728: ". . . I think this Act a very violent and extraordinary attaque upon the prerogative of the Crown for the right the Attorney General has to file Informations is delegated to him from the King and has been ever thought a most essential and necessary Power with Regard to the security of the Public Tranquility as well for the Service and protection of His Majesty's Revenue, and I apprehend that destroying that Power in the manner that is attempted by the Act, will be attended with very ill consequences. For if no delinquent is to be prosecuted without going through so Solemn an Enquiry whether it be expedient or Not, I believe it will be an encouragement to Wicked Men to perpetrate the Worst of Villanies, in hope of Justice being delayed which it must necessarily be in this form of proceeding that they may escape Punishment they justly deserve and which in policy ought to be as speedy as possible. Another reason against the passing the Act and which I beg leave to Submit to your Lordships' Consideration is that all prosecutions now depending are by the Act entirely quashed and discharged. What Consequence this may have to the Public Peace of the Colony, I can't tell but surely many inconveniences will arise by discharging those Prosecutions which I suppose just and not trivial and inconsiderable since they have been carried on by the Attorney General against whom there has been complaint which with submission Supposing there was any ground of the Accusation would be the most proper way of Proceeding rather than to attempt the restraining the Prorogative of the Crown in so Material a part of it. "The imposing a Fine upon the Attorney General if he does not pursue the directions of the Acts, is I apprehend an unprecedented Step and a High reflection upon the Crown. For can it be supposed His Majesty will appoint an Attorney General who is so unwilling to do his duty that he must by the fear and dread of Punishment be forced to put the laws in Execution which he ought strictly by his Employment to be supposed not only to observe himself but to see and demand a strict observance of them by others. For these reasons I am humbly of opinion the Act ought to be repealed."

[186] P.R.O., C.O. 5/1054/290.

Before proceeding to discuss the subsequent manifestations of hostility to the information, it should be pointed out that the procedure with reference to the framing and trial of informations did not differ markedly from the practice of a prepared indictment, save only that some of the cumbersome steps in connection with framing an indictment were avoided. There was, moreover, some effort made to integrate the two modes of initiation for, as we have seen, grand jury presentments were often made the basis of the Attorney General's informations in the Supreme Court where, for one reason or another, a fair trial could not be had at local Sessions or at Circuit. Sometimes the Attorney General framed informations on presentments in order to avoid the necessity of later resorting to certiorari on the indictments where it was apparent that in the end the Supreme Court would find it necessary to supervise the pleadings. It was in these cases that the court often took a hand in directing that an information be filed,[187] and doubtless if the grand juries' presentments had been complete and searching in matters concerning Crown rights, a great deal of the odium would have been removed from the ex-officio information. However, circumstances in the Province were such that the information was usually drawn up by the Attorney General on his own knowledge[188] or on the complaints of witnesses.[189] Occasionally, too, the Governor alone or in Council would direct the filing of an information,[190] and it is interesting to note that the Act of 1727 particularly conceded the Governor's right.

---

[187] Thus on Sept. 2, 1740, the grand jury presented Samuel Balding of Hempstead "for offering a sum of money to the high sheriff Uriah Huff of Oyster Bay to have such a jury as he thought fit to mention and desire the court to put it into form Ordered that the Attorney General file an information upon the said presentment" (*Ms. Mins. Cir. 1721–49* 104).

On June 4, 1742, the grand jury at Dutchess Oyer and Terminer and General Gaol Delivery presented the jail as insufficient, presented Augustine Hunt for administering an oath having no authority to do so, and presented Isaac Kip for a misdemeanor in office. The court thereupon "ordered the clerk of the circuits to serve coppys of the several presentments upon the Attorney General and that he file informations upon the presentments accordingly" (*Ms. Mins. Cir. 1721–49* 107). See also an information filed being "founded on a grand jury presentment" against Michael Keyser for false swearing (*Ms. Mins. SCJ 1766–69* [Engr.] 255, July 31, 1757). In King v. Simon Rumsey a presentment of the grand jury of Orange for an assault was delivered into the court and by the court delivered to the Attorney General with orders to proceed thereupon. Accordingly, the Attorney General filed an informa-

tion against the defendant "by order of the court" on the presentment (*Ms. Mins. SCJ 1764–67* [Rough] 85; *Ms. Mins. SCJ 1764–66* [Engr.] 285).

[188] It has been impossible to determine which informations were filed by the Attorney General on his own knowledge, but the complaints of the colonists against Attorney General Bradley referred to above, 372 n. 181, indicate that he probably filed the information against the Albany justices for an insufficient jail on his own initiative.

[189] As an example of a complaint of a witness for an information, see George Dennis' complaint against Lewis McDaniel, a justice of the peace, for maladministration (*H.R. Parch.* 6 A 1); also see *H.R. Parch.* 19 B 3, 19 C 3, 220 C 4, 46 D 10, 192 L 9, 177 D 3, 194 F 2, 197 E 6, 197 E 9, 13 E 3, for complaints of private individuals to the Attorney General requesting that he frame an information against the various persons complained against. Also see *H.R. Pleadings* Pl. K. 605 for a list of complaints in 1753.

[190] In 1702 the Council ordered prosecution of French and Wenham involved in the Bayard case (8 *Ms. Mins. Council* 302). In Queen v. Garret Oncklebagg, the Attorney General, on Sept. 5, 1707,

In language and form the information bore certain resemblance to the indictment. It opened with a memorandum, viz.:

> Be it remembered that John Tabor Kempe Esquire Attorney General of our Sovereign Lord the now King for the Province of New York who for our said Lord the King prosecutes, comes here into the Supreme Court . . . in his own proper person and for our said Lord the King giveth the court here to understand and be informed . . .[191]

after which the substance of the charge followed. The English courts had laid down the same requisites of certainty that obtained as to indictments, the same care in description of the defendant and the same precision with which the crime had to be alleged.[192] The defendant could plead exactly as to an indictment and of course trial was by jury.

We have already considered in the chapter on transfer jurisdiction some of the typical cases where information procedure was used. So far as Crown rights were concerned the device was indispensable in particular cases, but numerically the Crown information was employed in a mere fraction of all the cases where there is anything to be found on initiatory mechanisms of any kind. No attempt was ever made to use it in capital cases, and certainly before 1750 it was restricted largely to prosecutions involving fiscal or administrative matters.

It is possible to form a judgment on the question of whether or not a real grievance was involved in the dispute respecting informations by examining how frequently in point of fact the Crown information was used in the early eighteenth century and for what type of offense. In 1727, so far as we can judge from the English sources, the Crown informations were far commoner in England than in New York. Moreover, when we compare the total entries of indictments and Crown informations in New York, the relative consequence of the latter as a law enforcing device seems inconsiderable. Thus from 1691 to 1730 there appear to have been only about 80 Crown informations against 135 defendants compared with 292 indictments and presentments returned in the Supreme Court, the only court in which any Crown informations were brought,[193] but it must be recalled that minutes are missing for a number of

prayed that an information against the defendant be filed "it being by the Governor's special discretion" (*Ms. Mins. SCJ 1704/05–1709* 144). The Attorney General, on Dec. 19, 1727, was ordered by the Governor and Council to prosecute all suits involving the King's title to land (15 *Ms. Mins. Council* 200). For other examples the order re Van Tuyl,

1749 (21 *ibid.* 361); Peter Vrooman *et al.*, 1751 (23 *ibid.* 19); Rosekrans, 1771 (21 *ibid.* 251).
[191] H.R. Parch. 217 B 5.
[192] 2 Hawkins, *op. cit.* c.26 §4.
[193] Only indictments in the Supreme Court have been used, although the indictments in Sessions could be counted in establishing a ratio to test popular grievance.

years within this period. A survey of Crown informations from 1691 to 1727, in terms of offenses, discloses that they chiefly involved (as the Attorney General very properly maintained in his defense) Crown rights in cases of sedition, intrusion on Crown lands, obstructing royal surveyors, claim to a "royal fish" (a whale), extortion by officials, slandering a jury and maladministration by justices of the peace. There were only ten cases involving assault and battery, disorderly houses, malicious libel, and the like. There was one case of forgery, fourteen of riots and one of champerty. In their objections to Crown informations, the colonists complained of prosecutions for trivial offenses, but the majority of cases enumerated were for the most part not of a minor sort and they did involve Crown rights, a fact which supports the conclusion that the issue was basically political.

Colonial opposition to the Crown information was actively resumed in the year 1734 in the guise of a bill to regulate costs on prosecution by information. Bradley, who had felt the financial pinch of the earlier act before it was disallowed,[194] made haste to inform the Lords of Trade,[195] but his anxiety was groundless for the bill did not pass the Governor and Council. We do not know how constantly agitation was continued, but in 1743 it again flared up. According to William Smith Jr., the Attorney General had again been active in prosecuting magistrates for failure to repair jails and courthouses.[196] The assembly directed a bill to be brought in against such vexatious proceedings, but it did not pass. This was at the April session. In the fall of that year a bill regulating informations passed the assembly but failed in the Council.[197] The issue persisted and was one of the sources of irritation between the house and the Governor who was determined to support the Attorney General.[198]

Bradley died in August, 1751,[199] and was succeeded briefly by William Smith the elder.[200] In November, 1751 the Crown directed the commissioning of William Kempe as Attorney General. He arrived in New York in 1752, and in the following year over two hundred complaints and petitions were addressed to the Attorney General requesting that he file informations in cases of assault, battery, trespass and other misdemeanors.[201] Since the income of the

---

[194] Cf. his memorial to Governor Montgomerie, June 28, 1728, regarding his salary (P.R.O., C.O. 5/1092/69 [11]).

[195] 6 Doc. Rel. Col. Hist. NY 17, 18.

[196] 1 Smith, Hist. NY 453.

[197] Ibid. 460.

[198] Ibid. 468.

[199] 4 Letters and Papers of Cadwallader Colden

295. The date is incorrectly given in 6 Doc. Rel. Col. Hist. NY 17 n.

[200] 6 Doc. Rel. Col. Hist. NY 766.

[201] See, for example, the list contained in H.R. Pleadings Pl. H. 816:

   1. Israel Horsefield agt. Elijah Borton for assault. Q. if to be drawn

   2. Cornelius de Voes agt. John Pine et als for a

Attorney General was contingent upon his official activity, this must have been a gratifying welcome to the new incumbent. According to the historian Smith, however, Kempe "excited the disgust" of some leading merchants by lending too easy an ear to trifling complaints,[202] and an indictment was procured charging the Attorney General with maladministration. The "trifling complaint" specifically mentioned in the indictment was that of Mary Anderson at whose instance Kempe had prosecuted some of the blooded rakes of the metropolis who had attacked the girl and had subsequently proceeded to "frame" her mother.[203]

Kempe moved to quash the indictment against him, and a draft of his argument on the motion is extant.[204] He emphasized that an information was brought to punish breaches of the peace and was only an instrument to bring the question of guilt to a trial before a jury. He denied this procedure was a violation of the rights of Englishmen, "for it is no part of the liberty of the subject not to be prosecuted for his crimes by Information . . . unless it be for capitall offenses." He then cited the elaborate discussion in Shower's *Reports*[205] and proceeded to argue that the information was equivalent to an indictment or inquest, which was a mere record to apprise the King of an offense. The information was a suggestion to a court of record of crimes committed, made by the Attorney General whose duty it was to inform the court. There was no inconvenience to the subject for "here is a trial per pais, fair notice, liberty of pleadings dilatory as well as Bars, here's Subpoena and attachment; as much

misdemeanour in forging a warrant thereby arresting complaint.
3. Leopoldus Willigas and wife agt William Burnet for assault &c
4. Jacob Brower agt. Moses Gomez, the same
5. [Warden] Hutchins & Jonathan Hutchins agt. Edward Savage & Francis Welch, the same
6. Timothy Scandret agt. Stephen Hunt for Male Administration in ye Office of Justice of the Peace
7. Isaac De la Metre agt. Jacob Dikeman & others Riot and Assault etc.
8. Mr. Ramsay agt. Capt. Simonds in Admiralty [*sic*]
9. Jacob East agt. Mathias Knight and others Riot &c.
10. Joseph Montany agt. William Van Sise assault &c.
11. Nicholas Hatton agt. Philip Pell Assault etc.
12. J. Bryant agt. Stephen Baxter, same
13. Cornelius Boower agt. Andries Manuel, same
14. Gertrude Wilson agt. Mary Alison & al Riot

15. James Bailey agt. Philip Recheir Assault Ended
16. Sarah Churchill agt. John Debele For seizing goods before Rent due
17. Benajah Edwards agt. Jesse Wicks & Tappin Wood
18. James Hathwaite agt. Charles Evans Assault
19. Israel Pinckney agt. Roger Pell etc. forcibly carrying away a Letter of License & Assault
20. James Jackson agt. Stephn Dickson Forging warrant &c.
    Sybilla
21. Benigna ˄ Berkenmeyer ag. Jacob Freeze & al. Q.
22. John & Absm. Lequiers agt. [domine] Roberts Robbing Oyster Cove Q. Ended
23. George Sibbles agt. Wessels Assault
24. Eliz[th] Richards agt. Printz.

202 2 Smith, *op. cit.* 201.
203 Discussed *supra* 262 *et seq.*
204 H.R. *Pleadings* Pl. K. 421.
205 King v. Berchet *et al.* (1 *Show.* K.B. 106).

time for defence, no charge for the prosecutor makes up the record." The Attorney General prevailed, for on April 24, 1755, the Supreme Court ordered the quashing of the indictment.[206]

Before this case was settled, in December, 1754, a provincial statute was enacted regulating the use of informations.[207] With a wary eye upon the problem of royal allowance the legislators referred in the preamble to the English statute 3 and 4 William and Mary c.18, asserted that the objective of the new statute was to bring provincial practice into harmony with that obtaining in England, and proceeded to enact a close version of the English statute. The permission of the Supreme Court was required for the filing of informations, unless the informer posted a recognizance to prosecute. If the informer did not at his cost prosecute or if he obtained a nolle prosequi or if a verdict should pass for the defendant, the court could award costs to the defendant for which the recognizance would be liable unless in the opinion of the court there was reasonable cause. The act did not extend to informations ordered by the Governor and Council or by the Supreme Court. A brake upon reckless and blackmailing accusations was clearly intended, and when we consider that the Attorney General was accustomed to have some security for his own costs, the financial risk of informing was considerable. Nevertheless, such was the prevalence of private complaints to the Attorney General that a regular procedure was finally employed to handle such petitions, and we have found a printed blank form of complaint for a prosecution for this purpose.[208] In this request the complainant prayed that the Attorney General prosecute, at the same time undertaking for costs.

Whether or not the provincial legislators thought to include the ex officio informations initiated by the Attorney General is obscure. The English statute had put no restriction upon the Attorney General, but was directed at the Master of the Crown Office. Since there was no such officer in New York, the provincial act was meant to bind the Attorney General whenever he prose-

[206] Ms. Mins. SCJ 1754-57 (Engr.) 82, 87, 118, 155. Also see H.R. Pleadings Pl. K. 521.

[207] 3 Col. Laws NY 1007.

[208] This is contained in H.R. Pleadings Pl. K. 713. "To William Kempe Esqr. Atty Gen[ll] Sir: I desire you to prosecute at the suit of the King Henry Burchell of Dutchess . . . for Beating and abusing me . . . in New York City And if I do not prove, to the Satisfaction of the Court and Jury, at the Tryal of this Cause, that the said Henry Burchell Did Strike me first Or, if I make up or agree this Cause without your Consent thereto, first had under your Hand in writing on paying to you your Fees: Or if any Mistake has happened in the above-naming of the Christian or Sirname of the said Henry Burchell If I do not in that Case, within one Month next ensuing, deliver to you his true Christian and Sirname in writing, to be by you herein-above inserted and prosecuted, instead of such mistaken Name; I will, in any or either of these cases, pay you your Fees. Witness my Hand, this 15 Nov. 1752 John Waters Witness hereto Peter Silvester Witnesses present at the assault & batt John Ferguson."

cuted offenses as the Master might prosecute in England (viz. at the suit of an informer) but it could scarcely have been taken as an invasion of the authority of the Attorney General as such, and the later judicial records bear this out.[209]

After 1750 and until the Revolution the Crown information became a very common form of initiatory procedure and was employed not only on behalf of Crown interests, to punish recalcitrant officials, to prosecute customs actions, to test the right of officials to hold office, and to dispose of cases of difficulty or local prejudice, but also on behalf of private persons complaining of assaults, batteries, riots, forgery, perjury and attempted rape. Perhaps one of the reasons for the widespread use of informations, particularly between 1753 and 1766, was the troublous conditions existent during the French and Indian War and the political and economic unrest during the period prior to the Revolution. Land rioting was rife; armed resistance was made to the collection of rents; several boundary disputes were going on between New York and adjoining colonies; there was opposition both to the billeting of soldiers and to the collection of revenue for the defrayal of the expenses of the late war; public officials were becoming recalcitrant and local communities were seeking more independence. The information was the most effective weapon available to the Crown. There was nothing inherently unfair in the procedure, but it became inevitably associated in the colonists' minds with the suppression of those activities by which they were attempting to promote their liberties.

Summary Procedure

It is a circumstance worthy of remark that although the colonists had in 1727 protested vigorously against Crown informations, they nevertheless made no objections to the deprivations effected by the various sorts of common law summary proceedings employed in dealing with the vast morass of petty misdemeanors. In fact, as we have seen, the colonists themselves provided for a host of *qui tam* actions and also established a summary procedure for the trial of offenses less than grand larceny which was wholly new to the common law.

This partiality for summary procedure is not easy to explain, but we are disposed to attribute it to the sharp distinctions in social and economic status which prevailed in the colony. The democracy which royal governors bewailed was a political, not a social, democracy; and the generous imitation of

---

[209] Cf. particularly the *per curiam* opinion of the Supreme Court cited in 2 Smith, *op. cit.* 202; *infra* 657.

various incidents of oligarchical English local administration tended to enhance class differences. That there was a class which supplied much of the criminal business of the province, the records of the eighteenth century leave us in no doubt. Many a defendant in the city and sometimes in the country was a person without substance, but on the general circumstances which led him into the toils of the law the records are mostly silent. Vagrants[210] and slaves[211] are identified, but how the bulk of the group was recruited can only be surmised. It seems probable that the transported offenders and the indentured servants made considerable contributions.[212] Certainly the passion for common law due process among the propertied was such that the enactment of summary procedures would have been intolerable unless there was an element sufficiently numerous and not *sui juris* to constitute a problem.

Elsewhere we consider the summary procedures in regard to forcible entry, contempts, riots, nuisance, bastardy, and the like where never an indictment was used.[213] It is necessary here only to point out that in general the New York magistrate walked in the paths already well worn by the English justices when the Province was conquered.[214] In the usual case of petty crime the proceedings were gotten under way before a justice of the peace by means of sworn statements variously called depositions, affidavits, examinations or informations. Often the justices would examine the accused, and his denial or confession would be recorded. This part of the procedure was identical with the preliminary investigation of the magistrates in cases where a defendant would be put in custody or bound over for the grand jury, but if the matter were one

---

210 The problem appears as early as 1683 when the assembly legislated respecting vagabonds and idle persons coming into this province from other parts (1 *Col. Laws NY* 132) and cf. the Act of 1691 (*ibid.* 238). The preamble of the Act of 1721, indicating what may be described as the broadening base of vagrancy, speaks of "idle and necessitous persons come or brought into" the province from neighboring plantations, fleeing as a result of crime or because they were unwilling to work (2 *Col. Laws NY* 56).

211 The slaves were numerous and averaged about one-seventh of the population during the eighteenth century. In 1723, of a total population of 40,564, the census figures give 6,171 "Negroes and other slaves." In 1749, of a total of 73,448 there were 10,692 "black." In 1771, the total population was 168,007 with a total of 19,833 "blacks." The census figures are in 1 *Doc. Hist. NY* 465 et seq. The later figures do not account for Indian slaves.

212 We do not share the belief that there were no transported convicts in New York. It is stated by

McKee, A Century of Labor in 2 *Hist. State of NY* 306, "So far as is known there is not a single instance of an English convict who was transported to the colony for a major or for a minor offense." Again in his *Labor in Col. NY 1664–1776* (1935) 90–91, this writer states: "Of course it is possible that transported prisoners were brought to New York and misrepresented as voluntary redemptioners, but the written and printed records which survive lead to the belief that there were few or no 'transports' brought to the colony." In *Cal. Eng. Mss.* 527, is the entry of a master's certificate respecting the landing in New York of six men sentenced in Worcester to be transported for felony (1736). Cf. *ibid.* 525, the assignment of three other convicts to the same master.

213 Cf. *supra* 103, 122; *infra* 456.

214 See, for example, *Lancashire Quarter Sess. Recs.* 111, 157, 233, 289; *Manchester Sess.* 62–65, 67, 69, 138, 178, 179; 1 *Worcestershire Co. Recs.* xvii, 7, 347. There is a complaint of June 14, 1640, in the *Worcestershire Recs.* 686 (no. lxxvi [8]) regarding the procedure before justices.

which the justice, acting alone or in concert with one or two colleagues, was competent to determine, sentence would follow.

The few available records of this summary jurisdiction are not very informative, but apparently the justices acted on oral complaint. In Westchester on October 2, 1716, Dinah Kirkpatrick was complained of as a common disturber. Her husband was ordered to keep her home, and warned if she got at large she would be punished and he would be fined.[215] In Ulster, at meetings of the justices, a defendant to a complaint for taking property was ordered out of the county; a woman, and later a man, complained of as common disturbers were put under recognizance; and a negro charged with burglary was ordered whipped.[216] The most complete record of a single justice, that kept by Daniel Howel (1774-1779), does not indicate anything regarding the formulation of charges, but defendants were fined, put in the stocks or whipped without benefit of indictment.[217]

Occasionally, in General Sessions itself, summary jurisdiction was exercised upon mere complaint. In Orange, George Jewell was ordered to hang his dog because neighbors complained he was "injurious."[218] In Suffolk, Ebenezer Hulse was discharged from bail, but on an affidavit that he was a dangerous person, process was sent out to put him under recognizance;[219] and many years later, on the complaint of two men, David Marrow was sent to jail as an abusive and dangerous person to stay for twenty days unless released by consent of complainants.[220] John Brackett appeared at the Dutchess Sessions in October, 1753 and complained that Israel Veal had threatened to assault him. Witnesses were examined and Veal was fined 10s. and ordered committed until he paid.[221]

While the New Yorkers did not ask or expect any great formality in the case of minor offenses, carrying their indulgence to the point of permitting even

[215] Ms. Mins. Westch. Co. Sess. 1710-23 Special Session, Oct. 2, 1716.
[216] Ms. Mins. Ulster Co. Sess. 1711/12-1720 at meetings respectively on Aug. 18, 1716, Mar. 18, 1716/17, Nov. 30, 1717, Apr. 21, 1718. Cf. also meetings Aug. 1-5, 1729 (Ms. Files Ulster Co. Bundle G) where a negro against whom the peace was sworn was ordered in custody. In Dutchess, at a meeting April 24, 1749, one Ten Brook informed against some negroes for treasonable talk. The negroes were committed (Ms. Files Dutchess Co. 1755). Cf. also the record of the "Justices Court at Rhynbeck" Oct. 4, 1751, where complaint was made of a negro. His master promised "to take care of the niger until his wench is brought to bed" and then dispose of him.

[217] Daniel Howel's Book of Records (Pennypacker Coll., Easthampton).
[218] Ms. Mins. Orange Co. Sess. 1703-08 Oct. 29, 1706.
[219] Ms. Mins. Suffolk Co. Sess. 1723-51 Mar. 30, 1736. Compare the order putting a negro slave in jail (Ms. Mins. Albany Co. Sess. 1717-23, Oct. 5, 1720).
[220] Ms. Mins. Suffolk Co. Sess. 1760-75 Oct. 1, 1765.
[221] Ms. Mins. Dutchess Co. Sess. Liber B, Oct. 6, 1753. Cf. the earlier cases, King v. Ryckard and King v. Wm. Rogers, where the presentment was considered and the defendants fined (Ms. Mins. Albany Co. Sess. 1717-23, Feb. 4, 1717/18, Feb. 2, 1721/22).

petit larcenies to be heard summarily, nevertheless they particularly enacted that at the special courts held for the trial of crimes or conspiracy by negroes, a person should be appointed to prosecute and "preferr an Accusation in Writing specifying the time, place and nature of the offence as near as conveniently may be, to which accusation the Offender or Offenders shall be obliged to plead. . . ."[222] We have seen some examples of such accusations, and they are more or less in the idiom of the less technical presentments.[223] This provision is quite remarkable for it indicates an intention to put slave trials upon a slightly better level than the ordinary summary proceedings.

A word must be said in conclusion regarding the *qui tams* which appear in the sources as penal actions by private or official informers begun by bill, plaint, information or action of debt. In these cases the subject was deprived of a grand jury and usually of a trial jury as well. The tendency constantly to add new types of misdoing to the list of matter for which *qui tam* actions would lie was entirely in the eighteenth century tradition. The underlying philosophy was to enlist the busybody in the service of law enforcement by the bait of a share in the penalty, and to make the proceeding as little nuisance as possible. The summary trial before one or two justices out of Sessions was an obvious solution, especially as this had the weight of English usage behind it. The addition in some acts of proceeding by debt did not disturb the tradition since the New York justices possessed authority in petty civil litigation. And this had the advantage that a defendant substantial enough to pay the small charge for a six man jury could indulge his convictions that a trial jury was his right.

It is unfortunate that in the face of over three hundred acts of assembly containing some provision for the exercise of summary jurisdiction, the remaining records of out-of-Sessions justice are so few, and no certain conclusions either as to the number of cases or the extent of debt actions with a jury can be drawn. One is led, however, to infer from available case material and the statutory enactments that the colonists themselves as well as the Crown authorities realized that there was necessity for an expeditious accusation and trial procedure due to the inordinate amount of complaint and to the small amount of litigation which could be handled in Sessions and at Circuit. There was no question of raising constitutional issues[224] and no talk of the liberty of

[222] 1 *Col. Laws NY* 766.

[223] The accusation against Kip's negress for arson (*Ms. Mins. Albany Co. Sess.* 1717–23 June 8, 1722); Gilbert Livingston's accusation against Harry, April 10, 1730 (*Ms. Files Ulster Co.* Bundle C); Henry Livingston's accusation against Jack,

1741 (*ibid.* Bundle K). In *Ms. Mins. Dutchess Co. Sess.* Liber A, June 10, 1735 is Vanderbergh's accusation against Quacko. This last seems to be a combination opening and accusation.

[224] The constitutional questions regarding the Acts of 1732 (*infra* 606) were raised, it will

Englishmen, because the trial of these causes, being committed to local authorities, involved no collision with the agencies of prerogative and presented no threat of a kind which caused political uneasiness to the groups sharing in the government of the Province.[225] It was not the confidence man, the petty gambler or the wayward girl whose rights cried for the protection of a sworn inquest, but the delinquent justice, the merchant infringing the acts of trade, the evader of quitrents and the intruder upon Crown lands. The motives for the invocation of constitutional rights were not everywhere above reproach, yet the law has always owed more to the efforts to which men's self-interest impels them than is disclosed by the language even of such a treasured monument as Magna Carta.

be noted, by the Attorney General and not by the colonists.

[225] The interests of the groups supporting constitutional rights is reflected somewhat in the use of ideas taken from the land law. Cf. the recital in an act of Oct. 6, 1708 "to Relieve this Colony from Divers Irregularitys and Extortions" disallowed in 1709 (1 *Col. Laws NY* 622). The transition to an employment of real property concepts for purposes of constitutional argument is seen in Mulford's speech to the assembly on April 2, 1714 (cf. *supra* 313). Mulford said in part: "Gentlemen the ill measures that hath been taken, and the Foundation laid within this Colony, which may bring the Subjects within the same to be Tenants at will, both Persons and Estates, causeth me to make this Speech to this house, requesting them to consider well, what they do, and not sell a Birth-right privilege for fear, favour, affection or Lucre of Gain: But prove true to the trust reposed in them, not to make ill Presidents and Laws pernicious to the Publick. But to Endeavor[?] the Government may be carried on, for her Majestys benefit and the good of the Subjects according to the Laws and Constitution of the British Government: 'Tis not unnecessary to mention the ill Circumstances the Colony was under in the time when a Duty was settled on the Importation of Goods, for the Support of the Government, there was not any Port, or Officers appointed, where to make entry of their vessels, and get clearing when outward Bound except at New York where there was so many Officers and subtle fellows to inspect into every Critick in the Law. And if They were not fulfilled and observed in every particular Their vessels were seized. So that not any man was fit for Master of a vessell to go to New York except He were a Lawyer, and then They should not escape except it was by Favour. . . . ."

Mulford went on to complain of certain extortions and heavy taxes and then continued: "We have an undoubted Right and Property by ye Law of God & Nature settled upon the subject by act of Parliament wch is not to be taken from them by the Supreme power without due course of Law. The end of the Law is to secure our Persons and Estates, the end of Government to put the same in execution to that purpose that Justice may be done, according to the words of his Excellency's Instructions vizt You shall carry on the Government for our benefit, and the good of our Subjects, according to ye Laws and Custom of the Colony. . . .

"If we must be Inslaved, it were better to have it forced upon us, than for us to bring it upon our selves. . . . Much more might have been said but . . . although we are compared to a peevish Child that cryed for Salt Beef, for its own hurt, yet I hope you will have the sense of the burnt Child which dreads the fire, and not be like persons Non composmentis to wilfully run into the same" (*NY Misc. Mss. 1711–16* no. 23).

Another interesting document printed around 1715 is a "Memorial of aggrievances and appressions of the King's subjects in the Colony of New York in America" which complains against unequal representation and unequal taxation of the various counties. Here again it is stated that the people have a "property" in the government. The "Memorial" is reprinted in 3 *Doc. Hist. NY* 220. A complaint against the mercantile acts is to be found in the "case of the Inhabitants of New York," 1718 (*John Jay Papers* Box 3 no. 146 L).

CHAPTER VII

PROCESS

THE writers on criminal procedure in the seventeenth and eighteenth centuries devote so little attention to the matter of process that its function in relation to the whole problem of law enforcement is easily overlooked.[1] What is not directly apparent is how large process questions bulked in the practical business of bringing defendants to book, and how dependent the substantive body of law was upon the scheme of precepts by which a proceeding was kept in motion. What is completely obscured is the historic and still latent political significance of these forms—their inherent capacity for maintaining the authority, the peculiar prerogatives of the Crown in the preservation of order.

These considerations are of some consequence in a study of colonial dispositions respecting process particularly where, as in New York, the policy of the sovereign was to effect only an approximation of English legal institutions. Clearly, if in the criminal law substance was attendant upon form, the extent to which particular types of precepts became common form in the province would have a direct bearing upon the nature and extent of common law reception. As we shall presently see, the law in New York retained its utter provinciality only so long as the precepts were merely drafted *ad hoc* or followed the unartful specifications of the Duke's Laws. The common law gains footing only after the technical forms of English practice become established. The course of evolution here seems quite unplanned, which is the stranger because the exploitation of process as an instrumentality of royal policy has been an outstanding phenomenon in the growth of English law. There was hardly a form in the books that had not done its part of old in advancing the Crown's authority. And the virtue of these precepts in this regard was still sufficient when they came to be used in domains where the prerogative needed what ministration it could get.

If the Crown reaped benefits, both direct and collateral, from control over process and eventually from the employment of the accepted English forms, the colonists in turn derived security from the fact that the law was administered according to mandates whose use was governed by settled rules and whose scope was fixed with some degree of certainty. This security rested upon

---

[1] For reasons of convenience the discussion of final process is reserved for Chapter XI.

one of the few generalizations which the myriad decisions on points of process had produced, the idea of due process of law.

In the seventeenth and eighteenth centuries "due process" was an expression not yet endowed with the magic which it came to possess in American law after the Revolution. Nevertheless, it was by no means devoid of a certain constitutional significance, for it was a principle of long standing in England that litigants were entitled to established common law procedure, or that, in general, procedure must conform to accepted common law tests. The usual and current employment of the phrase in English practice was to designate the judicial order appropriate to a particular procedure[2] and this usage becomes the rule in eighteenth century New York.

Limited as the common law meaning of due process may seem, nevertheless, its migration to America and its establishment in the field of practice, in the countless situations where some type of process was needed, were conditions precedent to the subsequent transubstantiation of the expression and the enlargement of its constitutional function. Only when common law rules about precepts are completely seated is it possible to make political capital out of abuse, to transform the mere expectancy of the litigants into the indefeasible constitutional right of the citizen.

Process under the Duke's Laws

The eventual mutations in the meaning of due process lay far in the future when the first regulations respecting process were enacted by the conquerors of New Netherland. There was no question of introducing, at least with effectiveness, the fine array of precepts by which the King's judges at home maintained the majesty and power of the law, for James' new domain was far-flung and even in its center an unintegrated succession of villages scattered from Easthampton to Albany. Among a population largely alien and, where English-speaking, barely lettered, the fine distinctions between a *venire facias ad respondendum* and a subpoena to answer would not have survived even had there been judges capable of appreciating their savor. Of this the compiler of the Duke's Laws could not have been unaware, yet despite the fact that he was constructing a law book which overseers and country justices could assimilate, the directions about process are few and obscure. These directions are scattered through the code and they leave one mystified both as to the relation of civil

[2] Coke, *Book of Entries* (1651) 364b, 365; 3 *Dyer* 346b; *Benloe* 252 pl. 269; 1 *Anderson* 48.

and criminal process and as to the whole scheme of precepts from original to final process. This difficulty arises from the fact that instead of following the relatively lucid contemporary local court handbooks, a considerable part of the material on process was taken bodily from the Massachusetts code of 1660 —a document itself not too articulate.

We have indicated below certain characteristics of the Massachusetts law respecting process,[3] but we have no evidence that the new officials in New York were familiar with more than the bare language of the New England law book. Standing alone, the Massachusetts and the New York statutes are incomplete and scarcely calculated to answer the problems of either the trained or untutored officials who were charged with putting a new system into effect.

[3] The sections in the Massachusetts code of 1660 from which is derived a considerable part of the New York provisions respecting process were enacted in some particulars as early as the year 1641. The Massachusetts scheme of process is copied after that prevailing in English local courts (county courts, courts baron and borough courts). The typical course there was summons, attachment, distraint. (Cf. Wilkinson, *A Treatise Collected out of the Statutes, etc.* [1618] 151; Dalton, *Office and Authority of Sheriffs* [1682] 420; *Booke for a Justice of Peace* [1599] 96b.) The Massachusetts code gives an alternative of summons or attachment (*Col. Laws Mass.* [Whitmore ed. 1889] 124). The remarkable feature of the Massachusetts (and so of New York) "precedent" for the summons is that it is not addressed to any officer—the invariable rule in contemporary English procedure if the form books for the local courts are to be trusted. The Massachusetts summons is directed to the defendant, and entries in the early Essex County Court records indicate it was sometimes served by the plaintiff or his agent (1 *Records and Files of the Quarterly Court of Essex County Massachusetts* [1911] 53 [1643], 98 [1646], 147 [1648]). Cf. here *Thomas Lechford's Note-Book* (1885) 348 no. 12, entries which indicate the parties' responsibility for service of process. In 1 *Recs. Ct. of Essex Co. Mass.* there are some entries showing affidavit of service (*ibid.* 45 [1642]) or oral testimony to that effect (*ibid.* 139 [1647–48]). This conforms to the *Booke for a Justice* 96b, "And after absent the steward shall ask of the bailiffe howe he hath returned his precept," etc. In the code of 1660 (tit.: *Causes small Causes*) the law indicates the summons in causes involving no more than 40s. shall be directed to the marshal or constable (*Col. Laws Mass.* 132) but the "president" which dates from 1641 was not altered to conform, and the original process statute of that year seems to require only that attachments and replevins be directed to the constable (1 *Recs. Mass. Bay* 344).

How this manner of direct summons originated is puzzling, but we are disposed to attribute it to some form of local English aberration with which some emigrant official was familiar. The local practice, despite the books, was not uniform (cf. here 1 Bateson, *Borough Customs* [Selden Society] xiii), and there was authority for the proposition that local court summons by parole was sufficient (*Year-book* 14 Hy. VII, 8, 9). Winthrop was familiar with local court practice (1 Winthrop, *Life and Letters of John Winthrop* [1869] 62, and cf. the various entries in Adam Winthrop's diary [*ibid.* App.] regarding Adam's courtkeeping activities). It should be further pointed out that Massachusetts summons practice resembles the Chancery subpoena practice although the "president" does not resemble the subpoena itself. The Bay officials were aware that they had their own way of doing things; cf. the certificate of Winthrop (March 22, 1640) regarding service of a warrant "according to the custom of this Country" (*Thomas Lechford's Note-Book* 378).

Although the code of 1660 is not explicit on the process in criminal cases it appears that the usual form was a warrant directed to the constable on which a return was endorsed (cf. 2 *Recs. Ct. of Essex Co. Mass.* ix). A failure to return subjected the officer to fine (1 *ibid.* 84, 94). The form used in Essex County is strange as it corresponds with none of the forms in Dalton, *Countrey Justice* (1619) or Lambard, *Eirenarcha* (1614), the bibles of English local magistrates. It is nearest the *venire facias ad respondendum* in that it does not command the attachment or arrest of the defendant, but merely requires that the constable cause the defendant to appear. This was also the direction of the English precept for the peace (Lambard, *Eirenarcha* 86). Note, finally, Lambard's remark that "commonly an Enditment, or Information (being but an accusation or declaration against a man) is of none other force, but only to put him to answer unto it" (*ibid.* 519). He lists a venire facias first, then *dis-*

The first difficulty with the Duke's Laws is the free and indiscriminate use of the term "warrants." We shall consider presently in some detail the distinction which English law drew between "process" and "warrants."[4] At the moment it is necessary only to notice that process was the generic term for writs used *after* indictment while the precept used *before* indictment was called a warrant; and that whereas there were fixed forms of process (viz., venire, capias and the like) the warrant in Charles II's time was still an *ad hoc* instrument and the requisites of its form as yet unsettled. The distinctions of English law were not observed in the Duke's Laws for the term "warrant" is used to cover all forms of process, although the code distinguishes at various places between summons, attachment, warrants for appearance and subpoenas to testify. General rules are few. The Dukes' Laws provide that all warrants issue in the King's name, and in cases of felony or prison breach can be served even on Sundays and on those holidays sacred to the Stuarts when otherwise no process can be served. The justices of the peace or sheriffs are empowered to issue writs and warrants,[5] and the warrants of any justice will be effective in all the ridings.[6] All warrants issued under the hand and seal of the Governor are special warrants.[7]

The distinction between civil and criminal proceedings is blurred in the Duke's Laws. As we have already seen the prosecution of offenders by constables' presentment or individual complaint was a great deal closer to civil procedure than to the English procedure by indictment. This lack of distinction is patent in the section on "Actions" where rules of jurisdiction and proceedings for torts, debts and accounts as well as misdemeanors are scrambled together. In "actions" for assault, battery, breaches of the peace and the like, the justices of the peace are permitted to take bail or commit the defendants.[8] The section on "Bayle" indicates a much narrower discretion, since only persons committed by special warrant or for capital offenses are denied the right of bail.[9] By what process, however, the arrest was to be made is not clear. In the hybrid actions for breaches of the peace initiated by individual complaint, where both damages and fine or afflictive penalty were exacted, we may suppose that process, as in any civil action, was at the election of the complainant

---

tringas and if *nihil habet* returned, capias, etc. (*ibid.* 522, 523).

[4] *Infra* 413.

[5] 1 *Col. Laws NY* 13, 43, 63.

[6] *Ibid.* 43, provided the plaintiff resides in the riding where the justice lives or the cause arises there. This was an important deviation from Eng-

lish practice which limited the authority of the justice of the peace to the county where he was commissioned (Dalton, *Countrey Justice* [1677] 24).

[7] 1 *Col. Laws NY* 66.

[8] *Ibid.* 8.

[9] *Ibid.* 17.

by either summons or attachment. The book of laws gives forms for these.[10] It has no form of capias or warrant in criminal cases. That something of the sort was intended for cases initiated by presentment may be inferred from the provision that nothing was to be paid for warrants in criminal or capital causes,[11] and from the further reference to "warrants of appearance" to answer "all sorts of Actions at the Court or binding over to the Sessions or the Assizes for the good behaviour or the peace."[12]

The section on "Constables" throws some additional light on criminal process.[13] The constable who is employed by any justice for apprehending any person "shall not do it without a warrant in writing." He is also authorized to levy hue and cry after capital offenders, and to apprehend without warrant those "overtaken with Drink, Swearing, Sabbath breaking, Vagrant persons or night walkers," either where he sees them himself or on "present information." Even in these cases, however, a warrant is eventually to be issued, for the marshal is not to receive prisoners without a warrant; and where a known officer tenders a prisoner without a warrant he must oblige himself to deliver one within twenty-four hours.[14]

The Duke's Laws reveal nothing respecting the order of process and draw no distinction between original and mesne process. Even on the subject of final process the code is exasperatingly vague—no word respecting orders for executing capital punishments, a mere reference to the constable's duty to whip or punish anyone "to be punished by Order of Authority" where no other officer is appointed "unless they can get another person to do it."[15] The constable is ordered to collect fines[16] but by what process is not even hinted. It is possible, however, the compilers contemplated the process stipulated for the failure to pay rates and assessments: distraint of chattels, then of realty, and finally attachment of the body.[17]

It is obvious that with so little direction in the book of laws, the rustic ju-

---

[10] *Ibid.* 70.
[11] *Ibid.* 33 "Fees of Justice of Peace."
[12] *Ibid.* 32.
[13] *Ibid.* 28. The section is copied from the Massachusetts code of 1660 (*Col. Laws Mass.* 139). There were subsequently a few additions to the rules respecting process. In October, 1665, it was provided that search might be made by warrant or on a "sudden occasion" without warrant if the constable had his staff with him (1 *Col. Laws NY* 77 and cf. 73). In 1672, a requirement of security for hue and cry except in causes criminal and capital was enacted (*ibid.* 94).
[14] *Ibid.* 35.
[15] *Ibid.* 28.

[16] *Ibid.* 11.
[17] *Ibid.* 61 *Publicke charges.* In the *Ms. Mins. Ct. of Assizes* the entries indicate that the fine was considered a "public charge" (pp. 82, 85, 185). In October, 1665 it was enacted that "court fees" were to be collected by distress (1 *Col. Laws NY* 79). It seems to us unlikely that this term was meant to include the fine. So far as we are aware, the fine is never regarded even in English local court practice as a "fee." The Duke's Laws, moreover, draw the distinction between fine and amercement (*ibid.* 11), a fact which leads us to suppose familiarity with the English distinction in the manner of collection (Griesley's Case, 8 *Co. Rep.* 38a).

diciary was cast upon a sort of intellectual self-help in framing precepts to carry out its orders. To a certain degree the stream of written commands that flowed from the governor's office may have been a source of inspiration, but even these documents have an antic air as if the clerk had kissed the form book and had then forgotten it, for the warrants on even the same subject matter are almost invariably different.

The style of gubernatorial orders was set by Nicolls even before the Duke's Laws were compiled. The first warrant extant is one to search a Dutch ship. Thereafter are issued a variety dealing with the land squabbles of the English inhabitants, warrants for runaway negroes, summonses, *supersedeas* to local courts and even orders to take a recognizance.[18] These and later precepts were enrolled, but even this fact does not seem to have led to the establishment of set forms for the so-called special warrant.

Two important exceptions to the discursive precept were the forms of summons used by the Court of Assizes, and the subpoena to testify.[19] The first resembles the summons "president" in the Duke's Laws, and although it is not directed to any officer, is in substance a *venire facias ad respondendum*.[20] The address to the person summoned suggests the subpoena to answer an information. The subpoena used by the Court of Assizes is a mere order to appear and testify. No specific penalty is stipulated, but so far as we can tell from the burned record merely a general threat of the law's displeasure.[21] There is no indication whether or not the summons form was intended for criminal causes where no special warrant was used. It seems not unlikely that it was used in such cases, since no particular precept to be used against offenders was formulated,[22] and since the more important criminal jurisdiction was reserved to the Assizes.

In the Assize records of the first eight years of English rule, one defendant tried at Special Oyer and Terminer for the trial of a suspected homicide on a vessel, was merely summoned,[23] but we have found no other instances of this

---

[18] *Gen. Entries 1664–65* printed in *NY State Lib. Bull. Hist.* no. 2 (1899). In the remnant of *Ms. Gen. Entries 1665–72* are other orders and warrants. Cf. *infra* n. 23.

[19] *Ms. Mins. Ct. of Assizes 1665–72* 51.

[20] In the examples we have seen even the summons in civil process is directed to a constable or sheriff. The usual form appears to be an address at the foot of the precept. The formal "King to the Sheriff etc." of the English writs is abandoned. The officer is apparently supposed to make a return, although the very occasional insistence on this in par-

ticular cases seems to indicate a normal laxity in practice (e.g., 1 *Exec. Council Mins.* 218).

[21] Compare the forms of subpoena in Brownlow, *Writs Judiciall* (1653) 144.

[22] Unless a special warrant was invariably contemplated. The great variations in the wording of warrants under the Governor's hand suggest strongly that all his warrants were "special." Even the summons used in civil cases is constantly prefixed by a long whereas recital before it moves to the form set in the *Ms. Mins. Ct. of Assizes.*

[23] *Ms. Gen. Entries 1665–72* 543.

use. Among the surviving special warrants is one to attach the body, one to arrest, one to aid in apprehending an offender, and one to proclaim that a man surrender or suffer seizure of his estate.[24] In the remaining records for the period before 1672 most of the defendants had already been bound over by Sessions courts,[25] and one may infer their appearance was secured by mere summons, except where for some reason or other they were in custody.[26] There are some instances of the formal warrant for a hue and cry[27] after the practice then used in England,[28] and there is a variety of special warrants conforming to no identifiable English models.[29] In the Engel Hendricks murder case a posse appears to have been used. There is no relic of the process, only an account of wine and spirits consumed in bringing this poor wretch to the gallows.[30]

The failure of the Court of Assizes to evolve set forms of original process beyond the one mentioned may be attributed to the fact that it sat but once a year and was in the nature of a grand council of officials only a part of whose functions was judicial. Upon the Governor devolved the responsibility of making the necessary orders for the dispatch of interim business. This could have been effectively handled out of any contemporary English form book. Instead, the orders and warrants were heavily weighted with explanatory "whereas" clauses and the mandatory provisions seem to avoid expected words of art—the crisp and peremptory precision of English process. The New York precepts resemble in their elasticity and variation the royal orders in the close rolls of the thirteenth century and not the certain economy of the Register of Writs. We are disposed to believe that set forms were avoided as a means of keeping intact the gubernatorial prerogatives. As soon as a form is set, the subject will build his expectations upon it, for it has become "due process" by the fact of settlement. As long as the instruments of procedure are vagrant, only the most general claims of common right can come into existence.

The material for Assize and Council practice[31] under Andros is by no means

---

[24] *Exec. Council Mins.* 646, 800, 789, 309.

[25] E.g., *Ms. Mins. Ct. of Assizes 1665–72* 87, 145, 189.

[26] For example, *ibid.* 141, 184. See also the warrant of Nicolls to Hicks (1666) to arrest and imprison persons resisting payment of taxes and failing a proper prison to send them to jail in New York by *mittimus* (14 *Doc. Rel. Col. Hist. NY* 578).

[27] *Ms. Gen. Entries 1665–72* 547, 645.

[28] Lambard, *Eirenarcha* (1614) 185. There is a form in Dalton, *Countrey Justice* (1677) 484. This warrant probably has its origin in the requirements for examination and recognizance to prosecute where an injured person desired to bring an action

against a hundred upon the statutes of hue and cry.

[29] Our tests are necessarily the contemporary printed "precedents." It should be observed, however, that just as these vary in the several J.P. manuals, so there must have been a great variation in the private formularies of justices. Compare here the forms used by Sir Oswald Mosley printed in *Manchester Sessions* viii *et seq.*, and note the editor's comments on the variations.

[30] 2 *Rep. NY State Historian* 248.

[31] We include Council jurisdiction for the reasons indicated above. The chief collections of warrants are in the *Ms. Warrants Orders and Passes 1674–79* where the salvaged material covers the

lavish, but there are sufficient data to prove that in general the practice under Nicolls and Lovelace was followed. The order and warrant books indicate that there was a faint and gradual trend toward a settlement of form but there are enough warrants in draft form with interlineations and corrections to support the inference that the English precedent books were not yet being used.[32] As regards original process, the summons to appear is still in use,[33] there are more warrants of arrest[34] and, so far as it is possible to judge from existing minutes of Assizes, the physical apprehension of defendants has become usual. The table of sheriffs' fees of the year 1675, while somewhat fuller than that in the Duke's Laws, indicates that process has not become much more elaborate.[35]

The difficulties which beset a reconstruction of early Sessions practice arise not merely from the decay and dispersion of records but from the circumstance that there existed, until the time of Governor Dongan, considerable regional variation. That these differences were permitted to persist was due, we believe, to the prudent course of the several governors in easing as far as possible the introduction of English ways into communities predominantly alien. It was less the manner of law enforcement than the fact that the law be enforced which animated them. Possibly these considerations serve to explain why the matter of process is dealt with so casually in the Duke's Laws, and why no effort was made to correct this defect by subsequent amendment. In any event, the regime which regarded lightly the sacrosanct forms of the common law

years 1675–1677/78, and in the *Ms. Entries Letters Warrants 1680–83* of which only 82 damaged pages were saved.

[32] Compare, for example, the warrant to summon the Hempstead rioters, 1676 (25 *NY Col. Mss.* 228); the warrant for Heathcote (*infra* n. 49); the warrant of arrest for abduction, 1678 (27 *ibid.* 90); the warrant for Curtis, 1680 (29 *ibid.* 183); the warrant for William Taylor, 1680 (*ibid.* 112). The inference is most strongly supported where changes in the operative clauses, viz., the mandatory words, have been made.

[33] So the warrant re the troublesome pastor Fabricius (1675) in *Ms. Warrants Orders and Passes 1674–79* 123; the warrant for the constable and overseers of Hempstead, 1676 (*ibid.* 193). In the 1676 Assize minutes is a warrant to John Archer of Fordham Manor to answer an appeal of one Vervelen from a judgment fining him £20 for non-appearance (25 *NY Col. Mss.* 205). It should be noted that both this and the Fabricius warrant are addressed not to an officer but to the defendant. Cf. further, *ibid.* 228, a summons to rioters.

[34] Cf. the warrant to arrest Bayard, 1675 (*Ms. Warrants Orders and Passes 1674–79* 157); for Richard Jones, 1676 (*ibid.* 203); for Wm. Looker,

1676 (*ibid.* 226); for Benjamin Tuttell, 1676 (*ibid.* 227); for Adolph Meyer, 1677 (*ibid.* 265); for the constable and overseers of Flatbush, 1677 (*ibid.* 284); the warrant for Van Dyke, 1683 (*Ms. Entries Letters Warrants 1680–83* 61). There are warrants also in 25 *NY Col. Mss.* 237; 27 *ibid.* 9; 28 *ibid.* 129, 149; 29 *ibid.* 93, 112, 183, 184. Note further the general warrant of 1681 to arrest for riots in 14 *Doc. Rel. Col. Hist. NY* 762.

There are a few hue and cry warrants preserved in *Ms. Warrants Orders and Passes 1674–79* 124, 146, 173, 199, and in *Ms. Entries Letters and Warrants 1680–83* 7, 45.

For the practice of binding over by Sessions to answer at Assizes, cf. the Assize minutes of 1675 printed in 2 *Rep. NY State Historian* 386; 25 *NY Col. Mss.* 78. At the 1676 Assizes three of the defendants had been bound over (*ibid.* 181a); compare Andros' letters to the constable of Huntington in *Ms. Warrants Orders and Passes 1674–79* 155.

[35] 2 *Rep. NY State Historian* 433, 434. The table indicates no distinction between arrest in civil or criminal proceedings. An arrest costs 5s., an imprisonment 10s.

was equally indifferent to the administrative advantages of a uniform process, preferring the discretion implicit in the employment of the special warrant.

The difference in the procedure of these intermediate tribunals makes it necessary to describe this practice severally. In all cases our sources are chiefly the minute books, too often silent on points of process and only occasionally setting forth the text of a warrant. The judgment roll had not yet emigrated, and if a record (in the technical sense) was ever kept, no traces are left unless we can believe that the few scattered precepts in the *Colonial Mss.* are the salvage from such.

Of all the courts exercising inferior criminal jurisdiction the Mayor's Court of New York, being situated in the capital, was of the most consequence. Its character as a Sessions court before 1674 can be deduced only from the minutes, but upon the accession of Andros it is specifically so designated in the commissions.[36] Here, during the early period, despite the apparent intention of Nicolls to fashion the court after the English borough tribunals, the procedure, excepting for the introduction of jury trial,[37] remains much as it had been under Dutch hegemony.[38] It is only after English reoccupation that the records show a decided trend toward approximating English forms.

Under Nicolls and Lovelace the original process in minor cases was apparently the summons,[39] a device hardly to be distinguished from the Dutch "citation," particularly as the Dutch practice respecting defaults was continued.[40]

---

[36] *Supra* 64 n. 24.

[37] 5 *Recs. of New Amsterdam* 330.

[38] Cf. *supra* 329 regarding the similarity of prosecutions by schout and sheriff. The introduction of the English practice of security for good behavior is in the nature of an innovation. The Dutch had used bail (4 *Recs. of New Amsterdam* 240) but the notion of the process of good abearance or surety for peace was a good deal broader. The minutes sometimes refer to the security for good behavior as bail (5 *ibid.* 354, 6 *ibid.* 11).

[39] Sheriff v. Mills, 1666 (5 *ibid.* 341); Sheriff v. Smedes (*ibid.* 306). In Sheriff v. Moreau (*ibid.* 310) the defendant ran out of court. There follow three defaults and then a summons to appear "under pain of being called out by the sound of the bell" (*ibid.* 322). The entries *in re* Barton and Bloomer indicate as a result of special warrant, a public summons (6 *ibid.* 11, 21, 24). In Sheriff v. Corbyn (5 *ibid.* 311) the defendant was arrested by special warrant from the Governor, and cf. *ibid.* 318, where a servant is arrested. There are some entries in civil cases that indicate arrest is a mere service of process like attachment by pledges (*ibid.* 269) and others where actual corporal arrest was used.

[40] Dutch law in the seventeenth century proceeded by summons in cases where doubt existed as to the defendant's guilt, where there was a substantial question of fact in doubt, or where the offense charged did not involve capital punishment. This was the so-called ordinary procedure. In extraordinary procedure actual arrest was employed. This occurred where the offense was punished corporally, the offender was known, or his identity had been established by preliminary investigation or he had confessed (Damhouder, *Praxis Rerum Criminalium* [*Opera* 1646] c.3; 2 Van Leeuwen, *Commentaries on Roman-Dutch Law* Bk. 5 c.27, 541 *et seq.*). In the procedure by citation, defaults were allowed as in civil cases, the defendant upon the fourth default being adjudged contumacious, banished and his goods confiscated (Damhouder, *op. cit.* c.28). The citation was supposed to be served upon the defendant if he could be found; otherwise by public proclamation and by ringing a bell or blowing a horn (*ibid.* c.13). Van Leeuwen (*op. cit.* 545) regards the judgment upon the fourth default as one of guilt, but it is obviously interlocutory and for the contempt, since the defendant is allowed within six years to purge and be admitted to defend himself. Damhouder was used in New York. Mr. Augustus Van Cortlandt kindly showed us his ancestor's copy.

Roman-Dutch law drew no sharp lines between civil and criminal process in petty matters, and one may therefore suppose that the Mayor's Court rules of 1667/68 providing that all actions should be "brought in court" by summons, and allowing arrest only on failure to appear on the first court day or on intention to depart,[41] were designed for any type of cause.[42] The information in the minutes respecting process, however, is too vague to furnish support for much inference,[43] particularly because entries of criminal cases after 1667 are few.[44] It is clear, however, that where a serious crime was charged the actual apprehension of the defendant was effected; and where the Assizes had jurisdiction the practice was to bind over for appearance and good behavior, or in some cases to imprison until security was found.[45]

The effort to foster the Anglicanization of the province during Andros' first governorship is reflected in the changed character of the Mayor's Court practice after 1674. This is best evidenced by the conduct of civil litigation, for although the sources are somewhat more varied than those for the earlier period, the bulk of criminal business is slight. Indeed, it is not sufficient to support generalization respecting original process[46] beyond noting the relative increase in cases where persons were committed before trial. We have found only one entry (1675)[47] which indicates that a summons was used. The disappearance from the minutes of the earlier default entries together with the number of commitments noted[48] moves one to infer that the summons was falling into

[41] 6 *Recs. of New Amsterdam* 116.

[42] In a later order of October 12, 1672 (*ibid.* 393) the Mayor's Court cut the number of defaults previously allowed and provided that upon a "Legall arrest or Summons" failure to appear at the next court day entail judgment if the plaintiff had left a copy of his declaration at the city office four days before the sitting of the court. This ordinance was probably intended only for civil causes.

[43] But see the complaint against the carmen for abusive language (1670) where the offenders were merely summoned (*ibid.* 217). In 1667/68 two women were summoned for being in town without license (*ibid.* 101, 114).

[44] There are gaps in the minutes (*supra* 66 n. 49). Some entries indicate earlier proceedings not recorded in the extant minutes. It is possible a separate record of criminal business may have been kept. Cf. list of records in the clerks' hands, 1678/79. Some of these, e.g., the books of Nicolls and Lovelace's "placards," are lost (*Ms. Mins. Mayor's Ct. NYC 1677–82* 183b).

[45] 5 *Recs. of New Amsterdam* 338, 342, 354; 6 *ibid.* 11, 24, 132, etc. There is nothing to indicate a mesne process. In Sheriff v. Mol and Mannaet, one defendant is ordered imprisoned after trial had be-

gun, pending further investigation (5 *ibid.* 328).

[46] The total entries of criminal cases in the records 1674–83 are surprisingly few. It is possible that a special record was kept during this period, but a check of the presentments in the two declaration books leads us to think this was unlikely. It is possible that the pettiest cases were disposed of by a single justice or that the practice of meeting at individuals' houses occasionally recorded in the extant minutes (e.g., *Ms. Mins. Mayor's Ct. NYC 1677–82* Nov. 2, 1679) resulted in the loss of the records. It is clear from the remaining books that minutes of many sessions are missing. This can be determined not only by following the dates of supposedly consecutive sessions but also by reference to some earlier proceedings now not to be found. The variety of paper used in the minute book 1677–82 indicates that minutes were kept on loose octavos or quires, later bound.

[47] *Ms. Mins. Mayor's Ct. NYC 1674–75* fol. 10, Sheriff v. Jackson *et ux.*

[48] If any indication of process is noted it is ordinarily arrest or commitment, e.g., Case of P. J. Meade (*ibid.* fol. 26); Sheriff v. Morley (*ibid.* fol. 51); *Ms. Mins. Mayor's Ct. NYC 1677–82* fols. 7, 25, 125, etc. It is not always clear whether the de-

disuse. Two warrants of the years 1676[49] and 1677[50] are preserved that in the absence of further evidence we may take to be the usual form of arrest.

In any strict sense of contemporary common law practice these warrants are not "due process" in point of form. At the same time it is clear that however far from English models the clerks' pens may have strayed there already existed in the province a notion of due process in a more substantial sense. Thus the order in the case of John Tuder who had fleeced a yokel at play,[51] providing that any constable, sheriff or marshal might search Tuder's house at any time without warrant while Tuder stood bound to good behavior,[52] suggests that the normal rule of no search without a warrant was settled law.[53] It is further to be noted that this defendant was the first to appreciate the merits of attack on the forms of process. He objected (in a subsequent proceeding for resisting search) that the *mittimus* by which he had been sent to prison was not the same as that read in court. His objections were silenced when Matthias Nicolls, the secretary of the Province, "did there affirm that it was the same sense in every respect."[54]

fendant is already in court or if the order for commitment is a first process. Cf. *H.R. Ms. Wills* Liber 19B, 205. A girl had "enticed" a man to bed with her. The father made a disturbance. "She was immediately committed to my custody where I have kept her by her securities and do now present her." But see *Ms. Mins. Mayor's Ct. NYC 1677–82* 175 (Dec. 1679) where the court orders the sheriff to arrest one Phillips to answer "what shall be laid against him the next court." An entry in *Ms. Decl. Book Mayor's Ct. NYC 1675–77* fol. 182, indicates that in civil cases a "capias" is sometimes used.

[49] 25 *NY Col. Mss.* 237.
Wheareas George Heathcutt now of this Citty Merchant, hath this Morning in Presents of his honno[r] the Gouerno[r] and others, uttered Seditious Words against the Laws of this Gouernm[t] Alleadging hee had not the Priuilledge of an English man et alSoe that hee would proue there were [erasure] Duch Goods landed on shore here Contrary to Act of Parliament, &c. These are there-[fore] in his Ma[ties] name to require you to take the said George Heathcutt into yo[r] Custody and him safely to secure until hee doth giue in sufficient security [erasure] to the Value of One Thousande Pounds Sterling *to make his appearance at the next Co[rt] of Mayo[r] & Aldermen in this City* [*interlineation*; erasure] for w[ch], this shall to you bee a sufficient warrant Dated in New York this 10th day of October, 1676
W[m] Darvall May[or]
To the Sheriffe of New York.
This warrant was altered (as indicated) by the Governor's order.

[50] *Ms. Decl. Book Mayor's Ct. NYC 1675–77* fol. 334:
These are in his Majesties Name to require you to take into your charge and custody ye person of the said Edward Griffith, and him safely to keep untill he give sufficient security to Appeare at a Court to be held on Tuesday next (ye 23rd Instant) att ye Citty hall there to Answ[er] the afore and what may be alleadged against him on that behalfe—and for soe doeing this shalbe your sufficient Wartt. 19 Oct. 1677.
M. Nicolls.
It should be noted that the sheriff is given discretion over security. This does not conform to English practice where the discretion lay with the justices.
[51] *Ms. Mins. Mayor's Ct. NYC 1677–82* fol. 173b, Sheriff v. Tuder and Mann.
[52] *Ibid.* fol. 174b.
[53] 1 *Col. Laws NY* 73, 77. Tuder refused to permit his house searched without a warrant. This brought on another presentment but the case was dismissed for faults in the presentment. *Supra* 330.
[54] *Ms. Mins. Mayor's Ct. NYC 1677–82* fol. 175. On the trial, *infra* 566. At the Court of Assizes in 1680 Tuder offered a "bill" against Francis Rumbouts, late Mayor, which the grand jury voted, charging him and his associates with treason in that they had denied him a jury and had given judgment and execution without "his the said Tuders Lawful Tryall according to the Law of the land" (*Proc. Gen. Ct. of Assizes 1680–82* 13). Cf. *infra* 566.

Although the Mayor's Court of New York because of its situation was the most important tribunal exercising Sessions jurisdiction, and although it was peopled from time to time with officials who, as provincial councillors, also attended Assizes and presided at country Sessions, it does not appear to have been an exemplar. With the exception of the Sessions for the West and North Ridings which were both under supervision by the central authorities, all the intermediate tribunals in the country for one reason or another possessed individual characteristics. To a certain extent these differences were due to the difficulty of displacing familiar procedural customs through the intermediacy of a lay and untrained personnel, and to some extent they were, as we have indicated, deliberate. The Albany court is the strongest example in point.[55] The district was the last outpost against the combined French and Indian menace, and settled almost exclusively by Hollanders. The court, styled a "Cort of Commissaryes," but in terms of the extant jurisdictional scheme a combination of town and Sessions courts, was permitted to maintain its earlier

[55] The court at Albany because of its peculiar privileges is *sui generis*. It exercised the equivalent of both town court and Sessions jurisdiction in its district until 1672 when the settlement at Schenectady was given a town court (1 *Exec. Council Mins.* 146).

The records of the Albany court indicate a steady adherence to Dutch practice which is not much affected by English methods. Original process was ordinarily by citation (1 *Mins. Ct. of Albany, Rensselaerswyck, and Schenectady* [1668–73] 94 and compare the lists of citations and defaults *ibid.* 12, 17, 21, 22, 25, 26, etc.). It is not clear from the earliest records whether warrants were used, although in 1669 a plaintiff who claimed military privileges raised the issue that a special warrant alone properly lay (*ibid.* 133). In the later period it seems certain that written precepts were used (2 *ibid.* 332, 352; 3 *ibid.* 196, 231). These were also used to summon witnesses (2 *ibid.* 374; 3 *ibid.* 385). The records mention both a declaration book (2 *ibid.* 344) and an attestation book (*ibid.* 416, 421) but nothing is said of a process book. The same use of defaults already noted in connection with the Mayor's Court of New York and elsewhere obtained in Albany (1 *ibid.* 11, 12, 17, 22, etc.). In Dutch law a defendant was adjudged contumacious upon the fourth default and judgment passed against him. We have not noticed any criminal cases where this occurred, but if this rule obtained it would explain the absence of more severe process. Arrest and confinement appear to have been unusual. It is regularly used against servants (1 *ibid.* 168; 2 *ibid.* 308, 430; 3 *ibid.* 217). Occasionally there is notice of warrants to arrest freemen (2 *ibid.* 452; 3 *ibid.* 219). The peace officer also had

the right to seize contraband without warrant (2 *ibid.* 381) and upon flight the goods of the culprit were attached (3 *ibid.* 301). Apparently the search without warrant was allowed (2 *ibid.* 468). This was also contemporary Amsterdam usage (2 Van Leeuwen, *Roman-Dutch Law* Bk. 5 c.27, 548).

A few examples of process are entered in the court minutes. One of the earliest is a so-called *mittimus* (1679) which is actually an order to arrest in default of bail. This precept is not in the King's name (2 *Mins. Ct. of Albany* 415) but two years later, a similar document is so worded (3 *ibid.* 198). The existing warrants are not consistent on this point, and in general style they do not conform to the models used by other Sessions courts or by the Assizes (2 *ibid.* 452; 3 *ibid.* 79, 119 [civil cases], 93, 306 [inquests], 120, 181 [general warrant], 219, 300, 301). It should be noted, however, that by 1685 the *mittimus* in the form usual in the province is employed (3 *ibid.* 527, 554).

The Albany records have little to show regarding the process whereby the penalties exacted were enforced. The most usual penalty was the fine. There are examples of whipping (1 *ibid.* 277; 2 *ibid.* 121, 122, 430, 444); stocking (2 *ibid.* 182); confinement (1 *ibid.* 96; 2 *ibid.* 177); branding (2 *ibid.* 437); banishment (1 *ibid.* 277). The device of binding to good behavior was also used (1 *ibid.* 269, 323; 2 *ibid.* 177, 420; 3 *ibid.* 304, 396). The data are slight upon which to base conclusions respecting the adoption of English forms but it is reasonably clear that this did not proceed apace, despite the fact that the settlement had a copy of the Duke's Laws (2 *ibid.* 89) and that a Scot, Robert Livingston, was secretary of the court for a considerable period.

practices, and even after it acquired an English secretary and was citing substantive rules of the Duke's Laws its procedure moved in the grooves already worn under Dutch rule.

The plan of permitting existing judicial arrangements to stand was also tried down the Hudson in the Esopus and in the plantations along the Delaware. But as already stated it was abandoned at Esopus during Lovelace's regime, apparently because of the recurrent disturbances there, and a Sessions court established.[56] A similar change of policy was effected by Andros in respect of the Delaware lands when courts with an enlarged Sessions jurisdiction were commissioned in 1676.[57] In all of these courts Dutch practice lingered to a greater or less extent.

The circumstances that defeated standardization of courts exercising middle justice did not deflect the basic policy of maintaining a control over their proceedings. When the Duke's Laws were compiled, it had been Nicolls' design that a councillor would preside at Sessions. As we have noticed this practice was most consistently followed in the North and West Ridings.[58] Elsewhere it was possible to arrange only an occasional visitation.[59] Personal attendance was supplemented by the device of special instructions which in some instances are reminiscent of the charges laid upon English Assize judges before going on circuit.[60] Finally, through the medium of appeals to the Court of Assizes or petition to the Governor, a desultory supervision of the proceedings of Sessions was exercised, but this does not appear to have been directed to

[56] *Supra* 16 n. 78.
[57] *Supra* 18 n. 88.
[58] *Supra* 64 n. 23.
[59] By special commissions like that sent to Esopus in 1669 (1 *Exec. Council Mins.* 36) and that sent to the east end of Long Island in 1668/69 (14 *Doc. Rel. Col. Hist.* NY 617). It should be observed that despite the obstreperous behavior of the East Riding inhabitants, the Sessions there do not appear to have been regularly attended by a councillor. The court minutes which are very incomplete do not indicate the presence of councillors on the bench; but cf. the instructions to Capt. Manning cited *infra* n. 60. The order in the *Ms. Mins. Ct. of Assizes* 176, excusing East Riding constables from attendance, suggests that supervision was not regarded as vital.
[60] Two sets of these instructions are preserved: those for the June, 1670 Sessions at Jamaica (14 *Doc. Rel. Col. Hist.* NY 637) and those for the February, 1671/72 Sessions in the East Riding (*ibid.* 661). Compare the letter (1675) of M. Nicolls to the justices of the North and West Ridings ordering them to attend the Governor and

consult on matters of public good (*Ms. Warrants Orders Passes 1674-79* 169). It should further be noted that orders in particular matters were regulated by special warrant with which the printed sources are well peppered. The Newcastle court minutes indicate something of the supervision of the central authority in giving advice or orders (cf. *Recs. Ct. of New Castle* 98, 322, 421, 437). During the early period the significance of this guardianship lies chiefly in the strengthening of the general authority of the proprietor. It can scarcely be said to have led to an improvement in the legal capacity of justices of the peace, for the direction of the Governor and Council was in this respect essentially the blind leading the blind. Compare here the brave attempt of Governor Lovelace to assist Justice Wood of Long Island in a knotty case, "Tho but a batchelor yet I cannot conceive how ye crime of ye malefactor am't to a rape" etc. (*Ms. Gen. Entries 1665-72* 726). Even Matthias Nicolls, whom sympathetic biographers describe as a lawyer of parts, appears from his letter to the Newcastle magistrates (12 *Doc. Rel. Col. Hist.* NY 621) to have been essentially a fireside jurist.

matters of procedure, and in consequence there was no consistent attempt made to reduce the process of country courts to uniformity.

One may suppose because of the paternal surveillance of governor and councillors over the Ridings, particularly of the North and West, that the practice of these courts most closely approximated the intentions of the governing authorities regarding the functioning of Sessions. The materials here consist of minutes and a few warrants. Defendants came before Sessions either by transfer from town courts[61] which had already bound them to appear, on remit from Assizes,[62] by original process of the Sessions itself, or by special warrant of the Governor.[63] The earliest records throw little light upon the original process. There is some late evidence that a mere summons was used in minor charges,[64] and there are a few entries establishing the use of warrants to arrest or attach the body of persons accused.[65] In serious cases a special warrant from

[61] E.g., *Ms. Flatbush Town Recs.* Liber D, 179, 297, 403. There are also instances of remitting causes to town courts; cf. *Ms. Kings Co. Ct. & Rd. Recs. 1668–1766* 60 (chestnut tree cutter), 63 (abuse), 121 (fences); 25 *NY Col. Mss.* 57 (bastardy); 2 *Rep. NY State Historian* 250. We have seen an instance of what is in substance a *supersedeas* directed to a town court (1670) in *Ms. Gravesend Town Recs.* Liber III, 27.

[62] *Ms. Mins. Ct. Assizes* 88 (1660), 140 (1667), 144 (1667), 176 (1668); 2 *Rep. NY State Historian* 427 (1675); 25 *NY Col. Mss.* 197 (1676).

[63] In the printed sources most of the Governor's warrants returnable in Sessions deal with civil cases or general public affairs. For criminal cases of 1679 cf. 28 *NY Col. Mss.* 61, 110, 166. The last citation reads: Whereas Wynant Peters by misinformac'on & fals Suggestions hath obtained a patent from the Governo' for the upland at the Red Hook & parts Adjacent and upon pretence thereof hath encroacht upon the meadows there neglecting to erect or keep up any fence for the preservat'on thereof against his Hoggs and Cattle which proves prejudiciall to those concerned and is Against the Lawes of the Government; These are in his Ma^{tie*} name to require you to Summons the S^d Wynant Peters to make his appearance before the Justices at the Court of Sessions to bee held at Gravesend beginning on wendsday next the 17th Inst. and to answer what shall be alleadged against him on that behalf & that hee bring the originall patent with him; Hereof you are not to fail nor hee at your perills. Dated in New York this 10[?]^{th} day of December 1679.
By order of the Governour
Matthias Nicolls

[To] the Constable of Breucklyn
[or] his Deputy, who is to return
[t]his precept to the Court.

[64] In the *Ms. Suffolk Co. Sess.* 6, a defendant presented (1670) for a misdemeanor in calling a man a traitor is "called." 25 *NY Col. Mss.* 55 (1675) two defendants "called"; *ibid.* 252 (1676) a defendant "sent for" by warrant in a contempt case; 28 *ibid.* 23 (1678) Quakers illegally married, summoned. The defendants, not appearing, were subsequently "sent for" (*ibid.* 110 [1679]). *Ms. Kings Co. Ct. & Rd. Recs. 1668–1766* 348, contempt (1683). The minutes occasionally mention warrants without indicating of what nature (e.g., 2 *Rep. NY State Historian* 318 [1675]; 25 *NY Col. Mss.* 252, or the entry "to make appearance" is recorded, 29 *NY Col. Mss.* 88). There is nothing to indicate what form the mere summons took. One may suppose it did not differ materially from the form used by Assizes or in civil cases. For examples of the latter, cf. the two summons warrants signed by Matthias Nicolls (1678) in 27 *NY Col. Mss.* 121. An example of the subpoena to witnesses (1679) to appear at Sessions is in 28 *ibid.* 165.

[65] In the minutes are the following entries to show arrest: 27 *NY Col. Mss.* 129 (1678); 28 *ibid.* 110 (1679); *Ms. Kings Co. Ct. & Rd. Recs. 1668–1766* 179, 187 (1679), 214 (1680). There are not sufficient data to indicate the circumstances under which arrest was deemed proper. The following warrant (28 *NY Col. Mss.* 97) indicates the form used:
These are in his Majesties name to will and require you that you take into your Custody the body of Levy Grey and that he give in sufficient security for his appearance att the next Court of Sessions to be held the second Wednesday in June next in Jamaica upon Long Island to answer all such objections as there shall be declared against him by presentment made by the Deputy Constable of East Chester; And if he shall refuse to give in such security for his appearance and good behavior that then you forthwith deliver him into ye Custody of the Sheriff of the City of New York; So that he be att ye Next Court of Sessions for the North Riding

the Governor was sought.[66] Where there was any doubt regarding the jurisdiction of the court it was usual to bind the defendants over to Assizes[67] or to succeeding Sessions[68] and to commit until security was found.[69] The few warrants now extant do not conform to English precedents, and are substantially identical in point of form with Assize process.[70]

When the first attempt to extend the pattern of Sessions jurisdiction beyond the Ridings was made in relation to the Esopus lands, no thought was given to the matter of procedure, and it was not until June, 1673, that the Council formally ordered the Duke's Laws to be observed. During this interval the absence of any mandate or guide for the conduct of Sessions resulted in confusion over the limits of jurisdiction and led to an inevitable continuation of Dutch practice. The minutes of the court[71] disclose not only a failure to observe a particular "style" of Sessions,[72] but the greatest confusion among the officials themselves as to their competence and procedure.[73]

During the period between the conquest and the surrender of the province to the Dutch in 1673 the process of the Commissary Court and later of Sessions and the local courts with minor jurisdiction was substantially like that at Albany. Arrest was used when serious offenses were charged, but otherwise

---

of Yorkshire as above hereof faile nott dated this 24th of May Anno Domini 1679

John Pell

To the Deputy Constable
of East Chester.

Compare the warrant issued by the Mayor of New York cited *supra* n. 49. The precept, in 27 *NY Col. Mss.* 9b, addressed to the constable of Staten Island, appears to be a Sessions warrant. In one case in the East Riding a defendant was "brought before the court" to answer a charge of fornication before marriage (*Ms. Suffolk Co. Sess.* 7). This seems to have been an arrest.

[66] E.g., *Ms. Kings Co. Ct. & Rd. Recs. 1668–1766* 6, a case of adultery.

[67] *Ibid.* 35, a suspicion of adultery after a jury had found just cause (1670); 75, Quakers (1675); 179, misbehavior to girl; 2 *Rep. NY State Historian* 257, 341. *Supra* n. 25. Cf. the order in *Ms. Misc. Recs. Richmond Co.* 1 (1680) requiring security for appearance before Sessions in civil cases because the matter was "above the cognizance" of the town court.

[68] It is not always clear why this is done although there are cases where it seems to be due to doubts as to jurisdiction. Sometimes it is used because of circumstances such as sickness, or press of business and sometimes as a device to let the complaint lapse. Cf. *Ms. Kings Co. Ct. & Rd. Recs.*

1668–1766 11 (suspicion of receiving), 24 (fornication), 62 (abuse of wife), 111 (abuse of constables), 201 (assault), 204 (drunkenness); 27 *NY Col. Mss.* 252 (bastardy); 26 *ibid.* 159 (bastardy); 28 *ibid.* 23 (breach of peace). In some cases there is a commitment without indicating the conditions (2 *Rep. NY State Historian* 257; *Ms. Suffolk Co. Sess.* 32 ["misdemeanor"]).

[69] *Ms. Kings Co. Ct. & Rd. Recs. 1668–1766* 24 (fornication). Cf. here the *mittimus* in 28 *NY Col. Mss.* 61.

[70] There are a few precepts which are not related to criminal matters, but which are exhibits on the matter of skill in drafting. Compare here sheriff's warrant (1665) for a list of inhabitants and valuations (*Ms. Bushwick Town Recs.* 187–189); the warrant (1669) putting an idle fellow at work (*Ms. Gravesend Town Recs.* Liber IV, 25); the warrant (1670) re fines for neglect of training (*ibid.* 28); the order re constables (1670) in *Flatbush Town Recs.* Liber D II, 41; the civil capias (1678) in 28 *NY Col. Mss.* 23. There is a warrant (1681) regarding the collection of rates in the *Ms. Misc. Recs. Richmond Co.* 68. This volume contains minutes of the court of constable and overseers, 1680–82.

[71] In *Ms. Deeds Ulster Co.* Libers I–III.

[72] Cf. here Lambard, *Eirenarcha* (1614) 543.

[73] *Supra* 65 n. 26.

original process was merely a summons by the court messenger and seems to have consisted in reading the complaint.[74]

Upon the restoration of the Duke's authority in 1674 no immediate effort was made to conduct the Kingston Sessions in the provincial version of English usage. Although juries were sometimes impanelled[75] procedure otherwise seems for some years to have undergone no change.[76] In 1676 the leading English official, Justice Thomas Chambers, ex-carpenter and lord of Foxhall Manor, who had hitherto been entirely complaisant, raised the issue of the propriety of the form of prosecution by the sheriff. The matter was submitted to the Council which gave an equivocal reply and the minutes indicate that business was resumed thereafter as before.[77] It is not until the Andros regime was nearing its close that the first signs of English forms appear. Three civil summons are preserved[78] as well as warrants for arrest[79] and for the constable to appear with a defendant.[80] In view of the character of the minutes we are hardly justified in inferring that English process had ousted the Dutch, but the change was certainly under way.[81]

It is not easy to form a judgment on the relative dominance by 1683 of English over Dutch practice in the Kingston Sessions.[82] In those times the clerk responsible for the paper work of a court inevitably set its style. The conscientious La Montagne at Kingston, keeping his minutes in Dutch, may well

[74] *Ms. Deeds Ulster Co.* Liber I, 211 (1664), 256 (1665), 437 (1667). The Dutch rule respecting defaults is followed, e.g., *ibid.* 376, 378, 398, 434, 504; *ibid.* Liber II, 6.

[75] *Ibid.* Liber II, 444.

[76] The minute entries on process are scarce. Defendants were arrested in serious cases (*ibid.* 251 [1677/78]; 464 [1679]). In one case where the defendant absconded, the sheriff asked leave to attach his effects (*ibid.* 478 [1676]). There is nothing to show whether written summons was used in criminal cases, but as late as 1684 it was used in civil cases (*ibid.* Liber III, 191) where defendant asks a nonsuit because the complaint and summons did not agree. Cf. *infra* n. 78.

[77] *Ibid.* Liber II, 445. A civil action for battery had been tried by a jury and the sheriff then brought a complaint. "Captain Chambers Justice says that all fines are to be imposed by the higher authorities in behalf of the laws. He further says not to find in laws that any schout or sheriff can demand fines after the jury had rendered its verdict." The sheriff then proffered the terms of his commission. The court answered it was not annulling the commission but accepting it "as far as it extends." The Council's answer is in 13 *Doc. Rel.*

Col. Hist. NY 498. It merely stated the sheriff was to put the law in execution, apprehend and prosecute transgressors, but not be a judge in the case.

[78] *Ms. Deeds Ulster Co.* Liber II, 12; e.g., "Henry Paldu youw are in his Majst name sommened before the Session Coordt at Kingston upon the 28 April 1680 too answer an axsion of Cap. Thomas Delaval plaintiff in an axsion of 400 Sch. of wheat. W. Montagne Secr."

[79] *Ibid.* 252. "Too the Sheriff at Kingston. Mr. William Asforbie you are ordered in his Majst naem to aprehend the body of Cornelis Woutersen too bee put in Securyti to answer a case of William Fisher in the next Sessions courdt in an axsion of defamation. This will be your suffisiant warrant" (1679).

[80] *Ibid.* 252 (1679).

[81] This is indicated further by the fact that indentures in English begin and become more frequent from 1681 onwards (*ibid.* 576 *et seq.*).

[82] There is not much to indicate that the Duke's Laws were actually used in this jurisdiction, and except for a few letters from the governors giving advice (*ibid.* Liber I, 434, Liber II, 312, 416) the central authorities did not do much to further the extension of English practice.

by the mere alchemy of language and habit have transmuted quite English proceedings into something which on paper seems alien. At the same time it is clear from cases of assault and abusive words that an atmosphere more steadily hostile to the English than elsewhere existed in the Esopus region, and that the naturalization of procedure would be to this extent retarded. It needed the later Court of Oyer and Terminer with its grim common law procedure to bring home to the men of Ulster County the fact that conquest was complete.

In their remoteness from the center of government and their predominantly alien population the Delaware domains were in much the same situation as the upper Hudson settlements. Strangely enough, however, the minutes particularly of the Newcastle court where the clerk was English show a close correspondence with the Sessions practice of the Ridings and preserve but few of the peculiarities of Dutch procedure which is long dominant at Albany.[83] These Delaware jurisdictions have a brief existence as a part of the New York judicial development, but the light which the records throw upon practice under the Duke's Laws makes desirable some consideration of how the courts functioned.

So far as we have been able to determine the original process in criminal cases was either by summons[84] or by the equivalent of a capias.[85] There is too little evidence regarding the use of summons to settle the line when one process or the other was thought appropriate. In civil cases a form of "arrest" which

---

[83] The Upland records indicate that the Dutch practice respecting recording defaults and judgment after three or four defaults continued to obtain (*Recs. of Upland Ct.* 139). The practice at Newcastle seems much more Anglicized. Except for the few cases from the Whorekill printed in 12 *Doc. Rel. Col. Hist. NY*, the only minutes from the Southern Delaware are of the Deal court cited *supra* 335. These entries are not a sufficient basis on which to form any judgment, but cf. the ejectment pleadings (1679/80) in 12 *Doc. Rel. Col. Hist. NY* 636.

[84] *Recs. Ct. of New Castle* 289, a man charged with bigamy summoned; 302, a defendant charged with putting a stone in a bag of feathers apparently only summoned. The table of sheriff's fees (*ibid.* 43) mentions "arrest: serving a warrant 1s. 8d.; taking security 2s. 6d.; returning ye warrant 10d. For every summons before a magistrate 2s. 6d." The oath of the undersheriff, marshal and crier contains the clause to "execute and perform all warrants attachments summonses and the lyke" (*ibid.* 64).

[85] *Ibid.* 32, 91, 107, 294; *Recs. of Upland Ct.* 170. The text of warrants in *Recs. Ct. of New*

Castle 36, where the order is "him the said fenwike to bring by force before us"; and leave is given to pull down the house and fire on Fenwick. (Cf. *ibid.* 518.) In 26 NY Col. Mss. 81 is the following warrant signed by a Whorekill justice: Whereas this Day being the 7th day of August A° 1677, Complt. hath been made Before mee by mr. Edward Southein that John Roades hath taken away unleagally & unJustly Severall goods from his Supposed Landing belonging unto the Said mr Edward Southein— These are therefore in his Maties name to will & require yon to Bring Before mee the Body of John Roades upon Sight hereof to Answer the Complt of Mr. Edward Southein—hereof faile not at yor perill as yon will Answer the Contrary given under my hand this the day and year above written.—
                                        Helm Wiltbanck
[The] Constable for
Whorekill
            Binding over the party abovesaid to
            Remaine in Prison without—Bayle
            or mainprise to Answer the above-
            said action to the next Court.
To the Sheriffe of
our Jurisdiction.

was merely symbolic was used,[86] and it is conceivable that the summons in criminal cases was just that. From the minute entries as well as from surviving orders and warrants, however, there can be no doubt that physical apprehension of the defendant was frequently made.[87] Moreover, there seems to have been at Newcastle a lively appreciation of the nuances of due process. On one occasion the court denied the validity of a verbal commitment by an official not a peace officer;[88] it required a particular form of warrant for an entry upon closed premises to make an arrest,[89] and the court refused to issue new process while an earlier precept was outstanding.[90] What it failed to develop beyond the usual hue and cry[91] was any form of mesne process, the corollary, apparently, of its view that outstanding process remained in vigor until served.[92]

During the proprietary period the town organization occupies a position of some interest in the matter of process. Not only does it have a court which deals with petty offenses,[93] but it is used by Sessions and by the central authorities to perform certain functions connected with the general administration of justice. The constable is, of course, the spit-dog of the treadmill of government. His is the arduous task of serving precepts which may issue from any part of the province;[94] he must attend not only the annual Assizes[95] but his

---

[86] It should be observed that some civil cases speak of "arrest and non-appearance," e.g., *Recs. Ct. of New Castle* 51. This is apparently a merely symbolic arrest as appears by the case in *ibid.* 294. It is paralleled by the bastardy case where mere confinement to the house is regarded as imprisonment (*ibid.* 294). Compare there the curious entry (*ibid.* 51), "Whereas the defendant now is and has been a longt tyme absent out of the river so that the plaintiff cannot sue the defendants boddy he hath therefore attached of the Defendant in the plaintiffs owne hands one suit of black silk. . . ." This indicates to us that some service by way of attaching the plaintiff's person was regarded as a necessary first step. But see *ibid.* 70, 71.

[87] *Supra* n. 85. It should also be noted that binding to good behavior with an order to retain in custody is also used (*ibid.* 91), or bound and on breach to be imprisoned (*ibid.* 424). One case of imprisonment until sent to Assizes occurs (*ibid.* 104).

[88] Billop, the sub-collector of customs, had arrested and put an abusive citizen in the stocks. The minutes read: "There being no comittment for ye prisoner francis Jackson (for whose case the court was called) after debates the Court did not Judge ye verball comittment Lawfull," as Billop had no commission (*ibid.* 128).

[89] *Ibid.* 117. Apparently search could not be made ex officio as in Dutch law (cf. *ibid.* 104) although the constable and churchwardens were ordered to search false measures (*ibid.* 288).

[90] *Ibid.* 186, 187, an execution signed "against the boddy therefore it is improper to grant any other execution."

[91] Cf. the letter of Andros, Apr. 6, 1677 (*ibid.* 98); and the use after commitment a...¹ escape (*ibid.* 346).

[92] *Ibid.* 32, one defendant being apprehended, the warrants as to two others "to stand in force and bee executed if possible they can be found."
A further process problem of interest arose in a case where a justice was summoned as a witness. He told the sheriff that there were enough witnesses without him and the officer departed. The court, however, decided there was no lawful summons and that the justice could sit as a magistrate (*ibid.* 424).

[93] 1 *Col. Laws NY* 7 (Actions), 63 (Townships), 71, 74 (amendment of 1665), 91 (amendment of 1666). The Duke's Laws expressly exclude matters "criminal" from the ordinance power of the towns (*ibid.* 63) but do not clearly define the jurisdiction of the court over petty offenses although this is implicitly recognized in the provision that allows penalties up to 20s. to be laid. The enforcement of the law respecting innkeepers and ordinaries (including peace breach in taverns) is expressly the charge of the constable and two or more overseers (*ibid.* 40).

[94] *Ibid.* 43 (Justice of Peace), 28 (Constables).

[95] *Ibid.* 73 (amendment of 1665). *Ms. Mins. Ct. of Assizes* 175: Excuse of the East Riding constables

presence is required at his town court and he must not fail to be present with his staff at the Sessions.[96] The business of collecting rates is upon him,[97] and he does the distraining of the recalcitrant.[98] He must pursue the fleeing malefactor,[99] and he must present him. In company with the overseers he may have to examine persons for the Sessions or for the Council.[100] Whatever a justice of the peace may wish to pass on to him the constable cannot avoid.[101] Even his house is no sacred castle, for the law provides that he must give sanctuary to the distracted wives of his bailiwick.[102] Small wonder that scruples against taking the oath were often discovered.[103]

The constable's activities in behalf of the provincial government are merely those of an agent. The pattern is fixed from above and is nearly uniform in each riding. But within the scope of his local duties, as one of the responsible administrators of the town, what the constable does is the subject of certain variation. The Duke's Laws had laid down no detailed rules as to how the towns were to be ruled, and the governors wisely allowed some latitude in local administration, exercising supervision of town affairs chiefly through Sessions.[104] In the period immediately following the conquest, the records show that changes in town court procedure appear to be slight.[105] The local officers

from attendance at Assizes "as in ye Law they are required" (1668).

[96] 1 Col. Laws NY 7, 73 (Absence). And note the entries in the Sessions minutes for failure to have the staff of office (2 Rep. NY State Historian 328 [1675], 331 [1675]).

[97] 1 Col. Laws NY 61 (Publické Charges) and he also made the assessments (ibid. 14).

[98] Ibid. 61.

[99] Ibid. 29, 69; and compare the hue and cry warrant in Ms. Gen. Entries 1665–75 575 addressed to "Ye Constables or any other officers of ye towns within this government" (1670).

[100] Compare here Ms. Mins. Mayor's Ct. NY 1677–82 184, where testimony taken before the constable and overseer in Jamaica is submitted (Jan. 21, 1679/80); Ms. Flatbush Town Recs. Liber AA, 71, evidence taken on the order of justices of the peace (1678); ibid. 131, evidence in a fornication case (1679); arbitration by a warrant, Ms. Flatbush Town Recs. Liber C, 3; examination on order of Van Ruyven, J., ibid. Liber D, 107.

[101] A notion of the active life of a constable is indicated by the account of Tho. Lamberts, constable of Brooklyn (1672) in 1 Rep. NY State Historian 328. It opens:
"Feb. 15 A warr't for 3 horses 2 dayes
          1 more used
Ditto 18 A warrant T.L. 2 horses 2 days. . . ."

[102] 1 Col. Laws NY 46 (Marriages).

[103] Cf. the warrant of Nicolls to levy the fines imposed on those who refused to serve as constables (14 Doc. Rel. Col. Hist. NY 584 [1666]; Ms. Kings Co. Ct. & Rd. Recs. 1668–1766 177 [1679]; ibid. 209 [1680]). There are many entries in the West Riding Sessions records of presentments of constables for failure to attend to duties respecting highways, fences, etc. Cases where constables were abused are frequent. An entertaining sidelight on popular feeling about the office is a presentment (1679) of one Laud who, upon summons to testify, refused, saying "that hee did not value the constable's staff and could cut as good a stick out of the woods himself" (ibid. 198). The constable's staff was supposed to bear the King's arms.

[104] Town ordinances had to be confirmed at Sessions (1 Col. Laws NY 63 [townships], 82). Any justice of the peace might preside at the town court in the jurisdiction where he lived (ibid. 44).

[105] For purposes of comparison it is desirable to note briefly the characteristics of town court process in the English towns before 1664. Information about offenses and their trial is very slight in the printed records. Our conclusions respecting the procedure of these local courts is necessarily based in part upon the civil cases. Since the Connecticut law book was used in the eastern towns, the Connecticut rules of process were followed. These provided for a written summons to be followed by attachment of the person (1 Pub. Recs. Conn. 510, 511). Attachments of property were permitted only if the defendant was a foreigner about to abscond

naturally enough continued to conduct business in the manner to which they were used.[106] There was, to be sure, a drift toward imitating Sessions practice due to its supervision of town affairs and to the powers of judicial review. But up to the end of the town courts' existence there are still perceptible differences between localities and their practice.

At the present time the most complete records relate to the town courts of Western Long Island in the later county of Kings. Here the original process was by summons either by the constable or court messenger.[107] Whether a

or transfer his property "or any other just cause." In Southampton, summons preceded attachment (1 Recs. of Southampton 107) and security was taken as in Connecticut from the party suing an attachment (ibid. 63). The cases show nothing regarding process in criminal cases. The taking of security for good behavior was also known (ibid. 48, 125; 2 ibid. 7). At Easthampton a system of fines for non-appearance was instituted in 1651 (1 Recs. of Easthampton 17), "due warning" being set at twenty-four hours. The constable was allowed 6d. for serving every warrant and "travill or assistance" (ibid. 28). Two early and crude warrants of attachment of the year 1652 are preserved (ibid. 29; cf. also ibid. 44, 52). As in Southampton, security is taken when an attachment is sued (ibid. 30). Warrants were used to summon witnesses (ibid. 64, 77) and a jury (ibid. 65). Apparently the summons was the proper first process (ibid. 66, 153). There are a few entries respecting punishment: fines (ibid. 72, 87, 88) or a cleft stick on the tongue of a woman (ibid. 21). A mutilated warrant of execution in a civil case is preserved (ibid. 190, 191). The Records of the Town of Brookhaven (1880) contain practically nothing of interest. There is an entry of a fine (1 ibid. 8) and a curious use of "arrest" followed by "arrest" of the defendant's body. There are a few entries respecting punishment in 1 Huntington Town Recs.: "publick satisfackcion" or fine (p. 25); banishment (p. 27); "public satisfaction" (p. 29). In 1661 it was provided that "A warrant shall be 10s. 4d. ye making & 6d. serving. A Tachment 18s. 6d. ye making & 12d. ye serving. An Execution 2s. 6d. ye making and 2d. ye distress" (ibid. 34). In 1663 these costs were reduced (ibid. 47). The earliest town book of Hempstead is lost. The present first book (1 Records of the Towns of North and South Hempstead [1896]) contains an ordinance (1650) providing fines, corporal punishment, and banishment for failure to observe the Sabbath, and allotting one-half the fines to informers (p. 57). There is one entry rescinding an order of banishment (p. 86).

The English town of Gravesend was given a patent by Kieft in 1645 granting the right to hold court in debts and trespasses to 50 Holland guilders without appeal, with power to attach and sell on execution (Ms. Gravesend Town Recs. Liber VI, 4). The earliest table of fees does not indicate anything

regarding process, the only charges being for entering an action, writing a sentence, recording it, and for sworn testimony (ibid. Liber I, 14 [1647]). However, an entry of the same year shows that attachments were used (ibid. 17). Prosecution was by individual complaint for breaking the "common peace" (ibid. 19) or by the schout (ibid. 8, 90, 106, 107). The early entries show fines imposed (ibid. 19, 24), and in 1650 an ordinance was passed to deal with defamers and breakers of the peace threatening fine, imprisonment, "stocking" or standing at a public place. There are examples of fines (ibid. 61, 106), imprisonment (ibid. 61), standing at a public post (ibid. 60, 76). The most severe penalty is that imposed on one man for saying the Governor took bribes. He was condemned to have his tongue bored by a hot iron (ibid. 56–58). There are two examples of security for good behavior (ibid. 66, 120).

The Jamaica records contain nothing respecting criminal procedure (Records of the Town of Jamaica 1656–1751 [Frost ed.]). The Flushing records are said to have been destroyed by fire. The East Town records show that both summons and attachment were used but no indication of the order of proceeding (Mins. Westch. Ct. of Sess. 1657–96 12–15, 18, 19, 21—all civil). There are preserved crude warrants of attachment, of property, or person and property and of execution. Fine (ibid. 1, 9, 26), whipping (ibid. 5, 8) and banishment (ibid. 6) are the punishments in the few criminal cases recorded. It should be noted that the printed version incorrectly describes this court as a Court of Sessions. It was a town court. The first inhabitants of East Town came from New Haven but they do not appear to have lived by New Haven law (cf. on New Haven process New Haven Col. Recs. 1653–65 573, 585, 592, 615). There are two warrants of execution (civil) of Oct. and Dec., 1664 in Mins. Town Cts. Newtown (1940) 45, 46.

[106] The most striking indication of the small immediate effect which the English conquest had upon local judicial proceedings is to be observed in Ms. Flatbush Town Recs. Liber D, which begins in 1664 and runs to the year 1670. It is only after the lapse of some time that a definite change can be perceived.

[107] Ms. Flatbush Town Recs. Liber D, 59, an order of May 4, 1665, setting a fine of 5 glds. for fail-

written warrant was required we do not know, but we are disposed to believe it was not. In the Dutch towns the court allowed defaults but exacted fines for failure to appear. At Flatbush the sum of three guilders set in 1665[108] was increased to four guilders in 1669;[109] and ten years later it was stipulated that judgment was to follow a second failure to appear.[110] These rules are stated in a general form and apparently were intended to cover both civil and criminal cases. In one case, the defendant was committed after complaint heard[111] and in another, the defendant was "arrested," viz., ordered not to leave town until further notice.[112] At Gravesend and Bushwick apparently no difficulties in securing appearance arose. The most frequent penalty exacted by these courts was the fine.[113] However, there are cases where the convicted defendant was whipped[114] or put in the stocks.[115] There is no indication whatever of the process if any.

Among the English settlements on the Sound and on eastern Long Island, a very small amount of criminal business is entered in the town records. At Easthampton after 1664 there are only two indications of original process in criminal cases—one where the defendant was "brought . . . before the Court,"[116] the other where he was "warned by authority" to appear.[117] We have found nothing respecting original process at Southampton,[118] Oyster

---

ure to appear after being "warned," 231 (1667), 297, 339 (1668), 305, 371, 399 (1669); *ibid.* Liber D II, 135 (1672), 253, 273 (1678). The Gravesend records have only one case entry on process, a party warned into court (*Ms. Gravesend Town Recs.—Court Mins. 1662-99* Liber IV, 50). A table of fees, presumably of 1665, provides: entering action 15*d.*; judgment 1*s.* 6*d.*; execution, 1*s.* 6*d.*; orders 6*d.*, copies 6*d.*; entering attachments 9*d.* (*ibid.* 47).

The *Ms. Misc. Recs. Richmond Co.* contain presumably the complete records of the Constable and Overseers' Court of Staten Island between 1680 and 1682. Except for testimony in a bastardy case there is nothing relating to criminal cases in the book. On page 134 is a "List of warrants by the Justis to the town court." The causes listed are all civil and the warrants are not otherwise described.

[108] *Ms. Flatbush Town Recs.* Liber D, 59.

[109] *Ibid.* 377.

[110] *Ibid.* Liber D II, 325. Three English shillings were exacted for a first default.

[111] *Ibid.* Liber D, 187 (1666). This was an unusual case, actually without town court jurisdiction. A man had been presented for living with a concubine. The latter was then presented but failed to appear and so was ordered committed.

[112] *Ibid.* 371. This was a fornication case. The defendant confessed and then was ordered to be arrested.

[113] *Ibid.* 153 (1666) Sunday violation and contempt; 175 (1666) fence violation and contempt; 231 (1667) defamatory words; 305 (1668) fence violation; 375 (1669) defamatory words; 383 (1669) fighting. *Ibid.* Liber D II, 133 (1672) assault; 317, 363 (1678) defamatory words. *Ms. Gravesend Town Recs.* Liber IV, 14 (1666) Sunday violations; 16 (1666) contempt; 47 (1665) trespass in carrying off hay. *Ms. Bushwick Town Recs.* 247 (1666) an order of Council for the town court to fine for not giving seisin of lands.

[114] *Ms. Flatbush Town Recs.* Liber D, 179 (1666), living with a concubine. There is no indication of such punishments in the remaining records of the other adjacent towns.

[115] *Ibid.* 399 (1669), defaming a girl by refusing to marry her.

[116] 1 *Recs. Town of Easthampton* 330 (1670).

[117] *Ibid.* 423 (1678). Note also the crude warrant of attachment at 315 (1669), and the use of a warrant to summons in a civil case at 428 (1678).

[118] The absence in the Southampton town records of entries relating to town court litigation after 1664 suggests that a special book was kept for this business. A note signed by the constable in 1680 for £20 8*s.* 6*d.* due for "court fees and fines" indicates a court was exacting punishments (2 *Recs. Town of Southampton* 280 [1680]). The town clerk informed us in 1926 that all the extant records of the period had been published.

Bay[119] or Huntington.[120] At Hempstead the civil cases all speak of "warrants" initiating actions but there is no indication of how the defendant in criminal cases was proceeded against.[121] The information on punishments, however, is somewhat more detailed, although there is virtually nothing about the process whereby they were executed. A fine is the usual penalty,[122] although the stocks are sometimes used, probably more often than the records show.[123]

The scheme of process as it was worked out in New York before 1684 would have reduced an English cursitor or filacer to tears, but it appears to have functioned adequately. The lack of uniformity was an inherent weakness but the standard of professional skill at the bar was not sufficient to draw profit from this fact. True, objections to form were occasionally raised but there are no signs that a body of law about process was in the making. Most striking is the failure to exploit that vast mine of learning and objection, the *retorna brevium*. If any returns at all are endorsed upon process they are windy and technically vulnerable;[124] yet so far as we can judge they were the cause of no particular

[119] The town of Oyster Bay seems to have been singularly free of wrongdoing. In 1672 the fees were as follows: summons in town 6*d.*, a "warent" 12*d.*, attachment 2*s.* 6*d.*, out of town service 6*d.* per mile (1 *Oyster Bay Town Recs.* 223). Here both summons (*ibid.* 224, 225) and "arrest" (*ibid.* 203, 225) were used. Contemporaneously "arrest" was the term used in English local courts for attachment —the *duci facias* (Blount, *Law Dictionary* [1670] *s.v.* attachment).
The Oyster Bay men appear to have had a strict conscience about the dueness of process. In 1670 "the Towne of Oysterbay reaseavid a warrent from ye Constable haveing Date ye —— of 1670 wherein we doe not read ye Kings Name mentioned in [accordance] to law & it being a Scrupell to Sum to Act by ye Seade warrent we [deem] it not safe to proceed upon ye said Grounds untill ye said scrupell [receive] mor fully Sattisfacktion . . ." (1 *Oyster Bay Town Recs.* 217). In 1675 it was provided that summons or "arrest" must be four days before "courte day" (*ibid.* 225).
[120] The *Huntington Town Recs.* give a few accounts of costs. In the civil cases, these disclose either nothing as to process, e.g., p. 161 (1670), or show a summons was used, p. 325 (1681), or an attachment, p. 320 (1681). In a prosecution for Sunday violation the entry merely refers to constables' fees, p. 333 (1682).
1 *Recs. Town of Brookhaven* 21 prints one detailed account of costs (1666) in a civil case where summons was used. In an ordinance of 1674 it was provided that young men or maids who were out after nine at night were to be summoned to the next court and be punished at the discretion of the court.
[121] E.g., 1 *Recs. Towns of North and South*

Hempstead 282, 283, 335. There are occasional attachments (*ibid.* 336, 350). In 1671 a defendant "pleads he had no legall notice given him by his Adversary and was ignorant of his pretentions untill hee heard the same declared in court and therefore is unfitted to make his defence . . ." (*ibid.* 284). The idea of reasonable notice appears to have been well seated in the early settlements. It is worthy of remark because these infant communities were lawyerless.
[122] 1 *Recs. Town of Easthampton* 326 (contempt); 330 (breaking a pack); 369 (incontinence); 423 (breach of peace). 1 *Huntington Town Recs.* 202 (unjust detention); 333 (Sunday violation). There are no cases in the Brookhaven records but the ordinance of 1674 provides fines for drinking and racing horses in the town (1 *Recs. Town of Brookhaven* 34). 1 *Southold Town Recs.* 328, 329 similarly has ordinances stipulating fines but no cases are recorded. Some of the records of this town have been lost (*ibid.* xiv). 1 *Oyster Bay Town Recs.* 221 (false news). 1 *Recs. Towns of North and South Hempstead* 293 (abuse of authority); 271 (setting a fire).
[123] 1 *Huntington Town Recs.* 119 (defamatory words); 1 *Recs. Towns of North and South Hempstead* 339.
[124] Compare, for example, the sheriff's returns: 2 *Rep. NY State Historian* 225, 226 (1674); *Ms. Mins. Mayor's Ct. 1677–82* 231 (1680); *H.R. Ms. Wills Liber* 19B, 54 (1682), 71 (1683). At Newcastle there are some returns entered on the minutes themselves, e.g., the "non est inventus" (*Recs. Ct. of New Castle* 57). The lack of any precise information regarding returns is well illustrated in the directions to the sheriff regarding the warrant to arrest Van Dyke in *Ms. Entries Letters Warrants* 62

concern. Provincial justice does not appear to have malingered on this account, but the very absence of interest is evidence both of indifference to common law practice and of the lack of technical guides. Only a profound ignorance can explain the official failures to take advantage of the fiscal benefits inherent in the staggering array of common law process and the penalties upon misjudgment in their selection.[125]

The Introduction of Common Law Process

How well the Duke of York was acquainted with details of the situation in New York we do not know;[126] but Matthias Nicolls, Dyer and Andros were all in London immediately before the appointment of Colonel Thomas Dongan, and even if these men had not discoursed about procedure, the fantastic treason proceedings against Dyer must have given the Duke's advisers some insight into the *bizarrerie* of New York practice. It seems not unlikely that the particularity of Dongan's instructions respecting both the increase in revenue and the administration of justice were due to a desire to effect a greater conformity with English practice. The instructions[127] are emphatic upon the necessity of a "constant Establishment" for raising money to support and maintain the provincial government, an expression which may be understood to embrace the ordinary issues and profits of governmental machinery, since the instruction immediately preceding deals with laws for the raising of public revenue, and later deals separately and specifically with rents and customs. Moreover, the new governor is authorized to "elect and settle" courts of justice with the express proviso that "ye same be as nere answerable to ye law and Courts of Justice in England as may be."[128]

We have seen how the judicial system was reconstructed and how indictment procedure was introduced; it remains to examine how other practices were made "answerable" to the laws in England. For there can be no doubt that the early years of Dongan's administration saw a general acceptance of legal forms as used in England—a first and, we believe, a most significant step in the reception of the common law.

(Mar. 1683). The entries in the Assizes minutes indicate the court relied upon oral testimony of the officer serving if any question arose. Cf. 25 NY Col. Mss. 191, 196, 202.

[125] The table of fees in *Office of the Clerk of Assize* (1682) 247 is an example of the extremities to which the squeeze was exerted by the courts in England.

[126] Some details certainly came before the Duke in the course of the disputes between Lewin and Andros. Cf. especially the *Rep. to Commissioners of Duke of York's Revenue* (3 Doc. Rel. Col. Hist. NY 314) regarding the destination of fines and the alleged commitment of Tuder for demanding a jury.

[127] 3 Doc. Rel. Col. Hist. NY 331.

[128] 3 ibid. 333.

Were it not for the disastrous destruction of the major portion of the records for the early years of Dongan's regime,[129] the drastic nature of the shift in form could be easily demonstrated. The calendar of the lost manuscripts for these years lists a variety of precepts, such as capias, scire facias, habeas corpus, the like of which had not hitherto been used in New York.[130] Of the extant records the most persuasive proof of the change lies in minutes of the Court of Oyer and Terminer,[131] and the Sessions first held after the Judiciary Act of 1683. The proceedings in these tribunals appear for the first time enrolled in the approved and characteristic form of judicial record keeping in England. Indeed, in the case of the Albany Sessions it comes as something of a shock to view the utterly Anglicized style of the record which had theretofore been kept in Dutch and had radiated a sort of country comfort.[132] Into every type of paper which remembrances litigation and by which it is pursued crept the change to the new way—commissions,[133] indictments, process, to the final enrollment of proceedings. It is a change of major importance for it wiped out endemic experiment with forms, and once the frame of common law forms was set, the importation of English doctrine was made possible. It is a change of peculiar significance in criminal jurisprudence because in England this branch of the law had gravitated toward becoming essentially a jurisprudence of forms, a rigid structure of well-defined common law and statutory offenses—a mode of hard and fast proceeding from arrest to execution of sentence, unleavened by a real appeal jurisdiction and salted only by the vagaries of the twelve good men in the jury box. The adoption here of the forms signified the adoption of the substance.

In the bareness of evidence the circumstances inducing the change are diffi-

---

[129] Cf. supra 69 n. 77.

[130] Cf. Cal. Eng. Mss. 112 et seq. The term scire facias is used in the Newcastle records, but it is obviously a pseudo-learned flourish of the clerk (Recs. Ct. of New Castle 29, 40).

[131] 7 Ms. Mins. Council (Reverse) for New York County; Ms. Mins. Oyer and Terminer Ulster Co.; 35 NY Col. Mss. 86 (Albany Co.).

[132] The standard is not everywhere equal but it is particularly high in the earliest sets of Sessions minutes, those for New York (Ms. Mins. NYCQS 1683/84–1694), Albany (Ms. Mins. Albany Co. Sess. 1685–89) and Kings (Ms. Kings Co. Ct. & Rd. Recs. 1668–1766). The Westchester Sessions records begin in 1687. They are relatively crude and come from what we think to be a rough waste book. In the New York and Albany records, the causes which proceed to judgment are enrolled in the English style. There is a sample in Latin of the

form followed in Lambard, Eirenarcha (1614) 543. The earliest printed English version in a form book that we have seen is in Stubbs, Crown Circuit Companion (1768 ed.) 69. None of the most used handbooks of this period, such as Dalton, gives the form of enrollment. We are disposed to believe that a manuscript collection of precedents was brought over at this time. Even in the eighteenth century, the leaders of the New York bar continued to use ms. precedent books although their libraries contained the usual printed form books. Cf. Ms. Form Book Joseph Murray; Ms. Commonplace Book John Chambers; Ms. Precedent Book Wm. Livingston; Brevia Selecta (Van Cortlandt Mss.).

[133] Compare particularly the commission of 1685 to hold the Oyer and Terminer for Westchester (34¹ NY Col. Mss. 43) and the commissions to the New York justices (ibid. 74, 75).

cult to assess. The act settling the courts[134] beyond stipulating that summons shall be the process "of warning" in the town courts, simply establishes the office of clerk of the Sessions or Peace who is charged with drawing, entering and keeping records of "Indictments, informacons . . . and proceedings," and requires that all process be directed to the sheriffs to be executed by them or their deputies. The section dealing with the Court of Oyer and Terminer speaks of removal of actions by writ of error or certiorari—both forms new to the province. Beyond this the act is silent. An additional statute[135] deals at length with the proceedings on executions, adopts the extent, regulates the return and freezes the existing scale of fees.[136]

It will be observed that while the new legislation does not in terms adopt the English procedures, the acts are cast in terms of presuming its acceptance just as the Constitution of the United States assumes the existence of the common law. There is, however, no evidence of any administrative action to put the English forms into effect and from the dilemma of the Kings County authorities six months later[137] we may infer that it was probably in the spring of 1684 that the necessary steps in this direction were taken. For this there is some further basis for inference in a case in error at the Oyer and Terminer held in June, 1684, for Ulster County.

Thomas Chambers had recovered in civil action against one Richard Hayes in the March term of the Sessions. Hayes thereupon sued out a writ of error assigning as error *inter alia*[138]

That there was no legall process sued out by the s^d Thomas Chambers ag. the said Richard Hayes whereby to oblidge him to answer—Therefore the Court of Sessions their compulsion of the s^d Richard is Extrajudiciate and against the knowne practise and usage not only of the Courts of the Realm of England

---

[134] 1 *Col. Laws NY* 125.

[135] *Ibid.* 134, "An act for the due regulacon & proceedings on Execucons, Returnes of Writts & Confirming the Fees usually taken by the Officers etc."

[136] At the 1684 session an act was passed requiring substantial error for reversal of judgments and requiring that all original writs and process express the name of the party suing (*ibid.* 144). This assembly also enacted a "Bill" concerning arrests (*ibid.* 159), fixing the time when service of process was allowable and limiting the use of civil arrest in case of minors.

[137] *Ms. Kings Co. Ct. & Rd. Recs. 1668–1766* 360. The only administrative order respecting process that we have seen is in the entry in 1 *Mins. Com. Council NYC* 96 (Aug. 1683) requiring that writs and warrants issue in the Duke's name.

[138] *Ms. Mins. Oyer and Terminer Ulster Co. 1684* fol. 13. The judgment was reversed. In the "record" of Sessions, it appears that defendant claimed the "acct." and summons did not agree, that he had not been legally summoned, and that there was no declaration and craved a nonsuit "it not being granted he would not plead." Then comes the entry: "Whereas the extraordinary occasions of his honor the governor have hindered the summons the court doth order that he cannot deny to answer." This may point to the fact that writs issued from the Governor's office but this seems unlikely in the case of actions in Sessions. At this time Ulster was in Dongan's black books for petitioning to have the right to elect their own officers, and at the June Oyer and Terminer the petitioners were prosecuted for seditiously petitioning (*ibid.* fol. 1). The Sessions entry may have reference to these troubles.

~~but of this province~~ [*sic*]. Ffor by the Customs of all courts unless actions come regularly before them they can take no cognizance of them—so the method received of process in the s^d Court of Sessions being by Summons and in that accon no summons being served according to the Customs of that Court the deft. cannot be compelled to answr.

In view of the fact that the plaintiff in error rested upon the custom of Sessions, and that the reference to the practice in England was crossed out, we are disposed to believe that the changes in process were not known to the Ulster Sessions Court in March, 1684, and hence the plaintiff in error invoked the local custom to avoid the danger of a pleading directed to the "practice and usage" of English courts which by June were known, as the other proceedings at Oyer and Terminer clearly show.[139]

In the absence of any evidence that the adoption of common law forms of process and recordation was due to statute, ordinance or proclamation, we are disposed to attribute this event to the arrival of a craftsman trained to a much higher standard of performance than anyone theretofore resident in the Province.[140] In terms of our own notions of what makes a good lawyer, the only person connected with the government who could pretend to expertness was Thomas Rudyard who became Attorney General in 1684.[141] Rudyard, while

[139] The change must have been fairly complete by October, 1684 when the act to prevent arrests of judgment and superseding executions was passed (1 *Col. Laws NY* 162). After reciting the vexation caused by arresting and reversing judgments by writs of error and *supersedeas*, a time limit in bringing attaint and error was set. It was further provided no judgment was to be stayed or reversed for lack of form or by reason of lack of pledges to prosecute, default of entering pledges, or offering documents mentioned in pleading, or by reason of omitting *vi et armis* and *contra pacem* or other mistakes in forms. The act also provided that where any person in any action, real or personal, was barred by demurrer, confession or verdict such persons or their heirs should forever be barred "as to that or the like action."

The extent of reception is further indicated in the charter of New York City (1686) in the provisions respecting jurisdiction over petit larceny and misdemeanors "according to the Laws of England and the Laws of the said Province" and the introduction of the English practice respecting committal of felons by justices of the peace (1 *Col. Laws NY* 190, 191).

[140] The comments of writers that certain figures like Matthias Nicolls, Palmer or Graham were distinguished jurists or able lawyers are misleading, and if they are based on reliable evidence we have not seen it. No one who has written on the history

of New York (and this includes Hamlin, *Legal Education in Colonial New York*) appears to have grasped the fact that the ordinary English attorney *temp.* Charles II hardly measured up to the worst of present day American standards of training and skill. The attorney's education was primarily in the construction and use of the common forms and processes, and his work belonged to the clerical side of the law. His grasp and understanding of the theoretical aspects of the law were necessarily superficial. In the words of Dugdale (*Origines Juridicales* [1680] 320) the attorneys were "ministerial persons of an inferiour nature." The policy of excluding attorneys from the Inns of Court tended to sharpen the cleavage between them and the barristers. Cf. on the whole matter 6 Holdsworth, *Hist. Eng. Law* 431 *et seq.;* Bellot, Exclusion of Attorneys from the Inns of Court, 26 *Law Quar. Rev.* 137 *et seq.;* Christian, *A Short History of Solicitors* (1897).

There was undoubtedly the greatest variation in the qualities of attorneys for they ranged from the mere copyist to the accomplished conveyancer. Until Dongan's arrival there was no person in New York whom the records disclose to have approached the expertness of the really well-trained and capable English attorney. The fact that they may have been admitted to an Inn is not even presumptive evidence of learning.

[141] There is a notice of Rudyard in Whitehead,

Deputy Governor of East Jersey, had carried out a reform of procedure in that province along common law lines.[142] His pamphlets show him to have possessed a grasp of the law much more considerable than any of his provincial associates,[143] and he is known as a champion of the use of the English language in judicial proceedings.[144] The presence in Dongan's Council of John Palmer and of Lewis Morris who were similarly placed in East Jersey[145] strengthens the inference that change may have been induced from this direction. On the other hand, once the shift was decided upon, the task of instructing the local clerks of the peace in the correct rendition of writs and enrollments was an everyday affair of such dimensions that only a well-staffed secretariat could execute. Apparently John Spragg,[146] who became provincial secretary in 1683, maintained a large clerical establishment[147] and it is possible the management of the change was directed from this office.

The court minutes which are the chief sources of information about the details of procedural reform are necessarily unsatisfactory on details of form. We have already adverted to the introduction of the venire facias for the summoning of juries,[148] and the use of indictments which surviving examples show to have been in proper if simple form duly endorsed.[149] Similarly, the informa-

---

East Jersey under the Proprietary Governments (2 ed. 1875) 164 et seq. He was superseded in East Jersey as deputy governor in February, 1684. We have been unable to ascertain the date of his appointment in New York. Dongan mentioned it in a letter of August 27, 1684. Rudyard was succeeded by James Graham, Dec. 16, 1685 (Cal. Eng. Mss. 143).

[142] Discussed in Edsall, Journal of the Courts of Common Right and Chancery 1683-1702 (1937) 39 et seq., 128 et seq. The basic statute passed in 1682 is in Leaming and Spicer, Grants, Concessions and Original Constitutions of New Jersey 233. The detailed rules of March, 1682/83 are in 13 NJ Archives 37 et seq.

[143] Several of Rudyard's pamphlets are listed in Smith, Bibliotheca Anti-Quakeriana (1873) and in 2 Smith, A Descriptive Catalogue of Friends' Books (1867). Some indication of the quality of Rudyard's legal learning is to be found in An Appendix by Way of Defence and The Second Part of the People's Antient and Just Liberties Asserted, reprinted in 1 The Phoenix (1707) 322, 350.

[144] Cf. 1 The Phoenix 400. Not too much importance is to be attached to this fact as a basis of inference. Most of the forms in Dalton's Countrey Justice (1677) are in English, and contemporary Sessions records indicate widespread use of English precepts. A copy of Dalton is listed in the inventory (1689) of William Coxe who sat as justice of the peace in the New York Quarter Sessions; cf. H.R. Ms. Wills Liber 14A, 405.

[145] Cal. Council Mins. NY 7; 13 NJ Archives 4, 6, 8.

[146] There appears to be very little known about Spragg. The Grays Inn Admissions Register 1521–1887 336 describes him as "late of Uttoxeter, Co. Stafford, now of New York, Amer., Sec. to the Governor there." Spragg was admitted to the Inn on July 15, 1685, while he was in America. He does not appear to have been admitted to the bar. We have found no notice of Spragg's career after his return to England in 1687. A check of wills at Somerset House reveals that a John Spragg died in Barbados before May, 1701, the date of the act of administration, but there is nothing to identify this Spragg with the New York Secretary. It is worth noting that the will of William Spragg of Uttoxeter, probated May 16, 1645, contains a bequest to John Spragg, a minor son, "all my books manuscripts and paper 'draughts of presidents.'" This last item was courteously supplied us by the registrar of Lichfield Consistory.

[147] Cf. Dongan to the King, Mar. 2, 1686/87 (3 Doc. Rel. Col. Hist. NY 423).

[148] Supra 336. A sample of the form with the return endorsed on the face is in 35 NY Col. Mss. 80.

[149] E.g., ibid. 1a, 1b (Kings Co.); H.R. Parch. 196 L 7 (NY Co.). In the Oyer and Terminer minutes and the Sessions minutes of New York and Albany counties the indictments are set forth at large.

tion which was used rather liberally during the regime of Governor Dongan was also cast in the accepted phraseology of English practice including also the prayer for the issuance of due process.[150] With the present limited record resources it is nearly impossible to determine how closely the lines respecting process drawn by the English courts were followed, viz., the subpoena in informations, the *venire facias ad respondendum* for misdemeanors and the capias, *alias* and *pluries* for felonies.

The Oyer and Terminer minutes for New York County contain little on original process. In one case the record states that the defendant (indicted for larceny) was arrested by the sheriff.[151] The other entries relate to indictments for nuisance where the court orders appearance or the giving of security to appear.[152] There is nothing whatever on original criminal process in the Ulster Oyer and Terminer records.

The Sessions minutes are not more satisfactory, for neither in those for New York or for Albany, the most complete records for this period, are the process entries adequate.[153] On the civil side the usual entry "attached to answer" gives no clue to the form of process. Equally vague are the orders in certain criminal cases, viz., that the defendants "be sent for,"[154] or that they enter into recognizance for appearance,[155] or the two orders in combination.[156] In certain cases the sheriff is ordered that he "doe make persuit" where there had been prison breach,[157] or is ordered to "goe forthwith and apprehend the defendant as well by water as by land and abord shipp as well as on ashore and bring him forthwith"—a poetical mandate for a capias upon which the prosaic *non est inventus* was returned.[158] There are further orders, such as binding over defendants who had confessed felonies to Oyer and Terminer to receive sentence,[159] or committing for the next Gaol Delivery,[160] or exacting security for appear-

---

[150] *H.R. Pleadings* Pl. K. 459 (Info. v. Pink *Charles*); K. 456 (Info. v. Sloop *Lewis*); *Ms. Mins. NYCQS 1683/84–1694* 33, May 5, 1685 (Info. v. Rich. Pattishall).
[151] 7 *Ms. Mins. Council* (Reverse) 24 (King v. Paulus).
[152] *Ibid.* 32 (King v. Leisler; King v. Inhab. of Bevers Graft; King v. Inhab. of Nutstreet). Two other entries respecting process are the order that Alice Fisher, indicted for having a bastard, be rendered to the Court of Sessions to be prosecuted (*ibid.* 32); and the order for Hugh Ridell who had stabbed Vaughton to be brought to the bar with the cause of commitment which suggests a *mittimus* had been used (*ibid.* 50).
[153] Compare the record Nicolls v. Dyer, 1685 (*H.R. Mss. Papers* and *Ms. Mins. NYCQS 1683/84–1694* 10, 12 [1684]). In a separate minute of

the Sessions of August 4, 1685 (*H.R. Mss. Papers*) the *habeas corpus* [*ad respondendum*] to Oyer and Terminer is noted (Bryan v. Brewerton). The habeas corpus to remove causes to Oyer and Terminer was used as early as February, 1684, in the Mayor's Court (Phillips v. Melyne, *Ms. Mins. Mayor's Ct. NYC 1680–1683/84* Feb. 11, 1683/84).
[154] King v. Edmunds (*Ms. Mins. NYCQS 1683/84–1694* 142, Nov. 1, 1698); King v. Baton (*ibid.* 141, Nov. 1, 1688).
[155] King v. De Peu (*ibid.* 141, Nov. 7, 1688).
[156] King v. Farrell (*ibid.* 142, Nov. 1, 1688).
[157] King v. Thomassen (*ibid.* 2, Feb. 5, 1683/84).
[158] King v. Parcher (*ibid.* 141, Nov. 1, 1688).
[159] King v. Paulus (*ibid.* 32, Feb. 3, 1684/85).
[160] King v. Hellman; King v. Perkins (*ibid.* 141,

ance at a future Sessions.[161] The entries in the Albany minutes are fewer: the "sent for" formula,[162] binding to appear at Oyer and Terminer, or custody.[163] To the same effect are the scattered entries in Kings County—the notices of arrest or orders to take into custody.[164]

If we can put trust in the calendar of the burned volumes of the *New York Colonial Mss.* where various types of process are described by their technical names, e.g., scire facias, habeas corpus, capias,[165] we are led to infer that the common law baptism of the provincial writs having at last come about, the precepts themselves were in due form.

The changes just described were not effected without some temporary opposition on the part of the inhabitants, used to the informality of procedure under the Duke's Laws. The thoughts of those preoccupied with the liberties of Englishmen, and who longed for what the grand jurymen of 1681 had termed the "unparralleled forme and method of Government"[166] in England, had soared above the scrimshaw which made it function. It must consequently have come as a shock to the citizen who had believed liberties assured by the enactment of the "Charter of Liberties," to be nonsuited for want of form in his declaration, and to discover that a habeas corpus was not necessarily a writ for release. If the courts had been staffed with persons of juristic parts these shocks could have been eased. But the best of the judges of that period were mere attorneys not so well trained that they would prefer ends of justice to the facile solution which an insistence upon form invited.

The colonists' reaction was written in the Act of 1684 "to prevent Arrests of Judgments"[167] by which it was sought to terminate pettifogging about form and allow the judges discretion to have causes tried on their merits. The act is virtually a copy of the English statute 16 & 17 Car. II c.8, with the deletion of the section that had excepted criminal proceedings from the effects of the statute. It may be inferred from this excision that the New York act was intended to cover all forms of procedure. The evidence is wanting to prove that this provincial act accomplished the object for which it was designed, for an examination of even the civil actions does not disclose that the tendency toward imitating English technicalities abated. But the selection of this particular English statute for enactment in New York is generally significant in

---

Nov. 7, 1688); King v. Shaw (*ibid.* 147, May 1, 1689).

[161] King v. Square (*ibid.* 142, Nov. 1, 1688).

[162] *Ms. Mins. Albany Co. Sess. 1685–89* 28 (King v. Casperse); 57.

[163] *Ibid.* 22 (Info. v. Tounise).

[164] *Ms. Kings Co. Ct. & Rd. Recs. 1668–1766* 370, 384, 393, 397; and cf. *ibid.* 368, regarding a transfer to Oyer and Terminer by habeas corpus.

[165] *Cal. Eng. Mss.* 120 *et seq.*

[166] *Proc. Gen. Ct. of Assizes 1680–82* 16.

[167] 1 *Col. Laws NY* 162.

establishing how rapidly the procedural transformation had moved. What is no less striking is the abrupt abandonment of the attitude revealed by this provincial act when Jacob Leisler, a few years later, promoted a reversion to the early forms. The inhabitants were bitter in their complaints that common law forms were flouted and were eager to have the "due process" introduced by Dongan restored.

We have discussed the early history of process so meticulously not merely because of the light it casts upon the mechanics of transforming the legal system of the province from Dutch to English, but because by tracing procedural forms it is possible to ascertain when the common law itself, and the practices of English superior courts displace the replicas of English country practices. The evolutionary phase begun under Nicolls ends abruptly during Dongan's regime, and thereafter begins the phase of imitation, this tending inevitably toward an embrace of professional technicality. The historian's task ceases thus to be one of following a development and becomes one of ascertaining how many of the English forms were accepted and how they were employed. From the year 1691 onward, so far as any problem of development is concerned, it will be chiefly to observe how improvements in the skill of the bench and bar tended to accelerate the naturalization of common law forms.

Up to the present juncture we have dealt almost entirely with the process against defendants since there is little recorded respecting other varieties. But as the sources for the eighteenth century in New York become richer the process problem becomes more complex. We shall have to consider process relating to persons charged with or suspected of crime and also the process against officials, process to compel attendance by jurors, attachments for contempt and the process against witnesses.

The most important of these problems is that relating to defendants. Early commentators on the law had considered process properly to be only the mandates which issued after presentment or indictment.[168] The means of securing a person suspected or accused, but not yet indicted, were discussed as methods of arrest,[169] the reason being that until indictment no "process" in a strict sense was supposed to lie since process issued only upon matter of record. Any precept issued against a defendant before indictment was merely a "warrant." The practice of issuing warrants of arrest on mere suspicion was of questionable

---

[168] Compare Lambard, *Eirenarcha* (1614) 519; Cowell, *Interpreter* (1672) *s.v.* Process.
[169] Thus, in 2 Hawkins, *Pleas of the Crown,* the matter on warrants is in chap. 13 "Of Arrests by Public Officers." Process proper is discussed in his chap. 27.

validity but had become so general that the King's Bench early in the eighteenth century was reluctantly compelled to admit that justices' practice had become the law of the land.[170] Although it was not until the nineteenth century, when procedural reform blunted the old distinctions, that warrants were referred to as "process," for our purposes it will be convenient to accept this more modern conception and to consider the warrant as a species of "process."

At the opening of the eighteenth century in England the arrest of defendants who had not been taken red-handed was generally effected by hue and cry warrants or by warrants drawn "on surmise." Where it was necessary to commit a *mittimus* was used. After indictment, if the defendant was not already in custody the common law of process had developed on the basis of the seriousness of the offense. If the crime was a felony the actual securing and safekeeping of the defendant's person were requisite. Hence if he had not been taken before indictment an order to take him (the capias) issued, and if this failed upon due repetition (*alias* and *pluries capias*) his exaction and outlawry would be commanded. For minor offenses, which had come to be known as misdemeanors, first process was a mere summons—the *venire facias ad respondendum*. Recalcitrance, however, involved progressively more stringent process, distraint, capias and, finally, outlawry. This basic scheme was conditioned further by the matter of jurisdiction, for example, as in private courts where the extent of the franchise limited the court's mandate power, or in cases where summary jurisdiction was exercised by justices in special sessions or meetings. The Crown information, moreover, had its own initial process, the *subpoena ad respondendum* fashioned after Chancery practice.

It is a circumstance of considerable moment that even at the end of the seventeenth century there existed no adequate handbook on process, or even a chapter which attempted to make some system out of the welter of rules which appear in the abridgments and texts as a series of particularizations. More than any other branch of the law a knowledge of process depended upon a knowledge of actual practice. It is true that in the course of the eighteenth century the publication of Hawkins' and then of Hale's *Pleas of the Crown* provided some guide to the subject. But essentially the introduction overseas of English practice depended upon the range of the lawyer's previous experience at home, and upon the tempo at which the instruction of local officials could be executed.[171] Process was the one juncture in a proceeding at law where

---

[170] Regina v. Tracy (6 *Mod*. 179).

[171] Compare, for example, the handful of precedents enrolled in the late seventeenth century West-chester Sessions minute book (*Mins. Westch. Ct. Sess. 1657–96*) with the nearly contemporary process book kept by the Clerk in New York City (en-

the intelligent cooperation of inferior officers was essential, for no matter how sagely a cause was managed in court, the stupidity or ignorance of a sheriff or constable could cast a blight that might be irremediable. As we shall shortly see, the education of the peace officers was a problem most keenly sensed by the Supreme Court.[172] In the country Sessions where the bench had little training in the microscopia of the law the effects of mistakes were momentous only if a city lawyer were present to interpose his skill.[173] It was in these courts that vagary lingered and was slowly eradicated.

Most of the provincial variants were the result of ignorance, or were mere clerical malapropisms. They were not due to any desire to reform or simplify.[174] The colonists suffered from a defendant psychology, and were consequently prepared to endure useless technicalities for the insurance afforded by the due process guarantees explicit and implicit in the common law scheme. The function of process against persons suspected of or charged with a crime was to secure their attendance in court to answer what might be alleged against them, and eventually to enable the court, where defense failed, to render judgment and to have inflicted the sanctions provided by law. "Due process" was the sum of the glosses added to the authoritarian conception by many generations of defendants, and so secured by judicial decision and otherwise as to be an indisseverable part of it. Thus process could function only subject to such limitations as that notice be adequate both as to the pendency of proceedings and the nature of the charge, that certain types of precept were proper to certain offenses, and that the succession of processes was fixed. All of this was well understood by the colonists, who, as we have noticed, had experienced the disappearance of safeguards during Leisler's regime when common law forms were abandoned.[175] They understood also that in a government where prerogative was still lusty, ancient process and the precedents which had grown about it were their most certain protection in Crown cases.

Summary Process

The openhanded reception of common law process in all its ramifications involved of course an acceptance of its still unsettled problems. One of the most troublesome was the process in summary proceedings. This jurisdiction

---

dorsed *Mins. of Town Clerk 1701–06* but which is in reality a record of process issued in various civil cases). The difference in the range of knowledge is striking.

[172] *Infra* 454 *et seq.*

[173] Thus, for example, Queen v. Gilbert Living-

ston (*Ms. Mins. Ulster Co. Sess. 1711/12–1720* Sept. 2, 1712).

[174] Cf. the discussion of the mittimus *infra* 430.

[175] See, for example, the complaints in 3 *Doc. Rel. Col. Hist. NY* 644 *et seq.*, 665.

had long been committed to the lay justices of the peace, and there had never been any adequate control by the central courts. Even Blackstone, who could find perfection where none existed, was obliged to own that here process was very speedy and that the only check was the requirement of a summons.[176] Actually under the influence of the justices' manuals particular usages had developed in respect of certain types of jurisdiction,[177] a tendency which is manifest also in provincial New York.

As respects first process the colonial records from an early date onwards show that a summons was usual (even if no more than a verbal warning)[178] where courts proceeded summarily, except in nuisance cases where orders for abatement would be made without reference to the attendance of a defendant.[179] We have found some late evidence that the usual had become necessary as a matter of law. In 1773 the Supreme Court made an order to show cause why an information should not be filed against certain justices for convicting one Ward of stopping a road "without summoning him to make his defence."[180]

Practically, of course, since a large part of summary jurisdiction was only ultimately penal in purpose, and was concerned with compelling a defendant to do something or to forbear in certain conduct, his attendance was necessary.

---

[176] 4 Blackstone, *Commentaries* c.20, 282.

[177] Partly because of the arrangement of textual matter in terms of particular offenses and partly because of the specific sample forms.

[178] E.g., as appears from the way in which "warning" and summons are used in *Ms. Mins. Ulster Co. Sess. 1711/12–1720.*

[179] *Supra* 364. There are some early cases that show the defendant summoned, e.g., King v. Vincent (*Ms. Mins. NYCQS 1694–1731/32* 25, 26, May 4, 5, 1697). In New York City the Quarter Sessions in 1732 ordered the aldermen to inspect nuisances and cause their removal (*Ms. Mins. NYCQS 1732–62* 15, Aug. 3, 1732).

The following is a writ to abate used in 1771 in the case of the Oswego market (*Ms. Mins. SCJ 1769–72* [Engr.] 316): "George the Third . . . to our Sheriff of . . . New York Greeting Whereas heretofore . . . at our Court . . . by the Oath of . . . [24 named] Good and lawful Men . . . it was presented That a Certain street in the said City of New York . . . [that is Broadway] is a certain ancient Common Street . . . and that there . . . stands . . . a certain Building of the length of one hundred and fifty six feet . . . the Oswego Market By reason whereof the same Common Street . . . is greatly obstructed . . . so that the liege Subjects . . . could not . . . go . . . without great Danger of their Lives To the great Dam-

age and common Nusance, and to the endangering the Lives of all the Liege Subjects . . . And Whereas such were the proceedings . . . before us that by the Consideration of the same Court It was then and there ordered that unless the same Inquisition shod. be traversed within 20 Days that Our Writ issue to the sher' of . . . New York to abate the Nusance af[d] And now we having on our Behalf received in our Court before us that no Traverse of the said Inquisition . . . hath hitherto been had . . . and we being unwilling that such . . . enormous and intollerable Nusance should be longer sustained there We command you that without Delay you prostrate and abate the said Building and Nusance least any Damage . . . to any of our . . . subjects sho[d] happen in futur[e] and how you shall have executed this our prece[pt] make known to us at our City of New York . . . remitting to us this Writ Witness . . ." (*J. T. Kempe Lawsuits* L–O).

[180] King v. Barnes and Conner (*Ms. Mins. SCJ 1772–76* [Rough] 95). With respect to notice of trial after joinder of issue, cf. *infra* 612, and also the cases where the Attorney General or the court would order the matter (King v. Whey, *Ms. Mins. SCJ 1750–54* [Engr.] 253, 286; *H.R. Pleadings* Pl. K. 923; King v. Brush, *Ms. Mins. SCJ 1762–64* [Engr.] 21, 129).

Thus in poor relief cases orders to maintain, or for recognizance to secure maintenance[181] could be effectual only if the defendant was in court. Similarly the orders in bastardy cases,[182] those involving indentured servants,[183] and those for the disposition of vagrants[184] all would have been futile unless the defendant was haled before the magistrates. To this end the process against recalcitrants even in summary causes might run to a capias,[185] or the justices would issue a *mittimus* for commitment trusting apparently to luck that a constable would succeed in apprehending his prisoner.

It should be observed that although a magistrate in summary cases might proceed immediately to secure a defendant's arrest, this was only done occasionally for the summons was the rule. Probably in all cases the same form was used, for the records continually use the expression "common process." The variations occur in the final process chiefly because of the large discretion with which the justices were vested in the matter of orders. Here the pattern is much the same as that followed in England. There were certain limits to be observed in poor relief or in bastardy cases, and less rigid ones in the case of servants or vagrants, and here we believe that the manuals were influential where colonial statutes had not given directions. The act cited above dealing with bastardy and

181 E.g., Queen v. de la Montagne, ordered to take in wife and family (*Ms. Mins. NYCQS 1694–1731/32* 160, May 4, 1709); King v. Willson, ordered to give recognizance to save city against supporting his wife (*Ms. Mins. NYCQS 1732–62* 218, May 6, 1747).

182 A summons was first process, King v. Van Buren (*H.R. Parch.* 25 D 5); King v. Morin, ordered to give bond to save parish harmless (*Ms. Mins. NYCQS 1694–1731/32* 270, Aug. 3, 1714); King v. Sharpe, committed until sureties found (*ibid.* 17, 21, 25, Nov. 4, 1696, Feb. 3, 1696/97, May 4, 1697); Queen v. Onclebagg, ordered committed (*ibid.* 192, Feb. 7, 1710/11); King v. Laguill (*Ms. Kings Co. Ct. & Rd. Recs. 1692–1825* 28, 29); King v. Ketcham (*Ms. Mins. NYCQS 1760–72* 359). Cf. King v. Mary Lawrence, *supra* 102 n. 186.

An act of assembly of 1774 for the relief of parishes from bastards provided that on the examination and oath of the mother of a bastard, the justices might, on application made to them by the overseers of the poor or by any substantial householder, issue a warrant for the immediate apprehending of the person charged to be the father of the bastard in order to bring the reputed father before a justice of the peace. The justice before whom the reputed father was brought was authorized to commit the defendant to the common jail or house of correction unless the father should enter a recog-

nizance to appear at Quarter Sessions and abide and perform such orders as should be made by the court of Quarter Sessions "in pursuance of an act passed in the 18th year of the reign of her Majesty, Queen Elizabeth, concerning bastards begotten and born out of lawful Matrimony." The act also provided that the defendant be committed to jail or the house of correction might apply to the justices to have them summon the overseer of the poor or the substantial householder to show cause why the person should not be discharged. There was also an order in this statute allowing the churchwardens or overseers of the poor to seize the goods and chattels of the putative father or the mother in order to provide for the maintenance of the child in the event the parents ran away (5 *Col. Laws NY* 689).

183 E.g., the apprentice orders in *Ms. Mins. NYCQS 1694–1731/32* 338, 343, 374, 376, 535; *Ms. Mins. NYCQS 1732–62* 155; *Ms. Mins. NYCQS 1760–72* 115, 116. These orders might be to return to work, to discharge, to be committed or to be lashed.

184 *Supra* 108. The vagrants could be set at hard labor or merely confined (King v. Susannah Norton, *Ms. Mins. NYCQS 1732–62* 169, Aug. 1, 1744) or lashed (King v. Bridget Wilkins, *ibid.* 87, May 4, 1738; King v. Mary Carney and Elizabeth Hall, *ibid.* 178, Feb. 6, 1744/45).

185 As in King v. Sharpe, *supra* n. 182.

the various vagrancy statutes are examples of a disposition to make explicit the limits of magisterial authority.[186]

In one important class of cases, that relating to slaves, the colonists had to pick their own way. Although slaves were sometimes accorded the usual indictment process and trial available to free men—as in the Negro Conspiracy of 1712 where the defendants were all brought in by capias and were held in custody pending trial[187]—the usual practice was to try them summarily. There are a few cases in the late seventeenth century which show the commencement of this practice,[188] and in 1702 a provincial act specifically provided for summary trial in cases of assemblies of slaves, assaults on white women, trespasses and thefts.[189] This statute at one point explains that slaves are property and cannot without great loss or detriment to their masters "be subjected in all Cases Criminal to the strict Rules of the Laws of England." A variety of reviving acts as well as new statutes were enacted and eventually the law took final form in the act of assembly of 1730.[190] The method of apprehension of such culprits when complaint was made to one justice of the peace was by a warrant of the justice of the peace to the next constable to apprehend the offenders and cause the witnesses to come before him. If the justice of peace believed the slave guilty he was to commit him to prison and certify the cause to the next two justices of peace and they were to associate themselves with five freeholders for the trial of the cause. In one such trial, *King v. Jannean* (1738), Chief Justice De Lancey sat with New York City justices of the peace and five freeholders, and the jailer was ordered to set Jannean, the accused slave, at the bar. This would seem to indicate that Jannean had already been apprehended by a single justice's warrant and had been committed pending his trial before the justices and freeholders.[191] An example of the type of warrant used in slave cases is given below.[192]

[186] *Supra* n. 182. In certain cases no effort to deal with process appears to have been made. This is true of highway statutes which were enacted in great numbers. The orders of magistrates are also in vague language. Thus the Quarter Sessions order of 1692 regarding the duty of the carmen to repair the highways merely speaks of fines such as the Mayor may require for contempt (*Ms. Mins. NYCQS 1683/84–1694* 158, Nov. 1, 1692). Cf. also *Ms. Mins. NYCQS 1694–1731/32* 124, 132, May 7, Nov. 4, 1707; *Ms. Mins. NYCQS 1722–1742/43* 33, Feb. 5, 1723/24. We have seen no process used in highway cases, and it is possible when the statutes speak of "warning" inhabitants to repair mere oral warning is meant. The fines for nonper-

formance were exacted by a warrant of distress; cf., for example, 4 *Col. Laws NY* 510, 833.

[187] *Supra* 118.

[188] Cf. King v. Joe (*Ms. Mins. NYCQS 1694–1731/32* 28, June 10, 1697); King v. Tham (*Ms. Mins. Ulster Co. Sess. 1693–98* Jan. 7, 8, 1695/96).

[189] 1 *Col. Laws NY* 519. Cf. also *ibid.* 631 (1708), 761 (1712), 922 (1717).

[190] 2 *Col. Laws NY* 679 (1730).

[191] Meetings for the Trials of Slaves, July 20, 1728 (*Ms. Mins. NYCQS 1722–1742/43* [Rough] 348).

[192] "City of New York SS: Robert Lurting Esqr Mayor . . . to the Marshalls High Constable and all Other Constables . . . Greeting. Whereas

So far as we can judge from the rather scanty sources regarding the administration of summary jurisdiction, the colonists did not tolerate the growth of the abuses respecting process that existed in England. This may have been due to sensitivity about notice and hearing (early manifestations of which have already been noted), but it is more probable that the categorical statements in handbooks like Dalton's *Countrey Justice*[193] about the necessity of precepts were responsible. The same influence we believe is also to be seen in the handling of a second vexed problem—the warrant.

Process before Indictment

It has already been explained that the common law of process had developed on the basis that unless a person was taken in crime or by hue and cry, process lay only after indictment. Chiefly as a result of the statutes 1 & 2 Philip and Mary c.13[194] and 2 & 3 Philip and Mary c.10, which enlarged the powers of justices of the peace respecting suspected felons, warrants of arrest before indictment came into general use. Strictly speaking, these precepts were not due process in the accepted sense, and there was much controversy about them: whether a single justice could issue a warrant for an offense cognizable by two or more, whether a warrant to arrest on suspicion was proper, and what matter had to be incorporated in the text of a warrant.

It is important to observe that Sir Edward Coke, an authority most venerated in the colonies, had expressed various opinions not easy to reconcile. In his twelfth *Report,* published posthumously, he had reported that where a justice of the peace was given a certain jurisdiction he was impliedly given powers to make out warrants.[195] In his *Fourth Institute* he had denied explicitly that warrants to arrest on suspicion were lawful,[196] yet in his *Second Institute* he im-

Francis Sylvester . . . hath . . . Complained unto me, that yesterday . . . a . . . slave . . . Cato . . . Violently assaulted and abused his Daughter Susannah Sylvester . . . fourteen years . . . and attempted to Commit a Rape upon her body in Contempt of an Act of General Assembly . . . [the Act of 1730] These are Therefore in his Majesty's Name to Command you . . . that Immediately on sight hereof, You . . . Apprehend the Said Negro slave . . . & forthwith bring him before me or some Other Justice of the Peace . . . to be Examined touching the Premises and further to be dealt with According to Law And hereof fail not at your Perills, Given under my hand and seal . . . this 21st. day of January [1733/34] . . ."
Meetings for the Trial of Slaves (*Ms. Mins.*

NYCQS 1722–1742/43 [Rough] 329). The *mittimus* used is on page 330. For other meetings, *Ms. Mins. Ulster Co. Sess. 1711/12–1720* Apr. 21, 1718; *Ms. Mins. Dutchess Co. Sess.* Liber A, June 10, 1735; *Ms. Files Dutchess Co. 1755* Apr. 24, 1749, Oct. 4, 1751, Sept. 17, 1755 (the warrant listed in the costs); *Ms. Files Ulster Co.* Bundle D, June 19, 1741, Bundle F, June 22, 1728 (Indians—warrant ordered).
[193] *Supra* nn. 119, 121. Dalton, *Countrey Justice* (1677) 460.
[194] Discussed *supra* 94 *et seq.*
[195] Oath before Justices, 12 *Co. Rep.* 130, 131. The report was constantly cited for a good deal more than is explicitly stated in it.
[196] *Fourth Institute* 177.

pliedly recognized the sufficiency of such precepts if they were specific enough.[197] The conditions in the colonies were such that it would have been most imprudent to have harkened to the niggling of the lawyers. Fortunately, in 1705, Holt, C.J., had given his blessing to the justices' practice[198] on a basis broad enough to permit an untrammelled colonial development.

We have seen nothing to suggest that warrants were not regarded as due process in New York. By following Coke's admonition that they set forth with "convenient certainty" details of the matter charged, the difficulties which arose in England with respect to general warrants and the discretionary omission of the cause[199] did not develop. Probably, too, some effort was made to do things with exactness. When the jurisdiction of Orange County was detached from New York City and a separate General Sessions instituted, the records show the justices had some concern for proper handling of process. In April, 1704, the clerk was ordered to secure an opinion from the Attorney General whether a new sheriff could proceed on warrants issued to but not returned by his predecessor, and in 1707 the court refused a special warrant after an escape because the sheriff had previously applied to the Governor.[200] Some years later the Westchester Sessions doubting its power to issue a warrant for a contempt instructed the clerk of the peace to write the Attorney General.[201]

It was only occasionally that some question of law arose, usually with respect to an abuse of authority. The most important of these problems was over the hue and cry warrants. The records show that this device was not often used by the courts in the eighteenth century[202] although it had enjoyed a vogue during the proprietary period. Apparently the tradition had been established that such warrants, actually no more effective than the advertisements for wanted criminals that adorn contemporary post offices, were to be issued by the Governor. In any event the governors had the temerity to assert an exclusive prerogative in this matter to the exclusion of the courts. The matter is dealt with in Chief Justice Mompesson's report on maladministration:

[197] *Second Institute* 590.
[198] Reg. v. Tracy (6 *Mod.* 179).
[199] Cf. 2 Hawkins, *Pleas of the Crown* c.13, §§10, 25.
[200] *Ms. Mins. Orange Co. Sess. 1703–08* Apr. 24, 1704, Oct. 27, 1707.
[201] *Ms. Mins. Westch. Co. Sess. 1710–23* Dec. 5, 1710.
[202] Unless it was embraced within the usual order of "common process." But see *Ms. Mins. Cir. 1716–17* 31. Maritje Tyler presented for murder of her bastard child, the court orders a hue and cry be issued. The Sessions probably used the hue and cry

more generally than the minutes show; see the Ulster Co. warrant (1719), the Dutchess Co. warrant (1721) in *Book of Supervisors of Dutchess Co. 1718–22* 21, 46. Cf. also *Ms. Files Ulster Co.* Bundle F, Meeting of Justices, Aug. 20, 21, 1728. The ancient practice of actual hot pursuit persisted. Where an indictment for burglary was found against James Wilson, the court learning that the property stolen belonged to Isaac Sears and that he had "made fresh pursuit after the prisoner," ordered the property be restored after the indictment was confessed (*Ms. Mins. SCJ 1756–61* [Rough] 128, 129).

Huy and Cry. Of the same nature is the Governours granting Huy and Cry; by the Common law on a felony committed the Constable might and ought to levy huy and cry, so he may and ought to do still in some cases, and where the Justices of Peace by Stat. 4 E. 1. de Officio Coronatoris and 13 E. 1. C. 1. and other statutes, are informed to levy huy and cry, they are punishable if they doe it not, and so are the Constables where they are impowered to doe it; yet the Governour here reprimanded the Cheif Justice of this Province for granting a Huy and Cry after a person that burnt part of and then broke out of the Common Goal, the Governour claiming, the sole power of granting Huy and Crys. Upon what ground that motion was framed I know not, unless from a fee of 3s. in the blind table of Fees of this Province which the Assembly omitted in their late Bill of Fees, and the insisting on it is not only directly repugnant to the laws of England, but would tend to the escape of all fellons especially when the offences are committed at any distance from the Governour.[203]

It is apparent from other matter in Mompesson's report that the real dispute was not the hue and cry warrant but whether or not the Governor had the power at all to issue warrants. There had been wrangling in England over the powers of the Secretary of State or members of the Privy Council to issue warrants, they not being justices of the peace,[204] and the situation in New York more or less paralleled this controversy. The Governor's prerogatives in the matter had been settled during the period before 1690, but the extant sources are not illuminating on how far the displacement of the Governor's "special warrants" by common law process had resulted in any destruction of established custom. The records are even more obscure respecting related authority of the Council. The first really important occasion upon which this body undertook to issue process was in 1701/02 in connection with the Bayard case.

On January 16, 1701/02 a meeting was called to consider certain "treasonable addresses." The Council found on examination that Bayard and Hutchins were the principal ringleaders and accordingly "on consideration of the premises it is ordered that a messenger of the Council do summons the said Alderman Hutchins to appear before this Board." Bayard was also summoned and when he appeared on January 17, 1701, he was asked to deliver up the addresses. This he refused to do claiming he had done nothing illegal. The Council thereupon ordered that Bayard give security in £1000 with one surety to

---

[203] 5 *Doc. Rel. Col. Hist. NY* 410; compare 4 Blackstone, *Commentaries* 293, 294.
[204] The matter is discussed in Entick v. Carring-

ton (11 Hargrave, *State Trials* 313 at 317, 319) where the early cases are reviewed.

appear at the next Supreme Court to answer to an indictment or information there "to be exhibited against them at the King's Suite by the Attorney General."[205]

There is scanty evidence of abusive use of governors' warrants for apparently it was only on some extraordinary occasion that these were issued. On July 22, 1706, Lord Cornbury issued a warrant to the justices in Kings regarding illegal assemblages of negroes including the extraordinary command that if the negroes could not be taken they might be fired upon and killed.[206] This was followed on January 23, 1706/07 by a warrant to the sheriff of New York ordering him to arrest Francis Makemie and John Hampton who were preaching without a license,[207] and again in the same year a warrant to arrest Thomas Byerly, Collector of the Revenue, on a charge of embezzlement.[208] But two years later it was the Council which ordered the preparation of a writ *ne exeat* against Byerly.[209]

Altogether the proof now available of an abuse of prerogative is slight, and Mompesson's complaints were without result. Not only did the Governor continue to issue hue and cry warrants, particularly in cases where demands for extradition were made, but the executive arm (by which we mean the Council as well as the Governor) did not surrender its prerogatives with respect to process and continued now and then to fabricate its own precepts. We have mentioned the warrant used when the boundary dispute with New Jersey was raging,[210] and some years later in the controversy with John Henry Lydius

[205] 8 *Ms. Mins. Council* 208 *et seq.; Misc. Mss. Bayard;* cf. *supra* 83 *et seq.,* 231.

[206] *Ms. Conveyances Kings Co.* Liber 3, 70.

[207] "You are . . . Comanded to take into your custody the Bodies of Francis Makemie, and John Hampton (pretended Dissenting Protestant Ministers) for Preaching in this Province w[th]out quallifying themselves according to an Act of Parliament . . . [1 William & Mary] without any lycense first obtained and them safely to keep till they shall be discharged by due Course of Law, and for so doing this shall be your Sufficient Warrant." This is from a recital contained in the sheriff's return to a habeas corpus issued by Mompesson (*H.R. Parch.* 57 C 7) to learn the cause of commitment.

[208] ". . . You are hereby required and commanded to take into yo[r] custody the body of Thomas Byerly and him safely to keep until he find such security as I shall approve of to answere . . . on account of the Revenue" (*Misc. Mss. Wm. Blathwayt 1689–99*).

[209] 10 *Ms. Mins. Council* 654, May 19, 1709.

[210] *Supra* 299 n. 62. The difficulty one faces in coming to a conclusion about the frequency of executive warrants arises from the absence of entries in judicial records and the destruction of the executive manuscripts. Thus the papers in relation to an Orange County riot (43 *NY Col. Mss.*) were destroyed, and the *Cal. Eng. Mss.* 461, is not sufficiently explicit. The existence of a governor's warrant is, however, to be inferred from an entry in James Alexander's papers: "This day being the 21st of September The Sheriff made return of a warrant bearing date the 18th Day of July to him directed to take Thomas Swarthout . . . [and others] and having taken Bernardus Swarthout pursuant to the Govern[r]'[s] orders We do order that the Said Bernardus Be brought in order to be Examined, the Said Bernardus hath been Examined and He denys all the accusations alleged against in his Excell[cys] orders, but by no other proof but by his own mouth therefore ordered that the Said Bernardus give Security for his appearance at the Supream Court . . . [on the 2d Tuesday of October] to answer . . . pursuant to his Excellcys the Governour's orders" (*James Alexander Papers* Box 48). On Oct. 9, 1723, an information was filed against Bernardus Swartwout and others in the Supreme Court (*Ms. Mins. SCJ 1723–27* 23).

a conciliar warrant was again used after the sheriff of Albany had not been able to secure Lydius' attendance upon the Council.[211]

It is beyond our purpose to inquire into the relation of a Governor's own warrant and that ordered in Council, and when one was regarded as more appropriate than the other, for any exact conclusions involve a consideration of all types of precept ever used, civil and fiscal as well as criminal. Similarly, we cannot explore the causes which led the executive sometimes to ignore the Supreme Court which would have been the normal resort when judicial proceedings of any sort were contemplated. Probably the occasions when the executive assumed the initiative were usually due to a political complication, as when Colden was obliged to invent his writ of appeal. An example of what we regard as the normal (as against prerogative) way of handling a case of "high nature" is one which arose in 1765. In this year prosecutions were initiated by *qui tam* against a group of men for maintenance and selling pretended land titles. It was decided, however, that one of the group, Samuel Monroe, should be prosecuted by information and Kempe thought it advisable to apprehend the defendant by warrant before the information was filed. Accordingly, on March 7, 1765, Chief Justice Horsmanden issued a warrant the text of which is given below.[212]

[211] *J. T. Kempe Lawsuits* L–O. Note that on December 15, 1761, the sheriff attended the Council with the body of Lydius who said he had not previously appeared because he was unwell. Lydius defended his actions in surveying the lands contrary to the proclamation by saying he claimed title to the lands under a deed from the Governor of Massachusetts Bay, but the Council being of opinion that the deed vested no title in Lydius "Ordered . . . that the High Sheriff . . . do keep the said John Henry Lydius in Custody." On December 16, 1761, the sheriff again brought Lydius in and the latter was "discharged from his Contempt . . . and was also Discharged out of the Custody of the said Sherif upon his Entering into Recognizance before Mr. Justice Horsmanden . . . [in £5000 for his appearance at the next Supreme Court] to answer to an Information for his Contempt in Surveying . . . contrary to the Proclamation . . . and also to an Information . . . [for intrusion on Crown lands]" (*J. T. Kempe Lawsuits* L–O "Copy of Proceedings of Council—J.H.L. 10 Jan., 1762").

Compare also the order of Council to the Attorney General to prosecute George Klock for defrauding the Indians and the order by Lt. Gov. Colden on April 7, 1762, that Klock "stand committed" until he enter a recognizance in £3000 to be of good behavior to all especially the Canajoharie Indians and to appear to answer in the Supreme Court such information as filed against him.

In c. II n. 152 we referred to boundary riots.

An order made in Council on January 28, 1753, directing the sheriffs of Albany and Dutchess to apprehend the rioters who under color of grants from Massachusetts Bay or New Hampshire entered lands granted under the Great Seal of the Province of New York. Added to these warrants was a power to commit to jail and also "if need be to summon the aid of the Popl of the said counties." The latter is one of the few references to a *posse comitatus* we have found in our research (*NY Misc. Mss.* Box 7 [1741–57] no. 38). Cf., on the other uses of a *posse*, Moore's letter in 7 *Doc. Rel. Col. Hist. NY* 910–912; the affidavit of Yates in 4 *Doc. Hist. NY* 446 (1771); the affidavit of Griffin, *ibid.* 549 (1775). From an entry in *Ms. Mins. Westch. Co. Sess.* 1710–23 June 1, 1714, a *posse* was used in some sort of search for stolen goods.

[212] "By the Honorable Daniel Horsmanden . . . To the Sheriff . . . Greeting Whereas it appears before me that one Samuel Monroe . . . hath been Guilty of Divers Acts of Maintanance and illegally Sold . . . pretended . . . titles to . . . lands in the said county of Dutchess and under Pretence of Being Guardian to one Daniel Ninham and divers other Indians has maintained them in their Claims . . . and obliged himself to defend . . . [their] Titles . . . and whereas . . . [the Lieutenant Governor & Council have] ordered the Attorney General . . . to Prosecute. . . .

"These are therefore in his Majestys Name strictly to Charge . . . and Command you . . . to Ap-

Applications for warrants to the courts from officials like the Attorney General or the Governor, while in most circumstances the practical equivalent of an order, were essentially on the same footing as the complaints or affidavits of complaining witnesses upon the basis of which the judges exercised their authority. In the ordinary course of events the magistrate would determine on the basis of such complaints[213] or after examination whether a warrant should issue, and all judges, whether mere justices of the peace or members of the

prehend and take into Custody the said Samuell Monroe & Bring him before me in order to find suretys . . . to appear . . . [at the next Supreme Court on the 3d Tuesday April 15, 1766] to answer to such things as shall be objected against him on his Majesty's behalf . . . And if the said Samuell Monroe shall . . . refuse to give such Security, then you . . . are further . . . to take the said Samuell Monroe & Convay to Gaol . . . and deliver him to the Keeper thereof to be there kept until he shall find such security Hereby commanding you the said Keeper to receive him into your custody . . . until he shall find such Security Hereof fail not . . . at your Peril, and this shall be . . . a Sufficient Warrant for what you shall do herein by Virtue hereof Given under my Hand and Seal . . ." (*J. T. Kempe Lawsuits* P–R *sub nom.* Beverly Robinson). This is a copy of the warrant "taken from the original and examined this 14th October 1765." For a "draft of Judge's Warrant" in this case see *ibid.* Evidently Monroe was taken by virtue of the warrant of March 7, 1765, was unable to furnish bail, and was imprisoned by virtue of the "mittimus" provision in the warrant, because on October 8, 1765 we find Monroe writing to Attorney General Kempe from "New Gaol" to justify his taking "all lawful ways to aid the Indians in their claims" (*ibid.*). The warrant having been issued on March 7, 1765, the Attorney General, on April 27, 1765, filed an information in the Supreme Court against Monroe for a "high misdemeanor" (*Ms. Mins. SCJ 1764–66* [Engr.] 178), and in the filed pleadings is to be found a draft of the Attorney General's information against Monroe for a "great misdemeanor" which recites that the defendant, of evil name and fame, of dishonest conversation, had unlawfully, maliciously, turbulently and wickedly devised the exheredation of the King, intending to defeat the King's title to the Province of New York and to establish the Indians' right with force and arms. The information further recited that Monroe with force and arms unlawfully assembled, convened, consulted, conspired and confederated with others to bring about his illegal designs and machinations, and excited the Indians to claim certain lands in Dutchess County on the allegation that the lands had not been properly purchased from them. The information also stated that Monroe had gotten an instrument from the Indians making him their guardian (*H.R. Pleadings* Pl. K. 796).

[213] The persistence of this may be illustrated by an example in 1693 and one in 1770. "Whereas Complaint Came before me Nicholas Stillwell . . . [a justice of the peace] ag^t. James Kar . . . y^t. he . . . said he had murrdered . . . and he must murder another very quickly, or else he could not rest, wherefore the said Stillwell issued forth my warrant unto the Constable . . . to take the body . . . of the said Kar to answer before me . . . [and two other justices of the peace] the witness was examined before us upon their oaths & doth declare as followes. John Stillwell doth declare before us upon oath, that he did see such a like man in Clothes as Karr, at unseasonable time of ye night, he Came into his house . . . & he see such alike man goe into Kars house . . . John Stillwell's wife Came to James Kars door & Calld to him, & sayd are ye not ashamed to Come into peoples houses at such unseasonable time of the night . . . Whereas by Examinacon we did charge & Command you . . . [referring to the high sheriff] in their Maj^ties Names to take the body of James Kar . . . into y^r. Custody & him safely keep that we may have him at the next Court of Sessions to answer to the premises & this shall be yr sufficient warrant . . ." (*Ms. Kings Co. Ct. & Rd. Recs. 1692–1825* 19, 22).

The 1770 warrant, issued on an affidavit of one Rachel Bates, is as follows: "Province of New York ss: By the Honorable Daniel Horsmanden Esquire Chief Justice of the Supreme Court of Judicature . . . To all Sheriffs Constables and others his Majesty's Peace Officers . . . Whereas it appears to me on the Oath of Rachel Bates . . . that on the —— day . . . of December George Sullivan came to the House of her said [sick] Husband . . . and desired to see a certain bond given by —— Horsfield and the said John Bates to —— for the Sum of —— and that on delivery of the said Bond . . . to . . . George he . . . with a Pen knife did attempt to cut out of the said Bond the Name and Seal of the said —— Horsefield These are . . . to . . . require . . . you . . . upon Sight hereof to Apprehend and bring before . . . Judges of the Supreme Court of Judicature . . . the Body of . . . George Sullivan . . . to Answer the Premises . . . and in the mean Time to be of good Behavior hereof fail not at your Peril" (*H.R. Pleadings* Pl. K. 907). For further proceedings, *Ms. Mins. SCJ 1769–72* (Engr.) 441; *H.R. Pleadings* Pl. K. 355.

Supreme Court, possessed this authority. The magistrates seem to have regarded their function as discretionary, but the inhabitants at large did not, for complaints against the issue or refusal to issue warrants were constant, sometimes the outcries ascending even to the chambers of the Council.[214] One of the most flagrant examples of an abuse of discretion, the whitewashing of a suspected robber by Justice Vanderbergh of Dutchess[215] has already been adverted to and, as we have seen, the information became a useful instrumentality for holding abuse in check.[216]

Cases of resistance to warrants out of mere obstreperousness are rare although in general there is a vast amount of evidence bearing upon evasion of all forms of process by flight,[217] by simply ignoring summons, or by obstructing officers. In the case of flight a second and more stringent process might issue,[218] but if a person cited merely ignored the precept he might be charged with costs,[219] or in the case of refusing to obey a warrant issued pursuant to an order of the magistrates, a fine for a contempt would be exacted. The tradition had been early established that in relation to general county orders of the justices in Sessions warrants would issue for due performance.[220] The establishment of a rule that refusal to obey was a contempt was of great importance, and we find an early case (1693) where the court in Kings County acted on this principle.[221] Subsequent minute entries regarding fines for obstruction of

---

[214] For example, the complaints in 19 *Ms. Mins. Council* 24 (1739).

[215] *Supra* 321. *J. T. Kempe Lawsuits* C–F *sub nom.* Edwards, Apr. 30, 1763, endorsed "charge against John Edwards."

Frantz Rogen on January 4, 1771, filed a deposition complaining against a justice of the peace of Ulster County named Elsworth alleging various acts of champerty and maladministration connected with the granting of certain warrants. It seems that in October, 1765, the defendant's negro was "gaoled by the verbal order" of Elsworth for committing an assault and battery. The negro was tried and adjudged by Elsworth to be guilty of the offense, sentenced to sixty lashes, then to jail, the next day to twenty-five lashes and then to jail for ten days. Elsworth suggested to Rogen that he pay the court fees and get his negro. The constable thereupon released the negro but immediately thereafter served a warrant to bring him back before the justice of peace to find sufficient sureties for his appearance at the next General Sessions of the Peace for Ulster "and in the meantime that the said negro man keep the peace and be of good behavior." Rogen offered to go surety for his negro but this offer was refused because Elsworth wanted the negro to be bound in a £300 recognizance. Thereupon Rogen went to the justice of the peace Hornbeck and "desired of him a supersedeas . . . directed to the

sheriff bailiff constable and other officers . . . which . . . the deponent . . . delivered to the sheriff . . . upon . . . which the sheriff discharged the negro from his imprisonment." However, Elsworth again issued another warrant against the negro, and Rogen in his deposition alleged that all of these proceedings against the negro had been for the same offense for which the negro had been previously punished (*J. T. Kempe Lawsuits* C–F *sub nom.* DuMont and Elsworth). Cf. also the indictments in *Ms. Files Dutchess Co. 1726–40*, King v. Dubois (1740) granting warrants when not qualified; King v. William Scott (1740) granting illegal summons.

[216] *Supra* 379.

[217] For example, King v. Berkley, sent for by warrant and "is withdrawn" (*Mins. SCJ 1693–1701* 122); King v. Janneke Lourens (*Ms. Mins. Ulster Co. Sess. 1693–98* Sept. 6, 1698).

[218] Queen v. Catherine Springsteen (*Ms. Mins. Orange Co. Sess. 1703–09* Apr. 24, 1705, Oct. 29, 1706, Oct. 27, 1707); in re Evertsen (*Ms. Mins. Ulster Co. Sess. 1711/12–1720* Mar. 1, 1719/20).

[219] As in *Ms. Mins. Ulster Co. Sess. 1711/12–1720*, done at a "meeting" Dec. 27, 1718.

[220] On these ordinances *supra* 39.

[221] King v. Symonse (*Ms. Kings Co. Ct. & Rd. Recs. 1692–1825* 25).

rate collectors, fence viewers and the like, indicate the continuation of the rule.[222]

Some cases of resistance obviously reached the stage of a riot and appear thus in the records, but occasionally there was a one-man affair. John Van Zandt, a colonial recidivist, was informed against on January 24, 1756, for assaulting a constable in execution of his office and endeavoring to rescue a negro who had been taken by the constable. Alderman Stuyvesant had "by a certain precept or Warrant" commanded Constable William Richardson to apprehend a negro slave Dick (belonging to Van Zandt) for feloniously stealing an iron pot and a scythe. The warrant commanded the constable to bring the slave before Stuyvesant or some other justice of the peace "to be examined . . . and dealt with according to Law which said preceptor warrant was . . . delivered to . . . the Constable . . . in due fform of Law to be executed . . . And that the said . . . Constable . . . did take and arrest the said negro. . . ." But Van Zandt assaulted the constable and endeavored to rescue the slave out of Richardson's custody.[223]

It is apparent from the examples of warrants preserved, that in point of form an effort was made to comply with the directions in the justices' manuals and leave nothing to chance. Obviously it is impossible to say how far the usually meticulous recital of the details of a charge is to be accounted for by an apprehension that the conditions of due process would not be otherwise satisfied. But it is certain that Coke's admonition respecting "convenient certainty" was regularly followed. With the exception of the bench warrants ordered by General Sessions, virtually all the warrants issued by the justices of the peace that we have examined are extremely long-winded affairs setting forth at large the reasons for issuance, a feat of no mean dimensions when one comes ruefully to struggle with the penmanship, the spelling and the grammar of these docu-

---

[222] E.g., *Ms. Mins. Ulster Co. Sess. 1693–98* in re Hyman Rosa, Mar. 3, 1694/95; *Ms. Mins. Ulster Co. Sess. 1711/12–1720*, on cover (n.d.); *Ms. Mins. Westch. Co. Sess. 1710–23* Aug. 31, 1714.

[223] *Ms. Mins. SCJ 1754–57* (Engr.) 239. For the information see *H.R. Pleadings* Pl. K. 563, and *J. T. Kempe Lawsuits* V. Also see *H.R. Parch.* 69 L 10 for some further notes describing the case.

On December 16, 1765, Constable Abraham Hermanse of Kingston in Ulster County filed a deposition with the Attorney General alleging that one Rogen had interfered with him in the execution of his office, and the constable wrote a letter to one Mr. Morris (probably the clerk of the circuits) as follows: "I send you my Deposition. . . . My complaint is against Francis Peter Rogen for making

Resistance . . . [to the execution of a warrant against his negro] and for assaulting me. . . . And my Complaint against Abraham Van Remsen is that he would not assist Me in Executing my warrant and . . . against Abraham Tink is that he actual Laid hold of . . . Rogen in order to rescue said Rogen from me While I was conveying him Before the justice . . . I hope you will Lay . . . [the depositions] . . . before the Kings attorney and if there is a remedy to prosecute them . . ." (*J. T. Kempe Lawsuits* P–R *sub nom.* Rogen) *supra* n. 215. Compare also the case of Baltus Lydius who assaulted the sheriff of Albany (*Ms. Mins. SCJ 1764–66* [Engr.] 164, 178; *H.R. Pleadings* Pl. K. 798); King v. Solomon Davis—riotous rescue (*Ms. Mins. Orange Co. Sess. 1727–79* Oct. 28, 1740).

ments.[224] This meticulousness persists right up to the end of the colonial period. Quite exceptional are warrants like the one penned by that uncertain grammarian, Justice Henry Van Rensselaer,[225] commanding the defendants simply to answer the King,[226] a form which had been disapproved in England over a century earlier.[227]

As for the directions to the arresting officer, these vary according to circumstances. A common form is the order to apprehend and keep in custody until security for appearance is forthcoming. These warrants to oblige persons to find security for their appearance to answer were sometimes combined with the additional requirement that the defendants keep the peace, or be of good behavior. Oftentimes a complainant would "swear the peace" against someone and a warrant of the peace would be issued to apprehend the defendant and oblige him to find security to keep the peace. As we shall see, this happened ordinarily at the instance of women or when some timorous citizen was being bullied by a contentious neighbor. It is consequently diverting to find the case of a pavid sheriff. On August 4, 1725,

> William Dugdale . . . High Sheriff . . . having made Oath that he is in fear of his life or of some bodily hurt to be done . . . to him by David Provoost . . . and that he doth not require the Peace of him for any Malice Vexation or Revenge but for the Causes aforesaid. Ordered this Court Issue their Warrant to Attach the said David Provoost & cause him to find sureties for the Peace and for his Appearance at the Next session.[228]

What appears to be a peculiarity in provincial practice is the use of warrants to compel defendants to find security for appearance even after presentments or indictments for minor offenses. The normal expectancy, as we shall shortly see, would be issuance of the usual common law venire facias, but several cases have been found where after indictment it was ordered that "warrants" be issued—a very different thing from the usual order respecting "common process." These cases are all in General Sessions and are early. The expla-

[224] The country warrants are the real test of the necessity of recital. In *Ms. Files Ulster Co.* Bundle B, many warrants with long recitals may be found. Cf. especially, King v. Maria Tackert (1766), King v. Patrick McKay (1765), King v. William Boyd (1763); Bundle E, King v. Jacob Van Plarcom (1769); Bundle F, King v. James Crawford (1726), King v. Lambert Dolderbrink (1720/21), King v. Nicholas Schoonover [Schoonhoven, Schoonhaven] (1720/21); Bundle H, King v. Hugh Flanagan (1736). *Ms. Files Dutchess Co. 1740–50* IV, King v. John Simson (1746). In *File 1755* are many

elaborate warrants to levy under the Enlistment Act.
[225] Cf. the riot case discussed *supra* 201.
[226] *J. T. Kempe Lawsuits* V *sub nom.* Van Rensselaer.
[227] Boucher's Case (*Cro. Jac.* 8).
[228] *Ms. Mins. NYCQS 1694–1731/32* 453. It is to be noted that the defendant entered a recognizance of £100 with two sureties in £50 each to appear and meantime keep the peace, especially to William Dugdale, and not do him any harm (*ibid.* 454). Cf. further on the recognizance to keep the peace, *infra* 488 *et seq.*

nation, we think, is that the justices of the peace were not yet aware of the English rule that warrants were used before presentment and that a venire or capias was used afterwards.[229] Two 1718 cases in New York Quarter Sessions are to be explained by the fact that surety of the peace was required, for in the city Sessions[230] the procedure was by this time settled along conventional English lines.

Precepts ordering an officer to search must certainly have been in general use considering the great number of larcenies, robberies and burglaries that filled the calendars. Curiously enough, however, we have found only three recorded instances of search warrants. One is referred to in a constable's deposition at Westchester Sessions.[230a] Another reference is buried in certain depositions and examinations made before justices of the peace of New York City on January 3, 1722/23, regarding the larcenies committed by one George Borne.[231] Mary Lawrence in her deposition stated that on January 1, 1722/23 her shop windows were broken open, the hinges taken off, and there were feloniously taken out of her shop sundry pieces of calico, silk, muslin and so forth. "She applyed to Alderman Cruger for a warrant to search for said goods," and this warrant having been granted, a search was made and Mary

[229] Queen v. Uryon Springsteen (*Ms. Mins. Orange Co. Sess. 1703–07* Apr. 27, 1703); Queen v. Erwin Westerfield (*ibid.* Apr. 24, 1705); Queen v. Catherine Springsteen (*ibid.* Apr. 29, 1707); King v. Mary Jacobs (*Ms. Mins. Ulster Co. Sess. 1693–98* Sept. 4, 1694); King v. Van Nette (*ibid.*). (The instances of *mittimus* in this court after indictment and in Dutchess discussed *infra* 430.) Cf. also King v. Sarah Hillyard *et al.* (*Ms. Mins. Richmond Co. Sess. 1710–1744/45* Mar. 7, 1716/17). An example is the following from *NY State Lib. Mss.* 7460:

"Ulster County SS
Jacob Rutson A. Gaasbeek Chambers & Edw[d] Whittaker Esqs Justices of the peace for said County Assign'd To the Sherriffe of said County of Ulster Greeting Whereas Huybert Lambertson of Marbletown in the County aforesaid Stands Indicted at the last Court of Generall Sessions of the peace which was held at Kingston for the County aforesaid for that he the said Huybert on the tenth day of March in the Seventh year of our Soveraigne Lord the King that now is (by Common Justice being Comitted to the prison or Common Goal of this County did by force of armes break the said prison and feloniously thereout did make his Escape, You are therefore in his Majesties name Strictly Command & Required to take the body of the said Huybert Lambertson and him in Safe Costody keep untill he give in Sufficient Surety to the vallue of fifty pounds for his good behaviour untill and ap-

pearance at the next Cou[rt] of Gen[ll] Sessions of the peace to be held at Kingston afors[d] for the County aforesaid the first Tuesday in the Month of March next Ensueing then there to Answer to said Indictment & to stand too performe & fullfill what said Court Shall Injoyn and order therein hereof ffaile not . . ." (Jan. 11, 1721/22).

[230] Cf. King v. Codman *et al.*, 1718 (*Ms. Mins. NYCQS 1694–1731/32* 348, Aug. 6, 1718). In King v. Esther and George Stanton and two others where defendants were presented for threatening the life of Henry Feavour, the court "Ordered any of the Justices Issue their Warrt. to Oblidge the Defts to find Sufficient Sureties of the Peace & for their personall appearance at the Next Sessions" (*ibid.* 348). In the cases of King v. Gilliland *alias* Gillin, 1767 (*Ms. Mins. SCJ 1766–69* [Engr.] 317, 318) and King v. John Dowers, against whom two indictments for disorderly house were found on Oct. 30, 1767, the Supreme Court "Ordered the sheriff do take the defendant into custody . . . in order to plead to several matters and enter recognizances" (*ibid.* 321). These were probably orders for bench warrants.

[230a] Queen v. John Horton (*Ms. Mins. Westch. Co. Sess. 1710–23* June 1, 1714).

[231] *James Alexander Papers* Box 45, Quarter Sessions Papers. In the *Notes of Trial*, King v. Kelly, Oct. 24, 1764, one witness is reported to have mentioned a search warrant (*J. T. Kempe Lawsuits* K–L).

Lawrence's goods were found in a new chest in Widow Wheeler's house. John Jackson, the constable, was also sworn before the justice of the peace on January 3, 1722, and he stated that he was present at the search and that the widow said the goods belonged to a lodger. When the constable asked the lodger how the goods came into his chest, he said he did not know. The constable, therefore, carried the lodger (who was George Borne) before David Jamison, who ordered him to prison until he should be examined. George Borne was thereupon examined on January 3 before Justice Walter and he denied any guilt or complicity.

Whenever it was necessary to commit a defendant the warrant of arrest was complemented by a *mittimus,* an order to a jailer to keep a suspect in custody. This precept very often contained the direction that the custody was to last until the prisoner furnished sureties for appearance at court and to keep the peace,[232] a form most commonly followed after presentments, indictments or informations had been filed and the defendants had either pleaded not guilty or were being held until a plea was filed. If a recognizance was entered into, the defendant would be discharged from his *mittimus.*[233]

---

[232] The practice exists in the seventeenth century: King v. Kissimo, 1696 (*Ms. Mins. NYCQS 1694–1731/32* 17, Nov. 4, 1696); King v. Yechte, 1693 (*Ms. Kings Co. Ct. & Rd. Recs. 1692–1825* 23). For later cases, see King v. James Arden against whom the peace was sworn (*Ms. Mins. NYCQS 1694–1731/32* 529, Nov. 4, 1730). Compare King v. Nicholas Burger, discussed *infra* 460. William Walling in 1724 had been similarly committed for insolence to the grand jury (*Ms. Mins. NYCQS 1694–1731/32* 443–444, Aug. 5, 1724). See further King v. Baglin—disorderly house (*Ms. Mins. NYCQS 1732–62* 122, Aug. 3, 1740).

[233] For example, King v. Richardson—assault (*Ms. Mins. SCJ 1727–32* 102). After the recognizance had been entered, the order for discharge from the *mittimus* was given (*ibid.* 105). On June 7, 1729, Richardson and his surety appeared in the Supreme Court and "the Attorney General having nothing to charge the defendant with," he and his surety were discharged on their appearance (*ibid.* 124).

There is a steady stream of cases on this practice. Stephen Buckenhoven, presented in Quarter Sessions on May 7, 1701, for altering the tax rolls, appeared and was "put in custody" until he should give sureties for his appearance, but on Aug. 5, he was discharged on examination (*Ms. Mins. NYCQS 1694–1731/32* 64, 66). Richard Green, indicted for fraudulently tearing and destroying a £20 bond, pleaded not guilty and was committed until he give surety "to prosecute his traverse" (*ibid.* 88, May 3, 1704). Mary Barnes and John Kingston, indicted

for clipped coin, pleaded not guilty on May 1, 1705, and were committed until they should give security to prosecute their traverse. On May 2, 1705, Mary Barnes posted a bond of £40 and on August 8, she was found not guilty (*ibid.* 96, 97, 98, 99). Thomas Adams pleaded not guilty to an indictment for a breach of the peace on May 7, 1707, and was "committed to the sheriff's custody until he finds sureties to prosecute his traverse" (*ibid.* 124, 134). William Day pleaded not guilty, on Nov. 2, 1709, to an indictment for trespass and being ordered to be committed until he should give security to prosecute his traverse, he entered a recognizance in £20 with one surety in like amount (*ibid.* 168). Elizabeth Green and Catherine Elbertse, indicted on Aug. 2, 1710, for entertaining slaves, were brought in by the sheriff on Nov. 7, 1710, and pleaded not guilty, whereupon the court ordered that they be committed until they give security to prosecute their traverse "with effect" (*ibid.* 178, 185). It is to be noted that in this latter case Elizabeth Green being found guilty was sentenced to eight days in jail, while Catherine Elbertse pleading guilty was fined 12s. (*ibid.* 186). Thomas Banks pleading not guilty to an indictment for entertaining slaves was on Aug. 3, 1720, committed until he give security to prosecute his traverse, but he pleaded guilty and put himself on the mercy of the court, whereupon he was fined £5 and costs and ordered to be committed until the same were paid (*ibid.* 375). Jacobus Cosyne, presented for assault and battery, pleaded not guilty and the sheriff was ordered to take him into custody and he was to be committed

It appears from the minute entries that an opportunity was given to secure sureties before the *mittimus* issued, at least that seems the sense of the frequent orders in the alternative—recognizance or commitment. If bond were not posted the defendant would then be jailed. These orders were used not merely for the purpose of securing appearance, but were made also to compel acquiescence in the court's judgment, as well as to exact a recognizance to keep the peace after a release by proclamation, or after the infliction of a corporal punishment.[234]

It is unfortunate that there have not been preserved enough samples of the *mittimus* for us to form an opinion respecting their possible function as original process in the country districts. Judging from minute entries, the Albany, Ulster and Dutchess County justices[235] seem to have used the *mittimus* both to summon a defendant and to jail him, and it is possible that during the early eighteenth century the squires who were administering the law saw no reason for laboriously preparing a new paper to commit a man when one instrument would effectively summon him and put him in custody should this be necessary.[236] The evidence, such as it is, indicates that after Bradley became Attorney

until he should find surety to "stand and abide the determination of this court" (Kings Co. Oyer and Terminer and General Gaol Delivery, *Ms. Mins. Cir. 1721–49* 22, September 19, 1722). Jolin Mover, who pleaded not guilty to an indictment for assaulting a constable, was ordered to be committed until he give security to prosecute his traverse (*Ms. Mins. NYCQS 1732–62* 84, 87, Feb. 9, 1737/38, May 4, 1738). William and James Campbell pleaded not guilty to indictments for riot and burglary on Jan. 25, 1766, and were found not guilty of burglary. However, the Supreme Court ordered that these defendants be committed until they give recognizance of £30 each with one surety each in £30 for their appearance at the following term to answer for riot. On April 17, 1766, the defendants appeared and pleaded not guilty, but there are no further proceedings on this case (*Ms. Mins. SCJ 1764–67* [Rough] 134–136, 139). The Supreme Court on April 26, 1766, ordered the Attorney General to file an information against William Gilliland for passing a counterfeit New Jersey bill of credit and the court ordered that the defendant be committed until he give a recognizance in £100 with two sureties in £50 for his appearance at the next Supreme Court in July. On July 29 an information was read and filed against Gilliland and on July 30 he pleaded not guilty (*ibid.* 145, 147, 150). Cf. also King v. James Long, *infra* 508 n. 94.

[234] King v. Gardiner, 1739 (*Ms. Mins. SCJ 1732–39* 338, 344), sureties to abide the court's judgment. When an indictment for robbery had been filed against Peter McLean on July 29, 1763, and he was on Oct. 29, 1763, "set at bar," procla-

mation was three times made and although no prosecutor appeared against him, nevertheless the court ordered that he be committed until he find security in £100 for his good behavior for ten years (*Ms. Mins. SCJ 1762–64* [Engr.] 222, 296). Alex Forbes was found guilty of robbery and petit larceny on Oct. 29, 1773, and on Oct. 30, the court sentenced him to receive thirty-nine lashes at two different times, and in addition to be committed until he should give a recognizance in £100 with two sureties in £50 to keep the peace and be of his good behavior for twelve months (*Ms. Mins. SCJ 1772–76* [Rough] 134, 135, 137).

It should be noted that in cases of commitment on suspicion, the alternative of bail was not necessarily given: cf. King v. Moor (*Ms. Mins. Cir. 1716–17* 19); King v. Gardiner—murder (*Ms. Mins. Cir. 1721–49* 119); King v. Dean—theft (*ibid.* 92); King v. Talladay—accessory to grand larceny (*ibid.* 9). In King v. Dowers, Hannah Randall, a witness, ordered held for petit larceny (*Ms. Mins. SCJ 1764–67* [Rough] 240). See also the cases in *Ms. Mins. NYCQS 1694–1731/32* 251, Nov. 4, 1712, 433, Feb. 5, 1723/24, 459, Feb. 4, 1740/41.

[235] *Ms. Mins. Ulster Co. Sess. 1703–05* Sept. 3, 1703; *Ms. Mins. Ulster Co. Sess. 1711/12–1720 passim; Ms. Mins. Dutchess Co. Sess.* Liber A, May 20, 1723, May 18, 1725, Oct. 21, 1729, May 19, 1730, Oct. 19, 1731.

[236] For Albany cf. the orders in King v. Borghaert and Van Schaick (*Ms. Mins. Albany Co. Sess. 1717–23* Feb. 8, 1720/21); King v. John Warren (*ibid.* Feb. 7, 1721/22); King v. John Thomas

General a closer conformity with the pattern of English local justice became general.

Although we have considered the *mittimus* simply as one of the various types of process against defendants, contrived to assure the lawfulness of custody after arrest, it should be pointed out that it functioned likewise as an instrumentality in the administration of the law of bail, a matter we shall consider in the next chapter.

Process after Indictment for Misdemeanors

In England the usual first process after indictment for misdemeanor was the summons—*venire facias ad respondendum*. The New York clerks, however, were not usually so explicit but complicated matters for us by the cryptic form of their minute entries, viz., "common process ordered to issue" or "process to issue." Occasionally it is possible to discover by a later entry what this in fact was, but one cannot assume that the rules of the textbooks were followed. This was particularly true in the late seventeenth century where the choice of venire or capias seems to have been a matter of mere caprice. Thus in 1691 Ansell Levy was presented and "he not appearing upon proclamation three times made" a capias was awarded.[237] A few years later, some Sunday dice players were ordered taken into custody,[238] whereas the defendants charged with breach of an assize of bread were merely summoned.[239] As late as 1702 we find a capias used as first process in a false weight case.[240]

We do not know whether the *venire facias ad respondendum* emigrated

(*ibid.* Feb. 6, 1722/23, June 5, 1723). An example of a *mittimus* merely to jail Peter Mix and Johannes Lewis, Nov. 12, 1722 (*Redmond-Livingston Mss.* F. D. Roosevelt Library). The examination for horse stealing is attached. An example of the form used in Ulster in the 1720's is the warrant, Sept. 27, 1722, which recites that Mary Peerson has made oath against her husband. The constable is ordered to take him for security and if he refuses, to take him to jail. The sheriff is commanded to keep him until security is given (*Ms. Files Ulster Co.* Bundle G). Cf. also the warrant, Jan. 10, 1720/21, to the constable of Marbletown to take Nicholas Schoonover [Schoonhoven, Schoonhaven]. Cf. also the warrant to take and keep Lambert Dolderbrink, Jan. 10, 1720/21 (*ibid.* Bundle F); the warrant for Hugh Flanagan, Apr. 26, 1736 (*ibid.* Bundle H) to get security or put in jail.

[237] *Ms. Mins. NYCQS 1683/84–1694* 151, Aug. 5, 1691. Cf. King v. John Windower, who was presented on Oct. 5, 1694, for "speaking words coming under the crime of high misdemeanor" (*infra*

498); in this case the sheriff was ordered to take the defendant into custody "forasmuch as the Attorney General is not provided to present at present" (*Mins. SCJ 1693–1701* 64). Compare *Ms. Mins. Ulster Co. Sess. 1703–05* where the constable was sent after the local termagant, Hellegonda Van Slechtenhorst, Sept. 4, 1705.

[238] *Mins. SCJ 1693–1701* 93.

[239] *Ms. Mins. NYCQS 1694–1731/32* 30, 51, 53 Feb. 8, 1699/1700, May 1, 1700. Philip French was on Apr. 9, 1702 presented "for high misdemeanors," and the Supreme Court in this case "ordered the usual process issue" and that the defendant appear the following day—apparently venire facias is meant. There are no further entries on this case in the minutes (*Ms. Mins. SCJ 1701–04* 56).

[240] *Ms. Mins. NYCQS 1694–1731/32* 73, Nov. 4, 1702. Note that in this case the defendants, on February 2, 1702/03, protested that they were not guilty but nevertheless submitted to the mercy of the court and were fined 6s. (*ibid.* 75).

with capias during Dongan's governorship but on the basis of available evidence we are disposed to believe that it did.[241] The first reference we have seen to it is in the Westchester Sessions minutes for December, 1692 when one Horton was indicted for an unnamed offense and the court ordered process according to law to the next court of Sessions and "that the clerke issue forth a venire facias accordingly."[242] Mere acquaintance with the form, however, signifies nothing regarding familiarity with its uses. The process entries in the early country minutes are sadly few, but apparently even in misdemeanors the actual taking of a defendant was preferred over a mere summons to answer.[243]

By 1710, in both Richmond and Westchester counties, the records indicate that venire was the usual first process, but in Ulster the *mittimus* remains. This is also used in Dutchess after a separate Sessions Court was set up there in 1721, and disappears in the mid-thirties. James Livingston had procured for Henry Livingston, clerk of the peace, Jacob's *Law Dictionary*, the *Clerk's Instructor* and Bohun's *Declarations*,[244] a fact that may have helped to change the practice. The Ulstermen had seen the light about the same time, as the minute book for 1737–50 indicates.[245] The process entries in the Sessions minutes for Orange, Queens and Suffolk during the twenties indicate that defendants were summoned.

In the metropolis, the records show an understanding of the common law rule that following presentment a summons was sufficient for minor crimes. Beginning with the year 1693 there are scattered entries[246] to the effect that the

241 The *Cal. Eng. Mss.* has entries for vol. 33, NY Col. Mss., which indicate the cataloguer's "summons to answer" was probably a venire.

242 *Mins. Westch. Ct. of Sess.* 70. There is an earlier entry (*ibid.* 68) but the venire is dated 1693. In the *Ms. Mins. Ulster Co. Sess. 1693–98* the first entry is a presentment of theft and the following words "writ to answer" which may have been a venire facias.

243 Thus in Westchester, June 2, 1692, the court ordered precepts issued "to take them persons who are presented" (*Mins. Westch. Ct. of Sess.* 69) but in the following year a similar blanket order for precepts bears the marginal note "venire facias." This is not an official book or is at best a clerk's waste book, and has some curious comments by the compiler, as on page 78 respecting an arrest for abusive words. In Ulster, Sept. 4, 1694, a woman is arrested on an indictment for assault, and again on Sept. 7, 1697 a *mittimus* is issued in two assault cases. There is only one entry, King v. Lourens (March, 1697/98), where the use of mere summons is indicated (*Ms. Mins. Ulster Co. Sess. 1693–98*). In Queen v. De Witt (assault) the constable was "sent for" De

Witt. He was not found and a *mittimus* ordered (*Ms. Mins. Ulster Co. Sess. 1703–05* Sept. 4, 1705).

244 The bill dated Apr. 24, 1738, is in *Livingston Mss.* I.

245 It should be noted that in *Ms. Files Ulster Co.* Bundle F, is a *pluries capias*, May 8, 1735 (King v. Quick); Bundle M, a *pluries* Nov. 4, 1737 in the same case; and Bundle D a capias, Nov. 9, 1739, King v. Neeley. These indicate that the *mittimus* no longer is serving as the country capias.

246 King v. Griffit—false beam, 1693 (*Mins. SCJ 1693–1701* 49); Queen v. Rousby—fences (*Ms. Mins. NYCQS 1694–1731/32* 106, Nov. 7, 1703); Queen v. Boudinot—striking constable (*ibid.* 109–111, Feb. 27, 1705/06, May 8, 1706); Queen v. Fardon—misdemeanor, 1709 (*Ms. Kings Co. Ct. & Rd. Recs. 1692–1825* 160). In King v. Clarke, 1715/16, the court ordered the crier to inform the defendant (*Ms. Mins. NYCQS 1694–1731/32* 317). So in King v. Brown the defendant was "called" (*ibid.* 497, 498, Aug. 7, 1728). The Circuit minutes for 1716 show summons used in a riot case (*Ms. Mins. Cir. 1716–17* 2).

venire facias was the usual first process in offenses below the degree of grand larceny although we have seen only a few examples where it was used after indictments for petit larceny.[247] In the margin we quote examples of the writ used in the province.[248]

The practice respecting first process in misdemeanors after indictment had become so well-seated by the middle of the eighteenth century that the steps taken to summon Major Henry Pullen, indicted for assault and riot, seem a little strange. To this defendant, whom the local patriots detested, the Attorney General on June 28, 1769 wrote:

> Mr. Kempe presents his compliments to Major Pullen and acquaints him that the Grand Jury of the last term indicted him for riot and assault on Mr. Thody—that a writ should issue in course to compel his appearance at the next Supreme Court to answer the charge. Mr. Kempe has not yet issued the process being desirous of sparing Major Pullen the sheriff's visit on this occasion and therefore wishes he would direct some gentleman of the bar to enter his appearance and plead on the first Day of next Term.[249]

Apparently there was a particular due process for his Majesty's officers even if they did not behave as gentlemen.[250]

The accepted form of a sheriff's return of a venire facias was *venire feci* (that he had summoned the defendant as commanded) and the defendant

---

[247] E.g., King v. Francis Brown (*Ms. Mins. NYCQS 1732–62* 491, Nov. 6, 1760). At 3 P.M. the defendant evidently appeared, for the minute entries indicate that he pleaded not guilty, but was convicted and sentenced to thirty-nine lashes (*ibid.* 492). Also see King v. Ed. Dillon where, on an indictment for petit larceny, venire facias was ordered to issue for the defendant (*ibid.* 495, Feb. 4, 1761).

[248] King v. De Peyster (indictment for assault and battery 1756): "To . . . the Sherriff of . . . New York . . . We command you that you omit not by Reason of any Liberty within your Bailiwick but that the same you enter and cause William Depeyster . . . if he be found within your Bailiwick to come before us at our City of New York on the third Tuesday in April next to answer unto us upon certain articles exhibited against him in our Supreme Court . . . whereof he stands indicted and have you then there this Writ . . ." (*NY Legal Mss.* Box 43; *Ms. Mins. SCJ 1754–57* [Engr.] 222, 261).

King v. Snedeker, Coe, *et al.*—information for riotous assemblage, 1759: "George the Second . . . to our Sherriff of . . . Orange Greeting We command you that you omit not by Reason of any Liberty within your Bailiwick but that the same you enter and cause Theodorus Snedekar . . . William

Coe . . ., Guysbert Cuyper . . . and Michael Vander Vort . . . if they be found within your Bailiwick to come before us at our City of New York . . . in January next, to answer unto us upon certain Articles exhibited against them in our Supreme Court for our Province of New York at our Suit by Information of our Attorney General and have you then there this Writ . . ." (*H.R. Pleadings* Pl. K. 1050; *Ms. Mins. SCJ 1756–61* [Rough] 145, 165). The writ in this case was endorsed by the sheriff: "I have cause the defendants to come as commanded." The minute entries for April term, 1760, indicate that Alsop appeared for Theodorus Snedeker and pleaded not guilty (*Ms. Mins. SCJ 1757–60* [Engr.] 319). Also see the venire facias against James Ferguson (*J. T. Kempe Lawsuits* C–F), who had been informed against by the Attorney General for assaulting a constable and against whom process had been ordered to issue in 1761 (*Ms. Mins. SCJ 1756–61* [Rough] 248); the venire facias for Joshua Seaman, indicted (1774) for an assault and battery (*H.R. Parch.* 31 L 8) endorsed "not found," and cf. *Ms. Mins. SCJ 1772–76* (Rough) 184.

[249] *Ms. Kempe Letters* A–Z.

[250] Cf. the testimony in the "Notes for Trial," *J. T. Kempe Lawsuits sub nom.* Pullen.

might endorse the writ and promise his appearance at court. On his appearance the defendant personally, or by attorney, would pray that his appearance be entered and the rule to plead would then be made.[251] In some of the late cases where endorsement was made, the court seems to have treated this as the equivalent of the entry of appearance in court; at least the minutes in some cases seem to indicate this.

The matter of appearance was of considerable importance in English law, for a personal appearance of the defendant was required in misdemeanor cases at the Assizes and at Sessions. In the King's Bench, however, the rule had long obtained that appearance by attorney was sufficient when the defendant was only charged with a misdemeanor.[252] The appearance was also a condition *sine qua non* of the rule to plead, and on failure to comply judgment by default could be entered. These rules respecting appearance were not meticulously followed in New York, for we have found cases where vicarious appearances were allowed.[253] As late as 1761 in New York Quarter Sessions a defendant's "friend appeared for her" and the rule to plead was then made;[254] and in Dutchess at the October Sessions, 1763, the justices ordered an attorney's appearance should be accepted from time to time in the defendant's stead.[255]

One of the curious aberrations in provincial practice respecting the venire was the weird return *cepi corpus* (I have taken the body), the usual endorsement when a capias had been successfully served. So far as we are aware there was no precedent for such a return in English practice, and since a sheriff is the last person one would suspect of trying to establish new precedents, this anomaly must be ascribed to ignorance. On some of the writs thus endorsed is inscribed likewise the defendant's promise to appear, which shows clearly

251 Typical are the following cases: Queen v. Ellison—not repairing highway (*Ms. Mins. NYCQS 1694-1731/32* 106, 108, Nov. 7, 1705, Feb. 8, 1705/06); King v. Gerritson *et al.*—misdemeanor, 1730 (*Ms. Mins. SCJ 1727-32* 217, 233, 246, 271); King v. Stephen and Oliver De Lancey—assault (*Ms. Mins. NYCQS 1732-62* 146, 150, Nov. 4, 1742, Feb. 2, 1742/43); King v. De La Montagne —breach of peace (*ibid.* 208, 209, 212, Aug. 6, 7, Nov. 6, 1746); King v. Provoost—nuisance (*ibid.* 414, 421, Aug. 4, Nov. 2, 1751), renewed by certiorari and process issued (*Ms. Mins. SCJ 1756-61* [Rough] 90; *Ms. Mins. SCJ 1757-60* [Engr.] 114); King v. Van Zandt—assault, 1751 (*Ms. Mins. SCJ 1750-54* [Engr.] 45, 68); King v. Dye—no offense named, 1750 (*ibid.* 16); King v. Hunt—riot, 1751 (*ibid.* 45, 68); King v. Van Zandt—assault and attempted rape, 1754 (*ibid.* 341; *Ms. Mins. SCJ 1754-57* [Engr.] 84); King v. Wilks

et al.—riot, 1754 (*Ms. Mins. SCJ 1750-54* [Engr.] 348; *Ms. Mins. SCJ 1754-57* [Engr.] 42, 52); King v. Ferris—libel, 1754 (*Ms. Mins. SCJ 1750-54* [Engr.] 341; *Ms. Mins. SCJ 1754-57* [Engr.] 84); King v. Haring—riot, 1764 (*Ms. Mins. SCJ 1762-64* [Engr.] 362, 464; *Ms. Mins. SCJ 1764-66* [Engr.] 117); King v. Dowers—disorderly house, 1764 (*Ms. Mins. SCJ 1764-67* [Rough] 31, 134; *Ms. Mins. SCJ 1764-66* [Engr.] 76, 117). There are, of course, many more and later cases.
252 Cf. 1 Chitty, *Criminal Law* 411.
253 King v. Jacobs (*Ms. Mins. Ulster Co. Sess. 1693-98* Mar. 4, 1694/95); Queen v. Dirck (*Ms. Mins. Ulster Co. Sess. 1711/12-1720* Mar. 3, 1712/13).
254 King v. Hamilton (*Ms. Mins. NYCQS 1732-62* 517, Feb. 2, 1762).
255 King v. Henry and Mary Soper (*Ms. Mins. Dutchess Co. Sess.* Liber C, Oct. 18, 1763).

enough that no actual apprehension of the defendant had taken place. We have not seen, however, any evidence of efforts to take advantage of an incorrect return, an advantage which would scarcely have been overlooked in England. Some of these mistakes were undoubtedly covered by the clerk. In one case where the writ is returned *cepi corpus,* the minutes read "the sheriff returned *venire feci.*"[256]

In spite of the absence of any evidence that the colonial bar undertook to utilize the substantial body of precedents respecting bad returns, there was none the less a certain anxiety that writs be properly returned. This matter will later be considered in detail. For the moment, in relation to the venire facias it will be instructive to notice certain directions of Attorney General Kempe.

In New York Province the *subpoena ad respondendum,* the English first process upon informations, had been supplanted for reasons unknown by the *venire facias ad respondendum*[257] which differed in substance only by the omission of the threat of a mulct. An information had been filed against Sybrant Goose Van Schaick, Mayor of Albany, and others, and Kempe undertook to enlighten the Albany sheriff. He wrote:

> Enclosed I send you three several Sworne Processes of Venire Facias against Sybrant Goose Van Schaick Esq. Mayor of the City of Albany and others, which you will take care to execute. The Return to the Writs I have endorsed on each Writ, as I believe these processes have not been very frequent to your County—You will please to observe that on each Writ there is an Indorsemt. in the Words following "We and each of us promise to appear at the Return of this Writ and pray the Court that our appearance may be entered accordingly" This Indorsement the Defendants mentioned in the respective process must

---

[256] For some of these strange returns cf. King v. Sperham—perjury, 1756 (*H.R. Pleadings* Pl. K. 907). The defendant appeared by attorney (*Ms. Mins. SCJ 1754–57* [Engr.] 247, 261, 276). King v. John Brookman—assault, 1760 (*Ms. Mins. SCJ 1756–61* [Rough] 169; *Ms. Mins. SCJ 1757–60* [Engr.] 361 and see also *H.R. Parch.* 187 C 2); King v. Provoost—nuisance, 1760 (*Ms. Mins. SCJ 1756–61* [Rough] 185; *Ms. Mins. SCJ 1757–60* [Engr.] 361). King v. George De Bevois, an information for assault, *cepi corpus* returned on venire facias (*Ms. Mins. SCJ 1756–61* [Rough] 22, 1760; *Ms. Mins. SCJ 1757–60* [Engr.] 361, Aug. 1760). Also see King v. John Willett, Jr., on information for stopping a road, *cepi corpus* returned on venire facias (*Ms. Mins. SCJ 1756–61* [Rough] 185, Apr. 23, 1760; *Ms. Mins. SCJ 1757–60* [Engr.] 361, Aug., 1760). Likewise see King v.

John Lawrence, *supra* 282, the sheriff of New York returned "body taken" on venire facias (*Ms. Mins. SCJ 1757–60* [Engr.] 361). King v. Jonathan Valentine, no offense specified, 1765 (*H.R. Parch.* 176 L 10). King v. Thomas Clarke Jr. and John Kendal—riot, 1771 (*Ms. Mins. SCJ 1766–72* [Engr.] 355). There are many more examples. The case where the clerk made the *venire feci* entry on the writ returned *cepi corpus* (*H.R. Parch.* 191 C 7) is King v. Morrel and King—assault, 1771 (*Ms. Mins. SCJ 1766–72* [Engr.] 364).

[257] The form of the *subpoena ad resp.* in Brownlow, *Writs Judiciall* 144. It should be noted that in Dongan's time there were some cases of governor's warrants of arrest upon informations (3 *Doc. Hist. NY* 215, 217) but these were exceptional cases. We are disposed to think the venire crept in by way of the information for violation of the acts of trade.

sign, if they are found—You will also observe another Indorsement on each Writ, in the Words following "I have cause the Defendants within named to come before our Lord the King as I am by the within Writ commanded"—this last mentioned endorsement on each Writ, you must sign as Sherriff if the Defendts or any of them are found, and in case in such Case [sic] to fill up the Blanks left in the last mentioned Indorsement on each Writ, with the names of the defendants, or such of them as shall be found in your Bailiwick I am your very hum: Serv: J. T. Kempe Attorney General New York April 28th, 1760.[258]

Upon a sheriff's return to the writ of venire facias that he had summoned a defendant, it might occur that the latter, although properly served, and having acknowledged such service by endorsement, might, nevertheless, fail to appear. In such an event it was the practice in New York to issue a capias. Sergeant Hawkins indicates that upon default a second venire is proper,[259] but the tendency in England to resort to an arrest even as first process in misdemeanors[260] seems to be reflected in the Province. In any event there are a number of cases which establish the New York practice of capias as second process.[261]

There are other peculiarities of colonial practice respecting process in misdemeanors, one of which is the disappearance of distress infinite, the second process when the summons could not be served. We have found only a few cases where *distringas* was issued against a criminal defendant. On February 5, 1706/07, when an indictment had been found against George Norton, a butcher, for a breach of the peace, the New York Court of Quarter Sessions "ordered process issue against him" and on May 7, 1707, process having been evidently returned in the interim, the court "ordered a Distringas issue against the Defendt Returnable the next court."[262] No further orders for *distringas* in

---

258 *H.R. Pleadings* Pl. K. 288. The minute entries in King v. Sybrant G. Van Schaick, Eleanor Flood (wife of Patrick Flood) and Joseph Wells indicate that on April 23, 1760, an information was read and filed against these defendants and process was ordered to issue against them. With respect to Van Schaick an information for assault and battery was read and filed, while an information for a misdemeanor was filed against Eleanor Flood. From the Supreme Court minute entries of Aug. 1760, it would appear that the Attorney General's instructions to the sheriff were effectual in producing the desired result, for it is recited that "the sheriff of Albany on a venire facias returns that he has caused Sybrant Goose Van Schaick to come before the King as commanded who [Van Schaick] has endorsed his appearance. The like rule as to Eleanor Flood and Joseph Wells" (*Ms. Mins. SCJ* 1756–61 [Rough] 184, 185; *Ms. Mins. SCJ* 1757–60 [Engr.] 361).

259 2 Hawkins, *op. cit.* c.27 §11.
260 *Infra* 440.
261 King v. Robert Cross *et al.*, 1727 (*Ms. Mins. SCJ* 1723–27 253, 278; *Ms. Mins. SCJ* 1727–32 7). In the same year some of the justices of Albany informed against for insufficiency of the gaol did not appear on summons, "ordered that process issue" (*Ms. Mins. SCJ* 1727–32 279). Compare the entries in King v. Allison, 1731 (*ibid.* 303, 320); and see also King v. Little, 1743 (*Ms. Mins. NYCQS* 1732–62 155, 157, Aug. 3, Nov. 2, 1743); King v. R. Cornell, Rogers *et al.* (*Ms. Mins. SCJ* 1766–69 [Engr.] 188).
262 *Ms. Mins. NYCQS 1694–1731/32* 122, 124. On Aug. 5, 1707, this defendant appeared, confessed the indictment, prayed the mercy of the court, was fined 20*s.* with fees of the court and was ordered to be committed until he should make payment (*ibid.* 126, 128).

New York City have been found, but in 1755 at Orange General Sessions there is a sudden and brief spate of cases. At the April term the sheriff returned various defendants summoned on venire facias. All of them failed to appear and the court ordered *distringas*. On October 28, 1755, the sheriff returned the several defendants in custody on *distringas!* The defendants were ordered to the bar to plead and given time until the next court to prepare.[263]

The return in the Orange cases indicates that *distringas* was not usual nor was its function understood. The use of this writ depended upon a return to the venire that the defendant was sufficient, which meant either that pledges endorse the writ or that a notation of issues (viz., attachable values) be made. None of the books such as the anonymous *Compleat Sheriff* or Dalton's *Sheriffs,* both of which were read by provincial lawyers, makes clear how the return of sufficiency on a venire facias be made. Inevitably the bewildered peace officers resorted to a despairing *non est inventus,*[264] or, if there was any ground for doing so, the return of *nihil habet.*

The common law rule was that if a *nihil habet* (has nothing) were returned on a *distringas,* then capias should issue as third process. Despite the apparent disappearance of *distringas* as usual mesne process, the New York sheriffs often endorsed *nihil* on a venire, although we do not think this was treated as a necessary condition to the issuance of a writ to arrest, for there are only a few

[263] *Ms. Mins. Orange Co. Sess. 1727–79* King v. David Horton, King v. During, King v. Solomon Carpender, King v. Elinor Carpender.

[264] King v. Losie indicted for assault (*Ms. Mins. NYCQS 1732–62* Nov. 7, 1745, Nov. 8, 1749); King v. Thomas Lee, 1772 (*H.R. Pleadings* Pl. K. 1033); there were no minute entries to be found on this case.

Zachariah Rusler and five others were indicted for riot on October 28, 1774 (*Ms. Mins. SCJ 1772–76* [Rough] 207) and a venire facias issued against them was returned "not found." However, in addition to the sheriff's endorsement of "not found" on the writ, the defendants themselves endorsed the writ with their promise to appear (*H.R. Parch.* 187 E 2). There are no other entries to be found on this case.

Abraham Stutt, Thomas Baxter and William Finch were informed against in July and August Term, 1766, for riotous entry of a dwelling in Westchester and process was ordered to issue against them (*Ms. Mins. SCJ 1764–66* [Engr.] 444; *H.R. Pleadings* Pl. K. 1053). On May 2, 1767, "non est" was returned as to Abraham Stutt and on July 31, "non sunt" was returned as to all three defendants (*Ms. Mins. SCJ 1766–69* [Engr.] 188, 254). On April 28, 1770, other process having evidently been issued in the meantime, the sheriff of Dutchess returned Abraham Stutt taken, and he having en-

dorsed his appearance was given the usual rule to plead. On Aug. 4, 1770, judgment for want of a plea was rendered against Stutt (*Ms. Mins. SCJ 1769–72* [Engr.] 200, 245).

On Oct. 31, 1766, Elizabeth and Peter, free negroes, and one Smith were indicted for disorderly house. Elizabeth appeared in court on January 24, 1767, and was given the usual rule to plead but on May 2, 1767, judgment for want of a plea was rendered against her and on July 31, 1767, the sheriff returned "non est" on a *capias pro fine* which had evidently been issued against Elizabeth. At the same time (i.e., on July 31, 1767) "non est" was returned on the venire facias which had issued against Peter (*Ms. Mins. SCJ 1766–69* [Engr.] 27, 95, 186, 254). On April 29, 1769, on the motion of the Attorney General, the sheriff of New York was ordered to return the process in King v. Elizabeth and Peter by the following term or be amerced, but we do not know whether the "process" referred to was process to bring Peter or Smith in to answer, or process of *capias pro fine* against Elizabeth (*Ms. Mins. SCJ 1769–72* [Engr.] 24). There are no further proceedings on the case.

Also see "not found" returned on a venire facias issued on an indictment against Anthony Jeffrey and John Germond, Apr. 1771 (*H.R. Parch.* 183 D 4).

cases where a return of *nihil* was made on a venire facias,[265] and there are cases where the capias issued after a return of *non est inventus* on the venire.[266] If the capias was not served, an *alias* and *pluries capias* might issue. The *pluries capias* was the ultimate process in New York, for after an abortive experiment with outlawry (which we shall speak of in a moment) no scheme of exacting defendants was developed.

It is imprudent to attempt any generalizations regarding the order of process, for the provincial courts do not seem to have been able to carry through the articulation between the return of process and the next precept in the order that the common law prescribed, as peace officers seem to have been impervious to instruction. We have seen capias in misdemeanors where the defendant is returned "found," or returned "taken" and bearing endorsed, the defendants promise to appear,[267] suggesting that there was no actual taking into custody. Yet judging from a letter written by J. T. Kempe to Sheriff Willet of Westchester, February 16, 1767,[268] the endorsement of appearance seems to have been regarded by the local officers as a sort of *sine qua non* for any process. It is noteworthy that although elaborate rules of court for civil process[269] were in existence, the endorsements on indictments such as "run away" or "process issued returned . . . *non est* . . . gone to Pensicola—a soldier in the 26th Regiment"[270] suggest strongly that as to criminal process the venerated and rigid law of return of writs had become something easy and informal in the New World.

In these circumstances it is not surprising to come upon what appears to be an invention of the New York courts, the *alias* and the *pluries venire facias*, which were no more than repeated summons. We have seen no English forms for such writs, and no evidence of a practice in the motherland, only the hint in Hawkins that a new venire might issue on *default*, viz., after a failure to

---

[265] Queen v. Niewenhysen—assault (*Ms. Mins. NYCQS 1694–1731/32* 151 *et seq.*, Aug. 4, 1708); Queen v. Rideout—forcible entry (*ibid.* 135 *et seq.*, Feb. 4, 1707/08); King v. Welsh—assault (*ibid.* 543, 544, Nov. 4, 1731, Feb. 1, 1731/32); King v. Moore & Welsh—assault, return *nihil* (*ibid.* 542, 545, Nov. 1, 1731, Feb. 3, 1731/32).

[266] Cf. *supra* 436 n. 261, Queen v. Cordus, adultery (*Ms. Mins. NYCQS 1694–1731/32* 157 *et seq.*, Feb. 2, 1708/09); King v. Montague, Stephen and Oliver De Lancey, assault (*Ms. Mins. NYCQS 1732–62* 146, 150, Nov. 5, 1742, Feb. 2, 1742/43).

[267] *Ms. Files Dutchess Co. 1763–64* capias in King v. Bogardus. Cf. *Ms. Files Dutchess Co. 1726–40* capias in King v. Maxfield, "I have found the body." In Dutchess as early as 1736, the Common Pleas had a printed writ form with blanks for the operative words of either venire or capias (*Ms. Files Dutchess Co. 1726–40* Wood v. Walker). It was consequently easy to make mistakes. Cf. the printed *alias* of Common Pleas (1769) in *Ms. Files Ulster Co.* Bundle E. No printed Sessions forms have been found.

[268] *Ms. Kempe Letters A–Z.*

[269] *Ms. Rules for the Court of Oyer and Terminer* (Redmond-Livingston Mss.) Rules 4–6, 13.

[270] King v. Edward McCoy—disorderly house (*Ms. Mins. NYCQS 1762–72* 254, May 5, 1768); King v. Thomas Lee—disorderly house, 1771 (*H.R. Pleadings* Pl. K. 1033).

appear when the venire had actually been served. The New York practice, which develops after 1750,[271] had nothing to do with default, for the *alias venire* was issued after a return of *non est* on the first process, and if the *alias venire* were unavailing then the *pluries venire*. This was obviously patterned upon the ancient common law practice respecting the capias but it strikes one as a singularly ineffective device for securing appearance.

It is true that the renewed summons served to stave off discontinuance of process, an ever present hazard which is illustrated by the long periods which often elapsed before everyone was served in, let us say, a riot case, but this could have been accomplished by a capias. We strongly suspect, however, that this new form of process, if it was not inspired by a misreading of Hawkins, may have been contrived for the purpose of running up costs. On this latter point there is an instructive document in the manscripts of John Tabor Kempe respecting the schedule of costs in the case of *King* v. *Murray,* an information for assault and battery brought in the year 1758.[272]

[271] Cf. King v. Robinson—ind. riot, 1754 (*Ms. Mins. SCJ 1754–57* [Engr.] 42); King v. Catharine Turner—ind. disorderly house, 1755 (*ibid.* 200; *H.R. Pleadings* Pl. K. 1056, Pl. K. 898); King v. Levy—inf., 1756 (*Ms. Mins. SCJ 1754–57* [Engr.] 223; *Ms. Mins. SCJ 1757–60* [Engr.] 114; *H.R. Pleadings* Pl. K. 901, Pl. K. 399); King v. Henry Smith—inf. assault, 1757 (*Ms. Mins. SCJ 1756–61* [Rough] 86; *Ms. Mins. SCJ 1757–60* [Engr.] 114); King v. Hannah Robinson—ind. disorderly house, 1764 (*Ms. Mins. SCJ 1762–64* [Engr.] 427; *H.R. Pleadings,* Pl. K. 738); King v. Joseph Rodman—inf. riot, 1764 (*Ms. Mins. SCJ 1762–64* [Engr.] 362; *H.R. Pleadings* Pl. K. 736, K. 740, K. 750; *Ms. Mins. SCJ 1764–66* [Engr.] 76; *Ms. Mins. SCJ 1764–67* [Rough] 12; *Ms. Mins. SCJ 1766–69* [Engr.] 186). The Rodman case dragged on until 1772 when this *pluries venire* issued: "GEORGE the third by the Grace of God of Great Britain France and Ireland King Defender of the Faith and so forth To our Sheriff of our County of Westchester Greeting We command you as oftentimes We have commanded you that you omit not by Reason of any Liberty within your Bailiwick but that the same you enter and cause William Rodman late of the Manor of Pelham in the County of Westchester Yeoman if he be found within your Bailiwick to come before us at our City of New York on the third Tuesday in April next to answer unto us upon certain Articles exhibited against him in Our Supreme Court for our Province of New York at our Suit by Information of our Attorney General and have you then there this Writ WITNESS Daniel Horsmanden Esquire Chief Justice at our City of New York the Twenty fifth day of January in the Twelfth Year of our Reign. J. T. Kempe Attorney General. Clarke." This writ in

typical form was endorsed "not found James DeLancey Sheriff" (*H.R. Parch.* 186 B 2), and there are no further proceedings on the case.

Other cases are King v. Ambrose Jones *et al.*—inf. riot, 1765 (*Ms. Mins. SCJ 1764–66* [Engr.] 368; *H.R. Parch.* 194 H 5, 185 G 2; *Ms. Mins. SCJ 1766–69* [Engr.] 78); King v. Tanner—ind. assault, 1770 (*Ms. Mins. SCJ 1769–72* [Engr.] 147; *H.R. Pleadings* Pl. K. 373; *H.R. Parch.* 182 H 1); King v. Charingcross—ind. assault, 1772 (*Ms. Mins. SCJ 1769–72* [Engr.] 519; *H.R. Pleadings* Pl. K. 389; *H.R. Parch.* 183 D 3); King v. Robinson—inf. riot, 1771 (*H.R. Pleadings* Pl. K. 386; *J. T. Kempe Lawsuits* P–R); King v. Goven—inf., 1771 (*H.R. Parch.* no number); King v. Mason—ind. assault, 1772 (*Ms. Mins. SCJ 1769–72* [Engr.] 472, 474; *H.R. Pleadings* Pl. K. 387, 395; *H.R. Parch.* 183 C 9 [the *alias*], *H.R. Pleadings* Pl. K. 1049 [the *pluries*], *H.R. Parch.* 184 K 9 [another *pluries*]); King v. Hortwyck—ind. disorderly house, 1774 (*Ms. Mins. SCJ 1772–76* [Rough] 184; *H.R. Pleadings* Pl. K. 354; *H.R. Parch.* 183 C 8; *H.R. Parch.* no number; *H.R. Parch.* 35 L 10).

[272] The costs for the August vacation, 1758, indicate a charge of 6*s.* for a "draft of Venire facias Folio 4 at 1/6." For "copy and engrossing" the venire facias, the charge was 6*s.* plus 6*d.* more for the parchment used. The seal cost 2*s.* 3*d.* making a total of 14*s.* 9*d.* In October Term, 1758, a charge of 1*s.* was made for the sheriff's return "non est" and another shilling for the clerk's filing the return. For a "motion for alias Venire Facias" the charge was 5*s.* In Vacation, 1758, after the October Term, 6*s.* was charged for the draft of the *alias venire facias,* 6*s.* for copy and engrossing, 6*d.* for parchment, and 2*s.* 3*d.* for the seal. In January Term,

The same practices in returns which obtained respecting the *venire facias* were applied to the *alias* and *pluries venire facias,* that is to say, sheriffs would return *non est* if they had not succeeded in summoning the defendant, and if the process were served, the defendant's endorsement would be made upon it, and sometimes also the sheriff would make the additional return of *cepi corpus.*

The invention of an extended summons by means of repetition as an *alias* and *pluries venire* stands in sharp contrast to the equally unorthodox use of capias as a first process in misdemeanors. This had been resorted to rather freely in the late seventeenth and early eighteenth centuries both in New York City and in the country.[273] The practice had fallen into disuse as technical knowledge improved, but came to be revived during the disorders following the French and Indian War. It is this revival which seems so paradoxical since it occurs just after the first experiments with the *venire facias* had been made. For this particular aberration, viz., the use of capias, there was the example of contemporary usage in England. At this time it was customary in the King's Bench to require the arrest of defendants after indictments for misdemeanors. This was not done by capias but by bench warrant issued either by a justice at Sessions, or after Sessions, by King's Bench on certificate from the clerk of the peace.[274] This practice, eventually sanctioned by Act of Parlia-

---

1759, 1s. was charged for the sheriff's return "non est," another shilling for the clerk's filing the return, and 5s. for a "motion for pluries venire facias." In next Vacation, drafting, copying, engrossing and sealing the *pluries venire facias* cost 14s. 9d., and when, in April Term, 1759, the sheriff returned "non est" and the clerk filed the return, the charge was 2 shillings. In this term, also, there was a charge of 5s. for a "motion for continuation of process" and in next Vacation 14s. 9d. was charged for drafting, copying, engrossing and sealing a *pluries venire facias,* which was evidently the second *pluries venire* issued in the case. In July Term, 1759, the sheriff again returned "non est" on which the usual charges were made and there was again a motion for continuation of process. In next Vacation the usual charges were made for drawing up a *pluries venire facias* which was the third pluries issued in the case. In October Term, 1759, there is a charge of 5s. 6d. for "sheriff summoning" and 1s. for "clerk filing venire facias" as well as 5s. for "motion for rule to plead" (*J. T. Kempe Lawsuits* L–O sub nom. William Murray). While this bill of costs indicates that the sheriff had "summoned" the defendant, nevertheless the minute entries for October Term, 1759, state as follows: "Sheriff returns cepi corpus" as to William Murray (*Ms. Mins. SCJ 1757–60* [Engr.] 257).
    273 King v. Van Borson and Marschalk—ind.

not making proper assessments (*Ms. Mins. NYCQS 1694–1731/32* 17, 18, Nov. 4, 1696); King v. Cornelius Sebring—ind. selling unmerchantable flour (*ibid.* 38, May 4, 1698); King v. Cooley—ind. entertaining negroes (*ibid.* 40, Aug. 3, 1698); King v. Provoost—ind. false weights (*ibid.* 60, Feb. 5, 1700/01); King v. Jack—ind. peace breach, 1701 (*Ms. Kings Co. Ct. & Rd. Recs. 1692–1825* 74); Queen v. Roome—ind. entertaining slaves (*Ms. Mins. NYCQS 1694–1731/32* 73, Nov. 4, 1702); Queen v. Buckenhoven et al.—ind. assault on constable (*ibid.* 72); Queen v. Provoost—ind. false election returns (*ibid.* 72, Nov. 4, 1702); Queen v. Bickley—ind. keeping shop open against statute (*ibid.* 94, Feb. 7, 1704/05); Queen v. Sydenham—ind. forcible entry (*ibid.* 135, Feb. 4, 1707/08) —possibly a bench warrant; Queen v. Wood —ind. (*ibid.* 185, 190, Nov. 8, 1710, Feb. 6, 1710/11); Queen v. Young—ind. trespass (*ibid.* 167, Nov. 2, 1709); Queen v. Elbertse—ind. entertaining slaves (*ibid.* 174, 176, 177, May 3, Aug. 1, 2, 1710); Queen v. Wright—ind. assault (*ibid.* 174, 176, 177, May 3, Aug. 1, 2, 1710); King v. Peter, a negro—ind. entertaining slaves (*ibid.* 280, 285, Feb. 2, 1714/15, May 3, 1715); King v. Solomons —ind. assault and attempted stabbing (*ibid.* 411, Aug. 8, 1722).
    274 On this matter cf. 1 Chitty, *Criminal Law* 340. For the Sessions practice, *Crown Cir. Com-*

ment,[275] may have influenced the New York courts, although there is no direct evidence of the fact. There was, in any event, no exact imitation, for although there are some cases where the Supreme Court employed bench warrants, the use of capias seems to have been preferred.[276] The chief difference as a matter of convenience lay in the circumstances that the bench warrant was addressed generally to all peace officers and not, as the capias, to the sheriff of a particular county. As a matter of law, the bench warrant was, of course, not subject to the rules governing a capias; it had no limitations in respect to time of return[277] and was in particular not hampered by restrictions of form. In Dutchess County, beginning in the year 1767, a unique development takes place, for thenceforward the process entries are almost exclusively for bench warrants as first and sole process.[278] This development seems to be confined to this county, for although bench warrants are sometimes used at other county

panion (1768) 32. In Rex v. Freeman, 1731 (2 Barn. K.B. 28) it was said that the practice existed from time immemorial, a typical manner of justifying something questionable.
[275] 48 Geo. III c.58.
[276] Cf. King v. Dowers—ind. riot, 1767 (Ms. Mins. SCJ 1764–67 [Rough] 233); King v. Gilliland—ind. disorderly house, 1767 (Ms. Mins. SCJ 1766–69 [Engr.] 317, 318); King v. Clark—ind. assault, 1767 (ibid. 317, 318); King v. Pat Walsh & James Graham—ind. assault, 1769 (Ms. Mins. SCJ 1769–72 [Engr.] 106); King v. Burrel—ind. disorderly house, 1773 (Ms. Mins. SCJ 1772–76 [Rough] 128, 131). Also see the case of Catherine Johnson, indicted on Oct. 27, 1773, for disorderly house. In that case the Supreme Court, on October 28, "ordered the sheriff of New York do apprehend the defendant and bring her into court to be dealt with according to law" (ibid. 130, 131). Also see King v. Barberie Myers, indictment for disorderly house, ordered to be apprehended and brought to court to be dealt with according to law (ibid. 131, Oct. 27, 28, 1773).
[277] Cf. Mayhew v. Hill (2 Esp. 683).
[278] Ms. Mins. Dutchess Co. Sess. Liber D, beginning with King v. Jeremiah Jones (counterfeiting), Oct. 9, 1767. There are a number of these preserved in the county files. Typical is that in King v. Aaron Reade (Ms. Files Dutchess Co. 1767): "DUTCHES COUNTY: TO ALL CONSTABLES and Other his Majesties Officers within the County of Dutches and To every of them whom it may Concern. These are To will and require you, and in his Majesties Name to Charge and Command You upon sight hereof To bring before me or any other of his Majesties Justices of the peace for the County aforesaid the Body of Aaron Reade. To find Sufficient Surety for his personal appearance at the next General Sessions of the peace To be holden at poghkeepsie in and for Dutchess County on the Third Tuesday in May next to answer for an assault upon one John Maxfield and him did Beat wound and evilly entreat so that of his Life it was greatly dispaired and other harms to him Did to the great Damage of the said John Maxfield. WHEREOF he the said Aaron Reade Stands Indicted, and further To be Dealt withal according To Justice. HEREOF you are not To fail at your peril. GIVEN under my hand and seal in Dutches County the Thirteenth Day of January anno Dom. 1768—

Henry D. Burgh, Justice."
Cf. also King v. Ogle, et al.—ind. riot, 1767 (Ms. Mins. SCJ 1764–67 [Rough] 232). "By the Honorable Robert R. Livingston Esquire fourth Justice of the Supreme Court of Judicature for the Province of New York—To all Sheriffs Constables and other his Majesty's Peace Officers within the Province of New York and to every of them whom it may concern These are to will and require and in his Majesty's Name to Charge and command you and every of you upon Sight hereof to apprehend and bring before me or any other of the Judges of the Supreme Court of Judicature for the Province of New York the Bodies of Thomas Ogle . . . Thomas McDaniel . . . and Alexander McDaniel . . . for that they . . . with force and arms . . . in and upon one Cornelius Ryan unlawfully riotously and routously did make an Assault and him did beat his Majesty's peace whereof they stand indicted to the end that they . . . may find Sufficient Sureties for their . . . appearance at the next Supreme Court of Judicature . . . to answer . . . and further to be dealt with according to Law and to be in the meantime of good behaviour; Hereof fail not at your Peril" (J. T. Kempe Lawsuits L–O). See also the entry King v. Barnes (Ms. Mins. SCJ 1766–69 [Engr.] 322, 329, 380) and the warrant in King v. Wittmer and Haumaid—ind. forgery, 1774 (H.R. Pleadings Pl. K. 396).

Sessions[279] they do not become usual process. And in view of the decimation of records we can only guess that entry of a general order to apprehend was thus executed.[280]

About the class of cases which lay more or less between misdemeanors and felonies, the receivers of stolen goods, the colonists were in doubt. At common law receiving was not a felony, but beginning with the statute 3 Wm. & Mary c.9, a series of Acts of Parliament sought to cope with the problem, directing that receivers were to be treated as accessories after the fact, and then providing that they be tried for misdemeanor if the principal be not taken. Possibly under the influence of these changes in England, the New Yorkers invariably employed a capias as process against persons accused of receiving.[281] A similar policy existed in relation to petit larceny, for, as we have already indicated, if the defendant were not already committed or on recognizance before indictment, capias was usually issued.

Process after Indictment for Felony; Outlawry

One cannot be diffuse about the process after indictment for felony in New York, for ordinarily serious offenders were already in custody or on recognizance before a true bill was found, and the records consequently have relatively little information to yield. The colonists, once the capias was introduced, never used a venire in capital cases. The employment of a capias as initial process for persons indicted of felony is attested by a few early cases,[282] and we have found what may be described as a blank form of a capias used at Circuit in 1722.[283] To what extent the bench warrant may have supplanted the

---

279 King v. Patrick McKay, 1765 (*Ms. Files Ulster Co.* Bundle K); King. v. Burnet, 1772 (*ibid.* Bundle L).

280 It should be pointed out that many of the process entries in the minutes are too equivocal to use as evidence. This is particularly the case with the entries which show an order that process issue and the eventual return of *cepi corpus*. As we have seen, this return was used on venire facias and one cannot know what the process in fact may have been.

281 King v. Blanck—incitement to steal, 1697 (*Mins. SCJ 1693–1701* 113); Queen v. Anne White (*Ms. Mins. NYCQS 1694–1731/32* 94, Feb. 7, 1704/05); Queen v. Cure (*ibid.* 157, 159, Feb. 2, 1708/09, May 3, 1709). Also see Queen v. Clara Harris, also indicted for trading with slaves and buying stolen goods. Capias was awarded against her (*ibid.* 157, 159, Feb. 2, 1708/09). In Queen v. Mary Bosch, capias awarded on indictment for the

same offense (*ibid.* 175, May 3, 1710); King v. Arden and King v. Brown (*Ms. Mins. NYCQS 1732–62* 84, Feb. 10, 1737/38); King v. Elizabeth Clark (*ibid.*).

282 Cf. Queen v. Thomas—pres. possessing clipped money (*Ms. Mins. NYCQS 1694–1731/32* 72, Nov. 4, 1702); Queen v. John Moore and John Riggs—ind. murder (*ibid.* 203, Aug. 8, 1711); King v. Batterson—ind. (*ibid.* 297, Aug. 2, 1715).

283 *Misc. Mss. Ulster Co.*: "Ulster ss George by the grace of God . . . to the Sheriff and Constables of the County of Ulster or any of them Greeting We command you . . . that you take the body of —— and —— safely keep so that you have —— forthwith before our Justices of our Court of Oyer & Terminer & General Goal Delivery . . . to Answer us of a —— whereof —— stands indicted and have you then and there this writt Witness Lewis Morris Esqr Chief Justice of our Province of Newyork and first justice of our

traditional first process can only be conjectured, for too often the process entries are so cryptically phrased that either bench warrant or capias may have been used.[284]

If the capias could not be served, there would issue, as in England, an *alias,* and then a *pluries capias.* This practice was established early in the eighteenth century,[285] but the evidence of its persistence is slight.[286] The process normally had to be returned at a certain day, and if the return was negative the *alias* would issue. The repetition through a *pluries* was essential in order to found the procedure by outlawry. But in New York after some experimentation with this grimmest of all common law processes, the matter was abandoned until the eve of the Revolution.

The cases which came before the courts all involved misdemeanors, but as one of the colonial statutes on the matter dealt with felonies as well as with misdemeanors it will be convenient to consider the outlawry problem as a whole. The story in New York is very curious. Apparently no early effort had been made by the courts to introduce this procedure into the Province. In 1702 Philip French and Thomas Wenham were indicted in the Supreme Court of a "high misdemeanor," the offense being the signing of a so-called treasonable address in the Bayard case. Either innocently or to avoid trial, the two men, both leading citizens, left the Province. In this situation, as it was impossible to serve the defendants, a provincial act was passed outlawing them[287] but relieving them of the penalties if they appeared and gave security to answer. The act further provided that in the future in both civil and criminal cases if a resident served with process should wilfully depart the Province and should not within six months appear, proclamation should be made by the sheriff in the place of the defendant's residence, the same to be duly returned to the Supreme Court and recorded, and within twenty days after the return the persons against whom proclamation was made should be deemed outlawed "to all Intents and purposes according to the effect of outlawries within

said Court at Kingston the —— day of September in the ninth year of our Reign."

[284] In King v. Benjamin Chace and Jacob Mace —inf. forgery of bills of credit, process ordered and sheriff returns *cepi corpus* (*Ms. Mins. SCJ 1750–54* [Engr.] 274, 349).

[285] Cf. King v. Peter *et al.*—ind. larceny (*Ms. Mins. NYCQS 1694–1731/32* 49, 52, 53, Aug. 2, 1699, Feb. 8, 1699/1700); Queen v. Cordus—ind. adultery (*ibid.* 157 *et seq.,* Feb. 2, 1708/09).

[286] Most of the evidence relates to misdemeanors and here the difficulty is again with the form of entry. Thus in King v. Klock (inf. as common disturber of the peace, 1767) the sheriff returned *cepi,* but a rescue by Klock's son. The Supreme Court ordered a capias but whether or not this was an *alias* we cannot be certain (*Ms. Mins. SCJ 1766–69* [Engr.] 328). The capias was used as first process in informations for intrusion or conversion of King's goods (cf. 2 Hawkins, *Pleas of the Crown* c.27 §12 and King v. Van Rensselaer, *Ms. Mins. SCJ 1766–69* [Engr.] 329, 388).

[287] 1 *Col. Laws NY* 476–478. The act contained also regulations respecting service of process.

the Kingdome of England." Procedure for reversal of outlawry was also provided.

Governor Cornbury sent the act to England with some objurgatory comment about its injustice[288] and it was promptly repealed by the Queen on December 31, 1702, because of its repugnancy to English law owing to the shortness of time allowed defendants.[289] The statute accomplished its immediate aim in securing the appearance of French and Wenham,[290] and was seemingly responsible for a subsequent abortive attempt to introduce outlawry procedure on the English model.

The first case occurred in 1708 when Abraham Rideout was indicted in the New York Quarter Sessions for a forcible entry and breach of the peace.[291] The sheriff returned *nihil* on the venire facias and a capias was then ordered to issue. In August, 1708 a *non est inventus* was returned on this and an *alias capias* then issued which was likewise returned *non est* in November. A *pluries* then went forth. On May 4, 1709, the minutes of the Quarter Sessions have the entry "defendant was called upon the exigent and did not appear, First Default." There ensued at the next three terms further calls upon the exigent and on May 3, 1710, the "sheriff returns the exigent served and endorsed in hac verba that the defendant is not to be found in his bailiwick. Therefore it is ordered by the court that the said Abraham Rideout be outlawed according to the law and custom of England."[292]

The New York Sessions Court was obviously making an attempt to conform exactly to the traditional English ritual of outlawry, and the formal defect of a proclamation in Sessions in lieu of the county court, which the New Yorkers did not possess, was evidently not regarded as a real obstacle, especially as the proceedings were conducted under the eye of May Bickley, the Attorney General.

The Rideout case was the only one conducted to its conclusion, but two other cases were carried through the exigent. In 1708 Effio Niewenhysen was indicted in New York Quarter Sessions for assault and breach of the peace.[293] Again a venire facias was used and returned *nihil,* whereupon a capias, an

---

288 4 *Doc. Rel. Col. Hist. NY* 958, 999.
289 6 *Acts of Privy Council, Colonial* 20; *Cal. S.P. Colonial* 17–23, 77.
290 So, Atwood, C.J., in his defense of his conduct (13 *NYHS Colls.* [1880] 284).
291 *Ms. Mins. NYCQS 1694–1731/32* 135, 146, 150, 152, 160, 163, 166, 170, 174, Feb. 4, May 4, Aug. 3, Nov. 2, 1708, May 4, Aug. 2, Nov. 1, 1709, Feb. 7, 1709/10, May 3, 1710.

292 No *capias utlagatum* issued. In England, the justices did not have the power to issue this writ (Lambard, *Eirenarcha* [1614 ed.] Bk. 4 c.8).
293 *Ms. Mins. NYCQS 1694–1731/32* 151, 152, 163, 167, 168, 170, Aug. 4, Nov. 2, 1708, Nov. 1, 2, 1709, Feb. 8, 1709/10.

alias capias (probably) and a *pluries* were issued and returned *non est*. The court on Bickley's motion ordered an exigent which the sheriff returned *cepi corpus* and after a day's default the defendant appeared and supplied sureties, just one year after the return of the venire. Again, in February, 1709, the grand jurors in New York Quarter Sessions brought in a bill against Henry Cordus for living in open adultery, a most unusual prosecution. Here on the Attorney General's motion a capias was at once ordered. This, as well as a later *alias* and *pluries,* was returned *non est inventus* and the exigent was then ordered, November 1, 1709. Cordus appeared February 7, 1709/10 and offered security to appear and subsequently to plead.[294]

With these cases New York's first adventures with a process of outlawry ended. There is, so far as we are aware, no evidence why the experiment was so abruptly brought to a close, but differences in judicial machinery made impossible a literal compliance with the exact requirements of English procedure, a matter upon which the common law courts laid the greatest stress. The situation, moreover, in New York was such that the procedure was not practical. A man of substance would almost inevitably appear, as the records show, but for the footloose rogue it was easy enough to vanish into the woods or to evaporate into a neighboring province, to be barked at by futile hue and cry warrants, leaving nothing behind to forfeit.

It was not until the era of disorders just before the Revolution that process against defendants developed inadequacies which had not previously been sensed. We have seen how experiments with summons were made and how bench warrants out of the Supreme Court and even General Sessions met certain difficulties implicit in the restricted ambit of a warrant from the hand of a justice of the peace. It was precisely this problem which the provincial legislature sought to solve in 1771. In England a practice had developed known as the backing of warrants, that is, a warrant issued by a justice in one county was given force and effect in another county by the simple expedient of having it endorsed by a justice of the second county. This practice had been confirmed by statute in the reign of George II.[295] Apparently the New York justices were unwilling to try the backing of warrants on their own initiative and the New York provincial act sought to introduce the usage in language practically identical with that of the English statute.[296]

The procedure thus introduced assured a much greater cursiveness of pre-

[294] *Ibid.* 157, 159, 163, 167, 169, 170, Feb. 2, 1708/09, May 3, Aug. 2, Nov. 1, 1709, Feb. 7, 8, 1709/10.

[295] 23 Geo. II c.26 §11; 24 Geo. II c.55.

[296] 5 *Col. Laws NY* 209.

cepts, but it did not supply a severe enough remedy against the obdurate evader of process. It had been sought to bolster this weakness in the New York system by the device of governors' proclamations for arrest,[297] a clumsy and basically ineffective substitute for a really trenchant judicial process. The vanity of such measures came fully to light during the conflict over the Vermont lands, and accordingly, in March, 1774, the New York legislature took a bold step. A special act was passed[298] for the counties of Albany and Charlotte that imposed severe penalties for riot, and that enacted a version of the riot act provisions of the English statute 1 Geo. I St. 2 c.5 respecting proclamations and making it felony to interfere. The act then proceeded to state that, proof having been made that Ethan Allen and others were the principal leaders in the riots, proclamation for their arrest had been made and that "it is indispensably necessary for want of Process to Outlawry (which is not used in this Colony)" that provision be made for bringing such offenders in future to trial. The Governor with advice of the Council, as often as such persons should be indicted either in Charlotte or Albany for a capital offense or for any of the offenses in the act not made felony, might issue an order in council to require such persons to surrender within seventy days after the first publication of the order in two newspapers. The order was to be posted on the courthouses of the two counties and upon the door of two public houses. If the offender indicted of a capital offense did not surrender he should be convicted and attainted of felony and suffer death; the Supreme Court or Circuit Courts for the county might lawfully award execution. Persons indicted of lesser crimes were to be deemed guilty and the court when the indicted was found might lawfully proceed to judgment.[299]

The extraordinary act was temporary and expired of its own limitation December 31, 1775. It was savagely attacked by the Green Mountain Boys at a "convention" held April 26, 1776. In the pamphlet of their proceedings the following significant statement appears: "May it be considered that the legislative authority of the Province of New York had no Constitutional right or power to make such Laws and consequently that they are Null and Void from the Nature and Energy of the English Constitution therefore as they merit no place among the laws of the Realm of Great Britain. . . ."[300]

---

[297] Cf. supra 34, 291.
[298] 5 Col. Laws NY 647.
[299] See also the report of the assembly and the proclamation of Gov. Tryon (4 Doc. Hist. NY 525–527).

[300] The Proceeding of the Convention of the Representatives of the New-Hampshire Settlers 16. The document closes with the following verses:
"When Caesar reigned King at Rome,
Saint Paul was sent to hear his Doom,

This statute proved to be a futile gesture, for in spite of a £100 reward offered by the Governor, no one was able to take the offenders and an application for troops was finally addressed to General Gage.[301] The situation was clearly one where no process on earth would have availed. The authorities had had a foretaste of this sort of lawlessness when they had tried to round up the rebels for the Dutchess Assizes, and they should have realized that the provincial act was not only footless, but dangerous because of its oppressive character. During the preceding decade, there had been many episodes where process had been flouted yet nothing effective had been done to strengthen the executive power of the courts.

The "Incompleat" Sheriff

For all that official judicial records exhibit a long and well-seated understanding of technical nicety in the use of the law of process, there is evidence of a situation of equally long standing respecting the ignorance, stupidity and unconcern in the officers whose duty it was to see process served. We have already remarked upon the lack of consistency in the return of writs, and the task of instruction was never successfully completed. Two letters from sheriffs, dated 1729 and 1767, indicate how slowly an awareness of what a sheriff's duty consisted in had developed.

In 1729 Sheriff Goose Van Schaick of Albany wrote to Attorney John Chambers for advice as follows:

> Sir as I ame Sherrif of . . . Albany I am directed by Cerataine act of the genrall assembly Entituled an act for Continuing and enforcing the acts . . . to seize on the goods Chattells and the Real Estate of parsons adjudged Convict and make seal . . . in same manner as the sherrif is directed by another act for defraying the Cost and Contingent Charges of the trading house . . . whereby . . . I am first to seize on the personall Estate the quere is how I shall come at the parsonall Estate if the Convicted parsons keep theire doors lokt up . . . so that I cann nott enter . . . unless I Break their doors weither I may lawfully do it or nott

But *Roman Law* in a criminal Case,
Must have the Accuser Face to Face,
Or *Caesar* gives a flat Denial—
But here's a Law made now of late;
Which destines Men to awful Fate
And Hangs and Damns without a Trial,
Which made me view all Nature through
To find a Law where Men were ti'd,

By Legal Act which doth exact
Men's Lives before they're Try'd
Then down I took the sacred Book
And turn'd the Pages o'er
But could not find one of this kind
By God or Man before."

[301] 4 *Doc. Hist. NY* 534.

2 Secondly in what manner I ame to Enter and seize on the Reall Estate . . . to gett actuall possession . . .

4 And in Case I may Enter with Force on yᵉ Reall Estates . . .

7 And . . . if I am seized Either of parsonall or Reall Estate if it shall be Lawful to take Recognizance for the fine & forfeiture of the Convicted Parsons as directed by one of the aforementioned acts Because the act first above mentioned doth nott mention any thing upon that head. . . .[302]

Sheriff James Livingston of Dutchess was no less troubled in 1767 and he sought counsel of Duane, the Deputy Attorney General:

I have a prisoner in my custody for horse stealing, and have Recᵈ the Inclosed Letter, from the Justice who committed him I wish youᵈ be pleasᵈ to direct me how to proceed with the prisoner Whether I shoᵈ Carry him to the next Sheriff or whether I must carry him Clear to the place where the felony was committed or not and whether this letter is Sufficient forme to Convey him I take this liberty as you told me you acted for the Attᵉʸ Genˡ. Stevens who I told you was killed in apprehending a Traitor is still alive—But a person Stabᵈ my Deputy in the breast with a Sword after he was arrested & made his Escape and now hides and lurks in the County he denies he was taken . . . Shoᵈ be glad of yoʳ thoᵗˢ If he stands armed on his Defense whether he may not be shot at safely. . . .[303]

Occasionally the sheriff's troubles arose from a mixture of ignorance and timorousness. This is illustrated by an amusing correspondence between John Tabor Kempe and Harmanus Schuyler, sheriff of Albany, with reference to the serving of writs on John Henry Lydius and his son Baltus. On August 13, 1764, Attorney General John Tabor Kempe wrote to Harmanus Schuyler sending him "several processes at the suit of the King." One of these was a *"capias pro fine"* against John Henry Lydius convicted of intrusion on Crown lands and Kempe explained to the sheriff that "this writ is in the nature of an Execution to which no bail can be taken." Kempe also sent a capias against Lydius for a £5,000 debt on a forfeited bond. On December 10, 1764, Schuyler wrote to Kempe asking him how to serve execution on Lydius, since his doors were locked, and on December 31, 1764, Kempe advised the sheriff as follows:

---

[302] *Misc. Mss. Albany 1691–1799.*

[303] *James Duane Papers* Box 2, 1767–72. On May 1, 1761, J. T. Kempe was obliged to write to the sheriff of Dutchess suggesting that he keep Charles Hamilton and certain other defendants safely in jail and Kempe explained that "The Reason of my mentioning this to you, is because several

Criminals have broke Goal & made their Escape lately from some of the Counties, particularly last year one did from Westchester—and I should be very sorry should you be liable to be punished ~~as a Felon if they~~ [*sic*] so severely as the Law directs for the Escape of a Felon" (*J. T. Kempe Lawsuits* G–J).

If Mr. Lydius or his son cannot be taken . . . you must get assistance and go to the House . . . and tell the Persons in the House the cause of your coming and request . . . admittance. If they refuse . . . you must break open the Doors, which is Justifiable to serve a Capias Pro Fine . . . you have also a Scire Facias against John Henry Lydius which I presume you know how to serve,—I think the Capias pro Fine against Baltus Lydius is for £10 . . . and if he pays . . . he need not be carried to Gaol . . . but you cannot take Bail on the capias pro Fine against John Henry Lydius. . . .

Despite the Attorney General's careful instructions, the sheriff was unable to serve the writs and wrote to Kempe as follows on January 14, 1765:

Inclosed in this two writs an Execution in Sarifacas a John Henry Lidius. My debety has been to Lidius with two witnesses . . . Col. Lidius . . . looked out of the wender . . . my debety began to Read the Sairfacias . . . he sute the wender. I have not been able to get them yet. If you pleas to renue the Execution . . . I shall get Lidius and his Sun.

Kempe was very patient with Sheriff Schuyler, for on January 21, 1765, he sent the sheriff "a repitition of processes," but he warned that

if they should escape you must take the consequences . . . I have sufficient proof against you and shall take care to see that you shall make good to the Crown . . . why did you send the Writs by the post so late that . . . the King must have been delayed three weeks, why have you made no return on the Scire Facias . . . if you could not have returned Scire Feci you should have returned a Nihil. I have moved the Supreme Court against you as by the inclosed Rule of court . . . you will . . . shew cause . . . for in default I shall certainly issue the attachment . . . for the Public shall not suffer by the neglect of its officers . . . if it can be prevented by yr humble servt John Tabor Kempe.[304]

The rule of court referred to by Kempe was obtained in the following manner on January 19, 1765:

The Attorney General shewing to the court that he issued a capias pro fine against John Henry Lidius and . . . Baltus Lidius and sent them last vacation to Harmanus Schuyler Sheriff of Albany that the said Harmanus Schuyler had by letter to the Attorney General now read in Court acknowledged the Receipt of these Processes, and by the same letter Informed the Attorney Gen-

---

[304] *J. T. Kempe Lawsuits* L–O *sub nom.* John Henry Lydius is the source of all of the above quotations. On the process itself *infra* 729 *et seq.*

eral that the . . . [Lydiuses] both kept close with the Doors locked, and requesting the Attorney General's opinion how to proceed in the Execution of the said
Processes; that thereupon the said Atty General by Letter now read in Court
did direct him how to proceed in executing said Processes . . . [but the sheriff]
informed the Attorney General he had not executed the said writs . . . that he
did not think it safe, the said Lidius and his Son being resolute Fellows Whereby
the King is injured in his Suits and publick Justice delayed: and therefore the
Attorney General moved for an Attachment against Harmanus Schuyler for
this Neglect of his Duty and Contempt in disobeying the King's writs . . .
Ordered Harmanus Schuyler shew Cause . . . why an Attachment should not
issue. . . .

On April 20, 1765, Schuyler appeared in the Supreme Court "pursuant to the
Rule of last Term to shew cause why an attachment should not issue against
him: and the court having heard what he had to offer and judging it insufficient to excuse him therefore set a fine on him of [£20] which he paid in
court and was discharged."[305]

That there was some justification for the sheriff's fear of those "resolute
fellows," John Henry Lydius and his son Baltus, is evidenced by the fact that
on the very same day that he was fined for contempt, he, Sheriff Schuyler,
paid to the prothonotary in court a fine of £10 which he had collected from
Baltus Lydius[306] and at the same time filed an affidavit in the Supreme Court
"that the defendant did assault and wound the Sheriff in execution of his
office." The court thereupon "ordered that the said Sheriff take the Body of
the Said Baltus Lidius into his Custody for this Offense and him safely keep
until delivered by due Course of Law. And that the Attorney General file an
Information against . . . [the defendant] for the offense aforesaid."[307]

On April 27, 1765, the Attorney General filed an information against Baltus
Lydius for assaulting the sheriff of Albany in execution of his office, and accordingly a "judge's warrant" was issued against Lydius in April Term,
1765.[308] In the Supreme Court minutes of May Term, 1767, it is indicated that

---

305 *Ms. Mins. SCJ 1764–66* (Engr.) 117; *Ms.
Mins. SCJ 1764–67* (Rough) 57; also see *H.R.
Pleadings* Pl. K. 733.

306 In *ibid.* K. 748, there is to be found an
alias capias pro fine for £10 against Baltus Lydius,
and the return endorsed on the back of this writ by
Harmanus Schuyler, sheriff of Albany, is as follows: "The body in custody and I have got the
fine."

307 *Ms. Mins. SCJ 1764–66* (Engr.) 164.

308 "To all Sheriffs Constables . . . [&c]

Whereas it appears to me on the Oath of Hermans
Schuyler Esqr. Sheriff of . . . Albany that Baltus
Lydius . . . assaulted and wounded the said Harmanus Schuyler . . . in the due execution of his office. These are therefore To will and require and in
his Majesty's name to Charge and Command you
. . . upon Sight hereof to Apprehend and to bring
the said Baltus Lydius before me or any other of the
Judges of the Supreme Court of Judicature . . .
To the End that he . . . find Sufficient Sureties for
his . . . [illegible] appearance at the next Su-

the sheriff of Albany returned "non est"[309] and subsequently two writs of *pluries venire facias* which were issued against Baltus Lydius, and both of these were endorsed "not found."[310] Evidently process had been ineffectual to apprehend Baltus Lydius until November 30, 1770, when Deputy Attorney General Sylvester of Albany wrote to John Tabor Kempe as follows:

> Baltus Lydius . . . is lately taken at the suit of the Crown by process issued out of the Supreme Court and seems to be at a loss what it should be for and has applyed to me for assistance & direction—He says he paid the Sheriff long ago a £10 Fine for something he knows not from whence it originated—will you Please at your leisure give me a short sketch of the matter & the grounds of the present prosecution . . . with a Copy . . . of the Information if any fyled against him.[311]

Sheriff Schuyler was remiss in more cases than that of Lydius, and another example of his laxity may be seen in the case of *King* v. *William Snyder*. Snyder had posted a bond of £20 before a justice of the peace for his wife to appear at General Sessions to give evidence in a certain proceeding, but Mrs. Snyder did not appear in court and the default was recorded in Sessions and estreated to the Supreme Court. Thereupon the Attorney General commenced an action of debt against Snyder on the forfeited recognizance, claiming as the King's damages £30.[312] A capias was issued on August 4, 1764, to take Snyder for the debt, but this writ was endorsed by Sheriff Schuyler "not found."[313] However, a *pluries capias* dated January 19, 1765, bore the following return: "At the request and prayer of the plaintiff, I appoint . . . [one A.S.] to serve this writ Harmanus Schuyler Sheriff—I have taken the body Harmanus Schuyler Sheriff £1."[314] Sheriff Schuyler having returned the defendant taken, the Attorney General moved in the Supreme Court on April 27, 1765, that the sheriff bring in the defendant's body or be amerced 40s.[315] However, we have found a *pluries capias* of debt in 1767 on which Schuyler

---

preme Court of Judicature . . . in July next to answer . . . Hereof you are not to fail at your peril . . ." (*H.R. Pleadings* Pl. K. 798).

[309] *Ms. Mins. SCJ 1766–69* (Engr.) 186.

[310] *H.R. Parch.* 185 F 8 and 186 B 8.

[311] *J. T. Kempe Lawsuits* L–O. Sheriff Schuyler was probably not entirely blameless in his failure properly to execute his office, for on July 30, 1768, the following entry appears in the Supreme Court minutes: "The Defendant being Sherif of . . . Albany & not appearing in pursuance of an Order of this Court in October Term last nor having re-

turned any Process during the Term: It is ordered by the Court that an Attachment issue against him unless he shews Cause to the Contrary by the first day of next Term" (*Ms. Mins. SCJ 1766–69* [Engr.] 508). In *H.R. Pleadings* Pl. K. 787, is to be found the "agenda" for Apr. 18, 1765, and therein it is stated that the sheriff of Albany was to be obliged to account for fines, estreats, etc.

[312] *H.R. Parch.* 29 B 2.

[313] *H.R. Pleadings* Pl. K. 183.

[314] *H.R. Parch.* 185 E 9.

[315] *Ms. Mins. SCJ 1764–66* (Engr.) 177.

made the endorsement "not found,"[316] and on May 2, 1767, the Supreme Court
minute entries reflect that he returned "non est."[317] On January 23, 1768,
Schuyler returned the defendant taken and was ordered on the Attorney General's motion to bring Snyder's body in during the sitting of the court or be
amerced 40s.[318] On August 3, 1771, judgment for want of a plea was entered
against Snyder,[319] and the judgment roll indicates that the said William Snyder "although solemnly required came not nor doth he say anything in bar or
denial of the said action." The court therefore adjudged that the King recover
against Snyder his debt and £10 13s. for damages and costs. This judgment
was signed by Daniel Horsmanden, Chief Justice of the Supreme Court, on
December 3, 1771.[320] A writ of *fieri facias* was evidently issued against Snyder
on this judgment. Henry Ten Eyck had meantime become sheriff of Albany
and Kempe had new troubles. On May 3, 1772 the Attorney General moved,
and his motion was granted, requiring the sheriff of Albany to "amend his
return to the *fi. fa.* issued against the defendant by the first day of the next term
or attachment to issue against him."[321] Apparently Sheriff Ten Eyck did not
make the proper returns to the writs for on August 31, 1772, Kempe wrote
to him as follows:

> Having repeatedly in the case of the King against William Snyder, received
> from you Returns to the Fi Fa's issued against him for a debt due to his Majesty, "that you had not found Goods nor Chattels Lands or Tenements in your
> Baliwick whereon you could levy the Debt" and that Return being of no avail
> nor legal, I have put you under a Rule to amend your Return . . . or that an
> attachment issue against you. In all Cases of Executions you can make no other
> Return than 1: That you have levied the whole Debt 2. If part only is levied
> that you have levied to such an amount and that the Defendant has no Goods
> . . . whereon you can levy the Residue 3dly If the Defendant has nothing in
> your Bailiwick then the Return must be that the Defendant has no goods . . .
> in your Bailiwick whereon you can levy the Debt or any Part thereof. It is not
> sufficient to say you *have not found any* . . . nor even that you *cannot find any*
> —you must return the precept executed as far as deft has effects in your County
> or positively say that the Defendant has nothing in your Bailiwick, and this
> gives the Plaintiff a Remedy against you if he can prove Deft has any Thing in
> your Bailiwick . . . Silvester . . . will serve you with the Rule of Court, and
> deliver you the writ, the Return to which you are ordered to amend. . . .[322]

[316] *H.R. Parch.* 187 C 1.
[317] *Ms. Mins. SCJ 1766–69* (Engr.) 186.
[318] *Ibid.* 388.
[319] *Ms. Mins. SCJ 1769–72* (Engr.) 403.
[320] *H.R. Parch.* 29 B 2.
[321] *Ms. Mins. SCJ 1769–72* (Engr.) 524.
[322] *J. T. Kempe Lawsuits* S–U.

Kempe's remonstrances to the sheriff of Albany were of no avail, for on October 22, 1772, he was obliged to move against the sheriff in the Supreme Court and the court accordingly "Ordered that attachment issue against the Sheriff of Albany for not amending his return to the *pluries Fi Fa* pursuant to the rule made in this cause last term."[323]

We have described at length the Attorney General's troubles with Sheriffs Schuyler and Ten Eyck because the evidence is most detailed. Kempe had similar troubles with Sheriff Willet of Westchester, and went to great pains to explain the sheriff's duties. In this instance Kempe seems to have thought that Willet and his deputies were frightened men, for he intimates as much to them. Yet this does not seem to have had any effect.[324] In neither case have we to do with anything exceptional, because it is clear from the judicial records that similar difficulties had plagued the authorities throughout the eighteenth century. In the two series of records which are most complete, those for the Supreme Court and the New York Quarter Sessions, no return was made to the process ordered in one-fifth of all the cases where indictments, presentments and informations were filed.[325] Allowing even for a certain lack of vigor on the part of the Attorneys General or their deputies, it can hardly be questioned that the chief seat of delinquency or remissness was in the peace officers, the clerk of the peace or the Crown's officer charged with the execution of process. This conclusion is fortified by the fact that attachments for contempt as well as indictments and informations against sheriffs and other officers charged with the execution of process were numerous, so numerous in-

---

[323] *Ms. Mins. SCJ 1772–76* (Rough) 46.

[324] *Ms. Kempe Letters* A–Z, May 12, 1766, Feb. 16, 1767.

[325] We have noted 2,446 cases brought in the Supreme Court between 1693 and 1776, and 1,431 of the 2,446 cases were simply miscellaneous appearances of defendants on recognizances, orders for attachment, etc., and did not involve indictments, presentments or informations against the defendants. However, in approximately 1,015 of the 2,446 cases presentments, indictments or informations were made against offenders, and in 223 of the 1,015 cases, the only entries appearing on the cases were the indictments, presentments or informations, and the court's order that process should issue out against the offenders. In these 223 cases, no further entry appears in the minutes or pleadings regarding further proceedings, and it is to be assumed either that the Attorney General failed to continue the action or that the sheriff failed to make any return to the process.

In New York City Quarter Sessions from 1691 to 1776, we have noted 2,786 cases, of which 1,971

cases were miscellaneous appearances on recognizances or prosecutions for contempt, etc., and in these cases no presentment or indictment was made. In the remaining 815 cases where presentments and indictments were delivered into the Sessions, process was ordered to issue, but in 169 cases no return was made to the process, nor do any further proceedings appear in these cases. The offenses in which no return was made to process which had been issued, involved 96 cases of assault and battery, 32 cases of disorderly house, 9 of assaulting officers, 2 breaches of the peace, 4 market offenses, 4 nuisance cases, 4 fraud and deceit cases, 2 petit larcenies, 2 receivers of stolen goods, one riot and false imprisonment, one "libelling," one breach of the Sabbath, one breaking of a glass window, one taking and carrying away a fence rail, one against a justice of the peace for falsely imprisoning a litigant and three for breaking and entering houses. Six of these cases occurred between 1713 and 1723, 8 between 1724 and 1734, 9 between 1735 and 1745, 41 between 1746 and 1756, 53 between 1757 and 1767 and 52 between 1768 and 1776.

deed that it seems surprising that returns to process were so continuously mishandled.

Process against Officials

The peace officers when they took office presumably undertook to perform their duties well and faithfully, and the records show an effort to celebrate the fact with due formality.[326] But from the very beginning of English rule in New York the courts were periodically occupied with the problems of seeing that the solemn oaths were carried into effect, and the minutes are peppered with special injunctions or with general rules.[327] One of the chief difficulties,

[326] See, for example, the Supreme Court minute entry of Jan. 21, 1768: "Lewis Graham [of Westchester] . . . produced in Court a Deputization under the Hand and Seal of . . . high sheriff . . . appointing the said Lewis Graham Deputy Sherif . . . whereupon the said Lewis Graham was Sworn by the Court well and faithfully to Execute the said Office according to the best of his Skill and understanding" (Ms. Mins. SCJ 1766–69 [Engr.] 381). Also compare the following dated Feb. 1753: "George the Second . . . To Our Trusty Well beloved Benjamin Hinchman of Jamaica in Queens County Esqr. Greeting Know ye that We Reposing especial Trust and Confidence in your Loyalty and Integrity Have thought fit hereby to impower you . . . to Tender & administer unto, Adam Lawrence Esqr. High Sheriff of . . . Queens . . . the Oaths mentioned in An Act of Parliament [the Test Oaths etc.] . . . And to receive from him the declaration in the said Act mentioned to be made and Subscribed And also to Receive his Subscription to the said Oaths and declarations And to administer unto him an Oath for the due Execution and performance of his said Office of High Sheriff of Queens County And of what you do herein you are . . . to make Return into Our Secreties office for our Province of New York Witness . . . George Clinton." Hinchman's return to the writ was as follows: "By virtue of the within Writ . . . I did on Sixteenth day of February 1753 administer unto . . . Adam Lawrence . . . the Oaths . . . and received from him the declaration . . . and did receive his Subscription to the said Oaths . . . and administer unto him an Oath for the due Execution of the office . . ." (H.R. Parch. 194 K 1).

[327] At a Court of Quarter Sessions of the Peace for New York City on Feb. 7, 1705/06, "Ebenezer Willson Esqr. high Sheriff of the City and County of New York Called to Return the writts and precepts of this Court unto him directed and delivered [them] upon pain and Perill that shall fall thereon" (Ms. Mins. NYCQS 1705/06–1714/15 [Rough] 1, 2). See also the proclamation for the sheriff to return the precepts and other processes in Quarter Sessions, Feb. 4, 1706/07 (ibid. 10). The language

in Quarter Sessions ordering the sheriff to return process was the same throughout the colonial period, and in the New York Quarter Sessions minutes for May 5, 1772, the entry appears as follows: "Proclamation made, (to witt) John Roberts Esq. high Sheriff of . . . New York, Return the writs and precepts of this Court unto you directed and delivered Returnable here this day upon pain and peril that Shall fall thereon" (Ms. Mins. NYCQS 1772–91 I).

In the Supreme Court also, many rules were made for the sheriff to return process. On Sept. 5, 1706, the following Supreme Court order is entered in the minutes: "It is Ordered that Every Sheriff shall make and cause to be entered on record a sufficient Deputy to receive all manner of writs and process under the pains and penalties—mentioned in the Statute in that behalfe made in the 23rd year of King Henry the Sixth which last shall be duely put in execution" (Ms. Mins. SCJ 1704/05–09 85; also in manuscript volume entitled Rules of the Supreme Court, Extracts from Records of the Supreme Court, 1699–1783). The statute referred to in this order is probably 23 Henry VI c.9. On October 1, 1722, the Supreme Court made the following order: "Ordered that each sheriff [except in New York City] . . . shall appoint some sufficient person in the city of New York to be his deputy to receive and return all manner of writs and process returnable into this court and the names of each so appointed and his place of abode shall be given to the clerk of the court and by him entered on record. Ordered that each sheriff or deputy shall personally attend the Supreme Court in term time to dispatch those services which appertain to his office. Ordered by the court that the service of any rules of this court on the deputy appointed by such sheriff shall be as effectual as if served on the sheriff himself" (Ms. Rules of the Supreme Ct.). The following order was made on April 16, 1754, by the Supreme Court regarding sheriffs: "Ordered That the High Sherif of the City and County of New York or his Deputy or Deputies, The Clerk of this Court, High Constables, petty Constables . . . do from time to time

in the minds of the judges, was the laxity respecting the levy of issues, fines, forfeitures and amercements resulting from judicial proceedings. The delinquencies of the sheriffs finally became so intolerable that in 1763 the Supreme Court ordered that the clerk of the Supreme Court, all justices of the peace, the clerks of the circuits, of the peace and of Common Pleas courts and all town clerks, annually on the first day of the October term, deliver into the Supreme Court as a Court of Exchequer a true estreat upon oath of all fines, forfeitures et cetera, together with necessary particulars, so that further proceedings could be had.[328]

This order was subsequently supplemented in October, 1767, by a further order of the Supreme Court[329] because the sheriffs neglected "to return process in due season" and made return that supposed bail had been taken when none was given. The court forbade such offenses in the future and required that on the return day officers have the bail bond. It threatened attachment for contempt in cases of disobedience. This order was chiefly directed at returns of civil process, and is significant chiefly in that it tends to show the conduct of the peace officers was not due to any resistance to the enforcement of criminal law, but was due to generally slipshod behavior bordering on malfeasance.

The ordinary sanction imposed on the sheriff to compel him to make return of process was the threat of a forty shilling amercement. This was itself in the nature of process to compel the completion of return and was usually exacted upon the motion of the Crown prosecutor.[330] Sometimes the court

and at all times during the sitting of the Court, attend the Judges at their . . . coming to, staying at and departing from the said Court, with the Badges or Ensigns of their respective offices, as they will answer the contrary" (*ibid.*; *Ms. Mins. SCJ 1754–57* [Engr.] 3). On Apr. 24, 1755, the Supreme Court ordered that it be a standing rule of this court that the sheriffs and coroners of the several counties of the Province of New York do appoint by warrant to be filed in the clerk's office of the Supreme Court a person of the city of New York to receive writs, declarations, rules and other papers necessary to be served on the said sheriffs, and that the clerk of the court do serve the sheriffs of the several counties with copies of this rule and that upon any new commission issued to appoint any sheriff within this province he be forthwith served with a copy of this rule in the manner above recited (*Ms. Rules of the Supreme Ct.; Ms. Mins. SCJ 1754–57* [Engr.] 154, 155). On Apr. 30, 1763, the Supreme Court "Ordered by the Court that sherifs of the several Counties in this Province do henceforth, attend this Court in every future Term either in Person or by their respective Deputies on pain of such fine as the Court shall think proper

to impose for every Default and that this Order be published by the Clerk of the Court in one or more of the publick News Papers" (*Ms. Rules of the Supreme Ct.; Ms. Mins. SCJ 1762–64* [Engr.] 174).

[328] *Ms. Rules of the Supreme Ct.; Ms. Mins. SCJ 1762–64* (Engr.) 225–227. The Ulster clerk in 1763 prepared an elaborate table of all the cases where fines were exacted from 1693–1763. The Crown officials must have been staggered to read that in nearly all the cases the sheriff was responsible for collection and there was no information what had happened to the issues. This table is in *NYSL Mss.* 7460.

[329] *Ms. Mins. SCJ 1766–69* (Engr.) 327, 328.

[330] So in Queen v. James DePeyster and eight others, Attorney General Bickley on June 4, 1706, prayed on behalf of the Queen that unless the sheriff brought the bodies of the defendants into court on the Friday following, he be amerced 40s., and the motion was granted (*Ms. Mins. SCJ 1704/05–09* 60–61). In Queen v. Sharpe the Supreme Court on Mar. 16, 1709/10 ordered that the sheriff return the body tomorrow or be amerced 40s. (*ibid.* 249). On Oct. 15, 1723, an information was read and

would impose a larger amount and occasionally formal grand jury action would be taken. Thus, for example, the presentment of John Ayscough,[331] sheriff of New York, for illegally discharging one Barnabas Morgan who had been ordered whipped by the justices, and the presentment of the two city marshals who were charged with filling names in blank warrants and then extorting money.[332]

The usual practice, however, in New York Province, when the threat of amercement was ineffective, was to resort to attachment for contempt. The

---

filed against Joseph Brown *et al.*, and on motion of the Attorney General ordered that the sheriff of Orange and Dutchess counties bring in the bodies of the defendants or be amerced 40*s*. The sheriff of Orange returned *cepi corpus* and was ordered to have the defendants' bodies in court or be amerced 40*s*. (*Ms. Mins. SCJ 1723–27* 32, 51, 184). On Oct. 15, 1728, Edward Cablie and James Cannon were indicted and process ordered to issue against them. On Dec. 3, 1728, the sheriff of New York returned *cepi corpus*, and was ordered to have the defendants' bodies in court or be amerced 40*s*., but in this case "the sheriff declares the defendants in custody" (*Ms. Mins. SCJ 1727–32* 89, 103). In King v. Salisbury, the sheriff of Ulster on June 4, 1731, returned *cepi corpus* and was ordered to have the defendant's body before the court or be amerced 40*s*. However, in this case, the defendant appeared and his appearance was entered (*ibid.* 276). On Oct. 23, 1738, process was ordered to issue against Isaac Gardiner, and the sheriff of New York, on Apr. 20, 1739, returned *cepi corpus*. The court thereupon ordered the "common rule" which was probably the order that the sheriff have the defendant's body in court or be amerced 40*s*. However, in this case also, Smith appeared as attorney for the defendant and the Attorney General moved that the defendant be bound in recognizance or be committed. The defendant here entered a recognizance with one surety (each in £10) for his appearance (*Ms. Mins. SCJ 1732–39* 325, 338, 344). On Oct. 28, 1768, the sheriff of Dutchess returned Tim Brownel taken and he was ordered to bring the defendant's body or be amerced 40*s*. No other entries appear in this case (*Ms. Mins. SCJ 1766–69* [Engr.] 121).

In Queen v. Duxberry *et al.*, the high sheriff of Richmond failed to return a precept, and on Oct. 11, 1704, the Attorney General moved against him in the Supreme Court as follows: "Mr. Attorney prayse that ye high sheriff of Richmond be amerced for not returning the precept." The court evidently gave the sheriff another chance, because it was "Ordered if ye sheriff does not make his return sitting this court he be amerced 40*s*." (*Ms. Mins. SCJ 1701–04* 163). High Sheriff Boudewyn De-Witt of Ulster County was, however, given a much larger fine than was usually meted out on failure to return process, for on Oct. 7, 1699, the Supreme

Court ordered that he be "amerced £10 for that he hath not returned the writ to take the body of William DeMeyer at the King's Suit" (*Mins. SCJ 1693–1701* 174).

[331] *Ms. Mins. SCJ 1750–54* (Engr.) 253; *H.R. Pleadings* Pl. K. 598.

[332] The presentment charged the defendants with ". . . Receiving from Alderman George Brewerton Warrents and other precepts Blank Signed with the Name of the said George Brewerton and for filling up the said Blanks with the Names of Such persons as they Thought proper To Serve with the Same at their Discretion That a Warrant dated the fourteenth day of July in this present year One thousand Seven Hundred and Sixty nine to Take John Little of this City for Threatening & Abusing John Young, They the sd John Graham and William Scott having Taken the said John Little Did not Convey him to the Goal as Commanded, but Carrying him to Several Publick Houses did Exact on Various Pretences from the said John Little Divers Sums of Money To the Amount of Three pounds Current money of this City Obliging the said John Little to give a note of hand payable to Them or one of them for a Certain Sum Which He the Said John Little does not know the amount of And pray the Court of our Lord the King to put it into form Gerard G. Beekman Foreman." Endorsed on the back of this presentment were the names of the following witnesses: John Little, John Cox, James Mills, and Joseph Lynsen, and these additional remarks appeared at the end of the presentment: "Graham some time last winter in North Ward had a Blank Summons a Warrant, which he filled up in Mr. Lynsens Presence agt. one [blank] Carr a Taylor as he believes, for a Debt claimed of him by Graham As soon as it was filled up Graham desired Scott to go and serve it, who immediately went over to Carr with it—It was signed by Alderman Brewerton. There appeared in the Hands of Graham a great many more precepts or warrants, but he does not know they were Blanks." There are endorsed on the back of the presentment the following additional comments which were probably made by the Attorney General: "I cannot discover with any Certainty what the precepts were which Scott & Graham had blank nor that after they had filled up any, that they arrested any Person on any such ilegal Warrant nor is there

English practice here was various. The court could make a rule on the party to attend on a certain day to answer the matter complained of or could make a rule to show cause why an attachment should not issue or, if the offense was aggravated, could issue an attachment immediately. We have already noticed in connection with the education of Sheriff Schuyler the use of both the rule to show cause and the immediate issue of the attachment. There is no discernible distinction as to the reason for a choice of methods in New York, the matter being dependent upon motion by the Attorney General whose action was determined by the degree of his exasperation. The late seventeenth century cases show invariably a direct attachment for contempt,[333] and even as late as 1727 in *King* v. *Bronck et al.*, where process was ordered to issue against certain rioters, failure of the sheriff to make any return over three terms of the Supreme Court resulted in a peremptory order for attachment.[334]

We do not know just when the rule to show cause came into use, but we think it was employed initially in cases of complaints against justices of the peace, when for reasons of state a milder approach to the matter of dereliction was advisable.[335] Later it came to be more generally used. The difficulty of laying down any generalizations of policy, however, is illustrated by the Supreme Court's procedure in *King* v. *Bishop et al.*[336] where a *capias pro fine* issued in January, 1767, and on May 2, 1767, the sheriff was ordered to return the writ the following term or suffer judgment. The sheriff in August returned one defendant not found and Bishop taken but rescued. Thereupon the court ordered the sheriff to show cause why an attachment should not issue against him. Obviously the compliance with the first rule was regarded as not good enough.

In addition to the attachment for contempt to compel sheriffs to perform their duties we have seen some examples of a writ to distrain the goods of a sheriff out of office to compel him to bring in the body of a defendant or to sell goods attached under a *fieri facias* which he ought to have done while in office but had failed to do. This type of *distringas* was used as early as the year 1703[337] when in the case of *Queen* v. *Countess of Bellomont* the Attorney

Proof before me that any false Summons was served by either of them" (*H.R. Pleadings* Pl. K. 533). On Oct. 28, 1769, an information for extortion was filed against these defendants (evidently on the basis of the presentment) and process was ordered to issue. The Attorney General was given liberty to amend the information. On Jan. 20, 1770, the sheriff of New York returned the defendants taken and they were ordered to plead in twenty days or suffer judgment. On Apr. 28, 1770, on the Attorney

General's motion judgment for want of a plea was rendered against these two defendants (*Ms. Mins. SCJ 1769–72* [Engr.] 66, 122, 149, 200).

[333] *Infra* nn. 341, 344.

[334] *Ms. Mins. SCJ 1723–27* 219, 252, 280.

[335] *Infra* 463.

[336] *Ms. Mins. SCJ 1766–69* (Engr.) 94, 253, 501, 503.

[337] *Ms. Mins. SCJ 1701–04* 68.

General moved for and was granted a *distringas nuper vicecomitem* for a failure to return a writ. Many years later, Sheriff James Livingston, whom we have already encountered as a bewildered official, was on two different occasions distrained by this same writ, after his retirement, for failure to make returns of *fieri facias*.[338]

If the sheriffs, ordinarily persons of considerable standing in the commu-

[338] *Ms. Mins. SCJ 1769–72* (Engr.) 149, 245. In October Term, 1764, the Attorney General brought an action of debt on a recognizance which Peter Palmateer entered before the Mayor of Albany and two justices of the peace for his appearance at the next Court of Oyer and Terminer and General Gaol Delivery for Albany and to be of good behavior. This bond was in the amount of £1000 for Palmateer and £500 each for his two sureties, Valentine Perkins and Nathaniel Robinson, Jr. (see *H.R. Pleadings* Pl. K. 1030). On Jan. 17, 1765, the Supreme Court on reading the sheriff's acknowledgment of service of a declaration and rule to plead, and on the Attorney General's motion, gave judgment against defendants Palmateer and Robinson for want of a plea (*Ms. Mins. SCJ 1764–67* [Rough] 41). A *fieri facias* was issued against Peter Palmateer, and on July 29, 1769, Sheriff Livingston of Dutchess County returned to this writ that he had levied on the goods and chattels which remained in his hands (*H.R. Parch.* no number yet assigned). On Oct. 28, 1769, the Supreme Court minute entries contain the following regarding the return on the *fieri facias*: "The same Sherif of Dutchess returns fi: fa: and that he had levied on a House and Lot in Poghkeepsie and sundry Goods and Chattels which remained in his Hands for want of Buyers" (*Ms. Mins. SCJ 1769–72* [Engr.] 121). In the interim Sheriff Livingston went out of office, for on Jan. 20, 1770, the following Supreme Court entry appears: "The sheriff of Dutchess returns that he had distrained James Livingston late Sherif of . . . Dutchess by his Lands and Chattels in his Bailiwick to the value of twenty pounds. On Motion of same [Attorney General] Ordered that James Livingston [the late sheriff] bring the debt and costs levied by him in this Cause into Court . . . and that in Default the Issues now returned against him be forfeited and estreated, and another Distringas Issue." On Aug. 4, 1769, the court on the Attorney General's motion "Ordered an Alias Distringas on the late Sheriff of Dutchess" and as a result of this writ, the present sheriff of Dutchess on Oct. 26, 1770, returned that "he has distrained James Livingston . . . by all his Lands and Chattels as by the Writt he was commanded and had taken Issues thereof to the value of twenty Pound." On Aug. 3, 1771, the Supreme Court on the Attorney General's motion "ordered that another Distringas issue to the present Sheriff of Dutchess . . . to distrain James Livingston Esq' late Sheriff . . . to expose to Sale the Lands . . .

[etc.] levied by him on a fi fa agt the defendant [Peter Palmateer] in this cause" (*Ms. Mins. SCJ 1769–72* [Engr.] 149, 245, 292, 403).

The second case in which the *distringas nuper vicecomitem* was used, was that of King v. Henry Terboss and David Lyons. Lyons had entered a recognizance in £40 with one surety (Terboss in £20) for his appearance at Dutchess General Sessions of the Peace to answer for an assault and battery and in the meantime to be of his good behavior. Lyons and Terboss made default and their default was recorded in the Court of General Sessions. Demand was made upon Terboss for the amount of the bond and on his failure to pay, the Attorney General filed a narration in debt against him (*J. T. Kempe Lawsuits* S–U; *H.R. Parch.* 86 G 1 contains the narration). On Jan. 19, 1765, the sheriff of Dutchess returned Henry Terboss in custody and the latter was ordered to plead in twenty days or suffer judgment for want of a plea. On Apr. 18, the sheriff of Dutchess acknowledged the receipt of a copy of the declaration in debt on the bond and the rule to plead. Thereupon, on motion of the Attorney General, the court ordered that judgment for want of a plea be rendered against Terboss (*Ms. Mins. SCJ 1764–67* [Rough] 53). *H.R. Pleadings* Pl. K. 787 contains the rules indicating that a motion for judgment was made and judgment was entered on April 18, 1765. A *fieri facias* issued to the sheriff of Dutchess County, and he returned to this *fieri facias* that he had levied on a farm and sundry goods and chattels which remained in his hands for lack of buyers (*H.R. Parch.* no number yet assigned; for the minute entry see *Ms. Mins. SCJ 1769–72* [Engr.] 121). Since Sheriff Livingston of Dutchess had in the meantime gone out of office without making the proper returns, the following *distringas* was issued against him in the Terboss case: "George the Third To our Sheriff . . . Greeting We command you that you distrain James Livingston late Sheriff your Predecessor by all his Lands and Chattels in your Bailiwick, so that neither he nor any one for him meddle therewith until you shall have another Precept from us and that the Issues of the same you answer unto us so that he expose to Sale the Lands and Tenements Goods and Chattels . . . of Henry Terboss . . . to the Value of Twenty Pounds . . . [recovered against him and not sold for want of buyers] and have you then there this Writ." This writ was endorsed as follows: "I have distrained . . . James Livingston . . . by his Lands and

nity, were a constant source of aggravation to the courts, the troubles with constables were no less irritating. The constables were not minions of the sheriff but were responsible to the justices of the peace, whose "proper officers" they were. The magistrates dealt with them much more peremptorily since the constables were regarded as inferior officers, and since pains were taken to make the control over them more immediate by constant regulation in the orders of the justices in Sessions. These ordinances very often took the form of enjoining the performance of a certain duty and imposing a set fine in case it was not attended to, permitting a summary proceeding.[339] Apart from the fact that a close supervision over the constables was necessary when the shrieval office was inefficiently administered, the alertness of these officers was particularly essential to the functioning of the justice's summary jurisdiction since the

Chattels . . . in my Bailiwick, as I am by the within writ commanded, To the Value of Twenty Pounds Henry Rosekranz Jn. Sheriff of . . . Dutchess fees 20/" (*H.R. Pleadings* Pl. K. 1073). On Jan. 20, 1770, the minute entries indicate that the sheriff of Dutchess made the return that he had distrained to the amount of £ 20, and the court ordered that Livingston bring the debts and costs levied against him into the court and that in default "the issues now returned against him be forfeited and estreated and another distringas issue." On Aug. 4, 1770, an *alias distringas* issued against Livingston, and on Oct. 26, 1770, the sheriff of Dutchess returned that he had distrained Livingston as commanded and had taken issues thereof to the value of £ 20 (*Ms. Mins. SCJ 1769–72* [Engr.] 149, 245, 292). On the English practice, Tidd, *King's Bench Practice* (8 ed.) 313 *et seq.*

[339] In Kings County Sessions, numerous orders were issued obliging the constables to perform various duties on the threat of penalty of fine for their failure to do so. On Nov. 8, 1692, the court ordered that there be a good pair of stocks and a good pound in every town in Kings County which would be kept in "sufficient repaire." Furthermore, the court ordered that the clerk of the court issue warrants to the constables of every town to see the court order performed "as they will answer to the contrary at their peril" (*Kings Co. Ct. & Rd. Recs. 1692–1825* 9). On Nov. 12, 1707, the court "Ordered that all the Constables . . . that has not Each a p'. of good stocks erected . . . shall fforffeitt Each 18 shillings ffor the use of the poor . . . to be levyed on his goods & chattels by the sheriff . . . upon ffailure of payment . . ." (*ibid.* 154). Cf. also the order made in Kings Sessions on Nov. 12, 1695: "Ordered that the Constables of Every towne . . . shall every sunday . . . take Care for the apprehending of all sabbath breakers, and that they or the deputys goe with their staves . . . about their respective townes . . . as Constables and search all alehouses tavernes and other suspected

places for all prophaners and breakers of the sabbath day & them to apprehend and bring before any one of his Majesty's Justices . . . in ordr to be punished according to law, and in Case the Constables . . . shall refuse neglect or delay to performe the ordr . . . they shall . . . for every default forfeitt the summe of six shillings . . . to be disposed of to the use of the County" (*ibid.* 28).

The particularity with which the constables were ruled is illustrated by the fussing over their staffs of office. As late as 1772 in the lately formed county of Tryon, it was ordered that the constables "do provide themselves with pocket staffs as badges of their office . . . and that they be painted black with the King's arms" (*Ms. Mins. Tryon Co. Sess. 1772–76* Sept. 8, 1772; *Misc. Mss. Tryon Co.*). On May 10, 1698, at Kings Co. Sessions, all the constables appeared with their staves except the constable of Gravesend, who was fined 6s. for not having his staff, but when he pleaded that he had no notice thereof, the fine was remitted (*Ms. Kings Co. Ct. & Rd. Recs. 1692–1825* 42). On Sept. 11, 1717, the Court of Oyer and Terminer and General Gaol Delivery for Ulster County fined the constables 20s. each for not attending with staves suitable to their offices, but on the justices of the peace promising that in the future care would be taken that proper staves be used, the constables' fines were remitted (*Ms. Mins. Cir. 1716–17* 20). Cf. also the order that constables attending should have the benefit of the fines of non-attenders (*Ms. Mins. Dutchess Co. Sess.* Liber A, Oct. 16, 1745).

Non-attendance by constables was also punishable summarily as a contempt; cf. *Ms. Mins. NYCQS 1772–91* 153; *Ms. Mins. NYCQS 1732–62* 169. It should be remarked that the fines of constables for contempt were sometimes referred to as amercements, for on Nov. 6, 1695, James Spencer and Vincent Delamontagne, constables, were committed until they each paid the sum of 18s. which they were "amerced" for not attending the court (*Ms. Mins. NYCQS 1694–1731/32* 9).

practice developed of handling minor infractions of orders by punishment without any trial on the complaint of the constable.[340]

For the most part the erring constable was not honored with special process since it was sufficient to amerce him summarily. There are, however, some cases which resembled attachment for contempt; at least, the minuted orders seem to indicate the use of some process. Thus in 1707, Hendrick Wycoff, a constable in Kings County, was "ordered to appear . . . ffor contempt of authority in not coming before a justice of the peace to be sworne as constable when legally chosen . . . for constable." Wycoff appeared in court and "the contempt of Hendrick Wycoff being taken into consideration . . . Ordered ffor a ffine 30s. for the use of Her Majesty and to pay the costs of this court and . . . committed to the Sheriff's custody until the fine . . . be payd." Furthermore the court ordered that a warrant be issued to the present constable of Flatlands, John Hansen, to summon a town meeting for the choice of another constable.[341]

Volkert Briez, a Kings County constable, was "sent for" before the Kings County Sessions for contempt of their Majesties' authority for "tearing & burning an Execucōn directed to him as Constable . . . upon his examinacōn Confessed . . . mercy . . . Committed to the Common gaole . . . untill he shall pay five pounds . . . fine . . . Cost allowd £1."[342] Nicholas Burger, a constable of New York City, was on August 1, 1738, committed for his insolent behavior to the court and neglect of his duty. However, he was permitted at large on posting a recognizance in £10 with two sureties in £5 for his appearance at the next Quarter Sessions and for his good behavior in the mean-

[340] Thus John Nicoll, a justice in Dutchess, wrote to John Tabor Kempe, on Sept. 22, 1770: "I am Sorry . . . that you have been Plaged by a fellow who never fails being Troublesome . . . he was fined by me for Swearing on a Complaint of the Constable, and the fine Levied in manner as Directed by the act for the prevention of Immorality, To which I Strictly Adhered, If I should unfortunatly have Erred In my Construction of it, I have only fallen into the Common Error of this and the Adjacent Counties where it has been always Customary to Punish for breach of Sabbath Swearing or the neglect of Duty on the Roads on Complaint of the Constable and Road Master . . . without a formal Trial . . ." (J. T. Kempe Lawsuits C–F sub nom. King v. Henry Chase).

[341] Kings Co. Sess., Kings Co. Ct. & Rd. Recs. 1692–1825 153. On May 11, 1708, Wycoff was ordered by the Court of Sessions of Kings County to "stand for constable" for the ensuing year "according to the votes of the freeholders of Flatlands."

Apparently Wycoff was still somewhat reluctant to be the constable of Flatlands despite the town's vote of confidence, for he requested the court's permission to consider whether he would take the oath of constable. On the following day, Wycoff appeared in court and refused to accept the office of constable and refused to be sworn. The court then ordered that Oke Janse, the present constable of Flatlands, be continued until another constable could be chosen. The luckless Wycoff "for his contempt and refusing to serve as constable . . . when legally chosen" was fined £5 for the use of her Majesty and the court ordered that he be freed from being chosen constable of Flatlands for the ensuing year 1709. The office of constable of Flatlands was evidently undesirable, for on Nov. 9, 1708, Oke Janse was bound to court for contempt of authority, and having appeared was discharged when Major Stoothoff issued a warrant for the choice of another constable (ibid. 156, 157).

[342] Ibid. 25.

time. On November 10, 1738, he appeared, asked pardon of the court and was discharged. However, on August 4, 1742, he again appeared in court and "behaving Insolently to the Court order'd he be Committed for the Same." Again the recalcitrant constable was released without fine, for on August 5, 1742, "having Submitted himself to the Court and Ask'd pardon for his offences yesterday," he was discharged from his imprisonment and also from his recognizance on the payment of fees.[343]

To understand the full scope of the attachment for contempt and analogous measures used to fortify the process of the courts it is essential to recall the pivotal position of the country justice in local administration, to realize that his fiat was usually conveyed by warrant, and that in addition to constables a number of other officials were under the supervision of the local magistrates. In consequence, we find cases where town surveyors are fined and process to collect issued for not making returns to warrants for laying out highways;[344] county assessors who refuse to levy taxes according to justices' warrants are brought in for contempt;[345] and collectors of taxes are similarly proceeded against.[346] Sometimes, when the local machinery was inadequate the contempt proceedings would be undertaken in the Supreme Court, for there are a number of instances where a rule to show cause why attachment should not issue was ordered against highway commissioners, clerks of the peace and others.[347]

Related to the control over returns by sheriffs and constables is that exercised in respect to returns of writs of certiorari by the justices of Sessions. The use of attachments for contempt for this purpose has been spoken of in connection with transfer jurisdiction and procedure,[348] but it should be observed further that this particular device was also directed to inferior officers under circumstances which had nothing to do with the essential and proper power of a court to compel respect for its mandates. From the middle of the

[343] Ms. Mins. NYCQS 1732–62 89, 94, 140, 141. The presentment of constables for neglect was quite crowded out by the development of summary powers. Cf., however, the presentment by a Supreme Court grand jury in 1699 of the New York City constables for not keeping youths and negroes from playing in the streets on Sunday (Mins. SCJ 1693–1701 159).

[344] Thus, in 1695, the Brooklyn town surveyors were fined 12s. apiece for contempt (Ms. Kings Co. Ct. & Rd. Recs. 1692–1825 28). Cf. also the attachment vs. the Pres. of the Huntington Trustees (Ms. Mins. Suffolk Co. Sess. 1723–51 Mar. 29, 1743).

[345] Mins. Westch. Ct. of Sess. 1657–96 63.

[346] Ms. Mins. Westch. Co. Sess. 1710–23 Aug. 31, 1721; Ms. Mins. NYCQS 1694–1731/32 18, 24, Dec. 17, 1696, Mar. 4, 1696/97 (for Orange Co.).

[347] Cf. the proceedings against Commissioners Van Tyle et al. (Ms. Mins. SCJ 1754–57 [Engr.] 104, 105; Ms. Mins. SCJ 1750–56 [Rough] 234; Ms. Mins. SCJ 1754–57 [Engr.] 319, 329); the proceeding against Jackson et al. of Orange Co. (ibid. 171, Apr. 24, 1755); the proceedings against Daniel Corsen of Richmond (Ms. Mins. SCJ 1750–54 [Engr.] 95, 102, 154, 170, 334, 344).

[348] Supra 159.

fifteenth century, at least, and into modern times the Court of King's Bench had implemented its prerogative of general superintendence over the courts of the realm by attachment. The situations where this was used were often ones where error might be thought to have lain, but if there were some extraordinary or aggravating circumstance the King's Bench would resort to this more direct process.[349]

There are a number of cases in New York which illustrate how these King's Bench powers were manipulated. In 1755, one Cornhill filed an affidavit[350] against John Bailey as justice of the peace alleging that Bailey had issued a warrant to seize a certain person for a 6s. debt even though Cornhill had decided that he did not want to have this party arrested for debt as he had previously requested. On August 2, 1755, the Supreme Court, on reading Cornhill's affidavit, ordered that Bailey show cause why attachment should not issue against him, and this show cause order was "enlarged" from term to term on the following dates: October 21, October 30, 1755, January 24, April 29, 1756, January 21, 1757, and April and July, 1758. Thereafter no further proceedings appear and it can probably be assumed that the case against Bailey was dropped.[351] Again, in 1756, Lawrence Huff filed an affidavit against John Ferdon, a Dutchess justice, alleging that Ferdon gave judgment for the plaintiff when Peter Outwater sued Huff in a land action, although it was alleged that Outwater had offered no proofs whatsoever in support of his action.[352] On reading Lawrence Huff's affidavit, the Supreme Court on April 29, 1756, ordered that the defendant show cause by the following term why attachment should not issue against him.[353]

[349] Cf. 2 Hawkins, *Pleas of the Crown* c.22 §§25, 26. This jurisdiction is barely mentioned by Fox, *Contempt of Court* (1927) and is only superficially noticed by Holdsworth in 3 *Hist. Eng. Law*.

[350] H.R. *Pleadings* Pl. K. 576.

[351] *Ms. Mins. SCJ 1754–57* (Engr.) 176, 197, 204, 230, 261, 352; *Ms. Mins. SCJ 1757–60* (Engr.) 119, 139; also see *J. T. Kempe Lawsuits* B *sub nom.* John Bailey, for Stanford Cornhill's complaint against the defendant for maladministration in office; in this complaint Cornhill also alleged that defendant ordered a constable to serve a special warrant in a bedroom. The Kempe papers contain Cornhill's affidavit saying that he had personally served Bailey with a rule of the Supreme Court to show cause why an attachment should not issue against him. It may be that there was some doubt whether attachment for contempt or a Crown information should have been issued against Bailey, for in H.R. *Pleadings* Pl. K. 601, we find a draft of an information dated May 27, 1755, but nothing further seems to have been done on this.

[352] The facts are in a letter of John Bickerton to Wm. Kempe (H.R. *Pleadings* Pl. K. 909).

[353] *Ms. Mins. SCJ 1754–57* (Engr.) 261. We do not know what was the ultimate disposition of this case.

On July 31, 1755, Patrick Flood filed an affidavit against Isaac Van Alstyne, an Albany justice, for maladministration in the execution of his office. Van Alstyne had been most partial in all the decisions he made in cases against Patrick Flood. For example, when Flood sued one Daniel O'Connor for a debt of £1 1s. 5d., Van Alstyne allowed O'Connor to counterclaim for 9s. and ordered O'Connor to pay the balance of the debt to him, that is, to the justice of the peace. Flood was also ordered to pay 3s. 6d. to Van Alstyne for the warrant that Van Alstyne had issued against O'Connor, and then when Flood asked for the 12s. 5d. paid to the justice by O'Connor, Van Alstyne only gave him 6s. of this amount (H.R. *Pleadings* Pl. K. 222, 444, 611, 618–620, 653, 671, 719, 877; *J. T. Kempe Lawsuits* L–O). As a result of the many derelictions

It will be noted that the cases just cited occurred just after the information bill was enacted,[354] and it is conceivable that some uncertainty as to the possible effects of the new statute may have moved the Attorney General to experiment with a possible alternative to the information for maladministration. The act, however, proved to be no obstacle to the prosecution of justices and, as we have seen, the information was again resorted to to keep the justices in order.[355]

In situations where neither attachment nor information would lie against public officials the courts employed the writ of mandamus. Although this writ commonly was used to compel admission to office,[356] on two occasions it was brought to force an allowance of costs in criminal cases. On June 29, 1724, James Alexander, former Attorney General, and Lewis Morris, Chief Justice of the Supreme Court, brought an action against the justices and freeholders of the county of Ulster, and in the Supreme Court the following entry appears on that date:

> Upon ye Inform of ye Compl to this Court that ye Justices and Freeholders of ye County of Ulster have refused payment of the Costs of Several Indictments found by ye Grand Jury of that County where the Defts were found not Guilty Ordered that ye said Justices and Freeholders or some of them be Served with Copys of the said Bills of Costs, and if they Refuse to pay them that they shew Cause by the first Day of next Term why they did not pay them, and why a *Mandamus* shd not Issue to Compel them thereto. . . .[357]

in duty committed by Van Alstyne and alleged in Patrick Flood's affidavits, the Supreme Court on July 31, 1755, ordered that Van Alstyne show cause the following term why attachment should not issue against him. On Oct. 30, 1755, the rule was "enlarged" to the following term, and respites were also granted on the following dates: Jan. 24, Apr. 29, July 30, 1756, Jan. 21, Apr. 28, 1757, April, 1758. No further proceedings appear in the case, and since the last court order on the case, that of April, 1758, had granted the defendant time until the following term to show cause why attachment should not issue against him, it may perhaps be assumed that the defendant meantime was able to show cause and was accordingly discharged, even though the discharge had not been entered in the minutes (*Ms. Mins. SCJ 1754–57* [Engr.] 174, 201, 206, 230, 261, 284, 352; *Ms. Mins. SCJ 1757–60* [Engr.] 69, 119).

In 1752, proceedings by attachment were begun against Jacob Brinkerhoff, a Dutchess justice, but for what reason we do not know (*Ms. Mins. SCJ 1750–54* [Engr.] 124, 172, 334).

[354] There is a case in 1739 involving a show

cause order re attachment of four justices of the Orange County Common Pleas, but we do not know what the complaint was (cf. *Ms. Mins. SCJ 1732–39* 339, 346, 368 and *James Alexander Papers* Box 44, *James Alexander Supreme Ct. Reg. 1721–42* nos. 41, 42).

[355] *Supra* 175 *et seq.*

[356] Cf. the mandamus to the Mayor's Court in 1732 to allow Nathaniel Gilbert to practice as an attorney in that court (*Ms. Mins. SCJ 1727–32* 310, 326, 332, 337, 389); the writ itself is in *John Jay Papers* Box 5 no. 8; the mandamus in 1773 to the borough of Westchester to admit one Honeywell to the office of alderman, and another to admit one Leggett to the office of common councilman (*Ms. Mins. SCJ 1772–76* [Rough] 95, 101, 131, 163; *H.R. Pleadings* Pl. K. 730). On the New York practice note also the issuance of an *alias mandamus* in 1763, King v. Harmanus Gansevoort (*Ms. Mins. SCJ 1762–64* [Engr.] 89, 227). The rule to show cause why attachment should not issue was also used where return to mandamus was not made; cf. *J. T. Kempe Lawsuits* A *sub nom.* Albany.

[357] *Ms. Mins. SCJ 1723–27* 96.

The justices claimed they were unable to raise the money whereupon the court ordered that the supervisors of Ulster should be served with a copy.[358] The bill was in excess of £41 and the supervisors after voting £5 to the Attorney General resolved "to stand tryall."[359]

Apparently no further payment was made, but in 1735 Bradley experienced difficulties in the same county about securing his costs. In April, 1736, he filed his complaint and the supervisors were ordered to show cause why a mandamus should not issue against them for not paying the Attorney General. The case dragged on interminably under the clever generalship of William Smith, so that the mandamus to assess the bill of costs did not issue until 1739,[360] but an entry in James Alexander's Docket for 1742 indicates that the cause had even then not been settled.[361] The loss of the Supreme Court minutes for the period leaves us in the dark as to the final outcome.[362]

Jury Process

Were we bound to make our discussions of eighteenth century procedure conform to the literary and analytical conceits of eighteenth century text writers, it would be at the least a solecism to deal in a chapter on process with the variety of writs and precepts employed for the jury. The English convention of describing the dismal progress of a criminal proceeding step by step from arrest through execution, like some vast and over-detailed *Rake's Progress,* inevitably had the prisoner arraigned and pleading before the reader was given his first view "Of the Jury." Whatever the logic of this manner of

---

[358] *James Alexander Papers* Box 44 no. 16, *James Alexander Supreme Court Register 1721–42* no. 9.

[359] *Mins. Board of Supervisors Ulster Co. 1710/11–1730/31* 35. In January, 1730/31, the supervisors entered their opinion re a charge of £18 for sundry commissions of Gaol Delivery, that this was not a proper charge (*ibid.* 48).

[360] *Ms. Mins. SCJ 1732–39* 261, 275, 279, 281, 333, 342; *James Alexander Papers* Box 44 no. 42.

[361] *Alexander Supreme Ct. Docket* Apr. 20, 1742, in *Papers* Box 44 no. 39.

[362] In connection with these proceedings note the Supreme Court order, in March 1726/27, for a mandamus directed to the justices of Queens and to the vestrymen of Jamaica Parish to raise and levy all arrearages of salary of the recorder of Jamaica parish *nisi causa,* etc. (*Ms. Mins. SCJ 1723–27* 247).

The remedies to compel accountings by public officers are further illustrated by various early cases.

In 1709, the Attorney General filed an information against Byerly, the Queen's receiver general, alleging that the latter had failed to make a proper account, but the defendant pleaded that he had carefully accounted. The Attorney General joined issue and a jury was summoned, Lord Cornbury's commission was read in evidence, as well as the testimony of various witnesses, and the jury found for the defendant (*H.R. Parch.* 162 H 3; *Ms. Mins. SCJ 1704/05–1709/10* 250, Mar. 16, 1709/10).

In New York v. DeRiemer, Emott for the plaintiff prayed that a *capias ad computandum* be awarded against the defendant, and it may be presumed that this writ was in the nature of process obliging some New York officer to file an account. However, no rule was issued by the Supreme Court at this time, that is, on the first Monday of June (the 4th) 1705, but on Mar. 12, 1705/06, Jamison moved on behalf of the defendant to have the auditor's report filed and this motion was granted (*Ms. Mins. SCJ 1704/05–1709* 14, 49).

See also the case of King v. Samuel Heath, the deputy weighmaster, *supra* 310 n. 117.

composition may be, we find it convenient to deal at this point with the complicated problem of jury process.

The form for summoning grand juries to the Supreme Court was noted in the preceding chapter,[363] and it is necessary to advert here only to a peculiarity in the case of General Sessions where the precepts for summoning the court also contained a venire addressed to the sheriff commanding that he cause twenty-four freeholders to come before the justices to inquire of such things as they might be enjoined by the court to discover. Hawkins states[364] that since the summons for the Sessions had a clause for the summons of twenty-four men from every hundred, it was supposedly unnecessary to make any other precept for the return of a jury to try any issue joined, but in New York, as we shall see in a moment, venires did issue out of Sessions for trials of criminal cases.

In the margin are exemplified examples of precepts for the Sessions.[365]

[363] Supra 344 n. 59.

[364] 2 Hawkins, Pleas of the Crown c.41 §1, although he thinks practice and not the rules of the text writers was really determinative.

[365] On Oct. 25, 1712, the following precept for New York City and Co. issued: "City and County of New York ss Caleb Heathcote, David Jamison, William Smith, Johannes Jansen and Jacobus Kip Esqrs. five of her Majesties Justices for the Conservation of the peace in the City and County of New York and of divers thefts Trespasses and other Offences . . . perpetrated to hear & determine assigned To the Sheriff . . . Greeting . . . wee Command you that you Omitt not for any Liberty within your Bailywick but that you enter the same and Cause to Come before us . . . at the Next Court of General Sessions of the peace . . . twenty four honest and lawful men . . . everyone whereof hath at the least in Yearly Rents of Lands and Tenements forty shillings by the year then and there to Enquire . . . on the behalf of . . . the Queen . . . Also make known to all Coroners High Constables Petty Constables & Bayliffs . . . that they be then there . . . Furthermore Cause to be proclaimed . . . in Convenient places the aforesaid sessions . . . and be you yourself then there to do and execute those things which to your office pertaineth and have you there the names of the Jurors High Constables Petty Constables and Bayliffs . . . as well as this Precept. Given under our hands and seals in New York the 25th day of October [1712]. . . ." This precept bore the endorsement "The execution of this Writt appears by the panel annexed," and it was signed by the sheriff. Annexed was a panel of grand jurors bearing their names (Misc. Mss. NY Box 4 no. 8).

An example of a precept late in the eighteenth century is the following for August Sessions, 1769: "City and County of New York: Whitehead Hicks, Esqr. Mayor, Cornelius Roosevelt, Benjamin Blagge, Andrew Gauties & Abraham P. Lott Esqrs. five of his Majestys Justices for the Conservation of the peace in the said City & County of New York, and of divers felonies, imprisonments, Riotts, Routs, Oppressions, forestalling, regrating, Trespasses and other offences in the said City & County perpetrated to hear and Determine assigned to the Sheriff of the City & County aforesaid GREETING on behalf of our said Lord the King wee command you that you omit not by reason of any Liberty within your Bailiwick, but that you enter the same and cause to come before us and our associate Justices of the peace for the said City & County at the City Hall of the said City on the first Tuesday in August next (being the first day of the same month) Twenty four honest & Lawful men of the said City & County, everyone whereof hath at least in yearly rents of Lands & Tenements forty shillings, and then and there to enquire upon their oaths of such thing which on behalf of our said Lord the King shall be enjoined also make known to all Coroners, high & petty Constables & Bailiffs within the said City & County of New York that they be then and there to perform those things which on behalf of our said Lord the King, by reason ought to be done. Furthermore Cause to be proclaimed, throughout your bailiwick in Convenient places the aforesaid Sessions of the peace to be held at the day & place aforesaid and be you then and there to Execute those things which to your office appertains and have you then and there the Names of the Jurors, Coroner, high Constable, petty constables and Bailiffs aforesaid, as well as this precept given under our hands and Seals in the City & County of New York the Second day of May in the ninth year of his Majesty's Reign Anno Dom 1769. Whitehead Hicks Cornelius Roosevelt B. Blagge Andrew Gautier Abraham P. Lotte." The Sheriff's return and

The forms do not vary materially during the eighteenth century, and no question of the power of any common law court, even the early Special Sessions, to order an inquest seems ever to have been raised.[366]

For the summoning of petit juries there was the writ of *venire facias juratores* directed to the sheriff commanding him to cause twelve free and lawful men of the vicinage worth a certain amount per annum, to come before the court to recognize on their oath whether or not the defendant was guilty.[367] The venire conforms to English models except for the important particular of property qualifications, important not merely as an assurance of a certain type of juryman, but because it formed the basis of possible challenge. The policy of the Province respecting the qualifications of persons who were to do jury service was patterned on the English, that is to say, freeholding was taken as the basic standard. In the case of grand jurors, the English statutes were obscure as to the value of the holding and the New Yorkers in settling on 40s. yearly as a minimum were apparently relying upon the statement in *Coke on Littleton* (§464). But, just as in England it was usage to return the more substantial freeholders in a particular county, so in New York the grand jurors were consistently chosen from this group as the various records examined indi-

panel were annexed to this precept (*H.R. Pleadings* Pl. P. [no number yet assigned]).

Cf. also a precept for July 22, 1712 (*Misc. Mss. NY* Box 4 no. 8); precepts for Sessions, Nov. 1723 and Feb. 1724, May 1736, May 1753 and Feb. 1756 are in *H.R. Pleadings* Pl. P. (no number yet assigned). A precept for Aug. 1755 (*ibid.* Pl. P. 2770) and for Nov. 1762 (*ibid.* Pl. P. 2769). The precept for Feb. 1745 is in *NY Legal Mss.* Box 43. There are a great many such precepts in *Ms. Files Ulster Co.* and *Ms. Files Dutchess Co.*

[366] So a Special Sessions in May 11, 1697 ordered a venire for an inquest in a forcible entry case (*Ms. Mins. NYCQS 1694–1731/32* 26).

[367] For example, the venire in King v. Swan:

"GEORGE the third by the Grace of God of Great Britain France and Ireland King Defender of the Faith and so forth To our Sheriff of our City and County of New York Greeting We command you that you omit not by Reason of any Liberty within your Bailiwick but that the same you enter and cause to come before us at our City of New York immediately after the Reception of this Writ Twelve free and lawful Men of the Neighborhood of the North Ward of the said City and County of New York of which each of them shall have in his own Name or Right or in Trust for them or in their Wives Right a Freehold in Lands Messuages or Tenements or of Rents in Fee, Fee tail or for Life or a personal Estate of the Value of Sixty pounds free of all Reprizes Debts Demands or Incumbrances whatsoever by whom the Truth of the matter may be the better known and who to Godfrey Swan are in no wise related in any Degree of kindred to recognize upon their Oath whether or no the said Godfrey is guilty of the Murder and Felonies whereof he is Indicted because the same Godfrey in our Court before Us at our Suit of Good and Evil hath thereof put himself upon that Jury and have you then there the Names of the Jury and this Writ WITNESS Daniel Horsmanden Esquire Chief Justice of our Province of New York at the City of New York the Thirty first day of July in the fifth Year of our Reign   J. T. Kempe Attorney General   CLARKE." This was endorsed as follows: "The Execution of this Writ appears by the Pannel hereunto annexed," and appended was a list of jurors (*H.R. Parch.* 194 L 6). It will be noted that the summoning of a jury of the neighborhood extended to picking a jury from the very ward of the city, namely, in this case the North Ward.

For other venires for a petit jury, cf. King v. Wilks—murder, 1756 (*H.R. Pleadings* Pl. K. 887); King v. Tom and Cyrus—assault with intent to murder, 1765 (*H.R. Parch.* 196 L 10); King v. Eliz. Allen—trespasses and assaults, 1765 (*H.R. Pleadings* Pl. K. 747); King v. Zachariah Smith Allen—passing counterfeit bills of credit, 1776 (*H.R. Parch.* 191 H 8); King v. James and Mary Burn—burglary and grand larceny, 1765 (*H.R. Parch.* 70 D 10); King v. Elizabeth Stewart—petit larceny, 1773 (*H.R. Parch.* 186 E 4).

cate. This practice, indeed, seems to have acquired almost the force of a rule of law. When the proceedings against Alexander McDougall for seditious libel were pending, a notice appeared in the *New York Gazette* for April 2, 1770, in which it was stated that for years the sheriff had summoned a set of "principal gentlemen of the city in constant rotation," to serve as grand jurors, but he had abandoned this rule in McDougall's case, a deviation which was strongly protested.

The English statutes had long set for petit jurors a high property qualification. This policy, which rested upon the presumed higher responsibility and intelligence of propertied persons, had found expression in a series of statutes going back to the fifteenth century. In 1699 the colonists, perhaps under the influence of a recent English act, by statute fixed upon a house with ten acres freehold in the country, a dwelling house or personal estate of £50 in New York City and Albany.[368] This statute was continued and revived until the year 1741 when in a new and elaborate act the qualification was set at a freehold in lands, tenements or rents of the value of £60. In New York City (and later Albany) the alternative of a personal estate of like value would serve to qualify a man. As the preamble shows this was done to approximate somewhat the modern "blue ribbon" standard.[369] A body of fairly substantial persons was assured, but in the counties where the big manors were situated available jurymen were relatively few. The *List of the Freeholders of Westchester County* for 1763 contains a total of 801 names. In 1756 the total white population in that county was 11,919 of which 3,947 were males over 16 years of age. On the panels returned by the sheriffs in the Province the occupations of the persons summoned are sometimes stated. In the country the usual petit jury was made up of farmers and an occasional artisan—blacksmiths, shoemakers, breeches makers and the like. In the city, owing to the personal estate alternative the artisans predominated.

There are certain details respecting the summoning of trial juries in the Supreme Court which need explanation. Sometimes in cases tried at bar, the venire having gone out after issue joined, the record notes that the sheriff "did not return the writ" and he is accordingly again ordered to have a jury come. This procedure is the means of noting a continuance, to secure the further attendance of the defendant upon an adjournment, for having once attended,

---

[368] 1 *Col. Laws NY* 387. The English statute, 4 & 5 Wm. & Mary c.24.

[369] 2 *Col. Laws NY* 185. The Lieutenant Governor drew the assembly's attention to the desirability of following English statutes (1 *Jour. Gen. Assembly* 750). In 1746 the New York Act was made perpetual and the personal estate alternative extended to the city of Albany (3 *Col. Laws NY* 599).

the defendant could not again be required to attend unless a day was given. By a merely fictional failure of the sheriff to return the venire a reissuance "day was given to the defendants."[370] A typical example of this is the record in *King v. William Kelly and Waddell Cunningham,* informed against for riot in 1760.[371]

The quintessence of these fictional failures to return was evolved in relation to Circuit practice with reference to causes brought to issue in the Supreme Court but sent for trial to the Circuit at nisi prius. This was adverted to in the discussion of transfer jurisdiction and deserves some further examination. The English practice when a cause was removed to the central courts contemplated a venire for a trial at bar and a day there given the parties. When, however, the cause was to be tried at nisi prius, since the defendant had to be given a day, and since some time would elapse between the joinder of issue and the arrival of the justices in the country, the fictive failure to return the jury summoned was employed, whereupon in King's Bench *distringas juratores,* and in Common Pleas *habeas corpus juratorum,* became the real process for a jury summoned at nisi prius. But even this process could become a mere fiction if for any reason continuances were granted.[372]

The English textbooks of the early eighteenth century are none of them explicit on the point of whether any form of return at all was made on the venire facias when the cause was to be tried at nisi prius,[373] but it may be assumed that this part of the proceedings was then entirely fictitious, for the statute 3 George II c.25 specifically required return of a panel on every venire, although the *distringas* or habeas corpus was the writ by which the jury was actually summoned. The colonial records indicate a close following of English practices, and in 1741, the return provisions of 3 Geo. II c.25 were incorporated into the new colonial jury statute.[374] In one particular, however, the provincial courts appear to have wavered. Owing to the fact that the Supreme Court was

---

[370] Cf. 1 Tidd, *King's Bench Practice* 836 *et seq.*

[371] On Tuesday, July 29, 1760, the defendants pleaded not guilty "and of this they put themselves . . . upon the Country and the said Attorney General . . . requires likewise that the same may be enquired of by the Country." Accordingly the court ordered: "Therefore let there come a Jury thereof before our Sovereign Lord the King at the City of New York on the third Tuesday in October next, by whom &c. and who neither &c. to recognize &c. the same day is given to the said William and Waddell here &c." However, in October Term the following entry appears: "At which Day before Our Lord the King at the City of New York Came as well the said John Tabor Kempe Esquire who

prosecutes as the aforesaid William Kelly and Waddell Cunningham by their Attorney aforesaid, And the Sheriff did not return the Writ Therefore as before let there come a Jury thereof before our Lord the King at the City of New York on the Third Tuesday in January next by whom &c. and who neither &c. to recognize &c. the same day is given to the said William and Waddell here &c." (*H.R. Parch.* 139 C 3).

[372] On this cf. Duncombe, *Trials per Pais* (1739) 63 *et seq.*; Gilbert, *Hist. Com. Pleas* (3 ed.) 77 *et seq.*; 3 Blackstone, *Commentaries* 353 *et seq.*

[373] See, for example, 2 Hawkins, *op. cit.* c.41.

[374] 3 *Col. Laws NY* 185.

endowed with the powers of both Common Bench and King's Bench, it never seems to have settled definitely upon the form of effective jury summons for nisi prius trials using sometimes the more stringent *distringas* and sometimes the *habeas corpus juratorum*. Thus we find the habeas corpus used as early as 1700 and again as late as 1754. In the case of John Barnes, informed against for an assault committed in Westchester County, the record shows a venire, then a continuance, a fictional new venire, the nisi prius entry and finally the order "let the sheriff have their body's" (viz., a habeas corpus) and the notation of the issue of the writ.[375] On the other hand, in the preceding year when Josiah Rayner, William Reeves and James Lupton were informed against for riot,[376] a *distringas* was issued. The writ which is set forth below[377] shows

[375] The 1700 case in *Mins. SCJ 1693–1701* 200. King v. Barnes in *H.R. Pleadings* Pl. K. 214, and note that this document was entitled a nisi prius roll, and bore the following label: "Westchester County SS: Nisi Prius between our Lord the King and John Barnes, Returnable the 23rd September at Westchester County—Clarke Junr." We quote in part after issue joined: "let there come a Jury thereof before our Sovereign Lord the King at the City of New York on the third Tuesday in April next of which each &c. by whom &c. and who neither &c. to recognize &c. the same Day is given to the said John Barns here, &c." A continuance appears in the next entry on this case which was as follows: "At which day before our Lord the King at the City of New York came the asd. John Barns as before and the Sheriff did not return the Writ. Therefore let there come a Jury thereof before our Sovereign Lord the King at the City of New York on the last Tuesday in July next of which each &c. by whom &c. and who neither &c. to recognize &c. the same Day is given to the said John Barns here &c."

A continuance appears in the next entry on this case which was as follows: "At which day before our Lord the King at the City of New York came the asd. John Barns as before and the Sheriff did not return the Writ. Therefore let there come a Jury thereof before our Sovereign Lord the King at the City of New York on the last Tuesday in July next of which each &c. by whom &c. and who neither &c. to recognize &c. the same Day is given to the said John Barns here &c." Next in this case follows the nisi prius entry itself: "The Jury between our Lord the King and John Barns of a plea of Trespass and Contempt wherewith he stands charged on the Information of William Kempe Esqr: Attorney General of our said Lord the King for the Province of New York are respited before our Sovereign Lord the King at the City of New York, until the third Tuesday in October next unless before that time the Judges or Justices of our said Lord the Kings Supreme Court of this Province or some or one of them for the Tryal

of Causes brought to issue in the said Supreme Court should on Tuesday the Twenty third day of September now next ensuing at Westchester in the said County of Westchester according to the Form of the Ordinance and the Act of the Governour the Council and the Generall Assembly of this province in such Case made and provided [the act of assembly of 1741] sooner come, through the Default of the Jurors. Therefore let the Sheriff have their Body's &c [*sic*] the same Day is given to the said John Barns there &c. And be it known that a Writ of our said Lord the King for that purpose on the second day of August . . . at the City of New York is delivered of Record to the Sherriff of the County aforesaid in due Form of Law to be executed under the penalty attending the Neglect thereof."

[376] *Supra* 195.

[377] *H.R. Parch.* 210 E 6. "George the Second . . . to our Sheriff of . . . Suffolk Greeting We command you that you omit not by Reason of any Liberty within your Bailiwick but that the same you enter and distrain The Bodies of the several Persons named in the Pannel to this Writ annexed, Jurors summoned in our Court before Us . . . by all their lands and Chattels in your Bailiwick so that neither they or any . . . meddle therewith until you have another precept from Us that you answer for the Issues . . . so that you have their Bodys before Us . . . at . . . New York . . . in October . . . or before Our Judges . . . of our Supreme Court . . . or some or one of them if they . . . for the Tryal of Causes brought to Issue in our said Supreme Court should [come] before that time . . . [in] September . . . at . . . Suffolk according to the Form of the Ordinance and the Act of the Governour Council and General Assembly in such Case made and provided to recognize upon their Oaths whether or no [the defendants] . . . are guilty of the Trespass and Contempts whereof . . . they stand charged at our Suit by the Information of our Attorney General, . . . and have you then there this Writ. Witness. . . . ." This writ was endorsed with the command,

clearly the submission of the panel before the *distringas* issued, indicating thus a compliance with the English nisi prius practice, described some years later by Blackstone.[378] It may be added that the writ in the Lydius case was in the same form,[379] but as in most instances the writs are wanting and only the nisi prius rolls, *posteas* or judgment rolls are available (where the clerks usually contented themselves with a mere entry of "have the Jury etc.") it is difficult to say with any certainty exactly what process was used.[380] It seems, moreover, to have been the practice to issue the venire and the *distringas* at the same time,[381] although the latter in theory was founded on the supposed default of the jurors, and one can envision how easily the sheriffs, lackadaisical about returns, could have caused a confusion which needed the healing power of the clerk's *etcetera.*

The complexities of nisi prius practice were peculiar to this one phase of Circuit business and did not affect the trial of indictments originally found in the country and not transferred. The practice here had developed in reference to the particular commissions, justices of Gaol Delivery having in England the recognized right to have a panel returned on a mere award without precept, whereas justices of Oyer and Terminer were required to make a particu-

---

signed by John Chambers for the sheriff of Suffolk, to return twenty-four persons to "serve for the Tryal of the within authorized Issue." The further endorsement on this writ was made by the sheriff: "The Execution of this Writ appears in a certain Pannel to this writ annexed." Annexed and pinned to the writ was the following statement: "The names of the jury between . . . the King and Josiah Rayner and William Reeves the Younger Defendants in a Plea of Trespass and Contempt . . . [named jurors] Every One of the Jurors aforesaid by himself is attached by pledges John Doe & Richard Roe The Issues of every One of them X shillings . . . Sheriff." An exactly similar writ was used in King v. Richard and C. Lawrence (*J. T. Kempe Lawsuits* J–L; *Ms. Mins. SC] 1756–61* [Rough] 170, Jan. 19, 1760).

[378] 3 Blackstone, *Commentaries* 354.

[379] *Supra* 210 *et seq.* The sheriff of Albany was on Apr. 20, 1763, ordered to distrain the jurors "by all their Lands &c. And that he have their Bodies before our said Lord the King At the City of New York on the last Tuesday in July next, or before the Judges . . . of . . . the King's Supreme Court . . . or some or one of them if they . . . for the Tryal of Causes brought to Issue in the said supreme Court should before that time on . . . the Twenty third day of June . . . at . . . Albany . . . sooner come through the default of Jurors" (*H.R. Parch.* 219 D 4).

[380] Compare King v. Lent, Higby *et al.* (*H.R. Parch.* 140 B 4, Jan. and Apr. 1765). For other cases in which the sheriff is commanded to "have the jury &c.," see King v. Augustine Reynolds *et al.* —information for riotously taking negroes, July and Sept. 1763 (*H.R. Parch.* 189 G 2); King v. Anthony Van Schaick—information for preventing partition under the 1762 act for collecting quitrents, Jan., June and July 1764 (*J. T. Kempe Lawsuits* V); King v. Henry Livingston (*supra* c. III 176) information against defendant as a clerk of peace for failing to return recognizances from Dutchess Quarter Sessions into the Supreme Court as a Court of Exchequer (*H.R. Parch.* 91 A 4 and 217 B 5).

For further samples of writs for nisi prius juries or recitals of such writs see: King v. John Doty, 1772 (*ibid.* 120 C 8); King v. Jacobus Terboss *et al.*, 1765 (*ibid.* 77 D 9, 222 C 3); King v. Tobias and Van Velser, 1771 (*ibid.* 15 F 1); King v. Moses Fowler, 1733 (*ibid.* 113 F 2); King v. Moses Owen, 1763 (*ibid.* 153 H 1); King v. Jacobus Cosyne, 1733–35 (*ibid.* 35 B 4 and 192 B 5); King v. George Klock, 1762 (*ibid.* 228 B 2), and King v. Gilbert Ferris, 1754 (*ibid.* 52 E 4).

[381] See the correspondence between Kempe and Harmanus Schuyler in *J. T. Kempe Lawsuits* L–O *sub nom.* J. H. Lydius. In the Lydius case, a blank parchment was annexed to each writ for the panel to be entered, Kempe to Schuyler, May 24, 1762.

lar precept.[382] Since, however, the New York Circuit judges were commissioned both as justices of Gaol Delivery and Oyer and Terminer these distinctions were of no moment, for the judges could act under either commission.[383] Unfortunately we have found no jury process used at Circuit in criminal cases, but the record in *King* v. *Carlan* seems to indicate that a mere award was sufficient.[384] Moreover, it is apparent from a memorandum preserved in the *Notes on the July Assizes, 1766*,[385] a special commission for Dutchess County, that the manner of summons was regarded as of no special concern, but the summons six days in advance was deemed to be crucial, the reason, of course, being the creation of an opportunity to examine the panel for purposes of challenge, a privilege of which English law was by no means tender. It may be added that this memorandum is an interesting example of the colonial lawyers' employment of English statutes making changes in the law although these were not applicable to the dominions.

[382] 2 Hawkins, *Pleas of the Crown* c.41 §§1–5; Coke, *Fourth Institute* 164. On the English practice at the beginning of the eighteenth century, the remarks of Treby, C.J., in King v. Cook (4 Hargrave, *State Trials* 738, 744). The Assize judges sent out a general precept to the sheriff prior to the Session on the basis of which the necessary panels were prepared against their arrival. For the form, *Crown Circuit Companion* (1768 ed.) 5 *et seq.*

[383] Cf. Foster, *Crown Cases* 64.

[384] The defendant having pleaded not guilty of murder at an Albany Circuit, "the court immediately ordered that a jury come etc." (H.R. *Parch.* 169 K 5).

[385] *Notes on July Assizes Dutchess Co.* (*Misc. Mss. Dutchess Co. 1752–1870*) and see *supra* 87 for the trials.
"1. Gaol Delivery requires not precept to bring in a Jury but Justices of Oyer & Terminer must Comp: Jur: 56, 57.
"2. With respect to the time of summoning the Jury six days is fixed by St. 4 & 5 William & Mary c.24. upon which our act as to Qualification of Jurors & Time of Summoning them is planned— both Acts expressly require 6 Days Therefore qu:
"As to the Time of Summons since the Statute & the act (1) It is to be observed as before that our act is grounded on the Statute. That statute it is true as expressly requires six days summons as [does] our Act yet the Statute was for 3 Years . . . only; and by . . . 7 & 8 Wm 3 cap. 32 it is enacted that So much of the 4 & 5 of Wm. & Mary as relates to the returning of Jurors shall be in force with the same 7 & 8 W. for 7 Years and contains a proviso that 'no process of Venire Facias Hab: Cor: or Distas. for summoning attaching or distrayning of any Jury to appear shall give any longer fine

[time?] than was by law required before the making the said act but that where there shall not be 6 days between the awarding of such Writ, precept or process and return thereof every Juror may be summoned attached or distrained to appear at the day and time therein mentioned and appointed as he might have been before the making of the said act of 4 and 5 William III' (2) [. . . The second point indicates that 4 and 5 William & Mary and 7 and 8 William III were continued by 1 Anne St. 12 & 13 for seven years and by 10 Anne c.14 for eleven years to the end of the next session of Parliament when it was continued by 9 George I c.8 for 7 years and to the end of the next session of Parliament] Which brings us to the statute 3 George II c. 25 by which all the other acts are suffered to expire and the purport of this last statute is to establish the Qualifications of Jurors in civil causes in the same manner as by 4 and 5 William and Mary and that jurors in capital cases shall have the same qualifications. Whence it follows (a) That the Statutes leave the qualifications of Jurors in all criminal cases not capital as by the Common Law [*sic*] before 4 and 5 William and Mary, (b) In capital cases as by 4 and 5 William and Mary and (c) The time of summoning Jurors in all criminal cases as before that statute.
"But our Act of Assembly makes the time fixed at 6 days necessary because it is Broad as the clause establishing the Qualifications of Jurors to wit extends to all causes criminal and civil though it is planned on 4 and 5 William and 3 George II yet the penners of the act did not observe that the proviso of 7 and 8 William III left the summoning as at common law and the 3 Geo. II contains no provision as to the time of summoning."

The intimation of some writers that the precept for the convening of Sessions was sufficient for the summons of a petit jury by mere award is not borne out by the New York records where, as early as 1694, we find orders for the issuance of a venire facias for the trial of particular indictments.[386] An example of such a venire used in 1736 shows that it was issued in the name of the justices, being thus a mere precept,[387] whereas a later example from the year 1770 is in form a writ running explicitly in the King's name to the sheriff.[388] There are not enough surviving examples to enable us to determine what the ruling practice was, or whether the writ form at some time supplanted the precept.

The colonial legislature in New York provided for a special type of non-professional triers of facts for the trials of slaves, and also provided a certain informal type of process for summoning such bodies. Under the provisions of the Acts of 1712 and of 1730, for preventing and punishing slave conspiracies and regulating slaves, it was provided that on complaint to any justice of the peace against a slave supposed to have attempted or committed murder, rape, arson or mayhem, the justice might issue his warrant to a constable to apprehend the offender and if, on examination, he believed the slave

---

[386] King v. John and Garrett Hardenburgh—ind. nuisance (*Ms. Mins. NYCQS 1694–1731/32* 3, 4, Nov. 7, 1694). The year before in King v. Hutchins —ind. entertaining slaves, the entry is merely "come a jury before ye Justices" (*Ms. Mins. NYCQS 1683/84–1694* 160, May 2, 1693). The form of entry varies a great deal. See, for example, the following:
Mary Barnes and John Kingston, indicted for clipping coin, pleaded not guilty (*supra,* n. 233), putting themselves on the country. The memorandum entries indicate "a jury summoned" found the defendants not guilty (*Ms. Mins. NYCQS 1694–1731/32* 102, 103, 104, Aug. 8, 1705).
On May 3, 1715, Jacob Ten Eyck was indicted for vending bread of unlawful assize and pleaded not guilty. He put himself on his country and David Jamison who prosecuted did in like manner. Accordingly the Court of Quarter Sessions of New York County ordered: "Therefore let there Come a Jury thereof before the Justices of our said Lord the King for the Conservation of the peace . . . at the next Court . . . on the first Tuesday in August then next Ensuing Twelve honest and lawfull men of the neighbourhood of the Dock Ward of the City of New York aforesaid by whom &c.: And who Neither &c. to Recognize &c.: because as well &c: the same day is given as well to the said David Jamison who prosecuteth as to the said Jacob Teneyck." In this case, however, the defendant on Aug. 2, 1715, put himself in mercy, confessing the indictment and was fined £1 2s. (*ibid.* memorandum entry, 312, 313).

On Feb. 4, 1761, Edward Dillon was indicted and on his pleading not guilty the court "Ordered *venire* issue for his trial this afternoon." Dillon was found guilty and sentenced to receive 39 lashes on each of two different days (*Ms. Mins. NYCQS 1732–62* 495, 496).
Bridget McEwen was indicted for disorderly house on Nov. 3, 1767, and on Nov. 4 she pleaded not guilty. The next day the New York Court of Quarter Sessions made the following order: "the Court ordered the Sheriff to Return a Pannel of the Jurors for the tryal of this Cause, and the Sheriff thereupon Returned a pannel accordingly when the following Jurors were sworn vizt . . . [naming twelve]" (*Ms. Mins. NYCQS 1760–72* 226, 230, 233; cf. *infra* 514 n. 117).
On June 14, 1774, John Bollman pleaded not guilty to two indictments for assault preferred against him in Tryon County Sessions and the case being "At issue, on motion of . . . Lefferts, Prosecutor for the Crown, for the Sheriff to enter a Venire and Pannel in this cause the following jurors were returned and sworn . . . [12 named]." The defendant was tried, found guilty on one indictment and fined 40s. Thereupon, defendant put himself in mercy, confessing the other indictment, and was fined 20s. (*Ms. Mins. Tryon Co. Sess. 1772–76* quartos VIII & IX; *Misc. Mss. Tryon Co.*).
[387] King v. Daley and Stut—petit larceny (*H.R. Pleadings* Pl. K. 520; *Ms. Mins. NYCQS 1732–62* 62, 63, May 6, 7, 1736). This is what Foster calls a precept in the nature of a writ of venire facias.
[388] King v. Mary Curtin—petit larceny (*H.R.*

guilty, he might commit him to prison. The justice was then to certify the case to the next two justices of peace and require them to associate themselves with him. Then the justices were to issue their summons to five freeholders and at the same time appoint a prosecutor. There was to be no grand jury and the slave was to be obliged to plead to the accusations made against him.[389] An example of the process thus provided for is preserved in the records of *King* v. *Cato,* in which a slave was prosecuted for rape.[390]

The problem of a supply of jurors, when by reason of defaults or exhaustion of a panel by challenges, was handled variously. It was customary in England to return twice the number of jurors directed by the venire[391] so as to assure the actual appearance of the necessary twelve. If the panel was exhausted a Court of Gaol Delivery was competent to call for new panels, *ore tenus,*[392] and according to Hale, the King's Bench would under circumstances issue a new venire, presumably a new writ.[393] This practice appears to have disappeared during the eighteenth century due to statutory changes.[394] Nevertheless, we have found one New York case (of the year 1774) where the minutes state that "the cause went off for want of jurors" whereupon, on motion of the Attorney General, it was ordered that "the Venire in this cause be quashed and that a venire de novo issue."[395]

A more usual proceeding, however, where all the jurors did not attend upon a *distringas* or when so many had been challenged that a sufficient number for a jury was wanting, was for the writ of *tales* to issue—*undecim, decem* or *octo* depending upon the number still needed to bring the panel up to fighting strength.[396] This procedure was used in the New York Supreme Court at an

Pleadings Pl. K. 454; *Ms. Mins. NYCQS 1760–72* 309, 311, Feb. 9, 1770, May 3, 1770).

[389] 1 *Col. Laws NY* 766; 2 *ibid.* 684, 685.

[390] "To . . . [five named persons] Principal Freeholders . . . Pursuant to the Directions of an Act . . . of . . . Assembly . . . You and Each and Every of You are hereby summoned and Required to appear at the City Hall . . . in Conjunction with us to try hear and Determine if Cato . . . [a slave] be Guilty of attempting to Commit a Rape upon . . . Susannah . . . Sylvester . . . of which Offence he Stands Accused & hereof fail not Given under our hands and seals . . . the 23ᵈ day of January . . . [1733/34] James De Lancey Frederick Philipse Robt. Lurting . . . [and three others named]." Meeting of mayor and aldermen of New York City for trial of slaves under the act of assembly for conspiracy of slaves (*Ms. Mins. NYCQS 1722–1742/43* [Rough] in back of minute book, 332). It should be noticed that the pre-

cept used under the Act of 1712 was identical (King v. Kip's negress, *Ms. Mins. Albany Co. Sess. 1717–23* June 8, 1722).

[391] Coke, *Littleton* 155; 2 Hale, *op. cit.* 263, and on later practice, 1 Chitty, *Criminal Law* 505, 506.

[392] Per Treby, C.J., in King v. Cook (4 Hargrave, *State Trials* 744).

[393] 2 Hale, *op. cit.* 265. A *distringas* with a *tales* issued first if there were not enough jurymen to try the prisoner, and a new venire if the whole jury was charged off.

[394] Cf. Bacon, *Abridgement* Jurors, C; 1 Chitty, *op. cit.* 519.

[395] King v. Catherine Garrett—ind. perjury (*Ms. Mins. SCJ 1772–76* [Rough] 184, 201, 207). There are no minutes of subsequent proceedings.

[396] Cf. Alfred Denbawd's Case (10 *Co. Rep.* 102b, 103b); 2 Hale, *op. cit.* 266. It was held in King v. Perry (5 *Term Rep.* 456) that this procedure was necessary in trials at bar.

early date[397] and there are examples to be found as late as the year 1775.[398] Much rarer is the alternative measure established in England by statute and intended to expedite the dispatch of business, the so-called *tales de circumstantibus,* whereby the court would order the sheriff to add as many of the bystanders in court to the panel as to complete the necessary number.[399] The English practice required a particular warrant from the Attorney General for the *tales* to be prayed for the King,[400] but in New York it was granted simply upon motion of the Attorney General.[401]

It has already been indicated that jury process was normally directed to the sheriff, but when he was either directly interested or was related to one of the parties, process was then directed to the coroner. Thus in *King* v. *Tompkins,* informed against in 1735 for assaulting the high sheriff of Westchester, the court ordered the venire issued to the coroner of that county.[402] And much later, when George Harrison was indicted for riot, the Attorney General filed an affidavit alleging that the defendant was related to the sheriff and prayed the venire be directed to the coroner.[403] The family tie was obviously taken seriously in a jurisdiction where most of the officials were in one way or another connected with the large landowners. In an ejectment action an affidavit was filed where it is urged that, as the plaintiff's lessor was a second cousin to the sheriff's wife, a change of venue should be effected. No sooner was this accomplished than one Dirck Swart "a common Embraceour of Jurors . . . unlawfully and corruptly moved and persuaded" the jurors to a verdict for the plaintiff, for which offense an information was presently filed.[404]

---

[397] King v. Elwood, ind. murder, 1696, a "tales of 5" added (*Mins. SCJ 1693–1701* 91); King v. Baker, no offense indicated, 1702, a *tales* of 4 added on motion of the Attorney General (*Ms. Mins. SCJ 1701–04* 59); Queen v. Densworth a slave *et al.,* ind. burglary, 1704 (*ibid.* 150, 156).

[398] In King v. Darcus, 2 inds., grand larceny and stealing a gelding, Darcus was found guilty on the first indictment and prayed his clergy. On the second indictment, nine jurors were challenged and a sufficient number of jurymen not appearing the court ordered a larger panel of seventy-two jurors (*Ms. Mins. SCJ 1772–76* 107–111). Cf. also King v. Pat Smith, ind. petit larceny, 1775, where the court ordered a *tales* returned (*ibid.* 221, 243).

[399] Duncombe, *Trials per Pais* 68 *et seq.*

[400] A late form in 4 Chitty, *Criminal Law* 306.

[401] King v. Brazier, arraigned on a coroner's inquest for manslaughter in 1768. Twenty bystanders were ordered to be returned, but in fact only five were returned and the prisoner challenged three and the cause "remained" for want of jurors. Brazier was tried the next term and acquitted (*Ms. Mins. SCJ 1766–69* [Engr.] 555; *Ms. Mins. SCJ*

1769–72 [Engr.] 16). In King v. Mary Davis, indicted for petit larceny, the court seems to have ordered the *tales de circumstantibus* without motion (*Ms. Mins. SCJ 1772–76* [Rough] 242, 244).

[402] *Ms. Mins. SCJ 1732–39* 177, 200. In July, 1735, an information was filed against one Brown who pleaded not guilty. On January 24, 1735/36 a venire was ordered to issue to the coroner of Westchester (*Ms. Mins. SCJ 1732–39* 168, 200, 201). We do not know why the venire issued to the coroner in the latter case nor do we know the nature of the information filed against the defendant. In the case of John Allison, informed against on Apr. 24 and Aug. 7, 1733, for maintenance and false weights (*ibid.* 28, 49), the Attorney General moved that the venire issue to the coroner. For a Sessions example, King v. Gerritson (*Ms. Mins. Richmond Co. Sess. 1710/11–1744/45* Sept. 2, 1729 [defendant was sheriff's brother]).

[403] *Ms. Mins. SCJ 1756–61* (Rough) 180, 198; *H.R. Parch.* 136 E 7, and *H.R. Pleadings* Pl. K. 979 (the latter an affidavit by R.W. to "ground a motion" for the coroner to summon the jury).

[404] *J. T. Kempe Lawsuits* S–U *sub nom.* Dirck

Where the sheriff and coroner were both deemed to be interested it was possible to avoid a change of venue by application to have two elisors named by the court to pick the jury. This procedure, as we have seen, was used in the case of *King* v. *Van Rensselaer*,[405] and was again employed in 1772 when the sheriff of Dutchess was proceeded against on a charge of packing a jury.[406]

The colonial reception in such minute detail of the whole procedural paraphernalia which had developed about the petit jury may have owed something to the prevailing attachment to this most sacred incident of an Englishman's rights; that is to say, the colonists, always fearful of a diminution of their common law privileges, deemed these best secured by overlooking no particular, however adventitious. On the other hand, we have already seen in other relations how inexorably the imitative process, once set in motion, drove lawyers and judges to uncritical acceptance of whatever the books had to offer. The same blind forces we think were at work in the case of procedures relating to juries, for the records do not show that the popular political pieties about jury trial were translated into a constant readiness to preserve the institution by service. On the contrary, it was the courts with their *distringas* and *tales* that kept the citizen to the mark, for there is hardly a page in the minute books that does not note a delinquency of jurors, either grand or petit.

The reasons for the delinquencies are many and various. In 1706, one of the jurors summoned to serve on an inquisition of riot sought to avoid service by declaring "he would give his inquest beforehand in the cause by that means should find a way to gett off."[407] At Westchester Circuit in 1745, four petit jurors excused an absence by claiming they thought their attendance was not required until the second day of court, as at Sessions.[408] Sometimes a man claimed illness,[409] or business inconvenience,[410] and one man summoned stayed away because he was neither a freeman nor a freeholder.[411]

The courts treated as a contempt the various forms of jurors' delinquency, whether a mere failure to appear on summons, or leaving court before dis-

---

Swart. Although this information was filed by the Attorney General on the order of the Supreme Court on Oct. 31, 1767, and process ordered to issue against Swart on Jan. 23, 1768, nevertheless, no further proceedings appear in the case and it is not outside the realm of possibility that Swart's powerful patron arranged matters (*Ms. Mins. SCJ 1766–69* [Engr.] 326, 388).

[405] *Supra* c. IV 250. It is interesting to note that on July 30, 1768, that "common Embraceour of Jurors," Dirck Swart, who had been informed against for embracery on Oct. 31, 1767, was appointed one of the elisors in this case instead of Lucas Van

Veghte, who had been previously appointed (*Ms. Mins. SCJ 1766–69* [Engr.] 519).

[406] *Ms. Mins. SCJ 1769–72* (Engr.) 523, and compare the preliminary proceedings in Council, 26 *Ms. Mins. Council* 249, 251.

[407] In Queen v. Lawrence *et al.* (*Ms. Mins. SCJ 1704/05–1709* 100, 105, 108).

[408] *Ms. Mins. Cir. 1721–49* 343.

[409] *Ms. Mins. NYCQS 1772–91* 22, 23, Nov. 3, 4, 1772.

[410] *Ms. Mins. SCJ 1769–72* (Engr.) 173, 175.

[411] *Ms. Mins. NYCQS 1772–91* 22, 23, Nov. 3, 4, 1772.

charge,[412] or other irregularity. The proceedings were ordinarily summary, that is to say, a fine was imposed, usually in the sum of 13s. 4d., for a mere non-appearance, but frequently larger amounts were set.[413] If the person fined offered what the court regarded as a legitimate excuse the fine would be remitted. Very exceptionally, if the juror's delinquency amounted to a substantial contempt an attachment would issue.[414]

The fines not remitted at Circuit or Sessions were supposed to be estreated into the Supreme Court which would order the sheriff to levy distraint and collect the fines. A typical order is that made on April 28, 1770, to collect fines incurred for defaults at that term:

> That the Sheriff of . . . New York distrain the Goods and Chattels of the several Persons hereunder mentioned and named . . . and that he sell the same at publick Vendue, and that . . . he cause to be . . . levied . . . the several sums upon them . . . charged, the same being the Fines upon them . . . charged by this court in this present Term for their . . . Defaults and non-Attendance at this Court according to their Duty as Petit Jurors and Constables respectively.

The sheriff was to retain out of the proceeds of the sales his mileage fees at 6d. a mile and to take fines from the jurors not to exceed £3. The balance remaining was of course to be returned to the owners.[415]

Process against Witnesses

An examination of the process problem is not complete without some consideration of the process to bring in witnesses to testify. The *subpoena ad testificandum,* as we have seen, was one of the few forms of process mentioned in the Duke's Laws in the curious regulation which provided that a witness need not appear unless served with subpoena, and in the record book of the Court of Assizes a form is preserved.[416] The evidence of the use of subpoenas in the country Sessions during the eighteenth century is very scanty, for usually the recognizance to testify was there used. The minute entries indicate a mere verbal warning or an order to appear,[417] and the "notices of examina-

---

[412] E.g., *Ms. Mins. Cir. 1721-49* 281, 282 (1733).

[413] The examples are too numerous to list. For an instance of £3 and £5 fines (*Ms. Mins. SCJ 1754-57* [Engr.] 73, Oct. 16, 1754); £10 (*Ms. Mins. SCJ 1769-72* [Engr.] 121, Oct. 28, 1769).

[414] E.g., *Ms. Mins. SCJ 1704/05-1709* 108.

[415] *Ms. Mins. SCJ 1769-72* (Engr.) 196, 197.

[416] *Supra* 389.

[417] Cf. *Mins. Westch. Ct. of Sess. 1657-96* 75 (1693); as the names of the witnesses subpoenaed are given, we assume the notice was oral in the case of the other witnesses. In King v. Patrick Ker, the court ordered Jacob Turck "to appear" at Gaol Delivery (*Ms. Mins. Ulster Co. Sess. 1737-50* May 7, 1745). Cf. also King v. Dando (*Ms. Mins. Suffolk Co. Sess. 1723-51* Oct. 6, 1730). On May 15, 1739 the Queens court issued subpoenas for grand jury

tions" being filed leads us to think these were sometimes used in trials. On the other hand, the fact that the tables of fees for Sessions provide a charge for each subpoena[418] makes it likely the clerk would not ordinarily waive the opportunity to collect a few extra pence. An early form of a Sessions subpoena (dated 1692) is contained in the Westchester Sessions minutes.[419] It is considerably more elaborate than that used by the early Court of Assizes and closely approximates the English form,[420] although a penalty of only £50 instead of £100 is stipulated.

There are several examples preserved of the subpoenas used for trials at bar and at Circuit. New York practice evidently was made to conform at an early date with that prevailing in England.[421] The subpoena was issued for a number of witnesses with so-called tickets. The subpoena itself was served by giving the witness a view of it; the ticket was left with him. This procedure is described by John Tabor Kempe in a letter to Sir William Johnson instructing him how to make service in the case of George Klock charged with making Indians drunk and procuring them to sign deeds:[422]

witnesses (*Ms. Mins. Queens Co. Sess. 1722–87*). A bill of costs for a summary trial in *Ms. Files Dutchess Co. 1740–50* has an item "Order for Four Witnesses each 4s."

[418] 1 *Col. Laws NY* 641 (1709); *Ordinance of Fees* (1768) n.p. (Bar Assn. NY).

[419] *Mins. Westch. Ct. of Sess. 1657–96* 127.

[420] *Thesaurus Brevium* (1687) 304.

[421] For an example of a Supreme Court subpoena, *H.R. Pleadings* Pl. K. 182 (quoted *infra* n. 424). For the form of another such subpoena for a trial in the Supreme Court *en banc,* see *H.R. Parch.* 190 E 2. For a note of witnesses subpoenaed for April Term of the Supreme Court, 1762, in the case of King v. John Lawrence *et al.* (indicted for riot), see *H.R. Pleadings* Pl. K. 961, and for subpoena tickets written on paper and the subpoenas themselves written on parchment in the John Lawrence case, see *J. T. Kempe Lawsuits* G–J *sub nom.* Harrison. For a subpoena for witnesses to appear to give evidence against Peter Remsen, charged with slandering a juror, see *H.R. Parch.* 190 E 2. For a subpoena in King v. Godardus Van Solingen see *H.R. Pleadings* Pl. K. 903. For subpoenas and tickets in King v. Thomas Newton *et al.,* informed against for assault, see *J. T. Kempe Lawsuits* L–O.

The following is a Circuit subpoena: "George the third . . . To Elizabeth Robinson, Mary Robinson, Benjamin Birdsall . . . Greeting We command you and every of you firmly enjoining you (that laying aside all and all manner of Businesses and Excuses whatsoever) you . . . be before our Judges . . . of . . . our Supreme Court or some or one of them at the Court . . . to be held for the Trial of Causes brought to Issue in . . . Supreme Court on . . . the Nineth Day of September next at . . .

Jamaica in Queens County to testify all . . . you shall know in a certain Action . . . before us now depending undetermined between us and Thomas Tobias . . . in a Plea of Debt and on that Day by a Jury of the Country there to be tried and this you are in no wise to omit under the penalty of One hundred Pounds for every of you WITNESS Daniel Horsmanden Esquire Chief Justice of our Province of New York at Our City of New York the First Day of August the Twelfth year of our Reign Clarke J T Kempe Attorney General" (*H.R. Parch.* 183 E 4). For another subpoena to appear at Circuit in the case of King v. Snedeker *et al.,* informed against for riot, see *J. T. Kempe Lawsuits* C–F and also see *H.R. Pleadings* Pl. K. 378. For the subpoena to a witness to appear in the case of King v. Nicholas DeLavergne, a justice of the peace informed against for failing to return recognizances, see the one issued for a trial at Poughkeepsie in *H.R. Parch.* 184 H 10. Simon Rumsey was informed against for assault on the order of the Supreme Court of August Term, 1765 (*Ms. Mins. SCJ 1764–66* [Engr.] 285), and on May 19, 1767, J. T. Kempe sent one subpoena and four tickets for the defendant's trial at Orange County Circuit Court and in his letter to the sheriff directed that the sheriff fill in the names of the witnesses on the subpoenas. For a subpoena for witnesses to appear in King v. Robert Campbell and Archibald Livingston, who had been informed against for assaulting an undersheriff and who were to be tried at Orange County Circuit Court in June, 1764, see *H.R. Parch.* 186 D 3. Subpoenas for 1765 Nisi Prius are in *Ms. Files Ulster Co.* Bundle B.

[422] *J. T. Kempe Lawsuits* J–L. In these same papers there is a form of a subpoena to Goldsbrow

. . . I herewith enclose four subpoenas and sixteen tickets in the Case of the King agt. George Klock. I have not filled up the Subpoenas or Tickets with the Names of the Witnesses not knowing whether the Witnesses . . . are all . . . living . . . let the Names of such . . . as can be subpoenaed, be inserted in one of the Writs and on the Top of a Subpoena Ticket, and that Subpoena showed the witness in which his name is wrote, so that he may see the Seal, and the Ticket be delivered to him. . . .

The tables of fees, as early as 1709, indicate that subpoenas issued for no more than four witnesses, although it was not until much later that there is indication the English courts regarded this to be a rule of law.[423] That the mystical number four was not regarded as mandatory is apparent from a subpoena issued by the Supreme Court in 1774 where ten witnesses were named.[424]

Banyar for him to appear to testify at the Supreme Court or at the Albany Circuit in the George Klock case.

In King v. James Higby, Abraham Lent *et al.,* Kempe on May 28, 1765, sent instructions to William Clarke advising him how to serve subpoenas: "I now send you enclosed two Subpoenas and eight Tickets . . . [for the witnesses in the riot case] . . .—you will see I intend to try the causes the 11th June at poghkeepsie, . . . If you have any others . . . put their Names into one of the Subpoenas and write his name on the Ticket, and when you serve the subpoena on the witnesses you must show him the parchment in which his Name is mentioned, and the Seal of the Court and deliver the Witness one of the Tickets belonging to the Cause in which you Subpoena him or her. You need not give them any money as it is the Suit of the King—you must not put above the names of 4 witnesses in any one Subpoena. . . ." The formal subpoena on parchment was in the following language: "George the Third . . . to Zachariah Bush, Powel Vanderwoort, William Scuff and Frederick Scuff—Greeting: We command you that (laying aside all and all manner of business and excuses whatsoever) You and every of you be before our Judges or Justices of our Supreme Court or some or one of them at the Court before them some or one of them to be held for the Tryal of Causes brought to Issue in our said Supreme Court on Tuesday the Eleventh day of June next at Poghkeepsie in the County of Dutchess to testify the truth according to your knowledge on our part and behalf in a certain Cause before us now depending and then there to be tryed between us and James Higby Abraham Lent . . . of and concerning certain Trespasses and Contempts of which . . . the said James Higby . . . [et al.] stand Charged by the Information of our Attorney General and this you nor any of you are in no wise to omit under the penalty of £100 Witness Daniel Horsmanden

Esquire Chief Justice at our city of New York the twenty seventh day of April, in the fifth year of our Reign. Clarke. J. T. Kempe Attorney General." A subpoena ticket in this case, addressed to Mrs. Sarah Vanderwoort, was written on paper and was in the following form: "By virtue of a writ of subpoena to you directed . . . personally to be and appear before his Majesty's judges or justices of the Supreme Court or some or one of them to be held for the tryal of causes brought to issue in the said Supreme Court on Tuesday the 11th day of June next at Poughkeepsie in the County of Dutchess . . . to testify the truth according to your knowledge on the part of our Sovereign Lord the King in a certain cause now depending and then there to be tried between our Sovereign Lord the King and James Higby, Abraham Lent . . . [et al.] concerning certain trespasses and contempts whereof they stand charged by the information of his Majesty's Attorney General and hereof you are not to fail on pain of £100." This ticket was dated May 27, 1765. All of the above material is to be found in *J. T. Kempe Lawsuits* C–F.

In King v. John Henry Lydius, Attorney General Kempe in his letter to Sheriff Harmanus Schuyler of Albany on May 23, 1763, gave the instructions for serving subpoenas quoted *supra* 211.

[423] The text writers all cite the case in *Cowper* 846 (Doe v. Andrews) as authority. It is not a holding, but the argument of counsel is based upon the rule of four.

[424] Cf. the subpoena in King v. George Wittmer and John Haumaid who were indicted for forgery on Jan. 21, 1774: "GEORGE the third by the Grace of God of Great Britain France and Ireland King Defender of the Faith and so forth to Christopher Polonceaux, Charles Douilliard, Peter Bausher, Elizabeth Bausher, James Durand, Ann House, Solomon Simson, Mathew Kennedy, Patrick Kennedy and Philip House Greeting We command you and every of you firmly enjoining you that

The costs for subpoenas varied evidently due to mileage fees. In *King* v. *William Murray*, informed against on July 29, 1758, for an assault, the costs on the information and trial indicate that in vacation and April Term, 1760, the costs of a subpoena in this case were 4*s*. 3*d*., and the costs for four subpoena tickets amounted to 3*s*., while the charge for serving four witnesses amounted to 4*s*.[425] On the other hand, in the costs for putting off the trial in *King* v. *John Henry Lydius*, four subpoenas cost 17*s*. 3*d*. and fifteen subpoena tickets cost 11*s*. 3*d*. The "service" of these subpoenas cost 15*s*., but the cost for a messenger serving three subpoenas in Dutchess County ran to £3 3*s*., figured at a rate of 9*s*. a day for seven days. Furthermore, the cost of a messenger serving three subpoenas in Albany, which took him ten days in the Lydius case, totalled £4 10*s*. A *subpoena duces tecum* in this same case cost 6*s*. A "special" ticket for the *subpoena duces tecum* cost 3*s*. and service of this subpoena on Goldsbrow Banyar cost 1*s*. while there was another charge of 12*s*. for Mr. Banyar's bringing the record. Also included in these costs were travelling charges for ten days at 13*s*. 4*d*. a day, totalling £6 13*s*. 4*d*., but we do not know whether these travelling charges were incurred in connection with serving the subpoenas or whether they were the Attorney General's expenses.[426]

During the eighteenth century in England and also in New York the most usual means of securing the attendance of witnesses was to bind them over by recognizances to give evidence.[427] To this end it was customary, when necessary, to employ a warrant to get the witnesses before a justice of the peace.[428] We do not know how extensively such warrants were used in New York but there is preserved one addressed by Attorney General James Alexander to the high and petty constables of New York commanding them to bring in witnesses to be used in the case of *King* v. *Waldron*, indicted for stopping the King's Highway in Harlem:

(laying aside all and all manner of Businesses and Excuses whatsoever) you and every of you be before Us on Wednesday the Twentieth Day of April next at the City Hall in Our City of New York to testify the Truth according to your Knowledge on our Part and Behalf in a certain Cause before us now depending and then there to be tried between Us and George Wittmer and John Haumaid of and concerning certain Trespasses and Contempts of which they the said George Wittmer and John Haumaid are Indicted and this you nor any of you are in no wise to omit under the Penalty of one hundred pounds for every of you WITNESS Daniel Horsmanden Esquire Chief Justice for our Province of New York at our City of New York the Twenty second Day of January in the Fourteenth

Year of our Reign . . . J. T. Kempe Attorney General CLARKE" (*H.R. Pleadings* Pl. K. 182 and cf. *Ms. Mins. SCJ* 1772–76 [Rough] 145).

[425] *J. T. Kempe Lawsuits* L–O. *Supra* n. 272.

[426] *Ibid. Infra* App. 775 are the Lydius costs, and *ibid.* 775 the costs in King v. George Klock. In that case the cost for a copy of the instructions for the defendant to serve the subpoenas and tickets amounted to 5*s*. 6*d*. See *supra* 478, where we have quoted the Attorney General's instructions for serving subpoenas and tickets. The cost of sealing three subpoenas was 12*s*. 9*d*. and for twelve tickets was 8*s*.

[427] Cf. *infra* 511 *et seq.*

[428] There is a form in Dalton, *Countrey Justice* (1677 ed.) 483.

James Alexander . . . Attorney General . . . to the high constable and petty constables . . . of New York . . . New York SS: These are in the Kings Majestys name to Charge and Command you that presently upon Sight hereof you or Some of you do cause to Come before me the persons following to wit . . . [6 named yeomen] to the End that they . . . may be bound to make their personal appearance before the justices of the Supream Court at New York . . . then and there to testify their and every of their knowledges concerning a Certain misdemeanor whereof Samuel Waldron Stands indicted and is then and there to be tryd by a jury of the country and hereof fail not at your perils Given under my hand and seal at New York . . . [on June 7, 1722].[429]

When a prisoner or other person in custody was required to appear as a witness in any court the usual process in England was a *habeas corpus ad testificandum*.[430] Such process was used in the case of *King* v. *Kelly and Cunningham,* to which we have already referred,[431] to bring in George Spencer, the complaining witness, who was himself in custody,[432] and there are a few other cases where this writ was used.[433] In a number of instances, however, the minutes show merely an order to the sheriff to bring in a prisoner, and it is possible no formal process was used.[434]

---

[429] *James Alexander Papers* Box 44. Compare also a "subpoena" of June 10, 1721, in King v. Peter Bogardus, for Thomas Swartout and others to appear to testify at the Supreme Court in the King's suit against Bogardus on an information for oppression and extortion (*ibid.*).

When William Kasey complained against Ann and Godfrey Cunningham and others for an assault and battery, a letter was written to the Attorney General stating that Kasey could not get "all his evidences but if a subpoena or an order from you [i.e., the Attorney General] they will attend" (*J. T. Kempe Lawsuits* C July 1754). Evidently in this case the complainant thought that the Attorney General might be able to issue a summons or subpoena for witnesses. There is some evidence of informal practice respecting the means taken to compel witnesses to attend. Thus, in the late seventeenth century the Common Pleas of Westchester used what the clerk called a summons; cf. *Mins. Westch. Ct. of Sess. 1657–96* 120, and compare the following entry: "Dom Rex Joseph Horton witnesses summd Jonathan Hart Tho: Gague Bethiah Longstoff and Vollentine Vincent —— 9 br 30th 1693" (*ibid.* 125). The subpoena was in effect a summons and in one curious Circuit Court subpoena, this word is used in the body of the writ; cf. *J. T. Kempe Lawsuits* C–F *s.n.* Cole. In King v. Jane Smith (ind. larceny), the Supreme Court ordered that certain witnesses attend and "that one of the Constables summon the said persons" (*Ms. Mins. SCJ 1754–57* [Engr.] 218, 219).

[430] 3 Blackstone, *Commentaries* 130.

[431] *Supra* 282.

[432] *H.R. Pleadings* Pl. K. 960; *Ms. Mins. SCJ 1756–61* (Rough) 198, Oct. 21, 1760.

[433] In King v. Thomas Flood and others, indicted for assault and battery, the Attorney General on Oct. 18, 1763, made a motion that a *habeas corpus ad testificandum* issue to bring James Green in as a witness in the case, and this motion was granted (*Ms. Mins. SCJ 1762–64* [Engr.] 266). In King v. James Leary, the court "on motion of Mr. Attorney General ordered a habeas corpus to bring James Smith as a witness" (*Ms. Mins. SCJ 1756–61* [Rough] 198, Oct. 21, 1760).

[434] In King v. Nathaniel Cooley, indicted for assaulting a jailer in the execution of his office, the following minute entry appears on Oct. 28, 1773: "Mr. Attorney General suggesting that I . . . D . . . and Mary T . . . prisoners for debt in the custody of the sheriff of New York, are material witnesses for the crown, Ordered the said witnesses into court" (*Ms. Mins. SCJ 1772–76* [Rough] 131). George Brewerton Esqr. was informed against for maladministration in office and on May 1, 1772, "on motion of Mr. Attorney General Ordered the high sheriff of New York do bring into court John Graham now in his custody," charged in execution to be examined as a witness for the Crown on two informations against the defendant for maladministration in execution of his office as justice of the peace (*Ms. Mins. SCJ 1769–72* [Engr.] 520). On Apr. 28, 1774, the Supreme Court ordered the

Supplementary to the subpoena commanding the attendance of witnesses was the *subpoena duces tecum* which issued for the production of books and papers in the hands of third parties. Usually this writ simply consisted in adding a clause of requisition to the writ of subpoena. The occasions when such process would be used in criminal prosecutions were relatively rare. We have not noticed this writ employed in the first half of the eighteenth century, but doubtless it was even then used in civil cases. An example in a criminal prosecution where the *subpoena duces tecum* was necessary was the prosecution of Jacobus Terboss and nineteen other justices of the peace who were informed against in April, 1765, for maladministration due to their failure to return recognizances into the Supreme Court as a court of Exchequer.[435] The case was to be tried at nisi prius in Dutchess County, and a *subpoena duces tecum* issued to oblige Henry Livingston, the clerk of the peace of Dutchess County, to appear as a witness and to bring with him various writs and recognizances which were to be used in evidence against the delinquent justices.[436] Similarly, in the case of *King* v. *Wittmer and Haumaid* (1774), indicted for forgery in altering a document written in French, a *subpoena duces tecum* went forth to James Duane, William Smith and James Emott commanding them to bring certain documents.[437]

sheriff to bring before the grand jury as a witness a prisoner who was in the custody of the sheriff for debt (*Ms. Mins. SCJ 1772–76* [Rough] 179). In the case of King v. Alexander Perry, indicted for grand larceny on Apr. 20, 1765, the Supreme Court "Ordered the sheriff to bring into court John Newberry, a prisoner in his custody on mesne process to give evidence" (*Ms. Mins. SCJ 1764–67* [Rough] 59, 63).

In one hearing before the grand jury, the high sheriff, on Jan. 24, 1772, represented to the Supreme Court that Simon Stevens, a prisoner in his custody upon execution, was required to attend the grand jury as a witness. The court ordered the sheriff to bring Stevens as well as Fred Groome (also in the sheriff's custody) to attend the grand jury. The court furthermore made the order that immediately after the examination of these witnesses, they be at once remanded to prison (*Ms. Mins. SCJ 1769–72* [Engr.] 474).

[435] *Ms. Mins. SCJ 1764–66* (Engr.) 177, Apr. 27, 1765; *H.R. Parch.* 222 C 3, 77 D 9.

[436] The draft of the subpoena *duces tecum* was in the following language: "George To Henry Livingston Esquire Clerk of the peace for the County of Dutchess We command you firmly enjoining you that laying aside all and all manner of businesses and Excuses whatsoever you be in your own proper person before our Judges . . . of our Supreme Court or some or one of them at the Court before

them some or one of them to be held for the Trial of Causes brought to issue in our s^d Sup^r Court at Poghkeepsie in the County of Dutchess . . . [on June 9] to testify the truth according to your knowledge on our part . . . [in the case of King v. Jacobus Terboss and others] of and concerning certain Trespasses & Contempts of which they stand charged by the Information of our Attorney General And also that you . . . bring with you all the minuets of the proceedings of the Court of General Sessions of the peace for the said County of Dutchess . . . [from Jan. 1, 1750, to Jan. 1, 1765] and also all & every the Recognizance . . . for the personal appearance . . . [of several persons named] . . . at the said Court of General Sessions of the peace by whatsoever names they are called in the same recognizances . . . and also all . . . writs process and precipes, capias, alias capias and pluries from time to time issued by from and out of the said Court of Sessions and out of the office of the clerk of the peace . . . against them . . . their sureties or manucaptors or bail . . . and this you are by no means to omit under the penalty of £100 . . . Witness . . . [etc.]" (*J. T. Kempe Lawsuits* L–O sub nom. Henry Livingston). It will be remembered that Henry Livingston was himself informed against in 1767 for failing to return recognizances (*H.R. Parch.* 91 A 4).

[437] *H.R. Pleadings* Pl. K. 382 contains the *subpoena duces tecum* and the indictment for forgery is

We shall speak in a moment of the measures taken against recalcitrant witnesses, but as a necessary preliminary it is important to notice something of the measures taken to protect persons who were required to testify. In an age when the capias was freely used as first process in civil actions, and in a community where men did not scruple to resort to the law for unworthy ends, witnesses were often reluctant to attend court because of their fear of arrest. There is no direct evidence that this was a not unusual means of intimidation, but we strongly suspect this to have been the case. As to a fear of bodily violence there is no doubt at all. We have seen how in the case of witnesses appearing before the grand jury the courts would issue "protections,"[438] and the same practice obtained with reference to witnesses at trials. Thus, on two separate occasions that stormy petrel of the Cosby regime, John Peter Zenger,[439] was granted the Supreme Court's protection to enable him to testify and there are various other examples of this in the records.[440]

The recalcitrant witness does not appear to have been a problem until after 1750. The general use of recognizance to testify was, of course, an insurance against defaults, but there is some evidence which shows the courts to have been forbearing in the earlier period, and the failure of witnesses to appear resulted merely in a continuance. In *Queen* v. *Clara Harris* (1709), indicted at Sessions for trading with slaves and buying stolen goods, the trial was twice put off because of "the Queens evidence being upon the frontiers" and again because they were "out of the way."[441] And in the case of Henry Cordus, on trial for adultery (1710/11), who had narrowly escaped outlawry, the Sessions Court after various postponements granted a further continuance on the defendant's motion because of the absence of one of his material witnesses.[442]

---

entered on the Supreme Court minutes on Jan. 21, 1774 (*Ms. Mins. SC] 1772–76* [Rough] 145).

[438] Cf. *supra* 350.

[439] On June 7, 1731, on the motion of Mr. Murray, the Supreme Court "Ordered that John Peter Zenger have the protection of the court coming to, staying at and going from the court tomorrow to give evidence in a case between one Thomas Hall and one Magee" (*Ms. Mins. SC] 1727–32* 282). Likewise in King v. James Wallace, the Supreme Court on Oct. 13, 1732, ordered that John Peter Zenger have the court's protection in testifying (*ibid.* 360).

[440] In King v. William Norris and Charles Parca, indicted for petit larceny, the Supreme Court on Dec. 4, 1732, gave one Goodwin its protection "for being a material witness in this case" (*ibid.* 391–393). Cf. the orders in King v. Fowler and King v. Allison, *supra* 174, 185.

On Oct. 25, 1735, the Supreme Court "ordered a protection be granted to Thomas Griggs for his going to, stopping at and returning from Westchester to give evidence in behalf of the King to a court of Oyer and Terminer and General Gaol Delivery" (*Ms. Mins. SC] 1732–39* 190).

[441] *Ms. Mins. NYCQS 1694–1731/32* 157, 159, 163, 164, 167, 168, 174, Feb. 2, 1708/09, May 3, Aug. 2, 3, Nov. 1, 2, 1709, May 2, 1710.

[442] *Ibid.* 157, 173, 185, 191, Feb. 2, 1708/09, May 2, Nov. 8, 1710, Feb. 6, 1710/11. Cf. King v. Basford where a witness did not appear and nothing was done (*ibid.* 190, Feb. 6, 1710/11). In King v. Borghaert and Van Schaick, Collins moved for postponement as the witnesses could not be summoned in time (*Ms. Mins. Albany Co. Sess. 1717–23* June 4, 1721).

Even in the Supreme Court in 1733, in the case of *King* v. *Cosyne,* the failure of two witnesses to appear led the Attorney General merely to inform the court he could not proceed for "want of those evidences."[443]

The treatment of defaults and refusal to testify in criminal cases as contempts appears to us to have been another contribution of John Tabor Kempe. This must have been something of an innovation for in Kempe's brief in the case of *King* v. *Lawrence*[444] (the case involving the carting of George Spencer) is the marginal note "Attachment lyes for refusing to appear and give evidence" (citing 2 Lilly 449 and Stiles, *Practical Register* 672), suggesting that this rule, long established in England, was something of a novelty in the Province. In any event, it is worthy of remark that after 1760 there are a number of cases where the Supreme Court dealt sharply with reluctant witnesses who ignored process or who on appearance declined to give evidence.[445] There are no surviving examples of writs of attachment, but the minute entries of orders to take the persons into custody,[446] or a notice that a constable had "brought in" a defaulting witness,[447] are probably to be taken as executed by writ. Once present, the court either imposed a fine with imprisonment until paid or put the witness in contempt under recognizance.[448] Of course if the witness were already under recognizance this could be ordered forfeit.

Our account of the development of criminal process in New York has been overlong, especially as the subject is one which bristles with technicality, and which over the course of a century lacked all the elements of drama that sometimes lighten the otherwise lackluster face of procedure. But the prosaic anatomy is not without its uses, for not otherwise are the sinews of civil rights to be

---

[443] *Ms. Mins. SCJ 1732–39* 45. In 1751, a defendant having broken jail a material witness was released from his recognizance upon undertaking to appear on notice from the Attorney General, King v. McIntire (*Ms. Mins. SCJ 1750–54* [Engr.] 83).

[444] *H.R. Pleadings* Pl. K. 930.

[445] In the case of King v. Augustus Bradley, one John Crist was examined on Dec. 10, 1760, but stated that he would not give evidence in the case unless his evidence was taken immediately because he intended to leave the colony. J. T. Kempe therefore asked that a magistrate issue process to compel Crist to give his testimony (*J. T. Kempe Lawsuits* B).

[446] In 1764 the grand jury represented to the Supreme Court that John Lasher and others refused to take an oath to give evidence and the sheriff was ordered to take the recalcitrants into custody (*Ms. Mins. SCJ 1764–67* [Rough] 23). In the case of the murder of Eliz. Kaits (1767) two witnesses refused to attend the grand jury and were

ordered to be brought in to answer their contempt. They were put under recognizance (*Ms. Mins. SCJ 1766–69* [Engr.] 317, 319).

[447] On Oct. 27, 1767, Joseph Hildreth was brought into court. He had been subpoenaed but did not appear. He was fined 20s. and ordered committed until this was paid (*Ms. Mins. SCJ 1764–67* [Rough] 279). The estreats for 1767 show the fine paid for contempt in not obeying court process (*H.R. Parch.* 221 B 4).

In King v. Henry Klock a witness did not appear, and it was ordered her default be entered. In this case the witness was probably bound by recognizance and the entry of default was a warning of forfeiture (*Ms. Mins. SCJ 1766–69* [Engr.] 327).

[448] Cf. *supra* n. 446. One Martin who refused to testify was fined £10 and ordered committed until he paid (*Ms. Mins. SCJ 1762–64* [Engr.] 171). Note further the fines for contempt in refusing to testify in the trading with the enemy prosecutions, *supra* 243.

detected; and should contemporary judicial distaste for "substantive" due process become more pronounced, it will be prudent for the citizen to have at hand the record of the procedural expectations of his ancestors who made the phrase "due process" immortal in our constitutions.

CHAPTER VIII

RECOGNIZANCES

An adequate history of the system of suretyship in English as well as American law remains to be written. From the early and primitive days when men were pledged by oath to assure the keeping of the peace down to modern times, security devices have played a most important part in our law, notably in the criminal law and its administration,[1] where, in particular, the recognizance has been used for purposes preventive, compulsive, punitive and remedial.

Even in their remote beginnings suretyship devices were a feature of English local government, and they remained such through all the alterations effected both in their nature and scope, and through all the additions and changes in the machinery of local administration. This circumstance was a factor of consequence in the history of similar devices in America for, as we have seen, it was the local and the familiar legal institution which first gained footing overseas. The recognizance, as the most useful and the most exploited suretyship device in the seventeenth century, was therefore introduced into New York virtually at the moment of conquest; for it was, if not indispensable, at least peculiarly suited to the needs of a government in a province reduced by force and inhabited by persons of whose loyalty it was impossible to be sure.

In the previous chapter we noted how, during the proprietary period, the practice of taking sureties developed. The Duke's officers resorted to sureties for all manner of purposes: to bind men to be of good behavior, to compel appearance in court, to guarantee the prosecution of appeals, to enforce judgments, and as a form of final judgment.[1] The records of this period are not models of exactness, and the word "surety" is often employed in situations where probably only an informal arrangement was made, such as a mere promise to effect the appearance of a defendant. Nevertheless there is proof that at an early date the recognizance in the technical sense was being used, that is to say, an obligation in a sum certain, entered of record, conditioned upon doing some particular act.[2] This very rapidly becomes the usual method of exacting security.

---

[1] *Supra* 391 *et seq.* nn. 34, 48, 49, 65; *infra* 559.
[2] *Supra* 389 n. 18; *Ms. Mins. Ct. of Assizes 1665–72* 85, 86, 167; *Ms. Gravesend Town Recs.*

Liber 4, 32; for early forms of recognizances, 2 *Rep. NY State Historian* 255 *et seq.*

Although our sources before 1690 are not sufficiently ample to permit the reconstruction of a "law" of recognizances, or even to be certain that what was called a recognizance was always in fact an obligation of record, yet they show clearly enough how completely the recognizance had made itself at home and, in general, the paths of its future peregrinations. This, of course, runs into many directions, some of which lie quite outside the area which is here being explored. We cannot enter into discussion of the recognizance in civil procedure, nor its employment for such miscellaneous purposes as the bonding of public officers,[3] of shipping so that it would be conducted in accordance with statutory provision,[4] of alehouse keepers to keep good order and rule in their houses.[5] But since the recognizance was the instrumentality par excellence of the justice of the peace to assure the execution of his manifold duties, many of which had but a tenuous connection with his criminal jurisdiction, we cannot avoid some consideration of how the recognizance was used in the zone of half-shadow between matters civil and criminal.

No one has been sufficiently interested in the recognizance to have described how it crept into the many interstices of the justices' business. Probably from the time of its institution, the office of the justices as conservators of the peace carried with it authority to exact security. In any event the powers were made

[3] As an example of a recognizance used to insure the performance of their duties by public officers, see the following: "Be it remembered that on the fifteenth day of October . . . personally appeared be fore me . . . Adolph Brass, James Mills and Daniel Shatford and severally acknowledged themselves indebted to our sovereign lord the King in . . . [£1840] . . . [New York money] to be levied in their several Goods & Chattels Lands and Tenements to the use of our said Lord the King if failure be made in the Performance of the Condition following The Condition of this Recognizance is such that if the aforesaid Adolph Brass, James Mills or Daniel Shatford shall well and truely pay to the Treasurer of this Colony . . . [£920] . . . for which sum they . . . hath farmed the Excise on Strong Liquors Retailed in City of New York . . . then this recognizance is to be void . . . but in failure to remain in full Force and Virtue. Taken and acknowledged . . . before me Frederick Phillipse" (*Ms. Mins. SC] 1750–54* [Engr.] 3, Oct. 17, 1750). On Aug. 4, 1753, two recognizances by the managers of a lottery for founding a college (i.e., Kings College) were entered on the Supreme Court minutes. These recognizances were to insure the managers executing their trust in raising £1125 (*ibid.* 283). On Jan. 18, 1757, a recognizance was filed by two managers of the stamp office to execute the trust reposed in them, etc. (*ibid.* 336).

[4] Cf. *supra* 240.

[5] The earliest example we have seen, dated 1682, is a bond of one Lee and wife in the, as yet, uncatalogued papers in the Hall of Records (New York City). These are very rare documents as they were issued out of Sessions. Cf. also the order of Kings County Sessions for Nov. 8, 1692, that liquor retailers should have a license issued by two justices of peace and be bound in £10 by recognizances of two sureties for "their good order and rule in their house" (*Ms. Kings Co. Ct. & Rd. Recs. 1692–1825* 9). An interesting case in connection with liquor licenses is that of John Webb, 1712 (*supra* c. I n. 199). John Gardner, indicted on May 8, 1706, for entertaining negroes in his alehouse, had been treated more severely than Webb, for when he, on Aug. 6, 1706, confessed the indictment and prayed the mercy of the court, the New York Quarter Sessions made the following order: "Itt is . . . Considered that the said John Gardner be Suppressed from keeping an Alehouse Tavern or Victualling house or selling any manner of Strong Liquors by Retaile" (*ibid.* 110, 112). Samuel Shaw charged with being "a person of ill fame and a whoremonger" was ordered to desist keeping a tavern (*Ms. Mins. Dutchess Co. Sess.* Liber C, Oct. 16, 1759).

explicit in the reign of Edward III by statute[6] which authorized the justices to take sufficient surety and mainprize of "them that be not of good fame." From then on, the scope of this taking of sureties was gradually expanded. One of the most notable extensions out of the strictly criminal field was in relation to bastardy.[7] Here the recognizance served the multiple function of requiring the person charged to answer and, if found guilty, to save a parish harmless against the illegitimate child being a charge. Where exacted from the mother it was intended as a preventive of future misconduct.[8] This practice, as we have seen, was introduced in New York and the quasi-criminal quality of the jurisdiction is clear from the vigor of the process used.[9] In some instances, we find that a defendant would be discharged of his recognizance before trial on giving bond to indemnify the parish or save it harmless,[10] and in others, on a recognizance to appear the defendant was kept dangling by repeated continuances, the court thus keeping a watchful eye on him.[11] A similar practice existed in the cases of poor relief where husbands neglected

[6] 34 Edw. III c.1.

[7] 18 Eliz. c.3.

[8] On bastardy, *supra* 101 *et seq.*

[9] For example, one Sharpe was bound to appear to answer for begetting a bastard on Mehetabell Mahany, and when he appeared in Quarter Sessions on Nov. 4, 1696, he was ordered to be committed until he find sureties for his appearance at the following Sessions, whereupon he entered a recognizance in £100 with one surety to answer the charge. Sharpe appeared in court on Feb. 3, 1696/97, and a recognizance to assure support was ordered (*Ms. Mins. NYCQS 1694–1731/32* 17, 21). However, Sharpe neglected to enter the recognizance and a capias was ordered to take him into the sheriff's custody until he found sufficient sureties to perform the court's order (*ibid.* 25, May 4, 1697). Cf. also the case of Peter Morin against whom a warrant issued to compel him to give a bond (*ibid.* 270, Aug. 3, 1714).

[10] Thus, Jacobus Davis' plea to be discharged from his recognizance to answer for his supposed bastard gotten on Trintie Peterse was granted when, on Aug. 1, 1699, he gave "surety to save the city harmless" (*ibid.* 48). Also see Isaac De Costa, who had been continued on recognizance from Feb. 6 to Nov. 6, 1751, but was discharged on the latter date, "on producing a bond of having indemnified the parish against a bastard of Mary Tingle" (*Ms. Mins. NYCQS 1732–62* 289, 290, 294, 299–301, 305). Also see King v. Joseph Bary, discharged on Aug. 6, 1772, from his recognizance to appear to answer when it appeared to the court by the certificate of the churchwarden that the parish was indemnified (*Ms. Mins. NYCQS 1772–91* 16).

[11] In some of these cases, the defendant was continued on the recognizance for appearance through several terms and finally discharged. William Latham entered a recognizance for one justice of the peace on May 3, 1764, in £100 on condition that he "appear . . . at this present Sessions of the peace . . . and . . . then and there abide Such Order . . . as shall be made, for begetting a Bastard Child on the body of Anne King . . . which Child is now Chargeable . . . to the parish" (*H.R. Pleadings* Pl. K. 1000). Latham was continued on recognizance to the next Sessions on May 3, 1764, was continued on Aug. 7 and 8 and Nov. 6, but on Nov. 7, 1764, he was discharged (*Ms. Mins. NYCQS 1760–72* 106, 107, 111, 113, 114, 118, 119). Also see King v. Isaac Winn, where, on May 3 and 4, 1769, the defendant was continued on recognizance to answer for a bastard to the next Sessions and then continued through the following Sessions: Aug. 1769, Feb., May, Aug. and Nov., 1770, Feb., May and Aug., 1771, Feb., May and Aug. 1772. In November Sessions, 1772, this defendant was discharged (*ibid.* 279, 287, 295, 302, 308, 314, 323, 331, 338, 345; *Ms. Mins. NYCQS 1772–91* 2, 16, 23). One reason for such continuances is indicated in King v. Bartholomew Miller, who appeared in New York Quarter Sessions on Feb. 8, 1737/38, and was ordered to be continued on recognizance "untill Bridget Williams be delivered of her child which when born will be a bastard." In this case, Miller was discharged from his recognizance for his appearance on May 4, 1738 (*Ms. Mins. NYCQS 1732–62* 83, 86).

to support their wives,[12] and also in connection with the control over indentured servants.[13]

Surety of the Peace and Surety of Good Behavior

The role of the recognizance as a measure of preventive justice is only incidental in bastardy cases. It is in the so-called surety of peace and the surety of
good abearance that this audacious extension of the common law conception
of record as a means of forestalling crime can be appreciated. The early manuals derive the authority to bind for the peace from the first clause in the justices' commission, and the surety for good behavior from this clause plus the
statute of Edward III just cited. The two things, in the words of Lambard,
were of "great affinity," but the concept of good behavior as the courts interpreted it was much broader, and was pushed in response to the mutations of
social conscience to embrace even the incidents of what we now euphemisti-
cally describe as "night life." Indeed, an attentive reader of the case law, bound
to abear himself well, would feel safest if he remained home in bed out of
reach of temptation for "the sureties *de bono gestu* may be broke by the number of a mans company or by his or their weapons or harness."[14] As the two
types of surety were used in New York, the surety of the peace was confined
almost entirely to instances of "swearing the peace," and for preventive purposes. But the surety of good behavior, while used also for the prevention of
crime, was in most cases manipulated as form of process, as a species of parole
or even as penalty.

In New York the procedure for swearing the peace was patterned after the
English local practice, and did not run to the complicated and nearly obsolete
procedure by writ of *supplicavit* whereby the matter was engineered through
King's Bench or Chancery.[15] When a person was in fear that another would do
him some injury either to his person or property, he would appear before a
magistrate and make an affidavit embodying the facts of his complaint and
praying that the individual of whom he was in fear be bound to keep the
peace. The justice, so far as we know, more or less automatically would order
the defendant to keep the peace and would take sureties, making the matter

---

[12] E.g., the case of Thomas Willson (*supra*
108 n. 215), and of Vincent Delamontagne (*ibid.*).

[13] Thus Mary Bibby and Elizabeth Poole, indentured servants who deserted their masters, were ordered on Nov. 6, 1717, to be committed to jail until
they be bound for the term mentioned in their in-

dentures (*Ms. Mins. NYCQS 1694-1731/32* 338).
Cf. case of Anne Sewell (*supra* 109 n. 217).

[14] The distinctions are discussed in Lambard,
Eirenarcha Bk. 2 c.2; Dalton, *Countrey Justice*
(1677) cc. 70, 123.

[15] On this, Fitzherbert, *Natura Brevium* 79h.

of record. Usually the order to keep the peace would be coupled with a command to the principal to appear at Sessions to answer whatever should be objected against him and to do and receive what might be enjoined upon him. This procedure was used in almost the same way as complaints to the Attorney General for informations were used. Possibly in some instances, swearing the peace was simply a part of the procedure already described in Chapter VI, where it was pointed out that justices of the peace had the power to take depositions of complainants and examinations of defendants, and thereupon bind them over to the next Sessions where they were usually brought before the grand jury.

There are a great many cases of "swearing the peace" in the New York Sessions records, for the justices to whom complaint was made seem to have ordered a recognizance as a matter of course, trusting that at Sessions the impending trouble would be ironed out. The appearance at Sessions was necessary for the certification or return of the recognizance by the justice and for the party to report.[16] Although a peace recognizance commonly stated that the defendant was to appear to answer what might be objected against him, indictment was not necessarily contemplated. At least we have found but one instance, the case of Charles Richardson, where the peace having been sworn by Delanoy, the defendant was actually indicted and eventually discharged of the recognizance by confessing the indictment and paying a fine.[17] What usually happened was that the complainant did not appear and the defendant would then either be continued or discharged by proclamation.[18] The frequency of cases where no appearance was made by complainants raises a question whether this device was not often used for unworthy ends since it offered unique opportunity to the mean spirited to badger an adversary, and it is rare to find a discharge at the request of a complainant.[19]

[16] Dalton, *Countrey Justice* c.120.
[17] *NY Legal Mss.* Nov. 1751; *Ms. Mins. NYCQS 1732–62* 307, 311, Nov. 7, 1751, Feb. 6, 1751/52.
[18] Cf. the case of Richard Moore, discharged by proclamation when the complainant did not appear (*Ms. Mins. NYCQS 1694–1731/32* 13, May 5, 1696); Joost Van Luzie, who was bound over to keep the peace on the affidavit of Beletie Martin, appeared on paying fees (*ibid.* 285, May 3, 1715); Jacob Leisler and Francine Staats, bound over on April 22, 1715 on the complaint of Jane Jarvis (*NY Misc. Mss.* Box 4 [1711–16] no. 27), were discharged on May 3, 1715 upon paying fees (*Ms. Mins. NYCQS 1694–1731/32* 284). Cf. also the case of Reeliff Reeliffse (*ibid.* 371, May 3, 1720); Richard Talbot (*ibid.* 371, May 4, 1720); Hugh

Rainey *et ux.* (*ibid.* 408, Aug. 7, 1722); John Stockford (*ibid.* 458, Feb. 1, 1725/26); Joseph Penniman (*ibid.* 538, Aug. 3, 1731).

In some cases it is difficult to tell by the form of entry whether the case is one of the peace or not. Cf. King v. Pick (*Ms. Mins. Ulster Co. Sess. 1737–50* Nov. 6, 1739), and the discharges (*ibid.* Sept. 16, 1746 and Sept. 20, 1748).

[19] Misuse is recognized in the English statute 21 Jac. I c.8. Some of the New York complaints, such as "being a common disturber" (*Ms. Mins. Ulster Co. Sess. 1711/12–1720* Mar. 18, 1716/17) and a "quarrelsome neighbor" (*ibid.* July 8, 1718), seem to be what the English statute regarded as malicious complaint. For an example of discharge at request of a complainant, cf. the case of William

At the same time, evidence of the unruly and fractious temper of the settlers is so persistent and convincing, that one can hardly doubt the recognizance to keep the peace generally served a useful social end. Judging from some of the affidavits it was a boon to nervous women, whether, as Mary Anne Bickley, who was "in fear of her life or some bodily hurt by Charles King"[20] or, as Katherine Howard, who, bedevilled by a local fishwife, deposed and swore that Patience Ashton, Spinster,

> without any manner of provocation called the Deponent a great many abusive names, threatened the Deponent to beat her, to have her heart's blood, to do her business, called her Bitch, Whore, and an abundance of other scurilous names . . . threw mud stones and dirt against her door and challenged her [the Deponent] to come out saying she would sacrifice her body for the good of her soul . . . and that she is in fear of her life or of some bodily hurt . . . and that she doesn't require the peace of her for any malice, vexation or revenge but for the causes aforesaid and further saith not. . . .[21]

Similarly the instances of wives swearing the peace against their husbands who had beaten or abused them, occurring in an age when the dominion of the male was yet unchallenged, are solid evidence of the usefulness of this type of security.[22]

White (*Ms. Mins. NYCQS 1694-1731/32* 67, Feb. 3, 1701/02).

[20] *H.R. Pleadings* Pl. K. 970. Endorsed on the margin of this deposition is a note to the effect that Charles King had been bound in £30 with one surety in £15 to keep the peace. Cf. also Phebe Law's complaint of Sarah Hillyer, "a loose profligate woman" (*Ms. Mins. Rich. Co. Sess. 1710/11-1744/45* Mar. 4, 1717/18, Mar. 3, 1718/19).

[21] *NY Misc. Mss.* Box 5 (1718-30) no. 11. Patience appeared on Aug. 2, 1726 and was discharged next day, apparently because Katherine failed to prosecute (*Ms. Mins. NYCQS 1694-1731/32* 467, 468). Cf. Elizabeth Cronkhuyte's complaint vs. Katherine Kelly (*Ms. Mins. Albany Co. Sess. 1763-82* Oct. 8, 1773).

[22] Thus Jephthah Smith was bound on complaint of his wife and ordered discharged when no one appeared (*Ms. Mins. NYCQS 1732-62* 15, Aug. 3, 1732). Frederick Williams, on Feb. 7, 1739/40, was committed until he could find sureties when Mary his wife (who had previously had him committed) asked that the peace be continued. He was discharged May 7, 1740 (*ibid.* 111, 114, 115). Cf. also *H.R. Pleadings* Pl. K. 1045 (John Laurier, 1764); Pl. K. 461 (James McConnel, 1768) in the following language: "City & County of New York ss: Be it Remembered that on the twentieth day of August in the year of our Lord one thousand seven

hundred and sixty eight personally appeared before me Nicholas Roosevelt Alderman of the West Ward and one of his Majesty's Justices of the peace for the City & County of New York James McConnel & Robert McConnel both of the said City & Severally acknowledged themselves to be indebted unto our Sovereign Lord the King his heirs & Successors in manner following that is to say the said James McConnel in the sum of Sixty Pounds and the said Robert McConnel in the sum of thirty Pounds of good and lawfull money of New York to be raised and levied on their severall goods & Chattles Lands & Tenements to the use of our said Sovereign Lord the King his heirs & Successors in case default shall be made in the performance of the Condition following. The Condition of this Recognizance is such that if the above Bounden James McConnel shall and do personally appear at the next Court of General Quarter Sessions of the peace to be held for the City & County of New York on the first Tuesday in November next (being the first day of the same month) at the City Hall of the said City to answer unto such matters as shall be objected against him by Jane McConnell—of the said City, and to do and receive what shall be then & there enjoined him by the Court, and in the mean time to keep the peace of our Sovereign Lord the King, as well towards his said Majesty as all his liege People and more especially towards the said

Although, as we have remarked, there is some reason to suspect that the peace was often sworn out of malice, direct evidence is very slight. There is one pitiful petition from Thomas English to J. T. Kempe alleging the peace had been sworn against him by Judath Houper and he had been obliged to appear because of words with his wife. No one had appeared against him "although he has had to pledge the cloaths off his back this cold wether for to pay the charges."[23] Kempe does not seem to have done anything for English and there was not much relief available as the courts were reluctant to try the facts on affidavits;[24] indeed, until well into the eighteenth century the English courts admitted that they could not do otherwise than take the complainant's articles to be true.[25] In New York, however, there is one case where an extortion was involved and the parties were consequently indicted.

One Ambrose Bill appeared before Benjamin Blagge, an alderman and justice of the peace of New York City, and swore that he was in fear of his life of James Laman Smith, and averred, as was customary, that he sought the peace against Smith not out of malice or revenge but for his own safety; whereas "in truth and fact" (in the words of his indictment) Bill was not afraid of his life but swore the peace out of malice and revenge and not for his own safety.[26] Burger and Scandlin, constables, were also indicted for conspiring to have Smith arrested "by color of a certain warrant . . . called a peace warrant which they . . . pretended they had to apprehend and take . . . James Laman Smith." Smith was detained in prison for three hours and was only released after paying the conspirators six pounds eleven shillings to release him.[27] The prosecution, however, does not appear to have been carried through and we do not know what was done with the defendants.

Numerous recognizances to keep the peace have been preserved, and a typical example is quoted below.[28] The instruments vary but little in general

Jane McConnell then this Recognizance to be void otherwise to remain in full force & virtue.— Taken and acknowledged the day & year above written Before me Nich Roosevelt." This recognizance was endorsed "discharged." Cf. also the warrant for the arrest of a husband against whom the peace was sworn (*Ms. Files Ulster Co.* Bundle G, Sept. 27, 1722).

[23] *J. T. Kempe Lawsuits* C–F sub nom. English. Cf. also the letter of Michael Jacob (1773) regarding the false swearing of the peace by Jacob Moses (*J. T. Kempe Letters* A–Z).

[24] King v. King (2 *Ves.* 578).
[25] Lord Vane's Case (2 *Strange* 1202).
[26] *H.R. Pleadings* Pl. K. 11, K. 340.
[27] The "memorandum of oath before Alderman

Blagge" is contained in *J. T. Kempe Lawsuits* B sub nom. Bill, Dec. 31, 1774.

[28] "Dutchess County ss: Be it Remembered that on the Ninth day December in the fourteenth year of the Reign of our Sovereign Lord george the third by the grace of god of great Britain France and Ireland King defender of the faith &c. Daniel Hultz of Amenia Precinct in the said County yeoman came before me Roswell Hopkins Esqr. one of his Majestys Justices of the peace for the said County and Acknowledged himself to be indebted unto our said Sovereign Lord the King in twenty Pounds Current Lawful money of the Province of New york to be Levied on his goods and Chattels Lands and Tenements to the use of our said Sovereign Lord the King His Heirs and Successors in Case

form, and are usually conditioned upon appearance in Sessions, and meantime keeping the peace toward the King, his people and especially toward the complainant. Sometimes a special injunction was added not to do bodily hurt to the complainant or procure it to be done. A more stringent form was that which combined the undertaking to keep the peace with one to be of good behavior. As we have already remarked, an obligation to be of good behavior was more easily broken than one to keep the peace, infraction of which required some violent act, and there was no reason to combine the two except the lawyers' irresistible urge to cumulate. The colonial authorities understood that a distinction existed between the two types of surety, for Attorney General J. T. Kempe, writing to Alderman Mesier, remarks, "I reced the enclosed [affidavits] . . . but I want to know whether they were bound to keep the peace, or to their good Behaviour which includes that and something more, If the Recognizances are drawn up in Form be pleased to let me see them or a copy . . . if they are not yet drawn up in form be pleased to certify whether the Conditions of the Recognizances, are to keep the peace or to be of the good Behaviour."[29]

The recognizances binding both to peace and good behavior[30] do not any of them contain an injunction to observe the peace against a particular individual and are for this reason not to be regarded as exacted when some one swore out the peace. They fall rather into the class of recognizances of good behavior

Default shall be made in the Condition following.—
THE CONDITION of this Recognizance is such that if the above bounden Daniel Hultz shall personally appear at the next general Sessions of the Peace to be holden in and for the County of Dutchess to answer what shall be then and there Objected against him by Silas Hamblin on his Majestys behalf and shall in the meantime keep the peace towards the said Silas Hamblin and all other his Majestys liege People then this Recognizance to be Void or else to Remain in full force. Taken and acknowledged Before me Roswell Hopkins" (*H.R. Pleadings* Pl. K. 487). Cf. also *H.R. Pleadings* Pl. K. 486, a recognizance of Frederick Maybe (1775); *H.R. Pleadings* Pl. K. 311, a recognizance of Andrew Marley (1749); *H.R. Pleadings* Pl. K. 280, a recognizance of William Blake (1743).
[29] *J. T. Kempe Lawsuits* S–V *sub nom.* John Surnan.
[30] "City of New York ss: Be It Remembered that on this Twenty Seventh day of March in the Year of our Lord One Thousand Seven hundred and Seventy two personally appeared before me Daniel Horsmanden Esqr. Chief Justice of the Province of New York Jacques Rapalje and Garret Rapalje both of the City of New York and Acknowledged themselves to be Indebted unto our Sovereign Lord the King in manner following (that is to say) the aforesaid Jacques Rapalje in the sum of One hundred Pounds and the Said Garret Rapalje in the sum of Fifty Pounds to be Levied on their respective Goods and Chattels Lands and Tenements to the use of our said Lord the King his Heirs and Successors if default shall be made in the Condition following:—
The condition of the above Recognizances is such that if the above bounden Jacques Rapalje shall personally appear at the next Supreme Court of Judicature which is to be held at the City Hall in the City of New York on the third Tuesday in April next to Answer to what may be then and there Objected against him and abide such orders as the said Court shall make Concerning him and in the mean time keep the Peace and be of good behavior towards all his Majesty's liege Subjects then the above Recognizance to be void and of no effect otherwise to be and remain in full force and Virtue. Taken and Acknowledged the Day and Year abovesaid Before me Dan Horsmanden" (*H.R. Pleadings* Pl. K. 493; cf. also Pl. K. 488, Pl. K. 490, Pl. K. 492).

which were taken to assure the presence of defendants at Sessions and to prevent any misconduct before discharge.[31] Sometimes the bonds of this type would name the complainant, and include in the obligation answering the

[31] The following are sample cases where defendants were bound over to the good behavior: "Philip French Mercht. being bound to his good behaviour & for his personall appearance att this Court to doe & Receive as by this Court Should be Enjoyned him, personally Appeared and Nothing Appearing to the Court why he should Stand longer bound he was discharged from his recognizance" (*Ms. Mins. NYCQS 1694–1731/32* 5, Feb. 5, 1694/95).

On May 1, 1701, John Richardson with three sureties entered a recognizance in £20 each for Richardson to be of the good behavior. Richardson, Russel, Dale and Fuller, mariners, "jointly and severally enter into a recognizance in . . . £20 . . . to be levied &c [*sic*] if failure be made of the condition following, that is to say that if . . . John Richardson shall be of the good behavior towards his Majesty and all his liege people for a year and a day ensuing then this recognizance to be voide or else to remain in full force and virtue" (*NY Misc. Mss.* Box 3 no. 2).

Hendrick Metslaer, who was "bound to his behavior," appeared and no one appearing to prosecute him, he was discharged on Aug. 5, 1701 (*Ms. Mins. NYCQS 1694–1731/32* 66). Daniell Curtis, "bound to his behavior," was discharged when no one appeared to prosecute him on Nov. 4, 1702 (*ibid.* 72). On May 1, 1711, Samuel Kip appeared in his "proper person" and prayed discharge from his recognizance for the good behavior which was so ordered on the payment of fees (*ibid.* 199). Francis Cowenhoven, in Nov. 1712, entered a recognizance to be of his good behavior to the Queen and all her liege people and especially to his wife, and to appear at the next Quarter Sessions to do and receive all that should be enjoined upon him. Cowenhoven's recognizance was in £20 with two sureties in £10 each (*NY Misc. Mss.* Box 4 no. 6). Tryntie Cowenhoven, his wife, on Aug. 21, 1712, entered a recognizance to be of the good behavior toward the Queen and all her liege people, but more especially toward her husband, and to appear at the next Quarter Sessions to do and receive all that should be there enjoined upon her. Tryntie's recognizance consisted in two sureties bound in £20 each (*ibid.* Box 4 no. 14). These defendants both appeared in November Sessions, 1712 and were discharged (*Ms. Mins. NYCQS 1694–1731/32* 250, 251, Nov. 4, 1712). Thomas Arison, bound to his good behavior and appearance, appeared in Quarter Sessions on Feb. 2, 1713/14, and the court "ordered he and his bail continued" to the next Sessions. On May 4, 1714, Arison appeared and was ordered to be discharged from his recognizance of good behavior on the payment of his fees (*ibid.* 265, 267). Elizabeth Fairday appeared on recognizance for good behavior on May 8, 1717, and was discharged (*ibid.* 332).

"Thomas Brain . . . Chirurgeon Recognizes to our Lord the King in One hundred pounds . . . & Francis Harrison . . . and Lancaster Symmes . . . in . . . fifty pounds . . . upon Condition That . . . Thomas Brain do Personally appear at the Next General Quarter Sessions . . . to do and Receive all . . . and that in the meantime he be of the good behavior." On Aug. 7, 1717, Brain appeared in Quarter Sessions on this recognizance and was discharged on the payment of his fees (*ibid.* 334, 336). Elizabeth Grant, bound to her good behavior and appearance, was discharged on her appearance in Quarter Sessions on Aug. 4, 1719 (*ibid.* 361, 363). Susannah Smith, bound to her good behavior, was discharged on Aug. 5, 1719 (*ibid.* 363). John Walker, bound to good behavior, was also discharged on Aug. 5, 1719 (*ibid.* 361, 363). Likewise, Lucas Pieterse, bound to good behavior, was discharged on May 3, 1720 (*ibid.* 371). On Mar. 11, 1720/21, William Watson posted a recognizance in £20 for the appearance and good behavior of Ruth Tuck to the King and all his liege people, but we have seen no minute entries on this case (*NY Misc. Mss.* Box 5 no. 22). Mary Hare was discharged from recognizance for her good behavior on Aug. 2, 1721 (*Ms. Mins. NYCQS 1694–1731/32* 392). John Horne was discharged for good behavior on Feb. 7, 1721/22 (*ibid.* 398). Likewise John Gara was discharged from recognizance for good behavior on Aug. 5, 1725 (*ibid.* 452, 453). Winifred Mahany was bound in her good behavior by two sureties in £20 each, on Aug. 17, 1727 (*H.R. Pleadings* Pl. K. 1092).

Anthony Thorndale entered a recognizance in £30 before the recorder with one surety in £15 for his good behavior and appearance at the next Quarter Sessions, and when he appeared on Nov. 7, 1752, he was discharged (*Ms. Mins. NYCQS 1732–62* 324; *H.R. Pleadings* Pl. K. 890). Benjamin Halstead entered a recognizance for his good behavior in £200 with two sureties in £100 each "to answer such misdemeanors" as should be objected against him in Quarter Sessions (*H.R. Pleadings* Pl. K. 759). Halstead appeared in Quarter Sessions on Feb. 2, 1762, was continued to the third and fourth and then to the next Sessions. When he appeared on May 4, 1762, he was discharged (*Ms. Mins. NYCQS 1732–62* 517, 518, 521, 523). See *H.R. Pleadings* Pl. K. 858 for a recognizance for good behavior filed in May Sessions, 1775.

In all of the recognizances for good behavior above referred to, there were no other entries on these cases to indicate why the recognizance for good behavior was granted or to indicate that any indictment, presentment or other proceedings were had against these defendants.

latter at Sessions, and meantime not to do him harm; but these are stock precautionary phrases and from the absence of words of peace seem to indicate that no swearing of the peace had been done when the security was exacted.[32] The colonial justices preferred this surety of good behavior because it was a better safeguard, but we have seen cases where a mere obligation to observe the peace was ordered. So, in April, 1721, one Daniel Ebbetts filed an affidavit regarding two speeders in a sleigh. Since racing in the streets was a colonial pastime severely frowned on by the justices, Jenkins and Hendricks were accordingly bound over to the peace and were not discharged until nearly a year later, a prosecutor having failed to materialize.[33] There are some other recognizances of the peace of this type[34] but they are relatively few in number compared with those conditioned on good behavior and with those only requiring appearance.

We have already adverted to the fact that an order for a recognizance was a common incident to the preliminary proceedings before single justices, but it is virtually impossible to give any numerical estimate regarding the use of this device, as the country minute books in this detail were carelessly kept. It is equally impossible to ascertain any reasons of policy behind the choice of conditions of the security—peace, good behavior or mere appearance at Sessions. The subsequent proceedings offer few clues, for the party would appear and

---

[32] E.g., the following recognizance of John Jackson for good behavior, filed in February Sessions, 1748: "CITY OF NEW YORK ss: BE it Remembered that on the Fourth Day of January in the Seventeenth year of his Majesties reign Anno Domini 1748 Personally appeared before me John Marshall Alderman of Montgomery Ward of the Sd. City and one of his Majesties Justices of the Peace for the City & County of New York John Brandykin of the Sd City Vintner and Acknowledged himselfe to be Indebted unto our Lord the King his heirs & Successors in the Sum of Twenty Pounds Current Money of this Coloney of New York to be Raised on his Goods & Chatels Lands & Tenaments for the Use of our sd. Lord the King his heirs & Successors if Failure be made of the Condition following. THE CONDITION of this Recognizance is Such that if John Jackson of the Sd. City Marriner Shall Personally Appear at the next Generale Quarter Sessions of the Peace to be holden for the City & County aforesaid to Answer unto Such Matters as Shall be objected against him by Josiah Flemon of Sd City Cooper and to do and Receive what Shall then and there be Enjoynd him by the Court and in the meantime to be of Good Behaviour to his Majesty as All his Liege People Especially towards the Said Josiah Flemon and shall not do or procure to be Done any

hurt to him That then this Recognizance to be void & of none Effect or else to be and Remain in full force and Virtue. Taken and Acknowledged the Day and Year above Written before me. JOHN MARSHALL" (H.R. Pleadings Pl. K. 279).

[33] James Alexander Papers Box 46; Ms. Mins. NYCQS 1694-1731/32 398.

[34] Cf. also the following cases for sureties for the peace: Samuel Atchison, in £50 with one surety in the same (H.R. Pleadings Pl. K. 434); Richard Cornish, two sureties in £20 each, July, 1763 (ibid. Pl. K. 1011); Baltus Walshoven, £30 with two sureties in £15 each, Aug. 7, 1764 (ibid. Pl. K. 1038); David Roider, recognizance in £30, Aug. 7, 1764 (ibid. Pl. K. 1039); Placer Moore, £40 and one surety in £20 (ibid. Pl. K. 1039), discharged in Quarter Sessions on Aug. 8, 1764 (Ms. Mins. NYCQS 1760-72 112, 114); Elizabeth Cornish in £25 with one surety in £25, Aug. 7, 1764 (H.R. Pleadings Pl. K. 1044); John De Witt, £40 with one surety in £20, Aug. 4, 1767 (ibid. Pl. K. 1036), appeared and discharged in August Sessions, 1767 (Ms. Mins. NYCQS 1760-72 211); Peter Ennis, two sureties in £20, Aug. 5, 1767 (H.R. Pleadings Pl. K. 1012), appeared and discharged in August Sessions, 1767 (Ms. Mins. NYCQS 1760-72 211).

often be continued from day to day or from Sessions to Sessions until discharged, without any presentment, indictment or information being filed or other proceedings had. In the New York Quarter Sessions alone we have noted between 1691 and 1776 upward of sixteen hundred cases of appearance and discharge on recognizance without other proceedings. Only from the distribution of the cases is it possible to winnow some grain. Between the years 1691 and 1740 some 345 defendants, bound merely to appear, were so discharged, whereas 1133 such cases occur between 1750 and 1776. We have no doubt that the unquiet times before the Revolution were responsible for this extraordinary upswing as it was often impossible to secure indictments.

We would be cast less upon inference in dealing with these figures if there were available any means of establishing how substantial the reasons for requiring security may have been in particular cases which evaporate without prosecution. In the early decades of the eighteenth century the records are sometimes articulate, as in the case of the Ulster minutes for the years 1711/12 to 1720 where the reason for recognizance is entered, whereas the minutes of the same county for 1738–50 note merely the delivery of recognizances by a justice. Occasionally the clerk in New York City discloses something, as witness the case of Ann Butler. She was confined in 1729 for lack of security, discharged on May 7, but on November 5, 1729, the Sessions find her to be a woman of "ill name and fame and of very lewd life and conversation and an idle wandering person" who "keeps company and hath conversation with slaves" and is suspected of having seduced a slave to run away from his master after robbing him. It was hence ordered that she be committed to jail until she give surety for her appearance to answer what might be objected against her and in the meantime to be of her good behavior. On May 6, 1730, this woman was in court again and had evidently in the interim been ordered to be transported out of the province as a vagrant but had returned. The court, however, did not inflict the corporal punishment provided by the statute, but ordered Ann "transport herself out" of the Province again.[35]

Ann Butler was of the genus for whom the process of good abearance had originally been designed, and her inability to provide security was typically the unhappy situation of the ill famed. There is no evidence that facilities existed for persons with a criminal record to secure bail, but admitting even that such a one might occasionally be able to furnish a recognizance, it is apparent that the device was being used beyond its original purpose for the

[35] *Ms. Mins. NYCQS 1694–1731/32* 510, 517, 524.

number of cases where bond was entered into is out of all relation to the number of professional malefactors and their entourage. Therefore we see the quickened use of suretyship after 1750 as an effort to deal with disorders political in character and to bolster the sorry police establishment of the times.

The constant ordering of security when no further proceedings were taken does not appear to have been resented as an oppression, but the business of appearing and being continued on recognizance must have been a nuisance, especially provoking when the continuance was from day to day. In the margin we refer to some examples[36] which illustrate how this method of proceeding

[36] David Walker appeared on recognizance in Quarter Sessions on Feb. 5, 1750/51, was continued to the 6th and 7th, and then to the following Sessions. On May 7, 1751, he was ordered to be discharged but the rule was set aside and he was continued to the next Sessions. He appeared on Aug. 6, was continued on the 7th and 8th and then to the following Sessions. On Nov. 6, he was again continued to the following Sessions. On Feb. 4, 1751/52 he was continued to the following day when he was finally discharged (*Ms. Mins. NYCQS 1732–62* 288–290, 294, 299–301, 305, 308, 310). John Dilling appeared on recognizance on Aug. 8, 1764, and was discharged from his recognizance, but he appeared again on a recognizance on Nov. 6, 1764, was continued on the 7th and 8th and then to the following Sessions. He appeared on Feb. 5, 1765, was continued to the 6th and then to the following Sessions. He was continued through May 7, 8 and 9, Aug. 6, Nov. 6 and 7, 1765, Feb. 4, 5, May 6, 7 and Aug. 5, 1766. He was finally discharged on Aug. 6, 1766. In this case we have been unable to find any proceedings whatsoever against Dilling, either of indictment, presentment or even a complaint for the peace or good behavior (*Ms. Mins. NYCQS 1760–72* 113, 114, 118, 119, 121, 123, 125, 126, 128, 131, 132, 134, 137, 144, 147, 161, 163, 167, 169, 173, 176).

A similar practice was followed when indictments had been found against defendants, but here with better reason as there was sometimes difficulty in rounding up the witnesses. One curious case of this sort of continuance was that of John Stout who appeared on recognizance on Aug. 3, 1763, was indicted for petit larceny on Aug. 4, continued on recognizance on Nov. 1, 2 and 3, 1763, and finally discharged on the latter date. In the minute entries opposite the entry of Stout's discharge, there is the clerk's endorsement "Pd." which suggests some sort of composition, but we have been unable to find any other proceedings in this case (*Ms. Mins. NYCQS 1760–72* 82, 84, 88, 90, 92). Cornelius Lawler was continued on recognizance May 4, 5, Aug. 2, 3, 4, Nov. 1, 2, 3, 1763 and Feb. 7, 1764. On Feb. 8, an indictment for assault and battery was filed against Lawler and he was continued on recognizance to the next Sessions. On

May 1, he appeared on recognizance and was continued to the following day, and on May 2, 1764, the following entry appears: "Further appearance dispensed with." However, on the very next page of the minute book, also on May 2, we note the following entry: "Continued to the next session." Lawler appeared on Aug. 7, 1764, and was continued to the following Sessions. He was also continued through Nov. 6, 7, 8, 1764, Feb. 5 and 6, 1765, and on May 7, 1765, he was continued to the following Sessions but no further entries appear on the case (*Ms. Mins. NYCQS 1760–72* 75, 78, 81, 82, 88, 90, 92, 96, 103, 105, 106, 111, 118, 119, 121, 125–127, 131). See *H.R. Pleadings* Pl. K. 785 for the indictment for assault and battery against Lawler, filed Feb. 9, 1764.

Robert Midwinter was indicted on Aug. 8, 1765, for assault and battery and was continued on recognizance until the next Sessions. He was continued through Nov. 6, 1765, Feb. 5 and May 6, 1766. On May 7, 1766, he was discharged from his recognizance and no other proceedings appear against him (*Ms. Mins. NYCQS 1760–72* 140, 141, 144, 164, 167, 169). Also see Benjamin Ogden, indicted for assault and battery, and continued through May and August Sessions, 1765, and finally discharged on Aug. 6, 1765 (*ibid.* 133–135, 137; *H.R. Pleadings* Pl. K. 776). John West was indicted on Nov. 8, 1750 for a cheat and deceit in gauging a cask and on Nov. 9, process was ordered to issue against him. However, on Feb. 6, 1750/51, he was continued on recognizance to the following Sessions. He was also continued through May 7 and 8, and Aug. 6 and 7, 1751, and finally discharged on Aug. 8, 1751, with no further proceedings against him (*Ms. Mins. NYCQS 1732–62* 283, 284, 289, 294, 296, 299–301). John Willson appeared and was continued on recognizance on Feb. 3, 4, May 5, Aug. 4, 5, Nov. 3, 4, 1761 and Feb. 2, 1762. On Feb. 3, 1762, he was indicted for stealing. He was continued on recognizance May 4, 5, 6, Aug. 3, 4 and Nov. 2, 3 and 4, 1762. On the latter date he was ordered to be continued to the next Sessions, but no further proceedings appear against him (*ibid.* 495, 499, 505, 506, 508, 511, 512, 517–520, 523, 524, 526, 529, 530; *Ms. Mins. NYCQS 1760–72* 61, 62, 64).

operated. The examples cited are all taken from the Quarter Sessions in New York, but it is important to notice that the lavish use of the recognizance and the endless continuances is a phenomenon not peculiar to this city but was equally prevalent in the country. In certain localities the minute books are very striking. Thus the Suffolk General Sessions after 1740 apparently functions chiefly as a clearing house for recognizance business, and beginning in the 'sixties, the amount of this business in Dutchess, Orange and Albany constantly increases in bulk; indeed, in the last two counties it becomes the main occupation of General Sessions and leads one to think that an almost concerted effort at crime prevention was under way in many parts of the province.

The absence of any outcry against this expansion of preventive justice may be explained in part by the fact that the recognizance figured so largely in all sorts of contemporary occasions, civil as well as criminal, that the justices' experiments were not too obtrusive. Moreover, assuming a real ground of complaint existed against an individual, the alternative to security was commitment, which, in view of the then state of the jails, was a horror to be avoided. In the case of affrays and riots, since the colonists before the Revolution made great to-do about the illegality of commitment for what they perversely described as "peaceable assembly," the exaction of security could not have been resisted, for this would have involved questioning another sacred common law right—the right to bail—and in consequence the increase of recognizances was suffered in silence. This is a point which needs some further examination, for the uncertainties of the colonial courts respecting what offenses were bailable and what were not, had their effect upon the policies regarding recognizances generally.

The Power to Bail

The English law of bail in the eighteenth century was governed by three major considerations, the jurisdiction and powers of the judicial officer before whom a case came, the nature and quality of the offense and the reputation of the party. As set forth in the books, the welter of particular rules defied systematic treatment, and the constant concession of judicial discretion was a guarantee that nearly any possible generalization would always be studded with exceptions.[37]

The reaction of the colonial lawyers to the intricacies of the English law of

[37] The rules are best set forth in 2 Hawkins, *Pleas of the Crown* c.15, and Bacon, *Abridgment,* "Bail in Criminal Causes." Blackstone's account, built upon Hawkins, is oversimplified and at points misleading.

bail is not to their credit as inventors. Instead of adopting as a point of departure the admittedly unlimited discretion of King's Bench to bail even for treason or murder, the cases show that the debated powers of inferior judges served as a model for provincial policy, with a result that a confusion no less confused than that which prevailed in England characterizes the New York practice. It is possible, of course, that our conclusions may not be wholly fair as they are necessarily based upon the recorded orders of the court. Only exceptionally is there available any evidence to indicate how these orders were arrived at. Nevertheless, the exercise of discretion seems nearly always to be in terms of what a justice of the peace might do rather than a judge of King's Bench.

The cases in the treason group are not enough in number to support any generalization. Bayard and Hutchins, however, were not let to bail;[38] nor was James Batterson,[39] indicted for misprision of treason; nor John Windower presented for "words coming under the crime of high misdemeanor."[40] And much later, when William Prendergast was indicted for treason in connection with the Dutchess riots of 1765, the defendant was kept in custody. An army had been used to suppress these riots and no chances were taken.[41]

If these cases may be taken as showing a disposition to cleave to the ancient view that in treason a defendant was irreplevisable, the cases relating to the false coining (which in England was treated as a species of treason) were entirely without rule. In the early eighteenth century, Garret Onclebagg, the silversmith whose work is now the delight of collectors, was indicted for coining and uttering false money.[42] He was admitted to bail and eventually confessed the indictment. As he was only fined 20s. and ordered to give a recognizance to be of good behavior for a year, the offense, as we have already noticed, was then regarded in New York as no more than a misdemeanor.[43] In 1735, Catherine Johnson, a "prisoner" arraigned on an indictment for uttering false bills, was kept in custody,[44] whereas in 1769, Peter Lynch, who pleaded not guilty to an indictment for altering a New Jersey bill of credit, was at first

[38] Ms. Mins. SCJ 1701–04 41.
[39] Ms. Mins. NYCQS 1694–1731/32 297, Aug. 2, 1715.
[40] Ms. Mins. SCJ 1693–1701 64, Oct. 5, 1694. But in the case of Peter Clock [Chocke], 1695, a recognizance was allowed (ibid. 68, 73). In 1745, Patrick Ker, indicted for treasonable words, ordered kept in custody until the next gaol delivery (Ms. Mins. Ulster Co. Sess. 1737–50 May 7, 1745).
[41] Supra 87.
[42] Ms. Mins. NYCQS 1694–1731/32 70, 71, 77, Nov. 3, 4, 1702, Feb. 2, 1702/03.
[43] Supra 95 and note the 1745 statute (3 Col. Laws NY 511) making it a felony to counterfeit French, Spanish or Portuguese coin.
[44] Ms. Mins. SCJ 1732–39 158, 172. Compare King v. Boyce—passing counterfeit, bound to Supreme Court (Ms. Mins. Dutchess Co. Sess. Liber B, May 15, 1753).

committed, and later when the Attorney General admitted the evidence was insufficient to convict was allowed bail and subsequently acquitted.[45]

In the case of murder, the rule of commitment pending indictment, trial and sentence was general and obtained throughout the eighteenth century.[46] The reason for this seems to have been the fact that by the Statute of Westminster I c.15, persons taken for the death of a man, irrespective of the circumstances, were irreplevisable, and the text writers had indicated that even the superior courts, though not restrained by the statute, were always cautious of bailing persons for any homicide.[47] In the case of negroes, the colonists were inflexible in the commitments for murder[48] and carried the rule to include even persons who were accessories by merely being present at performance of the crime.[49] We have noticed a few exceptions in the case of white persons, but only a few. In 1698, John Fisher was indicted for murder, was admitted to bail, and was subsequently acquitted of murder but found guilty of homicide by misadventure.[50] The verdict indicates the reason for bailing,[51] but the mere circumstance of misadventure did not necessarily avail, for the Ulster justices, some years later, refused to release from custody an eleven-year-old boy who had killed another by accident.[52] There are some late cases which are none of them explicable as the facts available are meager. In 1768, Isaac Brazier had

[45] Ms. Mins. SCJ 1769–72 (Engr.) 104, 120, 143. Augustus Bradley, indicted on Apr. 30, 1761, for forging a bill of exchange, was bound in a £500 recognizance for his appearance to answer and in the meantime to be of good behavior (Ms. Mins. SCJ 1756–61 [Rough] 239). It is possible that in many of the counterfeiting cases the charge was one really sounding in deceit rather than a "high" offense. Thus Bernardus Bratt, John David and Michael Smith were on Apr. 22, 1766, indicted for a "deceit" in causing a Jersey bill of credit to be passed and also indicted for passing a Jersey bill of credit. When Michael Smith pleaded not guilty on Apr. 23, he was bound in a recognizance of £100 with one surety in £50 to appear. On Apr. 25 Smith was discharged from his recognizance and entered another recognizance to appear in the following term and in the meantime to be of good behavior. On Aug. 1, 1766, Smith was discharged because there was no prosecution (Ms. Mins. SCJ 1764–67 [Rough] 142–144, 154).

[46] Cf. King v. Lambris (Mins. SCJ 1693–1701 188, 189, 192). Queen v. Peter Mullinder (Ms. Mins. SCJ 1710–14 436, Mar. 12, 1712/13). It is to be noted that in this case, Mullinder on Mar. 13 was found guilty of manslaughter and on Mar. 14 pleaded his clergy which was granted (ibid. 437, 439).

Francis Shearman appeared on Oct. 12, 1704, and

pleaded "non cul." to an indictment for murder, and was thereupon committed to the custody of the sheriff. In this case likewise, the defendant was on Oct. 13 found guilty of manslaughter (Ms. Mins. SCJ 1701–04 166, 169).

James Wilks was indicted for murder on Oct. 27, 1755, and on Jan. 20, 1756, it is indicated that the "prisoner" pleaded not guilty. This prisoner was found guilty on Jan. 23 and sentenced to be hanged on Jan. 24 (Ms. Mins. SCJ 1754–57 [Engr.] 200, 218, 221–225). Godfrey Swan, indicted for murder, was also held a prisoner (Ms. Mins. SCJ 1764–67 [Rough] 82, 87, July 31, Aug. 1, 3, 1765).

[47] 2 Hawkins, Pleas of the Crown c.15 §33; Coke, Second Institute 186; 2 Hale, Pleas of the Crown 129, avers that King's Bench might bail.

[48] Cf., for example, Queen v. Peter the Doctor (Ms. Mins. NYCQS 1694–1731/32 248, Aug. 6, 1712); and cf. the account in Horsmanden, The NY Conspiracy passim.

[49] King v. Mary, a negress (Ms. Mins. NYCQS 1694–1731/32 21, Feb. 3, 1696/97).

[50] Mins. SCJ 1693–1701 132, 134, 137.

[51] Although the Statute of Gloucester expressly forbade it in such cases.

[52] Ms. Mins. Ulster Co. Sess. 1711/12–1720. But see King v. Aerie Roosa, an infant, bailed for £200 (Ms. Mins. Dutchess Co. Sess. Liber A, Oct. 17, 1727).

been allowed to post a bond in £500 with two sureties in £250 to appear, and a week later pleaded not guilty to an indictment for assault and battery and to a coroner's inquest for manslaughter. He was continued on recognizance until trial.[53] The English rule was that a man was not bailable if the offender was indicted for manslaughter, and here it is possible that the court elected to treat a coroner's inquest as not the equivalent of an indictment for purposes of bail. In the following year, John Goodwin, indicted for "attempting to murder," was a prisoner on execution in the custody of the high sheriff. The court ordered the execution discharged and exacted a recognizance with two sureties in £200 and two in £100 for appearance. On the other hand, Nathaniel Cooley, who was indicted in 1771 for wilfully burning the jail floor and for attempted murder, was committed pending trial.[54]

The provincial courts pursued a policy of great strictness with respect to grand larceny.[55] Indeed, in the records examined we have seen only one case where a defendant under indictment for this offense was admitted to bail. One John Bentley, indicted in New York Quarter Sessions in 1770, appeared on recognizance, was continued and finally, on motion of the clerk of the peace, committed before trial which eventually was had in the Supreme Court.[56] There is no hint as to why this person was bailed in the first place contrary to the usual practice, but the fact that he later appeared on recognizance in the Supreme Court indicates some irregularity from the very beginning.

Except for the three types of offense just mentioned, no further rules regarding the irreplevisable character of crimes seem to have existed, and the

---

[53] *Ms. Mins. SCJ 1766–69* (Engr.) 544, 555, 557, 574, 601, 607, 608; *Ms. Mins. SCJ 1769–72* (Engr.) 16.

[54] King v. Goodwin (*ibid.* 242, 244). It is to be noted that on Oct. 23, 1770, Goodwin was found guilty of an assault but not of an intention to murder and he was committed until sentence be given. On Oct. 26, he was fined £10 and committed until he should pay his fine and fees (*ibid.* 281, 288). Of interest in connection with the execution for which Goodwin was in custody of the high sheriff, is the indictment for attempted murder which was filed against him. This indictment recited that "a precept called capias ad satisfaciendum had issued out" against Fisher, commanding the sheriff to take Fisher to satisfy a plaintiff in a debt of £223 13s. 2d. Fisher, however, "with force and arms" discharged a pistol at the deputy sheriff and "feloniously and with malice aforethought" attempted to kill the deputy sheriff and also committed further assaults and batteries against him (*H.R. Pleadings* Pl. K. 559).

King v. Cooley (*Ms. Mins. NYCQS 1772–91* 80, 91, Feb. 5, May 4, 1774).

[55] The policy with respect to burglary and felonious breaking and entering was identical. Cf. King v. Mingo—entering and stealing (*Ms. Mins. NYCQS 1694–1731/32* 3, Nov. 6, 1694); King v. Morgan—entering and stealing, 1725/26 (*Ms. Mins. SCJ 1723–27* 181, 183); King v. William Prosser *et al.*—entering and stealing (*Ms. Mins. NYCQS 1732–62* 4, May 4, 1732); King v. Edward Lee—burglary, 1752 (*Ms. Mins. SCJ 1750–54* [Engr.] 160, 161).

For examples of commitments where grand larceny was charged, King v. Thomas Turner (*Ms. Mins. Ulster Co. Sess. 1737–50* May 7, 1745); King v. Mary Jeffers (*Ms. Mins. SCJ 1764–66* [Engr.] 85, 125; *Ms. Mins. SCJ 1761–67* [Rough] 59); King v. Ruyter (*Ms. Mins. SCJ 1769–72* [Engr.] 16).

[56] *Ms. Mins. NYCQS 1760–72* 303, 304, Feb. 9, 1770.

traditional distinction between felonies and misdemeanors was of no importance in this particular.[57] Thus where an indictment charged the felonious commission of a petit larceny,[58] defendant was bailed and there are even instances where in rape[59] and assault with intent to ravish,[60] sureties were ordered. In virtually all crimes of a "minor" nature it was usual to grant bail, even where petit larceny[61]—that bane of the colonists—was charged, and the notion of minor crime generously embraced matters as serious as attempted buggery,[62] receiving,[63] perjury,[64] riot[65] and criminal libel.[66]

To be sure, defendants in petit larceny cases were frequently committed,[67] but this seems to have been due either to their incapacity to furnish a recognizance or to the fact that they were persons of ill fame. There is occasionally an entry which makes this fact clear,[68] and now and then one finds upon the calendar a repeater; but on the whole the role which reputation played in determining judicial discretion is incalculable. Equally difficult to assess are factors such as the elements of aggravation in a particular case where a prisoner was indicted for a crime for which bail would normally be allowed,[69] or such as the temporary prejudice against a certain crime. We have noticed what we believe to be an instance of this last in the severity with which the court treated defendants in cases involving so-called cheats: where the acts were substantially what we today call forgery, defendants[70] were ordered into cus-

---

[57] Although in England the distinction was important, for in Rex v. Wyer (2 *Term Rep.* 77), it was said that King's Bench would not ordinarily bail in felony cases.

[58] King v. Isaac Moore (*Ms. Mins. NYCQS 1694–1731/32* 526, 527, Aug. 5, 1730).

[59] King v. Henry Klock, 1767 (*Ms. Mins. SCJ 1766–69* [Engr.] 326, 382).

[60] King v. Territt, 1771 (*Ms. Mins. SCJ 1769–72* [Engr.] 398–400). The bail here was in £500 whereas the bail in the Clock case (*supra* n. 40) only £20.

[61] E.g., King v. Sanders and Attkins, 1725 (*Ms. Mins. SCJ 1723–27* 142, 143, 146); King v. Catherine Christianse (*Ms. Mins. NYCQS 1732–62* 190, 192, 196, Nov. 5, 6, 7, 1745, Feb. 5, 1745/46). James Davis, indicted for feloniously stealing gun tackle worth 10*d.*, pleaded not guilty and the next day was called on his recognizance, tried, found not guilty and discharged (*Ms. Mins. NYCQS 1760–72* 108, May 3, 4, 1764).

[62] King v. Bastarr (*ibid.* 290, Aug. 4, 1769). Cf. *infra* n. 121.

[63] King v. Thomas Lawrence and Ellinor Blackington (*Ms. Mins. NYCQS 1694–1731/32* 459–461, Feb. 2, 1725/26); King v. Arden and King v. Brown (*Ms. Mins. NYCQS 1732–62* 84–87, Feb. 10, 1737/38, May 3, 4, 1738); King v. Eliz. Pym, 1769 (*Ms. Mins. SCJ 1769–72* [Engr.] 63, 64).

[64] King v. Gallaudet, 1769 (*Ms. Mins. SCJ 1769–72* [Engr.] 23, 62, 116, 117, 148).

[65] King v. Bishop *et al.*, 1766 (*Ms. Mins. SCJ 1764–67* [Rough] 141, 144); and compare the early case of rescue, Queen v. Oldfield and Hennyon (*Ms. Mins. NYCQS 1694–1731/32* 268, May 4, 1714).

[66] King v. McDougall, indicted in 1770 for libelling the assembly, was admitted to bail in £500 (*Ms. Mins. SCJ 1769–72* [Engr.] 193, 198); cf. *infra* nn. 87, 89.

[67] Cf. King v. Lydia Atkins (*Ms. Mins. NYCQS 1694–1731/32* 489, Feb. 6, 1727/28); King v. Jane Chambers (*Ms. Mins. NYCQS 1760–72* 115, 120, Aug. 8, Nov. 7, 1764); King v. Mary Curtin (*ibid.* 304, Feb. 9, 1770).

[68] So when Dick, a slave indicted of a felony, was allowed at large, the court upon the grand jury's representation that he was "a dangerous fellow" ordered he be taken (*Ms. Mins. SCJ 1727–32* 306, 341).

[69] E.g., in King v. James Collings *et al.*, indicted for an affray and assault, four of the offenders had attempted to rescue Collings who was being attached by a constable (*Ms. Mins. NYCQS 1694–1731/32* 397, Feb. 7, 1721/22).

[70] So in 1736, Miles Weeks, indicted for obtaining goods by a counterfeit letter, was committed

tody, and when convicted were severely punished. The reaction to a situation where the common law was on the one hand too severe (viz., counterfeiting) and on the other hand too lenient (viz., the alteration of private writings) is significant in illustrating how a mercantile community was attempting to secure an adjustment suited to its own necessities.

The attitude of the New York judges toward the matter of bail could be brought into somewhat sharper focus if the official minutes of response to the petitions of prisoners were less perfunctory. One of the earliest of such petitions was from "Peter the Doctor," a defendant in the Negro Conspiracy trials of 1712. He was indicted for murder and conspiracy on August 5, 1712, and was still in custody on October 14, 1712. He prayed that he be "joyned to his trial or be bayled this court."[71] The Supreme Court ordered that he be tried and he was acquitted on October 18. Occasionally the courts would grant bail upon motion or petition,[72] but as there is no insistence upon a right to bail in the various petitions of prisoners who languished in jail, sometimes without even being indicted, it is obvious neither defendants nor courts approached the matter in terms of right.[73]

The traditional means of bringing to a test the right to bail was by habeas corpus, but according to the records in New York this writ was infrequently employed. Early in the history of the Province the English authorities had stated that the Habeas Corpus Act of 31 Charles II did not extend to the dominions, and in 1698 Governor Bellomont laid before the Council a similar ruling made by the English authorities in 1695 with respect to a Massachusetts statute and which was apparently regarded as of sufficient importance to be

---

after confessing the indictment and pending sentence of thirty-nine lashes (*Ms. Mins. NYCQS 1732–62* 69, 70, Nov. 3, 4, 1736). Thomas Bell was indicted in 1738 for composing a "counterfeit" letter and committed. He was convicted, carted and given thirty-nine lashes (*ibid.* 93, Nov. 9, 1738).

[71] *Ms. Mins. SCJ 1710–14* 417, 429.

[72] Thus Matthias de Hart was presented for assaulting the surveyor of the port (*James Alexander Papers* Box 45) and admitted to bail (*Ms. Mins. NYCQS 1694–1731/32* 409, 412, Aug. 7, 8, 1722). Thomas Measie was ordered by the Supreme Court on Oct. 20, 1724, to be "admitted to Bayle" on the motion of Mr. Murray (*Ms. Mins. SCJ 1723–27* 111). Sometimes, on petition of the complaining witness, a prisoner would be allowed bail. In King v. Love (Lovett) and Wright, the complaining witness petitioned, thinking that bail would be subject to his suit (*J. T. Kempe Lawsuits W–Y sub nom. Walker*). William Love (Lovett) and John Wright appeared in the Supreme Court on Oct. 28, 1766, on

recognizance and were continued on Oct. 29 and 30, on which latter date an indictment for riot was filed against them (*Ms. Mins. SCJ 1764–67* [Rough] 174, 176, 177, 190).

[73] See the case of John Read (1729), in prison for eight months, discharged (*Ms. Mins. SCJ 1727–32* 156); Henry Lewis (1731) merely held on suspicion, discharged on payment of fees (*ibid.* 284); Jane Dun indicted for bigamy (1773) petitioned and was tried nearly a year later (*J. T. Kempe Lawsuits C–F; H.R. Pleadings Pl. K.* 41; *Ms. Mins. SCJ 1772–76* [Rough] 128 *et seq.*).

One Daniel Parish was evidently held in custody in the Dutchess County jail for some offense, because on July 28, 1770, Sheriff Henry Rosekranz wrote to Kempe asking that Parish be released "from our gaol" (*J. T. Kempe Lawsuits P–R*). On Aug. 4, 1770, the sheriff of Dutchess returned to the Supreme Court that he had Parish in custody. The latter was ordered to plead in twenty days after service of a copy of the declaration and "this rule"

communicated to other provinces.[74] Nevertheless, it would appear from one or two scattered references that the colonists believed that the statute was applicable.[75] The Supreme Court was endowed with the powers of King's Bench so there was no question of the authority to issue the writ, yet as the Habeas Corpus Act had implicitly affirmed the right to bail in misdemeanors, the problem whether the statute extended to the Province was not without importance. The question so far as we know was never litigated in New York. The frequent incompleteness of the records in habeas corpus cases may be mere accident, but it conveys an impression of furtiveness which leads one to wonder whether or not an issue was deliberately avoided.

Beginning with the year 1691 there is a sprinkling of early cases. The first case is not mentioned in the minutes and it is a unique example of an opinion signed by two Supreme Court judges. The opinion, dated May 17, 1697, recites that Fransa produced a writ of habeas corpus setting forth that he was committed to the New York jail by virtue of a mittimus signed and sealed by two justices of the peace for a breach of the peace against the form "of An Act of Parliament made in the fifteenth Year of King Charles the Second when no such Act was then made." At the hearing it appeared that the venire issued upon an information of forcible entry was grounded on the statute made 8 Henry VI. The offense was the dispossession of Penelope Attkins discussed in Chapter II. Fransa, it will be recalled, was fined 40s. and the mittimus was to order him kept in custody until the fine was paid. "Whereupon the Clerke writing the Mittimus Pursuant to sd. order by Misprision Inserted An Act made in the fifteenth Year of the Late King Charles the Second (by Copying the Mittimus after a printed President in a Booke Entituled Bonds Justice) in Stead of ye Statute of ye fifteenth Richard the Second, and being of Opinion

on the sheriff or on the defendant (in custody) or else suffer judgment. We do not know whether this case was a criminal case or not, but the case is entitled in the minute entries "King v. Daniel Parish" and was possibly a *qui tam* action (*Ms. Mins. SC] 1769-72* [Engr.] 246). In one unusual case the defendant's attorney secured a transfer from Albany to Tryon County jail, making no effort to get bail (King v. Bollman, March, 1774 [*Misc. Mss. Tryon Co.*]).

[74] The first ruling is in 3 *Doc. Rel. Col. Hist. NY* 357. For Bellomont's report cf. 8 *Ms. Mins. Council* 130. For the order respecting the Massachusetts statute which sought to enact the substance of 31 Car. II c.2, cf. 1 *Acts of Province of Mass. Bay* 99. Some years later (1703), in relation to a similar Bermuda act, the law officers of the Crown expressed a fear that justices of the peace would issue the writ and this might lead to abuse (*Cal. S.P. Colonial 1702-03* §1156).

[75] Cf. *infra* 504, 505. It is interesting to note that in the case of McCullogh v. Walker, in the New York Mayor's Court (1729), Murray argued against the English act to prevent vexatious arrests applying in the colony. Smith for the defendant countered with the argument that the Statute of Jeofails, the Statute of Limitations and the Habeas Corpus Act applied in New York. The memorandum of authority is in *Ms. Mins. Mayor's Ct. NYC 1729-34* (Engr.). The case is in the rough minute book under date Dec. 9, 1729. There is a superficial and badly informed discussion in Carpenter, Habeas Corpus in the Colonies, 8 *Am. Hist. Rev.* 16.

that it is a Bare Error in Clerkeship which by the Clerke might be Supplied, Amended doe not see Cause to Discharge him. . . ." The opinion is signed by Stephen Van Cortlandt and William Pinhorne.[76]

Two years later habeas corpus was used to determine bailability, but there is no indication of the court's action.[77] Indeed it is in only two of the early cases that we have the final order. In *Queen* v. *Whitehead et al.* (1706),[78] where the defendants were taken in an inquisition of riot, and *Queen* v. *Makemie and Hampton*,[79] committed for unlicensed preaching, there is an entry of the final order—in both cases, to admit to bail. There ensues a long period where the writ does not appear to have been used at all. Then in *King* v. *Zenger* it is invoked under dramatic circumstances.

Zenger had been taken in custody by virtue of a warrant issued by the Governor and Council. His friends obtained a writ of habeas corpus and on the return, Zenger's counsel, William Smith and James Alexander, insisted upon the right to bail on the basis of Magna Carta, the Petition of Right and the Habeas Corpus Act of Charles II.[80] They further insisted upon the right to moderate bail on the basis of a passage in Hawkins' *Pleas of the Crown,* the Habeas Corpus Act and the Bill of Rights. Zenger's affidavit was offered to the effect that excepting the tools of his trade and his clothes he was not worth £40. The court ordered that Zenger might be admitted to bail, himself in £400, with two sureties each in £200. This exorbitant sum it was impossible to raise and Zenger remained in custody until his trial.

It should be observed that although the Supreme Court was anything but well disposed toward Zenger, no exception was taken to the argument that the Habeas Corpus Act and the Bill of Rights applied to the colony so far as a right to bail is concerned, although the amount set by the Chief Justice is sufficient indication that he did not regard the restrictions respecting excessive bail to be binding. The case, therefore, settled nothing regarding the applicability of the statute.

After the Zenger case there is another long interval before the records again show a habeas corpus to secure a release on bail (and possibly to transfer the

---

[76] 41 *NY Col. Mss.* 66. For the forcible entry prosecution *supra* 124–125. On habeas corpus cf. also *supra* 155, 260.

[77] Nicoll, on behalf of Captain Shelly, moved for a habeas corpus (*Mins. SC] 1693–1701* 173).

[78] *Ms. Mins. SC] 1704/05–1709* 49, 57, 66, 76, 91, 92.

[79] *H.R. Parch.* 57 c.7.

[80] *Trial of John Peter Zenger* (London, 1765) 13. There are some notes on habeas corpus in the *Horsmanden Papers.* Horsmanden assisted the Attorney General. The *Argument on Habeas Corpus,* the *Argument on the Sufficiency of the Return* and the *Argument on Excessive Bail* are in 2 *Ms. Rutherford Collection* 11, 13, 17.

case)[81] and it is not until 1763 that a writ of habeas corpus explicitly grounded on 31 Charles II c.2 is brought. The circumstances were unusual and the minute entries are again exceedingly obscure.[82]

Waddell Cunningham had been presented for a violent assault and battery. As we reconstruct the case, Cunningham was already under recognizance, but subsequently his sureties wished to be released of their bond and have Cunningham committed. On the return of the writ marked as issued pursuant to 31 Car. II, defendant and sureties appeared and the latter declared they had surrendered Cunningham in discharge of themselves and prayed he be committed. The Court "doubting whether the surrender could be accepted order this minute of their offer to surrender him be made," and the recognizance was respited to the next term.[83]

The Cunningham case supplies an interesting sidelight on the lack of provincial familiarity with habeas corpus procedure. In England a *habeas corpus cum causa* (not *ad subjiciendum*) was available when sureties wished to be discharged, and the court was supposed to remand as a matter of course.[84] It was, moreover, only the *habeas corpus ad subjiciendum* which by statute had to be earmarked *"Per Statutum tricessimo primo Caroli II Regis."*[85] Here the petitioners confused the two writs, a mistake which in view of the then high standard of practice in New York we think could have happened only because the use of habeas corpus was unusual.[86]

It is with great hesitation that we have ventured to conclude that habeas corpus was not often resorted to, for the matter is one of the few phases of practice upon which the records are unreliable. Normally minutes were kept of a case only after presentment or indictment found or information filed, since it was only with these documents that the "record" in a criminal case began. If it should happen that a habeas corpus before indictment was sued,

[81] King v. Benjamin Ferguson, *supra* c. III n. 71.
[82] *Ms. Mins. SCJ 1762–64* (Engr.) 224, 225. An information based on the presentment was filed on Oct. 29, 1763. When it appeared on Jan. 27, 1764 that Forsey had begun a private action against Cunningham, the latter was fined £30 and discharged (*ibid.* 299, 358).
[83] It is not clear why the court doubted its power. Cf. King v. John McWilliams, where bail asked to be discharged and the defendant was then ordered in custody (*Ms. Mins. Ulster Co. Sess. 1737–50* May 1, 1749). In King v. Andrew Hamilton, indicted for riot and assault Aug. 1, 1766, the Supreme Court accepted a surrender and committed Hamilton (*Ms. Mins. SCJ 1764–67* [Rough] 155,

157). Cf. also King v. Hull (*Ms. Mins. Albany Co. Sess. 1763–82* Oct. 4, 1769).
[84] Tidd, *Practice of King's Bench* 405, 408, 417.
[85] 31 Car. II c.2 §3.
[86] For a possible example of the *habeas corpus ad deliberandum et recipiendum* used to remove a prisoner to take trial in the county where the offense was committed, cf. J. T. Kempe's letter to a local justice regarding the removal by habeas corpus of John Kelly and Henry Hill from Albany to New York to be tried at bar (*J. T. Kempe Lawsuits sub nom.* Kelly; *Ms. Mins. SCJ 1764–67* [Rough] 23, 24, 29, 34, for the trial of Kelly on an indictment for burglary).

there would be no reason to make a minute. This is clearly shown by the Zenger case where no whisper of the habeas corpus proceedings appears in the minutes because these took place anterior to the information. Similarly, in the case of Alexander McDougall, who, while proceedings were pending in the Supreme Court, was summoned before the assembly to answer for a libel upon it and committed for contempt, a habeas corpus was sued out but nothing can be found on this in the judicial records.[87] It should further be noted that if a writ of habeas corpus were issued out of term,[88] and were returned within the brief period set by the Habeas Corpus Act, the proceedings in chambers would not necessarily be minuted. Allowing even for these various possibilities, nevertheless, our conclusion rests chiefly upon the fact that the principal courts were ordinarily willing to bail except in treason, murder and grand larceny, if a defendant was able to furnish security and was of good fame. Furthermore, except in cases of political complexion like the Zenger and later the McDougall case, there was no disposition to set bail in excessive amounts.[89] In these circumstances, there was no occasion for complaints about a right to bail to grow and fester. Indeed, the most convincing evidence regarding the public attitude on the question is to be found in the series of acts permitting summary trial of persons charged with offenses less than the degree of grand larceny who were unable to supply bail within forty-eight hours—a substantial citizen could have his bail and with it his jury trial.[90] The historian alert for matters bearing upon the later bills of right will consequently forage fruitlessly in the records of bail administration in New York, for they yield but the slightest food for grievance even in the decades when a grievance could be plucked from any of the branches of government. Whatever may have been the experience in other colonies in the matter of bail, the most determined critics of the royal government in New York could find little from which to wring political advantage.

[87] See the account in Leake, *Memoir of the Life and Times of General John Lamb* (1850) 71 *et seq.*

[88] On this, Hands, *The Solicitor's Practice on the Crown Side of King's Bench* 72 *et seq.*

[89] In the McDougall case, bail was not denied but, as stated, set at £500 with two sureties in £250 each, and the defendant refused at first to be bailed. The Sons of Liberty attempted to play up McDougall as a second John Wilkes. There is an amusing account of their antics in Leake, *op. cit.* 69. Lieut. Governor Colden reported the bail to have been easily within McDougall's means (8 *Doc. Rel. Col. Hist. NY* 208).

In *William Smith Jr. Papers* Box 2 no. 204, is a letter on the McDougall case where *inter alia* it was said: "It seems necessary also that the magistrate should have the Power of committing offenders of this rash kind at discretion, and that while the matter is before him upon the question shall I commit or not it should be perfectly immaterial whether the accusation in the defamatory writing is true or false."

[90] In 1768, the assembly extended the summary procedure to felonious taking and asportation of goods to the value of £5 (4 *Col. Laws NY* 969) and by an amendment of 1774 provided that when an offender was in custody it was at his election to give bail and upon refusal he could be tried by three justices (5 *Col. Laws NY* 644).

The Recognizance in Relation to Trial

We have discussed the power and right to bail as if it were the thing unto itself that the eighteenth century text writers deemed it to be, whereas in fact the provincial records show bail to have been but an aspect of the much larger "law and practice of recognizances." It is only when one observes how security devices were used to fortify and insure the progress of a trial at all points, from the arrest of a defendant or the formulation of a charge against him, down through the final execution of sentence, that the bail problem falls into perspective. Even in the conditions of a defendant's bonds the variations show that from the standpoint of the courts the recognizance or bail is regarded not so much as a surrogate of imprisonment, as a device to assure the step by step functioning of the judicial process. This view was to a certain extent made inevitable by the state of the law respecting arrest by warrant before indictment and the lack of settled forms of such precepts, and it was also conditioned by the variety of process available after indictment. A person taken on a justice's warrant might merely be bound over to appear before the grand jury and in the event he was indicted, a new recognizance might be necessary. Similarly, it might be prudent, on appearance of a defendant merely summoned by a venire facias to answer an indictment for a misdemeanor, to require security that he would plead.[91] And, of course, after trial where a defendant might have been continuously at large it was often desirable to order security to abide the judgment,[92] in anticipation of the final process.

---

[91] E.g., Sarah Heard, indicted Feb. 3, 1719/20, for false swearing, appeared on Aug. 2, 1720 and pleaded not guilty. She was ordered committed till she give surety to prosecute her traverse, and she gave in a recognizance in £20 with William Taylor as her surety in £10 to appear and prosecute her traverse with effect (*Ms. Mins. NYCQS 1694–1731/32* 370, 374). John McLeod pleaded not guilty on Feb. 2, 1714/15 to an indictment for trading with slaves and was bound in £20 to appear at the next Sessions to prosecute his traverse with effect. But on May 3, 1715, he was continued on recognizance to the following Sessions and finally on Aug. 2, 1715, he was tried, found not guilty and discharged from his recognizance (*ibid.* 280, 285, 295). On Feb. 5, 1717/18, Edward Blagge was indicted for assault and battery, pleaded not guilty and was bound in £40 with two sureties in £20 each to appear and prosecute his traverse with effect the following Sessions, but when he appeared on May 6, 1718, he was continued on recognizance to the following Sessions and on Aug. 5, 1718, to the following day when the jury gave its verdict (*Ms. Mins. NYCQS 1694–1731/32* 342, 346–348). John Wallace, indicted Aug. 2, 1737, pleaded not guilty, was bound in £20 to prosecute his traverse with effect, appeared on Nov. 1, and his recognizance to prosecute his traverse with effect was "respited" to next Sessions. Likewise his recognizance was respited on Feb. 8, 1737/38, but finally on May 3, 1738, he was tried, found not guilty of the "misdemeanor" for which he had been indicted and was discharged from his recognizance (*Ms. Mins. NYCQS 1732–62* 77, 78, 80, 83, 86).

[92] So, George Wright Sr. and Jr., William Frost and Jacob Mott, on Nov. 30, 1726, were found guilty on an information for trespass and assault, and on Dec. 6, 1726, the court ordered that process issue to bring the defendants in to hear the court's judgment but on their attorney's motion the court ordered that no process issue for three weeks so that the defendants could enter recognizances "to answer such ffine as shall be imposed." On Mar. 15, 1726/27, the defendants appeared on recognizance and were ordered to appear the next day and on

An early case in New York is particularly interesting on these points. Henry Cordus, indicted for adultery, finally appeared after process had run to the exigent and was ordered committed unless he give bail to prosecute his traverse (Feb. 7, 1709/10). Cordus "recognized himself in £30 to appear next day." He appeared, pleaded not guilty and was then bound in £20 (with another as surety in £10) to appear and "prosecute his traverse with effect."[93] This succession of recognizances was unusual,[94] for ordinarily when a defendant appeared and was put on recognizance to plead and trial was put off, he was continued on his recognizance.

Judging from the specimens of recognizance used after 1750, it became usual to employ a form which covered all contingencies. The condition expressed was that the defendant would personally appear to answer what should be objected against him, to abide and perform what the court should enjoin upon him. This required appearance, pleading and performance of judgment, so that after appearance made no new recognizance had to be ordered, but the defendant if allowed at large would be continued on his recognizance or respited should some delay occur.[95]

Mar. 16 they were fined and ordered to be committed until their fine and fees were paid (Ms. Mins. SCJ 1723–27 224, 225, 235, 239, 243).

Isaac Gardiner having been found guilty, on the Attorney General's motion was ordered to enter a recognizance to "abide the court's judgment" or be committed, whereupon the defendant with one surety entered a recognizance in £10 each to abide the court's judgment (Ms. Mins. SCJ 1732–39 325, 338, 344, Oct. 23, 1738, Apr. 20, 24, 1739). Arnout Hendrikse, found guilty of keeping a disorderly house and selling strong liquor to slaves, on Mar. 15, 1730/31, entered a recognizance in £50 to abide the court's judgment and on Mar. 16 was fined £8 and was ordered committed until he paid the fine (Ms. Mins. SCJ 1727–32 259, 262).

[93] Ms. Mins. NYCQS 1694–1731/32 169, 170.

[94] But see Queen v. Jacobus Cornelisse (abusing the watch, 1702) where defendant appeared on recognizance and pleaded, and was then bound on a new recognizance to prosecute his traverse with effect (ibid. 72, Nov. 7, 1702). Cf. also King v. Lakeman, surety to prosecute traverse (Ms. Mins. Rich. Co. Sess. 1710/11–1744/45 Mar. 5, 1718/19); King v. Hillyer (ibid. Sept. 4, 1722); King v. Garrison, King v. Grant (ibid. Mar. 7, 1726/27); King v. Rolph (Ms. Mins. Rich. Co. Sess. 1745–1812 May 7, 1765). In King v. James Long (disorderly house, 1767), defendant appeared and was put under recognizance to answer and be of good behavior. On Jan. 23, 1768, when it appeared a material witness for the Crown was absent, a juror was withdrawn, and the defendant and sureties dis-

charged. The court thereupon ordered a new recognizance to answer next term (Ms. Mins. SCJ 1766–69 [Engr.] 322, 327, 379, 386).

[95] There are some early cases. See, for example, Queen v. Drommy (ind. bigamy, 1713) where a special verdict was found. The court, on Sept. 5, 1713, wished further to advise, so the defendant was continued on his recognizance to the following term. On Oct. 15, the court "will further advise till Saturday, defendant continued on his recognizance." On Oct. 16, "the court will further advise till next term, defendant continued on his recognizance." On Mar. 12, 1713/14, the defendant was continued on recognizance to the following term and on June 4 the defendant, brought to bar to receive judgment, produced a pardon and was discharged from his recognizance on the payment of fees (Ms. Mins. SCJ 1710–14 456, 457, 476, 480, 496, 499, 516, 538). On Sept. 2, 1713, Archibald Mott appeared on recognizance and confessed an indictment found against him, and the court "ordered that the defendant be continued on his recognizance till tomorrow" when judgment was given against him (ibid. 463, 466, 471).

After 1750 cases are legion. William Rogers, indicted on Aug. 3, 1769, for assault and battery, confessed the indictment and "the court will advise the next sessions." The defendant was continued on recognizance and appeared on Nov. 9, 1769, when he was fined and ordered to be discharged from his recognizance on the payment of fine and fees (Ms. Mins. NYCQS 1760–72 287, 288, 292, 297). James Rusthead was indicted on

The full scope of the recognizance device as well as the contemporary reliance upon it to keep a case in train can be seen in its use to bind complainants. This is the so-called recognizance *ad prosequendum*. There are examples of this as early as the year 1711,[96] and it was used consistently where persons were prosecuted by indictment until the time of the Revolution.[97] The reason why it was resorted to was, of course, the necessity of having a prosecuting witness. We do not know whether or not the English courts carried over into the misdemeanor field the textbook advice that courts could bind over persons to prosecute felonies;[98] but it is certain that in New York Province the magis-

May 3, 1739, for selling unwholesome meat and on Aug. 7, 1739, he appeared, confessed the indictment and prayed the mercy of the court, whereupon he was ordered to be continued on recognizance during the sitting of the court. On Aug. 9, he was ordered to be "discharged from his recognizance of the peace by proclamation paying his fees" (*Ms. Mins. NYCQS 1732–62* 101–103). Charles Nichol, Jr., appeared on recognizance on July 28, 1773, was indicted for petit larceny and pleaded not guilty on July 30. On July 31, 1773, he was ordered to be continued to the next term and when he appeared on Oct. 19, 1773, he pleaded *nolo contendere* which was entered, whereupon he was respited on his recognizance until the following Thursday. Appearing on his recognizance on Oct. 21, he was ordered to be fined £5 and committed until he paid the fine (*Ms. Mins. SCJ 1772–76* [Rough] 96, 107, 112, 117, 123).

[96] Cf. the recognizance of Abraham de Lucena, quoted *supra* 350 n. 81. On Nov. 11, 1711, Moses Hart and Moses Levy were each bound in £20, and each, with two sureties in £10 each, to appear at Quarter Sessions to do and receive all that should be enjoined on them and in the meantime to be of good behavior to the Queen and to all her liege subjects (*NY Misc. Mss.* Box 4 nn. 15, 17). De Lucena was not only bound as a prosecutor but he was also bound over as an accused, and on Nov. 10, 1711, gave in a recognizance in £20, with two sureties in £10 each, to appear in Quarter Sessions to do and receive all that should be enjoined on him and in the meantime to be of his good behavior (*ibid.* 11). See *Ms. Mins. NYCQS 1694–1731/32* 208, 209, for the trial, on Feb. 5, 1711/12, of Moses Levy and De Lucena, each indicted for assaulting the other.

Christopher Rousby on Feb. 3, 1712/13, entered a recognizance to prosecute Jeremiah Burroughs for receiving stolen goods and trading with Indian slaves. At the same time, the defendant himself was bound in recognizance to appear at the following Sessions and in the meantime be of good behavior. On May 5, 1713, Burroughs and Rousby were both continued on recognizance to the following Sessions (*Ms. Mins. NYCQS 1694–1731/32* 253, 259). On Apr. 20, 1736, a recognizance was

entered into by a certain complainant before Paul Richards, Esq., in £20 "for prosecuting to effect a bill . . . of indictment against Samuel Daley for stealing sundry boks . . . and against Thomas Stut as accessory thereunto." This recognizance was ordered to be filed (*Ms. Mins. SCJ 1732–39* 208). On June 7, 1762, Catherine Hordenbergh "personally came and appeared before me James Duncan one of his Majesties Justices of the peace . . . She Acknowledged her Recognizance of £50 to the King to give in her Evidence Against one David Smith and who was committed to the Said County gaol [i.e., the jail of Dutchess County] . . . on Strong suspecian of Stealing Sundry Goods from said Catherine Hordenbergh" (*J. T. Kempe Lawsuits* G–J).

[97] For a form of the recognizance: "City and County of New York ss: Be it Remembered that on the fourteenth day of January in the Year of our Lord one thousand seven hundred and seventy four personally appeared before me, Whitehead Hicks Esqr. Mayor, and one of his Majesty's Justices of the peace for the City & County of New York, John Watts of the said City, and acknowledged himself to be indebted unto our Sovereign Lord the King in the Sum of fifty Pounds Current money of New York to be raised and levied on his Goods and Chattels, Lands and Tenements to the Use of our said Sovereign Lord the King his Heirs and Successors, if Failure be made in the Performance of the Condition following—The Condition of this Recognizance is such, that if the above named John Watts shall and do personally appear before his Majesty's Justices at the next Supreme Court of Judicature to be held for the Province of New York at the City Hall of the said City on the Third Tuesday in January Instant, then and there to give Evidence against Daniel Hammond for a certain Felony by him lately committed in the said City and shall not depart the said Court without the Leave thereof then this Recognizance to be void, otherwise to stand and remain in full Force & Virtue Taken and acknowledged the Day and Year above written. Before me, WHITEHEAD HICKS" (*H.R. Pleadings* Pl. K. 228). See also the recognizance of John Duley (*ibid.* Pl. K. 342).

[98] Dalton, *Countrey Justice* c.164.

trates did not hesitate to take recognizances to prosecute for misdemeanors. In the procedure by information the recognizance to prosecute was made mandatory by the provincial Act of 1754,[99] and the Attorney General also took care to have security for costs.[100] It is possible that before this statute the Attorney General sometimes bound over a complainant, but it was probably not often done, for the failure to take this precaution was one of the grievances against information procedure as administered by Richard Bradley.

Closely related to this use of the recognizance was that exacted when a defendant sought to remove a cause by certiorari, and the recognizance *ad testificandum*. These were both intended, although in different ways, to forward the prosecution of a cause, the one in a forum other than that where the proceeding had been initiated, the second as a measure to assure the completeness of the Crown's prosecution of a defendant.

In the discussion of transfer jurisdiction we adverted to the fact that the removal of causes by certiorari at the instance of the defendants occurred only occasionally. In this the Province was more fortunate than the mother country where it had been necessary to attempt to stem such removals. The statute 21 James I c.8 had required a recognizance for the transfer of cases of riot, forcible entry and assault, and when this proved ineffective against the "divers turbulent contentious, lewd and evil disposed persons" who sought to dodge a trial in their home Sessions, a further enactment (5 Wm. & Mary c.11) extended

---

[99] 3 *Col. Laws NY* 1007.

[100] "Know All Men by these presents That We Henry Content of New Rochelle in the County of Westchester Drover and John Barheit of the same Place Yeoman are held and firmly bound unto John Tabor Kempe Esq[r] his Majesty's Attorney General for the province of New York in the Sum of One hundred pounds Current Money of the said Province of New York to be paid to the said John Tabor Kempe or to his certain Attorney, Executors, Administrators or Assigns, To which payment well and truly to be made We bind ourselves and each and either of our Heirs, Executors and Administrators firmly by the presents Sealed with our Seals Dated this Second Day of December in the fourth year of the Reign of our Sovereign Lord George the third by the Grace of God of Great Britain France and Ireland King Defender of the Faith &c and in the year of our Lord 1763. Whereas Complaint hath been made to the above named John Tabor Kempe Esq[r] his Majesty's Attorney General for the province of New York by Andrew Barheit of New Rochelle aforesaid Labourer in order for an Information to be exhibited by the said Attorney General in the Supreme Court of Judicature of the province of New York against Joseph Rodman of New Rochelle aforesaid Yoeman for assaulting and beating the said Andrew Barheit & Mary his wife now the Condition of this Obligation is such that if the said Andrew Barheit his Heirs Executors or administrators shall and do well and truly pay or cause to be paid to the said John Tabor Kempe, his Executors Administrators or Assignes, all such Costs Fees and Disbursements, as shall be by him laid out and expended, or certified to be due to him for his services in the said prosecution by One of the Judges of the said Supreme Court, and also such Fees and Charges as are usually paid in this Province by Clients to their Council for their Attendance in Westchester County on the Tryal of Causes brought to issue in the said Supreme Court, if the said Attorney General shall there attend for the Trial of the said Joseph Rodman then this obligation to be void and of none Effect, otherwise to be and remain in full Force & Virtue.

Signed   John Content   seal
              John Barheit

Sealed & delivered in
the presence of
    John Arthur
    Jarvis Daft."

(*J. T. Kempe Lawsuits* C–F.)

this requirement to all indictments at Sessions and increased the amount of the bond. This act did not apply to the dominions, but it is obvious from an early eighteenth century New York case that the court esteemed a recognizance as essential where a defendant sued out a certiorari,[101] and thereafter this was always required. Indeed, as we have seen in *King* v. *Ewing,* the failure to post a bond resulted in a *procedendo.*[102]

That the recognizance *ad testificandum* was akin to the bond to prosecute is apparent from the language of the instruments themselves.[103] Indeed, except for an endorsement on the recognizance or the minute entries, it would be difficult to distinguish one from the other. The recognizance to testify was very generally used in the Province after 1691. It cannot be averred with any certainty that it was regularly employed in the period of the Duke's Laws, for the minutes usually speak only of binding over to appear, and only occasionally is there mention of surety to prosecute.[104] Before Dongan's governorship, the subpoena alone seems to have been adequate, partly because even in criminal cases depositions were admitted in evidence.[105] Once, however, the recog-

---

[101] King v. Clarke, 1716 (*supra* 156 n. 72). The statute, 21 Jac. I c.8, having been enacted before the conquest of New York, could be regarded as applicable.

[102] *Supra* 158 n. 75.
Recognizances were also used in connection with the trial of the informations at nisi prius. Thus, when an information by the Attorney General was read against John Talman in the Supreme Court on Apr. 7, 1703, and the defendant pleaded not guilty, the Attorney General prayed that the defendant give sureties "to abide the Judgment of the court and to come to trial the next Supreme Court in Queens." The Attorney General's motion being granted, the defendant gave a recognizance in £200, with one surety in £50, for his appearance at nisi prius (*Ms. Mins. SCJ 1701–04* 69). Also see Queen v. Content Titus *et al.* (*ibid.* 70, Apr. 6, 1703).

[103] For example, the recognizance *ad testificandum* of John Berien, dated Sept. 7, 1770, to give evidence against Alexander McDougall, indicted for libel: "BE IT REMEMBRED That on the Seventh day of September in the Tenth Year of the Reign of our Sovereign Lord George the third by the Grace of God of Great Britain France and Ireland King Defender of the Faith &c. and in the Year of our Lord one thousand seven hundred and Seventy Personally appeared before me Daniel Horsmanden Esquire Chief Justice of the Province of New York John Berien of the City of New York Shopkeeper and acknowledged himself to be indebted unto our said Sovereign Lord the King in the Sum of one hundred Pounds Current money of the Province of New York to be levied on his Goods and Chattels, Lands and Tenements to the use of our said Lord the King his Heirs and Successors if failure be made in Performance of the Condition following THE CONDITION of this Recognizance is such, That if the above bounden John Berien shall and do Personally appear at the next Supreme Court of Judicature to be held for the Province of New York at the City Hall in the City of New York on the third Tuesday in October next and then and there in Behalf of Our said Sovereign Lord the King give such Evidence as he knoweth touching or concerning the making Printing and Publishing a certain seditious Paper and Libel lately Printed Published and Dispersed in the said City Dated New York Dec. 16th, 1769 and directed or Addressed To the Betrayed Inhabitants of the City and Colony of New York and signed or subscribed a Son of Liberty whereof Alexander McDougal of the said City of New York Mariner stands Indicted and shall not depart the Court without leave THEN this Recognizance to be void and of no Effect otherwise to be and remain in full force and virtue TAKEN and Acknowledged the Day and Year first above written BEFORE ME DANL. HORSMANDEN" (*H.R. Pleadings* Pl. K. 376). Cf. Thos. Cunningham's recognizance in King v. Greatrakes (*ibid.* Pl. K. 375, and cf. Pl. K. 466, Pl. K. 755).

[104] So, for example, in the minutes of the Court of Assizes 1676 (25 *NY Col. Mss.* 197) and in *Recs. Ct. of New Castle* 325, 346.

[105] E.g., the prosecution of Green for homicide at the 1676 Assizes (25 *NY Col. Mss.* 195); Sheriff v. Williams, a prosecution for larceny (*Ms. Mins. Mayor's Ct. NYC 1677–82* 150).

nizance to testify comes into use, its value as a time and trouble saving device is obviously appreciated.[106] The examining magistrate by putting witnesses under bond was able to assure their immediate presence at the next Sessions, and no further summons was necessary. Magistrates binding over witnesses were not restricted to insuring testimony in their own jurisdiction, but could exact an obligation to appear in superior courts.[107] The order to bond might also be given in General Sessions, for indictments there were usually tried at the term next following the finding of the bill.[108] The witness under recognizance, like the defendant, was subject to the risk that if he defaulted his bond would be forfeit,[109] and he must endure the irksome necessity of being on call at order.[110] It should be noticed, further, that the recognizance *ad testificandum* was, in the case of the Circuit where the term was very short, a particularly useful means of securing the witnesses' attendance and surer than the subpoena, the service of which involved trouble, mistakes and expense.[111]

[106] The cases cannot be fully listed, but cf. the proceedings against Mingo, a negro, for grand larceny, where the New York Quarter Sessions, refusing to take jurisdiction, committed the offender and bound over three witnesses to testify at the next Supreme Court (*Ms. Mins. NYCQS 1694-1731/32* 3, Nov. 6, 1694). In 1704, Teunis Frankhout was bound to testify against one Green indicted for destroying a bond (*ibid.* 88, May 3, 1704). In 1722, Henry Ten Brook and other witnesses before the grand jury discharged on payment of fees (*Ms. Mins. NYCQS 1722-1742/43* [Rough] 9, Aug. 8, 1722). Edward Man and Garrett Kettletas recognized themselves, on Apr. 21, 1735, in £20 to appear as witnesses against Catherine Johnson, indicted for false bills (*Ms. Mins. SCJ 1732-39* 158, 162).

[107] Cf. King v. Ker (*Ms. Mins. Ulster Co. Sess. 1737-50* May 7, 1745). Lawlis and Dunn were bound in recognizance on Dec. 5, 1765, before the coroner of New York City to appear in the Supreme Court to give evidence against John Dalton for the murder of John Marschalk (*J. T. Kempe Lawsuits* C-F *sub nom.* Dalton). See *H.R. Pleadings* Pl. K. 1065, for recognizances by four witnesses in £20 each to give evidence against John Kennedy for a felony, which recognizance was filed on Jan. 16, 1752.

[108] The Suffolk minutes have a great many such entries; cf., in particular, King v. Rev. James Lyons (breach of peace) where the defendant and six witnesses were all ordered bound over (*Ms. Mins. Suffolk Co. Sess. 1760-75* Oct. 1, 1765); Frans Cool bound Oct. 26, 1741 (*Ms. Mins. Dutchess Co. Sess.* Liber A).

[109] For example, King v. Francisco—estreat ordered (*Ms. Mins. Orange Co. Sess. 1727-79* Apr. 30, 1751); King v. Tooker—order nisi (*Ms. Mins.*

Suffolk Co. Sess. 1723-51 Oct. 4, 1737) explained and discharged Mar. 28, 1738; King v. John Verny —respite ordered (*Ms. Mins. Dutchess Co. Sess.* Liber F, Oct. 10, 1775).

[110] David Johnston, John Wollaston, Philip Van Horne and Thomas Cumming appeared on October 16, 1750, to give evidence and, on motion of Nicoll for the Attorney General, were ordered to be continued on their recognizances until the next term. On Jan. 16 and 19, 1750/51, Apr. 25 and Aug. 3, these witnesses appeared on their recognizances. On Aug. 3 Wollaston was discharged. The others were continued until on Oct. 19, 1751 when, with consent of the Attorney General, the court discharged them (*Ms. Mins. SCJ 1750-54* [Engr.] 1, 25, 29, 53, 67, 69, 83). Thomas Perry and six other witnesses appeared on Aug. 1, 1752, on recognizances to give evidence against Edward Lee for burglary, but the defendant having broken jail and escaped, the witnesses were discharged (*Ms. Mins. SCJ 1750-54* [Engr.] 160). In July, 1764, six witnesses were bound in £50 each before the coroner to give evidence in the Supreme Court against Frederick Locidon (Lowden) for murder (*H.R. Pleadings* Pl. K. 755). On Sept. 26, 1739, Justice Adam Seaman delivered in several recognizances of J. Washburne and others, bound over to give evidences against Jonathan Ogden for feloniously stealing a hog (*Ms. Mins. Cir. 1721-49* 99).

[111] In Queens Oyer and Terminer and General Gaol Delivery on Sept. 25, 1722, five named witnesses "appear on recognizances ad testificandum" (*Ms. Mins. Cir. 1721-49* 24). On June 13, 1736, Justice Glen delivered into Albany Oyer and Terminer and General Gaol Delivery a recognizance of James Steward, bound over to give evidence (*ibid.* 85). Also see recognizances *ad testificandum* to give evidence against Jonathan Dean in Queens

The employment of recognizances as a means of avoiding additional process, at least in the case of witnesses, had other practical advantages. Thus the table of fees of 1710[112] allowed the clerk of the Sessions 1s. 6d. for taking a recognizance and drawing it in form, whereas a subpoena ran to only 6d. for each "evidence." Furthermore, a recognizance taken by a clerk of the peace for an appearance in the Supreme Court assured him his fees, whereas these would accrue to the clerk of the Supreme Court if subpoenas were to issue. This may seem to be the slightest of small potatoes, but in an officialdom dependent on fees the farthing was never overlooked.

These considerations did not apply, however, to another process-saving use of recognizances—the surety to abide or perform judgment—since the charge for a *capias pro fine* and a recognizance was the same. This type of surety was intended primarily to afford an effective means of collection, and to avoid the cost of possible imprisonment and was used only when no corporal punishment was inflicted. The standard order upon judgment was that the defendant be committed until fine and fees were paid,[113] but if the defendant were already under recognizance he might be respited until these were paid,[114] although the court might nevertheless order commitment.

When a convicted defendant was allowed to give surety in the circumstances just described, the bond functioned as a species of bail to facilitate collection. But the courts also used the recognizance with a condition of good abearance as a form of additional sanction, a means of guarding against future misconduct of persons whom they regarded with mistrust. In other words the bond was at once penal and preventive. This practice had a direct bearing upon the development of imprisonment as a punishment in the colony and deserves, therefore, closer inspection.

The recognizances for good behavior or the peace, exacted as part of a sentence, seem to be an outgrowth of the early provincial practice of a submission and promise to behave. Probably, this informal method of dealing with defendants lingered on for a time as a part of the summary jurisdiction of the

---

Oyer and Terminer and General Gaol Delivery on Dec. 6, 1737 (*ibid.* 92).

[112] *An Ordinance for Establishing and Regulating Fees* 1710 (Broadside) 3.

[113] Cf. *infra* 736 *et seq.*

[114] For example, Henry Cordus, on being found guilty of adultery on Feb. 7, 1710/11, was fined £3 and fees of prosecution, and the court ordered that "upon performing this judgement he be discharged from his recognizance." On May 1, 1711,

Cordus and his surety were discharged from his recognizance for good behavior, evidently because the fine and fees had been paid (*Ms. Mins. NYCQS 1694–1731/32* 191, 199). Archibald Mott (*supra* n. 95) was on Sept. 3, 1713, fined £20 on a conviction on an indictment, and the court ordered "ye defendt continued upon his Recognizance untill he pay ye same," namely his fine and the court costs (*Ms. Mins. SCJ 1710–14* 471). Cf. King v. James Osborne (*infra* 723 n. 263).

justices, for we have noticed occasional examples,[115] and even one case as late as 1737 where in open Sessions a defendant bound over was given a discharge "on his promise that he will very well behave himself for the future."[116] Ordinarily, however, a bond was required, for once this procedure had become well seated, the justices rarely seem to have overlooked any occasion to demand surety. There are a great many cases where the defendant after conviction was bound over, but only occasionally is the alternative of imprisonment expressly set forth in the sentence.[117] Of course, a failure to post bond bore the implicit sanction of commitment; hence an impecunious or friendless defendant was inevitably headed for jail.

At common law, imprisonment was used primarily as a means of custody preliminary to trial, as temporary housing pending the infliction of a corporal punishment, or as a means of process to compel the payment of fine or the execution of a court order. During the Middle Ages an occasional statute would stipulate imprisonment as a direct form of punishment, but for the most part if a convicted defendant was incarcerated it was because he would not

[115] Volkert Briez on May 8, 1694, confessed on examination a contempt in destroying an execution directed to him as constable. On petition, the fine remitted upon promise to behave (*Ms. Kings Co. Ct. & Rd. Recs. 1692–1825* 25, 26). In 1703, John Lake, on examination, confessed to abusing and threatening a justice. On submission, discharged with costs and a promise to demean himself better in the future (*ibid.* 98). Isaac Springsteen, presented for false marking, said he did it by mistake so the court "thought fit to squash the indictment" (*Ms. Mins. Orange Co. Sess. 1703–08* Apr. 29, 1708).

[116] *Ms. Mins. NYCQS 1732–62* 34. Cf. King v. Conckling who "humbled himself" and was put on bond (*Ms. Mins. Westch. Co. Sess. 1710–23* June 3, 1718) and Solomon Jennings who misbehaved, the same (*ibid.* June 4, 1723).

[117] See, for example, Queen v. Onclebagg, ind. counterfeiting, submission to court, fined £20 and fees, committed until paid, surety for good behavior in £100 for a year (*Ms. Mins. NYCQS 1694–1731/32* 77, Feb. 3, 1702/03); Queen v. Flemming, ind. assault, breach of peace and abusing Mayor, confession of indictment, fined £5 and sureties for 12 months (*ibid.* 88, May 3, 1704); Queen v. Cornelia Burroughs *et al.*, inquisition of riot, 1706, fined and surety for one year (*Ms. Mins. SCJ 1704/05–1709* 86, 95); King v. Wood, presented, assault and wounding, 1726/27, confession of presentment, fined £9, committed until surety in £20 for good behavior for a year forthcoming (*Ms. Mins. SCJ 1723–27* 256); King v. Jane Allen, ind. assault on constable, confessed indictment, fined 40s. fees and surety for good behavior for

three months (*Ms. Mins. NYCQS 1694–1731/32* 523, May 6, 1730); King v. George and Mary Walker, ind. same offense, George convicted, fined £5 and surety for good behavior (*Ms. Mins. NYCQS 1732–62* 25, 30, May 2, Aug. 10, 1733); King v. Burger, ind. 1738, *nolo contendere*, fined 10s., surety of peace £10, discharged in three months (*Ms. Mins. SCJ 1732–39* 325, 327, 331); King v. Rayner, Reeves *et al.*, inf. riot, 1753, convicted, all fined and Reeves to give surety of good behavior for twelve months (*Ms. Mins. SCJ 1750–54* [Engr.] 249, 317); King v. Jones, ind. assault, 1758, confessed indictment, fined £5 and ordered committed for six months unless surety for good behavior for that period be found (*Ms. Mins. NYCQS 1732–62* 426, 429, Feb. 8, 9, 1758); King v. Dowers, ind. disorderly house, 1766, pleaded guilty, fined £5 and bound in £200 to good behavior for a year (*Ms. Mins. SCJ 1764–67* [Rough] 194).

An interesting case is King v. Douglas, ind. grand larceny, 1767, where the defendant was convicted, prayed his clergy, branded and required only to give a recognizance in £100 for a year (*Ms. Mins. SCJ 1764–67* [Rough] 211). In contrast, Bridget McEwen convicted in the same year of maintaining a disorderly house was given an hour in the stocks, and then discharged upon surety for good behavior for one year, otherwise to remain in jail during that time (*Ms. Mins. NYCQS 1760–72* 226, 233, Nov. 3, 5, 1767). In King v. Bishop *et al.*, inf. riot, 1767–68, a recognizance in £100 for five years was exacted (*Ms. Mins. SCJ 1764–67* [Rough] 145; *Ms. Mins. SCJ 1766–69* [Engr.] 94, 186–188, 253, 501, 503).

make fine or could not find sureties.[118] Largely owing to the influence of Star Chamber practice there is a quickened use of imprisonment as an independent sanction from the time of the Tudors onward;[119] yet in the early eighteenth century criminal law texts the conception of imprisonment as process still plays a more consequential role than imprisonment as punishment.

The status of imprisonment in New York is interesting, for the indications are that the process view was dominant. When a jail sentence was meted out it was most often ancillary, that is to say, it formed part of a complex sentence composed of fine, pillory or whipping and sometimes security after these punishments had been inflicted. In misdemeanor cases the range of judicial discretion was very considerable, but there was in New York City throughout the eighteenth century a strong predilection for corporal punishment. The cases on the permutations and combinations of punishment are interesting and so far as any rule can be extracted it appears that if a sentence was very severe corporal punishment no bond was exacted. Thus in 1727 David Wallace and David Willson were convicted of a cheat in passing counterfeit bills, and it was ordered "that on Dec. 12 . . . or, if foul weather, the next fair day thereafter the defendants shall stand in the pillory for one hour." They were then to be put in a cart and carted with a halter on their necks and be so placed as to be publicly seen. Wallace was then to get thirty-nine stripes and Willson twenty-eight. The sheriff of New York, having seen execution done, was to deliver them to the sheriff of Kings County, where they were to be imprisoned and pilloried an hour and Wallace was to get thirty-nine lashes, Willson twenty-eight. They were then to be delivered to the sheriff of Queens where the same punishment was to be meted out in Jamaica, and next they were to be sent to Westchester County for the same punishment. Then they were to be returned to New York where Wallace was to be imprisoned for six months and Willson for three months, whereupon they were both to be discharged upon payment of their fees.[120]

It may be that the expectation of Wallace and Willson surviving was so slight no bond was thought necessary. In other cases, however, where the corporal punishment was lighter, the court required recognizances for periods running as long as seven years. Thus, in 1755, James Gaines convicted for as-

---

[118] The subject has not been exhaustively studied, and the accounts in such works as Stephen, *Hist. of the Criminal Law*, are of no value. The statutes are conveniently listed in Dolsperg, *Entstehung der Freiheitsstrafe* (1928), but the discussion there is inconsequential.

[119] The effect of the establishment of houses of correction (on which cf. Leonard, *Early Hist. of Eng. Poor Relief* [1900] 113 et seq., 140 et seq.) was also profound.

[120] *Ms. Mins. SCJ 1723–27* 245, 268, 270; *Ms. Mins. SCJ 1727–32* 9–11, 24.

sault with intent to ravish an eight-year-old child was fined £10, given an hour in the pillory, six months in jail and, at the expiration of his sentence, was required to give a recognizance of good behavior for seven years.[121] Similarly, William Gilliland, convicted in 1767 of receiving and keeping a disorderly house, was sentenced to an hour in the pillory, twelve months' imprisonment and a bond of £100 for two years.[122] Nathaniel Cooley, found guilty in 1774 of "2 misdemeanors," attempted murder and attempting to fire the new jail, was ordered to be exposed for three hours in a cart, carted about the city, then to receive thirty-nine lashes and six months in jail and to be discharged only if he could find sureties for good behavior in the amount of £400.[123]

If it were possible to discover whether or not the defendants in cases like the one just cited had any real choice, we could be more certain whether or not the sentencing judge was merely giving the prisoner a disguised "stretch" of a good deal more than six months, for the security demanded was very substantial.[124] There was actually nothing to deter a court from imposing sentences of long imprisonment, but this was not the custom even when a recognizance was not part of the sentence, or when imprisonment alone was ordered.[125] It is chiefly for this reason, and despite the fact that the court would order a convicted defendant to be committed until all parts of the sentence were performed, that we are reluctant to believe the final recognizance of good behavior to have been a subterfuge to lengthen punishment. This use of the device seems rather to have been an attempt to provide something like a parole for those who enjoyed enough standing to supply the necessary sureties.

[121] Ms. Mins. SCJ 1754–57 (Engr.) 112, 115, 116, 200. The recognizance was filed on Oct. 27, 1755. Compare this sentence with that of John Bastarr convicted of attempted buggery—one hour in pillory, three months' imprisonment and recognizance for seven years (Ms. Mins. NYCQS 1760–72 295, 297, Nov. 8, 9, 1769).

[122] Ms. Mins. SCJ 1766–69 (Engr.) 317–324; compare King v. Carroe, disorderly house, 1767, fined £100, twelve months' imprisonment, recognizance in £200 with two sureties in £100 for two years (Ms. Mins. SCJ 1764–67 [Rough] 280; Ms. Mins. SCJ 1766–69 [Engr.] 316, 324).

[123] Ms. Mins. NYCQS 1772–91 91, 95, May 1, 6, 1774.

[124] In a few cases, the order of the court is phrased to indicate that protracted imprisonment was intended, as e.g., Queen v. Booby Dezere (1710) who was fined £8 and ". . . be imprisoned for one year and find sureties of his good behavior for two years and be kept a close prisoner till all is performed" (Ms. Mins. SCJ 1710–14 290, 292, 294).

[125] King v. Marks, selling bad meat, fine £3, jail three months (Ms. Mins. NYCQS 1694–1731/32 63–66, May 7, Aug. 5, 1701); Queen v. John Collison et al., riot, 1705, jail six months (Ms. Mins. SCJ 1704/05–1709 48); Queen v. Sydenham, forcible entry, fine £10, jail three months (Ms. Mins. NYCQS 1694–1731/32 146, May 5, 1708); Queen v. Green et al., entertaining negroes, jail eight days (ibid. 178, 186, May 2, Nov. 7, 1710); King v. Mosier, affronting justices, 1717, jail one week (Ms. Mins. Cir. 1721–49 44, 47); King v. McCarty, cheat, pillory fifteen minutes, jail one day (Ms. Mins. NYCQS 1732–62 59, 60, Feb. 3, 4, 1735/36); King v. Jones, grand larceny, 1764, clergy granted, branded, jail two months (Ms. Mins. SCJ 1762–64 [Engr.] 418–421, 428); King v. Lindsay, petit larceny, 1766, jail eight days (H.R. Pleadings Pl. K. 1071); King v. Margaret Erwin, petit larceny, 1771, jail one month (Ms. Mins. SCJ 1769–72 [Engr.] 438, 442, 448); King v. Keating, assault with intent to murder, 1771, guilty of assault only, jail two weeks (ibid. 352–362).

This quasi-parole use of recognizances was a logical extension of the powers respecting sureties for good behavior for persons of ill fame. The discretion vested in the justices was so considerable, where no specific charge was lodged against a suspected person, that it required no great searching of conscience to exert this discretion after a conviction since, in any event, the content of the court's powers in sentencing for misdemeanors was not clearly defined in the eighteenth century.

A much bolder use of the recognizance was in cases where proceedings against a defendant had at some stage failed, and the courts deemed it prudent to keep a finger upon him. This practice began at an early date. In 1698 when John Fisher was acquitted of a murder but convicted of "homicide by misadventure,"[126] he was compelled to enter into a recognizance in the amount of £100 for his good behavior for one year. The next case went considerably further. In 1703, Hannah Crosier was arraigned on three indictments for felony in stealing certain goods. She was acquitted absolutely, but the court on the following day ordered her discharge upon payment of fees and surety in £20 for good behavior for one year. That the court was not satisfied with the verdict is suggested by an order to the sheriff to restore the goods found in Hannah's possession to the proper owners.[127] There were a few cases in English reports which sanctioned the recognizance under these circumstances,[128] but we do not know if the court was aware of them. Throughout the remainder of the colonial period there can be found occasional orders for recognizances after acquittal.[129]

---

[126] Mins. SCJ 1693–1701 132–137. In English law forfeiture might be incurred in cases of this sort, depending on the terms of acquittal; cf. 1 Hale, Pleas of the Crown 492.

[127] Ms. Mins. SCJ 1701–04 74, 84, 88, 99. On Oct. 11, 1703, the defendant was given until the next term to appear on her recognizance. We also note that on Sept. 5, 1704, the Attorney General prayed that the defendant be called on her recognizance, and when she failed to appear, the court ordered that her recognizance be estreated (ibid. 118, 147).

[128] Cro. Jac. 507; Cro. Car. 292.

[129] An indictment for murder against Aaron Praal, Jr., was found ignoramus but was again recommended to the grand jury, whereupon an indictment for manslaughter was found, and Praal was tried but found not guilty. However, he was ordered to give in a recognizance in £100, with two sureties in £50 each, to be of his good behavior and keep the peace for a year and appear at the next Court of Oyer and Terminer and General Gaol Delivery in Richmond County. In this case, when the indictment for murder was found ignoramus, the coroner was indicted for a "breach of his office," and it may be a fair assumption that Praal had some influence in order to get off not only on the murder indictment but also on the one for manslaughter. The court may have felt that the petit jury's verdict on the latter charge was against the weight of the evidence and accordingly bound Praal in his good behavior (Richmond Oyer and Terminer and General Gaol Delivery, Apr. 24, 25, 27, 29, 1724, Ms. Mins. Cir. 1721–49 39–41).

Rachell Van Anthon, found not guilty on an indictment for murdering her bastard, was nevertheless ordered to give in a recognizance in £200, with two sureties in £100 each, to be of her good behavior for twelve months especially to all who gave evidence against her at her trial (Ulster Oyer and Terminer and General Gaol Delivery, Sept. 13, 14, 15, 1716, Ms. Mins. Cir. 1716–17 25, 26, 28–30).

Hartman Hine, found not guilty on an indictment for being an accessory to negro Jack in stealing a "skapple of wheat," was, despite his acquittal,

The provincial courts having elected to require sureties after a verdict of not guilty, no obstacles presented themselves in cases where the grand jury refused to indict, or where a proceeding failed because no prosecutor appeared and a discharge by proclamation was consequently necessary. We have found only a few examples of this practice but it is possible it was more freely used at Sessions than the records indicate.

Administrative Aspects

Since the recognizance played so considerable a role in colonial procedure and since in the gross a large amount of money was annually pledged, the mechanics of administration deserve some attention.

It should be noted in the first place that the recognizance was invariably in a sum certain and that as a rule defendants were bound with two sureties, a practice which probably stemmed from the recommendations of the manuals.[130] In the case of recognizances to give evidence, an undertaking of the witness alone was regarded as adequate, but it was exceptional to take a recognizance from a defendant alone without sureties.[131] In the case of slaves, the courts regarded an undertaking from the master to be sufficient,[132] and in one early case a husband was accepted as surety for his wife.[133] Apart from the sug-

---

ordered to give a recognizance in £30, with two sureties in £15 each, for his good behavior for a year. It should be noted that in this case the principal had been found guilty (Ulster Oyer and Terminer and General Gaol Delivery, Sept. 5–8, 1722, *Ms. Mins. Cir. 1721–49* 18–21).

Thomas Baxter, Jr., found not guilty on an indictment for felony, was ordered to give a recognizance in £20, with one surety in £10, to be of his good behavior and keep the peace for a year (Westchester Oyer and Terminer and General Gaol Delivery, Mar. 25, 26, 1724, *ibid.* 37–39). Cf. also King v. Sam Rose (*supra* 277).

In 1732 three defendants acquitted of larceny were put on recognizance (*Ms. Mins. NYCQS 1732–62* 4). In King v. James and Mary Burn (1765), the defendants were acquitted of grand larceny but one was obliged to give surety; the other had to answer another indictment (*Ms. Mins. SCJ 1764–67* [Rough] 41, 43); King v. Miller (*Ms. Mins. Cir. 1716–17* 3). In King v. McLean (*Ms. Mins. SCJ 1762–64* [Engr.] 222, 296), no prosecutor appeared but defendant had to give bond in £100 for ten years.

130 Thus Dalton, *Countrey Justice* (1677) c.120. It should be noted that on this point the rules about bail probably led to similar practices in the case of surety for the peace and other types of recognizance. On bail, cf. 2 Hale, *Pleas of the Crown* 125.

131 Cf. King v. Jacob Adams (*Ms. Mins. NYCQS 1694–1731/32* 48, 49, Aug. 1, 2, 1699). It is possible the personal recognizance was sometimes used in the country but the minute entries are usually too brief to justify inference one way or the other.

132 For example, King v. Quick and Butler, 1725 (*Ms. Mins. SCJ 1723–27* 164); King v. John Brown and Aeneas, 1771 (*Ms. Mins. SCJ 1769–72* 448). Cf. King v. Harry (*Ms. Mins. Dutchess Co. Sess.* Liber B, Oct. 15, 1751); a bond was taken from the master. But earlier, in King v. Quacko (*ibid.* Liber A, June 6, 1735) a mere promise to transport. In an Ulster bastardy case, the master promised to support if the girl was unable to, Meeting May 12, 1722 (*Ms. Files Ulster Co.* Bundle C). At a justices' Meeting in Dutchess, Oct. 4, 1751, a promise to transport is accepted (*Ms. Files Dutchess Co. 1755*).

An early example of a master's recognizance for the appearance of his slave: "Andries Moerschalk . . . recognizes to our sovereign Lady the Queen in fifty pounds . . . that his negro man slave called Diego shall be forthcoming when required to answer for murder or any other crime for which he may be accused within a year and a day from and after ye date hereof cognivit the 13 day of June 1712" (*NY Misc. Mss.* Box 4 no. 7).

133 King v. Hesther Blanck, 1697 (*Mins. SCJ 1693–1701* 113).

gestive effects of the advice in textbooks, there were practical reasons why mere personal recognizance was not regarded as adequate. In theory, the system depended upon an inexorable proceeding in case of default, and it was consequently essential that the obligation of suretyship be spread to assure collection from some source, and further that the recognitors be sufficient persons. In the country districts a certain temptation to be lax in the selection of sureties must have existed although some control was present in and by the periodic and purgative appearance of a Supreme Court justice on circuit. We have noted only one case where a country justice appears to have been deliberately indiscreet in his selection of recognitors in a riot case, for Mr. Justice Horsmanden wrote complaining[134]

> that you have taken the offenders securities the one for the other for their appearance at your next court of Quarter Sessions. The circumstances attending this riot appear very bad and you ought not to have taken the offenders themselves as securities . . . the Attorney General intends to prosecute the offenders in the Supreme Court according to their deserts . . . therefore cause the offenders to be bound with good security . . . in such sums as adequate to the enormity of the offense.

We have found nothing to indicate that sureties were carefully examined before an undertaking was accepted, for the anxieties of the central officials seem to have been directed chiefly toward insuring that the recognizances were properly filed. Since the justices of the peace were empowered to take security in all manner of cases out of Sessions, it was an essential step to assure the eventual collection of bonds in default that they be delivered over at the next ensuing Court of Sessions. Accordingly it was usual after the opening of Sessions to have proclamation made for "all justices &c. who have taken any recognizances, &c. to bring the recognizances thereof into court &c."[135] These would then be filed by the officer who had taken them[136] and the necessary entry be made.[137] Similarly, in Supreme Court the bonds were supposed to be delivered

---

[134] *Misc. Mss. Dutchess Co. 1752–1870.*

[135] *Ms. Mins. NYCQS 1705/06–1714/15* (Rough) 1, Feb. 7, 1705/06. Also see the order of Feb. 4, 1706/07: "Proclamation made for all Justices of Peace, Coroners or those that have any Inquisitions or Recognizances whereby they have lett any persons to Bail or taken any Examinations or Other things since the last sessions to put in the Records thereof into Court that the Queen's Justices may proceed thereon . . . Proclamation made (Vizt) all manner of persons that are bound over by Recognizance to prosecute and prefer any Bill of

Indictment against any prisoners . . . lett them come forth and prosecute or . . . forfeit their Recognizances" (*Ms. Mins. NYCQS 1694–1731/32* 121, 122). Cf. also the entry of May 5, 1772 (*Ms. Mins. NYCQS 1772–91* 1).

[136] See, for example, for Sessions, *Ms. Mins. Ulster Co. 1737–50* entries of May 6, 1740, Sept. 16, 1746, Sept. 20, 1748; for Circuit, *Ms. Mins. Cir. 1721–49* 78, 124; for the Supreme Court, *Ms. Mins. SCJ 1754–57* (Engr.) 199, 343.

[137] Obviously the entry did not mean an entry in the minute book but upon a special roll or in a

at the beginning of a term in order that proper action could be taken upon them,[138] and if any recognizances were outstanding the court might order certification by the official in whose hands it might be.[139] We think it probable that special files of recognizances were kept,[140] and we have direct evidence that at least one peace officer kept a book in which he entered them.[141]

According to an old rule the obligation was a matter of record as soon as taken and acknowledged, although not "made up" by the justice and only entered in his book.[142] This rule was obviously one to benefit the Crown where the Sessions records were faulty, and it was not calculated to correct the carelessness of clerks of the peace. We do not find that the requirements which had been laid down respecting recognizances under the Statutes Staple—that enrollment was essential to the validity of the recognizance—were carried over to criminal practice, certainly not in New York. The complaints against Peter Fauconnier that he had burned recognizances for customs duties[143] and the later charges against local officers for withholding estreats[144] indicate clearly an unremedied gap on the record side of recognizance administration.

Although the provincial authorities did not develop a means of checking outstanding recognizances by requiring meticulous registration, and naïvely persisted in trusting the justices to deliver the bonds in court, a very practical check existed in the form of the recognitors or persons bound. If the conditions of the bond were fulfilled they would expect its discharge and be certain not to incur the risk of a forfeiture.[145] It was in their interest consequently to keep a wary eye upon the peregrinations of the instrument by which they were

special docket, for there were an infinitely greater number of recognizances than are accounted for in the minute entries.

138 Cf. *Ms. Mins. SCJ 1750–56* (Rough) 4: "All justices of the peace, Coroners and others who have taken any Inqui: or Recognizances whereby they have let any person to Bail or done other things Let them put the records thereof in the Court that the King's Justices may proceed thereon."

139 *Ms. Mins. SCJ 1727–32* 158.

140 There are a great many still in the files of Dutchess and Ulster counties. Nearly all have the date of filing and only occasionally is the disposition endorsed on them. As the document was needed at Sessions it seems unlikely that the clerk would constantly riffle through the considerable mass of other court papers to find them. Scores of Ulster recognizances are bundled and tied without any other papers, a fact that suggests they originally were kept thus as the other papers are thoroughly scrambled. Cf. here Kempe's letter to Justice Haring. Justice David Smith had caused recognizances

to be delivered to Justice Abraham Haring in open court at Orange Sessions but "Having refused to permit them to be filed or any entry to be made of them whereby the persons so bound over were not called to appear" (*J. T. Kempe Lawsuits* G–J). Cf. also the unsigned statement in *H.R. Pleadings* Pl. K. 439 respecting a search in City Clerk Van Cortlandt's office.

141 In King v. Christopher, Alderman Filkin refused to discharge a recognizance to keep the peace after the disputants had composed the quarrel "because he had put it into his book but directed him [the complainant] to get Mr. Cortland the Town Clerk and settle with him" (*J. T. Kempe Lawsuits* C–F [*sub nom.* Christopher], L–O [*sub nom.* Lardner]). The only minute entry is in *Ms. Mins. NYCQS 1760–72* 295, Nov. 1769.

142 Brooke, *Abridgment* Record 58.

143 5 *Doc. Rel. Col. Hist. NY* 406.

144 *Supra* 175, *infra* 527.

145 Cf. the letter of Terboss to Kempe, Jan. 9, 1770 (*J. T. Kempe Letters* A–Z).

bound to the Crown.[146] Except for deliberate default, great care was normally exercised. Unusual is the experience of the three trusting yokels Mott, Teneick and Crum, who assumed too readily they had fulfilled the obligation of their recognizance by appearing at the first day of the court to which they had been bound over:

> Whereas we the Subscribers Were Laid Under Recognizance for B[r]eaking the peace: to Appear at the Last Supream Court held in . . . Orange Accordingly we Appeared & Answered to the first Call and Did Abide there till near the Breaking up of Court and None of Our Accusers Appeard . . . we through ygnorance Supposed We Were Dischard . . . we took advice of one who . . . advised us to go home: & if we would give him one Bowl of Grog he Would pay all Costs & Damages that we might Thereafter Sustain . . . Since we have been ynformed that we have forfited our Recognizance. . . .[147]

Although the chief concern of a person under recognizance was to observe the conditions, whether these were to appear in court, be of good behavior or the like, his second concern was to be rid of the obligation. It is impossible to discover from the minutes how frequently discharge was forced by defendants. Sometimes an entry is to the effect that "no cause appearing to the contrary"[148] discharge is ordered—suggesting a motion by the defendant. And occasionally we find explicit reference to a motion that the person at whose instance a defendant was bound show cause why the defendant should not be released.[149] A defendant could come to an agreement with a complainant[150] and secure discharge or he could sometimes wheedle the Attorney General into accepting a promise to appear in lieu of an existing bond.[151] Of course, in the cases where no prosecutor appeared the court would without motion order discharge.[152]

It was always possible to discharge recognizance by submitting to confinement, and we have seen cases where sacrificing defendants actually appeared

---

[146] There is a sardonic letter of John Taylor to Kempe (Jan. 26, 1773) telling of his experience with Alderman Gautier who promised to "fix" a default. Taylor, in his innocence, seems to have overlooked the necessary *douceur* and discovered too late a forfeiture had been entered (*J. T. Kempe Letters* A–Z).

[147] *Misc. Mss. Orange Co.*

[148] As in King v. Dunbar (*Ms. Mins. SCJ 1732–39* 167).

[149] Cf. King v. Fairley (*Ms. Mins. NYCQS 1694–1731/32* 47, Aug. 1, 1699); King v. Sophia a slave (1751), where the motion was made by attorney for the surety (*Ms. Mins. SCJ 1750–54* [Engr.] 82, 123, 127). There are many cases, as where defend-

ants were bound over to answer a grand jury, when they were discharged if no bill was found, but it is not apparent from the records whether or not this was done on the defendants' motion.

[150] King v. McKintosh (*Ms. Mins. NYCQS 1732–62* 249, 251–258, 264, 270, Feb. 9, 1748/49, May 3, Aug. 3, Nov. 10, 1749, Feb. 8, 1749/50).

[151] King v. John Bush, 1751 (*Ms. Mins. SCJ 1750–56* [Rough] 63).

[152] There are a great many of these cases. The discharge would be effective after proclamation; cf. Queen v. Brooke, 1713 (*Ms. Mins. SCJ 1710–14* 501); King v. De Groeff (*Ms. Mins. NYCQS 1732–62* 41, May 9, 1734).

and surrendered themselves in discharge of their bail.[153] More frequent, however, was the situation to which we have already adverted, where the sureties would seek to discharge their obligation by surrendering a defendant. The usual proceeding was simply to produce the defendant and request discharge,[154] the English procedure by habeas corpus having been used only in the case of *King* v. *Cunningham* referred to above.

It should be observed that although the principal and sureties were privileged to attempt discharge, the courts exercised an utter discretion which seems to have been limited only by a rule that when a recognizance was continued the sureties had the option to refuse to continue.[155] In the matter of defaults judicial discretion was equally unlimited, but it was not often exercised in favor of defendants. The justices' manuals[156] state that a recognizance might be respited on account of illness, and in 1714 King's Bench asserted its discretion in the matter of defaults in broad terms; but defendants had no right to respite.[157] Since the bond was the foundation of an ultimate fiscal right of the Crown, a strict fulfillment of the conditions of the obligation was the governing rule. It was not until 1764 that by Act of Parliament a procedure became available by petition in case of default due to inattention or ignorance.[158]

In New York Province, although there are not many cases, recognizances were sometimes respited because of illness,[159] storms,[160] absence on business[161] or military service.[162] During the first half of the eighteenth century, moreover, there are instances where the court saw fit to order respite when no ex-

---

[153] King v. David Jones (*Ms. Mins. NYCQS 1760–72* 217, Aug. 6, 1767); King v. Hull (*Ms. Mins. Albany Co. Sess. 1763–82* Oct. 4, 1769).

[154] In addition to the cases cited above, cf. King v. Wood (*Ms. Mins. NYCQS 1732–62* 28, Aug. 7, 1732); King v. Doran (*ibid.* 352, Aug. 8, 1771); King v. Mays (*Ms. Mins. NYCQS 1772–91* 28, Nov. 6, 1772); King v. Abner Collard (*Ms. Mins. Westch. Co. Sess. 1710–23* Dec. 6, 1720).

[155] King v. Van Tassel (*infra* 541).

[156] Sheppard, *Office of a Justice of the Peace* (1662) 84; cf. Dalton, *Countrey Justice* (1666) 210.

[157] Rex v. Tomb (10 *Modern* 278).

[158] 4 Geo. III c.10; *Crown Circuit Companion* (1768) 61 for the procedure.

[159] Queen v. Day (*Ms. Mins. NYCQS 1694–1731/32* 170, Feb. 8, 1709/10); Queen v. John Reade (*ibid.* 248, Aug. 5, 1712); King v. Daniel Vaughan (*Ms. Mins. NYCQS 1732–62* 92, Nov. 7, 1738); King v. Ellinor Wallace (*ibid.* 106, Nov. 6, 1739); King v. Coopman (*ibid.* 439, Aug. 1, 1758). In King v. Lent and Higby, the principals did not appear. On motion of Ludlow suggesting they had not had smallpox, although they were in town the court dispensed with appearance (*Ms.*

Mins. SCJ 1764–67 [Rough] 37). Caleb Miller respited for illness (*Ms. Mins. Orange Co. Sess. 1727–79* Apr. 25, 1727); Mary Willson because she was "in Travel" (*Ms. Mins. Queens Co. Sess. 1722–87* May 21, 1734).

[160] Queen v. Godfrey (*Ms. Mins. NYCQS 1694–1731/32* 88, May 3, 1704); King v. Osburn (*Ms. Mins. NYCQS 1732–62* 70, Nov. 4, 1736).

All recognizances respited at Dutchess Sessions Jan. 1, 1765, because of the snows (*Ms. Mins. Dutchess Co. Sess.* Liber C).

[161] Such as "being at sea" or in "pursuit of a felon."

[162] King v. John Westcomb (*Ms. Mins. NYCQS 1694–1731/32* 353, Nov. 4, 1718); King v. Barnes (*ibid.* 531–538, Feb. 2, 1730/31, May 4, 7, Aug. 3, 4, 1731); King v. Lawrence Sweine (*Ms. Mins. NYCQS 1732–62* 376–383, Nov. 4, 5, 1755, Feb. 3, 4, 1756); King v. Hanson (*Ms. Mins. NYCQS 1760–72* 298, Nov. 9, 1769); King v. Gilbert Smith (*ibid.* 320, Aug. 9, 1770); King v. John Kip (*ibid.* 365, Nov. 8, 1771); King v. Richard Williams (*Ms. Mins. Suffolk Co. Sess. 1723–51* Oct. 7, 1740); and the cases in *Ms. Mins. Dutchess Co. Sess.* Liber C, Oct. 20, 1760.

cuse at all was offered.[163] Frequently the court minutes in this period show a failure to appear, yet no default entered or even any further order; and sometimes a belated appearance at a session was treated as curing a default.[164] One gains the impression, especially from country minutes where the recognizance entries are sometimes sketchy, that a rather relaxed attitude prevailed.

In some counties the justices in General Sessions would upon default threaten estreat or forfeiture *nisi causa* but they seem to have been ready to hear and accept excuses, and there are actually very few cases before 1760 where an outright order of forfeiture was made.[165] There is some slight indication that discharges were sometimes handled at meetings of the justices or by the clerk of the peace, although this was certainly irregular.[166]

After 1760, judicial leniency disappears and it becomes usual upon default to order the recognizance forfeited. This tightening in practice may be attributed to the efforts of the Attorney General to put the administration of recognizances on a sounder footing. Governor Moore reported this fact in 1767 but added mournfully that "little advantage has been gained for the crown."[167] Nevertheless the minutes and estreats reflect the tightening up of administration and we shall see in a moment how this was accomplished.

Forfeiture and Collection

Recognizances could be forfeited in a variety of ways depending upon the condition of the obligation, as by failure to appear in court to answer or to give evidence, or in the case of recognizances for peace or good behavior, by misconduct. In the case of appearance the formality of proclamation was observed as a sort of fortification of the notice explicit in the terms of the bond.[168]

[163] King v. Ann Wilson (*Ms. Mins. NYCQS 1683/84–1694* 163, Aug. 1, 1693); King v. Petrus Brass (*Ms. Mins. NYCQS 1694–1731/32* 430–432, Feb. 4, 5, 1723/24); King v. Harris (*ibid.* 436–437, May 5, 6, 1724); King v. Daley, 1725 (*Ms. Mins. SCJ 1723–27* 147); King v. Sanders and Atkins, 1725 (*ibid.* 146); King v. Maynard (*Ms. Mins. NYCQS 1694–1731/32* 504, 506, Feb. 4, 5, 1728/29).

[164] As in King v. Peters (*ibid.* 438, 442, May 6, Aug. 4, 1724).

[165] *Ms. Mins. Dutchess Co. Sess.* Liber A: Francis Turner (estreat) Oct. 19, 1736; Lester *et ux.* (estreat) May 20, 1746. *Ibid.* Liber B: Peter Palmateer (estreat) May 15, 1758. *Ms. Mins. Orange Co. Sess. 1727–79:* Hern. Francisco (estreat) Apr. 30, 1751; Alex. Smith and others (rule *nisi*) Oct. 29, 1751. *Ms. Mins. Queens Co. Sess. 1722–87:* Sylvanus Wright (estreat) May 16, 1732. *Ms. Mins.*

Suffolk Co. Sess. 1723–51: Jonathan Titus (rule *nisi*) Sept. 30, 1729; Joseph Tooker (rule *nisi*) Oct. 4, 1737; Anthony Tooker (rule *nisi*) Mar. 29, 1743; Thomas Reed (rule *nisi*) Oct. 2, 1744. *Ms. Mins. Westch. Co. Sess. 1710–23:* Elias Conckling (rule *nisi*) June 3, 1718.

[166] John Machouria discharged at a meeting, Dec. 20, 1727, because he was leaving the county (*Ms. Files Ulster Co.* Bundle O). The recognizance of one Housecker (1755), discharged by the clerk at the instance of the sureties because he was dead (*Ms. Files Dutchess Co. 1755*).

[167] 7 *Doc. Rel. Col. Hist. NY* 906.

[168] The entries are legion. Cf. the entry in the case of Charles Priest, bound over to testify (*Ms. Mins. NYCQS 1694–1731/32* 262, Aug. 5, 1713); John and Nicholas Daley (*Ms. Mins. SCJ 1723–27* 147); Samuel Boyack and Stephen Bayard (*Ms. Mins. NYCQS 1732–62* 129, May 5, 1741); David

We have seen that unless the court granted a respite, defaults would be made a matter of record and the obligation ordered forfeit. This last order was essential to found the next necessary step, the estreat of the recognizance from inferior courts to the Supreme Court as a court of Exchequer, and upon estreat the debt to the Crown became absolute.[169] The process of estreating was to enter upon a roll an extract or summary of the recognizance, the fact of breach and the amount due. The mechanics of estreat in New York were seemingly a simplification of methods prevailing in England[170] with certain variations made necessary by institutional differences, for the whole administrative apparatus of the Exchequer was lacking in the Province.

The question of a "constant court of Exchequer" was raised in 1693 and the Council ordered Pinhorne, Nicoll and Graham to report. They replied that to set up such a constant court would not be serviceable to the Crown "nor in any ways advantageous to their Revenue." They were of the opinion that as a receiver and a surveyor general were appointed in the Province and as the Supreme Court had Exchequer powers this was sufficient.[171] This establishment was of course not the equivalent of the English, for there was wanting any articulation of the several agencies. Completely lacking were any systematic regulation and supervision of sheriffs' collections. This may have seemed very unimportant in 1693 when the Province was thinly populated. Nevertheless it is worth noticing that not a single forfeiture (an expression which included fine) appears in Receiver General Chidley Brooke's account for the Michaelmas quarter, 1696,[172] although the judicial records offer evidence to the contrary. The précis of the Ulster General Sessions records 1693–1763, prepared in 1763, indicates that the sheriff was responsible for issues and forfeitures and that it was not known whether the money was collected or what happened to it.[173] Obviously the colonial system was not "advantageous" to his Majesty's revenue.

We have already noticed that in the first half of the eighteenth century recognizances were occasionally ordered forfeit at country Sessions and we will consider in a moment various cases where bonds were put in suit. The

Navorro (*Ms. Mins. NYCQS 1732–62* 370, Aug. 5, 1755); James Hagan (*Ms. Mins. NYCQS 1760–72* 365, Nov. 8, 1771). The principal and sureties could be called only on the day on which they were bound to appear. Notice was required if called on another day (King v. Adams, *Cases Temp. Hardwicke* 237).
[169] Petersdorff, *Practical Treatise on the Law of Bail* (1824) 536.
[170] On the English procedure, cf. the forms in

Stubbs, *Crown Circuit Companion* (1768 ed.) 52 *et seq.* For an account of the mechanics, Gilbert, *Treatise on the Court of Exchequer* (1758) 83 *et seq.*; Hands, *Solicitor's Practice on the Crown Side of King's Bench* 80 *et seq.* It should be noted that the whole matter was overhauled in 22 & 23 Car. II c.22.
[171] 37 NY Col. Mss. 79.
[172] 41 ibid. 9.
[173] NY State Lib. Mss. 7460.

impression we have gathered from the records, however, is that prior to 1760 the proceedings against forfeited recognizances were haphazard, and this was due as well to the lack of coordination between the fiscal agencies and the courts as to the circumstance that of the available Crown officers who might have assumed responsibility no one in fact did so. In a letter addressed to General Monckton July 20, 1763, William Smith Jr. urged the necessity of an independent "Court of Exchequer," but it is apparent he had in mind not only the judicial but some of the administrative apparatus of Exchequer. Smith wrote: "For want of a Court of Exchequer all the fines imposed from the first settlement of the Colony and many forfeitures have been lost. No estreat of the fines was ever yet made from any of the courts. The Sheriffs generally, and the justices in the country sometimes have received them; and no account has been rendered to the Crown."[174]

Smith's statement is not correct, for some of the fines were collected and there are in fact some cases where recognizances taken in the country were put in suit in the Supreme Court. There is, however, no question but that indifference and irregularities prevailed, and the Attorneys General who should have paid some attention to the matter had not actively bestirred themselves. Under the very nose of Richard Bradley and his successor, William Kempe, the New York City Quarter Sessions Court was ordering the clerk of Sessions to put forfeited bonds in suit[175] and although the implication of this was that the Crown would not receive the issues, no effort was made to interfere.

A proceeding of this sort would have been unlawful in England where by statute 22 and 23 Car. II c.22 severe penalty had been placed upon collection of fines, amercements or recognizances except via process of Exchequer. It should be noticed, however, that a passage in Lambard's *Eirenarcha,*[175a] dutifully repeated in Dalton's *Office of Sheriffs,*[176] apparently condoned direct collection for satisfying the emoluments of justices of the peace. Authorities

---

[174] *Aspinwall Papers,* 9 *Colls. Mass. Hist. Soc.* (4 ser.) 477. And note also Smith's repeated references to the "indolence" of the Receiver General. Monckton left New York before this letter was written. In 1766 Governor Moore recommended a Court of Exchequer with four sessions per annum (7 *Doc. Rel. Col. Hist. NY* 827).

[175] In 1748 James Donnelly, indicted for beating the watch, did not appear. Judgment for want of a plea was entered and he was fined £6 and costs. The court then ordered the deputy clerk "has full liberty to put the recognizance in suit for the recovery of the same" (*Ms. Mins. NYCQS 1732–62* 240, 241, 244, 248, 251, 252, 268–270, Nov. 3, 1748, Feb. 7, 9, May 3, 1749, Feb. 6, 7, 1749/50).

On May 3, 1749, in the case of Edward Menzie, a similar order was made (*ibid.* 252, 264). Again in 1755 an order to put in suit the recognizance of Edward McGuire was made (*ibid.* 363, Feb. 6, 1755). On the same day an order to "put in suit" the recognizance of John Lewis was made (*ibid.* 347–348, 350, 354–355, 360–363, May 7, 8, Aug. 6, Nov. 5, 6, 1754, Feb. 4, 5, 6, 1755). The latest case occurred in 1759 when the recognizance of Mordecai Rietto was ordered to be put in suit (King v. John Cross, *ibid.* 448, Feb. 6, 1759). The recognizance in this last case is in *J. T. Kempe Lawsuits* C–F *sub nom.* John Cross.

[175a] Lambard, *Eirenarcha* Bk. 4 c.16.
[176] Dalton, *Office of Sheriffs* (1700) 328.

with such an attitude were undoubtedly more respected than the purport of an act which did not extend to the plantations. In the end, however, it was the trespasses of the New York Quarter Sessions which led to radical changes in the administration of forfeited recognizances, and it should be pointed out that the reforms were undertaken by John Tabor Kempe three years before the letter of William Smith Jr. was written.

The budding practice in the New York City Quarter Sessions was nipped in 1760. A bond to keep the peace had been ordered forfeit in the New York Quarter Sessions and the court ordered the Deputy Clerk, Augustus Van Cortlandt, to put the recognizance in suit. Kempe got wind of this order and on September 20, 1760, wrote to Van Cortlandt a peremptory letter: "Mr. Cortright's Recognizance being forfeited the penalty becomes the right of the Crown. It is my Duty to see that the King is not injured and must therefore insist that the Recognizance be put into my Hands for his Majesty's Interest."[177] The Deputy Clerk apparently did not comply with this request and the Attorney General then resorted to the expedient of removal by certiorari.[178] The case turned out to be important because a determined effort was made to have the Supreme Court accept an alleged practice at Westminster of granting a *quietus* when a default was due to ignorance or carelessness, a matter which will be discussed below.[179] We have noticed no further efforts of New York City Quarter Sessions to interfere and we consequently regard this first move to have been more or less conclusive.[180]

The next stage in the reformation of administration was an addition in 1763 to the rules of the Supreme Court:[181]

Whereas the Issues, Fines, Forfeitures and Amerciaments that have been due and answerable to our Sovereign Lord the King . . . ariseing in the Courts . . . and before Justices of the Peace by and before whom such Issues, fines, Penalties, forfeitures and Amerciaments have happened grown or been forfeited . . . have heretofore not been duly levied or if levied have not been accounted for to the Crown as Directed by Law, For Remedy whereof It is ordered by this Court that the [clerks of all the courts] . . . do on the first day of October Term . . . deliver into their Supreme Court as a Court of Exchequer

---

177 *J. T. Kempe Letters* A–Z.

178 In 1759, Cornelius and Lawrence Kortright, bound to the peace, failed to appear, and on Feb. 8 the Court of Quarter Sessions ordered the recognizance put in suit. On Nov. 4, 1760, the Attorney General produced a certiorari ordering the case moved to the Supreme Court (*Ms. Mins. NYCQS 1732–62* 448–450, 488).

179 *Infra* 548 *et seq.*

180 Typical is the entry in the case of Margaret Dennison, "ordered . . . default be Entered and that their said Recognizance be delivered into the Supreme Court in order that the Same may be put in suit by the Attorney General" (*Ms. Mins. NYCQS 1760–72* 284, May 4, 1769).

181 *Ms. Mins. SCJ 1762–64* (Engr.) 225–227.

upon Oath a true Estreat of all the said Issues, fines, Penalties, forfeitures and Amerciamants . . . due . . . the King . . . with the manner how . . . [such issues, etc.] became due . . . also of the time when and the Nature of the Writ Suit or Process . . . and betwixt what parties . . . with the names of the Persons . . . answerable for the same as well in the King's suit as in the Suit of the Party that such further proceedings may be had thereon as to the Justices of the said Court of Exchequer shall appear to be according to Law.

It cannot be doubted that the new rule was sufficiently published, for the court went to the pains of having the rule printed and circulated by the secretary of the Province.[182] What up to this time had been the process of collection in the country is extremely obscure. If the bond was in a small enough amount the local clerks could keep the whole business in the county by proceeding in the Court of Common Pleas. We have seen a *scire facias* brought by Livingston, the Ulster clerk, in 1724,[183] and years later his kinsman in Dutchess reported that he had found a writ brought by John Crooke (clerk in Ulster) on a forfeited recognizance.[184] Such proceedings were probably rare, for as we have said the orders of forfeiture are precious few. Nevertheless, in Dutchess County certain justices of the peace on May 15, 1764, caused a number of recognizances to be put in suit at the Dutchess Sessions and made no estreat thereof to the Supreme Court.[185] The obduracy of the Dutchess men did not cease here, for presentment was made in Sessions by the grand jury against Justice William Humphrey for taking five recognizances and not returning them into the Court of Sessions "which we conceive it was his duty to do. We therefore present him guilty of a misdemeanor and desire the court to put this in form."[186] Humphrey had actually returned the recognizances to the Supreme Court, and he accordingly wrote Kempe complaining about the presentment. Kempe replied on January 14, 1765, stating that Humphrey had acted correctly and would have been guilty of maladministration if he had returned the recognizances to the Court of Sessions. Kempe requested a copy of the indictment, promising a nolle prosequi if the facts were as stated.[187] This was duly sent and was subsequently read and "allowed" at Dutchess General Sessions.[188]

---

[182] Among the files of Ulster County were found the secretary's letter and the rare broadside print of the order, dated July 30, 1763, "at the Exchange." This document is now in the county clerk's safe.

[183] *Ms. Files Ulster Co.* Bundle G. Against Ben Wentwood for forfeited recognizance.

[184] "Petition of Henry Livingston" (*Ms. Files Dutchess Co. 1765–66*).

[185] *H.R. Pleadings* Pl. K. 795.

[186] *Ms. Files Dutchess Co. 1765.*

[187] *J. T. Kempe Lawsuits* G–J *sub nom.* Humphrey.

[188] *Ms. Mins. Dutchess Co. Sess.* Liber C, May 21, 1765. The nolle prosequi in the form of a warrant to the clerk of the court and under Kempe's hand and seal, dated March 11, 1765, is in *Ms. Files Dutchess Co. 1726–40.*

In the meantime, on October 27, 1764, another rule had been made in the Supreme Court providing that the issues, fines, etc. arising in the Supreme Court *en banc* should be estreated twice a year, that is, in October and April, by the clerk of the Supreme Court, and that the clerk should within twenty days after returning his estreats deliver to the sheriffs a duplicate of the certificate, estreat and schedule of any amount of money due from persons in each respective bailiwick.[189] A further rule was made that the clerk of the Circuit, the clerks of the peace and of common pleas, the town clerks and all the justices of the peace deliver to the sheriff of their county in July and October a true estreat or schedule of all fines, issues, amerciaments, forfeited recognizances, etc. "so that the sheriffs on their apposals in said court of Exchequer may be charged with the moneys received by them upon such schedules."[190] The sheriffs were furthermore ordered twice a year, that is, in April and October, to appear in the Supreme Court with their "profers and accounts for monies."[191]

By the spring of 1765, Kempe was ready to make what he no doubt believed was to be a salutary example, for on April 15 informations were filed against nineteen justices of Dutchess for maladministration in office. The details of this case have been related in the chapter on transfer jurisdiction and it will be recalled that Kempe suffered the discomfiture of securing no better than a judgment for want of a plea against two justices, for the rest were duly acquitted.[192] Nothing daunted, the prosecution against Henry Livingston, the

---

189 *Ms. Mins. SCJ 1764-66* (Engr.) 73.

190 The reference to apposals suggests some sort of approximation of English Exchequer practice was intended.

191 A few such accounts survive, e.g., *H.R. Pleadings* Pl. S. 1418 (Sheriff of Westchester, Oct. 1766); Pl. S. 1419 (Sheriff of Suffolk, Oct. 1769); Pl. S. 1420 (Sheriff of Westchester, Apr. 1768); Pl. S. 1421 (Sheriff of Westchester, Oct. 1766–Apr. 1767); Pl. S. 1422 (Sheriff of Suffolk, Apr. 1771).

For some sample estreats returned from the various courts, see the following: *H.R. Parch.* 192 A 2 (a return from Suffolk Sessions of the Peace for Mar. and Oct. 1764), 218 D 1 (an estreat of issues forfeited at Ulster and Dutchess Oyer and Terminer and General Gaol Delivery, 1765, 1766, 1767). *H.R. Pleadings* Pl. K. 449 contains an account of estreats of issues from Queens County Sessions of the Peace from 1757 to 1763, and this was filed on Oct. 18, 1763, probably as a result of the order of July, 1763. The offenses mentioned in this estreat were: an insult and assault and battery on justices of the peace, £6 and £10 fines; assaults, 5s., £1, £5 fines; disorderly gaming houses, 2s.

and £4 fines; and delinquent grand jurors, 16s. fines. Attached to this estreat is the following certificate: "City of New York ss.: Whitehead Hicks Clerk of the Court of General Quarter Sessions of the peace and Common-pleas . . . for Queens . . . Duly Sworn Deposeth . . . That the aforegoing Contains an Account or Estreat of all the fines and amerciaments . . . set by the . . . Sessions of the Peace as appears by the minutes of the said Sessions during the time . . . he . . . hath been Clerke . . . and that he knows of no fines or amerciaments . . . in the Court of Common Pleas." This deposition was taken before R. R. Livingston, justice of the Supreme Court, on Oct. 18, 1763. For other estreats from Sessions and Oyer and Terminer Courts, see the following: *H.R. Pleadings* Pl. K. 47, 361, 362, 364, 365, 369, 447, 448; *H.R. Pleadings* Pl. F. 335, L. 1533, L. 1429; *H.R. Parch.* 19 D 2, 156 L 10, 179 A 9. For returns of estreats from the clerk of the Supreme Court of Judicature returning issues, etc. forfeited in the Supreme Court *en banc* between the years 1765 and 1775, see *H.R. Parch.* 193 H 2, 192 G 10, 209 G 6, 221 B 4, 7 B 7.

192 *Supra* 176.

Dutchess clerk of the peace, was undertaken, for he, like the New York City clerk, had actually put the bonds in suit. After the informations were filed, Livingston prepared a petition[193] to Kempe in which he stated that he had been clerk since 1737 and that in 1753 the Dutchess court had ordered him to put certain forfeited bonds in suit. "Your petitioner . . . being not bred to the law was unacquainted with the manner of prosecuting forfeited Recognizances" and having found a writ used by John Crooke, nevertheless wishing to be better satisfied, wrote to Attorney Bartholomew Crannel, from whom he received a precedent. Twelve or thirteen people were "taken up," but the court saw fit to discharge them. Later, he had proceeded in the same way against the recognizances mentioned in the information,

> and as such writs are constantly issued with the name of an Attorney affixed, your petitioner to those writs in which the Crown was interested affixed the name of the Attorney General and received costs on each writ and at the discharge of the Defendants for the Attorney General which your Petitioner has offered but still has. The Attorney refusing to accept the same and insisting, when your Petitioner last conversed with him that he was obliged by Order of his Honor Lieut. Governor Colden to prosecute the said informations.

Livingston prayed a nolle prosequi, but Kempe was obdurate. Nevertheless, the Attorney General again fell short of his mark, for as we have seen the wily William Smith Jr. eventually entered a plea of *nolo contendere,* thereby cheating the Crown of the full force and effect of a jury verdict.[194]

In spite of the unsatisfactory outcome of the Dutchess cases, the eventual consequence appears to have been that the rules of the Supreme Court were respected. The Sessions Courts took care to send their estreats[195] and they looked coldly upon motions for respite.[196] The persons under bond became more wary, as the minute books indicate, and we have found one timorous fellow who forwarded a doctor's certificate after he had secured a respite for illness.[197]

The reforms thus instituted were a remarkable achievement since they were

[193] Petition dated Apr. 5, 1766 marked "Original sent to William Smith" (*Ms. Files Dutchess Co. 1765–66*).

[194] *Supra* 177.

[195] Cf. *supra* n. 191. The minute books, as e.g., *Ms. Mins. Suffolk Co. 1766–75* Mar. 29, 1769, have entries to show estreats had been sent in. Cf. also the apologetic letter, Aug. 1, 1774, of Christopher Tappan (Kingston) to Kempe: "The fines till very lately were so few and low and no forfeitures that

we have been rather remiss in sending up the estreats" (*J. T. Kempe Letters* A–Z). There are drafts of estreats in *Ms. Files Ulster Co.* Bundle K.

[196] Except at Albany, where, on June 6, 1764, Oct. 5, 1764, Oct. 2, 1765, respites granted or no defaults were entered (*Ms. Mins. Albany Co. Sess. 1763–82*).

[197] King v. Palmer, 1766 (*Ms. Files Ulster Co.* Bundle I).

initiated and carried out at a time when the first serious opposition to royal government manifested itself. It is significant therefore that only one further case of malfeasance by a local magistrate arose. In 1771 an information was filed against Nicholas DeLavergne, a justice of Dutchess County, for taking certain recognizances and failing to return, certify or bring them to Sessions to be recorded. The information further charged that DeLavergne had extorted some small sums of money from the persons bound, for the favor of not returning recognizances to Sessions. The case does not seem to have been prosecuted to a conclusion but we find that in 1774 the Council removed DeLavergne from office for maladministration.[198]

Having considered the provincial irregularities in the matter of collecting forfeited recognizances, we shall next consider the usual procedures when the cause reached the stage of suit. There were three methods used in New York, the *extendi facias, scire facias* and the action of debt. The questions regarding these several procedures all concern Supreme Court practice. They posit further the question of the reception of English Exchequer practice, for as a matter of English law collection of estreated recognizances on behalf of the Crown was properly the function of Exchequer.

It is in the first place to be recalled that soon after introduction of common law forms in New York, a court of Exchequer was established by Dongan (1685).[199] Although the single roll of its proceedings that we have seen furnishes little information about how it proceeded,[200] an entry in the minutes of New York City Quarter Sessions for August, 1691 is enlightening. It was there ordered in respect to certain defaulters, that, "being Legally summoned and called to this Court and not appearing Ordered that their General recognizances be Estreated into the Exchequer according to Law."[201] Since the recently enacted Judicature Act did not deal with this matter and since there is no evidence of any ordinance, it may be supposed the above entry reflects an established practice.

There is another important bit of evidence regarding the early introduction of Exchequer practice into the Province in the shape of two records which establish that the writ of extent[202] was used by the Supreme Court at the Octo-

[198] For the information, H.R. Pleadings Pl. K. 489. The Council proceedings are in 26 Ms. Mins. Council 388.

[199] Supra 27 n. 135.

[200] Of the year 1686 (H.R. Parch. 221 B 2), "Pleas held in his Majesties Court of Exchequer Holden in the Citty of New York etc."

[201] Ms. Mins. NYCQS 1683/84–1694 150, 151, Aug. 1, 1691. It should be noted that neither the Ulster County nor Westchester County Sessions minutes for this period cast any light upon the matter of collecting recognizances.

[202] On this, cf. 2 Tidd, King's Bench Practice 1095.

ber Term, 1691 for the purpose of collecting upon certain forfeited recognizances.[203] As these are the only occasions where the *extendi facias* appears to have been used for this purpose the matter deserves some comment. The recognizances in question were entered into for an appearance at the Supreme Court to answer certain charges in connection with Leisler's rebellion and to be of good behavior.[204] The two principals, Johannes Provoost and Jacob Mauritz, had been excepted from the act of amnesty[205] and had proceeded to Europe for the purpose of interceding with the Crown. During their absence they were "subpened to appear," and then their sureties, who also did not appear. The forfeiture being entered, the Attorney General moved that the recognizances be estreated and that the writ of extent be awarded.[206] The court accordingly awarded the writ, and the collection was thus effected.[207]

It is hardly to be doubted that the time-serving Joseph Dudley and his asso-

---

[203] *Infra* n. 206.

[204] Cf. the petitions of Provoost and Mauritz in 2 *Doc. Hist. NY* 238, 239.

[205] 1 *Col. Laws NY* 255.

[206] "Pleas held at the City of New York . . . October . . . [3 Wm. and Mary] Before Joseph Dudley Esqr. Chief Justice Thomas Johnson Stephanus Van Cortlandt, William Smith and William Pinhorne Esqrs. Justices of our Supream Court of Judicature within the Province of New York to hear try and determine &c. assigned Be it Remembered that on the first of October in the year of the Reign of William . . . the Third at New York . . . came there into Court James Graham Esqr. . . . Attorney General . . . and on behalfe of . . . the King and Queen brings forth a Recognizance of Johanne Provoost and Rip Van Dam in these words following viz. Bee it Remembered that on the 18th of April [3 Wm. and Mary] . . . yt Johannes Provoost . . . and Rip Van Dam . . . personally appeared before me Joseph Dudley Esqr. Chief Judge of their Majestys Supream Court of Judicature for the province of New York aforesaid and the said Johannes Provoost acknowledged himself to be indebted unto . . . The King and Queen in . . . £100 [Rip Van Dam in £50] . . . to be severally levyed upon their respective goods and Chattels lands and tenements To the use of . . . [King and Queen] their heirs and successours if default be made in the Condition following The Condiē of this above written recognizance is such that if the above-bound John Provoost shall personally appear before their Majesty's Justices of their Majesty's Supream Court of Judicature to be held . . . in October next . . . to answer unto such matters and things as shall be objected against him on their Majesty's Behalf and doe and receive that which by the said court shall then and there be enjoyned upon him and that he the said John Provoost in the meantime be of the good behaviour towards . . . the King and Queen and all their people that then this Recognizance to be void and of none effect or else to be and remaine in full force Capt' and Recogn' Coram J: Dudley and the said John Provoost being lawfully subpened to appear upon the said 1st Tuesday of October in [3 Wm. & Mary] . . . was then and there three times solemnly Exacted and required to come forth into Court . . . and save himself and his bayle Nevertheless the said John Provoost made default and appeared not And the said Rip Van Dam . . . being subpened was then and there three times solemnly Exacted and required to bring forth the said John Provoost whom he undertook to have there that day which he did not Moreover the said Attorney General on behalf of . . . the King and Queen did . . . grant that if the said John Provoost should at any time dureing the said terme appear yt he the said John Provoost should have the priviledge to save himself and his bayle Nevertheless the said John Provoost and Rip Van Dam on the last day of the said term . . . did not appear nor at any other intermediate term but made default By means whereof they became indebted unto . . . the King and Queen the said John Provoost in . . . £100 . . . and Rip Van Dam . . . in £50 . . . Whereupon the said Attorney General on behalf of . . . King and Queen moved that the said Recognizances be Estreated and that their Majestyes Writt of Extent be awarded against the said John Provoost for . . . £100 . . . and the summe of [blank] pounds [blank] for the costs of . . . the King and Queen on that behalf Expended &c. And against the said Rip Van Dam for . . . £50 . . . and the summe of [blank] pounds [blank] for the Cost of . . . the King and Queen . . . which was accordingly awarded Therefore command was given to the Sheriffe of the City and County of New York that he take etc. and that he cause to be extended &c." The record in the case of Mauritz and Jackson then follows (*NY Supreme Ct. Mss.* Box 36).

[207] Cf. the account in 2 *Doc. Hist. NY* 224.

ciates were intent upon making another example for the delectation of the anti-Leislerians who were in the saddle, but it is significant that when Provoost and Mauritz petitioned, years later, for compensation (since the Crown by Order in Council had granted an amnesty), there was no question raised regarding the propriety of the process used.[208] As was pointed out in Chapter I, the provincial assembly in 1683 had authorized the use of extent[209] for the execution of ordinary judgments and there was consequently no reason why the writ was not available to the Crown.

The disappearance of the extent as a means of realizing upon forfeitures is one of the minor mysteries of colonial practice.[210] The writ was used again in other Exchequer proceedings as late as 1729,[211] but we can find no trace of any further use to collect on recognizances. This may have been due to the fact that the administration of justice, in so far as it affected the fiscal interests of the Crown, definitely languished during the rapacious governorship of Fletcher. Indeed, judging from the curious totals of revenue from fines and forfeitures in those years it would appear that very little effort was made to collect upon forfeited recognizances.[212] And as the Supreme bench was peopled by three worthy citizens who were without the least training in the law the directive energy essential to the nurturing of budding Exchequer practice was wholly lacking.

After the initial efforts to use the *extendi facias* to recover forfeited recognizances were abandoned, the provincial authorities settled upon the *scire facias* and the action of debt. The *scire facias* was used in England in all cases where the King's debt was not endangered by insolvency.[213] It was a judicial writ based upon the record ordering the sheriff to warn the defendant to appear to show cause why the Crown should not have execution. If there was any doubt whether the recognizance was forfeit, the *scire facias* was the only proper mode of procedure irrespective of the solvency of the debtor.[214] When the

---

208 The provincial act of restitution is in 1 *Col. Laws NY* 384.

209 *Ibid*. 134.

210 There is one case where the extent may have been used. Robert Baker, William Harlow and John Sheppard were called on their recognizances on Oct. 13, 1705, and at their failure to appear, the Attorney General prayed their defaults be entered, which was done, and on Mar. 13, 1705/06, the Attorney General moved that if the defendants did not appear and plead within four days after the term, execution should issue against them. This motion was also granted, but we have found no further proceedings in the case and we do not know whether a *scire facias* or writ of extent was con-

templated (*Ms. Mins. SCJ 1704/05–1709* 46, 52).

211 Cf. King v. Heath, *supra* c. V n. 117.

212 1 *Doc. Hist. NY* 477. The fines and forfeitures for 1691 were £306 10s. The bulk of this was from the two recognizances discussed above (2 *ibid.* 224). In 1692 the amount was £60 8s., of which £45 was collected from Provoost (2 *ibid.* 224). In 1693, £229 17s. 5¾d.; in 1694, £15 7s.; in 1695, £264 17s. 4½d.

213 In which event an extent was available. On the procedure, cf. Tidd, 2 *King's Bench Practice* 1146, 1090.

214 Gilbert, *Treatise on the Ct. of Exchequer* 166.

writ was served, the sheriff returned *scire feci;* if not served he returned *nihil,* whereupon a second *scire facias* would issue. After two returns of *nihil,* the court would order a four-day rule to plead or an extent to issue. In the case of a forfeited recognizance to keep the peace, a more complicated procedure through the Crown office existed. The issue of breach was tried by a jury and the execution was by *fieri facias* or *capias ad satisfaciendum,* with a final estreat to Exchequer and extent if the judgment was not satisfied.[215]

Although the *scire facias* on forfeited recognizances was used in New York from 1694 down to the Revolution we do not know how exactly the details of English procedure were followed in New York for we have not sufficient details regarding the particular cases. Even at the end of the seventeenth century there existed no satisfactory texts regarding Exchequer practice,[216] and precedents were to be found only by ferreting in the Books of Entries. As late as the year 1754, Bartholomew Crannel, who sometimes deputized for the Attorney General, confessed to an unknown correspondent his inability to send a draft of a writ at the suit of the King upon a forfeited recognizance, "which I wo'd be glad to Send you taken from some book of precidents but I have looked over all that I have and Can't find any." Crannel goes on to say

it seems by the Books that the Method to recover the forfietures is to send the recognizance into the Exchequer upon which a Venire facias Issues against the Recognizees at the Return of which they must enter their Appearance and a Declaration must be filed against them.

I have from observing a precident in Rastal endeavoured to Draw a Venire or Summons which I have enclosed and believe will do

As to . . . whether Lands can be Seized and Sold by . . . fi fa . . . no . . . Doubt of it But care must be taken that the Judgment roll be correctly Drawn up and Docketted otherwise . . . no benefit by it, and besides the sherif can Sell no more than is necessary for paying the Execution nor ought he to Meddle with the Lands if there be Chattels sufficient. . . .[217]

The earliest instance of a *scire facias* proceeding at the suit of the Crown in New York, possibly upon a bond, occurs in the New York Supreme Court in 1694 when Emott for the Crown prayed a rule upon a *scire facias* for the defendant to show cause, and the court ordered that the defendant answer the

---

[215] Tidd, *op. cit.* 1092.

[216] Thus Brown, *Compendium of the Several Branches of Practice in the Court of Exchequer* (1688) has the briefest discussion of practice and contains largely forms; Fanshaw, *Practice of the*

Exchequer Ct. (1658) is too slight to have been of use.

[217] *Misc. Mss. Bartholomew Crannel.* This may be the letter to Henry Livingston; cf. *supra* n. 193.

following day or judgment be given for the Crown.[218] Thenceforward there are scattered references,[219] all too brief to form any conclusions regarding provincial practice. It appears, however, from a *scire facias* proceeding of the year 1722[220] in the Supreme Court, where execution was sought upon a judgment in the English Exchequer, that the New York bar at the time was not ignorant of English procedure, although a single record naturally does not offer lavish detail. A few years later occurred a case where the Crown attempted to collect on a forfeited recognizance that throws some additional light on the matter.

The case began with an action of debt upon a forfeited bond against Adam and Thomas Smith and Benjamin and Jacob Hicks. On June 13, 1727 the sheriff returned Adam Smith taken, and upon a sheriff's certificate to the Attorney General that Adam was in custody the court ordered he plead in twenty days after the service of the declaration or suffer judgment. At the same time the sheriff, having entered *cepi corpus* as to Benjamin Hicks and Thomas Smith, was ordered to bring in the bodies or be amerced. On December 5, 1727, the sheriff of Queens returned *cepi corpus* as to Jacob Hicks and was ordered to bring in the body or be amerced. In the meantime Jacob, evidently having been returned, was, together with Thomas Smith, served with a rule to plead in three weeks or suffer judgment. On this day the Attorney General alleging that he entered a judgment by default against Adam Smith, the court, evidently checking for such judgment, found that it did not appear to have been entered, and therefore ordered that in case it should later appear that such judgment had been entered, no execution should be issued until the following term. On March 15, 1727/28, the record was read and filed in connection with Thomas Smith and was ordered to be made a *concilium*. A few days later, the Attorney General was ordered to file his pleadings or defendant Adam Smith to be discharged. On June 11, 1728, the default judgment against Adam Smith was ordered to be set aside, and the sheriff of Queens was ordered to return a list of freeholders so that a special jury might be picked. At some juncture

---

[218] King v. Merritt (*Mins. SCJ 1693–1701* 53).
[219] Cf. *James Alexander Supreme Ct. Register 1721–42 sub nom.* Johannes Apple. In Nov. 1720, Jamison for the Crown had informed against Johannes Apple for a misdemeanor or contempt (*James Alexander Papers* Box 44 no. 8). The complainant was evidently Killian Van Rensselaer. At Jamison's request Alexander brought a *sci. fa.* on the recognizance, Mrs. Van Rensselaer having promised fees.

In the March Term, 1721/22 *James Alexander Supreme Ct. Register*, there is a reference to a *sci. fa.* on a recognizance of Garret Onclebagg and two sureties. The writ was returned served, and on motion for judgment *nisi causa*, Bickley for the defendant received time to plead. The plea was "condition performed" but no further entries have been found.

[220] *H.R. Parch.* 235 D 2; *James Alexander Supreme Ct. Register 1721–42* 4.

(possibly on another bond) a *scire facias* had also been issued to the sheriff of Queens against Adam Smith, and the sheriff not returning *scire feci,* the court on October 9, 1728 ordered judgment against Adam Smith. But on October 12, 1728, the rule on the *scire facias* was "enlarged" in favor of Adam Smith, the judgment by default evidently not having been entered. Three days later, defendant Smith was given a rule to plead in twenty days to the *scire facias* or else to suffer judgment. This proceeding then disappears from the minutes.

On June 9, 1729, in the action of debt on a recognizance of good behavior brought against Thomas Smith, Adam's surety, the court on the surety's demurrer to the declaration gave judgment for Thomas Smith. At the same time the court also gave judgment for Jacob Hicks in the action brought against him at the suit of the King. The next day Adam Smith was ordered to rejoin in twenty days or suffer judgment by default, but on October 21, 1729 (Adam evidently having filed his pleadings) the court ordered that the pleadings be made a *concilium* and that the same be argued the following term. On March 13, 1729/30, in a new proceeding on *scire facias* against Jacob Hicks and Thomas Smith, who were Adam Smith's bail, the court ordered that the defendants plead or suffer judgment, and on June 9, 1730, Jacob Hicks and Thomas Smith were ordered to file their plea to the *scire facias* in twenty days. Again on October 20, 1730, the sheriff of Queens returned *scire feci* as to Jacob Hicks and Thomas Smith, and they were ordered to plead by the following term. Evidently they demurred. On March 21, 1731/32, by consent it was agreed by the Attorney General and William Smith, attorney for Jacob Hicks and Thomas Smith, that Attorney Smith deliver the argument for the defendants to the Attorney General within a fortnight and that the latter should answer the argument in a fortnight after. Attorney Smith was then to reply to the Attorney General's argument on Thursday in the following term. There must have been delay for on June 13, 1732, in the case of Thomas Smith and Jacob Hicks, it was ordered that the King's counsel deliver the arguments to the defendants' counsel within that month or else that judgment be given for the defendants. On October 22, 1733, judgment was given for the defendants. We do not, however, know what happened in the case of Adam Smith.[221]

It is unfortunate that no relic of the arguments in this case survives, for the two proceedings against Adam Smith's bail seem to indicate a complete disre-

[221] *Ms. Mins. SCJ 1723–27* 279; *Ms. Mins. SCJ 1727–32* 22, 27, 37, 45, 68, 72, 83, 88, 127, 137, 158, 186, 214, 229, 321, 351; *Ms. Mins. SCJ 1732–39* 63.

gard of a notion of *res judicata* since there is no evidence that more than one bond was in suit. Conceivably the sureties raised the matter of *res judicata* by demurrer although this would have been a curious way to plead. The point of interest on *scire facias* practice is the latitude allowed defendants in the rule to plead compared with the severity of English Exchequer practice.[222]

There are a few other *scire facias* cases[223] from which some details may be culled, such as the proceedings against Joseph Taylor who had failed to appear at an Oyer and Terminer in September, 1751. Here, the defendant after a return of *nihil* on the *scire facias,* offered an affidavit to the effect he had been ill, and the Supreme Court ordered the recognizance discharged upon an undertaking that he pay costs.[224] Again, in the Lydius case, after the special verdict on an information for intrusion the court gave judgment for the Crown. The Attorney General then moved Lydius be called on his recognizance (for £5000) but both Lydius and his sureties defaulted.[225] A *capias pro fine*[226] issued in execution on the judgment in the intrusion case, and simultaneously a *scire facias* issued on the recognizance. On the latter the sheriff returned a

---

[222] It would appear from King v. John and James Killmaster (1739), that the twenty-day rule to plead was established practice in *scire facias* proceedings (*Ms. Mins. SCJ 1732–39* 360).

[223] For a provincial form of *scire facias,* cf. the following: "George the Second . . . to the Sheriff of . . . Dutchess Greeting Whereas at a Court of General Sessions of the Peace . . . in Dutchess [May 18, 1736] Before [nine justices of peace] . . . came Francis Turner . . . and acknowledged himself to be indebted unto us . . . in £12 . . . to be levied upon his goods and chattels, lands and tenements for the use of us . . . On failure of the performance of the following condition [to appear at the next General Sessions of the Peace to receive what should be enjoined him by the court and meantime to be of good behavior to us and all subjects, especially William Scott, justice of peace of Dutchess] . . . and whereas to us it doth appear of record that the said Francis Turner (being three times solemnly called in court at the last above-mentioned General Sessions of the Peace) Did not personally in the same court according to the form and effect of the recognizance aforesaid and because the said Francis Turner the aforesaid £20 hath not yet rendered to us: and we of the same £20 . . . being willing to be satisfied with all possible speed, as is just, We Command you that you omit not for any Liberty within your bailiwick; but that the same you enter and by good and lawfull means you make known to the said Francis Turner that he be before our justices of our Supreme Court at the City Hall . . . the third Tuesday in April next; and to shew if anything for himselfe he . . . can say wherefore we ought not to

have execution against him for the said £20 . . . to be levied &c . . . according to the form of the Recognizance . . . and have you then and there the names of those to whom you shall make it known and this writt. . . ." This writ was returned on Apr. 19, 1737, and the return was endorsed on the writ as follows: "By virtue of this writt to me directed I have made known unto . . . Francis Turner by Isaiah Ross and Joseph Crawford, good and lawful men of my bailiwick that the said Francis Turner be before the justices within mentioned and the day and place within written to shew if anything for himselfe he hath or can say wherefore our Lord the King ought not to have execution against him for the £20 . . . according to the form and effect of the within mentioned recognizance As by the within writt is Commanded me. James Willson Sheriff" (*McKesson Legal Papers* no. 17). The sheriff of Dutchess "having returned scire feci on the writ of scire facias," the Supreme Court on Apr. 26, 1737, "ordered . . . judgment . . . against the defendant unless he shew cause to the contrary sitting the court" (*Ms. Mins. SCJ 1732–39* 259).

[224] *Ms. Mins. SCJ 1750–54* (Engr.) 106, 148, 164.

In King v. Michael Showers, the defendant's recognizance was filed in the Supreme Court on Jan. 25, 1751/52. He evidently defaulted and process was ordered against him. On Apr. 30, 1752, the sheriff returned the first *scire facias, nihil* (*Ms. Mins. SCJ 1750–54* [Engr.] 106, 148).

[225] *Ms. Mins. SCJ 1764–67* (Rough) 11.

[226] *H.R. Parch.* 185 G 7.

nihil, and an *alias* issued on January 19, 1765.[227] This was also returned *nihil,* whereupon a rule to plead in twenty days was ordered. Lydius was not apprehended, and an action of debt was then begun against the sureties.[228] There was a demurrer which was overruled and judgment was given for the Crown.[229] The defendant's sureties were unable to pay and were committed.[230]

The desultory appearance in the records of *scire facias* proceedings for the Crown gives the impression that this method of realizing upon forfeitures was not popular. It is probable that the observation of Sir Henry Moore, that there were no fees in such a proceeding for the Attorney General, was equally true in the early eighteenth century, and that for this reason the prosecuting officer preferred to bring an action of debt.

The use of an action of debt to collect upon forfeited recognizances is a peculiarity of provincial practice which needs explanation. The first important case where this was employed was the proceeding in 1708 against Peter Fauconnier, who, it was claimed, had forfeited a bond of £8000 posted for the proper performance of his office as collector and receiver general. On September 8, 1708, a *capias* having been issued, the sheriff returned *cepi corpus,* and on September 11, the defendant appearing he was ordered to plead in fourteen days before the following term. Fauconnier demurred, asserting that he had well and truly executed his office and was not in law obliged to answer. Thereupon the Attorney General entered a nolle prosequi and the defendant went *sine die.*[231]

Fauconnier had been acting in the room of Byerly who had been suspended in 1705, but later was restored to office. Mompesson, the Chief Justice, had reported irregularities,[232] and a hot dispute over salary had brought the differences between the two collectors before the Council.[233] During September, 1708, the matter was before the Council which finally exonerated Fauconnier, and it was certainly on this account that the action was dropped. The result of the debt action, however, did not end Fauconnier's troubles, for in 1711 an action of account was brought for improper payment of salary. Again the defendant demurred but the court gave judgment for the Queen[234] on Septem-

227 H.R. *Pleadings* Pl. K. 749 contains the *scire facias* and the return. *Ibid.* 815 for the *alias sci. fa.*
228 H.R. *Parch.* 158 E 6, for the action for a £2,500 penalty brought against John David as one of the two sureties for John Henry Lydius. David demurred to the declaration, saying that the recognizance was forfeited for Lydius' failure to appear at the Supreme Court in August, at which time it did not appear from the recognizance that David was bound for Lydius' appearance.

229 *Ms. Mins. SCJ 1764–67* (Rough) 57, 110; *Ms. Mins. SCJ 1766–69* (Engr.) 29.
230 Cf. the petition of July 18, 1766, *Cal. Eng. Mss.* 764.
231 *Ms. Mins. SCJ 1704/05–1709* 183, 191.
232 5 *Doc. Rel. Col. Hist. NY* 406.
233 10 *Ms. Mins. Council* 185–218; 1 *Jour. Legis. Council* 253.
234 H.R. *Parch.* 103 B 5; *Ms. Mins. SCJ 1710–14* 340, 353, 370, 396, 416, 431, 451, 458, 468, 480.

ber 5, 1713. Fauconnier then brought error to the Governor and Council where on April 24, 1715, judgment was reversed.[235]

It does not appear that at any juncture the use of an action of debt for the Crown was attacked. By 33 Henry VIII c.39, bonds to the Crown were made Statutes Staple which, when payable within the year, were executed by *levari facias,* and if after a year, by *scire facias.*[236] Assuming that a bond did not in form comply with the statute and was actually a mere bond *in pais,* contemporary Exchequer practice was to issue a commission to find the debt. When returned the inquisition became a record on which a *scire facias* would issue.[237] Why the provincial authorities hit upon an action of debt as appropriate we do not know. True, there was old authority which justified the Crown's use of most of the forms of action available to the subject,[238] but assuming the bond was not of record, information for a debt was the traditional Crown remedy, for it offered definite procedural advantages over the ordinary civil action.

During the first half of the eighteenth century the action of debt was not often used in New York to collect on recognizances, and it may be conjectured from the Smith and Hicks case, discussed above, that there were some doubts whether or not it was the correct way of proceeding. From the standpoint of efficiency it was a maladroit selection. The whole point of having an obligation of record was to simplify and expedite execution. John Tabor Kempe, who was responsible for the spate of debt actions, must have been perfectly aware of this fact, yet he resorted to *scire facias* only exceptionally, and we have seen no cases where the Crown information for debt was here used. It is possible that colonial opposition to information proceedings was responsible for the neglect of this latter remedy, but it is more likely that the ordinary civil action of debt yielded a better financial return for official efforts.[239] Upon a proceeding by *scire facias* sureties were not liable to costs unless they appeared and pleaded nor were damages for the detention of the debt recoverable. Furthermore a judgment in debt could be executed against the debtor's body, and

---

[235] 11 *Ms. Mins. Council* 293.

[236] Gilbert, *Treatise on the Ct. of Exchequer* 102.

[237] Brown, *Practice in the Ct. of Exchequer* 364. It is not certain whether or not at this time the bonds of colonial officers fulfilled the conditions of St. 33 Hy. VIII c.39, but some years later Fane, in an opinion, indicated that they should (1 *Chalmers Opinions* 259).

[238] Theloall, *Digest des Briefs Originals* (1579) liber 1, c.3; Coke, *Third Institute* 136 n. h.

[239] *Supra* 537. Governor Moore's ordinance on fees of 1768 provided a fee of 18*s.* on *scire facias.* In all other actions (with a few named exceptions), the Attorney General was allowed the usual attorney's fees (in the N.Y. Bar Ass'n copy of Bradford, *Acts of NY* [1726]). The bill of costs in the recognizance proceedings against William Seton totalled £9 1*s.* 6*d.* (*J. T. Kempe Lawsuits* S–U).

this was not available in the case of *scire facias*. These were all considerations of some importance where sureties had to be proceeded against. We have not been able to ascertain to what extent actions of debt on bonds were used by Crown officers in eighteenth century England. But we infer that it was unusual for the Crown to resort to the ordinary civil action from the fact that upon one occasion Kempe noted upon a declaration his reliance upon a pleading precedent in a sixteenth century Book of Entries.[240]

There were certain peculiarities about the Crown's action of debt that need some explanation, for the civil procedure of New York Province is still territory that has never been scientifically explored. In England during the eighteenth century, practice in the King's Bench was dominated by the Bill of Middlesex procedure, and in the Common Bench by the so-called *quare clausum fregit*. These were both devices intended, among other things, to expedite process, so that it was usual to begin an action by a queritur[241] or praecipe,[242] viz., a complaint or brief statement of the action, whereupon a capias or precept in the nature of a capias would issue.[243] When the defendant was in custody, the plaintiff would then declare against him. An adaptation of this manner of initiating an action was used in New York.[244] We have found none of the initiatory complaints in recognizance cases, and it is even possible that a preliminary declaration was exemplified to secure process.[245] That the procedure was fashioned upon the King's Bench bill procedure is obvious from the references in the judgment rolls to the "bill" of the Attorney General, and from the fact that it was usual to declare against the defendant "in custody."[246]

---

240 Cf. the draft of a narration in debt on a bond against Nath. Marston (*J. T. Kempe Lawsuits* L–O). On the back is endorsed "Lilly's Ent. Rast Ent. 158.6. Robinsons Ent. 222." The Rastall reference is presumably to fol. 198. The Robinson reference is not in point. In the narration in King v. George Folliot (*ibid.*), there is a reference to "Lilly Ent. 145." This is in the second edition of the *Entries*, debt for the Crown on a bond.

241 Cf. Tidd, *Forms of Practical Proceedings in King's Bench, Common Pleas, and Exchequer of Pleas* (6 ed.) 62; Impey, *New Instructor Clericalis; Stating the Authority, Jurisdiction, and Modern Practice of the Court of King's Bench* (2 ed. 1785) 79 *et seq.*

242 Tidd, *Forms* 69; Impey, *New Instructor Clericalis . . . of Common Pleas* (1785) 155 *et seq.*

243 "The common course is now (to regain time) . . . to take out the *Capias* first, and bespeak your Precipe, and sue out the Original afterwards, although it be supposed in Law to be sued

out before . . ." (Trye, *Jus Filizarii* [1684] 59).

244 Sometimes called "Bill of Middlesex" and sometimes "New York Bill"; cf. the costs in McDonald v. Vance, 1769 (*J. T. Kempe Lawsuits* L–O). For a form see the *Ms. Precedent Book William Livingston* (*NY State Lib. Mss.* no. 1329). In this book is a full set of forms for debt on recognizances.

245 There are many praecipes preserved in the H.R. Mss. but none has been found in actions by the Crown. It is possible that none were used for there is no charge for a praecipe (otherwise inevitable) in the Seton case. In ordinary civil actions, a praecipe would be used, e.g. Duane v. Child; Child v. Johnson (*J. T. Kempe Lawsuits* C–F). On the procedure by bill, cf. especially the issue roll in Seton v. Dudley, 1759 (H.R. Mss. [no number]); an example of a provincial *latitat* in Dayton v. Parsons, 1772, is *H.R. Pleadings* Pl. K. 18.

246 For example, King v. Snyder (1768) the "bill" opens "John Tabor Kempe Esquire Attorney General of our Lord the now King for the Province

Invariably in these Crown actions, a capias[247] issued against the defendant, an aberration which is difficult to explain since the defendant-principal being already bound in sureties was already technically in custody. Indeed, the authorities seem generally to be agreed that in actions upon bail bonds given in civil actions a capias did not lie.[248] The Crown's action cannot therefore be regarded as an adaptation of debt proceedings upon civil bail, but, on the point of process, rests upon the generalization which a long line of English cases supported—that the Crown had right to the body of his debtor by way of process.[249]

After the defendant had been secured, he was declared against,[250] and it is to be noted that the Attorney General usually claimed damages in excess of the amount of the bond, in reliance upon the English statute 8 & 9 Wm. and Mary c.11 §8, which had conceded the right and against which the colonists had vainly attempted to legislate.[251] The course of action was in accordance with the usual common law procedure in civil cases, although it should be observed that defendants as a rule saw fit to demur, since there were frequently defects in the form of the recognizance,[252] a fact easy enough to understand when one reads the letters of country officials. The demurrers were sustained to an extent which bit deeply into the Attorney General's attempts to make the forfeitures a paying proposition, and the rolls of the courts between 1760 and 1776 show that many of the cases were hotly contested.

One of the most interesting of these forensic battles was the action brought against John and Hendrick Van Tassel. John Van Tassel had been bound in

New York who for the same Lord the King prosecutes complains of William Snyder in Custody &c. of a Plea that he render to our said Lord the King the Sum of Twenty Pounds . . ." (H.R. Parch. 29 B 2).

[247] "GEORGE the third by the Grace of God of Great Britain France and Ireland King Defend⁰ʳ of the Faith and so forth To our Sherriff of our City and County of New York Greeting, We command you that you omit not by Reason of any Liberty within your Bailiwick, but that the same you enter and take Laurence Kortright if he be found within your Bailiwick, and him safely keep so that you have his Body before us at our City of New York on the third Tuesday in April next to answer to us of a plea that he render to us the Sum of Forty Pounds of Debt and have you then there this Writ, Witness John Chambers Esquire second Justice at our City of New York . . ." (King v. Kortright, H.R. Pleadings Pl. K. 181). Cf. also H.R. Parch. 184 H 2 (King v. Lackey, 1761); ibid. 185 C 5

(King v. Kelly, 1769); ibid. 188 A 8 (King v. Ladner et al., 1772).

Alias capias was second process, H.R. Parch. 186 E 2 (King v. James McDugal and Isaac Hodge); ibid. 183 D 7 (King v. Romyn); ibid. 190 D 2 (King v. Winsent, 1775). This would be followed by a pluries, H.R. Parch. 69 L 8, 183 E 1 (King v. Rosa), H.R. Pleadings Pl. K. 701 (King v. Cranford et al.) and H.R. Parch. 187 L 9.

[248] 1 Tidd, King's Bench Practice 173; Petersdorff, Law of Bail 32, 226. The sureties, of course, were not "in custody" and hence capias would be available against them.

[249] Harbert's Case (3 Co. Rep. 11b); Sir Thomas Cecil's Case (7 Co. Rep. 18b).

[250] For examples, King v. Alberson, 1769 (J. T. Kempe Lawsuits A); King v. Seton, 1771 (ibid. S–U), and the drafts in H.R. Pleadings Pl. K. 1102, Pl. K. 1030.

[251] 2 Col. Laws NY 676 (1730).

[252] Moore to Shelburne, 1767 (7 Doc. Rel. Col. Hist. NY 906).

£20 with one surety, Hendrick Van Tassel, in £20, for his appearance at Westchester Sessions and to keep the peace in the meantime, especially to James Hammond. John had been continued and respited on recognizance through several Sessions, but in the interim had attacked Hammond, thrown stones at his door and threatened him, thereby forfeiting his bond. The Attorney General accordingly brought suit for £30 damages against Hendrick, the surety.[253] On January 19, 1765, capias having evidently been issued, the sheriff of Westchester returned *cepi corpus* as to Hendrick and was ordered to bring in the body or be amerced 40*s*.[254] To the narration Hendrick filed a demurrer, claiming that the declaration was not sufficient in law

> And for Causes of Demurrer in law, the said Hendrick Van Tassel according to the Statute shews to the Court . . . that, by the said Declaration the Recognizance is alledged to be forfeited because . . . John Van Tassel . . . with force and Arms . . . the Dwelling house . . . of one James Hammond did Attack . . . when from the Recognizance . . . it does appear that . . . Hendrick Van Tassel was only Bound as a Security for the said John Van Tassel.[255]

On October 31, 1765, the Attorney General filed a joinder in demurrer, praying judgment. Evidently between 1765 and 1767 the court held the matter under advisement.[256] On October 23, 1767, the record was read and filed and on motion of the Attorney General it was ordered to be made a *concilium*. The defendant was ordered to argue his demurrer on the following Thursday.[257] On October 29, 1767, on motion of Richard Morris, the court ordered that the rule for arguing the demurrer be "enlarged" to the following term.[258] No minute entries again appear on this case until January 17, 1769, when it is indicated that the Attorney General argued in reply to the defendant, and the court thereupon ordered that the defendant conclude his argument by the following term.[259] The concluding argument of the defendant on the demurrer has been preserved. It recapitulates some of the Attorney General's argument and is worth scrutiny because it raises the interesting question of the rights of both principal and sureties after a continuance:

[253] See a draft of the narration in H.R. *Pleadings* Pl. K. 1102, which gives the details.

[254] *Ms. Mins. SCJ 1764–66* (Engr.) 117.

[255] See the Roll of October Term, 1767, in H.R. *Parch.* 85 G 8 for further details.

[256] H.R. *Parch.* 85 G 8.

[257] For the "record," see H.R. *Parch.* 85 G 8, and for the minute entry of Oct. 23, 1767, see *Ms. Mins. SCJ 1764–67* (Rough) 271.

[258] *Ms. Mins. SCJ 1766–69* (Engr.) 317.

[259] *Ibid.* 601. Note that on Jan. 17, 1769, Kempe, in a letter to Judge Jones of the Supreme Court in connection with the bill of exceptions in King v. John Van Rensselaer, added the following: "P.S. I send an enclosed argument in King v. Hendrick Van Tassel on a demurrer to a declaration in debt on a forfeited recognizance" (*J. T. Kempe Lawsuits* V *sub nom.* Van Rensselaer).

For the Attorney General

In my first argument . . . I stated . . .

1st Whether the Court has a right to continue the Defendant upon this Recognizance from Court to Court so as to subject him to a forfeiture and [if so]

2dly whether from the tenor of this Recognizance it could be continued to any other purpose than as far as it related to the appearance of John Van Tassel [the principal]. . . .

The Attorney General had, in his argument, claimed the points were the same and that if he understood defendant's counsel then the question between them was whether the court to which a recognizance for the peace was returned could, on the appearance of the principal, keep the surety also bound to a future day without the consent of the latter expressly obtained.

The Attorney General had also answered the arguments of defendant by stating:

It has been the universal practice in England as well as here to continue such recognizances as the one in controversy in the manner this has been continued, and this power in the Courts to do this is by such Universal practice the daily acknowledged Law of the Land.

Therefore, since the court could continue a recognizance, so they could continue the recognizors, security and principal. The Attorney General was of the opinion that the sureties entered into the obligation subject to such continuances unless they refused in open court and delivered up the principal. If that was not done the consent of the security was implied.

The Attorney General had then urged the instance in the case of the security of John H. Lydius, which resolution "he hoped had settled this point." The defendant replied:

I cannot help differing with the Gentleman in the first place, that the practice of the Court in the continuance of such recognizances (if it is so which is not admitted) is the acknowledged Law of the Land, but on the contrary say if they have exercised a power which they have not and which is wrong in itself, their exercising it can never make it right or make it Law—2dly I insist that Recognizors enter into recognizances subject to no other Conditions than those expressed in the recognizance and that they are to be convicted or acquitted according to the Letter of them and not by any strained Construction—3dly I deny that it is the Business of the Security to deliver up the principal in Court when he wants to be discharged but on the contrary say it is needless, for if the Principal has done whatever the Security engaged he should do, he is by the very recognizance that bound him declared at Liberty the Condition being performed, and I am supported . . . by the constant practice of the Court, for . . . your Honours well remember it is the daily practice of the Court to call the Principals upon their recognizance and then they the Principals ask the continuance which is the fullest declaration of their consent, and I can see no reason why the Security (who is by no means bound to be in Court) should be in a worse state than the Principal and have the very nature of his contract altered without his consent [and as to delivering up the principal] . . . the Principal and the King's peace will be as well Secured by taking the Security's Consent in Court to the continuance, or if he is not there committing the Principal if he can't find other Security. . . . And as to the Instance urged [Lydius' case] I believe that and this are the only instances of Suits brought upon such Recognizances and I hardly think a single determination should be urged as the Law for we find different determinations by the Courts even upon the same point upon better information and fuller consideration. I must confess I did expect the Attorney General would have furnished some authorities in print from the Books, but I presume his Searches have been fruitless and I am the more inclined to think so, as in my opinion the Law is against him. I make no doubt your Honours will agree it to be Law, that all conditions are to be Construed in favor of the Person or Persons for whom they are made according to the plain Letter and meaning of them . . . [repeats condition of recognizance for John Van Tassel to appear at the Court of General Sessions of Westchester on the first Tuesday of November, 1763, and then and there to abide by what is enjoined by the court and meantime keep the peace to the people and especially James Hammond, etc.].

It is then alleged that John Van Tassel did appear, and as to the condition in regard to keeping the peace it says *in the meantime,* i.e. until November, 1763, and the declaration does not charge John Van Tassel with breaking the peace in the meantime or intervening time between taking the recognizance on October 18, 1763, and November. It is therefore concluded that the demurrer is good.

However, defendant had yet to meet the argument of the Attorney General, that on the basis of the Lydius case the principal is to *"abide by what should be enjoined him by the court."* This he did by pointing out that

in Lydius's case there was no such Clause, [and] it was admitted by Counsil for Bratt and David [Lydius' sureties] that if that recognizance had contained such a Clause there could be no doubt—had the Clause been as the Attorney General insists . . . the Gentlemen might have been right in their admission, but . . . they would have differed from him had such a Clause, as in this recognizance been in that . . . the words in this recognizance are, *then and there to abide and do what should be enjoined by the said Court,* . . . the words, *then and there,* . . . must refer to their antecedents of time and place . . . at the court of Sessions . . . of Westchester on the first Tuesday in November then next . . . the Court could not even enjoin any thing upon John Van Tassel which was not *then and there* to be done. . . . [Prayer for judgment.][260]

This argument is remarkable not because of book learning but because of the evidence it provides of the unusual reliance by the Crown upon a colonial practice precedent. The defendant did not prevail, for on October 26, 1769, the court gave judgment for the King.[261]

We have already adverted to the fact that the suit on a recognizance was sometimes an oblique method of determining whether a defendant had committed an offense. This issue was inevitably involved in cases where there had been a forfeiture for breach of a recognizance to observe the peace. The most interesting case of this sort was the proceedings against Thomas Tobias and William Van Velser Jr. begun in 1771, for here Tobias, the principal, breached his bond by an assault, and judgment was rendered against the surety when a jury at nisi prius in an action against the surety found the principal guilty of the assault. Tobias and Van Velser had entered a recognizance before Samuel Clowes, a justice of peace of Queens County, in £100 for the appearance of Tobias at Queens Sessions and for his good behavior in the meantime, especially to Elizabeth Robinson. However, while still bound on recognizance, Tobias threatened Elizabeth, assaulted her with a club at one time, another time threatened and assaulted two other persons with an axe, and toward Elizabeth "was of ill behavior against the form and effect of the recognizance and condition thereof."[262]

On April 27, 1771, a capias in debt on a forfeited recognizance in £100 was issued against Tobias, and the sheriff returned "In custody."[263] On August 3, 1771, Tobias was ordered to plead in twenty days "after service of a copy of the declaration and this rule on the sheriff or on the defendant in custody or suffer judgment."[264] Tobias then filed the following plea:

---

[260] *H.R. Pleadings* Pl. K. 1028.

[261] *Ms. Mins. SCJ 1769–72* (Engr.) 116. Evidently while proceedings were pending against Hendrick, process had been issued against the principal, John, for on May 2, 1767, the sheriff of Westchester returned *non est* against John (*Ms. Mins. SCJ 1766–69* [Engr.] 186). On May 1, 1773, a *pluries capias* in debt issued against John and this was returned "not found" (*H.R. Parch.* 183 D 2).

[262] See the summary of this part of the case in the Judgment Roll in King v. William Van Velser Jr. (*H.R. Parch.* 15 F 1).

[263] *H.R. Parch.* 185 E 2. He was respited on another recognizance at Queens Sess., May 21, 1771 because he was in New York jail (*Ms. Mins. Queens Co. Sess. 1722–78*).

[264] *Ms. Mins. SCJ 1769–72* (Engr.) 403, 404.

Thomas Tobias ads. John T. Kempe Esqr. Atty General who for our Sovereign Lord the King in this behalf prosecutes Plea in Debt on Recognizance in the penalty of £100 AND the said Thomas Tobias by John Morin Scott his Attorney comes & defends the force and Injury when . . . [illegible] and protesting that the declaration aforesaid of the said Attorney General for and in behalf of the said Lord the King is not sufficient in the Law and to which he said Thomas has no necessity by the Law of the Land to answer . . . [illegible] plea Nevertheless the said Thomas saith that as to the first second third fourth and fifth Breaches of the Condition of the Recognizances aforesaid above charged and supposed he the said Thomas Tobias is not thereof or of either of them guilty in manner and form as the said attorney general for and in behalf of the said Lord the King above against him hath complained and of this he puts himself upon the Country And as to the sixth Breach of the Recognizance aforesaid above charged and supposed the said Thomas protesting as before he hath protested saith that he by Virtue of the Recognizance aforesaid ought not to be therewith charged because he saith that as to the coming with force and arms and as to whatsoever else is against the peace of the said Lord the King and against the good behaviour of him the said Thomas he is in no wise thereof guilty and of this he puts himself upon the Country and as to the residue of the said Sixth breach above charged and supposed he the said Thomas saith that the said Attorney General his action aforesaid thereof for and in behalf of the said Lord the King ought not to have or maintain against him the said Thomas because he saith that the said Edmund Weeks the Younger at the time in which the said last mentioned breach is above supposed to have been made and committed at Oysterbay aforesaid in the County aforesaid upon him the said Thomas an assault did make and then and there would have beat wounded and evilly treated him the said Thomas had not he the said Thomas defended himself against the said Edmund Weeks the Younger and so the said Thomas saith that if any mischief or damage then and there happened to the said Edmund Weeks the Younger it was occasioned by the said assault of the said Edmund Weeks the Younger on him the said Thomas and in the defence of him the said Thomas & this the said Thomas is ready to verify wherefore he prays Judgment if the said Attorney General his action aforesaid thereupon for and in behalf of the said the Lord King ought to have or maintain &c.[265]

A trial of the issue was had at nisi prius,[266] for, on October 19, 1773, a *postea* was returned, read and filed in the Supreme Court *en banc,* and on motion of

[265] Unfortunately we do not have a citation to this document which was found in one of the bins in the Hall of Records. It may possibly be filed in *Pleadings* or *Parchments* (more likely the former),

and a check of the indices under Thomas Tobias or John Tabor Kempe may disclose the citation.

[266] See, for example, the subpoena to Elizabeth and Mary Robinson, dated Aug. 1, 1772, ordering

the Attorney General the court ordered judgment *nisi*. We take it that the verdict was for the King since the Attorney General moved for judgment.[267]

A narration in debt of £100 on a forfeited recognizance was also filed against William Van Velser Jr., who had been Tobias' surety, for the same breaches of the good behavior recognizance recited above. The Attorney General in his declaration, after reciting the facts given above, went on:

> Whereby an Action hath accrued to . . . the King to have and require of . . . the said William Van Velser Junior the aforesaid Sum of One hundred Pounds so by him . . . acknowledged to be due by him to . . . the King . . . Nevertheless the aforesaid William Van Velser Junior altho often . . . required . . . [the sum of £100] . . . to render hath hitherto refused and still doth refuse . . . to the Damage of . . . the King Two hundred Pounds And this for . . . the King the said Attorney General of . . . the King now is ready to verify &c. And therefore for . . . the King he brings Suit &c.[268]

Process evidently having issued against Van Velser, the sheriff of Queens on August 3, 1771, returned the defendant "taken" and was ordered to bring in the body or be amerced 40s.[269] The usual rule to plead was probably given to Van Velser, for he

> comes and defends the Force and Injury &c and Protesting the Declaration . . . is not sufficient in the Law and to which he . . . has no necessity nor by the Law of the Land is bound to Answer for Plea Nevertheless the said William saith that as to the first, second, third, fourth and fifth Breaches of the Condition of the Recognizance . . . the said Thomas Tobias . . . is not . . . guilty . . . and of this he puts himself upon the Country And the said Attorney General . . . in like manner &c.[270]

It is interesting to observe that the surety in this case pleaded that the principal was not guilty of the alleged breaches of the condition of the bond of good behavior. Van Velser, in his plea, went on to plead that as to the first part of the sixth alleged breach of the condition of the recognizance, Tobias was not guilty, and that as to the rest of the sixth breach (charging an assault on

---

them to appear at the Queens County Court for the trial of causes brought to issue in the Supreme Court to testify in the trial of King v. Thomas Tobias (*H.R. Parch.* 183 E 4). Also see the notes on trial, Sept. 16, 1773, at Jamaica, on debt on a forfeited recognizance in King v. Thomas Tobias (*J. T. Kempe Lawsuits* C–F *sub nom.* Dayton v. Parsons).

[267] *Ms. Mins. SCJ* 1772–76 (Rough) 114.
[268] For the facts so far related, see the Judgment Roll (*H.R. Parch.* 15 F 1).
[269] *Ms. Mins. SCJ* 1769–72 (Engr.) 404.
[270] Quoted from the Judgment Roll (*H.R. Parch.* 15 F 1).

Edmund Weeks Jr.), Tobias was not guilty because Weeks assaulted Tobias and the latter was obliged to defend himself.[271] The Attorney General replied to Van Velser's plea stating that he should be charged and also saying as to the sixth breach involving the assault on Weeks that Tobias "of his own proper cause" attacked Weeks. Issue having been joined, the usual jury process was ordered for a trial at nisi prius in Queens. The trial was had and the jury found the fact that Tobias, the principal, was guilty of the breaches of the recognizance. The jury also assessed the damages and the whole was made up as a *postea* endorsed on the nisi prius record.[272] On October 19, 1773, the *postea* was read and filed, and on motion of the Attorney General the court ordered judgment *nisi.*[273]

Tobias was not only bound on recognizance for his good behavior with William Van Velser Jr. as his surety, in £100 each, but another recognizance had been taken for his good behavior in £50, with John and Zebulon Doty sureties (in £25 each), for his appearance at Queens Sessions and for his good behavior in the meantime, especially to Elizabeth Robinson. Evidently the actions on the two forfeited recognizances were tried at the same time at nisi prius, for we have seen a *subpoena duces tecum* issued to the deputy clerk of Queens County commanding him to be before the judges at the Queens Circuit to testify in the action of debt in *King v. Tobias and Van Velser Jr.,* and to bring the recognizance of November 12, 1770, into which Tobias and Van Velser had entered. At the same time, the deputy clerk was ordered to bring in a recognizance of October 12, 1770, into which Tobias had entered with John and Zebulon Doty as his sureties.[274] A narration in debt on a bond against Tobias for the recognizance into which he entered with John and Zebulon Doty was filed because we have found Tobias's demurrer and plea of not guilty dated in April, 1772.[275] We have found also a *postea* in *King v. John Doty,* Tobias's

---

[271] H.R. Parch. 15 F 1.

[272] Ibid.

[273] Ms. Mins. SCJ 1772–76 (Rough) 114. From the *postea* (H.R. Parch. 15 F 1) the verdict: ". . . Thomas Tobias is Guilty of the Premises within laid to his Charge in Manner and Form as the said Atty General for our said Lord the King within against him complains and they assess the Damages of our said Lord the King by Occasion of the detaining the within mentioned Debt over and above his Costs and Charges by him about his Suit in this Behalf expended to Sixpence and for those Costs and Charges to Sixpence Therefore it is considered by the Court of our said Lord the King now here that our said Lord the King do recover against the said William Van Velser Jr. his said Debt and the

aforesaid Damages by the said Jury in Form aforesaid assessed and also forty three Pounds and Eight shillings for his Costs and Charges by this Court to our said Lord the King adjudged of increase by his Assent, which Damages in the whole * * * amount to Forty three pounds Eight Shillings and sixpence . . . And the said William in mercy, etc."

[274] This subpoena is contained on a parchment strip which has not as yet been catalogued in the Hall of Records, but can probably be found in the *Pleadings* or *Parchments* indices under King v. Thomas Tobias, or King v. Van Velser or King v. Doty. This subpoena bore the usual penalty of £100 and was dated July 31, 1773.

[275] H.R. Pleadings Pl. K. 257.

surety. This *postea* recites that a bill in debt had been filed against Doty for forfeiture of £25. Doty demurred and pleaded that Tobias was not guilty, but the *postea* shows that the jury at Queens Circuit found Tobias guilty of the premises.[276] On October 22, 1772, the Attorney General moved that the clerk of Assizes return the *postea* by the following Thursday. This motion was granted, but no further proceedings have been found.[277]

In the absence of any statistics regarding the issues upon execution of judgments where the Crown prevailed in suits upon recognizances, it is impossible to estimate how fruitful a source of revenue these forfeitures in fact were.[278] Governor Moore reported in 1766 that the jails were full of persons who were unable to satisfy the Crown for forfeited recognizances and he asked for authority to compound, for his instructions limited him to the compounding of fines under £10.[279] The English authorities were evasive[280] and no instructions were ever sent. It is possible, however, in view of the well-settled English practice, that there was some compounding with consent of the judges, for there are many more estreats for forfeitures than there are entries of actions.[281] The question whether the judiciary had these powers does not ever seem to have been raised, but the closely related question of the right to grant a *quietus* was argued in 1760 in the case of *King* v. *Cornelius and Lawrence Kortright.*

[276] H.R. Parch. 120 C 8. The *postea* was in the following language: "Afterwards . . . came . . . John Tabor Kempe Esquire . . . [and] John Doty . . . and the jurors of the Jury . . . say upon their oath that . . . Thomas Tobias is Guilty of the Premises within laid to his Charge in Manner and Form as the said Attorney General . . . within against him complains R. Morris clerk assizes" (*ibid.*). Also see H.R. Parch. 125 D 5 for the *postea* in King v. Zebulon Doty, Tobias's other surety. This *postea* also contains the jury's verdict that Tobias was found guilty.

[277] It is to be noted that process had evidently issued against John and Zebulon Doty and had been returned unsatisfied, for we have found an *alias capias* of debt issued against them. This latter writ was returned "in custody" (H.R. Parch. 191 F 2), and on Aug. 3, 1771, the minute entries reflect that the sheriff of Queens had returned John and Zebulon Doty in custody and they had been ordered to plead in twenty days or suffer judgment (*Ms. Mins. SCJ 1769–72* [Engr.] 404).

[278] It should be noted that the cases dragged out interminably in the courts. See, for example, the following cases where the records are the most complete: King v. Clewes *et al.* (*Ms. Mins. SCJ 1764–66* [Engr.] 76, 127; H.R. Parch. 12 L 2, 58 D 1; H.R. Pleadings Pl. K. 833, K. 850, K. 733).

King v. Snyder (*Ms. Mins. SCJ 1764–66* [Engr.] 177; *Ms. Mins. SCJ 1766–69* [Engr.] 186, 388, 403, 524; H.R. Parch. 29 B 2, 185 E 9, 187 C 1; H.R. Pleadings Pl. K. 183). A *fieri facias* issued in execution (*Ms. Mins. SCJ 1772–76* [Rough] 46). King v. George Caton and George Harris (*Ms. Mins. SCJ 1766–69* [Engr.] 285; *Ms. Mins. SCJ 1769–72* [Engr.] 59, 70, 104; H.R. Parch. 43 E 1, 185 B 8, 126 A 9; H.R. Pleadings Pl. K. 276, K. 329). King v. William Seton (*Ms. Mins. SCJ 1772–76* [Rough] 210; *J. T. Kempe Lawsuits* S–U sub nom. Seton, V sub nom. Van Veeder).

[279] 7 *Doc. Rel. Col. Hist. NY* 828: "Many miserable objects have languished for a great length of time in prisons here, not for crimes committed, but for having been so imprudent, as to become securities for others, who have not appeared at the time stipulated by the Recognizances, by which means they have been forfeited, and the securities thrown into gaol upon their inability to pay the whole sum, for which they became bound."

[280] *Ibid.* 845.

[281] For an offer to compound, see the letter of Michael Kayser to Kempe, May 1771 (*J. T. Kempe Letters* A–Z). In Governor Moore's letter (*supra* n. 279) was enclosed a memorandum of a New

Alderman Bogert found Cornelius Kortright and Francis Welsh

a fighting Near my doar upon which I Came out & Commanded the Peace, Soon After I Left them they went at it again & The Second fight . . . was Some Days After. . . . Soon After Law^r Kortright Came to my house with a cloak on him and a sword under it to Swear the peace ag^t Francis Welsh, I Endeavor to persuade Lawrence to dròp them disputes but On his Insisting to swear that his life was in danger I took his Oath & bound the s^d Francis over to the peace, . . . Soon after s^d Francis applied . . . to swear the peace agt Law^r & Cor^s Kortright, . . . upon which I swore s^d Francis & bound over the s^d Law^r & Cornelius Kortright to Appear at the the next General Quarter Sessions of the peace. . . .

Bogert then persuaded Welsh to drop the dispute but Lawrence Kortright

flew in a passion & told me I had no Right to bind him Over on s^d Francis Oath . . . as he had Complained first. . . .

The good alderman told Lawrence he was wrong and also told him that he would deliver in his, Lawrence's, recognizance on the next court day and that he should appear at Quarter Sessions

which I thought was Notice a Nuff, and I think taking a Recognizance to Appear at a Court at a certain time is a Sufficient Notice.[282]

Cornelius and Lawrence Kortright were continued on their recognizances through February 6, 7 and 8, 1759, but when they failed to appear on the latter date the Court of Quarter Sessions ordered that their default be entered and their recognizances put in suit.

It was this case which, as we have seen, opened Kempe's fight for proper estreats. On November 4, 1760, Kempe produced a writ of certiorari to move the case up to the Supreme Court, and, this being read and filed, it was ordered that return be made.[283] Suit was brought on the forfeited recognizance in the Supreme Court; Duane on behalf of the defendants moved for a *quietus*, arguing that the defendants failed to appear through ignorance and not through obstinacy. He also pointed out that there had been no indictment

York lawyer suggesting the Governor had power to compound (L.C. transcripts) as the courts did not.
[282] This affidavit of Alderman John Bogert is contained in *J. T. Kempe Lawsuits* J–L *sub nom.* Kortright.

[283] *Ms. Mins. NYCQS 1732–62* 448–450, 488. Cf. *supra* 526.

or information filed against them at Quarter Sessions "as appears by the certificate of the clerk of the peace." Duane further stated that he was "advised that it is the constant Practice of the Courts of Westminster, notwithstanding recognizances are forfeited & estreated for non appearance, to grant Recognizors Relief by Quietus if no obstinate or wilful contempt proved ag^t them." Duane also argued that the defendants were unable to make a legal defense or be otherwise relieved, and that it was a great hardship for them to pay the forfeiture since they were innocent of any crime except their failure to appear on their recognizance, which omission was only due to ignorance.[284]

Kempe answered Duane's arguments by stating that it was a well-founded maxim that ignorance of the law was no excuse, and that in this case there was no proof that the defendant was ignorant. To Duane's argument that the defendants had other business to attend to, Kempe very properly answered that all business must be laid aside to attend the King's courts. The Attorney General further pointed out that the mere fact that the defendants were not indicted was immaterial because the charge was a forfeiture of the recognizance by non-appearance. The Attorney General granted that if there was no obstinate contempt involved, the defendant's non-appearance might form grounds for the granting of a quietus as in "some extraordinary cases where the Act of God, or Imprisonment for Debt or some other cause not brought on the Def^t by his own wicked Act, have made it absolutely impossible for the Def^t to appear . . ." However, the impossibility of appearance could not be proven merely by the defendant's own oath, as in this case. Furthermore, the Attorney General pointed out that the defendants were not innocent, but were guilty of that contempt for which their recognizances had become forfeited.[285]

We do not know whether or not the *quietus* was granted in this case, but it is significant that the point was raised in the first of Kempe's actions to fix the Attorney General's rights to sue for forfeited recognizances. The most interesting feature of the argument is the reference to the alleged practice of the English courts at Westminster. This was conceivably a correct statement, although it was not until some years later that an Act of Parliament authorized the granting of a *quietus* on a recognizance forfeited owing to ignorance.[286] It is worthy of notice that in the same year this statute came into effect (May 1, 1764), the New York Supreme Court in fact did grant a *quietus*, although

---

284 *J. T. Kempe Lawsuits* G–J.
285 *Ibid.*

286 4 Geo. III c.10.

there is no evidence the judges were aware of the new act which, in any event, did not extend to the dominions.

In *King* v. *John Sealey and Alexander Jackson,* the Supreme Court, on October 16, 1764, on reading the defendant's petitions for a *quietus* and on motion of Kissam on behalf of the defendants, ordered "that the defendant be quieted and be discharged on the payment of costs to the Attorney General."[287] Again on August 4, 1770, one John Hagen filed a petition in the Supreme Court "setting forth his being arrested on a recognizance at the suit of the Crown and the great poverty and distress of himself and his family." This petition was read by the court and

it appearing to the Court that Joseph Munsell . . . (for whose appearance the Defendant had become bound) had not been indicted and that the publick Justice had not Suffered by the Non-Appearance of the said Joseph Munsell on the said Recognizance: It is ordered on Motion of Mr. Kissam on behalf of the Defendant, that the Defendant have a Quietus in this Suit and be discharged from further Prosecution thereof, he paying fees to the Attorney General.[288]

On October 26, 1771, the Supreme Court, on reading the affidavit of F. Child and the certificate of the clerk of the peace, ordered, on motion of Thomas Jones for the defendant, that *quietus* be granted and that Niel and Daniel McLean be discharged from the recognizance which they had entered into before Justice Brewerton for Niel's appearance at Quarter Sessions and which recognizance had been estreated "into this court."[289] Similarly, on April 30, 1773, the Supreme Court, on reading the certificate of the clerk of New York Quarter Sessions and on motion of Van Schaack and with the Attorney Gen-

---

[287] *Ms. Mins. SCJ 1764–67* (Rough) 15. John Neeley and Anthony Stephens on Oct. 20, 1764, were quieted and discharged on their petition for a *quietus* (*ibid.* 22). On Oct. 27, 1764, James Kain filed an affidavit, and on his motion for a *quietus* the court ordered that he and Johannis Cole Jr. be quieted and discharged on payment of costs to the Attorney General (*Ms. Mins. SCJ 1764–66* [Engr.] 100). In October, 1766, Moses Hetfield was granted a *quietus* on the motion of his attorney, Wickham (*Ms. Mins. SCJ 1766–69* [Engr.] 78). On Nov. 1, 1766, Joseph Crane, Jr. petitioned for a *quietus.* The Supreme Court, on reading two affidavits, certificates of the clerk of the circuits and a copy of a minute of the "court of Assize" being filed on motion of Duane, granted a *quietus* from Crane's forfeited recognizance (*Ms. Mins. SCJ 1764–67* [Rough] 193). On Oct. 25, 1767, Mr. Morris presented to the Supreme Court a petition of John

Barnes praying a *quietus,* and on reading an affidavit of Benjamin Blagge, which was filed, Morris moved for a *quietus.* However, "the court postpones consideration of this matter until another opportunity" (*Ms. Mins. SCJ 1764–67* [Rough] 277). On Jan. 22, 1768, John Barnes and his two sureties, John Cannon and William Karr, appeared in court and Barnes' petition for a *quietus* was read, Blagge's affidavit was filed and Morris moved that the court would grant a *quietus* from the recognizance forfeited by the defendants in the New York Quarter Sessions. The Supreme Court thereupon granted a *quietus* (*Ms. Mins. SCJ 1766–69* [Engr.] 382).

[288] *Ms. Mins. SCJ 1769–72* (Engr.) 259. On Jan. 17, 1771, on motion of Mr. Morris and by consent of the Attorney General, a *quietus* was issued in the case of King v. David Lyons (*ibid.* 315).

[289] *Ms. Mins. SCJ 1769–72* (Engr.) 465.

eral's consent, ordered that a *quietus* be entered on the estreated recognizance of Edward Agar *et al.*[290]

It is one of the ironies of our legal history that although so much of English law and practice respecting recognizances had become fixed in New York over the course of a century, quite without benefit of provincial legislative wisdom, yet it was not long after the Revolution that the whole matter was put upon a statutory footing,[291] as if the long and almost uninterrupted common law traditions of the colony were not themselves a sufficient warrant. Possibly the social and political upheavals incident to the long war with Britain had disrupted practices which the colonials' records show to have been an integral and indisseverable incident to the administration of criminal procedure; or possibly this was merely one of those gestures of legislative supererogation with which from time to time the statute books are fattened.

The establishment in colonial New York of the common law of recognizances, with some occasional innovations, was a real accomplishment of the law enforcing agencies of the Crown, for, as we have indicated, it made immediate a sense of responsibility which the King's writ alone would never have evoked. For our own time, colonial practice offers some food for reflection, especially when one views the small vestiges of the old law which successive revisions of the statutes have left,[292] and the impotent state to which the Court

---

[290] *Ms. Mins. SCJ 1772–76* (Rough) 90. The entry of the estreat as well as of the *quietus* in this case is contained in the following:

"King The
vs.
Thomas Clarke Jr.
Rachel Wyley
Edward Agar
John Taylor

City & County of New York ss: } An Extract of the two following Recognizances forfeited, and Set to our Lord the King, at the General Quarter Sessions of the peace of our said Lord the King, held at the City Hall in & for the said City & County of New York, on the first Tuesday in November 1772

1772 November the 3d Thomas Clarke Junr. of the City of New York Because he Came not to answer this day, to all and singular such things, which against him, on the part of our said Lord the King should be objected, as by a certain Recognizance taken on the 10th day of April in the year of our Lord 1771 before

Abraham P. Lott Esqr. one of the Justices of our said Lord the King Assigned to keep the peace, in the said City and County of New York, he undertook £ 50–0–0 Rachel Wyley Because she came not to answer this day to all and singular such things, which against her, on the part of our said Lord the King, should be objected, as by a Certain Recognizance taken, on the fifth day of October in the year of our Lord 1772 before Francis Filkin Esqr. one of the Justices of our said Lord the King, assigned to keep the peace, in the said City & County of New York she undertook — £ 30–0–0

Of Edward Agar & John Taylor of the said City Pledges of the said Rachel Wyley because they had her not to answer as above each in the Sum of . . . £ 15–0–0" (*H.R. Pleadings* Pl. K. 47).

[291] 2 *Laws of NY* (1785) c.9 Ninth Session (1786); c.8 Tenth Session (1787); 1 *Revised Laws of NY* (2 ed. 1807) 304 c.70 §5 (1801); 446 c.135 §6 (1801). See also People v. Van Eps, 1830 (4 *Wend.* 387) where the Supreme Court dealt with the matter of collection as if it were *res integra*.

[292] *NY Code of Criminal Procedure* §§89, 98, 99.

of Appeals reduced the so-called Public Enemy law.[293] "Them that be not of good fame" we still have with us, and better are the means of determining their fame than ever before,[294] yet it is only against the convicted criminal that there is now available the process of good abearance which a hard and un-sentimental generation devised in order that "the people be not troubled . . . or the peace blemished." One by one, old weapons of the law have been laid by as no longer meet for our defense although our own achievements in the prevention of crime are not so signal that we can lightly disdain the experi-ence of our forebears.

[293] NY *Penal Law* §722; People v. Pieri, 1936 (269 NY 315).

[294] Cf. the record set forth in the dissent of Finch, J., in People v. Pieri (*supra* n. 293).

CHAPTER IX

TRIAL: PART I

THE ineffable Blackstone, writing but a few years before the revolt of the American colonists, took occasion to record the objections of the age of enlightenment to the long abolished trial by ordeal: "One cannot but be astonished at the folly and impiety of pronouncing a man guilty unless he was cleared by a miracle, and of expecting that all the powers of nature should be suspended by an immediate interposition of Providence to save the innocent whenever it was presumptuously required."[1] To the children of an age certain only that perfection is beyond reach, these haughty words seem equally descriptive of the conventional trial of a felon in the English courts of the eighteenth century. Deprived of counsel, unless he were knowledgeable enough to claim a point of law against himself, deprived even of a view of the indictment, the hapless defendant was not privileged to have process to secure his witnesses, was often unable to cross-examine since depositions might be read in evidence and was cast largely upon the benignity of the presiding judge for aid in the conduct of a defense. When the jury was left to consider their verdict, if they could not agree by consultation in the box, the bailiff was sworn to keep the jury "without meat, drink, fire or candle." The wonder is that Providence intervened so often to effect an acquittal.

Although the complacency of most eighteenth century commentators on criminal procedure does not radiate the same self-satisfaction which glows in Blackstone's work, these writers do not hesitate to mark the improvements which their age had effected over the methods of an older day. The improvements in felony cases, due largely to the indulgence of a few judicial humanitarians, were slight enough, although in the case of misdemeanors, defendants enjoyed nearly as many safeguards as they do today, and a late seventeenth century statute[2] assured to persons indicted of treason privileges which no man charged with a felony could yet claim. It seems inconceivable that procedure in the trial of felonies could have been so little affected by the accepted *modus operandi* in each of the other two categories of crime, yet it is apparent from the records of important trials over the course of nearly a century that felony procedure was kept almost impervious. There was a weight of tradition

---

[1] 4 Blackstone, *Commentaries* 344.

[2] 7 Wm. III c.3 gave the right of counsel, and of having a copy of the indictment.

behind this attitude, the details of which are obvious even if today they seem to have been fatuous. For example, the deprivation of counsel is justified by the unrealistic excuse "that it requires no manner of Skill to make a plain and honest Defence . . . the Simplicity and Innocence, artless and ingenuous Behavior of one whose Conscience acquits him, having something in it more moving and convincing than the highest Eloquence of Persons speaking in a Cause not their own."[3] That a generation whose underprivileged were immortalized in the repellent gallery of Hogarth could have been cozened by such sentimentalities, is indeed extraordinary.

If the defendant on trial for felony in Blackstone's day was grievously circumstanced, his situation a hundred years earlier would have been somewhat more grim. Apart from the fact that until Holt's time judges generally demeaned themselves as if the avenging angel had invested them with the sword of justice, criminal procedure was still permeated with notions about royal prerogative which gave the prosecution incalculable advantages. Sir James Stephen has remarked that in the trials of the Restoration period the sentiment continually displays itself that the prisoner is an enemy of the King,[4] and there can be no doubt that this attitude was sustained by the reasoning justifying the rules which crippled the defense. The secrecy with which the indictment and the nature of the prosecution's evidence were guarded is defended by so liberal a lawyer as Sir John Somers as essential to the Crown.[5] The harsh rule that an accused's witnesses should not be sworn is grounded upon the absurdity that it was improper to have witnesses against the King.[6] There were other practices which had not even a shadow of justification, such as the near torture used to compel a defendant to plead,[7] and the questioning of the prisoner by the bench, as he conducted his defense, with the obvious design of forcing a confession.[8] The exception of criminal procedure from statutes of jeofails favored the continuation of oppressive rulings on pleading,[9]

---

[3] 2 Hawkins, *Pleas of the Crown* c.39 §2.

[4] 1 Stephen, *Hist. Criminal Law of Eng.* (1883) 397.

[5] Somers, *The Security of Englishmen's Lives* (1771 ed.) 31. Cf. also the discussion of the "king's interest" in the evidence (*ibid.* 43). But this tract is also noteworthy for its observations upon the public's interest in prosecution.

[6] 2 Hawkins, *Pleas of the Crown* c.46. The rule was changed by 1 Anne c.9.

[7] *Kelyng* (27) notes the "constant practice" at Newgate of tying a prisoner's two thumbs together with whipcord that "the pain of that might compel him to plead."

[8] This is distinctly the impression one gains from the trial of the Turners (6 Cobbett, *State Trials* 566), although it should be remembered that the law of evidence was still in a rudimentary state, and that the roles of the prisoner and the judge in the conduct of the trial gave great opportunity for rough handling. On the arbitrary conduct of Kelyng, C.J., cf. 6 *ibid.* 992.

[9] Thus a prisoner who had pleaded not guilty and was convicted produced a pardon, but the court (1662) regarded the plea as waiving the pardon (*Kelyng* 25).

and the persistence until 1670,[10] and possibly even later, of the notion that a jury could be fined for their verdict must certainly have been prejudicial to defendants.

What has been said respecting the conduct of felony trials *temp.* Charles II is based upon the proceedings in King's Bench and the Assizes. The misdemeanor cases which involved no matter of state seem to have been handled with fairness,[11] and defendants were in no worse case than they were a century later. But where a libel, a tumultuous assembly or the like was involved, trials were conducted with a malignant ferocity[12] that is almost unmatchable. Anyone familiar with the manners of the time is aware of the fact that the general problem of law enforcement was of proportions which inevitably hardened any tenderness for individual privileges. The mercies of the most benevolent judge, after a year of dealing with the footpads, highwaymen, contentious sectaries, unreconstructed rebels and the debauchees of his Majesty's court, must have been utterly benumbed.

To what extent the conduct of trials at Quarter Sessions resembled that in the superior courts it is impossible to say. If the case of Penn and Mead at Old Bailey is typical[13] the proceedings were exactly similar. The minute books of the country Sessions are too bare to furnish clues to the actual conduct of trials, but we suspect from this very fact that procedure was often more summary than the law warranted. That the trial of offenses was the least important function of the justices of the peace may be inferred from the fact that the manuals, until 1677,[14] deal with the matter very sketchily and chiefly in terms of what a justice might do rather than of what he might not do. A considerable part of criminal business could be disposed of summarily through the powers of examination, and even if a prosecution reached the stage of presentment, the defendant's confession of the indictment might then conclude the matter. The large number of such cases in the Surrey rolls 1663–1666[15] show this to have been usual, and the same practice obtained in Yorkshire where the trials in relation to the number of presentments were few.[16] The confession of the indictment most usually occurred after arraignment

---

[10] Bushell's Case, 1670 (*Vaughan* 143).

[11] This is the impression gained from an examination of Keble's *Reports,* although the brief and telegraphic style of the reports may be misleading on the trials as a whole.

[12] E.g., King v. Keach, 1665 (6 Cobbett, *State Trials* 702); King v. Crook, 1662 (*ibid.* 202).

[13] *Ibid.* 951.

[14] There is some discussion in Lambard, *Eire-narcha,* but of the seventeenth century compositions the first systematic account is in the 1677 edition of Dalton, *Countrey Justice.*

[15] *Surrey Quarter Sessions Recs. 1663–66* (39 Surrey Rec. Soc. Pub. [1938]).

[16] *Quarter Sessions Recs. 1657–77* (6 North Riding Rec. Soc. Pub. [1888]). These records are so edited that it is impossible to discover the actual disposition of presentments not brought to trial.

when the defendant was called upon to plead, and some samples of judicial browbeating[17] at this juncture in the trial indicate how the *cognovit* might sometimes be secured.

It is unfortunate that so little has been preserved regarding the actual conduct of trials in Sessions during Charles II's reign. The few cases which found their way into King's Bench by way of error, certiorari or habeas corpus rarely deal with matters of trial practice,[18] but on other points they tend to show a slapdash way of proceeding below in respect to such matters as the form of indictment that was probably characteristic of Sessions practice.[19] The directions for holding a Sessions in the 1677 edition of Dalton, and in the *Office of Clerk of the Peace*[20] are nearly identical with descriptions of how trials in superior courts should be conducted, but there is no reason to believe that these patterns represented what in reality went on, except in respect to the order of business. The truth is that it was only in certain specific points, such as the form of indictment, demurrer to the evidence, the form of sentence, that a defendant lucky enough to have counsel could make effective any objection. There were as yet few rules of evidence, and in Sessions cases no one seems to have dreamed of excepting either to the justices' conduct of a trial or even to the charge to the jury. Consequently there was room for arbitrary action by the court and for what we would today regard as the most prejudicial sort of error, the limits and extent of which no textbook or record would disclose. The picture of the trading lawyer-justice in *Hudibras*[21] may be caricature, but Butler was never up for *scandalum magnatum*, and in 1661 the King's Bench, with a saturnine appreciation of reality, decided that the words "buffle-head Justice" were not actionable.[22]

It is remarkable that in a century and among a people constantly exercised about fundamental rights and the liberties of Englishmen, so little energy was devoted to the protection of defendants at trial. But it is even more remarkable that in a new land, populated to some extent by the very victims of an almost

[17] Cf. Quaker trial at Exeter in Hamilton, *Quarter Sessions from Queen Elizabeth to Queen Anne* (1878); King v. Twyn Dover *et al.*, 1663 (6 Cobbett, *State Trials* 518); King v. Crook (*ibid.* 215).

[18] E.g., King v. Cook (1 *Lev.* 123) wrong form of judgment; Case of James (*T. Jones* 225) form of sentence; King v. Herham (2 *Keble* 132) notice; King v. Brown (*ibid.* 212) inquest and trial the same day; Le Roy v. Jadler (1 *Sid.* 99) the same. It should be noted that sometimes, as in Le Roy v. Summer (*ibid.* 270) the King's Bench, faced with a general bad practice, was compelled to countenance it.

[19] Cf. Le Roy v. Challenor (1 *Sid.* 159); Le Roy v. Temple (*ibid.* 192); King v. Coes (2 *Keble* 160); King v. Phittorn (*ibid.* 365); King v. Saunder (*ibid.* 537); King v. Grant (*ibid.* 358); King v. Fosse (*ibid.* 580); King v. Hayworth (*ibid.* 521); King v. Parker (*ibid.* 781); King v. Nichols (3 *Keble* 803).

[20] In the *Office of the Clerk of Assize* (1682) but printed in 1681.

[21] Butler, *Hudibras* (1822 ed.) Part 3, Canto 3.

[22] Bill v. Field (1 *Sid.* 67).

inexorable law, there was virtually no effort made toward a more merciful procedure. In New York from the time of the proprietor down to the Revolution, the common law manner of criminal trial, with all its shortcomings, remained the model for the colonists and, so far as we are aware, was never the subject of any attempted legislative improvement. What the modern lawyer views as inequities, the seventeenth and eighteenth century provincial simply assumed to be unalterable, and the few vagaries which found root in his courts were inconsequential.

Early New York Practice

Trial practice during the first two decades of English rule in New York is in the tradition of Sessions practice in England. Actually there is little reason to suppose that most of the first English officials were very familiar with that. The chief men were soldiers who like Colonel Nicolls had gone to the wars when they were young and who had knocked about the continent in long exile. Matthias Nicolls, the provincial secretary, had been admitted to Lincoln's Inn, but unless the ways of law students in Charles II's time were different from those of the modern species, his acquaintance with the conduct of trials must have been casual. The only person who certainly possessed judicial experience was Thomas Willett, but his knowledge had been acquired in Plymouth colony which had developed over some forty years its own idiosyncrasies.[23] Since, as we have seen, there was evidently at first no justice's manual available in New York from which pointers on trial might have been culled, the several courts were cast entirely upon the memory and imagination of the bench when the first prosecutions were initiated.

From the beginning, the paradigm for the several provincial courts in New York was the annual Assizes, for here the justices from all parts of the Duke's dominions assembled with the Governor and councillors. Here the Dutchmen from Esopus and Albany, and the transplanted Puritans from Long Island and Westchester sat with the newly arrived adventurers from England and learned how the King's Peace should be enforced. It was a queer procedure, as the record of the first important trial in 1665 discloses.[24]

Ralph Hall and his wife Mary, residents of Seatalcott, an outpost of New England culture, were accused of witchcraft. A jury was impanelled, ap-

---

[23] Goebel, King's Law and Local Custom in Seventeenth Century New England, 31 *Col. Law Rev.* 474.

[24] 4 *Doc. Hist. NY* 85.

parently with no thought of permitting challenge. The prisoners were brought to the bar and a presentment found by the constable and overseers of Seatalcott was then read, charging in one count the practice of "some detestable and wicked arts commonly called witchcraft and sorcery against one George Wood whereof the said Wood sickened and died." The second count charged the practice of the same arts upon the infant child of Ann Rogers causing the death of the child. At this juncture several depositions were read, "but no witnesses appeared to give testimony in court *viva voce.*" The clerk then called upon Hall to hold up his hand (viz., the arraignment) and summarizing the charges inquired, "What dost thou say for thyself—art thou guilty or not guilty?" Ralph and his wife pleaded not guilty "and threw themselves to be tried by God and the country." Thereupon their case was referred to the jury which returned the discursive verdict that "wee finde there are some suspitions by the Evidence of what the woman is charged with but nothing considerable of value to take away her life; but in reference to the man wee finde nothing considerable to charge him with." The court then bound Hall, body and goods, as surety for his wife's appearance from session to session and to be of good behavior.[25]

The vagarious quality of the procedure in this case is obvious—no challenge, written evidence only, examination of the evidence before pleading, no apparent presentation of testimony for the defense. Why the case was ever submitted to a jury, and why in the face of the verdict the defendants were put under recognizance can be explained only on the grounds of the superstitious unease that the witchcraft charge seems in these times to have begotten in otherwise reasonable judges.

A homicide was tried at this same session of the Assizes, but no further capital cases came before that court until 1668.[26] In the minor matters such as seditious words the court did not trouble to impanel a jury but upon examination of "proofs upon oath" or "testimoneys" permitted the defendant to make his defense and then proceeded to sentence.[27] This method of dealing with misdemeanors became characteristic of both Assize and Sessions practice. Obviously the manner of presentment, viz., by constable, or constable and overseers, gave an accusation an official quality which a grand jury presentment did not have. Since these constables' presentments were

[25] The recognizance was discharged in 1668 (*ibid.* 86).
[26] The 1665 minutes are burned, but the *Cal.*

Proc. Ct. of Assizes 1665–72 shows a trial in 1665 for homicide.
[27] *Ms. Mins. Ct. of Assizes* 81 (Barton and Bloomer, 1666), 84 (William Lawrence, 1666).

sometimes found after an investigation[28] that resembles the activity of the French *juge d'instruction,* the bench tended to treat the accusation as partly proven, and consequently to regard its own function as one of reviewing the evidence. The Duke's Laws had not made a jury mandatory in criminal cases, but had merely stipulated this body should not be less than six or more than seven, unless in capital cases the justices should think it proper to appoint twelve.[29] This had been altered in 1666[30] to require a jury of twelve at Assizes, but it is obvious from the various references to juries in the laws that the compilers were concerned primarily about the trial of civil actions and were not inclined to hem in the summary powers of justices.[31]

The Assizes had occasion again to try a capital case in 1668, when John Cooperstaffe was accused by David Dufour of homicide.[32] The "indictment" was "presented" by Dufour, a jury was impanelled and the prisoner then brought to the bar. The "indictment" was read, the prisoner arraigned and asked to plead. Cooperstaffe pleaded not guilty and then explained his version of the happening. The witnesses who had previously given their depositions were then sworn and gave evidence. The Governor "summes up all ye stances of ye tryall and gives the charge." The jury then withdrew and eventually brought in a verdict of not guilty.[33]

The procedure in the Cooperstaffe case approximates English practice more closely than the Hall case, but at the same term of the Assizes there was tried one of those early provincial hybrids which defy classification.[34] One Rider brought an action against Fittse Janssen and Marc Dale for money and goods to the value of £20 which the defendants were accused of having stolen from his house. Fittse was Rider's servant and she confessed to having taken the property at Dale's instigation. Dale "denyes ye fact" and as the action was civil in form, three witnesses were sworn for him. The case does not appear to have been submitted to a jury and the court ordered Dale to make satisfaction while Fittse was sentenced to be stripped to the waist and with a rod under each arm to stand on a barrel in public for a half hour with a paper on her breast in-

---

[28] See, for example, *Ms. Flatbush Town Recs.* Liber AA, 137 (1679), Liber D, 399 (1669).

[29] I *Col. Laws NY* 42.

[30] *Ibid.* 91.

[31] The Duke's Laws provided that a special verdict might be given and added the curious provision that when the jurors were in doubt they should have liberty in open court to take advice of any particular man on the bench or "any other whom they think fitt to Resolve and direct them" (*ibid.* 43). This curious provision was probably inserted on account of the preponderance of Dutch-speaking inhabitants. The oath for jurors is in *ibid.* 68.

[32] *Ms. Mins. Ct. of Assizes* 179 *et seq.*

[33] There was some qualification in the verdict but the ms. is burned at this point.

[34] Rider v. Janssen and Dale (*Ms. Mins. Ct. of Assizes* 186 *et seq.*).

scribed that "she received this punism't. for stealing and Purloyning her masters goods."[35]

In the year 1669, sometime after Francis Lovelace became governor, the provincial conceptions of how a criminal trial should be conducted underwent alteration. In that year three special Courts of Oyer and Terminer were held to try defendants charged respectively with a burglary, a murder and an insurrection. For these courts special instructions were drafted which indicate that at one time or another someone had seen a practice book.[36] The crier was to make proclamation, then the commission was to be read. The sheriff's return of the jury was to be read over. After being sworn the jury was to be counted over, but before they were sworn the prisoner was to be called, set at the bar and then informed that he might challenge them. The crier was to summon the prosecutor, and the trial was to begin by telling the jury to look at the prisoner who was to raise his right hand and have the indictment read to him. He was next to be asked to plead whereupon the witnesses were to be called. The instructions for the other two commissions were substantially identical except for the addition in the insurrection case of a direction to charge the jury.

These directions are a simplified version of the ritual given in *The Clerk of Assize*.[37] It is conceivable that a copy of this book was available, but this seems unlikely, since the formula giving the prisoner leave to challenge (an obvious detail to copy) varies considerably from the one printed in the handbook. What is more likely is that someone who knew how English trials were conducted had come to the Province and supplied a formula from memory. But the most noteworthy circumstance is the fact that in both the burglary and murder trials the commissioners were persons who also sat in the Court of Assizes, and were presumably familiar with the provincial way in which trials had been conducted. The directions consequently strike one as an implicit rejection of the earlier practice in capital cases, and were probably introductive of a new and better ordered procedure.

The records of the burglary trial held on April 7, 1669, are the most complete for this early period. Some of the depositions are preserved,[38] and ex-

---

[35] Where the defendant confessed the offense the court proceeded to sentence, as in the prosecution by Thos. Seabrooke against Bernard Smith (*ibid.* 184).
[36] 1 *Rep. NY State Historian* 234 (trial of Frizzell, Canada *et al.*); *ibid.* 243 (proceedings against Engel Hendricks). 1 *Exec. Council Mins.* 314 (trial of the Long Finn).
[37] T.W., *The Clerk of Assize, Judges, Marshall, and Cryer* (1660).
[38] 2 *Rep. NY State Historian* 228 *et seq.*

aminations of two defendants are drawn up in the form of interrogatories and answers. When the trial began one defendant confessed, but two of them pleaded not guilty. The witnesses were some of them sworn, but those who testified for the defense were not, and were all "examined," probably by the bench. When the jury retired they were given the depositions of the witnesses, an irregularity for which we have seen no precedent. Two of the defendants were convicted and sentenced to be branded and be imprisoned for a year and a day.

One further felony trial (for grand larceny) during Lovelace's regime yields some additional details regarding procedure.[39] The directions for the trial required the swearing of witnesses (apparently without distinction as to whom they were testifying for) and the court was cautioned that of the three defendants, two were to be admitted as witnesses but before conviction, and that the "prisoner" was to have liberty "to plead for himself." The minutes of the trial[40] show that one prisoner, Roger Essex, confessed the "indictment," one, Thomas Faulx, pleaded guilty to some of the thefts, and Ben Johnson, the principal defendant, pleaded not guilty, but in the course of the trial confessed to the larceny of certain goods. The jury brought in a verdict of guilty as to Johnson, and the court elected to treat the partial confession of Faulx as a complete admission. The judges then balloted for the punishment which in Johnson's case was thirty-nine lashes, an ear cut off and banishment, in Faulx's twenty-five stripes and banishment, in Essex's ten stripes.

The minutes of the Court of Assizes during Andros' regime are so fragmentary that it is difficult to reconstruct much regarding trial procedure. Apparently capital cases were tried in accordance with the procedure followed in the cases just summarized. At the 1675 Assizes,[41] one Scudamore was prosecuted for homicide. The prisoner was brought to the bar and the jury sworn. Two facts regarding the taking of evidence appear—that children were not put on oath and that the common law rule of not swearing defendants' witnesses was explicitly recognized. The jury was charged and returned a verdict of chance medley, whereupon the prisoner was discharged by proclamation. This case was followed by a prosecution of Daniel Lane for incest. Lane had absconded, but a jury was impanelled, proclamation was made for the defendant (who does not seem to have made an appearance[42]) and the court

---

[39] 2 Exec. Council Mins. 763.
[40] Ibid. 770.
[41] In 2 Rep. NY State Historian 386, 393, 394.

[42] The minutes do not record an appearance, and in 1683 Lane is referred to as an absconding criminal (Cal. Eng. Mss. 112).

proceeded to examine witnesses and depositions. The case was submitted to a jury but the minute does not indicate the verdict. It may be supposed since a jury was impanelled that incest was regarded as heinous. But to carry on a trial in the absence of a defendant was quite indefensible and was probably resorted to as a means of regularizing a proclamation of 1673[43] to the effect that unless Lane appeared he would be adjudged guilty of the offense and his estate confiscated.

The procedure at the Assizes of 1676[44] adds very little to our information. When the court opened the Governor delivered a charge to the constables regarding presentments, and two homicides were tried. In one case, only depositions were read; in the other, some witnesses were examined. The verdict in both cases was chance medley. At both the 1675 and the 1676 sessions, cases less than capital were handled without a jury, evidence was heard and the bench delivered its sentence.

There are unfortunately no further minutes extant of the regular Court of Assizes until the year 1680, but a minute has been preserved of the Special Assize Court held in January, 1676/77, for the trial of Captain John Fenwick charged with a forceful and riotous intrusion upon ducal lands in New Jersey.[45] Fenwick was brought to the bar, the jury was returned and the presentment, brought in the name of Sam Leete, the New York City clerk, was read. Fenwick was "prest to plead but pretends to appeale & saith he is ignorant of the Lawes and proceedings of this Governm't." Finally he pleaded not guilty. Various letters patent, deeds and depositions were read, and the prisoner making a "Long discourse" denied that New Jersey was under the jurisdiction of the court. The jury was charged and returned a verdict of guilty. Fenwick moved for an appeal, and also offered again to plead in his justification. But the court gave judgment sentencing Fenwick to costs, a fine of £40 and to remain in custody until he should give security in £500 to be of good behavior and not act in any public capacity.[46]

The remaining available minutes of the Assize Court throw little additional light upon trial procedure.[47] At the trial of Captain Dyer for treason,[48] when

[43] 1 Exec. Council Mins. 181, Document xcv.
[44] 25 NY Col. Mss. 181 et seq.
[45] 1 NJ Archives (1 ser.) 236 et seq.
[46] See also the Special Court of Assizes Oct. 26, 1676, to try the Hempstead rioters (14 Doc. Rel. Col. Hist. NY 726).
[47] There are some minutes of the 1679 term in 28 NY Col. Mss. 138a. Titus Serricks, bound over by the Gravesend Sessions (Ms. Kings Co. Ct. &

Rd. Recs. 1668–1766 179) for a confessed fornication, fined. Annecke Dircks bound over, ordered lashed and fined. In the remaining records for 1680–82 (except for the cases mentioned in the text) the only criminal proceedings are the trials of some negroes for prison breach and theft (Proc. Gen. Ct. of Assizes 34).
[48] Ibid. 12.

a grand jury was used for the first time, the defendant was arraigned and pleaded before the jury was called over. The indictment was read a second time and the witnesses sworn and examined. As we have seen, Dyer then questioned the law by which he was being proceeded against and the jurisdiction of the court, averring his authority was as good as the court's, since he had the Duke's commission as collector. This was a facer for the natives, and the court decided to send Dyer to England.[49]

The Assizes when convened at the regular fall session (1681) resumed the former way of proceeding. An "indictment" of Mr. Justice Moll of Newcastle for misdemeanors on the bench was presented by Abraham Mann who had been the Justice's victim. Moll, whose judicial ermine one writer describes as having the color and odor of skunk, pleaded not guilty. A jury was impanelled, evidence was taken and the jury found Moll guilty only as to some of the matter charged. But the court thereupon decided the indictment was vexatious, dismissed it and ordered Mann to pay costs. This was a remarkable way of proceeding; but judging from the ordinance passed respecting "causeless and vexatious" accusations against magistrates, the assembled justices suddenly became terror-stricken at the assaults upon their authority.[50]

It can scarcely be said that the Assize Court, beyond the example it set for the visiting officials, exercised a consistent influence in molding and developing the enforcement of the law in the province. Throughout its life it was overshadowed by the Governor and Council, for on this body the timid or distracted local justices could constantly unburden themselves for the immediate solution of difficulties. Nevertheless, it is obvious from the scanty sources at our disposal that the Assize Court and the special commissions performed the not unimportant service of introducing what amounted to a fairly close imitation of the common law trial of felonies, and to the extent that this ritual was made familiar to the New Englanders and Dutchmen who had earlier followed their own way, the ground was prepared for the eventually complete Anglicanization of the law. To be sure, the records are bare of technicalities; defendants did not object to the form of presentments, they did not challenge jurors; the pleas in bar were used as affirmative defense; there was no joinder of issue in misdemeanor, no objections to evidence, no quarrels with the bench's charge. The defendants were generally too ignorant to have heard of such possibilities and the judges were not much more sophisticated.

---

[49] The case of Rumbouts, discussed *infra* 566.	of *New Castle* 458, 496. The description of Moll
[50] *Proc. Gen. Ct. of Assizes* 23. Cf. also *Recs. Ct.*	is in Lewis, *Thomas Spry* (1932) 64.

Probably if we possessed accounts of country trials in contemporary England the proceedings would not seem very different.

Sessions practice in the Province was roughly similar to that at Assizes, although, as we have already pointed out, there was local variation.[51] Not many cases came to trial, and when the defendants did not confess, the courts usually proceeded summarily, that is to say, no jury was used but witnesses were examined and the bench decided whether or not the defendant was guilty. This method was pursued consistently in the New York City Mayor's Court,[52] where in the years immediately following the conquest it was exceptional for a jury to be impanelled.[53] Both parties would be heard—if the prosecutor did not have enough evidence he would be ordered to produce it. After this hearing, judgment would be pronounced. During the period 1665–1672, the Mayor's Court procedure does not appear from the records to have been very different from that at Albany where the Dutch customs prevailed, and it is possible that the actual conduct of trials was within the "peculiar lawes" mentioned by Nicolls' commission.[54] After the reoccupation in 1674 the tone of the records changes perceptibly, especially in civil cases, but preference for summary trial of criminal cases continues.[55] Apparently it was only when an offense of the degree of grand larceny[56] was presented, that a jury was deemed indispensable, and in one case a presentment for immoderate correction of a negro resulting in death was put to a jury which found natural death, yet the defendant was bound to Assizes.[57] There is little to wring from the minutes respecting procedure beyond the fact that defendants who would not plead were fined,[58] and that virtually no rules of evidence were followed. Depositions were admitted,[59] and defendants were not exempt from examination by the magistrates.[60]

---

[51] *Supra* 391.

[52] See, for example, 5 *Recs. of New Amsterdam* 290 (Sabbath breach, 1665), 310 (abusive words, 1665), 314, 317, 323 (theft, 1665), 328 (assault, 1665), 338 (disorderly house, 1666), 353 (theft, 1666); 6 *ibid.* 10 (whoredom, 1666), 11 (assault, 1666), 37 (smuggling, 1666), 49 (theft, 1666), 64 (receiving, 1667), 87 (smuggling, 1667), 113 (receiving, 1668), 142 (illicit sales to Indians, 1668), 194 (attempted arson, 1669), 220, 226 (excise, 1670), 279 (theft, 1671), 340 (disorderly conduct, 1671), 371 (seditious words, 1672).

[53] E.g., *ibid.* 93 (fornication), 196 (excise). It should be noted that in civil actions for assault a jury might be used, but apparently not when there was official prosecution.

[54] 5 *ibid.* 250, June 12, 1665.

[55] Cf. *Ms. Mins. Mayor's Ct. NYC 1674–75* 17 (disorderly conduct), 25 (Sabbath breach), 35 (swindling Indians), 63 (larceny). In one case no prosecutor appeared, and defendant was discharged on proclamation. In two cases the defendant confessed. In the volume of minutes for 1677–82 are many more cases of summary trial.

[56] *Ms. Mins. Mayor's Ct. NYC 1677–82* 149b (1679), 154 (1679), 270b (1680), 291 (1681), 302b (1682); *Ms. Mins. Mayor's Ct. NYC 1680–83* 200 (1683).

[57] *Ms. Mins. Mayor's Ct. NYC 1677–82* 64b (1677).

[58] *Ibid.* 173b (1679); *Ms. Decl. Book Mayor's Ct. NYC 1675–77* 335.

[59] *Ms. Mins. Mayor's Ct. NYC 1677–82* 150.

[60] *Ibid.* 227, 228.

The question of a right to a jury was finally raised in 1679 by John Tuder and Richard Mann in the gaming case already mentioned.[61] After the presentment was read the defendants demanded a jury, alleging "the court acted unlawfully by their going about to examine witnesses and not giving them the benefit of a jury."[62] The court, however, proceeded to examine witnesses and in the final sentence included a fine of 20s. for refusing to plead. Tuder took an appeal to the Assizes, and at the session where Dyer was indicted for treason, offered an indictment (which the grand jury voted a true bill) of Francis Rumbouts, the Mayor of New York, for treason in that "the defendant did plotte, contrive and practice Innovations in government, the subversion and change of the Knowne ancient and fundimental lawes of the Realm of England" which consisted in having denied a jury trial two years before. Rumbouts, brought to the bar, claimed he was unprovided to make a defense and was given until the next Assizes to do so. At the next session he pleaded the "insufficiency" of the indictment being grounded on an act of the Mayor's Court and produced his commission. He was thereupon "acquitted," apparently by the bench.[63]

It has already been noticed that except in the North and West Ridings the Sessions Courts each had a characteristic way of doing business.[64] The Duke's Laws contemplated some uniformity as necessary to the prestige of the courts, but beyond establishing a "stile" and the formalities of opening courts, failed to provide directions for trial.[65] The justices of the peace consequently had to control their own routine, and since defendants in criminal cases were never represented by counsel, country practice was not properly safeguarded against arbitrary official conduct, the occasional outrageousness of which is depicted in various petitions. Probably the most important effect of the lack of control was the extensive use of summary procedure. Unlike the practice in the Mayor's Court a jury was impanelled at the opening of a Sessions in the West or North Riding,[66] and this body, with an occasional change in personnel, functioned whenever a cause could not be disposed of otherwise. So far as the trial of crimes was concerned, however, this was a mere flourish, for although the jury was used consistently in civil litigation, it was most exceptional for an offender to be thus tried. And such is the penury of our sources that one cannot determine any rule for these exceptions. Even the grand lar-

---

[61] Supra 330, 394.
[62] Ms. Mins. Mayor's Ct. NYC 1677–82 173b.
[63] Proc. Gen. Ct. of Assizes 13, 16.
[64] Supra 395.

[65] 1 Col. Laws NY 27.
[66] See, for example, Ms. Kings Co. Ct. & Rd. Recs. 1668–1766 13 (1669), 226 (1680); 2 Rep. NY State Historian 244 (1674), 331 (1675).

ceny test which applied in Manhattan does not seem to have obtained elsewhere, for we find a jury once used in such a case and again, a summary proceeding to handle a closely similar state of facts.[67]

That the jurymen were a mere decorative frieze in the Sessions, when criminal business was before the court, was not alone due to an aping of the Assize
practice in misdemeanor cases, but is attributable to the curious way in which
the panel was constituted. The Duke's Laws had required that the sheriff
should first have the constable warn the overseers of the towns to attend as
jurors and only if the number were insufficient was the sheriff to be required
to return able and discreet men present at court or of the town where the court
was held.[68] The effect of this restriction was, of course, to put in the box at
least some of the very persons who had been responsible for a presentment, for
a criminal charge was frequently examined closely in the town before being
preferred at Sessions. Under these circumstances a defendant might well doubt
the advantage in putting himself upon the country.

This system whereby the semblance and not the substance of the Englishman's birthright was conferred upon the inhabitants reminds one of the grand
jury at the English Assizes, composed wholly or chiefly of justices of the
peace.[69] It was shrewdly calculated to constrict the circle of responsibility for
law enforcement and, strangely enough, was never protested. Indeed, the only
objections ever raised were by a magistrate at Kingston that the jurors returned
were not overseers.[70] All the indications are that the jury was not valued by
the rulers of the Province. In October, 1665, the town courts were by ordinance
relieved of summoning jurors on the ground that a bench of eight was equivalent;[71] the clerks consistently note the "acceptance" by the bench of jury verdicts; and the loose system of appeals where new facts could be presented set at
naught the traditional prerogatives of the men of the vicinage.

Since the jury trial of presentments was so unusual in the ridings, the Sessions there appear in the minutes chiefly as a sort of administrative clearing
house. Cases were turned over to one or two justices for disposal,[72] were re-

---

[67] Thus in 1674, defendants accused of stealing
a hog were given a trial by jury (25 NY Col. Mss.
28); but in 1679, a defendant accused of putting
his mark on another man's colt (viz., a form of
larceny) was tried summarily (28 ibid. 110).

[68] 1 Col. Laws NY 42.

[69] Webb, English Local Government; The Parish and the County 447.

[70] Ms. Deeds Ulster Co. Liber 3, 222. At the
Sessions for Sept. 7, 1681, Justice Lewis Dubois insisted that according to law the jury must be made

up of overseers, otherwise he would not sit. The
presiding justice said that the jury always had been
selected from freeholders by the sheriff and the rest
of the court agreed nothing could be said against
the jury. Dubois made a disturbance and was
ejected. The next day he again was ejected. He was
finally removed from the commission (ibid. 119).

[71] 1 Col. Laws NY 74.

[72] E.g., Ms. Kings Co. Ct. & Rd. Recs. 1668–
1766 56, 63, 75, 83, 355; 3 Rep. NY State Historian 342; 27 NY Col. Mss. 127.

manded to town courts,[73] or the prisoners were bound over to Assizes.[74] If none of these measures was expedient the court would generally try the offender summarily, that is to say, upon presentment by the constable, or on the complaint of an injured party and without formal arraignment, evidence would be heard; the defendant would be allowed to speak his piece and the court would proceed to judgment.[75] Sometimes the inquiry was very searching and lengthy, for the clerk (usually scrambling to keep abreast of the bench) was able in the rough minutes to indulge the native taste for setting out the "evidence." Two examples of this are an examination of a charge of false marking,[76] and a typically Puritan accusation of a youth for cursing his parents.[77] The bench was generally anxious to give a fair hearing, for it sometimes held over a case until more proof of a charge could be produced,[78] and on one occasion would not hear a presentment because of inadequate notice.[79] There is only one case where a defendant was convicted though absent—an escaped prisoner charged with theft—and here the court examining the proof of flight obviously regarded this as equivalent to a confession.[80]

The Sessions minutes yield little about rules of procedure. There does not appear to have been formal arraignment, and only where a jury was used do defendants appear to have pleaded. The witnesses were sworn, depositions sometimes examined, but the only traces of English formality are the orders for discharge by proclamation.

It is surprising that there was never an outcry by the querulous Long Islanders against this summary procedure. Possibly the long tradition of English peace administration in petty cases like disorderly conduct or bastardy was responsible for their inertia, but it may also be observed that frequently the Sessions sensibly punished only by exacting a recognizance, and if on occasion some indiscreet wench was peremptorily ordered flogged, the bigoted *émigrés* from New England would have been the last to protest.

---

[73] E.g., *Ms. Kings Co. Ct. & Rd. Recs. 1668–1766* 60, 122; 25 *NY Col. Mss.* 57, 252; 27 *ibid.* 127.

[74] *Ms. Kings Co. Ct. & Rd. Recs. 1668–1766* 35, 73, 179, 201; 2 *Rep. NY State Historian* 257, 344.

[75] This was the usual course in the East Riding; cf. *Ms. Suffolk Co. Sess. 1668–87* 6, 7 (1669/70), 30, 31 (1671/72). In the *Ms. Kings Co. Ct. & Rd. Recs. 1668–1766*, the cases are virtually all tried summarily: 18 (wounds, 1669), 50 (abuse, 1760), 73 (Quakers, 1675), 83 (breaking and entering, 1675), 111 (abusive words, 1677), 198 (abuse of constable, 1679), 201 (assault, 1679). The most detailed minutes on the procedure of examination are in 25 *NY Col. Mss.* 130 (1676), 133 (1675); 27 *ibid.* 127 (1678); 28 *ibid.* 110 (1679). In some instances there is a résumé of the evidence. A favorite form of entry is the "to be considered of," and then much later in the minutes a fine is noted. There is nothing to indicate in these cases that a petit jury functioned.

[76] 28 *NY Col. Mss.* 160.

[77] 27 *ibid.* 127.

[78] *Ms. Kings Co. Ct. & Rd. Recs. 1668–1766* 11; 25 *NY Col. Mss.* 252.

[79] 25 *NY Col. Mss.* 130.

[80] 27 *ibid.* 127.

In the other parts of the province where courts exercised Sessions jurisdiction, procedure at trial was little affected by the influx of Englishmen, except at Newcastle. Albany, of course, remained entirely in the Dutch tradition, and the Upland records show only the slightest sort of change. At Kingston there was a gradual assimilation of English usages, but juries were rarely used, and the occasional attempts to conform to the pattern set at the Assizes produced local tempests.[81] There was, of course, no substantial difference between the summary procedure used under Dutch law and under the Duke's Laws, and since this was the accepted way of trying misdemeanors the index of change is really to be found in civil cases. Yet even here jury trial was rather gingerly resorted to,[82] usually when one or the other party to an action requested it.

At Newcastle, owing chiefly to the fact that cases were tried which elsewhere would have been reserved for the Assizes, there are available more data respecting the procedure in criminal trials by jury. The trials were obviously conducted with a minimum of formality. The jury would be impanelled, the presentment read, the prisoner would plead, witnesses would be sworn and examined, a charge would be given and, after verdict, judgment.[83] There was no challenge, no formal arraignment, no question of law ever raised. Only one case shows an appreciation of the difference between summary procedure and jury trial. Witnesses had been examined when the defendants decided they wished a jury. The court thereupon impanelled a jury and required the witnesses to be sworn *de novo*.[84] Where the court proceeded summarily the procedure was identical with that in the ridings.[85]

In respect to its functioning as a criminal court the Sessions brought about little change in the administration of the law and accomplished little beyond further inuring the inhabitants to summary proceedings. Little was done to promote familiarity with the jury trial of crimes, and were it not for the fact that civil proceedings disclose a brave attempt to achieve a resemblance with what was fondly believed to be English practice, one would estimate the process of Anglicanization to have been much slighter than it actually was. Terms

[81] *Ms. Deeds Ulster Co.* Liber 2, p. 3 (1672/73), 445 (1676); Liber 3, p. 222.
[82] An example of this is the case of Nettleship v. Moll (*Recs. Ct. of New Castle* 10, 13). The defendant was a justice. After the jury had returned a verdict "billa vera for the plaintiff" (!) the defendant entered a "demur" against the sufficiency of the verdict. In Nettleship v. Tom (*ibid.* 13) the plaintiff insisted on a jury. He was awarded 5s. damages and costs but was compelled to pay for the jury as he had demanded it.

[83] Cf. Sheriff v. Gibson (rape, 1676) *ibid.* 16; Sheriff v. Bartelsea (arson, 1676) 19; Sheriff v. Johnson (rape, 1677) 85; Sheriff v. Gibson (receiving, 1677) 104; Sheriff v. Yeo (seditious words, 1680) 469.
[84] *Recs. Ct. of New Castle* 469 (1680).
[85] *Ibid.* 102 (abuse), 115 (peace), 128 (assault), 208 (buying stolen goods), 280 (bastardy), 287 (assault), 302 (false weights), 320 (bastardy).

like demurrer, motions for nonsuit, joining issue and the like are used in the civil business of Sessions, and although much of this was a meaningless use of technical jargon in the manner of the immortal Lawyer Evans Chew, the intention to do things in the common law way is certain. There are occasionally flashes in the minutes of recondite ideas: a midwife qualifying by production of her license gives testimony as to the condition of a girl charged with fornication;[86] the Sessions at Gravesend declares it is "not the practice of the governm't to oblige any to swear against himself";[87] evidence is examined to establish felonious intent.[88] But withal there is precious little to be found in the record of twenty years' activity to salt the amateurish patriarchalism of the bench.

With the changes in procedure that ensued after the Judiciary Act of 1683, provincial law administration launched into a new phase of common law reception. It is, of course, tempting to assume that the professional style of recordation bespeaks the acceptance of an equally professional mode of trial. Actually, however, in its blandness and correctness the "memorandum" entry is less informative than the rough minutes of the earlier period.

The most important revolution in respect of trial was the substitution of grand jury indictments in place of the presentments by constables or constable and overseers, and the abandonment of the restrictive rules regarding the personnel of the petit jury, for the sheriff was no longer bound to put the town overseers at the head of his panel but by statute was to summon men from the vicinage.[89] These changes alone were calculated to promote a different manner of trial, for the fact-finding and accusatory function was now definitely severed from the purely judicial.

The two remaining Oyer and Terminer records indicate a procedure entirely in the common law idiom, and if our identification of the handwriting in a set of instructions to the clerk of Oyer and Terminer is correct, a version of the directions as set forth in the *Office of the Clerk of Assize* was available.[90] In Ulster County, where a number of inhabitants were indicted for sedition, the Oyer and Terminer record shows an appearance and confession of

---

[86] *Ms. Kings Co. Ct. & Rd. Recs. 1668–1766* 179. It should be noted that the licensed midwife was supposed to extract confessions from unmarried mothers during labor. Cf. 2 *Mins. Ct. of Albany* 401; *Recs. Ct. of New Castle* 275.

[87] 2 *Rep. NY State Historian* 339.

[88] *Ms. Kings Co. Ct. & Rd. Recs. 1668–1766* 83.

[89] 1 *Col. Laws NY* 125, 127. This provision is specifically enacted both as to the Sessions Courts and the Oyer and Terminer.

[90] This is a four-folio fragment in the *Livingston-Redmond Mss.* The hand seems to be identical with that of the commission set forth *supra* 45 and with some of the deeds, *temp.* Dongan, enrolled in *Deeds Liber 3*, NY Sec. State Office.

the indictment followed by judgment.[91] One hardy soul pleaded not guilty, and the record then notes the joinder of issue, the summoning of the jury, the verdict and judgment.[92] The proceedings at the New York Oyer and Terminer of 1684 are substantially the same.[93] There is no indication whatever respecting the presentation of evidence or the details of trial, although one may suppose that a greater degree of formality now prevailed than theretofore.

In the Sessions records for New York City and Albany a similar tightening of procedure may be observed. Some orders respecting the conduct of trials in Sessions were probably issued, although we have seen nothing more specific than the direction that in New York City the recorder was to give a general charge.[94] But it is not to be credited that such a complete *bouleversement* of old established ways could have been achieved, as for example at Albany, without some thorough instruction. These records show in 1686 formal arraignment of prisoners and the formal entry of pleas, and the trial by jury in cases that would previously have been handled summarily.[95]

For the changes which occurred during Dongan's regime the most extensive sources relate to the New York Quarter Sessions. There can be no doubt but that in this court imitation of the common law ritual of trial was close. If a charge was brought to the stage of indictment,[96] the magistrates no longer followed the former method upon presentment of examining the evidence until the prisoner saw fit to confess or they were satisfied to convict or discharge. Now the defendant was arraigned, the indictment was read and he was required to plead.[97] If the defendant elected to put himself on the country, the formal joinder of issue took place, the petit jury was summoned and the trial then proceeded. The "memorandum" entry (viz. the formal record) never took notice of challenge[98] or anything concerning evidence. From some rough minutes of the August Sessions, 1685,[99] a faint idea of the practice may

---

[91] *Ms. Mins. Oyer and Terminer Ulster Co. 1684* fols. 1–4.

[92] *Ibid.* fol. 5.

[93] 7 *Ms. Mins. Council* (Reverse) fol. 1 *et seq.*

[94] *Supra* 70 n. 82.

[95] *Ms. Mins. Albany Co. Sess. 1685–87* 14 *et seq.*

[96] Of course, in certain cases when no indictment was necessary as e.g., bastardy, the court proceeded summarily, King v. Baton (*Ms. Mins. NYCQS 1683/84–1694* 141, Nov. 1, 1688); King v. Edmunds (*ibid.* 142, Nov. 1, 1688). In King v. Hattsel (*ibid.* 148, Aug. 1, 1689) a thief was examined and confessed. This does not appear to have been a trial.

[97] Cf. King v. Davies and Rynhout (*ibid.* 28,

Feb. 3, 1684/85); King v. Edmonds *et al.* (*ibid.* 71, Nov. 13, 1685); King v. Hubbart (*ibid.* 31, Feb. 3, 1684/85); King v. Kellerhouse (*ibid.* 82, Feb. 2, 1685/86); King v. Thomassen (*ibid.* 69, Nov. 13, 1685).

[98] It appears, however, from a civil case, Annett v. Read (*Ms. Mins. Mayor's Ct. NYC 1682–95* Jan. 15, 1683/84) where the plaintiff's attorney excepted to the array, that the provincials knew of the notion of challenge. On the improved knowledge of practice, cf. also Nicolls v. Dyer (1685) where a *tales* was granted when the jury did not appear (*H.R. Papers* Sessions of Aug. 1685).

[99] These are in the *H.R. Papers* (no number). The case discussed in the text is Ludgar q.t. v. the

be gathered from the trial of an information under the Navigation Acts. The statutes in question were read, and witnesses were sworn for both the informer and defendant. That a defendant's witnesses in a misdemeanor case should be sworn, establishes the eventual acceptance of English practice in misdemeanor cases. In the next year an entry of a defendant's appearance by counsel in another misdemeanor case[100] demonstrates further the progress of common law reception.

The most discursive document of this period is the account of the special Oyer and Terminer held in September, 1683, for the trial of certain piratical acts by the crew of the ship *Camellion*. This court sat before the procedural reforms were instituted, but it probably is fairly representative of what went on in succeeding years. One Edward Starkey was first put on trial for the piratical taking of the *Camellion*. The "indictment" was not found by a grand jury but was an ex officio complaint such as had been used for the past two decades. The Crown witnesses testified at some length and at one point a witness was cross-examined by the prisoner. The defendant's witnesses were not sworn. The petit jury found Starkey not guilty but he was required to give a recognizance in £200 for his good behavior for a year and a day. This was a test case, as the indictments against the other defendants were withdrawn by leave of court and an information then put in charging conspiracy and embezzlement. On this the remaining defendants were convicted, and all but one were sentenced to twenty lashes apiece, imprisonment for a year and a day and then to give security for good behavior.[101]

The muniments of civil litigation between 1683 and 1691 throw some light upon the rate at which the character of provincial procedure changed, but it must be borne in mind that until the beginning of the eighteenth century at least, there was a relative lag in the imitation of English criminal procedure chiefly because this was a matter with which the local bar, then more knowledgeable than the bench, had little to do. For this reason, one may hazard the guess that the criminal trial practice of the New York courts during the last decade and a half of the seventeenth century probably resembled that at Westminster in about the same degree as that of an English country Sessions. The development of trial procedure, beyond the minimum necessary for a record, was peculiarly the charge of the judges and the Crown prosecutors. The first

Pink *Charles.* The record entry is in *Ms. Mins. NYCQS 1683/84–1694* 56–59, Aug. 4, 1685. The information is in *H.R. Pleadings* Pl. K. 458.
   [100] *Ms. Mins. NYCQS 1683/84–1694* 112, May

3, 1686, King v. John Vincent. The entry ends after appearance noted.
   [101] *H.R. Ms. Wills* Libers 1 and 2, 306 *et seq.*

of such figures in New York with any pretensions to capacity were the execrated Chief Justice William Atwood and the Attorney General Sampson Sheldon Broughton, appointed in 1700.[102] It is consequently not mere accident that the Bayard treason trial of 1702, for all the peculiar things which there occurred, demonstrates how far advanced the process of copying common law methods was.

Eighteenth Century Practice

It would profit us little to attempt to establish the date when each particular incident of English trial practice first made its appearance in New York, and we shall consequently endeavor to depict in general the way in which trials were conducted in the province after the Judiciary Act of 1691 came into effect. So far as possible we shall indicate those particulars in which the practice of inferior courts may have differed from that in the Supreme Court.

The course of the typical criminal trial in New York during the eighteenth century can be plotted with the *Office of the Clerk of Assize* or the *Crown Circuit Companion* in one hand and with Hawkins' *Pleas of the Crown* in the other, for the information yielded by the standard record even in combination with minute books is an accumulation of rules unmitigated by the vistas of human passion that unfold in the accounts of contemporary English trials. Except for a few cases where public interest stimulated an attempt to preserve a running account of proceedings, as in the Bayard, the Makemie, the Zenger and the Negro Conspiracy trials, there is regrettably little to help us visualize the courts at work. The general run of crime in the Province was not of a character to excite curiosity as to how an offender was dealt with in the courts, and if there was morbid inquisitiveness it was not pandered to by reams of evidence in the public prints. The spectacle of prisoners pilloried or stripped and whipped about the town was sufficient satisfaction of such appetites.

To a certain extent the failure of the New York criminal trials to titillate the pamphleteers was due also to the circumstance that in this field few forensic battles were fought, chiefly because counsel was only occasionally employed in criminal cases. Attorneys appeared for defendants in Dongan's time,[103] but it is apparent from the sources that the restrictions of English law

---

[102] 4 *Doc. Rel. Col. Hist. NY* 667. Broughton had a law library of sorts, for the inventory of his estate lists lawbooks and manuscripts (*H.R. Ms. Wills* Liber 5 & 6, 433). Columbia Law Library has a copy of Kelyng's reports with Broughton's autograph—not a book which would set a good example for a provincial Attorney General.

[103] Cf. *supra* 572. At the New York Co. Oyer and Terminer of 1684, Swinton appeared to move for bail for a prisoner accused of stabbing (7 *Ms. Mins. Council* [Reverse] 51).

respecting the right to counsel were followed. That is to say, only on points of law could counsel appear in felony cases, and there is no evidence that the colonial judges indulged prisoners beyond this limit as sometimes occurred in England.[104] In misdemeanor cases, the liberty of defendant to be represented at all stages of the proceedings was respected, and in the provincial court minutes are numerous instances where counsel made appearances, entered pleas, argued motions and the like.[105]

The acceptance in New York of the old rules about counsel necessarily circumscribed the role of the bar in molding a distinctive provincial law. The character of the prosecutions likewise had its effect, for the records show that barring certain of the information proceedings where the significant issue was not the particular crime but the collateral political implications, the type of case where a smart defense engineered by a skilled technician was possible was limited. Furthermore, the usual defendant was quite unable to afford legal advice, and was thus cast upon the good offices of the judges for help in conducting his case.[106] In the country it was exceptional for a defendant to be represented, although now and then when some local nabob was in the toils of the law a lawyer would appear to lend aid. As a result, with the Crown usually represented by a competent Attorney General or a deputy familiar with the routine of securing a conviction, the trial end of criminal law enforcement was a rather one-sided affair. The exactness with which the details of English usage were reproduced in New York may consequently be attributed to the fact that it was largely the achievement of appointed officials who followed the books and did their duty by the King; that its shortcomings were suffered was because it was little subject to the batterings, the snares and stratagems of defense counsel.

---

[104] In the Leisler trial the defendants were allowed counsel (P.R.O., C.O. 5/1037 fol. 1), an indulgence which the records do not show to have been beneficial. As this trial was not conducted with any proper regard for rule the case cannot be regarded as a precedent. In the Bayard case the court, under the misapprehension apparently that the statute 7 Wm. III c.3 applied to the dominions, assigned counsel and allowed the defendant the privileges extended by that statute. This case likewise had no significance as a precedent.

[105] Examples have already appeared in various cases discussed in previous chapters. In the borderline case of King v. Peterson, indicted (1734/35) for cursing the Governor, counsel was assigned (*Ms. Mins. SCJ 1732–39* 147, 189). Cf. also King v. Brewer (*Ms. Mins. SCJ 1723–27* 280); King v.

Fleet (*Ms. Mins. SCJ 1727–32* 136, 145); King v. Albany Justices (*ibid.* 133); King v. Cosyne (*ibid.* 230); King v. Colos et ux. (*Ms. Mins. SCJ 1732–39* 28); King v. Gardiner (*ibid.* 325, 338); King v. James Tuthill (*Ms. Mins. SCJ 1750–54* [Engr.] 328). In King v. Buchanan (1756), counsel appeared by virtue of a warrant of attorney (*Ms. Mins. SCJ 1754–57* [Engr.] 222, 240).

[106] We have seen nothing to indicate in criminal cases a practice of defense *in forma pauperis*, nor was help forthcoming for complainants. George Spencer, the informer (*supra* 241), discovered that his adversaries had retained all the counsel available and petitioned the court for aid. The court assigned J. T. Kempe and John Alsop but Spencer was to pay the fees (*Ms. Mins. SCJ 1756–61* [Rough] 186).

Although the general run of criminal cases in New York was of such a character that there was little scope for effective action by counsel at trial, it was nevertheless possible for the lawyers to play a role in negotiating clients out of trouble even after a case had passed the stage of pleading. This is a phase of practice the dimensions of which could be accurately estimated only if a greater bulk of lawyers' papers were available. As it is, the judicial records in most instances offer only the slightest handhold for guesses. There are, for example, the numerous occasions where the defendants were discharged by proclamation because of failure of prosecution, a blunt form of entry that offers no clue to the circumstances. There is furthermore the nolle prosequi already discussed,[107] where counsel were in some cases undoubtedly busy; indeed, Governor Moore's schedule of fees provides a charge for drawing a nolle prosequi in the table of attorney's fees.[108] An equally numerous group of cases are those where prosecution was dropped or a merely nominal penalty was inflicted because the defendant had come to an agreement with the complaining witness. These cases were frequently managed by confessing the indictment or pleading *nolo contendere,* at the same time advising the court of the settlement, a method which we believe reflects expert advice.[109] Such arrangements could of course be made by the Attorney General, for we have found a power to compound given by a complainant to William Kempe.[110] But a cautious and propertied defendant if he could settle would certainly retain counsel to make his bargain.

---

[107] *Supra* 367 *et seq.*

[108] *An Ordinance for Regulating . . . Fees* (1768) 2. The attorney was to get 3*s.* for "drawing a noli prosequi," the Attorney General to receive 10*s.* for entering it.

[109] For example, in King v. Nathan Levy *et al.* (*Ms. Mins. NYCQS 1694–1731/32* 515–518) the Attorney General, on reading the indictment "and understanding that satisfaction has been made to James and Martha Long [the victims] . . . sayeth that he further for . . . the King . . . will not prosecute." On Aug. 6, 1734, John Thorn was indicted for assaulting a constable, but on October 22, 1734, the Attorney General informed the court that Constable Hendrick Slyck and the defendant, Thorn, "were come to an agreement." He also stated that Thorn had been in jail for six weeks and therefore the court let Thorn off with a fine of 1*s.* which he paid to the sheriff and was discharged (*Ms. Mins. SCJ 1732–39* 122, 137). In King v. Edward Gatehouse, the defendant was, on Aug. 1, 1739, found guilty on an indictment for an unnamed offense, but on Aug. 7, 1739, "inasmuch as the defendant has made up with the prosecutor and

made proper acknowledgements to and asked pardon of the sheriff . . . the court fines the defendant 10*s.*" (*ibid.* 334, 347, 355). Nicholas Burger on Oct. 23, 1738, submitted to the mercy of the court because he did not wish to contend with the King, and on Oct. 24, the court fined the defendant 10*s.*, "he having before agreed with the prosecutor and he giving security for his good behavior . . . especially towards Lucas VanVeghten and Mary VanVeghten" (*ibid.* 325, 327). Cf. King v. Johannes Bradt (*infra* 727 n. 383). On Aug. 1, 1752, Thomas Wenman confessed an indictment for usury and put himself on the mercy of the court, but on Oct. 25, 1753, on the motion of the Attorney General for judgment, the court ordered that the defendant be fined 3*s.* 4*d.*, "he having agreed with ye prosecutor" (*ibid.* 160, 317). Adam King, confessing an indictment for a deceit in selling half a load of hay as a full load, was fined 13*s.* 4*d.*, "he having agreed with the prosecutor" (*ibid.* 317, 342, 351). There are numerous other examples.

[110] In King v. Newton *et al.* (*Ms. Mins. SCJ 1750–54* [Engr.] 209, 280). The power is in *J. T. Kempe Lawsuits* L–O.

The most informative document available on these matters is the *Supream Court Register* kept by William Smith Jr. for the years immediately following his admission to the bar. Smith, under the heading of a case, would enter a promise to pay and have it signed by the client. He took care to keep a journal of his work, possibly to let the client know how the fees were earned. Some of these cases show negotiations with the Attorney General and how matters were manipulated.[111]

Appearance and Arraignment

In the ordinary course of events, once an indictment had been found and there was no way of avoiding trial, proceedings were gotten under way only when a defendant's appearance had been secured and the fact of this appearance was entered. It was to effect this end that much of the complicated structure of process and recognizance existed, for English law demanded that in felony and treason cases a defendant personally appear, and in misdemeanors allowed appearance by attorney only when the case was in King's Bench. These requirements were followed in New York, the only relaxation being that sometimes the Sessions courts did not exact the appearance of the defendant himself.[112] The entry of appearance was made in the minute book but, as we have seen in regard to recognizances, this part of the clerk's duty was often haphazardly executed.

In the English Quarter Sessions the appearance of the defendant, if he came on a venire facias or pursuant to a recognizance, was the opportunity for him to traverse the indictment if it was for some minor trespass, a step which in the words of Lambard was "to denie the point of the indictment."[113] The procedure in England was to appear with sureties, when the clerk of the peace would read the indictment and the defendant would then make his traverse, the real object being thereby to forestall trial until the next Sessions.[114] This manner of delaying proceedings obtained in New York but it was not confined to Sessions. Cases first appear in the early eighteenth century, and occur occasionally thereafter. Apparently the traverse was offered in open court and

---

[111] William Smith Jr., *Ms. Supream Court Register A*. For an example, *infra* 742 n. 380.

[112] Cf. Queen v. John France where the father appeared ([1705] *Ms. Kings Co. Ct. & Rd. Recs. 1692–1825* 148); King v. Anne Hamilton where a "friend" appeared (*Ms. Mins. NYCQS 1732–62* 517, Feb. 2, 1762). *Supra* 434 nn. 253–255.

In the case of defendants unable to speak English, interpreters were sometimes sworn, but it is not

apparent that they did more than enter the plea; cf. King v. John and Garrett Hardenburgh (*Ms. Mins. NYCQS 1694–1731/32* 4, Nov. 7, 1694); King v. Domingus Crea, 1722 (*Ms. Mins. Cir. 1721–49* 30, 31); King v. Weght, 1776 (*Ms. Mins. SCJ 1775–81* [Engr.] 61, 63).

[113] Lambard, *Eirenarcha* Bk. 4 c.13.

[114] 1 Chitty, *Criminal Law* 486.

it would be then ordered that the defendant continue on his recognizance or a new engagement to prosecute the traverse with effect would be exacted.[115] This procedure was actually the equivalent of an imparlance, but the traverse served also as a blanket notice that in some manner or other the indictment would be attacked. In the form in which the traverse was sometimes entered in New York it was treated as a plea of not guilty, but it is obvious from English usage that the defendant's eventual move when the case came up for trial might be something different. The intendment of the expression "traverse" in Sessions can be best understood with reference to the rule that a traverse is normally tried at the next succeeding session of the court. Having made a traverse, a defendant, who usually never appeared with an attorney, was able to seek counsel and come in with a motion to quash and then, failing this, to plead the general issue. This appears most clearly in the Dutchess General Sessions records, and an entry of October 15, 1751, when one Ricketson was given sixty days to plead "saving all advantages and exceptions to the indictment," indicates how the matter was understood.[116] It is also to be observed that in cases where defendants were entitled to traverse on appearance, the entries fail to

[115] George Norton, a butcher, indicted on Aug. 1, 1704, in N.Y. Quarter Sessions for selling corrupt flesh "denys the Indictment and traverses the same," whereupon he was bound in £20, with Bartholomew Trout as a surety in £10, "to prosecute his traverse with effect" (*Ms. Mins. NYCQS 1694–1731/32* 90).

Bartholomew Trout, indicted in N.Y. Quarter Sessions on Aug. 3, 1709, for an assault and breach of the peace, appeared on Nov. 1, 1709 "in his proper person and prays time to traverse . . . at the next sessions," whereupon he gave in a recognizance in £20 to "prosecute his traverse with effect the next sessions" (*ibid.* 164, 167).

An indictment for entertaining slaves having been brought in against Mary Lyndsey on May 3, 1710, in N.Y. Quarter Sessions, the defendant on Aug. 2, 1710 "appears in her proper person and pleads not Guilty and Traverses the Indictment till the Next Court Joseph Berry and James Wright her suretys severally Recognize . . . in twenty pounds . . . that the Def^t do personally Appear at the Next General Sessions and prosecute her Traverse with Effect" (*ibid.* 175, 177).

On Feb. 7, 1710/11, John Basford "was called upon his recognizance and appeared and pleaded not guilty" to an indictment for using false weights whereupon he was ordered to enter a recognizance in £20 to "prosecute his traverse with effect the next sessions" (*ibid.* 190, 191).

In King v. William Gilbert "on motion of Jamison the defendant appears Ppio Psona Indictment read the defendant pleads not guilty and traverses the Indictment" (*Ms. Mins. SCJ 1723–27* 126, Mar.

10, 1724/25). Likewise in King v. Hannah Carlisle, "Vernon Ɖ defendt Ordered defendants appearance be entered. Defendant pleads not guilty and traverses the indictment" (*ibid.* 126, Mar. 10, 1724/25).

Abraham Priso and his wife, indicted for a misdemeanor in buying iron from slaves, "plead not guilty and traverse ye Indictment till next term" (*ibid.* 143, June 5, 1725).

Samuel Brown, indicted in N.Y. Quarter Sessions for assault, "pleads not guilty and traverses the indictment" (*Ms. Mins. NYCQS 1732–62* 41, May 9, 1734).

The same or another Samuel Brown, under indictment for a misdemeanor in receiving stolen goods, on May 3, 1738, "traverses the Indictment and pleads not guilty" whereupon he was, on May 4, bound in £20 "to appear and prosecute his traverse with effect" (*ibid.* 86, 87).

Note also some country entries: King v. Pudney (*Ms. Mins. Queens Co. Sess. 1722–87* May 16, 1727); King v. Sarah Hillyer, who pleads not guilty and traverses (*Ms. Mins. Richmond Co. Sess. 1710/11–1744/45* Sept. 4, 1722); King v. Cornelius Wynants (*ibid.* Sept. 25, 1744, Mar. 19, 1744/45); King v. Lawrence (*Ms. Mins. Richmond Co. Sess. 1745–1812* Sept. 22, 1761); King v. Abner Winant (*ibid.* May 4, 1773); King v. Richard Johnson (*ibid.* Sept. 27, 1774); King v. Abner Reeves (*Ms. Mins. Suffolk Co. Sess. 1723–51* Oct. 4, 1737); King v. Israel Smith (*Ms. Mins. Suffolk Co. Sess. 1760–75* Mar. 28, 1775).

[116] *Ms. Mins. Dutchess Co. Sess.* Liber B. Compare King v. Van Wogelom where defendant

notice that there was formal arraignment, indicating clearly the defendant was not yet called to answer.

The trial of a defendant who was in custody, as in cases of treason or felony, or who was taken in misdemeanors on a capias, generally began by arraignment, that is to say, the prisoner was brought to the bar, the indictment read to him and he was asked if he were guilty or not guilty. This formality, important in the Middle Ages, had become no more than an occasion for identification and for the announcement of the defendant's answer to the charge against him.[117] As we have seen, this ceremony was introduced into New York shortly after the conquest, and the records indicate that it was not peculiar to felony trials but was also used in misdemeanor cases whenever the defendant was in custody.[118]

In only one particular was the matter of arraignment of real importance and that was in regard to the accessories to a crime, for in felony cases the common law did not allow arraignment of an accessory until the principal was

pleaded not guilty and his attorney "enters plea of traverse" (*Ms. Mins. Richmond Co. Sess. 1710/11–1744/45* Sept. 22, 1741).

[117] 2 Hale, *Pleas of the Crown* 216 *et seq.*

[118] The following are a few examples of arraignment entries. On Aug. 11, 1701, John Wood was arraigned at a Special Court of Oyer and Terminer and General Gaol Delivery held in New York City on an indictment for felony whereupon he "accordingly was arraigned and pleaded not guilty and put himself upon God and his country" (*Ms. Mins. SCJ 1701–04* 2).

James Stewart and two others had been brought into the Supreme Court on an inquisition of riot delivered into the court by two New York justices of peace, and on Oct. 13, 1705, "the Defendts now all arraigned and all pleaded not guilty and puts themselves upon God and their country Ordered to be brought to trial at two . . . in the afternoon" (*Ms. Mins. SCJ 1704/05–1709* 42).

At Westchester Oyer and Terminer and General Gaol Delivery for Aug. 9, 1721, William Moras, who was under indictment for feloniously taking goods worth £27, was "brought to the barr and arraigned on his arraignment [*sic*]," whereupon he pleaded not guilty and "puts himself upon God and his country" (*Ms. Mins. Cir. 1721–49* 3).

When Jacob Blackwell was indicted for felony at Albany Oyer and Terminer and General Gaol Delivery for Aug. 25, 1722, the court "ordered the sheriff take him," whereupon he was "brought to the barr pleaded not guilty and put himself upon God and the country" (*ibid.* 16).

In King v. Moses Susman, "on an indictment . . . for stealing Gold and Silver money . . . the prisoner arraigned pleads not guilty" (*Ms. Mins. SCJ 1723–27* 273, June 12, 1727).

On June 5, 1730, Ellenor Floyd "on an indictment for . . . murthering her bastard child . . . arraigned . . . for her tryall puts herself upon God and the country" (*Ms. Mins. SCJ 1727–32* 201).

On May 7, 1734, Samuel Brown appeared in New York Quarter Sessions on an indictment for petit larceny, and on May 9, "the Defendant was Arraigned on an Indictment of Petty Larceny . . . put himself upon God and the Country and pleaded not Guilty" (*Ms. Mins. NYCQS 1732–62* 39–41).

At Queens County Oyer and Terminer and General Gaol Delivery for Sept. 15, 1734, "Henry Hinton being brought to the Barr was arraigned upon the Coroner's Inquest for accidentally shooting Ezechiel Weeks upon which he confessed the fact" (*Ms. Mins. Cir. 1721–49* 71).

On June 17, 1735, at Albany Oyer and Terminer and General Gaol Delivery "the Grand Jurry find a bill for murder against Alexander Frasier . . . Ordered that the prisoner be brought to the Barr . . . The prisoner being brought to the Barr was arraigned upon two indictments for murder and for his tryall put himself upon God and the country" (*ibid.* 80, 81).

Margaret Grass was indicted in the Supreme Court for a capital felony and, on Apr. 22, 1736, "The Attorney Gen[11] moves for the prisoner to be brought to the Barr upon her arraignment and being Come she pleaded Not Guilty and her Tryall to be on Saturday next" (*Ms. Mins. SCJ 1732–39* 210).

On Oct. 24, 1774, Bridget Kennedy, "arraigned" on an indictment for larceny, pleaded not guilty (*Ms. Mins. SCJ 1772–76* [Rough] 199).

attainted. This rule was applied in New York as early as 1693. In a case involving a burglary by some negroes, two were arraigned as principals, one confessed the indictment and the other pleaded not guilty. The confession of one principal was treated as sufficient and three other negroes involved as accessories were thereupon brought to the bar.[119] Thereafter, the rule regarding accessories was consistently followed;[120] indeed, in 1739 a defendant was ordered released on the ground that the principal offenders had not been taken.[121]

Pleading

In felony cases the most important incident of arraignment was the announcement of the defense, for the ancient rule of answer *instanter* still applied during the eighteenth century. In misdemeanors tried in the Supreme Court, however, it was customary to give a rule to plead, either upon appearance or later. This, when resorted to in New York, was usually a twenty-day rule after which a judgment for want of a plea might be entered.[122] If the defendant or his attorney did not enter a plea during the interval the prosecutor was entitled to sign judgment by default, and we have seen one such document.[123] From the minutes of the courts, however, it is apparent that this for-

[119] *Mins. SCJ 1693–1701* 42.
[120] Cf. Queen v. Mary and Tom, slaves (*Ms. Mins. SCJ 1704/05–1709* 84, 90); King v. Betty and Frank, slaves (*Ms. Mins. NYCQS 1694–1731/32* 362–365); King v. Moras (*Ms. Mins. Cir. 1721–49* 9, 12).
[121] King v. Anne Hall (*Ms. Mins. SCJ 1732–39* 341, 365).
The colonial act respecting accessories and receivers of 1773 (5 *Col. Laws NY* 543) enacted the substance of various English statutes.
[122] Numerous instances have been set forth in previous chapters. The following cases indicate the consistency of the practice.
In Queen v. John Theobalds and in four other cases on Mar. 16 and 18, 1709/10, the sheriff was ordered to bring in the bodies or be amerced 40s. However, Regnier appearing for the defendants, they were ordered to plead in fourteen days before the following term or suffer judgment (*Ms. Mins. SCJ 1704/05–1709* 249, 251). Likewise, see the similar rule in Queen v. John MacCanon, on Mar. 18, 1709/10, Jamison appearing for defendant (*ibid.* 249, 251). In Queen v. Willet, George appeared for the defendant who was ordered to plead in fourteen days before the following term or suffer judgment (*Ms. Mins. SCJ 1710–14* 459, 487, June 6, Sept. 5, 1713). On Apr. 23, 1733, the sheriff of New York returned *cepi corpus* as to one Colos, and when Smith appeared for the defendant he was

ordered to plead in twenty days or suffer judgment (*Ms. Mins. SCJ 1732–39* 28). In King v. Nicholas Brittain, on an indictment removed to the Supreme Court from Richmond County, Smith on Jan. 23, 1738/39, appeared for the defendant who was ordered to plead in twenty days or suffer judgment. In this case, it is interesting to note that on Apr. 17, 1739, the court ordered that unless the defendant show cause to the contrary in four days, judgment would be given against him. However, on Apr. 20, judgment was stayed in the cause on motion of Smith for the defendant (*ibid.* 332, 336, 339). On Oct. 20, 1756, an indictment was filed against William McKim for an assault and battery committed on Charity Caston and on Jan. 21, 1757, the defendant was ordered to plead in thirty days or suffer judgment. On Jan. 22, 1757, Smith appeared for the defendant but no further proceedings appear in the case (*Ms. Mins. SCJ 1754–57* [Engr.] 309, 314, 349, 362). In July term, 1757, the sheriff of Queens returned *cepi corpus* as to Samuel Fish who endorsed his appearance on the writ and was thereupon ordered to plead in a month or suffer judgment (*Ms. Mins. SCJ 1757–60* [Engr.] 56). In King v. Silas Bayly and in King v. Jesse Harris, the sheriff of Westchester returned *venire feci* and the defendants were ordered to plead in twenty days or suffer judgment (*Ms. Mins. SCJ 1766–69* [Engr.] 592, Nov. 5, 1768).
[123] King v. Haring *et al.* (1764): "I sign judg-

mality was not necessarily observed in New York, the courts merely ordering the entry of default either as a matter of course or upon motion.[124] If the court did not require defendant's presence for sentence the judgment and amount of the fine would then be noted and occasionally the clerk ordered to issue *capias pro fine.* That the rule to plead was no mere idle threat is evidenced by the fact that in the Supreme Court, between 1693 and 1776, judgment by default was entered in fifty-four cases and in the New York Quarter Sessions between 1691 and 1776 in seventeen cases.

One of the strange quirks of Sessions practice was the eventual adoption of the rule to plead. This begins in the 1740's and was actually a diminution of the indulgence which allowed traverse on appearance and trial of the cause at the next Sessions. Some of the orders simply state that defendant plead in so and so many days, without adding "or suffer judgment." Possibly defendants were reluctant to plead, or the recognizance did not have a condition "to answer," or the justices may have been setting about to secure a manner of plea more specific than the imprecise "traverse." We are disposed to think that the practice grew up in imitation of the Supreme Court usage, and that the local jurists were not entirely aware of what they were about. In some counties a twenty-day period, in others a forty and still others a sixty-day grace was stipulated.[125]

How the rule to plead or judgment to follow drifted into criminal practice has never been satisfactorily explained, but it seems to be derived from the procedure used in civil cases. In other words, since the petty cause involving a fine depended largely upon the activity of a complainant, the medieval conception that the King must be answered was abandoned for the more rational notion that failure to comply with the court's rule to plead was treated exactly as a default in answering a plaintiff in civil proceedings.[126] The colonists, how-

---

ment agt each and every Def[ts] for want of a plea John Tabor Kempe Esq. Attorney General" (*H.R. Pleadings* Pl. K. 757).

[124] As in King v. Grimes on motion of the clerk (*Ms. Mins. NYCQS 1732–62* 329, 339, 348, Feb. 7, 1753, Nov. 7, 1753, May 8, 1754); King v. Doughterman (*ibid.* 351, 357, 360, Aug. 7, Nov. 6, 1754, Feb. 4, 1755); King v. de Grote (*Ms. Mins. NYCQS 1760–72* 321, 327, 337, 350, Aug. 9, Nov. 7, 1770, Feb. 8, 1771, Aug. 8, 1771); King v. Griffiths (*ibid.* 360, Nov. 7, 1771); King v. Gomez, 1767 (*Ms. Mins. SCJ 1764–67* [Rough] 140; *Ms. Mins. SCJ 1766–69* [Engr.] 95); King v. Ferguson and Cooley, 1766 (*Ms. Mins. SCJ 1764–66* [Engr.] 178, 284, 368, 443; *H.R. Parch.* 193 L 9, 182 K 10). There are many other examples.

[125] King v. William Smith, 60 days (*Ms. Mins. Dutchess Co. Sess.* Liber A, Oct. 20, 1741); King v. Ricketson, 60 days (*ibid.* Liber B, Oct. 15, 1751); King v. Constable, 40 days (*Ms. Mins. Albany Co. Sess. 1763–82* Oct. 2, 1765); King v. Berry, 40 days (*ibid.* Jan. 21, 1766); King v. De Noyallis, King v. Snedeker, 20 days (*Ms. Mins. Orange Co. Sess. 1727–79* Oct. 26, 1762); King v. Mersereau (*Ms. Mins. Richmond Co. Sess. 1745–1812* May 4, 1762); King v. Hicks (*ibid.* Sept. 28, 1762). New York City cases, *supra* n. 124.

[126] On the civil procedure, 1 Tidd, *Practice of King's Bench* 474 *et seq.*, 562. The Supreme Court was familiar with this; cf. the rule of 1699 (*Mins. SCJ 1693–1701* 166).

The criminal practice was limited to cases of fine

ever, appear to have viewed the defendant's default as the equivalent of a confession, for there are some "memoranda" entries (viz., enrolled judgments) where the defendant is recorded as pleading guilty, whereas the rough minutes show only a judgment for want of a plea.[127] This inference of confession the English authorities applied in misdemeanor cases only to obstinate refusals to plead,[128] for it was clearly understood that the defendant suffered default judgment chiefly to save the expense of trial and was not therefore to be treated as contumacious. There was no occasion for this distinction to be made in New York since the courts only once, and at an early date, had to cope with a direct refusal to plead in a minor case. William Bickley and Daniel Latham were presented on February 7, 1704/05, for working on the thirtieth day of January "in contempt of the statute" and capias was ordered to issue against them. On May 1, 1705, Bickley "acknowledged" he kept his shop open on January 30 but did not know it was an offense against the law. He submitted to the mercy of the court and was fined 6s. and fees. Latham, however, "appeared in his proper person and the Indictment being read he refused to plead." In this case, the defendant's refusal to plead was not taken *pro confesso,* but the court "Ordered that he stand committed till he find sufficient surety for his . . . appearance . . . to answer."[129]

The refusal to plead was equally unusual in the New York felony prosecutions. Until 1772,[130] the *peine forte et dure,* that humane invention of the Middle Ages to compel a defendant to answer a felony indictment, was a part of English common law procedure. This was still in use during the reign of Charles II,[131] although it came to be supplanted by the less obnoxious persuasion of thumb tying.[132]

---

as the defendant had to be present when a judgment of corporal punishment was inflicted (2 Hawkins, *Pleas of the Crown* c.48 §17).

[127] Cf. King v. Mathew Morris, indicted for disorderly house (*Ms. Mins. NYCQS 1732–62* 402, 403, 408, 409, 415, 416, 417, Feb. 3, May 5, Aug. 5. 1757); King v. John Cox, indictment for a nuisance and fire hazard in keeping a yard filled with tar next to a dwelling; King v. Heyman Levy, indictment for a nuisance and fire hazard in keeping a shingle yard near dwellings; King v. Samuel Louden, indictment for nuisance in maintaining a vessel aground in Rotten Row (*ibid.* 414, 415, 420, 421, 429–433, Aug. 4, Nov. 2, 1757, Feb. 9, 1758). It will be noted that these are all inferior court cases.

[128] 2 Hawkins, *op. cit.* c.30 §10; 3 *Middlesex County Records* (Sessions Rolls), 348, 352–354 (1663) *passim.*

[129] *Ms. Mins. NYCQS 1694–1731/32* 94, 96. There were no further proceedings in this case and we do not know whether Latham finally did appear to answer. In King v. Caleb Miller, defendant did not appear to plead and process was threatened. He was already under bond (*Ms. Mins. Orange Co. Sess. 1727–79* Oct. 1727).

[130] By statute 12 Geo. III c.20, the *peine forte* was abolished and it was provided that where a prisoner stood mute he should be convicted and judgment awarded as if convicted by verdict or confession. The act extended to the plantations.

[131] Cf. 3 *Middlesex Co. Recs.* (Sessions Rolls) 350 (1664), 372 (1665).

[132] *Supra* n. 7. Barrington, *Observations on the Statutes* (1767) 59.

The *peine forte* was not incorporated in the law of New York for the reason, we think, that the judges who sat in judgment upon Jacob Leisler saw fit to employ a modification of it on that unhappy man, and this one experience with the great mercies of the *peine* was sufficient. The attentive reader will not have forgotten that in *King* v. *Leisler et al.*, the defendants Leisler and Milborne objected to the jurisdiction of the court, but the bench seeking and securing the advice of the Governor and Council held this to be "noe plea."[133] The judgment roll sent to London, however, says nothing of this, but recites, "And the said Jacob Leisler on the above Presentment being arraigned before the said Justices of our said Lord and Lady the King and Queen the Day and year first above sc., to the same maketh no Defense but although solemly Required any Answer to the same to make utterly Denyes and is mute to the same."[134] The minutes, which note the overruling of the plea, recount that on the next day (April 1) Leisler was brought to the

> barr and again arraigned on the Indictment for treason the president remembers him of the favour done him and advises him to plead, who continues his generall talke refusing to plead and prays he may further advise with his Councell, butt the Kings Councell prayed Judgm^t unless the prisoner will plead, and he was ordered tyed up and putt in irons in order to his suffering the Judgmt of the law to be given by this court. . . .[135]

The judgment roll entry taken in connection with the minutes (and in particular, the minute for April 15 which shows a third arraignment and demand for a plea) establishes that the bench, by the order to tie and iron and delaying the pronouncement of sentence, was in effect attempting to compel a plea. Assuming Leisler's objection to the jurisdiction was correctly held to be "noe plea," the proper procedure would have been to impanel a jury to determine whether or not the prisoner stood mute from malice or act of God.[136] The failure to do this was an accumulation to the disgrace which the bench had already assumed, and now that the record is available the names of Joseph

---

[133] Cf. *supra* c. II 83. The minutes (P.R.O., C.O. 5/1037/1) read: "Jacob Leisler was brought to the barr who prayed oyer of the Com̃on wch was read and refusing to hold up his hand read a small paper offering that forasmuch as he had been in power here he ought not to plead till such time as that power was determined being told that if on his tryall he would offer to justifye the Indictmt by such power it would properly come before the Court and be determined he sayd he is a subject of the King and honours the Comĩcon whereupon the opinion of the bench was asked wch was unanimous that whatsoever had been said was heard of grace and did in itselfe the most favourable accepted amount to noe plea in law or fact. . . ." The ruling of the Governor and Council is in 2 *Doc. Hist. NY* 207.

[134] P.R.O., C.O. 5/1082/4. The same entry as to Milborne.

[135] P.R.O., C.O. 5/1037/2.

[136] On this 2 Hawkins, *op. cit.* c.30 §9, and note the old authorities cited by him to the effect that the jury must be used in treason cases. At least one of

Dudley and his associates may be inscribed in the calendar of infamy where they belong.[137]

Only one case has been found where a defendant in fact stood mute. At the Suffolk Oyer and Terminer and General Gaol Delivery (1723), Elizabeth Horton was indicted for murdering her child. At the arraignment Elizabeth stood mute. The court then, in accordance with the ancient practice of determining by inquest whether the prisoners stood mute through obstinacy or any other cause, had a jury sworn. Two witnesses were produced for the Crown, and the jury returned the verdict, "that the prisoner at barr does not stand mute through malice or obstinacy and also find that before and at the time of committing the fact she was mad and is so at the present time."[138]

When a defendant was given his opportunity to answer or object to the charge against him which in felonies was upon arraignment, and in misdemeanors when the indictment was known, there were various courses available. If he wished to avoid pleading at all he might move to quash, a matter which we shall consider in connection with motions generally.[139] At Sessions, as we have seen, the traverse would leave the defendant free to move to quash at the next term.

In New York, defendants ordinarily would either plead the general issue or confess the indictment. The records show also a scattered use of other pleas, to the jurisdiction, in abatement, in bar, and very rarely a demurrer. In felony cases, since the defendant became aware of the exact charge only when the indictment was read to him upon arraignment, this plea was offered orally when the clerk or the court asked him whether he was guilty or not. In New York, oral pleading was at first the rule in misdemeanors, but as the eighteenth century wore on it became usual to use written pleadings to such an extent that when certain defendants in 1766 orally pleaded not guilty to an indictment for riot the clerk thought the fact worth special notice in the minutes.[140]

The written pleas by attorney that have been preserved vary considerably in form. They are sometimes a quite informal statement,[141] such as "I plead

the judges, Thomas Johnson, and the Attorney General, Thomas Newton, had law training.

[137] On the Commission: Joseph Dudley, Thomas Johnson, Sir Robert Robinson, Chidley Brooke, William Smith, William Pinhorne, John Lawrence, Captain Gaspar Hickes, Major Richard Ingoldesby, Colonel John Youngs and Captain Isaac Arnold.

[138] Ms. Mins. Cir. 1721–49 67, 68.

[139] Infra 599 et seq.

[140] On Apr. 17, 1766, W. and J. Campbell, appearing on recognizance, "pleaded Ore Tenus not guilty" (Ms. Mins. SCJ 1764–67 [Rough] 139).

[141] Cf. King v. Van Zandt (1753), "New York Supreme court John Van Zandt adv. the King Plea for William Kempe. I plead not guilty for the defendant, William Smith" (J. T. Kempe Lawsuits V). This was evidently in response to a demand "Mr. Smith I demand a plea W. Kempe Attorney General" (ibid.).

not guilty for the defendant" signed by the attorney and sometimes the words *"modo et forma"* are added.[142] In certain cases the form of civil pleading is followed, viz., the recital that the defendant comes by his attorney,[143] but most frequently the plea is offered directly by the attorney and a warrant of attorney by the defendant is appended.[144] One of the very elaborate forms found is that used by William Smith Jr. in the important prosecution of John Van Rensselaer for intrusion.[145]

For the most part our information respecting pleading comes from the minute books or from the endorsements on indictments, and these are neither of them loquacious sources. Owing to the circumstances that oral pleading was the rule in felony cases, and further that traditionally the mass of misdemeanor cases were handled at Quarter Sessions by a lay or nearly lay bench, English criminal procedure had remained little affected by the technical achievements

---

[142] Cf. King v. Ferris (1754): "Gilbert Ferris adv. our Lord the King On Information by the Attorney Gen[l] I plead for the Defendant Not Guilty modo et forma &c W[m] Smith Atty for Defend[t] City of New York Ss Gilbert Ferris puts in his place W[m] Smith his Attorney at the suit of our Sovereign Lord the King in the plea af[dn]" (*ibid.* C–F); King v. Alexander Ennis (1761): "I plead not guilty modo et forma &c Thomas Jones Att[ey] for the Deft Queens County Ss Alexander Ennis puts in his place Thomas Jones his Attorney at the suit of John Tabor Kempe Esq[r] Attorney General . . . who for our said Sovereign Lord the King . . . prosecutes . . . on an Information for an Assault and Battery &c" (*ibid.*). This latter plea was filed Aug. 10, 1762.

[143] On Apr. 27, 1765, Joshua Smith was informed against by the Attorney General for intrusion on Crown lands (*Ms. Mins. SCJ 1764–66* [Engr.] 178) and he pleaded not guilty in August Term, 1765 (*ibid.* 284). His plea "Received Aug. 3, 1765 in court" was as follows: "And the said Joshua Smith by John Morin Scott his Attorney Comes and defends the force and Injury when &c And protesting that the Information aforesaid of the aforesaid Attorney General . . . is not sufficient in the Law for him . . . the Information to have or maintain for plea nevertheless the said Joshua Saith that he is not Guilty of the premises above to him imposed in manner and form as in the Information aforesaid above is Supposed and of this he puts himself upon the Country and the aforesaid Attorney General for the said Lord the King in like manner &c Scott Attorney for the Defendant

"Ulster County Ss Joshua Smith puts in his place John Morin Scott his attorney at the Suit of our Lord the King in the plea aforesaid" (*J. T. Kempe Lawsuits* S–U).

Peter Remsen, informed against for slander in charging a juror with giving a false verdict (*Ms.*

Mins. SCJ 1766–69 [Engr.] 448, Apr. 25, 1768) filed the following plea: "And the said Peter Remsen Comes by Thomas Smith his Attorney and having heard the Information Aforesaid he saith that he is not thereof Guilty and of this he puts himself upon the Country Thomas Smith for the Deft. City and County of New York Ss: And the Said Peter Remsen Puts in his place Thomas Smith his Attorney at the Suit of Our Lord the King in the Plea Aforesaid" (*H.R. Pleadings* Pl. K. 172). Cf. also *H.R. Parch.* 228 B 2; *H.R. Pleadings* Pl. K. 479.

[144] *Supra* n. 142.

[145] "And the said John Van Rensselaer Esq[r] comes here by William Smith Jun[r] his Attorney to this by favor of the Court specially admitted and prays hearing of the Information af[d] & to him it is read, which being read & heard and by him understood he complains that by Colour of the Premises in the said Information specified he will be greatly vexed & disquieted & this very unjustly, because protesting that the Information aforesaid & the Matter in the same contained is not sufficient in the Law & to which he hath no Necessity nor by the Law of the Land is held to answer for Plea nevertheless as to the Force & Arms & any Disherison & Exhereration of our Lord the King in the Information af[d] specified as also as to the whole further Trespass & Contempt in the Information aforesaid above specified & by him supposed to be done or any Part thereof the said John Van Rensselaer Esq[r] saith that he is not thereof guilty in Manner & Form as by the Information aforesaid above is supposed and of this he puts himself upon the Country &c[a] Smith Jnr P Defend[t] . . . And the said John Van Rensselaer Esq[r] puts in his Place William Smith Junr. his Attorney at the Suit of the Attorney General of our Lord the King of the Plea af[dn]" (*J. T. Kempe Lawsuits* V).

of civil practice. Furthermore, for the requirements of a record it had become settled in England that an entry by the clerk on the indictment of plea and verdict was sufficient. Thus, if a prisoner confessed, the abbreviation *cogn.* (*cognovit*) was written on the indictment. If he pleaded not guilty, the abbreviation *po. se* (*ponit se super patriam*) was used, followed by the verdict, *culp.* or *non culp.* as the case might be.[146]

The New York clerks in the last decade of the seventeenth century introduced the jargon of endorsements into their minute books, but not a sufficient bulk of indictments prior to 1750 is available for us to be certain English practice in this respect was followed, although this seems likely. Judging from the early minute book specimens the clerk did not understand this particular bit of abracadabra, for we find instances where it is noted that the defendant "non cul. po. se" but the jury's verdict was guilty,[147] and as late as the year 1735 it appears that in New York the entry *non cul.* was used to designate the pleading and not the verdict.[148] After the year 1750, when the evidence becomes more ample, it is obvious that English usage in respect to the entry of pleas had become established in the Supreme Court, for the indictments are endorsed with the correct formula.[149]

[146] The information respecting this is in *Office of the Clerk of Assize* (1682) 39, 151, 158; *Crown Circuit Companion* (1768 ed.) 11. It may be observed that Blackstone seems to have been quite ignorant of clerks' practice (4 *Commentaries* 339). Evidently his explanation misled later antiquarians; cf. the difficulties of Jeaffreson in 1 *Middlesex Co. Recs.* introd., later cleared up in vol. 2. A comprehensive list of clerical abbreviations is appended to the introduction of vol. 3 of the *Middlesex Co. Recs.*

[147] *Mins. SCJ 1693–1701* 51, 52, Dec. 15, 1693. In this printed version of the Supreme Court minutes the entries appear as "Jefferson non vul. pro se Clifford non vul pro se," revealing on the part of the editors an ignorance not only of Latin and of law, but also an inability accurately to decipher the handwriting of clerks in early New York courts. The original manuscript minutes of the Supreme Court for the period reveal the words to be "non cul. p°. se." In some typewritten notes by the editors of the printed edition (the notes being on file in the NY Hist. Soc. Library), we find an explanation of the basis on which the editors rested their transcription. These notes opine that "non vul." meant "non vulnerabile" or "non vulnerabilem" which was translated by them as a plea of not vulnerable!

For further examples, King v. Le Reaux, 1695 (*ibid.* 76, 77); King v. Elwood, 1696 (*ibid.* 91); King v. Fisher (*ibid.* 132–134); Queen v. Shearman, "Defendt appeared pleads non cul," 1704

(*Ms. Mins. SCJ 1701–04* 166, 169). In the Negro Conspiracy cases of 1712, the abbreviations are correctly used in Queen v. Mars (*Ms. Mins. NYCQS 1694–1731/32* 228, 234–239, May 30, 1712; *Ms. Mins. NYCQS 1705/06–1714/15* [Rough] 99, June 10, 1712) yet in Queen v. Furnis, Kitto and four others, there is a marginal entry of *non culp.* against the plea although jury returned guilty (*Ms. Mins. NYCQS 1694–1731/32* 234, 236, June 10, 1712).

[148] King v. Lasher, 1734/35 (*James Alexander Papers* Box 44, *NY Supreme Ct. Docket*) "Plead non cul po se paid it to the Attorney General." Cf. *Ms. Mins. SCJ 1732–39* 104, 142.

[149] See, for example, King v. Lyons (1759), an indictment for manslaughter in killing an opponent in a boxing match (*H.R. Pleadings* Pl. K. 1079), and cf. *Ms. Mins. SCJ 1756–61* (Rough) 158, 163; King v. Bentley (1770), indicted for grand larceny (*H.R. Pleadings* Pl. K. 477); King v. Steel (1770), indicted for grand larceny (*H.R. Pleadings* Pl. K. 561; *Ms. Mins. SCJ 1769–72* [Engr.] 193–195). Lewis Jones pleaded not guilty to three indictments for passing counterfeit Jersey money and was tried and acquitted on all three indictments (*ibid.* 181, 184, 187, Apr. 21, 23, 25, 1770). In Jones' case, each of the three indictments was separately endorsed with the abbreviations, *Po. se non cul.* (*H.R. Pleadings* Pl. K. 262, 315, 383).

On Apr. 22, 1771, Adam Smith pleaded not guilty to an indictment for grand larceny (*Ms. Mins. SCJ 1769–72* [Engr.] 352) and endorsed on one of

This cabalistic form of endorsement upon indictments was not used in the country. A great number of Sessions indictments for Dutchess, Ulster and Suffolk counties have been examined and no trace of the city practice can be found. Occasionally an indictment will be marked "Quashed," "discharged," "process issued and returned," "defendant paid fine and costs," but the settled practice was for the clerk to enter in the minute book the fact that defendant had traversed, or had pleaded not guilty or confessed. It therefore appears that the ends of public recordation were regarded to be sufficiently served by the remembrancing of proceedings in this form, although a proper case "record" for the purpose of judicial procedure was traditionally only by way of the endorsement of indictments.[150]

The clerk's notations upon indictments establish only the pleading of guilty or not guilty (and in England, standing mute), for as far as we are aware no other plea, such as one to the jurisdiction, in abatement or in bar, was so entered. For light on these pleas one is consequently cast upon minutes or upon surviving pleas filed in misdemeanor cases. It has already been remarked that there are not many examples of the use of these pleas in New York, but we shall consider here those we have found.

The plea to the jurisdiction has been discussed in connection with the Leisler case and the conflicts problems, and it is not necessary to recapitulate.[151] This

the copies of the indictment is the notation, "Po. se" (*H.R. Pleadings* Pl. K. 263). He was tried and found guilty on Apr. 24, 1771 (*Ms. Mins. SCJ 1769–72* [Engr.] 355) and endorsed on the indictment of record is the abbreviation, "Po. se cul." (*H.R. Pleadings* Pl. K. 317). Smith, having been granted his clergy for this offense, was again arraigned on Jan. 23, 1772, on two indictments, one for grand larceny and one for petit larceny to both of which he pleaded not guilty. He was tried and convicted on both indictments and sentenced to be hanged (*Ms. Mins. SCJ 1769–72* [Engr.] 471, 472, 477). Endorsed on his indictment for petit larceny was the clerk's notation, "Po. se cul." (*H.R. Pleadings* Pl. K. 496), while the same notation appears on his indictment for grand larceny (*ibid.* Pl. K. 374).

In October Term, 1771, William Johnson, pleading not guilty to an indictment for petit larceny, was tried and found guilty (*Ms. Mins. SCJ 1769–72* [Engr.] 445–447). Endorsed on the indictment record was the notation, "Po. se cul." (*H.R. Pleadings* Pl. K. 560).

Sam Doren was tried and found not guilty on an indictment for highway robbery (*Ms. Mins. SCJ 1769–72* [Engr.] 471, 473, Jan. 23, 1772), and endorsed on the indictment is the abbreviation, "Po: se Non cul." (*H.R. Pleadings* Pl. K. 529).

Jacob Moses was indicted in Quarter Sessions for receiving stolen goods and the indictment was delivered into the Supreme Court where Moses was tried and found guilty (*Ms. Mins. NYCQS 1772–91* 7, May 8, 1772; *Ms. Mins. SCJ 1772–76* [Rough] 23, 26, 28, 29, 38, 53, 54, July 28–30, Aug. 1, Oct. 27, 1772). Endorsed on the indictment in the Moses case is the notation, "Po. Se: Cul." It would seem that in this case a new indictment had been drawn up in the Supreme Court for the "Po. se Cul." endorsement is on an indictment filed in the Supreme Court on July 30, 1772 (*H.R. Pleadings* Pl. K. 505) and not on the indictment filed in Quarter Sessions on May 8, 1772 (*ibid.* Pl. K. 528).

Zachariah Smith Allen pleaded not guilty to two indictments for passing a counterfeited Pennsylvania bill of credit (*Ms. Mins. SCJ 1775–81* [Engr.] 62, 63, Jan. 19, 1776) and the two indictments were endorsed "Po. se" (*H.R. Pleadings* Pl. K. 240, K. 241) but this case was evidently never tried.

[150] The notations come into use after the Revolution, but in English. For example, cf. *Ms. Files Suffolk Co.* Indictments 1773–1839, People v. Hubbs, People v. Kechem (1794).

[151] *Supra* 313 *et seq.*

plea was practically an anomaly in Sessions courts, because the justices of the peace as a rule were careful not to take cognizance of cases beyond their jurisdiction, and owing to the broad powers of the Supreme Court, it was offered there only in a handful of cases. Nearly every one of these cases was politically important and they are consequently illustrations less of a law on such pleas than of the diplomatic maneuverings of the judges and Crown officers.[152] The vigorous manner in which the Supreme Court defended the judges' commissions in the Zenger case[153] undoubtedly had the effect of discouraging any further use of the plea where the substantive powers of this court might have been involved. Consequently, we find that when it was next put forward, in *King* v. *Gardener et al.,* the objection is addressed to the locus of the crime, viz., New Jersey. The defendant's plea is set forth below,[154] but the judicial minutes do not disclose the eventual disposition of the case.

John Henry Lydius, in the information proceeding against him for intrusion, attempted to raise a similar question of jurisdiction on the ground that the lands in question lay out of New York Province, but as we have seen he had already pleaded the general issue. The contemporary English rule that matters of jurisdiction were admitted by this plea was urged by the Attorney General and the case went to the jury.[155]

The plea in abatement was rarely used in New York; in fact we have found only two clear examples. This plea was founded on some defect apparent on

[152] So in King v. Le Reaux, King v. Mulford, King v. Broughton, *supra* 302, 313, 317.

[153] *Supra* 49.

[154] "And the said Richard Gardener comes and by protestation Saith That he is an Inhabitant and . . . one of [the] . . . Justices of the peace of . . . New Jersey and a Deputy Surveyor . . . and that the doing of his Duty in . . . Sussex . . . and the pretended crimes laid in the said Indictment are the same for plea Nevertheless he saith That the place where the Crimes laid in the first Indictment were committed doth lie within . . . New Jersey . . . and yet are triable in . . . New Jersey . . . and not anywhere else . . . and this he is ready to verify . . . wherefore he does not understand that the court of our Lord the King here will further take Cognizance . . . J. Alexander of Council for the Defendant The said Richard Gardener being one of the people called Quakers on his Solemn affirmation according to Law Saith that the matters of his protestation and plea aforesaid are true to the best of his Knowledge . . . Affirmed the third day of August before me Jno Chambers" (*J. T. Kempe Lawsuits* G–J 1754).

Other defendants in this same action, namely Anthony Van Natta and Abraham Van Acken, also filed a plea to the jurisdiction and Anthony Van

Natta said that he and the other defendants, in order to apprehend Joseph Westbrook and Jacobus Swartout for "sundry Riots that they . . . had been guilty of in New Jersey . . .," did assist the justices of peace in apprehending the rioters "as it was Lawful for them to do. . . ." In the plea to the jurisdiction it was further pointed out that Westbrook and Swartout were apprehended and bailed by the authority of New Jersey. The defendants in the Supreme Court action "For plea Nevertheless They say that the place where the crime laid in the said Indictment was Committed doth lye within and is part . . . New Jersey and that all Crimes Committed within . . . New Jersey have been and yet are Triable in the Courts of . . . the King . . . of New Jersey and before his Majesty's Justices there . . . and not anywhere else out of the said province . . ." (plea, Anthony Van Natta, Joseph Westbrook and Abraham Van Acken adv. the King, *J. T. Kempe Lawsuits* W). Documents relating to the troubles are in 78 *NY Col. Mss.* 53 *et seq.* Smith's *Supream Court Register A* does not show the final disposition. Probably there was a *nolle pros.* as a result of the Council's "line of peace" (23 *Ms. Mins. Council* 138).

[155] *Supra* 212.

the face of the indictment, or upon a fact extrinsic which rendered the indictment insufficient. But it was a plea of little advantage to the prisoner as a new indictment could be framed to meet the defect. Furthermore, it was more usual to object by way of motion to quash.

The first occasion when the plea in abatement was used in a criminal prosecution was in 1693 at the Westchester Sessions, when Gabriel Leggett, indicted for stealing a hog, appeared and "pleaded ye Indictmt for yt their wanted a sufficient addition in ye Inditemt According to ye Statute." The court took the matter under advisement and apparently overruled the plea, for Leggett later pleaded a pardon.[156]

It was not until 1757 that such a plea was again offered. On January 20, Godfrey Batcar was arraigned in the Supreme Court on a coroner's inquest for the murder of John Webb. Upon his arraignment "The prisoner . . . pleads that his Sirnam is Betcke and not Batcar and that he is not Guilty of the Murder, and is not the Person named in the Inquest, and therefore prays Judgment whether he should be put to answer further." The court did not rule on this plea but on the following day discharged the prisoner for lack of prosecution.[157]

The pleas in bar listed by eighteenth century writers are four in number: *autrefoits convict, autrefoits acquit, autrefoits attaint* and pardon.[158] A considerable body of learning had developed in England about these pleas indicating a frequent use, but again we have found in New York only a few examples. With reference to previous conviction there are two cases, but we cannot be sure that the defense was made by plea. Jacob Bratt, Francis Wessells and William Shakerley were presented in New York Quarter Sessions on August 4, 1697, for making and selling bread contrary to the laws of the city. We have not found any minutes of a further prosecution, conviction or punishment for this offense, but when these same defendants were presented on February 8, 1699/1700, for vending bread of unlawful assize, they were, on May 1, 1700, "discharged from the presentment of the Grand Jurors having been fined before for the same fact."[159] Many years later, George Klock Jr. appeared in the Supreme Court to answer for a contempt in rescuing his father from the sheriff but "It appearing to the Court by the Examination of the Defendant taken in Court on Oath that the Defendant had been indicted in the Court of . . . [General Sessions] . . . for Albany for the Rescue aforesaid and had been

---

[156] *Mins. Westch. Ct. of Sess. 1657–96* 86.
[157] *Ms. Mins. SCJ 1754–57* (Engr.) 339, 342.

[158] Cf. 2 Hawkins, *op. cit.* c.35; 2 Hale, *op. cit.* 240.
[159] *Ms. Mins. NYCQS 1694–1731/32* 30, 51, 53.

fined the sum of ten pounds for the same and had paid the said Fine: on Motion of W. Smith Jr. the Court orders that the Defendant be discharged."[160] The minute entry in this case indicates that the fact of previous conviction was raised by motion, since the formal plea of *autrefoits convict* required production of the record, viz., the indictment duly endorsed, and the informal method of establishing the fact of conviction by examining the defendant on oath, could only have been followed if the question was raised on motion.

Of a plea of *autrefoits acquit* the judicial records show no sign,[161] and this, as well as the infrequency of *autrefoits convict,* we think can be attributed to the solicitude of royal officials that there be no double prosecutions.[162] Indeed, the only important occasion where an issue of double jeopardy was raised was in connection with the Cunningham case discussed in the chapter on appellate jurisdiction.[163]

Only two cases of pardon being pleaded in bar have been found. The first of these occurred in 1693 when Gabriel Leggett supplemented his plea in abatement by pleading the pardon of a general act of assembly.[164] This act was a pardon for those active in the Leisler rebellion, and Leggett alleged the offense had been committed in Andros' time. The court took the view that the crime was not within the purview of the act and adjudged that Leggett should pay costs and give a recognizance for good behavior. The other case in which a pardon was pleaded before conviction was that of Dick, a slave, who had been indicted for felony on December 7, 1731, in the Supreme Court.[165] On October 12, 1732, Warrell on behalf of the prisoner showed a "warrant" from Rip Van Dam, late President of the Council, addressed to Attorney General Bradley, "directing him to discharge the prisoner from all prosecution." Despite this "warrant," Dick was evidently held in custody until December 5, 1732, for on that date, "The prisoner arraigned pleads the King's Pardon on which he produced in Court." The court thereupon ordered that he be discharged on payment of his fees.[166]

---

[160] *Ms. Mins. SCJ 1766–69* (Engr.) 504, 505, July 28, 1768.

[161] A petition of Gloriana Ginderell (*J. T. Kempe Lawsuits* G–J) recites that she had been sued for a pig, alleged to be falsely marked, and the verdict of the jury had been in her favor. She was again sued and pleaded *autrefoits acquit,* but Justice of the Peace Bleecker overruled the plea. This seems to have been one of the provincial borderline civil actions. Note further that Bleecker was later prosecuted for maladministration in connection with another highhanded act. He was fined £10 (*Ms. Mins. SCJ 1762–64* [Engr.] 298, 343;

Ms. Mins. SCJ 1764–67 [Rough] 11; *H.R. Pleadings* Pl. K. 794).

[162] Thus in King v. Henry Slyck defendant was discharged in Quarter Sessions from presentments because he was under indictment for the same offenses in the Supreme Court (*Ms. Mins. NYCQS 1732–62* 60, 62, Feb. 3, 1735/36, May 6, 1736). Cf. the motion in King v. Allison (*supra* 187).

[163] *Supra* 244.

[164] *Mins. Westch. Ct. of Sess. 1657–96* 86.

[165] *Ms. Mins. SCJ 1727–32* 306, 358, 395.

[166] There are occasional examples of so-called special pleas. Thus Hendrick Claaese Van Vegte, a

No comment is necessary respecting the plea of not guilty, further than to remark that the records indicate some variation as to the manner in which it was offered, viz., a mere not guilty, or not guilty *modo et forma,* or the addition of the ancient phrase "and puts himself on the country." The English authorities of the eighteenth century seem to have regarded the joining of issue in indictments for capital cases as immaterial.[167] Since the pleading was oral no formal issue was made up preparatory to trial, although the plea of not guilty and an entry of "the like" (*similiter*) for the Crown were stated in the record. The jury was conceived to be an inquest into the truth of the charge which made an issue immaterial. On the other hand, in indictments for misdemeanors or informations, an issue had to be made up.[168] The English method of making a record and of entering a joinder of issue was introduced by the clerk of the Court of Oyer and Terminer in 1684,[169] and early rolls of the Supreme Court show the continuation of the practice.[170] The New York

Kings County justice of peace, was presented for a breach of the peace "ffor Coming into Broockland Church . . . with his pen & Ink . . . taking up of people's names and taking one particular mans hatt up; and in disturbance of the minister and people in the service of God." Vegte, in justification of his actions, made the following answer: "Hendrick Vegte . . . ffor plea to the presentmt. saith that in obedience to . . . the Governor's order and a duty Incumbent . . . in his office ffor the preservation of the peace he did goe into the Church . . . to take notice of the persons that were guilty of the forcible Entry made into said Church that day . . . by breaking of said Church doore open with fforce and armes and fforceably entring . . . and that he is in noe manner of way guilty of the breach of the peace, yt. was done in pursuance of his Excellencys order and his duty as a Justice of the peace, all which never the les is humbly submitted to . . . this Court. . . ." The court "ffinding the said Hendrick is no manner of way guilty . . . by doeing of his duty, doe order that the said Hendrick be Cleared and discharged" (*Ms. Kings Co. Ct. & Rd. Recs. 1692–1825* 163, Nov. 15, 1710).

Another case in which special matter was evidently pleaded in justification was that of the indictment against the Oswego market in 1771. In this case, the market having been presented on Jan. 18, 1771, as a nuisance, the Attorney General moved for a writ directed to the sheriff of New York to "prostrate without delay the Oswego Market." The Mayor of New York City, on behalf of the corporation, moved for time to consider whether the city should defend against the indictment, and the court thereupon ordered that "unless the said Indictment is traversed within twenty days . . . a Writ to abate the same Nusance do issue to the Sheriff." On Apr. 27, 1771, the Attorney General

moved for the writ to prostrate the Oswego market "for want of a Traverse to the said Inquisition." However, the court declared it would "further advise . . . [of a plea] Tendered which the Court had not time to Consider." Thus far we have referred to the minute entries on the case (*Ms. Mins. SCJ 1769–72* [Engr.] 316, 318, 363), but what the plea was is disclosed in *H.R. Pleadings* Pl. K. 1016. This "Plea" had recited that the defendants (the Mayor, Aldermen and Commonalty of New York City) protested that the indictment against the market was not sufficient in law and that the defendants had "no necessity to answer." However, "for plea nevertheless," the defendants stated that the City of New York was on an island and that the street on which the alleged nuisance was committed was a common highway. The defendants claimed that they had the right to license the said market by prescription and custom and also by rights given under the city charter. In answer to this "plea" the Attorney General had evidently filed a demurrer, for we have found a "Draft of Demurrer" dated Apr. 13, 1771 (*ibid.* Pl. K. 912). Evidently the court agreed with the Attorney General, and despite the defendant's plea, the sheriff of New York was, on Aug. 3, 1771, ordered to prostrate the Oswego market as a nuisance (*Ms. Mins. SCJ 1769–72* [Engr.] 404). Writ *supra* 416 n. 179.

167 Per Holt, C.J., in Queen v. Tutchin (6 *Mod.* 268, 281); Rex v. Oneby, 1727 (2 *Strange* 766, 775); Rex v. Royce, 1767 (4 *Burr.* 2085); King v. Dowlin, 1793 (5 *T.R.* 313, 319).

168 Queen v. Tutchin (6 *Mod.* 281).

169 Cf. *Ms. Mins. Oyer and Terminer Ulster Co.* fol. 4 (June 1684).

170 For example, King v. Joseph Smith and King v. Le Reaux (*H.R. Parch.* 209 G 9 [1697]).

Quarter Sessions adopted the practice almost at once,[171] but it did not spread to the country for some time. Not until 1700 did it reach Kings County,[172] and the contemporary Sessions minutes of Ulster and Westchester dispense with any notation of this formality. So far as we know, no questions ever arose in New York regarding the manner of entry in the record or the necessity of an issue in misdemeanors, but English forms seem to have been consistently and trustingly followed.

The confession of the indictment presents a variety of problems, some of which have to do with the form in which this was made, and others with the matter of sentence. As a matter of form, confession could be made by a plea of guilty or, in non-capital cases, by a refusal to contend with the King—the *non vult* or *nolo contendere*. In misdemeanors the question of choice in the manner of pleading was important, because the *nolo contendere* was looked on as a mere implied confession, the object of which was to obtain the indulgence of the court in setting a lower penalty than if the case went to trial.[173] *Nolo* was not used in capital felonies where the plea of guilty, "the highest Conviction that can be,"[174] left the judge no option but to proceed to sentence, although for tactical reasons a prisoner might confess in order to plead his clergy or to secure a pardon as an approver.[175]

The New York cases indicate that in capital cases the confession of the indictment led to no mitigation of the sentence.[176] But in cases which were clergiable there are a number of examples where defendants rather stupidly abandoned the chance of an acquittal, by confessing and praying their clergy.[177] Since even in the event of conviction by verdict, a defendant could

[171] King v. Davies (*Ms. Mins. NYCQS 1683/ 84–1694* 28, Feb. 1684/85); King v. Edmonds (*ibid.* 71, Nov. 13, 1685).
[172] *Kings Co. Ct. & Rd. Recs. 1692–1825* 74: "MR. Abraham Governr. ffor the Diffendant and pleas Nott gilty in manner and fform and Stand Indited and off this Putts them Selves uppon the Country and the Procecuter in Like manner."
[173] 2 Hawkins, *op. cit.* c.31 §3.
[174] *Ibid.* §1.
[175] 2 Hale, *op. cit.* 226.
[176] Thus Henry Lewis, arraigned at a Special Court of Oyer and Terminer and General Gaol Delivery on Aug. 11, 1701, confessed the murder of Henry Bredsted, and the court "ordered the Sheriff bring the Prisoner to the Barr to receive Judgment of Death which was accordingly done Sentence of Death passed upon the Prisoner" (*Ms. Mins. SCJ 1701–04* 1, 2, 3). In King v. James Wilson on indictment for burglary and felony the "Defendant pleads guilty" and being asked why sentence of

death should not be passed against him and "saying nothing against it" ordered hanged (*Ms. Mins. SCJ 1756–61* [Rough] 128, 130, 131, Jan. 17, 20, 1759).
In the case of Lewis, a negro belonging to Peter Barberie, it is possible that a confession worked a mitigation of the sentence. Lewis was indicted on June 4, 1725, "for taking two guns, two pair of pistoles [*sic*] five shirts a bag w'th Bullets one powder horn and a pair of thread stockings belonging to his said [*sic*] to the value of three pounds" and on June 8, "the Indictm't for feloniously stealing of goods to the Value of three pounds belonging to his Master being read the Deft confesses himselfe guilty of the felony Whereupon it is Ordered by the Court that he be whipped before the City Hall at the carts taile, and there receive Nine Lashes . . ." (*Ms. Mins. SCJ 1723–27* 142, 143, 146). It is not clear why the court elected to treat the felony as non-capital.
[177] Jane Smith, indicted on Oct. 27, 1755 for

have clergy, this manner of pleading seems extremely peculiar. We have likewise seen cases where confession was made when the prisoner to get his pardon turned King's evidence, a question to be discussed later.

As a matter of textbook law the confession of indictments in non-capital cases was mere choice between a *cognovit* and a *non vult,* but the cases in New York are by no means so easily classified, for the records disclose the manner of a confession to have been as manifold as the roads to salvation. Generally the motive was to secure leniency, but the variety in formulating the plea was due at first to ignorance of exact English usage, and perhaps even to a provincial resistance against the limitations of criminal pleading.

It is quite evident that until the second decade of the eighteenth century, the colonists did not know the plea of *nolo contendere,* at least by its technical name. Lambard[178] had described what he called a "confession after a manner," as "onely a not denying in which the partie doth cunningly, and (after a sort) take the fault upon him, without plainly confessing himselfe guiltie thereof." This description was taken by later writers to be a *nolo contendere,* but it is apparent from English Sessions records that such implied confessions were entered as "submissions," whereupon a fine would be imposed.[179] The New York records of the proprietary period furnish examples of "submissions," but

feloniously stealing a silver can, pleaded not guilty on Jan. 20, 1756, but on Jan. 23, "The prisoner withdraws her Plea not Guilty, and pleads guilty to the indictment, and on her prayer . . . the Court allowed her the benefit of her clergy. Ordered . . . burnt in the brawn of the left thumb to Morrow in the face of the Court." On Jan. 24, 1756, this was done and she was discharged (*Ms. Mins. SCJ 1754–57* [Engr.] 200, 218, 222, 225).

On Jan. 23, 1756, Andrew Wells confessed indictments for grand and petit larceny "and the prisoner praying his clergy . . . ordered burned in the brawn of the left thumb." On Jan. 24 he was branded and discharged (*ibid.* 222, 225).

Alexander Douglas, indicted on Apr. 24, 1758 for manslaughter, pleaded guilty on Apr. 26 and, on being asked what he had to say why sentence of death should not be passed against him, prayed the benefit of his clergy which was allowed by the court and he was burned in the brawn of the left thumb (*Ms. Mins. SCJ 1756–61* [Rough] 97, 100). Moses Vintner pleaded guilty to an indictment for manslaughter and prayed the benefit of his clergy upon which he was ordered to be burned in the brawn of the left thumb and discharged (*ibid.* 217, 219, Jan. 21, 23, 24, 1761). For the case of Elizabeth Clarke, *infra* 754. Benefit of clergy was also granted to Sarah Gillet when she confessed an indictment for grand larceny and prayed her clergy. But she was again indicted for grand larceny a year

and a quarter later, and this time she pleaded not guilty, was tried and found guilty. Her prayer for clergy made after conviction was refused because of a record of a previous allowance of clergy, and she was accordingly sentenced to be hanged (*Ms. Mins. SCJ 1764–67* [Rough] 231, 241, Apr. 28, May 1, 1767; *Ms. Mins. SCJ 1766–69* [Engr.] 505–507, July 28–30, 1768). Pompey, a slave belonging to Anthony Shackerley, on confessing an indictment for grand larceny and praying his clergy, was accorded benefit of clergy (*Ms. Mins. SCJ 1764–67* [Rough] 231, 241, Apr. 28, May 1, 1767). On John Dailey, *supra* 148 n. 44. Phoenix Jewet confessed an indictment for grand larceny and prayer for clergy was allowed (*Ms. Mins. SCJ 1772–76* [Rough] 145, 147, Jan. 21, 22, 1774). Robert Curry confessed two indictments, one for petit larceny and one for horse stealing, and, when the Attorney General moved for judgment, Curry "pleads his cleargy" whereupon "the court orders that the Prisoner receive thirty nine lashes." The lashing was evidently a punishment for the petit larceny, but the minutes contain no indication as to whether Curry was branded (*ibid.* 216, 221, Jan. 18, 21, 1775).

178 Lambard, *Eirenarcha* Bk. 4 c.9.

179 See, for example, *Surrey Quarter Sessions Recs. 1659–61* 45; 2 *Minutes of Proceedings in Quarter Sessions . . . County of Lincoln 1674–95* 251, 342, 354.

toward the end of the seventeenth century we come upon a more prolix form, that is to say, a denial of guilt, but nevertheless a submission to fine.[180] In other instances we find defendants pleading guilty and craving mercy, possibly intending thereby to obtain lenient treatment, but the courts generally treated the offenders no differently from those who confessed without asking special favor.[181]

Although the plea of *nolo contendere* came into use during the first quarter of the eighteenth century, it was at first only rarely used in the Supreme Court. After the middle of the century, examples become more numerous.[182] The

[180] King v. Urian Nagell—seditious words, 1693 (*Ms. Kings Co. Ct. & Rd. Recs. 1692–1825* 19); King v. Haselbury—horse stealing, 1696 (*ibid.* 31–33); Queen v. Buckenhoven—assault on a constable, 1702/03 (*Ms. Mins. NYCQS 1694–1731/32* 72, 73, 76, 77, Nov. 4, 1702, Feb. 3, 4, 1702/03); Queen v. Onclebagg—false coining (*ibid.* 71, 74, 77, Nov. 4, 1702, Feb. 2, 3, 1702/03); Peter Delancey—assault on a constable (*ibid.* 535, 536, May 6, 7, 1731); King v. Pinhorne—affray (*Ms. Mins. NYCQS 1732–62* 67, 69, Aug. 5, Nov. 3, 1736). In Ulster, Hyman Rosa (obstructing officers) puts himself on the court's mercy and is fined (*Ms. Mins. Ulster Co. Sess. 1693–98* Mar. 3, 1694/95); Jan de Witt (abuse) does the same (*ibid.* Mar. 3, 1695/96).

[181] King v. Eliz. Moore and Mary Vincent—petit larceny (*Ms. Mins. NYCQS 1694–1731/32* 20, Feb. 2, 1696/97); King v. Fortune, a negro slave—receiving (*ibid.* 41, Aug. 3, 1698). Compare also the following cases where the plea of guilty apparently did not effect a mitigation. On Aug. 4, 1724, Andrew Anderson, on an indictment for stealing "one pair of Spectacles and the Case thereof of the value of ten pence," was arraigned "and pleaded Guilty and prays the Mercy of the Court" whereupon the court ordered that "the said Andrew Anderson shall return to the place from whence he came and there . . . at the Publick Whipping Post . . . shall be stripped from the waste upwards and whipped fiften lashes upon the Naked Back untill he shall bleed once twice or thrice According to the Discretion of the Justices" (*ibid.* 443). On Feb. 6, 1727/28, Lydia Atkins was indicted "for feloniously stealing a Callicoo Gown of the Goods of Martha Ludlow of the value of ten Pence." She "confessed the Indictment & Pleaded Guilty and prayed the Mercy" and on Feb. 7, "The Prisoner was brought to the Barr being Convict of Petty Larceny by her own Confession . . . Therefore it is Considered by the Court that she return to the place from whence she came . . . and that she be carried from thence to the Publick Whipping Post . . . and there be stripped from the middle upwards and then Receive . . . seven Lashes upon the Naked back" (*ibid.* 489, 491). Patrick Hay stole a pocketbook worth 10*d.* from Nicholas

Vechte and, on pleading guilty to an indictment for the offense and praying mercy, he was sentenced to twenty-five lashes (*ibid.* 533, Feb. 3, 1730/31). Martha Cash received the following sentence on pleading guilty and praying mercy for stealing two remnants of printed calico: "It is Considered . . . that the offender shall Return to the place from whence she came and . . . be Carryed out and tyed to the tail of a cart . . . Stripped from the Waste upwards and there Receive three Lashes on the Naked back . . . and thence be drawn to the Meal Market and there Receive three Lashes . . . Burgess Path . . . five Lashes . . . Coenties Market . . . three Lashes . . . Broad Street . . . three Lashes . . . Duke Street . . . five Lashes . . . Beaver Street . . . three Lashes . . . and thence to the place from whence she Came" (*Ms. Mins. NYCQS 1732–62* 3, May 3, 4, 1732). John McCune and John Fitzgerald submitted to the court's mercy on indictments for petit larceny and were each sentenced to thirty-nine lashes and to leave the city (*Ms. Mins. NYCQS 1760–72* 273, Feb. 9, 1769). King v. David Rose—assault (*Ms. Mins. Suffolk Co. Sess. 1723–51* Mar. 1725); King v. Denton—assault (*Ms. Mins. Orange Co. Sess. 1727–79* Apr. 25, 1727); King v. Patrick Cunningham (*ibid.* Oct. 31, 1738); King v. Davis—riotous rescue (*ibid.* Oct. 28, 1740); King v. Sylvanus Wright—assault (*Ms. Mins. Queens Co. Sess. 1722–87* Sept. 18, 1722); King v. Van Cliff—assault (*ibid.* Sept. 24, 1725); King v. Adam Smith (*ibid.* Sept. 17, 1728); King v. Andries Peck—speaking against reformed religion (*Ms. Mins. Dutchess Co. Sess.* Liber A, Oct. 21, 1729); King v. Knickerbocker—concealing burglary (*ibid.* May 15, 1739); King v. Freeling—offense not given (*Ms. Mins. Albany Co. Sess. 1717–23* Oct. 4, 1721).

[182] King v. Hunt *et al.*—trespass, 1721 (*Ms. Mins. Cir. 1721–49* 6–8); King v. Jacobus Bruin, 1722, 10*s.* (*ibid.* 21, 22); King v. Eltinge (*Ms. Mins. Ulster Co. Sess. 1737–50* Nov. 2, 1742); King v. Van Zandt—assault (*Ms. Mins. NYCQS 1732–62* 150, Feb. 3, 1742/43); King v. Green *et al.*—riot, 1763 (*Ms. Mins. SCJ 1762–64* [Engr.] 91, *Ms. Mins. SCJ 1764–67* [Rough] 68); King v. Leary—assault, 1763 (*Ms. Mins. SCJ 1762–64* [Engr.] 157); King v. Dowers—riot, 1763 (*Ms.*

gradual discovery and spread of this plea are interesting. In Suffolk it appears first in 1729 when a defendant says he is not willing to hold plea with the King and confesses. And subsequently the form of entry is "Confesses himself guilty of the fact but being unwilling to contend with the king submits to the mercy of the court."[183] In Richmond, the formula "rather than contend confesses and submits" is first used in 1727[184] but in Dutchess, Orange and Ulster it is not discovered until the forties.[185] This plea becomes a great favorite in the country Sessions; indeed, in both Richmond and Albany counties it crowds the out-right *cognovit* from the records. Possibly this remarkable predilection for the plea *nolo* may be attributed to the fact that it was usual merely to fine even in cases where a corporal punishment might on outright confession have been inflicted. In the case of persons of status the plea was a favorite, for obviously less stigma attached to a generous refusal to contend with the King than to a plea of guilty, and it is consequently not surprising that there are a number of cases where officials under charges avoided embarrassment by resorting to this evasive plea.[186]

Interesting in connection with the early efforts to find a formula which would avoid the effects of an outright plea of guilty are cases where defend-ants made discursive answers when they believed they had an excuse but could not deny the act with which they were charged. There was no plea of confes-sion and avoidance in criminal law, yet the colonists for a time struggled

---

Mins. NYCQS 1760–72 84, Aug. 4, 1763); King v. Gerrit Underdonck, 1764 (*Ms. Mins. SCJ* 1764–67 [Rough] 5); King v. Quackenbush—riot, 1765 (*ibid.* 40); King v. McCarty—assault (*Ms. Mins. NYCQS 1760–72* 180, 195, Aug. 6, Nov. 6, 1766); King v. Clark—riot, 1767–68 (*Ms. Mins. SCJ 1766–69* [Engr.] 317, 318, 374); King v. Driskill —assault on customhouse officer, 1768 (*ibid.* 454, 457); King v. William Mahawn—assault (*Ms. Mins. NYCQS 1760–72* 273, 277, Feb. 9, 10, 1769; *H.R. Pleadings* Pl. K. 731); King v. Day, 1771 (*Ms. Mins. SCJ 1769–72* [Engr.] 341); King v. Bausher —disorderly house (*Ms. Mins. NYCQS 1760–72* 350, 359, 360, Aug. 7, Nov. 7, 1771); King v. William Pelton (*ibid.* 360, 362, Nov. 7, 8, 1771); King v. Herkimer, 1772 (*Ms. Mins. Tryon Co. Sess.* Quarto 1); King v. Webb and Baker—riot, 1773 (*Ms. Mins. SCJ 1772–76* [Rough] 132, 137); King v. Charles Nichol Jr.—petit larceny, 1773 (*ibid.* 107, 117, 123); King v. Adam Taylor—as-sault (*Ms. Mins. NYCQS 1772–91* 80, 90, 91, Feb. 5, May 4, 1774).

There are a few cases of corporal punishment on *nolo* pleaded, e.g., King v. Joseph Lace, indicted for attempt to ravish an infant. Defendant pleaded *nolo* but was sentenced to forty lashes (*Ms. Mins. Al-*

bany Co. Sess. 1763–82 Oct. 2–5, 1764); King v. McNeal—attempted rape (*Ms. Mins. Dutchess Co. Sess.* Liber E, Oct. 10, 1774), pillory.

[183] The first case is King v. William Green (*Ms. Mins. Suffolk Co. Sess. 1723–51* Sept. 30, 1729). The formula cited, King v. Richard Satterly (*ibid.* Oct. 2, 1732). Subsequently the regular *nolo con-tendere* appears.

[184] King v. Buddin (*Ms. Mins. Richmond Co. Sess. 1710/11–1744/45* Mar. 7, 1726/27).

[185] King v. Lawrence Huff (*Ms. Mins. Dutchess Co. Sess.* Liber A, Oct. 20, 1747); King v. James Hart (*Ms. Mins. Orange Co. Sess. 1727–79* Apr. 28, 1747). For Ulster, *supra* n. 182.

[186] King v. Peter Vrooman, a justice of the peace informed against for neglect of his duty, 1752 (*Ms. Mins. SCJ 1750–54* [Engr.] 164, 195); King v. Mills, a jailer informed against for extortion (*Ms. Mins. NYCQS 1732–62* 527, May 4, 1762; *Ms. Mins. NYCQS 1760–72* 65, Nov. 4, 1762); King v. Henry Livingston, clerk of the peace (*supra* 177, 529); King v. Alex. Colden, 1755 (*Ms. Mins. SCJ 1754–57* [Engr.] 117, 144, 146); King v. Van Rensselaer, a justice of the peace, 1766 (*supra* 202).

against the unhappy choice between guilty and not guilty. These cases all occur during the period when practice in the inferior courts was still not conducted utterly by common law standards, and involve mostly infractions of local ordinances. For example, two assessors in the North Ward of New York City, indicted for not duly assessing the inhabitants of the ward, appeared and prayed their discharge because "the not assessing of Cornelius Plevier was wholy through Ignorance omitted and not wilfully."[187] The court took the matter under advisement and the case then disappears. Again in *Queen* v. *Nicholas Roosevelt* (1702),[188] the defendant indicted for "falsely and maliciously returning himselfe Alderman . . . Contrary to the plurality of voices to the utter Overthrow of the Liberties and Priviledges of this City," appeared and protested rather naïvely that he "is not acquainted with the Constitutions of this Corporation" and declared his error was committed ignorantly and not by design. He submitted to a fine which was set at £5 plus the usual fees.[189]

[187] King v. Tymon Van Borson and Andries Marschalk (*Ms. Mins. NYCQS 1694–1731/32* 17–19, Nov. 4, 1696, Feb. 2, 1696/97).

[188] *Ibid.* 72, 77, Nov. 4, 1702, Feb. 2, 1702/03.

[189] Indicted for nuisance, John Hardenburgh, on Nov. 7, 1694, "personally Appeared & pleaded to the Indictment of Nuisance that he was ignorantly Guilty of the Matter Alleadged . . . and that itt was not with his privity. Whereupon the Court taking the premises into serious Consideration Order that the said John Hardenburgh doe pay the sum of thirty Shillings as a fine with Costs of Court, & thereupon be discharged" (*Ms. Mins. NYCQS 1694–1731/32* 3, 4).

John Vincent was presented on May 4, 1697, for a nuisance in keeping tan pits for leather dressing "which is a Common Nuisance to the Neighbourhood by the unwholesome & Stinking Smell" and, on May 4, he appeared and said "that he did not know that the throwing down of his water in the streets was any Nuisance and prays the Mercy of the Court promising for the future to give no Occasion of Offence. . . . Ordered . . . discharged from further prosess upon the said presentment paying fees" (*ibid.* 25, 26).

Elias Nean and Ezekiel Grazeillier were bound over on Aug. 30, 1700, for "Nuisance" in packing and selling unmerchantable flour (*NY Misc. Mss.* Box 3 no. 19) and on Nov. 5, 1700, they "appeared in Court and declared they did not design any fraud by packing flower not Merchantable, but did believe the same was good . . . and pray the Court to remitt any prosecution . . . for the future they will be careful." The court, even before these defendants had been indicted, ordered that they be discharged on payment of their fees (*Ms. Mins. NYCQS 1694–1731/32* 56).

Cornelius Lodge, presented for false weights, "in-

formed the Court that his wife used a yard not his" and prayed the court's mercy whereupon he was fined 6s. and costs. Cf. also the plea of Richard Potter (*supra* 106 n. 203). On Nov. 4, 1702, Caleb Cooper, presented for false weights, appeared in court and offered an elaborate excuse for his offense. He "Acknowledged there was found in his house . . . [a seven pound weight which was] . . . a small matter too heavy which he lately bought of Thomas Burroughs pewterer but protests he knew not it was . . . [overweight and believes he is a loser thereby not a gainer] and prays the Court will Consider his Reputation and submits himselfe to a fine." The court, taking the matter under advisement, "consider him not guilty of a designed fraud but on his submission fine him six shillings and costs" (*ibid.* 73).

William Bickley, "Indictment Agt. the Defendt. for prophaneing Christmas day . . . Confesses that he did keep open Shop on the said day but that he did itt Conscientiously and not Contemptuously and submits himself to the discretion of the Court" whereupon he was fined 20s. and fees (*ibid.* 86, Feb. 2, 1703/04). The case of Gabriel Sprung is cited *supra* 365 n. 149.

Albertus Ringo, presented for selling drink to negroes, confessed the presentment, praying the court's mercy. He protested "he was ignorant that it was the breach of any law and prays the Court to be favourable in the fine," whereupon he was fined 50s. and costs (*Ms. Mins. NYCQS 1694–1731/32* 51, Feb. 8, 1699/1700).

On Nov. 6, 1711, in Queen v. Elizabeth Ranger, "The Grand Jurors brought in a Bill agt. the Defendt for Entertaining and trading with Negro slaves, the Defendt. in Custody being brought into court Confesses the Indictment & prays the mercy of the Court for that the Negro man called Diego

It is hardly to be doubted that irrespective of the form in which a defendant acknowledged his guilt he was ordinarily motivated by the hope of lenient treatment. To what extent this manner of pleading really accomplished the defendant's purpose it is difficult to determine, for in theory the courts had a more or less unlimited discretion in fixing the punishments for misdemeanors. In some cases, the standing and reputation of the defendant were taken into consideration, as, for example, in the two early counterfeiting cases involving Gabriel Ludlow and William Fowler, although, as we have already noted, political and economic issues over the currency may also have been involved.[190] Even the poverty and size of the defendant's family were occasionally taken into account, but here again the eternal question of the burden of poor relief may have been more moving than a desire to be merciful.[191] In a few cases, a real effort was made to determine the merits of the prayer for leniency when the courts would hear evidence or examine affidavits in support of the accused's petition.[192] This practice where *nolo* was pleaded suggests an effort to supply the want of a plea of confession and avoidance in minor cases. Ordinarily, however, when a defendant confessed the indictment, the court would proceed to sentence without hesitating over considerations that might have

assured her he was a free man. . . . It is therefore considered by the Court that the Defendt. pay a fine of twenty Shillings to the use of our Lady the Queen with full Charges of prosecution and that she stand Committed till she pay the same" (*ibid.* 205).

[190] *Supra* 95 n. 168, 113.

[191] Mary Callachan, indicted for stealing two iron pots worth 10*d.*, confessed and was sentenced to twenty lashes but remitted because she had two small children and was pregnant (*Ms. Mins. NYCQS 1732–62* 164, 167, May 3, 1744). Edward Anderson confessed an indictment for stealing a cloak, handkerchief and pair of shoes worth 10*d.*, sentenced to twenty-one lashes, remitted because he was born in the city and had a wife and two children (*ibid.* 445, Nov. 9, 1758). Regnier Quackenbush (1765) pleaded *nolo* to an information for riot, was fined 10*s.* 8*d.* because of his poverty (*supra* n. 182). John Driskill (1768) pleaded *nolo* to an indictment for assault on a customhouse officer, fined 13*s.* 4*d.* for the same reason (*supra* n. 182).

[192] In Queen v. Darby Donavan (1713), defendant confessed an indictment for assault and battery. "Affidavit of James Bussey and Jansen Read read on ye behalf of ye prisoner. John Chollwell sworn on behalf of ye prisoner" (*Ms. Mins. SCJ 1710–14* 478). In King v. Alexander Colden, defendant pleaded *nolo* to an indictment for assault and battery; ". . . the court having considered what was offered by the defendant in mitigation . . ." fined 5*s.* 4*d.* (*Ms. Mins. SCJ 1754–57* [Engr.] 117, 144, 146). Justice Van Rensselaer and Hendrick Rowe, when informed against for riot, pleaded *nolo*, were given leave by the court to produce affidavits in mitigation (*supra* n. 186). Similarly affidavits offered by Van Rensselaer in the information for maladministration. James Reed, indicted in 1770 for assault on a constable, appeared and on "Motion of Mr. Jay ordered that his Appearance be entered and . . . [to appear Thursday] and have then leave to examine Witnesses in Mitigation of his Fine" (*Ms. Mins. SCJ 1769–72* [Engr.] 239, 277, 288). Thos. Cheesman, indicted in 1771 for assault and battery, withdrew his plea of not guilty rather than contend with the King. The court stated it would consider the fine at the next Sessions. On Nov. 6, "This court having heard the witnesses" both for Crown and defendant set the fine (*Ms. Mins. NYCQS 1760–72* 350, 355). Cf. also the entry in King v. Fling, "The Court will hear evidence at the next session to assess fine" (*Ms. Mins. NYCQS 1772–91* 25, 35, Nov. 6, 1772, Feb. 3, 1773). The country courts also heard evidence in mitigation. Cf. King v. Vandenberg (*Ms. Mins. Albany Co. Sess. 1763–82* Jan. 1767); King v. Jonas Bolton *et al.* (*ibid.* June 7, 1775); King v. Neal Shaw (*Ms. Mins. Charlotte Co. Sess. 1773–1800* Oct. 18, 1774); King v. Mowl (*Ms. Mins. Dutchess Co. Sess.* Liber E, Oct. 5, 1773); King v. John Campbell (*Ms. Mins. Queens Co. Sess. 1722–87* Sept. 18, 1770); King v. Wm. Steed (*ibid.* May 18, 1773).

counted for the offender. This can, in most instances, be deduced from the severity of the sentence in cases where some corporal punishment was adjudged. But where fines were imposed, since there was no standard scale for fixing penalties, nothing can be inferred from the few cases where the record explicitly indicates they were exceptionally light. Most illuminating on the disposition of at least one court is the obdurate attitude of the New York City magistrates in dealing with petit larceny, for an examination of the cases shows that they were equally severe whether the defendant was convicted by jury verdict or on his own confession.[193]

Before leaving the subject of pleading, it is well for us to speak of one of its most striking aspects in New York. In the city Quarter Sessions between 1691 and 1776, we have counted 248 cases where defendants confessed, 17 where judgment was suffered for want of a plea, and only 94 where defendants pleaded not guilty and were tried.[194] A sampling of country Sessions records shows a similar disproportion of confessions.[195] On the other hand, in the Supreme Court *en banc,* where the records are less complete, the count for the years 1693–1776 discloses confessions in 91 cases (15 in order to secure benefit of clergy), not guilty pleaded in 429 cases, judgment for want of a plea in 54, and 5 cases where the prisoners were sentenced without any indication of plea or even trial.[196] The most obvious inference, of course, is that in Sessions, since the bulk of the cases were minor misdemeanors, defendants to avoid expense

---

[193] In New York City Quarter Sessions between 1691 and 1776, there were seventeen such cases where the defendant was found guilty on a jury trial, and the punishments were as follows (the numbers in parentheses represent the number of cases in which such punishment was used): 7 lashes (1); 15 lashes (5); 21 lashes (2); 39 lashes (3); 39 lashes and carting (3); 39 lashes, exposed in a cart, carted and banished from the city (1); 40 lashes (1); 39 lashes twice and carted (1). On the other hand, we have seen thirty-three cases of petit larceny in N.Y.C. Quarter Sessions between 1691 and 1776 where the defendants confessed the indictments, and it would seem that the punishments were, if anything, more severe than in the cases where the offenders were found guilty on a jury trial. The following are the punishments meted out to those confessing indictments for petit larceny: 6 lashes (1); 7 lashes (1); 9 lashes (2); 15 lashes (1); 15 lashes until the offender bleed once, twice or thrice in the discretion of the magistrates (1); 18 lashes (1); 20 lashes (3); 21 lashes (2); 21 lashes and banished from the city (2); 21 lashes with birch rods (2); 26 lashes (1); 31 lashes (1); 31 lashes and one day in jail (1); 39 lashes (3); 39 lashes and banished from city (2); 39 lashes and carting (1);

39 lashes, carting and banished from city (3); 39 lashes, exposed in cart two hours, carting and leave the city (2); exposed in public cage two hours and transported out of city (1); exposed five minutes in a cart and banished from city (1); eight days in jail (1). These figures do not include the summary convictions under the Act of 1732 and its continuations.

[194] These figures are exclusive of special Sessions cases and the summary convictions for nuisances.

[195] For example, in Ulster County between Sept. 1712 and Sept. 1720, exclusive of summary cases, sixty-six defendants pleaded guilty and three not guilty (*Ms. Mins. Ulster Co. Sess. 1711/12–1720*). In the same county for the years 1737–50 there was a similar proportion of the *nolos* accounted as guilty pleas (*Ms. Mins. Ulster Co. Sess. 1737–50*). In Tryon County in the years 1772–76 there were thirty-six confessions and only five pleas of not guilty (*Ms. Mins. Tryon Co. Sess.*).

[196] At Oyer and Terminer and General Gaol Delivery for all counties for the years 1716, 1717 and 1721–49 there were nineteen confessions and fifty-nine pleas of not guilty (in twenty-eight of which the defendants were acquitted).

were more likely to plead guilty than in the Supreme Court where chiefly felonies or the more serious misdemeanors, whether prosecuted by information or indictment, were involved. It is also possible that the toll of confessions was increased by some dickering with Crown officials, especially in the country, to relieve the pressure of trials at the over-brief Sessions. In the case of the petit larcenies there is some reason to believe that the defendants were "taking a plea," for sometimes the stolen articles enumerated in the indictment were obviously of much greater value than the classic 12d. which marked the borderline between grand and petit larceny.[197] There are also a few cases which point rather more definitely to negotiations with the prosecuting official. In them, the defendant having pleaded not guilty would relinquish his plea and pray mercy or "submit," and usually was only lightly fined.[198] It is possible, of course, that these cases are to be treated as examples of pleading *nolo,* but they all occur after the period of invertebrate pleading, when even in the country the anatomy of pleading was well understood.

It is proper at this juncture to consider the demurrer, for in the early eighteenth century at least, the general demurrer in criminal cases was still regarded as a confession of the facts, and the prisoner, when the court ruled against him, was barred from pleading over, but was sentenced.[199] In misdemeanors, there was no doubt as to the correctness of the practice, but in 1724 Sergeant Hawkins bluntly cast doubt upon the authorities which supported the rule in felony cases.[200] Many years later, Blackstone,[201] with an Olympian disregard of Hawkins' text, urged as the latter's opinion that a prisoner be allowed to plead over to the felony, and then, curiously perverting the views of Hale, suggested that demurrers were seldom used since the same advantages might be taken upon a plea of not guilty or by motion in arrest of judgment.[202]

[197] Samuel Daley was charged with stealing books worth 10d. from his master, William Bradford (*Ms. Mins. NYCQS 1732–62* 62, 65, May 6, 7, 1736). Anne Wright accused of stealing a teakettle worth 10d. (*ibid.* 145, 147, Nov. 3, 1742). James McKensey, stealing a shirt and stock worth 10d. (*ibid.* 140–143, Aug. 4, 5, 1742).
[198] King v. Banks—entertaining slaves (*Ms. Mins. NYCQS 1694–1731/32* Aug. 2, 3, 1720) £5; King v. Isaac Solomons—assault and attempt to stab his wife (*ibid.* 411, 415, Aug. 8, Nov. 7, 1722) 5s. and costs; King v. Judith Peters—disorderly house (*ibid.* 442, 446, Aug. 4, Nov. 4, 1724) 40s. and costs; King v. Dowers—disorderly house, 1767–68 (*Ms. Mins. SCJ 1766–69* [Engr.] 321, 322, 460) £3; King v. Lieutenant William Jones—riot (*Ms. Mins. NYCQS 1760–72* 271, 273,

277, Feb. 8–10, 1769; *H.R. Pleadings* Pl. K. 515) £3; King v. Stone—offense not specified, 1772–73 (*Ms. Mins. Tryon Co. Sess.* Quarto 1, 1–2) 1 dollar; King v. Welsh—assault (*Ms. Mins. NYCQS 1772–91* 2, 4–6, May 2, 4, 1762) 20s.; King v. Brown—assault, 1774 (*Ms. Mins. Tryon Co. Sess.* Quarto 1, iv and vii).
[199] Coke, *Second Institute* 178; 2 Hale, *op. cit.* 257, 315.
[200] 2 Hawkins, *op. cit.* c.31 §5. His doubts had already been forecast by Hale.
[201] 4 Blackstone, *Commentaries* 334.
[202] 2 Hale, *op. cit.* 257, argues a confession by demurrer to be willful for the prisoner might have the advantages of exception to the sufficiency of the indictment before plea of not guilty or after conviction.

It is not surprising that the demurrer, being deemed so two-edged a weapon, was very rarely resorted to in New York; indeed, we have found only three cases, all of them early, where defendants demurred to indictments. The earliest occurs in 1693 when at Westchester Sessions, Nicoll, counsel for Gabriel Leggett, demurred to the sufficiency of an indictment and the demurrer was sustained.[203] Again, in 1702, Sophia Thomas, indicted for having clipped money in her possession, demurred to the indictment. The Attorney General joined, and after argument the court found the indictment insufficient.[204] A year later, a defendant charged with a similar offense was similarly successful.[205] Of course, as we have already seen in the quasi-criminal actions on provision bonds and the suits on recognizances, the demurrer was freely used,[206] and it was likewise sometimes employed by the Attorney General in demurring to pleas,[207] but obviously the device was too risky for defendants under indictment.

The sufficiency of an indictment could also be tested by a motion to quash, although this, if successful, was not as effective as the demurrer to set a defendant at large for he could always be indicted anew. The motion to quash was consequently used chiefly to delay proceedings. In New York Province this afforded certain strategic advantages in dealing with the Crown officers, for in a number of cases where indictments were quashed no further proceedings have been found.

The motion to quash comes into general use early in the eighteenth century although in 1697, in *King* v. *Le Reaux,* what amounted to such a motion was made after verdict.[208] In 1701, in the case of *King* v. *Peter Ponton,*[209] Emott moved for the defendant that a presentment for felony be quashed for "being uncertain" and the motion was granted. In the next year, in the treason case against Bayard,[210] this same attorney and his associate Nicoll vainly sought to derail proceedings by a similar motion before the arraignment. It was claimed that the indictment was not found by twelve men and a variety of authorities were cited to establish the point. Atwood, C.J., ruled, however, that there could be no averment against the record, that the grand jury was an inquest of office which could be found by a number less than twelve. Counsel then objected that the jury had not been returned by a precept under the seals of the

203 *Mins. Westch. Ct. of Sess. 1657–96* 85.
204 *Ms. Mins. NYCQS 1694–1731/32* 72, 78, Nov. 4, 1702, Feb. 3, 1702/03.
205 Queen v. Anna Vanderspigel (*ibid.* 78, 79, Feb. 3, 1702/03, May 4, 1703).
206 *Supra* 240 *et seq.;* 540.
207 As in King v. Mulford (*supra* 302).
208 Cf. *supra* 313.
209 *Ms. Mins. SCJ 1701–04* 17.
210 14 Howell, *State Trials* 479.

commissioners, but this the Chief Justice brushed aside and the trial proceeded.

From the time of these cases onward, the motion to quash appears off and on in the records,[211] and it should be noted that sometimes the court would quash on its own initiative.[212] There is not a great deal to indicate what the particular rules of practice were, beyond the fact that the motion was sometimes made after pleading,[213] and that in general it was founded upon errors such as the absence of freeholders[214] on the grand jury, the failure to state a particular statute and the like.[215] The motion would then be argued. The best example of such an argument is that of William Kempe when he was indicted

[211] In Queen v. Onclebagg, Bickley on behalf of the defendant prayed that the inquisition might be filed, and his motion having been granted, Bickley moved on Oct. 7, 1703, to quash the inquisition. This was argued on Oct. 8 and 13, and on the latter date the inquisition was ordered to be quashed (*Ms. Mins. SC] 1701–04* 111, 116, 122, 129). On Oct. 11, 1701, Bickley on behalf of Johann De Peyster, David Provoost and Nicholas Roosevelt moved to quash a grand jury presentment against them for falsely and deceitfully returning an alderman, two constables and assistant collectors, when the majority had voted for the opposite parties. Bickley's motion was granted (*ibid.* 20, 21).

An indictment found at Quarter Sessions against Fortune, a negro, was delivered into the Supreme Court by Judge Walter, and on motion of Murray, the court ordered that the indictment be quashed and the defendant discharged (*Ms. Mins. SC] 1723–27* 93). On Mar. 15, 1727/28, John Little appeared in person on a certiorari removing an indictment of rescue found at Orange County General Sessions, and this indictment being read and exceptions taken by the defendant, the court ordered that the indictment be quashed and the defendant discharged from his recognizance (*Ms. Mins. SC] 1727–32* 34).

Of interest is the following memorandum which appears in *H.R. Pleadings* Pl. K. 727: "John Livingston for Fraudulently branding of two flasks unmerchantable flour knowing them to be so Quashed . . . Michael Lawrier for Fraudulently repacking of Pork Quashed . . . Samuel Dunscomb . . . [for fraudulently repacking pork] Quashed . . . Anthony Ten Eyck for fraudulently selling unmerchantable Pork Quashed." The indictment against John Livingston for branding unmerchantable flour was found on Apr. 26, 1753, and on Aug. 4, 1753, the defendant was ordered to plead in twenty days or suffer judgment. However, on Apr. 17, 1754, the minute entries indicate that the indictment was quashed (*Ms. Mins. SC] 1750–54* [Engr.] 249, 253, 286; *Ms. Mins. SC] 1754–57* [Engr.] 6). We note, however, from the *J. T. Kempe Lawsuits* S–U *sub nom.* Ten Eyck, that Livingston had pleaded not guilty, evidently prior to the quashing of the

indictment. Cf. further *infra* n. 213 as to the other defendants.

[212] E.g., King v. Matt. Dubois (*Ms. Mins. Dutchess Co. Sess.* Liber A, May 20, 1740); King v. Balthazar Van Kleek (*ibid.* Oct. 19, 1742). The Dutchess court very frequently quashed on its own motion. King v. Wm. Cole (*Ms. Mins. Orange Co. Sess. 1727–79* Oct. 25, 1737); King v. Allison (*ibid.* Oct. 30, 1744); King v. Roger James (*Ms. Mins. Richmond Co. Sess. 1710/11–1744/45* Mar. 7, 1720/21); King v. Glowrie Delamatre (*Ms. Mins. Ulster Co. Sess. 1737–50* May 3, 1743).

[213] On Oct. 25, 1753, an indictment for fraudulently repacking pork was found against Michael Lourier [Lawrier] (*supra* n. 211). On Jan. 15, 1754 defendant pleaded not guilty, and on Apr. 17, 1754, on motion of Nicoll, the court ordered that the indictment be quashed (*Ms. Mins. SC] 1750–54* [Engr.] 316, 342; *Ms. Mins. SC] 1754–57* [Engr.] 5). On Aug. 4, 1753, an indictment had been found against Samuel Dunscomb for fraudulently repacking pork, and on Oct. 25, 1753, the defendant was ordered to plead in twenty days or suffer judgment. On Jan. 16, 1753, he pleaded not guilty, but on Apr. 17, 1754, the indictment was quashed (*Ms. Mins. SC] 1750–54* [Engr.] 292, 316, 344; *Ms. Mins. SC] 1754–57* [Engr.] 5). On Apr. 26, 1753, Anthony Ten Eyck had been indicted for branding and disposing of unmerchantable pork (*supra* n. 211), and on Aug. 4, 1753, Smith Jr. appeared for the defendant, who was ordered to plead in twenty days. However, on Apr. 17, 1754, on hearing the arguments on both sides and on motion of Smith Jr., the court ordered that the indictment be quashed (*Ms. Mins. SC] 1750–54* [Engr.] 250, 252, 286; *Ms. Mins. SC] 1754–57* [Engr.] 5). It is to be noted that in the latter case the defendant had evidently pleaded not guilty (*J. T. Kempe Lawsuits* S–U).

[214] King v. Neeley (*Ms. Mins. Ulster Co. Sess. 1737–50* May 6, 1740). In King v. Roger James (*supra* n. 212) the indictment was quashed because not found by a majority and the foreman's signature was defaced.

[215] Queen v. Livingston (*Ms. Mins. Ulster Co. Sess. 1711/12–1720* Sept. 20, 1712). In King v.

for maladministration.[216] In a few cases, the Attorney General forestalled a motion to quash by moving to amend or qualify the indictment or information because it was insufficient.[217]

While the motion to quash is essentially an aspect of pleading it may also be viewed in relation to motion practice in general. The reader will already have had occasion to observe in cases heretofore cited how constantly motions were used at all junctures in a criminal proceeding. Indeed, the records give the impression that the inertia of sheriffs, juries, prosecutors and judges was such that it was nearly impossible for a case to be propelled to judgment without incessant motions on the part of the Crown or the defendant. Only in the country Sessions do the justices themselves appear to have dispatched business without this stimulus. There are, for example, the motions that process issue, and that process be returned, the motions for arraignment, and for the defendant to plead, motions for a struck jury, and for the discharge of the prisoner unless the Attorney General bring the case for trial, and finally the motions for new trial and to arrest judgment.

In the present state of our knowledge concerning contemporary English criminal practice it is not possible to determine how far the liberal use of motions in New York was inspired by the usage in the motherland. None of the criminal law textbooks deals with the question except parenthetically, and, so far as we are aware, Edward Wynne was the first writer to appreciate the important role of motions in trial.[218] Wynne, indeed, claims to have formed a new notion of practice, for he conceives a judicial procedure as a series of stages

---

Roper (*Ms. Mins. Suffolk Co. Sess. 1723–51* Sept. 1728) the reason was "manifest error." In King v. Gale (*Ms. Mins. Orange Co. Sess. 1727–79* Oct. 1756) an indictment for Sabbath breach was quashed because defendant was an assemblyman and had to go to New York.

In the country it does not appear that a notice of a motion was necessarily given. Cf. King v. Green (*Ms. Mins. Suffolk Co. Sess. 1723–51* Mar. 25, 1729), where King's counsel on exceptions to the indictment asked for time. In King v. Faulkner (*Ms. Mins. Queens Co. Sess. 1727–87* May 18, 1731), Murray, "allowed" as defendant's attorney, moved to quash and motion granted. Cf. also King v. Joans (*Ms. Mins. Orange Co. Sess. 1727–79* Oct. 1728).

In *Ms. Files Dutchess Co. 1763–64* is a notice from Cary Ludlow (defendant's attorney in King v. Bogardus, indictment for perjury), addressed to Henry Livingston or any other person prosecuting pleas of the Crown and dated Sept. 28, 1763, stating that he intended to move to quash. Possibly by this time, country practice required notice.

[216] *Supra* 377.
[217] See, for example, King v. John Allison (*supra* 184); King v. Jacobus Cosyne on an information for words against the King: ordered that the "Information be amended by adding these words, viz. [on and concerning our said Lord the King] [*sic*] between the words (uttered) and (these)" (*Ms. Mins. SCJ 1732–39* 158, Apr. 17, 1735, *supra* 360); King v. Isaac Monro "On motion by Mr. Attorney Generall That the indictment for the misdemeanor be qualified for insufficiency thereof, it is ordered accordingly" (*Ms. Mins. SCJ 1723–27* 118, 121).

On Aug. 1, 1738, on an indictment found in Orange County and removed by certiorari into the Supreme Court, the Attorney General moved that the indictment might be quashed for want of sufficiency and that he might be admitted to file an information on the merits of the case (*Ms. Mins. SCJ 1732–39* 317).

[218] Wynne, *Eunomous* (5 ed.) Dialogus II §§23–39. First edition 1767.

with the motion as an essential instrument to secure an orderly progression from stage to stage. He concedes, however, only a few motions as necessary in Crown cases, and if this is a correct exposition of Crown practice in his day it is apparent that the New Yorkers, probably under the influence of civil procedure, had gone much further than their compatriots in making the progress of criminal procedure contingent upon motion. It is apparent also from Attorney General Jamison's accounts with the clerk of the Supreme Court in 1713 and 1714[219] that even by this time there was a free use of motions in criminal causes. Undoubtedly the practice was indulged for the purpose of enhancing bills of costs. And it has for the scholar the one advantage that the entry of motions in the minute books makes it possible to clothe the otherwise bare skeleton of the "record" itself with some useful detail.

[219] 59 NY Col. Mss. 100.

CHAPTER X

TRIAL: PART II

O NCE a defendant had exhausted all means of avoiding an answer to the Crown's charges against him, if indeed he saw fit to try evasion and, not wishing to confess, was put to denying his guilt, it was by no means a foregone conclusion in provincial New York that he would be tried by a petit jury. We have had occasion from time to time to remark upon the extent of summary jurisdiction in New York, and it is desirable at this point, now that we have the defendant ready for trial, to review the situations where petit juries would not be summoned. This is a matter of immediate present-day interest since the several constitutions of the state from 1777 onward have all contained the provision that trial by jury as "heretofore used" or guaranteed should remain inviolate.[1] These words are a direct reference to the pre-Revolutionary practices which, musty though they be, it behooves the citizen to know.

The Charter of Liberties of 1683[2] which the Crown rejected had provided that all trial should be by twelve men, "as neer as may be peers or Equals" of the neighborhood in the county "where the same should arise and grow." The Act of 1691 (later disallowed), declaring the rights of the New Yorkers, repeated this language.[3] Both enactments exempted faults and misdemeanors in contempt of courts of judicature from affeerment by juries. The Judicature Acts of 1691 and 1692 also contained provisions that no man's rights or property should be determined (except as facts were admitted or there had been default) unless the facts be found by verdict of twelve men of the neighborhood. This safeguard was also contained in Bellomont's judiciary ordinance. Although the jury of the vicinage was revered as a constitutional fundamental, like all fundamentals it was subject to vicissitudes for, as we have seen, summary jurisdiction was expanded, and the colonists took great pains to require a property qualification for jurors.[4] With one detail, however, there was little tampering, viz., the necessity of trial by the vicinage. Indeed from the viewpoint of the inhabitants this was the chief *raison d'être* of the circuit and nisi

---

[1] Article 41 of the 1777 constitution provided: "Trial by Jury in all cases in which it hath heretofore been used shall be established and remain inviolate forever." The constitution of 1821 had a substantially similar provision (Art. 7 §2). In 1846 the constitution permitted a waiver of jury in civil cases (Art. 1 §2), repeated in 1894. The amended constitution of 1938 (Art. 1 §2) permits a waiver in non-capital cases.

[2] 1 *Col. Laws NY* 113, 114.

[3] *Ibid.* 246, 247.

[4] *Supra* 467.

prius system.[5] Early in the eighteenth century the question of trial by twelve men of the neighborhood was made an issue under circumstances that we think made a lasting impress on provincial law.

On the motion in arrest of judgment in the Bayard case[6] (which has already been discussed) the objections embraced a claim that one juror was an alien, and a claim that the jury should have been summoned from the ward where the alleged offense was committed. The court, however, shortly overruled these objections. The same points were raised by Mrs. Hannah Hutchins, wife of John Hutchins, who was convicted at the same Oyer and Terminer. In a petition to the Lieutenant Governor[7] she complained that her husband's trial had been by a jury of Dutchmen

unacquainted with the Liberties of Englishmen and also strangers to yoᵣ petitioner's husband, his life and conversations and . . . consequently not of his vicinity as the Law in such cases Implyes and directs. May it therefore please

[5] *Supra* 77, 144 n. 33, 172.

[6] 14 Howell, *State Trials* 511 *et seq.*

[7] In the transcript of Eng. Mss. XLV 96, *Bayard Papers.*

In his petition and "appeal" to Queen Anne, Nicholas Bayard stated among other things that he had been "convicted by an illegal petty jury of Aliens and Dutch unduly returned and very ignorant of the English Laws and Language" (the petition, *supra* c. IV n. 38). Among the affidavits taken by John Bridges and Samson Shelton Broughton, under the Queen's order of reference for the collection of evidence in connection with the Bayard appeal, are statements of some of the petit jurors who had joined in the verdict declaring Bayard guilty of high treason. Thomas Sanders and Isaac Stoutenbergh, two of the trial jurors, made oral statements as follows, confirming the allegations made by Bayard in his petition: ". . . these Depon⁺ˢ doe owne their great Ignorance of the Laws of England at that time not knowing what was High Treason . . . the Foreman . . . Did assert it was High Treason . . . to disturb the peace good and quiet of this Government and that Colonell Bayard had disturbed the peace by the addresses and eight or nine jurors were for clearing . . . Bayard but were perswaded by the foreman." It is to be noted, however, that the deponents, Sanders and Stoutenbergh, appeared before Broughton and Bridges "and owned and sayd the above-written papers that had been read to them was true but would not swear to the same" (Eng. Mss. XLVI 152, *Bayard Papers*).

Two other witnesses examined by Bridges and Broughton, George Stanton and Robert Anderson, testified that Hutchins had specifically demanded the right to trial by a jury of Englishmen: ". . . upon his Tryall the deponants heard the said Alder-

man Hutchins desire . . . the benefit of the Act of Parliament . . . and that the Jury might have it read to them but was refused him That the said Hutchins . . . told the Judge that as he was . . . an Englishman born he hop'd that he might have the liberty of being tryed by a jury of his own country men which the Judge over ruled and would not allow him" (*ibid.* 174). One John Ellison deposed that Chief Justice Atwood and the Solicitor General challenged every Englishman on the jury panel.

When Bayard was reprieved, pending his appeal, the erstwhile "traitor" turned on his enemies and attempted to have De Peyster, Provoost and others arrested "for being Justices on the Bench at his triall and . . . for being of the grand jury that indicted him." Thereupon De Peyster and Provoost petitioned the Queen "for relief of those miseries," alleging that Bayard and Hutchins were arraigned and tried under an act of assembly and that "Your petitioners . . . behaved themselves . . . allowing to the said Bayard and Hutchins to make use of the advantages and Privileges Established by law as by the records of the said Trialls nor was any jury picked for that purpose they had their challenges allowed, above the number of eighty being summoned and neither of them excepted against so many as the law allows neither were they [the jurors] so ignorant and mean as is pretended for every one was a good and substantiall freeholder . . . but some of them [the jurors] being examined before a committee of the House of Representatives did conceive they were not obliged to answer all questions . . . relating to that affair by reason your Majestie had . . . [granted] an appeal upon the hearing whereof your petitioners are certain your Majestie will be fully informed of the facts" (*Misc. Mss. Atwood*).

Yo^r Honor to . . . grant that . . . [he] . . . may have Englishmen or at least [persons] of English extraction to be of his jury who may properly be said to be of his neighbourhood and none other.

The impact of the Bayard case upon New York politics outlasted the lifetime of the participants, and it may be that publication of the proceedings and especially their inclusion in the *State Trials* kept alive recollections respecting the issues over the jury. In any event, it is striking that through the rest of the colonial period the visne was treated with tenderness so that only on a few occasions was a venue changed, and then specifically because the neighborhood was prejudiced against a defendant.

Beyond the circumstances of particular cases, beyond even the colonists' own legislation lurked the deep-seated feeling—and feeling it was—that the common law was controlling in this fundamental matter of the jury, and that nothing could avail to diminish the rights of Englishmen, even if expatriate, in respect thereto. Periodically there swept up storms when violent assertions in terms of right were made, as in William Smith's objections to the quitrent bill of 1755;[8] in the lawyers' protest against the £5 Act;[9] in the assembly's resolutions regarding the *Forsey* v. *Cunningham* appeal,[10] and its solemn resolve of March 8, 1775.[11] At the same time, it should be observed that in spite of their anxiety to protect the ramparts of democracy, the colonists were disposed to maintain the structure as it was. In other words, they made little effort to restrict the field of summary jurisdiction and require jury trial for petty offenses. The only perceptible brake upon the then current expansion of summary powers is the tendency to permit an action of debt as an alternative to information for the recovery of penalties and to allow in such cases a six-man jury if a party was willing to pay the costs.

The field where one might look for some attempt to have jury trial expanded was in relation to contempts, not indeed, where officers of the law were involved, but where private individuals offended the courts.[12] Curiously enough,

---

[8] The bill permitted disseisin on certificate of a Crown officer that rents were owing. No jury or any legal process was provided. Smith grounds his argument on Magna Carta, c.29 (2 *Jour. Legis. Council 1743–75* 1199).

[9] *Ibid.* 1325 *et seq.* (1758).

[10] *Supra* 235 n. 37; 2 *Jour. Gen. Assembly NY* 768, 795, 806.

[11] 3 *ibid.* 63.

[12] On officers cf. *supra* 454. In 1692 Harmanus Smack declared "that what the Justices of this court decided was by force and not according to the law."

Ordered taken in custody but submitted (*Ms. Kings Co. Ct. & Rd. Recs. 1692–1825* 10); cf. King v. Bibou, 1693 (*ibid.* 19) and King v. Mary Richardson, 1693, who paid a fine (*ibid.* 12). King v. Tiebout, 1695, also fined (*Ms. Mins. NYCQS 1694–1731/32* 10, 11, Feb. 4, 1695).

We have (*supra* c. V 303) referred to the case of Simon Smith, chaplain of the fort, who, on being presented for marrying Elizabeth Buckmaster to Adam Baldridge without a license, "did contemptuously utter severall scurrilous expressions to the scandal of his function the abuse of ye grand jurors

despite evidence of a persistently disrespectful attitude toward official persons and despite the already blooming American penchant for blunt and trenchant expression of opinion, the colonists endured without complaint the exercise here of summary jurisdiction, possibly because the cases where the courts became exasperated enough to act were relatively infrequent, and usually the defendants made a speedy and humble submission.

The New Yorkers accepted without cavil the heavy inheritance of English statutes which empowered the justices of the peace to proceed summarily in cases of riot and forcible entry, poor relief, bastardy, nuisances and the repair of highways, bridges and jails. And, as remarked, the fecundity of their own summary legislation denotes an absence of constitutional scruple. Against the boldest of their innovations—the less-than-grand-larceny statutes of 1732—no jury-loving native voice was heard. Indeed, it was a Crown officer who first commented upon the threat which these acts presented to constitutional safeguards.

In 1769 a complaint was made to the Governor regarding three Suffolk justices of the peace who, under this act, had railroaded the servant of a substantial citizen. Attorney General Kempe warned the justices that there had been much complaint regarding the way the provincial statute was enforced by them. He pointed out that the act was intended only for vagrants and other disorderly persons unable to maintain themselves in jail, to prevent their im-

and diminution to the dignity of the court" (*Mins. SCJ 1693–1701* 173, 174, Oct. 7, 1699). The recalcitrant Smith was about to be discharged from his recognizance in New York Quarter Sessions on Feb. 5, 1700/01 on the payment of fees, "upon which the said Simon Smith refused to pay the said fees and gave the court very abusive language telling them he would pay none, that they had no Authority to Compell him, that he would finde a Law for them and that he Cared not for their illegall proceedings & several Other abusive and Scurolous language that he cared no more for the Mayor than Another Man." In this instance the Court of Quarter Sessions ordered that Smith be "Committed till he find sufficient sureties for his Appearance att the next Sessions and that in the meantime he be of good behavior" (*Ms. Mins. NYCQS 1694–1731/32* 60). At Suffolk Oyer and Terminer on Aug. 20, 1717, "John Mosier [was ordered to be] committed into ye sheriffs Custody and to suffer a weeks Imprisonment for affronting the Kings Justices in Going to Hold court." However, on Aug. 21, Mosier was ordered to be released out of prison on the payment of the sheriff's and other fees (*Ms. Mins. Cir. 1716–17* 44, 47). Cf. also King v. Walling who was insolent to the grand jurors (*Ms. Mins. NYCQS 1694–1731/32* 443, 444, Aug. 5, 1724). At the Ul-

ster court for the trial of causes brought to issue in the Supreme Court, the court summarily ordered, on Sept. 2, 1729, that John Tenbroek be fined £10 and committed to the sheriff's custody until he pay his fine, for "having privately given victuals to the jury" in a civil case. However, Tenbroek, on his submission, was discharged and the court ordered that his fine be remitted (*Ms. Mins. Cir. 1721–49* 257).

At Queens Oyer and Terminer and General Gaol Delivery for Sept. 4, 1733, there is this entry: "James Dickenson comeing into court and telling of them the [sic] would not do him justice Ordered the sheriff take him into custody." On Dickenson's petition he was discharged later that same day (*ibid.* 65, 66).

On Mar. 25, 1735, the Westchester court for the trial of causes, etc. ordered that one Robert Williams be committed to jail for striking the sheriff at the court door while the court was in session (*ibid.* 300). Cf. also King v. Dawson (*Ms. Mins. NYCQS 1732–62* 86, May 3, 1738); King v. Kidney, 1749 (*Ms. Mins. Cir. 1721–49* 348); King v. Townsend, 1750 (*Ms. Mins. SCJ 1750–54* [Engr.] 27); King v. Barrett and Fitzgerald, 1764 (*Ms. Mins. SCJ 1762–64* [Engr.] 353, 429); King v. Aaron Ackerman, 1774 (*Ms. Mins. SCJ 1772–76* [Rough] 207).

prisonment from being a charge on the county, and "must not be extended beyond that, as it destroys the trial by Jury."[13] Again on June 9, 1769, in reply to a request for instructions Kempe expatiated as follows:

It may be not improper to presume that the whole scope of that act is of a very extraordinary nature and appears upon very little reflection to be destructive of that Grand Bulwark of our Freedom & Safety, the tryal by Jury, inasmuch as it is calculated to enable magistrates to punish the subject criminally without the judgment of their peers and thereby throw down that barrier against the arbitrary power of the Crown which it is the peculiar happiness of our constitution to have established. Nor is it less extraordinary in this, that it leaves the inferior magistrates in their Discretion to inflict infamous punishments for offences which by the Equity of our laws cannot even by the King himself or by the highest Courts of Judicature be so punished. Too great Tenderness & caution there cannot be used in Proceedings under this act not only because it may at least be doubted whether the Act be not in itself void for its repugnancy to the Laws and the first Principles of the Constitution . . . but because [an infamous punishment ruins the offender's life].

Kempe went on to give explicit instructions as to how the act should be administered, prefacing these with the statement that the act must be strictly construed in the most confined sense. The preamble, he thought, was the key to the construction for it pointed to the specific persons against whom the act was directed, and this, to save the county the expense of imprisonment until the next General Sessions should meet, and to enable the resident poor to get back to work so that their families would not be a charge upon the county.

It is remarkable that such tenderness for jury trial should have been felt in this particular quarter, for the King's Attorney General was almost the last person one would have expected to hold a brief for the jury. On the other hand, except for the derisive handling of Justice Peters by the rioters in Dutchess and later of Benjamin Hough by the Cumberland County rebels, we have seen no evidence of organized opposition to the enormous cumulation of provincial acts conveying summary powers to the justices in all manner of petty misdemeanors. The situation exemplifies that curious and typical American trait of enthroning a principle but allowing practice to be quite thoroughly bemired.

We have several times remarked upon these petty misdemeanor statutes, and although it is beyond our purpose to embroider upon their details, we

18 *J. T. Kempe Letters* A–Z. To Benajah Strong, Selah Strong and Richard Woodhull.

must indicate their bearing upon jury trial. The provincial assembly legislated here entirely without plan, and there seems to be no relation between the objective of a statute and the sanction. The hit-or-miss character of the legislation is indicated by a group of statutes passed between the years 1710–14. In 1710,[14] an act to prevent the burning of woods was implemented by a summary one-witness information proceeding before a single justice, one half the penalty to go to the person grieved. In 1711[15] the Bill of Credit Act provided that collectors failing to endorse a bill of credit should forfeit £5, one half to the informer who could sue in any court. In 1712[16] an act conveyed to John Rosevelt [sic] and another the monopoly of making linseed oil, and threatened would-be competitors with a fine of £200 which the monopolists could collect by debt in any court of record. In 1713[17] the Excise Act penalized persons selling liquor to slaves 40s. for every sale, the sum to be recovered before any justice of the peace. In 1714,[18] an act to license peddlers provided that persons forging licenses should be liable to £50 forfeit to be recovered by action of debt, bill, plaint or information in any inferior court, one half to go to the informer.

The above sampling is typical,[19] and an examination of the colonial acts at large discloses that frequently the statutes were so loosely drawn that it is not possible to decide whether a civil action or an information was intended. Since the New York magistrates had a petty civil as well as a criminal jurisdiction, such distinctions may have seemed immaterial. Yet clearly if the legislature had been exercised about abridgment of jury trial, the debt action with an optional six-man jury would have been stipulated in these penal laws more often than it was. Curiously enough, the only provincial comment was adverse to such actions. When the statutory limit of the justices' civil jurisdiction was raised, their competence over penal actions automatically extended to statutes with equivalently higher penalties. William Smith Jr. objected to this because the actions for penalties were regarded as too intricate for the average justice

---

[14] 1 *Col. Laws NY* 716.
[15] *Ibid.* 739.
[16] *Ibid.* 752, and compare the lampblack monopoly to John Parmiter (*ibid.* 755).
[17] *Ibid.* 788.
[18] *Ibid.* 807.
[19] Compare with legislation of a session chosen at random: Fortification Act—refusal to work on Oswego Fort, 6s. per diem recoverable before any two J.P.'s of Albany County (3 *ibid.* 145); Excise Act—sale of liquor without license, £5 recoverable "in a summary way" before two magistrates (3 *ibid.* 156); Poor Relief for New York—£5 for failure to declare value of goods brought into the city, recoverable in any court of record by action of debt, bill, plaint or information (*ibid.* 181); Wells and Pump Act—40s. for injuries to pumps recoverable before magistrates (*ibid.* 184); Gambling Act—£20 for keeping gambling devices or permitting gambling, recoverable by bill, plaint or information in any court of record (*ibid.* 194); act to prevent deer-killing out of season—30s. per deer recoverable before one justice by anyone who "shall inform and sue" (*ibid.* 196); act for return of stray cattle—20s. for penning recoverable before a justice of the peace (*ibid.* 202).

of the peace. But we have seen no comment respecting the non-use of juries in the *qui tam* actions before justices of the peace, and the almost complete absence of records here, coupled with the very limited sources bearing on the summary jurisdiction, generally renders it impossible to determine whether or not the bark of the statutes was worse than the bite of practice.

One other exception to jury trial must be mentioned, but this was one foisted on the colonists by Act of Parliament. The statute 11 and 12 Wm. III c.7 for the suppression of piracy stipulated exactly how the commissioners for the trial of pirates were to function. There was to be no indictment by grand jury but the Register of the Commission was to read "articles" against the prisoner who was to plead guilty or not guilty. Witnesses were to be examined viva voce in the defendant's presence and his cross-examination was to be conducted through the President of the court. The defendant was allowed witnesses and had the right to be heard "what he can say for himself." The court was to deliberate and a vote was to be taken by individuals, judgment being rendered according to the "plurality of voices."

Trials under the commissions issued pursuant to 11 and 12 Wm. III c.7 were unusual occurrences. It is clear from the account given by William Smith Jr. of the trials of Joseph Andrews in 1769 and of William Wood in 1774, that the procedure required by the act was followed, although in the Andrews case Smith records his objections that the commissioners failed to adhere to the rules of civil law respecting evidence necessary to convict.[20]

Between the welter of statutes permitting summary trial and the case of the sea robber who became a rare defendant once the sanctuary of privateering was understood, lay the solid earth of normal expectancy—the trial jury for the sufficient defendant in felony cases and in what may be described as the pedigreed misdemeanors, those of ancient legal lineage too serious to be committed to Special Sessions. The Supreme Court records show that defendants were invariably accorded jury trial in capital causes and misdemeanors prosecuted by information or indictment if they pleaded the general issue. No cases have been found in Oyer and Terminer where a jury was not used if the defendant pleaded not guilty, and the few isolated instances of reference of

---

[20] Andrews was charged with piracy and several murders. His companion had been tried and convicted in the West Indies. Cf. 4 *Ms. Journal William Smith Jr.* May 17, 1769; *New York Gazette or Weekly Postboy* May 22, 1769; 26 *Ms. Mins. Council* 140. Wood was charged with piracy in murdering the captain of the schooner *Mercy* and robbing him of his goods. The evidence showed merely that the captain disappeared during the night and two sailors next looted his chest. As the elements of piracy were missing Wood was acquitted. Smith states "the Commission & Stat. of 11 & 12 Wm 3 Cap. 7 as I conceived gave no authority but in cases of Piracy" (4 *Ms. Jour. Wm. Smith Jr.* Oct. 15, 1774). There are notes also in *Wm. Smith Jr. Mss.* Box 3 folder 8.

indictments to justices out of Sessions seem all to be cases where no plea had been proffered and the case was within some summary statute.

The Time of Trial

The necessity of a jury and the measures taken to assure its presence as well as the rules about time of pleading all had a bearing upon the time of trial. In England, since the sheriff was supposed to have a panel of forty-eight on hand for the Assizes, the circuit rule was that trial of felons took place immediately upon arraignment.[21] The "immediately" must in New York be qualified to "promptly," for at Circuit a day's respite was frequently allowed.[22] The record of a trial reads as if the cause proceeded at once, but actually this did not accurately represent the facts. For example, in *King* v. *Manas Carlan,* the record indicates trial immediately upon arraignment, but the Oyer and Terminer minutes show that after Carlan had pleaded he complained that he could not get his witnesses. Thereupon the court, having ordered subpoenas, postponed the trial until the next day.[23]

Proceedings at bar in the Supreme Court show a similar practice,[24] but it is important to observe that, in general, trials in that court were regulated by a rule of March 15, 1704/05:

> General rules to be observed. First day of each Terme for grand jury and the Doggett. Second day for tryalls. If yt be not sufficient for all ye Tryalls, those remaining to be tryed the Last day but one by special order—notice of tryall

---

[21] 2 Hale, *Pleas of the Crown* 28; 4 Blackstone, *Commentaries* 351.

[22] On Sept. 12, 1716, at Ulster Oyer and Terminer and General Gaol Delivery, Rachell Van Anthon, indicted for murdering her bastard child, filed a prayer through her attorney, Bickley, that she be tried "this court" or be discharged. This was ordered accordingly, and on Sept. 13 she was arraigned and found not guilty (*Ms. Mins. Cir. 1716–17* 26–28). George Brown, indicted for felony at Westchester Oyer and Terminer and General Gaol Delivery on Sept. 5, 1738, pleaded not guilty and the court "ordered that he prepare for his tryal tomorrow." Brown was tried on the following day and found guilty (*Ms. Mins. Cir. 1721–49* 94, 95).

[23] *Ibid.* 119; H.R. Parch. 169 K 5.

[24] Ann Clay, indicted on Apr. 8, 1703, in the Supreme Court for felony, was arraigned and put herself upon God and her country, whereupon the court ordered that she "be tryed tomorrow," and on the following day she was tried and acquitted (*Ms. Mins. SCJ 1701–04* 85). John Douglas was indicted on Jan. 23, 1767, in the Supreme Court for

grand larceny and pleaded not guilty. On Jan. 24 he was tried and found guilty (*Ms. Mins. SCJ 1764–67* [Rough] 208, 211). Catherine Fagen Cooper was arraigned on two indictments for "larceny from the person privily" and pleaded not guilty on Apr. 26, 1769. She was tried on Apr. 27, 1769, and found guilty on both indictments (*Ms. Mins. SCJ 1769–72* [Engr.] 16, 18). On Apr. 23, 1770, Thomas Clay, Jacob Osborn and John Galloway pleaded not guilty to an indictment for burglary and on Apr. 24 Clay and Osborn were tried and found guilty (*ibid.* 182, 185). On Jan. 22, 1773, James Alexander pleaded not guilty to an indictment for counterfeiting and endorsement on a bill of exchange and publishing the same, and on Jan. 23 he was tried, found guilty and sentenced to thirty-nine lashes and to the pillory (*Ms. Mins. SCJ 1772–76* [Rough] 67, 70, 71). William Elkins and Abraham Stokes pleaded not guilty on Jan. 19, 1776, to an indictment for petit larceny, and on Jan. 20 they were tried and found guilty (*Ms. Mins. SCJ 1775–81* [Engr.] 63, 64, 65).

within forty miles of this citty to be eight days exclusive, above forty miles fourteen days—. . . Third day for argumentt. fourth day for Judgemt of the Court.[25]

Translated into practice this rule meant that trials took place the second day of the term, and a defendant in a felony case, if already in custody, would be tried the day after indictment. In trials at bar, a venire would have to issue immediately upon general issue pleaded. If the return was to be forthwith,[26] the trial would proceed as soon as the panel was delivered, otherwise on the return day set in the writ. Of course, if a cause was sent down for trial at Circuit, a delay would ensue. The summoning of jurors in such cases has already been discussed.[27]

The provision for notice to non-residents has reference to the trial of misdemeanors. We have already seen that in England, at Quarter Sessions, it was not the practice to try at the same Sessions where an indictment was found, but the defendant would traverse and the case would come up at the next ensuing Quarter Sessions unless the defendant consented to an immediate disposition. A similar rule prevailed at Assizes although judges of Oyer and Terminer and Gaol Delivery were conceded to have the power to compel immediate trial.[28] In King's Bench, first by rule of court[29] and later by statute,[30] a non-resident defendant had to be given notice by the prosecutor when trial was to take place, and possibly a defendant could also take it upon himself to notify the prosecutor he was ready for trial[31] although we have only seen Quarter Sessions precedents of this practice.[32]

In New York Province, the courts in general pursued the policy of trying misdemeanors at the next or a later term after indictment,[33] although occa-

---

[25] *Ms. Mins. SCJ 1704/05–1709 7.*
[26] Cf. the venire, *supra* 466 n. 367.
[27] *Supra* 468.
[28] 2 Hale, *op. cit.* 28.
[29] *Rules and Orders of King's Bench* (2d ed. 1747), Mich. 4 Anne, note c.
[30] 14 Geo. II c.17 §4.
[31] It is so stated to be assize practice in Stubbs, *Crown Circuit Companion* 16. We have seen nothing to show such a practice in King's Bench. In a Crown information brought by the Attorney General there was no way a defendant could bring on trial.
[32] *Ibid.* 39, 43.
[33] For example, when William Barclay was indicted (Nov. 6, 1706), on two bills, one for suffering tippling in his house, and the other for maintaining unlawful games, he did not plead until Feb. 4, 1706/07, and his trial was set for the May Sessions. However, on May 6, 1707, his recogni-

zance to prosecute his traverse with effect was continued until the following Sessions. Evidently the case was continued through two more Sessions, for we find that he was not in fact tried until Feb. 4, 1707/08, when he was found guilty on both indictments (*Ms. Mins. NYCQS 1694–1731/32* 118, 122, 124, 135). Mary Lyndsey was indicted on May 3, 1710, for entertaining slaves and she pleaded not guilty on Aug. 2, 1710. The minute entry indicates that she "traverses ye indictment till the next court." On Nov. 7, 1710, the court ordered that her trial come on the following morning, and on Nov. 8 she was tried and found guilty (*ibid.* 175, 177, 185). When an information was filed against Arnout Hendrikse on Nov. 30, 1730, for keeping a disorderly house, and he pleaded not guilty, the court ordered that he "prepare for tryall next term." On Mar. 15, 1730/31, he was tried and found guilty (*Ms. Mins. SCJ 1727–32* 244, 259). Benjamin Davis, who was indicted on July 28,

sionally the country minute books show that a trial would take place the same day an indictment was found.[34] No examples of notice of trial by defendants have been found, and except for judicial action which could be secured by motion, there was little a defendant could do to bring an outstanding prosecution to trial. The notice required by the Supreme Court rule just quoted seems at first to have been treated as notice by the court itself,[35] but after the middle of the eighteenth century, this was taken over by the Attorney General as the examples given below demonstrate.[36] Possibly this was another of the innovations for which the Kempes, father and son, were responsible, but the sources before 1753 are not of a character to warrant certainty upon the point.

While it is apparent that during the course of the eighteenth century, the

1758, for disorderly house, was not tried until Apr. 20, 1759, when he was found guilty (*Ms. Mins. SCJ 1756–61* [Rough] 105, 137, 138). For the country, cf. the following typical cases: King v. Poillon, indicted for assault Sept. 2, 1718, tried Mar. 3, 1718/19 (*Ms. Mins. Richmond Co. Sess. 1710/11–1744/45*); King v. Egberts, indicted Mar. 17, 1740/41, tried Mar. 16, 1741/42 (*ibid.*); King v. Honeywell, indicted June 3, 1712, tried June 7, 1713 (*Ms. Mins. Westch. Co. Sess. 1710–23*); King v. Knapp, indicted June 5, 1711, tried June 2, 1713 (*ibid.*).

[34] *Ms. Mins. Richmond Co. Sess. 1745–1812* King v. Lawrence *et al.* (riot), Sept. 22, 1761; King v. Van Gelder (offense not stated), Sept. 24, 1771. *Ms. Mins. Westch. Co. Sess. 1710–23* King v. Herrick (offense not stated), Dec. 5, 1710. *Ms. Mins. Ulster Co. Sess. 1693–98* King v. Sarah Ward (pound breach), Sept. 7, 1697; King v. Bosselyn (receiving), Mar. 1, 1697/98. *Ms. Mins. Suffolk Co. Sess. 1723–51* King v. Richard Thomas (petit larceny), Oct. 3, 1732; King v. Reeves (assault), Oct. 4, 1737. Generally, however, the cases would go over until a following session unless the indictment was confessed.

In the Supreme Court, misdemeanors were also sometimes tried in the term the indictment was found; cf. example of William Chambers who pleaded not guilty to an indictment for misdemeanor on Oct. 14, 1709, and it was ordered that the case "come to trial tomorrow by consent." However, it will be noted that Chambers was not in fact tried until Mar. 16, 1709/10, when he was found not guilty (*Ms. Mins. SCJ 1704/05–1709* 244, 248). Jane Fielding pleaded not guilty to an indictment for disorderly house on Jan. 20, 1768, but was tried and found guilty only three days later (*Ms. Mins. SCJ 1766–69* [Engr.] 380, 386). Booby Dezere pleaded not guilty to an indictment on Sept. 8, 1710, and was ordered to be committed for want of sureties. The defendant asked to come to trial the following day, and the Attorney General consented to this. On Sept. 9, Dezere was tried and found guilty. He was fined £8, imprisoned for a year and ordered to give surety for his good behav-

ior for two years (*Ms. Mins. SCJ 1710–14* 290, 292, 294).

[35] The evidence is not too convincing, but it would seem that before the rule was issued the court gave notice; cf. King v. De Meyer, 1701 (*Ms. Mins. SCJ 1701–04* 11); Queen v. Provoost, 1703, defendant "to take notice of tryal on Friday" (*ibid.* 120, 130, 168). In King v. Roch, 1753, the court gave notice of trial (*Ms. Mins. SCJ 1750–54* [Engr.] 215); King v. Jack, a slave, 1735, notice given in court (*Ms. Mins. Cir. 1721–49* 82).

[36] On Jan. 16, 1753, Thomas Newton, John Smith and Francis Boggs were informed against by the Attorney General for assault, and after they had pleaded not guilty, the following "copy of notice of Tryal" was issued by the Attorney General: "Sir Please to take notice that I intend to bring this matter to Tryal on Wednesday . . . August 1 W. Kempe Attorney General July 23, 1753" (*Ms. Mins. SCJ 1750–54* [Engr.] 209, *J. T. Kempe Lawsuits* L–O).

Josiah Rayner *et al.* were informed against for riot and for destroying sheep by poison, on Apr. 27, 1753 (*supra* 195). On Aug. 25, 1753, William Smith, their attorney, was served with the following notice of trial:

The King agt Josiah Rayner and William Reeves the Younger

Notice of Tryal

New York Supreme Court

Sir/

Pray take Notice that I intend to bring the above cause to tryal at the next court for the tryal of causes brought to issue in the Supreme Court to be held . . . in Suffolk at Southold . . . Tuesday the 11th day of September next.

Dated the 25th day of August 1753
I am Sir Y' Humble Servant
William Kempe
Attorney General

To William Smith Esqr
Attorney for Defendants

The notice of trial was endorsed as follows: "Copy served on Mr. Smith the day within written Mr.

Attorney General or his deputy obtained an increasing authority in determining when a trial of an indictment was to be had, it was the court which in the end had the authority to settle the matter. The law had not developed to the point that a defendant, except perhaps in felonies, was entitled to a speedy trial, but it is obvious from the cases that any unreasonable delay was a basis

J. T. Kempe" (*H.R. Pleadings* Pl. K. 422 [notice], Pl. K. 1008 [affidavit of service]).

The following is a notice of trial in the case of Thomas White, who was up for an undesignated offense:

The King
    agt.   } Copy of Notice of Trial
Thomas White

January 24, 1767

The King
    agt.   } New York Supreme Court
Thomas White
Sir

Be pleased to take Notice that I intend to bring the above cause to Trial at the Supreme Court of Judicature to be held for the Province of New York at the City Hall of the City New York on Friday the Twenty fourth day of April next Dated this Twenty fourth day of January 1767

I am
Your Humble Servant
J. T. Kempe

To James Duane Esquire   }
Attorney for the Defendant

This copy of notice of trial was endorsed: "Served Copy on Mr. Duane the same day in Court" (*H.R. Pleadings* Pl. K. 44).

On May 14, 1764, J. T. Kempe notified Kissam, acting as attorney for Robert Campbell, John Peterse Smith and Archibald Livingston (*supra* c. III) that he intended to bring the action against them to trial at the Court for the Trial of Causes to be held in Orange County (*H.R. Pleadings* Pl. K. 777 and 1063). On October 13, 1766, a notice of trial was given by the Attorney General in the case of Hannah Robinson, who had been indicted for disorderly house on Apr. 27, 1764. This notice of trial stated that the trial was to take place on Oct. 29, 1766, but the minute entries fail to reveal that any trial was had in the case (*J. T. Kempe Lawsuits* P–R; *Ms. Mins. SCJ 1762–64* [Engr.] 427). On Sept. 10, 1764, J. T. Kempe notified Whitehead Hicks, attorney for Moses Owen, who was informed against for perjury, that a trial would be held (*J. T. Kempe Lawsuits* L–O). In King v. Peter Vandewater, J. T. Kempe on June 11, 1765, notified the defendant's attorney, Crannel, that a trial would be held at the court for the trial of issues at Poughkeepsie in Dutchess County (*J. T. Kempe Lawsuits* V). In the case of King v. Higby, Lent *et al.*, informed against for riot (*supra* c. III 198) a notice of trial was served on the defendants' attorney for trial at Poughkeepsie, and a copy of the notice of trial contained in *J. T. Kempe Law-*

suits G–J, was endorsed "served by Jarvis 17th day of May, 1765." See also the notice of trial at nisi prius in Ulster dated May 13, 1767, in the case of King v. David Moore and Samuel Wickham, informed against for intrusion on Crown lands (*ibid.* L–O). Also see the notice of a trial to be held at New York City on Oct. 29, 1766, in the case of William Pitts, who had been indicted in the Supreme Court on Oct. 22, 1765 for assault. This notice of trial was dated Oct. 13, 1766 (*ibid.* P–R; *Ms. Mins. SCJ 1764–67* [Rough] 125).

In the case of James Livingston, indicted in the Supreme Court on July 27, 1769, for assault and battery, J. T. Kempe on Oct. 19, 1769, notified the defendant's attorney, Thomas Smith, of a trial to be held at bar, after Smith had pleaded not guilty for the defendant on Oct. 18. But on Oct. 23, 1769, the defendant withdrew his plea and confessed the indictment, whereupon he was fined 6s. 8d. and discharged (*J. T. Kempe Lawsuits* L–O; *Ms. Mins. SCJ 1769–72* [Engr.] 64, 111). Major Henry Pullen was indicted for riot and assault on Apr. 21, 1769, in the Supreme Court (*Ms. Mins. SCJ 1769–72* [Engr.] 11). On Oct. 16, 1769, William Smith Jr., his attorney, by grace of the court specially admitted, pleaded not guilty on the defendant's behalf, whereupon, on that same day, the Attorney General notified Smith that the trial was to be held in the Supreme Court *en banc* on Oct. 24, 1769. Endorsed on a copy of the notice of trial was the following statement: "Served the above day" (*J. T. Kempe Lawsuits* P–R). On Oct. 24, 1769, Pullen was tried and found guilty and on Oct. 28 was fined £10 which he paid to the prothonotary (*Ms. Mins. SCJ 1769–72* [Engr.] 114, 119). See also the notice of trial in the case of Caren Smith, dated Oct. 16, 1769, setting the trial for Oct. 24. This notice of trial was served on Oct. 16. The defendant here had been indicted on July 27, 1769, for assault and battery. However, before the day set for trial, that is, Oct. 24, Smith appeared on Oct. 19, and submitted himself to a fine (*J. T. Kempe Lawsuits* S–U; *Ms. Mins. SCJ 1769–72* [Engr.] 64, 104).

In Quarter Sessions, notices of trial were evidently not very formal, and as an example we have the cases of John Mordecai, indicted on Feb. 7, 1771, in New York Quarter Sessions for petit larceny. He pleaded not guilty and the court "ordered that he prepare for his tryal tomorrow" (*Ms. Mins. NYCQS 1760–72* 332). County practice is obscure. In King v. Robinson (*Ms. Mins. Albany Co. Sess. 1763–82* Jan. 20, 1773) notice of trial is mentioned.

for complaint and that the court would intervene. The most drastic remedy here was the issuance of a special commission of oyer and terminer where a defendant could not be tried before the end of a term or where too great a period would ensue before the regular circuit was held in the country. We have seen one case, *King* v. *Lambris,* where such a commission was issued because counsel for a defendant indicted for murder moved to have the court recommend a petition for a special commission from the Governor to insure a speedy trial, a request which seems to have been granted because such a commission did issue.[37] But probably such applications were usually handled by petition of the defendant or by the prosecutor without intervention of the court.[38]

Ordinarily delay in coming to trial was handled by the defendant moving the court that his cause be tried, and the entries which occur now and then, especially during the period when Richard Bradley was Attorney General, indicate clearly enough that the New York defendant did not have the privilege in misdemeanors of forcing trial by means of notice to the prosecutor, but was entirely dependent upon the good offices of the court.[39]

[37] *Mins. SCJ 1693–1701* 188, 189, 192, 193.

[38] On the special commissions *supra* 83.

[39] Queen v. Husk indicted for felony Sept. 4, 1713, continued until June 1, 1714, when on petition court ordered trial (*Ms. Mins. SCJ 1710–14* 476, 488, 495, 506, 517, 522). Jacobus Cosyne, informed against for various assaults on Oct. 20, 1730, pleaded not guilty but was not tried, and on June 13, 1732, the court ordered that he be tried the following term or discharged. On Oct. 11, 1732, he was discharged when the Attorney General failed to bring on his case (*Ms. Mins. SCJ 1727–32* 208, 228, 230, 351, 354). On June 13, 1732, Jacob Remsen prayed (*supra* 155 n. 69) that he be tried on Wednesday of the following term or be discharged, and on Oct. 11, 1732, he was discharged when the Attorney General failed to bring up the case. Bradley's deputy, Evert Wendell, on an information for illegally turning Caspar Van Hoesen out of the possession of his lands, was continued from Apr. 21, 1735 until Apr. 24, 1738, and on the latter date moved, through his attorney Murray, to have the Attorney General bring on the cause or be discharged. On Aug. 4, 1739, Wendell was discharged, the Attorney General having sent his (Wendell's) counsel word that he would proceed no further (*Ms. Mins. SCJ 1732–39* 162, 190, 204, 211, 226, 270, 343, 350). One DeWitt, in an unspecified Crown action, pleaded not guilty on Oct. 27, 1735, and on Jan. 21, 1735/36, on motion of Murray for the defendant, the court ordered that unless the cause was brought to trial the following term, "the defendant be discharged nisi causa ad contrarium." On Apr. 22, 1736, the defendant was discharged (*ibid.* 191, 197, 210). Informed against for perjury Dominicus Vanderveer pleaded not guilty, and on July 30, 1752, the court ordered that unless the Attorney General bring the cause to trial the next Circuit Court at Kings County, the defendant should be discharged (cf. *supra* 168 n. 114). John Carey and four others were on January 16, 1753, informed against for an assault and, the case evidently not having been brought on by Oct. 24, 1754, the court "ordered that unless this cause be tried the next court in Dutchess the defendant be discharged." No further minutes or papers appear in this case, and we do not know whether the case was tried or whether the defendants were discharged (*Ms. Mins. SCJ 1750–54* [Engr.] 209; *Ms. Mins. SCJ 1754–57* [Engr.] 96). Samuel Gerritson, Sr. and seven others were on January 19, 1754, informed against for misdemeanor, and the case was evidently delayed from term to term, until finally on Oct. 28, 1756, the court ordered that unless the Attorney General tried the case before or at the following Circuit Court for Kings County, the defendants be discharged. In the October term, 1759, it is recorded that these defendants were discharged (*Ms. Mins. SCJ 1750–54* [Engr.] 348; *Ms. Mins. SCJ 1754–57* [Engr.] 40, 41, 177, 200, 220, 283, 320; *Ms. Mins. SCJ 1757–60* [Engr.] 263). On Aug. 1, 1754, John Lawrence Jr. and three others were informed against for assault, and on Jan. 25, 1755, the case not having been tried yet, the court ordered that it be tried the following term or the defendants be discharged. On Apr. 18, 1755, the defendants were tried and acquitted (*Ms. Mins. SCJ 1754–57* [Engr.] 49, 53, 118, 125, 145, 146). John Coe, Theodorus Snedeker and numerous other defendants were on Oct. 25, 1759, informed against

The situation in respect to postponements of trial was somewhat different. The Attorney General had the privilege of countermanding a notice of trial once given, apparently without having to obtain leave of court. Thus in *King v. Gilbert Ferris,* informed against for attempting to poison his wife, the Attorney General decided to amend the information and, as a means of securing the consent of defendant's counsel, wrote peremptorily: "I desire to know if you can consent to the amendment. If not I hereby countermand the Notice of trial given in this cause for the 24th inst."[40] If, however, the defendant wished to secure a postponement, he had to apply to the court by way of motion. From the entries which mention the reasons for such motions it appears these were usually made on account of the difficulties in securing "evidences." And there are even occasions when at the moment of trial the Attorney General was obliged to apply for a continuance for the same reason.[41] During the first part

for riot, but on Aug. 4, 1764, "information having been filed five years past and not brought on to Tryal On motion of Mr. Duane for the defendants Ordered that they be discharged" (*Ms. Mins. SCJ 1756–61* [Rough] 165; *Ms. Mins. SCJ 1764–67* [Rough] 12).

[40] *Ms. Mins. SCJ 1750–54* (Engr.) 341; *Ms. Mins. SCJ 1754–57* (Engr.) 41, 83; for the letter from William Kempe to Smith, see *J. T. Kempe Lawsuits* C–F. See also King v. Whey (1753) presented for selling unmerchantable pork (*Ms. Mins. SCJ 1750–54* [Engr.] 247, 253, 286; *H.R. Pleadings* Pl. K. 923).

[41] King v. Leconto, deft., indicted for breach of the peace (*Ms. Mins. NYCQS 1694–1731/32* 30, Aug. 4, 1697); King v. De Meyer, 1701 (*Ms. Mins. SCJ 1701–04* 11, 27). Toby, Francisco, Juan and Diego, indicted on Mar. 14, 1706/07, for running away with a sloop, were to appear on Oct. 16, 1707, but the court ordered that the trial be put off until the next term (*Ms. Mins. SCJ 1704/05–1709* 115, 152). John Wood was indicted for assault on Nov. 8, 1710, trial put off because Queen's witnesses were absent; later discharged since no one appeared to prosecute him (*Ms. Mins. NYCQS 1694–1731/32* 185, 190, 198, 203, Feb. 6, 1710/11, May 1, Aug. 8, 1711). Henry Cordus, indicted on Feb. 2, 1708/09 for adultery, pleaded not guilty in Quarter Sessions on Feb. 8, 1709/10 and was ordered to appear at the following Sessions. On May 2, 1710, his attorney, Wileman, moved that the trial be put off until the following Sessions. Bickley, the Attorney General, consented to this and the court accordingly continued the defendant till the following Sessions. When defendant appeared on Aug. 2, 1710, Attorney General Bickley advised the court that the Queen's "evidences" had not appeared in response to a subpoena, and the court "ordered that the trial be put off till the next Sessions." Defendant appeared on Nov. 8, 1710, but prayed that the trial be put off until the next court, "his attorney being out of town who has his papers

whereby to make his defense." Defendant's motion was granted and again the trial was put off. On Feb. 6, 1710/11, the court put the trial off until the next day on the defendant's allegation that a material witness was absent. Cordus was finally tried and found guilty on Feb. 7, 1710/11 (*ibid.* 157, 170, 173, 176, 185, 191). See also Queen v. Clara Harris (*supra* 442 n. 281). John Moore pleaded not guilty on Oct. 11, 1711, to an indictment for murder, but when the case came on for trial on the next day, the witnesses, called on their recognizances, failed to appear, and on consent of the Attorney General the trial was put off. However, the case was finally tried on Mar. 12, 1711/12 (*Ms. Mins. SCJ 1710–14* 343, 346, 358).

Johannis Dissier appeared at Albany Oyer and Terminer and General Gaol Delivery on Sept. 4, 1716, and "the trial of the cause put off untill ye next court of Oyer and Terminer and General Gaol Delivery for Albany on payment of costs by the defendant to the King's Attorney General" (*Ms. Mins. Cir. 1716–17* 22). At Albany Sessions the trial of Coenrat Borghaert and Elias Van Schaick was put off when Collins for the King so moved because witnesses "could not be summoned to appear this court" (*Ms. Mins. Albany Co. Sess. 1717–23* June 7, 1721). The trial of Judith Peters for keeping a disorderly house and selling liquor to negroes contrary to the act of assembly was put off on May 6, 1724, on the prayer of the defendant with the consent of the Attorney, "her husband being gone to sea in the Greyhound" (*Ms. Mins. NYCQS 1694–1731/32* 438). After the jury was called on Aug. 6, 1733, for the trial of Jacobus Cosyne for assaulting a sheriff, two witnesses were three times called and failed to appear, whereupon "the Attorney General informed the court that he could not proceed to trial for want of those Evidences and therefore prayed this Cause be put off till next term" (*Ms. Mins. SCJ 1732–39* 45). In the case of John James, indicted for killing a Cayuga Indian, the petit jury called at Albany Oyer and

of the eighteenth century these motions were handled informally but eventually the practice developed of grounding them on an affidavit. As we have seen, John Henry Lydius in this way succeeded in staving off his trial on an information of intrusion. An amusing example of such an affidavit is one executed by John Morin Scott, who, when a notice of trial was served on him, discovered his client had vanished into the wilds of Dutchess County.[42]

That defendants were given the privilege of having trial put off was a development related to the growing indulgence of the eighteenth century toward persons accused. Indeed, there is little authority before Mansfield's time to justify such a course, and we consequently think that the practice of the New York courts, possibly under the influence of civil practice, was in this respect somewhat advanced.[43] The dangers of too generous an attitude became obvious, to the Attorney General at least, when an attempt was made to put off trial by the defendants who had been indicted for riot in the carting of George Spencer, a case already discussed at length.[44] Kempe's notes[45] start off with the antiquated proposition that "the King shall never be delayed in his suit," and he then goes on to argue:

> 2dly: The Case of the Crown and a common person is greatly different. In private Causes a Man sues for a private Injury [illegible word] and if he is delayed by the Deft in Instances of this Nature he shall be paid his Costs [two

Terminer and General Gaol Delivery on July 1, 1733, was discharged with the prisoner's consent because his "evidence" failed to appear (*Ms. Mins. Cir. 1721–49* 61). In the case of Johannes Bradt, on an information for an undesignated offense, his attorney, Murray, "informed the Court that he had forgot to give Notice to the Defendant of the Rule of last Term [to plead] and, it appearing to the Court that it will not delay the Tryal on motion of Mr. Murray Ordered that the Defendants Recognizance be respited til the first day of next Term" (*Ms. Mins. SCJ 1750–54* [Engr.] 106, Jan. 25, 1751/52).

[42] *H.R. Pleadings* Pl. K. 45.

McDougal	
ads.	to
The King	put off Tryal
	Scott Atty.
	Filed 18 Oct 1758

Margaret McDougal	
the Wife of Angus	
McDougal	New York Supream Court.
ads	
The King	

City of New York ss: John Morin Scott Attorney for the above Defendant being duly sworn depos-

eth and saith that the abovesaid Angus McDougal some Time before July Term last informed this Deponent that he was then immediately going to remove with his family from this City of New York to Poghkeepsie in Dutchess County which this Deponent verily believes he the said Angus did he this Deponent never having seen him the said Angus or his said Wife to his the Deponents Knowledge since that Time. That since the receipt of the Notice of Trial in this Cause the said Deponent has caused Inquiry to be made concerning the said Angus & his wife and has been informed that he lives with his Wife and family either at Poghkepsie or the Fish Kills in the County aforesaid That Poghkepsie is about forty Miles distant from this City of New York as is also the place heretofore Shewn to the Deponent for the Fish Kills and further this Deponent saith not

Sworn this 18th day   Jn° Morin Scott
of October 1758
  Before Me
    Dan. Horsmanden

Cf. *Ms. Mins. SCJ 1756–61* (Rough) 97, 142.

[43] Compare here the remarks in Foster, *Crown Cases* (2 ed.) 2.

[44] *Supra* 280 *et seq.*

[45] *H.R. Pleadings* Pl. K. 960 fol. 2.

illegible words] Harm done—Prosecutions by the Crown are of a publick nature, to punish offences ag^t the publick—and Delays in such Cases are the greatest detriment, not to a single individual but to the whole Community for if any delays are permitted in the prosecution of offenders,—(the Chief end of whose punishment is to deter others) it encourages others to commit crimes when they see other offenders Escape punishm^t.

3dly: If Trials in criminal prosecutions be permitted to be put off after this manner by the Defend^t it will be in the power of any Criminal to put off his Trial for ever, for if once why not [illegible] . . .

4^thly: It is unprecedented for any thing I can find in the Books there not being one Instance fallen under my observation Tho I have made diligent search.

5th: There are a number of Instances where it has been desired in Cases where the life of the Defendants have been concerned and I know of no Instance in such Case where it has been granted & if in such Case where the life is concerned it shall not be granted a fortiori it shall not where the Risque of the Def^t is not so great

6^thly I concive [sic] the Court will act with the greatest Caution in a case of this Kind, as it may be drawn into Example & that it will not without being fully satisfied of the practice by any means permit this Tryal in which the publick is so much concerned to go off.

7^thly—I think in Cases where the Crown and consequently the publick is concerned, the Court ought to know by affadavit what he can prove, that it may appear whether he is material Witness or no. for the def^t may believe what he can depose is material when it really is not—If Plaintiff knows he is a material Witness he must know what he can swear, or he cannot know whether he is a material Witness or no.

Challenges

We have not been able to discover exactly how the maneuvering respecting time of trial, especially when countermanded or put off, affected the issuance of process for a petit jury. The methods of summoning at Circuit were elastic enough to cope with postponements, but for a trial at bar obviously the only possible way was for the venire to go out only when Crown and defendant were present and ready to proceed. The details respecting the jury process have already been discussed,[46] and there remains to be considered only the matter of challenge. This is unfortunately one aspect of trial procedure on which little detailed information is available. For example, in *King* v. *Lambris*

---

[46] *Supra* 466 *et seq.*

(1700) the minutes of the special Oyer and Terminer commissioned to try the defendant for murder state merely that the prisoner challenged nine of the panel.[47] The printed version of the Bayard case[48] indicates that eighty jurors were challenged before twelve were sworn, and contains otherwise only a notice of the brief passage between Bayard's counsel and the Solicitor General over the question of peremptory challenge. Emott insisted that the Crown could not challenge without cause, but Weaver claimed the Crown should show cause only if there were not enough on the panel to serve and in this he was sustained by Atwood, C.J. The Solicitor General also resorted to the device of examination; one juror accepted by Bayard was examined by Weaver on a *voir dire* to ascertain if he had been approached by the prisoner's friends, but as to another juror Atwood later ruled that a peremptory challenge must be made before such an examination and not afterward.

Various "Notes on Trial" like those kept for the Dutchess Assizes have notations regarding either the number of challenges, or show which jurors were challenged by each side, but none of these notes and none of the few entries in judicial minutes on the matter indicates how far the considerable body of English learning on challenge was used in the Province.[49] In felony cases, the deprivation of counsel necessarily militated against the free use of challenge, although, remarkably enough, some of the negroes on trial for the 1741 conspiracy had wit enough to object to a juror.[50] On the other hand, the records show certain details of practice, some of which, the *tales* and *tales de circumstantibus,* have already been considered.[51] And it may be again pointed out that because of challenges on a few occasions, it became necessary to discharge the jurors already sworn and hold over the trial of the defendant.[52] In one rare instance the court, not satisfied to dismiss a challenged juror, resorted to a practice already used in civil cases and had an inquiry made into whether or not a juror was biassed. This occurred at the nisi prius trial of John Allison on an information for maintenance and false weights.

[47] *Mins. SCJ 1693–1701* 193.
[48] 14 Howell, *State Trials* 486.
[49] For example, in Queen v. Makemie a juror was challenged (*Ms. Mins. SCJ 1704/05–1709* 130), but the printed account of the trial (4 Force, *Tracts* no. 4) does not throw any light on the matter.
[50] King v. Bastian, Francis (Bosch's) Albany, Curacoa Dick, negroes (June 9, 1741); cf. Horsmanden, *The NY Conspiracy* (2 ed. 1810), 135. At the trial of the whites, John Hughson, Sarah his wife, and Margaret Sorubiero, for receiving, two

jurors were challenged May 6, 1741 (*ibid.* 48). At the later trial of these for a conspiracy, Hughson challenged sixteen peremptorily. The account remarks, "At Hughson's challenging among others a young gentleman, merchant of the town, Peggy seemed out of humour and intimated that he had challenged the best one of them all; which occasioned some mirth to those within hearing of it" (*ibid.* 110).
[51] *Supra* 473 *et seq.*
[52] Cf. King v. Brazier (*Ms. Mins. SCJ 1769–72*

On June 5, 1735, a witness was sworn to prove that one of the persons on the panel, having differed with the defendant, ought not to be a juror. The court thereupon ordered that the three jurors who had already been picked should be sworn to try whether Thomas Smith, Jr., the challenged juror, "ought to be an indifferent man." However, in this instance the defendant himself "allowed" that Smith be sworn as a juror.[53]

An approximation of challenge in open court was achieved in the selection of special juries. It has been pointed out that struck juries, when permitted, had the advantage of saving considerable expense, and if the case was tried at bar, avoiding the nuisance of transporting a large number of prospective jurors to the capital. These advantages were possibly what induced the remarkable provision in the provincial act of 1741 for the regulation of juries, that in the Supreme Court it should be lawful upon motion by the Crown or by any prosecutor or defendant "in any Indictment or Information, in the nature of Quo Warranto depending," to order and appoint a struck jury, the procedure for selection to be as theretofore.[54] The language here is so broad as to include indictments for felonies, a practice never indulged in England.

The manner in which the special jury was picked served also to eliminate the time-consuming process at trial of settling upon twelve presumably satisfactory men. Motion was made in advance of trial for a struck jury and if granted, the venire which merely ordered the return of the book of freeholders would issue.[55] The procedure in the Zenger case illustrates how the matter of challenge was handled. On July 29, 1735:

On Motion of Mr. Chambers Ordered that the Secondary do strike forty Eight ffreeholders out of the ffreeholders Book promiscuously in presence of the Attorney General and the Defendants Attorney and if Either party shew any Legall Cause why any of them shou'd not be put on the Said List to be by him Nominated that he hear the same and Judge thereof according to the practice in Such Cause and after the Prothonotary has so struck forty Eight ffreeholders

[Engr.] 16, 19, 20); King v. John Armstrong (*Ms. Mins. SCJ 1775–81* [Engr.] 86).

[53] *Ms. Mins. Cir. 1721–49* 295. This was approved criminal practice (cf. 2 Hale, *op. cit.* 275) but in New York was first used in a civil case where two witnesses were sworn to try if a certain juror "be an indifferent person to be a juryman in this cause," and they found that he was an "indifferent" person (*Ms. Mins. SCJ 1710–14* 330). In the civil case of John Wright v. Henry Vaughan at the Dutchess Court for the Trial of Causes Brought to Issue in the Supreme Court, the plaintiff and defendant on Sept. 9, 1729, agreed to bring the trial on at bar by a jury out of Westchester County, when it was found that the jury were parties concerned in the action (*Ms. Mins. Cir. 1721–49* 257).

[54] 3 *Col. Laws NY* 291.

[55] In the *Kempe Letters* A–Z is a book of Albany freeholders. In the *Van Cortlandt Mss.* is a Westchester County list. From a letter of Beekman to Livingston, May 1, 1744, it appears the tax list might be used (*Misc. Mss. Beekman*).

that Each Party strike out Twelve thereof And that the remaining Twenty-four be returned to try the Cause.[56]

The struck jury was used either on motion of the defendant or the Attorney General, and in spite of the colonial act was a device used only in cases of misdemeanor. This act apparently contemplated such juries only for trials at bar, and we cannot find that such juries were used at Circuit where striking would have been a desirable time-saver if a case threatened to be complicated and long drawn out. There are not many criminal cases where a struck jury was used, but it should be observed that it was employed in some of the most important quasi-political trials of the eighteenth century.

Preparation for Trial

The jury having been selected and sworn, the stage was at length set for the presentation of the Crown's case against the accused. The skill and thoroughness with which this was done varied considerably from court to court, from case to case and from counsel to counsel. In the country Sessions it is apparent that ordinarily little preparation of the Crown's case was made in advance of trial, for often a deputy Attorney General was not appointed until a defendant was about to be tried, and very probably preparation amounted to no more than collecting complaints and depositions and the summoning of witnesses. On the other hand, with respect to prosecutions in the Supreme Court, there is

[56] *Ms. Mins. SCJ 1732–39* 163, 168, 169. Cf. also the citations on challenge and struck jury in King v. Zenger (2 *Ms. Rutherfurd Collection* 27). Cf. also King v. DeWitt (*Ms. Mins. SCJ 1732–39* 191). In the case of Edward Gatehouse on an indictment for an unspecified offense, the Attorney General, on Apr. 20, 1739, moved for a struck jury and the court ordered that the coroner of New York deliver a book of freeholders to the clerk of the court, who should strike out forty-eight men and then each of the parties to be at liberty to strike out twelve of the remaining jurors. The remaining twenty-four jurors were then to be returned by the coroner to try the case (*ibid.* 334, 338). Moses Gomez, Napthali Hart Myers *et al.* were informed against for assault and battery. Wm. Smith, Jr. moved for a struck jury on July 31, 1756, and the court ordered that "the sherif of . . . New York return a Book of the Freeholders of the said City and County, into the Secretary's Office on or before the first Wednesday in October next, and that on the day following the Clerk in the presence of one of the Judges of this Court, strike forty eight names out of the said Book that each party strike twelve names out of the said

forty-eight and that the remaining twenty four be returned to try this cause, and if either party neglect giving their attendance that the clerk strike for the absent party." These defendants were tried and found not guilty on Oct. 20, 1756 (*Ms. Mins. SCJ 1754–57* [Engr.] 300, 308). On an information against Theodorus Snedeker, John and William Coe and others for riot and assault, the Attorney General in April Term, 1760, moved for a struck jury and the court thereupon ordered that the sheriff of Orange County return a list of the freeholders of the county into the office of the clerk of the court, who, on May 20, 1760, was to strike a jury in the usual manner. We do not know what happened to this case in the interim, but on Aug. 4, 1764, the defendants were ordered to be discharged, since an information had been filed against them for the past five years and they had not been brought to trial (*Ms. Mins. SCJ 1757–60* [Engr.] 311; *Ms. Mins. SCJ 1764–67* [Rough] 12). See also King v. McDougall—seditious libel (*Ms. Mins. SCJ 1769–72* [Engr.] 193, 198). In *H.R. Pleadings* Pl. K. 602 is a copy of an order to strike the jury (Oct. 17, 1770).

evidence running over many years to show the care which Crown officers took in getting their cases ready for trial. As this is a phase of practice which has been little noticed it deserves some further remark.

In the New York archives, both public and private, are preserved scores of so-called "briefs," sometimes labelled "memoranda for trial," from which it is possible to reconstruct a considerably more detailed picture of particular cases than either minutes or records supply, and which likewise afford a basis for judging the degree of technical skill in the Province.

The most interesting briefs in criminal cases are those prepared by various Attorneys General and in particular those of John Tabor Kempe. These briefs vary a great deal in form and content. The most elaborate are outlines of the prosecution's whole plan of attack, and cover what was to be said in the Crown's opening, the details of proof, descriptions of each witness's testimony and arguments with citations on the points of law which might be involved. Sometimes a brief is a mere summary of the evidence. Thus in *King v. Stevens*,[57] James Alexander states succinctly that the grand jury of New York City had indicted the defendant for counterfeiting and that he had pleaded not guilty. There follows a detailed statement of what each of the witnesses, presumably in the order in which they were to be called, was going to say. On the other hand, William Kempe had very little testimony to offer against John Van Zandt, informed against for an attempted rape.[58] His brief opens with the gist of the information and then proceeds with a dramatic account of Van Zandt's attack on Mary Mitchell, her resistance and final successful outcry which brought in defendant's brother. He then tells a long story about an attempt of someone to break in later in the night, with an appropriate marginal note: "Not directly to ye point." He apologizes for having only Mary Mitchell as a witness of the attack by remarking sententiously, "As crimes of this nature are attempted on Women when alone so it cannot be expected that any other Witnesses of the Fact can be produced than Mary Mitchell herself." He explains that circumstantial evidence is to be offered and sets out the evidence in detail of the brother and some neighbors.

In the prosecution against Alexander McDougall for seditious libel the problem was somewhat different, and in the elaborate brief which he prepared, J. T. Kempe devotes himself chiefly to an analysis of what the defense would have to establish. The Attorney General first summarized the indictment, which

---

[57] *James Alexander Papers* Box 46 (1744).   [58] *H.R. Pleadings* Pl. K. 925.

sets forth that the Deft. being a person of turbulent . . . mind and Seditious Disposition unlawfully . . . and Maliciously . . . intending to . . . scandalize as well the Honble Cad. Colden Esqr as the Council and General Assembly . . . and to bring the said Governor Council and General Assembly into the utmost Hatred . . . and Contempt . . . and to represent the said General Assembly as corrupt and the Members . . . as . . . degenerate . . . and to raise most unreasonable Fears in the minds of his Majesty's Subjects . . . did unlawfully . . . Malitiously and Seditiously write . . . and publish . . . a certain . . . false seditious . . . Malitious . . . Libel . . . The Tenor of which . . . is in the Words . . . following (Prout the Libel) To the great scandal . . . of the Lieutenant Governor the Council and the general assembly . . . that is to say the three Branches of the Legislature To the great scandal of . . . James DeLancey . . . and family . . . and Henry Pulleine to the great Disturbance of the public Peace . . . In manifest contempt of . . . the now King and his Laws to the Evil . . . Example . . . and also against the Peace. . . .[59]

The Attorney General next in his brief referred to the defendant's plea of not guilty and entered some notes on the evidence in support of the charge, including a deposition of James Parker, deceased. Kempe then took up seriatim various accusations and the evidence that he would use in support of them. Kempe's notes then went on:

If the Defendt should be permitted by the Court to justify by proving the Truth of the Libel—These are the Proofs it will be necessary for him to make— Selected in the Order the charges stand in the Libel

1 That the inhabitants . . . are Betrayed
2 That the Representatives in General Assembly are . . . lost to all sense of duty. . . .
3 That they have betrayed the trust in passing the Vote to give the Troops £1000. . . .
4 That they have betrayed the Liberties of the people
. . . . .
9 Have deserted the American Cause
. . . . .
11 Their Conduct repugnant and subversive of the means used to withstand the Tyranny of the British parliament
. . . . .
20 The Lieutenant Govr that he might make Hay while the Sun Shines and get a full Salary flattered the Ignorant Members . . . to emit a paper Currency . . . to impose on the people &c.

[59] J. T. Kempe Lawsuits L–O.

In the first thirty-one headings the Attorney General attempts to make Mc-Dougall's arguments look ridiculous and tries to show that the various points which McDougall would have to prove, in order to defend the libel by showing that it was true, could not be demonstrated. Kempe, in his brief, then indicates that the defendant would not only have to prove the truth of the allegedly libelous matter, but would also have to defend himself against the charge of sedition, and Kempe pointed out that McDougall, by advising the people to rouse themselves against unjust oppressors, was really guilty of sedition.[60] In an appendix we have set forth the elaborate and interesting brief prepared for the case of *King* v. *Sullivan* (1773) and likewise the brief prepared by James Alexander outlining the defense in *King* v. *Zenger*.

The Opening

In England the trial of the issue began properly after the prisoner had been called to the bar with the clerk's injunction to the jury respecting its task, at which time the indictment was again read.[61] If the case was important, counsel for the prosecution would "open the indictment," that is to say, would address the jury and explain what the Crown was attempting to prove.[62] It is by no means clear how consistently this procedure was followed in New York. At the trial of Abraham Gouverneur for murder in 1691, the record sent to London uses the expression "the Attorney General opened the Indictment,"[63] and some early eighteenth century minute entries employ the same expression.[64] In the printed accounts of the Zenger case[65] the "opening of the information" is stated, and similarly the "opening of the indictment" by the Attorney General in the Negro Conspiracy trials. It would appear from these latter cases that the clerk might make a summary of the indictment, not necessarily reading

---

[60] For other examples cf.: King v. Thomas Newton, John Smith and Francis Boggs, information for assault, January term, 1753 (*J. T. Kempe Lawsuits* L–O *sub nom.* Newton) prepared by William Kempe, and another by the same hand, King v. Pell, 1754 (*H.R. Pleadings* Pl. K. 441); King v. Josiah Rayner, William Reeves and James Lupton, informations for riot and for destroying sheep by poison, April term, 1753 (*H.R. Pleadings* Pl. K. 578, 984, 1099); King v. John Willet, indicted for illegally exporting pork, October term, 1753 (*J. T. Kempe Lawsuits* W–Y); King v. John Lawrence, George Harrison and others for riot, Nov. 1759 (*H.R. Pleadings* Pl. K. 930); King v. Robert Campbell and Archibald Livingston, information for assaulting an undersheriff, rescuing a prisoner and riot, Oct. 1763 (*ibid.* Pl. K. 1061); King v. Peter Remsen, information for slandering jurors,

Jan. 1767 (*ibid.* Pl. K. 1100). In other sections of this work, it will be noted that we have quoted frequently from briefs of the Kempes.
[61] *Crown Circuit Companion* 13; 2 Hale, *op. cit.* 293.
[62] 4 Blackstone, *Commentaries* 354; 1 Chitty, *Criminal Law* 555.
[63] P.R.O., C.O. 5/1037 fol. 8.
[64] Queen v. Booby Dezere, Sept. 9, 1710 (*Ms. Mins. SCJ 1710–14* 292); Queen v. Wm. Bradford, Oct. 17, 1712 (*ibid.* 424); Queen v. Peter the Doctor, 1713 (*ibid.* 427); Queen v. Joseph Berry, Sept. 4, 1713 (*ibid.* 472). In the latter case the entry was as follows: "Upon an Indictment for counterfeiting ye Bill of Credit of ye government Prisoner brought to ye Barr. Jury Sworn. Attorney Generall opens ye indictment. Witnesses sworn."
[65] *The Trial of John Peter Zenger* (1765) 11.

it *in extenso,* and that the Attorney General would then give his own summary of the bill and make his address.[66] The evidence of the briefs supports the inference that counsel for the Crown usually did not fail to make this summary, so that in felony cases a prisoner would hear the indictment or its purport three times.

Examples of the opening speech of the prosecution are relatively rare. The Solicitor General in the Bayard case is reported to have spoken for about an hour, but only a slight indication of what was said is preserved.[67] In *Queen* v. *Makemie,* another fully reported case, no record of the Attorney General's remarks was kept, although Nicoll, counsel for the defendant, makes some slighting references to a discourse about the laws of Henry VIII which Mr. Attorney had delivered.[68] The earliest complete specimens of opening to the jury that we have seen are those delivered by James Alexander at the trial of Michael Slaughter, who had been indicted for a misdemeanor in promising aid to and taking a reward from William Moras for an escape.[69] Moras had been tried and convicted for a highway robbery. The Attorney General, Alexander, opened the case against Slaughter at Westchester Circuit as follows:

> Michael Slaughter stands indicted for promiseing his assistance to the felon Wm. Moras to Escape out of the hands of Justice & taking a reward for so doing, this Crime Looks very like that of an accessary for he who comforts and conceals a felon is an accessary to the felony & shall have Sentence of death if his book save him not & this crime that the prisoner at the bar has been guilty of does not seem to be less criminal than comforting & concealing a felon. But as we ought to be tender of the life of man and if there be the Least doubt we ought to solve it in favour of Life, I have therefore drawn the Indictment against him no way to touch his Life but only as a Trespasser or as guilty of a misdemeanor for which he is to suffer such a fine only as the Court in their wisdom shall think fitt. The proof of the fact on the inditement will be very short and plain from his confession. Deliverance Brown saw him call out the felon to speak with him. Wm. Richison, Richard Ogden heard him confess.

Another opening of Alexander's was that delivered at the trial of the Indian squaw Beck indicted July 26, 1722, at Suffolk Circuit for firing the barn of

[66] Horsmanden, *The NY Conspiracy:* King v. Hughson *et al.* 48; King v. Roosevelt's Quack and Phillipse's Cuffee, 80; King v. Hughson *et al.* (second trial) 110, which indicates, although not convincingly, that a summary was read; King v. Bastian *et al.* 134; King v. Quash *et al.* 145; King v. Ury, 289.

[67] 14 Howell, *State Trials* 487.
[68] Cf. 4 Force, *Tracts* no. 4.
[69] King v. Moras (*Ms. Mins. Cir. 1721–49* 3, 4); King v. Slaughter (*ibid.* 4–7). The opening is in *James Alexander Papers* Box 60. Slaughter was fined £3.

her master, John Hedges, at Easthampton. Beck had pleaded not guilty and the case came to trial the following day.[70]

> You have heard that the prisoner at bar stands indicted for malitiously and feloniously burning the barn of her master, John Hedges and that upon the indictment she has been arraigned and upon her arraignment has pleaded that she is not guilty & put herself for her tryal upon God and her Country which Country Gentlemen of the Jury you are and that issue you are sworn to try.
>
> The Crime for which the prisoner Stands indicted you are Sensible Gentlemen is of the Highest nature and of the utmost ill Consequence to Society The Lives nor goods nor chattels of any persons are not in Safety if Such go unpunished and Some Do Say with very good reason that had there been more inquiry into a Like accident which happened to Mr Hedges before this which all of you know or have heard of & the person guilty punished for it as the law decrees [?] that its probable he might have Escaped the Like accident now of having his barn again burned.
>
> Gentlemen in Such Crimes as this you cannot Expect to have Such Evidence as can positively Swear they Saw Such & Such a person do the fact No, for none can you expect would be so foolish & mad to call witnesses to their Crimes . . . Its by minute Circumstances only that Such Crimes are Commonly discovered such as words dropping from the person Suspected before the fact committed . . . [At this point the Attorney General goes into detail regarding the facts of the case] . . . And which appearing to you I have no doubt but you will find the prisoner guilty & thereby have her punished according to her deserts and Struck a terror into others from Committing the Like Crimes which now I'm Sorry to hear are come so much in practice.

A number of the forensic masterpieces of Richard Bradley were included by Horsmanden in his account of the Negro Conspiracy trials of 1741. Allowing even for the public excitement of the time, these speeches seem unduly passionate, and are the equal of some of the better vituperation of the Prince Albert period of American jurisprudence. The passage describing the white defendant Hughson is typical:

> Gentlemen, This is that Hughson! whose name and most detestable conspiracies will no doubt be had in everlasting remembrance, to his eternal reproach; and stand recorded to latest posterity.—This is the man!—this that grand incendiary!—that arch rebel against God, his king and his country! that

[70] This document, which appears to be a draft of the Attorney General's opening, is in *James Alexander Papers* Box 59, among wills, deeds, indentures, etc. of Smithtown, L.I. For the minute entries see *Ms. Mins. Cir. 1721–49* 13. It is also to be noted that the prisoner was acquitted (*ibid.*).

devil incarnate, and the chief agent of the old abaddon of the infernal pit and regions of darkness.[71]

The style of John Tabor Kempe seems pallid in comparison, chiefly because the samples which we possess of his openings are in the dull form of notes, unwarmed by the figures which the heat of the moment enkindled. For example, at the Dutchess Assizes for July, 1766, when William Prendergast was tried on an indictment for high treason, the "notes" on the trials summarize Kempe's opening:

1. That sometime since there was a discontent in some tenants in the county on account of the Tenure of their farms—This he says had it been no more would not be treason.

2. That Messrs Robinson &ca having sued a number of their Tenants in Ejectment the prisoner with a great number of others combined to put out those who had been put in by the Landlords and restore the possession to the others that they should prevent suits for rents to prevent the execution of Justice by officers on account of their opposition to the law and to deliver the gaols of those who should be imprisoned for any of the causes afd—In execution of this Scheme.

3. That they formed themselves into companies, chose leaders, of which the prisoner was one, armed themselves and assembled to put their design in Execution.

4. By making Proclamation forbidding all officers to Execute their offices on the days of their meeting and restor'd possession by force.

5. That they associated with disaffected persons in other counties.

6. That accordingly they armed themselves in a great Multitude under the prisoner's command and did proceed to deliver some prisoners in the Gaol of New York.

7thly. They assumed regal power by Erecting Courts and laws and trying and punishing a justice of Peace for doing the duty of his office.

8. Rescued a prisoner from Poghkeepsie Gaol who was committed for debt.

9. Came to a resolution to oppose the King's Troops [and] did in two instances by firing on them and wounding one of the wounded men dead.

10. That in further Execution of legislative authority They ordained that if any person was sued or proceeded agt. to Execution for other Debts than for rent his cattle should be valued and delivered at the Valuation to the plaintiff in Satisfaction of his Debt.[72]

---

[71] Horsmanden, op. cit. 113.
[72] Misc. Mss. Dutchess Co. 1752–1870. The notes on the trial next indicate that the "Witnesses for the Crown" were called (ibid.).

Whether or not it was usual in country Sessions to address the jury, we do not know. One specimen of rustic eloquence is set forth in the Dutchess County Sessions records for 1735. Quacko, a "negro fellow," was on trial before three justices and five freeholders for an attempted rape. The clerk of the peace, Henry Vanderburgh being appointed to prosecute, stated:

> Being appointed by your honours to prosecute the prisoner pursuant to an Act of Assembly; I beg Leave with submission to Acquaint your Honours that this Prisoner Quacko a negro man Belonging to Mr. Hendrick Scherer stands accused for Viellely atempting to ravish force and Deflower one Arriantye Janging, widdow of Rhynbeck. The said prisoner on the third day of the Instant month about the twelfth hour of the same day at Rynebeck on the Kings Highway with force did throw down the said Arriantie and attempt to stop her mouth and to Ravish force deflower the said Arriantie was prevented by persons speedly coming to her releaffe. This is the case which I shall proceed to prove to your Honours by severall witnesses and don't Doubt your Honours speedy Justice for so wicked an offence agt. an Act of General Assembly in that case made and provided.[73]

After the opening, it was the practice next to put in the evidence for the Crown. The witnesses were called and sworn. Following the direct and cross-examination of the Crown's witnesses, the defendant's witnesses were called. In the first year of Anne, an Act of Parliament had at long last authorized the swearing of the defendant's witnesses in felony cases,[74] but the act did not extend to the plantations. Nevertheless the minute entry in the case of *Queen v. Ann Bowen* (1707/08)[75] establishes the early application of the statute in New York. The persistence of this practice is, however, poorly attested, for usually no notation was made of the swearing of witnesses. At the trial of the whites during the negro plot excitement, the defendants' witnesses in *King v. Hughson et al.* were not sworn, but in *King v. Ury* they were.[76] Possibly the swearing of defendant's witnesses was discretionary with the court,[77] for in

[73] *Ms. Mins. Dutchess Co. Sess.* Liber A, June 6, 1735. Under the statute of 1730 a written statement of the complaint against a negro was required. The above sample is actually a combination of such a complaint and an opening. Quacko was sentenced to thirty-nine stripes at Poughkeepsie and eight days later, forty more stripes at Rhinebeck. His master was to transport him out of the county within twelve months.

[74] 1 Anne St. 2 c.9 §3.

[75] *Ms. Mins. SCJ 1704/05–1709* 165.

[76] King v. Hughson *et al.* (Horsmanden, *op. cit.* 117). The account notes merely that defendant's witnesses were "called," but the Crown witnesses were "called and sworn." For King v. Ury, *ibid.* 301.

[77] In King v. James Wilks (1755), an indictment for murder, Thos. Sperham, a witness for the defendant, was examined. The court ordered an information to be brought against him for perjury. Obviously he was sworn.

the colonial Act of 1767 which sought to extend to New York various Acts of Parliament, the statute of Anne establishing the privilege was specifically mentioned.[78]

Evidence

The energies devoted by English courts and, after them by the commentators, to detailed rules of process and to the form of indictments stand in sharp contrast to their indifference respecting the problems of proof. We have earlier remarked on the fact that in the late seventeenth century criminal trials were hampered by few rules of evidence, and although the business of examination and cross-examination in the hands of some was already masterful art, little thought was devoted to questions of limitation. The law of evidence, such as it was, appears in the books still in the primitive stage of a mere catalogue of single rules. Indeed, there is little to distinguish treatise discussion like Duncombe's *Trial per Pais,* Nelson's *Law of Evidence* and the chapter in Hawkins' *Pleas of the Crown* from the sections in the abridgments of Bacon and Viner or the scrapple served up in the justices' manuals. The first work of any analytic merit is Baron Gilbert's book published in 1754,[79] but his examination of criminal cases is slight, and beyond emphasizing the relation of proof to issue is not a great improvement over other works.

If the quality of the evidence literature in the eighteenth century was not such as to be especially illuminating to the provincial lawyers, the quality of the New York records is, for our inquiry, somewhat less so. The shortcomings of the latter, of course, are due to the character of criminal records in general, and the persistence of ancient traditions respecting what need be committed to writing. The failure of an error procedure to develop in the colony, and the almost utter abandonment of the bill of exceptions assured the continued fugacity of oral proceedings. However obnoxious a judicial ruling respecting some question of admissibility might be, no objection would be made of record for this would serve no practical end.[80] It is true there are still stored reams of depositions and examinations, there are pages upon pages of counsel's summaries of testimony prepared in advance of trial, but the *posteas* and judgment rolls are nearly always silent on what was said or proffered at

---

[78] 4 *Col. Laws NY* 953. This act was disallowed.
[79] The book was used in New York not long after publication. It had appeared anonymously and to distinguish it from the earlier anonymous book of Nelson it was referred to in New York as the "New Law of Evidence."
[80] The case of King v. John Van Rensselaer, discussed *infra*, is a rare exception to the rule.

trial, and the judicial minutes at best ordinarily furnish only a list of documents or the names of those who testified.[81]

The nature and limitation of our sources are such that the usages in New York with respect to problems of proof will have to be discussed chiefly in terms of trial practice rather than in terms of a "law of evidence" as this is today understood. This means, of course, that we shall have to consider various matters which have no bearing upon the use of excluding rules but which have significance for the procedural system at large. The first of these matters has to do with certain practical considerations, peculiar to the colony, arising out of the mystical regard in which the jury was held, and the grudging view which this same jury often took of the law-enforcing efforts of the royal officials. These attitudes, on the one hand, had the effect that on some occasions matters were left to the jury which in England would have been the province of the court; and, on the other hand, that the prosecution had a much greater

[81] Ordinarily the minute entries did not contain any statement regarding the swearing in of witnesses except to list the names of the witnesses and sometimes to add the word "sworn" after their names. Usually the witnesses and evidence for the Crown were listed first, followed by the listing of the defendant's witnesses and evidence. Thus on the trial of Frederick Platt for murder at a Special Court of Oyer and Terminer and General Gaol Delivery for Westchester on June 5, 1700, at 2 P.M., "Court opened by proclamation Dom Rex ver Fredrick Platt Jury Sworne, Witnesses pr Dom Rex James Mott Robt Blowman John Horton Edward Rogers John Desburg Witnesses pr Deft Ben: Desborough William Barnes" (*Mins. SCJ* 1693–1701 196). At New York Quarter Sessions for Feb. 4, 1707/08, William Barclay was tried on indictments for suffering tippling and unlawful games in his house and the "Jury Sworn. Evidence ꝑ Dom Reg . . . [four named] . . . Evidence ꝑ Deft . . . [two named] . . . Constable sworn [to go out with the jury]" (*Ms. Mins. NYCQS 1694–1731/32* 135). See also Queen v. Rebecka Butler, June 3, 1714 (*Ms. Mins. SCJ 1710–14* 530); King v. Rachell Van Anthon, Sept. 14, 1716 (Ulster Oyer and Terminer and General Gaol Delivery, *Ms. Mins. Cir. 1716–17* 28); King v. Josiah Raignier, June 27, 1728 (Suffolk Oyer and Terminer and General Gaol Delivery, *Ms. Mins. Cir. 1721–49* 50); King v. George Walker, Aug. 9, 1733, "Jury Sworn. Evidence for the King . . . [three named] . . . Evidence for the Defendt . . . [two named]" (*Ms. Mins. NYCQS 1732–62* 29); King v. Catherine Johnson, Aug. 1, 1735: "On tryall for uttering false Bills . . . [three named] . . . called on their recognizances appear . . . [six named] . . . witnesses pro Rege The Jury return & finds the Prisoner guilty"

(*Ms. Mins. SCJ 1732–39* 172); King v. John Van Zandt, Oct. 17, 1753: "On tryal for an assault Jury sworn vizt . . . [twelve named] . . . Evidence ꝑ Rege . . . [three named] . . . Smith ꝑ Deft Witnesses for Deft . . . [two named] . . ." (*Ms. Mins. SCJ 1750–54* [Engr.] 305); King v. Newton, Smith and Boggs, Aug. 3, 1753, on an information for assault, ten witnesses were called for the Crown, only two of whom were marked sworn and four witnesses were called for the defendants (*ibid.* 280); King v. Gomez, Levy, Myers *et al.*, Oct. 20, 1756, "On Information for an assault and battery On tryal Jury sworn Vizt . . . [twelve named] . . . Mr. Attorney General Mr Nicoll Mr Scot pro Rege Mr Smith Mr. Lodge Mr. Smith Jr Mr. Livingston for Defts Evidence ꝑ Rege . . . [four named] . . . for Deft . . . [five named witnesses] . . ." (*Ms. Mins. SCJ 1754–57* [Engr.] 308); King v. Elizabeth Frances, Feb. 9, 1764, "The Defendant being indicted for feloniously Stealing . . . linnen cloath . . . of the Value of Ten pence, plead not guilty The Jurors Sworn to Try this Cause are . . . [twelve named] . . . Evidences ꝑ Rege . . . [two named] . . . Constable Sworn to Attend the Jury The Jury being Returned Say they find Elizabeth Frances Guilty of the felony" (*Ms. Mins. NYCQS 1760–72* 101); King v. Edward Welch, Nov. 2, 1774, "On three several Indictments for Assault and Battery . . . At Issue for Trial Jurors drawn and sworn vizt . . . [twelve named] . . . Witnesses pro Rege . . . [three named] . . . Witnesses for Deft . . . [five named]" (*Ms. Mins. NYCQS 1772–91* 114).

At the trial of Hannah Bond on Nov. 7, 1739 for disorderly house, four witnesses for the King were "sworn" and one Crown witness "Edward Burling affirmed." He was probably a Quaker (*Ms. Mins. NYCQS 1732–62* 107).

burden of persuasion than would have been the case in a less troubled environment. The first of these effects will be considered later in connection with the charge and the verdict, but the second, since it bears on the otherwise obscure question of the burden of proof, will be dealt with at this point.

It was well settled in the eighteenth century that the prosecutor was under the obligation to prove the material portions of the indictment or information[82] and that this had to be done with a greater degree of certainty than was required in civil cases.[83] This was probably the extent of the Crown's burden in the routine felony prosecutions in New York, but it is obvious that the Crown's burden was enhanced in any case which engaged local sympathies or ran counter to popular prejudices. The problem was met by an increasing cultivation of the preliminary examinations before justices of the peace and the collection of affidavits, depositions and confessions out of which the Crown's case would be constructed.

The importance of this preliminary work is brought out in a letter of Richard Bradley to Evert Wendell of Albany respecting a forcible entry case. Bradley, as we have seen,[84] instructed his deputy to bind over Jan Halenbeck and his wife to testify and if he could find others who saw the riot to bind them likewise.

> Have they not sons or daughters or white servants who saw it? If they have, such are the best evidence . . . Pray bind them all to give evidence for the King on the information fyled last October term . . . Nelson's Justice will show you the fforme, or if you or the justices are not pfect in the form, let them be bound in twenty or ten pounds each to give evid. and minutes only taken and copys of the minutes sent mè and I'll put them into form and send them to you and the 2 justices may signe them when I send them to you, but the minutes of which you send me the copys must be first signed by the two justices before you send me the copys and let the recognizance for evidence be taken for the first Tuesday in June . . . But let 3 or 4 of the best evidences . . . be bound in forty pounds apeece with a surety for each . . . in twenty pd. which is the common course.[85]

---

[82] The rule develops from the distinctions between what is substantial and what is circumstantial, the Crown being obliged by its proof only to the former (Coke, *Fourth Institute* 135, 230; Duncombe, *Trials per Pais* [7 ed. 1739] 471; 2 Hale, *op. cit.* 291 *et seq.*).

[83] Regina v. Muscot, 1714 (10 *Mod.* 192). Parker, C.J., contrasting a prosecution for perjury with a property case remarked: ". . . to convict a man of perjury a probable, a creditable witness is not enough; but it must be a strong and clear evidence and more numerous than the evidence given for the defendant."

[84] *Supra* 193 n. 204.

[85] Letter of Attorney General Richard Bradley to Evert Wendell, deputy Attorney General, Jan. 21, 1726 (*Misc. Mss. Bradley*). In Evert Wendell's *Ms. Account Book* there is a compilation of rules of evidence taken out of Nelson and Dalton.

Similarly instructive is a letter of J. T. Kempe to Justice Douw respecting the evidence in *King* v. *Kelly:*

> I have by this Post sent to the Sherriff of Albany a *Habeas Corpus* to bring John Kelly . . . to New York . . . to be tried for the Robbery . . . The Goods found must be sent down, as also such Persons in Albany as are material, either to prove the finding the Goods on the prisoners, or their Confession of the Fact if they made any, In General such Witnesses as are any wise material . . . should be bound over in their own Recognizances without securities to appear here to give Evidence ag^t the prisoner at the next Supreme Court—The Examination of the Prisoners should also be sent, and the Depositions of the Witnesses, for I presume both were taken on the first commitment of the Offenders.[86]

It may be inferred from this letter and from the comprehensive investigations made in other cases of a similar type[87] that what had been at first practiced mainly in the unpopular prosecutions like those for riot or maladministration, had become a normal incident of preparation, an inference borne out by surviving briefs and "notes of evidence" drawn up in advance of trial.[88] From the little we have found of the manner in which a defense was made when the prisoner was without counsel, these elaborate preparations were not motivated by any anxieties over defendant's evidence. We believe consequently that they were due to the fact that the Crown had to overcome not only the presumption of innocence but the unpredictable renitence of New York juries.

The relation of the quantum of proof to the requirement of certainty was one that called for the exercise of a delicate discretion. The freemen in the jury box had to be persuaded but not bewildered. Sometime in the 1750's James Alexander offered some advice on this matter:

> Lengthening a cause by a multiplicity of evidence not necessary, puts those things necessary out of the remembrance of the jury, and brings things into darkness and obscurity. This is an artifice of those who have a bad cause to

[86] Letter dated Aug. 13, 1764 (*J. T. Kempe Lawsuits* J–L).

[87] See the elaborate set of examinations for King v. Borne (grand larceny) in *James Alexander Papers* Box 45, and cf. *Ms. Mins. Cir. 1721–49* 27. For later examples, King v. Noble (1766) charged with threats against a justice (*H.R. Pleadings* Pl. K. 683, 685, 704); King v. Morel (1771) charged with breaking windows (*J. T. Kempe Lawsuits* L–O).

[88] As in King v. Elizabeth McCarthy (*J. T. Kempe Lawsuits* L–O). Elizabeth was indicted for murder on Oct. 23, 1770, tried on Oct. 25 and found not guilty on Oct. 26 (*Ms. Mins. SCJ 1769–72* [Engr.] 279, 286, 287). King v. John Kelly, on indictment for burglary, where the evidence of seven witnesses is given (*J. T. Kempe Lawsuits* J–L); the notes of evidence in King v. Marinus Willet for assault and battery (*ibid.* W–Y); note of evidence in King v. Godfrey Swan for murder (*ibid.* S–U), and notes of evidence in King v. Gilbert Ferris for attempting to poison his wife (*ibid.* C–F).

manage. But those who have a good cause ought to be cautious how they offer any piece of evidence but what's necessary and pertinent; all those that are not so ought to be winnowed out and blown away as chaff from corn—[88a]

In the prosecutions for misdemeanor where the defendant was represented, since the Crown was faced with a contest on somewhat equal terms, the necessity of producing a strong case was even more emergent. This was especially true where the charge was brought by information. Since this manner of proceeding was in bad odor, and since there was frequently a suspicion of the Crown's motives, the Attorney General had cast upon him a burden substantially different in character from that which the law had weighed out for him.

The misdemeanor cases where an able defense was offered supply us with some slight data regarding provincial ideas about burden of proof. The first of these cases was *King* v. *Zenger*. Here the Attorney General had offered in evidence the offending newspapers which the defendant admitted he had both printed and published. The information had charged that "falsely seditiously and scandalously" Zenger had published certain libels. Hamilton for the defense insisted that the falsehood be proved.[89] Bradley relying on Holt's charge in *Tutchin's Case* insisted that this was immaterial, and that he would not prove a negative. Hamilton thereupon remarked: "We will save Mr. Attorney the trouble of proving a negative and take the *onus probandi* upon ourselves and prove those very papers that are called libels to be true." The Chief Justice then interposed that he could not be admitted to give the truth of a libel in evidence and that he could not justify a libel. To this Hamilton rejoined that "justify" meant justification by plea, and that under the general issue in a criminal case the defendant could always be admitted to give in evidence the truth of the fact that went to his acquittal. He proceeded to cite various cases, but the court on the basis of some Star Chamber cases ruled against him.

Not until many years later do we again come upon discussion of the apportionment of the burden of proof. In the intrusion proceedings against Lydius it will be recalled[90] that John Tabor Kempe had insisted in his brief that the proof of title rested with the defendant and that it did not lie with the King to prove a conveyance from the Indians. Since the Crown was in possession "it lies with the defendant to prove that the King was out of possession twenty years before the suit for intrusion was begun." Again in the brief prepared for

---

[88a] Sedgwick, *Memoir of the Life of William Livingston* (1833) 51.

[89] *The Trial of John Peter Zenger* (1765) 20 *et seq.*
[90] *Supra* 212; *J. T. Kempe Lawsuits* L–O.

the McDougall libel case, discussed in this chapter,[91] Kempe outlined the proofs necessary for the defendant to make in the event he was allowed to justify the truth of the libel, showing clearly that he understood how the burden of producing evidence could pass from the Crown to the defendant.

We do not know how typical were discussions of this sort at the trial of misdemeanors sufficiently important to provoke the attention of the Attorney General.[92] But they illustrate a tendency, perceptible also in England,[93] for rules used in civil litigation to be applied in criminal cases where the pressure of analogy made the precedents persuasive, and where counsel was on hand to use the advantage. The felony trials remained impervious to this tendency. Only rarely do the books imply that in Crown cases the burden of proof could shift,[94] for they speak of defense in terms of rebuttal,[95] or in the language of pleading[96] which Hamilton found objectionable. And it may be observed that even these descriptions lack reality; for beyond denial, witnesses to character or attempts to discredit identification, the prisoner in the dock of the Supreme Court or at Old Bailey in London was usually helpless to ward off the noose.[97] It is striking that in so many extant *Notes on Trial* no indication whatever of defendants' evidence appears.

It is important to notice that the inadequacies of the defense in felony cases were due chiefly to the harsh rules about a view of the indictment, deprivation of counsel and limited subpoena privilege, and not to undue advantages which the use of preliminary examinations gave the Crown. The justices' manuals usually contained an admonition that evidence which went against the Crown should be taken as well as that which was against the defendant. In New York this was carried further and the right of confrontation by the defendant (if he had been taken) was accorded. This practice probably developed during the early eighteenth century,[98] chiefly because it was a convenient way to wrest

[91] *Supra* 622.

[92] We have seen no sign of this sort of thing in country Sessions trials.

[93] Stephen in 1 *Hist. of the Criminal Law* 440 speaks of rules of evidence passing from the civil to the criminal courts after 1688. He is not explicit on how this was effected but it is certainly more apparent in misdemeanor cases than in felonies.

[94] As Foster, *Crown Cases* 255, in relation to the defense in homicide cases.

[95] Compare here Bathurst, *Theory of the Law of Evidence* (1760) 116, 117 and Mansfield's remarks in Rex v. Almon (5 *Burr.* 2686).

[96] Coke, *Littleton* 283a; Nelson, *Law of Evidence* 287 §43.

[97] Compare the accounts of defense in the negro plot cases in Horsmanden, *op. cit.,* and the accounts in the eighteenth century trials in the Old Bailey *Sessions Papers.*

[98] At a meeting of justices of Ulster, Dec. 18, 1723, an affidavit was taken of Jurian Toppan respecting the passing of a counterfeit coin. One defendant being present was sworn and stated where he had obtained the dollar. He was ordered committed. The other person complained of was also present but no statement was taken from him. The first utterer of the coin was ordered to be taken on a hue and cry warrant (*NY State Lib. Mss.* 7460 no. 20). This is the only early evidence we have seen of the defendant being present at examinations.

a confession from a prisoner. By 1741 it was evidently established usage, for it was followed during the Negro Conspiracy scare. In the introduction to his opus on this lamentable episode, Mr. Justice Horsmanden explains the procedure: "The witnesses were always examined apart from each other first, as well upon the trials as otherwise and then generally confronted with the persons they accused who were usually sent for and taken into custody upon such examinations."[99] The body of Horsmanden's book shows that King's counsel then went to work on the suspects and endeavored to secure a confession. The expression "generally confronted" suggests that there was no compulsion felt to have the prisoner present and nothing is said about cross-examination.

Confrontation at a preliminary hearing inevitably raised the question of a right to cross-examine. This appears in the charges against Henry Van Rensselaer, an affair discussed in Chapter III. The worthy justice, it will be recalled, brought four "evidences" to three friendly justices and had them examined. According to Van Rensselaer's own version:

> After Exsemined we bound them over to the next Sessions to give their Evidence and we concluded to grant a warrant . . . to lay them unther Recognizer & when we meeted I found the Justice Frese & Van Dyck of an Other Opinion & they Desire to Journ to an other [day] to Exsemned more Evidences & . . . we . . . had Mr. Quackenbush & Ten Eyck to Exsemned moor Evidences Conserning the Riots but not [?] to try the Cause . . . & then there was Jerime Hogenboom . . . [and other rioters] . . . whome made Great impedent to Exsemned which we Justices order them to be Silence or Else to be find and order them to put to Question to a Justices & they accordly did.[100]

The complaint against Van Rensselaer's actions in these examinations was voiced by one Mueller in a letter of April 11, 1766 to Attorney General Kempe: "Van Rensalaer makes it a continual practice to examine his evidences but we hope there will come a time when both partys will be heard." Eleven of the rioters wrote a "Situation of the proceeding of Henry Van Ranssalaer against a Number of persons at Claverack on a supposed Riot" in which they averred that, in response to a warrant issued by Van Rensselaer, Freeze and Van Dyke, they had appeared, denied their guilt and were later released when three out of four justices sitting with Van Rensselaer found the charges wholly unsupported. Despite the action of a majority of the justices, Van Rensselaer persisted in his charges and ordered the defendants to appear again. It was also

---

[99] Horsmanden, *op. cit.* 7.   [100] *J. T. Kempe Lawsuits* V.

charged that "During the Course of the Examination of the Witnesses Mr. Ransalaer would not admit any of the prisoners to ask or propose one Single Question to the Witnesses nor suffer anyone to do it in their Steed." The complainants asserted that

the several violent and arbitrary steps . . . [taken by Van Rensselaer] . . . manifestly tending to the subversion of the invaluable privilege of English Subjects they conceive aught not to pass unnoticed; and as the Law undoubtedly wisely guardid against the enormous abuse thereof by its Ministers—they Submit the above State of their Case to those whose province it is, to take cognizance thereof.[101]

The "violent and arbitrary steps" complained of by Van Rensselaer's accusers were obviously his practice of examining witnesses of his own choosing alone, and his refusal to permit the prisoners to cross-examine these witnesses. The colonists apparently expected that the preliminary proceedings should be an impartial inquiry into the facts and should approximate the amenities of a trial. The Dutchess matron who stirred up the Attorney General against the "Skimmiltoners" was bitter that she had not been allowed to offer evidence in her defense before indictment, "the judges being against me and siding with the rioters (being their relations) would not take any notice of me."[102]

The royal officials in New York do not seem to have admitted any right to cross-examination at a preliminary hearing, although it was insisted upon at summary trials. This question was raised by one Smelliger who had been sentenced to be whipped for petit larceny by Charles Clinton, James McClaghry and Samuel Sands, justices of Ulster County, without an opportunity to examine witnesses, and the Attorney General wrote to one of the justices that it was not "justifiable to sentence him without examining witnesses in his presents that he might cross-examine them."[103] To the ordinary man there was probably not much reason to distinguish between a summary trial and a preliminary examination; hence the claim that the latter should be conducted with an equal regard for the defendant's rights.[104]

101 *Ibid.* V. As we have seen (*supra* p. 201), judgment for want of a plea was entered against all three of the justices on the informations against them for maladministration in this affair (*Ms. Mins. SCJ 1764–67* [Rough] 141, 145, 157, Apr. 19, 26, Aug. 2, 1766).
102 *Supra* 198.
103 *J. T. Kempe Lawsuits* S–U *sub nom.* Smelliger.

104 An episode which occurred in Dutchess County in 1766 indicates something of the popular reaction to the preliminary examinations. Rioters seized Samuel Peters, a justice of peace, and forced him to swear never to officiate in his office against them. The crowd was angry because Peters had had the temerity to declare the peace against them and had begun an examination of witnesses. The tables were turned when Peters was seized by the rioters

The circumstances under which a preliminary hearing was held had a bearing upon the use of the written depositions, affidavits and examinations at trial. The English writers were categorical that when life was in jeopardy, testimony must be viva voce in the presence of the prisoner, but they admitted that by virtue of the statute 1 & 2 Ph. and M. c.13, informers' examinations could be read if the informer was dead or unable to travel or was kept away by procurement of the prisoner.[105] In one important case, it had been ruled that examinations could be read at the defendant's request to impeach the credibility of a witness.[106]

The casual way in which any remembrance of evidence was noted in court makes it difficult to determine how far the sworn examination was employed in New York. We have remarked upon the fact that during the proprietary period depositions were used at the trial of felonies,[107] and the evidence prior to 1750 indicates that this practice continued. The most striking example occurred when the witness Samuel Clowes was being examined during the Bayard treason trial. The Solicitor General read from Clowes' examination before the Council, insisting the witness reconcile his earlier and later statements and Clowes, though a lawyer, raised no objection. The presiding judge, moreover, repeatedly demanded of other witnesses why their stories varied from their preliminary depositions.[108]

At Suffolk Sessions in 1723, a material witness having deposed he was about to go to England, the court ordered his affidavit taken "which affidavit is to be allowed as evidence at trial."[109] In 1733, at the trial of John Hogan for murder, a "Surgeon's opinion read how the victim came to his death,"[110] and in 1741 at the Negro Conspiracy trials the examinations were on various occasions

---

for he was then ordered to hold court for the mob and swear in witnesses. Any witnesses who failed to testify as the mob demanded were threatened with jail, bread and water, and those convicted in these mock trials were to be dragged through mud and water. The Sons of Liberty were then to tie the alleged offenders "to a white oak tree" and to whip them "as long as the mob thought proper." Then the victims of the mob's vengeance were to be "carried out of the County and kicked as long as they [the rioters] thought proper." When the rioters were finally apprehended and tried at the Dutchess Assizes of 1766, Peters testified against them and said that "he is convinced . . . the true reason of their abusing him was that he had taken the aforesaid examinations." Peters also testified that he had been admonished by the mob and that they said to him: "We will teach you not to go

about taking evidence against us" (*Misc. Mss. Dutchess Co.*).

[105] 2 Hawkins, *op. cit.* c.46 §96.
[106] King v. Strafford (2 *State Trials* 622).
[107] *Supra* 565.
[108] 14 Howell, *State Trials* 488.
[109] *Ms. Mins. Suffolk Co. Sess. 1723–51* fol. 3, King v. Abigail Tonesen (receiving).
[110] *Ms. Mins. Cir. 1721–49* 39. It may be noted here that "surgeon's" evidence was often proffered, but the later cases show viva voce testimony, e.g., King v. Gaines (*Ms. Mins. SCJ 1754–57* [Engr.] 115). In Kempe's papers are various depositions by physicians: King v. Haup—assault with intent to ravish (*J. T. Kempe Lawsuits* S–U); King v. Dawson—murder, 1766 (*ibid.* C–F); King v. Domine—assault with intent to ravish (*ibid.*); King v. Dalton—murder (*ibid.*).

introduced into evidence, although the witnesses also testified.[111] A year later in Dutchess "three affidavits were read against" Robert Wattson.[111a]

It is probable that examinations were proffered more frequently than the records show, for although the early instances of trials being put off for want of material witnesses implies a regard for viva voce testimony, the conditions of travel in a county as huge as Albany, for example, must often have made the use of depositions necessary.

In this connection it should be noticed that in 1746 a provincial statute was enacted for the "greater ease and benefit of all Persons whatsoever in the taking affidavits to be made use of & Read in the Supream Court of this Colony, in all matters & causes whatsoever Depending in the said Supream Court, or in any wise Concerning the Proceedings of or in the Same"; that the Chief Justice and a puisne judge of the court "Shall and may" commission persons in the several counties to take affidavits to be "read and made use of" in the Supreme Court.[111b] We have seen one such commission for Ulster County (1763) but have no evidence that the commissioners took affidavits in criminal cases.[111c] In spite of the broad language of the act, it seems to us very doubtful that it was intended to embrace Crown cases (intrusions or revenue causes excepted), since the word "examination" is consistently used in the sources for the written statements sworn to by witnesses in criminal cases. Indeed, the only instances where the word affidavit is used in such a relation are the Dutchess and Suffolk cases mentioned above.

We have found no instances after 1750 where examinations were used except with the explicit permission of the court. In a great number of cases the examinations are preserved and no mention is made in the minutes that the witnesses appeared and testified.[112] But it cannot be inferred that these exami-

111 King v. Comfort's Jack et al. (Horsmanden, op. cit. 124, 125); King v. Bastian et al. (ibid. 134, 136).

111a Ms. Mins. Dutchess Co. Sess. Liber A, May 18, 1742.

111b 3 Col. Laws NY 546.

111c Ms. Files Ulster Co. (Co. Clerk's Safe) Commission to Charles Clinton, John Hardenbergh and Levi Paulding.

112 John Willet was indicted in the Supreme Court on Oct. 25, 1753, for illegally exporting pork (Ms. Mins. SCJ 1750–54 [Engr.] 317), and this indictment was subsequently quashed (H.R. Pleadings Pl. K. 727). In this case the filed papers contain a "memorandum of witnesses statements" (ibid. 669).

We have several times adverted to the trials of John Lawrence, William Kelly et al., for riot (Ms. Mins. SCJ 1756–61 [Rough] 224, 225, 228, Apr. 22–24, 1761), and although the minute entries contain no reference to the King's witnesses being sworn, we find in H.R. Pleadings Pl. K. 980, that George Spencer was examined on oath as a witness against the defendants before two aldermen in New York City on Nov. 9, 1759. In this case, however, the minutes show defendants' witnesses sworn. See also ibid. K. 961, for witnesses subpoenaed; ibid. K. 425, for notes on trial reciting the evidence offered; ibid K. 978, for notes on trial and the examination of witnesses. Cf. J. T. Kempe Lawsuits J–L sub nom. William Kelly, for a list of witnesses.

In the Dutchess County riot cases, not only were there entries of the evidence in the minutes on the

nations were put in evidence. Their preservation in the files is due to the fact that they were used both in the preparation of the Crown's case and at trial for the purpose of guidance and check on direct and cross-examination.

The cases where the court gave leave to use examinations at trial are all misdemeanors, where no examination had yet been had. The earliest instance (1736) occurred in Suffolk County where on the representation of Clowes for the King that a Crown witness was "a very ancient man" it was ordered he be examined and his evidence so taken be read at trial, "three days notice being given Defendant of such Examination."[113]

Many years later, in *King* v. *John Lawrence Jr. et al.* informed against for assault, the Supreme Court on January 25, 1755 ordered on motion of the Attorney General that he "be at Liberty to examine Witnesses before one of the Judges of this Court giving two days previous notice thereof to the Defendants Attorney and that the Examinations so taken be read at the Tryal saving legal Exceptions to the Defendants."[114] Again at the Tryon County Sessions for September, 1774, Robert Brown, having pleaded not guilty to an indictment for assault and battery, was ordered continued until the next Sessions and in the meantime "Jeremiah Heberus be examined as well on the part of the defendant as on the part of the crown and that his testimony shall be admitted as evidence on the tryal provided he be examined in the presence of the prosecutor and the defendant."[115] An order for preliminary examination of a different character was made at Albany Sessions on January 20, 1773, in the case of *King* v. *Moses Robinson* when, after the cause had been put off for want of the Crown's only witness, the defendant moved and the court granted leave to examine his witnesses and "to introduce their opposition or evidence on the

---

trial (*Misc. Mss. Dutchess Co.*) but the *J. T. Kempe Lawsuits* C–F *sub nom.* John Caine also contain affidavits, depositions and the like against the various rioters.

Phillip Fell was convicted and granted clergy on an indictment for grand larceny (*Ms. Mins. SCJ 1764–67* [Rough] 133, 137, 138, Jan. 23, 25, 1766), and in the *J. T. Kempe Lawsuits* B are to be found the examinations on oath of John Blakelock and Rinear Staats, who deposed before a New York City alderman in Nov. 1765, that Fell had stolen Blakelock's pocketbook, had given it to Staats and later confessed to Staats that he had stolen it. It is to be noted that John Blakelock testified and the examination of the prisoner (Nov. 13, 1765) was used. For the case of John Carey *et al.*, *supra* n. 39.

[113] *Ms. Mins. Suffolk Co. Sess. 1723–51* Oct. 5,

1736. Cf. Overseers of Southold v. David Gardiner (*Ms. Mins. Suffolk Co. Sess. 1760–75* Mar. 27, 1770).

[114] *Ms. Mins. SCJ 1754–57* (Engr.) 118. The case came on for trial on Apr. 18, 1755 and the defendants were acquitted (*ibid.* 146).

In *H.R. Pleadings* Pl. K. 691 there is a paper which evidently refers to a rule for examination either of witnesses or parties to an action, which is as follows: "On motion of Mr. Attorney General Ordered that Mr. John Kiese, Mr. Nathaniel Lawrence . . . be admitted to a Counsel Examination and that Messrs. —— [*sic* blank] be their examiners." We do not know what case this rule for examination refers to, nor do we know any facts other than that quoted.

[115] *Misc. Mss. Tryon Co.*

trial."[116] This examination presumably was done then and there, and at the trial in June, 1773, the defendant was acquitted.

The examinations in these cases were basically no different from a properly conducted examination before a magistrate. Sir Matthew Hale had justified the use of examination at trial on the ground that act of Parliament authorized the taking of informations, that the judges were judges of record, and that they were judges of the crimes upon which informations were taken.[117] This reasoning was ignored by Gilbert in his insistence upon the best evidence rule,[118] but no one seems to have been the least bothered by the hearsay quality of the affidavits, informations and the like.

The confession was one type of evidence secured in advance of trial that was on a somewhat different footing from other preliminary examinations. The confession of defendants actually put on trial will be later discussed in relation to the privilege against self-incrimination, but at this place it is desirable to refer to the confessions of accessories.[119] This method of securing proof for the Crown was probably as favored a police device as it is today. The usual bait for turning King's evidence was a pardon,[120] and the most spectacular demonstration of the efficacy of this lure is again to be found in Horsmanden's account of the negro plot.

Under the terms of the provincial Act of 1730[121] the testimony of a slave was competent at the trial of another slave for conspiracy, but when the prosecutions were first begun in 1741, the Crown officials, under the impression that the matter was routine, made little effort to secure confessions from the slaves, but had two of the first and most important convicted negroes executed at

---

[116] *Ms. Mins. Albany Co. Sess. 1763–82* Jan. 20, 1773.

[117] 2 Hale, *op. cit.* 285.

[118] Gilbert, *Law of Evidence* (1769 ed.) 60–61, where he discusses depositions generally, and 141 where he sets forth by his test of "utmost evidence," restrictions on the use of examinations.

[119] Cf. the justification in Gilbert, *op. cit.* 139.

[120] Various colonial statutes provided an incentive for defendants not only to give testimony against their codefendants by promising them a pardon, but also offered the additional inducement of an informer's reward. Thus, for example, the act of assembly of Nov. 25, 1751, to prevent injury to glass lamps in New York City, enacted that "if Two or more Persons having been jointly Concerned in committing the offense . . . and one or more of them Shall within the Space of one Month . . . inform against any or all the Rest Concerned . . . so as to Convict him her or them

. . . the Person . . . So informing Shall not be Liable to the Payment of the Forfeiture here in before appointed, but Shall Notwithstanding his . . . offense . . . be Intituled to the Reward herein before allowed to Informers" (3 *Col. Laws NY* 855). The act of assembly of Mar. 24, 1772, for the prevention of private lotteries, provided that any justice of peace suspecting that any persons were running a lottery might summon the suspects to examine them "and in order that such persons may not be excused from answering any Questions which shall be asked them by the said justice by Colour of any Plea or Pretense that they may thereby incur any Penalty . . . it is hereby declared that they shall upon being examined . . . and declaring all they know . . . be exempted from any such Penalty and from all prosecutions" (5 *ibid.* 354). Also see *ibid.* 642.

[121] 2 *Col. Laws NY* 684.

once. As panic began to spread and the citizenry became convinced a plot of huge dimensions existed, a very determined drive for negro testimony was begun, first by pardoning two convicted slaves,[122] and later by means of a governor's proclamation[123] assuring a pardon to all who would confess. By this means, in Horsmanden's brutal phrase, "many negroes began to squeak,"[124] and counsel for the Crown were hard put separating the sheep who were to testify from the goats who were to die.[125] It is not clear from the account of these trials whether or not the confessions were consistently put in evidence, but presumably they were on the same footing as any other type of examination. In the case of the confessions of the negroes Quack and Cuffee, taken at the stake, these statements were repeatedly used and proved at various trials by the deputy secretary Moore who took them.[126] Mr. Justice Horsmanden comments that the value of these confessions lay in the fact that the testimony of the other witnesses "was by them . . . confirmed in the midst of flames which is the highest attestation"!|[127]

One of the most interesting pieces of generalship at these trials was in connection with proof against John Ury, the so-called priest. The star witness for the Crown throughout the trials had been the white servant, Mary Burton, but by the time Ury's indictment was reached, her credit was considerably diminished among the soberer inhabitants.[128] As slave testimony was not admissible against Ury, the prosecution endeavored to wrest a confession from Sarah Hughson who had been convicted early in the proceedings but who had not been executed. With remarkable steadfastness, for the pressure upon her was terrific, she had endured the "condemned hole" from June 4 until July 27 awaiting sentence, and finally on promise of a pardon furnished the testimony essential to Ury's conviction.[129]

The circumstances in 1741 were exceptional, but we have seen other instances where pressure was attempted to secure confessions by promise of pardon as in the prosecutions for trading with the enemy in 1763.[130] On one occasion at a trial for counterfeiting in 1773, Judge Robert Livingston, faced

---

[122] Horsmanden, *op. cit.* 134, 146.
[123] *Ibid.* 167.
[124] *Ibid.* 205.
[125] *Ibid.* 206, 235, as to how this was done.
[126] *Ibid.* 114.
[127] *Ibid.* 102.
[128] Cf. Horsmanden's long account attempting to bolster the credibility of this witness (*ibid.* 365 *et seq.*) and his introductory remarks (*ibid.* 11).
[129] *Ibid.* 285.
[130] *Supra* c. IV 243. Thomas Norton pleaded

guilty to an indictment for grand larceny on Oct. 27, 1767, but on Oct. 29 was granted a pardon and ordered bound in a recognizance in £100 to give evidence against Samuel Ashcraft, his co-defendant. Norton was evidently granted the pardon in order that he might give evidence against Ashcraft, but when Ashcraft's trial came up on Oct. 31, 1767, Norton failed to appear, and Ashcraft was discharged for lack of prosecution (*Ms. Mins. SCJ 1764–67* [Engr.] 318, 327).

with the absence of the single material witness whose testimony was essential, rescued one defendant from liquidation by giving him a pardon and taking his deposition whereby the conviction of other defendants was assured.[131]

The amount of scrivening energy devoted to preliminary examinations is remarkable considering the stress that came to be laid upon oral testimony at trial. But it was a general law-enforcing purpose which these papers performed rather than a function in the judicial process proper. In other words, they facilitated the task of Crown officers in getting ready and conducting a prosecution, but were only exceptionally a part of the case itself, in the sense of data to be weighed by the jury in reaching a verdict. At the precise juncture in a prosecution when a witness's words acquired immediate significance in settling the issue of a defendant's guilt, they were no longer worth committing to paper because no useful procedural end would be served by so doing. They became matters for the ear of God and the country and not for the record.

If the perpetuation of common law traditions respecting oral proceedings, and the meticulous observance of the economies of a criminal "record," had the consequence, grievous for us, that statements respecting testimony are rarely to be found in minutes of the provincial courts or the records of trials, the clerks were equally indifferent to rulings which the courts might make in the course of hearing evidence, an attitude which the historian of the law finds equally deplorable. It is small consolation that in this respect the New York sources are not much worse than those of England, where the bulk of our information is derived from the execrably reported State Trials[132] which too often were ex parte accounts on which little trust can be rested. The reports of Assizes or King's Bench in the eighteenth century reveal the most casual interest in rules of evidence, and even a search of the dismal pages of the Old Bailey Sessions Papers discloses that only rarely was there occasion to determine a question of admissibility or the like.[133] Doubtless in respect of matters of proof, practice was better defined than the sources tell. Inevitably, however,

---

[131] Livingston to Gov. Tryon, Mar. 9, 1773 (*Gratz Coll.* [Pa. Hist. Soc. Mss.]) and his letter, Nov. 10, 1772, re James Brown who turned King's evidence (*loc. cit.*).

[132] So far as we are aware there has been no critical examination of the *State Trials* at large as sources, but obviously the reports of Penn's trial and the Popish Plot cases are anything but reliable stenographic reports. These are no doubt, in Baron Gilbert's phrase, "the utmost evidence" of the actual proceedings in court, but it is nevertheless miraculous to think of a body of law being

grounded upon such unreliable accounts. How far this was done is obvious from the citations to Hawkins' chapter on evidence in the first edition of his *Pleas of the Crown*.

[133] The eighteenth century accretions to the law of evidence as they affected criminal trials are conveniently discovered in the margins of Curwood's edition of Hawkins (1824). To be sure, rulings in civil cases affected criminal proceedings, but even in these cases the formulation of rules seems to have been of relatively small interest to reporters.

these practices, since they related to matters normally not committed to writing, let alone made of record, were in a very explicit sense unwritten law. This is characteristic of any first instance jurisprudence that does not live under the threat of the undoing hands of appellate tribunals, for such in general was the quality of English criminal justice.

Judging from provincial citation, New York practice developed under the guiding constellation of Duncombe's *Trials per Pais,* Hawkins' *Pleas of the Crown,* Nelson's *Law of Evidence* and eventually Gilbert's treatise. It is not apparent how influential these collections of precedents were, for the accounts we have seen of trials establish little concerning the effects of textbook learning. From the three types of documents relating to the evidence in particular prosecutions—the preliminary examinations, counsels' summaries of evidence in briefs and the occasional notes taken at trials—one important generalization can be established: that in general a good deal of testimony which would today be excluded as hearsay was regarded as admissible in the eighteenth century. This fact, however, signifies nothing regarding the influence of commentators, for although they murmur a few pieties about hearsay, it is clear that the implications of the term had been exploited little beyond its most obvious lay meaning. A second important generalization which the New York documents yield is that in spite of the progressive professionalization of the law the standards of what was admissible in evidence did not become much more strict. The pervasiveness of the eighteenth century attitude can best be illustrated by examples from three trials.

It will be recalled that in *Queen* v. *Bayard* the nub of the charge was the addresses which the defendant had procured certain citizens and soldiers to sign and which the prosecution claimed were treasonable. These documents were not put in evidence[134] but most of the testimony revolved about them. The Crown's first witness, Samuel Clowes, after giving an account of his association with Bayard and his connection with the addresses was questioned more nearly regarding his own signing.

Sol. Gen.: Mr. Clows, pray tell us, what was the reason why you did not sign the other two addresses?

---

[134] Bayard, in petitioning and appealing to the Queen, complained that the addresses were not produced. "Yo[r] Petitioner was Committed by . . . the governor and council . . . for High Treason under pretence that your Pet[r] had signed . . . scandalous libells . . . and . . . [he was] . . . brought to tryall before Special Commissioners appointed for that purpose . . . and . . . the pretended libells . . . were only adresses to . . . [the King, Commons and Governor Cornbury] . . . and were not produced at the tryall for the judgment of the court and . . . no full proof that the pet[r] signed or caused any others to sign 'em" (*Bayard Papers 1698–1710*).

Clows: I think I am not at this time obliged to tell that, being that it does not at all affect the matter.

Mr. Atwood: Yes but it does; you must tell us.

Clows: One of the chief reasons was because I then thought that the saying the assembly had given a gift to the lieutenant governor, to tempt him to pass their acts, was a reflection upon the lieutenant governor; but it is my judgment now, that it was no reflection at all upon him.

Sol. Gen.: How! and do you not think so now.

Mr. Atwood: He only speaks it as his judgment.[135]

The negro trials of 1741 contain a great many examples of the admission of hearsay. We mention but one of the most remarkable taken from the trial of the Hughsons.

John Schultz . . . called and sworn

Schultz said "that Cuffee (Phillipse's negro) being carried with Quack immediately after their conviction into prison, where Hughson and his wife were, as he came in said to Hughson, we may thank you for this, for this is what you have brought us to; and Cuffee owned the next day to the witness that he had said so."[136]

Our third example is taken from the trial of the Dutchess rioters twenty-five years later, the notes of which reveal some very curious things, especially at the trial of William Prendergast.[137]

Witness for the Crown James Dickenson Sworn To give an account of the origin of the mob says Prisoner [William Prendergast] came with a party of his men to witnesses house and told him he was his prisoner—Asked him by what authority—he answered by the King's, demanded to see his authority. Did not shew it but ordered him to pay £80 for one of his gang then present. Witness refused—prisoner with threats said he should, but at length went away. Says he understood that the Design of Mob was to compel their Landlord to alter their

---

135 14 Howell, *State Trials* 488, 489.

136 Horsmanden, *op. cit.* 117.

137 The next quotations are all from the notes on the July Assizes of 1766, Dutchess County (*Misc. Mss. Dutchess Co. 1752–1870*).

In the notes for the Dutchess Assizes of Aug. 14, 1766, we find the trial and testimony for and against Edmond Green and four others indicted for assaulting Hannah Hobby and causing a miscarriage. Here also the testimony on direct and cross-examination is given *in extenso*. Also see the trials of Daniel Taylor and three others for breaking and entering the house of John Genong and of Alexander McArthur and three others for murder (*ibid.*).

In the trial of Robert Campbell and Archibald Livingston at Orangetown at the court for the trial of causes brought to issue in the Supreme Court held in Orange County on June 6, 1764, are to be found similar notes for trial and examination and cross-examination of witnesses for the Crown and the defense (*H.R. Pleadings* Pl. K. 1064, *supra* c. III 181). Also see the "notes and evidences on the trial" of Roper Dawson on Jan. 24, 1766, in the Supreme Court *en banc*. Dawson had been indicted on Jan. 22, 1766 for murdering John Mackenzie by stabbing him in the right side of the abdomen between the third and fourth ribs. Thomas Wallace was sworn as a witness for the

rent—The reason assigned by the prisoner for demanding the £80 was on acct. of the Improvement of a farm . . . CROSS EX^d asks whether he appeared to be in joke or earnest about the £80 but answered he seemed much in Earnest, struck his stick on the floor—spoke very ugly . . . COURT—Have you rec^d any injury from the Mob—Answers he had his apple trees Girdled and his barn set on fire believes it to have been done by the Mob who were angry for his endeavour to oppose it.

In answer to the prisoner—sayd never heard him declare people should not recover their just rents nor officers from doing their duty, never threatened but relating the £80.

A number of witnesses were next examined and the testimony for the Crown closed as follows:

Elisha Collared sworn—Heard Isaac Perry say they were determined to prevent Regulars from doing any damage to mob or to take them—Saw several of the mob go to Quaker Hill to engage the Regulars—heard some of the mob say passing by his house that they were going to meet to fight the regulars.

Here the King's counsel rested. The first witness for the prisoner, John Akins, stated "never heard a bad character of the prisoner except as to the mob affair—has not heard he was a projector but heard he was a promoter of the mob and the principal head." Cross-examined, "says Saturday about the middle of the afternoon they resolved to deliver themselves up. He tried to persuade them to deliver up their arms to him, some of them did. . . ." The rest of the testimony was in a similar vein of hearsay.

If these reports can be relied upon and are, as we think, typical, it is understandable why there is not much information available about objections to the admission of evidence. What has been found on this point relates chiefly to the competency of witnesses and to the admissibility of documents. We shall speak first of the question of competency.

King, as was also Gamaliel Wallace (*J. T. Kempe Lawsuits* C–F; for the minute entry see *Ms. Mins. SCJ 1764–67* [Rough] 132, 133, 134). This indicates two examinations of the deceased were used. They were apparently admitted as dying declarations. On Apr. 21, 1769, Major Henry Pullen, Esq. was indicted for riot and assault and was tried and found guilty on Oct. 24, 1769 (*Ms. Mins. SCJ 1769–72* [Engr.] 11, 114). In the *J. T. Kempe Lawsuits* P–R *sub nom.* Pullen, are the notes on his trial and the Attorney General's opening indicates that the indictment charged the defendant with riot and assault and also for a simple assault and battery. The witnesses for the King having been examined, the King's evidence closed and the wit-

nesses for the defendant were sworn. Also see the trial of Benjamin Ferris on Sept. 9, 1773, at White Plains on an inquisition for forcible entry and detainer (*J. T. Kempe Lawsuits* C–F). John Kelly was tried on Oct. 24, 1764, in the Supreme Court on an indictment for burglary and found guilty (*Ms. Mins. SCJ 1764–67* [Rough] 23, 29). In the *J. T. Kempe Lawsuits* J–L, are to be found the notes of evidence taken on the trial of this defendant. Also see the notes on the trial of Stephen Tippet and three others on an indictment for burning Cornelius Bogardus' fence (*H.R. Pleadings* Pl. K. 435; for the minute entries, see *Ms. Mins. SCJ 1772–76* [Rough] 167, 170).

At the trial of Nicholas Bayard for treason the defendant called David Jamison, then clerk of the Council. The Solicitor General made no objection, but the Chief Justice interposed by saying: "Mr. Jamison has refused to purge himself of signing these addresses and is *particeps criminis* for which reason he cannot be allowed as evidence."[138] The defendant does not appear to have excepted to this ruling, although the witness was not even under indictment. As Jamison had already infuriated Atwood by attempting to take notes of the proceedings it was doubtless prudent to be silent.

The question of the competency of a person convicted and sentenced for a felony but in receipt of a pardon, was raised by John Ury when the Crown offered Sarah Hughson as a witness. The Attorney General, citing "Hawkins' title Pardon ch. 37 §48," retorted that as Sarah's pardon had been pleaded and allowed, the law admitted her capacity to testify. Whereupon the court so ruled.[139]

There are two cases in the New York records involving the testimony of infants below the age of nine years. In 1755, at the trial of James Gaines, indicted for assault with intent to ravish Margaret Bennet (a child), four women and three men, one of them a physician, gave evidence for the Crown. Then "Mary Bennet An Infant eight years of Age and going in her ninth, was examined upon the Authority of Justice Hale, Vide his Summary of Pleas of the crown under title Evidence—page 263 which was cited in this case and Read where it is said that the examination of Infants of nine years is allowed in some cases."[140] The entry reads as if objection had been raised, but in a case eleven years later the court seems to have proceeded of its own motion. John Domine (1766) was indicted for a similar offense on an infant aged eight and one-half years, and the infant "being first examined by the court was sworn." The cases are worthy of notice since there was precedent to the contrary in the English books.[141]

Although the judicial records indicate that questions of competency seem to have engaged the bar more often than other questions, it is from an argument which may never even have been delivered that some insight into provincial grasp of these matters is derived. This argument is part of a brief prepared by John Tabor Kempe for the information proceedings, already dis-

[138] 14 Howell, *State Trials* 503.

[139] Horsmanden, *op. cit.* 295. It may be noted that Horsmanden (*ibid.* 251) in a note comments upon the competency of the masters and owners of slaves. These had been allowed to testify which the learned Justice thought to be too great an indulgence because they were interested.

[140] *Ms. Mins. SCJ 1754–57* (Engr.) 112, 115, 116.

[141] King v. Domine (*Ms. Mins. SCJ 1764–67* [Rough] 190, 191). Cf. also King v. Tom, a slave (*Ms. Mins. SCJ 1762–64* [Engr.] 294). For the English rule, Rex v. Travers (2 *Strange* 699).

cussed, against some of the metropolitan nabobs for trading with the enemy.[142] Kempe states that "it is not improbable that it may be insisted that some of the witnesses may be improper" because they were interested witnesses and were *"particeps criminis."* With reference to the argument that the witnesses were interested, Kempe proposed to point out that while in certain types of crimes a witness could be disqualified because he was interested (for example, forgery, frauds, perjury, usury, etc.), nevertheless in the informations filed for this offense no one could be disqualified as a witness because he was interested since the witness in accusing others need not accuse himself of the crime. Kempe also pointed out that even if the witness were an interested witness, nevertheless, "not every kind of interest disqualifies." For example, if the interest was so small that it would not bias the witness, then he would not be disqualified (citing 2 *Bac. Ab.* 290, 291). A witness would not be disqualified where the interest was only remote or contingent (citing 1 *Salk.* 286). Thus where a man was charged with a crime, his heir could be a witness even though forfeiture of estate and corruption of blood would ensue on conviction (citing "N. L. Evid., 136, Brownl, 47"). A witness could be sworn to give evidence to his own detriment (citing 2 *Salk.* 691, N. L. Evid. 122, Viner's *Abridgement,* Tit. Evidence 95 or 195.2). But the witness could not be sworn to derive an interest to himself (citing N. L. Evid. 124). To the defendant's argument that no one could be compelled to swear against his own proper interest, Kempe intended to point out that a witness could be sworn against his own interest, saying that the "court of Chancery every day compels the party on oath to discover his own frauds." With reference to the defendant's possible argument that these witnesses could not be sworn because they were *particeps criminis,* Kempe proposed to quote "2 Hawk. P.C. 432" by which he would endeavor to show that every *particeps criminis* might be a witness for or against his accomplices if he had not been indicted himself.

In this document it is not merely the citations which are illuminating, showing as they do familiarity with the most important available literature, but the fact that objections in a case of moment might be argued with learning and thoroughness. As a matter of practice, it appears from the case of *King* v. *Van Rensselaer* that when the question of interest was raised the witnesses were examined on their *voir dire.* Kempe had offered several of the defendant's tenants who lived on the disputed tracts and, after they had declared their interest, requested that each might be sworn to give evidence of the possession

---

[142] *H.R. Pleadings* Pl. K. 1023. Cf. *supra* 242.

of the others with a saving as to their giving evidence respecting their own possession. This Judge Jones refused. Thereupon the Attorney General made the formal offer of proof which included an allegation that the witnesses had shown writings respecting their tenancy and an offer of general reputation regarding the matter. At this point defendant's counsel objected. The court sustained the objection and the Attorney General excepted.[143]

We shall speak in a moment of the anomalous position of the defendant's testimony but it remains to be seen how the informer was handled. So far as we can judge there was no limitation upon such testimony until after the provincial information statute which bound the informer for costs. The evidence question was brought up in *King* v. *Gomez et al.*, one of the few cases reported by William Smith Jr. This was an information for assault on Solomon Hayes and the question was whether an informer bound for costs could be a witness.

> The Attorney General offered Solomon Hayes on trial for a witness. We objected that he had recognized for the costs pursuant to the Act of Assembly and insisted upon the following book cases. Law of Evid. Gilbert 121, 122. Trials p. pais 226. 1 Sid 237. Hard. 331. Hayes wife was also offered. *Per Curiam.* The objection is unanswerable. The prosecutor is evidently interested and the wife by necessary consequence. C.J. said that since the statute of Wm. III of which our act is nearly a copy a nominal prosecutor was inserted in the information to elude the very objection now made. Trial went on and verdict for defendants.[144]

Nothing can be inferred from these examples regarding the frequency of such arguments over objections to evidence. Clearly, however, this would occur only when a defendant was represented by counsel at all stages of a trial, viz., in misdemeanor cases. In prosecutions for felony such interchange would be most unlikely for we cannot recall any instance where a prisoner was indulged with the aid of counsel at this most crucial juncture in his trial, and few defendants would be knowledgeable enough themselves to imagine objections and to argue them through.

The significance of an equality in professional representation in Crown cases is exemplified still further in cases where written evidence in some form was introduced. The scope of this type of proof was very broad in the eight-

[143] "Crowns First Exception," *J. T. Kempe Lawsuits* V *sub nom.* Van Rensselaer.
[144] *Ms. William Smith Jr. Papers* V 2. Cf. also 2 Smith, *History of NY* 242. The report adds: "Note In this cause I had a rule for a struck jury but I doubt whether the defendant's on any infor- mation except such as are in the nature of a quo warranto is entitled to a struck jury and yet the reason for this security to the subject is stronger in cases on information than on indictments. See our jury act and the clause relating to struck juries" (Minute entries, *supra* nn. 56, 81).

eenth century, chiefly because it was not then thought of in terms of any hearsay rule, and it is therefore desirable, before speaking of the cases where objections were raised, to review the types of written "evidences" which are mentioned in the minutes.

The most striking feature of provincial practice here is the range of matter
that was included in the class of "public documents." Foremost were the acts
of assembly which were often read in evidence, obviously because the court did
not take judicial notice of them.[145] Even when an indictment or information
was based on such an act, they might be read in evidence. Thus Michael Burton and Arnout Hendrikse were tried on March 15, 1730/31, on an indictment
for keeping a disorderly house, and part of the evidence of the Crown consisted in two acts of assembly which were read in court.[146] An information was
filed against James Tillet for encroaching upon and obstructing the King's
highway in Queens County, and the defendant was tried at the Queens Court
for the Trial of Causes brought to issue in the Supreme Court on September 4,
1734. An "Act of Assembly" of 1730 respecting highways was read in evidence for the Crown but the jury found the defendant not guilty.[147]

This practice was presumably based on the rule expressed in the books that
although a general act of Parliament is "taken notice of by the judges or jury
without being pleaded . . . particular laws which do not concern the whole
Kingdom . . . must be brought before them to judge thereon."[148]

The conglomeration of documents used in the prosecutions of the Queens
and Albany justices for failure to repair the county jails is an interesting example of what were obviously regarded as "public documents" proper to be
used in evidence. It will be recalled that the Queen's justices were tried in 1724
on an information.[149] After the jury had been sworn, "on motion of Mr. Attorney General, Act for repair [of] Gaols read, information read, rule of court
read, minutes of the justices read, representation of the grand jury read."[150]
Similarly on August 20, 1729, when the justices of the city and county of Albany were tried upon two informations filed against them in the year 1723 for
failure to repair the jails of that county, after the sheriff and several other witnesses had testified, the following evidence was offered on behalf of the
Crown: the act of assembly for repairing jails; a minute of a presentment by

[145] There are examples of this in the early minutes of the Supreme Court; cf. *Mins. SCJ 1693–
1701* 97, 189.
[146] *Ms. Mins. SCJ 1727–32* 259.
[147] *Ms. Mins. Cir. 1721–49* 281; *H.R. Parch.
171 C 6.*

[148] Gilbert, *Law of Evidence* (1769) 40, 41, and
the cases there cited.
[149] *Supra* 170.
[150] *Ms. Mins. SCJ 1723–27* 83, 84.

the grand jury at Albany Oyer and Terminer for 1722; the commission of peace for the justices of Albany of 1719 and the minutes of the Albany Sessions of December, 1722. The defendants offered the following testimony in their defense: a receipt from the Attorney General, the charter of the city of Albany and the act confirming the charters and grants of the Province of New York.[151]

There is a sprinkling of cases where other types of judicial documents were read in evidence. Thus at the trial of Michael Slaughter for jail break (1721), the *mittimus* for his commitment was read,[152] and at the trial of Daniel Taylor and three others for breaking and entering (1766), a "bench warrant admitted" in evidence for the Crown.[153] On numerous occasions coroner's inquests would be read in evidence.[154]

The sources give no indication respecting the authentication or proving of these documents, but under the prevailing generous view of what constituted a record,[155] it seems likely that no particular proof was required if the document had some connection with a judicial proceeding. Probably courts required only that an original be exemplified. This question was raised in *Queen* v. *Makemie* when the Attorney General offered a copy of the Queen's instructions to Cornbury, justifying on the ground that the Governor was out of the Province. This was a matter of consequence since the indictment was based in part on Makemie's violation of the instructions. The defendant's counsel objected vigorously to the use of a copy, but eventually agreed to accept the copy in order to avoid postponement of the trial.[156] The printed account of the trial does not indicate that any authentication of the copy was required beyond signature by the Governor.

With respect to other types of writings recorded in a public office and in particular deeds, the instances where these were used in criminal prosecutions indicate that the instrument itself and not the "record" entry was admissible.

[151] *Ms. Mins. Cir. 1721–49* 252. When Richard Albertson was tried at the Queens Court for the Trial of Causes brought to issue in the Supreme Court on Sept. 2, 1740, for maladministration in the office of justice of peace, in setting aside a verdict which was arrived at by a six-man jury under the 40-shilling court act, the Attorney General offered in evidence for the Crown a presentment of the grand jury and also had a clause of the act of assembly for the trial of causes of 40s. which was read in evidence for the King (*Ms. Mins. Cir. 1721–49* 322).

[152] *Ms. Mins. Cir. 1721–49* 5.

[153] *Misc. Mss. Dutchess Co.*

[154] E.g., King v. Lambris—murder, 1700 (*Mins. SCJ 1693–1701* 173); King v. John Reeves—murder, 1738/39 (*Ms. Mins. Cir. 1721–49* 97); King v. Koole *et al.*—manslaughter, 1754 (*Ms. Mins. SCJ 1754–57* [Engr.] 81–83).

[155] Cf. Coke, *Littleton* 283a. In Thurston v. Slatford (1 *Salkeld* 284) a "record" of Sessions was held admissible.

[156] *Narrative of a New and Unusual American Imprisonment,* 4 Force, *Tracts* no. 4, 25, 26; *Ms. Mins. SCJ 1704/05–1709* 123. Cf. also Queen v. Riggs, and Queen v. Moore indicted for murder (1711/12) where the Queen's instructions were read (*Ms. Mins. SCJ 1710–14* 358, 359).

Indeed, it was only by particular statute that such entries could be made competent proof.[157] Possibly early practice was less careful, but it was strict toward the end of the colonial period.[158] The recital of the evidence for the defendant in *King* v. *Van Rensselaer* indicates the manner in which such evidence was offered. It is to be noted further that in this case the defendant offered two surveyors to give their opinions as to the construction of the royal grants. Kempe objected alleging the courts were the judges of the construction of the King's grants and that no private opinion was proper evidence. The court overruled the objection and permitted one Vroman who was a surveyor to express his opinion on the boundaries that were in issue.[159]

[157] Cf. the recital in an act of assembly, Apr. 3, 1775 "for admitting in Evidence an ancient Record of the Office of the Town Clerk for the City and County of New York" (5 *Col. Laws NY* 844). In the Act of 1762 respecting quitrents, the book entries of certain allotments were made evidence of such partitions (4 *ibid.* 597).

[158] In King v. Ben Ferris, oral testimony regarding a lease was used (*J. T. Kempe Lawsuits* C–F).

[159] *H.R. Pleadings* Pl. K. 281: "Whereupon William Smith Junr. Council for the Defendant gave in Evidence to the Jurors aforesaid certain Letters Patent under the great Seal of the Province of New York, to Killian Van Rensselaer the son of Johannes Van Rensselaer and Killian Van Rensselaer the son of Jeremias Van Rensselaer dated the 4th day of November 1685, (Prout the Letters Patent) and also certain other Letters Patent under the Great Seal of the said Province to the said Killian Van Rensselaer son of the sd Jeremias Van Rensselaer bearing date the 20th day of May 1704, (Prout the Letters Patents) and also a certain Deed Poll from the said Killian the son of Jeremias Van Rensselaer to Henry Van Rensselaer bearing date the first day of June in the third Year of the Reign of her late Majesty Queen Anne (Prout the Deed) and also did give in Evidence to the Jurors afsd, two certain Instruments in writing not sealed, not as Evidence of Title under which the defendts claimed the Lands in Question but only an explanatory of the Boundaries of the said Tract of Land called Claverack, one of which said writings bears date the 27th day of May 1649, and is in the Dutch Language (Prout) and also a Translation of the said last mentioned Instrument of Writing (in the words following Prout) and also the other of the said Writings bears date the 15 of June 1670 and is in the Dutch Language (Prout) and also a Translation of the sd last writing in the words following (Prout) . . . and did further offer to give in Evidence by Two persons surveyors their opinions of the Construction of the King's Grants where the same were defective in Description, for the want of a Line or Lines to close and perfect the Boundaries of the Tracts mentioned in such Grants and the

Council for the Deft did further alledge and offer to give in Evidence that the Rights which the ancestors of the Defendt claimed under the Dutch Governmt while this Country was in the hands of the States General of the united Provinces were considerably contracted & diminished by divers grants of large Tracts made by the English Governors to other persons out of the first Tract described in the sd Letters Patent before the granting the sd first mentioned Letters Patent, and insisted that for this Reason the most Liberal Construction of the Letters Patent afd ought to be made in favour of the Deft respecting the extencion of the said second Tract of Land in the sd Letters Patent mentioned and did further offer to give in Evidence by the Testimony of the said Surveyors that there were many Grants from the Crown for Lands in this Province passed in early days defective for the want of a closing Line or Lines to perfect the descriptions thereof Whereupon the sd Atty General did object to the giving of any or either of the matters afd in Evidence to the Jury afd. alledging that the Kings Courts are to judge of the Construction of the King's Grants that no private opinion of any other person whatever relative to the sd Construction was proper Evidence to be given to the sd Jurors, and alleging further that it was impossible that any Diminution of the first mentioned Tract by such prior Grants as afd could tend to elucidate the Boundaries of the sd second Tract described in the sd. Letters Patent and further also alledging that any Evidence that other Grants of the Crown were imperfect could not be material or proper to be given in this issue and that . . . [illegible] each and every of the matter afd so offered as Evidence could only tend to prejudice the Jurors afd and to mislead them from the true Points in Issue and therefore prayed the Court that no such Evidence or any part thereof might be given to the sd Jurors Nevertheless the sd Justice overruled the sd objections and did permit Isaac Vroman one of the sd Surveyors . . . [to say] That it was the opinion of the said Isaac Vroman that a closing Line of the sd Tract last mentioned in the sd Letters Patent and now in controversy ought to be supplied by a

The intrusion proceedings against John Henry Lydius throw some further light upon the technicalities of evidence relating to title. Here Lydius had only an Indian deed and a supposed grant from Gov. Shirley of Massachusetts to support his claim to the lands. As to the first, Kempe states in his brief that this "should not be given in evidence it being contrary to the Constitution for a subject to derive title but through the Crown." As to the Massachusetts grant, it was to be excluded "on a plea of not guilty as it tends to prove that the lands lie out of the province." This should have been pleaded to the jurisdiction, because what could be pleaded in abatement could not be given in evidence on the general issue. The Shirley grant could not be offered to establish a royal grant since a Massachusetts Bay title denied the jurisdiction of the court of New York.[160]

The cases just discussed, criminal only in a technical procedural sense, dealt with matters where, on the civil side, rules of evidence were many and well understood, and where, consequently, aberrations could not occur especially as the defense in both cases was ably represented. By this time provincial practice was conducted on a high level of skill, but we doubt, nevertheless, whether questions of evidence were given meticulous attention in a routine felony prosecution.

There are occasional references in the sources to letters offered in evidence, but in most instances details are wanting.[161] In the prosecution of John Ury, the alleged priest, we have an example of how this evidence was offered and used. Just before the Crown rested Joseph Murray, who was acting as King's counsel, stated that he had a letter from General Oglethorpe of Georgia, the contents of which he described. "I only offer this," continued Murray, "by way of inducement and illustration of what is strictly evidence and what I think by law I may: it is to show in general that there was a plot; [and cited some authorities out of the *State Trials*]." The court required counsel to prove

Line run from the place so alledged to be the head of Kinderhook Creek, along the South side of the sd Creek as the Creek runs to the place of Begining at Major Abraham Stats, and that he the said Isaac Vroman thought such Construction reasonable, and that the sd Isaac Vroman had surveyed divers Tracts of Land Granted by the Crown which were defective for want of a Line or Lines to close."

160 *J. T. Kempe Lawsuits* L–O; *supra* 212.

The embarrassments incident upon the rule that original deeds must be offered is illustrated by the troubles of Kempe in trying to get a satisfactory bill of exceptions in the Van Rensselaer case. He complained he had been unable to set forth the evi-

dence in his bill of exceptions because this was all in the defendant's hands. He obtained a rule for producing it, but only part was returned, the defendant alleging that the balance had been returned to the Patroon of Rensselaerswyck (*Misc. Mss. Claverack*).

161 King v. William Norris, 1732 (*Ms. Mins. SCJ 1727–32* 393); King v. Shakemaple, 1723 (*ibid.* 116). In the Lydius case, Kempe proposed to use a letter of the defendant to the Governor (*J. T. Kempe Lawsuits* L–O). In King v. Recarrick, "evidences and papers" were read (*Ms. Mins. NYCQS 1683/84–1694* 150, Aug. 4, 1691); and in King v. Zenger, newspapers "which owned by the Defendant" were offered (*Ms. Mins. SCJ 1732–39* 177).

Oglethorpe's hand, and parts of the letter were then read, the substance of which was that a Spanish prisoner had disclosed that Spaniards were sending priests into the north to burn magazines and towns.[162] Nothing illustrates more vividly the curiously formalistic nature of the contemporary law of evidence than this solemn establishment of a signature for the purpose of admitting what strikes us as a particularly incompetent piece of testimony. It was introduced apparently in reliance upon Hawkins' statement[163] that although what a stranger is heard to say is no manner of evidence for or against a prisoner, yet it could be used by way of inducement or illustration of what is properly evidence.[164]

The testimonial capacity and the privilege of a defendant have been reserved to the end of our discussion of evidence chiefly because the problem has ramifications which extend beyond the limits of ordinary jury trial procedure. It is a problem that has little to do with maxims, and, as our sources read, bears no relation to the copybook pieties of superior courts from which the standard accounts of the privilege against self-incrimination have been constructed. It is a problem which for the eighteenth century must be viewed and approached in terms of administration and not in terms of procedure. For although contemporary writers ring their changes upon the principle that persons interested cannot be witnesses, and the tag *nemo tenetur prodere seipso* is occasionally mentioned, the trials reveal that the chief concern of prosecutors and judges was that the defendant should talk, and in this should be encouraged and not hindered.

With reference to trials before juries it is essential to distinguish the situation of the defendant charged with felony from that where he was charged with a misdemeanor. In the former case, since he was conducting his own defense he

---

[162] Horsmanden, *op. cit.* 297. In the Lydius case, Kempe proposed to use one Dr. Young to prove the handwriting (*J. T. Kempe Lawsuits* L–O).

[163] 2 Hawkins, *op. cit.* c.46 §44.

[164] The records supply some further details respecting practice. A defendant, for example, was permitted to offer witnesses as to his character, cf. King v. Beck, an Indian (*Ms. Mins. Cir. 1721–49* 13); King v. Ury (Horsmanden, *op. cit.* 301 et seq.). In King v. Sullivan indicted for destroying a bond, Kempe had a list of witnesses to the defendant's character (*J. T. Kempe Lawsuits* S–U). In the case of John Dalton indicted for murder of John Moschelck, one Winson filed an affidavit stating he and his fellow officers could testify to Dalton's character. One Lawlis also made a deposition ". . . he heard the Philadelphia . . . man say that he could

lick ten Irishmen; one John Dalton a soldier being in Company and being an Irish-man resented the words . . . the said Dalton was very quiet and no way quarrelsome in any respect until the Philadelphia man had threatened so much." A fight started; Moschelck threw Dalton out and in the ensuing struggle Moschelck was stabbed (*J. T. Kempe Lawsuits* C–F). Dalton was acquitted (*Ms. Mins. SCJ 1764–67* [Rough] 135).

Witnesses were not allowed to read their testimony but could use prepared statements to refresh their memories. King v. Ury (Horsmanden, *op. cit.* 305).

A judge was competent to testify, King v. Borne: "John Cruger Justice sworn to give evidence came down from the bench" (*Ms. Mins. Cir. 1721–49* 27).

was directly vulnerable to questioning from the bench, and, as we have pointed out, the English *State Trials* demonstrate how an adroit judge in the course of a defendant's activities as counsel could carry on a virtual examination of the accused and often secure damaging admissions.[165] The same thing could of course occur where a defendant acted as his own counsel in misdemeanors.

We cannot be certain how far these methods were used in New York, but certainly the opportunity existed. There is one example of a defendant's examination in court, the case of *Queen* v. *Maķemie*. The defendant here had waived the examination of Crown witnesses because he was willing to own the preaching which was charged to have been without license. Thereupon, the Attorney General put, and the defendant answered, a number of questions as to his activities.[166] The bench did not caution the defendant (who was represented) and it appears that although the general issue had been pleaded, the plan of the defense was essentially the strategy of the demurrer, viz., to admit the facts and challenge the applicability of the statutes upon which the indictment was based.

This was an early case and there is little in later sources to show how far either Attorney General or judge could go in interrogating a prisoner. The business of incrimination did not, of course, have to proceed by way of questioning, for there were no restrictions placed upon comments by the prosecution as to what an accused might say in addressing a jury. Under the circumstances of a defendant acting as his own counsel it was a simple matter for a lawyer to treat what had been said *arguendo* as if it were testimony to be weighed in conjunction with the Crown's evidence. This is strikingly illustrated by the way in which the pathetic address of John Ury to the jury was handled by the elder William Smith in his closing for the prosecution.[167]

The most dangerous juncture at a trial for the defendant-counsel was the moment when the Crown introduced a confession taken by a justice at a preliminary hearing. These were admissible by virtue of the same English statutes[168] which made available the examinations of informers. Although a confession could only be introduced if not made under oath, it would serve to convict without corroborating evidence, if the defendant had pleaded not guilty in open court.[169] Obviously if a defendant had any remarks to make about his ear-

---

[165] *Supra* 555.

[166] *Narrative of an Unusual American Imprisonment*, 4 Force, *Tracts* no. 4, 26.

[167] Horsmanden, *op. cit.* 315 *et seq.*

[168] 1 & 2 Ph. & Mary c.13; 2 & 3 Ph. & Mary c.10.

[169] 2 Hawkins, *Pleas of the Crown* c.46 §§3–5. Hawkins says where the defendant pleads, the confession is not taken as a conviction since the petit jury must try it. Gilbert, *Law of Evidence* 140, says because "the trial ought to be solemn and of record that determines the fate of life and death."

lier words, he would likely find himself answering questions from the bench. In the situation where he had made more than one preliminary statement and had contradicted himself, the introduction of all the "confessions" would tempt him to unguarded speech, or he might even be asked to explain. An example of this occurred at a special Sessions in 1742 for the trial of a negro. The defendant had made several "confessions" which were introduced, but as these were contradictory, he was asked if he had made the confessions as read. He replied that he had. He was then asked to repeat what he had first said—the portions, indeed, which were incriminating.[170]

This case of course concerned a slave, but we have not noticed any special tenderness for white persons charged with felony, and it is not unlikely that similar tactics were used against them. There are numerous cases where the minutes reveal the reading at trial of a prisoner's confession. It had to be proved by the magistrate who took it, but otherwise no further formalities were observed. An early example of the use of these confessions is *Queen* v. *De Hart*. The defendant was tried at the Supreme Court on September 8, 1705 on an indictment for larceny and the mayor of New York was sworn in evidence for the King. In addition, the Crown offered as evidence "The prisoner's Examination taken before ye Mayor" and, the jury having deliberated for half an hour, a verdict of "guilty to the value of 10 pence" was brought in.[171] On August 10, 1721, William Moras was tried at Westchester Oyer and Terminer and General Gaol Delivery on an indictment for feloniously taking goods and chattels worth £27. Seven witnesses were sworn to give testimony for the King and "the confession of the prisoner taken before Samual Purdy, Justice of Peace" was read in evidence for the Crown. Moras was convicted and sentenced to be hanged.[172]

In the margin are cited some other instances where the minutes state that confessions were put in evidence,[173] but in none of these cases have we any

This rule obtained in New York; cf. Livingston to Tryon, Nov. 10, 1772 (*Gratz Coll.* [Pa. Hist. Soc. Mss.]). "Brown could have been convicted on his own confession," but turned King's evidence.

[170] Horsmanden, *op. cit.* 336.

[171] *Ms. Mins. SCJ 1704/05–1709* 30. The case, perhaps, is an unusual one, since the usual sentence of thirty-nine lashes was not meted out, but the defendant was only fined £4 (*ibid.* 37).

[172] *Ms. Mins. Cir. 1721–49* 3, 4. Sam, a negro, was tried on an indictment for felony and burglary on Dec. 17, 1726, at Westchester Oyer and Terminer and General Gaol Delivery; five Crown witnesses were sworn, the "prisoner's examination read" in evidence for the prosecution, and Sam was found guilty by the jury and sentenced to be hanged (*ibid.* 47, 48).

[173] See, for example, King v. David Wallace and David Willson—counterfeiting, 1727 (*Ms. Mins. SCJ 1723–32* 9–11, 24); King v. George Brown—felony, 1738 (*Ms. Mins. Cir. 1721–49* 94, 95); King v. De Goede—grand larceny, 1755 (*Ms. Mins. SCJ 1754–57* [Engr.] 112, 114, 147, Jan. 23, 24, Apr. 19, 1755); King v. Sarah Gillet—grand larceny, 1768 (*Ms. Mins. SCJ 1766–69* [Engr.] 505, 506). Note also that endorsed on an indictment found against Darcus for burglary in April term, 1771, was the notation: "Witnesses: Prisoner's Ex-

indication how the defense was made or whether the confession was the basis for any examination of the defendant. Numerous confessions have been found which from the minutes do not appear to have been offered at trial; but sometimes an indictment will bear a note that a confession was part of the evidence.[174] In some cases where the Crown had a confession to use, the defendants in open court either confessed the indictment or pleaded *nolo contendere*.[175] Since it was quite a matter of chance that the indictment was endorsed with a notation respecting a confession, or that the confession itself is

amination [R.F. a named witness]," and also the notation, "Po: se cul" (*H.R. Pleadings* Pl. K. 348). King v. John Quain, Robert Fall and John Harriott —grand larceny (*Ms. Mins. NYCQS 1772–91* 175, Feb. 8, 1776; *Ms. Mins. SCJ 1775–81* [Engr.] 85, 86). Clergy was granted to Quain and Fall but we do not know what Harriott's fate was (*ibid.* 87).

[174] William Steel was indicted for grand larceny in April term, 1770, and endorsed on his indictment as "Witness" was "Criminals Examination." He was subsequently tried, convicted and granted clergy, but the minutes do not indicate whether or not his examination was read in evidence (*Ms. Mins. SCJ 1769–72* [Engr.] 193–195, 197, Apr. 27, 28, 1770).

Also see the case of Catherine Longworth, convicted and sentenced to hanging for housebreaking (*Ms. Mins. SCJ 1769–72* [Engr.] 471, 473, 477, Jan. 23, 24, 25, 1772). Endorsed on her indictment were the names of two witnesses and a reference to "Prisoner's Examination" but the minute entries contained no reference to the use of the examination in evidence; for the indictment see *H.R. Pleadings* Pl. K. 496.

In October, 1772, John Forster was indicted, tried, convicted and sentenced to thirty-nine lashes for petit larceny (*Ms. Mins. SCJ 1772–76* [Rough] 48, 49, 55, 60, Oct. 23, 24, 28, 31, 1772) and, while the minute entries do not record the use of his examination in evidence against him, we have nevertheless found among miscellaneous filed papers the following incriminating statement dated Oct. 20, 1772: "City of New York Ss: John Forster . . . being examined and on his Examination say [*sic*]; that this day, about Eleven O Clock in the fore noon he Entered the Cabben of a Wissil said to belong to Captain Robert Elder then lying at Cruger Wharf, and did then, and there take out of the said Cabben, the following goods to wit, two check Shirts, one D⁰ piller case, one towell, seven pair of Stocking, and one handkerchief and carried them from the said Cabben about forty or fifty yᵈˢ when he was apprehended by the Said Captain Elder. John Forster. Taken before Andrew Gautier." Not only did Forster's examination appear among the papers but the following affidavit by Elder is also to be found: "Deposition of Captain Elder agt John Forster. City of New York Ss: Captain Robert Elder . . . Marriner. being Duly

Sworn, and Saith that this Day. his Vessell was Robbed. of two check Shirts. one D. Pilliber, one towel Seven pair of Stocking & one handkerchief. and that the Said Goods were found In the possession of one John Forster of the Said City Taylor, & that the said goods are his [Elder's] property. Robert Elder. Sworn on the 20th day of october, 1772 before me Andrew Gautier. Robert Elder Bound to Prosecute" (*H.R. Pleadings* Pl. K. 457). It is also to be noted that endorsed on Forster's indictment which was filed on Oct. 23, 1772, is the following: "Witnesses: Captain Robert Elder and Prisoners Examination. Po: Se Cul" (*ibid.* Pl. K. 495).

On July 26, 1774, Christopher Henniger deposed on oath before a New York alderman and justice of peace that he saw John Stanworth break into a cellar. On the same day we find a record of the "Examination of John Stanworth . . . Charg'd upon the oath of Christopher Henniger with having . . . open'd the cellar," which examination was taken before the same alderman and signed by Stanworth. In the examination the accused said he did not unlock the cellar but may have gotten drunk "and tumbled into it" (*ibid.* Pl. K. 271). Stanworth was indicted, tried and convicted on July 29, 1774, and sentenced to be hanged the following day (*Ms. Mins. SCJ 1772–76* [Rough] 181, 183, 185), but neither in the minutes of the trial (*ibid.* 183) nor on the indictment itself (*H.R. Pleadings* Pl. K. 352) do we find any reference to the examination of July 26, 1774.

[175] Cf. King v. Lasher *et al.*—obstructing a highway, 1764 (*Ms. Mins. SCJ 1764–67* [Rough] 31, 41, *H.R. Pleadings* Pl. K. 739). King v. Catherine Johnson—grand larceny, 1766 (*Ms. Mins. SCJ 1764–67* [Rough] 135, 139; the examination is in *J. T. Kempe Lawsuits* J–L). King v. Thomas Norton and King v. Sam Ashcraft—grand larceny, 1767 (*Ms. Mins. SCJ 1764–67* [Rough] 279, *Ms. Mins. SCJ 1766–69* [Engr.] 318, 327; the examination is in *J. T. Kempe Lawsuits* A and L–O). King v. Juba, a slave—petit larceny, 1772 (*Ms. Mins. SCJ 1772–76* [Rough] 29, 37; the indictment *H.R. Pleadings* Pl. K. 470). King v. Edward Mathews—assault, 1771 (*Ms. Mins. SCJ 1769–72* [Engr.] 318, 403; the indictment *H.R. Pleadings* Pl. K. 385).

still available, the few cases just cited seem to us to possess a significance quite disproportionate to their number. They suggest that where a confession was available a case would not reach the stage of trial. This has possibly some bearing upon the extraordinary preponderance of guilty pleas in the inferior provincial courts and may explain the striking fact that after 1750 in some counties a jury trial of a criminal cause at Sessions was often a mere annual event. If this conjecture is correct it follows that the locus for the dispatch of a great deal of criminal business was the hearing before the justice, and the preliminary examination under the circumstances of limited professional aid for an accused appears as a standing impairment of privilege.

We think that the existence before the Revolution of a privilege of defendants is an illusion. The fruit grown from the seed of the maxim *nemo tenetur prodere seipso* was an exotic of Westminster Hall, and of it neither the local justices in England nor in New York had eaten, or if they had, they took good care to keep their knowledge to themselves.[176] The summary powers of justices were so considerable that there was a constant tendency to dispose of cases as they arose rather than to save them for Sessions. And in one county the justices seem to have exercised entire discretion whether or not they would handle petty offenders summarily or let them be tried at General Sessions.[177] The encroachments of the psychology of summary procedure upon the General Sessions is reflected in provincial minute books where the meetings of justices, the Special Sessions and the General Sessions of the Peace are indiscriminately entered, for often the lines that distinguish the procedure at one type of sitting from another are indistinct.[178] Moreover, down to the outbreak of revolt we find occasional entries at the formal General Sessions which demonstrate that the ancient practice persisted of questioning a defendant upon his arraignment and securing his submission.[179] It is obviously idle to imagine that

---

[176] The handbooks were not particularly helpful here; cf. Dalton, *Countrey Justice* (1677) c.165 §6. "The Offender himself shall not be examined upon Oath: for by the Common Law, *nullus tenetur seipsum prodere*. Neither was a man's fault to be wrung out of himself (no not by examination only) but to be proved by others until the Stat. 2 & 3 Ph. & M. c.10 gave Authority to the Justices of the Peace to examine the Felon himself."

[177] Cf. *Ms. Mins. Suffolk Co. Sess. 1723–51* 13, Mar. 1728: "Ordered that the Justices of the peace respectively in breaches of the peace may amerce the offender as a fine to the King six shillings and eight pence or bind them over to the court according as the nature of the offence shall require." In

an order of Mar. 27, 1744 the justices in the several towns were ordered to see that certain presentments were prosecuted according to the crimes therein specified.

[178] E.g., *Ms. Mins. Westch. Co. Sess. 1710–23; Ms. Mins. Ulster Co. Sess. 1711/12–1720; Ms. Mins. Albany Co. Sess. 1763–82.*

[179] Probably all the "humble submissions" were so handled. Cf. further King v. John Stanton, a free negro, presented for assault, where "the court examines the matter" and discharges (*Ms. Mins. Westch. Co. Sess. 1710–23*); Queen v. Pearce, presented for assault, where the defendant "owned he had done a foolish action" but denied evil intent (*Ms. Mins. Ulster Co. Sess. 1710/11–1720* Sept.

a "principle" which even Baron Gilbert forbears to mention, should have been cosseted in our own courts.

That a privilege against self-incrimination did not develop in a jurisdiction where the inhabitants were constantly rummaging in the storeroom of common law liberties, was the fault of neither the judiciary nor the bar, but was due to a prevailing indifference which is reflected in the general temper of provincial legislation. There had been great to-do in England during the early seventeenth century over the ex officio oath in ecclesiastical procedure, and although some disgruntled subjects had protested in 1640 that the secular adaptation of this proceeding involved a similar infraction of fundamental right,[180] nothing had come of the protest. The failure to carry over notions about self-incrimination to temporal justice is apparent in the unending stream of penal statutes where the usual procedure stipulated was information to a magistrate and conviction by the oath of one or two witnesses or by the defendant's confession alone. As we have already seen this was a favorite device in New York recurring as it does with regularity in the provincial penal statutes.

Imperviousness to the safeguards for defendants is exemplified still further in the colonial acts which institute an oath of purgation. The first act where this was used was in a statute to prevent the supply of liquor to Indians in Albany County.[181] It was provided that wherever a person was suspected of an infraction the mayor, recorder or any two justices of the town or county of Albany could summon such person and tender to him "on oath whether he she or they hath sold, given or other ways disposed of any of ye liquors . . . to an Indian." If the person suspected confessed upon oath or refused the oath he should be taken as convicted and subject to certain penalties. At the following session, in an amendment to the act for the encouragement of seamen, a similar procedure was introduced for tavern keepers who, to defeat the statutory limitation on the credit allowed seamen, took any bonds, bills or specialties from such seamen.[182]

In 1712, following the negro plot scare, the drastic act for the suppression of conspiracies[183] naïvely incorporated a provision that a person who knew or was suspected of knowing an entertainer of slaves and did not report to a magistrate would be tendered an oath and so purge himself. If he refused or

---

1713, Mar. 2, 1713/14); King v. McNess, presented for nuisance, pleaded not guilty but "on interrogation" submits (*Ms. Mins. Charlotte Co.* [*Washington*] *Sess. 1773–1800* Jan. 10, 1775).
[180] 1 *Worcestershire County Records* 684.

[181] 1 *Col. Laws NY* 658. The form of oath is in a renewing statute, *ibid.* 890.
[182] *Ibid.* 681.
[183] *Ibid.* 764.

failed to discover the entertainer he was subject to £2 fine or jail until he satisfied the fine.

This new procedure having secured the confidence of the legislators was employed thereafter until the very eve of the Revolution. It was extended to persons abusing Indians,[184] to persons suspected of trading with the French,[185] to persons accused of selling liquor to Indians without license,[186] to persons taking and not declaring goods for Oswego,[187] to tavern keepers suspected of selling liquor to apprentices and receiving property in payment,[188] to shipmasters required to report copper imported into the province,[189] to persons suspected of disaffection,[190] to persons suspected of taking articles in pawn from Indians,[191] to persons concealing an insolvent's assets,[192] to persons suspected of conducting a private lottery.[193]

The parallel between this purgation procedure and the ecclesiastical forms against which the English Puritans had so bitterly inveighed is strikingly illustrated in the act against gaming of 1774[194] which gave an action of debt against persons winning at play and stipulated that a person sued or liable to be sued should "be obliged and compellable to answer upon oath such bill or bills as shall be preferred against him for discovering the money won at play."

It must not be supposed that in these various acts the provincial assembly was making experiment with something new. Long before New York was settled, English magistrates administering the bastardy statute were compelling women to disclose under oath the parentage of the bastard and, as we have seen, this practice was used in New York,[195] even though the woman might be committed or punished. Furthermore, the putative father might also be obliged to affirm or deny under oath his alleged paternity. There is also some slight evidence to show that even in circumstances where there was no statutory warrant whatever, a defendant might be allowed to "swear off" a charge. Thus, in 1701/02 William Fowler accused of uttering chipped coins was allowed to purge himself,[196] and much later, in 1763, a Dutchess justice allowed John Edwards, complained of for a robbery, to take oath that he was innocent.[197]

[184] *Ibid.* 828 (1714).
[185] *Ibid.* 99 (1722).
[186] *Ibid.* 245 (1725).
[187] *Ibid.* 710 (1731).
[188] *Ibid.* 954 (1737).
[189] *Ibid.* 962 (1737).
[190] 3 *ibid.* 424 (1744).
[191] 4 *ibid.* 349 (1759).
[192] 5 *ibid.* 130 (1770).

[193] *Ibid.* 354 (1772). We have not listed all the various reenactments. Cf. Jackson's adverse report, 5 *Acts of the Privy Council, Colonial* 381.
[194] *Ibid.* 623.
[195] *Supra* c. II nn. 187, 311; c. VII n. 182.
[196] *Ms. Mins. NYCQS 1694–1731/32* 68, Feb. 4, 1701/02.
[197] *J. T. Kempe Lawsuits* C–F; *Ms. Mins. SCJ 1762–64* (Engr.) 175, 176.

On the basis of the evidence here assembled, the conclusion is inescapable that so far as New York Province was concerned there was no attempt made to privilege a defendant or to treat his testimony as incompetent; but on the contrary, a great deal was done to make sure that in one form or other his testimony would be secured and that it would count against him. The shadowy protection offered by the rule that a confession could not be under oath,[198] was quite offset in the cases where he could be convicted on a confession alone and by those where he was required to trap himself by a purging oath. This indifference to any privilege against self-incrimination probably embraced witnesses generally although we have found but one case. Here witnesses were arrested after giving incriminating testimony. There is no particle of proof to show that they were aware such testimony ought not be compelled or that they were in any way cautioned by the court.[199] Whatever may be the colonial background of the later constitutional protection, it derives, as far as New York is concerned, from a very tardy realization that such protection was desirable.

The Closing and the Charge

The evidence being in, the defendant's case was brought to a close by an address to the jury. In a letter written by James Alexander shortly before his death the requisites of a proper "speech to a jury" were set out:

. . . every part of it ought to be connected with the evidence by reference to such a deed which says so and so—such a writing so and so—such witness declared so and so. These are constantly to be the premises upon which the speech is to be founded, and when the premises you reason upon are fixed, proceed in reasonable observations and consequences—but referring to or relying upon things not given in evidence, though perfectly known to you is departing from the evidence in the cause, and flying at random, which must be destructive to a good cause but a bad one has occasion for it.

To use an argument unsupported by the evidence is murdering a cause, for the opposite side will drop all your material arguments well supported and insist on

[198] Only in this detail do the colonists seem to have been particular. The confessions are never under oath and even the examinations before the Council are not. Cf. the examination of Bernardus Swartwout (*James Alexander Papers* Box 48) and of John Baptist Van Eps (*Misc. Mss. Albany Co. 1691-1729*) charged with spreading false reports among the Indians.
[199] Cf. Queen v. Ann Clay (1703), where a Crown witness stated defendant had passed certain

goods out of a window to him. He was ordered into custody (*Ms. Mins. SCJ 1701-04* 85, 88). In a few cases, witnesses were proceeded against for perjury. In King v. Wilks (1756), Thos. Sperham, a defendant's witness, ordered to be informed against (*supra* n. 77). See also King v. Elizabeth Van Sice (*Ms. Mins. SCJ 1764-67* [Rough] 64, 69) and King v. Garrett (*Ms. Mins. NYCQS 1772-91* 95, May 6, 1774; *H.R. Pleadings* Pl. K. 309).

those not supported and refer the jury to those as specimens of your arguments.[199a]

Most of the early examples of defendants' closing, however, contain little or no comment on the evidence. Neither Nicoll nor Emott in their closing for Colonel Bayard[200] dwelt upon the glaring omissions in the Crown's case, but devoted themselves to a discussion of the law. The same tactics were followed in *Queen* v. *Makemie* where the counsel hammered away at the inapplicability of certain acts of Parliament,[201] and in *King* v. *Zenger* where Hamilton with great guile expounded his notions of the jury's function in libel cases.[202] The only non-professional closing we have seen are the remarks of John Ury on trial for conspiracy and for being a priest, a rather pathetic and earnest explanation of his situation and an attempt to discount the late boiling of stories against him.[203]

For the latter years of the colonial period we have seen only rough notes of closings. For example, in *King* v. *Robert Campbell and Archibald Livingston* informed against for assaulting an undersheriff (a case discussed in Chapter III), the summation of Kissam for the defense is outlined:

The Several Circumstances in which the evidence clashes—Question which witnesses ought to be believed—Charge of a high crime—Consequences bad to the Deft:—They are to be fined at the *Discretion of the Crown*—Charged in the Information that the Defts knew—Law never meant that an officer should treat a prisoner ill—Campbell put away the pistol—The Weight of the Evidence should be given to the 5 Witnesses.[204]

Another closing of this same attorney is outlined in the trial notes of *King* v. *John Taylor* who was prosecuted for an assault on Joan Griffiths. Taylor was a marshal who had been active against disorderly houses. Joan, who had been in trouble on this account, came to Taylor's house and lured away one Captain Wiley whom Taylor sought to rescue from the temptress and in the execution of this design Joan was beaten. The Crown put Joan on the stand and

[199a] Sedgwick, *Memoir of the Life of William Livingston* 49 n.
[200] 14 Howell, *State Trials* 495 *et seq.* These remarks are published as if they were an opening for the defendant, for the account shows Bayard calling some character witnesses after counsel finished. We think there must have been a mistake in the printing for the general character of the speeches indicates clearly and certainly that they were the summation for the defendant.

[201] 4 Force, *Tracts* no. 4.
[202] *The Trial of John Peter Zenger* 21 *et seq.*
[203] Horsmanden, *op. cit.* 299, 311. Ury opened with a speech but the court broke in, "Mr. Ury if you have any witnesses to examine it is more proper you should do that now, and make your defence afterwards." Later Ury read again what he had stated at the opening of this defense.
[204] H.R. *Pleadings* Pl. K. 1064.

two others who had little to tell. The defense put on several witnesses who contradicted the prosecution's version. Kissam's remarks are reported as follows:

> Taylor a Marshall—Diligent in suppression of bad Houses—The Bawdy Houskeepers his Enemies—Mrs. Griffiths denies striking Taylor—Mrs. Griffiths seems under prejudices—Voher [a defense witness] cold dispassionate sensible—Voher proves she made the first assault—Voher the most credible Evidence—If the blow was not given in the Entry—He was justifiable in kicking her in the Entry. She lugged him by the hair. Dun and Griffiths (Crown witnesses) the only material evidence.

Duane, Kissam's co-counsel, made a few additional remarks, and it may have been his unfortunate statement that it was "not a matter of importance striking such a woman" which caused a verdict of guilty.[205]

By far the most elaborate notes on a defense closing are those taken on William Smith Jr.'s speech in the case of *King* v. *Van Rensselaer,* the intrusion case discussed in Chapter IV. Smith began with some remarks about the "Heavy Arm of the Crown," and spoke of the antiquity of the Van Rensselaer patent referring to the fact that there were "many Patents in like Circumstances." He went on to define what the Crown had to prove and then explained why the Crown had intended a large grant to the Van Rensselaers. The confirmation of the Dutch grants was gone over, the rights under the capitulation of 1664 and the fact that this was a grant to a whole family. The evidence regarding the description and the survey was examined at great length and then the Livingston grants were discussed and the conveyances from the Indians. The arrangement of the arguments was skillful, for first every freeholder whose rights depended on a royal patent was made uneasy about the "heavy arm," then everyone whose metes and bounds depended on a natural landmark, and the spectre of the Indian deed was produced as a final touch to terrify the juror whose title may have been derived from such a source.[206]

The closings for the Crown seem in general to have laid much stress upon the evidence—distinguishing, emphasizing and commenting. At the Bayard trial, Weaver ignored the law cited by defendant's counsel and limited himself to summing up the evidence "as to matter of fact." Bickley's summation in *Queen* v. *Makemie* is a mere abstract, and in *King* v. *Zenger,* Richard Brad-

---

[205] "Notes on Trial, King v. Taylor," 1771 (*J. T. Kempe Lawsuits* S–U).
[206] "Notes on Mr. Smith Jr.s Argument" (*J. T.*

Kempe Lawsuits V). These are four legal cap pages of closely written notes. Unfortunately a mouse has ravaged the margins.

ley's speech is briefly reported as brushing aside the defense's references to *Sir Edward Hale's Case* and *Bushel's Case* and insisting that since the printing and publishing of the paper were confessed the jury could do nothing but convict.[207]

The cases just mentioned were all "state trials" upon which considerable preparation was lavished. There has fortunately been preserved the summation by James Alexander in a routine felony case tried at Circuit (1721), *King* v. *Moras* in which the defendant was indicted for feloniously taking £27. Moras had taken the money from one Merrit and had turned over £25 to Isaac Jacobs who escaped to Connecticut. Alexander said:

> . . . the Prisoner . . . has never offered to give any account where he got the bags its the greatest presumption & probability that he was the person who stole it
>
> But Mr Lyon tells you further that upon the jews frighting him with takeing him up he gave him money to Let him go which he never would have done had not he been guilty
>
> This as I said Gentlemen is fuller proof than has been in a ~~hundred~~ 1000 criminal cases where the criminal has been found guilty. But Seeing there's Evidence by his confession that puts all past any dispute we'll insist on this no longer but give you his own Confessions Deliverance Brown, Richard Ogden Andrew Merrit John Lyon Jun[r] Justice Purdie
>
> After so particular & full Evidence Every part of it almost proveing the fact Laid in the Inditement I think it needless . . . [to repeat it] . . . so shall conclude with the 13th verse of the 7th chapter of Joshua in the case of . . . the thief. Thus Saith the Lord god of Israel there is an accursed thing in the midst of thee O Israel thow canst not Stand before thine Enemies untill ye take away the accursed thing from amongst you.[208]

Horsmanden published three summations of the elder William Smith at the negro plot trials in 1741. That in *King* v. *Ury* has already been referred to and it may be added further that Smith also dwelt largely on the heinousness of the papists and seems to have revelled in exciting the Protestant prejudices of his audience. In *King* v. *Roosevelt's Quack and Phillipse's Cuffee*, the evidence was again commented upon and in a most prejudicial manner. The Crown's case had been opened with an inflammatory address by Attorney

---

[207] King v. Bayard (14 Howell, *State Trials* 503); Queen v. Makemie (4 Force, *Tracts* no. 4). The remarks are devoted chiefly to answering the objections that the Acts of Parliament did not ap- ply. King v. Zenger (*The Trial of John Peter Zenger* 46).

[208] *James Alexander Papers* Box 60; cf. *supra* 368 n. 163.

General Bradley, but the final remarks of Smith were supercharged. The same combination of passions characterizes the opening and closing of the prosecution in the case against the Hughsons.[209]

For the second half of the eighteenth century the chief source of information regarding the closing speech for the Crown is in the various notes taken on trial. Many of these are in J. T. Kempe's handwriting and it is obvious that the purpose of noting the purport of each witness's testimony was for the necessary comment, just as the précis of defense counsel's remarks was for rebuttal. No complete verbatim account of any closing either by William or by J. T. Kempe has been found. In some cases, as *King* v. *Campbell and Livingston* and *King* v. *Major Pullen,* only the briefest sketch for summing up was jotted down. More elaborate notes made at the trial of Cockrain for murder at the Albany Circuit, 1770, give some notion of J. T. Kempe's technique.[210]

1 Heinousness of Murder
2 Legal Idea of Malice
3 Consequence to the prisoner. to the public
4 Whether Murder or not depends on temper of Mind
 Intention
 Circumstances—previous & at the Time
 Circumstances previous
  a had differences
  b 2 days before he & negro pursued with a knife & club
  c Swore he would crack his Backbone &c.
 Circumstances at the Time
  1 Went into the Woods under the pretence of forewarning him from cutting &c.
  2 Spoke softly
  3 Nevertheless took away his axe
  4 Could not suppose he would yield his property peaceably
  5 Quarrel of necessity
  6 Killed him on spot
  7 Evidence of the attack & beating
 Circumstances just after the Death
  1 Threatened Vanderburgh . . .
  2 Take away your Master, You deserve to be as he is
  3 Sometime after this repeated it

---

[209] King v. Ury (Horsmanden, *op. cit.* 316); King v. Roosevelt's Quack and Phillipse's Cuffee (*ibid.* 92); King v. Hughson *et al.* (*ibid.* 119).

[210] *J. T. Kempe Lawsuits* C–F.

4 Owned he had given him a good dressing
5 Left him there—If not dead he must have froze to Death
The Manner of the beating
    Defense
1 Behaved civil
2 Van Alen attacked first
3 Fell over a log
4 Died by the fall
5 Did not beat him to hurt him
6 Gave him but 2 or three blows & whipped his Backside
7 To affront & not to hurt him much
8 Took possession of his horse.

It will be observed that in this case Kempe touched upon the legal elements necessary to establish murder. In certain cases it was customary for King's counsel to deal elaborately with the law if such questions arose. Thus at the trial of Roper Dawson[211] for murder a special memorandum covering a great number of authorities was prepared, apparently to forestall a manslaughter verdict. The use of such authorities is illustrated by Kissam's closing at the trial of William Prendergast for treason at the Dutchess Assizes in 1766.[212]

Kissam Sums up—Observes the Charge in the Indictmt distinguishes between Express and constructive levying of War Observes that the evidence will amount to the last and from the Evidences raises the particular points of fact evincive of a Constructive levying of War. Then produces the following authorities

Foster p. 211 Note the generality of the whole / id 213 / Poph: 122 / Kieling 19 / Foster 118 / Kieling 75 / Hawkins.

He then proceeded to deal with the evidence:

1. A Resolution of the Mob to rescue persons out of all Gaols who were imprisoned for the Mob or for Rents. This fact proved by Moss Kent, George Hepburn James Livingston, Eliphalet Stephens. Several other witnesses to this point but as to Generality of Resolution not so full. 2. This design tho not expressly avowed by the prisoner yet it appears he acted in two Gaol deliveries with the very Mob some of whom had avowed the Generality of their Design and of which he appears to be a leader. This point proved by Tenbrook James Livingston as to the Gaol delivery effected at Poghkeepsie, Eliphalet Stephens Samuel Tower as to gaol delivery at New York 3. The revenging himself agt

Justice Peters for executing his office The witnesses to this fact are Justice Peters, George Hughson, Reuben Garlick. 4. Making proclamations forbidg. all officers to execute any process.

It seems to us highly unlikely that the closing speeches after 1750 were as arid as they appear in the notes taken at trial. Those were the days when revolution was smoldering and was soon to be fanned by the stirring speeches of the Liberty Boys. We can be sure that counsel were not ignorant of the American passion for oratory, and so, for example, when it is drily noted that Thomas Smith, defending Patrick Walsh for an assault, said the defendant "will be in the Mercy of the King's judges,"[213] there was surely a proper and heartwarming embellishment of the theme.

No evidence has been found that counsel for the defendant was accustomed to request the court to charge in a particular form. Indeed, the only example of such a request is in the exceptions which J. T. Kempe vainly endeavored to get Judge Jones to seal in the case of *King* v. *Van Rensselaer*.[214] In this case the question of guilt turned on the interpretation of the grants, the location of the landmarks and the completeness of the survey. Kempe

> did request the said Justice to give in charge to the Jurors afores^d. that the Law is that where a Grant of the Crown for Lands is doubtfull and will admit of two Constructions such Construction Shall take place as will pass the least Land, and the said Atty General did further insist that the said several Grants to Killian Van Renselaer and Killian Van Renselaer so given in Evidence of on the part of the Def^t as to the second Tract of Land therein described & now in Question are void in Law for uncertainty in the Boundaries thereof and requested the sd Justice to charge the said Jurors that the said Grants from the Crown last mentioned were void in Law as to the said Tract therein mentioned now in Question for uncertainty in the Boundaries of the same Tract therein mentioned. And the said Atty General did further request the said Justice to direct the said Jurors to find their verdict specially as the Matters of Law which would arise thereon were of Great difficulty and Importance.

These charges Jones declined to make in this form, and we shall shortly see how he did charge.

The absence of proof on requests to charge is not necessarily conclusive, but if it was usual, so careful and attentive a prosecutor as John Tabor Kempe would have made some memorandum, for there was little he did not remem-

---

[213] *J. T. Kempe Lawsuits* W–Y.   [214] *J. T. Kempe Lawsuits* V *sub nom.* Van Rensselaer.

brance even in routine cases. We are disposed to believe that the rather elaborate legal arguments offered in some of the summations took the place of the formal request to charge. In consequence, counsel, performing the double task of persuading in a single speech the judge as to the law and the jury as to the tenor of the evidence, might undermine the effect of what the court eventually might choose to say. Unfortunately, the specimens of charges that we have seen are poor examples. Atwood's charge in the Bayard case is a mere paraphrase, but it clearly overstepped the bounds of a mere summing up and the statement of the law was incorrect.[215] The charge of Mompesson, C.J., in *Queen* v. *Makemie* is a masterpiece of irresolution. The case hinged on whether certain acts of Parliament applied in the colonies and whether the Queen's instructions were a "law" upon which an indictment could be founded:[216]

> Gentlemen, You have heard a great deal on both sides, and Mr. Attorney says the fact is confessed by the Defendant, and I would have you bring it in specially, for there are some points I am not now prepared to answer; How far Instructions may go, in having the force of a Law, especially when not published, or made known: And there is one objection made by Mr. Makemie, and that is the Oath of Supremacy of England is abolished; & how far it will go in this matter, I confess I am not prepared to answer; if You will take upon you to judge of Law, you may, or bring in the fact specially: This is the first Instance I can learn, has been a Tryal or Prosecution of this nature in America.

Equally remarkable is the charge of De Lancey in *King* v. *Zenger*. At the outset of his argument, Hamilton had trapped the Chief Justice into the remark, "All words are libellous or not as they are understood. Those who are to judge of the words must judge whether they are scandalous or ironical, tend to the breach of the peace or are seditious: there can be no doubt of it."[217] When it came to the charge, De Lancey remarked that Hamilton had taken pains to show that juries should pay little attention to what the judge might say. "I shall, therefore, only observe to you that as facts or words in the information are confessed the only thing that can come before you is whether the words as set forth in the information make a libel. And that is a matter of law, no doubt which you may leave to the court." He then read from Holt's charge in *Tutchin's Case*[218] which concluded that the jury was to consider whether the words tended to beget an ill opinion of the government.[219]

[215] 14 Howell, *State Trials* 503.
[216] 4 Force, *Tracts* no. 4, 44.
[217] *The Trial of John Peter Zenger* 28.

[218] 14 Howell, *State Trials* 1128 (1704).
[219] *The Trial of John Peter Zenger* 47.

A few other examples of charges have been found. Two are printed in Horsmanden's account of the negro plot. At the trial of the Hughsons, the court remarked it was not necessary to recapitulate the evidence, and said merely that if the jury could not credit the witnesses for the Crown, it should acquit; but if the evidence against the prisoners "seems to be so ample, so full, so clear and satisfactory, if you have no particular reasons in your own breasts, in your own consciences to discredit them," it should find them guilty.[220] The other charge was in the case of five Spanish negroes who had claimed to be free. The court stated that one of the indictments was grounded upon an act of assembly which made the testimony of one slave against another "legal evidence." The court proceeded to explain that from the decree of the Admiralty Court and the evidence of the vendue master it appeared the defendants were slaves and no evidence to the contrary had been offered. If the jury decided they were slaves, it was to consider the negro testimony. In any event, if they were free or slave, the main question was whether they were guilty of the second indictment of conspiring to burn the town and destroy the people. To prove the charge there was only one witness, Mary Burton, "nevertheless one witness is sufficient and if you give credit to her testimony you will no doubt discharge a good conscience and find them guilty; if you have a sufficient reason in your own minds to discredit her testimony, if you can think so you must then acquit them" but all the prisoners were equally involved in the testimony.[221]

We do not know how consistently the judges kept notes on trials for the purpose of making a charge. The trial notes in Kempe's handwriting we have assumed were taken to furnish the basis for the Crown's closing. Other notes in unidentifiable hands may possibly have been the notes taken by the judges. In one case, however, *King* v. *Caleb Pell,* where Pell was prosecuted for a cheat, the trial notes are in Judge John Chambers' hand, and a charge is written out. He charged as follows:

The Defendant is prosecuted as a cheat on his father by imposing upon him to Sign a deed for Land to him instead of a power of attorney and the Question is if he be Guilty or not. On the part of the Deft it is proved there was such a deed and the deed speaks for itself and as the witness one Edward Barton and Thos Fisher. If you believe Fisher, Barton understood it to be a deed for land & so did he. On the part of the Crown Several circumstantial evidences are introduced in order to prove the cheat by which the father acted. The credibility and character of the Evidence are your proper province and therefore if upon the

[220] Horsmanden, *op. cit.* 120.   [221] *Ibid.* 160.

whole you are fully satisfied in your consciences that the deft. did impose on his father you ought to find him guilty otherwise not.[222]

In the case of *King* v. *Van Rensselaer* we possess only Kempe's version of the parts of the charge to which he objected and which Judge Jones did not think was a correct version. We quote the charge as reported, and although without the grants themselves it is in particulars nearly meaningless, the direction to the jurors to supply lines which Jones thought proper seems curious indeed:[223]

That the Line from Wahankaseck on Hudsons River in the said Grants mentioned should run Twenty four Miles on an Easterly Course, because such distance and Line is certain & observed in his said Charge that the place called Wawanaquaseck was a Heap of Stones that might be removed and therefore an uncertain Boundary. And the said Justice did further give in Charge to the s[d] Jurors That it was the Opinion of the sd. Justice that from the Termination of the said 24 Miles a Line should be drawn to the Head of Kinderhook Creek and that the same is the Head of the Creek by Major Abraham Staats's meant by that Boundary in the said Grants, and that another Line should be supplied by the said Jurors from the Head of the said Kinderhook Creek to the Mouth of the Creek by Major Abraham Staats on Hudsons River, as a closing Line of the second Tract mentioned in the s[d] Grants under which the Def[t] claims Title and that tho' there appeared to him a little uncertainty as to the s[d] last mentioned Line, yet as there are a Number of Patents for Lands in this Province, which are imperfect in their description, and as Isaac Vrooman and another Surveyor had Sworn that as to many of such Tracts so imperfectly described they had in Surveying the same supplied a closing Line from the last Boundary therein mentioned respectively to the place of Beginning, he the said Justice could not adopt an Opinion that such Grants were void for such uncertainty in Description, And the s[d] Justice did further give in Charge to the s[d] Jurors, that tho by Law the Kings Grants are void for uncertainty and that tho where the Kings Grants are capable of two Constructions, such Construction ought by Law to prevail as will pass the least Land to the Subject, yet that in the present Case it was his Opinion that the Grants under which the Def[t] claims the Lands now in Question are sufficiently certain as to the Bounds of the said second Tract aforesaid, and that there is no uncertainty as to what is meant in the said Grants by the Head of the said Creek by Major Abraham Staats as aforesaid. . . .

222 *John Chambers Mss.* Box 1.
223 *J. T. Kempe Lawsuits* V *sub nom.* Van

Rensselaer. Jones denied he told the jury to supply the line (*Misc. Mss. Claverack*).

These specimens of charges are a slight foundation upon which to build any generalizations. If they are at all typical it is obvious that the jury derived most of its guidance as to the weight and effect of the evidence and as to the law from the arguments of counsel. Under these circumstances it is understandable that, as in the Makemie and the Zenger cases, the jury might encroach upon the judicial function and settle whether as a matter of law a particular accusation was a crime. The charge in *King* v. *Caleb Pell* is certainly no proof that the judges had become more instructive as the century advanced and with Horsmanden serving as Chief Justice until 1778, the presumptions are against a change.

Verdict

After the charge, the jury was left to deliberate on its verdict, a process which might be accomplished without going from the bar.[224] Usually, however, the jury withdrew and a constable was sworn to attend. The constable's oath required:[225]

> You shall well and truly keep every person sworn of this inquest together in some private and convenient Room without Meat, Drink, Fire or Candle light. You shall suffer no person whatever to speak to them or any of them, neither shall you yourself speak to them or any of them unless to . . . [know] if they are agreed on their verdict.[226]

The common law apparently proceeded on the theory that conscience-searching best went forward with a little fasting. Any relaxation of the ancient ritual even during the course of a trial needed a rule of the court. Thus in *King* v. *Van Rensselaer*, the court made the following rule on October 25, 1768:

> It appearing to the Court that the Jury would not be able to go through the Trial of this Cause without Rest and Refreshment, and the Parties on both sides agreeing to an Adjournment of the Jury and that they should be committed to the Care of the Elizors, the Court ordered that they be adjourned until nine o Clock tomorrow.[227]

224 E.g., King v. Wright (*Ms. Mins. SCJ 1764–67* [Rough] 273, 274); King v. Welch (*Ms. Mins. NYCQS 1772–91* 114, Nov. 2, 1774).

225 On the flyleaf of *Ms. Mins. SCJ 1756–61* (Rough).

226 *Ms. Mins. SCJ 1750–56* (Rough) 1 has another oath: "You shall go out with such jurors as shall have leave of the Court and suffer no Person

to speak to them but take Care that they return immediately to Court so help you God." The oath in the text is the time-honored one used at English trials.

227 On the following day, that is, Oct. 26, 1768, "the jury called over and appearing, the court proceed to the trial of this cause" (*Ms. Mins. SCJ 1766–69* [Engr.] 557, 558). It will be remembered

Once the jury had left the bar it might be sent for if it had been out overlong, but the court was supposed to leave the jurors to their own devices. No evidence except that written and under seal could be taken out,[228] and if their recollections had to be refreshed this had to be done in open court.[229] In the Makemie case the act of assembly was taken out by the jury,[230] but no other proof of such a practice has been found. At the trial of Colonel Bayard, the jury was sent for and as no verdict had been reached, further directions were asked. The foreman read from some notes he had taken of the evidence, but the defense denied the evidence had been given and asked the Chief Justice to satisfy the jury "of the truth of the evidence." Atwood replied he could give a further charge as to the law, but if the jury had any trouble with matters of fact "they might find the prisoner guilty or he could move in arrest of judgment." Emott, for the defense, protested violently to this remark, but Atwood silenced him and thereupon "renewed" his charge to the jury.[231]

The proceedings in the case of Hutchins were equally prejudicial. According to an affidavit of Clowes, a witness, Atwood sent a constable

to ask the Jury if they were agreed, or if they had anything to say to ye Court. The Constable brought word they were not agreed. . . . Nevertheless the Judge . . . ordered the Jury to come to him. Mr. Emott opposed it saying it was unprecedented but was overruled. . . . The Judge told them [the jury] he had before informed them . . . to send no Message to him notwithstanding which there had been sollicitation made to him from them for [a copy of] an act of Parliament [viz., the Bill of Rights] . . . which act could be of no use to them he opined. He opened ye matter to them largely and sumed up the evidence in doeing of which he said Mr. Clewes said . . . that these things had rendered the government vile and cheap . . . Mr. Emmet opposed his giving a new charge to the jury which put the Judge in a great passion. He threatened Emmet with prison y[t]. Emett said Clewes did not say [that these things had rendered the government vile and cheap]. . . .

At this point, Clowes broke in,

No I never said so. Chief Justice in a passion: I know not . . . whether . . . you are afraid to give your evidence . . . but every time you come you swear less and less as I can shew you. S. Clewes: I beg yr Honors Pardon that cannot be

---

that in the Attorney General's report of Feb. 10, 1773, to the Governor and Council in connection with this case, he stated that the trial lasted ten days (*Misc. Mss. Claverack*).

228 2 Hale, *op. cit.* 307.
229 *Ibid.* 296.
230 4 Force, *Tracts* no. 4.
231 14 Howell, *State Trials* 505 *et seq.*

shewed to me. I am certaine. My evidence has allways been the same. I am an Englishman and afraid of no man. I never said that these things *has* rendered the government so [i.e., vile and cheap]; neither did I ever say positively that ye speaker [of the Assembly] *was* an alien (tho yr Honor said both in yr charge) what you may do by implication I know not but I never said so.

In the affidavits of George Stanton and Robert Anderson respecting Hutchins' trial it was stated

that Alderman Hutchins pray'd the Judge that if anything of matter of law offered in his favor that he [the Judge] would be of Councill for him and inform the Jury in his behalf. That instead of soe doing the said Atwood pleaded more in his charge to the jury against the said Hutchins than the King's Councill had done upon the whole tryall.[232]

The records show various occasions where the jury was sent for and then sent back for further deliberation,[233] and sometimes, as in *King* v. *Lawrence,* the foreman would state that it was desired to bring in a special verdict.[234] So far as we can ascertain, however, there never again in provincial New York occurred episodes like that in the Hutchins case.

In the *posteas* and judgment rolls, jury verdicts are stated in set formulae. In the minute books, however, since the verdict was delivered orally and the clerk catechised the foreman in the case of acquittal as to flight, and in case of conviction as to goods and lands,[235] the verdicts are entered in the most various of

---

[232] Eng. Mss. XLVI, 158 *et seq., Misc. Mss. Bayard.* John Ellison and James Wright, an undersheriff, filed affidavits in which they stated substantially that after the jurors were sent out a constable was sent to inquire whether they were agreed on a verdict, and although a negative reply was received together with a request for another half hour to deliberate, nevertheless Chief Justice Atwood called the jury back and "gave them a very severe charge against the prisoner . . . told them they could do no less than bring him in guilty for they had a very good example before them . . . Coll. Bayard who was condemned some little time before for the same crime that Hutchins was now tryed for." Atwood threatened that if the jurors did not find Hutchins guilty "on the president of Bayards Tryal" he would fine or otherwise punish them.

[233] E.g., King v. Baker, 1702 (*Ms. Mins. SCJ 1701–04* 61, 62); Queen v. Sam, a slave, *et al.* (*Ms. Mins. NYCQS 1694–1731/32* 213, Apr. 12, 1712); King v. Bergen *et al.,* 1717 (*Ms. Mins. Cir. 1716–17* 39); King v. Jaef, 1746 (*Ms. Mins. Cir. 1721–49* 118). An amusing case in which the

jury failed to agree on a verdict was a long ejectment case at the Albany Court for the Trial of Causes brought to issue in the Supreme Court held on Sept. 18 and 19, 1721: "The time being expired for holding ye court by his Majesty's ordinance it was not adjourned but on Tuesday morning the judge went into the courthouse to receive the verdict and the jury, asked whether they had agreed on their verdict, answered that there were an abundance of papers read which they did not understand, so they left it to the judge, who finding the ignorance and obstinacy of the jury to be Verry great and the court not having been oppened at Albany in the time appointed by the ordinance, he thought it impracticable to force the jury to agree. Therefore he rose up without saying anything to them and ordered me to make this entry in the minutes" (*Ms. Mins. Cir. 1721–49* 253).

[234] *Ms. Mins. SCJ 1756–61* (Rough) 225.

[235] Stubbs, *Crown Circuit Companion* 14. *Nulla bona,* or *cat.* [with the amount] *retraxit,* or *nec retraxit,* as the return might be, was supposed to be endorsed on the indictment.

ways, especially in the late seventeenth and early eighteenth centuries before the clerks had become completely familiar with the English forms. Some of these entries are set forth below.[236] It may be observed at this point that in cases sent down for trial at nisi prius, it was the formula written in the *postea* that was before the Supreme Court at bar when it came to pronounce the final judgment.[237]

[236] At the trial of George Recarrick in Aug. 1691, in New York Quarter Sessions, "The jury brings in the Defendant not Guilty of the tresspasse in the Indictment Charged" (*Ms. Mins. NYCQS 1683/84–1694* 150, Aug. 4, 1691). On the trial of Garrett Hardenburgh, on an indictment for nuisance, "the jury finde for the defendant. Ordered the defendant be discharged paying fees" (*Ms. Mins. NYCQS 1694–1731/32* 4, Nov. 7, 1694). William Elwood was tried on Apr. 8, 1696, on an indictment for murder, and "the jury finde the prisoner not guilty nor that he did flee. Delivered by proclamation three times made" (*Mins. SCJ 1693–1701* 91). David Provoost Jr. was tried at New York Quarter Sessions in June, 1703, and "the jurors say upon their Oath that the Defendt is not Guilty of Making a false return of Alderman . . . Therefore . . . the Defendt. be discharged . . . paying fees" (*Ms. Mins. NYCQS 1694–1731/32* 81, June 1, 1703). In Queen v. Justus Bush (1710), although the defendant was tried on an indictment "The Jury ffind ye Defendant to be discharged from his recognizance paying fees" (*Ms. Mins. SCJ 1710–14* 289). On Sept. 14, 1716, Rachell Van Anthon was tried on an indictment for murdering her child, and "the jury find the prisoner not guilty of the murder whereof she stands indicted nor that she did fly for it to their knowledge" (*Ms. Mins. Cir. 1716–17* 28). Frank, a free negress, was tried and convicted as an accessory to a felony, and the jury used the following language: "The Jury find the defendant guilty of the felony whereof she stands indicted. Nulla Bona nec Retraxit" (*Ms. Mins. NYCQS 1694–1731/32* 362, Aug. 5, 1719). James Morgan was tried for feloniously breaking in and stealing several parcels of plate from Cornelius Wynekoop, and on June 13, 1726, "the jury find the defendant not guilty and that he did not fly for it and ordered the prisoner be discharged paying fees" (*Ms. Mins. SCJ 1723–27* 200). On Dec. 16, 1726, at Westchester Oyer and Terminer and General Gaol Delivery, the following verdict was brought in against Benjamin Willson on three indictments for felony: "The jury appear and find the prisoner guilty of three indictments for felony and that he had no lands or tenements goods or at the time of the felony committed or at any time since to their knowledge" (*Ms. Mins. Cir. 1721–49* 47). Philip Griffin and Thomas Jolly were tried on an indictment for felony "and the jury being sworn and charged with them find them not guilty of the felony whereof they stand indicted on evidence appearing against them nor

that they did fly for it. Discharged" (*Ms. Mins. Cir. 1721–49* 91, June 25, 1737). An indictment for manslaughter committed in a boxing match being found against Isaac Lyons, he pleaded not guilty, and was placed on trial. "The jury . . . find the prisoner not guilty and that he did not fly for it to their knowledge . . . Discharged" (*Ms. Mins. SCJ 1756–61* [Rough] 158, 163, Oct. 21, 1759). David and Elizabeth Smith were tried on two indictments for burglary and on both indictments "the jury returned to the bar say they find the prisoners not Guilty and that they did not fly for it to their knowledge" (*Ms. Mins. SCJ 1764–67* [Rough] 234, Apr. 29, 1767). Margaret Hunter pleaded not guilty to an indictment for petit larceny and on Aug. 6, 1773, the case was "At issue for Tryal on plea not guilty . . . The Jury without Going from the Bar Say that Margaret Hunter . . . not Guilty of the felony . . . that She had no Goods nor Chattels and that She did not fly for it" (*Ms. Mins. NYCQS 1772–91* 64).

On an indictment for passing counterfeit, the jury found George Weght not guilty and that he did not fly for it (*Ms. Mins. SCJ 1775–81* [Engr.] 61, 63, 64, Jan. 18, 1776), and endorsed on his indictment was the following: "po. se non cul. nec retraxit" (*H.R. Pleadings* Pl. K. 333).

[237] Cf. the *postea* entry in King v. Lent, Higby *et al.*: "Whereupon it was proceeded to the taking of the Jury aforesaid by the Jurors aforesaid now here appearing who to say the truth concerning the within contained being Elected, tried and Sworn say upon their Oath, that as to the Trespasses and Contempts in the Information within Specified and by them the said Isaac Lent, . . . [etc.], within Supposed to be done and committed or any part thereof they the said Isaac Lent, James Higby, Andrew Mick, John Van Vleck the Younger and Peter Vandewater are thereof in no wise guilty, neither is either of them Guilty, in manner and form as they the said Isaac Lent, James Higby, Andrew Mick, John Van Vleck the Younger and Peter Vandewater for their discharge of the premises within, by pleading have alledged And the Jurors aforesaid on their Oath aforesaid, do further say, That as to the Assault and Battery in the Information within Specified, and by them the said Peter Johnson and Abraham Lent within Supposed to be done and Committed, they the said Peter Johnson and Abraham Lent and each of them are thereof Guilty in manner and form as by the said Information is within supposed, and as to the Riot and the rest of the premises in the Information

There is considerable learning in the books on the so-called partial verdict, that is to say, where the jury would convict on one count and acquit on another. The writers include here cases where the offense charged embraced one of a minor degree and the jury verdict discharged on the higher crime and convicted for the inferior. Similarly classified are the cases where several were joined in an indictment and the verdict was different as to the several defendants. We shall consider here instances of this sort as well as the verdicts where defendants were arraigned upon more than one indictment.

So far as can be determined there was no consistent policy followed in New York respecting the use of counts as against a multiplicity of indictments. The country indictments usually stated a single count but the Supreme Court practice was entirely eccentric, and it is possible that the difficulty of securing convictions frequently moved the Attorney General to prefer two or three indictments to the risk of an omnibus instrument.

In 1737, Henry Slyck was arraigned on two indictments, one for entertaining apprentices and the other for giving them credit. He was convicted on the first and acquitted on the second.[238] Again, in 1767 William Gilliland pleaded not guilty to two indictments, one for a disorderly house, the other for receiving, and was convicted only on the former.[239] Where the indictment or information had several counts, the jury usually seem to have picked out the least serious charge to convict on. Thus Elizabeth Allen, informed against for assaulting Jane Doughty causing her to bring forth a dead child, was convicted only of the assault.[240] Samuel Smith, tried on an information for forgery and a cheat, was found guilty only of the forgery.[241] This judicious choice of evils was made in some of the riot cases, for as early as 1717 two defendants were acquitted of a riot and convicted of trespass.[242] A similar verdict was returned in a case which occurred in 1753[243] and one in 1774.[244]

The verdicts in cases of this type are illustrative of one of the most impor-

---

within Specified and by them the said Peter Johnson and Abraham Lent, within Supposed to be done and Committed, or any part thereof, they the said Peter Johnson and Abraham Lent, are thereof in no wise Guilty, neither is either of them Guilty" (*H.R. Parch.* 140 B 4).

[238] *Ms. Mins. SCJ 1732–39* 258.

[239] *Ms. Mins. SCJ 1764–67* (Rough) 323. In King v. Cooley, two indictments for attempted arson of the jail and for attempted murder evidently committed in a jail break, the defendant was convicted on both indictments (*Ms. Mins. NYCQS 1772–91* 80, 91, Feb. 5, May 4, 1774).

[240] *Ms. Mins. SCJ 1764–67* (Rough) 64.

[241] *Ibid.* 239 (forgery at this time less severely punished than cheats). Cf. also King v. Sullivan indicted for fraudulently getting a bond and for defacing it, convicted on the second count (*Ms. Mins. SCJ 1772–76* [Rough] 78; *H.R. Pleadings* Pl. K. 355).

[242] *Ms. Mins. Cir. 1716–17* 39.

[243] King v. Newton *et al.* (*Ms. Mins. SCJ 1750–54* [Engr.] 280).

[244] King v. Tippet *et al.* (*Ms. Mins. SCJ 1772–76* [Rough] 167, 170). Cf. also King v. Walsh and Graham, 1769 (*Ms. Mins. SCJ 1769–72* [Engr.] 113).

tant aspects of the jury's prerogative—the power to effect a mitigation in the severity of the law by verdicts which would let off an obvious offender with penalties less than the worst of the charges against him would make inevitable. This power was not confined to the selection of a relatively innocuous count on which to return a conviction, but extended, as indicated above, to a finding of an offense less in degree than that charged in the indictment. The importance of this rule in the case of felonies was obvious, since it was possible thus for the defendant to pray clergy and escape the rigor of the otherwise inevitable judgment of life and limb. The rule was essential where a homicide, by misadventure or in self-defense, was involved since the limitations of criminal pleading required that facts in extenuation or excuse be put in evidence and the jury give its verdict thereon.

The New York practice followed the English[245] in that the jury's verdict was stated in terms of guilty of homicide *se defendendo* or *per infortunium*. John Fisher was indicted in April term, 1698, for murder, but on April 7, 1698, "the jury . . . finde the prisoner not guilty of murder but homicide and by misadventure and that he did not flea for it."[246] Huybert Vandenberg was tried on an indictment for murder on March 12, 1713/14 and "the jury find the defendant not guilty of murther but guilty of Chance Medley onely."[247] Jacob Koole and two others were indicted for manslaughter and were tried on October 22, 1754, when

the jurors find that the prisoners are not guilty nor is either of them guilty of the Felony charged in the indictment . . . nor did either of them flie for it. But the Jurors say that the prisoners did on the day charged in the indictment . . . shoot and discharge a gun . . . into some Reeds . . . to kill a Bear . . . not knowing or mistrusting that the said Cornelius Vanck was in the said Reeds . . . [and that the said Cornelius was killed by three wounds] . . . by misfortune and that the prisoners nor either of them had any goods or chattels to their knowledge at the time of the crime charged in the indictment. . . . Ordered discharged. . . .[248]

---

[245] 2 Hawkins, *op. cit.* c.47 §4.
[246] *Mins. SCJ 1693–1701* 134. It is also to be noted in this case that the defendant was obliged to give a bond with two sureties in the sum of £100 for his good behavior for a year and a day (*ibid.* 137). Cf. also King v. Smith (*H.R. Parch.* 209 G 9, *Mins. SCJ 1693–1701* 120).

John Moore was tried on Mar. 12, 1711/12 on an indictment for murder, and "the jury find the

prisoner not guilty of murder but guilty of killing John Griffith by misadventure whereupon the prisoner is discharged paying his fees" (*Ms. Mins. SCJ 1710–14* 358). Note that in this case the defendant was not obliged to post a bond for a year and a day.

[247] *Ms. Mins. SCJ 1710–14* 516.
[248] *Ms. Mins. SCJ 1754–57* (Engr.) 82.

A curious case was that of Frederick Locidon (Lowden?), who was arraigned on an indictment of "killing se defendendo," and was also arraigned on a coroner's inquest for manslaughter. He was tried on August 3, 1764, and "the jury without going from the bar find the prisoner not guilty of manslaughter but guilty of homicide in his own defense and that he did not fly for it to their knowledge," whereupon the court ordered him discharged.[249] We have noticed many cases where defendants indicted for murder were merely convicted of manslaughter. Peter Mullinder was tried on March 13, 1712/13, on an indictment for murdering Henry Clarke and "The Jury find the defendant guilty of manslaughter and that he had no goods or chattels lands or tenements at the time of the felony committed or since to their knowledge."[250] Patrick Kreamer was arraigned on a coroner's inquest for the murder of Martinus Cregier, and was also arraigned on an indictment for manslaughter. He was tried on both charges and "the jurors find the prisoner not guilty of murder on the coroner's inquest and guilty of manslaughter on the indictment and that he had no goods or chattels to their knowledge."[251]

Another situation where mitigation could be effected were those cases where grand larceny was charged. It had long been settled in England that where an indictment charged the stealing of goods of a certain value above 12*d.*, the jury might find the defendant guilty but could find the value of the goods to be less than 12*d.* Verdicts of this sort were usual in New York, and there is evidence that the colonists added some variations as where persons indicted for burglary were merely found guilty of felonious stealing.[252]

[249] *Ms. Mins. SCJ 1764–67* (Rough) 7, 8, Aug. 2, 3, 1764.
    John Dalton was tried for murder on Jan. 25, 1766, and "the jury find the prisoner not guilty of murder but guilty of homicide in his own defense and did not flie for it and no goods. Ordered discharged" (*ibid.* 135).
[250] *Ms. Mins. SCJ 1710–14* 437. On Mar. 14, 1712/13 the defendant was granted benefit of clergy (*ibid.* 439).
[251] *Ms. Mins. SCJ 1754–57* (Engr.) 50, 51, Aug. 2, 1754. The defendant was granted the benefit of his clergy (*ibid.* 51).
    Bryan Mullen was tried on an indictment for murder, but the jury found him not guilty of murder but guilty of manslaughter and that he had no goods or chattels, etc. He was granted the benefit of his clergy and discharged (*ibid.* 149, 150, 153, Apr. 22, 24, 1755).
    Roper Dawson was on Jan. 24, 1766, tried on an indictment for murder, and "the jury being returned to the bar find the prisoner not guilty of

murder but guilty of manslaughter," and that he had no goods or chattels, etc. (*Ms. Mins. SCJ 1764–67* [Rough] 134). Dawson was also granted his clergy (*ibid.* 136, Jan. 25, 1766).
    Josiah Murphy was tried on an indictment for manslaughter and a coroner's inquest for murder, and the jury, "sworn on both indictments," found him not guilty on the first "indictment" for murder, but guilty of manslaughter, and on the "second indictment" the same (*Ms. Mins. SCJ 1772–76* 128–136).
[252] Cf. Hawkins, *op. cit.* c.47 §6. Queen v. Densworth and John Allen (*Ms. Mins. SCJ 1701–04* 150, 156, 171, 172); King v. George Borne and King v. Ann Sawyer (*Ms. Mins. Cir. 1721–49* 28, 29). Borne convicted of burglary, Ann guilty only to 10½*d.*
    Ned, a negro, was tried at Albany Oyer and Terminer and General Gaol Delivery on July 1, 1733, and was found guilty of felony but not of burglary, and that the goods involved were worth £5. On July 3 he was sentenced to thirty lashes

The jury's finding with respect to a convicted prisoner's property may also have something to do with the alleviation of the law's severity. The return as to flight, chattels and tenements was essential to establish the royal forfeitures, and the year and day in felony cases. In New York, however, we have found only three cases where the jury found goods. In 1733, Edward King was convicted of murder and the jury at Circuit found "he had no goods chattels lands or tenements at the time of the murder but what are in the coroners hands."[253] A convicted counterfeiter in 1756 was found to have a horse and saddle valued at £5,[254] and John Allen, indicted in 1775 for "larceny from the person privilly was found to have a Jersey bill of credit, a *Johannis* and a guinea, of goods and chattels."[255] The failure otherwise to find chattels is not completely explained by the fact that felons were often from the poorest class. We think it likely that owing to the feeble growth of exchequer powers in New York, the juries, as a persistent matter of policy for the purpose of relieving the families of felons and the general burden of poor relief, deliberately avoided finding forfeitures. We shall speak of this again in the next chapter.

Not infrequently the juries in New York would return special verdicts, and apparently, as we have seen in the Makemie and Zenger cases, it was regarded as the privilege of the jury to decide whether or not it would so do.[256] Instances of special verdicts appear early in the eighteenth century. Thus, in the case of Daniel B. Hewitt who was indicted and tried on March 13, 1704/05 for prison break, the jury found a special verdict, and evidently the court found the law

and was ordered to receive an additional thirty lashes a week later (*ibid*. 60, 61).

At Suffolk Oyer and Terminer and General Gaol Delivery on Sept. 11, 1734, Joseph Adams was arraigned on three indictments for "felony." He was tried and the jury found him not guilty of stealing a horse or two powder horns from Stephen Reaves, but guilty of stealing a vest from Nathan Hanick and that the vest and buttons were worth 12d. Adams was thereupon sentenced to thirty lashes (*ibid*. 73).

At Albany Oyer and Terminer and General Gaol Delivery William Mitchell was indicted on June 25, 1737, for sheep stealing, and on June 28 he was tried, and after the Chief Justice charged the jury and a constable was sworn with the jury, "they withdrew and in a short time brought the prisoner in guilty of petit larceny to the value of ten pence." Mitchell was sentenced to twenty-five lashes on each of two separate occasions (*ibid*. 91). Cf. also King v. Hester Crutch, 1730 (*Ms. Mins. SCJ 1727–32* 204, 207); King v. Darcus, 1771 (*Ms. Mins. SCJ 1769–72* [Engr.] 352, 353); King v. McNamara (*Ms. Mins. SCJ 1769–72* [Engr.] 358, 359,

361); King v. Hammond (*Ms. Mins. SCJ 1772–76* [Rough] 143–145, 147). Mary Dailey was indicted and tried on Oct. 26, 1767, for burglary. In that instance, "the Jury find the prisoner not guilty of burglary but guilty of grand larceny and that she had no goods or chattels, lands or tenements at the time of the felony committed or since to their knowledge." On Oct. 31 she was granted benefit of clergy, burned and discharged and it may be that the jury, by convicting her of a clergiable felony and acquitting her of a non-clergiable one, was attempting here to effect a mitigation (*Ms. Mins. SCJ 1764–67* [Rough] 275; *Ms. Mins. SCJ 1766–69* [Engr.] 326).

[253] *Ms. Mins. Cir. 1721–49* 64, 65.

[254] King v. Owen Sullivan (*Ms. Mins. SCJ 1754–57* [Engr.] 255).

[255] *Ms. Mins. SCJ 1775–81* (Engr.) 250, 253. The finding here may be the stolen goods.

[256] It may be noted here that two cases of a private verdict have been found. King v. John Thompson (*Ms. Mins. SCJ 1723–27* 140, 141); and King v. Hannah Carlisle (*ibid*. 140, 141).

to be for the King because Hewitt was sentenced to twelve months' imprisonment and two years on his good behavior.[257] Paroculus Parmyter was tried on an indictment for champerty and maintenance on September 4, 1706, and the jury found a special verdict. This was ordered to be argued in the following term and on October 12, 1706, a *"Cūr. advisar. vult"* was entered but on March 15, 1706/07, the defendant was called three times and failed to appear.[258] On June 6, 1713, John Drommy was tried on an indictment for bigamy and the jury found the following special verdict: "The jury find the prisoner to have been married in Ireland and afterwards married in New York his first wife being then living according to the indictment but whether he be guilty of felony within the Statute in the Indictment mencōned they submit to the court." On October 15, 1713, "on ye special verdict Jamison ₽ Dom⁹. Reg⁹. opens ye matter Bickley ₽ defend. The Court will further advise till Saturday." On October 16, 1713 and March 12, 1713/14, *curia advisares* were again entered but when the prisoner was brought to the bar to receive judgment on June 5, 1714 he pleaded the Queen's pardon and was discharged.[259]

It seems probable that the jury was sometimes constrained to render a special verdict because it was confused by the legal arguments of counsel and its doubts were not helped by the charge. From the sample charges we have quoted this can be readily understood, and a verdict rendered in an assault case at Quarter Sessions in 1718 is suggestive. Here the jury "find a violent Presumption that the Deft is Guilty of the offences whereof he Stands Indicted and pray the Advice of the Court if a Violent Presumption be Sufficient Proof in Law and leave it to the Court to determine, Cur⁹ Vult-Advisare."[260]

If the minutes are to be trusted, the special verdicts in the early cases were so badly drawn that it was probably difficult to proceed on them. We have found a customs information case in 1733 where, with leave of the court, the Attorney General was allowed to amend the special verdict before the final rule for argument was made.[261] It cannot be asserted, however, that in criminal

[257] *Ms. Mins. SCJ 1704/05–1709* 6, 9, 10.
[258] *Ibid.* 84, 94, 108, 121.
[259] *Ms. Mins. SCJ 1710–14* 456, 457, 476, 496, 499, 516, 538.
[260] *Ms. Mins. NYCQS 1694–1731/32* 342, 347, 348, Feb. 4, 1717/18, Aug. 5, 6, 1718; *H.R. Parch.* 198 B 2.
[261] James Wallace was tried on Oct. 14, 1732, and "The Jury returning to the bar find a special verdict, and afterwards the value of the goods in the Information except the three pieces of Calico to the value of thirty four pounds N. York

money." On Oct. 16, the following minute entry was made: "The Jury find a Special verdict in this cause as signed by Counsel on both sides pro ut and delivered the same in Court as their verdict & withall say if the Law be for the plt then they find for the plt and if the Law be for the Defendant then they find for the defendant." On Dec. 5, 1732 Smith, on behalf of the defendant, moved, and it was ordered, "that the record in this cause be made a consilium by the first day of next Term And that it be argued within the next term or the defendt be discharged." The rule was "enlarged" on Mar. 13

information cases a like practice obtained, especially as the books were explicit that the court could not amend such verdicts.[262] In later practice, this stricture was observed, but as we have seen in *King* v. *Lawrence*,[263] the Attorney General faced with a defective special verdict sought to withdraw a juror and moved for a *venire facias de novo*.

The problem of an insufficient verdict arose again in the Lydius intrusion case where the defendant's counsel, fearing the court might undertake to notice judicially facts not appearing in the verdict, insisted the court could not do this. Kempe's reply to this argument was as follows:[264]

> As to the Principle itself it is certainly the Law in General, that the Judges shall not presume a Fact not found in a Special Verdict, and adjudge upon it, but this holds as to meer facts only of which the jurors are only to answer and does not extend to such things as arise by the operation of law . . .
>
> For the Judges must take Notice of divers facts . . . not mentioned in the pleading such as the . . . existence of Publick Stat: the Common Law of the Land, the policy of the Constitution &c and in short all things of a publick Nature that are not matters in pais . . .
>
> The policy of our Constitution (of which the Judges must Judicially take Notice . . .) vests the original Property of all Lands in the Crown . . . The parting with it by the Crown is a matter in pais, and the court consequently is not to suppose it unless . . . found. The Jury have not found any Letters Patent of the Crown . . . [when] the def[t] first entered . . . The Original Property of the Crown then being recognized, and no Grant of the Crown found the Kings Right stands unimpeached . . . [No possession need be found in the King] . . . because the King is by the Operation of Law always in Possession . . . and this being merely a matter of Law was improper to be found by the Jury. . . .

There can be no doubt that in the last years of the colonial period, the Crown officers maintained an attitude of great correctness toward the jury verdict, respecting its integrity in the trial process at large. In the early eighteenth century it was the custom in some of the country courts for the bench to note

and Mar. 20, 1732/33. On Apr. 23, 1733, the Attorney General was granted leave to amend the special verdict and a rule was made for argument in the following term. On Jan. 22, 1733/34 the court granted the Attorney General's motion that, unless Smith argue by the first day of the next term, "he be foreclosed of Speaking any further to it." On Apr. 22, 1734, the court granted a similar motion by the Attorney General: "Unless Smith deliver his argument or Authorytys in Writing to M[r] Atty the next week he be precluded from speaking any further in this cause." Evidently Smith finally delivered in his argument for, on Jan. 21, 1734/35, the Attorney General replied to Smith and on Jan. 22, 1734/35 the court gave judgment for the King (*Ms. Mins. SCJ 1727–32* 364, 369, 396; *Ms. Mins. SCJ 1732–39* 5, 17, 18, 27, 81, 101, 143, 146).

[262] 2 Hawkins, *op. cit.* c.47 §9.
[263] *Supra* 283 n. 225.
[264] *J. T. Kempe Lawsuits* L–O.

its agreement with the verdict[265] as if its consent were essential to the finality of the jury's finding. This disappears, partly because the common law ritual became better known, but partly also because freeholder opinion and conviction made the jury an instrumentality of great independence, the more to be reckoned with as the judges were many of them men of small or mediocre parts. This was perhaps the most interesting outcome of the tedious process of making trial practice conform to English models, for it contributed largely to the feeling in Revolutionary times that of all incidents of criminal justice trial by jury should remain inviolate.

[265] Cf. King v. Englebert Nott and Okey Johnson, 1693 (*Ms. Kings Co. Ct. & Rd. Recs. 1692–1825* 12); Queen v. Umprah Clay, 1703 (*ibid.* 91–92); Queen v. Hannah Taym, 1710 (*Ms. Mins. Westch. Co. Sess. 1710–23* 3); Queen v. Honeywell, 1713 (*ibid.* 27).

CHAPTER XI

FINAL PROCEEDINGS

THE proceedings after verdict in a criminal cause, fraught with such consequence for Crown or defendant, were inconsiderable in early common
law, and even in the seventeenth century were barely touched by innovation.
The books reflect the practical attitude—the battle was done; to collect the
spoils, to free or dispatch the prisoners was a mere quartermaster's task of
which the captains of the law were disdainful. The judicial function at this
juncture, viewed in the words of the oyer and terminer commission, is seen as
one of bringing matters to an end.[1] And the concluding rituals are so highly
formalistic that they give the impression the court is concentrated more upon
a nice rounding off of a record than upon the ethical implications of passing
judgment upon a fellow man. This impression gains in substance when one
takes into account the prevailing notion that a judgment is but the sentence of
the law pronounced by the judge upon matter in the record.[2] At this vital
point the judge is a mere prolocutor, and since the law, as well as stipulating
what must be said, attaches certain consequences to the pronouncement, the
acts and orders thereafter are similarly done in a ministerial capacity.

The character of final proceedings had been determined at an early period
in the history of the common law. The conception of the judgment had its
origin in the times when the *iudicium* lay with a higher power (still invoked
in the offer of trial by God as well as the country), and the exigent rule that
the sentence be kept in a precise formula derives from the formulary procedure of the trials by ordeal and battle. The orders and precepts for execution
were the fruits of years when fiscal-administrative occupations were a large
part of the judicial office. It is, moreover, significant that the routine of procedure after verdict was developed when the jurisdiction of the royal courts was
confined largely to felonies. This routine was hardly disturbed even after misdemeanor business grew in volume and importance, and when, by statute and
otherwise, the judges acquired a limited discretion in dealing with minor offenses. This had the result of promoting a certain uniformity but it tended also
to perpetuate a rigid medieval system where there was no reason for it.

As the procedure stood in Hale's day, the steps which followed an acquittal
were usually brief. The judgment would be that the prisoner should be dis-

---

[1] Lambard, *Eirenarcha* Bk. 4 c.15.   [2] 3 Blackstone, *Commentaries* 395.

charged of the premises and should depart without day.[3] He was usually charged fees, and sometimes he might be put under recognizance for a specified period if the judges were suspicious of him.[4] In the case of a verdict of conviction the procedure was necessarily more elaborate. This moved through three stages when a corporal punishment or death was to be inflicted. The first stage was the *allocutus* when the defendant was called to the bar and, in case of felonies, had to be asked[5] if he had anything to say why judgment should not be rendered. At this moment the prisoner could claim his clergy, produce his pardon, move in arrest or offer matter in mitigation. The second stage was the judgment itself, preceded preferably, as the handbooks advise,[6] by an exhortation to the prisoner. The final stage was the making of orders and precepts for execution. In the case of crimes where the only punishment was a fine, the defendant did not have to be present and the court might proceed forthwith to judgment.[7]

Just as other parts of a trial were affected by the rarity of an error proceeding, so the immutability of the scheme just outlined was thereby fostered. Furthermore, the requisites of a record once having been fixed, the addition or subtraction of anything vital was, as a practical matter, excluded, especially where it was the foundation of fiscal rights.[8] How despotically the record governed is obvious from the rule that the motion in arrest must be based upon a fault in the record, and the similar restriction of relief by way of new trial to the *venire facias de novo*.[9] Obviously there was little foothold for a defendant to avoid the inexorable penalty which awaited him even when he had been treated unfairly or unjustly in the conduct of the trial, and there was equally not much room for judicial tergiversation. Such evasion of the strict path of duty as occurred was in relation to the judgment and this was not always in the direction of justice and mercy. In the case of the so-called express judgments with a fixed sentence, that is to say, where, as in the old common law felonies, time-honored formulae had to be followed and where statute precisely stipulated the sentence there was no choice. However, there were a variety of offenses where it was at the option of the bench whether fine or corporal punishment should be meted out and here the judges could manufac-

---

[3] 2 Hale, *Pleas of the Crown* 391.
[4] *Ibid.* 394; *supra* 514 *et seq.*
[5] Rex v. Speke (*Comberbach* 144); Batsomb's Case (3 *Mod.* 265).
[6] So the *Office of the Clerk of Assize* (1682) 63.
[7] Queen v. Templeman (1 *Salkeld* 55).

[8] It eventually became usual to insert in the record a notice of the *allocutus*, but in Rex v. John Ward (2 *Lord Raymond* 146), its omission was held immaterial. This is a striking illustration of the dominance of the old rules about form.
[9] *Supra* 279.

ture their own forms of judgment.[10] Projecting the authority thus possessed, the courts, and particularly the justices of the peace, proceeded to stretch the "crooked cord of private opinion which the vulgar call discretion,"[11] and assumed not only to set the amount of fines even when these were supposedly exactly stipulated by statute,[12] but also, in despite of long tradition, to imprison as well as fine for offenses where the law contemplated a single penalty.[13] These aberrations, which were under way in Lambard's time,[14] had a lasting effect, for the latter practice was countenanced eventually even in the sacred purlieus of the King's Bench.

It should be observed that although in the field of misdemeanors judicial discretion was in certain instances free to construct the formula of judgment, through the circumstance that within limits the choice of penalty lay with the judge, the rules respecting execution were not directly tampered with. This was due to the fact that the form of execution depended upon the record entry, that is to say, judgment being entered in a particular form, a fixed method of execution upon body or goods, and this only, was lawful.[15] Since, in the case of a fine a *capiatur* was entered, if the defendant was not in custody, the *capias pro fine* issued of course, even if a fine was not set in accordance with a statute. And similarly, if both fine and imprisonment were adjudged, the same writ went forth because this was the only process which lay.[16]

The gradual multiplication of cases where discretion in choosing a penalty was exercisable brought about no basic change in the *ordo iudiciorum* after verdict, although it may have had some effect upon notions of punishment, especially since the bench was presumed to take into account circumstances such as the baseness of the offense, the behavior and the age and standing of the defendant.[17] It is significant, however, that none of the favorite justices' manuals, such as Dalton, Nelson or Burn, discusses this; indeed, so far as they speak of judgment the emphasis is upon exact observance of statutory standards. These were not, even in the eighteenth century, of a sort to encourage the

---

[10] It should be noted that Hawkins (2 *Pleas of the Crown* c.48) divides judgments into those by express sentence to the punishment proper to the crime and those without such sentence (outlawry and abjuration). Judgment by express sentence he divides into those where the sentence is fixed and stated and always the same for the same species of crime (as e.g., murder); and where the sentence is discretionary and variable according to circumstances (as e.g., petit larceny). What he does not make clear is that by statute or practice (as in the case of petit larceny) there were certain limits set upon the exercise of discretion.

[11] Coke, *Littleton* 227 b.
[12] Lambard, *Eirenarcha* Bk. 4 c.16. In the case of fines at the will of the King, the law regarded the judges as exercising the discretion for the Crown. Since the fine was in medieval law a bargain to secure release from imprisonment, the court was here acting in a ministerial-fiscal, not in a judicial capacity.
[13] Cf. here Fox, *Contempt of Court* 171 *et seq.*
[14] Lambard, *op. cit.* Bk. 4 c.16.
[15] Coke, *Third Institute* 211.
[16] Godfrey's Case (11 *Co. Rep.* 42, 43b).
[17] 2 Hawkins, *Pleas of the Crown* c.48 §4.

germination of the equity which one would suppose was implicit in the grant of a limited discretion.[18] The records in England show that in its way as harsh and nearly as stereotyped a judgment became the rule in misdemeanors as in felonies.

Final Proceedings under the Duke's Laws

If the age of reason had nearly run its course before the criminal procedure in England engaged its censures, the preceding age of revolt had been more froward. Since the process of judgment and the penalties which were an end of criminal law involved certain ethical considerations, these matters had felt the impact of Puritan dissatisfaction with the world as it stood in the early seventeenth century. The effects of Puritan remonstrance were not lasting in England,[19] and they survived but little longer in the New England plantations where the spirit of dissent first was free to put its reforms into law.[20] It was, curiously enough, with some of these reforms that the New York provincial law made its début, through the circumstance that the Duke's Laws were in part compiled out of the New England Codes. The express penalties of the ferocious "Capitall Laws"[21]—the death sentence for the person who denied the true God, for the child who should strike his parent, for the sexual pervert and for the adulterer—are the donative of Massachusetts Bay at the new altar of justice *in partibus barbarorum*. Similarly, the large discretion left to the magistrates in the establishment of penalties for offenses not specially mentioned[22] as well as for crimes described in the code,[23] reflects, albeit less surely, the same influence, for such discretion was a characteristic of the judicial systems in New England and had proceeded far beyond the limited discretion to that date conferred in England.[24] In this detail the necessities of a theo-

---

[18] Compare here *The Eirenarch* (1774) 32, where the writer, after suggesting the magistrate's office should be a "petty chancery," immediately runs to cover with a cautionary footnote.

[19] Robinson, Anticipations under the Commonwealth of Changes in the Law, in 1 *Select Essays in Anglo-American Legal History* 483 as to the reforms in criminal law.

[20] Discussed in Goebel, King's Law and Local Custom in 17th Century New England, 31 *Col. Law Rev.* 416.

[21] 1 *Col. Laws NY* 20.

[22] As adopted at Hempstead the code gave the Assizes the discretion to settle the punishment of offenses not specified, this to be not contrary to the "known" laws of England, but Nicolls sent out amending orders to the magistrates: "it Is also left to the Discression of the Court to appoint smaller

matters or punishments for smaller offences of that kind" [viz., stealing] (*ibid.* 73).

[23] E.g., all amerciaments and fines (*ibid.* 11); assaults (*ibid.* 15); fornication (*ibid.* 35); fires (*ibid.* 36); lying (*ibid.* 45).

[24] There is a discussion of the basis of this in 31 *Col. Law Rev.* 440 n. 45. Provisions in the Massachusetts Code of 1660 (*Colonial Laws of Massachusetts* [Whitmore ed.]): barratry, 125; disobedient servants, 136; firing woods, 151; cursing, 194; reproaching courts, 143; fornication, 153; idlers, 158; obdurate Sabbath breach, 189; wife beating, 171; drinking after sunset, 190. Although the discretion of magistrates was governed by the direction that in the event of a defect of law in a particular case, recourse should be had to the word of God (*ibid.* 121), this is scarcely to be viewed as a limitation on the magistrates. The unbridled dis-

cratic state piloted by a small and compact group corresponded entirely with those of a military governor of a conquered province. And Colonel Nicolls, who had his own opinion of the Levites in the Bay Colony, must have smiled sardonically that in giving the transplanted New Englanders in his province what they were used to, he was preparing for them a mirror for magistrates such as they would in the end most resent; for he saw the office not as a secular priesthood finding dooms by the books of Moses, but as an English justice of the peace judging by the statutes.

Although it is apparent both from Nicolls' correspondence and from the measures taken to secure a centrally controlled judiciary that an approximation of the English system was desired, the achievement fell short of the ideal in matters of detail because, among other things, no exact information was available on such dull particulars as process and the rules governing the conduct of trials. As respects final proceedings, clearly defined notions of what constituted a record, the established relation of the execution to the judgment, and even the necessity of a precept for the executing officer in addition to the order entered by the court were all absent, and this operated to produce what can only be described as the opposite of the clean-cut way in which English trials were terminated.

Perhaps the most striking thing about early New York Assize proceedings is the manner in which judgment was formulated. At the prosecution of the Halls for witchcraft, the court in the face of an equivocal verdict, as we have seen, "sentenced" the husband to be surety for his wife[25] and ordered the two to be of good behavior. The ancient and nearly indispensable words of judgment, "it is considered," are wanting,[26] in fact there is no indication that the bench was acquainted with the conventional formulation of judgment. But that the court, although ignorant of English precedent, conceived sentence

cretion was given by Thomas Hooker as a main reason for the exodus to Connecticut (1 *Colls. Conn. Hist. Soc.* 11), but the legislation of that colony was similar in tone. In 1642, capital laws copied after those in the Massachusetts Body of Liberties were adopted (1 *Pub. Recs. of Conn.* 77) and a broad grant of discretion was given in the case of incorrigibles and those who practiced ways of "uncleanes and lasivious caridges." For examples of discretion in the code of 1650 (*ibid.*): barratry, 512; pilfering, 514; taking cattle, 516; revealing court secrets, 520; fires, 526; fornication, 527; idleness, 528; defaming magistrates, 539. This colony likewise had the direction respecting the word of God (*ibid.* 509).

The brethren in New Haven, who had obvi-

ously studied the Massachusetts laws, put in their code of 1656 the rule respecting the word of God (*Records of the Colony of New Haven* [Hoadly ed.] 572), and further gave explicit discretion to fix penalties in all cases, past or present, where the laws were silent (*ibid.* 597). Further examples of grant of discretion in particular cases: barratry (574); larceny (575); breach of peace (586); fines (589); fornication (590); heresy (590); unlicensed sale of liquor (595); persistent drunkenness (597); aggravated lying (599); mayhem (601); profanity (606); Sabbath breach (608).

[25] *Supra* 559.
[26] Coke, *Fourth Institute* 70; cf. Rex v. Chandler (1 *Lord Raymond* 583).

should be delivered in form is apparent from the judgments delivered in the later cases of Barton and Bloomer,[27] Arthur Smith,[28] Richard Woodhull[29] and William Lawrence.[30] These cases were all heard without a jury and the judgments entered in much the way that one would find them in a Sessions Order Book of an English county rather than in the grudging terseness of a judgment roll.[31]

We have surmised, on the basis of provincial instructions for holding an Oyer and Terminer prepared in 1669, that from some source a more exact imitation of the English order of business at a trial came into use.[32] It is apparent, however, from the way that the sentences are formulated in the felony cases that no consistent forms of judgment were in use. In the prosecution of Engle Hendricks for murder, the minutes read: "All the bench condemne her. Sentence of death pronounced ag'st her by Mr. Whitfield President—That shee was to goe to the place from whence shee came & from thence to the place of Execucon there to hang by the Neck untell shee be dead—So Lord have mercy upon her soule. . . ."[33] On the other hand, in the judgments in the case of Frizzell *et al.* for burglary,[34] of David DuFour for harboring,[35] of Thomas Faulx and others for grand larceny[36] the sentences are mere travesties of the conventional English formula, although it is obvious the court was trying to approximate it. This is indicated in certain judgments where it is recited that "having taken into consideration the facts and the nature of the crime and so forth do give judgment. . . ."[37] Here is a palpable effort to render the traditional "all and singular the premises being seen and by the justices here fully understood it is considered. . . ."

There is no evidence that during Andros' governorship the concluding proceedings were brought, as a matter of recordation, into closer conformity with English precedents. Indeed, in a case tried at the 1675 Assizes,[38] and in two cases at the succeeding session,[39] verdicts of chance medley were returned for homicides *per infortunium* and the defendants were discharged by proclamation, although at common law it was the practice to let the defendant at mainprise to purchase his pardon. This was, of course, a senseless rule and the colo-

[27] *Ms. Mins. Ct. of Assizes* 81.
[28] *Ibid.* 83.
[29] *Ibid.*
[30] *Ibid.* 84.
[31] The justificatory recital before the actual order in some of these cases is similar to the style of some of the warrants, cf. *supra* 426.
[32] *Supra* 561.
[33] 1 *Rep. NY State Historian* 246.

[34] *Ibid.* 240.
[35] *Ibid.* 250.
[36] 2 *Exec. Council Mins.* 771.
[37] Cf. the judgment in the case of Barton and Bloomer (*Ms. Mins. Ct. of Assizes* 81), and that against Fenwick (1 *NJ Archives* [1 ser.] 237).
[38] 2 *Rep. NY State Historian* 394.
[39] 25 *NY Col. Mss.* 190, 205.

nists were obviously finding a sensible alternative. The judgments upon convictions in this period are in the same idiom as those during the first occupation of the Province.

With respect to execution and the process used, the data are meager, but presumably the precepts were drawn in conformity with the ordering portion of the judgment. Thus, where a fine for abusing a justice was adjudged, it was ordered that this be levied out of the goods and chattels,[40] a command which would have foreclosed the normal English proceeding by capias. In the instances prior to 1674 where an afflictive sanction was imposed, the sentence is explicit,[41] but the only process we have seen is the precept for the execution of the infanticide Engle Hendricks.[42] Probably some written warrant for execution was deemed essential, but for the period 1664–73, a strange mélange has survived the ravages of time—an order for transportation,[43] an order to burn certain libels,[44] a warrant to levy for fines[45] and a *mittimus* for an indefinite imprisonment,[46] the very title of which, "Warrant for ye clapping of Wm. Douglas in prison," indicates how little the terminology of even English local practice was known in New York.

Whether or not there were any judicial writs which became *de cursu* during the Andros regime is a matter open to doubt. It was usual to make a record of precepts which were issued by the central authorities, and the warrant book for the years 1674–79 contains only one example of final process.[47] The minutes of 1675 and 1676 state "The Formes of Warrants Summons and Subpoenas &c as heretofore." This may have reference to fixed forms of final process but, if so, there is no direct evidence on the point. On the contrary, we have seen two special precepts—one to levy upon the property of Cornelius Steenwyck convicted of sedition,[48] and a warrant for the execution of a degrading punishment.[49] There had been a total forfeiture of chattels adjudged in the Steenwyck case and a special writ was obviously thought essential. It is entirely possible, since the criminal business of Assizes was not considerable, that

---

[40] *Ms. Mins. Ct. of Assizes* 143.
[41] *Ibid.* 185, 188, 190.
[42] 1 *Rep. NY State Historian* 247.
[43] 1 *Exec. Council Mins.* 322.
[44] 2 *ibid.* 485.
[45] 14 *Doc. Rel. Col. Hist. NY* 584.
[46] 1 *Exec. Council Mins.* 325. Compare here the release of Ralph Hall from a recognizance (1668) in 1 Smith, *Hist. of NY* 511, with the forms in Dalton, *Countrey Justice* (1677) c.176.
[47] In 1676, the Quaker Thos. Case was arrested

and committed by the Governor for preaching; cf. the warrant for him and his companion Ann Rogers in *Ms. Warrants Orders and Passes 1674–79* 193. Case suffered execution on his earlier bond for good behavior and was required to give new security (25 *NY Col. Mss.* 196²). There may, of course, have been some other books now lost where other warrants were entered.
[48] In the Assize minutes (2 *Rep. NY State Historian* 429).
[49] 14 *Doc. Rel. Col. Hist. NY* 686 (1674/75).

executions were normally drawn *ad hoc*. The unfortunate destruction of the Assizes book for this period makes any certain conclusion impossible.[50]

While the sources relating to the jurisdiction of superior courts testify to an effort, however badly guided, to walk the way of common law practice, the records relating to the Sessions courts show nothing of the sort. In so far as there is anything English with which the final proceedings of these inferior tribunals can be compared it is the antic summary jurisdiction of the justice of the peace. Owing possibly to the rare use of juries for the trial of the minor offenses entrusted to the New York Sessions, the judgment appears usually in the form of an order. It was thus that in England summary proceedings before magistrates were disposed of whether in Sessions or out. There, by the middle of the seventeenth century, signs point to the application of a *terminus technicus* to summary orders—the "conviction"[51]—an expression which included cases where presentment was made by a justice and where by confession or examination and without jury trial a penalty was ordered by Sessions or by single or double justices. The magistrates were supposed to keep a record of convictions,[52] but it was not until Holt's time that King's Bench commenced to lay down requirements. Even then it is significant that neither the *ideo consideratum est* of the judgment[53] nor the Latin language was made requisite[54]—in other words, criteria different from those essential to common law judgment were established. This was more than mere fussing over form. The "conviction" or order was assailable by motion to quash or by certiorari while the judgment was subject only to writ of error.

The characteristics of the "conviction" have been noticed not because the procedural particulars were of the remotest concern to the homespun justices in the wilderness, but because it is possible thereby to discover a prototype for the New York Sessions records through their resemblance to the so-called justices' Order Books[55] of England. When the clerk in the West Riding of New

[50] The printed Assize records, 1680–82, have nothing of the sort entered. The material collected by Paltsits from the then unburned manuscript and printed in his *Exec. Council Mins.* shows *ad hoc* precepts in so many civil cases that it seems most probable this was also the case in criminal procedure.

[51] Dalton, *Countrey Justice* (1677) 406. The summation of eighteenth century change is in 1 Burn, *Justice of the Peace* (11 ed.) *s.v.* Conviction.

[52] Cf. the form in Dalton, *op. cit., s.v.* Guns.

[53] Dr. Groenvelt v. Dr. Burwell *et al.* (1 Lord Raymond 469); Rex v. Chandler (*ibid.* 583).

[54] Rex v. Lomas (*Comb.* 289); but cf. Rex v. Chaveney (2 *Ld. Raymond* 1368).

[55] For a specimen cf. *Surrey Rec. Soc.* vol. 36. Unfortunately, when Jeaffreson edited the Middlesex records he threw in entries from Sessions rolls, Gaol Delivery rolls and order books indiscriminately. Although the order book entries are tagged there is no way of knowing if all the book was used. No study has been made of the status of the order book or what normally was supposed to be entered there.

York made his entries for a conviction upon presentment, for contempt and for bastardy,[56] in a manner almost identical with these books, he was obviously unfamiliar with the dark art of Quarter Sessions enrollment, but apparently possessed some inkling of how the transgressions of recusants, conventiclers, alehouse keepers, gamesters, poachers and lewd fellows were booked.

The manner of noting the determination of Sessions courts did not differ essentially from the Dutch practice.[57] In the New York Mayor's Court where sentences of banishment,[58] whipping[59] and fine[60] were imposed or where a defendant was put under recognizance,[61] the words "order," "condemn" or "decree" are used indiscriminately during the first decade of occupation. During these years, moreover, there is no sign that any forms of process were used in execution. After the English again assumed control in 1674, the minute books occasionally use the expression "doe sentence"[62] but usually cleave to the peremptory word "orders," whether a whipping, branding or banishment was inflicted.[63] Not infrequently the fact that the order has been executed is noted on the minutes, a circumstance which leads one to conjecture that no special process was used. On the other hand, we have seen a pair of precepts of 1679[64] and 1680[65] ordering a levy on goods and in default to take the body of the defendant. Since imprisonment was often used to compel security to enforce the payment of fines or restitution[66] it is likely that some warrant was given the

---

[56] *Ms. Kings Co. Ct. & Rd. Recs. 1668–1766* 18, 47, 130, 217, 302.

[57] Cf. 5 *Recs. of New Amsterdam* 64, 77, 85 (1664); *Ms. Flatbush Town Recs.* Liber B, 107, 119, 163. It is worth noting that in the English-speaking jurisdiction at Gravesend the forms of entries closely resemble the later riding recordings (*Ms. Gravesend Town Recs.* Liber I, 56, 60, 76).

[58] 6 *Recs. of New Amsterdam* 194; or threatened banishment (*ibid.* 87, 101, 340).

[59] *Ibid.* 194.

[60] E.g., *ibid.* 100, 113, 123, 142, 159, 233. Sheriff v. Carpyn (6 *ibid.* 87, 88).

[61] E.g., 5 *ibid.* 297; 6 *ibid.* 155 (together with fine and corporal punishment).

[62] "Doe order and pass sentence" of whipping: *Ms. Mins. Mayor's Ct. NYC 1674–75* fol. 63 (stealing); "doe sentence" to stand at whipping post, *ibid.* (false oath).

[63] *Ms. Mins. Mayor's Ct. NYC 1677–82* fols. 11 (stealing), 131 (stealing), 141 (drawing knife), 227 (stealing and contempt), 227b (receiving), 228 (stealing), 260b (bastardy); *Ms. Mins. Mayor's Ct. NYC 1680–83* fols. 250 (stealing). Branding: *Ms. Mins. Mayor's Ct. NYC 1677–82* fol. 227 (stealing and contempt). Standing at whipping post: *Ms. Mins. Mayor's Ct. NYC 1674–75* fol. 62 (perjury); *Ms. Mins. Mayor's Ct. NYC 1677–82* fols. 11 (receiving a negro), 49 (suspicion of theft),

228 (accessory in stealing). Banishment: *Ms. Mins. Mayor's Ct. NYC 1677–82* fols. 131 (stealing—banished for a year and a day), 183 (stealing—banished for a year and six months), 196, 227 (stealing). In some cases the banishment is threatened for another offense (*ibid.* 183, 197). In one case (*ibid.* 196) a penalty is threatened on the sheriff if he does not "attend to" the banishment.

[64] *Ms. Mins. Mayor's Ct. NYC 1677–82* fol. 136b:

"To the Sheriffe of the said Cittie
These are in his Maj[ties] name to charge and command you that unless the said Richard voluntarily performs ye judgment of court above mencion—that then you levy the same upon his goods and chattell and for want thereof to take into your custody the body of ye said Richard until he satisfy the same."

The offender, Richard Pattishall, had landed passengers without license.

[65] H.R. *Ms. Wills* Liber 19b, 31, a warrant in the case of an illegal combination of coopers.

[66] *Ms. Mins. Mayor's Ct. NYC 1677–82* fols. 7, 175, 250. There are numerous entries binding defendants over for hearing by the Governor at the Assizes, e.g., *Ms. Mins. Mayor's Ct. NYC 1674–75* fol. 24; *Ms. Mins. Mayor's Ct. NYC 1677–82* fols. 13, 25, 60, 64b, 125.

sheriff. On certain cases, such as bastardy, where the city was to be held harmless, the orders were implemented by recognizance.[67]

As we have already indicated, the practice in the ridings was from the first patterned upon the English summary procedure, and the judgments are entered in the records as orders. Usually the defendants were fined,[68] and although there appear to be no surviving writs of execution, there is collateral evidence that fines were collected by distress.[69] Occasionally persons convicted were sentenced to be whipped or put in the stocks,[70] and there is at least one instance where the record suggests that only an oral command to the officer was the warrant for an immediate stocking.[71] The recognizance of good abearance also occurs as a final sanction and was probably executed in court without precept.[72]

[67] Ibid. 197, 260b. It should be noted further that in the case of servants, additional years of service are added as a penalty (Ms. Mins. Mayor's Ct. NYC 1674–75 65; Ms. Mins. Mayor's Ct. NYC 1677–82 244b). The judgment sometimes includes a requirement that the defendant "ask forgiveness" (ibid. 178), and compare the complaint in the Ms. Declaration Bk. Mayor's Ct. NYC 1675–77 133, and the petition (ibid. 123). The judgment includes an order for restitution (Ms. Mins. Mayor's Ct. NYC 1677–82 183, 226b, 230, 340b), treble value or whipping. In the case of Tuder and Mann (supra 566), the court ordered repayment of the amount won at play. Despite the form of the judgment, Morris, op. cit. 742, states this "appears to be an action for the recovery of money." The cause was initiated by presentment from the text of which (H.R. Ms. Wills Liber 19b, 309) its character as a criminal case is obvious.

In some of the cases where a money penalty is inflicted, costs are added (Ms. Mins. Mayor's Ct. NYC 1677–82 183, 224b, 246). In one case where the defendant was found not guilty the city clerk, prosecuting for the Crown, was assessed the costs (ibid. 44); in one case, the complaining witness pays the costs (ibid. 270b). Sometimes even after acquittal the defendant is charged costs (ibid. 226b, 302b). There are numerous entries directing a portion of the fine to be paid the sheriff.

[68] The records of the early period are very scant. Cf., however, Ms. Kings Co. Ct. & Rd. Recs. 1668–1766 18, overthrowing stocks (1669), and the various entries where fines set are remitted, ibid. 6 (unlicensed sale of liquor), 9 (order of town court), 38 (defamation). In some cases, a defendant is ordered to do certain things or be fined at a later Sessions (ibid. 6, 37, 40, 48, 56, 64). In one case of mayhem the defendant was ordered to pay the surgeon's bill and compensation to the injured party (ibid. 18). In the East Riding a defendant in 1670 is fined £3 for calling an official a traitor (Ms. Suffolk Co. Sess. 1668–87 6). Other fines: fornication before marriage (ibid. 7); taking goods

under attachment (ibid. 31); forging a warrant (ibid. 7); abusing a justice (ibid. 38). In this last case the defendant was required to make a public acknowledgment of his "evil and abusive carriage." The acknowledgment was made a matter of record. After 1674 the records show the following respecting fines: Ms. Kings Co. Ct. & Rd. Recs. 1668–1766 76 (no offense indicated); 130 (abuse of constable); 177 (refusal to serve as constable); 198 (abuse of constable); 201 (assault); 209 (drunkenness); 217 (Sunday violation); 281 (pound breach); 328 (pound breach). In 25 NY Col. Mss. 129 (misdemeanor), 130 (hog stealing), 133 (abuse of justices); 27 ibid. 129 (frivolous complaint); 28 ibid. 110 (escape), 160 (marking another's colt). Some sentences are in the alternative are given, viz.: Ms. Kings Co. Ct. & Rd. Recs. 1668–1766 279 (assault—submission or fine); 302 (bastardy—security or whipping); 25 NY Col. Mss. 252 (fine or whipping); 28 ibid. 110 (fine or stocks); 1 Rep. NY State Historian 342 (fine to be half if submissive).

[69] Ms. Kings Co. Ct. & Rd. Recs. 1668–1766 25 (1669), 36 (1674), and compare the petition of the Quakers (1680) fined for violating the law respecting marriage, in 14 Doc. Rel. Col. Hist. NY 752.

[70] Whipping: Ms. Suffolk Co. Sess. 1668–87 30 (later commuted by fine); Ms. Kings Co. Ct. & Rd. Recs. 1668–1766 63, 302; 25 NY Col. Mss. 252 (in the last case as an alternative punishment). Stocks: Ms. Kings Co. Ct. & Rd. Recs. 1668–1766 302; 28 NY Col. Mss. 160 (as an alternative).

[71] Ms. Kings Co. Ct. & Rd. Recs. 1668–1766 301.

[72] Ibid. 18, 40, 50, 302, 355; 28 NY Col. Mss. 110. It should be noted that there are numerous entries where a part of the penalty is "submission" or "acknowledging fault publickly," a typical Puritan sanction. There are some cases where the final determination is left to a single or two justices (cf. Ms. Kings Co. Ct. & Rd. Recs. 1668–1766 75, 128, 355) or remitted for final action to a town court

In the Esopus jurisdiction, the records being kept in Dutch, the early statements of the court's determination are entered as they had been prior to the conquest, although in the years immediately before the Judicature Act of 1683 the judgments appear as orders.[73] The common penalty was the fine.[74] Indeed, the infliction of a severer sanction was so unprecedented that in 1672/73 a sentence of flogging caused a flurry because there was no one to execute it. Difficulties were finally resolved by the drawing of lots for the office of executioner.[75] The binding from Sessions to Sessions occurs, and one example of the form used has survived.[76] There are no examples of final process of execution in criminal cases.[77] In 1680, the court ordered a jail built for drunken Christians and Indians,[78] but there is no indication that any formalities were employed to people this place of durance.

At Newcastle, thanks to the diligence of the clerk, the relative prolixity of the records shows perhaps more clearly than elsewhere in the Province the inferior justice's conception of the judicial function. The order form of giving judgment prevails, and on some occasions is set forth in the same length[79] as the more elaborate Assize judgments. The influence of Assize example is apparent also in the formal clearing by proclamation after acquittal by jury.[80] As a rule the sentences ran to fines[81] or whipping,[82] but the stocks were sometimes used[83] and there are a few cases of banishment.[84] No samples of final

(*ibid.* 34, 63; 25 *NY Col. Mss.* 252; 27 *ibid.* 127). We have seen one entry of clearing by proclamation (25 *ibid.* 252).

[73] *Ms. Deeds Ulster Co.* Liber III 172, 224, 236, 241.

[74] E.g., *ibid.* Liber I 211 (1664), 378 (1666), 519 (1669). *Ibid.* Liber II 48, 49, 59 (1675), 456 (1677), 477 (1676), 529 (1681), 594 (1682).

[75] *Ibid.* Liber II 2–4 (Feb. 1672/73).

[76] *Ibid.* Liber I 622; *ibid.* Liber II 280: "Whereas Suveryn Ten Houdt has been bound by the now court of Sessions to behave well till the next session upon the penalty of hundred sch. of wheat, Therefore I the undersigned, Suveryn Ten Houdt promise to comport myself well and peacefully. In case it shall be found differently I shall pay on behalf of his Majesty the quantity of hundred sch. of wheat. In testimony of the truth. I have subscribed to the present with my hand this April 30, 1680. "Annulled by the Court of Session has behaved well."

[77] In *ibid.* Liber III 186, is a warrant to the sheriff to arrest one Roelef Swartout on execution in a civil case. We have seen no warrants for the levying of fines. In some cases, as *ibid.* Liber II, 594, where a man is forbidden to discharge his gun in the house under a penalty, the entry of the order would be sufficient. There is a curious case in

1665 where the schout pays the penalty for the defendant and later brings suit against the defendant for the advance (*ibid.* Liber I 241, 257).

[78] *Ibid.* Liber III 217, burghers imprisoned for debt were to be kept in the church loft.

[79] *Recs. Ct. of New Castle* 102, 226, 287, 320, 328.

[80] *Ibid.* 16, 85.

[81] *Upland Ct. Recs.* 54 (assault), 59 (assault), 61 (assault), 95 (list of fines), 181 (defamation), 194 (sale of liquor to the Indians). *Recs. Ct. of New Castle* 19, 20 (attempted arson), 113 (challenge to duel), 102 (abuse), 203 (receiving), 226 (threatening magistrates), 287 (slander of court), 302 (contempt), 320 (sending away pregnant maid).

[82] *Ibid.* 88 (assault), 130 (breaking stocks and contempt), 320 (bastardy), 327 (theft), 386 (runaway servant), 440 (bastardy), 492 (theft).

[83] *Ibid.* 287 (assault), and cf. 128 (where stocks are used for temporary detention).

[84] *Ibid.* 289 (for having a bastard), 327 (theft), 440 (for having a bastard). Cf. here Andros' letter of May 12, 1680, "It being neither practice nor Lawe of oʳ nation or contry to bannish thous vagabonds coming first to a place lent out afore settlement or (generally) six weeks residence" (*ibid.* 421).

process have been discovered, but it was customary to enter on the minutes that a sentence had been executed.[85] Fines were ordered collected by distraint on chattels.[86] The bench at Newcastle seems to have ruled with considerable severity;[87] there is no disposition to set penalties in the alternative, and the Delaware court offers the only example we have seen of vicarious punishment. One Ralph Hutchinson had sent off a servant who had been presented. He was fined 150 guilders "wch is for the well deserved punishment wch otherwayes should have ben Inflicted on hur ye sd. Mary for her having a Bastard. . . ."[88]

The fact of most immediate importance with respect to final proceedings in the years following the Judicature Act of 1683, is the introduction of the common law form of judgment in addition to the already accepted form of "conviction" in summary proceedings. This is attested as well by the Oyer and Terminer records for New York and Ulster counties as by the Sessions records of New York City and Albany. This change is evidenced by the fact that when common law form of enrollment comes into use, words of consideration and judgment become of course in indictment procedure[89] in lieu of the mere "order" heretofore favored. Furthermore, the records of Oyer and Terminer by the regular and correct use of the *ideo capiatur*[90] indicate that the second important step, a reception of the time-honored relation of judgment and execution has been taken, that with the common law form of judgment the stringent execution of sentence has arrived.[91] No longer in the face of a *capiatur* can the defendant convicted expect to escape with a mere distraint, but his body becomes the security for satisfaction.[92] Owing to the unfortunate

---

[85] E.g., *ibid.* 88.

[86] Cf. the order regarding ringing of service (*ibid.* 101; also 302). *Upland Court Recs.* 193, a general order permitting execution.

[87] This is most evident in the bastardy cases, viz., a pregnant girl is ordered to leave in eight days or be severely punished. Persons are forbidden to harbor pregnant women without notifying a magistrate (*Recs. of Ct. of New Castle* 389). In another case, evidence was offered that the putative father had beaten the accused spinster so that the child was born dead with broken limbs. The woman was sentenced to twenty-one lashes but no action was taken against the man (*ibid.* 263, 320). Subsequently the severe sentence of thirty-one lashes was pronounced against this woman for having another bastard (*ibid.* 440), but a fine of £5 was later accepted.

[88] *Ibid.* 321.

[89] *Ms. Mins. O. & T. Ulster Co.* fol. 1 *et seq.*; 7 *Ms. Mins. Council* (Reverse) fols. 1, 13, 24; *Ms. Mins. NYCQS 1683/84–1694* 29, 35, 72.

[90] *Ms. Mins. O. & T. Ulster Co.* fol. 1 *et seq.*, and note the distinction with the *misericordia* entry in civil cases. 7 *Ms. Mins. Council* (Reverse) 5, 28, 29, etc.

[91] The remaining court records before 1691 offer no examples of capital punishment. At the Oyer and Terminer the most severe penalties exacted are whippings: 7 *Ms. Mins. Council* (Reverse) 1, 2 (grand larceny); 29 (larceny and escape). The same is true of Sessions: *Ms. Mins. NYCQS 1683/ 84–1694* 31 (larceny); 69 (burglary); 148 (larceny). The *Ms. Mins. Albany Co. Sess.* have no penalties higher than fine or custody. The pardon for Henry Thompson convicted of burglary establishes that branding was sometimes a part of the sentence (34¹ *NY Col. Mss.* 78). One entry in the *Cal. Eng. Mss.* 134 shows an execution of a slave for arson.

[92] E.g., *Ms. Mins. NYCQS 1683/84–1694* 29, Feb. 3, 1684/85 (King v. Davies); 82, Feb. 2, 1685/86 (King v. Kellerhouse). The judgment in information cases against the losing informer is

destruction of the *Colonial Manuscripts* where so many specimens of process were preserved, no examples of final process in criminal cases for this period have to our knowledge survived.

The attentive reader of the *State Trials* is well aware of the fact that on the inscrutable face of the common law memorandum entry there appears little of what in fact transpired in court, and equally that in the court minutes, however hastily noted, the shortcomings of judicial knowledge are only occasionally betrayed. Consequently, although our best evidence might lead one to the conclusion that during Dongan's governorship the practice in New York was brought into close conformity with the English, this was probably true only in the limited sense that the forms were employed and the way toward an understanding of their correct use was open. It is inconceivable that except for following a new ritual, Oyer and Terminer judges like Matthias Nicolls, or the rural magistrates who had held court under Andros, were by a turn of the hand educated and indoctrinated in the sophisticated ways of Westminster or the Old Bailey. There are no proceedings of Dongan's day sufficiently detailed to enlighten us, and the first trials of which we possess more than the record or minutes, those of Jacob Leisler and his associates, can be viewed as representative of the state of provincial law only with considerable reservation since they were conducted under the dark aegis of two Massachusetts men, the presiding judge, Joseph Dudley, and the Attorney General, Thomas Newton, who was later to add to his laurels at the Salem witchcraft trials.

In these cases, as we have seen, we possess both the records and the minutes as well as certain collateral documents and affidavits.[93] It has been related how Leisler vainly pleaded to the jurisdiction, how Dudley and his associates, "their duty not weighing or regarding," pavidly and contemptibly accepted an opinion of Sloughter and his Council and overruled the plea, and how by a modified *peine forte et dure* the court strove to force a plea. The minutes disclose further that in despite of common law practice to give judgment forthwith or on the next day,[94] Leisler was kept in irons from March 31 to April 17, 1691, before he was brought up for judgment. He, Milborne and Beekman were

---

"mercy," and against the convicted defendant, confiscation and mercy (*ibid.* 35, 95, 97, May 5, 1685, Aug. 2, 1686). The Albany Sessions uses the mercy formula for fines (*Ms. Mins. Albany Co. Sess. 1685–89* 20) or orders commitment until the fine is paid (*ibid.* 14, 18, 22).

[93] Cf. *supra* 83, 582.
[94] 2 Hale, *Pleas of the Crown* 403. It is to be noticed that the trial was by special commission and presumably the rule of the statute 14 Hy. VI c.1 would apply.

then asked if they had anything to say why judgment of death should not be pronounced, to which it was answered "they conceive untill the King determine ye power by which they acted they should not answer." Thereupon the sentence was pronounced that they

be carryed to the place from Whence they Came and from thence to the place of Execucon, that there they shall be severally hanged by the Neck and being alive their bodys be Cutt Downe to the Earth that their Bowells be taken out and they being alive burnt before their faces that their heads shall be struck off and their Bodys Cutt in four parts and which shall be Deposed as their Maj^ties shall Assigne and the said Jacob Leysler, Jacob Milburne and Gerrardus Beekman are in Mercy &c.[95]

Thus the judgment roll. The minutes state merely that sentence of death was passed upon the prisoners,[96] but it appears that Leisler and Milborne were merely hanged because the other parts of the sentence were respited by the Governor.[96a]

The trials of Leisler and his comrades are instructive, not only because they are a standing caveat against assuming that currency of common law forms meant familiarity with substance, but because they show that provincial practice had not yet achieved even the existing deplorable English standards of fairness. To be sure, state trials in this period are a notoriously bad fundament on which to base a norm, but in England they were responsible for a lot of law, and in respect to the Leisler cases it is significant that none of the petitions for the reversal of attainder or for pardon attempted to impeach the proceedings of the Oyer and Terminer Court.[97]

In the next New York case where we have more than a record version of events, *King* v. *Bayard,* technical proficiency shows great advance, to the extent even of using the common law's own weapons for combatting the prejudice and overbearance of the bench. The sources, however, for the first ten years of the Supreme Court's existence throw little light on the rate at which lawyers and judges became more knowledgeable, for although the rolls in various cases[98] speak the formal language of Westminster, the judicial min-

[95] P.R.O., C.O. 5/1082 fol. 5. Note that a similar sentence was pronounced in King v. Prendergast convicted of treason at the Dutchess Assizes, 1766 (Moore to Shelburne, Oct. 11, 1766, P.R.O., C.O. 5/1098 fol. 257).
[96] P.R.O., C.O. 5/1037 fol. 10.
[96a] 2 Brodhead, *History of NY* 648.
[97] Cf. the petitions in 1 *NY Hist. Soc. Colls.* (1868) 333, 336, 339, 340. The petition of Jacob

Mauritz and others (*ibid.* 342) states merely that Sloughter in "an arbitrary and illegal manner" had caused Leisler to be imprisoned, accused, tried and condemned. This is the manner in which Leisler Jr.'s petition (2 *Doc. Hist. NY* 240), puts the matter. This can hardly be construed as an attack on the proceedings in the court itself.
[98] E.g., the records in *H.R. Parch.* 209 G 9 (1696).

utes, beyond establishing the fact that clergy, the motion in arrest and other paraphernalia are in use, are vexatiously brief. For these critical years as well as the decades following, the reconstruction of the proceedings at and after judgment is perforce made from sterile materials. But there was not a great deal to learn about proper concluding proceedings, a fact which will become apparent as we now move to consider the practice from 1691 onward.

Proceedings Preliminary to Judgment

In the years immediately following the establishment of the Supreme Court, final proceedings in New York were patterned after the directions in handbooks which conveyed little information beyond the main points of the ritual.[99] There were, however, various details of practice accounted of some importance that were unavailable except through communication by persons experienced in the routine of the English courts. And these came to be adopted in the Province as the quality of the immigrant bar improved. The first of these practices of which we shall speak is the motion for judgment.

In criminal cases it was necessary for the court to pronounce judgment when the indictment had been confessed, when the defendant defaulted on a rule to plead, and when a verdict had been rendered. This step was not one that in all circumstances was taken automatically on the initiative of the bench where the case had been tried, but owing to discrete rules which had developed respecting particular jurisdictions and commissions, and to differences in the handling of capital and non-capital cases, practice in England was various. The King's Bench in all cases required the prosecutor to enter a rule for judgment *nisi causa*. This was apparently a development from the nisi prius practice where after trial the *postea* was made up and delivered to King's Bench for the judgment *en banc*.[100] At the Assizes, in felonies, judgment could be rendered by the court unless the case was sent down from King's Bench.[101] Similarly, in cases brought to issue and tried at Quarter Sessions that bench would pronounce judgment.[102] So far as we are aware, no motion for judgment was there necessary except where judgment by default was taken. The evidence respecting the varieties of English practice in the eighteenth century is not ample and is particularly obscure on the Sessions practice.

99 This was probably true even of the period 1684–91, as indicated by the manuscript directions for the clerk of Oyer and Terminer in *Livingston-Redmond Mss*.
100 The practice is well attested in the case of trials at nisi prius; cf. Rex v. Francklyn (2 *Barnard*.

88); Hands, *Solicitor's Practice* 12. The rule in the case of trials at bar is supported by certain state trials.
101 2 Hale, *Pleas of the Crown* 29, 34.
102 2 Hawkins, *Pleas of the Crown* c.8 §31.

The earliest example we have found in New York of a motion for judgment is in the Leisler case, but here without a ruling, the prisoner was ordered to be chained and returned to prison.[103] Except for some prosecutions for violation of the Acts of Trade, the motion does not appear again in the Supreme Court minutes for some time, although we have found it in a bill of costs of 1702.[104] Possibly the clerks did not see fit to minute such motions and it may be the court usually delivered judgment without intervention by counsel. In a felony trial in 1709[105] we find the Attorney General moving for judgment, possibly because the defendant was a woman and there may have been some hesitancy over the sentence. But it is only when the circuit system is well grooved in the ways of the English Assizes that it is obvious the King's Bench rules have become guiding. English practices with respect to the filing of *posteas* and the motion for judgment are exactly copied in New York.[106] There are occasional entries of motions where the trials were held at bar[107] but it cannot be certainly stated that the court required the prosecutor to move for a rule. Sometimes, where the defendant defaulted the Attorney General or his deputy would move for judgment[108]—here clearly because the court's action

[103] P.R.O., C.O. 5/1037 fol. 2.

[104] Brooke q. t. v. Barquenteen Orange; Idem v. Iron Barrs (*Mins. SCJ 1693–1701* 59 [1694]). The bill of costs is in Queen v. De Meyer (45 *NY Col. Mss.* 113).

[105] On June 11, 1709, "Mr. Attorney prays Judgement against the prisoner [Margaret Smith convicted of felony] and the prisoner having said nothing why Judgement should not pass against her Judgement is pronounced against her that she be brought to the place whence she came from thence to the place of Execution where she is to be hanged . . . on July first" (*Ms. Mins. SCJ 1704/05–1709* 222, 223). Margaret later produced a pardon, Sept. 10, 1709 (*ibid.* 235, 236).

[106] The usual motion for judgment *nisi causa* occurred when the *postea* was returned from Circuit into the Supreme Court. Thus when the jury at Orange Circuit on June 3, 1735, found John Allison not guilty on informations for cheating and for maintenance, the *postea* was returned into the Supreme Court on July 29, 1735, and having been read and filed, the court ordered judgment "nisi ad contrarium in quattor diebus" (*Ms. Mins. Cir. 1721–49* 295; *Ms. Mins. SCJ 1732–39* 167). Likewise when James Tillet (Phillip?) was acquitted at Queens Circuit on Sept. 4, 1734, on an information for blocking the King's highway, the *postea* was returned into the Supreme Court on Oct. 16, 1734, and was read and filed on behalf of the defendant's attorney. Then on his motion judgment was ordered for the defendant unless cause was shown to the contrary in four days (*Ms. Mins. Cir. 1721–49* 281; *Ms. Mins. SCJ 1732–39* 126). Cf. King v.

Brittain (*supra* 165 n. 122); King v. Higby, Lent and others (*supra* 199).

In King v. Henry Livingston, clerk of the peace (*supra* 176) the Attorney General, on June 11, 1767, before Judge Jones, moved to bring on the case at Circuit, whereupon William Smith Jr. for the defendant changed the defendant's plea to *nolo contendere*. On July 31, 1767, "the defendant appeared at bar and agreeable to the postea submitted to a fine . . . ordered fine be . . . fifty shillings" (*H.R. Parch.* 91 A 4; *J. T. Kempe Lawsuits* L–O; *Ms. Mins. SCJ 1766–69* [Engr.] 259).

[107] E.g., King v. Van Zandt, 1756 (*Ms. Mins. SCJ 1754–57* [Engr.] 239); King v. George Elms, 1770 (*Ms. Mins. SCJ 1769–72* [Engr.] 275).

[108] For example, on Oct. 29, 1763, "On Information for an Assault and Wounding by shooting Elisha Smalley: Judgment by Default being entered in this Cause by Rule of last Term, On motion of Mr. Attorney General that the Court would set a fine on the Defendant, who has Engaged for the Costs of Prosecution, the Court sat [*sic*] a fine of Ten pounds on the Defendant" (King v. Baltus Lydius, *Ms. Mins. SCJ 1762–64* [Engr.] 295). Cf. also King v. Simon Grimes, who was indicted for keeping a disorderly house, was returned taken by the sheriff on Nov. 7, 1753, and ordered to plead in twenty days or suffer judgment. On May 8, 1754, "on motion of the clerk of the peace, Ordered judgment be entered against the defendant for want of a plea" (*Ms. Mins. NYCQS 1732–62* 329, 339, 348).

On Aug. 4, 1757, the sheriff returned Margaret Currio taken on an indictment for disorderly house,

was contingent upon the vigilance of the prosecuting authority. There are also instances where the indictment had been confessed when motions for judgment were made,[109] although there seems to be no good reason why this was necessary. The country courts needed no such prod to dispatch their business, for we can recall no instance where such motions were made in inferior courts outside of New York City.

The King's Bench practice with respect to motions for judgment is connected with its allowance of four days after confession or verdict within which the defendant could move in arrest and eventually for a new trial.[110] Anciently, the *allocutus*—when the prisoner was asked if he had anything to offer why sentence should not be pronounced—was the occasion for proffering reasons in arrest. The four-day rule based on civil procedure appears to have been due to allowance of counsel where points of law were raised in felony cases, and such practices as affidavits in mitigation in misdemeanors. The rationale of this appears in *King* v. *Bayard,* where immediately after verdict counsel prayed time to offer reasons in arrest.[111] The Chief Justice ordered these be offered the next morning, and at that time gave the Solicitor General a day to peruse the reasons. As in the case of demurrer, questions of law could not be answered offhand.

Colonial practice in respect to the motion in arrest, the motion for a *venire de novo,* and the motion for a new trial has already been discussed.[112] We cannot be sure from the minutes that in the Supreme Court the four-day rule was constantly adhered to, but the occasion for the defendant's last stand was always possible at the *allocutus* which in New York was a part of the ritual even when sentences less than capital were imposed.[113] Apparently, from the few

whereupon she was ordered to plead in twenty days or suffer judgment. On Nov. 2, 1757, Margaret was "discharged from recognizance and on motion of the clerk for judgment judgment entered for want of a plea" (*ibid.* 415, 421).

[109] For example, on Nov. 6, 1728, "Upon Motion of the Clerk of the Peace for Judgment agt. the Defendant [Mary Brown who confessed keeping a disorderly house] . . . Considered by the Court that the Defendant do pay a fine to our Lord the King of five pounds for Committing the said Offences with full fees of Prosecution" (*Ms. Mins. NYCQS 1694–1731/32* 502).

In King v. James Burns, the defendant confessed an indictment for petit larceny, and on Feb. 7, 1765 "on motion of the Clerk of the peace for Judgmt. agt. the Defendt . . . ordered . . . carried to the place from whence he Came . . . and thence to the Publick Whipping Post . . . [where he was to get thirty-nine lashes] and then to be

Transported from this City, and if ever found in it thereafter to be taken up and receive the Like punishment" (*Ms. Mins. NYCQS 1760–72* 127, 129).

[110] 2 Hawkins, *Pleas of the Crown* c.48 §1.

[111] 14 Howell, *State Trials* 505.

[112] Cf. *supra* 272 *et seq.*

[113] For examples of the ritual, Queen v. Barker, 1711 (*Ms. Mins. SCJ 1710–14* 346, 347); King v. Margaret Grass, 1736 (*Ms. Mins. SCJ 1732–39* 212, 213); King v. Richard Roch, 1753 (*Ms. Mins. SCJ 1750–54* [Engr.] 217, 221); King v. McDaniel and Kilfoy (*Ms. Mins. SCJ 1754–57* [Engr.] 341–342); King v. Cooley (*Ms. Mins. NYCQS 1772–91* 91, 95, May 4, 6, 1774).

The case of William Elkins and Abraham Stokes is a curious one, for the defendants were convicted of petit larceny and "The Prisoners being set at the Bar, and Asked why Sentence of Death should not be passed on them, and having nothing to Say the Court gives Sentence, that the Prisoners severally

cases where special verdicts were rendered, the practice was to have argument on the law before the prisoner was brought to the bar for sentence. The court would then advise upon its judgment, a process which might consume more than a single term.[114] During the early eighteenth century there are various entries in the minutes of the Supreme Court indicating advisement, sometimes probably to give a prisoner opportunity to secure a pardon, and sometimes when there were circumstances which pointed to possible mitigation.[115] When the practice of allowing affidavits in mitigation on a plea of *nolo* was established the giving of judgment was often postponed until another term.[116] Included also in the proceedings preliminary to judgment were the claim of benefit of clergy and the proffer of pardon, both of which were made when the prisoner was asked whether he had anything to say why judgment should not be rendered. These matters will be discussed in connection with mitigations.

Judgment

It was usual in New York to render judgment in the presence of the defendant.[117] This was mandatory at common law upon convictions where afflictive

receive twenty Lashes each . . . at the private Whipping Post in the Bridewell" (*Ms. Mins. SCJ 1775–81* [Engr.] 64, 65, Jan. 20, 1776).

[114] Thus, Queen v. Paroculus Parmyter—indicted for champerty in 1706 (*Ms. Mins. SCJ 1704/05–1709* 84, 94, 103, 108, 121); Queen v. Drommy—bigamy, 1713 (*Ms. Mins. SCJ 1710–14* 457, 496, 499, 516, 538).

[115] King v. Tymon Van Borson and another, assessors presented for failing to assess the inhabitants of the north ward, prayed their discharge on Feb. 2, 1696, stating that their failure to assess was "through ignorance," whereupon the following entry was made: "Cur⁹ advisare vult." No further proceedings appear in the case (*Ms. Mins. NYCQS 1694–1731/32* 17, 19). On Feb. 1, 1714/15, John Wood confessed an indictment for assault and battery and prayed the mercy of the court, whereupon the following entry was made: "cur⁹ advisare vult." On Feb. 2, the defendant was fined 13s. 4d. (*ibid.* 278, 279).

When the jury found a "violent presumption" that Edward Blagge was guilty of the assault and wounding for which he was indicted and prayed the court's advice if this was sufficient proof in law, the court took the case under advisement by a "cur⁹ vult advisare" (*ibid.* 348, Aug. 6, 1718).

[116] Thomas Cheeseman entered a *nolo contendere* on an indictment for assault and battery on Aug. 9, 1771, and the court stated that it would consider the fine the next Sessions. On Nov. 6, 1771, the court heard the witnesses for the Crown and defendant and considered the evidence sub-

mitted, whereupon it ordered that the defendant be fined ten shillings (*Ms. Mins. NYCQS 1760–72* 350, 355).

Abraham Van Wyck, on Apr. 27, 1772, entered a *nolo contendere* on an indictment for breaking a window, and, appearing on his recognizance on May 2, 1772, was discharged from his recognizance. As to the judgment on the indictment, the court wished to advise further, but no further minute entries on the case appear (*Ms. Mins. SCJ 1769–72* [Engr.] 514, 522).

On Aug. 6, 1773, judgment for want of a plea was entered against Thomas Burling on an indictment for nuisance in keeping a liquor still in a neighborhood where large quantities of flax were dressed, thus creating a fire hazard, and "the court will consider fine next court." However, no further proceedings appear in the case (*Ms. Mins. NYCQS 1772–91* 37, 61).

Edward Welch was convicted by jury verdict on three indictments for assault and battery on Nov. 2, 1774, and the court stated that it would consider the fine. On Nov. 4, Welch was ordered to pay the forty-shilling fine (*ibid.* 114, 119).

On final proceedings against Joshua Bishop *et al.* in August 1766, cf. *supra* 203.

[117] In this connection should be noted a very exceptional case, King v. Jacob Lewis, informed against for assault and battery. Lewis appeared by attorney and a rule to plead was given. After one imparlance Lewis appeared and pleaded not guilty. At Queens *nisi prius*, Sept. 1735, he failed to appear and an inquest by default taken, the jury re-

punishments were to be meted out,[118] and there had once been a time in England when this was essential in misdemeanors generally. The absconder then, as later, was outlawed. The original reason for insistence upon the presence of a person to be sentenced to a penalty of life or limb the English courts had long forgotten, but in the eighteenth century it was explained that in offenses of a gross nature it was desirable to have the defendant brought up for the sake of example, the notoriety of his appearance conducing to deter others.[119] Although there was no relaxation of attitude if a corporal punishment was involved, the rules respecting fine had been undergoing modification since the end of the seventeenth century, a change which led to a more flexible conception of judgment in misdemeanors. The attendance of the defendant who was only to be fined was held to be dispensable, and this chiefly because the courts abandoned the old notion that a fine was a ransom from imprisonment—a notion that had earlier made the defendant's presence essential to bargain the amount.[120] To some extent this relaxation was also due to the exploitation of the rule to plead or suffer judgment, the effectiveness of which would have been destroyed if in a prosecution for a merely finable offense notice beyond the original process had been required.[121] King's Bench consequently, upon default on a rule to plead and after the prosecutor had signed judgment, would order it to be entered, at which time the fine would be set.[122] *Capias pro fine* would issue if the defendant refused to pay the sum imposed.

Some of these developments were known in New York and we shall have more to say about provincial practice in connection with execution.[123] At the moment it is only necessary to notice that in misdemeanor cases the Supreme Court became more anxious than its prototype, the King's Bench, to have a defendant at the bar for sentence, since it would order judgment to be entered but would set the fine only after an effort to get the defendant into custody by a capias.

These proceedings where it was sought to secure the defendant's presence show that although the Supreme Court did not follow King's Bench prac-

---

turning a conviction. On the return of the *postea,* Smith appeared for Lewis, but on motion for the Crown, judgment *nisi* was ordered. The next term the court fixed the fine at £20. This is the only instance of an inquest by default we have seen (*Ms. Mins. SCJ 1732–39* 79, 120, 122, 141, 185; *Ms. Mins. Cir. 1721–49* 297; *H.R. Parch.* 12 H 7).

[118] Rex v. Harris and Duke, 1697 (1 *Ld. Raymond* 267).

[119] Rex v. Hann and Price, 1765 (3 *Burr.* 1786–87).

[120] Fox, *Contempt of Court* 172, 184, 196.

[121] This is to be inferred from the opinion in Rex v. Simpson, 1717 (1 *Strange* 44) where a summary conviction before a justice was sustained despite defendant's absence, on the ground that opportunity to appear was sufficiently accomplished by the summons.

[122] Hands, *Solicitor's Practice* 15; Rex v. Robinson (2 *Burr.* 801).

[123] Cf. *infra* 722 *et seq.*

tice it nevertheless regarded such a judgment in a misdemeanor case as interlocutory.[124] This was possible because the civil practice of signing judgment[125] was applied to misdemeanors, but the judgment so signed did not become final until enrolled. We have found some examples of the prosecutor signing judgment in New York,[126] and there can be no doubt from the evidence that the distinction between entering and enrolling judgment was observed, at least by the middle of the eighteenth century.

These details, which may strike the reader as hopeless technicalities, were important for several reasons. In the first place, they make clear that there was a recognized difference between the pronouncement of judgment and the recordation thereof.[127] In the second place, they serve to explain why in misdemeanors, judgments were sometimes altered after pronouncement, although once of record no alteration was possible.[128] Finally, the interlocutory charac-

[124] Rex v. Robinson (2 Burr. 801).

[125] Cf. Tidd, King's Bench Practice 566, 568.

[126] In King v. Petrus Haring et al., on an information for riot, the Attorney General, on July 31, 1764, moved for judgment for want of a plea and the court so ordered (Ms. Mins. SCJ 1764–67 [Rough] 3). In H.R. Pleadings Pl. K. 757, is to be found a "note of signing judgment" for July term, 1764, the original of which was "delivered" on July 31, 1764, and in this "note" is the following statement signed by J. T. Kempe as Attorney General: "I sign judgment against each and every defendant for want of a plea."

In King v. Matthew DuBois and fourteen other justices of peace, Attorney General J. T. Kempe on May 23, 1767, filed the following: "On information for maladministration as justices of peace: I sign judgment against all these defendants for want of pleas." However, on May 26, 1767, a similar paper in this case was endorsed: "Withdrawn" (J. T. Kempe Lawsuits C–F).

In several cases we have found notes indicating that judgment for want of a plea was signed but it is not indicated who signed the judgment, although we assume the Attorney General did. In King v. Richardson, endorsed on an indictment for fraudulently packing beef and pork of less than standard measure, is the following: "Judgment signed the 30th day of April 1754 for want of a plea" (H.R. Pleadings Pl. K. 555); also see King v. Alice McKim, information for trespass, Apr. 10, 1754 (ibid. Pl. K. 658); King v. John Pell Jr., information for violent breach of peace and assault, Apr. 10, 1755 (ibid. Pl. K. 950).

[127] The jury having found a verdict against Jane Chambers for petit larceny and the clerk of the peace having moved for judgment on the verdict, the court ordered that she be given fifteen lashes (Ms. Mins. NYCQS 1760–72 121, Nov. 7, 1764). Endorsed on the indictment against Jane (H.R. Pleadings Pl. K. 811) is the statement that she

pleaded not guilty and "judgment entered."

When the clerk of the Assizes (viz., Circuit) returned the postea against Rayner, Reeves and Lupton, finding them guilty of riot, their attorney on Oct. 20, 1753, filed reasons in arrest of judgment. On Oct. 25, the court gave its opinion that these reasons were insufficient, whereupon it was ordered that the judgment stand confirmed (Ms. Mins. SCJ 1750–56 [Rough] 165).

Likewise, when Smith filed reasons in arrest of judgment in King v. Gilbert Ferris, on Nicoll's motion on behalf of the Attorney General for judgment nisi causa on the postea, the court, on Jan. 23, 1756, heard the reasons in arrest of judgment but was "of opinion that Judgment be entered according to verdict." On Jan. 24, 1756, on the Attorney General's "motion for judgment on the verdict" the court fined the defendant £80 (Ms. Mins. SCJ 1754–57 [Engr.] 223, 240).

Ellinor Franshaw, on arraignment for petit larceny, "pleads guilty Ordered . . . twenty one lashes on her bare back and then to leave the city" (Ms. Mins. NYCQS 1760–72 139, Aug. 7, 1765). Endorsed on the indictment in this case is the following entry: "Defendant being arraigned pleads guilty sentenced to twenty one lashes tomorrow Judgment entered" (H.R. Pleadings Pl. K. 812).

[128] For example, in King v. Samuel Gerritson and others (supra c. III 178), two informations were filed on Jan. 19, 1754, against the defendants for "misdemeanor." Process was issued against the defendants and, on Apr. 25, 1754, the sheriff of Kings County having returned cepi corpora, the defendants endorsed the writ, whereupon their appearances were entered and they were ordered to plead in twenty days or suffer judgment. On Aug. 2, 1755 judgment for want of a plea was ordered and capias pro redemptione ordered to issue. On Oct. 27 the sheriff of Kings County was ordered to return the writs of capias pro redemptione by the following term, but on Jan. 22, 1756 "on reading

ter of misdemeanor judgments was the chief reason why defendants were able to move in arrest or present evidence in mitigation.[129]

The pronouncement of judgment after verdict was, according to the records, a mere rehearsal of the traditional formulae. It is apparent, however, from the few printed accounts of trials that the judge sometimes preceded the actual sentence by certain hortations which are not always to the modern taste. In Bayard's case Atwood confined himself to a few scathing remarks,[130] but at the trial of the negroes in 1741, Mr. Justice Horsmanden and his colleague Phillipse delivered a variety of rather gruesome excoriations of the poor wretches whom they were committing to the stake or to the scaffold.[131] This was one of the extraordinary judicial conventions of the time, induced perhaps by the belief that the judge, since he was ordering the taking of a life, had a duty to save a prisoner's soul by exhorting him to find the way to repentance, or perhaps by the belief that a proper painting of a convict's wickedness would have a deterring effect upon the audience.

In the case of judgments on motion or on demurrer, one would anticipate some sort of reasoned opinion, but although such opinions were undoubtedly delivered, as witness the remarks of De Lancey on the exceptions to the judges' commissions, and the few cases reported by William Smith Jr.,[132] the surviving records are nearly bare of even the slightest hints regarding reasoned decisions. Occasionally in the Sessions minutes reasons will be briefly noted. Thus, in Orange County an indictment for Sabbath breach was quashed because the

the affidavits of Peter Vandervoort . . . [and another] ordered the judgments in these two causes against the defendants be set aside on the payment of costs," and the defendants were thereupon again ordered to plead in twenty days or suffer judgment (*Ms. Mins. SCJ 1750–54* [Engr.] 348; *Ms. Mins. SCJ 1754–57* [Engr.] 40, 177, 200, 220). See also King v. Adam Smith *et al.* (*supra* 534).

For a country case where judgment was altered, cf. King v. Harris and Hickey where the defendants were on confession sentenced to 40s. or twenty lashes each. The next day the "rule" against Hickey was declared void and he was sentenced to twenty lashes at once and banishment (*Ms. Mins. Ulster Co. Sess. 1737–50* Nov. 7, 8, 1738).

[129] Apparently the "entry" was in the minutes, although according to English practice the indictments were also endorsed in the city. The country Sessions indictments were usually endorsed only if quashed. For city practice cf. the cases of Jane Chambers and Ellinor Franshaw (*supra* n. 127). Hugh McCuen on Nov. 7, 1764, confessed an indictment for assaulting some city watchmen and was fined 5s. (*Ms. Mins. NYCQS 1760–72* 121). Endorsed on his indictment was the notation

"Judgment entered" (*H.R. Pleadings* Pl. K. 763). On May 4, 1764, Philip Bergen confessed an indictment for assault and battery and was fined 5s. (*Ms. Mins. NYCQS 1760–72* 109). Endorsed on his indictment was this statement: "This judgment omitted being entered" (*H.R. Pleadings* Pl. K. 766). In King v. John Stewart and Thomas Everitt, on an indictment for grand larceny where the defendants were convicted and granted clergy, we have seen among J. T. Kempe's papers "Notes in order to make up Roll—Grand Larceny 26th October Indictment found 27th tried and found guilty Tuesday," etc. (*J. T. Kempe Lawsuits* S–U). In *H.R. Parch.* 165 K 9, is to be found the judgment roll which was finally made up in the Stewart and Everitt case.

[130] 14 Howell, *State Trials* 516.

[131] Horsmanden, *The NY Conspiracy* 51, 93, 150, 319.

[132] *William Smith Jr. Papers* Bk. V. It should be noted that in certain causes not criminal we possess opinions, some rather extended; cf., for example, the opinions in Fauconnier v. The King, 11 *Ms. Mins. Council* 294 (1715), and Cunningham v. Forsey, 29 *ibid.* 9 *et seq.* (1765).

defendant as a member of the assembly was obliged to go to New York;[133] in Queens, on a plea of *nolo* to an indictment for gaming, the fine was set at 2*s*. because the defendant had not made a practice of suffering gaming in his house;[134] in Dutchess a conviction before three justices was set aside on motion, not because the magistrates had acted contrary to duty but because it was "informal."[135] There is little in these country records to indicate a grasp of the law beyond a familiarity with the procedural machinery, yet even the occasional entries in the Supreme Court minutes are not much more informing.[136] It seems incredible that in cases like the proceedings against William Kempe, the prosecutions for trading with the enemy, or the great suit against Lydius, the elaborate arguments and the abundant citation were coolly brushed aside with a mere announcement of judgment. But unless the work of some diligent, but as yet unknown, reporter comes to light we shall remain ignorant of the exact scope of judicial opinion in this era.

The defects in our sources respecting the reasoned judicial opinion are due in part to the circumstances that throughout the colonial period English decisions were treated as the primary source of reference, and it was only on rare occasions that a provincial case was regarded as worth citing. Furthermore, in spite of the care taken by counsel in preparing evidence and arguments in advance of trial, the tradition that judicial bodies caused to be remembranced only what had utility for purposes of record or review was strictly followed, with the result that public recordation was held to the minimum necessary for these ends. It is only necessary to recall that it was not until 1865 that the English introduced official reports, to realize how fortuitous was the preservation of judicial wisdom even in the mother country.

Punishments

But if a solemn observance of the economies of common law recordation has blighted inquiry into the quality of judicial thought, it at least has pre-

---

[133] King v. Sam Gale (*Ms. Mins. Orange Co. Sess. 1727–79* Oct. 1756).

[134] King v. Stephen Henman (*Ms. Mins. Queens Co. Sess. 1722–87* Sept. 15, 1761).

[135] King v. Margery Hally (*Ms. Mins. Dutchess Co. Sess.* Liber A, Oct. 16, 1739; *Ms. Files Dutchess Co. 1726–40*).

[136] In Queen v. Samuel Clear, the defendant made a motion in arrest of judgment which was argued on both sides between Oct. 13, 1703 and Sept. 5, 1704, but on Sept. 7, 1704, "The opinion of ye court is that the action is discontinued by the death of the defendant" (*Ms. Mins. SCJ 1701–04*

126, 130, 147, 154). For King v. Waddell Cunningham, *supra* c. VIII 505. In c. X we have referred to the court's decision to allow the testimony of an infant of eight years in the prosecution of James Gaines for attempted rape (*Ms. Mins. SCJ 1754–57* [Engr.] 115, Jan. 24, 1755). Stephen Tippet and others were convicted by jury verdict of pulling down and burning Cornelius Bogardus' fence but "the court orders that the defendants be discharged of their recognizances being of opinion that the offence is not fineable" (*Ms. Mins. SCJ 1772–76* [Rough] 156, Apr. 29, 1774).

served details essential to a view of punishment, because an entry of the explicit sentence for fiscal and other reasons was one of the essentials. The picture here is one that is in some respects severe and in others capriciously lenient. Colonial practice was built upon a fairly exact copy of the English with all its harshness and its stylized compassion.[137] This imitation involved acceptance of the distinction between fixed and discretionary penalties, which, as we have seen, carried limitations; that is to say, in respect of felonies the unalterable judgment of life, with attainder and forfeiture implicit, was adopted, and the so-called discretion available in the case of lesser offense portended only a choice between bodily afflictive sanction or a fine. It is in relation to the finable offenses that in New York we discover signs of indulgence and this, indeed, chiefly in relation to prosecutions by Crown informations which were viewed with a jaundiced eye. When Blackstone wrote his fourth book he estimated that in England there were 160 offenses to which the felony punishment attached by act of Parliament.[138] Many of these were crimes established by statutes which did not extend to New York Province. The records here show that the extreme penalty was adjudged in rather a restricted number of offenses, and the tally is increased considerably by the inclusion of cases involving slaves.

There are unfortunately no satisfactory and complete records on which to base statistics.[139] The New York Quarter Sessions records are continuous from

[137] Viz., benefit of clergy, verdicts under 12d. in larceny prosecutions, etc.

[138] 4 Blackstone, Commentaries 18. Cf. the comment of Stephen, in 1 Hist. Criminal Law 470, where he indicates that by proper computation the number of statutory non-clergiable offenses was actually much smaller than Blackstone averred.

[139] Although it is impossible to give accurate statistics on punishments it is worth indicating the prevalence of particular forms. Taking due note of the fact that several distinct punishments might be meted out to a single defendant the records show about 446 penalties in the Supreme Court, 342 in Quarter and Special Sessions in New York City between 1691 and 1776, 60 in the Courts of Oyer and Terminer and General Gaol Delivery, 1716–17 and 1721–49, about 70 in the meetings of Mayor and Aldermen of New York City between 1733 and 1743. The total of punishments is less than the total of pleas, because in many cases the minute entries, after showing that the defendant had pleaded, contain no further proceedings. Furthermore, the total of punishments is less than the total of convictions and confessions, because in some cases the minute entries show no further proceedings. Out of 446 cases in the Supreme Court of Judicature where punishments were meted out be-

tween 1693 and 1776 (with certain years completely missing), there were 351 convictions, 75 confessions and 20 default judgments. Eighty-seven defendants were sentenced to be hanged after being convicted for the offenses of murder, counterfeiting, burglary, highway robbery, horse stealing, sacrilege in stealing, felony, pickpocketing and grand larceny. Among these 87 cases were some of slaves hanged for attempted rape and attempted murder. We have also included in this total 19 cases of slaves hanged in connection with the 1741 slave conspiracy. In connection with the same slave conspiracy, there were 13 slaves burned alive and 57 slaves transported. We have seen 78 cases in the Supreme Court in which clergy was granted to criminal defendants (15 on confessions and 63 on convictions). The majority of these grantings of clergy were grand larceny cases (about 50), and manslaughter was also a crime for which clergy was commonly granted. Not many instances of clergy granted in the early period have been found, and in fact there were only 2 cases of clergy up to 1693, then one in 1712, one in 1730, one in 1750, 10 between 1754 and 1758, one in 1761, one in 1762, 60 between 1764 and 1776 and one undated (cf. infra 751). We have found 11 cases in which the pillory was used: 2 on confessions of perjury

1691 to the Revolution, there are gaps in the Supreme Court and Circuit records, all of the country Sessions are incomplete, and there is but fragmentary information available on the summary convictions before single, double or triple justices. Missing also are records of particular special oyer and terminer commissions. On the basis of the available records, all of which we have consulted, we have counted 140 cases where the death penalty was adjudged. Thirty-nine of these involved slaves. The greatest carnage resulted from the trials incident to the alleged conspiracies of 1712 and 1741. Sixteen

and 9 on convictions for coining, deceitfully passing counterfeit, attempted counterfeiting, cheating in counterfeiting New York bills of credit, disorderly house and cheating in counterfeiting a bill of exchange. In 2 cases, one of grand larceny and one of receiving stolen goods, defendants, on being convicted, were sentenced to wear labels expressing their offense. Two defendants convicted of a cheat in counterfeiting New York bills of credit were, among other things, ordered to wear halters for a stated period of time. There were 20 cases in which imprisonment was used as a punishment, and the imprisonment lasted anywhere from eleven days to a year and a day. Imprisonment was used as a punishment for attempted rape, petit larceny, jailbreak, riot, disorderly house, cheating, defacing a bond and cheating in counterfeiting New York bills of credit. In only one of these 20 cases was there a confession, and that was for disorderly house, and in the other 19 cases the defendants were convicted by jury verdict. In 62 cases the lash was liberally applied, the punishments ranging anywhere from 13 to 117 lashes for any individual defendant. In 9 of the cases the defendants confessed, and in the other 53 cases the defendants were convicted by jury verdict. The offenses for which the lash was used in the Supreme Court involved coining, attempted counterfeiting, burglary, horse stealing, pickpocketing, being an accessory to a felony, grand larceny, attempted rape, receiving stolen goods, perjury, jailbreak, disorderly house, riot, trespass and cheating in counterfeiting a bill of exchange. In 6 cases defendants convicted by jury verdict were sentenced to be placed in a cart and drawn around town. The offenses involved pickpocketing, grand larceny, attempted rape, receiving stolen goods, petit larceny and jailbreak. The good behavior was used either as a substitute for, or as a complement to, other punishments in 13 cases (4 involving confessions and 9 convictions). The good behavior security was demanded for a period anywhere from three months to seven years, and the offenses for which this security was demanded, probably as a sort of parole, were deceit in passing a false Jersey bill of credit, attempted rape, petit larceny, jailbreak, riot, destruction of sheep by poison and disorderly house. There were 136 fines meted out (53 on confession, 63 on conviction and 20 on default). The fines ranged on confession from one shilling to a hundred pounds for offenses including petit larceny, disorderly house, riot, assaulting officers, attempted rape, seditious words, libel, usury, maladministration of office, assault and battery, deceit, obstructing the King's highway and misdemeanor. The fines on jury convictions ranged from six pence to a hundred pounds and were meted out for seditious words, attempted wife poisoning, attempted rape, petit larceny, riot, forcible entry, assault and battery, disorderly house, entertaining slaves, nuisance, cheating, maladministration of office, false swearing, refusal to aid officers, etc. In some cases defendants were pardoned as the Council minutes show, but the pardons were not entered in the judicial minutes.

In the Courts of Oyer and Terminer and General Gaol Delivery in the years 1716–17 and 1721–49, there were 60 punishments meted out. In all, 25 defendants confessed judgments, 30 were convicted, 4 were acquitted and one was discharged on his indictment being found *ignoramus*. In 15 cases, defendants convicted of murder, burglary and felony were hanged. In 9 cases, defendants were lashed (one on confession and 8 on conviction) for crimes including petit larceny and enticing a slave away. The lashes extended from fifteen to sixty lashes for one defendant. In 13 cases, defendants were obliged to give surety for their good behavior for periods ranging from three months to a year and a day. One of these defendants was obliged to give surety for his good behavior although an indictment for felony against him had been found *ignoramus*. In 4 cases of the 13 in which defendants had to give surety for their good behavior, involving murder, manslaughter, felony and petit larceny, the defendants were acquitted. In 6 of the 13 cases where they had to give surety for their good behavior, defendants confessed indictments for trespass and assault, and in 2 of the 13 good behavior cases, defendants were convicted for jailbreak and petit larceny. Four defendants confessing or being convicted of assault, riot and petit larceny were discharged despite their guilt. In 27 cases (21 involving confessions and 6 involving convictions), the defendants received fines ranging from five shillings to forty pounds. The offenses in these cases comprised riot, maladministration of office, jailbreak, promising a felon aid in his escape, assault and trespass.

slaves were burned alive, one was hanged in chains until he was dead from lack of sustenance and one was ordered broken on a wheel and to continue languishing until death. Others of the slaves of our total of thirty-eight were mercifully sentenced to death by hanging. There are records between 1691 and 1776 of 101 cases of white persons sentenced to be hanged for murder, "felony," burglary, counterfeiting and horse stealing. Missing in our tabulation are the minutes of the Supreme Court for the years 1715–23 and 1740–50, and most of the Circuit cases after 1750; hence there is no reliable basis for conjectures as to probable figures.

Except for the two outbreaks of public hysteria in 1712 and 1741, it is patent that there prevailed in New York Province if not a greater compassion at least a greater reluctance to take life than was the case in England. This is the more remarkable because the people who fell into the toils of the law are revealed by examinations and depositions often to have been brutal and debased, and one would expect that years of dealing with such specimens would have not disposed the judges to depart from the rigors of English practice. They were, to be sure, inclined to order the whip, but it is not true, as a lay historian has stated, that "the number of criminals hanged in the city [viz., New York] was appalling."[140]

In the capital felony cases involving whites the courts, in pronouncing sentence of death, adhered to the time-honored English formula for judgment (which included the order *suspendatur per collum quosque mortuus fuerit*) —at least the minute entries so indicate.[141] This form of judgment was supposedly unavoidable on conviction, yet there are cases, some of them occurring shortly before the Revolution, where the judges of the Supreme Court took the law into their own hands and merely sentenced the defendants to be whipped.[142] There is nothing in the records to explain why this was done, and

---

[140] Peterson and Edwards, *New York as an Eighteenth Century Municipality* (1917) 308.

[141] E. Wilkins was sentenced for murder as follows: "The prisoner being asked what he could say for himselfe why judgment should not pass against him and having said nothing but what he said before, the court pronounced judgment against him that he be carried to the place from whence he came from there to be carried to the place of execution . . . and hanged by the neck till he be dead" (*Ms. Mins. SCJ 1704/05–1709* 46, Oct. 13, 1705). James Wilks was convicted of murder, and on Jan. 24, 1756, the following entry appears: "On motion of Mr. Attorney General for judgment the prisoner was set at bar and being asked what he had to say why sentence of death should not pass and saying

nothing—the court pronounced sentence as follows: That the prisoner be carried from hence to the place whence he came and thence to the place of execution there to be hanged by the neck until he be dead" (*Ms. Mins. SCJ 1754–57* [Engr.] 223, 224). The formula is in Coke, *Third Institute* 211.

[142] Arraigned on an indictment for felony, Philip Dennis, having pleaded not guilty, was tried and found "guilty to ye value of forty pounds." Dennis did not plead his clergy, but was only sentenced to receive thirty-nine lashes to be divided into three lashes at each of thirteen named places (*Ms. Mins. SCJ 1710–14* 492, 495, 500, Oct. 15, 16, 1713). Lewis, a negro belonging to Peter Barberie, confessed an indictment for taking two guns, two pair of pistols, five shirts, a bag with bullets, a

there was certainly no statute which authorized such an alteration in the law. The provincial assembly in 1768 had provided that persons charged with the felonious taking of personalty to the value of £5 could be proceeded against "as offenders in petty larceny now are . . ." except where the crime was not clergiable. But in two instances where whipping was ordered the offense clearly did not fall within the purview of this statute although the judges may have supposed the enlargement of their discretion was greater than the express letter of the law.[143]

In the case of slaves who were sentenced to the stake or to be broken it should be noticed that the provincial statutes gave to the Special Sessions or meetings a very wide discretion in the specification of penalties. The formula of judgment where these brutal penalties were ordered was consequently a colonial invention but one which followed the pattern of the treason and felony formulae of the mother country.[144]

The afflictive penalty most favored in the Province was whipping, which the existing records show to have been imposed in upward of 250 cases, although it is obvious from the few extant summary trial records that if more such were available the total would be greater. The offenses for which this sentence was pronounced included petit larceny, perjury, coining, attempted rape, jailbreak, receiving, assaulting officers or justices, common assaults, cheating, fraud, kidnapping, vagrancy and disorderly houses. The number of lashes given to any individual ranged anywhere from five to one hundred and fifty, although in general there is evident a predilection for thirty-nine, just under the Scriptural monition. The selection of this penalty was governed by factors which are

powder horn and a pair of thread stockings belonging to his master and worth three pounds. He was merely sentenced to be lashed (*Ms. Mins. SC] 1723–27* 142, 143, 146, June 4, 8, 1725). John, alias Edward King, was convicted on indictments for burglary and grand larceny and was merely sentenced to receive thirty-nine lashes on a Monday and thirty-nine more lashes the following Monday. In the first place, it would seem that on the grand larceny charge, to avoid hanging, King should have had to plead his clergy, and furthermore, on the burglary charge, he should have been sentenced to be hanged, since the offense was not clergiable (*Ms. Mins. SC] 1769–72* [Engr.] 170, 174, 182, 198, Apr. 17, 18, 23, 28, 1770). Mary Daily was convicted of grand larceny, but instead of pleading her clergy, was sentenced to twenty-one lashes and discharged (*Ms. Mins. SC] 1769–72* [Engr.] 193–198, Apr. 27, 28, 1770). If this Mary is the one mentioned *supra* 675 n. 252, she was not entitled to clergy a second time.

[143] 4 *Col. Laws NY* 969.

[144] For the slave cases in 1712 cf. *supra* 118. Two particularly vindictive punishments which we have not included in the tally given in the text above (as the public records are missing) are mentioned in a letter from Christopher Bancker to Abraham De Peyster, Jr., on Jan. 23, 1716/17: "A negro . . . was executed December 27 . . . first hanged on the gallows till Dead Dead Dead and afterwards hanged in Gibbits where he was to remain for forcing a little girl of 13 years to lay with him. On the 24th of December at Schoharie . . . [one Trucax] was murdered . . . by a negro man and woman . . . they were executed the second of instant. The negro man was burned half an houre until dead and then hanged in gibbits where he is to remain and the wench was burned one houre and afterwards the ashes" (*Misc. Mss. Bancker* Box 1).

quite outside our ken, for the cases cannot be worked into a semblance of consistency. It was a favorite of the Suffolk justices, and just before the Revolution the Dutchess bench succumbed to the lure of the lash.

Defendants convicted of petit larceny were usually sent to the whipping post but there are instances where fine or imprisonment was adjudged.[145] Similarly, the same fate awaited slaves convicted of crimes less than capital, but here again there are exceptions.[146] Probably the whipping sentence depended chiefly upon whether or not the crime was of a type so prevalent that the sentence was designed to operate *in terrorem,* and upon the type of offender before the court. In most cases the evidence adduced for conviction is wanting, so that there is no way of fixing how far the circumstances of a particular offense entered into consideration as a matter of course. In matters like riot and disorderly houses it was usual to fine; when we come here upon sentences of lashing, it is obvious there were aggravating circumstances.

One metropolitan flourish was the sentence of carting which appears to have been used rather infrequently for we have found that only twenty-five persons were sentenced to be placed in a cart and drawn around town. This punishment was usually coupled with lashing or other punishments, and was meted out for such offenses as petit larceny, counterfeiting, grand larceny, attempted rape, receiving stolen goods, jailbreak, attempted murder, attempted arson, cheating and violent wounding. This penalty was similar to stocking and pillory in that public exposure provoked the real indignities at the hands of the sadistic onlookers. It was used somewhat more often than the pillory for we have found only sixteen instances where the latter was used. To be sentenced to the pillory and the cart had the serious consequence that the person suffering either was thereby rendered infamous.[147] There is late seventeenth century authority to the effect that it was the nature of the crime and not the punishment which destroyed the convict's capacity,[148] but the writers of justices' manuals continued to state the old rule.[149] It is possible that in New York this latter conception still obtained for the judges were sparing of the cart and the pillory. Pillory was so unusual in Dutchess that, unlike the stocks, it

---

[145] Queen v. De Hart (*Ms. Mins. SCJ 1704/05–1709 37*) £4 and custody until paid; King v. Garr, King v. Simonson (*Ms. Mins. Richmond Co. Sess. 1710/11–1744/45* Sept. 26, 1738, Mar. 20, 1738/39); King v. Harris (*Ms. Mins. Suffolk Co. Sess. 1760–75* Oct. 4, 1763, Oct. 2, 1764).
[146] Queen v. Densworth, a slave (*Ms. Mins. SCJ 1701–04 150–172*); King v. John Brown and

Aeneas, a slave (*Ms. Mins. SCJ 1769–72* [Engr.] 441, 447).
[147] Coke, *Third Institute* 219; Coke, *Littleton* 6b.
[148] King v. Davis and Carter (5 *Mod.* 74); King v. Ford (2 *Salkeld* 690).
[149] Cf. Nelson, *Office and Authority of a Justice of the Peace* (1711) *s.v.* Pillory; 3 Burn, *Justice of the Peace* (1770 ed.) *s.v.* Pillory.

was not standing ready; for in 1774 when Archibald McNeal was sentenced to a half hour in that instrument, the clerk adds "to be put in as soon as the sheriff has his pillory ready."[150] If ignominy alone was thought desirable there was available exposure at the whipping post or in the stocks which were maintained the length and breadth of the Province. The latter appears only rarely in the judicial records but was used chiefly, we suspect, for the summary convictions of drunk and disorderly persons.[151]

Another instrumentality peculiar to New York City was the cage which the Common Council minutes show to have been a constant object of municipal concern, but which is mentioned rarely in the judicial records. Ann Cannon in 1751 confessed an indictment for petit larceny, and the New York Court of Quarter Sessions "ordered she be set in the publick cage for two hours" and leave the city within forty-eight hours.[152] In another case it appears as the *locus* of a whipping.[153] Probably this object was used chiefly for persons convicted summarily. In three cases, labels indicating the culprit's offenses were ordered to be placed on them as part of their punishment.[154] Two defendants were,

[150] *Ms. Mins. Dutchess Co. Sess.* Liber E, Oct. 14, 1774.

[151] The situation respecting the stocks is puzzling for they are rarely mentioned in the provincial acts of assembly (cf. 1 *Col. Laws NY* 356, Sabbath breach [1695]; *ibid.* 617, immorality [1708]; 2 *ibid.* 304, act re stocks in Schenectady [1726]). In both the 1695 and 1708 acts, the stocks were to be used if there was no property on which to levy for the fine. Judging from the general trend of colonial penal legislation, imprisonment was usually threatened once there were jails available. It should be noted that during the proprietorship stocks were sometimes the alternative for fine; cf. the North Riding Sessions of 1679 (28 *NY Col. Mss.* 110); and the entry in *Ms. Deeds Ulster Co.* Liber 3, 151 (1684). Except for the Sabbath breach statute mentioned above, there is almost no evidence that this custom continued, but it should be noted that in 1774 Justice Howel of Suffolk Co. ordered Jonathan Cook to three hours in the stocks for refusal to pay a small fine (*Daniel Howel's Book of Recs.*). It is possible the stocks were used as a sanction for violating local ordinance; cf. the order of the Westchester justices (1693) in *Mins. Westch. Ct. Sess. 1657-96* 83. We have seen no sentences to the stocks in the early minutes of this county although on Dec. 2, 1712, Abraham Underhill who had abused a justice of the peace was ordered to pay 30s. and to repair the stocks and whipping post (*Ms. Mins. Westch. Co. Sess. 1710-23*). As it seems unlikely an instrument of justice would be kept in repair unless it was used we are therefore disposed to believe that the stocks were used in cases of summary convictions where the offender

was not substantial enough to pay a fine or to furnish recognizance. In New York City the stocks were used. Peterson and Edwards (*op. cit.* 196, 308) seem to doubt this, but in 1767 the Quarter Sessions Court sent Bridget McEwen, convicted of keeping disorderly house, to an hour in the stocks (*Ms. Mins. NYCQS 1760-72* 233, Nov. 5, 1767).

[152] King v. Ann Cannon, alias Doleman (*Ms. Mins. NYCQS 1732-62* 289, 290, Feb. 6, 7, 1750/51).

[153] King v. Joe, a slave. Joe was summarily convicted on the information of Jacobus Van Cortlandt, a justice of the peace, after an examination of various witnesses. The court being satisfied that Joe was guilty of petit larceny, ordered that he "forthwith by the Common whipper . . . att the Cage be Stripped . . . from the Middle upwards and then and there . . . be tyed to the tayle of a Carte and . . . shall be Drove round the City and Receive . . . att the Corner of each Street nine lashes" (*Ms. Mins. NYCQS 1694-1731/32* 28, June 10, 1697).

[154] Elizabeth Pym was convicted in the Supreme Court of knowingly receiving stolen goods, and was sentenced to be whipped around the town at the cart's tail "with a Label on her forehead signifying that she is a receiver of stolen Goods, and that she receive Ten Lashes on the Bare Back at each of the Three most publick places in Town" (*Ms. Mins. SCJ 1769-72* [Engr.] 63, 64, 66, 69, July 27-29 1769).

Ann Gough was convicted of grand larceny but instead of being sentenced to be hanged or of claiming her clergy, she was sentenced to be carted around the town "with a label on her breast ex-

among other punishments, sentenced to having a halter put around their necks.[155]

It is a circumstance worthy of notice that after 1750, the minute books of the country Sessions show the most sparing use of corporal punishment for, in general, fines are the usual penalty. This may be partly accounted for by the fact that after 1750 it was rare that a traverse of an indictment was pushed to trial. Usually the defendants confessed or pleaded *nolo,* and unless the offense was an extremely grievous one[156] only a fine would be inflicted. At the same time it is not improbable that where proceedings were summary before single or double justices, the sentences were more severe. Our only direct proof here is in Suffolk County where the *Book of Records* of Daniel Howel for the years 1774 to 1776[157] contains a number of instances of both stocking and lashing in conviction on summary proceedings, whereas the contemporary minutes of the General Sessions show merely the imposition of fines on persons there tried. It may be supposed that a similar practice prevailed in other counties, but the records of summary proceedings, if in fact kept, have long since vanished. The explanation of the difference (if it was as general as we suggest) probably lies in the character of the defendants dealt with in Special Sessions, especially under the "offenses less than grand larceny" laws. These persons were vagrants or persons without substance and were accordingly in the callous spirit of the time given the least expensive available punishment.[158]

pressing her crime," and she was afterwards to get twenty-one lashes. The sheriff was ordered to see that execution of this sentence was carried out (*ibid.* 107, 111, 120, Oct. 20, 23, 28, 1769).

In Queen v. Bartholomew Vank and Thomas Roberts, defts. were convicted of "coining" and had labels placed on their heads with the words "ffor counterfeiting dollars" (*Ms. Mins. SCJ 1704/05–1709* 54, 57, 62, 68, 72).

[155] *Supra* 515 n. 120.

[156] Whipping ordered in King v. Abigail Scot, King v. John Field—petit larceny (*Ms. Mins. Suffolk Co. Sess. 1723–51* Mar. 1726); King v. Thos. Story (*ibid.* Oct. 1743); King v. Thos. Pepper—entering county house (*Ms. Mins. Ulster Co. Sess. 1737–50* May 5, 1741); King v. Joseph Lace—attempted rape (*Ms. Mins. Albany Co. Sess. 1763–82* Oct. 2–5, 1764).

[157] Pennypacker Collection (Easthampton Lib.).

[158] Compare the recital in the Act of 1732 (2 *Col. Laws NY* 745). The most complete data on the enforcement of these laws are in the records of "meetings" of Mayor and Aldermen of New York City for the trial of offenses less than the degree of grand larceny between 1733 and 1743. About seventy punishments were meted out when these defendants were summarily convicted of offenses

comprising counterfeiting, pickpocketing, receiving stolen goods, vagrancy, fraud, assault, kidnapping and petit larceny. Three defendants were sentenced to the pillory for a quarter hour for the crimes of counterfeiting and petit larceny. One defendant was exposed at the whipping post for a quarter hour for petit larceny. One servant was jailed until his master should give orders for his release after he was convicted of the crime of petit larceny. Three defendants were sentenced at hard labor (two for petit larceny and one for a cheat in counterfeiting a Spanish dollar). Sixty-seven were whipped anywhere from 5 to 117 times and their offenses involved counterfeiting, kidnapping, cheating, petit larceny, pickpocketing, receiving stolen goods, vagrancy and wounding. Two were carted for counterfeiting and petit larceny. Thirty-one were ordered to leave the city or province for counterfeiting, petit larceny and vagrancy, and one of these was ordered to remain in Westchester for six months. The others were for the most part ordered never to return on the pain of being lashed when apprehended. One defendant convicted of petit larceny was discharged when the magistrates were satisfied that he bore a good character in the community.

Imprisonment was not favored in the country because it was costly, and although banishment was sometimes resorted to, for we have counted over fifty such sentences,[159] this also involved outlay. It cost the Dutchess taxpayers 6s. 6d. to get rid of Margrit King in 1736, and 10s. in 1738 for "Transporing a vagabond."[160]

We have already spoken of imprisonment as punishment in connection with the matter of recognizance, and have commented upon the fact that it was usually ancillary to some other penalty.[161] In the Sessions, when fines were set it was frequently stated in the minutes that the prisoner was to be in custody until the fine was paid. Very infrequently was a sentence of imprisonment alone inflicted. In New York City, judging from some late lists of prisoners in jail still preserved, imprisonment was used as a punishment for convictions on summary trial.[162] The Supreme Court and city Quarter Sessions minutes show further that these courts now and again, upon conviction at the regular terms, would use an outright jail sentence.

The fine, as we have indicated, was the sanction par excellence of provincial criminal justice. It was imposed in the greatest variety of non-capital cases—adultery, assaults, attempted poisoning and rape, coining, frauds, lotteries, petit larceny, riots, usury and numerous other offenses. It is in relation to this penalty that certain tendencies toward leniency are perceptible. In General Sessions the fines were usually trifling unless an offense like an assault upon an officer was involved. The picture which the extract of fines for Ulster from 1693 to 1763 portrays is typical of inferior jurisdictions. Starting with a single case of a farthing, a penny, and threepence, there are eight at sixpence, eleven at 1s., five at 4s., two at 5s., five at 6s., thirteen at 10s., two at 20s., three at 30s. and one at 40s. During these seventy years there are nine cases of fines ranging from £3 to £15. After the French and Indian War there are indications of somewhat increased rigor in the counties where there were disturbances.[163]

[159] For example, *supra* 296 n. 53. In the country the justices seem to have desired only that the undesirable be banished from the county. Cf. King v. Alice Kerney (*Ms. Mins. Dutchess Co. Sess.* Liber A, May 19, 1741); King v. Hickey (*Ms. Mins. Ulster Co. Sess. 1737-50* Nov. 7, 1738); King v. Robert Nugent, out of Long Island (*Ms. Mins. Suffolk Co. Sess. 1760-75* Oct. 7, 1760). Horsmanden lists seventy negroes transported to Newfoundland, Madeira, the West Indies and elsewhere as commutation of sentences imposed at the slave trials in 1741 (*The NY Conspiracy* App.). Cf. *H.R. Parch.* 149 B 3, bonds and list of transported negroes.
[160] *Old Misc. Recs. of Dutchess Co.* 127, 188.

[161] *Supra* 515.
[162] *Ms. Accounts of James Mills* (Keeper of City Gaol), *NY City Clerk Ms.* file no. IV, 3. Account Dec. 12, 1769—Mar. 12, 1770; Account Sept. 13, 1770—Dec. 12, 1770; Account Dec. 13, 1770—Mar. 12, 1771; Account Mar. 13, 1771—June 12, 1771.
[163] The Ulster list is in *NY State Lib. Mss.* 7460. Compare for example, in Richmond County at the September term, 1729, eight defendants pleaded *nolo* to indictments for assault, five were given fines of 6s., one of 8s., one of 20s. and one of 6d. Two pleading the same to indictments of housebreaking were each fined 6s. Two defendants ("misdemeanor") were discharged by proclamation and

The Supreme Court judges were also disposed toward small fines and we have already noticed that even in cases of riot the penalties were frequently inconsequential. Naturally the policies at Circuit where court was held by the city and country judges reflect the prevailing tendencies. The one exceptional occasion of heavy fining was the special "Assize" at Poughkeepsie in 1766 where one fine of £200, one of £50, one of £40, several of £20, £10 and £5 were imposed. But even here in many of the ninety-four cases the penalties ran only to amounts less than 20s. The estreats for Circuit in the following years indicate the average penalty ranged between £10 and £1, but in many instances fines less than a pound were imposed.[164]

The scale of fines in New York was appreciably less than in England and is perhaps to be explained by a greater spirit of moderation in the New World. Possibly also the penalties were set with some reference to the financial capacity of defendants and the desire to keep them off the books of the overseers of the poor. In some cases, as we shall see, a small fine was set because a settlement was made with the complainants.

Escheat and Forfeiture

Something of the same indulgence which prevailed in respect of fines seems also to have come into being with regard to the application of the economic sanctions implicit in the judgment of felony and treason—the escheat and forfeiture. It is necessary to preface our examination of the New York practice here with some brief account of the English rules. In the case of treason all lands of inheritance and all rights of entry to lands in the hands of a wrong-

one (housebreaking) was tried and acquitted (*Ms. Mins. Richmond Co. Sess. 1710/11–1744/45*). The scale remains much the same for some time although beginning in 1763, stiffer fines are set in assault cases, viz., King v. Hicks (May 1763) £5; King v. Kelsey (May 1765) £5; King v. Hicks (Sept. 1766) £3. The "base" seems to be 20s. at this time on either *nolos* or *cognovit*, although in King v. Johnson (Sept. 1773) a six-penny fine for a confessed assault was set (*Ms. Mins. Richmond Co. Sess. 1745–1812*). In Queens County between 1722 and 1773, the fines for assaults run 5s., 20s., 30s., and in one case, King v. Abraham Bond, where the defendant had insulted Clowes, £6 and £2 1s. 6d. costs were inflicted (*Ms. Mins. Queens Co. Sess. 1722–87* Sept. 1758). The fines in Orange were also trifling, but in one riotous rescue a very exceptional £40 fine was imposed, King v. Davis (*Ms. Mins. Orange Co. Sess. 1727–79* Oct. 29, 1740). In forcible entries cf. the cases in 1748 and

1749 in Dutchess where assaults confessed are fined 1s.–12s. but forcible entries £9 and £10 (*Ms. Mins. Dutchess Co. Sess.* Liber A).
[164] On Supreme Court fines in riots, cf. *supra* c. III 204 and as to general range of fines, *supra* n. 139. The Oyer and Terminer fines 1716–49 are referred to in that note. For the later period, *H.R. Parch.* 218 D 1, 179 A 9, 211 C 2. A sampling shows the following: Dutchess, 1771, £10 (assault on sheriff); Ulster, 1771, £2 (assault on constable); Dutchess, 1772, £1 (assault), £2 (non-attendance of constable at court); Albany, 1772, 6s. 8d. (assault), £1 (killing a horse); Westchester, 1772, two at £1 (non-attendance of constables at court); Queens, 1772, three at 10s. (assaults); Tryon, 1772, £1 (petit larceny), three at £1 (non-attendance of constables at court), two at £1 (absence of petit jurors); Albany, 1773, £3 (assault); Orange, 1773, 6s. 8d. (assault).

doer of which he was seised forfeited to the Crown upon attainder.[165] The Crown was similarly entitled to the forfeiture of chattels upon conviction. Where an offender was attainted of felony, however, such rights in lands escheated to the lord of whom the lands were held, subject to the royal prerogative of a year and a day.[166] The chattels, however, were forfeit to the King upon conviction.[167] If an offender was acquitted but the jury found flight, there was likewise a forfeiture of chattels.

The actual application of these rules in the case of lands was a matter of great complexity because of the ramifications of real property law and the disturbing effect of various statutes. During the reign of Henry VIII it had been sought to broaden the whole base of royal rights in a revised statute of treasons,[168] but by judicial decision exceptions continued to come into existence. From the administrative point of view, the most important effect of this statute was the rule that in treason cases the Crown acquired a right of entry without inquest of office,[169] although it was probably in many cases impracticable to proceed without a special inquisition.[170] This was the case when wholesale forfeitures took place after the Rebellion of 1715 and the matter was handled by statutory commissioners.[171] The rule of immediate entry does not seem to have extended to cases of felony, where the Crown had only a year and day and waste. The requirement that a petit jury make a return respecting the lands, tenements and chattels of a convicted offender when rendering a verdict,[172] was possibly intended to simplify the settlement of Crown rights. The lord to secure his escheat applied for a writ of escheat ordering conveyance.[173]

The machinery for collecting chattel forfeiture was grounded on a statute of Edward III's reign[174] that required a sheriff, when an *alias capias* issued after indictment, to seize the goods of the accused. A later statute provided that the property of persons arrested or imprisoned on suspicion of felony would not be seized before conviction or attainder.[175] But just as the warrant of arrest came into use in despite of the law so, as Lord Hale reports,[176] peace officers constantly made seizures of chattels, and Dalton states[177] that an officer might

[165] Coke, *Third Institute* 19; 1 Hale, *op. cit.* 240 et seq.; 2 Hawkins, *op. cit.* c.49 §1.

[166] Coke, *Littleton* 13, 391.

[167] Foxley's Case, 5 *Co. Rep.* 109.

[168] 26 Hy. VIII c.13, and cf. also 33 Hy. VIII c.20 §3.

[169] Dowtie's Case (3 *Co. Rep.* 9b, 10b); 1 Hale, *op. cit.* 240.

[170] Viz., the inquisition of instruction, Gilbert, *Historical View of the Ct. of Exchequer* 132–134.

[171] 1 Geo. I st. 2 c.50.

[172] *Office of the Clerk of Assize* 50; *Crown Circuit Companion* 14.

[173] Fitzherbert, *Natura Brevium* (1794 ed.) 144 H; Viner, *Abridgment, s.v.* Escheat.

[174] 25 Edw. III c.14.

[175] 1 Rich. III c.3.

[176] 1 Hale, *op. cit.* 366.

[177] Dalton, *Countrey Justice* (1677 ed.) c.165.

take sureties against embezzlement, or might seize and appraise chattels, turning them over to the town for safekeeping until conviction or acquittal. The courts on several occasions stated categorically that a defendant was entitled to his chattels for his maintenance prior to conviction,[178] and consequently no royal rights attached as a result of these extra-legal seizures.

The collection of the chattel forfeitures depended upon further administrative action after trial. These items were by st. 22 & 23 Car. II c.22 supposed to be included in estreats to the Exchequer whence process for collection would issue.[179] Presumably the court depended for this upon the finding respecting lands and chattels made by the jury when rendering a verdict, upon a coroner's roll, or a return by a sheriff, although the latter would normally account directly to the Exchequer. There are signs that by the eighteenth century, these "casual revenues" were most casually handled[180] except in the treason cases where the wealth and position of the offenders made the forfeitures something worth exertion. Blackstone, usually mute on practical questions of law enforcement, remarks that juries rarely found flight because forfeiture was deemed too severe a penalty.[181] And a half century later, a former Chief Baron of the Exchequer informed a Parliamentary committee that for "long years" the Crown's year and day in escheats had been abandoned, and that chattel forfeiture was insignificant because most felons had nothing to forfeit.[182]

The reception in New York of the economic sanctions incident upon treasons and felonies was clearly intended by the Crown, for these are mentioned in the 1686 instructions to Dongan,[183] and directions continued to be made thereafter regarding the matter.[184] That these plans were never successfully carried out was due to a variety of factors, not the least of which was the failure to set up in New York an establishment comparable to the English Exchequer whereby the exaction of forfeitures would be assured. Furthermore, the fact that these revenues, since they appertained to the Crown, were specifically within the jurisdiction of the Receiver General[185] and their disposition thus

---

[178] Fleetwood's Case, 1611 (8 Co. Rep. 171); —— v. Chillender, 1657 (Hardres 97); Jones v. Ashurst (Skinner 357).

[179] The sample of estreats from Assizes (1779) in 4 Chitty, Criminal Law (1816) 485, does not, however, contain any forfeitures.

[180] The lack of system in the enforcement of economic sanctions is indicated by a case mentioned in Parliament when Romilly's bill respecting attainder of felony and treason was under discussion. In the reign of George II a woman had been convicted of murder, and not until 1813 did the

Crown make a claim of escheat (28 Hansard, Parl. Debates clxviii).

It should further be noted that cases involving forfeitures are rare, and abridgments like Bacon and Viner contain mostly very old law.

[181] 4 Commentaries 386.

[182] Report from the Select Committee on Criminal Laws (1819) 49.

[183] 3 Doc. Rel. Col. Hist. NY 371.

[184] 1 Labaree, Royal Instructions 331.

[185] Cf. the 1687 instructions to Plowman, Receiver General (3 Doc. Rel. Col. Hist. NY 501).

not subject to the assembly, tended to promote the same indifference which prevailed with regard to quitrents.

All our evidence bearing upon the forfeiture or escheat of lands relates to the prosecutions arising out of the Leisler Rebellion. The first cases are those of Leisler, Milborne, Beekman, Gouverneur and others who were indicted for treason or felony. As to all the defendants convicted at that bloody assize, the juries returned no lands, tenements or chattels to their knowledge. There was no finding in the case of Leisler and Milborne, the judgment being given as if they had stood mute. The conclusion of the record states, "and let the sheriff etc.," which we suppose to have been a direction to make inquest of lands and chattels. Despite the petit jury finding as to some defendants, it appears that there ensued a general forfeiture of lands and chattels, and there is collateral proof that this was effected by a writ of inquiry.[186] The applications for the reversal of the attainders of Leisler, Milborne and Gouverneur were made particularly to secure a restoration of estates,[187] and when the Act of Parliament was finally passed[188] Leisler's widow was restored by a writ of possession issued by Governor Bellomont.[189] Beekman, who had been convicted of treason, was reprieved, and later by Order in Council ordered discharged from recognizance and his wife was granted the use of his chattels pending the settlement of his case.[190] The other convicted defendants were long kept from their estates and only restored by an act of assembly in 1699.[191]

Beyond the slight evidence that a writ of inquiry issued we have found no records which show how the forfeitures in these cases were carried out, although Mary Milborne speaks in a petition of the plundering of her husband's house.[192] The sheriff does not appear to have accounted to any court,[193] and nothing can be inferred from the Supreme Court proceedings by extent against the forfeited recognizances of Provoost and Mauritz.[194] Judging from

---

[186] For the jury finding, P.R.O., C.O. 5/1087, King v. Gouverneur (fol. 3); King v. Coerten et al. (fols. 6, 8); King v. Beekman (fol. 6); King v. Gouverneur, murder (ibid. 5/1082 fol. 4). In George Farewell's bill for his services in the trials of 1691 is the item "Attending the jury in Execuçon of the writt of Enquiry for three days drawing & Engrossing the returne thereof Examinacon of the Witnesses ec. In all wch Mʳ Emott assisted for my part 02.10.0" (37 NY Col. Mss. 118).

[187] The petitions, Orders in Council, etc. are in 1 NY Hist. Soc. Colls. 331 et seq.

[188] The act is in 2 Doc. Hist. NY 249.

[189] 1 NY Hist. Soc. Colls. 390. The widow was apparently not excluded from the estates in the interim; cf. her petition (2 Doc. Hist. NY 224).

[190] 37 NY Col. Mss. 87. This was by writ of the Governor to the sheriff of Kings reciting that as security had been taken that the chattels be forthcoming according to inventory, Magdalena Beekman was to have use of them. Cf. also the recognizance of Beekman re chattels in 2 Doc. Hist. NY 210.

[191] 1 Col. Laws NY 384.

[192] 2 Doc. Hist. NY 250.

[193] Ibid. 224. The sheriff's accounts were extracted from "the audited account of the Revenue."

[194] Supra 530 et seq.

the petitions for recourse directed to the Governor it seems likely that the orders emanated from that quarter.

Barring an alleged escheat taken and pocketed by Governor Fletcher in the case of a Richmond County suicide,[195] no further sanctions were taken against the lands of criminals until the treason cases of Bayard and Hutchins. It was charged by Lord Cornbury that Chief Justice Atwood and Receiver Weaver had caused the prosecutions in order that the debts of the Province might be satisfied from the forfeitures.[196] This happy means of balancing a budget did not succeed, for the Order in Council reversing the sentences included "all issues and proceedings" upon the sentences, and the subsequent acts of assembly specifically restored both defendants to their property.[197] Inquisition was probably contemplated, as Hannah Hutchins petitioned that no office be found until the Queen's pleasure be known and that she be permitted to keep her husband's shop open.[197a] No direct evidence, however, has been found to indicate the measures taken either to seize or release the forfeited property in these cases. At this time the Province already had an escheator general[198] but from the records it appears that this officer's activities were confined to occasions where a decedent was without heirs or to seizure of property of deceased aliens.[199] There was a succession of such officials[200] eventually succeeded, it would appear, by county escheators.[201] On only one occasion was the escheator particularly empowered to deal with forfeitures—when by act of assembly the threat of forfeiture was employed to compel Robert Livingston to submit certain accounts.[202] A subsequent repealing statute recites the fact that an inquest of office had been found by the escheator general upon order of the Lieutenant Governor, and eventually Livingston was restored by an order of the New York Council.[203]

With these episodes the escheat of lands as an incident of punishment seems to have come to an end. It is possible that inquests of office and escheats there-

[195] 4 Doc. Rel. Col. Hist. NY 423.
[196] Ibid. 1011, 1013.
[197] 1 Col. Laws NY 531 (1703), 590 (1705).
[197a] 45 NY Col. Mss. 99.
[198] George Sydenham appointed in 1698 (Cal. NY Col. Commissions 5).
[199] Cal. Council Mins. 180, 181, 292; cf. also Cal. Eng. Mss. 266, 311, 346. The escheat of aliens' lands was foreclosed by the Act of 1715 (1 Col. Laws NY 858). Cf. also Ms. Deeds Westch. Co. Liber C, Nov. 23, 1698; 42 NY Col. Mss. 130 (re Thomas Williams' estate). Williams died without heirs.
[200] Barne Cosens was appointed in 1702 (Cal.

Council Mins. 165); Augustine Graham in 1712 (Cal. NY Col. Commissions 16); Thomas Farmer in 1720 (ibid. 18).
[201] Cf. the appointment of John Colden for the County of Albany in 1750 (ibid. 30). We have seen no other notices of such appointments but surmise from this that the administration of escheats was changed. There is no escheator general listed in Tryon's report of 1774 (8 Doc. Rel. Col. Hist. NY 454).
[202] 1 Col. Laws NY 461.
[203] Ibid. 687; 8 Ms. Mins. Council 340; Cal. Council Mins. 178; Cal. Eng. Mss. 319.

upon may have taken place without entry in judicial records, since the Governor and Council assumed the power to deal with escheats for reasons other than crime. No accounts of the Receiver General for the eighteenth century relating to escheats earlier than Archibald Kennedy's first statements have been found. These return the pitiful sum £35 6s. 8d. in escheats (presumably of all sorts) for December, 1721—June, 1726[204] and £15 for fines and forfeitures from August, 1722 to March, 1727.[205] From a petition of 1733 it appears that Kennedy found great difficulty in collecting fines and forfeitures and requested instructions for accounting by sheriffs.[206] This petition suggests that the collection of casual revenue was entirely a matter between the Crown's fiscal officer and the local authorities, and the silence of the judicial records until Kempe's time, except where forfeitures under acts of trade were sued for, indicates that little help came from this direction. The reason for this probably is to be found in the fact that New York juries almost invariably reported no lands, tenements or chattels upon conviction. This finding was itself the equivalent of an inquest of office[207] and unless there was a subsequent information the court would not be likely to make further inquiry.[208]

The situation with respect to chattel forfeiture was upon much the same footing. In 1697 Joseph Smith, convicted of manslaughter, forfeited his chattels.[209] He petitioned that whereas by the "strict rules" of the common law his goods and chattels were forfeit, yet for the support of his family he prayed leave to keep them. This was referred to the judges who reported favorably that they thought the petitioner's goods would be found very inconsiderable and that Smith's family was an object of mercy. Apparently no effort at inquisition or appraisal had been made. Thereafter, except for the treason prosecutions in 1701, the seizure of goods was very rare. As was stated in the preceding chapter, only three instances have been found where juries reported chattels,[210] and we are disposed to think that this incident of felony judgment had virtually disappeared by 1766. In that year one Roper Dawson was convicted of manslaughter and the jury made the usual return of no chattels.[211] Dawson, however, was a merchant and not without means. Opinion of coun-

---

204 *Cal. S.P. Colonial 1726–27* no. 164.
205 *Ibid.* no. 620.
206 *Cal. S.P. Colonial 1733* no. 39.
207 1 Hale, *op. cit.* 362.
208 The Crown in ordinary inquests of office had a right to a *melius inquirendum*, Paris Stoughter's Case (8 Co. Rep. 168a).
209 Cf. the petition for pardon and report thereon in 41 NY Col. Mss. 121.

210 *Supra* 675. It should be noted that in 1706 Susannah Walgrave petitioned for the goods of her husband, a suicide. The sheriff was ordered to turn these over to her, taking security to pay them over if upon representation to the Queen "her pleasure is to this effect" (51 NY Col. Mss. 182).
211 *Ms. Mins. SCJ 1764–67* (Rough) 134.

sel was sought respecting the seizure of his goods, and this fact, plus the ancient authorities cited,[212] leads us to believe that the provincial lawyers were facing the problem as one novel to them. Dawson's property was evidently forfeited, for some years later he petitioned, praying pardon of the forfeiture and a grant and restitution of his goods and chattels "by the said Felony conviction and Judgment forfeited and now belonging to the crown." Lieutenant Governor Colden laid the matter before the Council and stated he was willing to accede if this was not contrary to the royal instructions regarding fines and forfeitures. The Council was unanimously of the opinion that the Crown had invested in the Governor the authority of pardon (except treason and murder) and that where a pardon issued before conviction the forfeiture was also pardoned. Consequently the Governor could restore the party here as this would not be within the limitation of the instruction.[213] It should be noticed finally that no inquisitions on forfeitures have been found, and in none of the many estreats of issues, fines and forfeitures of the Oyer and Terminer and Supreme Courts are there any entries to suggest that there had been forfeiture for felonies.[214]

The disappearance of escheat and forfeiture in felony cases is attributable chiefly to the fact that most of the felons convicted were so meanly circumstanced that there was nothing to forfeit. Even if any of these wretches had been landholders, the incentive for Crown officers to require escheat was wanting. Underpopulation was a problem that troubled the governors until well after the French and Indian War, for the pattern of tenure was such that the acquisition of a freehold was not easy.[215] There would have been little point in enforcing a sanction against heirs while complaining that the sons of settlers were leaving for other colonies to secure freeholds.[216] In the counties where feudal tenures prevailed, the year and day would in most instances have been nearly valueless, and would have been virtually unenforceable against the great lords like the Van Rensselaers, the Phillipses or the Livingstons who dominated provincial politics. Similarly unenforceable would have been claims to leaseholds under the prerogative of *catalla felonum*.[217]

<hr />

[212] *NY Hist. Soc. Mss. Colls., Misc. Mss. C.*: "Mr. Cortland's Opinion Concerning R. Dawson's effects."

[213] 26 *Ms. Mins. Council* 180, Mar. 14, 1770; *Cal. NY Col. Commissions* 77.

[214] *Supra* 528 n. 191.

[215] On this, Hunter's letter of 1710 (5 *Doc. Rel. Col. Hist. NY* 180); of 1715 (*ibid.* 459); Morris' complaint of 1733 (*ibid.* 953); Johnson's descrip-

tion of 1763 (7 *ibid.* 576). 1 Smith, *Hist. NY* 276, 310.

[216] Colden (1732) in 1 *Doc. Hist. NY* 247.

[217] 1 Hale, *op. cit.* 250. It should be stated that wherever we have had reason to suspect a convicted felon held lands we have attempted to ascertain through the registers of deeds in various counties whether or not any record of escheat existed. We have found no such records, and we have

In relation to the forfeiture of moveables other considerations were no less weighty. No jury of freeholders on whom the burden of poor relief rested was likely to find chattels and thus cast upon the county the support of a convict's wife and family. We have seen in other connections how this matter of support influenced the administration of the law and there is no reason to believe that it was less influential in the matter of forfeiture. That these considerations were more important than Crown right appears from an entry in the New York Quarter Sessions minutes for 1720 where the court ordered that four and one-half ounces of plate having been found in the dwelling of Thomas Codman recently executed for felony were to be delivered to Hannah Anderson as she "is very sick and weak, in a very Dour condition and a great object of charity."[218] And in Dutchess County in 1746 it was ordered by Sessions that a piece of fustian twenty-four and one-half yards long left by "Jacob Volkenburgh a felon lately in gaol" be sold at vendue at 2s. 4d. per yard to defray the charges of keeping him.[219]

There has been observed only one consistent exception to the usual return of *nulla bona*—the finding and valuation by New York City coroners' juries of instruments of death, which were of course forfeited as deodands, a strange example of the force of superstition in overcoming the frugality or prejudice of the burghers.[220]

The return of stolen goods stood upon a different footing, for some solicitude existed that these should not fall into wrong hands. This feeling is amusingly illustrated by an early episode in Westchester where a malefactor had fled leaving a portmanteau and a horse. The local justices, instead of proceeding to have this property forfeited to the Crown, ordered it to be held by the sheriff until someone should claim it.[221]

The usual proceeding after a criminal prosecution for larceny, burglary or the like was the formal order by the court for restitution. Such orders were made in the proprietary period[222] and appear frequently in the records of the eighteenth century.[223] The English practice depended upon a statute which

been advised by several expert title searchers that no such records have ever come to their attention.

218 *Ms. Mins. NYCQS 1694–1731/32* 384, 385, Nov. 2, 1720.

219 *Ms. Mins. Dutchess Co. Sess.* Liber A, Oct. 21, 1746.

220 *Ms. Mins. Coroner NY Co. 1748–58 passim.* The Governor probably had the disposal of the deodand. Cf. *Cal. Eng. Mss.* 823, where a horse (the deodand) is granted to the decedent's widow. The documents are burned. Note, finally, that in

qui tam actions under the Acts of Trade, the goods in question would be forfeit. These were *in rem* proceedings, cf. the cases cited *supra* c. IV nn. 48, 49, 56.

221 *Ms. Mins. Westch. Co. Sess. 1710–23* 12.

222 E.g., *Ms. Mins. Mayor's Ct. NYC 1674–75* 26; *Ms. Mins. Mayor's Ct. NYC 1677–82* fols. 226b, 230.

223 King v. Jonsen, 1692 (*Ms. Kings Co. Ct. & Rd. Recs. 1692–1825* 8); Queen v. Hannah Crosier, 1703 (*Ms. Mins. SCJ 1701–04* 88, 99); at this

718   LAW ENFORCEMENT IN COLONIAL NEW YORK

required that the injured party or someone by his procurement give evidence against the offender as a condition of restitution which would be effected by writ.[224] The judicial records do not show that this statute was followed in New York for it does not appear that prosecution was necessary to found a claim. It is true that on one occasion it was ordered (Suffolk Circuit, 1728) that property stolen by an Indian in the hands of the sheriff was to be restored to one Conklin, the owner, on condition that he "oblige himself that if the said Indian be apprehended he will produce the goods in court to convict him."[225] But the courts might merely order property held until claim was made[226] or the goods would be petitioned for, sometimes by persons who did not prosecute.[227] Only one instance of the use of a writ of restitution has been noticed;[228] apparently a court order on the record was deemed sufficient.

Infamy

It remains to speak of a final incident of conviction in treasons and felonies, and of certain sorts of degrading punishment—the infamy. In case of serious crime this loss of "lawfulness" had been an implicit consequence of judgment since the days of the first Norman kings,[229] and in the course of the Middle Ages had come to be attached to lesser offenses if the sentence was to the pillory, the cart or the like. How much weight the New Yorkers attached to this

Sessions, Ann Clay was acquitted of larceny but the goods in question were ordered returned to the owner (*ibid.* 99); Queen v. Margaret Smith, 1709 (*Ms. Mins. SC] 1704/05–1709* 219); King v. Ben Willson, 1726 (*Ms. Mins. Cir. 1721–49* 48); King v. Lewis, a slave, 1725 (*Ms. Mins. SC] 1723–27* 146). King v. Ned (1733), indicted for burglary but convicted only of felony and sentenced to receive thirty lashes (*Ms. Mins. Cir. 1721–49* 61); King v. Richard Combs, 1740 (*ibid.* 101); King v. Benjamin De Goede (*Ms. Mins. SC] 1754–57* [Engr.] 138, Jan. 25, 1755); King v. John Jones (*Ms. Mins. SC] 1762–64* [Engr.] 421, Apr. 27, 1764). Richard Roch was convicted of "privily and secretly stealing from Theophilus Elsworth a pocketbook and bills of credit of the value of 180 pounds," and was sentenced to death. The court also "ordered that the Money in the hands of Stephen Van Cortlandt Esqr. found upon [Roch] . . . be delivered . . . to Theophilus Elsworth . . . on his giving a receipt for the same" (*Ms. Mins. SC] 1750–54* [Engr.] 215, 221, Jan. 18, 20, 1753). Also see King v. Edward Lee (*ibid.* 161, Aug. 1, 1752).
[224] 21 Hy. VIII c.11.
[225] *Ms. Mins. Cir. 1721–49* 49, 50.
[226] King v. Willson, 1726 (*ibid.* 48).
[227] Cf. the petition of Anne Muggleson to Gov-

ernor Burnet, 1722 (*James Alexander Papers* Box 46) and the following: "Adolphus Phillipse Esqr. informed the Court that there were Some goods belonging to Adolph Banker George Jewell and Evert Aarkon three of his Tenants that were taken upon a felon lately escaped out of the County Gaol of Westchester wh[ch] goods are in the hands of Joseph Hunt Esq[r] the Mayor of the Burrough of Westchester that they are perishable goods . . . & prayed this Court would order that the said goods might be delivered to the Owners. Ordered with the consent of his Maties Attorney General that Such of the goods be delivered to y[e] persons claiming them as they Shall make Oath that truly belongs to them or any of them Saving one yard of the said Linnen to be retained" by the Mayor for the trial of the felon if taken (*Ms. Mins. SC] 1723–27* 214, 215).
[228] King v. Makelowne, 1701 (*Ms. Mins. SC] 1701–04* 2, 3).
[229] 1 Goebel, *Felony and Misdemeanor* (1937) 275, 413, 414. The eventual introduction of the trial jury resulted in the infamy being attributed to conviction in felonies, but the infamy incident to pillory and the like depended upon the judgment, until the theory developed that it was the turpitude of the offense and not the manner of punishment which resulted in infamy.

incident of infamy is not too well documented. During the troubled years following Leisler's execution, the evidence indicates that acceptance of the implications of attainder met political resistance. Governor Fletcher reported in 1693 that some of the persons convicted and reprieved in the treason trials had been elected to the assembly, an action which Fletcher had refused to countenance.[230] Nevertheless, in 1698, Myndert Coerten and Gerardus Beekman were elected from Kings County. These men had been pardoned but the attainder had not been removed. The assembly refused to seat them.[231] In contrast with the voters' disregard of the effects of being attainted, it appears from a 1693 petition of Gerardus Beekman that a person who was infamous was unable to protect himself from his traducers and was cast upon the mercies of the authorities for special protection.[232]

The anti-Leislerians learned nothing from the experiences of their enemies. Nicholas Bayard having escaped the gallows undertook, pending his appeal, to bring action against the judges who had tried him and the grand jury. The Crown law officers reported that persons attainted were incapable of bringing actions and further that such actions would not lie even after reversal of attainder.[233] Bayard sought also to secure the passage of an act disabling the judges from ever being judges, jurors, witnesses, executors or administrators. The act did not pass but the principals were worried enough to petition the Queen to be relieved from Bayard's machinations.[234]

The subsequent history of infamy in the Province is apparently one of tacit acceptance of the ancient rules. We have seen that the courts observed the rule which disqualified persons attainted as witnesses,[235] and it appears likewise that such persons were popularly regarded to be without capacity to own property. In 1696, Gabriel Leggett, it will be recalled, was convicted of stealing a hog from Thomas Williams who had been attainted of treason. Leggett assigned as error the fact that the complainant was incapacitated to be the owner of any goods or chattels whatever.[236] And years later the New York merchants, petitioning for the *nolle prosequi* of an indictment against Isaac Jacobs for felony, averred that the larceny in question had been from a felon.[237]

There does not appear to have been much disposition by the provincial legis-

[230] 4 *Doc. Rel. Col. Hist. NY* 54. It is amusing to note that on Oct. 14, 1692, the New York City common council refused to allow the election of a councilman who was under bond for good behavior because he was "therefore not fitt or qualified to Serve in that office of Trust" (1 *Mins. Com. Council NYC* 288).

[231] 1 *Jour. Gen. Assembly NY* 85, 86, 88.
[232] 2 *Doc. Hist. NY* 235.
[233] 4 *Doc. Rel. Col. Hist. NY* 1032.
[234] *Misc. Mss. Atwood.*
[235] *Supra* 645.
[236] *Supra* 259.
[237] *Supra* 368.

lature to make a specific penalty of infamy. The election law of 1699 expressly extended the penalties of st. 5 Eliz. c.9 to persons committing frauds,[238] a statute which, among other things, disqualified perjurors to be witnesses. The tendency, however, in colonial penal legislation was in the illimitable expansion of the *qui tam* action or, as in the case of counterfeiting, the application of the omnibus "felony without benefit of clergy" punishment. Nevertheless, at the very eve of the Revolution, a gaming statute provided that persons winning more than £10 deceitfully at cards, dice or the like should forfeit five times the sum so won and "shall be deemed infamous and suffer such corporal Punishment as in Cases of wilful Perjury."[239]

Execution of Afflictive Sanctions

The execution of sentences was a matter that depended upon the crime and whether or not the prisoner was in custody. In the case of a capital offense, the prisoner was in custody at the time of sentence, and although anciently a warrant was necessary for execution, this practice had been virtually abandoned by the English courts at the time New York was settled. It was considered that a defendant being in the sheriff's custody an open pronouncement of the judgment was the only necessary direction for execution, and in King's Bench the mere entry of the *praeceptum est marescallo quod faciat executionem* was sufficient and nothing more was usual.[240] At the English Assizes the clerk made out four calendars of the convictions, one signed by the clerk and delivered to the judge, the second signed by the judge and left with the clerk, the third delivered to the sheriff and the fourth to the jailer. The executions took place in accordance with the sentences set forth in the calendar.[241]

The early minutes of the Supreme Court do not disclose whether or not this tribunal adopted the King's Bench practice, but the surviving judgment rolls where sentence of death was not imposed, follow so closely the particulars of English enrollment[242] that it seems probable the Supreme Court merely gave an oral direction to the sheriff in capital cases. None of the contemporary oyer and terminer records contain orders respecting execution and no writs or warrants have been found.[243] From other sources it is established that the sher-

---

[238] 1 *Col. Laws NY* 407.
[239] 5 *Col. Laws NY* 621.
[240] 2 Hale, *op. cit.* 31, 409.
[241] *Office of Clerk of Assize* 56, 74; Stubbs, *Crown Circuit Companion* 15.
[242] E.g., the roll in King v. Johannes Provoost (*NY Supreme Court Mss.* Box 36); King v.

Le Reaux, King v. Joseph Smith (*H.R. Parch.* 209 G 9).
[243] The proceedings in King v. Leisler and the other persons tried in 1691 contain merely the sentence. Neither the printed account of King v. Bayard, nor the minute book has any directions.

iff was responsible for hangings. In 1697, Sheriff Tuder presented the New York City Council with a bill for £12, the cost of executing a negro,[244] and in the following year his successor brought in to Quarter Sessions an "Acct. amounting to the sum of thirty nine pounds sixteen shillings for Executing three Murderers (Vizt.) Samuell Lowen, John Suterbury & Thomas Verwin for the hangman for Negroes for Carmen and Carting for Iron worke and for hanging the dead bodies in Irons."[245]

A dozen years later there commence occasional minute entries which give explicit directions to the sheriff in cases of capital crimes.[246] Rules of the Supreme Court required the presence of the latter[247] and for this reason, perhaps, the clerk did not always enter an explicit reference to the sheriff. The judgment roll would in any event be the only document which would have to contain such a precept. The rule of 1727 forbidding any executions until the roll was made up and signed,[248] indicated clearly enough the official status of the roll as against the minute book.

The system of having execution depend upon the oral command or the entry of this in the roll provided no check upon the sheriff, although the fact that executions were paid for was probably enough insurance that they would be carried out. In 1722, the Supreme Court ordered among other things that "the service of any rules of this court on the deputy appointed by the sheriff shall be as effectual as if served on the sheriff himself."[249] Whether or not this had reference to the introduction of any calendar of executions is doubtful.[250] Many years later in the case of *King* v. *Domine* who was sentenced to

244 2 *Mins. Com. Council NYC* 11.

245 *Ms. Mins. NYCQS 1694–1731/32* 36, May 3, 1698. Cf. the Minutes of the Ulster Supervisors, Oct. 10, 1730, where the sheriff's bill of £3 for a hanging and 6s. for fetters was presented (*Ms. Files Ulster Co.* Bundle I).

246 Queen v. Claus (*Ms. Mins. NYCQS 1694–1731/32* 212, Apr. 11, 1712). There was no express direction to the sheriff in the cases of the other negroes sentenced at the special court: King v. Ben Willson and King v. Sam (a slave) sentenced to be hanged (1726) and a special guard assigned "for the security of the prisoners" until execution (*Ms. Mins. Cir. 1721–49* 48); King v. Negro Ned (1733) sentenced to thirty lashes in Albany, thirty more in Schenectady and an additional thirty the following week in Albany, "which punishment he is to receive at the most publick place in each respective town between the hours of 10 and 12 which sentence the high sheriff of the county is to see executed" (*ibid.* 61); Wan, a slave, was sentenced for burglary as follows: "That the prisoner be carried from hence to the place from whence he

came and thence to the place of Execution and there hanged by the Neck until he be dead. Ordered that the prisoner be executed on Friday the first day of November next between the Hours of 10 and 12 in the Forenoon And that the sheriff see Execution done accordingly" (*Ms. Mins. SCJ 1750–54* [Engr.] 89, Oct. 24, 1751); the sheriff was ordered to see execution done on John McDaniel and Simon Kilfoy, sentenced to be hanged for highway robbery (*Ms. Mins. SCJ 1754–57* [Engr.] 338, 339, 341, 342, Jan. 19, 20, 1757); King v. John Williams and another, 1767, for grand larceny and burglary (*Ms. Mins. SCJ 1764–67* [Rough] 205, 207, 208, 211); King v. Jack, a slave, 1770, for burglary (*Ms. Mins. SCJ 1769–72* [Engr.] 279, 280, 282, 288); King v. Francis Burdet Personel, 1773, for murder (*Ms. Mins. SCJ 1772–76* [Rough] 102, 106–108, 111).

247 Rules of Sept. 5, 1706, Apr. 16, 1754, Apr. 30, 1763, Oct. 31, 1767 (*Ms. Rules Supreme Ct.*).

248 *Ms. Mins. SCJ 1723–27* 276, June 13, 1727.

249 Cf. *supra* 454 n. 327.

250 In *Ms. Files Ulster Co.* Bundle L is a parch-

three cartings and thirty-nine stripes on each trip, it was "ordered sheriff see execution done accordingly, see the file of rules,"[251] from which it may be inferred that a calendar was used. No such calendars have been found for the Supreme Court, but there are preserved several later "List[s] of rules" of the Dutchess General Sessions setting forth the offenders' names and the penalties, signed by the clerk of the peace. These seem to be the provincial equivalent of the English calendars, and are the only evidence available respecting the Sessions practice of warrant for executing corporal punishments.[252]

In cases where imprisonment or fine was to be the sentence, the procedure varied depending upon whether the defendant was present in court or not, and if present, whether he was in custody or under recognizance. We have already remarked upon the fact that in the eighteenth century imprisonment was just coming into vogue as a form of punishment and that custody was chiefly used as a means of compelling the liquidation of a fine.[253] Except for a few cases where imprisonment was part of a compound sentence,[254] the provincial courts ordinarily treated the misdemeanors not worthy of corporal punishment as something to be penalized only with a fine.[255] The evidence in the Sessions records is overwhelming on this point. Even in respect to the serious or quasi-political misdemeanors tried in the Supreme Court the same attitude prevailed. In consequence the procedure for execution is essentially a procedure to secure payment of a penalty.

Execution of Pecuniary Sanctions

The problem of enforcing a pecuniary sanction was considerably simplified in New York by the lavish exploitation of the recognizance. Country minute books covering the last decade of the seventeenth century show that the summons to answer misdemeanors was almost invariably fortified by an undertaking to answer, and in the eighteenth century it is an extremely rare occur-

ment order (1725) in the case of Nicholas Schoonover [Schoonhaven] (*supra* 268). This may be the form of "rule" then used.

It should also be noted that the mutilated last page of *Ms. Mins. NYCQS 1705/06–1714/15* is a list of persons condemned at the special court for the trial of the 1712 negro conspirators "received sentence today" and may from its appearance be a memorandum for such a calendar.

[251] *Ms. Mins. SCJ 1764–67* (Rough) 190–195 (1766).

[252] *H.R. Pleadings* Pl. K. 365 (Jan. 1774); K. 362 (Oct. 1774), K. 364 (Jan. 1775), K. 363 (Oct. 1775). These are not estreats. This is clear

from the heading and from K. 362 where there is a sentence of whipping (King v. McNeal *et al.*) which would not be included in an estreat. For a copy of a Dutchess Common Pleas rule attached to a referee's report cf. West v. Gonsalis (*Ms. Files Dutchess Co. 1767*).

[253] *Supra* 514 n. 115.

[254] *Ibid.* n. 116.

[255] We have found one case where in General Sessions a man was ordered imprisoned for twenty days merely on the complaint of two men that he was a dangerous person, King v. Marrow (*Ms. Mins. Suffolk Co. Sess. 1760–75* Oct. 1, 1765).

rence when a defendant appears without having given security.[256] Similarly in the two periods when a capias was used as first process in misdemeanors, the defendant being in custody, the control over his person was sufficient to make final process unnecessary.

In the early years when a defendant present on a venire facias merely gave security to answer, the recognizance was discharged by appearance.[257] In this event an order to pay a fine and to stand committed until he did so would require a *mittimus* to jail him. We have not seen any samples of such documents but the table of fees for 1710 provides a charge for *mittimus*.[258] The court also might, as it did, exact a recognizance to abide judgment.[259] If a defendant was already in custody the mere order to commit sufficed, and the 1710 ordinance as well as Sir Henry Moore's ordinance of 1768 provides a sheriff's fee for "every person committed."[260]

The country records are usually silent on measures taken to collect fines, although now and again the bench will order "discharge" on payment of fine or confinement until payment or giving surety.[261] In most instances the penalties were so small that they could be paid immediately. In the New York City Quarter Sessions and in the Supreme Court, orders to commit until fine and fees were paid are relatively frequent,[262] probably because the capias was there a more usual form of process and a greater number of city defendants could not furnish bail. These records too will occasionally state that the penalties were paid in court and the defendant was discharged.[263]

---

[256] Cf. Queen v. Gilbert Livingston (*Ms. Mins. Ulster Co. Sess. 1711/12–1720* Sept. 2, 1712); King v. Louw (*ibid.* Sept. 1, 1715). In the cases where the entries show under the same date an indictment and a confession or a *nolo*, with no indication of process or recognizance, it is possible that the defendant sometimes was merely summoned, but more likely he was present on a justice's warrant.

[257] *Supra* 507 *et seq.*

[258] *An Ordinance for Regulating and Establishing Fees* (Broadside, 1710) 4.

[259] *Supra* 507 n. 92.

[260] *An Ordinance for Regulating . . . Fees* (1710) 4; (1768) no page.

[261] Cf. *Ms. Mins. Suffolk Co. Sess. 1723–51* Sept. 1725; King v. Stringham (*ibid.* Mar. 1728); King v. Harris (*Ms. Mins. Ulster Co. Sess. 1737–50* Nov. 7, 1738); King v. Stokes (*ibid.* May 1, 1744). Some of the indictments preserved in the Dutchess County Clerk's Office (*File 1740–50*) are endorsed "discharged," e.g. King v. Hoffman, King v. Henry Schuyler, King v. Evert Vosburgh (all of 1744).

[262] *Supra* 512 n. 109. Thomas Adams, sentenced to a £5 fine and the charges of prosecution on being convicted of a breach of the peace, was ordered to "stand committed till he pay the same" (*Ms. Mins. NYCQS 1694–1731/32* 124, 134, 136, May 7, 1707, Feb. 4, 1707/08).

Also see Queen v. Dorothy Wright (*ibid.* 177, 178, Aug. 2, 1710); King v. Judith Peters (*ibid.* 446, Nov. 4, 1724) and King v. William Richardson (*Ms. Mins. SCJ 1732–39* 283, Oct. 25, 1736). Jacobus Cosyne was committed to the county jail until he paid a fine of £10 for assaulting Abraham Laquire and £40 for assaulting Antoinette Laquire; he was also to find sureties for his good behavior for a year and discharge the costs of his prosecution before he was released (*Ms. Mins. Cir. 1721–49* 22–24, Kings Co. Oyer and Terminer and General Gaol Delivery, Sept. 18, 1722). In the case of Mary Canada, who confessed an indictment for aiding one Shute in getting out of jail, the defendant was fined 40s. and was ordered to be committed to the common jail without bail or mainprise for one month and until she should pay her fine and fees (*Ms. Mins. NYCQS 1732–62* 111, Feb. 7, 1739/40).

[263] In Queen v. William Day, on a conviction for

The collection of fines in the cases where one or two justices proceeded summarily, or where the *qui tam* action was brought before the magistrates on one of the innumerable penal statutes is a matter that is extremely obscure owing to the fact that so few records of these proceedings have been preserved. And even when the estreating of fines was put upon a regular basis the return of such issues was apparently evaded or at least rendered negligible. The English practice in case of summary conviction was by distress or imprisonment, and the offender might be kept in custody or required to give security pending the return on the warrant of distress. If there was not sufficient goods the defendant could then be committed. Information about this procedure and the requisite forms were available in manuals, like Nelson's *Justice of the Peace*, which were in use in New York, but we suspect the provincial justices proceeded without much regard for English methods.[264] A case which shows the adaptation of these summary methods to a defendant who confessed an indictment for breach of the assize of bread is in the New York Quarter Sessions records,[265] but from the scanty available sources of country practice we find in Suffolk County that Justice Howel set an offender who refused to pay a fine in the stocks,[266] and Justice Terboss of Dutchess issued a warrant of execution to levy on a defendant in a penal action incorporating instructions that in "de-

---

trespass and assault, "It is Considered by the Court that the Defendt pay a fine of twelve shillings to our sovereign Lady the Queen with the Charges of Prosecution and that he stand Committed till he pay the same. The Defendt. having paid the fine and fees Ordered he and his security be discharged from their Recognizance" (*Ms. Mins. NYCQS 1694–1731/32* 178, Aug. 2, 1710). In the case of Johannes Bradt (*infra* 743), on Oct. 26, 1752, "the sheriff of Albany by receit produced in Court acknowledges that he has received thro' the hands of the Attorney General the Sum of five pounds being the fine assessed . . . to be paid by the . . . defendant for which he stands charged to the King" (*Ms. Mins. SCJ 1750–54* [Engr.] 124, 164, 194).

James Osborne, convicted on an indictment of keeping disorderly house, was fined £20 which he was "to bring into Court the first day of the next Sessions, and if the said fine be not paid forthwith that he stand committed till the same be paid. The Defendt. being Called . . . ordered he be continued on his Recognizance till next Sessions." The following Sessions "Deputy Sheriff produced the fine of Twenty pounds Imposed on the Defendt. Ordered he bring the Same into Court the next sessions" (*Ms. Mins. NYCQS 1760–72* 100, 109, Feb. 9, May 4, 1764).

On Apr. 17, 1765, "the court sets a fine of three shillings four pence on Edward Ackerson, paid to

the prothonotary and ordered discharged" (*Ms. Mins. SCJ 1764–67* [Rough] 51).

Elizabeth Allen, convicted of assault, was on Apr. 27, 1765 fined 6s. 8d. and ordered committed until she paid the fine and gave security in £25 of her good behavior for three months. This fine was paid to the prothonotary in court (*ibid.* 69, Apr. 27, 1765).

George Clark entered a *nolo contendere* on an indictment for riot and misdemeanor and was fined 6s. 8d. which he "paid to the prothonotary in court. Ordered discharged" (*Ms. Mins. SCJ 1766–69* [Engr.] 374, Jan. 19, 1768).

Henry Pullen, convicted on an indictment for riot and assault, was on Oct. 28, 1769, fined £10 which he paid to the prothonotary in court and was discharged of his recognizance (*Ms. Mins. SCJ 1769–72* [Engr.] 119).

Peter and Elizabeth Bausher entered a *nolo contendere* on an indictment for disorderly house, were fined 20s. and fees and ordered committed until paid. However, the defendants paid the fine "to the clerke in court" (*Ms. Mins. NYCQS 1760–72* 359, Nov. 7, 1771).

[264] E.g., Nelson, *Justice of the Peace* (4 ed. 1711) 216.

[265] King v. Thurman (*Ms. Mins. NYCQS 1694–1731/32* 295, 296, Aug. 2, 1715).

[266] *Daniel Howel's Book of Records* 1, 2 (1774). There is no mention of a warrant.

fault of distress" the defendant was to be jailed.[267] Both these cases occurred shortly before the Revolution and suggest that throughout the century the practice of country justices was neither uniform nor in accordance with the books.[268]

We have spoken thus far of execution when the defendant was present at judgment. The situation when he was absent presented difficulties, especially if the offense was one where corporal punishment might be inflicted. Until Holt's time it was assumed that a defendant had to be present even if only a fine was to be imposed,[269] but as already stated, it was ruled early in Anne's reign that if a clerk was present to undertake for a fine the defendant did not need to appear.[270] If a corporal punishment was to be adjudged the defendant's presence was indispensable.[271] The New York practice eventually was brought into conformity with these rules, but probably only after the lapse of some years. In 1705, the Supreme Court ordered on an inquisition for a riot that the defendants be imprisoned for six months without bail. When called, however, the defendants did not appear and the Attorney General moved that a default be entered. In the March term following (1706) it was ordered execution issue if the defendants did not appear in four days. This case is quite exceptional, for thereafter the court does not appear to have given judgment for imprisonment unless the defendant was present.[272]

The most usual situation where a defendant might be fined *in absentia* was on a default judgment after a rule to plead. Here, as has been shown, it was possible to collect by putting the recognizance in suit, although this involved further litigation.[273] Moreover, to achieve the ends of criminal law enforcement it was often desirable to proceed with the salutary business of setting a fine on the defendant himself, for it was obviously better policy to put a convicted offender in jail for not paying a penalty, than to have him confined on a second proceeding for not discharging a debt. This was why the *capias pro fine* was used even when a defendant's recognizance to abide judgment was still in force. The writ had originally the purpose of taking the defendant to

---

[267] Green v. Cooper, 1770 (*H.R. Parch.* 24 G 1) and cf. *supra* 266.

[268] The practice in England was meticulous respecting the succession of precepts. The only combination warrant of this sort we have seen is in *The Young Clerks Vademecum* 79 (to levy or put in stocks). This book was printed in Belfast and reprinted by Hugh Gaine in New York, 1776. There is no such precedent in the much used Burn, *Justice of the Peace* (1770 ed.).

[269] Per Attorney General (*arg.*) in Queen v. Potter (2 *Ld. Raymond* 937).

[270] Queen v. Templeman (1 *Salkeld* 55).

[271] Rex v. Harris & Duke (1 *Ld. Raymond* 267).

[272] Queen v. Wilkins, Warner *et al.* (*Ms. Mins. SCJ 1704/05–1709* 46, 52).

[273] *Supra* 530 *et seq.*

imprison him until he made fine, viz., bargained for his release; but by the end of the seventeenth century it was used principally to take him after the fine was set by the court.[274]

The process entries in the judicial minutes during the early 1700's are so scanty that it cannot be stated categorically that a *capias pro fine* issued invariably for final process, although nothing else can be inferred from the use of the traditional phrase in the enrolled judgments "that he be taken to satisfy" for a fine. In the Sessions Courts there was probably little use of the *capias pro fine* before the middle of the eighteenth century, because until then the rule to plead with judgment on default was not used there. The inferior courts on default confined themselves to entering default, orders to estreat recognizances *nisi causa* and the final order to estreat.[275] The earliest express order for a *capias pro fine* in the New York Quarter Sessions minutes occurs in 1754.[276] The country minutes show simply that forfeiture of recognizance is the usual final step on default, but these records are not to be trusted implicitly in details relating to process. We know from the *Register of Costs* kept by James Duane when acting as deputy Attorney General in Richmond County that *capias pro fine* was used in nearly every case where he appeared.[277]

The Supreme Court did not develop a consistent policy with respect to defendants in misdemeanors absent at the time of judgment, for at the very eve of the Revolution it was sometimes attempting to compel their appearance and sometimes merely ordering proceedings on the recognizance. During the early eighteenth century this court was lenient in the matter of defaults,[278] and in many a case the last order of record will be a continuance.[279] Now and then an order for estreat of the recognizance will be made and occasionally execution will be ordered,[280] by which a capias must be understood.[281] Most of the orders in case of constables' or jurors' defaults contain no directions to levy, but we know from estreats that distraint was made.[282] The silence of the minutes

274 In Duke's Case (*Holt* 400) the *capias pro fine* is described by Holt as a writ "which is to bring him into court to pay money."

275 E.g., *Ms. Mins. Westch. Co. Sess. 1710–23* June 3, 1718, June 2, 1719; *Ms. Mins. Suffolk Co. Sess. 1723–51* Sept. 30, 1729, Oct. 3, 1738; *Ms. Mins. Queens Co. Sess. 1722–87* May 16, 1732. In Orange County, there is an occasional order on default that "process issue," King v. Caleb Miller (*Ms. Mins. Orange Co. Sess. 1727–79* Oct. 1727); King v. Bron (*ibid.* Oct. 1728). The first reference to a capias in Dutchess is King v. De Graff (*Ms. Mins. Dutchess Co. Sess.* Liber A, Oct. 16, 1744).

276 King v. Grimes (*Ms. Mins. NYCQS 1732–62* 348, May 8, 1754).

277 *James Duane Ms. Register A.*

278 *Supra* 522 nn. 158, 159.

279 Typical is King v. John Daley (*Ms. Mins. SCJ 1723–27* 147 [1725]).

280 Queen v. Hannah Crosier (*Ms. Mins. SCJ 1701–04* 147, Sept. 5, 1704); King v. Dykos et al. (*Ms. Mins. SCJ 1723–27* 211 [1726]).

281 Queen v. John Sheppard (*Ms. Mins. SCJ 1704/05–1709* 52, Mar. 13, 1705/06); Queen v. Harlow (*ibid.*); King v. Adam Smith et al. (*Ms. Mins. SCJ 1727–32* 27) execution stayed.

282 The entries usually merely note the mulct, but sometimes an order for the sheriff to levy as in *Mins. SCJ 1693–1701* 88, 114; *Ms. Mins. NYCQS 1694–1731/32* May 4, 1726. In case of jurors' de-

as to further steps upon judgment for want of a plea does not mean process did not issue. For example, James Mills, the jailer of New York, was indicted in 1752 for permitting a prisoner to escape, and in 1757 judgment for want of a plea was entered.[283] There is no record of execution issuing, but in a contemporary lawyer's cost book it appears that a *fieri facias* was issued.[284] After ten years the sheriff succeeded in returning that he had levied.[285]

About the middle of the eighteenth century, when the judicial records are fuller and more numerous, we come upon a peculiarity in final process which does not obtain in the inferior courts—the use of a *capias pro redemptione*. The New York form of this writ corresponds with the *capias pro rege* in the Register of Writs[286] and commands that the defendant be taken "to satisfy us of his redemption for a certain transgression." Some of the surviving examples of these New York writs are endorsed *capias pro fine,* but this is a generic description, for the *capias pro fine* proper orders the defendant be taken "to satisfy us of his fine" and this form is also used in New York. The difficulties of distinguishing between these two types of final process are enhanced by the fact that in the judicial minutes the clerk will sometimes write his entry *capias pro redemptione* and sometimes *capias pro fine* and in the latter situation the process actually used turns out to be a *capias pro redemptione.*[287]

This mixing of genus and species can be explained by the use of collections like Rastall's *Entries*[288] and Brownlow's *Writs Judicial*[289] where the forms are collected without clear indication of the conditions for selection. None of the textbooks used in the Province explain precisely how the court was to proceed upon default judgments; indeed, these works preserve an almost contemptuous silence in respect of misdemeanor practice generally. The eighteenth century case law offers no satisfactory clues, and even that indefatigable collector of marginalia, Joseph Chitty, leaps lightly over this stage of process.[290]

It is stated by Blackstone that where a defendant is convicted of a misde-

---

faults, the colonial Act of 1699 directed distraint (1 *Col. Laws NY* 387).

[283] *Ms. Mins. SCJ 1750–54* (Engr.) 160, Aug. 1, 1752; *Ms. Mins. SCJ 1757–60* (Engr.) 73, Oct. 13, 1757.

[284] King v. Mills in *Ms. Cost Book Jan. 1764—Jan. 1768.* This book was kindly loaned us by the owner Mr. Augustus Van Cortlandt. It is in the handwriting of his ancestor Augustus Van Cortlandt.

[285] *Ms. Mins. SCJ 1766–69* (Engr.) 338, Oct. 31, 1767.

[286] *Registrum Brevium* (1687) "Brev. Jud." fol. 19.

[287] For example, in King v. Elms (riot), the minutes speak of a *capias pro fine* (*Ms. Mins. SCJ 1769–72* [Engr.] 275, Oct. 18, 1770) but the writ (H.R. Parch. 184 E 4) was a *pluries cap. pro redemptione.*

[288] Collected under *Fine pro Rege.*

[289] Collected under *Capias ad satisfaciendum.*

[290] 1 Chitty, *Treatise on Criminal Law* 695, 811.

meanor "a capias is awarded and issued to bring him in to receive his judgment,"[291] a remark which has been used by the law dictionaries as the sole reference to the *capias ad audiendum judicium*.[292] In early nineteenth century England, a capias "to satisfy us concerning his redemption" was the process to bring in a defendant for a fine.[293] This is identical with the old Latin writ in the Register and is probably what Blackstone had reference to. This late English form corresponds to the *capias pro redemptione* of New York practice.

The New York cases show that the *capias pro redemptione* might be used to get a defendant in court because the bench might wish to inflict an added sanction or because it was willing to hear matter in mitigation. There was, however, no impediment in the way of a judicial fixing of the fine in default cases since an element of contempt was present. Where the court saw fit to assess the penalty if the defendant was not found on a *capias pro redemptione*, a *capias pro fine* would issue.

The course of procedure is illustrated by the various stages in the prosecution of Baltus Lydius upon an information for assault and battery. The information was filed on October 30, 1762 and process ordered to issue. On July 26, 1763, the court ordered judgment for want of a plea "and *capias pro redemptione* to issue."[294] At the next term of the Supreme Court, the Attorney General moved that a fine be set upon the defendant, and the court accordingly assessed the fine at £10. Apparently a *capias pro fine* then issued, for on January 19, 1765, viz., nearly three years after the fine was set, an *alias capias pro fine* was issued.[295] This writ is set forth below.[296]

291 4 Blackstone, *Commentaries* 375. Attorney General Kempe secured a copy of this volume in 1771. The practice we are speaking of was used in New York long before this volume appeared.
292 A search of the English form books has failed to yield a writ of this name. We have, however, seen three Supreme Court cases all in the spring term, 1754, where such a writ was ordered. John Pell informed against for a violent breach of the peace, Alice McKim informed against for an assault and battery, and Robert Richardson indicted for fraud in repacking pork, all failed to file pleas pursuant to rule of court. In each case, judgment for want of a plea was signed and filed and it was ordered "a *capias ad audiendum judicium* issue" (*Ms. Mins. SCJ* 1750–54 [Engr.] 275, 315–317, 349; *Ms. Mins. SCJ* 1754–57 [Engr.] 42). No further proceedings occurred and no copy of the writs has survived.
293 Corner, *Practice on the Crown Side of Queen's Bench* (1844) 152, 243, form cl.
294 The writ issued has not been found. See, however, the writ used against William Cox (King v. Moore, Wickham and Cox, *Ms. Mins. SCJ* 1764–

66 [Engr.] 178, 284) where a rule to plead had been issued in an information for intrusion and presumably a default, although this is not entered. *H.R. Parch.* 193 B 9:
"George the third . . . To our Sheriff of our County of Ulster Greeting We Command you that you omit not by reason of any Liberty within your Bailiwick but that you take William Cox of the Wallkill Precinct in the County of Ulster Yeoman if he be found within your Bailiwick and him safely keep so that you have his Body before us at our City of New York on the third Tuesday in April next to satisfy us of his Redemption for a certain Transgression upon us done in intruding upon our Lands with Force and Arms in Contempt of us our Laws and Dignity whereof he is Convicted . . . ."
[Endorsed] "he is not found
                    Abraham Low   Sheriff."
295 *Ms. Mins. SCJ* 1762–64 (Engr.) 65, 215, 295.
296 *H.R. Pleadings* Pl. K. 748:
"George the third by the Grace of God of Great

The materials available for the years after 1750, despite discrepancies in terminology, establish that although a judicial order made before fine assessed might be called *capias pro fine,* the process itself is *pro redemptione.* That this form alone was proper until fine set is obvious from the fact that upon failure to take the defendant a *pluries capias pro redemptione* would issue. Thus in the case of John Sloomer indicted for assaulting a constable, the defendant was returned, his appearance endorsed and a rule to plead given October 26, 1770. On January 18, 1771, a judgment for want of a plea was entered, and a similar entry again made on August 3, 1771. No further minute entries appear but we have found a *pluries capias pro redemptione* dated January 23, 1773, on which the defendant was returned not found.[297]

The reluctance of the New York courts to assess fines in a defendant's absence has already been remarked upon; indeed, the cases where we can be sure this was done are rare. Obviously if a defendant could not be taken on a *capias pro redemptione* there was nothing to be gained by setting a fine and issuing a *capias pro fine.* A more appropriate measure would consequently be the proceedings upon the recognizance.

The most striking illustration of the order in which the means of satisfying the Crown was selected is, of course, the case of John Henry Lydius, to snare whom a staggering array of process became outstanding. It will be recalled that the defendant appeared for trial and upon a special verdict the court "gives judgment for our sovereign Lord the King." The same day, August 4, 1764, there was issued a *capias pro redemptione* which Kempe in his instructions to

Britain France and Ireland King Defender of the Faith &c. To our Sheriff of our City and County of Albany Greeting We Command you as before we have Commanded you that you omit not by reason of any Liberty within your Bailiwick but that you take Baltus Lydius of the City of Albany Gentleman if he be found within your Bailiwick and him safely keep so that you have his Body before us at our City of New York on the third Tuesday in April next to satisfy us of his Fine of Ten pounds by our Court before us on him imposed by the Judgment of the same Court for certain Trespasses and Contempts whereof he is Convicted and have him then there this Writ Witness Daniel Horsmanden Esquire Chief Justice for our Province of New York at our City of New York the Nineteenth day of January in the fifth Year of our Reign.   Clarke"
J. T. Kempe Attorney General
[Endorsed] "the Body in Custody
          I have got the Fine
          Har Schuyler Shireff."
[297] *Ms. Mins. SCJ 1769–72* (Engr.) 147, 291, 321, 403. For the *pluries,* see *H.R. Parch.* 182 K 2.

Other cases are King v. Honeywell *et al.*—assault, Apr. 24, 1755 (*Ms. Mins. SCJ 1750–54* [Engr.] 341, *Ms. Mins. SCJ 1754–57* [Engr.] 41, 155); King v. Gerritson *et al.,* 1755–56 (*ibid.* 177, 200, 220); King v. Bemper, 1757–59 (*ibid.* 348, *Ms. Mins. SCJ 1756–61* [Rough] 69, *Ms. Mins. SCJ 1757–60* [Engr.] 256); King v. John Smith, 1759 (*Ms. Mins. SCJ 1757–60* [Engr.] 257); King v. Thomas Brookman, 1759 (*ibid.* 256); King v. Gilbert Wessells—disorderly house, 1759 (*Ms. Mins. SCJ 1756–61* [Rough] 142, *Ms. Mins. SCJ 1757–60* [Engr.] 256); King v. Lynch—riot, Oct. 1760 (*Ms. Mins. SCJ 1756–61* [Rough] 198, *H.R. Pleadings* Pl. K. 960 [the capias]); King v. McDaniel and Wise—assault, 1763 (*Ms. Mins. SCJ 1762–64* [Engr.] 176, 298); King v. Bishop, Wright *et al.* (*supra* 203 n. 237); King v. Ferguson and Cooley—intrusion, 1765–71 (*Ms. Mins. SCJ 1764–66* [Engr.] 178, 186, 284, 368, 443, *H.R. Parch.* 182 K 10 [*pluries capias*]); King v. Joseph Tidd—riot, 1770 (*Ms. Mins. SCJ 1769–72* [Engr.] 274); King v. Mitchener—assault, 1773–74 (*Ms. Mins. SCJ 1772–76* [Rough] 84).

the Albany sheriff described as a "writ in the nature of an execution to which no bail can be taken." At the same time a *scire facias* on the forfeited recognizance and a capias in an action of debt on the bond were dispatched.[298] The sheriff's adventures attempting to serve these writs have been recounted, and the subsequent repetition of process. No fine was set in the intrusion judgment, and the final writ issued on this, although it is referred to as a *capias pro fine,* was a *pluries capias pro redemptione.*[299]

A somewhat different series of steps was taken in *King* v. *Paul Gallaudet.* The defendant was convicted on October 26, 1769, on an indictment for perjury. He was apparently not present at judgment, for the Attorney General moved and it was ordered that "the sheriff of New York, his deputy and all other peace officers do apprehend the said Paul Gallaudet and keep him in safe custody to be dealt with according to law." The form of this order indicates a bench warrant was intended. The defendant did not appear and on January 20, 1770, after proclamation, his default was entered and the recognizance ordered estreated. The sureties also made default and an action of debt was presumably filed, for a *pluries capias* in debt was issued January 23, 1773, but it was returned not found.[300]

There is no indication that the Supreme Court attempted to exploit its powers as a court of Exchequer by fixing fines, estreating them and then using a *levari facias* to collect. If the defendant had been present at judgment a *capias pro fine* would issue if a fine was not paid[301] and, except for the distraint used against officers, other process for collection has been found in very few cases.[302] In most cases, of course, if the defendant was present and solvent the fine was paid forthwith to the prothonotary of the Supreme Court.[303] The court sometimes directed this officer to turn over the fine to the Receiver General, and eventually in 1764 made a general rule to this effect.[304]

---

[298] *Supra* 218, 448, 536.

[299] *H.R. Pleadings* Pl. K. 1058: "George the Third . . . that you take John Henry Lydius of the City of Albany Esquire . . . at our City of New York on the Third Tuesday in October next to satisfy us of his Redemption for a certain Transgression upon us done in intruding upon our Lands with force and Arms in Contempt of us our Laws and Dignity whereof he is Convicted and have you then there this Writ Witness Daniel Horsmanden Esquire Chief Justice of our Province of New York the fourth Day of August in the fourth Year of our Reign. . . ."

[300] *Ms. Mins. SCJ 1769–72* (Engr.) 117, 148,

Oct. 26, 1769, Jan. 20, 1770. The estreat in *H.R. Parch.* 209 G 6. The capias in *H.R. Parch.* 182 K 1.

[301] Cf. King v. Gilbert Ferris (*Ms. Mins. SCJ 1754–57* [Engr.] 240, Jan. 24, 1756); King v. Van Zandt (*ibid.* 239); King v. Grimes (*Ms. Mins. NYCQS 1732–62* 329, 339, 348, Feb. 7, Nov. 7, 1753, May 8, 1754).

[302] There are the instances where, by statute or ordinance, distraint was provided, as the assize of bread. For example, King v. Thurman (*Ms. Mins. NYCQS 1694–1731/32* 29, Aug. 2, 1715).

[303] E.g., King v. William Willson (*Ms. Mins. SCJ 1762–64* [Engr.] 285, 295, Oct. 29, 1763). There are many such entries in the estreats.

[304] *Ms. Mins. SCJ 1762–64* (Engr.) 360.

Fees and Costs

The offenders convicted of offenses less than capital were not discharged of what is sententiously described as their "debt to society" by submission to corporal punishment, imprisonment or fine, but they had yet to satisfy the instrumentalities of justice for its price, and they might have to satisfy a prosecutor for his costs. The eighteenth century bureaucracy was one which still lived by a system of fees, for even where, as in the case of the judges of the Supreme Court, a salary was paid, this scarcely sufficed for bread and meat—the side dishes and the gravy were furnished by those who enjoyed official service.

During the period with which we are concerned we shall see that there prevailed considerable confusion respecting the two terms "fees" and "costs." Fees were properly the sums due for official services such as the issuance or return of a writ. The fees were stipulated in set tables or schedules, and in New York these tables contained niggardly lists of items for which attorneys might charge. Costs were in theory the allowance to a party for expenses incurred in a suit, and a bill of costs normally included fee items as well as charges for services by counsel other than those enumerated in the scheduled charges. The propriety of such unscheduled items was the source of bitter controversy during the colonial period, for there was considerable public pressure to limit lawyers to what the fee ordinances stipulated. Bills of costs had to be "taxed," viz., allowed by the court, but the judges were on the side of the angels for they soon conducted this task on a *quantum meruit* basis.

In New York the fee system was put into formal operation by the Duke's Laws[305] which established an explicit but rather simple table of charges. Some subsequent modification of the scale was made, and in 1683 the assembly confirmed the existing arrangements.[306] The criminal records during the proprietary period indicate, first, that the courts did not draw any distinction between fees and costs, and, second, that they did not invariably order a convicted defendant to pay such charges.[307] Apparently, these were viewed primarily as an additional punishment, for in some cases only half the "costs" would be ordered paid by a defendant.[308]

---

[305] 1 *Col. Laws NY* 32.
[306] *Ibid.* 134.
[307] Cf. *Ms. Mins. Mayor's Ct. NYC 1674–75* 26; *Ms. Mins. Mayor's Ct. NYC 1677–82* Sheriff v. John Williams, fol. 154; Sheriff v. Eliz. Robinson, fol. 244b; Sheriff v. John White, fol. 246; *Ms. Suffolk Co. Sess. 1668–87* 32; *Ms. Mins. Ulster Co. Sess.,* in *Deeds* Liber III, Constable v. DeWitt, 241.

After the procedural changes in 1684 the records show no change, viz., *Ms. Mins. Albany Co. Sess. 1685–89,* King v. Rosie, 18; King v. Casperse, 20; King v. Van Loon, 26; 7 *Ms. Mins. Council,* King v. Whitty, 13; King v. Van Dyke, 29.

[308] Sheriff v. Mary Henries (*Ms. Mins. Mayor's Ct. NYC 1677–82* fol. 183) or as in Sheriff v. Anderson (*ibid.* 192) one-half the fine to the sheriff.

We shall speak presently in greater detail of costs, but at this point it is important to notice that English contemporary practice ordinarily required the payment of fees by defendants even where they were acquitted or discharged by proclamation.[309] A pious maxim that no officer would take reward for doing his duty[310] had yielded to the practical argument that fees were perquisites allowed for labor and trouble and, where established by usage, were not assailable. Indeed, it was said in the middle of the seventeenth century that the court would see that officers had their proper recompense and would treat as contempt a refusal to pay.[311] For the most part the English fees were regulated by ancient usage and, as the tables in practice books show, were taken for virtually every gesture in the course of a proceeding. In comparison, the New York table of fees established in 1665 was a very modest affair.

In 1686 a direction that the Governor and Council of New York fix the fees was included in the royal instructions and was thereafter a standing order.[312] After the Leisler Rebellion, in 1693, a table was fixed by the Governor and Council[313] which remained in force until 1709 when the assembly enacted a bill which the Crown disallowed.[314] An acrid dispute developed over the power to establish these charges, the assembly taking the position that it had an inherent right to dispose of freeholders' moneys because it was elected.[315] Governor Hunter and his Council, however, proceeded to pass an ordinance in 1710[316] which set a scale substantially higher than in the earlier provincial act. This remained, so far as criminal proceedings were concerned, the legal basis of all charges until the ordinance of Governor Moore (1768). It may be remarked as to both these ordinances that they were less complex and lower in scale than the comparable tables in the *Crown Circuit Companion*.

Owing to the fact that for years after 1691 the New York courts, or at least the record keepers, persisted in confusing costs and fees, it will be well to summarize briefly the English law. The enforcement of criminal law in England depended upon a "prosecutor," viz., the complainant, but since a proceeding upon indictment was a King's suit, the prosecutor had to defray his own charges because it was a rule that the King neither pays nor receives costs.[317] Sergeant Hawkins, however, states it to have been the constant practice in King's Bench for the court to induce defendants to make satisfaction to prose-

---

309 *Office of the Clerk of Assize* 72, 73.
310 2 Coke, *Institutes* 210.
311 *Per* Rolle, C.J., 1650 (1 Lilly, *Abridgment* [1719] 598).
312 1 Labaree, *Royal Instructions*, no. 521.
313 *A Catalogue of Fees* (1693).

314 1 *Col. Laws NY* 638.
315 5 *Doc. Rel. Col. Hist. NY* 359.
316 *An Ordinance for Regulating and Establishing Fees* (1710).
317 King v. Gohaire (1 *Barn.* 275); Hullock, *Law of Costs* (1792) 548.

cutors for costs and damages by "intimating an inclination" to mitigate the fine. This court could likewise give the injured prosecutor a third of the fine.[318] This proceeding was imitated by the justices in Quarter Sessions.[319] In summary proceedings there was no power to award costs.

The most important alteration of this scheme was effected by statute 21 Jac. I c.8 and the policy continued by statutes 5 & 6 Wm. & Mary c.11, both of which required a defendant removing indictments in certain causes by certiorari into King's Bench to give security for the prosecutor's costs. The purpose of these acts was to discourage the wholesale removal of causes, but inevitably some change was wrought in the whole conception of costs.

The information stood upon a somewhat different footing. Here the basic rule in informations *qui tam* on penal statutes (the so-called popular actions) was that an informer was not entitled to costs unless the statute awarded them.[320] But as these statutes multiplied, in more and more of them was inserted the added incentive of costs. Conversely, the defendant was protected by statute 18 Eliz. c.5, which awarded him costs where an informer delayed or discontinued or verdict was passed against him. The informations brought by the Attorney General ex officio were governed by the rule restricting costs in the Crown case unless there was a private informer.[321] As we have seen by statute 7 & 8 Wm. & Mary c.18, such informers were required to give security for costs to force the prosecution of their complaints.[322]

It should be observed that the English rules respecting costs had nothing to do with the matter of the defendant's own fees. These were due officials under all circumstances unless the defendant was allowed to defend *in forma pauperis*. This liability for fees was carried to such an extreme that a defendant discharged on habeas corpus was not released until the jailer was satisfied of his fees.[323]

Practice respecting costs and fees in criminal cases is obscure enough in England, and although there are considerable data available in New York, the basic principles of application are hard to ascertain. We must, however, begin with the premise that in New York the private prosecutor was not at first a factor of consequence except in the *qui tam* and information proceedings. In the second place, it is obvious that the Attorney General had a much more diffused au-

[318] 2 Hawkins, *op. cit.* c.25 §3.
[319] *Crown Circuit Companion* 41.
[320] 2 Hawkins, *op. cit.* c.26 §57.
[321] Cf. Queen v. Corporation of Bewdley (1 *Peere Williams* 207, 227 n).
[322] *Supra* 370.
[323] 2 Rolle, *Abridgment* 32. On the anxiety respecting fees, compare King v. Fry, 1775 (1 Leach, *Crown Cases* 129).

thority than in England since he would appear in the Supreme Court, at Circuit and at General Sessions, or act in the latter by special deputy.[324] This office, moreover, was on a strange financial basis. A salary of a mere £50 was reported in 1693,[325] and £70 in 1699.[326] By 1707 it had risen to £150.[327] The salary appears for a long time to have been on a precarious footing,[328] and even after Monckton cajoled the assembly into making provision for Kempe, the appropriation was for "extraordinary services."[329]

The nominal sum paid by way of salary to the Attorney General was fixed, of course, in the expectation of income from fees. These were determined in reference to particular services and did not extend to all activities normally included in an attorney's bill of costs.[330] In England such items would be borne by a prosecutor; but in New York where the onus of proceeding in indictments was upon officials, the Attorney General would either be out of pocket or he would have to find some means of compensation.

We do not know how at first the expenses of Crown prosecution were either calculated or met. The earliest "complete" accounts preserved relate to the trial of Jacob Leisler and his associates. George Farewell, who was of counsel for the Crown, put in a bill for unspecified services charging £1 10s. each in the cases of Leisler, Milborne, Delanoy (two charges), Gouverneur, Beekman, Coerten, Williams, Brazier and Edsall. He added a charge of £2 for making up the record. Thomas Newton who conducted the prosecutions had the same notion of a *prix fixe* charging a flat £10 "To the Indicting and prosecuting" of the several defendants whether for treason or merely riot. This he

[324] *Supra* 319, 366.

[325] 1 *Doc. Hist. NY* 199. Livingston in 1692 states it was £100 (4 *Doc. Rel. Col. Hist. NY* 253).

[326] 4 *Doc. Rel. Col. Hist. NY* 599.

[327] 7 *ibid.* 908.

[328] Nanfan informed the assembly in 1701 that the King paid the Attorney General £150 (1 *Jour. Legis. Council* 158). The Council voted Broughton some money in 1703 (3 *Ms. Mins. Council* 354). Bickley, Cornbury's Attorney General, died holding unpaid warrants that the assembly took care of in 1714 when outstanding claims were settled (*Acts of the Assembly 1691–1725* [1728] 101). It appears, however, from a memorial of Rayner, Bickley's successor, that Rayner's compensation was paid out of direct revenues of the Crown (5 *Doc. Rel. Col. Hist. NY* 161). Bradley, in a memorial of Jan. 4, 1727/28, states that Broughton and Rayner were paid "from home out of the Privy Purse" and complains bitterly that more than £800 was owing him which he could

not get (P.R.O., C.O. 5/1072/64). His memorial to the New York Council was merely "referred" (15 *Ms. Mins. Council* 313). In 1730 the assembly voted him £150 as compensation for six years (2 *Col. Laws NY* 696) and in 1732 he was voted £60. Spenser (2 *Hist. State of NY* 174) states that after 1709 no provision for salary was made by the assembly. This is obviously not accurate. In a memorial of Kempe to Monckton, July 22, 1763 (39 *Mass. Hist. Soc. Colls.* [*Aspinwall Papers*] 480) it is stated that from 1733 onward Bradley was paid £150 a year by the English Exchequer.

[329] 2 *Jour. Legis. Council* 1488. Thus several appropriation bills beginning 1762 contain a provision of £140 to J. T. Kempe for "extraordinary services" (4 *Col. Laws NY* 627, 734, 800, 849, 912, 963, 1026). Cf. also the memorial cited *supra* n. 328.

[330] Such as time in conference, on which compare Wm. Smith Jr. journal entries and bill in *King v. John Carey, Wm. Van Wyck et al.* (1753) in his *Ms. Supream Ct. Register A* 55, 331.

represented to be double the usual amount because the trials were at a special Oyer and Terminer. The total sum claimed was £300.[331]

Upon the reorganization of the judiciary, changes in scale were made, but the notion of a flat charge remained. Governor Fletcher's schedule of fees set a fee of £1 10s. for "criminal causes"[332] and £3 for "capitall causes." There is no indication how this was to be collected. In Hunter's Ordinance these flat fees were abandoned for a series of particular charges, and in 1768 the number and variety of these were increased. Where a defendant in a misdemeanor case was convicted, any item identifiable as a fee could be put on him. "Cost" items such as conferences or travel were not provided for. Capital cases, on the other hand, were prosecuted without any foreseeable means of compensation. Officials repeatedly stated during the eighteenth century that in such cases, expenses (and this undoubtedly includes fees) were borne by the Attorney General. Indeed, Governor Monckton's recommendations for an Attorney General's salary were made with specific reference to this difficulty. These statements are, however, too broad for it appears that compensation was expected from the county when a felony case was tried at Circuit. We have seen the difficulties over Alexander's bill raised by the Ulstermen in 1725, yet in 1726/27, Bradley was paid £1 19s.,[333] and Dutchess in 1735/36 allowed the Attorney General £10 for his costs at Circuit and the trial of James Cain for felony,[334] and in 1745/46 Lewis Morris Jr. (who was evidently deputizing for the Attorney General) was allowed by Dutchess £7 12s. for fees and £7 10s. for prosecuting a murderer.[335] The responsibility of the county was asserted in vigorous terms by Bradley, writing to a correspondent in Ulster County in February, 1735/36:[336]

> Your people deal very ungenerously with me and betray their ignorance as well as sordidness when they give for their reason of their resolution not to pay me that my bill of costs is not signed by a Judge (I suppose they mean because it was not taxed wch is never done in criminal cases as these were). Do they think I can come as far as Sopus; spend my money & time for nothing to serve them and give them my fees too; who ever they are that are of that opinion are manifestly very dishonest & unjust men. My bill is according to the ordinance of

[331] Farewell's bill which included also charges for drafting certain acts is in 37 NY Col. Mss. 118; Newton's bill in ibid. 119.
[332] Catalogue of Fees 11.
[333] Supra 463; Mins. Board of Supervisors, Ulster Co. 1710/11–1730/31 39.
[334] Old Misc. Recs. Dutchess Co. 107, "allowed on his bill of costs."
[335] Ms. Book of Taxes Dutchess Co. Liber C, 336, 337.
[336] Misc. Mss. Richard Bradley.

Fees wch if they refuse to pay me, I hope they will not take it amiss if I use all legal means to pay my selfe. They have forgot sure that I forgave their county above £200 at one time. Is this their requital of so great a kindness. It never lies me in less than ten pounds to come as far as Sopus, reckoning my expenses and loss of business at home etc. and I must lose my fees too. Is this their conscience? . . . Your county formerly pd me a bill by your hands for such like service and did not object to want of a judge's hand then nor anything else.

We do not know how the liability of the county for prosecution charges at Circuit came to be fixed. The principle is recognized in an act compensating Bradley (1730) by which, because his prosecutions had been for the benefit of New York City, part of his compensation was put upon the corporation,[337] in all probability because the grand jury of New York County had recommended relief.[338] And in 1732 the acts providing for the trial of causes less than grand larceny specifically made the county liable. It is not improbable that the notion of local liability stems from English conceptions of the grand jury's powers in respect of county finances.[339] Since the presentments are made by this body and the services of the Attorney General in putting them in form are requested in the presentment, the work is thus undertaken at the instance of county representatives. There is, indeed, a hint to this effect in James Alexander's *Supreme Court Register*.[340]

In the case of misdemeanors punished by imprisonment, whipping or fine, it was usual to award the Attorney General or his deputy their fees and eventually even, under certain circumstances, costs. The early developments are by no means clear because for some years the Supreme Court minutes are nearly bare of any details and the country clerks are obviously unaware of the distinction between costs and fees. The records of Kings County Sessions disclose the greatest variation. J. J. VanDitmars is discharged by proclamation on May 19, 1697, "paying fees of court,"[341] but his co-defendants (who were tried) when fined a year later are ordered to pay also £10 14s. 6d., "The cost of this and the former court."[342] Mary Richardson at this Sessions is fined and ordered to pay "cost of court."[343] In October, 1693, Urian Nagell is fined and pays no costs for seditious words, but John Bibou is discharged without fine and pays "officers fees."[344] At succeeding Sessions "cost of court" is the usual expression and

[337] 2 *Col. Laws NY* 697.
[338] *Ms. Mins. NYCQS 1694–1731/32* 527, Aug. 5, 1730.
[339] 1 Webb, *English Local Government; Parish and the County* 448 *et seq.*

[340] *James Alexander Supreme Ct. Register* 50.
[341] *Ms. Kings Co. Ct. & Rd. Recs. 1691–1825* 4.
[342] *Ibid.* 12.
[343] *Ibid.*
[344] *Ibid.* 19.

probably meant only the fees. At the riot inquest against John Rapalje and others in 1696 "all cost and charges expended about the enquiry" are charged the defendants.[345] Sometimes these are particularized as in the case of Jurrian Bries (1700) who was discharged on paying 17s. to the sheriff and 11s. to the clerk,[346] and John Leake and Reine VanSickelen who paid to the clerk "18s. with cost, cost allowed 5s. to the constable."[347]

In other country Sessions the clerks likewise note that the convicted defendant must pay "costs" as well as a fine,[348] and in Westchester it appears that costs meant simply fees, for Gabriel Leggett convicted of larceny (1694) is charged: "Costs 3:16:6: to ye Clark 1:7:7½: to ye Sherife 00:11:00: Cryer and Marshall 0:3:10½: Attorney Pr. Dom. Rg. 1:10:0: Court fee 00:04: 00."[349] The New York City Quarter Sessions has no similar clue to the meaning of the clerk's language—indeed the variety of expressions is similar to that used in Kings County. Defendants are charged costs and fees indiscriminately, although after 1703 the usual entry is a charge for fees.[350] Occasionally it is adjudged that the defendant pay all costs and charges of prosecution[351] "or fees of prosecution."[352] In these cases, it is possible more than the usual clerk's, sheriff's and Attorney General's fees were intended, and that the court would direct the defrayment of the private prosecutor's expenses. Unfortunately, no bills of costs are available for these cases.

Fees even in the routine prosecution were substantial. In 1711, Elizabeth Ranger was indicted for entertaining negro slaves. She confessed the indictment and was fined 20s. with full fees. A marginal notation shows these to have been "Clerk 1:19:0: Sheriff 0:05:0: Cryer 0:11:9: Attorney General 0:18:0"—a total of £3:03:9.[353]

Sessions practice with respect to fees during the eighteenth century is most

[345] Ibid. 38.
[346] Ibid. 62.
[347] Ibid. 67.
[348] Ms. Mins. Ulster Co. Sess. 1693–1698: King v. Barent Cool (bastardy), "costs"; King v. Pieterse, "charges," Mar. 3, 1694/95; King v. a Negro, "costs," Sept. 3, 1695; King v. Bosselyn, "costs," Mar. 2, 1697/98.
[349] Mins. Westch. Ct. of Sess. 1657–96 125. At Queens Sessions, May 21, 1706, Derick Cokefaire confessed an indictment. Discharged paying "fees," committed until paid (51 NY Col. Mss. 131).
[350] Ms. Mins. NYCQS 1683/84–1694: King v. Anna Cuyler, "cost of suite" and King v. John Joort, "cost of suite," 151, Aug. 5, 1691; King v. Hardenburgh, "fees," 154–155, Feb. 2, 1691/92. Ms. Mins. NYCQS 1694–1731/32: King v. Anne Sewell, "fees," 9, Nov. 6, 1695; King v. Vincent, "fees,"

25, May 4, 1697; King v. Davis, "court costs," 48, Aug. 1, 1699; King v. Ringo, "court costs," 51, Feb. 8, 1698/99; Queen v. Cooper, "costs," 73, Nov. 4, 1702; Queen v. Bickley, "fees," 86, Feb. 2, 1703/04.
[351] King v. Hutchins (Ms. Mins. NYCQS 1683/84–1694 160, May 2, 1693). In King v. Gabriel Ludlow (Ms. Mins. NYCQS 1694–1731/32 42, Oct. 12, 1698) the defendant, up for passing counterfeit, was ordered to pay "the costs of this Special Sessions."
[352] Queen v. Cordus (ibid. 191, Feb. 7, 1710/11). Cf. also Queen v. Laurier (ibid. Feb. 2, 1708/09); Queen v. Elbertse, "charges" of prosecution (ibid. 177, Aug. 2, 1710); Queen v. Dorothy Wright (ibid. 177, Aug. 2, 1710).
[353] Ms. Mins. NYCQS 1694–1731/32 205, Nov. 6, 1711. The fees are entered in the margin.

clearly defined in the New York City records where a defendant upon acquittal or discharge by proclamation nearly always pays fees,[354] and where an
order to pay a fine almost invariably is coupled with fees.[355] The direction to
keep in custody frequently covers both items, a fact which suggests that the
payment of fees was regarded as a part of the punishment. In *King* v. *Grimes*
(1754)[356] where the defendant was fined £3 with full fees, the clerk was ordered "to issue a *capias pro fine* for recovery of same." We have found one
case, *King* v. *Pelton* (1771) where on a plea of *nolo* the fine was paid in court
and the defendant permitted to "engage to pay fees of prosecution."[357] The
country clerks were not nearly so painstaking about entries respecting fees, but
we have no doubt they were exacted. These country records continue sporadically to mention costs, but unless the New York Sessions Courts were breaking
with the English rule that Sessions Courts could not award costs, this word
can be taken to mean fees. For example, at Dutchess Sessions, October, 1729,
Jan Niemant was fined 1s. to the King for an assault and an additional 15s.,
6s. to the poor and the remainder to the clerk and justices for costs. Andries
Peck for speaking against the reformed religion was fined 6s. to the King and
£3 14s. for all costs and charges.[358] Two years later John Van den Bogart is fined 6s. to the poor and the "charges of the clerk."[359] In this county,
moreover, there are a number of cases where the court directs costs or fees to be
paid from the fine.[360] In Suffolk County, the terms "costs" and "fees" are used
interchangeably,[361] and there is some indication that the same usage obtained

[354] There are many entries; cf. the following
typical cases: Queen v. John Breasted—bill ignoramus (*Ms. Mins. NYCQS 1694–1731/32* 65, Feb.
6, 1710/11); King v. Mariana Vincent—discharge
from recognizance (*ibid.* 410, Aug. 7, 1722); King
v. John Wood—discharge on promise to behave
(*Ms. Mins. NYCQS 1732–62* 34, Nov. 7, 1733);
King v. Edw. Menzie—assumed bastardy liability
(*ibid.* 264, Nov. 10, 1749); King v. George Clarke
—discharge on recognizance (*Ms. Mins. NYCQS
1760–72* 225, Nov. 3, 1767); King v. Jas. Bary—
assumed bastardy liability (*Ms. Mins. NYCQS
1772–91* 16, Aug. 6, 1772).
[355] The following are typical: King v. John
Wood, confessed (*Ms. Mins. NYCQS 1694–1731/
32* 279, Feb. 2, 1714/15); King v. Judith Peters,
confessed (*ibid.* 446, Nov. 4, 1724); King v. Jane
Allen, confessed (*ibid.* 523, May 6, 1730); King v.
Joseph and Edward Anderson, confessed (*Ms.
Mins. NYCQS 1732–62* 163, May 3, 1744); King
v. Jas. Donnelly, jugt. for want of plea (*ibid.* 252,
May 3, 1749); King v. John Smith, confessed
(*ibid.* 458, Aug. 9, 1759); King v. Cheeseman,
confessed (*Ms. Mins. NYCQS 1760–72* 355, Nov.
6, 1771).

[356] *Ms. Mins. NYCQS 1732–62* 348, May 8,
1754; cf. also King v. De Graff (*Ms. Mins. Dutchess Co. Sess.* Liber A, Oct. 16, 1744) same order.
[357] *Ms. Mins. NYCQS 1760–72* 362, Nov. 8,
1771.
[358] *Ms. Mins. Dutchess Co. Sess.* Liber A, Oct.
21, 1729.
[359] *Ibid.* Oct. 19, 1731. Cf. also King v. Mathew
Dubois—discharged paying "fees" (*ibid.* 20, 1740);
King v. Peter Simson—discharged paying all
"charges" (*ibid.* May 18, 1742).
[360] King v. Jonathan Hoegg—forcible entry
(*ibid.* Oct. 18, 1748); King v. Ben Busch—forcible
entry (*ibid.* Oct. 17, 1749); King v. Joseph Boyce
—passing counterfeit (*Ms. Mins. Dutchess Co.
Sess.* Liber B, May 15, 1753); King v. Thos.
Young—blasphemy (*Ms. Mins. Dutchess Co. Sess.*
Liber C, May 16, 1758). In this county, discharge
on proclamation cost 4s. 6d.; King v. Lewis Can-
nel (*Ms. Mins. Dutchess Co. Sess.* Liber D, Oct. 3,
1769).
[361] E.g., King v. Green, costs (*Ms. Mins. Suffolk Co. Sess. 1723–51* Sept. 30, 1729); King v.
Sayre, fees (*ibid.* Mar. 29, 1730). In Albany some
confusion obtains between 1717 and 1723. E.g.,

in Queens.[362] The best confirmation of this confusion of terms is in a record kept by a lawyer. James Duane, deputizing for Kempe in Richmond from 1755–57, kept an account of fees, for he had to pay half to the Attorney General, and in two cases he refers to these as "costs."[363] If lawyers like Bradley and Duane used the term so loosely it is not likely the clerks of the peace would be more meticulous.

In view of the course usually taken by a prosecution in Sessions it is difficult to see how there could be anything but fee charges. The rarity of an actual jury trial in the country has been remarked upon, most of the indictments being usually confessed, *nolo* pleaded, or the defendants kept upon recognizance for a salutary period. Where the actual "cost" figure is given, in most cases it can be broken down with the aid of the table of fees into items such as the draft of indictment, process charges, clerk's and crier's fees. Even in the occasional cases where a charge exceeds what one can thus readily reconstruct, it is possible more processes were used than the clerk made note of in the minutes. The fees in Duane's *Register* for Richmond cases run from 29s. to £1 15s. and the average was roughly the same in most of the country courts. In the case of recognizances the fee ordinances set the several charges, but a defendant's bill depended entirely upon the number of continuances. For example, in 1751, Thomas Richardson was discharged[364] paying 11s. 3d.—which included the standing fee in Dutchess County of 7s. 6d. for discharge,[365] 1s. 9d. for filing affidavits and two continuances at 2s., whereas the surety of Johannes Housecker in 1764 paid £2 2s. to be rid of responsibility for his principal who had been bound over in 1755 and had left the county.[366]

There can be no doubt that the practice of exacting fees from defendants had a profound effect upon the recourse to trial of an issue. We have found only early bills for trials in General Sessions courts[367] and it was not the practice to enter such items in the minutes. They were probably less than the bills in

King v. Ryckard, fees (*Ms. Mins. Albany Co. Sess. 1717–23* Feb. 4, 1717/18); King v. Borghaert, costs (*ibid.* Oct. 4, 1721); King v. Van der Leyden (*ibid.* Oct. 30, 1722).

[362] E.g., King v. Joseph Connell, costs (*Ms. Mins. Queens Co. Sess. 1722–87* Sept. 20, 1763); King v. Gilbert Lawrence, fees (*ibid.* May 19, 1767).

[363] *James Duane Ms. Register A* 13, King v. Peter Egbert "fees 29/ rec'd (1756) these costs"; *ibid.* 17, King v. Simonson (costs); *ibid.* 12, King v. Anna Beddell (fees).

[364] *Ms. Files Dutchess Co. 1740–50* King v. Thomas Richardson.

[365] *Ms. Mins. Dutchess Co. Sess.* Liber A, May 15, 1744.

[366] *Ms. Files Dutchess Co. 1755.* The endorsement on the recognizance reads: "Nov. 1, 1763 Hend Teeter told me ye complainant was long since dead and ye defendant moved out of the county & prays court to discharge me. Entry recog. £—3— Cryer & Bellringer & continuance—2.9. 17 Continuances—17—& for Bellringer—12.9. Discharge May, 1764—6.6."

[367] *Supra* 737.

the Supreme Court some of which are set out in the Appendix[368] and somewhat in excess of summary trial bills. The details of such a special "meetings" account are reproduced in the margin.[369] In this case, *King* v. *Jack*, a slave (1755) accused of abusive behavior, the charges amounting to £4 were ordered divided between the complainant and the slave's master. Since no jury was used in the case and since there were no pleadings, motions or other such fee items, the amount was relatively modest. But clearly no defendant to a minor charge in General Sessions cognizant of the usual light fines would balk at pleading *nolo* or confessing an indictment. If he could thereby escape with only the additional fees of twenty or thirty shillings he would hardly run the risk of conviction by a jury and the sizable bill that this manner of trial would entail.

It is difficult to believe that the Supreme Court dealt differently with defendants in the matter of fees than did the inferior courts, yet for the years prior to 1750, the judicial minutes lead one to think that this may have been so. Entries ordering a defendant to pay fees upon acquittal or discharge by proclamation are frequent,[370] but there is only an occasional such order upon conviction. These minutes were not carefully kept, as witness the paucity of process entries, and the failure to mention fees or costs may mean nothing. When the Supreme Court judges went on circuit, defendants who were fined were usually ordered to pay fees and there is no reason why a different rule should have obtained in trials at bar. There was no public fund to pay the process, the return, the appearance, the indictment and the succession of other charges, yet

---

[368] See King v. Klock, King v. Lydius, *infra* 775 *et seq.*; King v. Van Schaick, *infra* 777. A Supreme Court bill in King v. Mary Nicholls (1746) amounting to £14 7s. 6d. is in *H.R. Pleadings* Pl. K. 965.

[369] The trial was held at Poughkeepsie, Sept. 17, 1759 (*Ms. Files Dutchess County 1755*). The costs:

Constable summoning 4 witnesses and returns	£0	14	6
Bring son to gaol	0	10	0
Prison fees of Jack and son	0	8	0
Turck for Warrant and Examination	0	3	0
Lawrence Van Kleek for do.	0	3	0
To King Exam. of Jack and son last Saturday	0	3	0
The same this day	0	3	0
Order for four witnesses each	0	4	0
copying do	0	4	0
Swearing two witnesses each 1/	0	2	0
Record and filing	0	4	6
Constable for bringing Jack to gaol	0	12	0
Reading two affidavits	0	2	0
Justices attending two days	0	2	0
Ct.	0	2	0
Clerk and attendance		£3.17.0	
		3	
		£4. 0.0	

[370] E.g., King v. Jacobs, 1694 (*Mins. SCJ 1693–1701* 56); Queen v. Ann Clay, 1703 (*Ms. Mins. SCJ 1701–04* 99); Queen v. William Lawrence *et al.*, 1706 (*Ms. Mins. SCJ 1704/05–1709* 103); Queen v. John Wiley, 1706 (*ibid.* 91); Queen v. Cornelia Burroughs *et al.*, 1706 (*ibid.* 95); Queen v. Jonas Wood, 1707 (*ibid.* 145); Queen v. Thomas Burroughs, 1707 (*ibid.* 145); Queen v. Moore, 1711 (*Ms. Mins. SCJ 1710–14* 358); Queen v. Sarah Wiggins, 1711/12 (*ibid.* 368); Queen v. Eliz. Howe, 1712 (*ibid.* 382); Queen v. Husk, 1713 (*ibid.* 530); Queen v. Drommy, 1713 (*ibid.* 538); King v. Grace, 1725 (*Ms. Mins. SCJ 1723–27* 136); King v. Ellenor Floyd, 1730 (*Ms. Mins. SCJ 1727–32* 206).

it seems extremely unlikely that the bill was footed by an Attorney General who could not even be sure his own salary would be paid. And in the absence of any regulation we do not believe either that any official waived fees or that complainants carried such burdens. On the other hand, some entries as to costs or fees are peculiar. In one early case, the clerk notes that the fine included the costs,[371] in another, one Donavan who confessed an indictment for assault was fined 3s. 4d. plus 4 "dollars" for Attorney General's fees and costs of court.[372] Defendants sentenced to corporal punishment sometimes had to pay fees and there is a spattering of the orders to pay "costs" which may only mean the fees.[373]

Collateral evidence on liability for costs and fees is not extensive but it all points to the burden being upon the defendant. The assembly, in 1708, attempted to legislate against taking fees upon acquittal but this act was disallowed.[374] The Committee on Grievances brought in the same complaint again in 1713, but nothing came of it.[375] No mention is made of fees upon conviction. This matter, however, came to issue in the agitation over the information bill (1727) when it was charged that Bradley was bringing proceedings for fees and charges and to get unreasonable compositions.[376] Bradley admitted that costs to the amount of £45 in the Albany justices' case had been given him "on their own Motion and pressing Solicitations . . . and . . . were not two thirds of the Fees then justly due, there being twenty-six Defendants."[377] This evidence indicates that the court was awarding costs in information cases, even if the minutes do not show it. James Alexander in 1739 notes in his *Register* that in *King v. Vincent Mathews et al.* (1739) the matter of costs was raised by motion.[378] Since motions were very often not entered by the clerk it is possible that this may be the explanation why so little is to be discovered in the judicial records.

There are not sufficient data upon which to base any judgment whether or

[371] Queen v. Tiebout, "fined ten pounds and committed till payment in which fines ye costs are included" (*Ms. Mins. SCJ 1701–04* 127, Oct. 3, 1703).
[372] Queen v. Donavan (*Ms. Mins. SCJ 1710–14* 478).
[373] Queen v. Vank and Roberts (1706) in addition to pillory (*Ms. Mins. SCJ 1704/05–1709* 72); Queen v. Isaac Marquese (1706) fine and fees (*ibid.* 108); Queen v. Mott (1713) fine and cost of court (*Ms. Mins. SCJ 1710–14* 471); Queen v. William Roberts (1713) imprisonment and fees (*ibid.* 437–440); Queen v. Dennis (1713) whipping and fees (*ibid.* 500); King v. David Wallace and David Willson (1727) imprisonment, pillory, whipping and fees (*Ms. Mins. SCJ 1727–32* 10); King v. Norris and Parca (1732) whipping and fees (*ibid.* 395); King v. Catherine Johnson (1735) whipping and fees (*Ms. Mins. SCJ 1732–39* 195).
[374] 1 *Col. Laws NY* 622.
[375] 1 *Jour. Gen. Assembly* 336. It should be noticed that in 1717 the New York grand jury was taken into custody by the assembly's sergeant at arms for an address which offended the assembly. They paid fees when discharged! (*Ibid.* 411.)
[376] *Ibid.* 566.
[377] *Ibid.* 570.
[378] *James Alexander Supreme Ct. Register* 44 "Jan 1739/40—moved for opn. of court for costs had rule *nisi causa.*"

not the words fees and costs were used interchangeably in the Supreme Court. Bradley, as we have seen, confused the two terms, obviously for the reason that the Ordinance of 1710 purported to contain everything that could properly be taxed as costs and all these items are essentially fee items. It appears, however, from a letter written by Horsmanden, C.J., in 1767, that for a long time the fee ordinance had not been followed and that the judges had made allowances for services on a *quantum meruit* basis.[379] The significance of this is that the charges for advocacy had moved from a mere fee to a cost basis. The bill of defendant's counsel and his journal entries in *King* v. *John Carey, William Van Wyck et al.*, reproduced in the Appendix, indicates how matters stood in the early 'fifties.[380]

The problem of costs had always presented two distinct issues—costs as between attorney and client, and costs as between parties litigant. In criminal causes the rule that the Crown neither gave nor received costs purported to eliminate any issue as to the Crown's representative, and a strict application of the rule would have restricted the Attorney General to the acceptance only of fees, except in proceedings on relation of an informer. Thus, an indictment proceeding in theory would involve a question of costs only as between the defendant and his counsel, and a matter of fees as between Attorney General and the complainant or the defendant as the court might determine. As we have seen, the complainant's costs were treated in England as matter of equity in the determination of the penalty. In the absence of evidence prior to 1750 that this latter practice was consistently followed, we are disposed to believe that the Attorney General stayed on a fee basis in indictment proceedings and benefited by the broadened base of charges only in informations. It is regrettable that no accounts are available, and Bradley's statements are of no great help. Obviously, if it is true that only £150 had been his rewards up to December 24, 1730, for eight years of prosecutions, he had been remunerated not even on a fee basis, and his claim to £1878 owing, judged from the roster of cases tried, is far in excess of mere fees.[381]

After the year 1750 there is much more information available. The first significant exhibit is, of course, the printed blank of the year 1752 whereby complainants requesting a prosecution at the suit of the King obliged them-

---

[379] 1 *Colden Letter Books* 373. This was in response to a general inquiry sent out by the Lieutenant Governor pursuant to a royal order intimating fees were extortionate. The evasion of the 1710 Ordinance began early. In the back of Augustus Van Cortlandt's copy of the *New York Laws*

1751 is a table certified by Henry Wileman (*circa* 1725) of allowances for travelling expenses.
[380] *William Smith Jr. Ms. Supream Ct. Register A* 55. Cf. Appendix 780, Bills of Costs.
[381] *Cal. S.P. Colonial 1730* 419.

selves to pay the Attorney General's fees. The document is so phrased as to cover either a proceeding by indictment or by information.[382] The second important item is the Information Act of 1754 which required, except in ex officio informations, security to prosecute and an authorized award of costs to the defendant if the case was not pursued or if he secured a verdict, unless the Supreme Court thought there was reasonable cause. Taken in conjunction these two documents served to put upon prosecuting witnesses a considerable financial responsibility. On the other hand, it is at this time that we first find enough cases to establish that the Supreme Court had adopted the King's Bench practice of setting a low fine as a means of inducing a defendant to settle the prosecutor's costs. This line of cases begins after the arrival in New York of Attorney General William Kempe. Johannes Bradt had been informed against in June, 1751, and after his pleading *nolo contendere* his cause was continued until August 1, 1752 when "the defendant having agreed with the prosecutor the court assess on the defendant a fine of £5."[383]

It is possible that the missing records for the years 1740–50 would show earlier examples, but another case occurring about this time suggests that this procedure is an innovation since the intervention of the Governor was sought. Peter Vrooman was informed against for neglecting his duty as a justice of the peace in not arresting a felon, for rescous and for assaults on the arresting officer. Vrooman petitioned the Governor stating he was willing to contend but not willing to pay the charges of the prosecutor and humbly prayed a nolle prosequi. This availed him not, for "by Order of his said Excellency it is entered accordingly and ordered by the Court that unless the Defendant pay the Costs of the prosecution in a month Attachment do issue."[384]

There are a number of entries after these episodes stating that the defendant had agreed with the prosecutor,[385] and in some cases there is an additional notation to the effect that defendant be discharged paying fees.[386] Probably in

[382] *Supra* 378 n. 208.
[383] *Ms. Mins. SCJ 1750–54* (Engr.) 164, Aug. 1, 1752. Cf. the three earlier cases *supra* 575 n. 109.
[384] *Ms. Mins. SCJ 1750–54* (Engr.) 195, Oct. 26, 1752.
[385] Cf. King v. Wenman (*supra* 575 n. 109); King v. Adam King (*Ms. Mins. SCJ 1750–54* [Engr.] 317); King v. Hannah Ferris (*Ms. Mins. SCJ 1754–57* [Engr.] 10, Apr. 19, 1754); King v. Wendell Ham *et al.*, riot (*ibid.* 9, Apr. 18, 1754); King v. Alex Colden, assault (*ibid.* 146, Apr. 19, 1755); King v. Ann and Godfrey Cunningham, assault (*ibid.* 154, Apr. 24, 1755); King v. James Thompson, assault (*Ms. Mins.*

SCJ 1756–61 [Rough] 86, Oct. 26, 1757); King v. Jas. Buchanan, assault (*Ms. Mins. SCJ 1754–57* [Engr.] 240, Jan. 24, 1756); King v. Waddell Cunningham, assault (*Ms. Mins. SCJ 1762–64* [Engr.] 358, Jan. 27, 1764); King v. Robert Campbell *et al.*, riot (*Ms. Mins. SCJ 1764–67* [Rough] 42, Jan. 17, 1765); King v. Haring *et al.*, riot (*ibid.* 35, Oct. 27, 1764); King v. Alex Jackson (*ibid.* 15, Oct. 16, 1764). Cf. also the *qui tam* case, Ogden q.t. v. John Allison *et al.* (*Ms. Mins. SCJ 1766–69* [Engr.] 312, Oct. 27, 1767).
[386] For example, King v. Whiley (*Ms. Mins. SCJ 1754–57* [Engr.] 1, Apr. 16, 1754); King v. Ferris (*ibid.* 240, Jan. 24, 1756); King v. Van Zandt

these cases the fines may merely have been criers', sheriffs' or jailers' fees, because the Attorney Generals' bills to the prosecutor included all the essential fees connected with trial, and it may be assumed a settlement in consideration of a small fine embraced these charges. In some cases this appears from the records, as in *King v. Caleb Pell* informed against for forging a deed. Here, the court, "it appearing that defendant hath made satisfaction to the party injured and hath agreed with the prosecution," fined £15.[387] Since William Smith Jr. notices he was consulted as to what was to be offered the Attorney General, the agreement with the prosecutor may be taken to mean the settlement of Kempe's charges.[388]

In some cases where composition was made before trial the Attorney General would also have to be satisfied. Jacob Dyckman and another were informed against for a riot, but the case was settled after a plea had been entered.[389] The prosecutor was paid £6, the Attorney General 15s., and defendants' counsel's bill of costs amounted in addition to £4 10s. 3d.[390] Probably numerous cases which disappear from the records were settled in this way, but we have not enough data to be certain where the line was drawn between a case that was regarded as fit or unfit for settlement. John Tabor Kempe wrote to Sir William Johnson in 1763,[391] "it is not a practice with me to compound offences unless the injured party is made satisfaction even in petty trespasses and never have I compounded one where the publick is concerned." The distinction which Kempe seems to have drawn was between causes where the Crown was immediately concerned, the felonies, intrusions, revenue and political riot cases, and those where an enraged burgher had had his windows broken, or been submitted to indignities at the hands of some mob. His record is one of singular devotion to his office, for he went to trial in numberless hard cases which it might have been much more advantageous to settle.

In the last years of the colonial period the matter of costs seems to have exercised the bar. An elaborate scheme prepared for civil cases is preserved in the Smith papers, and in 1764 some of the younger lawyers entered into an agreement respecting the matter.[392] Nothing was arranged regarding criminal cases, but these were a minor part of a lawyer's practice.[393] The mat-

---

(*ibid.* 239, Jan. 24, 1756); King v. Ben Birdsall (*Ms. Mins. SCJ* 1766–69 [Engr.] 255, July 31, 1767); King v. Domine (*ibid.* 195, Nov. 1, 1766).
   [387] *Supra* 183 n. 166; *Ms. Mins. SCJ* 1754–57 (Engr.) 118.
   [388] *William Smith Jr. Ms. Supream Ct. Register A* 123.

[389] *Ms. Mins. SCJ* 1754–57 (Engr.) 45, July 30, 1754.
   [390] *William Smith Jr. Ms. Supream Ct. Register A* 113.
   [391] 4 *Papers of Sir William Johnson* (1925) 3.
   [392] *William Smith Jr. Papers Miscellanea.*
   [393] This is apparent from the *Supream Court*

ter was put on a new footing by the Ordinance of 1768 wherein certain additions increased the fees in criminal cases. The most significant addition was the special table of "Attorney General's Fees in the Supreme Courts where a Defendant voluntarily compounds with the Attorney General in order to obtain a *nolo prosequi* or mitigate his fine,"[394] a series of charges which meant some increase in compensation. Similar provision was made as to fees of the clerk of the peace and clerk of the Supreme Court. This ordinance dealt with no matter of administration other than to require taxation of costs in all cases and to authorize the judges to disallow bills containing charges for "unnecessary service," a provision which suggests that the *quantum meruit* practice of the Supreme Court was not abolished but a certain discretion left. The delicate point of settlement with officials was left untouched, and judging from Colden's correspondence with his son who was clerking at Albany, this was a source of great controversy.[395] The Supreme Court clerk conducted his business at least partly on a credit basis. There are some early term accounts[396] preserved, and one of May Bickley's running over several years.[397] The most remarkable of these accounts is James Duane's with George Clarke, Jr., Clerk of the Supreme Court, that ran from October, 1754 to January, 1774 and totalled £335 13s. 3d.[398] At Clarke's death only £15 had been paid on this. The judges do not appear to have attempted to regulate the matter, for the only rule we have seen is one of 1764 respecting prompt settlement of the term fee of the judges, a move which may have been induced by the state of Joseph Murray's account with De Lancey, C.J.[399]

After the promulgation of the Ordinance of 1768 the Supreme Court ordered it "be the rule for taxing costs in this court against the loser except for judgment entered before the Ordinance."[400] This rule, in spite of its form, was certainly not intended to cover criminal cases, prosecuted by indictment or by

Register of William Smith Jr. and particularly from the *Ms. Cost Books* of William Livingston, the two volumes of which cover the years 1749–1772.

[394] The Bar Association copy was used. No page numbers.

[395] 9 *Cadwallader Colden Papers* (68 *NYHS Colls.*) 4, 5, 14, 15, 16, 35. Colden informed his son that the city clerk used a quarterly or half-yearly system. Augustus Van Cortlandt's *Ms. Account for Clerks Fees in the Mayor's Ct.*, which Mr. Augustus Van Cortlandt kindly permitted us to examine, carried credit accounts of long standing, e.g., Thomas Hicks, fols. 130–136.

[396] 52 NY Col. Mss. 71–73 (1707), 105 (1708), 136 (1708); 54 *ibid.* 100.

[397] *Account with the Clerk of the Supreme Ct.*

1713–15, De Peyster Mss. For a later example see *Samuel Jones Papers 1721–1823* fol. 1, Jan. 1762—Oct. 1763.

[398] *James Duane Mss.* III. Even the crier ran a credit business. Cf. Richard Wenman's account with Kempe running over many years (*J. T. Kempe Lawsuits* V *sub nom.* Wenman).

[399] *Ms. Mins. SCJ 1764–67* (Rough) 34. The *Ms. State of Account* between the estate of De Lancey and the estate of Joseph Murray, Mar. 20, 1761, covering judges' fees from Oct. 1733 to July term, 1756, and amounting to £168 10s. (*De Lancey Family Mss.*). Another document sets out the cases.

[400] *Ms. Mins. SCJ 1766–69* (Engr.) 508.

ex-officio information, and indeed, the case of *King* v. *Van Rensselaer* tried shortly thereafter establishes that it was not. The Council in 1763 had recommended that the costs of the Lydius intrusion case be taken out of the quitrents, and again in 1767 made a similar request.[401] This was certainly a relief for the Attorney General but it did nothing to increase a sense of obligation in the legislature or even in the courts. It was in any event a financial arrangement available only if the Crown consented, and hence to be invoked only in cases where Crown interests were directly at stake. The records are otherwise inconclusive on the "cost" problem after 1768, for the misdemeanors where a conviction was obtained were more frequently punished with whipping or imprisonment. There are only a few cases of fines, usually insignificant, which suggest that prosecutors' costs were paid.[402] The considerable number of cases where prosecution was not continued probably signifies compounding, although the minutes do not so state.[403]

There can be no doubt that the matter of costs had a very direct bearing upon the efficacy of law enforcement. We have from time to time adverted to the charges in particular cases, and in the Appendix we reproduce the bill in *King* v. *Van Schaick*[404] which is typical of a litigation that dragged out over several terms. A defendant who compromised had in addition to the prosecutor's bill his own attorney's account which was usually considerably less since it did not include the items like the costs of drawing indictment or process charges.

It may be observed that the New York bills of costs in criminal cases are generally less than those in England if the samples in Palmer's *Attorney's Bills of Costs* (1792) may be taken as typical. Probably the most striking feature of the bills for prosecution is the fact that the Attorney General's services were poorly remunerated. It will be noticed from the Van Schaick bill (in the Appendix) that most of the items represent out-of-pocket expenses. If the Attorney General's charge of £4 for "a long letter" seems high, he obviously

[401] For the Council proceedings on the bills in the John Van Rensselaer case cf. 26 *Ms. Mins. Council* 127, 135, 137. Duane received £100, and on Dec. 2, 1768 Agent Munroe's bill of £433 9s. 2d. was approved. The vote in the Lydius case is discussed in the Council's letter to Monckton, June 25, 1763 (P.R.O., C.O. 5/1098 fol. 437). The vote on Apr. 22, 1767 (26 *Ms. Mins. Council* 94).

[402] *King* v. *George Elms*, riot, 20s. (*Ms. Mins. SCJ* 1769–72 [Engr.] 275, Oct. 18, 1770); *King* v. *Day*, 6s. (*ibid.* 341, Apr. 16, 1771); *King* v. *Ben Burrows*, assault, "half a mark" (*Ms. Mins. SCJ* 1772–76 [Rough] 262, Oct. 27, 1775).

[403] There are a few specific references in *King* v. *James Armstrong* (assault); the complainant wrote to Kempe the "differences" had been settled (*J. T. Kempe Lawsuits* P–R *sub nom.* Pierson); cf. *H.R. Pleadings* Pl. K. 482, indictment *King* v. *Spicer* (1770) marked "settled"; Pl. K. 521, indictment *King* v. *Joseph Campbell* (1770), "settled." Note also *King* v. *Esselstyne* where on reasons of failure to return a certiorari, the defendant was discharged on payment of reasonable costs (*Ms. Mins. SCJ* 1772–76 [Engr.] 220, Jan. 21, 1775).

[404] *J. T. Kempe Lawsuits* V. *Infra* 777.

did a lot to earn the £1 9s. retainer. Where the Attorney General could get an undertaking from an informer it was possible for him to come out whole, but in ex-officio prosecutions he was in a difficult position. After some correspondence Kempe managed to induce Sir William Johnson to pay the Klock bill,[405] but in the Van Rensselaer case he was obliged to memorialize the Council.[406] In *King* v. *Bache* where judgment had been for the defendant on the demurrer, a writ of error was brought to the Governor and Council and, judging from a notice sent to defendant's counsel, error proceedings were discontinued in a way which gave Kempe hope of securing his costs although judgment had been against the Crown in the Supreme Court.[407] The concurrent prosecution of Forman went to the Council on error and a *nolle pros.* was entered, contingent upon Forman's paying prosecution costs. This defendant ignored the order and having conveniently become insolvent referred the Attorney General to his assignees.[408] The financial hazards being what they were, it is not surprising that after some years of New York practice William Kempe died with virtually no assets,[409] and that his son John Tabor resorted eventually to a form of recognizance from complainants whereby the principal and the sureties bound themselves to pay all costs expended or certified, and such fees "as are usually paid in the province by clients to the council for attendance."[410] What is even more remarkable is that there were so many people sufficiently irate to prefer complaints of misdemeanor and take the risk of no compromise and the still greater gamble that a jury would convict.

It may be remarked, in conclusion, that except for cases where the payment

---

[405] *J. T. Kempe Letters* A–Z, Letter of May 23, 1766. Cf. also 4 *Papers of Sir William Johnson* 668, 700, 744. For the bill of defendant's attorney, *infra* 775 *et seq.*

[406] *Cal. Eng. Mss.* 774. These papers are lost.

[407] Cf. *supra* 246. The notice is in *H.R. Pleadings* Pl. K. 328:

"The King agt. Theophilact Bache } NEW YORK SUPREME COURT

Sir

Be pleased to take Notice that I intend to get the Costs in the above Cause (a Copy whereof is herewith sent you) taxed by Mr. Chief Justice at his Chamber Situate in the East Ward of the City of New York on Tuesday next at four of the Clock in the afternoon of the same day Dated this 30th day of April 1767

I am
Your humble Servant
Attorney General[1]

To
Thomas Jones Esquire
Attorney for the Defendant"

[408] Kempe to John H. Cruger, Feb. 1, 1769 (*J. T. Kempe Letters* A–Z). There were two bills, one for £136 14s. 6d., the other £32 9s. 11d. The difference Kempe explains on the ground that things had been left out of the second in "favor" Forman and that the bills having been drawn to be certified on a *quantum meruit*, he had asked the judges to settle them on a narrow footing. Note also Kempe's statement in a letter to Gov. Moore, Apr. 3, 1767, that some prosecutions for illegal trade had to be dropped because there was no money to support witnesses during trial (P.R.O., C.O. 5/1098 fol. 555).

[409] *J. T. Kempe* to Oliver De Lancey (*J. T. Kempe Letters* A–Z).

[410] For example *H.R. Pleadings* Pl. K. 735; *J. T. Kempe Lawsuits sub nom.* Rodman.

of fees was exacted from a defendant corporally punished, the Supreme Court did not pursue a policy of ordering confinement until such charges were paid, a particular in which its practice differed from that at Sessions. We have found no explanation of this, and it can only be attributed to a certain indifference. John Tabor Kempe complained bitterly to Governor Moore that "there is no way of compelling offenders of any Sort even when of ability and convicted, of defraying the charges of bringing them to Justice, nor will the Courts here appropriate any part of the Fines laid for offences to this service, nor often recommend it to them to pay the costs previous to affeering the Fines. When there is an acquittal of the person charged or the Offender is poor nothing can be hoped for and not often is anything to be obtained on conviction."[411] This situation was not remedied and so the financial risks continued to be shared by the complaining witness and the Attorney General.

Mitigations and Pardon

"Nothing is more common than to hear those who have taken only a Superficial View of the Crown Law, charge it with numberless Hardships and undistinguishing Rigour; whereas those, who have more fully examined it, agree that it wants nothing to make it admir'd, for Clemency and Equity as well as Justice, but to be understood."[412] Thus the excellent Sergeant Hawkins introduced his *Pleas of the Crown* in the reign of the first George. Our disagreement with these sentiments has been constantly registered in this volume, and it is but just that we should finally direct our attention to what quality of mercy the law of crimes possessed.

We have in the course of the preceding pages indicated certain particulars where the severity of an otherwise pitiless jurisprudence had been tempered in practice. This has been, of course, most noticeable in the case of prosecutions for misdemeanors where the allowance of counsel had produced the effect of a much greater protection for defendants than where they were on trial for felonies. The most noteworthy of these mitigations, which long tradition had made of course, was the scaling down of fines on a plea of *nolo contendere* or where the defendant agreed to assume the costs of prosecution. In the administration of justice in New York, moreover, it is necessary also to regard the manipulation of the recognizance device, especially in the inferior courts, as an

---

[411] P.R.O., C.O. 5/1098 fol. 558.
[412] Hawkins, *op. cit.* introd. The views of Blackstone were similar, and it is worth noticing that Sir William Holdsworth, in 11 *Hist. Eng. Law* (1938) 580 *et seq.*, entertains views only slightly less rosy.

easement of the relentless consequences of indictment. No one who has examined the records of the General Sessions Courts for the decade before the
battle of Lexington can fail to be struck by the manner in which the binding
for appearance and for good behavior has crowded out the confessed indictment and the jury trial as a measure for keeping the King's peace. The recognizance was probably resorted to less in a spirit of compassion than in a desperate
effort to cope with marching insurgence, but the practice cannot be dismissed
as mere aberration of emergency when it is as usual in the placid county of
Suffolk as in the turbulent county of Albany. Unquestionably the compelling
of regular estreats and the suits upon forfeited bonds[413] caused a revaluation of
the recognizance as law-enforcing device, and direction of attention to the
matter of deterrence. The diet of the inferior courts had become unbalanced
by superabundance of assaults, batteries, routs and riots. It could not be corrected by active prosecution there because juries would not convict.[414] At best,
it might be kept slightly in hand by the ancient machinery for assuring good
abearance, leaving to an occasional Oyer and Terminer the task of acting *in
terrorem.*[415]

Aside from this change in the complexion of the records making the enforcement of the law at the end of the colonial period seem unexpectedly
clement, the evidence of a New Testament attitude toward misdemeanants is
not overwhelming. In the General Sessions there prevailed in most counties
an atmosphere of leniency, but only rarely is an act of mercy discoverable. The
early patriarchal conceptions of judging, where upon submission an apology
or act of reparation was ordered, soon are supplanted by the stereotyped common law discretion which could only swing pendulum-like between a fine or
a whipping. The form in which mercy is most often manifested is by an order
to get out of the country.[416] The only place where the old ways lingered was in
Dutchess. Here in 1764 Benjamin Tidd was let off charge of criminal libel by
retracting his statement that Thomas Davenport had had criminal conversation with Tidd's negro wench;[417] and Thomas Young, indicted for blasphemy,
escaped with a mere £10 fine[418] by making a recantation "humbly begging
the pardon of God Almighty, the World of Mankind and the present Court

---

[413] *Supra* 526 *et seq.*
[414] 2 *Colden Letter Books* 77, 141, 144.
[415] *Supra* 91 n. 157.
[416] For example, King v. Nugent (*Ms. Mins.
Suffolk Co. Sess. 1760–75* Oct. 7, 1760); King v.
Alice Kerney (*Ms. Mins. Dutchess Co. Sess.* Liber A, May 19, 1741); King v. Thos. Pepper (*Ms.
Mins. Ulster Co. Sess. 1737–50* Nov. 4, 1740, May

5, 1741). For New York City cases, cf. *supra* 593
n. 180. Some of the cases where indictments were
quashed were possibly acts of grace. Usually there
is no indication whv the quashing was done.
[417] *Ms. Mins. Dutchess Co. Sess.* Liber C, May
15, 1764.
[418] *Ibid.* May 18, 1758.

of Sessions."[419] The mercy in these cases consisted in not holding the defendants for the Circuit where the causes would normally have gone.

In contrast with General Sessions, the scanty records of summary "meetings" show a proportionately less rigid method of disposing of cases. In Ulster County a woman suspected of theft is sent out of the county;[420] in Westchester a woman charged with being a common disturber is ordered to be kept home by her husband;[421] in Dutchess a complaint about an unruly negro is diagnosed as a neighbors' quarrel and the complainant and master made to divide the costs.[422] There are numerous instances of a mere taking of surety, with no further mention of the case in the records. In New York City in the meetings for the trial of offenses less than grand larceny there are some examples of remission of punishment. Nicholas Lynch, summarily sentenced to twenty-one lashes for petit larceny, had his sentence suspended on condition of leaving the city,[423] and a similar rule was made in the case of Daniel Norris because of "his being in drink."[424] Duncan McDowell charged with petit larceny alleged his son had found the goods, and was discharged because he had a good character.[425] Two women, one accused of petit larceny, and the other of receiving, had their sentences remitted for circumstances not related.[426] There are unfortunately not enough records to form a trustworthy opinion about the rigor of summary proceedings, but it is apparent from the way in which masters' abuse of indentured persons was dealt with that the provincial magistrates had their humane moments.[427]

There is a scattering of acts of grace in the Circuit records. Mansfield Hunt, a youth, pleaded *nolo* to an indictment for riot at the Westchester Oyer and Terminer in 1721, and it was ordered that he "being a youth be remitted to the correction of his father."[428] At the Ulster Circuit in the next year Augentie Brass who confessed to an indictment for carnal copulation with a negro was discharged "paying fees," "it appearing to the court that she was seduced under promise of marriage and something out of her sences."[429] William Smith, at the Orange Circuit in 1775, was discharged after confessing an indictment of assault and battery because the court thought he had acted in self-defense after

[419] Ms. Files Dutchess Co. 1756.
[420] Ms. Mins. Ulster Co. Sess. 1710/11–1720 Meeting of Aug. 18, 1716.
[421] Ms. Mins. Westch. Co. Sess. 1710–23 Meeting of Oct. 2, 1716.
[422] Ms. Files Dutchess Co. 1755 Meeting of Sept. 15, 1755.
[423] Ms. Mins. NYCQS 1722–1742/43 (Rough) 371, 372, Mar. 20, 1740/41.
[424] Ibid. 372, Mar. 27, 1741.
[425] Ibid. Mar. 27, 1741.
[426] Ibid. Meeting of May 19, 1742.
[427] For example, Ms. Mins. NYCQS 1694–1731/32 376, Aug. 3, 1720, 535, May 5, 1731; Ms. Mins. NYCQS 1732–62 Aug. 4, 1762; Ms. Mins. NYCQS 1772–91 11, May 8, 1772; Ms. Mins. Richmond Co. Sess. 1710/11–1744/45 Sept. 5, 1721.
[428] Ms. Mins. Cir. 1721–49 6, 7.
[429] Ibid. 18, 19.

provocation.[430] In 1764, Augustine Reynolds and others, convicted on information for riotously taking away and imprisoning certain negroes, were given only a small fine because they had restored the negroes and because they were poor.[431]

The discretion which judges possessed in misdemeanor cases was not in essence so narrow but that the springs of mercy might have flowed more freely than in the thin trickle which we have noted. But in the case of felonies, it was so strictly limited by the law to the stylized forms of mitigation that no spirit of forbearance could avail except in the provided channels.

We have spoken of the grooves in which the jury might exercise its charity: the verdict in thefts for amounts under the 12d. boundary between grand and petit larceny, and the privilege of finding manslaughter, self-defense or accident upon indictments for murder.[432] These prerogatives the juries in New York did not hesitate to assert, and to these old and established powers of mitigation may be added, perhaps, the avoidance in New York of the incidents of felony judgment by the persistent finding of no goods or tenements.[433] Of considerably greater significance than these possible interferences of the jury, but connected therewith in the case of verdicts for crimes of a less degree when murder, burglary, arson, highway robbery and certain others were charged, is the mitigation obtained by benefit of clergy.[434]

Devised for the protection of clerks and to safeguard ecclesiastical jurisdiction, benefit of clergy was made available after 1350[435] to any man who could read, and the legislature, as Blackstone fatuously remarks, "in the course of a long and laborious process, extracted, by noble alchemy, rich medicines out of poisonous ingredients. . . ."[436] Specifically this medicine was a nostrum for the noose, until Queen Anne's reign available only to those who could pass a test slightly less exiguous than that now required in New York of prospective voters. This trial by book the Parliament in 1706 declared "by experience is found to be of no use" and enacted that clergy could be allowed without the reading requirement.[437] The benefit which the privilege involved where allowed was a branding and under certain circumstances also an imprisonment or whipping.

The body of exceptions and distinctions which prevailed in regard to clergy

430 *Ibid.* 45.
431 *H.R. Parch.* 178 H 4; *Ms. Mins. SCJ 1762–64* (Engr.) 349.
432 *Supra* 674 *et seq.*
433 *Supra* 715 *et seq.*
434 For a compact discussion, 1 Stephen, *Hist.*

Criminal Law 457 *et seq.* The most detailed account of the later seventeenth century rules is in 2 Hale, *op. cit.* c.44 *et seq.*
435 25 Edw. III st. 3.
436 4 Blackstone, *Commentaries* 371.
437 5 Anne c.6.

are the bewildering marginal glosses written by the judges about the school-man's text that a Mosaic standard of guilt could not be disintegrated, but might be circumvented by exception. Some of these rules came into use in New York, but for the most part they were ignored or there was no occasion for them to be applied. Benefit of clergy itself could not be jettisoned because it was so deeply seated in law and was tolerable as respects crimes like homicide or grand larceny because it was then the only available means of dealing humanely with degrees of responsibility.

The first provincial cases we have found occurred in 1693 when two defendants found guilty of some felony prayed clergy—the entry: "Jefferson legit clerice, Clifford legit clerice."[438] The next case found occurred at an Albany Oyer and Terminer, Nov. 19, 1706, where John Woodcock, indicted for murder, was convicted of manslaughter and prayed clergy, but in 1713 a prisoner similarly convicted, after praying his clergy, produced a pardon. He accordingly was discharged without branding.[439] Clergy was not again invoked until 1730,[440] and thereafter we have no recorded instances until 1750. From this time forward the cases increase, there being a total of seventy-three cases in the years from 1754 to 1776. The form in which the minute entries are made indicates that the colonists had accepted the abolition of the reading test, although the statute of Anne did not extend to the plantations.[441]

There is no apparent reason why the prayer of clergy was so little used in the first half of the eighteenth century. There are numerous cases where it might have been invoked, and since there is no reason to think that the judges did not advise felons convicted of clergiable offenses of their rights or that the advan-

---

[438] *Mins. SCJ 1693–1701* 52.

[439] Queen v. Woodcock, *Oyer and Terminer Minutes* (51 NY Col. Mss. 184). The pardon case is Queen v. Peter Mullinder (*Ms. Mins. SCJ 1710–14* 439, Mar. 14, 1712/13). In 1704, Densworth a slave and John Allen were indicted for felony and burglary. Densworth was convicted "to the value of 9s."; on motion of the Attorney General he was burned in the face, and ordered imprisoned for a month. There is no sign clergy was claimed (*Ms. Mins. SCJ 1701–04* 150, 156, 171, 172).

[440] King v. Mulatto Will (*Ms. Mins. SCJ 1727–32* 282, June 7, 1731).

[441] Richard Salter and Benjamin DeGoede were convicted of felony and "on Motion of Mr Attorney General for Judgment the Court will Consider thereof until next Term." In the following term "The Prisoners were set at the Bar, and being severally asked what they had to say why Judgment of death should not pass against them . . . prayed their Clergy, whereupon . . . judgment that the prisoner should be burned in their hands

on the brawn of their left thumbs, which was accordingly done . . . and the prisoners . . . discharged on paying their fees" (*Ms. Mins. SCJ 1754–57* [Engr.] 114, 116, 138, 147, Jan. 24, 25, Apr. 19, 1755).

For a judgment roll entry, King v. Campbell convicted of grand larceny (*Ms. Mins. SCJ 1764–67* [Rough] 251, 257, July 30, 31, 1767; H.R. Parch. 170 L 7):

"And upon this it is required of the said John Campbell if he hath or knows anything to say for himself why the Court here ought not to proceed to Judgment and Execution of him upon the Premises aforesaid Who thereupon for himself saith that he is a Clerk and prayeth the Benefit of Clergy to be allowed him in this Behalf Therefore it is considered that the Aforesaid John Campbell be burnt in his left hand according to the Form of the Statute in such Case made & provided And immediately he is burnt in his left Hand and is Delivered according to the Form of the Statute."

tages were not known, it seems possible that at least some of the felons may already have borne the tell-tale brand inflicted in England. It seems hardly credible that a person convicted of grand larceny would run the risk of a sentence to be hanged or to receive thirty-nine lashes in preference to branding on the thumb unless there were some practical obstacle and a second plea of clergy was such an obstacle. This does not by any means explain the omission of the plea in all cases, and since practice by 1700 was on sound professional basis the temporary desuetude of clergy, just as its sudden revival after 1750, remains something of a mystery.[442]

The English rules respecting what were and what were not clergiable offenses appear to have been carefully observed. In this connection it may be noticed that since statutes had made many alterations in the law of clergy, nice questions might be raised by the form of an indictment, viz., whether or not it stated an offense in terms which brought a case within a statute. One such case was *King v. Catherine Longworth,* indicted for "house breaking." She was sentenced to be hanged, but apparently the Attorney General thought a prayer of clergy was going to be proffered for he prepared a memorandum to establish that the housebreaker was ousted of clergy.[443] There is no evidence that the question was argued.

[442] Questions of clergy may have been raised although the minutes do not so indicate. James Morgan was indicted and acquitted of feloniously breaking in and stealing several parcels of plate from Cornelius Wynekoop (*Ms. Mins. SCJ 1723–27* 181, 200, Mar. 11, June 13, 1726). Endorsed on certain examinations of witnesses is the following: "Stat. 39 El. Ch. 19; 3 and 4 William and Mary Ch. 9; 10 and 11 William the Third, Ch. 29, 12 Anne Ch. 7. See for 'em Woods Inst. take away clergy 394" (*H.R. Pleadings* Pl. K. 600).

[443] Cf. the memorandum, *J. T. Kempe Lawsuits* L–O:

"January Term 1772 the King vs Catherine Longworth—note of statutes ousting clergy in cases of robbing Dwelling Houses

23 H. 8 c.23 Where the owner his wife and tenants . . . are put in fear

25 H. 8 c.3 Extension of above act to those who stand mute or challenge above 20 jurors

1 Edw. 6 para. 10 Giving Clergy in some other offenses denies it to this . . . if any person be in the House and put in dread

6 Edw. 6 c.10 1 Edw. 6 repealed as far as it allows clergy when taken away by 23 H. 8.

5 & 6 Edw. 6 c.9 Recites that three doubts had arisen upon the statute

See Keyling's Reports 67. 68. 69. &c. Hawkins Pleas 354

1. Whether Clergy was taken away for robberys

in dwellings the master &c. not being in the Room where the things were taken.

2. If they were asleep and

3. whether it extended to Robberies in . . . Tents Ferries Markets &c.

Takes away Clergy in Robberys committed dwelling houses . . . the owner . . . his wife [&c.] . . . being anywhere within the precinct of the Dwelling House whether . . . sleeping or not

3 & 4 W & M c.9 Principals and accessories ousted of clergy for *taking* goods &c. *any persons* being therein and put in fear.

39 Eliz. 15 Recites that felonious persons, understanding that robbing offenses in the daytime, no person being therein, is not penall as where some person is therein, were emboldened to commit robberies in breaking and entering houses no person being therein, ousts Clergy for taking above 5/ out of any dwelling house &c. *although no persons shall be therein* adjudged that this Statute extends only to larcenies accompanied with breaking the House

4 & 5 W & M c.9 Takes away from accessories the Benefit of Clergy as well where no person is in the house as where there are persons therein.

12 Anne c.7 Stealing in a dwelling House to the amount of 40/ although the house be not broken and although the owner or any other person be

As we have intimated, it was a rule that a person could only once have allowance of clergy and if he were again convicted of felony he would be sentenced to be hanged. There were a number of cases in New York where this happened. Thus, Elizabeth Clark confessed an indictment for grand larceny on April 25, 1767 and on May 1 was allowed clergy. In the following October she was again convicted of grand larceny, and when she sought clergy the record of the previous conviction was brought in against her and she was sentenced to be hanged.[444] The effect of the single allowance of clergy was to create a sort of first offender rule, a not inhumane conception, and the fact that the court might, after branding, order imprisonment up to a year prevented the mandatory allowance from operating entirely in defeasance of sensible law enforcement. In New York, the prisoners were usually discharged upon branding, paying fees, although there are examples of additional imprisonment or the taking of surety for good behavior.[445]

The ultimate mercy of the law for the felon was the pardon which traditionally was a matter of royal prerogative. Consequently the powers of the courts were limited to recommendation or to stay of execution pending some notice of executive pleasure. The prerogative was delegated to the Governor by the terms of his commission as to all offenses except treason and "wilful murder." This officer was likewise vested with a power of reprieve,[446] which the language of the instrument seems to limit to the cases reserved

. . . not in the house and aiders therein are ousted of clergy
As to what is a Breaking see 2 [1?] Hawkins 102 §4.5
What is an Entry   See II Hawk 103 §7."

The minute entries are in *Ms. Mins. SCJ 1769–72* (Engr.) 471–477, Jan. 23–25, 1772.

[444] *Ms. Mins. SCJ 1764–67* (Rough) 225, 228, 241, 272, 274; *Ms. Mins. SCJ 1766–69* (Engr.) 325. The record produced is *H.R. Parch.* 133 D 3. See also King v. Sarah Gillet (*supra* 592 n. 177). King v. Stewart (*Ms. Mins. SCJ 1764–67* [Rough] 278; *Ms. Mins. SCJ 1766–69* [Engr.] 326, Oct. 31, 1767) clergy granted. (*Ibid.* 607, Jan. 21, 1769) clergy denied (*H.R. Parch.* 165 K 9). King v. Adam Smith, clergy allowed for grand larceny, Apr. 27, 1771; sentenced to thirty-nine lashes and carting, Aug. 3, 1771; convicted of grand larceny and sentenced to be hanged, Jan. 25, 1772 (*Ms. Mins. SCJ 1769–72* [Engr.] 352, 355, 362, 398, 400, 401, 402, 471, 472, 477). For the judgment roll read when clergy was refused, see *H.R. Parch.* 127 E 6. King v. John Daley, convicted of grand larceny on Jan. 22, 1773, and on Jan. 23 "prayed his Clergy and the Record of a former Conviction of a felony and his being allowed his Clergy in that Case being read, and the prisoner not gain-

saying but that he is the same John Dailey [*sic*] mentioned in the said record," the court sentenced him to be hanged (*Ms. Mins. SCJ 1772–76* [Rough] 69, 70). King v. John Bryan, granted clergy on a conviction of grand larceny on July 29, 1775; refused clergy on Jan. 20, 1776, because the Attorney General "offered to the Court a Record of a former Conviction and Allowance of Clergy, which being Read and the Prisoner not gainsaying the said Record, but admitting his being the same Person," he was accordingly sentenced to be hanged (*ibid.* 247, 248, 254; *Ms. Mins. SCJ 1775–81* [Engr.] 63, 65). For the judgment record which was read against John Bryan, see *H.R. Parch.* 120 F 10.

[445] As in King v. John Jones (*Ms. Mins. SCJ 1762–64* [Engr.] 418, 421, 428, Apr. 23–27, 1764). In King v. John Douglas, a recognizance for a year was exacted (*Ms. Mins. SCJ 1764–67* [Rough] 208, 211, Jan. 24, 1767).

Cross, *Benefit of Clergy in American Criminal Law* (61 *Proc. Mass. Hist. Soc.* 154) finds nothing on New York. Obviously he did not know where to look.

[446] See, for example, the commission of 1686 to Dongan (3 *Doc. Rel. Col. Hist. NY* 379); to Fletcher (*ibid.* 830); and to Clinton (6 *ibid.* 192).

to the Crown, but which in fact was exercised in cases where the Governor himself had the right to pardon.[447] There are indications of some cooperation between the executive and the judiciary on this matter. As we shall see in a moment, judges recommended pardons and if a King's pardon for murder was thought desirable it was essential to have advice for the necessary reprieve. In the case of James Wilks, convicted of murder, Chambers and Horsmanden explained the defendant was drunk and had a mistaken idea of the law.[448] Smith, Livingston and Jones suggested a reprieve for a negro convicted of rape because the only evidence was that of a child of eight.[449] Godfrey Swan the judges thought was a lunatic and should be reprieved.[450] An unusual case was a request from the Governor and Lieutenant Governor of Connecticut for a reprieve of Felix Meigs, late of that province, in order that information could be sweated out of him about a ring of counterfeiters.[451]

It should be noticed in connection with reprieve that, as a practical matter, the courts themselves had worked out what amounted to a coordinate power since it was possible to respite the imposition of sentence,[452] or in sentencing to omit directions as to the time of execution. There was further one situation where reprieve at the direction of the court was grantable as a matter of law. This was the unusual circumstance where a woman convicted of felony who claimed to be pregnant would have execution stayed until after she was delivered. On April 26, 1736, Margaret Grass, convicted of felony, "being called and asked why sentence of death should not pass against her, pleaded her

[447] A week's reprieve granted in Council to Jonathan Jordan (*Cal. Council Mins.* 271 [1719]) and cf. also *Cal. Eng. Mss.* 751 (1704). For the form of reprieve, "By the Honorable Cadwallader Colden Esq. his Majesty's Lieutenant Governor . . . To Henry Ten Eyck Jr. Esq. High Sheriff of . . . Albany and to all officers and others whom these presents may Concern Greeting Whereas at the last court of Oyer and Terminer and General Gaol Delivery held in and for the County of Albany in . . . New York, one John Snyder was indicted, tried and convicted of a certain Burglary by him committed, for which he now lies under sentence of death to be executed on 4 Mar. next I have thought fit to reprieve and I do by and with advice of His Majesty's Council . . . Reprieve the said John Snyder until the 4th of February . . . next And you are hereby commanded to stay execution until the 4th of February on which day you are to see execution done according to the Sentence so given as aforesaid For which this shall be to you . . . sufficient warrant Given under my hand and Seal at arms at Fort George . . . 27 Oct. 1774 . . . Cadwallader Colden By his Honor's Command Samuel Bayard Jr. D. Secy." (*Misc.*

Mss. Albany 1691–1799 folder 1770–79). Compare the similar document of Gov. Tryon in the case of the negro Peet, July 17, 1773 (*ibid.*).

[448] Cf. a letter to Governor Hardy, Feb. 4, 1756, *Gratz Coll.* (Pa. Hist. Soc.); 25 *Ms. Mins. Council* 108; 82 *NY Col. Mss.* 63.

[449] 25 *Ms. Mins. Council* 497.

[450] 26 *ibid.* 20.

[451] *Ibid.* 316. Compare *ibid.* 155, John Jubeart, convicted of counterfeiting, reprieved to get evidence.

[452] Toby and three other Indian slaves were convicted of felony, Mar. 12, 1707/08. The next day judgment was respited to next term but nothing further appears (*Ms. Mins. SCJ 1704/05–1709* 165, 168). In King v. Rose (1728) judgment was respited and the prisoner put under recognizance (*Ms. Mins. Cir. 1721–49* 51). In King v. Middleton, McMurray, Pearson and Porter, convicted of highway robbery, Middleton was sentenced to be hanged. Judgment respited as to the others. There are no further entries (*Ms. Mins. SCJ 1756–61* [Rough] 211–215, Oct. 27–30, 1760). See also King v. Valentine Ruyter (*Ms. Mins. SCJ 1769–72* [Engr.] 16–18, 23, Apr. 26, 27, 29, 1769).

Belly and said she was with child." It was ordered a jury of matrons examine her. On the following day this jury reported Margaret was quick with child, so the "court think proper to reprieve her until October." On August 3 the defendant produced a pardon and was discharged.[453] Many years later, Frances Malone, convicted of stealing from the person privily, made a similar plea before sentence. Respite was ordered and at the following term she was ordered to be hanged,[454] but she secured a pardon conditional on leaving the Province.[455]

The fact that pardon was an act of prerogative excluded any judicial interference and left the courts only a mere advisory function. It is true the records speak of "allowing" a pardon[456] upon proffer but this signified no more than that the mandate was in proper form. Ordinarily the limit of the court's power was merely to see that the proper order was made and entered. Where a defendant secured a pardon in advance of trial, he could as we have seen plead it and be discharged.[457] And after conviction, as we have noticed in connection with reprieve, if there was any reason to suppose a pardon might issue, the court would not sentence until a later term, although sometimes the prisoners were sentenced and subsequently there was a second *allocutus* at which time the pardon was produced[458] and discharge then ordered.

In England it was the custom to present gloves when a pardon was proffered, and it had even been held that the judges might insist on this presentation before allowing the pardon.[459] We have seen only one case where the minutes explicitly mention the gift of gloves—*Queen* v. *Berry and Mark* where the former made the gift but the latter was excused because of his poverty. The judges were evidently bent on a rule, for the minutes state the ceremony was "according to ye custom as in ye 4th Edw. 4th fol. 106. Siderfin 452; King v. Webster Sir Thomas Jones Report 56."[460] It is possible this silly custom persisted, but there is no evidence on the point.

[453] *Ms. Mins. SCJ 1732–39* 212–215, 229, Apr. 23, 26, 27, Aug. 3, 1736.

[454] *Ms. Mins. SCJ 1764–67* (Rough) 251, 254, 257, 258; *Ms. Mins. SCJ 1766–69* (Engr.) 325, July 31, Oct. 31, 1767.

[455] *26 Ms. Mins. Council* 108. Mary Jeffers, convicted of felony and in jail, petitioned the Supreme Court, Oct. 22, 1765, that she was pregnant and near delivery. Recommended the city officials take her into the workhouse until she was fit to be put back in jail (*Ms. Mins. SCJ 1764–67* [Rough] 85, 125).

[456] For example, Queen v. Margaret Smith, the pardon "being read is allowed" (*Ms. Mins. SCJ 1704/05–1709* 222, 235, 236); King v. George

Brown, 1738 (*Ms. Mins. Cir. 1721–49* 94–96); King v. Mary Clarke, 1752 (*Ms. Mins. SCJ 1750–54* [Engr.] 104–106, 131, 132).

[457] *Supra* 589.

[458] Queen v. Berry and Mark (*Ms. Mins. SCJ 1710–14* 466, 472, 475–477, 500); Queen v. Margaret Smith (*supra* n. 456); King v. Mary Clarke (*supra* n. 456); King v. Eliz. Herbert (1750–51) is an example of a term delay in sentence (*Ms. Mins. SCJ 1750–54* [Engr.] 13, 15, 29). Early fee bills show a charge by the clerk for reading the royal pardon and filing it; cf. Jamison's account in *59 NY Col. Mss.* 100.

[459] *2* Hawkins, *op. cit.* c.37 §71.

[460] *Supra* n. 458.

One would expect that for record purposes a pardon would always be noted on the court minutes, but this was not invariably done. There are a number of instances where the minutes of the Governor and Council show that pardon was granted but no mention is made in any court record. In some of these cases the pardon was contingent on leaving the Province. The failure to have a record seems, in these particular instances, unaccountably remiss. So, as we just noticed, Frances Malone, who pleaded her belly and later was sentenced to be hanged, secured such a pardon, and in the same year William Johnson convicted of felony for sacrilege in stealing prayer books from St. Paul's was pardoned with the same condition, but the Supreme Court minutes do not mention these pardons.[461] The vagaries of the clerks defy, however, any explanation, for while they sometimes ignore the necessary they meticulously record the useless. When George Brown was pardoned in 1738, he was ordered to get out or be punished as a vagrant. The clerk appended an Aesopian note to his record: "N.B. he departed the province the next day crossing Hudsons River and going to the ferries as he crossed the river he threw his pardon into it and in a day after Robbed two men upon which he was taken tryed and hanged in about a fortnight after pleading his pardon."[462]

Except as to the crimes reserved by the Crown, prerogative of pardon was presumably to be exercised by the Governor himself; yet as the eighteenth century wore on, pardon cases came to be handled in Council as a matter of routine. This practice originated in the seventeenth century[463] but was only occasionally used during the first half of the eighteenth century.[464] Some of the entries in the Council minutes show clearly enough that it is only advice which is sought, but obviously the Governor did not even have to do this, for in the case of Gunner Parks[465] he acted without consultation. In the few cases that we have found where fines were remitted pursuant to the Governor's powers in this matter, it appears that the Council was consulted.[466]

The advisory function of the judges, already mentioned in connection with reprieve, is poorly attested during the early period of provincial history, but there is considerable evidence when pardon cases came to be regular Council

[461] 26 Ms. Mins. Council 102 (Johnson), ibid. 108 (Malone).
[462] Ms. Mins. Cir. 1721–49 94–96.
[463] Cf. the 1697 case of Joseph Smith (41 NY Col. Mss. 121; 8 Ms. Mins. Council 127); Vandenbergh's negro in 1698 (42 NY Col. Mss. 72).
[464] William Barker, 1711, tabled (55 NY Col. Mss. 1; 11 Ms. Mins. Council 17); Burgher's negro, 1719 (Cal. Eng. Mss. 441; Cal. Council Mins. 271); William Smith, 1720 (62 NY Col. Mss. 75;

Cal. Council Mins. 275); John Connor, 1731 (16 Ms. Mins. Council 75); Negro Dick, 1732 (ibid. 238); Margaret Grass, 1736 (17 ibid. 106); Jack and Bastian, 1741 (19 ibid. 114); John Stevens, 1744, rejected (ibid. 276).
[465] Supra 305.
[466] Catharine Carroe [Crow] (89 NY Col. Mss. 58; 26 Ms. Mins. Council 110); Patrick Walsh (26 Ms. Mins. Council 207); John Graham (ibid. 171).

business. As a rule pardons were sought by petition and where there was cause the judges would write in support.[467] Sometimes outsiders would intervene as in the case of one Van Ornem, convicted of burglary, where three hundred New Yorkers petitioned,[468] and Fred Tobias, convicted of stealing a hog, in whose behalf certain Common Pleas judges of Orange certified that the verdict was against law and unsupported by evidence.[469] The judges' reasons are not always given, but sometimes the insufficiency of the evidence is mentioned,[470] the mental deficiency of the convict[471] or the absence of malice.[472] The French and Indian War, it may be remarked, was a great stimulus to the springs of mercy, for during this period the pardoning power was used as a means of recruiting his Majesty's armed forces. Chief Justice Horsmanden in 1762 represented to the executive that three fellows convicted of grand larceny were to be burned in the thumb, "that the court therefore had deferred judgment apprehending that the great want of men at present might incline his Honour to think fit a pardon for the Kings Service."[473] There are numerous other examples.

One important use of pardon was to qualify or induce persons to be King's evidence. The case of Sarah Hughson in the negro plot cases has already been mentioned.[474] She had already been convicted of felony when pardoned, but the force and effect of a pardon were not limited to this situation, for it could be effective to prevent prosecution. Thus Isaac Jacobs was pardoned while he was still out of the Province,[475] and one Richard Maeslyes, languishing in the Dutchess jail under suspicion of counterfeiting, was pardoned before any proceedings were undertaken.[476] There are various examples available of persons involved in crimes pardoned when they turned King's evidence. Thus Thomas Griffiths was pardoned for testifying for the Crown against Van Ornem,[477] one Hubbs was pardoned on condition of making a confession regarding a jail break. In a counterfeiting case Justice Livingston writes the Governor that he

---

[467] In addition to cases cited *supra* nn. 448, 449, 450 and *infra* nn. 470, 471, cf. James McBride, 1755 (82 *NY Col. Mss.* 38; 25 *Ms. Mins. Council* 126); Nat. Freeman, 1762 (*J. T. Kempe Lawsuits sub nom.* Lydius in a postscript to a letter; 25 *Ms. Mins. Council* 452); Deborah Tonge, Eliz. Dunt, Eliz. Floyd, 1766 (26 *Ms. Mins. Council* 68); William Johnson, 1767 (*ibid.* 102); Richard Hudnett *et al.*, 1769 (*ibid.* 145); John Ryan and Hannah Hyatt, 1770 (*ibid.* 186); Thomas Clay, Jacob Osburn, 1770 (*ibid.* 186); William Davison, 1771 (*ibid.* 254); Catherine Longworth, 1772 (*ibid.* 271); Eliz. Donaghue and Neptune, 1773 (*ibid.* 376); John Stanworth, 1774 (*ibid.* 407); Nicholas Bassong *et al.*, 1775 (*ibid.* 441).

[468] 25 *Ms. Mins. Council* 418.
[469] 26 *ibid.* 312. See also the case of John Snyder for whom the mayor, recorder and aldermen of Albany petitioned, *ibid.* 410.
[470] Frances Malone, 1767 (*ibid.* 108).
[471] John Hennessy, 1769 (*ibid.* 155); Michael Myers, 1774 (*ibid.* 406).
[472] Wilks, 1756 (De Lancey, Chambers and Horsmanden to Gov. Hardy, Feb. 4, 1756, *Gratz Coll.* [Pa. Hist. Soc.]).
[473] 25 *Ms. Mins. Council* 444, May 4, 1762.
[474] *Supra* 640, 645.
[475] *H.R. Parch.* 223 A 4.
[476] 25 *Ms. Mins. Council* 283 (1759).
[477] 26 *ibid.* 353, 361 (1773).

had pardoned William Hurlburt in order to get his evidence.[478] Actually this was only a promise to intercede for subsequently the Governor's pardon was issued. A similar arrangement was made with James Brown in a receiving prosecution in order to secure conviction of Jacob Moses.[479]

Some of the pardons are enrolled in the surviving colonial book of commissions,[480] but we are not sure whether this was a practice of long standing. Where a murder was pardoned by the King, the colonial authorities were notified and the sheriff of Middlesex and the mayor and recorder of London were directed to place the name of the beneficiary of royal grace in the calendar of persons included in the general pardon for those confined and pardoned at Newgate.[481] This was a remarkable way of making a public notification effective in America, and it seems likely a document was given the person pardoned although we have no evidence of the fact.

In general, the pardon power seems to have been exercised not ungenerously, and if in the expected eighteenth century tradition money sometimes passed hands, no trace of any such transactions has been found. There are, in any event, too many instances of poor persons being pardoned for suspicions to attach to the execution of this prerogative. Whether the practice in England was one of equal disinterestedness we do not know, but one may fairly well doubt whether the justices of King's Bench ever troubled to write the Crown to save some wretch from the gallows because he had been drunk. The century which saw the introduction of the bitter common law of crime into New York was not the most benign epoch in the history of human charity, and the community where this law was put into effect was undisciplined. In the spirit of the times and in most cases justifiably if the examinations before magistrates are to be credited, the vengeance of the law was sternly taken. But the courts were not invariably callous, and when at commencement of trial the clerk recited "God give thee a good deliverance," a defendant could cherish some hope that his fellow men would fairly help.

We have come to the end of our record and the moment to move for judgment is upon us. The record itself speaks with more authority than any words

---

[478] Livingston to Tryon, Mar. 9, 1773, *Gratz Coll.* (Pa. Hist. Soc.); 26 *Ms. Mins. Council* 334.
[479] Livingston to Tryon, Nov. 10, 1772, *Gratz Coll.* (Pa. Hist. Soc.); 26 *Ms. Mins. Council* 325. A previous confession of Brown was already available (cf. *supra* 151 n. 53). Cf. King v. Ashcraft and Norton (*supra* 640 n. 130).

[480] For example, the pardons of Falmouth and Jack, Nov. 22, 1770 (*Ms. Book of Commissions 1770–89* 3); Hulburt, Jan. 28, 1773 (*ibid.* 73); Bassong, Aug. 5, 1775 (*ibid.* 173).
[481] E.g., 25 *Ms. Mins. Council* 126 (Wilks); 429 (Pearson).

we can add, but since in our introduction we took issue with various assumptions about colonial law that have been propagated by others, it is essential that we refer once more to the various hypotheses and conclusions of which these opposing opinions are composed. Once more it must be asked: what place is left for the theory of the frontier; when was our American law formed?

The attentive reader will have observed that even if one is not prepared to agree that there was an English model for nearly every device employed in New York in the years immediately following the conquest, the forms and rules of Westminster Hall itself had secured a firm footing in the superior courts by the year 1691; and if it be conceded that our General Sessions must be compared not with the King's Bench but with English Quarter Sessions, and that reception can be tested by Dalton's manuals as well as by Coke's *Institutes,* the last of any reasonable doubt must vanish. We have not pretended that throughout the last two decades of the seventeenth century technical proficiency in the Province was equal to the English, but such relative inexpertness can scarcely be laid to the frontier. The state of practice in the early eighteenth century demonstrates that it is upon the degree of transplantation of culture that the improvement of knowledge depends. Where then did the forest, the Indian danger and the license of open spaces produce the effects which are claimed for it? Surely, the magistrates of Albany and Ulster were not less in humanity than the bench in Yorkshire; surely the defendants who stood at the bar of the Supreme Court or of New York Quarter Sessions were no more degraded than the procession which passed through Old Bailey. And if one would explain provincial riots as a repercussion of the backwoods way of life, how is the tumult before the Houses of Parliament after the South Sea crash to be explained, the London riots of 1768, or the later episode when Mansfield's house was burned? Certainly the fact that the inhabitants of the northern English counties were not environed by redskins did not make the events there in '45 less savage than the uprising in Dutchess of '66. The truth is, when one comes to matters of law breaking and of law enforcement, the European world was then no more and no less brutal than the American. And if American problems are to be seen in true perspective, they are better viewed from Newgate than from the salon of Strawberry Hill.

To what extent the quality of Americanism can be attributed to the law practiced in New York, is a question not to be answered by quotation of the colonists' own words. They took the law still warm from the devout hands of Coke and Hale, but they were fully and not too happily aware that what they made of it was an imitation, and the limitations put upon their freedom of choice was one reason for political insistence upon identity of common law and fundamental law. This is far from any claim that provincial law was identical in all its ramifications with English law. New York possessed a much simpler and more rational judicial organization than did England, and whatever rules and practices were received had to be accommodated to this system. The colonists remade the justice of the peace into a judge of civil as well as of criminal causes, they jettisoned outlawry and escheat and, in the various ways which we have recounted, effected minor accommodations. These achievements were recognized to be something discrete and substantial, inferior, if at all, only to the fundamental law from which they were derived, because this fundamental law was conceived as something right, above and beyond the pronouncements of official persons. That is why, immediately after independence had been declared, the provincial Congress could speak of the laws of the state as if the renunciation of the sovereign had been no more than the removal of a symbol—the law stood.

Perhaps the strongest arguments of those who cherish the belief that our American law begins in 1783 are colonial reliance upon English judicial opinion and the absence of native reporting. These are small matters when placed against the stout body of practice, the independent character of which is evidenced by the special collections of manuscript precedents kept by lawyers who had large libraries of English books. What is done in the conduct of a litigation or a prosecution is the real life blood of a legal system, and persistence in the ways of practice is as true a type of precedent as the consistent pursuit of doctrine.

In the end the measure of Americanism is to be found in the impalpable transfigurations of the settler's spirit and so his use of his intellectual heritage. These changes were described by the cultivated Crèvecoeur, himself an Orange County farmer,[482] and they are told with no greater sensibility than in the poet's lines:[483]

> The homesick men begot high-cheekboned things
> Whose wit was whittled with a different sound
> And Thames and all the rivers of the Kings
> Ran into Mississippi and were drowned.

---

[482] Crèvecoeur, *Letters from an American Farmer* (1904 ed.) 48 "What is an American."

[483] Stephen Vincent Benét, 1 *Selected Works* 4 (New York, Farrar and Rinehart, 1942) "John Brown's Body."

APPENDICES

APPENDIX A. SOURCES

LOCATION AND ABBREVIATIONS

The following lists are not designed to be a complete bibliography of all materials examined or cited, but primarily to serve as a guide to the location of manuscripts and to abbreviations of these and the printed sources most frequently used in this volume. We have not included manuscript collections which were searched but were found to contain nothing bearing upon our problem.

MANUSCRIPT SOURCES

These sources are listed alphabetically by the operative word (county, court, surname, or town), which is set in small capital letters. Abbreviations used in footnotes are set in italics. The following abbreviations of locations are used:

CU—Columbia University Library
HR—Hall of Records, New York County
NYHS—New York Historical Society Library
NYPL—New York Public Library, Manuscript Division
NYSL—New York State Library, Albany, New York

P.R.O. Adm.
ADMIRALTY Papers (Public Record Office, London)
Deeds ALBANY County Liber III (Albany County Clerk's Office, Albany, N. Y.)
Misc. Mss. Albany
Miscellaneous Manuscripts ALBANY
1691–1799 (NYHS)
Ms. Mins. Albany Co. Sess.
Minutes ALBANY County Court of Sessions
1685–89 (Albany County Clerk's Office)

Minutes ALBANY County General Sessions of the Peace
1717–23 ⎫
1763–82 ⎬ (Albany County Clerk's Office)
James ALEXANDER Papers (NYHS)
James ALEXANDER, Supreme Court Register
1721–42 (NYHS)
Calendar of Proceedings of Court of ASSIZES
1665–72 (NYPL)
Ms. Mins. Ct. of Assizes
Minutes of Court of ASSIZES, 1665–72. This is now bound with Ms. General Entries 1665–74 (NYSL)
Miscellaneous Manuscripts ATWOOD (NYHS)

Miscellaneous BANCKER Papers (NYHS)

Miscellaneous Manuscripts BAYARD (NYHS)
BAYARD Papers
1698–1710 (Bound volume, NYHS)
Miscellaneous Manuscripts BEEKMAN (NYHS)
BILLS Which Failed to Become Laws
1685–1776. 3 vols. (NYSL)
Miscellaneous Manuscripts William BLATHWAYT (NYHS)
Misc. Mss. Bradley
Miscellaneous Manuscripts Richard BRADLEY (NYHS)
BREVIA Selecta. (In Miscellaneous Manuscripts Van Cortlandt, NYHS.) This is the Precedent Book of John Van Cortlandt
BUSHWICK Town Records
1660–1825 (Kings County Hall of Records, Brooklyn, New York)

Miscellaneous Manuscripts CANAJOHARIE (NYHS)
Miscellaneous Manuscripts Andrew CANON (NYHS)
John CHAMBERS Manuscripts (NYSL)
HR Chancery
CHANCERY Files (HR)
Ms. Mins. Charlotte Co. Sess.
Minutes CHARLOTTE County General Sessions of the Peace
1773–1800 (NYSL)

Ms. Mins. Circ.
Minutes CIRCUIT, 1716–1717 (HR). Cf. *supra* 80
n. 122

Minutes CIRCUIT, 1721–49 (New York Bar Association). Cf. *supra* 80 n. 122
Miscellaneous Manuscripts CLAVERACK (NYHS)
Book of COMMISSIONS, 1770–89 (NYSL). This is
volume six of the series. Cf. *infra* Printed Sources,
Cal. Col. Com.

Conn. Archives
CONNECTICUT Archives (State Library, Hartford,
Connecticut)
Miscellaneous Manuscripts CORNBURY (NYHS)
Ms. Mins. Council
Manuscript Minutes of the Governor and COUNCIL of New York Province (NYSL)
Miscellaneous Manuscripts Bartholomew CRANNEL
(NYHS)

Minutes of the DEBATING CLUB, 1768–74 (NYHS)
DE LANCEY Family Manuscripts (Museum of the
City of New York)
F. A. DE PEYSTER Manuscripts (NYHS)
James DUANE Manuscripts (NYHS)
James DUANE Manuscript Register A (NYHS)
DUKE's Laws, Huntington, L. I., copy (Huntington
Town Clerk)
DUKE's Laws, Van Cortlandt copy (CU)
Files DUTCHESS County (Dutchess County Clerk's
Office, Poughkeepsie, New York). These files
cover the years from 1726 through the Revolution. They are here cited by the dates on the file
drawers. The documents are not filed in any
chronological order
Miscellaneous Manuscripts DUTCHESS County
1752–1870 (NYHS)
Ms. Mins. Dutchess Co. Sess.
Minutes of the DUTCHESS County General Sessions of the Peace
Liber A—1721–50 ⎫
Liber B—1750–57 ⎪
Liber C—1758–66 ⎬ (Adriance Library,
Liber D—1766–71 ⎪ Poughkeepsie,
Liber E—1771–75 ⎪ New York)
Liber F—1775–82 ⎭
Book of Taxes, DUTCHESS County, Liber C (Adriance Library, Poughkeepsie, N. Y.)

General ENTRIES, 1665–72 (NYSL)
ENTRIES Letters Warrants, 1680–83 (NYSL)

FLATBUSH Town Records
Libers A, AA, B, C, D, DII (King's County Hall
of Records)

GRATZ Collection (Pennsylvania Historical Society,
Philadelphia)
GRAVESEND Town Records
Libers III, IV, VI, VII (King's County Hall of
Records)

HORSMANDEN Papers, 1714–47 (NYHS)
Daniel HOWELS Book of Records (Pennypacker
Collection, Easthampton Public Library)
Town Records of HUNTINGTON. Court Records
(Huntington Town Clerk's Office)

JAY Papers (NYHS)
Samuel JONES Papers, 1721–1823 (NYPL)

John Tabor KEMPE Lawsuits (NYHS)
KEMPE Letters, A–Z (NYHS)
Ms. King's Co. Ct. & Rd. Recs.
KING's County Court and Road Records
1668–1766 ⎫
1692–1825 ⎬ (King's County Hall of Records)
Conveyances KING's County
Libers I, II, III (King's County Hall of Records)

LIVINGSTON Manuscripts (NYHS)
LIVINGSTON Papers (NYPL)
Redmond-LIVINGSTON Manuscripts (Franklin D.
Roosevelt Library, Hyde Park, N. Y.)
Cost Books William LIVINGSTON (NYPL)
Precedent Book William LIVINGSTON (NYSL)

McKESSON Legal Papers (NYHS)
Accounts of James MILLS (New York City Clerk's
Office, Municipal Building, New York)
Miscellaneous Manuscripts MORRIS (NYHS)
Precedent Book Joseph MURRAY (CU)

Minutes Coroner, City and County of NEW YORK
1747–58 (CU)
Ms. Mins. NYCQS
Minutes of the General Quarter Sessions of the
Peace for the City and County of NEW YORK
1683/84–1694 ⎫ (Office of the Clerk of General Sessions, Criminal Courts Building, New York)
1694–1731/32 ⎬
1732–1772 ⎪
1772–1791 ⎭
1705/06–1714/15. Rough Minutes ⎫
1722–1742/43. Rough Minutes ⎬ (HR)

Account of Clerk's Fees in the Mayor's Court, NEW
   YORK City (in private hands)
Ms. Decl. Book Mayor's Ct., N.Y.C.
   Declaration Book, Mayor's Court, NEW YORK
   City, 1675–77 (HR). Cf. also H. R. Wills, Liber
   19B, in which a later Declaration Book is en-
   rolled
Ms. Mins. Mayor's Ct. NYC
   Minutes of the Mayor's Court, NEW YORK City
   1674–75 ⎫
   1677–82 ⎪
   1680–83 ⎬ (HR)
   1682–95 ⎪
   1724/25–29 ⎪
   1729–34. Engrossed Minutes ⎭
Minutes of the Meeting of the Mayor, Deputy
   Mayor and Aldermen of NEW YORK City, 1733–
   43. Bound with Ms. Mins. NYCQS 1722–42/43
   (Rough)
Minutes Town Clerk NEW YORK City, 1701–06
   (HR). This is a book of process issued
NY Col. Mss.
   NEW YORK Colonial Manuscripts (NYSL). Cf.
   infra, Printed Sources, Cal. Eng. Mss.
Ms. Deeds NY Sec. of State
   Deeds and Letters Patent NEW YORK Province
   (Office of the Secretary of State, Albany)
NY Legal Mss.
   NEW YORK Legal Manuscripts (NYHS)
NY Misc. Mss.
   Miscellaneous Manuscripts NEW YORK (NYHS)
NYSL Misc. Mss.
   Miscellaneous Manuscripts NEW YORK State Li-
   brary (NYSL)

Miscellaneous Manuscripts ORANGE County
   (NYHS)
Deeds ORANGE County, Liber A (Orange County
   Clerk's Office, Goshen, N. Y.)
Ms. Mins. Orange Co. Sess.
   Minutes of the ORANGE County General Sessions
   of the Peace
   1703–08 (in Orange County Deeds, Liber A)
   1727–79 (Orange County Clerk's Office)

H.R. Papers
   PAPERS not yet classified (Hall of Records, New
   York County)
H.R. Parch.
   PARCHMENTS (Hall of Records, New York
   County)

H.R. Pleadings
   PLEADINGS (Hall of Records, New York County)
P.R.O. P.C. 1
   PRIVY COUNCIL Papers (Public Record Office,
   London)
P.R.O. P.C. 2
   PRIVY COUNCIL Register (Public Record Office,
   London)

Ms. Deeds QUEENS County, Liber A (Queens
   County Register's Office, Jamaica, N. Y.)
Ms. Mins. Queens Co. Sess.
   Minutes QUEENS County General Sessions of the
   Peace, 1722–87 (Queens County Clerk's Office,
   Jamaica, N. Y.)
Miscellaneous Manuscripts QUEENS County
   (NYHS)

Deeds RICHMOND County, Libers A, B, C (Rich-
   mond County Clerk's Office, St. George, Staten
   Island, N. Y.)
Ms. Mins. Richmond Co. Sess.
   Minutes RICHMOND County General Sessions of
   the Peace
   1710/11–44/45 ⎫ (Richmond County Clerk's
   1745–1812 ⎭ Office)
Miscellaneous Records RICHMOND County (Rich-
   mond County Clerk's Office)
RUTHERFORD Collection (in private hands)
First Book of Minutes of the Parish of RYE, Book
   of Vestrymen and Churchwardens, 1760–95
   (NYHS)

Journal William SMITH Jr. (NYPL)
William SMITH Jr. Manuscripts (NYPL)
William SMITH Jr. Supream Court Register A
   (NYPL)
STILLWELL Manuscripts (NYHS)
Deeds SUFFOLK County, Liber A (Suffolk County
   Clerk's Office, Riverhead, N. Y.)
Files, SUFFOLK County: Indictments, 1773–1839
   (Suffolk County Clerk's Office)
Ms. Mins. Suffolk Co. Sess.
   Minutes SUFFOLK County General Sessions of
   the Peace
   1723–51 ⎫ (Suffolk County Clerk's Office)
   1760–75 ⎭
Ms. Suffolk Co. Sess. 1668–87
   SUFFOLK County Sessions Minutes and Papers,
   1668–82 (Suffolk County Clerk's Office)
Miscellaneous Manuscripts SUFFOLK County
   (NYHS)

Miscellaneous Manuscripts SUPREME COURT (NYHS)

Ms. Mins. SCJ

Minutes SUPREME COURT of Judicature of the Province of New York

1701–04 (NYHS)

1704/05–1709. This volume actually runs to March 18, 1709/10 but is endorsed "1709" (HR)

1710–14 (HR)

1723–27 (HR)

1727–32 (HR)

1732–39 (HR)

1750–54. Engrossed Minutes (HR)

1750–56. Rough Minutes (HR)

1754–57. Engrossed Minutes (HR)

1757–60. Engrossed Minutes (HR)

1756–61. Rough Minutes (HR)

1762–64. Engrossed Minutes (HR)

1764–67. Rough Minutes (HR)

1766–69. Engrossed Minutes (HR)

1769–72. Engrossed Minutes (HR)

1772–76. Rough Minutes (HR)

1775–81. Engrossed Minutes (HR)

Cf. *infra* Printed Sources, *Mins. SCJ* 1693–1701

Rules of the SUPREME COURT, 1699–1783, in Ms. Moot Papers (NYHS)

Ancient Records of SUSSEX County (Pennsylvania Historical Society, Philadelphia)

Miscellaneous Manuscripts TRYON County (NYHS)

Ms. Mins. Tryon Co. Sess.

Minutes TRYON County Sessions, 1772–76 (NYHS). These are rough minutes written in paper books which we designate as *Quartos,* and are filed in *Miscellaneous Manuscripts Tryon County.* These Minutes are fuller than the *Ms. Minutes General Sessions of the Peace 1772– 1789* (Montgomery County Clerk's Office, Fonda, N. Y.)

Deeds ULSTER County, Libers I–III (Ulster County Clerk's Office, Kingston, N. Y.)

Files ULSTER County (Ulster County Clerk's Office). These papers are bundled without regard to date or subject matter and bear paper slips A, B, C, etc.

Ms. Mins. O. & T. Ulster Co. 1684

Oyer and Terminer and General Gaol Delivery Record ULSTER County, 1684 (Ulster County Clerk's Office)

Ms. Mins. Ulster Co. Sess.

Minutes ULSTER County General Sessions of the Peace

1693–98 ⎫
1703–05 ⎭ (Ulster County Clerk's Office)

1711/12–1720 (NYSL)

1737–50 (Ulster County Clerk's Office)

Miscellaneous Manuscripts ULSTER (NYHS)

Cost Book August VAN CORTLANDT, 1764–68 (in private hands)

Miscellaneous Manuscripts VAN CORTLANDT (NYHS)

WARRANTS Orders and Passes, 1674–79 (NYSL)

Evert WENDELL's Account Book (NYHS)

List of Freeholders WESTCHESTER County in *Misc. Mss. Van Cortlandt* (NYHS)

Deeds WESTCHESTER County, Libers A, B, C, D (Westchester County Clerk's Office, White Plains, N. Y.)

Ms. Mins. Westch. Co. Sess.

Minutes WESTCHESTER County General Sessions of the Peace 1710–23 (in Westchester County Deeds Liber D). Cf. *infra* Printed Sources, *Mins. Westch. Ct. of Sess.*

H.R. Ms. Wills

WILLS, court proceedings, and miscellaneous papers enrolled in the libers for the registration of wills (Clerk of the Surrogate's Court, Hall of Records, New York County)

PRINTED SOURCES

Here are listed (alphabetically by first word) only those works most frequently cited containing provincial or local New York source materials. References to sources of other provinces as, e.g., *Public Records of Connecticut,* will be found in the notes *supra.*

English law reports are not included here. They are cited in the footnotes by the common abbreviations. Citations to English statutes are to the 1763–71 edition of the *Stat-*

utes at Large and after 10 Geo. III to Pickering's *Statutes at Large*. We cite by regnal years in the manner current in the eighteenth century. This has been done to avoid the confusion which would result from attempting to reconcile the style of colonial lawyers' citation with the changes in regnal years made in the Record Commission's *Statutes of the Realm*.

Acts of the Privy Council, Colonial Series (1908–12). 6 vols.
Book of the Supervisors of Dutchess County, N. Y. 1718–1722 (1908?), vol. I
Cal. Col. Com.
Calendar of New York Colonial Commissions, 1680–1770 (NYHS 1929)
Cal. Council Mins.
Calendar of Council Minutes, 1668–1783 (New York State Library Bulletin 58, 1902)
Cal. Eng. Mss.
Calendar of Historical Manuscripts in the Office of the Secretary of State, Albany, New York, Part II English Manuscripts, 1664–1776 (1866)
Cal. S.P. Colonial
Calendar of State Papers, Colonial Series, America and West Indies. (London, 1860–)
Col. Laws NY
The Colonial Laws of New York from the Year 1664 to the Revolution. 5 vols. Albany, 1894
Doc. Hist. NY
The Documentary History of the State of New York (E. B. O'Callaghan ed., 1850–51). 4 vols.
Doc. Rel. Col. Hist. NY
Documents Relative to the Colonial History of the State of New York (E. B. O'Callaghan ed., 1853–87). 15 vols.
Exec. Council Mins.
Minutes of the Executive Council of the Province of New York 1668–1673 (Paltsits ed., 1910). 2 vols.
General Entries, 1664–65. (New York State Library Bulletin 2, 1889)
Huntington Town Records (Street ed., 1887). 3 vols.
Jour. Gen. Assembly NY
Journal of the Votes and Proceedings of the General Assembly of the Colony of New York. Vols. 1 and 2 (1764–66); vol. 3 (1820)
Jour. Legis. Council
Journal of the Legislative Council of the Colony of New York, 1691–1775 (1861). 2 vols.

Labaree, Instructions
Labaree, Royal Instructions to British Colonial Governors, 1670–1776 (1935). 2 vols.
Laws and Ordinances of New Netherland, 1638–74 (E. B. O'Callaghan ed. 1868)
Minutes of the Board of Supervisors of Ulster County, 1710/11–1730/31 (Historical Records Survey 1939)
Mins. Com. Council NYC
Minutes of the Common Council of the City of New York, 1675–1776 (1905). 8 vols.
Mins. Ct. of Albany
Minutes of the Court of Albany, Rensselaerswyck and Schenectady, 1668–85 (A. J. F. Van Laer ed. 1926–32). 3 vols.
Mins. SCJ 1693–1701
Minutes of the Supreme Court of Judicature, April 4, 1693 to April 1, 1701 (45 *NYHS Colls.*) Cf. *supra* Manuscript Sources, *Ms. Mins. SCJ*
Minutes of the Town Courts of Newtown, 1656–1690 (Historical Records Survey 1940)
Mins. Westch. Ct. of Sess.
Minutes of the Court of Sessions (1657–1696) Westchester County, New York (Dixon Ryan Fox ed. 1924). These minutes pp. 1–38 are of the town courts 1657–1678/79; the minutes pp. 39–59 of the Court of Sessions 1687–88; the minutes pp. 60–128 of the Westchester Court of General Sessions of the Peace 1691–1696. Cf. *supra* Manuscript Sources, *Ms. Mins. Westch. Co. Sess.*
NYHS Colls.
New York Historical Society published collections
Old Misc. Recs. Dutchess
Old Miscellaneous Records of Dutchess County (1902)
Oyster Bay Town Records, 1653–1704 (1916–24). 2 vols.
Proc. Gen. Ct. of Assizes
Proceedings of the General Court of Assizes, 1680–82 (45 *NYHS Colls.*)

Recs. Town of Brookhaven
Records of the Town of Brookhaven, Suffolk
County, N. Y. Vol. I, 1655–1798 (1880)
Recs. Town of Easthampton
Records of the Town of Easthampton, Long
Island, Suffolk Co., N. Y. (188?–1905). 5 vols.
Recs. of New Amsterdam
Records of New Amsterdam, 1653–1674 (Fernow ed. 1897). 7 vols.
Recs. Ct. of New Castle
Records of the Court of New Castle on Delaware (Colonial Society of Pennsylvania 1904)
Recs. Towns of North & South Hempstead
Records of the Towns of North and South

Hempstead, Long Island, N. Y. [1654–1777]
(1896–1901). 5 vols.
Recs. of Southampton
First-Third Book of Records of Southampton,
Long Island, N. Y. (1874–1878). Vols. 1–3
Rep. NY State Historian
Report of the State Historian of the State of
New York (Colonial Series) I and II (1897–98)
Southold Town Records (J. W. Case ed. 1882–84).
Upland Ct. Rec.
Record of Upland Court; from the 14th of November 1676 to the 14th of June 1681 (Edward
Armstrong ed. in Memoirs of the Historical Society of Pennsylvania, vol. 7 [1860] 9–203)

APPENDIX B. COMMISSIONS

DRAFT OF AN OYER AND TERMINER COMMISSION, 1705

(50 *New York Colonial Manuscripts* 61)

Know yee that wee have assigned you or any three of you (whereof wee will & requ[ire] the Said Roger Mompesson & Robert Milward to be one) our Justices to inquire [by the] oath of honest & lawfull men of Queenes County aforesaid & by other wayes meanes & methods (as well within Libertyes as without) whereby the truth may be the better known of whatsoever [Tr]easons Misprission of Treasons Insurrections Rebellions Murders ffelonyes Homicides Killings Burglaryes Rapes Assaults batteryes woundings unlawfull meetings & assemblys words spoken abettings misprissions Retaynings false Allegeances Trespasses Riotts Routs and falsityes Contempts evill doings neglects Concealm̄ts maintenances oppressions Champtertyes Deceipts and other misdoings Offenses Misdemeanors & Injuryes whatsoever And alsoe of all accessaryes thereunto—within the County aforesaid (as well within Libertyes as without) by whomsoever & howsoever had done perpetrated & com̄itted & by
any
what person or persons & to any person or persons when where how & in what manner [a line inked out] And of all other Articles & Circumstances the premisses or any of them howsoever concerning And the same Treasons & all other the premisses to hear and determine according to the law and custome of our Kingdome of England & our said province of New Yorke Therefore wee com̄and you that att Such certaine dayes & places as you or any three or two of you (whereof wee will & require either of you the said Roger Mompesson & Robert Milward to be one) to this purpose Shall appoint you doe dilligently make Inquiry upon the Premisses and all & Singular the premisses hear & determine & these things you Shall doe and pforme in manner & forme aforesaid Doeing therein that which to Justice belongs according to the law & custome of our Kingdome of England & of our said province of New Yorke Saveing to us all Amerciam^{ts} & other things upon that Account to us belonging Wherefore wee have comanded our Sherriffe of Queens County aforesaid that all Such certaine dayes & places as you or any three or two of you (whereof wee will & require either of you the Said Roger Mompesson & Robert Milward to be one) to him Shall make know[n] to cause to come before you or any three of you (whereof wee will & require either of you the Said Roger Mompesson & Robert Milward to be one) Such & soe many honest and lawfull men of his Bayliwick (as well within Libertyes as without) by whom the truth in the premisses may bee the better known and inquired into In Testimony whereof wee have caused these our Letters to be made patents & the Seale of our Said Provin[ce] to our Said Letters patents to be affixed The Same to continue and be in force for the Space of one whole yeare to be accompted from the date herein & noe Longer Witness our Right Trusty & well beloved Cousin Edward Viscount Cornbury Capt Generall & Govern^{r} in Cheife in & over our Said Province of New Yorke & Territoryes depending thereon in America & Vice Admirall of
att our ffort att New York aforesaid
the Same ^ this Tenth—day of Aprill In the ffourth yeare of our Reigne & Anno Dm̄ 1705

DRAFT OF A GAOL DELIVERY COMMISSION, 1705

(50 *New York Colonial Manuscripts* 68)

Know yee that wee have assigned you or any three of you (whereof wee will and require either of you the said Roger Mompesson or Robert Milward to be one) our Justices our Gaole at Jamaica in Queens County aforesaid of the prisoners therein being to deliver Therefore wee comand you that att a certaine day which you ~~or~~ any three or two of you (whereof wee will and require either of you the said Roger Mompesson or Robert Milward to be one) to this purpose shall appoint you come to Jamaica aforesaid that Gaole to deliver Doeing therein what to Justice belongs—according to the law & Custome of England & of our said province of New Yorke Saveing to us all amerciaments & other things From thence to us belonging Wherefore wee have comanded our Sherriffe of Queenes

County aforesaid That att a certaine day which you or any three or two of you (whereof wee will and require either of you the said Roger Mompesson or Robert Milward to be one) to him Shall make known that he cause to come before you or any three of you (whereof wee will and require either of you the said Roger Mompesson or Robert Milward to be one) all the prisoners in our said Gaole and their Attachments In Testimony whereof wee have caused these our Letters ~~patents~~ to be made patent and the Seale of our Said province to our Said Letters to be affixed—The Same to continue and be in force for ye Space of one whole yeare to be accompted from the date of these prsents & noe longe[r] Witness our Right Trusty & well beloved Cousin Edward Viscount Cornbury Capt Generall & Governer in Cheife in & over our Said province of New Yorke & Territoryes depending thereon in America and Vice Admirall of the Same & att our ffort att New York afores[aid] this Tenth day of Aprill. In the ffourth yeare of our Reign Anno Dñi 1705

COMMISSION OF THE PEACE, ORANGE COUNTY, 1702/03

(Ms. Deeds Orange Co. Liber A fol. 4 et seq.)

Anne by the grace of God of England Scotland France and Ireland Queen Defender of the ffaith &c To our well beloved and ffaithfull William Smith Peter Schyler Sampson Shelton Broughton Gerrardus Beekman William Lawrence Rip van Dam John Bridges and Caleb Heathcote of our Counsill of our Province of New York and William Merritt John Merrett Danll. Honan Cornelius Kuyper Teunis van Howton Thomas Burroughs and Michaell Howden Esqrs greeting Know Yee that wee have assigned you and every of you joyntly and severally our Justices to Keep our peace in our County of Orange in our Province of New York And to keep or cause to be kept all laws and Ordinances made for the good of the peace and for the conservacon of the same and for the quiet rule and Government of our people in all and every the Articles thereof in our said County according to the force forme and effect of the same and to chastise and punish all persons offending agt. the forme of those laws and ordinances or any of them in the County aforesaid as according to the forme of those Laws and Ordinances shall be fitt to be done and to cause to come before you or any of you all those persons who shall threaten any of our people in their person or in burning their houses to ffind sufficient security for the peace or for the good behaviour towards us and our heires and if they shall refuse to find such security than to cause them to bee kept safe in prison till they find such security. Wee have assigned you and every three or more of you whereof any of you the said William Smith Peter Schuyler Sampson Shelton Broughton Garrardus Beeckman William Lawrence Rip van Dam John Bridges and Caleb Heathcote William Merrett John Merrett Daniell Honan and Cornelius Kuyper and Teunis van Howton wee will to be our Justices to enquire by the oaths of good and lawfull men of the County aforesaid by whome the truth may be known of all and all manner of petet larcenys, thefts, trespasses, fforestallings, regrettings and extorcons whatsoever and all and singular other misdeeds and offences of which Justices of the peace may or ought lawfully to enquire by whomesoever and howsoever done and perpetrated or which shall happen hereafter howsoever to be done or attempted in the County aforesaid and of all those who in the County aforesaid have either gone or riden or that hereafter shall Presume to goe or ride in Company with armed fforce against the peace to the Disturbance of the people and alsoe of all those who in like manner have lain in wait or hereafter shall presume to lye in wait to maim or kill our people and alsoe of Inholders and of all and singular other persons who have offended or attempted or hereafter shall presume to offend or attempt in the abuse of weights or measures or in the sale of victualls against the forme of the Laws and Ordinances or any of them in that behalfe made for the comon good of this Province and the people thereof in the County aforesaid and alsoe all Sheriffs Bayliffs Constables Goalers and other offices whatsoever who in the execution of their offices about the premises or any of them have unlawfully demeaned themselves or hereafter shall presume unlawfully to demeane themselves or have been or hereafter shall be careless remiss or negligent in the County aforesaid and of all and singular articles circumstances and of all other things whatsoever by whomsoever and howsoever done or perpetrated in the said County or which shall hereafter happen howsoever to be done or attempted in any wise

more fully concerning the truth of the premissess or any of them. And to inspect all Indictments whatsoever soe before you or any of you taken or to be taken or made or taken before others Late Justice of the peace in the County aforesaid and not as yet determined and to make and continue the process thereupon against all and singular persons so Indicted or which hereafter shall happen to be Indicted as aforesaid and all and singular other the premises according to law. And Therefore wee command you and every of you that you dilligently intend The keeping of the peace Laws and Ordinances and all and singular other the premisses and att certaine dayes and places which you or any such three or more of you as is aforesaid shall in that behalfe appoint or by Law shall be appointed you make enquirys upon the premises and hear and Determine all and singular the premises and performe and fullfill the same in forme aforesaid doeing therein that which to Justice appurteineth according to the Laws Statutes and Ordinances aforesaid Saveing to us the Amerciaments and other things to us thereof belonging And wee command by virtue of these presents the Sheriff of the County aforesaid that at certain dayes and places which you or any such three or more of you as is aforesaid shall Make known unto him or shall be by Law appointed as aforesaid to cause to come before you or any such three or more of you as aforesaid such and soe many good and Lawfull men of his Bayliwick by whome the truth in the premisses may be the better Known and Inquired off. In Testimony Whereof wee have caused the Grate seale of our Province of New York to be hereunto affixed. Wittness our right Trusty and right well beloved Cowzin Edward Viscount Cornbury Capt. Generall and Governor in Cheif of the province of New York &c att Fort William Henry this eight day of March in the first yeare of our Reign Anoque Dom. 1702.

Entered the 8th of Ocbr 1703

₰ Wm Huddleston Cl.

COMMISSION OF THE PEACE, SUFFOLK COUNTY, 1772

(Ms. Book of Commissions 1770–89 66–68)

George the Third by the Grace of God of Great Britain France and Ireland King Defender of the Faith and so forth. To our beloved and faithful Cadwallader Colden and Daniel Horsmanden Esquires, Sir William Johnson Baronet, John Watts, Oliver DeLancey, Charles Ward Apthorpe, Roger Morris, William Smith, Henry Cruger, Hugh Wallace, Henry White and William Axtell Esquires Members of our Council for our Province of New York—John Tabor Kempe Esquire Attorney General of our said Province, and to William Smith, Samuel Landon, Nathaniel Woodhull, Isaac Post, John Chatfield, Richard Miller, Thomas Youngs, Robert Hempstead, Jonas Williams, Thomas Helme, Daniel Wells, Parker Wickham, Thomas Cooper, Benajah Strong, Jonathan Thompson, Selah Strong, William Phillips, Phineas Fanning, John Moss Hobart, Richard Woodhul, Samuel Hunting, Barnabas Terrill, Benjamin Browne, James Reeves Junior, John Woodhull, Thomas Dearing, Gilbert Smith, Abraham Gardiner, Maltby Gelston, Frederick Hudson, Daniel Smith, Nathan Fordham, David Baker, Timothy Carle Junior, and David Gardiner Esquires Greeting. Know Ye, that We have assigned you and every of you jointly and severally our Justices to keep our Peace in our County of Suffolk in our Province of New York in America and to keep and to cause to be kept all Laws and Ordinances made for the Good of our Peace and for the Conservation of the same and for the quiet Rule and Government of our People in all and every of the Articles thereof in our said County as well within Liberties as without according to the Form force and Effect of the same and to chastise and punish all Persons offending against the Form of those Laws and Ordinances or any of them in the County aforesaid, as according to the Form of those Laws and Ordinances shall be fit to be done, and to cause to come before you or any of you all those Persons who shall threaten any of our People in their Persons or in burning their Houses to find sufficient Security for the Peace for their Good Behaviour towards us and our People, and if they shall refuse to find such Security, then to cause them to be kept safe in Prison till they find such Security. We have also assigned you and any three or more of you whereof any of you the said Cadwallader Colden, Daniel Horsmanden, Sir William Johnson Baronet, John Watts, Oliver DeLancey, Charles Ward Apthorpe, Roger Morris, William Smith, Henry Cruger, Hugh Wallace, Henry White, William Axtell, John Tabor Kempe, William Smith, Samuel Landon, Nathaniel Woodhull, Isaac Post, John Chatfield, Richard Miller, Thomas Youngs, Robert Hempstead, Jonas Williams, Thomas Helme, Daniel Wells, Parker Wickham, Thomas Cooper, Benajah Strong, Jonathan Thompson, Selah Strong, William Philips, Phineas Fanning, and John Moss Hobart We will to be one our Justices to enquire by the Oaths of good and lawful Men of our County aforesaid by whom the Truth may be the better known of all and all manner of Felonies Trespasses, Forestallings, Regratings, Ingrossings, and Extortions whatsoever and of all and singular other Offences and Misdemeanors of which Justices of the Peace may or ought lawfully to enquire by whomsoever and howsoever done and perpetrated or which shall happen hereafter howsoever to be done or attempted in the County aforesaid And also of all those who in the County aforesaid have either gone or ridden or that hereafter shall presume to go or ride in Companies with armed Force against the Peace to the Disturbance of the People and also of all those who in like manner have lain in wait or hereafter shall presume to lye in wait to maim or kill any of our People And also of Innholders and of all and singular other Persons who have offended or attempted or hereafter shall presume or attempt to offend in the abuse of Weights or Measures or in the Sale of Victuals against the form of the Laws and Ordinances or any of them in that behalf made for the common good of our said Province and the People thereof in our County aforesaid. And also of all Sherifs Bailiffs Constables Goalers and other Officers whatsoever who in the Execution of their Offices about the Premises or any of them have unlawfully demeaned themselves or hereafter shall presume unlawfully to demean themselves or have been or hereafter shall be careless remiss or negligent in our County aforesaid and of all and singular Articles and circumstances and all other Things whatsoever by whomsoever and howsoever done or perfected in our said County or which hereafter shall happen to be howsoever done or attempted in any wise more fully concerning the Truth of the Premises or any of them and to inspect all Indictments whatsoever before you or any of you taken or to be taken or made or taken before others late Justices of the Peace in the County aforesaid and not as yet determined and to make and continue the Process thereupon against all and singular the Persons so indicted or which shall happen hereafter to be indicted before you until they be apprehended render themselves or be outlawed and to hear and determine all and singular the Felonies Trespasses Forestallings Regratings Ingrossings Extortions unlawful Assemblies and Indictments aforesaid, and all and singular other the Premisses according to Law. And therefore We Command you and every of you that you diligently attend the keeping of the Peace, Laws, and Ordinances and all and singular other the Premisses aforesaid and at certain Days and Places which you or any such three or more of you as is aforesaid shall in that behalf appoint, or by Law shall be appointed, you make inquiries upon the Premisses and hear and determine all and singular the Premisses, and perform and fulfill the same in form aforesaid, doing therein that which to Justice appertaineth according to the Laws and Customs of that Part of our Kingdom of Great Britain called England and the Laws and Customs of our said Province of New York, Saving to us our Amerciaments and other Things to us thereof belonging. And we Command by virtue of these Presents the Sheriff of our County aforesaid for the Time being that at certain Days and Places which you or any such three or more of you as is as aforesaid shall make known unto him or shall be by Law appointed as aforesaid he cause to come before you, or such three or more of you as aforesaid such and so many good and lawful Men of his Bailiwick as well within Liberties as without by whom the Truth of the Premisses may be the better known and inquired of. In Testimony whereof We have Caused these our Letters to be made Patent and the Great Seal of our Province of New York to be hereunto affixed. Witness Our trusty and wellbeloved William Tryon Esquire our Captain General and Governor in Chief in and over our said Province of New York and the Territories depending thereon in America Chancellor and Vice Admiral of the same; At our Fort in our City of New York, the Seventeenth Day of November one thousand seven hundred and seventy two in the Thirteenth Year of our Reign. Clarke.

APPENDIX C. BILLS OF COSTS

KING V. JOHN HENRY LYDIUS

Below are the "Costs for putting off trial" in the prosecution of John Henry Lydius for intrusion on Crown lands, a case discussed *supra* 210. The original of this document is in *J. T. Kempe Lawsuits* L–O *sub nom.* Lydius.

Notice of trial copy and service	2/6	
Copy for judge	2/6	
Drawing venire	12/0	
Sheriff for service 4 subpoenas	17/3	
15 tickets	11/3	
[total]		2/ 4/ 6

Service	15/	
Messenger serving 3 subpoenas in Dutchess 7 days @ 9/ pr. day	3/ 3/0	
Messenger serving Subpoenas in Albany 10 days @ 9/	4/10/0	
Subpoena duces tecum	6/	
Special ticket	3/	
Service on Mr. Banyar	1/	
Mr. Banyar bringing Record	12/	
Traveling charges 10 days @ 13/4	6/13/4	
[total]		16/13/ 4

Two witnesses from Dutchess 8 Days each @ 4/6	3/12/0	
Dr roll	3/	
Copy and engrossing	3/	
Parchmt	6/	
Sealing roll	2/3	
[total]		10/ 0/ 3

Drawing Brief	9/
Motion for Tryal	5/
Counsel prepared for Trial	12/

Traveling Charges 17 days @ 13/4 [sic]	11/17/8 [sic]	
Copy of Pannel	2/	
[total]		13/ 5/ 8

Clerk of Assizes bill	12/ 9/2	
[grand total]		54/ 2/11

[To this total bill was added an additional £3 12s., but it was not stated what this expense was, and the final grand total came to £60 10s., making in all an expense of more than £270 as the costs for simply putting off a trial (*ibid.*). The clerk of the Circuit's bill, referred to in the above bill of costs, was itemized as follows:]

Entering cause in Judge's book	17/6
Fileing roll	3/0
Read affidavit to put off trial	1/0
Fileing same	1/0
Traveling charges 17 days @ 13/4 per day	11/6/8
	12/9/2

[The costs for process dated June 26, 1762, were as follows:]

4 subpoenas	9/0
distringas	2/3
bringing record	12/0
traveling charges	6/13/4
sealing roll	2/3

KING V. GEORGE KLOCK

This is the final bill of costs in the case of *King* v. *George Klock* taxed by Robert R. Livingston, Judge of the Supreme Court. The case is discussed *supra* 218–220. The document was found, curiously enough, in *James Alexander Papers* Box 19A. Alexander, so far as we know, had no connection with the case and was dead at the time of the trial.

New York Supreme Court

George Klock
adᵛ
The King
} Costs

January Vacation 1762

Retaining fee	£ 1. 9.0
Warrant of Attorney &c	0. 2.3
Paid Mr. Banyar for Copy of Information	1.16.0
£ 0.10.0 Perusing & Considering of Information	0.10.0
Fee on Defense	0. 5.0

4. 2. 3

April Term 1762

Motion that Defendᵗˢ Appearance be entered	0. 5.0
Rule inde	0. 3.0
Motion and Rule that Defᵗˢ appearance be respited till the last Day of this Term	. 8.0
0. 3.0 Motion & Rule that Defᵗ be discharged but Court over-ruled	. 8.0
Motion and Rule to respite to next Term	. 8.0
Term fee	0. 5.0

1.17. 0

Vacation

Met Wᵐ Smith Junʳ to Consult about Plea on perusal of Information	.10.0
Dʳ Plea fol. 2 @ 1/6	0. 3.0
Copy for Attorney General	0. 1.6

0.14. 6

July Term 1762

Motion and Rule that Defᵗ appearance be entred & Respite allowed till first of next Term	. 8.0
Term fee	0. 5.0

Vacation

Copy of Issue fol. 54	2. 6.0

October Term 1762

Motion and Rule that Defᵗ appearance be entred & Respite allowed till first of next Term	. 8.0
Term fee	0. 5.0

January Term 1763

Motion & Rule for Entring Defᵗ Appearance & to respite Recognizance till first of next Term	. 8.0
Term fee	. 5.0

4. 5. 0

April Term 1763

Motion & Rule that Defᵗ Appᶜᵉ be entered and Recognizance respited till first of next Term	. 8.0
Term fee	5.0

0.13. 0

Vacation & July Term

Dᵣ Brief and Copy	0. 9.0		
Copy for Council	0. 3.0		
Council prepared for Tryal	0.12.0		
Copy of Transcript	2. 0.6		
£.0.13.0		3. 4. 6	

	Carried forward	£14:16: 3	
Dᵣ Notice of Tryal &c	£ 0. 1.6		
Dᵣ & Copy of Instructions for Defᵗ in Serving Subpenas & Tickets	0. 5.6. [?]		
Sealed 3 Subpoenas 12/9. 12 Tickets 8/.	1. 0.9		
Travelling Charges 17 Days 13/4	11. 6.8		
Copy of pannel 2/. Copy for Council 2/.	0. 4.0		
Council on Tryal	2. 0.0		
Motion & Rule that Clerk of the Circuit Return Record tomorrow	0. 8.0	15: 5:11	
Motion and Rule that Postea be read and filed	0. 8.0		
Clerk for entring Judgment	0. 2.3		
Dᵣ Judgment	0. 6.0		
Copy and Engrossing on Roll	0. 6.0		
Docketting Judgment	0. 1.0		
Dᵣ Costs and Copy	0. 9.0		
paid Judge for Certifying	0. 6.0		
Attending thereon	0. 2.0		
Term Fee	1. 5.0		
Clerk of the Circuits fee as pᵣ Bill	1. 3.0	3:13: 3	
		£33.15. 5	
Deduct		13. 0	
		£33. 2. 5	

I do certify that the fees in this Bill amounting to thirty three Pounds two Shillings & five Pence are charged according to the usual allowances in such Cases—New York 4 Octobᵣ 1763

Robert R. Livingston

KING V. SYBRANT VAN SCHAICK ET AL.

Van Schaick was informed against for an assault and battery. The trial was scheduled for nisi prius but a nolle prosequi was entered. It will be noticed that pursuant to its powers under the Information Act of 1754 the Supreme Court first refused to permit the information to be filed. The Attorney General was compelled to memorialize the Governor, and eventually filed affidavits to ground the information. Cf. *supra* 436 n. 258. The document is in *J. T. Kempe Lawsuits* V.

July—Octᵣ [*sic*] Vacation 1759

Retaining Fee	£1. 9.0
Examining & taking Complaint of Patrick Flood in writing fo. 16	1. 4.0
Drawing same in form of an affidt.	12.0
Drawing affidt. of Thomas Morrell fo. 16	1. 4.0
Drawing affidt. of Bradley	10.—

Aug. 1759

Long Letter to Mr. Van Schaick containing the whole substance of Flood's cmplaint	4. — —

Jany Term 1760

Dr Information fo. 31 @ 1/6	2. 6.6
Copy and Engrossing	2. 6.6
Parchment	5.—
Motion to file Information which the Court at that time refused	5.—
Motion for reading the Affidavits, and that the Court would order the Information to be filed	5.—
Clerk for reading the Affdt. of Patrick Flood	3.—
Term Fee	5.—

Vacation

The Court having last Term refused to permit the Information to be filed last Term, Drew a long Petition to the Govr setting forth the whole Compl^t and the courts Refusal fo. 15	}	1: 2:6
Copy		11.3
Copy presented the Govr.		11.3

8: 1:0

April Vacation [sic] Term 1760

~~Motion to file Information~~ [sic]

Motion to read Affdts. in order to ground Motion for filing Information	— 5.0
Clerk reading and filing 4 Affts.	—12.—
Altering and mending Information	— 5.—
Clerk reading and filing Information	— 3
Motion for Process	— 5.—
Rule thereof	— 3
Term Fee	5.—

1:18:0

£15:18:0

[Page 2 of "costs"]

Brought over	£15..18..0.

Vacation

Dr Venire fa: fo. 4 @ 1/6	6.—
Copy Engrossing & Seal	8.3.

July Term 1760

Sheriff for summoning	
Clerk filing Venire Facias	1
Motion for Rule to plead	5.—
Rule thereon	3.—
Term Fee	5

Vacation

Copy Plea	2.—
Drawing up Issue fo. 39	2.18.6
Copy and engrossing	2.18.6
Parchmt. 6/ filing Roll 3/	— 9.—

Octr Term 1760

Term Fee and Continuance	— 6.6

Jany: 1761

Term Fee and Continuance	– 6.6

April Term 1761

Term Fee and Continuance	– 6.6

July Term 1761

Term Fee and Continuance	– 6.6

Octr. Term 1761

Term Fee and Continuance	– 6.6

Jany. Term 1762

Term Fee and Continuance	– 6.6

April Term 1762

Motion for a struck Jury	5.–
Motion that the Sherriff return a Book of the Freeholders by the 18th May	5.–
Rule for a struck Jury	3.–
Term Fee and Continuance	6.6

Vacation May 6th: 1763 [*sic*]

Copy Rule for struck Jury to send the Sherriff	– –
Letter to the Sherriff	5.–
Dr Notice of striking Jury Copy & Service	2.6
Copy for Judge &c.	1.6

	Carried forward	. . . .

[Page 3 of "costs"]

	Brought over	£ [*sic*]

20th May.

10	Attended at Brocks before Mr. Justice Horsmanden to strike the Jury, when after having gone through the pannel it was found the Sherriff had not returned it }	£ – –
4:1.6	Dr Nisi Prius Roll fo 54	4.01.6
4:1.6	Copy and Engrossing	4.01.6
6	Parchm^t	6.–

July Term 1762

Term Fee and Continuance	6.6

Octr Term

Term Fee and Continuance	6.6

Jany Term 1763

Term Fee and Continuance	6.6

April Term 1763

Term Fee and Continuance	6.6
Entring noli prosequi	10.–
Clerk entring the like	4.–
Dr Judgment	6.–
Copy and Engrossing on Roll	6.–
Clerk for Judgmt	2.3
Filing Roll	1.–
Dr. Bill of Costs and Copy	6.–
Copy for Deft.	3.–
Three Term Fees and Continuances from April 1763 to Jany. 1764	19.6

KING V. JOHN CAREY ET AL.

The defendants were informed against for an assault on January 16, 1753. This case disappears from the minutes after a rule by the Supreme Court on October 24, 1754, that the cause be tried at the next Circuit in Dutchess County or the defendants be discharged (cf. *supra* 614 n. 39). The journal entries below are extremely suggestive as to the possible disposition of the many other cases which disappear from the minute books without indication of any settlement. The entries are taken from *Wm. Smith Jr. Supream Court Register A* 55.

King v. John Cary Wm. Van Wyck *et al.* { Inf. of Wm. Kempe for Riot and Assault

Journal Entries	*Costs*
Jan. vac. 1753	**Jan Vac 1753**

27 Mar Rec^d letter from Defdt containing state of case with 40/ advised Mr. Theodor Van Wyck of N.Y. & one Burras that a composition be made with Atty General	Retaining fee 27 March 5 Deft 20/ each	7 10 0
	Warrant of Atty	2.3
	Term fees	5 0
28 at Mr. Theod. Van Wycks request waited upon Atty General to agree on Terms he said he must write to Informer	Council to Mr. Van Wyck & Mr. Burras for composition	1. 8 0
25 April rec'd letter fo Informer one Gale—D^r. Letter to Defdt & sent letter to Gale from Atty General Inclosed.	**28 Do**	
Recd Letter from Father of Defdt dated 31 March 1753.	Waiting upon Atty General at Theodorus Van Wycks request to agree on terms	10 0
Letter & warrant from same of Van Wyck of N.Y. & one Humphrey on 13 April 1753 without date 10. 5.3	Dr Letter of Directions & Copy to Defdt endorsing one from A.G. to one Gale the informer	— 10.0

April Term 1753	**April Term**	
My appearance for Defts entered. Mr. Kempe had rule to Plead in 20 days	Motion that appearance be entered	5.0
	& for 5 appearances	5.0

Vac	**Vac.**	
1 May at Instance of Mr. Kempe Mr. Gale being at his House spent morning to receive proposals of accomodation—but none agreed on—4 July Rec^d from Mr. Kempe copy of Information 12 July rec'd Dem'^d of Plea. 13 Do sent plea and letter to Mr. Kempe	Copy of Information fol 9	6.9
	1 May	
	Attended at the Atty General spent the whole morning about term of accomodation	1. 0.0
	30 Do	
	Dr a copy of letter to Atty Gen	10.0
	Dr Plea & Copy to file	4.6
	fine inde	1.0
	Copy of issue fol 13	9.9
	Jan & April & July 1754	
3. 7.0	Term fee	15.0

Oct. Term 1754

Rule that unless case be tried at next court for trial of Causes in Dutchess the Defdt be Discharged—I mentioned this to Atty General who agreed to the rule

July Vac

N B a circuit held in Dutchess Ergo Ds discharged 10 June 1760 accepted 18.6.s in full

Oct. Term

Motion for trial next circuit in Duch	5.0
Clerk for Rule	3.0
Term fee	5.0

1755, 1756, 1757

12 Terms	3. 0.0

Jan April July 1758

Term fee	15.0
Dr Costs & Copy	9.0
Copy to be	3.0
Attending	5.0
paid Judge for a certificate	6.0
——— Copy of taxed bill for deft.	3.0

6.19.0

20.11.3 Taxed at £20.6.3   4 July 1760 Copy sent to Mr. Theod Van Wyck to be for'd. to Defdts in Dutchess Co.

APPENDIX D. BRIEFS

KING V. JOHN PETER ZENGER

The following brief is in 2 *Ms. Rutherfurd Collection*, fol. 35. It is in two columns in the handwriting of James Alexander. The brief was written after the text of the information was available but before the attempt to except to the judge's commissions. It should be noted that the final argument of Andrew Hamilton followed this outline in many particulars.

[Page 1]

Zenger ads Dom { Information for Lybelling
Regis { Method proposed for Defense

As its notorious that journals have been sold at Zenger's house, that many people have paid himself for them and even some of jury, also his sons and servant may possibly be compelled to declare their knowledge of his printing them etc. I think it may give an ill turn to the minds of the jury to Lay any Stress on want of proof of his printing or publishing, and I think better acknowledge them, but think stress of the Defense ought to be on this point.

Whether those parts of the journals in the information be Lybells or not
   That they were Lybell perhaps will be produced 1 Hawkins 194 that its no justification of a Lybell that the contents thereof are true.
Supported by the Star Chamber cases on margine; & possibly Sundry cases in King Charles the Second & King James 2ds time may be produced to prove the same doctrine.
               Answer
The Destruction of the Star Chamber and the Revolution succeeding these two

Quere if should except to the Ch. justice from judging because
1st he was one who supported the argument agt. Zengers journals in the Conference between the Council and assembly
2dly on the argument on Zengers habeas corpus he said on this very case that a jury would go near to perjure themselves if they found Zenger not guilty, and submitt whether he be an indifferent judge to try the Cause.
Support this by 3d Cook 29 Institutes safety of prisoner consisteth in indifferency of the Court, the judges ought not to deliver their opinions beforehand of any criminal case that may come before them judically etc.

If Except Quere if in writing or viva voce

[Page 2]

Reigns and the manifest partiality and Exorbitancy of these Reigns as the judges then being at Discretion of the Ministry and pushed and willed for its purposes Leaves no stress on those authorities, on the contrary as in state tryalls vol 4, 290 things in ill Reigns are to be markt out as Rocks for us to avoid rather than patterns to be imitated
   That they are not Lybells.
What a Lybell is even by Star Chamber Law
   1 Hawkins 193 a malitious Defamation in printing or writing or any Defamation whatsoever
   Now if whats printed be true it cannot be a Defamation for Defamation must be charging another with something false and Scandalous or more nearly to the word, giving another fame than whats agreeable to truth, but giving ones true fame cannot be a Defamation
2d The information itself and all indictments and informations for Lybells that ever were do plainly point out whats requisite to make a paper a Lybell viz. to be false malitious Seditious and Scandalous but if a paper [continued on page 3]

But here I think it may not be amiss to give a short view of the exorbitancy of those times and the extraordinary [?] doctrines there propagated by the judges with the cures that have since been applied to those things
Abr. State tryalls vol 1st bottom of page 182 to end of common plea and observe on it, here we see plays strained up to the government and writing against them to be writing against the government and a horrible punishment inflicted for it and numerous were the instances of such Cruelties of that Court of Star Chamber from which the Chief of the Doctrine of Lybells was wrought
   But this terrible Court of Star Chamber was made an end by the Stat. 17 Car 1st fo. 1107 read part of 1st 2d and 3d par. circumflexed but vid. ye preamble and n.b.
   But in King Charles the 2d and King James the 2ds time the Court of Kings Bench began to exercise the same cruelties as the Court of Star Chamber had done
   At State tryalls vol 3 fol. 854 S.S. Bernardiston

[Page 2 cont.]

[First column]

fin'd 10,000 etc but this was reversed see State Tryalls vol 5 page 716 [illegible matter]
But the judges (then at the Kings mere will) once in KJ 2ds time did openly claim the whole authority of the Star Chamber and the right to inflict like punishments as Comberback 36
  but declaration of Lords and Commons put an end to those things and enacted they should never be drawn into consequence.
Stat. 1 W. and M.
  State Tryalls vol 2d 546 Brewsters Tryall
Ld C.J. to say Kings abusing his power the people may resist it expressed truth without more etc.
but after the revolution that Doctrine was so far from being law that the Canbury [?] Dr. Sacheverel suffered for asserting — whose Tryall State Tryall vol 5 page 686 If King invade the peoples there of supreme power its lawful to oppose a past fame

[Second column blank]

[Page 3]

[In margin]
Subpoena Geo. Clark
  to p. the Destruction
  of the Indian deed.*

be not proved to be these, but on the Contrary to be true, twelve upon their oaths could never justly find a Defendant guilty of such information.
            with this agrees
State Tryalls vol 4 363 b (Bishops tryall) Sir Robt. Sawyer as to falsity and that it was malitious and seditious are all matters of fact and no proof offered up
ibid. 390 b Justice Powell to make it a Lybell it must be false and malitious and it must tend to Sedition and I see nothing to prove falsehood and malice
S.T. 3. vol 851 Bernardiston Tryal 851 no proof of seditious intent but Chief Justice Jeffreys said law supplies proof but Wms. of council for defendant insisted on proof of malice
ibid. 854 a verdict against Bernardiston but state tryals vol 5 page 716 that judgment reversed by House of Lords on writ of error and gave their reasons
State tryals vol 5 page 544 Mr. Serg. Darnell of council agt. Tutchin says will you say they are true from which may be inferred that if he would have said so and proved so then they would not have been Lybells seeing they were not false

[Second column blank]

[Page 4]

[In margin in another hand]
See ye [two illegible words] of ye L.C. Ju. Holt in severall parts of ye page where to attaint ye Deft. may call Witnesses to prove ye content of ye Libell

State tryals vol 5 page 448 Fullers Case L.C.J. Holt can you make it appear that books are true
ibid 449 if you can offer any matter to prove what you have writt Let us hear it
            Objection
A Lybell not to be justified upon an indictment or information tho the Contents be true and for this may be cited
many books as Hobart 253 and Cooks reports 125 both Star Chamber cases. 3d Salkeld 225 Holt says Deft may justify in an action not in an indictment for a Lybell if words be true

[Second column blank]

* This refers to the newspaper statement "See men's deeds destroyed."

[In margin, Alexander's
hand]
Witness
  Geo Clark
  Cornelius Van Horne
  Capt. Morris
  Rip Van Dam
  Joseph Scott
  Jere. Tothill
  Richard Ashfield

I say that this must mean that a Deft cant plead the justification of the words on an indictment, but cannot mean that deft cant give it in Evidence that they are true.

For to suppose it would make the law contradict itself.

As suppose an action is brought for a Lybell and Deft justified by pleading that what he wrote was true as it was Lawful for him to do and proves his justification and is acquitted. Shall Deft for same thing be condemned on

[Page 5]

an information or indictment when it was admitted before that it was lawful for him to do it

I think its absurd to say it and to take off the absurdity tho he cant plead the justification he may give the matter of it in evidence

and agreeable to this is the general cases before listed

Also

Law of evidence 111 when a man cannot take advantage of special matter in pleading, he shall take advantage of it in evidence Co. Lit. 283 example 1 Hawk. cap 29 sect 25

1 Hawk. cap. 62 Sect 3 in battery may give it in Evidence that other first assaulted him but in an action for it he must plead it.

2d Hawkins Cap 46 Sect 44 it seems agreed that son assault demesn may be given in evidence on the general issue in an indictment but not in an action of battery

Also in murder Deft shall not justify by se defendendo, per infortunium etc but must give it in evidence

[Second column blank]

[Page 6]

[In margin]
Quere if plea to jurisdiction of Chancery in the Equivalent case late filed may not be given in evidence to prove this. Especially as by the King's Council it was admitted true by coming to hearing thereon without denying the facts thereof by replication.

As to that part of no 13 in the information that question may be put without any Lybell or accusation agt. the present administration seeing no time is prefixed for the many past proceedings, and I shall now assign some past proceedings before this Govt and from which it might be collected, viz.

1 the erecting a Court of Chancery in Coll Hunters time and the Exchequer in the present Gov.s time without Consent in general assembly which is a thing notorious and the Consequences of that thing has been again and again Resolved to be oppressive by the acts of the General assembly which are also notorious

Judges Justices Sheriffs and Coroners in whose hands are our Laws our Liberties and Properties, were before this govr came appointed by the govr. alone contrary to the Royal instructions and Consequently our Lives Liberties and Properties were at the mere will of a Govr. before this Govr came, and I think no man will say but that this is a State of Slavery and so no Lybell on the present administration as charged.

But that paper is very modest for afterwards the Contrary question is put and only proposes a fair inquiry into facts who is right or not not pretending to assert the truth of one side or other of the question

[Second column blank]

[Page 7]

[In margin]
George Clark was present at destroying deed, the proceedings at Albany are always entered on minutes of council and this was so entered Quere if cant compel clerk of council to give evidence of it. The New York Gazette may be insisted on for a proof because the information says that no. 13 means govr etc but from the face of it it appears to be directed to the writters of Paragraph in the Gazette the week before and consequently the Govr. etc. were writers of that paragraph, also because the Gazette is printed by the Kings printer of New York who is paid a yearly salary of £50 drawn by the Govr.

As to that part of no. 23 in the information the facts are that they see mens deeds Destroyed, judges arbitrarily displaced new Courts Erected without consent of the Legislature by which it seems to me tryals by juries are taken away when a govr pleases men of known estate denied their Votes

If these facts be true then are the facts asserted in that paper not false malitious seditious etc as in the information

As to destroying Albany deed Richard Ashfield and Jeremiah Tuthill to prove as per depositions of Albany people also the New York Gazette No which confesses it and endeavors to justify it

Judges arbitrarily Displaced to wit the late Chief Justice of this court, Vincent Matthews to prove the new Commission to Orange County, but if he does not then in General leave it to every mans knowledge whether not only this but former Governours have displaced judges at their pleasure (which is doing it arbitrarily)

[Second column blank]

[Page 8]

[In margin]
The preface to the argument of Van Dam's council signed by Van Dam also the further proceedings of Van Dam by which it appears to have been adjudged on Demurrer for want of Equity that the King might sue in Equity without any Equity, which is taking away juries in all Civil causes of the King if Govrs please

As to erecting new courts
Govr Hunters Erecting Court of Chancery as before and for other instances leave it to juries own knowledge from Van Dams case
As to men of known estates denied their votes the Journal no. 9
Lewis Morris Junr Jas Tothill to prove truth of that account of Westchester election

As to the question put upon these facts it seems rational to follow from the facts,

[Second column blank]

[Page 9]   to conclude with an Encomium on the Liberty of   [Second column blank]
the press the Danger of Cramping it, we see most
nations in the world were reduced to Slavery and
arbitrary power, the freedom of the press is one of
the greatest preservatives agt. that. No proof that
the journals informed agt. were false malitious
Scandalous and seditious as charged in the information and how can they upon their oaths say they
were so without saying which they cannot say that
Deft. is guilty as in the information set forth.
Should the attorney Genll. show authorities
which I do not know that he can, that other parts
of the same journals may be given in evidence there
is one article in no. 13 immediately before that in
the information which is a hearsay that proved not
true, but I think its unreasonable to put deft. on
proving anything out of the information, at least
without notice that

[Page 10]   it will be insisted on, but however here is an affi-   [Second column blank]
davit of Abraham Vanhorn one of the council who
heard that matter from a man who said he was
come from Road Island, which I think is enough
to justify an article of hearsay news, and there's
nothing in that article thats scandalous seditious or
malitious nor false as there its set forth viz. only
we hear for once it was heard, as by that affidavit
will appear if necessary to be produced

KING V. JOHN LAWRENCE JR. ET AL.

This is the trial brief used in the assault case discussed *supra* 262–263. The document, it will be noticed, seems to contain William Kempe's opening as well as his analysis of the testimony and of the legal points involved. The document is in *H.R. Pleadings* Pl. K. 501.

The King
agt.
Jn°· Laurence   } Brief
& others

The King agt. { John Lawrence the younger
Charles Arding
Cornelius Levingston   } On the Information of the Attorney General for
and   an assault on Mary Anderson
Hendrick Oudenaarde }

The Information sets forth that John Lawrence the younger Charles Arding Cornelius Levingston and Hendrick Oudenaarde on the r5th June in the 27th year of the Reign of the present King with fforce and Arms at the City of New York aforesaid, that is to say in the South ward of the same City, in and upon One Mary Anderson in the peace of God and our said Lord the King then and there being did make an Assault, and her said Mary Anderson then and there did beat wound and illtreat so that of her life it was greatly dispaired, and other Wrongs to the said Mary Anderson then and there did to the great Damage of the said Mary Anderson, and against the peace of the King

To this the Defend.ts have pleaded Not guilty and thereupon Issue is joined.

Although this prosecution is no more than for an Assault, yet in the Course of the Evidence it will appear to be attended with such Circumstances, as will shew it to be for a Crime of no ordinary Nature no less than a fforce and Violence offered to the person and Chastity of one Mary Anderson, a young Girl at the time of the Violence offered but barely turned 14 years of Age, A Crime that deserves the severest Reprehension, and a most severe punishment in Order to put a stop to such inordinate and lewd practises: For were Crimes of this nature suffered to pass unregarded and without punishment it is to be feared, that the Honour of no Mans ffamily the Honour and Chastity of No mans wife or Daughter would be long secure from the brutal Attempts of lustfull and licentious people. It is true the Attempt for which this prosecution was commenced was against a poor and helpless Orphan, but the poor have as much right to have their Honour and Virtue protected as the greatest.

Hugh Wallace	Elizabeth Anderson the Mother of Mary is the Widow of one Mr Anderson of the Kingdom of Ireland of a good Family and of a genteel Imployment, but upon his
W^m· Crampshire	Death was reduced to low Circumstances, but having an only Brother at Boston in New England, one Captain James Dalton a man in good Circumstances, she made known her Case to him, and he ordered her to send her Daughter to him, who is intitled to a considerable fortune after the Death of a Relation in Ireland, and he would take Care of her, but she not caring to part with her came to a Resolution to go herself with her Daughter to her Brother at Boston, and accordingly took a passage for herself and Daughter on Board a Vessell bound for Philadelphia in her way thither, but being taken sick spent the greatest part of that little Substance she brought with her, so that not having sufficient to pay their passages, was constrained to bind her Daughter as a servt to pay the Man untill she could go to Boston to her Brother to get money of him to redeem her, which she did and redeemed her Daughter, and about April last removed to New York by her Brothers Directions, where he might have a Better Opportunity to assist her in some little way of Business there which he advised her to put herself into to maintain herself & Daughter And accordingly on her Removal hither she hired a small shop or shed with a Chamber over it not a foot wide in a good Neighbourhood of Mr Reed, and sold Bread Beer Candles Cheese in small Quantitys by the penny Lemmons Oranges Limes potatos and other such small Commoditys, and was generally esteemed an honest industrious Woman, and the Daughter a sober and virtuous Girl 'til this matter happened, and the Defendts to damp this prosecution against them, endeavoured to blacken their Characters—It becomes necessary to relate so much of the Circumstances of these unfortunate people, because no Schemes have been left unattempted, no Falshoods nor Inventions omitted to blacken their Character, nor no practices untryed to deterr the carrying on this prosecution agt. the defendts. upon a presumption it is presumed that these poor destitute Creatures were friendless and had no Body to protect them, and indeed it has hapned unluckily for them that Captain James Dalton has been at sea ever since this matter has been in agitation but will no Doubt on his Return make a just Scrutiny into this matter, and call those that have been guilty or the Occasion of any unjust or inhuman Treatment of his Sister and Neice to a severe Acct for it.

Now to come to the matter immediately relating to the Cause of this prosecution.

Elizabeth Anderson	It will appear upon the Evidence of the said Elizabeth Anderson, and her Daughter, that soon after she came here the Defendts Lawrence and Arding frequently
Mary Anderson	came to her Shop on pretence to buy fruit, but by their Behaviour she mistrusted they had ill designs upon her Daughter Mary, and therefore the Mother whenever she saw y^m coming towards the Shop was carefull to send her Daughter up-

stairs out of the way. They being disappointed by the Mothers Care, and lodging or boarding together at Mrs. Ferraras took the Opportunity when she was from Home and out of Town to send her Negro Wench about 10 o'Clock at night as of a Message from her Mistress to Mrs. Andersons Shop with Orders to send some China Oranges over to her house, Accordingly Mrs. Anderson not mistrusting any ill Design sent her daughter Mary

Mary Anderson

The Negro wench let her in and went into the parlour where the Defendts were and told them the Oranges were come, and Mary Anderson being then in the Entry hearing the Defendts ask the Wench, who was come with them, the Mother or the Daughter, and the Wench saying the Daughter they said that is well, send her in and she hearing this, and not hearing Mrs Ferraras Voice in whose Name the Oranges were sent for, a little alarmed her, however she went into the Room where she saw the 4 Defendts siting round a Table with a Bowl of punch before y^m, they said nothing to her for some little time, but held down their heads and sneered and winked upon One another, And thereupon she said Gentlemen did you not send for Oranges, and one of them saying they were not the Oranges they wanted she turned to go away, But the Defendts Levingston and Oudenaarde jumped up, and hastned to the Door, and prevented her going out, And Arding laid violent hands upon her and endeavoured to force her into a Room adjoining to the parlour where was a Bed, but she laying fast hold of the Door with one hand and the staple of the Lock with the other resisting with all her might and screaming Levingston and Ourdenard laughed and sang to make a Noise, that she might not be heard, But Arding finding it difficult to force here into ye Room let her go, when Lawrence immediately seized on her, and suddenly pushed her out of the parlour into a long Entry then dark that leads to his Store, and Oudenaarde followed with a Candle, but the Defendt Lawrence damned him and bid him get back again saying he had light enough for what he wanted w^{th}out a Candle, and then having her alone in the Entry by himself, he offered her silk for a Gown out of his Store if she would comply with his Desires, but she refusing he pulled down his Breeches and used Violence towards her, So that to save herself from his Attempt she was obliged to stoop and pull the hind part of her petty coat forwards between her legs, and hold the same in her Teeth, And after he had strugled with her for some time he let her go, and she got away and went Home.

That when she came home she was greatly disordered, and her Mother had much ado to keep her from fainting but told not her Mother what had happened to her til Monday Morning, when Mr. Levingston called to the Daughter & asked her if she had been to the Kings Attorney. And the Mother hearing the Question insisted she should discover what had happened to her.

Elizabeth Anderson
Mary Anderson

Upon the Discovery to her Mother of what had happened to her, her Mother brought her the same day to the Attorney General, and relating what had happened made a Complaint against the Defendts Lawrence Arding Levingston and a fourth person whose name the Daughter knew not, and prayed a prosecution against them, And the Attorney General telling them he hoped that they had related nothing but the Truth and had not made this Complaint for the sake of getting money from them, Mrs. Anderson the mother replyed she did not, and that her Design in it was only to prevent her Daughters Ruin, And that if the Gentlemen would give her an Assurance not to meddle with her Daughter for the future, she was willing to pass by what had been done.

Elizabeth Anderson Mary Anderson Elizabeth Crampshire	This the Defendts were acquainted with but took no farther Notice of it than threatning to be revenged of both Mother and Daughter, and said they would have them whipped, and accused the Mother of buying stoln Goods, of Entertaining Negros, of keeping a Bawdy house and being a Common Disturber of ye Neighbourhood And in Order to draw her in to be guilty of these offences, that they might have a handle agt her, Two young Fellows Servts to one Mr Cunningham, sent by Defendts as supposed, came to her to offer her some Cloaths to buy wch one of them told her he had of his sisters, and among the rest a Cloke, which because she refused to buy he offered to give her, but she refusing his present, The other told her he had something for her in her own way; that he would let her have some potatos at 1 sh. a Bushell but she must not speak of it; but she telling him she would buy no potatos of him, They both on a sudden pretended to be very Drunk, and swore they would not go out of the Shop without some punch, she told them she sold none, but they seeing some in a small Bason on the Countor she had made for her own Drinking, swore they would have that, and to get rid of them she gave it to them, and as soon as they had got it, they threw down two shillings on the Counter to pay for it, and called in some Negros at the Door to drink of it, but one of y^m owing her a shilling for other things they had had of her she kept that, but returning the other shilling drove them and the Negros out of the shop, for which they gave her a violent Blow in the Face
Eliz. Anderson Mary Anderson	Notwithstanding which, Mr. Cunningham the next day sent for her and accused her of harbouring his servts and threatned to have her punished for it, unless she desisted to prosecute the Defendts.
Eliz. Anderson Jno: Provoost Esqr	Another time a Negro came to her and offered to sell her some Cheshire Cheeses, but under pretence of having them weighed, she decoyed him to Alderman Provoost and delivered him and the Cheeses to the Alderman
Wm. Cordoso heard Nell Hill say it. Thos Dalton Marg^t Dalton Nell is a person of bad Character James Ternan,— Mary Anderson saw Nell drinking with Arding and Lawrence several times	Lawrence and Arding procured several people in particular a Fellow called blind Callahan an infamous Fellow to come before her Door in the Night to mobb and abuse her, and Lawrence and Arding hid in their sloop as he was going away called him to go back and mob her again, and they would give him the other half Dollar, This One Nelly Hill heard as she was passing by and declared it But is since it seems gained over by the Defendts and Arding gave her Directions when he subpoenad her to go to Mr Levingston to refresh her Memory with what she had said that she might swear the same things again, And this if material can be proved by Thos Dalton Has since been treated with liquor in order to swear on this Trial by Arding and Lawrence
Mary Anderson saw French fling the Stones.	One French likewise a Bro of Mrs Farraras has been very busy in abusing her continually flinging Stones at her Door in the night, and in raising Disturbances, and notwithstanding they accused her of being the Occasion of the Disturbances, they themselves created, and even procured her to be committed for them
	After many Attempts to hurt her they at last so far prevailed as to procure her to be punished by the Recorder and Aldermen in a summary way for petit Larceny
Elizth: Anderson Mary Anderson	The Case was this, A poor Woman a stranger to her that seemed to be in great Want came to her shop, and made a Complaint that she was almost starved having eat nothing for 3 days and Mrs Anderson out of Compassion gave her some Victuals which as soon as she had tasted, she pretended to faint, and when she

came to, complained grievously that she had a sick husband at Home and three Children a starving for want of ffood, and desired Mrs Anderson would let her have some Bread and cheese some small Beer and other necessarys, and offered to pledge a petty coat she had on 'til she paid for it, But the Daughter mistrusting this might be another Trick whispered to her mother and told her so, desiring her not to take the pettycoat, but the Mother replyed she did not believe so, but that the Woman was really in Want, and let her have the things and took the petty coat, and a few days after the Woman came again and she let her have more necessarys to the Value of the pettycoat and more, and the Woman not coming afterwards to redeem it, and supposing she never would, she made Use of it and wore it as her own, And one Charles Sulivan a person of ill Character meeting with her near his house at Freshwater, as she was one day returning from the Attorney Generals, where she had been to acquaint him with the plots that were laid to intrap her, he invited her into his house to rest herself, and when there asked her how she came by the pettycoat she had on she told him (tho falsly) she spun it herself, and brought it out of Ireland with her, But he claiming it and saying it was stole out of his house, and she knowing that the Defendts had accused her of buying stolen Goods, was terrified and immediately confessed she had recd it of a Woman as a pledge, pulled of the pettycoat and gave it him, and begged of him not to speak of it, but he threatned to prosecute her for the Theft (tho he acknowledged she was never in his house before) unless she produced the Woman she had it of, and took the Silver Buckles out of her Shoes and her Scarlet Cloke clasped with a Silver clasp from her Back 'til she should find the Woman, And the next day wanting her Cloke, she went to Sulivan and pledged a gold Ring to him from her finger for her Cloke 'til she should find the woman, But upon a diligent Enquiry after her, She found that Sulivan knew the woman that had robbed him; and that she was run away for it and Sulivan had been in pursuit of her, upon this she thought

French went to him

Sulivan had used her ill, and informed the Alderman of the whole matter *And thereupon Sulivan* as there is reason to believe, was encouraged by the Defendts to

Bych^r: Sharp
W^m: Darlington

prosecute Mrs. Anderson for stealing ye pettycoat upon the presumption of Theft, the same being found upon her; But to take away this presumption Mary Anderson related and offered to prove how her Mother came by the pettycoat in manner as before related, and other proofs were offered that the pettycoat was stole by the Woman before mentioned, But the Recorder gave no Attention to it, told Mary Anderson of her prosecuting the Defendts and threatned her; And ordered Mrs. An-

This will be proved by
Gab: Lash

derson to be whipt; And Arding and Lawrence gave the Executioner Money to whip her severely and she was whipped most inhumanly, till she fell several times into Convulsions, and continued in them, and in a violent Fever and delirious many days afterwards, that it was generally thought she would have dyed.

Mary Anderson

That the Defendts were promoters of this punishment will appear from many Circumstances and particularly from hence, that the Day before Mrs Anderson was sentenced to be whipt, they insulted the Daughter and told her, Wee shall see your Mother's Back tomorrow, and yours too Miss polly in a little time; and are yet daily insulting and threatening her; and on Tuesday last to terrify her from giving Evidence against them, threatned her with the pillory a Friday and whipping.

John Christie

The Defendts. among other Aspersions say that Mrs. Anderson was whipped at Philadelphia, and have got, tis said some people of bad Characters to swear it, But were this Fact, as it is not, this will not justify their Attempt upon the Daughter; and when Mrs. Anderson was stript here to be whipped, her Back appeared fair and even without any Tear or Blemish, of sufficient proof of ye Falsity of it.

Note—It is to be supposed that the Defendts will insist that Mrs. Anderson having undergone a publick punishmt. by whipping is thereby become infamous and disqualified to be a Witness

Hawkins in his pleas of ye Crown Ch: 46 Sect 19 Title Evidence says That it seems agreed that a Conviction and therefore a fortiori an Attainder or Judgmt. of Treason, Felony, &c and also Judgmt for any Crime wtsoever to stand in the pillory or be whipt or branded in a Court which had a Jurisdiction are good Causes of Exception agt. a Witness—But he says Sect 20th that it is agreed that no such Conviction or Judgmt can be made use of to this purpose unless the Record be actually produced in Court

And this Conviction and Attainder must be by Judgmt in a Court of Record either by process of Outlawry or on a Conviction by the Verdict of 12 Men, or by pleading guilty, as appears by Cowels Interpreter under the Word Convict, and the Books there quoted, where it is said that a Convict is he that is found guilty of an offence by Verdict of a Jury Stamfords pla: Coron and under the word Attainder he says that Attainder is larger then Conviction, Conviction being only by the Jury Attainder is not before Judgmt. and for this he quotes Perkins Grants Nu: 27–29

But the Maior Recorder and Aldermen proceeding in a Summary way by Witnesses without a Jury, upon the Act of Assembly intitled an Act for the speedy punishing and releasing such persons from Imprisonmt. as shall commit any criminal offence in the City and County of New York under the Degree of Grand Larceny, are no Court of Record, and in the 2d place had no power by Vertue of y^t Act of Assembly to order Mrs Anderson to be whipt. For that Act gives them power only where a person shall commit an Offence under the Degree of Grand Larceny and being taken and committed to Gaol shall not within 48 hours give Bail to answer at ye Sessions then they may hear and determine the Offence, and the Offender being convicted by Confession or on the Oath of one or more credible Witnesses, they may in their Discretion order such corporal punishmt. not extending to life or Limb as they shall think proper and discharged the offender

Now by the natural Construction of this Act the Offender committed and not giving Bail, must be understood to be committed for the Crime for wch such punishmt is to be inflicted but Mrs Anderson was not in Gaol or commited for the Crime for which she was punished, but only for being a common Disturbance to ye Neighbourhood.

KING V. GEORGE SULLIVAN

This brief is interesting because of what it shows respecting provincial knowledge of the law of attempt. On October 23, 1771, George Sullivan was indicted for defacing a bond and, on a second count, for attempting to destroy the same. He was tried on April 21, 1773, and was found guilty on the first count. On May 1, 1773, the Supreme Court ordered that he be imprisoned for the space of one month and fined £5, which he thereupon paid to the prothonotary in court (*Ms. Mins. SCJ 1769–72* [Engr.] 441; *Ms. Mins. SCJ 1772–76* [Rough] 78, 92). The indictment is to be found in *H.R. Pleadings* Pl. K. 355. The brief which follows is in *J. T. Kempe Lawsuits* O–S.

April Term 1773

The King
V⁸   } Brief
Geo. Sullivan

The Indictment charges that the Defendt on 17 Decr: in the 11 yʳ of the King [1770] at the East Ward fraudulently got into his hands from one Rachel Bates a Bond signed and sealed by one John Falkner, Israel Hersfield Junʳ and one John Bates dated 26 Day of Oct. 1768, by which they were bound to David Jones Esqr. in £251.13.4 for the Payment to him of £126.16.8, on or before 25 Day of Decr. next after the Date of the Bond with lawfull Interest. vizt. under Colour of pretence that he would inspect the said writing and immediately redeliver it to the said Rachel and that the said George afterwards on the same Day did with open knife cut & destroy the Bond, with an Intent unlawfully and wickedly to deceive and defraud the said John Bates of the Sum mentioned in the condition of that Bond with the Interest, which the said John Bates had before that time paid and discharged to the said David Jones out of his own proper Monies, the same being the proper Debt of the said John Falkner & Israel Hersefield, and Bates being bound as afsd at their Request & as their Security

2. Count for an attempt to destroy this Bond with open knife with the same Intention as above charged—

Plea Not Guilty—

Witness Rachel Getfield
Thomas Jones

If the first Count is proved there will be no Dispute about the Criminality of the act, if the 2d Count is only proved then it will be insisted on.

That as it only charges an *attempt* not compleated, it is not punishable, that the *Intent* to commit a Misdemeanor is not Criminally punishable, inasmuch as the Fact was not committed. That if it had, it would *only* have been a *Misdemeanor*. The attempt therefore to do a *misdemeanor* must be a *less* Offence than committing it, and cannot therefore be a *Misdemeanor* which is of the lowest class of offences punishable by Law.

1—*Intent* particularly regarded. This only constitutes the Essential Differences of actions—The same acts are criminal or not according to the *Intent* of the agent.

Acts abstractedly considered are entirely indifferent—On this principle The acts of Idiots Madmen &c are not punished because no *Intention* can be imputed to them. On this principle also the Law punishes Actions done under some Circumstances, when the same acts under other Circumstances are justifiable, & perhaps Virtuous—. A man is killed—If with malice tis *Murder*—If no premeditated malice it is *manslaughter*—If it happens by Chance, tis *excusable Homicide.* If in the Execution of a Duty as fighting agt. an Enemy it is a Virtue.

2. Hence the *bare Act* is not punished, but the Intent with which that act was done, upon this Maxim *Intentio tua ponit nomen operi tuo.*

3. . . . [These dots appear in the original] I admit that a *naked Intent* uncoupled with an act was never punished by our Laws, nor perhaps by any other, nor *can be,* It being only an *affection of the Mind,*—Some act therefore is necessary to manifest the Intent. It has been held that *a Discovery* of a Treasonable Intent to kill the King, tho by *words only or writing* is a sufficient overt act.

In other Offences there must be some *act* done *leading to* the *Execution* of the Intent, or otherwise the Intent never was punishable.

3 Coke Inst. 5.

4. Anciently by the Laws of England, as it is now in most Parts of Europe whenever an *Intent* to commit an offence was coupled with *an act* leading to the Execution of it, or in other words if an *attempt* to do it was made, there the Maxim *Voluntas reputabitur pro Facto* obtained and the offender received the same punishment, tho he failed in the *attempt,* as if he had fully executed his Intent, as a proof of which see 3 Coke Inst. 5.

5. At present the Rigor of the ancient Law hath so far abated, as not to punish an attempt to commit a Felony as a *Felony committed,* and this I take to be the meaning of the Maxim That Voluntas non reputabitur pro facto, perhaps the Maxim may go farther and mean that in no species of Offences shall the *ineffectual attempt* to commit a crime, be punished *equally* as if the Offence itself had been *perpetrated.* But it surely cannot mean that a Man may lawfully and without Fear of Punishment *attempt* to commit as many wicked Actions under the Degree of Felony as he pleases. The Maxim cannot mean that an *attempt* shall not be punished *at all,* but not equally as if the Attempt had succeeded, and this I take it in *Felonies* only. I find it applied to no other instance.

6. The *Good Order & Security of* Society requires that it should not be *safe* for a man even to *attempt* the Commission of Crimes. It must in the nature of Things be an Offence agt. the wellbeing of Society. If so what should prevent the Law's power of punishing? How comes it that an *attempt* to commit a *Misdemeanor* is not a *Misdemeanor,* what is it then? It *is an offence,* and must be classed among Misdemeanors, for it can be classed among no other species of Crimes agt. the public.

7. The Maxim, *voluntas non reputabitur pro Facto,* holds only in Felonys—I find it mentioned in *no other* Instance—

8. The Maxim that *Voluntas reputabitur pro Facto* holds in Treason. The Reason is that from the Enormity of the Offence, every Act leading to it is to be considered as Treason also, it can be classed among no other species of offences, and the public Security requires such severity—From this Consideration there can be no *accessories* in Treason, all are Principals from *necessity,* and every act expressive of the Intent, involves the agent in the Guilt of Treason.

2 Hawk: 310. Sect. 2.
315. Sect. 16.
Dalton 350. 352.

The like Law of Misdemeanors from *necessity,* it is the *lowest* general Class of offences, every Person concerned is guilty of something which is an *offence* and must be a principal even if he does only such Things as would make him an accessory before the Fact in ~~Felony~~ Cases of Felony—and every Act done showing the Criminality of the agent makes him Guilty of a misdemeanor and this the public security also requires, or crimes might be attempted with Impunity.

Consent alone makes a Man a principal in Trespass as well as in Treasons, and the Maxim that Voluntas reputabitur pro Facto is thus proved to take place in *Misdemeanors* as well *as Treasons*—But be this as it may, & should the Contrary Maxim hold, for the reasons before given it can mean no more, than that the punishment for an *attempt,* may be less than for the actual Perpetration of the offence.

9. Were there no authorities tending to shew that an attempt to commit a misdemeanor is punishable, yet Reason and the General Law or Nature of Society would be sufficient to shew that it must be so. When any thing is prohibited by the Law as *Criminal*, the *attempt* to commit it is also prohibited as *Criminal*. It is a Maxim *Quando aliquid prohibetur, prohibetur et omne per quod devenitur ad illud.*

110 fol: 13.
101 fol: 98.
Dyer 95 a.b.
Viner Title Intent D
pag 451.

10. There are not wanting Cases to confirm this Doctrine.

    1. An *Attempt* to maintain a suit is punishable, tho the Suit be not actually maintained. Yet maintenance itself is but a misdemeanor.

5 Mod. 207 .   .   .   .
1 Sid. 186

    2. An Intention to fight a Duel.

INDEX OF PROVINCIAL NAMES AND CASES

Crown cases are listed by names of defendants and are indicated by the abbreviations K.v. and Q.v. In the early records the clerks were still using the Latin style *Dominus Rex v.* but this form was abandoned. For reasons of convenience, all citations in this volume have been Englished. When there are several defendants the case is indexed by the name which appeared first in the clerk's first minute book entry or in the indictment or information. Brackets are used to indicate footnote numbers.

GENERAL INDEX

Brackets are used to indicate footnote numbers

Attorney General (*cont.*)
applies for warrants, 424
as Master of Crown Office, 371
assisted by bar, 88
authority in New York, 733–34
authority over prosecutions, 319
commissions to, 50
compensation recommended by grand jury, 736
compromise by, 193
consulted on process problem, 420
costs of, 735
countermands notice of trial, 615
defends jury trial, 607
deputies of, 193, 319, 347, 360
discretion over time of trial, 613
efforts to collect forfeitures, 526, 528, 540
expenses and rewards of, 742, 747–48
favors multiple indictments over single with counts, 673
fees, 366 [154], 734
frames informations, 150
income from informations, 377
instructs deputy, 630
management of provocation, 347, 366
moves for special jury, 620
nolle pros by, 154
opens indictment or information, 623–24
policy re prosecution, 744
prepares indictments, 352, 354
presentment of, 363
prosecution of, 317, 318, 377
refuses interference in K. v. Parks, 304
salary of, 734
security for costs to, 510
warrant for witnesses, 480
See also Index of Provincial Names and Cases: Alexander; Bickley, May; Bradley, Richard; Broughton; Graham, James; Jamison, David; Kempe, J. T.; Kempe, William; Rayner, John; Smith, William
Attorneys. *See* Counsel
autrefoits acquit, 588–89
autrefoits convict, 241, 588–89

Backed warrants, 296, 445–46
Bail
and habeas corpus, 502–06
availability, 495
characteristics of English law, 497
colonial policy, 497–98

Bail (*cont.*)
commitment alternative, 514
courts' attitude toward, 502
excessive, 504, 506
for cheats, 95, 98 [174], 501
for forgery, 501
for grand larceny, 500
for homicide, 499–500
for murder, 499
for rape, 501
for treason, 498
in misdemeanors, 501
in small felonies, 501
part of law of recognizances, 507
power to, 497–506
right to, 502–06
surrender in discharge of, 522
See also Recognizances
Bail bonds. *See* Recognizances
Banishment, 298–99, 688, 690–91
Bar, trials at. *See* Supreme Court; Trial at bar
Barretry, in General Sessions, 98 [176]
Bastardy, 129, 338, 417
and poor relief, 103–04
appeals in, 102, 269–71
certiorari to review, 264–65
complaints, 338
in Dutchess County, 101
in General Sessions, 101–04
jurisdiction based on English acts, 100
presentment of, 102
procedure re, 102
process, 103–04
recognizances, 103, 487 [9–11], 689
use of purging oath, 658
Bayard Case
exemplifies progress of common law reception, 573
landmark of provincial law, 85
motion in arrest of judgment, 274–76
See also Index of Provincial Names and Cases: Bayard, Nicholas
Belly, plea of, 755–56
Bench warrants, 440–42, 450, 730
Benefit of clergy, 591–92
allowed but once, 753–54
and jury verdicts, 751
branding and, 752, 753
creates first offender rule, 754
desuetude of, 752
device for grading responsibility, 752

Debt, action of *(cont.)*
to collect recognizances, 534–35
Declaration of Rights (1774), xvii
Defendants
and counsel, 573–74
and recognizances, 507
appearance by, 507–08
chaining of, 692, 695
closing speech, 660, 662
commitment of, 501
for fines, 723
confessions by, 634, 653–56
cross-examination by, at preliminary hearing, 634–35
detention on suspicion, 343
discharge, 341, 367–69, 429
by proclamation, 575
by warrant, 589
of accessories, 579
on payment of fines, 723
procedure, 343
examination of, 340, 565
examined by court, 565
exceptions to witnesses not being sworn, 627–28
fees
due by, 733
of, on discharge, 342–43, 732
fines *in absentia,* 725
hazards of conducting own defense, 652–53
impediments upon, at trial, 554–58, 633
in felony trials, 627, 633
indictment read to, 623
liability for costs, 74
liability for fees, 732, 739
limitations on, in felony trials, 633
motions for discharge, 343, 521
motions for trial, 614
motion to postpone trial, 615–16
oppression of, 634–35
presence at judgment, 697–99
privilege of postponing trial, 616
privilege to move for special jury, 620
promises to behave, 513–14
purgation oaths of, 657–58
questioning, 652–53, 656
recognizances upon acquittal, 517
representation in misdemeanors, 632
right to certiorari, 155
right to confrontation, 633
right to counsel, 554–55, 557
right to jury, 603–10

Defendants *(cont.)*
subpoena privilege, 633
surrender of bail, 522
testimonial capacity of, 652–59
undertake for costs, 536
weakness of evidence, 631
witnesses not sworn, 555, 562, 572, 627
See also Process against defendants
Delaware plantations, 396
courts in, 18 [88], 68
pattern of jurisdiction in, 65, 68
trials in, 569
Demurrer. *See* Pleading and pleas
Deodands, 717 [220]
Depositions. *See* Confessions; Examinations
Discharge
by proclamation, 369, 575
of grand jury, 347
Discretion, judicial, 681–82
Disorderly house, 100–01
raid on, 114 [244]
Distringas juratores, 468, 469 [377], 470, 473
Distringas super vicecomitem, 458 [338]
Dominion of New England
courts of, 21
influence on New York, 24–25
New York included in, 10, 21–23
Due process, 380, 385, 394, 401, 405 [119, 121], 415, 481
instructions re, 7
Duke's laws, 269
appeals, 256
civil and criminal proceedings under, not clearly distinguished, 387
commissions, 44
constables, 388
effect of New England codes, 61, 684
enactment, 16
establish style of courts, 566
extension in Province, 16 [78], 18 [88]
fees, 731
jury provisions, 567
magisterial discretion, 684
on jurisdiction, 61
petit jury not mandatory, 560
process scheme, 385
prosecution, 328
provisions as to Sessions, 64
provisions for Assizes, 19
resolution abrogating, 25
Sessions Courts, 18

Nuisance (*cont.*)
  summary procedure, 364
  writs to abate, 416 [179]

Oath
  of constable at trial, 669
  of grand jury, 345
  of office, 454–55
    refusal, 402 [103]
  of purgation, 657–58
Officials
  plea of *nolo* by, 594 [186]
  royal, prosecution of, 318
  See also Process, against officials
Orange County
  Allison affair in, 183 *et seq.*
  and New Jersey boundary troubles, 314 [123],
    422
  assault case in, 181 *et seq.*
  Circuit extended to, 74, 142 [18]
  Cowboys in, xviii
  hue and cry warrant, 295 [48]
  ordinance for circuit in, 142 [18]
  plea of *nolo* in, 594
  recognizance business in, 497
  Supreme Court for, 28
Orders
  county, 38, 40, 425
  justices of peace, 106, 425
Orders in Council, 12, 224, 228, 231–32, 237
Ordinances
  county, 38, 425
    supplementary, 40
  justices' power and grand jury, 302
  local, 36–42
    and grand jury, 71, 361–63
    infractions of, 595
    prosecutions, 106
  provincial, 36 *et seq.*
    Albany Circuit of 1768, 143
    authority of Council, 11, 32
    authority of Governor, 11, 32–33
    Chancery of 1701, 27 [135]
    Circuit terms of 1761, 143
    extending Supreme Court term of 1741, 86
    Fee of 1710, 32 [164], 623, 732, 735, 742
    Fee of 1768, 477, 723, 732, 745
    Fee Schedule of 1693, 575, 732, 735
    Judiciary of 1699, 29, 33, 112, 239, 603
    Judiciary of 1704, 30

Ordinances (*cont.*)
  provincial (*cont.*)
    miscellaneous local courts, 32 [164]
    Nisi prius of 1715, 30, 36, 74, 79, 142
    Orange County Circuit of 1704, 74, 142 [18]
    Registration of Title of 1723, 32 [167]
    Special Supreme Court term of 1701, 300
  town, 37 [184]
    confirmation, 269
    confirmed by Sessions, 36
Oswego market, 416 [179]
Outlawry, 414, 443–45
Overseers
  and constable, 69
  as jurymen, 567
Oyer and Terminer and General Gaol Delivery,
    Court of (1683–1688)
  and appeals, 238
  Circuit feature of, 20
  error in, 256 [121], 408
  established, 19
  instructions for clerk, 570
  jurisdiction, 20
  original jurisdiction, 70
  process in, 411
  records of, 691
  remands cases, 166
Oyer and Terminer and General Gaol Delivery,
    Courts of (1692–1776), a name for Circuit
    Courts, 143. *See also* Circuit Courts
Oyer and Terminer, Commissions of
  for the trial of Admiralty causes at Old Bailey,
    306
  for the trial of offenses on the high seas, 308–
    09, 357, 572
  special, 62, 82 *et seq.*, 618
    common law rule for judgment, 692
    early, 561
    early uses, 85 [136]
    final ritual in early, 685
    for Dutchess riots, 88
    Governor's prerogative re, 91
    limitations of, 274
    precept for grand jury, 344
    prosecutions in early, 332
    provision for, in New York City, 75
    relation to Circuit, 90
    to expedite trials, 90
    under Duke's laws, 19
    under Leisler, 24
    used for political causes, 83

Proclamations, judicial
  discharge by, 341–43, 369, 562
    rules, 342
  to grand jury, 344–45
  writ of, 236, 300, 315
Prohibition, writ of, 236, 300, 315
Proprietor
  and change in provincial law, 406
  authority of, 5
  powers of, 6
  rights merge in Crown, 8
  rights of, 2–4
Prosecution
  discontinuance of, 367
  management of, 366
  of royal officials, 318
  of slaves, 382
  payment of costs, 196, 463–64
  summary, 380–81
  See also Complaints; Indictments; Informations
Protections, 185, 316, 350, 482 [439]
Provincial law
  and Acts of Assembly, 31
  and Acts of Parliament, 13–15
  as affected by process, 384, 406
  Bayard Case a landmark of, 85
  characteristics, 60
  diversity, xxxv
  charter as source of, 5–7
  colonial demands, 5
  commission as source, 8–9
  common law forms introduced, 69
  common law process introduced, 406 et seq., 691
  development of, 59–60
    before Revolution, xvii
  effects of early, 569
  Exchequer practice in, 530
  mentioned in commissions, 48
  policy on bail, 497–98
  policy on counterfeiting, 95–97
  summary procedure, 419
  tacit adoption of English statutes, 14
  variants in forcible entry, 125
Provision Act, 240–41
Provision bonds, 241, 244
Public works, 107
Punishment
  afflictive, 697–98
  cage, 707
  capital in New York not excessive, 704
  carting, 706

Punishment (cont.)
  composite sentence, 516
  corporal, 562, 597, 698, 701–10
  discretion in, 702
  early, 560
  effect of extending judicial discretion, 682
  English capital, 702
  execution of, under Duke's laws, 386
  fines, 698, 709–10
    imprisonment to collect, 688, 709, 722, 723
    payment in court, 723
    theory of, 698
  fixed and discretionary penalties distinguished, 702
  hanging, sentence, 704 [141]
  imitation of English, 702
  imprisonment, 514–15, 572, 709
  in country Sessions (1665–1683), 689–90
  in New York City Mayor's Court, 688
  in Sessions Courts, 688–91
  in Supreme Court, 702 [139]
  in town courts, 402–05
  infaming effect, 706
  labeling, 707
  of slaves, 704
  pillory, 706–07
  predilection for corporal, in New York City, 515
  recognizances, 515–17
  statistics on, 702 [139]
  stocking, 689–90, 706–07 [151], 708
  vicarious, 691
  whipping, 705–06, 708
  See also Escheat; Forfeiture; Infamy
Purgation, oaths of, 657–59

Queens County
  costs in, 738, 739
  fines in, 710 [163]
  justices prosecuted, 170
  riot in, 123
Qui tam actions, 338, 340, 379, 423, 609, 724
  appeal of, 237
  for forfeiture, 238 [56]
  nature of, 236

Rape
  attempted
    prosecutions in General Sessions, 106 [206]
    prosecution of slaves, 120 [267]

Taxes, collection of, 39–40
Torture, 555
Town
  supervision of, 402
  unit under Nicolls, 38
Town courts, 17
  abolished in 1691, 26
  Act of 1683, 20
    Amendment of 1685, 20
  initiate Sessions, 403
  procedure, 401–05
    before conquest, 402 [105]
Town meetings, justices preside at, 134
Trade
  Acts of. *See* Acts of Trade
  illicit, 240
  power to regulate, 245–46
  regulation of, 40–41, 131, 240
Trading with enemy, prosecutions for, 240–49
Traffic
  ordinances, 37, 39
  regulation, 484
Transfer
  by certiorari, 151, 154–61
    defendant's rights, 155
    procedure upon, 158–59
    recognizance for costs, 156
    record removed, 160
    return, 159
  by habeas corpus, 155–56
  by hand, 147–51
    enrollment, 150
    in country, 150
    procedure, 147
    types of, 148
  from General Sessions to Circuit, 82
  See also Indictments, transferred
Treason, 274
  appeal in, 224, 231
  bail in, 498
  colonial statute, 84 [132]
  first indictment for, 566
  incident of infamy in, 718
  incidents of judgment, 710 *et seq.*
  pardon prerogative, 755
  prosecutions for, 334
  sentence for, 693
  trial of, 83–85, 88–89, 554, 563–64
  use of conciliar warrant in, 421
  where tried, 83 *et seq.*

Treaty
  of Breda, 2
  of Westminster, 2
Treby, C.J., 471 [382], 473 [392]
Trial
  affected by fee charges, 739
  appearance at, 576
  arraignment, 559, 561, 564, 570, 578–79
    function of, 578–79
    on indictment and inquest, 675
    repeated, 582
  at Sessions, 565–70
  challenge
    examination on *voir dire,* 618
    for cause, 618
    peremptory, 618
    trial of challenged juror, 619
  characteristics
    of English, 554–58
    of New York practice (1683–1691), 570
  charge to jury, 665–69
    exceptions to, 251, 253, 665
    re-charging, 670
    requests for, 665
  closing speech, 659–65
    and evidence, 659–60
    comment on evidence, 661–62
    defendant's, 660, 662
    for Crown, 661–65
    matters of law, 660, 663–64
  conduct of, 620–23
  confrontation, 633
  Crown witnesses sworn in felonies, 627
  defendants examined at, 340, 565, 652–53
  delay in, 611
  depositions and examinations at. *See* Evidence
  effect of indictment procedure, 670
  effect of jury selection, 570
  evidence. *See under* Evidence; Examinations; Witnesses
  examination of witnesses. *See under* Witnesses
  felony and rules of evidence, 633
  final proceedings at
    allocutus, 681
    characteristics of, 680
    English rules, 680 *et seq.*
    influence of English practice, 684
    upon fine or imprisonment, 722
    See also Judgment
  indictment read, 564, 583, 623